Sociology

Third Canadian Edition

A Down-to-Earth Approach

Brief Contents

To a new and hopeful generation
of sociology students

Betty Freidan (1921–)
The Feminine Mystique

Simone de Beauvoir (1908–1986)
The Second Sex

Immanuel Wallerstein (1930–)
The Modern World System

Jean Baudrillard (1929–)
Simulations

Dorothy Smith (1926–)

2000

Robert Park (1864–1944)
Introduction to the Science of Sociology

C. Wright Mills (1916–1962)
The Power Elite

Roland Barthes (1915–1980)
The Pleasure of the Text

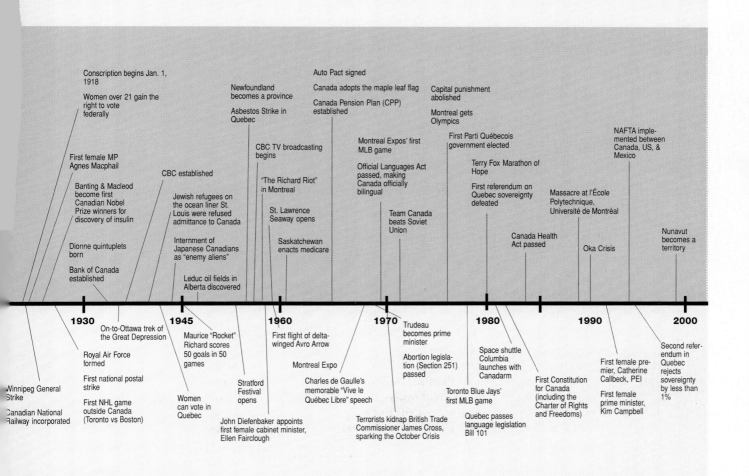

Conscription begins Jan. 1, 1918

Women over 21 gain the right to vote federally

Newfoundland becomes a province

Asbestos Strike in Quebec

Auto Pact signed

Canada adopts the maple leaf flag

Canada Pension Plan (CPP) established

Capital punishment abolished

Montreal gets Olympics

First female MP Agnes Macphail

Banting & Macleod become first Canadian Nobel Prize winners for discovery of insulin

CBC established

CBC TV broadcasting begins

"The Richard Riot" in Montreal

St. Lawrence Seaway opens

Montreal Expos' first MLB game

Official Languages Act passed, making Canada officially bilingual

First Parti Québecois government elected

Terry Fox Marathon of Hope

First referendum on Quebec sovereignty defeated

NAFTA implemented between Canada, US, & Mexico

Massacre at l'École Polytechnique, Université de Montréal

Jewish refugees on the ocean liner St. Louis were refused admittance to Canada

Internment of Japanese Canadians as "enemy aliens"

Leduc oil fields in Alberta discovered

Saskatchewan enacts medicare

Team Canada beats Soviet Union

Canada Health Act passed

Oka Crisis

Nunavut becomes a territory

Dionne quintuplets born

Bank of Canada established

1930

On-to-Ottawa trek of the Great Depression

Royal Air Force formed

First national postal strike

First NHL game outside Canada (Toronto vs Boston)

1945

Maurice "Rocket" Richard scores 50 goals in 50 games

Women can vote in Quebec

Stratford Festival opens

John Diefenbaker appoints first female cabinet minister, Ellen Fairclough

1960

First flight of delta-winged Avro Arrow

Montreal Expo

Charles de Gaulle's memorable "Vive le Québec Libre" speech

1970

Trudeau becomes prime minister

Abortion legislation (Section 251) passed

Terrorists kidnap British Trade Commissioner James Cross, sparking the October Crisis

1980

Space shuttle Columbia launches with Canadarm

Toronto Blue Jays' first MLB game

Quebec passes language legislation Bill 101

First Constitution for Canada (including the Charter of Rights and Freedoms)

1990

First female premier, Catherine Callbeck, PEI

First female prime minister, Kim Campbell

2000

Second referendum in Quebec rejects sovereignty by less than 1%

Winnipeg General Strike

Canadian National Railway incorporated

Third Canadian Edition

Sociology

A Down-to-Earth Approach

James M. Henslin
Southern Illinois University

Dan Glenday
Brock University

Ann Duffy
Brock University

Norene Pupo
York University

PEARSON

A and B

Toronto

National Library of Canada Cataloguing in Publication

Sociology : a down-to-earth approach / James M. Henslin ... [et al.]. —
3rd Canadian ed.

Includes bibliographical references and index.
ISBN 0-205-38304-1

1. Sociology. I. Henslin, James M.

HM51.H3974 2004   301   C2003-900169-5

ISBN 0-205-38304-1

Vice President, Editorial Director: Michael J. Young
Senior Acquisitions Editor: Jessica Mosher
Marketing Manager: Judith Allen
Senior Developmental Editor: Martina van de Velde
Editorial Coordinator: Söğüt Y. Güleç
Copy Editor: Linda Cahill
Proofreader: Gail Copeland
Production Manager: Wendy Moran
Page Layout: Joan M. Wilson
Permissions Research: Sandy Cooke
Photo Research: Tricia Yourkevich
Art Director: Julia Hall
Cover and Interior Design: Amy Harnden
Cover Image: Joanne Tod, *Union Picnic sur l'Herbe*, 1985

Statistics Canada information is used with the permission of the Minister of Industry, as Minister responsible
for Statistics Canada. Information on the availability of the wide range of data from Statistics Canada can be
obtained from Statistics Canada's Regional Offices, its World Wide Web site at **http://www.statcan.ca**, and its
toll-free access number 1-800-263-1136.

1 2 3 4 5   08 07 06 05 04

Printed and bound in the USA.

Contents

Part four   Social Institution 235

Chapter 10   Bureaucracy and Formal Organizations   235

Chapter 11   The Economy: Money and Work   259

Chapter 14   Education and Religion   331

Education: Transferring Knowledge and Skills   332

List of Features

Mass Media in Social Life

Perspectives

Sociology and the New Technology

Liberal and Conservative Views on Social Issues

Welcome to sociology! I've loved sociology since I was in my teens, and I hope you enjoy it, too. Sociology is fascinating because it holds the key to so much understanding of social life.

If you like to watch people and try to figure out why they do what they do, you will like sociology. Sociology pries open the doors of society, so you can see what goes on behind them. *Sociology: A Down-to-Earth Approach* stresses how profoundly our society and the groups to which we belong influence us. Social class, for example, sets us on a path in life. For some, the path leads to better health, more education, and higher income, but for others it leads to poverty, dropping out of school, and even a higher risk of illness and disease. These paths are so significant that they affect our chances of making it to our first birthday, as well as of getting in trouble with the police. They even influence how our marriage will work out, the number of children we will have—and whether or not we will read this book in the first place.

When I took my first course in sociology, I was "hooked." Seeing how marvelously my life had been affected by these larger social influences opened my eyes to a new world, one that has been fascinating to explore. I hope that this will be your experience also.

From how people become homeless to how they become presidents, from why people commit suicide to why women are discriminated against in every society around the world—all are part of sociology. This breadth, in fact, is what makes sociology so intriguing. We can place the sociological lens on broad features of society, such as social class, gender, and race-ethnicity, and then immediately turn our focus to the small-scale level. If we look at two people interacting—whether quarreling or kissing—we see how these broad features of society are being played out in their lives.

We aren't born with instincts. We don't come into this world with preconceived notions of what life should be like. At birth, we have no ideas of race-ethnicity, gender, age, or social class. We have no idea, for example, that people "ought" to act in certain ways because they are male or female. Yet we all learn such things as we grow up in our society. Uncovering the "hows" and the "whys" of this process is also part of sociology's fascination.

One of sociology's many pleasures is that as we study life in groups (which can be taken as a definition of sociology), whether those groups be in some far-off part of the world or in some nearby corner of our own society, we constantly gain insights into our own selves. As we see how *their* customs affect *them*, effects of our own society on us become more visible.

This book, then, can be part of an intellectual adventure, for it can lead you to a new way of looking at your social world—and in the process, help you better understand both society and yourself.

I wish you the very best in college—and in your career afterward. It is my sincere hope that *Sociology: A Down-to-Earth Approach* contributes to that success.

James M. Henslin, Professor Emeritus
Department of Sociology
Southern Illinois University, Edwardsville
henslin@aol.com

Preface

To study sociology is to embark on a fascinating journey into a new world of perception and understanding. It is an exploration of other worlds and ideas far from your own—as well as a quest to understand your own world and ideas. Since this book is designed to help you on this journey, we'd like to show you how it is organized, and then review its themes and features.

The Organization of this Text

The text is organized into five parts. Each has a broad focus and is designed to help you acquire the sociological perspective. This will enable you to better analyze social relations—and the particular corner of life in which you find yourself.

Part I focuses on the sociological perspective which we introduce in the first chapter; in Chapter 2 "What Do Sociologists Do?") we present the methods used by sociologists.

Part II builds on this foundation as we continue our sociological exploration of the significant influence social groups have on our lives. We present an overview of culture, introduce socialization, and contrast macrosociology and microsociology.

Part III focuses on social inequality, which has such a tremendous impact on our lives. Because social stratification is so significant—and to understand social life we need to know that it penetrates every crevice of our existence—we first take a global focus, which presents an overview of the principles of stratification, then turn the sociological spotlight on social class. After establishing the broader context, we focus on gender, the most global of the social inequalities. Following this, we examine the inequalities of race, ethnicity, and age.

In Part IV, we turn to those engulfing social arrangements called social institutions. Social institutions are so significant that without understanding them we cannot understand life in society. First we examine the impact of bureaucracy and formal organizations. Then we turn to an analysis of the economy and politics, currently our overarching institutions, which exert such an incredible amount of control over our lives. Following this, we look at four other social institutions that also play a significant role in our lives—the family, education and religion, and medicine.

In Part V, you will gain insight into why your world is changing so rapidly, as well as catch a glimpse of what is yet to come. This concluding part opens with social deviance and social control, which students often find to be among their favourite topics in sociology. The next chapter examines population, urbanization, and the environment, which have such an impact on us all. Lastly we look at the fascinating areas of collective behaviour and social movements.

Themes and Features

Perhaps the single greatest goal of the introductory sociology course is to see the connection between the individual and society, to understand how social forces shape our behaviour. To help students reach this goal, there are four central themes: down-to-earth sociology, diversity, technology and society, and contrasting liberal and conservative perspectives on social issues.

Let's look at these themes in more detail.

Down-to-Earth Sociology

Why shouldn't sociology be presented in a manner that conveys its inherent excitement? Without any doubt, sociology is the most enticing of all the social sciences. Yet textbooks often make sociology seem dull, and thereby fail to reach students.

The choice of subtitle for this book, *A Down-to-Earth Approach*, is deliberate, for our goal is to share sociology's excitement as we embark on our fascinating journey. To note how the basic substance of sociology penetrates our everyday lives is to make visible the influence of the social on who we are. We know that you already have an awareness of the influence of the social on your life, and we are going to build on this awareness.

This down-to-earth approach is present in the vignettes that open each chapter. Many of these lively vignettes are based on James Henslin's personal sociological experiences. To stimulate your sociological imagination, we use examples that you can relate to. Threaded through these examples are the central insights provided by sociology's major perspectives. As we apply symbolic interactionism, for example, you will see how symbols create social life. As we examine functionalism, you will see how people's actions have both manifest and latent consequences. And you will have no difficulty seeing the far-reaching implications for your own life of the conflict perspective's view that groups compete for scarce resources. In this Canadian edition, the inclusion of feminist theories complements the three major theoretical perspectives of the discipline while postmodernism brings a fresh, new perspective to some of the issues raised in this text.

Down-to-Earth Sociology boxes underscore this approach. They focus on such topics as Sociological Findings and Common Sense (Chapter 1), Careers in Sociology (Chapter 1), Expressing Yourself Online (Chapter 3), Exploring Myths About the Poor (Chapter 6), Boys' Conflicted World: the Struggle for Expression and Self (Chapter 7), The Inuit Expulsion (Chapter 8), and Youth Unemployment and Crime in Canada (Chapter 16).

We have attempted to reinforce this down-to-earth theme through a writing style that is also "down-to-earth," that is, one that is accessible and inviting. We have tried, then, to avoid unnecessary jargon so you won't have to endure linguistic torture in order to grasp basic ideas. These ideas are of utmost importance in your sociological journey, and to introduce them we try to use concise explanations, clear (but not reductive) language, and relevant examples.

Cultural Diversity and Globalization

Any attempt to explain Canadian society must pay keen attention to its diverse populations, for ours is truly a multicultural society. It also must explore the many implications of the globalization of the world's societies.

Discussions of diversity, such as the Perspectives box in Chapter 8 (Over Half a Century of Citizenship), help you apply your growing sociological imagination to fundamental changes occurring in our society. They also will help you see connections among key sociological concepts, such as culture, socialization, norms, race, gender, and social class. As your sociological imagination grows, you will better understand the social structure of our society—and your own place in it.

Global interconnections profoundly affect our lives. The dawn of a global economy—new to world history—influences the kinds of skills and knowledge you need in order to make a living, the types of work that will be available to you, and the variety and costs of the goods and services you consume. This new global economy, which has married our fate with that of other nations, also determines other essential aspects of your life, such as whether you will experience war or peace.

Global matters are considered in regard to stratification, social institutions, technology, social change, and the environment. Perspectives boxes entitled "Cultural Diversity Around the World" address such aspects as international corporations (Chapter 10), the rise of nationalism (Chapter 12), and urbanization in the least industrialized nations (Chapter 17).

Sociology and the New Technology

One of the most profound social forces that you face is the accelerated rate of technological change. In just a single generation, computers have become integrated in our daily lives; alternative, or niched, media outlets have proliferated, including online services and the Internet; "sci-fi"-like technologies are being used to aid reproduction; distance learning is becoming common. Topics selected both for their relevance and timeliness include Global Village or Big Brother? (Chapter 3), Cybercommunications and the Creation of Electronic Communities (Chapter 5), Gender and Reproductive Technology (Chapter 7), and Technology and the Dilemma of Medical Rationing (Chapter 15).

French sociologist Jacques Ellul feared that technology was destroying civilization while Canadian Marshall McLuhan celebrated the "global village." The emerging sociological theory of technology, rather than regarding technology as an out-of-control force that drives culture and on which all social change depends, emphasizes that individuals and groups—with all their values and special interests—shape technology. In addition to the impact of technology on our daily lives, this edition introduces the student to the growing influence of environmental sociology in Canada, not only on the discipline of sociology but in our daily lives as well (Chapter 18).

Critical Thinking

Thinking Critically about Social Controversy is another important feature of this text. These sections, which address pressing and often controversial social issues, underscore the significance of sociology for understanding the events that are challenging our ideas and changing our lives. They consider interesting issues ranging from Are Sex Offenders Sick? (Chapter 2) to Why Canadian Mothers Work for Pay (Chapter 13). These Thinking Critically sections make excellent points of departure for class discussions, since they contrast several points of view or theoretical interpretations about areas of social controversy. Critical Thinking Questions at the end of each chapter ask you to further apply such insights.

The Mass Media and Social Life

These sections stress how the mass media affect our behaviour and permeate our thinking. We consider how they even penetrate our consciousness to such a degree that they influence how we perceive our own bodies. As students consider this theme, they should begin to see the mass media in a different light, which should further stimulate their sociological imagination.

We have included a series of boxed features called Mass Media in Social Life to make it more prominent for students. Among these are an analysis of the influence of computer games on images of gender (Chapter 4), the worship of thinness—and how this affects our own body images (Chapter 5), how gender is portrayed on television in the popular cartoon, *The Simpsons* (Chapter 7), and stimulating greed to stimulate the economy (Chapter 11).

The Canadian Edition

The Third Canadian Edition is a substantial revision aimed at making content current, relevant, and of increased interest to Canadian students, particularly in the areas of feminism, postmodernism, social issues, gender coverage, and the mass media. By enhancing topic coverage in these areas while retaining the best features of the previous edition, it appeals to instructors who teach social action-oriented mainstream courses to university and college students.

Features

- A timeline covering Canadian and sociological events
- A thorough but concise text of 18 chapters
- Current perspectives: an emphasis on "inclusivity," i.e., including the diversity of Canadian experience, integrating feminist and postmodernist perspectives to address the needs of many users
- Challenging as well as informative content that draws on issues that are "in the news," such as employed mothers, violence against women, problems of poverty and homelessness
- The latest Canadian data, examples, studies, issues, and photos
- Enhanced pedagogy to make content more accessible and engaging

Chapter Highlights

Chapter 1 What Is Sociology?

- Careers in Sociology
- Recent trends in feminism such as postmodern feminism and queer theory
- Inclusion of macro and micro dimensions of postmodernism

Chapter 2 What Do Sociologists Do?

- qualitative interviews
- feminist methodology
- diagrammatic representation of the quantitative and qualitative research strategies

Chapter 3 Culture

- overview of values in Canada
- sex and morality among Canadians
- up-to-date survey results about Canadian attitudes to the September 11, 2001 terrorist attacks in the United States

Chapter 4 Socialization

- the role of the new technology in socialization; for example, gender messages in computer games and popular music
- socialization as an important key to exploring gender inequalities and serious issues such as violence against women
- generational issues for young Canadians, notably, the tendency for more young Canadians to remain in (or return to) their parental home in their twenties and early thirties and the growing tendency of young Canadians to participate in the paid labour force

Chapter 5 Social Structure and Social Interaction

- Postmodernism as both macro and micro sociological perspectives
- The application of feminist perspectives in both micro and macro sociological analysis

Chapter 6 Social Inequality: Global and National Perspectives

- the difference between wealth and income
- the average Canadian family with regard to relative wealth and earned income
- consequences of class in regard to physical and mental health and access to services

Chapter 7 Inequalities of Gender

- data and analysis on Canadian women's educational achievements and changes in the occupational structure
- women in sports
- males and masculinity, including the conflicted world of boys

Chapter 8 Inequalities of Race and Ethnicity

- the three major classifications in Canada: native peoples, the "Two Charter Groups," and immigrants
- multiracial feminism and inquality

Chapter 9 Inequalities of Age

- the latest trend in the research literature—to locate aging in the life course—while also integrating critical perspectives on aging, notably, aging from a feminist perspective
- making use of recent trends so that aging is discussed both in terms of traditional concerns such as social isolation and physical impairment, and also in terms of seniors' empowerment and a positive perspective on the aging process
- issues concerning seniors that are currently receiving considerable media attention; notably, generations in conflict, poverty amongst seniors, and elder abuse

Chapter 10 Bureaucracy and Formal Organizations

- volunteerism among Canadian seniors
- the Canadian Establishment
- scientific management and lean production

Chapter 11 The Economy: Money and Work

- corporate concentration in Canada
- work in Canadian society, for example the highest and lowest paying jobs in Canada

Chapter 12 Politics: Power and Authority

- the Canadian parliamentary system, including the evolution of the political party system
- the social basis of the Quiet Revolution in Quebec and the rise of the sovereignty movement in Quebec
- women, equity, and the right to vote
- feminist perspectives on gender reform, resistance, and rebellion

Chapter 13 The Family: Initiation into Society

- critical, feminist perspectives on family studies
- diversity in Canadian families—including racial and ethnic differences, one-parent families, childless families, blended families, gay and lesbian families
- up-to-date Canadian figures on age of first marriage, family structures, and fertility rates
- landmark national census figures on the division of domestic labour in Canada
- up-to-date Canadian data and analysis of high profile issues, such as family breakdown and family violence

Chapter 14 Education and Religion

- the educational attainment of Canadians and the relationship between education and social class
- school leavers and inequality of access to education.
- characteristics of religion in Canada
- female spirituality and feminist themes in Christianity and Judaism

Chapter 15 Medicine: Health and Illness in Canada

- health care in Canada
- the development of the sociology of health in Canada.
- feminist perspectives on sexism and the gendered experience of health and illness

Chapter 16 Social Deviance and Social Control

- youth unemployment and crime
- feminist theories and male violence against women
- feminist theories and issues of public policy in Canada

Chapter 17 Population, Urbanization, and the Environment

- feminism and the population debate
- Canadian immigration policy
- demographic profiles of Canada from 1851 to 1996

- urban patterns in Canada
- the environmental paradigm
- discussion of ecofeminism and the environment

Chapter 18 Social Movements and Social Change

- the pros and cons of trade unions in Canada
- feminist and postmodern theories of social change

In-Text Learning Aids

Sociology: A Down-to-Earth Approach includes a number of other pedagogical aids to help your learning. These include:

Chapter Outlines provide a useful preview of what's ahead.

Learning Outcomes summarize what the student will learn in each chapter.

Opening Vignettes pique interest and alert you to key topics. Many are based on James Henslin's own experiences.

Focus Questions at strategic points in the chapter draw attention to important aspects of the topics and issues being discussed.

In Sum appears at various spots in the chapter to help review important points before going on to new materials.

Interactive Chapter Summaries reinforce the important concepts and issues discussed in the chapter. A question-and-answer format enhances learning.

Critical Thinking Questions encourage students to apply the knowledge they have gained.

Key Terms: Learning new terms can be difficult. To help you, key terms are highlighted and introduced within a context that explains or illustrates them. They are listed together at the end of each chapter along with page numbers. To learn sociology, it is necessary to learn the sociologists' basic vocabulary, and these terms provide working definitions of the most important sociological concepts.

HandsOnSociology CD-ROM Icon: This icon connects relevant text material with material found on the *HandsOnSociology CD-ROM.*

Using the Internet: Because the Internet has become such a significant aspect of our culture, and because it contains such a vast amount of sociological information, at the end of each chapter a set of useful Weblinks helps you use the Internet to explore ideas from the chapter. Pay a visit to our Companion Website at **www.pearsoned.ca/henslin**.

Comprehensive Glossary: Complete and with clear definitions, it is designed to bring together the important concepts and terms introduced in the text, organizing them into a single, accessible format.

Supplements for the Student

Study Guide Plus. This guide provides learning objectives, key terms, self-tests, and glossaries. Students who need special language assistance will find a glossary for potentially confusing idioms and colloquialisms.

FREE Companion Website. An extensive Web site has been developed for this text at **www.pearsoned.ca/ henslin**. Features of the Web site include chapter outlines, learning objectives, key points, key terms; practice tests (interactive multiple-choice, true-false, fill-in and essay questions); essay development; Web destinations; and Resources on the Net.

HandsOnSociology CD-ROM with Interactive Exercises. This exciting new CD-ROM is provided free with every new text. The CD-ROM contains animated multimedia tutorials and a census update area. The tutorials take some of the most challenging topics in an introductory sociology course, such as Malthusian theory, and present them in an accessible manner using animations and audio clips, while the census update material provides analysis and explanation of statistics from the 2001 Census of Canada.

Research Navigator™. *Research Navigator*™ is the easiest way for students to start a research assignment or research paper and comes with access to three exclusive databases of credible and reliable source material including EBSCO's ContentSelect™ Academic Journal Database, New York Times Search by Subject Archive, and "Best of the Web" Link Library. iSearch guides combine a print guide to the academic use of the Internet with online access to the database. iSearch guides are available <u>free</u> when packaged with a new Pearson text. Contact your representative for bookstore order codes.

Supplements for the Instructor

Instructor's Manual. This useful teaching aid provides chapter summaries, learning objectives, and detailed lecture outlines, suggestions for introducing the chapter, discussion questions, class activities, student projects, and Internet activities.

Instructor Resource CD. This exciting new CD-ROM contains PowerPoint slides, lectures, text graphics (figures and tables), and the *Instructor's Manual* and *Test Item File* for the Third Canadian Edition.

Pearson Education Canada Custom Videos for Sociology (with User Guide). Carefully selected video clips complement the text and include guidelines on how to use them in the classroom. A synopsis of each video shows its relation to the chapter and dis-

cussion questions help students focus on how concepts and theories apply to their own lives.

PowerPoint Presentation. This *PowerPoint Presentation* provides graphic and text images for complete multimedia presentations in the classroom. The presentation is available through the password-protected Instructor Central Web site for downloading. Your sales representative will arrange access.

Test Item File. The *Test Item File* contains more than 2000 questions in multiple choice, true-false, short answer, and essay formats.

Pearson TestGen. The *Pearson TestGen* is a special computerized version of the *Test Item File* that enables instructors to view and edit the existing questions, add questions, generate tests, and print the tests in a variety of formats. Powerful search and sort functions make it easy to locate questions and arrange them in any order desired. TestGen also enables instructors to administer tests on a local area network, have the tests graded electronically, and have the results prepared in electronic or printed reports. Issued on a CD-ROM, the *Pearson TestGen* is compatible with Windows and Macintosh systems.

Transparencies. The *Allyn & Bacon Transparencies for Introductory Sociology* (ISBN 0-205-32616-1) package includes more than 125 colour acetates featuring illustrations both from the sixth U.S. edition of the text and from other sources.

The Sociology Digital Media Archive III. Want more electronic presentations in your classroom? This CD-ROM (ISBN 0-205-37548-0) contains hundreds of graphs, charts, and maps to supplement your lectures and illustrate key sociological concepts. It also includes 40 topical lectures with 20–50 PowerPoint slides each. If you have full multimedia capability, you can use the DMA's video segments and links to sociology Web sites.

Online Course Management. CourseCompass, powered by Blackboard and hosted nationally, is Allyn and Bacon's own course management system. CourseCompass helps you manage most aspects of teaching the introductory course. It features pre-loaded content for Henslin, Third Canadian Edition including the *Test Item File* and an e-book version of the text. For colleges and universities with WebCT™ and Blackboard™ licenses, special course management packages are available in these formats as well.

Acknowledgments

The gratifying response to earlier editions indicates that my efforts at making sociology down to earth have succeeded. The years that have gone into writing this text are a culmination of the many more years that preceded its writing—from graduate school to that equally demanding endeavor known as classroom teaching. No text, of course, comes solely from its author. Although I am responsible for the final words on the printed page, I have received excellent feedback from instructors and students who have used this book.

I am also indebted to the fine staff at Allyn and Bacon. I wish to thank Karen Hanson, who first saw the merits of this project and gave it strong support; Jeff Lasser, who has been especially helpful in consultation and who has continued the development of supplemental online sites; Hannah Rubenstein, who made vital contributions to earlier editions of the text on which this one is based; Judy Fiske for constantly hovering over the many details—and supporting my many suggestions; Kathy Smith for creative copy editing; Myrna Engler for ingenuity in photo research—and a willingness to "keep on looking"; and Dusty Friedman, who has done an outstanding job of overseeing both the routine and the urgent. It is difficult to heap too much praise on such capable people, whose efforts have coalesced with mine to produce this book. The students are the beneficiaries of our combined efforts, whom we constantly kept in mind as we prepared this edition.

I wish you the very best in your teaching. It is my sincere desire that *Sociology: A Down-to-Earth Approach* contributes to that success.

—JMH

First and foremost, I wish to acknowledge Arlene Mahood whose early intervention at Prentice Hall made it possible for all of us (Dan, Ann, and Norene) to participate in this project. I also wish to thank Ann and Norene for agreeing to be joint authors in the rewriting of this book; and Moira Russell, Documents Librarian of Brock University, for her invaluable technical assistance.

It is often the case that an author acknowledges the "invaluable contribution" made by his/her spouse or partner. In this case, no such salutary statement will be made. Instead, the revisions to the original text were written during long periods of solitary confinement in my basement office. On numerous occasions, I was "liberated" from my work by Rick, my spousal partner. These interruptions may have caused some at Pearson Education to fret, but they prevented me from becoming a morose recluse.

—DG

I wish to thank Dusky, Hermana, and Mayra for their loving support.

—AD

To my family members, John, Jennifer, and Gregory Barkans—thank you for your ongoing support and patience during the long hours I spent at my desk. Sorry I had to miss some important games. I would also like to thank Chris Eyles for sharing his story and Mark Thomas for his invaluable research assistance.

—NP

The Canadian authors would like to thank the following reviewers for their help in developing this edition of *Sociology*: Debra Langan, York University; Mary Knight, Durham College; Sue Ferderber, Algonquin College; Laurie Forbes, Lakehead University; René Gadacz, Okanagan University College; Tami M. Bereska, Grant MacEwan College.

James M. Henslin, who was born in Minnesota, graduated from high school and junior college in California and from college in Indiana. Awarded scholarships, he earned his Master's and doctorate in sociology at Washington University in St. Louis, Missouri. After this, he was awarded a postdoctoral fellowship from the National Institute of Mental Health, and spent a year studying how people adjust to the suicide of a family member. His primary interests in sociology are the sociology of everyday life, deviance, and international relations. Among his more than a dozen books is *Down to Earth Sociology: Introductory Readings* (Free Press), now in its eleventh edition. This book of readings reflects some of these sociological interests. He also has published widely in sociology journals, including *Social Problems* and *American Journal of Sociology*.

While a graduate student, Jim Henslin taught at the University of Missouri at St. Louis. After completing his doctorate, he joined the faculty at Southern Illinois University, Edwardsville, where he is Professor Emeritus of Sociology. He says, "I've always found the introductory course enjoyable to teach. I love to see students' faces light up when they first glimpse the sociological perspective and begin to see how society has become an essential part of how they view the world."

Henslin enjoys spending time with his wife, reading, and fishing. His two favourite activities are writing and travelling. He especially enjoys living in other cultures, for this brings him face to face with behaviours that he cannot take for granted, experiences that "make sociological principles come alive."

Dan Glenday was educated in Quebec (BA (Distinction) at Sir George Williams University, now Concordia University, and MA at McGill University) and Ontario (Ph.D. at Carleton University). He has taught at the University of Toronto, Queen's, Eastern Michigan University, and is now at Brock University where he is a full professor of Sociology and founder and director of the Centre for Labour Studies.

His most recent books include *Canadian Society: Meeting the Challenges of the Twenty-first Century*, Oxford; 2000 (with Ann Duffy) and *Good Jobs, Bad Jobs, No Jobs: The Transformation of Work in the 21st Century*, Harcourt Brace, 1997 (with Ann Duffy and Norene Pupo).

Ann Doris Duffy was educated in Ontario (BA, MA, Ph.D. at McMaster University). She is currently a full professor in the Department of Sociology at Brock University, where she is also actively involved in the Women's Studies and Labour Studies programs as well as in the Master's Program in Social Justice and Equity Studies. In 1995 she received an Ontario College and University Faculty Associations' Teaching Award. Her research interests include women's employment, family violence, and aging. She has co-authored and co-edited a number of books, including *Few Choices: Women, Work and Family; The Part-Time Paradox; Good Jobs, Bad Jobs, No Jobs: The Transformation of Work in the 21st Century; Family Violence: A Canadian Introduction;* and *Canadian Families: Diversity, Conflict and Change*. Professor Duffy is currently preparing a book on the experiences and concerns of women at mid-life to be published by Oxford University Press.

Norene Pupo, (Ph.D. at McMaster University, 1985), is an associate professor at the Department of Sociology, York University, as well as the director of the Centre for Research on Work and Society of the same university. Professor Pupo has researched and published in the areas of women and work, part-time employment, women and social policy, and unions and economic restructuring. She has co-authored *The Part-time Paradox* and *Few Choices: Women, Work and Family,* and has co-edited *Good Jobs, Bad Jobs, No Jobs: The Transformation of Work in the 21st Century*, and is currently working on a manuscript on Canadian unions' responses to economic restructuring. In addition, she has been an expert witness on issues related to employment insurance and has presented papers at numerous scholarly conferences and actively participates in graduate student supervision.

A Great Way to Learn and Instruct Online

The Pearson Education Canada Companion Website is easy to navigate and is organized to correspond to the chapters in this textbook. Whether you are a student in the classroom or a distance learner you will discover helpful resources for in-depth study and research that empower you in your quest for greater knowledge and maximize your potential for success in the course.

[www.pearsoned.ca/henslin]

Enter

PEARSON
Jump to...   http://www.pearsoned.ca/henslin   Home Search Help Profile

Companion
Website

Home >

Companion Website

Sociology: A Down-to-Earth Approach, Third Canadian Edition, by Henslin, Glenday, Duffy, and Pupo

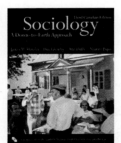

Student Resources

The modules in this section provide students with tools for learning course material. These modules include:

- PowerPoint Presentation
- Glossary
- Practice tests including multiple-choice, true and false, and essay questions
- Web Destinations
- Resources on the Net

In the quiz modules students can send answers to the grader and receive instant feedback on their progress through the Results Reporter. Coaching comments and references to the textbook may be available to ensure that students take advantage of all available resources to enhance their learning experience.

Instructor Resources

This module links directly to additional teaching tools. Downloadable PowerPoint Presentations, Electronic Transparencies, and an Instructor's Manual are just some of the materials that may be available in this section.

part one

What Is Sociology?

The Sociological Perspective

Learning Outcomes

After you have studied this chapter, you will be able to

■ describe what makes sociology different from the other social sciences

■ explain why sociology is a science

■ discuss the five major sociological theories

■ state what one can do with a degree in sociology

Even from the dim glow of the faded red-and-white exit sign, its light barely reaching the upper bunk, I could see that the sheet was filthy. Resigned to another night of fitful sleep, I reluctantly crawled into bed—tucking my clothes firmly around my body, like a protective cocoon.

The next morning, I joined the long line of disheveled men leaning against the chain-link fence. Their faces were as downcast as their clothes were dirty. Not a glimmer of hope among them.

No one spoke as the line slowly inched forward. When my turn came, I was handed a Styrofoam cup of coffee, some utensils, and a bowl of semiliquid that I couldn't identify. It didn't look like any food I had seen before. Nor did it taste like anything I had ever eaten.

My stomach fought the foul taste, every spoonful a battle. But I was determined. "I will experience what they experience," I kept telling myself. My stomach reluctantly gave in and accepted its morning nourishment.

The room was strangely silent. Hundreds of men were eating, but each was sunk deeply into his own private hell, his head aswim with disappointment, remorse, bitterness.

As I stared at the Styrofoam cup holding my solitary postbreakfast pleasure, I noticed what looked like teeth marks. I shrugged off the thought, telling myself that my long weeks as a sociological observer of the homeless were finally getting to me. "That must be some sort of crease from handling," I concluded.

I joined the silent ranks of men turning in their bowls and cups. When I saw the man behind the counter swishing out Styrofoam cups in a washtub of water, I began to feel sick at my stomach. I knew then that the jagged marks on my cup really had come from a previous mouth.

How much longer did this research have to last? I felt a deep longing to return to my family —to a welcome world of clean sheets, healthy food, and "normal" conversations.

Source: Based on the personal experiences of James Henslin.

The Sociological Perspective

Why were these men so silent? Why did they receive such despicable treatment? What was James Henslin doing in that homeless shelter?

Sociology offers a perspective, a view of the world. The sociological perspective (or imagination) opens a window onto unfamiliar worlds, and offers a fresh look at familiar worlds. In this text you will find yourself looking at your own world in a different light. As you look at other worlds, or your own, the sociological perspective casts a light that enables you to gain a new vision of social life. In fact, this is what many find appealing about sociology.

The sociological perspective has been a motivating force in the lives of all the authors of this text. Ever since we took our first introductory course in sociology, we have been enchanted by the perspective that sociology offers. We have thoroughly enjoyed both observing other groups and questioning our own assumptions about life. We sincerely hope that the same happens to you.

Seeing the Broader Social Context

The **sociological perspective** stresses the social contexts in which people live. It examines how these contexts influence their lives. At the centre of the sociological perspective is the question of how people are influenced by their **society**—a group of people who share a culture and a territory.

To find out why people do what they do, sociologists look at **social location**, where people are located in a particular society. Sociologists consider their jobs, income, education, gender, age, and ethnicity. Take, for example, how growing up identified with a group called females or a group called males affects our ideas of what we should attain in life. Growing up as a male or a female influences not only our aspirations, but also how we feel about ourselves and how we relate to others in dating and establishing households and at work.

Sociologist C. Wright Mills (1959) put it this way: "The sociological perspective enables us to grasp the connection between history and biography." Because of its history, each society has certain broad characteristics—such as its ideas of the proper roles of men and women. By biography, Mills referred to the individual's specific experiences in society. In short, people don't do what they do because of inherited characteristics, such as instincts. Rather, *external* influences—our experiences—become part of our thinking and motivations. The society in which we grow up, and our particular corners in that society, then, lie at the centre of our behaviour.

People around the globe take their particular world for granted. Something inside us Canadians tells us that hamburgers are delicious, small families attractive, and designer clothing desirable. Yet something inside some of the Sinai Desert Arab tribes used to tell them that warm, fresh camel's blood makes a fine drink and that everyone should have a large family and wear flowing robes (Murray, 1935; McCabe, Terrence, & Ellis, 1990). And that something certainly isn't an instinct. As sociologist Peter Berger (1963) phrased it, that "something" is "society within us."

Although obvious, this point frequently eludes us. We often think and talk about people's behaviour as though it were caused by their gender, their ethnicity, or some other factor transmitted by their genes. The sociological perspective helps us escape from this cramped personal view by exposing the broader social context that underlies human behaviour. It helps us see the links between what people do and the social settings that shape their behaviour.

The Growing Global Context

As is evident to all of us—from the labels on our clothing to the components in our cars—our world is becoming a global village. Communications used to be so slow that in the War of 1812 the Battle of New Orleans was fought two weeks after the United States and Great Britain had signed a peace treaty. The armed forces there had not yet heard that the war was over (Volti, 1995).

Today, in contrast, instantaneous communications connect us with remote areas of the globe, and economic agreements such as NAFTA (North American Free Trade Agreement) and membership in the WTO (World Trade Organization) connect Canada not only with the United States and Mexico but also with France, Japan, and Korea. At the same time that we are immersed in such global interconnections, however, we continue to occupy little corners of life, marked by differences in family background, religion, job, gender, ethnicity, and social class. In these corners, we learn distinctive ways of viewing the world.

One of the beautiful—and fascinating—aspects of sociology is that it is able to analyze both parts of our current reality: the changes that incorporate us into a global network and our unique experiences in our smaller corners of life. In this text, we shall examine both of these vital aspects of the contemporary experience.

Sociology and the Other Sciences

To satisfy their basic curiosities about the world around them, humans gradually developed **science**, systematic methods used to study the social and natural worlds, as well as the knowledge obtained by those methods. **Sociology**, the scientific study of society and human behaviour, is one of the sciences that modern civilization has developed.

A useful way of comparing these sciences—and of gaining a better understanding of sociology's place—is to first divide them into the natural and the social sciences.

The Natural Sciences

The **natural sciences** are the intellectual and academic disciplines designed to comprehend, explain, and predict the events in our natural environment. The natural sciences are divided into specialized fields of research according to subject matter, such as biology, geology, chemistry, and physics. These are further subdivided into even more highly specialized areas, with a further narrowing of content. Biology is divided into botany and zoology, geology into mineralogy and geomorphology, chemistry into its inorganic and organic branches, and physics into biophysics and quantum mechanics. Each area of investigation examines a particular "slice" of nature (Henslin, 1997b).

Sociologists have a particular interest in the social consequences of material goods, group structure, and belief systems—as well as how people communicate with one another.

The Social Sciences

People have not limited themselves to investigating nature. In the pursuit of a more adequate understanding of life, people have also developed fields of science that focus on the social world. These, the social sciences, examine human relationships. Just as the natural sciences attempt to objectively understand the world of nature, the **social sciences** attempt to objectively understand the social world. Just as the world of nature contains ordered (or lawful) relationships that are not obvious but must be discovered through theoretical advances and controlled observation, so the ordered relationships of the human or social world are not obvious. However, unlike nature, humans create and re-create their second nature—society. Fortunately, or unfortunately for some, there are several theoretical perspectives that help us understand ourselves, our society, and those countries and nations around us. Each theory is based on controlled and repeated observations.

Like the natural sciences, the social sciences are divided into specialized fields on the basis of their subject matter. These divisions are anthropology, economics, political science, psychology, and sociology.

Political Science. *Political science* focuses on politics and government. Political scientists study how people govern themselves: the various forms of government, their structures, and their relationships to other institutions of society. In studying a constitutional government, such as Canada's, political scientists also analyze voting behaviour.

Economics. *Economics* also concentrates on a single social institution. Economists study the production and distribution of the material goods and services of a society.

Anthropology. *Anthropology*, in which the primary focus has been preliterate or tribal peoples, is the sister discipline of sociology. The chief concern of anthropologists is to understand *culture*, a people's total way of life. Culture includes (1) the group's artifacts, such as its tools, art, and weapons; (2) the group's structure, that is, the hierarchy and other patterns that determine how its members interact with one another; (3) the group's ideas and values, especially how its belief system affects people's lives; and (4) the group's forms of communication, especially language.

Psychology. The focus of *psychology* is on processes that occur within the individual. Psychologists are primarily concerned with mental processes: intelligence, emotions, perception, and memory.

Sociology. *Sociology* has many similarities to the other social sciences. Like political scientists, sociologists also study how people govern one another, especially the impact of various forms of government on people's lives. Like economists, sociologists are concerned with what happens to the goods and services of a society—but sociologists place their focus on the social consequences of production and distribution. Like anthropologists, sociologists study culture; they have a particular interest in the social consequences of material goods, group structure, and belief systems, as well as in how people communicate with one another. Like psychologists, sociologists are also concerned with how people adjust to the difficulties of life.

Given these overall similarities, then, what distinguishes sociology from the other social sciences? Sociology is the study of human group life. Unlike political scientists and economists, sociologists do not concentrate on a single social institution. Unlike anthropologists, sociologists focus primarily on industrialized societies. And unlike psychologists, sociologists stress factors *external* to the individual to determine what influences people. The Down-to-Earth Sociology box on page 7 revisits an old fable about how members of different disciplines perceive the same subject matter.

The Goals of Science

The first goal of each science is to explain why something happens. The second goal is to make generalizations, that is, to go beyond the individual case and make statements that apply to a broader group or situation. For example, a sociologist wants to explain not only why Mary went to university or became a renowned astrophysicist but also why people with her characteristics are more likely than others to go to university or to become astrophysicists. To achieve generalizations, sociologists look for patterns, recurring characteristics, or events. The third scientific goal is to predict, to specify what will happen in the future in the light of current knowledge.

To attain these goals, scientists need to examine evidence with an open mind, in such a way that it can be checked by others. Secrecy, prejudice, and other biases, with their inherent closures, go against the grain of science.

Sociologists and other scientists also move beyond common sense, those ideas that prevail in a society that "everyone knows" are true. Just because "everyone" knows something is true does not make it so. "Everyone" can be mistaken, today, just as easily as when common sense dictated that the world was flat or that no human could ever walk on the moon. As sociologists examine people's assumptions about the world, their findings may contradict common-sense notions about social life. To test your own "common sense," read the Down-to-Earth Sociology box on page 8.

Sometimes the explorations of sociologists take them into nooks and crannies that people would prefer remain unexplored. For example, a sociologist might study how people make decisions to achieve material success or work for Greenpeace. Because sociologists want above all to understand social life, they cannot cease their studies because

Focus Question
Why is sociology different from the other social sciences?

It is said that in the recent past, five wise men and women, all blindfolded, were led to an elephant and asked to explain what they "saw." The first, a psychologist, feeling the top of the head, said, "This is the only thing that counts. All feeling and thinking take place inside here. To understand this beast, we need study only this."

The second, an anthropologist, tenderly touching the trunk and the tusks, said, "This is really primitive. I feel very comfortable here. Concentrate on these."

The third, a political scientist, feeling the gigantic ears, said, "This is the power centre. What goes in here controls the entire beast. Concentrate your studies here."

The fourth, an economist, feeling the mouth, said, "This is what counts. What goes in here is distributed throughout the body. Concentrate your studies on this."

Then came the sociologist (of course!), who, after feeling the entire body, said, "You can't understand the beast by concentrating on only one part. Each is but part of the whole. The head, the trunk and tusks, the ears, the mouth—all are important. But so are the parts of the beast that you haven't even mentioned. We must remove our blindfolds so we can see the larger picture. We have to see how everything works together to form the entire animal."

Pausing for emphasis, the sociologist added, "And we also need to understand how this creature interacts with similar creatures. How does their life in groups influence their behaviours?"

We wish we could conclude this fable by saying that the psychologist, the anthropologist, the political scientist, and the economist, dazzled on hearing the wisdom of the sociologist, amid gasps of wonderment, threw away their blindfolds and, joining together, began to examine the larger picture. But, alas and alack! On hearing this sage advice, all stubbornly bound their blindfolds even tighter to concentrate all the more on the single part. And if you listened very, very carefully you could even hear them mutter, "The top of the head is mine—stay away from it." "Don't touch the tusks." "Take your hand off the ears." "Stay away from the mouth—that's my area."

Focus Question
What makes sociology a science?

people feel uncomfortable. With all realms of human life considered legitimate avenues of exploration by sociologists, their findings sometimes challenge cherished ideas.

As they examine how groups operate, sociologists often confront prejudice and attempts to keep things secret. It seems that every organization, every group, nourishes a pet image that it presents to the public. Sociologists are interested in knowing what is really going on behind the scenes, however, so they peer beneath the surface to get past that sugar-coated image (Berger, 1963). This approach sometimes brings sociologists into conflict with people who feel threatened by that information—which is all part of the adventure, and risk, of being a sociologist.

The Development of Sociology

Just how did sociology begin? In some ways it is difficult to answer this question.

Simple assertions of truth—or observations mixed with magic or superstition or the stars—are not adequate. All science requires the development of theories that can be proved or disproved by systematic research.

This standard simplifies the question of the origin of sociology. Sociology is clearly a recent discipline. It emerged about the middle of the nineteenth century when European social observers began to use scientific methods to test their ideas. Three factors combined to lead to the development of sociology.

The first was the Industrial Revolution. By the middle of the nineteenth century, Europe was changing from agriculture to factory production. This brought social upheaval, violently changing people's lives. Masses of people were forced off the land. They moved to the cities, which greeted them with horrible working conditions: low pay; long, exhausting hours; dangerous work; foul smoke; and much noise. To survive, families had to permit their children to work in these same conditions, some of them even chained to factory machines to make certain they did not run away.

The French Revolution and, to a lesser extent, the American Revolution helped spark the idea that individuals possess inalienable rights. These ideas challenged the traditional order. Religion lost much of its force as the unfailing source of answers to life's perplexing questions. As a result, the political systems in Western countries slowly began to give way to more democratic forms.

Tradition provides a ready answer: "We do this because it has always been done this way." Traditional societies discourage original thinking. Since the answers are already provided, why search for explanations? Sweeping change, however, does the opposite: By upsetting the existing order, it encourages questioning and demands answers.

The second factor that stimulated the development of sociology was imperialism. The Europeans had been successful in conquering many parts of the world. Their new colonial empires, stretching from Asia through Africa to North America, exposed them to radically different

Some findings of sociology support common-sense understandings of social life, while others contradict them. Can you tell the difference? If you want to enjoy this quiz fully, complete *all* the questions before looking at the next box to check your answers.

1. **True/False** The earnings of Canadian women have just about caught up with those of Canadian men.

2. **True/False** When faced with natural disasters such as floods and earthquakes, people panic and social organization disintegrates.

3. **True/False** Revolutions are more likely to occur when conditions remain bad than when they are improving.

4. **True/False** Most people on welfare are lazy and looking for a handout. They could work if they wanted to.

5. **True/False** Compared with men, women touch each other more while they are talking to one another.

6. **True/False** Compared with women, men maintain more eye contact while they are conversing.

7. **True/False** The more available alcohol is (as measured by the number of places to purchase alcohol per 100 people), the more alcohol-related injuries and fatalities occur on Canadian highways.

8. **True/False** Couples who live together before they marry usually report higher satisfaction with their marriages than couples who do not live together before they marry.

9. **True/False** The reason that people discriminate against minorities is prejudice; unprejudiced people don't discriminate.

10. **True/False** Students in Japan are under such intense pressure to do well in school that their suicide rate is about double that of U.S. students.

---

cultures. Startled by these contrasting ways of life, they began to ask why cultures differed.

The third impetus for the development of sociology was the success of the natural sciences. Just at the time when the Industrial Revolution and imperialism moved people to question fundamental aspects of their social worlds, the **scientific method**—objective, systematic observations to test theories—used in chemistry and physics had begun to transform the world. Given these successes, it seemed logical to apply this method to the questions now being raised about the social world.

Auguste Comte

This idea of applying the scientific method to the social world, known as **positivism**, was apparently first proposed by Auguste Comte (1798–1857). With the French Revolution still fresh in his mind, Comte left the small, conservative town in which he had grown up and moved to Paris. The changes he himself experienced, combined with those France underwent in the revolution, led Comte to become interested in the twin problems of social order and social change (which he called "social statics" and "social dynamics"). What holds society together? he wondered. Why is there social order instead of anarchy or chaos? And once society becomes set on a particular course, what causes it to change? Why doesn't it always continue in the direction it began?

As he pondered these questions, Comte concluded that the right way to answer them was to apply the scientific method to social life. Just as it had revealed the law of grav-

Auguste Comte (1798–1857), who is identified as the founder of sociology, began to analyze the bases of the social order. Although he stressed that the scientific method should be applied to the study of society, he did not apply it himself.

ity, so, too, it would uncover the laws that underlie society. This new science, or positivism, not only would discover social principles but it would also apply them to social reform. Comte called this new science *sociology*—"the study of society" (from the Greek *logos*, "study of," and the Latin *socius*, companion, "being with others").

Comte had some ideas that today's sociologists find humorous. For example, as Comte saw matters, there were only six sciences—mathematics, physics, chemistry, biology, astronomy, and sociology—with sociology far superior to the others (Bogardus, 1929).

Comte insisted we cannot be dogmatic about social life, but that we must observe and classify human activities in order to uncover society's fundamental laws. Because he developed this idea and coined the term "sociology," Comte is often credited with being the founder of sociology.

1. **False.** Over the years, the income gap has narrowed, but only slightly. On average, full-time working women earn only about 65 percent of what full-time working men earn; this low figure is actually an improvement, for in the 1970s women's incomes averaged about 60 percent of men's.

2. **False.** Following such disasters, people develop *greater* cohesion, cooperation, and social organization to deal with the catastrophe.

3. **False.** Just the opposite is true. When conditions are consistently bad, people are more likely to be resigned to their fate. Rapid improvement causes their aspirations to outpace their circumstances, which can increase frustrations and foment revolution.

4. **False.** Most people on welfare are children, the old, the sick, the mentally and physically handicapped, or young mothers with few skills. Less than 2 percent meet the common stereotype of an able-bodied male. See also "Exploring Myths About the Poor" in Chapter 6.

5. **False.** Men touch each other more during conversations (Whyte, 1989).

6. **False.** Female speakers maintain considerably more eye contact (Henley, Hamilton, & Thorne, 1985).

7. **False.** In California, researchers compared the number of alcohol outlets per population with the alcohol-related highway injuries and fatalities. They found that counties in which alcohol is more readily available do not have more alcohol-related injuries and fatalities (Kohfeld & Leip, 1991).

8. **False.** The opposite is true. The reason, researchers suggest, is that many couples who marry after cohabiting are less committed to marriage in the first place—and a key to marital success is firm commitment to one another (Larson, 1988).

9. **False.** When racial discrimination was legal in the United States, sociologists found that due to business reasons and peer pressure some unprejudiced people did discriminate (LaPiere, 1934). For these same reasons, some prejudiced people do not discriminate, although they want to.

10. **False.** The suicide rate of Japanese students is about one-half that of U.S. students (Haynes & Chalker, 1997).

Karl Marx

Karl Marx (1818–1883) not only influenced sociology but also left his mark on world history. Marx's influence has been so great that even that staunch advocate of capitalism the *Wall Street Journal* has called him one of the three greatest modern thinkers (the other two being Sigmund Freud and Albert Einstein).

Like Comte, Marx thought that people should take active steps to change society. Marx, who came to England after being exiled from his native Germany for proposing revolution, believed that the engine of human history is **class conflict**. He said that the *bourgeoisie* (the controlling class of *capitalists*, those who own the means to produce wealth—capital, land, factories, and machines) are locked in inevitable conflict with the *proletariat* (the exploited class, the mass of workers who do not own the means of production). This bitter struggle can end only when members of the working class unite in revolution and throw off their chains of bondage. The result will be a classless society, one free of exploitation in which all individuals will work according to their abilities and receive according to their needs (Marx & Engels, 1848/1967).

Marxism is not the same as communism. Although Marx stood firmly behind revolution as the only way for the workers to gain control of society, he did not develop the

Karl Marx (1818–1883) believed that the roots of human misery lay in the exploitation of the proletariat, or propertyless working classes, by the capitalist class, those who own the means of production. Social change, in the form of the overthrow of the capitalists by the proletariat, was inevitable from Marx's perspective. Although Marx did not consider himself a sociologist, his ideas have profoundly influenced many in the discipline, particularly conflict theorists.

political system called *communism*, which was a later application of his ideas (and rapidly changing ones at that). Indeed, Marx himself felt disgusted when he heard debates about his insights into social life. After listening to some of the positions attributed to him, he even declared, "I am not a Marxist" (Dobriner, 1969b, p. 222; Gitlin, 1997, p. 89).

Unlike Comte, Marx did not think of himself as a sociologist. He spent years studying in the library of the British Museum in London, where he wrote widely on history, philosophy, and, of course, economics and political science. Because of his insights into the relationship between the social classes, especially the class struggle between the "haves" and the "have-nots," many sociologists today claim Marx as a significant early sociologist. He also introduced one of the major perspectives in sociology, conflict theory, which is discussed later in this chapter.

Emile Durkheim

Emile Durkheim (1858–1917) grew up in eastern France and was educated in both Germany and France. At the beginning of his academic career, sociology was viewed within the university as an offshoot of history and economics (Coser, 1977). Durkheim sought recognition for sociology as a separate academic discipline and did so when he received the first academic appointment in sociology in France at the University of Bordeaux in 1887.

Durkheim also had two other major goals (Giddens, 1978). One was to study how individual behaviour is shaped by social forces. In one of his most enduring studies, he compared the suicide rates of several European countries. Durkheim (1897/1966) found that each country's suicide rate was different, and that it remained remarkably stable year after year. He also found that different groups within a country had different suicide rates. For example, unmarried Protestant males killed themselves at a higher rate than Catholics, Jews, females, and the married. From his research findings, Durkheim drew the highly insightful conclusion that suicide is not simply a matter of individuals here and there deciding to take their lives for personal reasons. Instead, social factors underlie suicide.

Durkheim identified social integration, or the degree to which people are tied to their social group, as a key social factor in suicide. He concluded that people with weaker social ties are more likely to commit suicide. This factor, he said, explained why unmarried Protestant males have higher suicide rates. Durkheim argued that Protestantism encourages greater freedom of thought and action; males are more independent than females; and the unmarried lack the ties and responsibilities of marriage. In other words, because their social integration is weaker, people with these characteristics have fewer social ties that keep them from committing suicide.

Although strong social bonds help protect people from suicide, Durkheim noted that in some instances strong bonds encourage suicide. This type of suicide, which Durkheim termed altruistic suicide, can occur when some people kill themselves following the death of a dearly loved spouse. Their own feelings are so integrated with those of their mate that they prefer death rather than life without that person.

The French sociologist Emile Durkheim (1858–1917) contributed many important concepts to sociology. When he compared the suicide rates of several countries, he discovered an underlying social factor: People are more likely to commit suicide if their ties to others in their communities are weak. Durkheim's identification of the key role of social integration in social life remains central to sociology today.

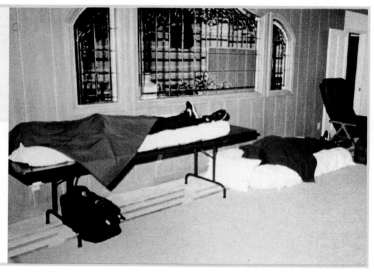

Sociologists analyze almost all aspects of human behaviour, from the joys of marriage and college graduation to the despair that leads to suicide—or, in some instances, the hope that leads to suicide. Hope was the unusual motivation for suicide for 39 members of the Heaven's Gate cult, who thought they would be beamed aboard a spaceship. Emile Durkheim was the first sociologist to study suicide, and his 1897 study remains a classic in sociology.

Emile Durkheim used the term anomie to refer to feeling rootless and normless, lacking a sense of intimate belonging—the opposite of what sociologists mean by community. Durkheim believed that modern societies produce feelings of isolation, much of which comes from the division of labour. In contrast, members of traditional societies, who work alongside family and neighbours and participate in similar activities, experience a high degree of social integration—the opposite of anomie.

A hundred years later, Durkheim's study is still quoted because of its scientific rigour and excellent theoretical interpretations. His research was so thorough that the principle he uncovered still applies: People who are less socially integrated have higher rates of suicide.

Durkheim's third concern was that social research be practical. He thought of sociologists as similar to physicians. They should diagnose causes of social ills and develop remedies for them. For example, Durkheim concluded that the new individualism or selfishness was a characteristic of capitalism and not pathological, but a normal, healthy expression of a changing society. When individualism goes too far, however, it then poses the danger of what Durkheim called anomie, a breaking down of the controlling influences of society. Under these conditions, people become detached from society and are left with too little moral guidance. This is dangerous, for their desires are no longer regulated by social norms (Coser, 1977). Durkheim

suggested that sociologists intervene: To prevent anomie, they should create new social groups to stand between the state and the family. These groups, such as professional associations, even trade unions, would help meet the need for a sense of belonging that the new, impersonal industrial society was eroding.

In sum, perhaps Durkheim's major contribution was his thorough sociological approach to understanding human behaviour. Suicide, for example, appears to be such an intensely individual act that psychologists should examine it, not sociologists. Yet, as Durkheim illustrated, if we look at suicide only in individualistic terms, we miss its *social* basis.

Max Weber

Max Weber (1864–1920) (Mahx VÁY-ber), a German sociologist and a contemporary of Durkheim's, also held professorships in the new academic discipline of sociology. With Durkheim and Marx, Weber is one of the most influential of all sociologists, and you shall come across his writings and theories in the coming chapters.

One of Weber's most important contributions to sociology was his study of the rise of capitalism. How, he asked, did capitalism come about—and why did some countries adopt it with enthusiasm, while others lagged behind? Weber suspected that religion might be the key. As background, we need to understand that the typical approach to life at this time was not to strive "to get ahead," but to work only enough to maintain one's usual way of life. Weber (1904/1958) theorized that the Roman Catholic belief system encouraged Catholics to cling to this traditional way of life, while the Protestant belief system, especially Calvinism, encouraged people to embrace change. For Catholics, the accumulation of material objects was taken as a sign of greed and discontent. Protestantism, in contrast, while also denouncing greed, pushed people to work hard, to save money, and to invest it. Thus, Weber theorized, Protestantism, which overtook Catholicism as the dominant religion in some European countries after the Reformation of the 1500s, led to the development of capitalism.

Max Weber (1864–1920) was another early sociologist who left a profound impression on sociology. He used cross-cultural and historical materials to determine how extensively social groups affect people's orientations to life.

To test his theory, Weber compared Roman Catholic and Protestant countries. In line with his theory, he found that the Protestant countries were much more likely to have embraced the new economic system called capitalism. This theory was controversial when Weber developed it, and it continues to be debated today (Dickson & McLachlan, 1989; Zou, 1994).

The Role of Values in Social Research

Weber also raised another issue that remains controversial among sociologists when he declared that sociology should be **value-free**. By this, he meant that a sociologist's values, personal beliefs about what is good or worthwhile in life and the way the world ought to be, should not affect his or her social research. Weber wanted **objectivity** to be the hallmark of sociological research.

Objectivity as an ideal is not a matter of debate in sociology. On the one hand, all sociologists agree that objectivity is a proper goal, in the sense that sociologists should not distort data to make them fit preconceived ideas or personal values, and that research reports must accurately reflect actual, not desired findings. On the other hand, it is equally clear that no sociologist can escape values. Like everyone else, sociologists are members of a particular society at a given point in history and are therefore infused with values of all sorts, and these inevitably play a role in their research. For example, values are part of the reason that one sociologist chooses to do research on the Mafia, while another turns a sociological eye on kindergarten students. To overcome the distortions that values can cause, sociologists stress **replication**, that is, the repetition of a study by other researchers to see how the results compare. If values have unwittingly influenced research findings, replication by other sociologists should uncover this problem and correct it.

Despite this consensus, however, the proper role of values in sociology is still hotly debated (Seubert, 1991; Hewa, 1993). The problem centres on the proper purposes and uses of sociological research. Regarding the *purpose* of sociology, some sociologists take the position that sociology's proper role is to advance understanding. Sociologists should gather data on any aspect of social life in which they are interested. Others are convinced that it is the responsibility of sociologists to explore harmful social arrangements of society—to investigate what causes poverty, crime, war, and other forms of human exploitation. (See Figure 1.1.)

Regarding the *uses* of sociology, those who say that understanding is sociology's proper goal take the position that the knowledge gained by social research belongs to the scientific community and to the world. Accordingly, it can be used by anyone for any purpose. In contrast, those who say that the goal of sociology should be to explore harmful social arrangements say that sociologists should use their studies to alleviate human suffering and make society a better place to live.

Although the debate about the proper role of values in social research can be more complicated than the argument summarized here—perhaps sociologist John Galliher (1991) best expresses the majority position:

> Some argue that social scientists, unlike politicians and religious leaders, should merely attempt to describe and explain the events of the world but should never make value judgments based on those observations. Yet a value-free and nonjudgmental social science has no place in a world that has experienced the Holocaust, in a world having had slavery, in a world with the ever-present threat of rape and other sexual assault, in a world with frequent, unpunished crimes in high places, including the production of products known by their manufacturers to cause death and injury as has been true of asbestos products and continues to be true of the cigarette industry, and in a world dying from environmental pollution by these same large multinational corporations.

Verstehen and Social Facts

Weber and *Verstehen*

Weber also stressed that one cannot understand human behaviour simply by looking at statistics. Those cold numbers may represent people's activities, he said, but they must be interpreted. To understand people, he said that we should use **Verstehen** (a German word meaning "to understand"). Perhaps the best translation of this term is "to grasp by insight." By emphasizing *Verstehen*, Weber meant we must pay attention to what are called **subjective meanings**, the ways in which people interpret their own behaviour. We can't understand what people do, Weber insisted, unless we look at how people themselves view and explain their own behaviour.

The Purposes of Social Research

To advance understanding of human behaviour **versus** To investigate harmful social arrangements

The Uses of Social Research

Can be used by anyone for any purpose **versus** Should be used to reform society

Figure 1.1 The Debate over Values

To better understand this term, let's return to the homeless in the opening vignette. Why were the men so silent?

Verstehen can help explain this. When Henslin interviewed men in the shelters (and, in other settings, homeless women), they revealed their despair. As someone who knows—at least on some level—what the human emotion of despair is, you are immediately able to apply it to their situation. You know that people in despair feel a sense of hopelessness. The future looks bleak, hardly worth plodding toward. Consequently, what is there worth talking about anyway? Who wants to hear another hard-luck story?

By applying *Verstehen*—your own understanding of what it means to be human and to face various situations in life—you gain an understanding of people's behaviour, in this case the silence, the lack of communication, among the homeless that Henslin observed.

Durkheim and Social Facts

In contrast to Weber's use of *Verstehen*, or subjective meanings, Durkheim stressed what he called **social facts**. By this term, he meant the patterns of behaviour that characterize a social group. (Note, however, that Weber did not disagree about the significance of social facts, for they are the basis of his conclusions about Protestantism and capitalism.) Examples of social facts in Canada include June to August being the most popular months for weddings, June 1 being the most popular date for moving in Montreal, suicide being higher among Native peoples and more recently Quebec teenagers, and more births occurring on Tuesdays to Thursdays than any other days of the week.

Durkheim said that we must use social facts to interpret social facts. In other words, each pattern reflects some underlying condition of society. People all over the country don't just coincidentally decide to do similar things, whether getting married or committing suicide. If that were the case, in some years middle-aged people would be the most likely to kill themselves, in other years, young people, and so on. Patterns that hold true year after year, however, indicate that as thousands and even millions of people make their individual decisions, they are responding to conditions in their society. It is the job of the sociologist, then, to uncover social facts and then to explain them through other social facts.

How Social Facts and *Verstehen* Fit Together

Social facts and *Verstehen* go hand in hand. As a member of Canadian society, you know that summer weddings are related to the end of the school year and how these months, now locked in tradition, common sentiment, and advertising, carry their own momentum. As for suicide among Canada's Native peoples or the recent burst in suicides among Quebec's teenagers, you probably already have a sense of the greater despair that many Native peoples or some teenagers feel.

Sexism in Early Sociology

Attitudes of the Time

As you may have noticed, all the sociologists we have discussed are males. In the 1800s, sex roles were rigidly defined, with women assigned the roles of wife and mother. In the classic German phrase, women were expected to devote themselves to the four K's: "*Kirche, Küchen, Kinder, und Kleider*" (church, cooking, children, and clothes). To dare to break out of this mold risked severe social disapproval.

Most women received no education beyond basic reading and writing, and many not even that. A few women from wealthy families, however, insisted on pursuing higher education, which at that time was reserved almost exclusively for men. A few even managed to study sociology, although deeply entrenched sexism in the university stopped them from obtaining advanced degrees or becoming professors. In line with the times, their own research was almost entirely ignored.

Harriet Martineau

A classic example is Harriet Martineau (1802–1876), who was born into a wealthy English family. When Martineau first began to analyze social life, she would hide her writing beneath her sewing when visitors arrived, for *writing was "masculine" and sewing "feminine"* (Gilman, 1911/1971, p. 88). Martineau persisted in her interests, however, and she eventually studied social life in both Great Britain and the United States. In 1837, two or three decades before Durkheim and Weber were born, Martineau published *Society in America*, in which she reported on this new nation's family customs, race and gender relations, politics, and religion. In spite of her insightful examination of U.S. life, which is still worth reading today, Martineau's research met the fate of the work of other early women sociologists and, until recently, was ignored. Instead, she is primarily known for translating Comte's ideas into English.

Interested in social reform, Harriet Martineau (1802–1876) turned to sociology, where she discovered the writings of Comte. An active advocate for the abolition of slavery, she travelled widely and wrote extensively.

Sociology in Canada and the United States

Sociology in Canada

The establishment of sociology as an academic discipline in Canada followed a different course from the history of sociology in the United States. Sociology in Canada is the story of the "Two Solitudes" (MacLennan, 1946), or Quebec sociology and sociology in the rest of Canada.

Quebec sociology owes its early development in the late nineteenth and early twentieth centuries to conservative European, mainly French, developments. The first known study of a Quebec family was done by a man named Gaudrée Boilleau who was a student of the conservative French sociologist Frédéric LePlay. The sociology of Leon Gérin, the preeminent Quebec sociologist of this period also was deeply influenced by LePlay's sociology of the family. Gérin spent his "career" as a sociologist studying the rural family in Quebec (Glenday & McMullan, 1970). Until the arrival of Everett Hughes at McGill University in the early 1940s, sociology in Quebec concentrated on the microcosm of the individual and the family in rural Quebec society.

Sociology in the rest of Canada was influenced by two cultures, the British and U.S. traditions. The British tradition was centred at the University of Toronto while the U.S. influence was positioned at McGill University. To most historians of sociology, Carl Dawson is credited with introducing sociology to an English-speaking audience in Canada. Even though sociology courses had been offered at the University of Manitoba and in the Maritimes, Canada's first major program in sociology began in 1922 at McGill University under Dawson's leadership. The University of Chicago program, the leading centre of U.S. sociology in this period, was the model Dawson used to establish sociology at McGill University. Dawson was instrumental in bringing several Chicago-trained sociologists to McGill University, of whom the most notable for the development of sociology in Quebec and Canada was Everett Hughes. Until the early 1960s in Canada, Dawson's own work on rural settlements

in western Canada helped to establish the prevalence of community studies in early Canadian sociology.

The centre for British influence in the field was the University of Toronto. Unlike France or the United States for that matter, the British tradition did not have room enough for a separate department of sociology among the social sciences. On the contrary, until the 1960s, when an independent department of sociology was established at the University of Toronto, any sociology done there was through the auspices of the Department of Political Economy. There was a healthy disdain for the U.S. brand of sociology among the sociologists, political economists, and historians that dominated the department. They criticized the U.S. treatment of sociology as little more than the study of social problems like poverty and delinquency and its lack of theoretical and research rigour.

For several years, the head of the Department of Political Economy was Harold A. Innis. Innis was an economic historian who created the model of economic development known as the staples theory of international trade. The staples approach was particularly useful when studying the development of Canada as a distinct economy and society. Like most colonies, Canada's usefulness, first to the French and later to Great Britain and the United States, was its abundance of natural resources. These staples such as furs, fish, timber, mineral ores, oil, and so on were, for the most part, exploited by "foreign" capitalists.

According to Innis, the staple exports created the conditions for the economic development of Canadian society. For example, companies involved in the building of Canada's railways and canals became necessary to ship the staple out of the country cheaply. In other words, the conditions for the development of a more complex Canadian society were dependent on the number and kind of staple exports.

Samuel D. Clark, working alongside Harold Innis, became the lead sociologist among the group of social scientists working at the University of Toronto during the late 1930s and 1940s. Clark built on the work of Innis by showing how the staples approach helped shape our society over the previous two-and-a-half centuries or from the French Regime to the mid-twentieth century. It is especially interesting to note that a distinctive sociology of English and French Canada was evolving during this period and is exemplified by the fact that S. D. Clark's important study entitled *The Social Development of Canada* (1942) was published at about the same time as Everett Hughes' *French Canada in Transition* (1943).

The 1960s, however, witnessed a large influx of American-trained sociologists in universities across Canada. Their interest in the discipline did not rest either in the development of a distinctive sociology in Canada or in community studies or historical sociology; it lay in a sociology of social problems and in rigorous research methods, especially statistical research methods. Therefore, by the early 1970s, if not earlier, the demise of a uniquely Canadian sociology led to the dominance of U.S. theories,

Wallace Clement (1952–present) is considered by many to be Canada's preeminent sociologist. His many books include *The Canadian Corporate Elite, Continental Corporate Power* and *Relations of Ruling: Class and Gender in Postindustrial Societies* (with John Myles). Wallace Clement is discussed in Chapters 8, 11, and 12.

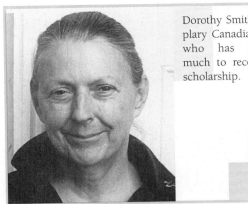

Dorothy Smith, an exemplary Canadian academic who has contributed much to recent feminist scholarship.

Jane Addams (1860–1935), a recipient of the Nobel Peace Prize, tirelessly worked on behalf of poor immigrants. With Ellen G. Starr, she founded Hull-House, a centre to help immigrants in Chicago. She was also a leader in women's rights (women's suffrage) and in the peace movement.

practices, and academics within Canada's departments of sociology.

This influence has been somewhat counterbalanced by the impact of feminism, and to a lesser extent postmodernism, in the sociology departments of most Canadian universities. Among the feminist scholars, Margrit Eichler and Dorothy Smith stand out as exceptional contributors to their field. Margrit Eichler (1988b) is widely recognized for her work in nonsexist research methods, while Dorothy Smith (1987, 1999) is best known for her studies of feminist theory, especially her work on the everyday world of women and men. We will have more to say about feminist theories in the next section of this chapter.

Sociology in the United States

The Beginnings. Sociology first took root at the University of Chicago and at Atlanta University, then an all-black school.

At first, sociology in the United States was dominated by the department at the University of Chicago, founded by Albion Small (1854–1926), who also founded the *American Journal of Sociology* and was its editor from 1895 to 1925. Members of this first sociology department whose ideas continue to influence today's sociologists include Robert E. Park (1864–1944), Ernest Burgess (1886–1966), and George Herbert Mead (1863–1931), who developed the symbolic interactionist perspective examined later.

Early Women Sociologists. The situation of women in North America was similar to that of European women, and their contributions to sociology met a similar fate. Denied faculty appointments in sociology, many turned to social activism (Young, 1995). Paradoxically, until recently, due to the fact that some worked with the poor as social activists because they couldn't get appointments as professors of sociology, they were regarded as social workers. (Young, 1995). Among the early women sociologists in the United States were Jane Addams, Emily Greene Balch, Isabel Eaton, Sophie Germain, Charlotte Perkins Gilman, Alice Hamilton, Florence Kelley, Elsie Clews Parsons, and Alice Paul.

Jane Addams. Jane Addams (1860–1935), who like Harriet Martineau came from a background of wealth and privilege, is the most outstanding example. On one of her many trips to Europe, she was impressed with work being done to help London's poor. From then on, Addams tirelessly worked for social justice (Addams, 1910/1981). She founded Hull-House in Chicago's notorious slums, which was open to people who needed refuge—to immigrants, the sick, the aged, the poor. At her invitation, sociologists from nearby University of Chicago were frequently visitors at Hull-House. Her efforts at social reform were so outstanding and so effective, that in 1931 she was a co-winner of the Nobel Peace Prize, the only sociologist to win this coveted award.

W. E. B. Du Bois. With the racism of this period, African-American professionals also found life difficult. The most notable example is provided by W. E. B. Du Bois (1868–1963) (Lemert, 1994).

Du Bois' writings, numbering almost 2000, preserve a picture of race relations of that period. Frustrated at the lack of improvement in race relations, he turned to social action. Along with Jane Addams, Florence Kelley, and others from Hull-House, he founded the National Association for the Advancement of Colored People, or NAACP (Deegan, 1988). Continuing to battle racism both as a sociologist and as a journalist, Du Bois eventually embraced revolutionary Marxism. Dismayed that so little improvement had been made in race relations, at the age of 93 he moved to Ghana, where he is buried (R. Stark, 1989).

Social Reform Versus Social Theory. Like Du Bois, many early North American sociologists combined the role of sociologist with that of social reformer. During the 1920s and 1930s, for example, Park and Burgess not only studied prostitution, crime, drug addiction, and juvenile delinquency, but they also offered suggestions for how to alleviate these social problems.

Then, during the 1940s, sociology in the United States took a different direction. In tandem with its rise as the dominant force in the capitalist world, the United States also faced the Communist threat to its influence in the developed European nations and less developed world. In this milieu of U.S. superiority, greater emphasis was given to gaining the academic respectability of sociology, and the focus shifted from social reform to social theory. Talcott Parsons (1902–1979), for example, developed abstract models of society known as structural functionalism that exerted great influence on sociology and political science. These models of how the parts of society harmoniously work together did little to stimulate social activism among its adherents either at home or abroad. Consequently, Parsons had his critics, among whom was C. Wright Mills.

C. Wright Mills (1916–1962), however, deplored the theoretical abstractions of this period, which he said were accompanied by empty research methods. Mills (1956) urged sociologists to get back to social reform, seeing imminent danger to freedom in the coalescing of interests of the power elite—the wealthy, the politicians, and the military. After his death, the turbulence in United States and Canadian societies in the 1960s and 1970s, fuelled by the Vietnam War, also shook the dominance of structural functionalism in U.S. sociology. As U.S. supremacy in the world weakened, interest in social activism revived, and Mills' ideas became popular among a new generation of sociologists.

Robert Merton (b. 1910) stressed the need for sociologists to develop **middle-range theories**, explanations that tie together many research findings but avoid sweeping generalizations that attempt to account for everything. Such theories, he claimed, are preferable because they can be tested. Merton (1949/1968), for example, explains how U.S. society's emphasis on attaining material wealth encourages crime and delinquency.

The Present. Since the 1970s, U.S. sociology has not been dominated by any one theoretical orientation or by any single concern. Some sociologists are content to study various aspects of social life, interpret their findings, and publish these findings in sociology journals. Others direct their research and publications toward social change and actively participate in community affairs to help bring about their vision of a more just society.

John Porter (1921–1979) was one of the leading sociologists in Canada during the post–World War II period. His book *The Vertical Mosaic* stands today as a benchmark in scholarship and practical public policies. John Porter is discussed in Chapters 8 and 12.

George Herbert Mead (1863–1931) is one of the founders of symbolic interactionism, a major theoretical perspective in sociology. He taught at the University of Chicago, where his lectures were very popular. Though he wrote very little, after his death his students compiled his lectures into an influential book, *Mind, Self, and Society*.

What Do Sociologists in Canada and the United States Do Now?

During the past two decades, the activities of sociologists have broadened. Once, just about the only occupation open to a graduate in sociology was teaching. Although most sociologists still enter teaching, the government has now become their second-largest source of employment. Many other sociologists work for private firms in management and planning positions. Still others work in criminology and demography, in social work, and as counsellors. Sociologists put their training to use in such diverse efforts as tracking the spread of AIDS and helping teenage prostitutes escape from pimps. Later we shall look more closely at some of these careers open to sociology graduates.

At this point, however, let's concentrate on a better understanding of sociological theory.

Theoretical Perspectives in Sociology

Facts never interpret themselves. In everyday life, we interpret what we observe by using common sense, placing any particular observation or "fact" into a framework of more-or-less-related ideas. Sociologists place their observations into a conceptual framework called a theory. A **theory** is a general statement about how some parts of the world fit together and how they work. It is an explanation of how two or more facts are related to one another. By providing a framework in which to fit observations, each theory interprets reality in a distinct way.

Sociologists in Canada use five major theories: symbolic interactionism, functional analysis, conflict theory, feminist theories, and postmodernism. Let's first examine the main elements of these theories. (See Table 1.1.)

Symbolic Interactionism

We can trace the origins of symbolic interactionism to the Scottish moral philosophers of the eighteenth century, who

Table 1.1 Major Theoretical Perspectives in Sociology

Perspective	Usual Level of Analysis	Focus of Analysis	Key Terms
Symbolic interactionism	Microsociological—examines small-scale patterns of social interaction	Face-to-face interaction; how people use symbols to create social life	Symbols Interaction Meanings Definitions
Functional analysis (also called functionalism and structural functionalism)	Macrosociological—examines large-scale patterns of society	Relationships among the parts of society; how these parts are functional (have beneficial consequences) or dysfunctional (have negative consequences)	Structure Functions (manifest and latent) Dysfunctions Equilibrium
Conflict theory	Macrosociological—examines large-scale patterns of society	The struggle for scarce resources by groups in a society; how dominant elites use power to control the less powerful	Inequality Power Conflict Competition Exploitation
Feminist theories	Microsociological—individual and small groups Macrosociological—patterns of patriarchy	Individuals in face-to-face interaction, predominately women	Patriarchy Sexism Gender Division of Labour
Postmodernism	Macrosociological—language and culture Microsociological—describing the socially constructed postmodern individual	Texts—documents, film, photos, video, collages, and so on	Signifier Text/Intertext Indeterminacy Angst or anxiety Polymorphous/Androgynous

Sources: Various, including *The Condition of Postmodernity* (p. 43), by David Harvey, 1989, Oxford, England; New York: Blackwell.

noted that people evaluate their own conduct by comparing themselves with others (Stryker, 1990). In the United States, a long line of thinkers added to this analysis, including the pioneering psychologist William James (1842–1910) and the educator John Dewey (1859–1952), who analyzed how people use symbols to encapsulate their experiences. This theoretical perspective was brought into sociology by sociologists Charles Horton Cooley (1864–1929), William I. Thomas (1863–1947), and George Herbert Mead (1863–1931). Cooley's and Mead's analyses of how symbols lie at the basis of the self-concept are discussed in Chapter 4.

Symbolic interactionists view *symbols*—things to which we attach meaning—as the basis of social life. First, without symbols our social relations would be limited to the animal level, for we would have no mechanism for perceiving others in terms of relationships (aunts and uncles, employers and teachers, and so on). Strange as it may seem, only because we have symbols can we have aunts and uncles, for it is these symbols that define for us what such relationships entail. Second, without symbols we could not coordinate our actions with others; we would be unable to make plans for a future date, time, and place. Unable to specify times, materials, sizes, or goals, we could not build bridges and highways. Without symbols, there would be no books, movies, or musical instruments. We would have no schools or hospitals, no government, no religion. In short, as symbolic interactionists point out, symbols make social

life possible. Third, even the self is a symbol, for it consists of the ideas that we have about who we are. And it is a changing symbol, for as we interact with others, we constantly adjust our views of the self on the basis of how we interpret the reactions of others.

Symbolic interactionists analyze how our behaviours depend on how we define ourselves and others. For example, if you think of someone as an aunt or uncle, you behave in certain ways, but if you think of that person as a boyfriend or girlfriend, you behave quite differently. It is as though everyday life is a stage on which we perform, switching roles to suit our changing audiences. Symbolic interactionists primarily examine face-to-face interaction, looking at how people work out their relationships and make sense out of life and their place in it.

In Sum

Symbolic interactionists explain change in terms of the changing symbols (or meanings) associated with particular institutions such as the family, the economy, or the university.

Functional Analysis

The central idea of **functional analysis** is that society is a whole unit, made up of interrelated parts that work together. Functional analysis, also known as *functionalism* and *structural functionalism*, is rooted in the origins of sociology (J. H. Turner, 1978). Auguste Comte, for example, viewed society as a kind of living organism. Just as a biological organism has interrelated tissues and organs that function together, he wrote, so does society. Like an organism, if society is to function smoothly, its various parts must work in harmony.

Emile Durkheim also saw society as composed of many parts, each with its own function. When all the parts of society fulfill their functions, society is in a "normal" state. If they do not fulfill their functions, society is in an "abnormal" or "pathological" state. To understand society, then, functionalists say that we need to look at both *structure* (how the parts of a society fit together to make the whole) and *function* (what each part does; how it contributes to society).

Continuing the work of Durkheim, Robert K. Merton used the term *functions* to refer to the beneficial consequences of people's actions that help keep a group (society, social system) in equilibrium. In contrast, *dysfunctions* are consequences that undermine a system's equilibrium.

Functions can be either manifest or latent. If an action is intended to help some part of a system, it is a *manifest function*. For example, suppose the tuition at your university is doubled. The intention, or manifest function, of such a sharp increase may be to raise faculty salaries and thus recruit better faculty. Merton pointed out that people's actions can also have *latent functions*, unintended consequences that help a system adapt. Let us suppose that the tuition increase worked, that the quality of the faculty improved so greatly that your university gained a national reputation overnight. As a result, it was flooded with new applicants and was able to expand both its programs and its campus. The expansion contributed to the stability of your university, but it was unintended. Therefore, it is a *latent* function of the tuition increase.

Sometimes human actions have the opposite effect, of course, and hurt the system. Because such consequences are usually unintended, Merton called them *latent dysfunctions*. Let's assume that doubling the tuition backfired, that half the student body couldn't afford the increase and dropped out. With this loss of income, the university had to reduce salaries. It managed to get through one year this way, but then folded. Because these results were not intended and actually harmed the social system (in this case the university), they represent a *latent* dysfunction of the tuition increase.

In Sum

From the perspective of functional analysis, then, the group is a functioning whole, with each part related to the whole. Whenever we examine a smaller part, we need to look for its functions and dysfunctions to see how it is related to the larger unit. This basic approach can be applied to any social group, whether an entire society, a university or community college, or even a group as small as a family.

Conflict Theory

Conflict theory provides a third perspective on social life. Karl Marx, who developed conflict theory, witnessed the Industrial Revolution that transformed Europe. He saw that peasants who had left the land to seek work in urbanizing areas had to work at wages that barely provided enough to eat. The average worker died at age 30, the wealthy at age 50 (Edgerton, 1992, p. 87). Shocked by this suffering and exploitation, Marx began to analyze society and history. As he did so, he developed **conflict theory**, concluding that the key to all human history is class struggle. In each society, some small group controls the means of production and exploits those who do not. In industrialized societies the struggle is between the **bourgeoisie**, the small group of capitalists who own the means to produce wealth, and the **proletariat**, the mass of workers exploited by the bourgeoisie. The capitalists also control politics, so that when workers rebel the capitalists are able to call on the power of the state to control them (R. C. Angell, 1965).

When Marx made his observations, capitalism was in its infancy and workers were at the mercy of their employers. Workers had none of what we take for granted today—the right to strike (for unionized workers only!), minimum wages, eight-hour days, coffee breaks, five-day work weeks, paid vacations and holidays, medical benefits, sick leave, unemployment compensation, government pension plans. His analysis reminds us that these benefits came not from generous hearts, but from workers who forced concessions from their employers.

Some current conflict sociologists use conflict theory in a much broader sense. Ralf Dahrendorf (b. 1929) sees conflict as inherent in all relations that have authority. He points out that **authority**, or power that people consider legitimate, runs through all layers of society—whether small groups, a community, or the entire society. People in positions of authority try to enforce conformity, which in turn creates resentment and resistance. The result is a constant struggle throughout society to determine who has authority over what (J. H. Turner, 1978).

Another sociologist, Lewis Coser (b. 1913), pointed out that conflict is especially likely to develop among people who are in close relationships. Such people are connected by a network of responsibilities, power, and rewards, and to change something can easily upset arrangements that they have so carefully worked out. Consequently, we can think even of close relationships as a balancing act—of maintaining and reworking a particular distribution of responsibilities, power, and rewards.

In Sum

Unlike the functionalists who view society as a harmonious whole, with its parts working together, conflict theorists see society as composed of groups fiercely competing for scarce resources. Although alliances or cooperation may prevail on the surface, beneath that surface is a struggle for power. Marx focused on struggles between the bourgeoisie and proletariat, but today's conflict theorists have expanded this perspective to include smaller groups and even basic relationships.

Feminist Theories

There are, at present, at least three variants of **feminist theories**: Marxist feminist theories, liberal feminist theories, and non-Marxist radical feminist theories. While they differ in important ways from one another, especially when it comes to their programs for changing society, there are common characteristics in all three approaches that we will outline after briefly describing each approach.

Marxist Feminist Theories. Marxist feminists share the view of Marxists that class or economic position is more fundamental than gender in explaining inequality. Like Marxists, they point out that women's position in society is a consequence of the property relations of capitalism. Women and men are viewed as property but the exploitation of women includes their (that is, women's) objectification into roles that serve men's interests. Marxist feminists argue for revolutionary changes to the world economy as the only way to change both men's and women's exploitation by capitalism. In the present, Marxist feminists see one of their goals as combating the "false consciousness" of women's groups like Real Women that dignify women's traditional role of subservience and exploitation in the traditional family.

Liberal Feminist Theories. Liberal feminists claim that legal restraints and customs are at the root of the subservience of women in society. While they recognize the importance of class, ethnicity, or race as valid criteria in understanding women's inequality, our society's laws and customs stand out as the principal factors. Liberal feminism has been criticized for being exclusionary—that is, preserving middle-class women's position in the university and society at the expense of women of colour or women from poor backgrounds. Moreover, liberal feminists have created controversy for their opposition to prostitution and soft pornography as exploiting women. On the other hand, liberal feminists have been at the forefront of changes in the existing structure that have gone far toward breaking down prejudices—changes such as pay equity, provision of day care for working mothers, better education for women, and opening women to nontraditional career options.

Radical Feminist Theories. Radical feminists believe that it is patriarchy that oppresses women. Patriarchy is a system characterized by power, dominance, hierarchy, and competition. It is not just patriarchy's legal structures and gender socialization that must be changed, but our society's cultural and social institutions that keep women "in their place" must be transformed. Institutions such as the traditional family, the church, and the academy are often singled out for restructuring. While many radical feminists point to women's biology (e.g., child-bearing) as a critical factor in women's relegation to second-class status, they endeavour to support those initiatives that can overcome whatever socially constructed negative effects biology may have on both men and women.

Recent developments in feminist theory include lesbian feminism, men's feminism, and postmodern feminism and queer theory. Lesbian feminism argues that if heterosexual relationships are exploitative by nature, then why bother with men at all? Men's feminism applies feminist theories to the study of men and masculinity. The last theory undermines previous theories of two sexes, two sexualities, and two genders and offers a view of equality based on many sexes, sexualities, and genders that cannot be played against one another (Lorber, 1998, p. 174).

What Is Common to Feminist Theories. These three feminist theories have a number of things in common.

1. Biological sex differences do account for gender, but gender differences are not simply derived from biology; they are products of complex social, historical, and cultural factors. The degree of weight given to biology differs fundamentally across feminist theories.

2. The gender division of labour is a hierarchical one with men's roles dominant and better rewarded and women's roles subordinate and less valued.

3. The present relations between the genders are so intertwined that changes in one area affect many other aspects of social life. Social issues such as abortion or homosexuality are related to the "liberation of women" from the structures of subservience in society. Gains or losses in the struggle for women's rights influence the direction of change in other areas such as gay and lesbian rights.

4. The knowledge of science, ourselves, and our society has been largely derived from men's experiences because they have held positions of authority in the social order. The contributions made by women and other "invisible" minorities must be uncovered and communicated for all to benefit.

In Sum

The three variants of feminist theories are Marxist, liberal, and non-Marxist radical theories. All feminist theories share, at least, four characteristics.

Postmodernism

Postmodernism as a theory of present-day society could be viewed as the logical rejection of modernity. Modernity, as a sociological concept, was first employed by Max Weber to describe the society or civilization that had emerged from feudalism, otherwise known as industrial capitalism. It was the society based on the Enlightenment ideas of reason, science, and human freedom. Modernity meant that change was possible because human beings could act collectively. In addition, science could make society materially better while reason promised to unmask the prejudices based on religious or other irrational ideas and lead all humanity toward personal freedom.

C. Wright Mills was the first sociologist to argue that we were living in a "post-modern period," by which he meant a society where "the ideas of freedom and of reason have become moot; that increased rationality may not be assumed to make for increased freedom" (1959, p. 167). The advent of two world wars, nuclear weapons, the Cold War, and so on meant that personal freedom was not automatically linked to progress, reason, science, capitalism, or communism. Quite the contrary. Many horrors were and continue to be visited on humanity in the name of reason, science, capitalism, and communism.

Postmodernism as a theory of present-day society recognizes diversity where modernity pushes sameness. Postmodernism points out cultural and sexual differences while modernity looks for uniformity of tastes and habit. In other words, the culturally homogenized world promised by modernity with the spread of capitalism into every nook and cranny in the world economy is being replaced by a view of present-day society as a cultural collage where people can live in their own cultural and social space as free individuals. For some analysts, such as David Harvey (1989), postmodernity as a theory of cultural diversity in an otherwise culturally homogeneous capitalism is made possible because of the computer revolution. That is, computers and other forms of information technologies contribute to the economic viability of small businesses based in culturally distinct communities. Instead of assimilation or marginalization, information technologies make cultural diversity a reality. In an age of conglomerates, it is increasingly possible to make a comfortable living working at home or starting a small business because the Internet is the link to a world market.

The computer is also the site where image is dominant and the symbol supreme. Jean Baudrillard (1983, 1993, 1995), the French theorist of postmodernity, is noted for his developmental theory of the symbol. In preindustrial societies, the sign or symbol is passed on in festivals, rites of passage, and rituals. It is often expressed as an exchange of gifts. In industrial capitalist societies, societies Baudrillard labels productionist, the sign or symbol and the real world are the same. Statements such as "clothes make the man/woman"

Focus Question
What are the five major sociological theories?

capture the essence of the link between the real world and the sign. That is, the clothes someone wears confer her/his status in society. The rise of postmodernity breaks the link between the symbol and the real world. The symbol becomes autonomous. In the world of cyberspace, for example, the image is more important than the real world. Young people today play video games in a world of their own choosing. For postmodern theorists, the world of the image, symbol, and sign is steadily encroaching on modernity.

The major criticisms of postmodernism centre on its preoccupation with surface reality. In addition, postmodern theorists often view society as a closed system in which events happen but seemingly under no one's control. Why some images, symbols, or signs are more important than others are questions of power and are usually left unasked by postmodern theorists.

In Sum

Postmodernism emphasizes cultural diversity in opposition to the cultural homogeneity promised by modernism. Information and communications technologies help make cultural diversity a reality. A conception of power, however, is absent from most postmodern theories.

Levels of Analysis: Macro and Micro

A major difference between the theoretical orientations described above is their level of analysis. Functionalists and conflict theorists focus on **macro-level analysis**; that is, they examine large-scale patterns of society. In contrast, symbolic interactionists and postmodernists usually focus on **micro-level analysis**; that is, they analyze **social interaction**, or what people do when they are in one another's presence. Feminist theories cross both levels of analysis. (See Table 1.1.)

Let's return to the example of homelessness to make this distinction between micro and macro levels clearer. In studying the homeless, symbolic interactionists would focus on what they say and what they do. They would analyze what homeless people do when they are in shelters and on the streets, focusing especially on their communications, both their talk and their **nonverbal interaction** (how they communicate by gestures, silence, use of space, and so on). The observations made earlier about the despair and silence of the homeless, for example, would be areas of interest to symbolic interactionists. Unfortunately, postmodern theories have difficulty grasping the reality of homelessness.

This micro level, however, would not interest functionalists and conflict theorists. They would focus instead on the macro level. Functionalists would examine how changes in the parts of society are related to homelessness. They might look at how changing relationships in the family (smaller, more divorce) and economic conditions (higher rents, inflation, fewer unskilled jobs, loss of jobs overseas) cause homelessness among people who are unable to find jobs and do not have a family to fall back on. For their part, conflict theorists would stress the struggle between social classes, especially how the policies of the wealthy push certain groups into unemployment and homelessness. That, they would point out, accounts for the disproportionate number of Native Canadians who are homeless. Feminists would be capable of understanding the plight of homeless women and of explaining the disproportionate number of homeless women with children as due to patriarchy.

Putting the Theoretical Perspectives Together

Which theoretical perspective should we use to study human behaviour? Which level of analysis is the correct one? As you have seen, these theoretical perspectives provide different and often sharply contrasting pictures of our world. No theory or level of analysis encompasses all of reality. Rather, by focusing on different features of social life, each provides a distinctive interpretation. Consequently, it is necessary to use all five theoretical lenses to analyze human behaviour. By putting the contributions of each perspective and level of analysis together, we gain a more comprehensive picture of social life.

Applied and Clinical Sociology

Sociologists Paul Lazarsfeld and Jeffrey Reitz (1989) divide sociology into three phases. First, as we have already seen, when sociology began it was indistinguishable from attempts to reform society. The primary concern of early sociologists was to make the world a better place. The purpose of analyzing social conditions was to use the information to improve social life.

During the second phase, the goal of sociologists was to establish sociology as a respected field of knowledge. To this end, sociologists sought to develop **pure** or **basic sociology**, that is, research and theory aimed at making discoveries about life in human groups.

During the third phase, there has been an attempt to merge sociological knowledge and practical work. Dissatisfied with "knowledge for the sake of knowledge," many sociologists use their sociological skills to bring about social change, to make a difference in social life.

Efforts to blend sociological knowledge and practical results are known as applied sociology. This term refers to the use of sociology to solve problems. Today's applied sociologists work in a variety of settings, recommending practical changes that can be implemented. A business firm may hire a sociologist to solve a problem in the workplace; sociologists may do research for government commissions or agencies investigating social problems such as pornography, crime, violence, or environmental pollution. The following Down-to-Earth Sociology box describes careers in sociology: what sociologists do with their degrees.

Some applied sociologists not only make recommendations for change on the basis of their findings but also themselves become directly involved in solving problems. This type of applied sociology is called clinical sociology. Clinical sociologists who work in industrial settings may try to improve working conditions to reduce job turnover. Others work with drug addicts and ex-convicts, while still others are family counsellors who try to change basic relationships between a husband and wife or between children and their parents. Figure 1.2 below contrasts basic and applied sociology.

The Future.   Sociology has now come full circle. From an initial concern with improving society, sociologists switched their focus to developing abstract knowledge; now, sociologists are again seeking ways to apply their findings. These efforts have gained momentum in recent years.

Figure 1.2   Comparing Basic and Applied Sociology

Source: Based on "Basic and Applied Sociological Work: Divergence, Convergence, or Peaceful Co-existence?" by J. R. De Martini, 1982, *The Journal of Applied Behavioral Science, 18*, 2, pp. 203–215.

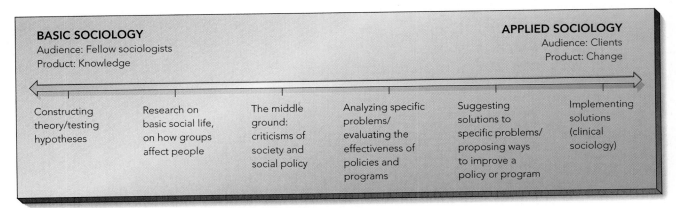

Contrary to popular misconceptions, sociologists put their skills to work in a variety of settings, not just the university. They can be found counselling children, consulting for business and/or governments, or improving relationships in the workplace.

Pat Eklund graduated with an undergraduate degree in sociology and several hundred hours of "time" spent as an intern in a local correctional facility. According to Pat, "That time and those experiences in prison [as an intern] have been the springboard for my career in criminal justice. I was being prepared in ways that I did not know or understand at the time, and I am even now still discovering the lessons I learned then." Underlying these experiences was his sociological perspective. "I am always looking for why things happen, what is underneath someone's behaviour. This is where my degree in sociology has proved invaluable," concluded Pat.

Mary's interest in sociology included writing a departmental honours thesis. Her real interest was theory. While practical applications were interesting, abstract modelling was her passion. Because of circumstances, Mary was unable to pursue her studies in graduate school. Instead, Mary worked at a variety of jobs including a stint as a computer consultant for businesses implementing new hardware and software. In one of her jobs, Mary often conducted training seminars on abuse for police officers. She used her sociological training to develop models for identifying abusive situations. Without

the models, the police officers may not have recognized the potential for abuse in certain situations. According to Mary, "The problem is that people experience so much of their lives as a kind of chaos. They don't really see how the things that happen are interconnected. ... If you are going to have a real effect on people's lives, then making them aware of the larger picture—the model—is a real gift."

Dave Blume and Bob Chase both earned undergraduate degrees in business. In addition, both Dave and Bob earned second degrees in sociology. According to Dave, "the competition in the business world can be very intense. You have to give potential employers a reason to select you over other candidates who have the same business degree that you do. Sociology, with its focus on groups, organizations, and human interaction is a natural complement to business. And, it is a degree which is increasingly well received in the business world." Bob adds, "People socialized in some of the older business patterns are just so inflexible that they cannot adjust. Sociology prepares you for understanding change and anticipating it. The degree is a real asset."

According to Donna, the choice was sociology because in many ways it defined her own life. "It seemed that my whole life has been spent working with people in groups—my work, my children, and their groups like girl scouts and other organizations. I have had to learn how to get along with many different people in many different settings.

Further, sociology helped me gain a better understanding, a better feel for what was happening." Donna focused her course work on the sociology of politics and power and started her own career as an independent consultant and trainer. Donna's consultations and training sessions often take the form of workshops that cover a wide variety of topics, including cultural diversity, women, and organizational creativity and power and organization. According to Donna, "My sociology comes into play in two ways. First, the discipline helps me see and understand the issue, such as cultural diversity in the workplace. Secondly, the discipline also helps me administer the seminars themselves. You have to carefully manage them or you'll lose the participants." One way to run such seminars is to involve the participants in the phenomenon being examined. The objective is to demonstrate that the real task is to effectively communicate what they want others to do.

For some, this kind of work seems a bit difficult to grasp. To help you understand, Donna suggests an aggressive career development approach. She observes that "Workshops like I do are an ongoing part of the business and government worlds. Simply because you haven't heard about them doesn't mean that they do not exist. You could begin by contacting convention bureaus and getting a list of industry conventions or annual meetings which have come to your city. Then ask for convention schedules. You will see for yourself the array of workshops offered. But this is only a start."

Many departments of sociology offer courses in specialties such as gender and workplace issues, criminology and family violence, and even internships, at both the graduate and the undergraduate level.

These changes are taking sociology closer to its starting point. They provide renewed contact with the discipline's roots, promising to invigorate it as they challenge us to

grasp a vision of what society can become—and what sociology's role can be in that process of change.

Focus Question
What can you do with a degree in sociology?

Summary and Review

THE SOCIOLOGICAL PERSPECTIVE

What is the sociological perspective?

The **sociological perspective** stresses that people's social experiences—the groups to which they belong and their particular experiences within these groups—underlie their behaviour. C. Wright Mills referred to this as the intersection of biography (the individual) and history (social factors acting on the individual). pp. 4–5.

SOCIOLOGY AND THE OTHER SCIENCES

What is science, and where does sociology fit in?

Science is the application of systematic methods to obtain knowledge and the knowledge obtained by those methods. The sciences are divided into the **natural sciences**, which seek to comprehend, explain, and predict events in the natural environment, and the **social sciences**, which seek to understand the social world objectively by means of controlled and repeated observations. **Sociology** is the scientific study of society and human behaviour. pp. 5–7.

THE DEVELOPMENT OF SOCIOLOGY

When did sociology first appear as a separate discipline, and what factors contributed to its emergence?

Sociology emerged as a separate discipline in the mid-1800s in western Europe, during the onset of the Industrial Revolution. Industrialization brought social changes so sweeping they affected all aspects of human existence—where people lived, the nature of their work, and interpersonal relationships. Early sociologists who focused on these social changes include Auguste Comte, Herbert Spencer, Karl Marx, Harriet Martineau, Emile Durkheim, and Max Weber. pp. 7–12.

THE ROLE OF VALUES IN SOCIAL RESEARCH

Should the purpose of social research be only to advance human understanding or also to reform society?

All sociologists concur that social research should be **value-free**: The researcher's personal beliefs should be set aside in order to permit objective findings. But sociologists do not agree on the uses and purposes of social research. Some believe its purpose should be only to advance understanding of human behaviour; others, that its goal should be to reform harmful social arrangements. p. 12.

VERSTEHEN AND SOCIAL FACTS

How do sociologists use *Verstehen* and social facts to investigate human behaviour?

According to Weber, to understand why people act as they do, sociologists must try to put themselves in their shoes. He used the German term **Verstehen**, "to grasp by insight," to describe this essentially subjective approach. Emile Durkheim, although not denying the importance of **Verstehen**, emphasized the importance of uncovering "social facts" that influence human actions. **Social facts** are objective social conditions that influence how people behave. Contemporary sociology uses both approaches to understand human behaviour. pp. 12–13.

SEXISM IN EARLY SOCIOLOGY

What was the position of women in early sociology?

Only a few wealthy women received advanced education, and their writings were largely ignored. Harriet Martineau is an example. p. 13.

SOCIOLOGY IN CANADA AND THE UNITED STATES

What universities in Canada were considered the historical centres of sociology in English-speaking Canada? How were they different?

McGill University and the University of Toronto. Sociology in English-speaking Canada was influenced by two traditions, the British and the U.S. The British influence was centred at the University of Toronto while the U.S. influence was positioned at McGill University.

Canada's first major program in sociology began in 1922 at McGill University under the leadership of Carl Dawson. The University of Chicago program, the leading centre of U.S. sociology in this period, was the model that Dawson used to establish sociology at McGill University. Dawson was instrumental in bringing several Chicago-trained sociologists to McGill University.

The British tradition treated sociology as a branch of political economy. Unlike McGill, an independent department of sociology was not established until the 1960s at the University of Toronto. Any sociology done there was under the auspices of the Department of Political Economy. There was a healthy disdain for the U.S. brand of sociology among the sociologists, political economists, and historians that dominated the Department of Political Economy. Their main criticisms were that U.S. sociology was practised as little more than the study of social problems such as poverty and delinquency and that it lacked theoretical and research rigour. pp. 14–15.

How recently were academic departments of sociology established in the United States?

The earliest departments of sociology were established around the turn of the twentieth century at the universities of Chicago and Atlanta. During the 1940s sociology was dominated by the University of Chicago. Today, no single university or theoretical perspective dominates. In sociology's early years, the contributions of women and minorities were largely ignored. pp. 15–16.

THEORETICAL PERSPECTIVES IN SOCIOLOGY

What is a theory?

A **theory** is a general statement about how sets of facts are related to one another. A theory provides a conceptual framework within which facts are interpreted. p. 16.

What are the major theoretical perspectives?

Sociologists make use of five primary theoretical frameworks to interpret social life. **Symbolic interactionism** examines how people use symbols to develop and share their views of the world. Symbolic interactionists usually focus at the micro level—on small-scale patterns of human interaction. **Functional analysis**, in contrast, focuses on the macro level—on large-scale patterns of society. Functional theorists stress that a social system is made up of various parts. When working properly, each part contributes to the stability of the whole, fulfilling a function that contributes to a system's equilibrium. **Conflict theory** also focuses on large-scale patterns of society. Conflict theorists stress that society is composed of competing groups struggling for scarce resources.

Feminist theories focus on both the microsociological and the macrosociological. All three variants of feminist theory stress the importance of biology and patriarchy in determining the position not only of women but also of men in society.

Postmodernism concentrates on both the macrosociological and the microsociological levels of analysis. Postmodern theorists are concerned with analyzing the importance of symbols, signs, and images in present-day society.

Because no single theory encompasses all of reality, at different times sociologists may use any or all of the five theoretical lenses. With each perspective focusing on certain features of social life and each providing its own interpretation, their combined insights yield a more comprehensive picture of social life. pp. 16–21.

APPLIED AND CLINICAL SOCIOLOGY

What is the difference between pure (or basic) and applied sociology?

Pure (or basic) sociology is sociological research whose only purpose is to make discoveries. In contrast, **applied sociology** is the use of sociology to solve problems. pp. 21–22.

Critical Thinking Questions

1. Do all sociological theories believe in progress, that is, the view that all societies advance from one stage of civilization into the next?

2. Why is symbolic interactionism regarded as microsociology?

3. Why are functionalism and conflict theories considered to be macrosociology?

4. Why are feminist theories and postmodernism both microsociological and macrosociological?

Key Terms

Weblinks

All URLs listed are current as of the printing of this book. URLs are often changed. Please check our Web site **www.abacon.com/ henslin** for updates.

Current Research in Social Psychology (CRISP)

www.uiowa.edu/~grpproc/crisp/crisp.html
A peer-reviewed electronic journal covering all aspects of social psychology, sponsored by the Center for the Study of Group Processes at the University of Iowa.

Sociology Internet Resources

www.wcsu.ctstateu.edu/socialsci/socres.html
A useful page put up by the Department of Social Sciences at Western Connecticut State University.

World Wide Sociology Webring

www.geocities.com/~wwsociology/
The World Wide Sociology Webring (WWSW) is being developed for the purpose of bringing together sociologists and students from colleges around the world to develop a community where the free exchange of ideas may take place. This webring will also be a place where published and unpublished papers can be made available to all doing research in the social sciences.

Dead Sociologists' Society

raven.jmu.edu/~ridenelr/DSS/DEADSOC.HTML
A list of the various theorists, some biographical information, and a summary of their work can be found in the Dead Sociologists' Index, or you can look at the Dead Sociologists Gallery or the original chart from which the site was developed.

Chapter 2

What Do Sociologists Do?

Learning Outcomes

After you have studied this chapter, you will be able to

■ understand the seven research methods and their limitations

■ make use of the Data Liberation Initiative in Canada

■ read a table

■ describe the eight steps in a research model

■ discuss the ethical issues surrounding research on human participants

Carol Meredith and Barclay McKie were 19 years old when they first met in Wetaskiwin, Alberta. On July 28, 1997, barely a month after she had decided to leave her husband and almost 10 years after they had first met, Meredith was sexually assaulted by McKie and dropped off at a shopping mall near Calgary, Alberta. A warrant was issued for McKie's arrest and Meredith fled 600 kilometres northeast of Calgary to her sister's home in Cold Lake, Alberta. According to RCMP officials, on July 31, 1997, less than nine hours after she had arrived at her sister's home, a man beat her sleeping brother almost to death, attacked her, and dragged her by the hair for half a block down one of Cold Lake's busiest streets and shoved her into a brown van. Six days later, she was found dead from a blow to the head in a van some 30 kilometres from the town. The day before Meredith was discovered, Barclay McKie was arrested as he tried to buy a bus ticket to Edmonton, Alberta.

At approximately the same time as Meredith's murder, Statistics Canada released its 1996 crime figures that showed incidents of wife assaults *declined* by 18 percent since 1993 from 14 420 to 11 829 cases per year! Feminists and public-shelter advocates across Canada dismissed these figures since they could show that women and children seeking shelter in Alberta alone rose 10 percent between 1996 and 1997 to 20 139 individuals. What could account for these disparities in the research findings? First of all, Statistics Canada relied on *reported* cases to the police while workers in the field relied on reporting who came into their front doors asking for help!

Second, the decline in reported cases may be due to a much-applauded public policy of zero tolerance for domestic violence. How? Under zero tolerance, many women who might previously have called the police to defuse a domestic incident may no longer call for fear of losing their men to prison, thereby leaving them in a potentially escalating dangerous environment.

This case illustrates the importance of understanding the nature of social problems and how they are researched. It also helps us understand the relationship between what Robert K. Merton called the manifest function of a good public policy (in this case zero tolerance of family violence) and its unintended consequences of helping to make matters more difficult to understand and cope with.

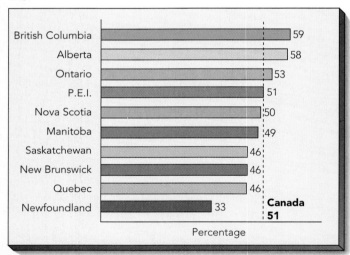

Figure 2.1 Proportion of Women 18 Years and Over Who Have Ever Experienced Violence, by Province, 1993

Source: Statistics Canada, *The Daily*, November 18, 1993, p. 2 (Catalogue no. 11-001).

What Is a Valid Sociological Topic?

Sociologists do research on just about every area of human behaviour. On the macro level, they study such broad matters as the military (Moscos & Butler, 1997), race relations (W. J. Wilson, 1996), and multinational corporations (Kanter, Wiersema, & Kao, 1997). On the micro level, they study such individualistic matters as pelvic examinations (Henslin & Biggs, 1997), how people interact on street corners (W. H. Whyte, 1989, 1997), and even how people decorate their homes at Christmas (Caplow, 1991). In fact, no human behaviour is ineligible for sociological scrutiny whether that behaviour is routine or unusual, respectable or reprehensible.

Because sociologists find all human behaviour to be valid research topics, their research runs from the unusual to the routines of everyday life. On the macro level, they study how voting patterns are related to religion, and on the micro level they study tattoo contests, such as this one in New York's East Village. Their analyses range from such intensely individual acts as suicide to such broad-scale social change as the globalization of capitalism.

What happened to Meredith and McKie, as an example of family violence, is also a valid topic of sociological research.

Common Sense and the Need for Sociological Research

First, why do we need sociological research? Why can't we simply depend on common sense, on "what everyone knows"? As noted in Chapter 1, common-sense ideas may or may not be true. Common sense, for example, tells us that spouse or partner abuse has a significant impact on the lives of the people who are abused.

Although this particular idea is accurate, we need research to test such ideas, because not all common-sense ideas are true. After all, common sense also tells us that if a woman is abused she will pack up and leave her husband or same-sex partner. There are also cases of partner abuse in gay male relationships. Research, however, shows that the reality of abuse is much more complicated than this. Some women and gay men do leave right away, some even after the first incident of abuse. For a variety of reasons, however—the main one being that they feel trapped and don't see viable alternatives—some put up with abuse for years.

This brings us to the need for sociological research, for we may want to *know* why some put up with abuse, while others don't. Or we may want to know something entirely different, such as why men are more likely to be the abusers. Or why some people abuse persons they say they love.

Regardless of the particular question that we want to answer, the point is that we need to move beyond guesswork and common sense. We want to know what really is going on. And for accurate answers, we need sociological research. Let's look, then, at how sociologists do their research.

Seven Research Methods

Sociologists use seven **research methods (or "research designs")** for gathering data: surveys, participant observation, qualitative interviews, secondary analysis, documents, unobtrusive measures, and experiments. To understand these strategies better, note how the choice of method depends on the questions we want to answer.

Surveys

Let's assume that your resources allow you to investigate alcohol and marijuana consumption only on your university campus. Let's also suppose that your university enrollment is large, making it impractical to **survey**, or question, all the students who are enrolled. Now you must select a **sample**, individuals from among your target **population**. The total number of students in your university campus is your population, the target group that you will study. How you choose a sample is critical, for the choice will affect the results of your study.

For example, to survey only first-year students, or only seniors, or only those enrolled in introductory sociology courses, or only those in advanced physics classes, will produce unrepresentative results in each case. To be able to generalize your findings to the entire campus, you must

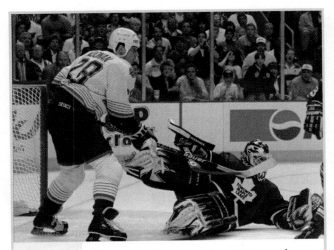

Because sociologists usually cannot interview or observe every member of a group they wish to study, such as the spectators at this hockey game, they must select a sample that will let them generalize to the entire group. The text explains how samples are selected.

select a sample that is representative of the campus (called a "representative sample"). What kind of sample will allow you to do this?

The best is a **random sample**. This does not mean that you stand on some campus corner and ask questions of whomever happens to walk by. *In a random sample, everyone in the population has the same chance of being included in the study.* In this case, since the population is every student enrolled in your university, every student, whether first-year or graduate, must have the same chance of being included in the sample. Equally, such factors as a woman's or man's major, her or his age, her or his grade point average, or whether she or he is a day or evening or full- or part-time student must not affect her or his chance of becoming part of your study.

How can you get a random sample in this case? First you need a list of all the students enrolled in your university. You then would assign a number to each name on the list and, using a table of random numbers, determine which of these students become part of your sample. (Random numbers are available on tables in statistics books, or they can be generated by a computer.)

Because a random sample represents the population—in this case all students enrolled at your university—you can generalize your findings to all the students on your campus, whether they were included in the sample or not.

Asking Neutral Questions. After you have decided on your population and sample, your next task is to make certain that your questions are not biased to one point of view or another. Your questions must allow **respondents**, people who respond to a survey, to select appropriate responses to standardized questions. Otherwise, you will end up with biased answers—and biased findings are worthless. For example, if you were to ask "Don't you agree that men who beat their wives deserve a prison sentence?" You would be tilting the answers toward agreement with the position being stated. For other examples of flawed research, see the Down-to-Earth Sociology box.

Questionnaires and Structured Interviews. Sociologists not only strive to ask questions that reduce bias, they also are concerned about how **questionnaires**, the list of questions to be asked, are administered (carried out). There

are two basic techniques. The first is for the respondents to fill them out. Such **self-administered questionnaires** allow a large number of people to be sampled at relatively low cost.

In some cases, **structured interviews** work best. Both self-administered questionnaires and this type of **interview** use **closed-ended questions**. Each question is followed by a list of possible answers. The advantages of structured interviews are that they are faster to administer, and they make it easier for the answers to be *coded* (categorized) so that they can be fed into a computer for analysis. The primary disadvantage is that the answers listed on the questionnaire may not include all the respondent's opinions.

Establishing Rapport. Research on spousal abuse also brings up another significant issue.

It is vital for researchers to establish **rapport** ("ruh-pour"), a feeling of trust, with their respondents, especially when it comes to sensitive topics, areas about which people feel embarrassment, shame, or other deep emotions. Here, feminist researchers in Canada have been in the forefront of not only including women in research but also of recognizing the importance of validating the experiences of women. Nowhere is this more important than in the study of violence against women.

We know that once rapport is gained (e.g., by first asking nonsensitive questions), participants will talk to researchers about personal, sensitive issues.

Participant Observation (Fieldwork)

In the second method, **participant observation (or fieldwork)**, the researcher participates in a research setting while *observing and recording* what is happening in that setting. Simply put, the researcher spends a great deal of time with the people he or she is studying. The research with the homeless mentioned in Chapter 1 is an example of participant observation. Moreover, this was a well-established research technique in the early history of sociology in Canada, when it was also known as "community studies." Sociologists and anthropologists would spend at least a year in a small town or village in rural Quebec, Ontario, the Maritimes, or the Prairies, to help them understand the social, religious, political, and economic life of its inhabitants. Examples include Everett Hughes'

Improperly worded questionnaires steer respondents toward answers that are not their own, producing invalid results.

The methods of science lend themselves to distortion, misrepresentation, and downright fraud. Consider the following information. Surveys show that:

- Canadians overwhelmingly prefer Toyotas to Chryslers.
- Canadians overwhelmingly prefer Chryslers to Toyotas.
- Canadians think cloth diapers are better for the environment than disposable diapers.
- Canadians think disposable diapers are better for the environment than cloth diapers.

Obviously such opposites cannot all be true. In fact, both sets of findings are misrepresentations, although each does come from surveys conducted by so-called independent researchers. These researchers, however, are biased, not independent and objective.

It turns out that some consumer researchers load the dice. Hired by firms that have a vested interest in the outcome of the research, they deliver the results their clients are looking for. There are four basic ways of loading the dice.

1. *Choose a biased sample.* For example, if you want to "prove" that Canadians prefer Chryslers to Toyotas, you can interview unemployed union workers who trace their job loss to Japanese imports. The answer is fairly predictable. You'll get what you're looking for.

2. *Ask biased questions.* Even if you choose an unbiased sample, you can phrase questions in such a way that most people see only one logical choice. When the disposable diaper industry paid for the survey cited above, the researchers used an excellent sample, but they worded the question this way: "It is estimated that disposable diapers account for less than 2 percent of the trash in today's landfills. In contrast, beverage containers, third-class mail, and yard waste are estimated to account for about 21 percent. Given this, in your opinion, would it be fair to ban disposable diapers?"

Is it surprising, then, that 84 percent of the respondents said that disposable diapers are better for the environment than cloth diapers? Similarly, when the cloth diaper industry funded a survey, they worded the questions to load the dice in their favour.

3. *List biased choices.* Another way to load the dice is to use closed-ended questions that push people into the answers you want.

Consider this finding: "Canadian university students overwhelmingly prefer Levis 501 to the jeans of any competitor." Sound good? Before you rush out to buy Levis, what if you found out that the researchers asked a sample of Canadian university students which jeans would be the most popular in the coming

year, and their list of choices included no other jeans but Levis 501!

4. *Discard undesirable results.* Researchers can simply keep silent about results they find embarrassing, or they can even continue to survey samples until they find one that matches what they are looking for.

As stressed in this chapter, research must be objective if it is to be scientific. Obviously, none of the preceding results qualifies. The underlying problem with the research cited here—and with so many surveys bandied about in the media as fact—is that survey research has become big business. Simply put, the vast sums of money offered by corporations have gone unquestioned by many university administrators and academics in Canada. In an era of "tight money," with the proportion of government financing of higher education shrinking, the potential exists for the commercial corruption of social research.

The beginning of the corruption is subtle. Paul Light, dean at the University of Minnesota, put it this way: "A funder will never come to an academic and say, "I want you to produce finding X, and here's a million dollars to do it." Rather, the subtext is that if the researchers produce the right finding, more work—and funding—will come their way." He adds, "Once you're on that treadmill, it's hard to get off."

Sources: Crossen (1991); Goleman (1993); F. Barnes (1995).

---

study of the effects of industrialization on traditional institutions in Drummondville, Quebec, otherwise known as *French Canada in Transition* (1943) or John Jackson's study of high schools and language conflicts in Tecumsch, Ontario (1975).

How else other than by participant observation could it be possible to study the subcultures of motorcycle gangs, jazz or blues musicians, or professional wrestlers?

Let's suppose that your interest is in learning about the world of professional wrestling. You may want to know if the time spent becoming a professional wrestler has changed the hopes, dreams, and self-concept of the men or women you will come to know, or how it has affected their relationship

with their wives or husbands or partners. Participant observation can provide detailed insight into such questions.

Now let's go back to your campus again, assuming for the sake of argument that it has a crisis intervention centre. Such a setting lends itself to participant observation, for here you may be able to observe victims of spousal abuse from the time they first report the attack to their later participation in counselling. With good rapport, you may even be able to spend time with victims outside this setting, observing other aspects of their lives. Their statements and other behaviours may be the keys that help you unlock answers about how the abuse has affected their lives.

As you may have noticed, the researchers' personal characteristics are extremely important in fieldwork. Their sex, age, race, personality, and even height and weight can affect their findings (Henslin, 1990a). For example, could a male researcher conduct participant observation of women who have been beaten by their husbands? Given the sensitivity of the topic, which specifically centres on the emotions of women who have been brutally victimized by men, female sociologists are better suited to conduct such research, and thus more likely to achieve valid results.

To some sociologists, participant observers face a problem with **generalizability**, being able to apply their findings to larger populations. But this is a concern only for those who are wedded to a nineteenth-century view of science. These kinds of qualitative research are rich in description and often provide significant theoretical insight.

> **Focus Question**
> What is the difference between description and explanation?

Qualitative Interviews

A **qualitative or field interview**, commonly referred to as a **structured conversation**, is the third research method. A researcher begins by creating an interview schedule or a list

Because spouse abuse occurs between two people who have an intimate relationship, it often is considered a private matter. When the abuse occurs in public, however, it usually is seen in a different light.

of questions about the topic he or she wants information about. For example, when interviewing gay and lesbian couples about their different lifestyles, both parties, the researcher and the person being interviewed, should view themselves as participants in a conversation, but it is a conversation in which the interviewer is asking most of the questions and a conversation that is tape-recorded. However, the interviewer should not be afraid to stop and listen when his or her participant strays from the guided tour of questions. A qualitative or field interview is like taking a journey into a new territory, seeking help from those who know what to see and do, what to look for, and what not to expect along the route.

In recent years, a number of feminist writers have argued for a distinctive feminist methodology (Eichler, 1988b; Stanley & Wise, 1993). The traditional claim made by most social scientists has been that knowledge about our social world can be objective. However, for many feminist sociologists, sexist value judgments explicitly or implicitly inform the choice of study, how to investigate the particular social phenomena, and even the interpretation of the findings.

Many feminist methodologists reject the emphasis on control and the impersonal nature of scientific research. Instead, they are drawn to qualitative techniques, principally interviewing. (However, this does not mean that it is not possible to do quantitative research in a feminist way.) The interview, from a feminist point of view, is like a conversation between equals. This is made possible when the interviewer and interviewee are the same gender. This technique allows women to "tell their own stories" in a manner that is non-exploitative and descriptive. Increasingly, sociologists in Canada, both men and women, acknowledge the contributions made by feminist sociologists in qualitative research interviewing.

Secondary Analysis

In **secondary analysis**, a fourth research method, researchers analyze data that have already been collected by others. For example, if you were to examine the original data from a study of women who have been abused by their husbands, you would be doing secondary analysis. Ordinarily, researchers prefer to gather their own data, but lack of resources, especially money and time, may make that impossible.

Data Liberation Initiative (DLI). To avoid many of the methodological pitfalls of secondary analysis such as the reliability and validity of the data collected, many researchers in Canada use Statistics Canada databases for their secondary analysis. The recent creation of the Data Liberation Initiative (DLI) has proved invaluable to students and faculty alike. The DLI, begun in 1996 as a five-year pilot project, is a cooperative effort of the Social Sciences and Humanities Research Council of Canada, the Canadian Association of Research Libraries (CARL), the

Canadian Association of Public Data Users (CAPDU), the Canadian Association of Small University Libraries (CASUL), Statistics Canada, and other government departments. It provides low-cost access to Statistics Canada data files and databases to Canadian university faculty, staff, and students for teaching and research purposes. Each university pays an annual fee and is able to download files and make them available for use by students and faculty.

DLI databases include, among others, the Canadian Socioeconomic Information Management System (CANSIM), the National Population Health Survey, and the Labour Force Historical Review. Other available social surveys from the DLI include the General Social Survey (GSS), Canada's Alcohol and Other Drugs Survey, Family Expenditure and Food Expenditure Surveys (FAMEX and FOODEX), School Leavers Survey, and many more. These are large files of anonymous survey responses that can be analyzed using statistical packages.

A complete list of available files is given on the DLI Web site along with a list of DLI contacts at each Canadian university and other background information on the program (see the Weblinks section of this chapter).

Documents

The use of **documents** (written sources) is a fifth research method sociologists use. To investigate social life, they examine such diverse sources as books, newspapers, diaries, bank records, police reports, household accounts, immigration files, and records kept by various organizations.

To study spouse abuse, you might examine police reports and court records. These could reveal what proportion of complaints result in arrest and what proportion of the men arrested are charged, convicted, or even put on probation. If these were your questions, police statistics would be valuable (see recent *Juristat* data).

Sociologists use different methods of research to answer different questions. Among the methods that could be used to study spouse abuse is to examine the documents kept by shelters for battered women, which log the number of calls and visits made by victims.

A crisis intervention centre, for example, might have records that provide other key information. Diaries kept by abuse victims would yield important insights into their reactions, especially how their attitudes and relationships with others change over time.

Of course, we are presenting an ideal situation in which the crisis intervention centre is opening its arms to you. In actual fact, the centre might not cooperate at all, neither asking victims to keep diaries nor even letting you near its records. Access, then, is another problem researchers face constantly. Simply put, you can't study a topic unless you can get access to it.

Unobtrusive Measures

The sixth method is **unobtrusive measures**, observing the behaviour of people who do not know they are being studied. For example, social researchers studied the level of whisky consumption in a town that was officially "dry" by counting empty bottles in trash cans, and the degree of fear induced by ghost stories by measuring the shrinking diameter of a circle of seated children (Webb, Campbell, Schwartz, & Sechrest, 1966). A sociology student studied gender differences by recording all the graffiti in every public restroom in two towns (Darnell, 1971). An example of commercially applied social research is the outfitting of shopping carts with infrared surveillance equipment. After tracing the customers' paths through a store and measuring their stops, retailers use their findings to change the location of their items (M. J. McCarthy, 1993). Another technique for studying the social makeup of small towns or villages is to visit and spend some time examining the community's graveyards. Important insights into the history, infant mortality, ethnic makeup, and so on can come from using this technique.

Experiments

The seventh method, the **experiment**, is useful for determining cause and effect. Let's suppose you develop the hypothesis that the consumption of alcohol creates attitudes that favour wife beating. You can conduct an experiment to test this hypothesis.

After randomly selecting male volunteers, your next step is to measure the **dependent variable**, the men's attitudes toward spouse abuse. In one group, called the **experimental group**, you introduce the **independent variable**; that is, you give them a specified amount of alcohol. The other men, the **control group**, are not exposed to the independent variable; that is, they are not given alcohol. You then measure the dependent variable (attitudes toward spouse abuse) again in both groups. In this way, you can assume that any changes in attitude in the experimental group can be attributed to the independent variable—the alcohol—which only that group received.

Sociologists seldom use this classic method of the natural sciences, because most sociologists are interested in broad features of society and social behaviour, or they are interested in the *actual workings* of some group in a *natural setting*. Neither of these interests lends itself well to an experiment.

Sometimes experiments are not conducted rigorously, which increases the likelihood that variables will be confused. This is not necessarily a bad thing. As described in the Down-to-Earth Sociology box, in the 1920s Elton Mayo did a set of famous experiments that uncovered a surprising third variable.

Focus Question
What are the seven major research techniques used by sociologists?

Focus Question
What is the difference between an independent and a dependent variable?

Deciding Which Method to Use

How do sociologists choose from among these methods? Four primary factors affect their choice. First and foremost concerns the purpose of the research, the questions that the sociologist wishes to answer. Some methods are better for answering some questions and not others. Participant observation, for example, is good for uncovering the meanings people give to their behaviour, while surveys work better at revealing attitudes toward public issues such as abortion, gay adoption, the Young Offenders Act, or Quebec independence. Second, resources or sources of funding are crucial. Sociologists must match methods to available resources. For example, although they may want to conduct a survey, they may find that finances will not permit it, and instead they turn to the study of documents. The third significant factor is access to subjects. If people in a sample live in remote parts of the country, researchers may have to mail them questionnaires or conduct a telephone survey even if they would prefer face-to-face interviews. Fourth, the researcher's background or training comes into play. Sociologists, after graduate school, generally use the methods in which they have had the most training.

Down-to-Earth Sociology   The Hawthorne Experiments

Research from the 1920s, known as the Hawthorne experiments, became a classic in sociology. This research drives home how necessary it is to accurately identify independent and dependent variables.

The managers of the Hawthorne plant of the Western Electric Company near Chicago wanted to know how different levels of lighting would affect productivity. Several groups of women participated in what are known as the Relay Room Experiments. In the control room the level of lighting was held constant, while in the experimental room the lighting was varied. To everyone's surprise, output increased in *both* locations. In the experimental room, productivity remained high even when the lights were dimmed to about the level of moonlight, so low that workers could barely see what they were doing!

To solve this mystery, management called in a team of researchers headed by Elton Mayo of the University of Chicago.

This team tested 13 different work conditions. When they changed the workers' pay from hourly wages to piecework, productivity increased. When they served refreshments, output again went up. When they added two five-minute rest periods, productivity jumped. When they changed the rest periods to two ten-minute periods, again output increased. When they let the workers go home early, they found the same result. Confused, the researchers restored the original conditions, offering none of these added benefits. The result? Even higher productivity.

The situation grew even more confusing when men were observed in what is known as the Bank Wiring Room Study. Here, the researchers did not change the work conditions at all. They simply observed the men while they worked and interviewed them after work. Instead of there being no change in productivity, as might have been expected, productivity *dropped*.

None of this made sense. Finally, Mayo concluded that the results were due to the research itself. The women, aware that they were being studied and pleased at the attention paid to them, responded by increasing their efforts. The men, in contrast, were suspicious about why the researchers were observing them. They feared that if they had higher productivity, they would be expected to produce more each day, or that higher productivity might even cost some of them their jobs. Consequently, they decreased their output.

The Hawthorne research is important for what it revealed about the research process itself. Today, researchers carefully monitor the *Hawthorne effect*—the change in behaviour that occurs when people know they are being studied.

Sources: Based on Roethlisberger & Dickson (1939), Mayo (1966), Baron & Greenberg (1990).

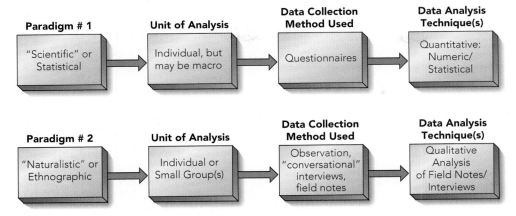

Figure 2.2 Two Common Social Research Strategies or Paradigms

Thus, sociologists who have been trained in **quantitative research methods**, which emphasize measurement, numbers, and statistics, are likely to use surveys. Sociologists who have been trained in **qualitative research methods**, which emphasize observing, describing, and interpreting people's behaviour, lean toward participant observation or qualitative interviews. Figure 2.2 illustrates the two common paradigms for social research. In the next Down-to-Earth Sociology box, you can see how a combination of quantitative and qualitative methods is used in applied sociology. The Thinking Critically about Social Controversy box illustrates how significant the choice of research method is, and how sociologists can find themselves in the midst of controversy for applying rigorous research methods.

Focus Question
What is the difference between qualitative and quantitative research?

A Research Model

As shown in Figure 2.3, eight basic steps are involved in scientific research. Be aware that this is an ideal model. In some research these steps are collapsed, while in still others one or more steps may even be omitted. Besides, there are different types of research sociologists do—*scientific or theoretical* (research with limited practical application), *applied*

Down-to-Earth Sociology

Applied Sociology: Marketing Research as a Blend of Quantitative and Qualitative Methods

If a company is going to survive in the highly competitive business world, it must figure out what consumers need and want, and then supply it, or else convince people that what they need or want is what the company already is producing.

What Marketing Research Is

To increase sales, manufacturers try to improve the "position" of their products. "Position" is marketing jargon for how customers think about a product.

This is where marketing researchers come into play. They find out what customers think they want, how

they select and use products, and what images they hold of a product or service.

To do this, marketing researchers use a combination of qualitative and quantitative techniques. An example is "focus groups," groups of about 10 people who have been invited to discuss a product. A moderator leads a discussion before a one-way mirror, where other team members observe or videotape the session. To control for regional variations, other focus groups may be held at the same time in other cities. Sociologist Roger Straus points out that his training in symbolic

interactionism is especially useful for interpreting these results.

Marketing researchers also use quantitative techniques. For example, they may conduct surveys to determine what the public thinks of a new product. They also gather sales data from the bar codes found on almost all products. They use statistics to analyze the data and prepare tables and graphics that summarize the findings for clients.

Sources: Based on R. A. Straus (1991) and communication with R. A. Straus, 1993.

What could be simpler, or more inoffensive, than counting the homeless? As sometimes happens, however, even basic research can be difficult to do and politically controversial.

In 1997 the United Way of Greater Toronto, in a report entitled "Beyond Survival: Homelessness in Metro Toronto," called for the creation of a Task Force on Homelessness. In January 1998, the newly elected mayor of Toronto, Mel Lastman, created the Homelessness Action Task Force. An interim report was published in July 1998, and the final report, "Taking Responsibility for Homelessness," was released to the public in January 1999.

Which method or methods would be the most suitable to, first, count the homeless in Toronto, and, second, suggest remedies? Surveys? Interviews? Secondary analysis? Focus groups? To survey a population, for example, you first need to know the size of the population or the geographical space it occupies. Since no one knew the exact number of homeless persons in Toronto, nor what constituted the geographical space in which they were all located, a survey was ruled out. In fact, the exact number of homeless was one of the questions the Task Force wanted to investigate!

The first research task was to establish an operational definition of the homeless. The Task Force settled on the following:

- those who are "visible" on the streets or staying in hostels
- the "hidden" homeless, who live in illegal or temporary accommodation
- those at risk of soon becoming homeless

What did the members settle on as their research method(s)? They chose a multi-method approach that included

- an extensive review of the existing literature on the homeless in North America and Europe
- close to 200 hours spent by each member visiting local sites and listening to presentations made by professionals and community stakeholders
- consultation with homeless people through individual interviews and focus groups

- interviews with 17 homeless Aboriginal people as part of the task force's research to develop a distinct strategy for Toronto's Aboriginal population
- work with municipal staff familiar with the homeless

What were some of the main findings from the investigations? First, the more important causes for the new wave of homelessness in Toronto isolated by the Task Force were

- the increase in both the incidence and the depth of poverty brought about, in large part, by changes in the structure of the labour market
- restrictions and cutbacks in income security programs such as employment insurance and social assistance (the shelter component of welfare is too low to cover typical rental payments in Toronto)
- the removal of support for social housing development by both the provincial and the federal government
- spousal abuse, reported to be the main cause of homelessness for over one in four women using the hostel system
- physical or sexual abuse, which accounts for almost three out of four young people who are homeless
- severe mental illness or addictions, which are the significant cause(s) of homelessness among single adults

- distinct problems of the one in seven street homeless who are Aboriginals

Thus, the "typical" homeless person is no longer the single, alcoholic adult male! Youth under the age of 18 and families with children are the fastest-growing groups of the homeless. Together these two groups accounted for almost half the people using hostels in Toronto in 1996.

What about other Canadian cities? While members of the Task Force did not have a comprehensive knowledge of homelessness in other Canadian cities, they did analyze the causes of and responses to homelessness in the larger metropolitan areas. They discovered Toronto was not unique. In Calgary, the homeless population includes employed and unemployed people. In Montreal and Vancouver, homeless youth are the major problem. The root causes of homelessness in all big Canadian cities are the same: poverty, a lack of affordable housing, abuse, mental illness, and addictions. Experts in major Canadian cities told the Task Force that the federal government's withdrawal from social housing was a primary cause of the rise in homelessness in the last five years.

There is also widespread consensus on what is needed to combat the problem. First and foremost, there must be programs to preserve the existing stock of low-cost housing while increasing the supply, in all major Canadian cities.

Research sometimes lands sociologists in the midst of a dispute. Most people would agree with the figures released by the Toronto task force on the homeless, but the solutions offered generate controversy. Recognizing the need for publicly funded social housing is one such controversial remedy for homelessness.

Figure 2.3 The Research Model

Source: Adapted from *Sociology*, 3rd edition (Figure 2.2), by R. T. Schaefer, 1989, New York: McGraw-Hill.

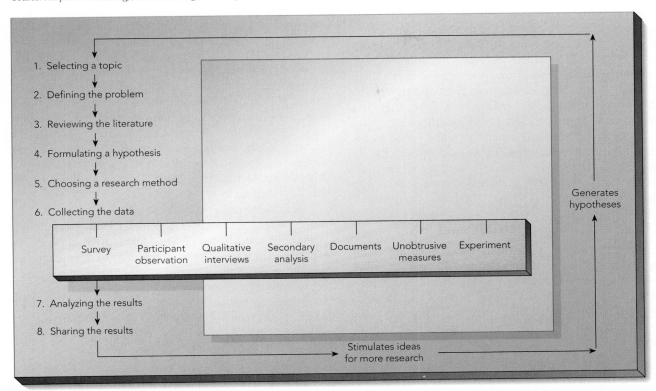

(research that has a direct practical significance in either public policy or commerce), and *evaluative* (research that measures the value of what other researchers/analysts have already done and executed).

1. Selecting a Topic

The first step is to select a topic. What do you want to know more about? Always try to select a topic in which you have a personal interest. Many sociologists simply follow their curiosity. They become interested in a particular topic, and they pursue it: studying the homeless, women, and part-time work (Duffy & Pupo, 1996); examining how new technologies are changing the workplace (Glenday, 1997, 1995); or understanding the makeup of the Canadian economic and political elites (Porter, 1965; Clement, 1978; Olsen, 1980). Some sociologists choose a topic because funding is available to study it, others because social problems such as domestic violence, young offenders, or corporate crime have become pressing social issues and the sociologist wants to gather data that will help people better understand it and perhaps contribute to public policy solutions.

Because sociologists find all human behaviour to be valid research topics, their research runs from the unusual to the routine. Their analyses range from such intensely individual acts as suicide to such broad-scale social change as the globalization of capitalism.

2. Defining the Problem

The second step is to define the problem, to specify exactly what you want to learn about the topic. For example, you can start with a general interest in how or why the homeless grew in numbers over the 1980s and 1990s in the major cities of Canada and the United States. Or you may want to compare the similar job ghettos of gay men and women. Or you may want to know what can be done to reduce spouse abuse. Sociologists conduct research on any aspect of social life that interests them.

3. Reviewing the Literature

The third step is to review the literature to see what has been written on the problem. This is an extremely important step in the research process if sociologists are to distinguish themselves from such nonscientists as newspaper or television reporters. Reading research reported by others helps narrow down the problem, pinpointing particular areas to examine. Reviewing the research may also provide ideas about what questions to ask.

4. Formulating a Hypothesis or Research Question

The fourth step is to formulate a **hypothesis** or research question: a statement of what you expect to find according to predictions from a theory and what others have found from your literature review. A hypothesis predicts a relationship between or among **variables**, factors that change, or vary, from one person or situation to another. For example, the statement "The more strongly religious people are, the more racist their attitudes will be toward visible minorities in Canada" is a hypothesis. Hypotheses need **operational definitions**—precise ways to measure their variables. In this example, we would need operational definitions for three variables: religiosity or how religious a person is, racist attitudes, and visible minorities.

A research question generally seeks theoretically informed, in-depth descriptions of sociological events, issues, or places. More often than not, sociologists use qualitative research methods such as semi-structured or conversational interviews.

5. Choosing a Research Method

The means by which sociologists collect data are called **research methods** (or research designs) that can be further classified into two broad categories—quantitative and qualitative methods. Sociologists use seven basic research methods, outlined in an earlier section. They select the one(s) that will best answer the particular questions they want to answer.

6. Collecting the Data

The next step is to gather the data. Sociologists take great care to assure both the validity and the reliability of their data. If you are using a quantitative method such as a questionnaire, **validity** is the extent to which operational definitions measure what they are intended to measure. Our operational definition must make sense and be precise enough that there is little question about what we are measuring. For example, just how should we measure religiosity—is the number of times a year a person goes to a place of religious worship an accurate reflection of how religious that person is? Wouldn't we also want to know what religion means to him or her, a much more difficult matter: possibly a question best answered by qualitative methods?

The term **reliability** refers to the extent to which different studies come up with similar results. If one study shows that 1 percent of the women in a certain city have been the victims of spouse or partner abuse, while another study finds that the fraction is 10 percent, you can see why sociologists would use the term "unreliable" to describe both these studies.

Focus Question
What is the difference between reliability and validity in sociological research?

7. Analyzing the Results

After the data are gathered, it is time to analyze them. To do this, sociologists use qualitative and quantitative techniques. *Qualitative* analysis is especially useful for data gathered by participant observation and in-depth interviews. Sociologists classify statements people have made in qualitative interviews in order to identify the main themes. This process can also be used to uncover themes in movies, music videos, television programs, newspapers, or any visual or written document. The goal is to faithfully reproduce the world of the people being studied. In Henslin's research on cab drivers, for example, he (1967, 1993) tried to picture the world as cabbies see it, so anyone reading the analysis would understand not just what cabbies do but also why they do it.

Quantitative analysis involves statistically analyzing relationships between variables, sometimes known as number-crunching (see Table 2.1). Quantitative analysis is especially useful to test hypotheses. The computer has become an especially powerful tool for quantitative analysis because statistical packages such as Microcase and the Statistical Package for the Social Sciences (SPSS) can analyze huge amounts of information and identify basic patterns in an instant.

8. Sharing the Results

In this step, the researchers write a report to share their findings with the scientific community. The report includes a review of the preceding steps to help others evaluate the research. It also shows how the findings are related to the literature, the published results of other research on the topic. When research is published, usually in a scientific journal or a book, it then "belongs" to the scientific community. Table 2.1 illustrates how published research is often displayed. These findings are available for **replication**; that is, others can repeat the study to see if they come up with similar results. In this way, scientific knowledge builds slowly as finding is added to finding.

Ethics in Sociological Research

In addition to choosing an appropriate research method, sociologists must also bear in mind the matter of ethics. Their research must meet their profession's ethical criteria, which centre on basic assumptions of science and morality (Canadian Sociology and Anthropology Association, 1995). Research ethics require openness (sharing findings with the scientific community), honesty, and truth. Ethics clearly forbid the falsification of results, as well as *plagiarism*—stealing someone else's work. Another basic ethical guideline is that research subjects should not be harmed by the research. Ethics also require that sociologists protect the identity of people who provide information, which some-

Table 2.1 How to Read a Table

Those with "Too Much Power," 1975 Through 1995 in Percentages
(Based on The Project Canada Surveys, 1975, 1980, 1985, 1990, 1995)

	1975	1980	1985	1990	1995
The rich	80	82	74	77	74
Corporations	83	84	73	72	69
Politicians	—	70	65	76	63
The media	—	54	52	58	59
Labour unions	74	79	66	54	59
Americans	72	61	52	58	54
Lawyers	—	49	—	—	50
Interest groups	—	—	—	27	45
Religious groups	—	20	20	28	27
Professors	—	14	—	—	10
Average Canadians	—	—	—	<1	<1

Source: *The Bibby Report* (p. 113), by Reginald Bibby, 1995, Toronto: Stoddart. Copyright © 1995. Reprinted by permission of Stoddart Publishing Co. Limited.

A table is a concise way of presenting information. Because sociological findings are often presented in tabular form, it is important to understand how to read a table. Tables contain six elements: title, headnote, headings, columns, rows, and source. When you understand how these elements work together, you know how to read a table.

1. The title states the topic of a table. It is located at the top of the table. What is the title of this table? Please determine your answer before looking at the correct answer below.

2. The headnote is not always included in a table. When it is, it is located just below the title. Its purpose is to give more detailed information about how the data were collected or how data are presented in the table. What are the first six words of the headnote of this table?

3. The headings tell what kind of information is contained in the table. Are there any headings in this table?

4. The columns present information vertically arranged. What does the first column tell you?

5. The rows present information arranged horizontally. Read the sixth row, "Americans." Did Canadians still think Americans had too much power in 1995?

6. The "Source" of a table, usually given at the bottom, provides information on where the data shown in the table originated. Often, as in this instance, the information is specific enough for you to consult the original source. What is the source for this table?

Some tables are much more complicated than this one, but all follow the same basic pattern.

Answers

1. The title reads "Those with 'Too Much Power,' 1975 Through 1995 in Percentages."

2. The first six words of the headnote are "Based on The Project Canada Surveys."

3. Yes. The headings are "1975" etc. beginning at column 2.

4. The first column tells you the groups, occupations, and organizations judged as having "too much power," ranked in order of highest to lowest score from all the Project Canada surveys.

5. Yes, although the percentage of Canadians is decreasing.

6. Reginald Bibby, *The Bibby Report* (Toronto: Stoddart, 1995), p. 113.

times is intimate, potentially embarrassing, or otherwise harmful to them. Finally, although not all sociologists are in agreement about this, it generally is considered unethical for researchers to misrepresent themselves.

When it comes to doing sociological research, there is also the question of where the money comes from and if there are any "strings attached." For example, virtually all research foundations in Canada such as the Donner Foundation or "think tanks" such as the Fraser Institute have a political agenda. What ethical questions are raised when spokespersons for these organizations stipulate the general orientation the research should take? Unfortunately,

Ethics in social research are of vital concern to all sociologists. As discussed in the text, sociologists may disagree on some of the issue's finer points, but none would approve of slipping LSD to unsuspecting subjects just "to see what would happen," as was done to U.S. servicemen in the 1960s under the guise of legitimate testing.

this question is being asked less frequently these days. Instead, the brunt of the questions on ethics in sociological research deal with the responsibility of individual sociologists. The examples that follow represent some of the ethical considerations individual sociologists can be confronted with when doing their research. First, to illustrate the extent to which they will go to protect their respondents, consider the research conducted by two U.S. sociologists, Mario Brajuha and Rik Scarce.

The Brajuha Research

Mario Brajuha, a graduate student at the State University of New York at Stony Brook, was doing participant observation of restaurant work (Brajuha & Hallowell, 1986). He lost his job as a waiter when the restaurant where he was working burned down. The fire turned out to be of "suspicious origin," and during their investigation detectives learned that Brajuha had taken field notes. They asked to see them. When Brajuha refused, the district attorney subpoenaed the notes. Brajuha still refused to hand them over. The district attorney then threatened to send Brajuha to jail. By this time, Brajuha's notes had become rather famous, and unsavory characters, perhaps those who had set the fire, also began to wonder what was in them. They, too, demanded to see them—accompanying their demands with threats of a different nature. Brajuha unexpectedly found himself in a very disturbing double bind.

For two years Brajuha refused to hand over his notes, even though he had to appear at numerous court hearings and became filled with anxiety. Finally, the district attorney dropped the subpoena. When the two men under investi-

gation for setting the fire died, so did the threats to Brajuha, his wife, and his children.

The Scarce Research

In 1991, a group calling itself the Animal Liberation Front broke into a research facility at Washington State University, released animals, and damaged computers and files. Rik Scarce, a doctoral student in sociology at the university who was doing research on radical environmental groups, was summoned before a federal grand jury investigating the break-in. Scarce was not a suspect, but law enforcement officers thought that during his research Scarce might have come across information that would help lead them to the guilty parties.

Scarce answered scores of questions about himself and topics related to the raid, but he refused to answer questions that would violate his agreements of confidentiality with research subjects. He cited the American Sociological Association's Code of Ethics: "Confidential information provided by research participants must be treated as such by sociologists, even when this information enjoys no legal protection or privilege and legal force is applied" (1989 version).

A federal judge did not agree, and put Scarce in the Spokane County Jail for contempt of court. Although Scarce could have obtained his freedom at any time simply by testifying, he maintained his laudable ethical stance and continued to refuse, in his words, "to be bludgeoned into becoming an agent of the state." Scarce served 159 days in jail. The longest any scholar before this had been held in contempt was one week (Scarce, 1993a, 1993b, 1994).

The Humphreys Research

Sociologists agree on the necessity to protect respondents, and they applaud the professional manner in which Brajuha and Scarce handled themselves. Let's look at the Humphreys case, which forced sociologists to rethink and refine their ethical stance.

Laud Humphreys, a classmate of Henslin's at Washington University in St. Louis, was an Episcopal priest who decided to become a sociologist. For his Ph.D. dissertation, Humphreys (1970, 1971, 1975) decided to study social interaction in "tearooms," public restrooms where some men go for quick, anonymous oral sex with other men.

Humphreys found that some restrooms in Forest Park, just across from the campus, were "tearooms." He first did participant observation, just hanging around these restrooms. He found that in addition to the two having sex, a third person—called a "watchqueen"—served as a lookout for police and other unwelcome strangers. Humphreys then took the role of watchqueen, watching not only for strangers but also watching what the men did. He systematically recorded these encounters, and they became part of his dissertation.

Humphreys became curious about the regular lives of these men. Impersonal sex in tearooms was a fleeting encounter, and the men must spend most of their time doing other things. What things? With whom? And what was the significance of the wedding rings that he saw on many of the men? Humphreys then hit on an ingenious technique. After observing an encounter, he would leave the restroom and record the licence number of the man's car. Through the help of a friend in the St. Louis police department, Humphreys then obtained each man's address. About a year later, Humphreys arranged for these men to be included in a medical survey conducted by some of the sociologists on the Washington University faculty. Disguising himself with a different hairstyle and clothing, and driving a different car, he visited these men at their homes. He then interviewed them, supposedly for the medical study.

Humphreys said that no one recognized him—and he did obtain the information he was looking for: family background, education, income, health, religion, and even their relationship with wife and children. He found that most of the men were in their mid-thirties and had at least some college education. Surprisingly, the majority were married, and a higher proportion than in the general population turned out to be Roman Catholic. Moreover, these men led very conventional lives. They voted, mowed their lawns, and took their kids to Little League games.

Humphreys also found that, although most of the men were committed to their wives and families, their sex lives were far from satisfactory. Many reported that their wives were not aroused sexually or were afraid of getting pregnant because their religion did not allow them to use birth control. Humphreys concluded that these were heterosexual men who were using the "tearooms" for an alternative form of sex, which, unlike affairs, was quick (taking no time away from their families), inexpensive (zero cost), and non-threatening (the encounter required no emotional involvement to compete with their wives). If a wife had discovered her husband's secret sex life, of course, she would have been devastated. However, Humphrey's research findings have done much good to dispel the myth that only gay men would engage in such behaviours in public washrooms!

This study stirred controversy among sociologists and nonsociologists alike (Goodwin, Horowitz, & Nardi, 1991). Humphreys was severely criticized by many sociologists, and a national columnist even wrote a scathing denunciation of "sociological snoopers" (Von Hoffman, 1970). Concerned about protecting the identity of his respondents, Humphreys placed his master list in a safety deposit box. As the controversy grew more heated, however, he feared that the names might be subpoenaed (a court case was being

threatened), and he had the list destroyed. Humphreys had a contract to remain at Washington University as an assistant professor, but he was fired before he could begin teaching. (Although other reasons were involved, his research was a central issue. There was even an attempt by one professor to have his doctorate revoked.)

Was this research ethical? That question is not easily decided. Although many sociologists sided with Humphreys and his book reporting the research won the highly acclaimed ASA C. Wright Mills Award, criticisms mounted. At first Humphreys vigorously defended his position, but five years later, in a second edition of his book (1975), he stated that he should have identified himself as a researcher.

How Research and Theory Work Together

As discussed, sociological research is based on the sociologist's personal interests, access to subjects, appropriate methods, and ethical considerations. But the value of research is related to sociological theory. On the one hand, as sociologist C. Wright Mills (1959) so forcefully argued, research without theory is of little value, simply a collection of unrelated "facts." On the other hand, theory unconnected to research is abstract and empty, unlikely to represent the way life really is.

Research and theory are both essential for sociology. Every theory that sociologists develop must be tested. Thus, theory stimulates research. And as sociologists research, they often come up with surprising findings—findings that, in turn, stimulate the development of theory to explain them.

The Real World: When the Ideal Meets the Real

Although one can list the ideals of research, real-life situations often force sociologists to settle for something that falls short of the ideal. See the following Thinking Critically about Social Controversy box for a look at how two sociologists confronted the ideal and the real.

This is exactly what sociology needs more of: imaginative, and sometimes daring, research conducted in an imperfect world under less than ideal conditions. This is really what sociology is all about. Sociologists study what people do whether those behaviours are conforming or nonconforming, whether they are pleasing to others or disgust them and arouse intense anger. No matter what the behaviour studied, systematic research methods together with the application of social theory take us beyond common sense. They allow us to penetrate surface realities so we can better understand human behaviour and, in the ideal case, to make changes to help improve social life.

Thinking Critically about
Social Controversy

Are Sex Offenders Sick? A Close-up View of Research

Two sociologists, Diana Scully and Joseph Marolla, were not satisfied with the typical explanation that rapists are "sick," psychologically disturbed, or different from other men. They developed the hypothesis that rape, like most behaviour, is learned through interaction with others. That is, some men learn to think of rape as appropriate behaviour.

To test this hypothesis, Scully and Marolla would have liked to interview a random sample of rapists. But this was impossible, for there is no list of rapists, which would have enabled the researchers to give all of them the same chance of being included in a sample.

However, when they had the opportunity to interview convicted rapists in prison, they jumped at it. They sent out 3500 letters to men serving time in seven prisons in Virginia, the state where they were teaching. About 25 percent of the prisoners agreed to be interviewed. They matched these men on the basis of age, education, race, severity of offence, and previous criminal record. This resulted in a sample of 98 prisoners who were convicted for rape and a control sample of 75 nonrapists—men convicted for other offences.

To prevent bias that might result from the sex of the interviewer, Marolla and Scully each interviewed half the sample. It took them 600 hours to gather information on the prisoners, including their psychological, criminal, and sexual history. To guard against lies, they did what is called a "validity check"; in this case, they checked what the individuals said against their institutional record. They used 12 scales to measure the men's attitudes about women, rape, and themselves. They also presented nine vignettes of forced sexual encounters to measure the circumstances under which the men defined a situation as rape or viewed the victim as responsible.

Scully and Marolla discovered something that goes against common sense: that most rapists are not sick, that they are not overwhelmed by uncontrollable urges. They found that the psychological histories of the rapists and the nonrapists were similar. Rapists, they concluded, are emotionally average men who have learned to view rape as appropriate in various situations. Some rape spontaneously, while others plan their rapes. Others use rape as a form of revenge, to get even with someone, not necessarily the woman.

Scully and Marolla also found support for what feminists had been pointing out for years, that power was a major element in rape. Here is what one man said:

> Rape gave me the power to do what I wanted to do without feeling I had to please a partner or respond to a partner. I felt in control, dominant. Rape was the ability to have sex without caring about the woman's response. I was totally dominant.

To discover that most rape is calculated behaviour, that rapists are not "sick," that the motivating force is power rather than passion—the criminal pursuit of pleasure rather than mental illness—is extremely significant.

Connecting Research and Theory

Such findings go far beyond simply adding to our storehouse of "facts." As was indicated in Figure 2.3, research stimulates both the development of theory and the need for more research.

Sources: Scully & Marolla (1984, 1985); Marolla & Scully (1986); Scully (1990); Foley, Evancic, Karnik, King, & Parks (1995).

Summary and Review

WHAT IS A VALID SOCIOLOGICAL TOPIC?

Any human behaviour is a valid sociological topic, even disreputable behaviour. Spouse abuse is an example. Sociological research is based on the sociologist's interests, access to subjects, appropriate methods, and ethical considerations. pp. 28–29.

COMMON SENSE AND THE NEED FOR SOCIOLOGICAL RESEARCH

Why isn't common sense adequate?

Common sense does not provide reliable knowledge. When subjected to scientific research methods, common-sense ideas often are found to be very limited or false. p. 29.

SEVEN RESEARCH METHODS

How do sociologists gather data?

Sociologists use seven **research methods (or research designs)** for gathering data: **surveys, participant observation, qualitative interviews, secondary analysis, documents, unobtrusive measures,** and **experiments**. pp. 29–34.

How do sociologists choose a particular research method?

Sociologists choose their research method on the basis of the research questions to be answered, their access to potential subjects, the resources available, their training, and ethical considerations. pp. 34–35.

A RESEARCH MODEL

What are the eight basic steps of scientific research?

1. Selecting a topic
2. Defining the problem
3. Reviewing the literature
4. Formulating a **hypothesis** or research question
5. Choosing a **research method**
6. Collecting the data
7. Analyzing the results
8. Sharing the results

pp. 35–38.

ETHICS IN SOCIOLOGICAL RESEARCH

How important are ethics in sociological research?

Ethics are of fundamental concern to sociologists, who are committed to openness, honesty, truth, and protecting their subjects from harm. In addition, most research foundations and think tanks in Canada have political agendas that can seriously undermine the ethical neutrality of sociological research. The Brajuha research on restaurants, the Scarce research on the environmental movement, and the Humphreys research on "tearooms" were cited to illustrate ethical issues of the personal responsibility of sociologists. pp. 38–41.

HOW RESEARCH AND THEORY WORK TOGETHER

What is the relationship between theory and research?

Theory and research are interdependent. Sociologists *must* use theory to interpret the data they gather. Theory without research is not likely to represent real life, while research without theory is merely a collection of unconnected facts. p. 41.

What happens when the ideal meets the real?

As illustrated by the Scully-Marolla research on rapists in prison, real-life situations often force sociologists to conduct research under real-life conditions. Although conducted in *the natural social world*, social research stimulates sociological theory, more research, and the potential of improving human life. p. 41.

Critical Thinking Questions

1. Can someone who is heterosexual study homosexuals? Describe the steps you would take before developing your research hypothesis or research question.

2. Why would anyone want to study the personal records of dead people?

3. When is it appropriate to lie to a research subject?

4. Can you generalize from a case study? If not, why do sociologists continue to employ this research technique?

Key Terms

closed-ended questions 30
control group 33
dependent variable 33
documents 33
experiment 33
experimental group 33
generalizability 32
hypothesis 37
independent variable 33
interview 30
operational definitions 38
participant observation (or fieldwork) 30
population 29
qualitative or field interview 32
qualitative research methods 35
quantitative research methods 35
questionnaires 30
random sample 30
rapport 30
reliability 38
replication 38
research methods (or "research designs") 29
respondents 30
sample 29
secondary analysis 32
self-administered questionnaires 30
structured conversation 32
structured interviews 30
survey 29
unobtrusive measures 33
validity 38
variables 38

Weblinks

All URLs listed are current as of the printing of this book. URLs are often changed. Please check our Web site **www.abacon.com/henslin** for updates.

Data Liberation Initiative (DLI)

www.statcan.ca/english/Dli/dli.htm
Go to the DLI Web site and locate your university's DLI contact person(s).

Canadian Sociology and Anthropology Association

artsci-ccwin.concordia.ca/socanth/csaa/csaa.html
Go to the CSAA Web site and locate the Professional Code of Ethics. What does the CSAA code of ethics say about an organization's ethical responsibilities to its researchers and research participants?

Canadian Socioeconomic Information Management System (CANSIM)

(Locate CANSIM from your university's DLI database.)

NESSTAR Home Page

www.nesstar.org/
NESSTAR (Networked Social Science Tools and Resources) is an infrastructure for data dissemination on the Internet. The site's Explorer software offers an end-user interface for searching, analyzing, and downloading data and documentation. The Publisher software offers tools and resources for making data and documentation available online.

CASS Home Page: An ESRC Resource Centre

www.scpr.ac.uk/cass/docs/fr_casshome.htm

CASS is an ESRC (Economic and Social Research Council) Resource Centre run jointly by the National Centre for Social Research and the University of Southampton, with the University of Surrey. It provides short courses in survey methods and is developing a survey Question Bank for use by social scientists and social researchers in the academic world, government, market research, and the independent and voluntary sectors.

Resources for Methods in Evaluation and Social Research

redrival.net/evaluation/

Lists free resources for methods in evaluation and social research. The focus is on how to do evaluation research and the methods used: surveys, focus groups, sampling, interviews, and other methods. Most of the links are to resources that can be read over the Web.

Office for Human Research Protections (OHRP)

ohrp.osophs.dhhs.gov/

On the OHRP Policy and Assurances Page are presented regulations, ethical principles, IRB Guidebook, OHRP/OPRR Reports, FAQs, and other materials relevant to the protection of human research subjects.

part two

The Individual, Social Groups, and Society

Culture

Learning Outcomes

After you have studied this chapter, you will be able to
- explain what makes humans different from all other animals
- understand why language is so important for human culture
- state in what ways Canadians outside of Quebec differ from Quebecois
- state the relationship between biological differences and cultural differences

I stood in the oppressive heat of the Moroccan-Algerian border, I had never felt heat like this before. The sweat poured off me as the temperature soared past 110 degrees Fahrenheit.

As we were herded into the building—without air conditioning—hundreds of people lunged toward the counter at the rear of the building. With body crushed against body, we waited as the uniformed officials behind the windows leisurely examined each passport.

When I had arrived in Morocco, I found the sights that greeted me exotic—not far removed from my memories of *Casablanca*, *Raiders of the Lost Ark*, and other movies that over the years had become part of my collective memory. The men, women, and even children did wear those white robes that reached down to their feet. In spite of the heat, every woman wore not only a full-length gown, but also a head covering that reached down over the forehead and a veil that covered her face from the nose down. All you could make out were their eyes—and every eye the same shade of brown.

And how short everyone was! The Arab women looked to be on average five feet, and the men only about three or four inches more. As the only blue-eyed, blonde, six-foot-plus person around, wearing jeans and a pullover shirt, in a world of white-robed short people, I stuck out like a sore thumb. Everyone stared. No matter where I went, they stared. It was so different from home, where, if you caught someone staring at you, the person would immediately look embarrassed and glance away.

And lines? The concept apparently didn't even exist. Buying a ticket for a bus or train meant pushing and shoving toward the ticket man (always a man—no women were visible in any public position), who just took the money from whichever outstretched hand he decided on.

And germs? That notion didn't seem to exist here either. Flies swarmed over the food in the restaurants and the unwrapped loaves of bread in the stores. Shopkeepers would considerately shoo off the flies before handing me a loaf. They also had home delivery of bread. I still remember a bread vendor delivering an unwrapped loaf to a woman standing on a second-floor balcony. She first threw her money to the bread vendor, and he then threw the unwrapped bread up to her. Only, his throw was off. The bread bounced off the wrought-iron balcony railing and landed in the street filled with people, wandering dogs, and the ever-present burros. The vendor simply picked up the loaf and threw it again. This certainly wasn't his day, for again he missed. But the man made it on his third attempt. And the woman smiled, satisfied, as she turned back into her apartment.

The situation had become unbearable. Pressed body to body, the man behind me had decided that this was a good time to take a nap. Determining that I made a good support, he placed his arm against my back and leaned his head against his arm. Sweat streamed from my back at the point that his arm and head touched me.

Source: The personal experience of J. Henslin.

What Is Culture?

What is culture? The concept is sometimes easier to grasp by description than by definition. For example, suppose you meet a young woman who has just arrived in Canada from India. That her culture is different from yours is immediately evident. You first see it in her clothing, jewellery, makeup, and hairstyle. Next you hear it in her language. It then becomes apparent by her gestures. Later, you may hear her express unfamiliar beliefs about the world and opinions about what is valuable in life. All these characteristics are indicative of **culture**, the language, beliefs, values, norms, behaviours, and even material objects that are passed from one generation to the next.

In Southeast Asia, for example, a Canadian would be surrounded by a culture quite alien to her or his own. Evidence would be everywhere. The **material culture** Henslin witnessed in Morocco—such things as jewellery, art, buildings, weapons, machines, and even eating utensils, hairstyles, and clothing—provided a sharp contrast to what he was used to. There is nothing inherently "natural" about material culture. That is, it is no more natural (or unnatural) to wear gowns on the street than it is to wear jeans.

Technology is central to social life. From these two forms of transportation, it becomes evident how technology limits or expands human activities and, ultimately, how it plays a significant role in the types of societies we develop. The photo on the left is of a Tajik man in China, near Tashkurgan.

Henslin also found himself immersed in a contrasting **nonmaterial culture**—ways of thinking (beliefs, values, and other assumptions about the world) and doing (common patterns of behaviour, including language, gestures, and other forms of interaction). Here again, no particular custom is "right." People simply become comfortable with the customs they learn during childhood, and uncomfortable when their basic assumptions about life are challenged.

Culture and Taken-for-Granted Orientations to Life

To develop a sociological imagination, it is essential to understand how culture affects people's lives. While meeting someone from a different culture may make us aware of culture's pervasive influence, attaining the same level of awareness regarding our own culture is quite another matter. *Our* speech, *our* gestures, *our* beliefs, and *our* customs are usually taken for granted. We assume that they are "normal" or "natural," and we almost always follow them without question. As anthropologist Ralph Linton (1936) said, "The last thing a fish would ever notice would be water." So it is with people: Except in unusual circumstances, the effects of our own culture generally remain imperceptible to us.

Yet culture's significance is profound; it touches on almost every aspect of who and what we are. We came into this life without a language, without values and morality, with no ideas about religion, war, money, love, use of space, and so on. Yet at this point in our lives we all have them. Sociologists call this "culture *within* us." These learned and shared ways of believing and of doing (another definition of culture) penetrate our beings at an early age and quickly become part of our taken-for-granted assumptions concerning normal behaviour. *Culture becomes the lens through which we perceive and evaluate what*

is going on around us. The rare instances in which these assumptions are challenged, however, can be upsetting. Our Canadian values and norms, or our nonmaterial culture, can fail us and leave us feeling embarrassed or out of place. For example, if you are travelling and participating in the cultural life of Southeast Asia—living and experiencing their culture—there will be many occasions when you will be introduced to new ways of handling your experiences with food, dress, relationships with women, even polite conversation. You will feel uneasy when, for example, someone is talking to you no more than five centimetres from your face. Not only that, you can smell his/her breath and it's not pleasant! But you feel you can't move away; you are somehow locked into this social encounter. When this happens—when your nonmaterial culture fails to make sense of your surroundings—the disconnection you experience is known as culture shock.

An important consequence of culture within us is **ethnocentrism**, a tendency to use our own group's ways of doing things as the yardstick for judging others. All of us learn that the ways of our own group are good, right, proper, and even superior to other ways of life. As sociologist William Sumner (1906), who developed this concept, said, "One's own group is the center of everything, and all others are scaled and rated with reference to it." Ethnocentrism has both positive and negative consequences. On the positive side, it creates in-group loyalties. On the negative side, ethnocentrism can lead to harmful discrimination against people whose ways differ from ours.

The effects of culture on our lives fascinate sociologists. By examining more explicitly just how profoundly culture affects everything we are, this chapter will serve as a basis from which you can start to analyze your previously unquestioned assumptions of reality and thus help you gain a different perspective on social life and your role in it.

In Sum

To avoid losing track of the ideas under discussion, let's pause for a moment to summarize, and in some instances clarify, the principles we have covered.

1. There is nothing "natural" about material culture. Arabs wear gowns on the street and feel that it is natural to do so; Canadians do the same with jeans.

2. There is nothing "natural" about nonmaterial culture; it is just as arbitrary to stand in line as it is to push and shove.

3. Culture penetrates deep into the recesses of our spirits, becoming a taken-for-granted aspect of our lives.

4. Culture provides the lens through which we see the world and obtain our perception of reality.

5. Culture provides implicit instructions that tell us what we ought to do in various situations. It provides a fundamental basis for our decision-making.

6. Culture also provides a "moral imperative"; that is, by internalizing a culture, people learn ideas of right and wrong. (Canadians, for example, believe it is unacceptable to push and shove to get ahead of others in a line.)

7. Coming into contact with a radically different culture challenges our basic assumptions of life.

8. Although the particulars of culture differ from one group of people to another, culture itself is universal. That is, all people have culture. There are no exceptions. A society cannot exist without developing shared, learned ways of dealing with the demands of life.

9. All people are ethnocentric, which has both functional and dysfunctional consequences.

Practising Cultural Relativism

To counter our tendency to use our own culture as a standard to judge other cultures, we can practise **cultural relativism** by trying to understand a culture on its own terms.

For example, many Canadians may appear to have strong feelings against raising bulls for the sole purpose of stabbing them to death in front of crowds shouting "Olé!" According to cultural relativism, however, bullfighting must be viewed strictly within the context of the culture in which it takes place—*its* history, *its* folklore, *its* ideas of bravery, and *its* ideas of gender roles.

As a Canadian you may still regard bullfighting as wrong, of course, if our culture, which lies deep within you, has no history of bullfighting. We all possess culturally specific ideas about cruelty to animals, ideas that have evolved slowly and match other elements of our culture. Consequently, practices that once were common in some areas—cock-fighting, dog-fighting, bear-dog fighting, and so on—have been gradually weeded out (Bryant, 1993).

Many Canadians outside Quebec perceive "la fête nationale du Québec" with suspicion. To most French-speaking Quebecois and those who have inherited Quebec culture, "la fête nationale du Québec" is a colourful and joyous time for family and friends. Cultural relativism requires the suspension of our own perspectives in order to grasp the perspectives of others, sometimes much easier said than done.

Although cultural relativism is a worthwhile goal and helps us to avoid cultural smugness, this view has come under attack. In a provocative book, *Sick Societies* (1992), anthropologist Robert Edgerton points out that some cultures endanger their people's health, happiness, or survival. He suggests that we should develop a scale to evaluate cultures on their "quality of life." He also asks why we should consider cultures that practise female genital mutilation, gang rape, or wife beating, or that sell daughters into prostitution, as morally equivalent to those that do not. Cultural values that result in exploitation, he says, are inferior to those that enhance people's lives.

Edgerton's sharp questions and incisive examples bring us to a point that will come up repeatedly in this text—disagreements that arise between scholars as they confront changing views of reality. It is such questioning of assumptions that keeps sociology interesting.

The material culture in which we are reared becomes a taken-for-granted part of our lives. It is no more natural or unnatural for the Arab women in one photo here to wear gowns, veils, and head coverings in public than it is for Canadian women in the other photo to appear on the beach in scanty attire. For Canadians, the scene above appears strange, and for some distressful, for they see this clothing as a sign of female subservience in a male-dominated society. For many Moroccans, the scene on the right is not only strange, but distressful, as they consider it a sign of moral depravity.

Components of Symbolic Culture

Sociologists sometimes refer to nonmaterial culture as **symbolic culture** because a central component is the symbols that people use to communicate. A **symbol** is something to which people attach meaning and which they then use to communicate. Symbols are the basis of culture. They include gestures, language, values, norms, sanctions, folkways, and mores. Let's look at each of these components of symbolic culture.

Gestures

Gestures, the use of one's body to communicate with others, are useful shorthand ways to give messages without using words. While people in every culture of the world use gestures, their meaning may change completely from one culture to another. Canadians and Americans, for example, communicate a succinct message by raising the middle finger in a short, upward stabbing motion. We wish to stress "Canadians and Americans," for that gesture does not convey the same message in South America or most other parts of the world.

Among Mexicans, for example, their rudest gesture—placing the hand under the armpit and moving the upper arm up and down means "Your mother is a whore," absolutely the worst possible insult in that culture.

Gestures thus not only facilitate communication but, since they differ around the world, can also lead to misunderstandings, embarrassment, or worse. In Mexico, for example, raising your hand to a certain height to indicate how tall a child is may result in laughter. Mexicans use several hand gestures to indicate height, and there are separate ones for people, animals, and plants. (See Figure 3.1).

To get along in another culture, then, it is important to learn the gestures of that culture. In many cultures, for example, you would provoke deep offence if you were to offer food or a gift with your left hand, because the left hand is reserved for dirty tasks, such as wiping after going to the bathroom. Left-handed Canadians visiting Arabs, please note!

Now suppose for a moment that you are visiting southern Italy. After eating one of the best meals in your life you are so pleased that when you catch the waiter's eye, you smile broadly and use the standard North American "A-OK" gesture of putting your thumb and forefinger together and making a large "O." The waiter looks horrified, and you are struck speechless when the manager asks you to leave. What have you done? Nothing on purpose, of course, but in that culture that gesture refers to a part of the human body that is not mentioned in polite company (Ekman, Friesen, & Bear, 1984).

Is it really true that there are no universal gestures? There is some disagreement on this point. Some anthropologists claim that no gestures are universal. They point out that even nodding the head up and down to indicate "yes" is not universal, since in some parts of the world, such as areas of Turkey, nodding the head up and down means "no" (Ekman et al., 1984). However, ethologists—researchers

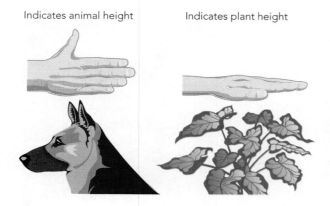

Indicates animal height

Indicates plant height

Indicates human height

Figure 3.1 Gestures to Indicate Height, Southern Mexico

who study biological bases of behaviour—claim that expressions of anger, pouting, fear, and sadness are built into our biology and are universal (Eibl-Eibesfeldt, 1970, p. 404). They point out that even infants who are born blind and deaf, who have had no chance to learn these gestures, express themselves in the same way. Although this matter is not yet settled, we can note that gestures tend to vary remarkably around the world.

Language

The primary way people communicate with one another is through **language**—a system of symbols that can be strung together in an infinite number of ways for the purpose of communicating abstract thought. Language itself is universal in the sense that all human groups have language, but there is nothing universal about the meanings given to particular sounds. Thus, as for gestures, in different cultures the same sound may mean something entirely different or may have no meaning at all. As the first Down-to-Earth Sociology box illustrates, symbols can take on unique meanings within a unique culture—in this case the culture of online communication. The second Down-to-Earth Sociology box points out differences between French-speaking Quebecois and English-speaking Canadians that exist in many areas of social life, including mores around teenagers and sex at home.

The significance of language for human life is difficult to overstate, as will become apparent from the following discussion of the primary ways language allows culture to exist.

Language Allows Human Experience to Be Cumulative. By means of language one generation is able to pass significant experiences on to the next, allowing that next generation to build on experiences it may not itself undergo. Hence the central sociological significance of language: *language allows culture to develop by freeing people to move beyond their immediate experiences.*

Without language, human culture would be little more advanced than that of the lower primates. People would be limited to communicating by some system of grunts and gestures. You can grunt and gesture, for example, that you

want a drink of water, but in the absence of language how could you share ideas concerning past or future events? There would be little or no way to communicate to others what event you had in mind, much less the greater complexities humans communicate—ideas and feelings about events.

Language Provides a Social or Shared Past and Future. Even without language, an individual would still have memories of experiences. Those memories, however, would be extremely limited, for people associate experiences with words and then use words to recall the experience. With language, events can be codified, that is, attached to words and then recalled so they can be discussed in the present.

Language also extends our time horizons forward. When people talk about past events, they share meanings that allow them to decide how they will or should act in similar circumstances in the future. Because language enables people to agree with one another concerning times, dates, and places, it also allows them to plan activities with one another.

Think of the difficulty, perhaps impossibility, of conveying just a slight change in this simple sentence: "I can't make it tomorrow."

Language Allows Shared Perspectives or Understandings. When humans talk with one another, they are exchanging ideas about events, that is, exchanging perspectives. Their words are the embodiment of their experiences, distilled and codified into a readily exchangeable form, intelligible for people who have learned that language. Talking allows people to arrive at the shared understandings that form the essence of social life.

Language Allows Complex, Shared, Goal-Directed Behaviour. Common understandings further enable people to establish a *purpose* for getting together. Suppose you want to go on a picnic. You use speech not only to plan the picnic (who will drive; who will bring the hamburgers, the potato chips, the soda; where you will meet; and so on) but also to decide on reasons for the picnic, which may be anything from "because it's a nice day and it shouldn't be wasted studying" to "because it's my birthday." Only because of

Talking online has become a favourite activity of millions of people, young and old, who use their computers to communicate with others on an everyday basis. Teenagers who rehash the day's events with friends, grandmothers who keep in touch with grandchildren in different provinces, hobbyists who correspond about special interests, businesspeople who seal their deals with the click of a "send" button: All of them love the speed of online communications. They send an e-mail or post a note in a chatroom, and in an instant people thousands of miles away, across the country or in distant lands, can read and respond to it.

Although online communication allows for the speedy transmission of words and ideas, it doesn't allow its users to convey the nuances that are transmitted during face-to-face talk, especially the gestures and tones of voice that people use to monitor and communicate sub-messages. To make up for this, users have developed symbols that are meant to convey humour, disappointment, sarcasm, and other indications of mood or attitude. Although not as rich in number or as varied or spontaneous as the non-verbal cues of face-to-face interaction, these symbols are useful. Here are some of them. If you tilt your head to the left

as you view them, these symbols will be clearer.

:-)	Smile
:-))	Laugh
:-D	Laugh or big grin
:-(	Sad
:-((	Very sad
;-)	Wink, wink-know what I mean?
:-X	My lips are sealed
:-P	Tongue in cheek
:-'	Tongue in cheek
>:-)	Feeling in a devilish mood
:-0	WOW! (What a surprise!)

Some correspondents also use the following abbreviations, which add a touch of whimsy and make their correspondence even more succinct:

ILY	I Love You
LOL	Laughing Out Loud
OTF	On the Floor (laughing)
ROTF	Rolling on the Floor
ROFLWTIME	Rolling on Floor Laughing with Tears in My Eyes
IMHO	In My Humble Opinion

AFK	Away from Keyboard
BAK	Back at Keyboard
BRB	Be Right Back
TTFN	Ta-Ta for Now
WB	Welcome Back
BTW	By the Way
GMTA	Great Minds Think Alike
WTG	Way to Go!
J/K	Just Kidding
D/L	Downloading
OIC	Oh, I See
UGG	You Go, Girl!
IAB	I Am Bored
L8R	Later
CUL8R	See You Later
TTYL	Talk to You Later

As e-mail advances, such shorthand may become increasingly unnecessary. We now have the means to include video in our e-mail: Just click the link, and your image appears. The recipient is also able to hear your voice. As miniaturized video transmitters become inexpensive, live or stored verbal messages—which include facial cues—may replace much correspondence. E-mail itself is unlikely to be replaced, however, and some system of symbols to substitute for gestures will continue.

language can you participate in such a common yet complex event.

Language and Perception: The Sapir-Whorf Hypothesis. In the 1930s, two anthropologists, Edward Sapir and Benjamin Whorf, became intrigued when they noted that the Hopi Indians of the southwestern United States had no words to distinguish between the past, the present, and the future. In contrast, English, as well as German, French, Spanish, and so on, specify carefully just when something takes place. From this observation, Sapir and Whorf concluded that the common-sense idea that words are merely labels people attach to things was wrong. Language, they concluded, has embedded in it ways of looking at the world. The French have a unique phrase to convey this meaning: 'prise de conscience.' The Germans have 'weltanschauung.' There is nothing like this in the English language. Therefore, when we learn a language, we learn not only words, but also a certain way of thinking and perceiving (Sapir, 1949a, 1949b; Whorf, 1956).

The implications of the **Sapir-Whorf hypothesis**, which alerts us to how extensively language affects us, are far-reaching. *The hypothesis reverses common sense*: It indicates that, rather than objects and events forcing themselves onto our consciousness, it is our very language that determines our consciousness, and hence our perception, of objects and events. Inuit, for example, have many words for snow. As Inuit children learn their language, they learn distinctions between types of snowfalls that are imperceptible to non-Inuit speakers. Other Canadians might learn to see heavy and light snowfalls, wet and dry snowfalls, and so on, but not having words for "fine powdery," "thicker powdery," and "more granular" snowfalls actually prevents us from perceiving snow in the same way as Inuit do.

Over the past 15 years, the National Magazine/Maclean's Poll has reported that Canadians are generally tolerant and liberal.

But what about parents, teens, and sex? Would Canadian parents permit their 18-year-old son with a steady girlfriend to have sex in their home? Two out of three Canadians said no. But one province stood out as an exception—Quebec. In Quebec, 57 percent, or almost three times the result of any other province, said they would allow their 18-year-old to have sex at home! Topping this, 42 percent of Quebecois would allow their 18-year-old *gay* son with a steady boyfriend to have sex at home—that's between three and six times higher than any other province in the nation (B.C.=7% yes; Ontario=13% yes).

Let's hear from two parents who participated in the most recent poll for their explanations.

Pierre (fictitious name) and his wife Céline (fictitious name) have raised two children: a daughter, 21, and son, 18. The family talks openly about sex. Both kids have been allowed to have sex at home with their steady partners since they were 17. Their father, Pierre, explains why.

> I have no control over my kids' sexual life. If I say no, they'll do it somewhere else. If I say yes, it feels safer.

Their children say most of their friends enjoy the same policy at home. The son doesn't have a girlfriend now—but when he did—she would stay the night.

> During the day we're around the house with my parents, but at night, we go into my bedroom and close the door.

For Pierre and his wife, the freedom they allow their teenagers sends a strong message: that the house belongs to all of them…that it's a safe haven from the chaotic world of teenage life. Céline says:

> School, work, and friends demand so much from my kids. They are faced with all kinds of rules and limitations. When they're at home, I want them to feel safe, secure, and natural.

It's a different story in southwestern Ontario, where the teenage daughters are younger: 13 and 15. Their father, John (fictitious name)—a teacher—was surveyed and answered no to the question: If his girls were 18, would he allow them to have sex in the house?

His wife, Ann (fictitious name), agrees, because, she says, the older sister has to set an example. The older sibling says many of her friends are having sex, but she's not ready. And when the time does come, she agrees with the house rules.

I wouldn't feel comfortable having sex in my parents' house, especially when they are home. It has to do with the whole respect thing my parents talk about.

On other matters of sex and teenagers, the mother says:

> I would encourage my daughters to talk to me if they ever decide to have sex with someone. I would want to talk to them about birth control. This way, I'll know that they are sexually active, but it wouldn't bother me as much as if it was in my house.

Clearly, on the issue of teenagers and sex in the home, many French-speaking Quebecois are more tolerant than most Canadians. Why is this so? One explanation centres on the differences in the role of the family in Quebec society compared to the how the family is experienced in Ontario or the rest of Canada. In Quebec, the family is seen as a refuge against a hostile world while in Ontario, the family offers other rewards. (For a discussion of the nature of the Quebec family see Gerin, 1928. For a broader view of the role of the family in the social and political life of society, see Todd, 1995, 1998).

Source: Adapted from *The National Magazine/ Maclean's* Poll, 1998. Retrieved September 25, 2002 from **www.tv.cbc.ca/national/pgminfo/poll/ index.html.**

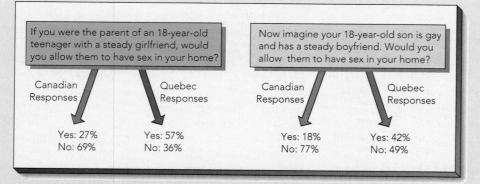

Figure 3.2 Differences Between Quebec and the Rest of Canada on Matters of Parenting, Sex, and Teens

Although Sapir and Whorf's observation that the Hopi do not have tenses was incorrect (Edgerton, 1992, p. 27), we still need to take their conclusion seriously, for the classifications that we humans develop as we try to make sense of our world do influence our perception. Sociologist Eviatar Zerubavel (1991) gives a good example. Hebrew, his native language, does not differentiate between jam and jelly. Only when Zerubavel learned English could he "see" this difference, which is "obvious" to native English speakers. Similarly, if you learn to classify students as "dweebs," "dorks," "nerds," "brains," and so on, you will perceive a student who asks several questions during class in an entirely different way from someone who does not know these classifications.

In Sum

The sociological significance of language is that it takes us beyond the world of apes and allows culture to develop. Language frees us from the present by providing a past and a future, giving us the capacity to share understandings about the past and to develop common perceptions about the future, as well as to establish underlying purposes for our activities. Consequently, as in the case of the picnic, each individual is able to perform a small part of a larger activity, aware that others are carrying out related parts. In this way a series of separate activities becomes united into a larger whole.

Language also allows us to expand our connections far beyond our immediate, face-to-face groups, so that our *individual* biological and social needs are met by extended networks of people. This development, in turn, leads to far-flung connections with our fellow humans extending outward from our family and local community to worldwide networks of production and distribution. Although language by no means *guarantees* cooperation among people, language is an *essential* precondition of collaboration. Without language, the extended cooperative human endeavours on which society is based simply could not exist (Malinowski, 1945; Hertzler, 1965; Blumer, 1966).

In short, our entire way of life is based on language, although, like most aspects of culture, its *linguistic base* is usually invisible to us.

Learning a language means not just learning words but also acquiring the perceptions embedded in that language. Precisely because language is such a primary shaper of experience and culture, difficulties arise between people who live among each other but do not share a language.

Focus Question

Why is language so important to human culture?

Values, Norms, and Sanctions

To learn a culture is to learn people's **values**, their ideas of what is desirable in life. When we uncover people's values, we learn a great deal about them, for values are the standards by which people define good and bad, beautiful and ugly.

Every group develops expectations concerning the right way to reflect its values. Sociologists use the term **norms** to describe those expectations, or rules of behaviour, that develop out of a group's values. They use the term **sanctions** to refer to positive or negative reactions to the ways in which people follow norms. **Positive sanction** refers to an expression of approval given for following a norm, while **negative sanction** denotes disapproval for breaking a norm. Positive sanctions can be material, such as a money reward, a prize, or a trophy, but in everyday life they usually consist of hugs, smiles, a clap on the back, soothing words, or even handshakes. Negative sanctions can also be material—a fine is one example—but they, too, are more likely to consist of gestures, such as frowns, stares, harsh words, or raised fists. Being awarded a raise at work is a positive sanction, indicating that the norms clustering around work values have been followed, while being fired is a negative sanction, indicating the opposite.

Folkways and Mores

Norms that are not strictly enforced are called **folkways**. We expect people to comply with folkways, but we are likely to shrug our shoulders and not make a big deal about it if they don't. If someone insists on passing you on the left side of the sidewalk, for example, you are unlikely to take corrective action. However, if the sidewalk is crowded and you must move out of the way, you might give the person a dirty look.

Other norms, however, are taken much more seriously. We think of them as essential to our core values, and we insist on conformity. These are called **mores** (MORE-rays). A person who steals, rapes, and kills has violated some of society's most important mores. As sociologist Ian Robertson (1987, p. 62) put it,

A man who walks down a street wearing nothing on the upper half of his body is violating a folkway; a man who walks down the street wearing nothing on the lower half of his body is violating one of our most important mores, the requirement that people cover their genitals and buttocks in public.

It should also be noted that one group's folkways may be another group's mores. For example, to walk down the sidewalk in a nudist camp with the entire body uncovered would conform to that subculture's folkways.

A **taboo** refers to a norm so strongly engrained that even the thought of its violation is greeted with revulsion. Eating human flesh and having sex with one's parents are examples of such behaviours (Benales, 1973; Read, 1974; Henslin, 1997c).

The violation of mores is usually a very serious matter. In this case, it is serious enough that the police at this international rugby tournament have swung into action to protect the public from seeing a "disgraceful" sight at least as designated by this group. Yet, unlike the reactions to most violations of mores, this scene also shows barely suppressed laughter.

Subcultures and Countercultures

> We can make epistemically subjective statements about entities that are ontologically objective, and similarly, we can make epistemically objective statements about entities that are ontologically subjective (Searle, 1995, p. 8).

Our best guess is that you are unable to decipher the meaning of this statement. It might as well be written in Greek for all it means to most of us. Philosophers, however, write like this, and to them the author's intent is clear. Philosophers form a **subculture**, *a world within the larger world of the dominant culture*. Every subculture has some distinctive way of looking at life. Even if we cannot understand the preceding quote, it makes us aware that the philosopher's view of life is not quite the same as ours.

Canadian society contains thousands of subcultures. Some are as broad as the way of life we associate with teenagers, others as narrow as those we associate with bodybuilders or philosophers. Ethnic groups also form subcultures: Their values, norms, and foods set them apart. So might their religion, language, and clothing. Occupational groups also form subcultures, as anyone who has hung out with cab drivers (F. Davis, 1959; Henslin, 1993), the police (Pepinsky, 1980), factory workers (Halle, 1984), artists (McCall, 1980), or construction workers (Haas, 1972) can attest. Even sociologists form a subculture, who, as you are learning, use a unique language for carving up the world.

Consider this quote from another subculture:

> If everyone applying for welfare had to supply a doctor's certificate of sterilization, if everyone who had committed a felony were sterilized, if anyone who had mental illness to any degree were sterilized then our economy could easily take care of these people for the rest of their lives, giving them a decent living standard but getting them out of the way. That way there would be no children abused, no surplus population, and, after a while, no pollution. (Zellner, 1995, p. 58).

Welcome to the world of the "survivalists"—where the message is much clearer than that of the philosophers, and much more disturbing.

The values and norms of most subcultures are compatible with the larger society to which they belong. In some cases, however, such as these survivalists, the group's values and norms place it in opposition to the dominant culture. Sociologists use the term **counterculture** to refer to groups whose values and norms place them in opposition to mainstream culture. Heavy-metal adherents who glorify Satanism, hatred, cruelty, sexism, violence, and death are an example of a counterculture. Note that motorcycle enthusiasts who emphasize personal freedom and speed and affirm cultural values of success are members of a subculture. In contrast, the members of an outlaw motorcycle gang who also stress freedom and speed but add the values of despising women and selling drugs and prostitution, form part of a counterculture (Watson, 1988).

Countercultures do not have to be negative. Skinheads who are members of SHARP (Skinheads Against Racial Prejudice) or SARS (Skinheads Against Racism) counter the negative image presented by neo-Nazi skinhead groups in Canada such as the Western Guard. Unfortunately, the neo-Nazi groups are given more press and media coverage than SHARP or SARS.

Values in Canadian Society
An Overview of Canadian Values

As you well know, Canada is a **pluralistic society**, made up of many different cultural groups. Canada has numerous religious, racial, and ethnic groups, as well as countless interest groups centring on such divergent activities as collecting Barbie dolls and hunting deer. However, the study of national cultural values is of interest to many sociologists, not just in Canada, but in the United States, Europe, and many other countries as well. (R. M. Williams, 1965, studies the U.S.; Lipset, 1990, contrasts Canadian with U.S. cultural values; Hofstede, 1980, 2001, examines masculine and feminine characteristics of many different national cultures.)

For 20 years (since 1983), the TV show *The National Magazine* and *Maclean's* magazine have polled Canadians on a wide variety of topics from taxes to sex, politics, and morality, to what the next 50 years will bring us in the way of medicine and whether we will be visited by extraterrestrial life. This annual "snapshot" of values in Canada is reported in both *Maclean's* and CBC's *The National Magazine*. (Also on the Internet—see the Weblinks section at the end of this chapter.) One of the latest polls, in 1998, was conducted by Allan Gregg of Decima Corporation.

The members of SHARP (Skinheads Against Racial Prejudice) counter the negative image presented by neo-Nazi skinhead groups and provide evidence that countercultures do not have to be negative.

should behave, only 40 percent of Canadians said they strongly agree! Moreover, 63 percent of Canadians said a politician should *not* resign if it was discovered that he or she has had an extramarital affair. However, 80 percent of Canadians said lying under oath was grounds for dismissal. At this moment in our history, the attitudes of most Canadians on the issue of politics and sex are quite different from those of our U.S. neighbours.

Another view of sex and politics is afforded by the recent election of Glen Murray, the openly gay activist, as mayor of Winnipeg, a major metropolitan centre in Canada (there are openly gay mayors in other, smaller communities such as Wolfville, Nova Scotia). Together with Svend Robinson, the long-time federal politician and gay activist, they are just a few examples of a growing tolerance of diversity among more and more Canadians.

Tables 3.1 and 3.2 provide further evidence of the liberal moral values of most Canadians. Table 3.1 sets the tone by showing that a majority of Canadians feel questions of sex and morality are personal matters and that we, as a society, should accept these differences and not impose our moral codes on others. Granted, there are variations across this vast land of ours. And Quebec stands apart from the rest of the country on issues of personal morality and sex. Virtually twice as many Quebecois (or 50 percent) as Canadians in other regions of the country (from a low of 18 percent in B.C. to a high of 26 percent in the Maritimes) believe that the more permissive attitude on sexual matters is a good thing!

Figure 3.2 (page 54) showed the differences between Quebec and the rest of the country on matters of parenting, sex, and teens. Quebec is much more accepting of teenagers, whether gay or straight, having sex at home with a steady partner than any other province or region of the country. Why is this so? In the Down-to-Earth Sociology box earlier in this chapter, two different explanations were provided. Clearly, these represent marked differences in the

What are Canadians telling the pollsters about what is important and what is not? When it comes to politics and sex, most Canadians, unlike Americans, really don't want or feel the need to know what their politicians do in bed and with whom. When asked whether they expect politicians and other leaders to set an example of ideally how we

The study of national cultural values has become much more interesting for sociologists, as Canadian society has grown in complexity and created a mosaic that envelopes its two-founding-nations status.

Table 3.1 Sex and Morality in Canada, 1998—Percentage Who Agree Strongly

	Canada (%)	B.C. (%)	Prairies (%)	Ontario (%)	Quebec (%)	Atlantic (%)	Men (%)	Women (%)
"It is important that we accept others' rights to different lifestyles and how they live their lives"	64	56	54	60	81	63	63	65
"No one has the right to impose their morality and ways of doing things on others"	57	49	46	55	70	57	56	57
"A person's sex life whether they are married and have affairs is their business and should not be a reason for judging them"	49	34	38	46	70	46	48	50
"I expect politicians and other leaders to set an example of ideally how we should all behave"	40	36	46	41	39	38	41	40

Source: Adapted from *The National Magazine/Maclean's* Poll, 1998. Retrieved September 25, 2002 from **www.tv.cbc.ca/national/pgminfo/poll/index.html**.

Table 3.2 Canada as a Permissive Society: Good or Bad Thing?—Percentage Permissive

	Canada (%)	B.C. (%)	Prairies (%)	Ontario (%)	Quebec (%)	Atlantic (%)	Men (%)	Women (%)
"Over the past 10 to 20 years would you say Canadians' attitudes on sexual matters have become permissive?"	70	78	70	70	70	64	67	73
Respondents who indicated that it is a good thing that attitudes on sexual matters have become more permissive	29	18	20	24	50	26	36	23
Respondents who indicated that it is a bad thing that attitudes on sexual matters have become more permissive	29	36	43	30	17	28	25	33
Respondents who indicated that they are not sure that attitudes on sexual matters have become more permissive	41	46	36	45	34	46	39	43

Source: Adapted from *The National Magazine/Maclean's* Poll, 1998. Retrieved September 25, 2002 from **www.tv.cbc.ca/national/pgminfo/poll/index.html**.

perception about the character of the home in Quebec and the rest of the country.

When it comes to other differences in values and beliefs, Quebec is a paradox. That is, there are values that Quebecois share with the rest of Canada and there are those they do not.

This should not be surprising. Quebecois live within a language frontier that generates a sense of collective belonging. Moreover, Quebec has its own flag, its own media and star system. In a recent study of Canadian identity, Graves, Dugas, & Beauchamp (in press) summarized their findings by saying that the factors that influence a feeling of attachment to the country as a whole were different in Quebec. Overall, Quebecois held a lower attachment to Canada than did people in the other provinces of Canada. When compared to Ontario, where attachment to the province and a belief in liberal political culture reinforce attachment to Canada, the opposite was the case for Quebec. A weak attachment to the province and conservative political values stimulate attachment to Canada. What Quebecois share with the rest of Canada are the positive attitudes about the role of the state in their lives.

Just as interesting is the fact that when Quebecois look outside, they tend to "skip" Canada and adopt a continental or global view. Table 3.3 tells us that Quebecois are more jealous of their personal liberties than the average Canadian since they are less likely to give up some personal freedom to combat terrorism. This is just one indicator of the well-documented "hedonist-individualist" streak that separates Quebec from the rest of Canada. Allan Gregg, a well-known Canadian pollster, once stated that when he asked Canadians whether they agreed or disagreed with the following statement: "eat, drink, and be merry, for tomorrow you may die," 77 percent of Quebec teenagers agreed compared to only 17 percent of teens in British Columbia (Aubin, 2001-2002).

Table 3.4 describes some aspects of Canada's relations with the United States after September 11, 2001. First of all, it is interesting to note that fewer Canadians than in 1990 would want to become American citizens. The differences between men and women are especially pronounced. Almost half of all Canadians feel that we are not especially close friends to the Americans. However, a greater percentage of Quebec respondents reported being like best friends to the Americans. But, a significantly larger percentage of Quebecois felt that the September 11 terrorist attacks were aimed solely at the United States. Once again we are witness to the complex set of values and beliefs held by Canadians and Quebecois.

Focus Question
In what ways do Canadians outside of Quebec differ from Quebecois?

Native Peoples in Canada

The multicultural aspect of recent Canadian history is often viewed as a positive value. Many ethnic groups celebrate their differences and their similarities as Canadians at numerous festivals, carnivals, and celebrations every year in Canada. On the other hand, Native Canadians have very little reason to rejoice and make merry. Their present status as Canadians has been enshrined in the *Indian Act* of 1876. As Table 3.5 clearly shows, the *Indian Act* has served to isolate Natives from mainstream Canadian society by keeping them on reserves. More importantly, and in many ways because the federal government controls their social life, Native peoples in Canada are afforded few opportunities for meaningful employment or for starting business ventures that respect their diverse cultures. Neither are the living conditions on many reserves healthy. Nor are there opportunities for young people to explore their place in their way of life. The combination of adverse social, psychological, and economic conditions serves to heighten susceptibility to illness and poor health. It is little wonder, then, that Native peoples report the highest incidences of death due to respiratory disease, accidents, violence, and poisoning (Jarvis & Boldt, 1983; Department of Indian Affairs and Northern Development, 2001). As indicated in the Mass Media and Social Life box, the incidents of "starlight tours" in Saskatoon, Saskatchewan, highlight the continuing plight of Native peoples in Canada.

Value Contradictions and Social Change

As you can see, not all values fall into neat, integrated packages. Some may even contradict one another. The **value contradiction** of group superiority violates freedom, democracy, and equality. There simply cannot be

Table 3.3 Quebec and the Rest of Canada: Points of Difference

	Quebec	Rest of Canada
More Likely to Support:		
Canada re-evaluating its Israeli-Palestinian policies	63%	49%
Being concerned the war on terrorism will spread	73%	61%
The feeling that we are becoming more like Americans	50%	41%
Less Likely to Support		
Canadian involvement in Afghanistan	65%	83%
More funding for the Canadian military	48%	74%
Giving up some freedoms to combat terrorism	47%	63%
The idea that Canada could become a terrorist target	39%	64%

Source: Adapted from "Where the Solitudes Meet," by Benoit Aubin, December 31, 2001–January 7, 2002, *Maclean's* (Toronto Edition), 114 (53), p. 32.

Table 3.4 Canada-U.S. Relations After September 11, 2001

| | Responses in 1990 | Responses after September 11, 2001 | | | | | | | |
	1990	Canada	Quebec	Ontario	Atlantic	Prairies	B.C.	Men	Women
If you were given the opportunity to become a citizen of the U.S. and live and work there, would you?									
(% who said "Yes")	30	25	30	24	20	23	21	31	19
How would you describe our relations with the U.S.?									
Like family	—	10	8	12	11	10	4	—	—
Best friends	—	23	29	22	19	19	18	—	—
Friends but not especially close	—	47	42	49	51	49	51	—	—
Cordial but distant	—	18	18	16	14	20	25	—	—
Openly hostile	—	1	2	—	2	—	1	—	—
Were the September 11 attacks aimed at the U.S. alone or at Western democratic countries like Canada?									
(U.S. alone)	—	49	66	44	41	41	46	—	—
How long do you think the war against terrorism will last?									
A few months	—	9	10	9	8	10	6	9	9
1 year	—	14	11	14	17	14	15	13	15
2–3 years	—	21	22	22	18	16	21	17	24
4–5 years	—	9	11	8	8	10	10	10	9
6 years or more	—	40	42	41	39	43	38	47	34

Source: Adapted from "Where the Solitudes Meet," by Benoit Aubin, December 31, 2001–January 7, 2002, *Maclean's* (Toronto Edition), *114* (53), p. 26.

Perspectives

Pro Wrestling 101 at Memorial University

Starting in January 2000, students at Memorial University in St. John's, Newfoundland, were able to study professional wrestling. The course has been offered through the Department of Folklore where it easily fits with other courses in popular culture—courses dealing with subjects such as comic books and soap operas. What would the course cover? Certainly one important topic is the business of pro wrestling, which includes topics like the burgeoning profits of the major federation, the WWE, the recent public stock offerings of the WWF, now the WWE, the meagre salaries of most of the pro wrestlers, and especially the episode of Jesse "The Body" Ventura, former Governor of Minnesota, who was once ostracized from pro wrestling when he tried to unionize pro wrestlers and introduce health and pension plans.

Another is the sociology of pro wrestling—the dramaturgical approach to the study of pro wrestling with its front- and backstage behaviours. Before each match, the stage management and preparation takes place in the backstage away from the audience while the antics of the ring are its front-stage presentation to the public.

Grades are based on exams, of course, and a term paper. Topics range from issues dealing with the presentation of gender (masculinity and femininity) in pro wrestling to permitting a student to create a wrestling character complete with his or her own distinct personality and address why the character would appeal to an audience.

Source: Adapted from *Canada AM*.

---

full expressions of freedom, democracy, and equality along with racism and sexism. Something has to give. One way Canadians sidestepped this contradiction in the past was to say that the values of freedom, democracy, and equality applied only to certain groups. The contradiction was bound to surface, however, and so it did, as is evident from the internment of the Japanese during World War II and the women's liberation movement during the 1960s and 1970s. However, most Canadians who live and work with many different subcultural groups continue to extend the values of freedom and equality and, as we saw earlier when discussing values in Canadian society, tolerance to more and more groups. As a result, we are reducing the emphasis on only one national group superiority.

As society changes, then, some values are challenged and undergo modification. Such change may be gradual, with people slowly adjusting their behaviours and ideas, or

known, on too many occasions, to ask the proverbial question "What is the Canadian identity?" It is also true that our geography has helped define us as a nation—at least when we have tried to unite the country from east to west. Note that Canada's national motto—*A mari usque ad mare*—from sea to sea—is stamped on all our paper currency.

But could it be that we are losing what distinctiveness we possess as Canadians as we become more closely tied economically to the United States—that is, as our trade, capital, and people move north and south? Reginald Bibby, who surveyed Canadians over two decades, arrives at some startling conclusions. While maintaining that Quebec has succeeded in retaining its language and culture, Bibby claims that multiculturalism has done little to advance a sense of ourselves as a distinct nation. He goes further and asserts that Canadians outside Quebec have "a questionable sense of where they have come from, have few heroes, [exhibit] a passive acceptance of being inferior to the U.S. [, and] in lieu of having our own 'Canadian culture,' our tendency has been to fill the void with American culture, resulting in an intensified 'Americanization of Canadian life'" (Bibby, 1995, p. 50). What do you think? Are there unique Canadian values worth preserving?

"Ideal" Versus "Real" Culture

Many of the norms that surround cultural values are only partially followed. Consequently, sociologists use the term **ideal culture** to refer to a group's ideal values, and *norms* to refer to the goals they hold out for themselves. The idea of success, for example, is part of ideal culture. North Americans glorify academic progress, hard work, and the display of material goods as signs of individual achievement. What people actually do, however, usually falls short of this cultural ideal. Compared with their capacities, for example, most people don't go as far as they could in school or work as hard as they can. Sociologists call the norms and values that people actually follow **real culture**.

Cultural Universals

With the amazing variety of human cultures around the world, are there any **cultural universals**—values, norms, or other cultural traits that are found everywhere?

Anthropologist George Murdock (1945) sought to answer this question. After combing through data gathered by anthropologists on hundreds of groups around the world, he drew up a list of customs concerning courtship, cooking, marriage, funerals, games, laws,

music, myths, incest taboos, and even toilet training. He found that although such activities are present in all cultures, *the specific customs differ from one group to another.* There is no universal form of the family, no universal way of disposing of the dead. Similarly, specific games, rules, songs, stories, and methods of toilet training differ from one culture to another.

Even incest is defined differently from group to group. For example, the Mundugumors of New Guinea extend the incest taboo so far that for each man, seven of every eight women are ineligible marriage partners (M. Mead, 1935/1950). Other groups go in the opposite direction and allow some men to marry their own daughters (La Barre, 1954). In certain circumstances, some groups require that brothers and sisters marry one another (Beals & Hoijer, 1965). The Burundi of Africa even insist that, to remove a certain curse, a son have sexual relations with his mother (Albert, 1963). Such sexual relations were allowed only for special people (royalty) or in a special situation (such as that of a lion hunter before a dangerous hunt), and no society permits generalized incest for its members.

In short, although there are universal human activities (speech, music, storytelling, marrying, disposing of the dead, preparing food, and so on), there is no universally accepted way of doing any of them. Humans have no biological imperative that results in one particular form of behaviour throughout the world.

Focus Question
Do biological differences explain cultural differences?

Animals and Culture

Let us digress for a moment to follow a fascinating and related issue: Do animals have culture? Do they have language?

Do Animals Have Culture?

According to our definition of culture as a learned way of life passed on to others, it would seem that animals could not have culture. The basic sociological question is this: Are there any behaviours that animals learn, and then pass on to others?

The answer begins with an observation by Japanese anthropologists. In 1953, they saw a young monkey pick up a sweet potato covered with sand, dip it in water, and wash off the sand with her hands. A month later, her playmates began to wash their sweet potatoes. Several months later, her mother followed suit. In 10 years, 75 percent of the troop were doing this (Hanson, 1973). At a minimum, then, animals do learn from one another, and a learned behaviour can be adopted by other animals.

The solution to our question continues with a chance meeting in 1957 between Louis Leakey, a world-renowned anthropologist and paleontologist, and Jane Goodall, a secretary from London. Leakey, who had been collecting fossils in an area of Tanzania in Africa, asked Goodall if she would like to study some chimpanzees living on the shores of a lake. Leakey explained that because the remains of early humans were often found on lakeshores, an understanding of chimpanzee behaviour might shed light on the behaviour of our Stone Age ancestors (Van Lawick-Goodall, 1971).

Goodall accepted the invitation. When the chimps became accustomed to her and allowed her to join them, Goodall slowly figured out how they communicate. Eventually she was even able to participate in their gestures, hoots, and facial expressions. For the next 30 years, Goodall lived in the remote jungle (J. Walters, 1990). Today she is on a globe-spanning crusade to promote conservation and improve conditions for captive chimps (J. J. Miller, 1995).

What did Goodall learn that might help us decide whether animals have culture? She observed that these wild chimps made and used **tools**; that is, they modified objects and used them for specific purposes. Until this observation, it was assumed that only humans used tools. The chimps would first pick a blade of grass, then strip off its leaves and lick one end. Next they would poke the sticky end into a

Jane Goodall's research demonstrated that animals have a primitive culture; that is, they teach one another behaviour that is transmitted across generations. Such culture is very limited, however, because, unlike humans, animals do not have language.

nest of termites. After waiting a bit, they would pull it out covered with termites, then savour the taste as they licked off the stick.

Stimulated by Goodall's discovery, scientists began trying to determine the extent of **animal culture**—learned, shared behaviour among animals (Eibl-Eibesfeldt, 1970).

From one of the more humorous footnotes to these scientific endeavours, we learn that even the mating behaviour of some animals is learned. Zookeepers around the world have been dismayed that their gorillas will not mate, and they have had to replenish their supply of these animals from the wild. Then zookeepers in Sacramento, California, noticing that the gorillas appeared to want to mate, concluded that maybe they just didn't know how (Stark, 1989). Taking a long shot, they showed the animals a movie of two adult gorillas mating. The lesson turned out to be a success.

On a rudimentary level, animal culture exists. Although this principle has been established, we do not yet know the particulars. What animals? What specific behaviours? The initial answers, enticing though they may be, only point to further provocative questions.

Focus Question
What makes humans different from all other animals?

Do Animals Have Language?

A related question that has intrigued scientists and nonscientists alike is whether animals have language. Do those barks and meows your pets make constitute language?

Social scientists think of language as more complex than mere sounds. They view language as symbols that can be infinitely strung together to communicate abstract thought. Animal sounds, however, appear to be closer to a baby's cries. Although a baby will cry when in pain, this cry of distress, even though it brings a parent running, is not language. The cry is merely a biological response to pain, similar to reflexes.

Social scientists also point out that animals do not even have the vocal apparatus necessary to utter the complex sounds that make up language. When Allen and Beatrice Gardner (1969), psychologists at the University of Nevada, learned from Goodall's research that chimps in the wild use many more hand signals than vocal signals, they decided to teach chimps gestures instead of words (Fleming, 1974). Their first pupil was Washoe, a female chimpanzee born in the wild in 1966.

The Gardners taught her American Sign Language, in which hand gestures correspond to individual words. For example, they taught her the sign for "open," using three doors in the house trailer she lived in. After learning that gesture, Washoe transferred it to all the trailer's doors and drawers—then to containers, the refrigerator, and even to the water faucet.

Within a year, Washoe had become inventive and was putting signs together in the equivalent of simple sentences. She even made up combinations, such as joining the sign for "give me" with "tickle" to indicate that she wanted to be tickled. At the end of four years, Washoe could use 160 signs.

Do animals have the capacity for language? Such experiments have persuaded some scientists that they do. Others, however, remain unconvinced. For the answer to this question, then, we must await further evidence.

Technology in the Global Village

New Technologies

The gestures, language, values, folkways, and mores we have discussed are all part of symbolic or nonmaterial culture. But culture, as you recall, also has a material aspect, a group's things, from its houses to its toys. Central to a group's material culture is its **technology**. In its simplest sense, technology can be equated with tools. In its broader sense, technology also includes the skills or procedures necessary to make and to use those tools.

We can use the term **new technology** to refer to the emerging technologies that have a significant impact on social life. For people 500 years ago, the new technology was the printing press. For us, these new technologies are computers, satellites, and various forms of the electronic media.

The sociological significance of technology is that its importance goes far beyond the tool itself. *The type of technology a group has sets the framework for its nonmaterial culture.* Technology influences the way people think and how they relate to one another, a focus of the box on Sociology and the New Technology. Consider gender relations. Through the centuries and throughout the world, it has been the custom (a group's nonmaterial culture) for men to dominate women. Today, with instantaneous communications (the material culture), this custom has become much more difficult to maintain. For example, when women from many nations gathered in Beijing for a U.N. conference in 1995, satellites instantly transmitted their grievances around the globe. Such communications may create discontent, or sometimes a feeling of sisterhood, and taken together women will agitate for social change.

Cultural Lag and Cultural Change

A couple of generations ago, sociologist William Ogburn (1922) coined the term **cultural lag**. By this, Ogburn meant that not all parts of a culture change at the same pace. When some part of a culture changes, other parts lag behind.

Ogburn pointed out that *a group's material culture usually changes first, with the nonmaterial culture lagging behind*, playing a game of catch-up. For example, when we get sick, we could type our symptoms into a computer and get an immediate printout of our diagnosis and best course of treatment. In fact, in some tests computers outperform physicians (Waldholz, 1991). Yet our customs have not

"COOL! A KEYBOARD THAT WRITES WITHOUT A PRINTER."

Technological advances are now so rapid that the technology of one generation is practically unrecognizable by the next generation.

caught up with the technology, and we continue to visit doctors' offices.

Sometimes nonmaterial culture never does catch up. Instead, we rigorously hold onto some outmoded form, one that once was firmly needed, but long ago has been bypassed by new technology. A striking example is our nine-month school year. Have you ever wondered why it is nine months long, and why we take off the summers? For most of us, this is "just the way it's always been," and we've never questioned it. But there is more to this custom than meets the eye, for it is an example of cultural lag.

In the nineteenth century, when universal schooling came about, the school year matched the technology of the time, which was labour-intensive. For survival, parents needed their children's help at the critical times of planting and harvesting. Although the invention of highly productive farm machinery eliminated the need for the school year to be so short, generations later we live with this cultural lag.

Technology and Cultural Levelling

Except in rare instances, humans always had some contact with other groups. During these contacts, people learned from one another, adapting some part of the other's way of life. In this process, called **cultural diffusion**, groups are most open to a change in their technology or material culture. They usually are eager, for example, to adopt superior weapons and tools. In remote areas of South America one can find metal cooking pots, steel axes, and even bits of clothing spun in mills in North America. Although the direction of cultural diffusion today is primarily from the West to other parts of the world, cultural diffusion is not a one-way street, which can be seen in architectural designs, food (bagels, falafel, Thai, and so on), and leisure items such as the hammock.

With today's technology in travel and communications, cultural diffusion is occurring rapidly. Air travel has made it

Sociology and the
New Technology

Information and Communications Technologies (ICTs):
Global Village or Big Brother?

A sign over a photocopy machine:

> WARNING! This machine is subject to
> breakdowns during periods of critical
> need. A special circuit in the machine
> called a "critical detector" senses the
> operator's emotional state, in terms of
> how desperate he or she is to use the
> machine. The "critical detector" then
> creates a malfunction proportional to
> the desperation of the operator. Threat-
> ening the machine with violence only
> aggravates the situation. Keep cool and
> say nice things to the machine. Nothing
> else seems to work. Never let the
> machine know you are in a hurry.

All over the country, users of copiers
have laughed at some version of this
attempt to turn frustration into humour.
This sign comes close to a point of view
called **technological determinism**, the
idea that technology is the single greatest
force in shaping our lives. Like the preceding warning, some technological
determinists believe that machines have
become an independent force that is out
of human control (D. Chandler, 1995).
For them, technology is more important
than anything else—politics, economics,
religion, or any other social factor—in
creating the kind of society we live in.

Two Canadian analysts, Harold Innis
and Marshall McLuhan, both at the University of Toronto, examined the effects
of technological revolutions on our culture. For Innis, oral cultures were limited in their size; that is, in terms of their
population density. However, the ability
to write made human geographical
expansion possible because a literate
group could keep in touch through writing. In Innis' mind, bureaucratic empires
became possible when people could
check the records and develop standards
of judgment.

Marshall McLuhan built on Innis by
portraying communications technologies
as extensions of the human body. Just as

a pole increases the reach of your arm, so
too do the new and varied ways we communicate with one another today extend
the power of our senses. But not all senses share equally in their extension. Literacy may amplify one's eyes, McLuhan
observed figuratively, but it shrinks one's
ears. A computer, for example, extends
the power of our brain and, ironically,
our ears with the use of computer games
and access to new music over the Web,
but not our sense of touch or smell. The
more we use microelectronics-based
technologies, whether a cell phone, a
computer, or a Walkman, the smaller our
world becomes. We are living in what
McLuhan coined "the Global Village."

Sherry Turkle takes McLuhan several steps further by arguing that information and communications technologies
help create separate virtual realities that
play on our fantasies, both sexual and
nonsexual.

Instead of stressing how technology
shapes culture, other analysts stress that
culture shapes technology. This view,
called the **social construction of technology**, emphasizes how values and special interests shape the development and
use of technology (Bijker, Hughes, &
Pinch, 1987). For example, in the 1500s
guns were imported to Japan (Volti,
1995). The Japanese copied them, modified their design, and manufactured
them. The use of guns, however, threatened the Samurai, the warrior class that
used swords and followed ancient rituals
in hand-to-hand combat. Suddenly, from
a distance, anyone with a gun, even cow-
ards and social inferiors, could kill the
best-trained and bravest Samurai. The
Japanese government then centralized
the production of guns and sold them
only by licence, which they refused to
grant. People and culture—in this case
the Samurai and adherence to Japanese
rituals of bravery—dominated technology.

Marshall McLuhan.

In short, the *social constructionists*
emphasize how people control, influence, or use technology. The *technological
determinists*, in contrast, emphasize how
technology affects people's customs,
lifestyles, relationships, and even ideas.

For Your Consideration

The technological determinists and the
social constructionists bring us to a significant issue: Does technology free us,
or is it yet another force of society that
programs us? In other words, are we in
control of technology, or is technology in
control of us?

Perhaps the truth consists of a combination of these views; perhaps technology both liberates and constrains. If so,
can you provide examples from your own
experience of how people mold technology, and how it, in turn, molds us?

In today's world, the long-accepted
idea that it is proper to withhold rights on
the basis of someone's sex can no longer
hold. What is usually invisible in this revolutionary change is the role of technology, which joins the world's nations into a
global communication network.

possible to journey around the globe in a matter of hours.
In the not-so-distant past, a trip from Canada to Africa was
so unusual that only a few hardy people made it, and newspapers would herald their feat. Today, hundreds of thousands make the trip every year.

The changes in communication are no less vast. Communication used to be limited to face-to-face speech. Today's
electronic communications transmit messages across the
globe in a matter of seconds, and we learn almost instantaneously what is happening on the other side of the world.

Although today's cultural diffusion moves primarily from the West to the East, it is not entirely one-way. These children are trading Pokémon cards. Pokémon originated in Japan and swept across North America.

more. One result is **cultural levelling**, a process in which cultures become similar to one another as expanding industrialization brings not only technology but also Western culture to the rest of the world. Japan, for example, has adapted not only Western economic production but also Western forms of dress and music. These changes, superimposed on Japanese culture, have turned Japan into a blend of Western and Eastern cultures.

Cultural levelling, occurring rapidly around the world, is apparent to any traveller. The Golden Arches of McDonald's welcome today's visitors to Tokyo, Paris, London, Madrid, and even Moscow, Beijing, and Hong Kong. In Mexico, the most popular piñatas are no longer of donkeys but of Mickey Mouse and Fred Flintstone (Beckett, 1996). In the Indian Himalayan town of Dharmsala, a Buddhist monk and two Indian boys, sitting on benches in a shack with a dirt floor waiting for a videotaped U.S. movie to begin, watch a Levis commercial on MTV. "Thanks to MTV," says an Indian girl in Calcutta, "I can wear a miniskirt to a disco" (Brauchli, 1993b).

Although the bridging of geography and culture by electronic signals does not in itself mark the end of traditional cultures, it inevitably results in some degree of cultural levelling—North American culture with French, Japanese, and Bulgarian accents, so to speak.

In fact, travel and communication unite us to such an extent that there almost is no "other side of the world" any-

Summary and Review

WHAT IS CULTURE?

All human groups possess **culture**—language, beliefs, values, norms, and material objects passed from one generation to the next. **Material culture** consists of objects (art, buildings, clothing, tools). **Nonmaterial (or symbolic) culture** is a group's ways of thinking and patterns of behaviour. p. 49.

What are cultural relativism and ethnocentrism?

People are naturally ethnocentric; that is, they use their own culture as a yardstick for judging the ways of others. In contrast, those who embrace **cultural relativism** try to understand other cultures on those cultures' own terms. pp. 49–50.

COMPONENTS OF SYMBOLIC CULTURE
What are the components of nonmaterial culture?

The central component is **symbols**, anything to which people attach meaning and use to communicate with others. Universally, the symbols of nonmaterial culture are **gestures**, **language**, **values**, **norms**, **sanctions**, **folkways**, and **mores**. pp. 51–52.

Why is language so significant to culture?

Language allows human experience to be goal-directed, cooperative, and cumulative. It also lets humans move beyond the present and share a past, future, and other common perspectives. According to the **Sapir-Whorf hypothesis**, language even shapes our thoughts and perceptions. pp. 52–55.

How do values, norms, folkways, mores, and sanctions reflect culture?

All groups have **values**, standards by which they define what is desirable or undesirable, and **norms**, rules or expectations about behaviour. Groups use **positive sanctions** to show approval of those who follow their norms, and **negative sanctions** to show disapproval of those who do not. Norms that are not strictly enforced are called **folkways**, while **mores** are norms to which groups demand conformity because they reflect core values. p. 55.

How do subcultures and countercultures differ?

A **subculture** is a group whose values and related behaviours distinguish its members from the general culture. A **counterculture** holds values that at least in some ways stand in opposition to those of the dominant culture. p. 56.

VALUES IN CANADIAN SOCIETY
What are the values of Canadian society?

Although Canada is a **pluralistic society** made up of many groups, each with its own set of values, tolerance and liberal moral values dominate. For Canadians, sex and morality means acceptance and tolerance. While adultery is not the basis for a politician's resignation, lying under oath is. There are differences in values between Quebecois and the rest of Canada.

Some values come together (**value clusters**) to form a larger whole. **Value contradictions** (such as equality and racism) indicate areas of social tension, which are likely points of social change. Changes in a society's fundamental values are opposed by people who hold strongly to traditional values. Leisure, physical fitness, self-fulfillment, and concern for the environment are emerging core values. **Ideal culture** is a group's ideal values and norms, and their goals. **Real culture**, people's actual behaviour, often falls short of their cultural ideals. pp. 56–63.

CULTURAL UNIVERSALS

Do cultural universals exist?

Cultural universals are values, norms, or other cultural traits found in all cultures. Although all human groups have customs concerning cooking, funerals, weddings, and so on, because the specific forms these customs take vary from one culture to another there are no cultural universals. p. 63.

ANIMALS AND CULTURE

Do animals have culture?

To the extent that some animals teach their young certain behaviours, animals also have a rudimentary culture. No animals have language in the sociological sense of the term, although some experiments indicate that some animals may have a limited capacity to learn language. pp. 63–65.

TECHNOLOGY IN THE GLOBAL VILLAGE

How is technology changing culture?

Ogburn coined the term **cultural lag** to refer to a group's nonmaterial culture lagging behind its changing technology. With today's technological advances in travel and communications, **cultural diffusion** is occurring rapidly. This leads to **cultural levelling**, whereby many groups are adopting Western culture in place of their own customs. Much of the richness of the world's diverse cultures is being lost in the process. pp. 65–67.

Critical Thinking Questions

1. Are all cultures equally valid? Can you think of a culture (e.g., Nazism) that you would find unacceptable? Why do you feel the way you do?

2. Do the media influence our culture, or does the expanding cultural diversity in our society influence the changes we find expressed in the media?

3. Is sexual orientation simply the product of a person's cultural upbringing? What role does biology play in our sexual preferences?

4. Why do many teenagers rebel against authority? Is there such a thing as a teenage subculture?

Key Terms

animal culture 64
counterculture 56
cultural diffusion 65

cultural lag 65
cultural levelling 67
cultural relativism 50

cultural universals 63
culture 48
ethnocentrism 49
folkways 55
gestures 51
ideal culture 63
language 52
material culture 48
mores 55
negative sanction 55
new technology 65
nonmaterial culture 49
norms 55
pluralistic society 56
positive sanction 55
real culture 63

sanctions 55
Sapir-Whorf hypothesis 53
social construction of
    technology 66
subculture 56
symbol 51
symbolic culture 51
taboo 55
technological determinism 66
technology 65
tools 64
value cluster 61
value contradiction 59
values 55

Weblinks

The National Magazine/Maclean's Poll

www.tv.cbc.ca/national/pgminfo/poll/index.html

Since 1983, the TV show *The National Magazine* and *Maclean's* magazine have polled Canadians on topics from taxes to sex, politics, and morality. Here you can see the results.

Culture and Tradition: The Canadian Graduate Student Journal of Folklore and Ethnology

www.ucs.mun.ca/~culture/

Canada's longest-running, bilingual folklore journal, published for nearly 20 years in both French and English. It is currently run by graduate students in Folklore at Memorial University of Newfoundland. Topics covered include the traditional arts, music, cuisine, architecture, beliefs, cultural psychology, and sociological structure of regional ethnic, religious, and industrial groups in Canada.

Multicultural Home Page

pasture.ecn.purdue.edu/~agenhtml/agenmc/

Covers a wide range of information: geographical, historical, arts, weather, recipes, tourist information, and so on. The page was developed by students interested in sharing information about their home countries.

The Ancient World Web

www.julen.net/ancient/

A searchable, categorized ongoing collection of links.

Tables of Contents for All Issues of Postmodern Culture

jefferson.village.virginia.edu/pmc/

Postmodern Culture, an electronic journal of interdisciplinary criticism, is published by Johns Hopkins University Press with support from the University of Virginia's Institute for Advanced Technology in the Humanities.

Socialization

Chapter 4

Learning Outcomes

After you have studied this chapter, you will be able to

■ understand how human behaviour is shaped by the social environment

■ understand how gender identity is created

■ understand the stages of socialization

■ balance your grasp of socialization with an understanding of our ability to be active participants in the social construction of the self

The old man was horrified when he found out. Life never had been good since his daughter had lost her hearing when she was just two years old. She couldn't even talk—just fluttered her hands around trying to tell him things. Over the years, he had gotten used to that. But now … he shuddered at the thought of her being pregnant. No one would be willing to marry her; he knew that. And the neighbours, their tongues would never stop wagging. Everywhere he went, he could hear people talking behind his back.

If only his wife were still alive, maybe she could come up with something. What should he do? He couldn't just kick his daughter out into the street.

After the baby was born, the old man tried to shake his feelings, but they wouldn't let loose. Isabelle was a pretty name, but every time he looked at the baby he felt sick to his stomach.

He hated doing it, but there was no way out. His daughter and her baby would have to live in the attic. For more than six years the little girl was kept locked away.

When the newspapers reported this case, sociologist Kingsley Davis decided to find out what happened to Isabelle after her discovery. We'll come back to that later, but first let's use the case of Isabelle to give us some insight into what human nature is.

Genes or Environment?

For generations, one of the big issues every sociology student has been introduced to is an exploration of the "nature versus nurture" debate. Two competing viewpoints on the nature of human existence have struggled against one another. Are people's fates, likes and dislikes, behaviour dictated by inborn characteristics—in other words, genetic material—or are our destinies created by the culture, historical period, family, and friendship group we just happen to belong to? A sampling of newspaper headlines indicates that this intellectual contest is raging on into the new millennium: "A New Study Supports Nurture over Genes"; "Parenting Strongest Influence on Kids, Study Finds" (*Toronto Star*, September–December 1999); "Divorce is Inherent Mating Behaviour" (*The Saturday Post*, 2002, p. SP6). Although researchers now know much more about both the human genome and social influences, the newspaper items speak to our continuing fascination with the complex and unclear relationship between the two.

One of the most important contributions of modern sociology has been an exploration of the ways in which social forces and the **social environment** "create" human experience. In this sociologists have built upon a line of inquiry which has fascinated men and women for centuries. We have long been intrigued by the prospect of children reared away from civilization, away from the influence of families and friends. The ancient legend of Romulus and Remus, the twin babies reared by wolves who grew up to found Rome, speaks to this captivating puzzle. Rudyard Kipling's story of Mowgli, who is abandoned in the jungle and reared by wild animals, echoes the same concerns. In actuality, few instances of "wild" or **feral children** have been documented in history.

Focus Question
How does the genetic explanation of human development measure up against the environmental perspective?

Feral and Isolated Children

Over the centuries, the discovery of feral children has been reported from time to time. Supposedly, these children were abandoned or lost by their parents at a very early age and then raised by animals. In one instance, a feral child, known as "the wild boy of Aveyron," was studied by the scientists of his day (Itard, 1962). This boy, who was found in the forests of France in 1798, walked on all fours, and pounced on small animals, devouring them uncooked. He could not speak, and he gave no indication of feeling the cold. Other reports of feral children have claimed that on discovery, these children acted like wild animals: They could not speak; they bit, scratched, growled, and walked on all fours; they ate grass, tore ravenously at meat, drank by lapping water; and showed an insensitivity to pain and cold (Malson, 1972).

There have been several well-documented instances of children who were reared in extremely deprived and isolated circumstances. Among the most well-known is the case of Isabelle, recounted at the beginning of this chapter, which was investigated by the prominent U.S. sociologist Kingsley Davis. Born in the early 1930s to a deaf-mute mother, Isabelle was confined to the dark attic of her grandfather's house until she was discovered at about six-and-a-half years of age. Unable to speak, she communicated with her mother through gestures. Malnutrition and lack of sunshine had left her legs so deformed by rickets that she could only get around by skittering along on the floor. Her reaction to strangers, especially men, was that of a fearful and hostile wild animal. On an intelligence test she scored almost zero (Davis, 1940/1997).

Amazingly, when Isabelle was taken out of her deprived environment and given intensive language training, she was transformed. In only two months, she was able to speak in short sentences. In about a year, she could write a few words, do simple addition, and retell stories after hearing them. Seven months later, she had a vocabulary of almost 2000 words. It took only two years for Isabelle to reach the intellectual level normal for her age. She then went on to school, where she was "bright, cheerful, energetic, and participated in all school activities as normally as other children" (Davis, 1940/1997, p. 127).

As discussed in the last chapter, "language" is a key to human behaviour. In order for human interaction to occur, there needs to be a shared system of communication. This language system may take various forms—spoken, spoken and written or, as with American Sign Language, signed. Without language, people have no mechanism for developing thought and self-awareness. Unlike animals, humans have no instincts that take the place of language. If an individual lacks language, he or she lives in a world of internal silence, without shared ideas and experiences, without connections to others. Without language, there can be no culture—no shared way of life—and culture is the key to what people become. Each of us possesses a biological heritage, but this heritage does not dictate specific behaviours, attitudes, or values. It is our culture that superimposes the specifics of what we become onto our biological potential.

However, biology may establish certain time limits on our ability to acquire language and make connections to others. A more recent instance of an isolated and deprived child suggests there are limits on our receptivity to our social environment. Genie was discovered in 1970 by California authorities. She was the child of an abusive, older father and a partially blind mother completely dominated by her husband. From about the age of two until she was $13\frac{1}{2}$ years old, Genie had lived her life locked in a small room. When removed from this abusive and deprived environment, her behaviour was much like that of a wild animal. She could not speak or chew; she could not stand upright or straighten her arms and legs. Her intelligence score was that of a one-year-old. She defecated and urinated wherever she happened to be.

Unfortunately, unlike Isabelle, intensive training was not able to bring Genie back to a "normal" level of development. She learned to walk and to use simple, though garbled, sentences but her language use was primitive and she did not learn to use the bathroom. At the age of 21, she was placed in a home for adults who cannot live alone (Pines, 1981). From Genie's sad life, it appears that biology may set a limited time within which social connections and language acquisition must occur. If bonding and learning to communicate with others does not occur prior to age 13, the biological window of opportunity may close.

Deprived Animals

A final lesson can be gained by looking at animals that have been deprived of normal interaction. In a series of experiments with rhesus monkeys, psychologists Harry and Margaret Harlow demonstrated the importance of early learning. The Harlows (1962) raised baby monkeys in isolation. They gave each monkey two artificial mothers. One "mother" was only a wire frame with a wooden head, but it did have a nipple from which the baby could nurse. The frame of the other "mother," which had no bottle, was covered with soft terrycloth. For their food, the baby monkeys nursed at the wire frame. But when the Harlows (1965) frightened the babies with a large mechanical bear or dog, the babies did not run to the wire-frame "mother"; instead, they would cling pathetically to their terrycloth "mother." The Harlows drew the significant conclusion that infant-mother bonding is due not to feeding but rather to what they termed "intimate physical contact." To most of us, this phrase means cuddling.

It is also significant that the monkeys raised in isolation were never able to adjust to monkey life. Placed with other monkeys when they were grown, they didn't know how to enter into "monkey interaction"—to play and to engage in

Like humans, monkeys need interaction to thrive. Those raised in isolation are unable to interact satisfactorily with others. In this photograph, we see one of the monkeys described in the text. Purposely frightened by the experimenter, the monkey has taken refuge in the soft terrycloth draped over an artificial "mother."

pretend fights—and the other monkeys rejected them. Neither did they know how to engage in sexual intercourse, in spite of futile attempts to do so. The experimenters designed a special device, which allowed some females to become pregnant. After giving birth, however, these monkeys were "ineffective, inadequate, and brutal mothers ... [who] ... struck their babies, kicked them, or crushed the babies against the cage floor."

In one of their many other experiments, the Harlows isolated baby monkeys for different lengths of time. They found that monkeys isolated for short periods (about three months) were able to overcome the effects of their isolation. Those isolated for six months or more, however, were unable to adjust to normal monkey life. In other words, the longer the isolation, the more difficult it is to overcome. There also may be a critical learning stage that, if missed, may be impossible to overcome, as apparently was the case with Genie.

Because humans are not monkeys, we must be careful about extrapolating from animal studies to human behaviour. The Harlow experiments, however, support what we know about the effects of isolation on children.

Focus Question
What is the impact of deprivation and isolation on humans and on other animals?

In Sum

There is considerable scientific evidence that society and social experience make us human. It seems likely that if babies could be raised in isolation from human contact they would mature into full-size adults but would not develop into "human beings" as we understand them. In particular, without the use of language or other symbol systems, humans reared in isolation would not experience or grasp relationships between people, would not be able to share the knowledge of others, and would be unable to chronicle their own history.

The Social Development of the Self, Mind, and Emotions

At birth we have no idea that we are separate beings, no idea even that we are he or she. How do we develop a **self**, the picture we have of how others see us, our view of who we are? The process by which we learn the ways of society (or of particular groups), is called **socialization**. This is what sociologists have in mind when they say "Society makes us human."

Cooley and the Looking-Glass Self

Back in the 1800s, Charles Horton Cooley (1864–1929), a symbolic interactionist who taught at the University of

Michigan, concluded that this unique aspect of "humanness" called the "self" is *socially created*; that is, our sense of self develops from interaction with others. He coined the term **looking-glass self** (1902) to describe the process by which a sense of self develops, which he summarized in the following couplet:

Each to each a looking-glass
Reflects the other that doth pass.

The looking-glass self contains three elements:

1. *We imagine how we appear to those around us.* "Others think I am clever."

2. *We interpret others' reactions.* We come to conclusions about how others evaluate us. "People like me because I am clever."

3. *We develop a self-concept.* On the basis of our interpretations of the reactions of others, we develop feelings and ideas about ourselves. "I like myself, since others view me as likeable."

The development of the self does not depend on accurate evaluations. Even if we grossly misinterpret how others think about us, those misjudgments become part of our self-concept. Note also that although the self-concept begins in childhood, *its development is an ongoing, lifelong process.* The three steps of the looking-glass self are a part of our everyday lives, and as we monitor how other people react to us, we continually modify the self. The self, then, is never a finished product, but is always in process, even into old age.

Mead and Role-Taking

Another symbolic interactionist, George Herbert Mead (1863–1931), who taught at the University of Chicago, added that play is critical to the development of a self. In play, children learn **taking the role of the other**, that is, putting themselves in someone else's shoes to understand how someone else feels and thinks and anticipating how that person will act.

Young children attain this ability only gradually. Mead suggests *taking the role of the other* is an essential part of learning to be a full-fledged member of society. At first, we are able to take the role only of *significant others*, individuals who significantly influence our lives, such as parents or siblings. Later we develop *the capacity to take the role of the generalized other*, which is essential not only for extended cooperation but also for the control of antisocial desires (G. H. Mead, 1934; Coser, 1977; Mackie, 1987). In a simple experiment, psychologist J. Flavel (1968) asked 14-year-olds and 8-year-olds to explain a board game to some children who were blindfolded and to others who were not. The 8-year-olds gave the same instructions to everyone, while the 14-year-olds gave more detailed instructions to those who were blindfolded. The younger children could not yet take the role of the other, while the older children could.

To help his students understand what the term *generalized other* means, Mead used baseball as an illustration. The text explains why team sports and organized games are excellent examples to explain this concept.

As they develop this ability, at first children are able to take only the role of **significant others**, mother, father, sister, or brother. By assuming their roles during play, such as dressing up in their parents' clothing, children cultivate the ability to put themselves in the place of significant others.

As the self gradually develops, children internalize the expectations of larger numbers of people. The ability to take on roles eventually extends to being able to take the role of an abstract entity, "the group as a whole." To this, our perception of how people in general think of us, Mead gave the term **generalized other**.

Taking the role of the other is essential if we are to become cooperative members of human groups whether the family, peers, or work. This ability allows us to modify our behaviour by anticipating the reactions of others, something Genie never learned.

Prominent Canadian sociologist Marlene Mackie uses Mead's three stages of "learning to take the role of the other" to explain how we learn our gender roles (1987, pp. 124–137).

1. *Imitation/preparatory stage.* Children under 3 can only mimic others. They do not yet have a sense of self as separate from others, and they can only imitate people's gestures and words. This stage is not actually role-taking but it prepares the child for it. In particular, the child is learning things have names and he or she has a name—Susie or Bobby. Later, the child learns that boys and girls usually have different kinds of names and that, indeed, boys and girls are treated differently by caregivers. For example, research indicates that parents "interact more with girls" and play a more protective role with them. Boys are expected to spend more time

alone and to move out into the world. Toddlers do not understand these early experiences in gender terms, but they clearly set the stage for subsequent developments.

2. *Play stage.* During the second stage, from the age of about 3 to 5 or 6, children pretend to take the roles of specific people. Girls will play at being mother or teacher while boys pretend to be hockey players or firefighters. At this stage, younger children often have an imperfect understanding of gender roles; they may think that hair length or urination posture determines who is a boy/man and who is a girl/woman. One researcher recounts the story of a 5-year-old girl who said she couldn't tell how many boys and girls were at a party since the children were bathing in the nude. Similarly, these young children often do not yet understand that gender is a constant; that is, boys do not grow up to be mommies. However, they do understand that gender is important in their social reality and they quickly acquire greater sophistication. They learn that there are "boys' toys" and "girls' toys" and they learn which ones they should "prefer."

Caregivers, parents, and peers directly and indirectly convey the message that boys and girls are significantly different, that it is critically important that you know whether you are a boy or girl and, finally, that you learn to act appropriately as a boy or a girl. Playing out these gender roles becomes an increasingly important mechanism for learning these social lessons. In this process boys and girls learn to step outside themselves and construct "the self as a gendered being."

3. *Game stage.* This third stage, organized play, or team games, begins roughly at age 7 and lasts through to puberty. The significance for the development of the self is that to play the games, the individual must be able to take on multiple roles. Mead used the analogy of a baseball game. In order to play baseball, it is important to know not only what to do when you go up to bat but also what to expect from the other players in the game- what will the catcher, first base, umpire, and so on be doing in the game. Without the knowledge of the entire game and these diverse roles, it is impossible to play in any meaningful sense. Similarly, boys and girls learn that gender roles are complexly related to one another. The role of "being a girl" hinges on some other who will be "acting the role of boy." Girls, for example, typically learn through their same-sex play activities to function well in small, intimate groups, to converse, to be empathic, and to show affection. Boys, in contrast, learn through their games and sports to coordinate with others, to cope with interpersonal rules, to work as a group as well as an individual, and to deal with competition and criticism.

Many analysts comment that this is not a simple, positive process for either boys or girls. Boys, for example, are more likely to grow up to be emotionally out of touch.

However, it is girls who, many feel, bear the brunt of this process. Girls are often learning to take a subordinate role—to be the audience and not the actors—not only to the males in their lives, but also in terms of access to society's rewards (Nelson & Robinson, 2002).

Mead also wanted to allow for human freedom of choice in his framework. He introduced the two concepts the "I" and the "me." The "*I*" is *the self as subject*, the active, spontaneous, creative part of the self as in "I throw the ball." In contrast, the "*me*" is the *self as object*, made up of attitudes internalized from our interactions with others as in "They made me do it." Mead stressed that the individual is not only a "me," like a computerized robot passively absorbing the responses of others. Rather, the "I" actively makes sense of those responses and acts.

Mead also drew a conclusion that some find startling—that *not only the self but also the human mind is a social product*. Mead stressed that we cannot think without symbols. But where do these symbols come from? Only from society, which gives us our symbols by giving us language. If society did not provide the symbols, we would not be able to think and would not possess what we call the mind. While our understanding of thought processes and the development of the brain have changed dramatically in light of more recent research, Mead's thesis that how we think is, at least in part, a product of social experiences remains sound (Covell & Howe, 2001).

> ## Focus Question
> In what ways can the complexities of gender socialization be usefully compared to the learning of a game, such as baseball?

Piaget and the Development of Reasoning Skills

Essential to the human mind is the ability to reason. How do we learn this skill?

This question intrigued Jean Piaget (1896–1980), a Swiss psychologist, who noticed that younger children would give *consistent* wrong answers on intelligence tests. This might mean, he thought, that younger children follow some sort of incorrect rule in figuring out answers. Perhaps this is how we all learn to reason.

To find out, Piaget set up a laboratory where he could give children of different ages problems to solve (Piaget, 1950, 1954; Phillips, 1969). After years of research, Piaget concluded that children go through four stages as they develop their ability to reason. At each stage, children develop new reasoning skills. (As we review these stages, it may be helpful to mentally substitute *reasoning skills* for Piaget's term *operational*.)

1. *The sensorimotor stage (from birth to about age 2).* During this early stage, the infant's understanding is limited to direct contact with the environment. It is based on sucking, touching, listening, seeing. Infants do not think in any sense that we understand. During the first part of this stage, they do not even know that their bodies are separate from the environment. Indeed, they have yet to discover that they have toes. Neither can infants recognize cause and effect. They do not know that their actions cause something to happen.

2. *The preoperational stage (from about age 2 to age 7).* During this stage, children develop the ability to use symbols. They do not yet understand common concepts, however, such as size, speed, or causation. Although they can count, they do not really understand what numbers mean. Nor do they yet have the ability to take the role of the other. Piaget asked preoperational children to describe a clay mountain range and found that they could do so. But when he asked them to describe how the mountain range looked from where another child was sitting, they could not do so. They could only repeat what they saw from their view.

3. *The concrete operational stage (from the age of about 7 to 12).* Although reasoning abilities are more developed, they remain *concrete*. Children can now understand numbers, causation, and speed, and they are able to take the role of the other and to participate in team games. Without concrete examples, however, they are unable to talk about such concepts as truth, honesty, or justice. They can explain why Jane's answer was a lie, but they cannot describe what truth itself is.

4. *The formal operational stage (after the age of about 12).* Children are now capable of abstract thinking. Without concrete examples, they can talk about concepts, come to conclusions based on general principles, and use rules to solve abstract problems. During this stage, they are likely to become young philosophers (Kagan, 1984). For example, if shown a photo of a slave, a child at the concrete operational stage might have said, "That's wrong!" Now, however, he or she is more likely to ask, "If the United States was founded on equality, how could people have owned slaves?"

Freud and the Development of Personality

Along with the development of the mind and the self comes the development of personality. Let's look at a theory that has influenced the Western world.

In Vienna, Sigmund Freud (1856–1939), a physician, founded *psychoanalysis*, a technique for treating emotional problems through long-term, intensive exploration of the subconscious mind.

Freud believed that personality consists of three elements. Every child is born with the first, an **id**, Freud's term for inborn drives for self-gratification. The id of the new-born is evident in cries of hunger or pain. The pleasure-seeking id operates throughout life, demanding the immediate fulfillment of basic needs: attention, safety, food, sex, aggression, and so on.

But the id's drive for immediate and complete satisfaction runs directly against the needs of other people. As the child comes up against norms and other constraints (usually represented by parents), he or she must adapt to survive. To help adapt to these constraints that block his or her desires, a second component of the personality emerges, which Freud called the **ego**. The ego is the balancing force between the id and the demands of society that suppress it.

The ego also serves to balance the id and the **superego**, the third component of the personality, more commonly called the conscience. The superego represents *culture within us*, the norms and values we have internalized from our social groups. As the *moral* component of the personality, the superego gives us feelings of guilt or shame when we break social rules, or pride and self-satisfaction when we follow them.

According to Freud, when the id gets out of hand, we follow our desires for pleasure and break society's norms. When the superego gets out of hand, we become overly rigid in following those norms, finding ourselves bound in a straitjacket of rules that inhibit our lives. The ego, the balancing force, tries to prevent either the superego or the id from dominating. In the emotionally healthy individual, the ego succeeds in balancing these conflicting demands of the id and the superego. In the maladjusted individual, however, the ego cannot control the inherent conflict between the id and the superego, and the result is internal confusion and problem behaviours.

Sociological Evaluation. What sociologists appreciate about Freud is his emphasis on socialization; that is, the social group into which we are born transmits norms and values that restrain our biological drives. Sociologists, however, object to the view that inborn and unconscious motivations are the primary reasons for human behaviour, for this denies *the central principle of sociology*: that social factors such as social class, religion, and education underlie people's behaviours (Epstein, 1988; Bush & Simmons, 1990). Feminist sociologists have been especially critical of Freud. Although what we just summarized applies to both females and males, Freud assumed that what is "male" is "normal." He even analyzed females as inferior, castrated males (Hamilton, 2000; Chodorow, 1990; Gilligan, 1982).

> **Focus Question**
> In what ways have Cooley, Mead, Piaget, and Freud contributed to our understanding of socialization?

Global Considerations: Teen Smoking and Socialization

Smoking cigarettes provides a useful example of the power and complexity of socialization. Certainly, there is no evidence that people have any inborn drive to inhale tobacco smoke. Considerable evidence documents the numerous health risks attached to smoking. It is estimated that globally 100 million deaths were attributable to tobacco use during the twentieth century (Lu, 2002). Enormous effort and expense have been expended to educate the public about these risks. Yet, around the world young men and women, almost all under 19 years of age, become "smokers." In Canada, between 27 and 30 percent of teenagers

Although males are socialized to express less emotion than females, such socialization goes against their nature. In certain settings, especially sports, males are allowed to be openly emotional, even demonstrative, with one another. Shown here is Scottie Pippen embracing an exhausted Michael Jordan after a Chicago Bulls victory against the Utah Jazz.

Unsubtle ad campaigns: Young people are subjected to powerful social and commercial pressures that promote smoking as a socially desirable activity.

Source: Mayes, *St. Catharines Standard*, Nov. 24, 1999 (A10). Reproduced courtesy of Malcolm Mayes/Artizans.com.

and 36 percent of young people aged 20 to 24 are smokers ("More Inuit Children Smoke," 2002, p. A6; Carey, 2000). To understand this behaviour it is important to recognize the powerful historical, social, and commercial pressures that create smoking as a socially desirable activity.

Smoking is a habit which, while it is biologically reinforced through physical addiction, must first be learned. Historically, smoking was a male-dominated behaviour until the early twentieth century. Popular magazines played an important role at that point in encouraging young women to take up smoking by presenting smoking as a glamorous, "modern," and rebellious behaviour (Tinkler, 2001). Today, along with the mass media, peers play an important role in introducing smoking to young men and women and creating a social context in which smoking is linked with positive social characteristics (Maxwell, 2002). Researchers in the United Kingdom report, "Smokers are seen by their peers as fun-loving and non-conformist and cigarettes as a passport to an exciting and popular lifestyle" (Lucas & Lloyd, 1999). Needless to say, these messages are reinforced by cigarette advertisements that associate smoking with youthful, attractive, slender young men and women. Similarly, in China, where one-third of the world's cigarettes are consumed, young people seek to emulate the teenage smoker since she or he is seen as "cool" and "fashionable." Further, the use of American cigarettes, a very costly commodity, is an important mechanism for conveying to others that you are not only "hip," but also affluent

(Cheng, 1999). Clearly, for many young people worldwide, the pressures from the social and commercial environment are much more powerful than any concerns they may have about their health and well-being.

> **Focus Question**
> According to the socialization perspective, why do some people become smokers and how do some people learn to become non-smokers?

In Sum

Prominent social theorists have attempted to explain how we develop a sense of self, a mind, and a set of emotions. Through this ongoing work we have developed an appreciation for the complex process of socialization that occurs in every culture and at every historical moment. Our fundamental sense of self—what we desire, who we love, how we experience sadness—is rooted in our socialization experiences (Massey, 2002; Requena, 2001).

Socialization into Gender

One of the key ways in which Canadian society channels behaviour is through **gender socialization**. By expecting different attitudes and behaviours from us *because* we are male or female, the social group nudges boys and girls in separate directions in life. This foundation of contrasting attitudes and behaviours is so thorough that, as adults, most of us act, think, and even feel according to the guidelines laid down by our culture as appropriate for our sex.

How do we learn gender messages? Because the significance of gender is emphasized throughout this book, with a special focus in Chapter 7, for now let's briefly consider the influence of just the family and the mass media.

Gender Messages in the Family

Our parents are usually the first significant others who teach us our part in this symbolic division of the world. Sometimes they do so self-consciously, perhaps by bringing into play pink and blue, colours that have no meaning in themselves but have social associations with gender. But our parents' own gender orientations are so firmly established that they also teach us **gender roles**, the behaviours and attitudes considered appropriate for our sex, without being aware of what they are doing.

A classic study illustrates how deeply ingrained these orientations are. Psychologists Susan Goldberg and Michael Lewis (1969) asked mothers to bring their 6-month-old infants into their laboratory, supposedly to observe the

Parents are so ensconced in their gender roles that they'll often pass on behaviours and attitudes to their kids without even thinking about it.

infants' development. Secretly, however, the researchers also observed the mothers. They found that the mothers kept their female children closer to them. They also touched and spoke more to their daughters. By the time the children were 13 months old, the girls stayed closer to their mothers during play. When Goldberg and Lewis set up a barrier to separate the children from their mothers, who were holding toys, the girls were more likely to cry and motion for help, the boys to try to climb over the barrier. Goldberg and Lewis concluded that in our society mothers unconsciously reward daughters for being passive and dependent, but sons for being active and independent.

These lessons continue throughout childhood. On the basis of sex, children are given different kinds of toys. Preschool boys are allowed to roam farther from home than their preschool sisters, and they are subtly encouraged to participate in more rough-and-tumble play—even to get dirtier and to be more defiant (Gilman, 1911/1971; Mackie, 1987; Henslin, 1997a; Nelson & Robinson, 2002). This process that begins in the family is completed as the child

is exposed to other aspects of society (Nelson & Robinson, 2002; Thorne, 1990). Teachers, for example, expect male and female students to be different. They then nurture the "natural" differences they find, with the result that boys and girls often develop different aspirations in life. The advent of the "feminist classroom," of course, seeks to change this traditional gender socialization pattern (Maher & Tetreault, 2001).

Gender Messages in the Mass Media

The **mass media**, forms of communication directed to large audiences, reinforce cultural expectations of gender. Of the many ways they do this, let's examine advertising, television, and video games.

Advertising. Although advertising uses a mix of gender images, it continues to perpetuate stereotypes by portraying males as more dominant and rugged and females as more sexy and submissive. The buffed male model, unsmiling, posed in the wilderness or on a deserted beach comes to mind. Semi-clad female bodies whose assets are intended to sell a variety of products from automobiles to hamburgers are at the other end of the spectrum of stereotypical, culturally molded images.

Despite growing public awareness of this kind of stereotyping, it persists. Men are still less likely to be portrayed cooking, cleaning, washing dishes, or shopping; women are more likely to be shown caring for an infant (G. Kaufman, 1999). Further, a review of research indicates that this sex-role stereotyping in television commercials is a global phenomenon, since it has endured for 25 years on five continents (Furnham & Mak, 1999).

Young people who spend a lot of time playing video games are subjected to many disturbing and skewed gender messages from the games' characters.

Television. Television reinforces stereotypes of the sexes. On prime-time television, male characters outnumber female two to one. They also are more likely to be portrayed in higher-status positions (Vande Berg & Streckfuss, 1992). Viewers get the message, for the more television people watch, the more they tend to have restrictive ideas about women's role in society (Signorielli, 1989, 1990).

The exceptions to the stereotypes are notable and a sign of changing times. One program, perhaps the most stereotype-breaking of all, is *Xena: Warrior Princess*, a popular television series imported from Australia. Portrayed as dominant and possessing magical powers, Xena overcomes all obstacles and easily defeats all foes whether male or female.

While Xena may suggest a shift in attitude toward strong women, Australian researchers suggest that media images of the "new man" are mostly smoke and mirrors. The *Blokus domesticus*, the "sensitive new-age guy," is more rhetoric in the popular media than reality—a rhetoric that only appears to respond to women's demands for change while actually masking the lack of real movement, for example, in men's role in household responsibilities (McMahon, 1998).

Video and Computer Games. Playstation, Game Cube, Gameboy, X-Box, and numerous other game systems, along with a wide variety of computer games, have become part of most young Canadians' lives. Even university students, especially males, relieve stress by escaping into video and computer games. The gender messages embedded in these games are disturbing. An analysis of 33 popular Nintendo and Sega Genesis games finds that when females do appear in such games (they are frequently absent) they are often presented as sex objects. The majority of the games include aggression as part of the strategy or object of the game. Almost half included violence directed at others and almost one-quarter depicted violence directed at women (Dietz, 1998).

Focus Question

What are some of the media images in films and popular music that currently influence young men and women's ideas about masculinity and femininity?

Mass Media in Social Life

Heroes for Girls: From Snow White and Sleeping Beauty to Pocahontas and Xena—Are We Making Progress?

The mass media not only reflect gender stereotypes, but also play a role in changing them. Sometimes they do both simultaneously. The images of Lara and of Xena the Warrior Princess reflect women's changing role in society and, by exaggerating the change, also mold new stereotypes.

If there is one outstanding area in which the mass media have been subject to critical scrutiny, it is in their portrayal of women. As extensively documented in the latter part of the twentieth century, television, movies, school textbooks, and magazine advertisements tended to present women in a narrow and stereotyped fashion. In many instances, females, even in cartoons and children's picture books, were simply absent. When images of women did appear in the mass media, they were often restricted to young, white, attractive, and sexualized individuals. Not only their appearance but also their activities were stereotyped, with traditional locations, such as the home, predominating. As a result of these critical analyses, there has

been considerable effort to assure a more realistic and varied portrayal of women and girls (Nelson & Robinson, 2002).

Although much has indeed changed, research suggests that progress has been at best uneven. For example, a recent examination of children's picture books reported that, although the inclusion of females as main characters in these books and their titles has greatly improved since the 1970s, the female images are often stereotyped (Gooden & Gooden, 2001). Girls, for example, are still more likely to be described as nurturers and care-takers than adventurers, more likely to take care of the lost puppy than to rescue it from harm. Even in very contemporary forms of mass media, such as computer clipart (Print Shop or Microsoft Office), females are less visible than Caucasian males and more frequently depicted in inactive/nurturing and undesirable roles. For example, illustrations depicted females more often in passive positions, sitting and reclining, and assigned them the role of "audience" to the male figure (Milburn,

Carney, & Ramirez, 2001).

However, in other areas of the mass media there appear to have been tremendous changes in the portrayal of girls and women. The Disney heroine, for example, has moved from *Snow White and the Seven Dwarfs* (1937) to *Sleeping Beauty* (1959), *Pocahontas* (1995), *Mulan* (1999), and *Lilo and Stitch* (2002). In contrast to the traditional heroine who was restricted to her role as "selfless nurturer" and romantic, the more contemporary heroine is an active and even aggressive participant in the story. In the 1995 Disney film, Pocahontas, for instance, is first seen as she paddles alone in the wilderness. She is presented as self-sufficient, lively, and strong. Later, in defense of her romantic counterpart, John Smith, she rebels against her father and her community. Similarly, Mulan (1999) is portrayed as a headstrong young woman who disobeys her parents, leaves her family home, and successfully impersonates a male soldier (Dundes, 2001). Similarly, the "pleasantly plump" heroines, Lilo and her older sister Mele, in *Lilo and Stitch* (2002) break the mold of the Barbie-shaped heroines in Disney films. Perhaps most commented upon in recent analyses has been the introduction of women as female action heros. *Xena* and *Lara Croft: Tomb Raider* (2001) present a novel image of femininity in that they are openly and physically aggressive (Calvert, Kondla, Ertel, & Meisel, 2001).

Clearly much has changed in the mass media's portrayal of women and girls. However, it is important to critically scrutinize the new images that are being offered. For example, while the modern female Disney heroes may no longer be "docile," they tend to be motivated by the traditionally female "ethic of care." Pocahontas sacrifices her own desire to accompany John Smith to England in order to remain and nurture her community. Mulan leaves home in order to protect her aging father from military duty, and her self-sacrifice is ultimately rewarded, as in many Disney classics, with a matrimonial happy ending (Dundes, 2001). Even Xena's ground-breaking role has been challenged. In Sandra Calvert, Tracy Kondla, Karen Ertel, and Douglas Meisel's recent research on young adults' perceptions of Xena, it was clear that her impact on gender roles was complex. The researchers found that although some young men and women, who themselves have more masculine personality traits, may see her as a role model, most do not. Most young men and women indicate they "like" Xena when she is in a program in which she plays a somewhat feminine role, being nurturing rather than using brute force. Finally, young women were more likely to want to be like her when they thought of her as physically attractive. In short, despite the apparent nontraditional message in Xena, she was adopted as a role model only by those males and females who already valued masculine characteristics. The majority of young men and women experienced the program in a manner consistent with traditional gender stereotypes (Calvert et al., 2001).

The mass media not only reflect gender stereotypes, but also play a role in changing them. Sometimes they do both simultaneously. The images of Lara and of Xena the Warrior Princess reflect women's changing role in society and, by exaggerating the change, also mold new stereotypes.

Popular Music. Popular songs also convey gender socialization messages. While many, of course, romanticize women and their relationship with men or portray loving relationships between men and women, it is alarming to find that, like many video games, some popular music promotes anti-female and pro-violence themes. Lisa Sloat's research into the depiction of female sexuality by male songwriters in contemporary music reveals many hit and less popular songs in which women are portrayed as obsessive, evil, and dangerous and deserving of degradation and violence (1998). It appears that young men and women are receiving, at best, mixed messages about both women's role in society and violence against women.

Absorbing Gender Messages: The Peer Group.
When sociologist Melissa Milkie (1994) studied a group of junior high school boys, she found that much of their talk centred on the latest movies, videos, and television programs. Of the many images presented in these media, the boys would single out sex and violence. They would joke and laugh about what they had seen, repeat lines, and act out parts for the amusement of one another.

If you know boys in their early teens, you've probably seen something like this yourself. You may have been amused, or even shaken your head in disapproval. Like a good sociologist, however, Milkie peers beneath the surface. She concludes that the boys were using media images to discover who they are as males. In the experience of these boys, and so many like them throughout our society, to be male is to be obsessed with sex and violence. Not to joke and laugh about murder and promiscuous sex would have marked a boy as a "weenie," a label to be avoided at all costs. I should add that this was a normal group of young teenagers, who were in the process of learning what it is to be a male in our society.

Contradictions and Complexities in Gender Socialization

Of course, the gender messages presented through the family, mass media, and so on are complex and sometimes confusing. Many analysts are now arguing that the male role is particularly unclear and "in crisis" (Faludi, 1999). This is reflected in contemporary movies, for example, where male characters range from the sensitive protagonist in *American Beauty* (1999) to the macho seducer in *Magnolia* (1999) to the bare-knuckled fighter in *The Fight Club* (1999) (Goodwin, 2000). Certainly, when young men embrace the male models of physical aggression and dominance, they are likely to find themselves penalized in institutions, such as education, which prioritize obedience and conformity.

Undesirable outcomes may result from as innocuous a behaviour as a gendered style of walking. Emulating a favourite hip-hop artist's "stroll" may have unintended negative consequences. LaVonne Neal found that boys who used a stylized "stroll" as part of their "cool" pose were rated by teachers (who based their evaluations only on tapes of the boys walking) as lower in achievement, higher in aggression, and more likely to need special education (Emerson, 2001). Similarly, emulating the high-risk behaviour of male movie celebrities or musicians—drugs, fast cars, guns, smoking—can put young men at increased risk for personal injury, addiction, and other health problems (Nelson & Robinson, 2002, p. 387). In short, following the lead of prominent gender role models may, in fact, have negative consequences.

We must also keep in mind when discussing gender socialization that there are going to be important differences depending on social class, racial and ethnic background, sexual orientation, and so on. Indeed, some contemporary analysts are arguing that these differences are so profound and there are such multiple patterns of masculinity and femininity that the socialization model should be abandoned (Connell, 2002, p. 77). Certainly, we need to remain conscious of the diversity of gender experiences. For example, researchers often forget to acknowledge that disability dramatically influences gender socialization. We do know that the disabled are much less likely to find role models in the mass media, and when such models do appear, they are often presented as unrealistic, unidimensional figures. Within this general invisibility, there are important male/female differences in the socialization of the disabled. Analysts suggest, for instance, that disabled women are less likely to be sex-role stereotyped (for example, less likely to be portrayed primarily in terms of their physical attractiveness to men) but are also more likely than the male disabled to be represented as asexual (Ferri & Gregg, 1998). With advances in postmodern feminism,

more attention is focusing on the diversity of gender socialization experiences, including those of the disabled girl/woman, but much remains to be done (Hillyer, 1997). In short, gender socialization must be approached as a complex, multi-faceted social process.

Focus Question
Is it possible for the family to socialize a disabled young woman to be completely gender-neutral—that is, not to be guided by the current division between male and female? Why or why not?

In Sum

Biological sex is one of the most important "sorting" principles in society. We learn to divide the world into male and female and to locate ourselves within this gendered reality. Although we may differ in our notions of masculinity and femininity and may select quite different gender orientations—from Martha Stewart to Xena, the Warrior Princess—we organize our lives around gender.

Depending on our particular culture and the historical period we are born into, being a woman may be an important source of **social inequality** in our life. As men, we may benefit from a variety of privileges and obligations. Often these patterns of inequality are perpetuated through media images, with male images being more dynamic and interesting while females play a primarily supporting role.

Agents of Socialization

Social institutions, organizations, groups, and individual people all influence our self-concept, emotions, attitudes, and behaviour and are called **agents of socialization**. Of the many agents of socialization that prepare us to take our place in society, we shall examine the family, religion, day care, school, peers, sports, mass media, and workplace.

The Family

Around the world, the first group to have a major impact on humans is the family. Unlike some animals, we cannot survive by ourselves, and as babies we are utterly dependent on our family. Our experiences in the family are so intense that they have a lifelong impact on us. They lay down our basic sense of self, establishing our initial motivations, values, and beliefs (Gecas, 1990). The family gives us ideas about who we are and what we deserve out of life. It is in the family that we begin to think of ourselves as strong or weak, smart or dumb, good-looking or ugly, or somewhere in between.

As Canadian-born sociologist Erving Goffman puts it, the family is a "socialization depot" (1977, p. 314). This is particularly true in terms of learning what it means to be masculine and feminine. Through our parents and siblings, we witness the daily acting-out of gender roles. Not only do we learn to model this behaviour, we are often explicitly instructed as to what boys and girls should and should not do. For example, girls have earlier curfews, are more likely to have chores inside the home, and so on. Interestingly, research indicates that it is the father who plays "the more critical role in emphasizing appropriate sex typing" (Mackie, 1991, p. 109). Fathers, more than mothers, treat sons and daughters differently and, by instruction and example, more actively encourage gender differences (Mackie, 1991).

Canadian families, of course, do not produce uniform male and female results. As Marlene Mackie points out in her review of the research literature in Canada, there are important variations in families' approaches to gender socialization. For example, there is considerable evidence that working-class families are more traditional and conservative in their views of women's roles. Children growing up in this context, for example, are more likely to believe that women are responsible for the lion's share of the household work and that women are better suited to housework and child care than men. Similarly, there are important ethnic differences between Canadian families that may translate into noteworthy differences in how boys and girls are expected to behave as well as in how the family functions. Quebecois families, once considered among the most traditional, now appear to have embraced a much more liberal stance than the rest of Canada on gender issues, gay rights, authority within marriage, and women's work outside the home (Edwards & Mazzuca, 1999a). In Canadian Filipino families, notions of "family reputation" appear to play an important role in encouraging academic success amongst adolescents (Salazar, Schludermann, Schuldermann, & Huynh, 2001). As immigration to Canada continues, ethnic diversity will be an increasingly important ingredient in understanding family socialization.

> ## Focus Question
> Why does the socializing influence of the family lessen as the child grows up?

Religion

Religion plays a significant role in the socialization of many Canadians. It especially influences morality, becoming a key component in people's ideas of right and wrong. Over one-third of Canadian children (under 12 years of age) attend religious services at least once a month. More than half of Canadian children attend at least occasionally. However, attendance is affected by various family charac-

teristics. In general, children whose mothers are employed, married (as opposed to single), and better educated are more likely to attend religious services (Jones, 1999). In short, there is evidence that religion plays an important part in children's socialization. However, it must be pointed out that there is also evidence Canada is becoming a more secular nation given that the number of Canadians reporting regular attendance at religious services (at least once a month) dropped from 41 percent in 1988 to 34 percent in 1998 (Clark, 2000, p. 23). However, for the many Canadians who are involved in a religious community, clearly religious teachings, rituals, and structures affect socialization. For example, many feminists argue that religion—Protestant, Roman Catholic, Jewish, Muslim, and so on—continues to play a key role in gender socialization. Specifically, religions historically have created, and today often reinforce, the marginalization of women in society and assign important social roles to men (Ehlers, 2000).

Day Care

Globally, day care for children is on the upswing. In Italy, 85 percent of four-year-old children spend some time away from their parents in care and education programs. Throughout Europe the figures are remarkably similar: 82 percent in Germany, 75 percent in Finland, 71 percent in Portugal, 79 percent in Spain, and 98 percent in Belgium (T. Henry, 1995).

In Canada, almost one-third of all children (under age 12) were in child care and about one in eight Canadian households paid for child-care services at some point (Cheal et al., 1997; "Childcare services industry," 2002, p. 1). This, in part, reflects the dramatic increase in the number of employed mothers. Almost two-thirds of mothers of young children are in the paid labour force. As a result, many young children spend some portion of their day in the care of others. Given the lack of government support for employed parents, the overwhelming majority of these children are cared for by sitters, by relatives, and in licensed day-care homes. Only a small minority (about 10 percent) are in licensed day-care centres. The exception is Quebec, which in 1997 decided to implement by 2001 a universal child-care program for every child at $5 per day. However, demand for these spots has dramatically exceeded availability and by 2000, there was a two-year wait to get on waiting lists for these $5-a-day spots (Montgomery, 2000, p. A17).

Despite the ongoing shortage of licensed day-care centres throughout Canada, Canadian children are increasingly likely to spend some portion of their early childhood being cared for by persons other than their parents (Monsebraaten, 1998; Orwen, 1999; Burke, Crompton, Jones, & Nessner, 1994).

> ## Focus Question
> Overall, does day care have a positive or negative socializing impact on young children?

Given this shift in child-rearing patterns, it is not surprising that day care remains contentious. Some condemn the trend to day care as a reflection of our growing materialism and loss of family values; others counter that parents have little choice but to take paid work and that day care in fact benefits many children. As you would expect, much depends on the quality of day care: High-quality care (safe, small numbers, warm interaction, with low turnover of well-trained staff devoted to an appropriate program) benefits children while low-quality care has negative effects.

However, even with the current unevenness in quality and problems of accessibility, some argue that day care is tending to benefit Canadian society. Canadian demographer David Baxter, for example, argues that day care children are more likely to be "cookie-sharing kids" than self-centred individualists, and as a result Canadian crime rates have dropped consistently throughout the 1990s (Carey, 1999a). Others point out the particular advantages of day care for children coming from deprived, dysfunctional, or abusive homes. Other groups of children may also derive specific benefits from access to preschool programs. The Wabnong site of the Aboriginal Head Start program in Scarborough, Ontario, reveals, for example, the potential of specific day-care programs to address ethnic and racial issues and to encourage cultural awareness, self-knowledge, and pride in minority children (Green, 1999).

The School

If asked how schools socialize students, you might stress the formal knowledge and skills they transmit, such as reading, writing, and arithmetic. As part of the **manifest functions**, or intended purpose, of formal education, transmitting such skills is certainly part of socialization. The increased popularity of "private" schools and home-schooling in North America is, of course, altering the manifest functions for some children, for example, by embracing a pointedly religious or "elite" curriculum. Our schools' **latent functions**, the unintended consequences that help the social system, are also significant. Let's look at this less visible aspect of education.

At home, children learn attitudes and values that match their family's situation in life. At school, they learn a broader perspective that helps prepare them to take a role in the world beyond the family. At home, for example, a child may have been the almost exclusive focus of doting parents, but in school the child learns *universality*—that the same rules apply to everyone, regardless of who their parents are or how special they may be at home.

Sociologists have also identified a *hidden curriculum* in our schools. This term refers to the latent function of education, namely the inculcation of values that, though not explicitly taught, form an inherent part of a school's "message." For example, the stories and examples used to teach math and English grammar may bring with them lessons in gender inequality and help to create a "chilly climate" for girls and women (Nelson & Robinson, 2002).

Peer Groups

As a child's experiences with agents of socialization broaden, the influence of the family lessens. Entry into school marks only one of many steps in this transfer of allegiance. One of the most significant aspects of education is that it

Schools are one of the primary agents of socialization. One of their chief functions is to sort young people into the adult roles thought appropriate for them, as well as to teach them the attitudes and skills that match those roles. What sorts of attitudes and adult roles do you think these junior high school girls are being socialized into? Is this a manifest or a latent function? Is it a dysfunction?

Many adults who wish to reduce gender distinctions prefer that grade-schoolers of both sexes participate in the same playground activities. In spite of the sometimes not-so-subtle suggestions of teachers, however, grade-school children insist on separating by sex, where they pursue different interests and activities and develop contrasting norms.

exposes children to **peer groups**, individuals of roughly the same age who are linked by common interests, for example, friends, clubs, gangs, and "the kids in the neighbourhood."

Sociologists Patricia Adler, Steven Kless, and Peter Adler (1992) document how the peer group provides an enclave in which boys and girls resist the efforts of parents and schools to socialize them their way. Observing children at two elementary schools in Colorado, they saw children separate themselves by sex and develop their own worlds with unique norms. The norms that made boys popular were athletic ability, coolness, and toughness. For girls, they were family background, physical appearance (clothing and ability to use makeup), and the ability to attract popular boys. In this children's subculture, academic achievement pulled in opposite directions: For boys, to do well academically hurt popularity, while among her peers getting good grades increased a girl's standing.

Of course, peer groups can form around and support "deviant" sets of values. The trend toward increasing female youth violence and "girl gangs" may be seen as one example of such group influence. There is evidence suggesting that girls are now more likely to engage in violent attacks on other girls and that this behaviour is reinforced by peer group values. However, it is also important to keep in mind that minority racial status, poverty, inner-city residence, and residence on a rural reserve are all related to the likelihood that a girl will be charged with a criminal offence (A. Duffy, 1996).

You know from personal experience how compelling peer groups are. With the cardinal rule seeming to be "conformity or rejection," anyone who doesn't do what the others want becomes an "outsider," a "nonmember," an "outcast." For preteens and teens just learning their way around in the world, it is not surprising that the peer group is king. For example, considerable sociological research documents that in Canada and globally our peer subculture has a strong influence on our adolescent sexual behaviour;

that is, whether or not we intend to use condoms, engage in casual sex, and so on (Maticka-Tyndale, 2001; Selvan, Ross, Kapadia, Mathai, & Hira, 2001).

As a result, the standards of our peer groups tend to dominate our lives. If your peers, for example, listen to rap, heavy metal, rock and roll, country, folk, gospel, classical, hip hop, or any other kind of music, it is almost inevitable that you also prefer that kind of music. Peer influences also extend to behaviours that violate social norms. If your peers are university-bound and upwardly striving, that is most likely what you will be; but if they use drugs, cheat, steal, or, for some young men, abuse their girlfriends, you are likely to do so, too (Haynie, 2001; Totten, 2000).

Sports

Sports are also a powerful socializing agent. Everyone recognizes that sports teach not only physical skills but also values. In fact, "teaching youngsters to be team players" is often given as the justification for financing organized sports.

The Workplace

Another agent of socialization that comes into play somewhat later in life is the workplace. Those initial jobs that we take—part-time work after school and in university—are much more than a way to earn a few dollars. From the people we rub shoulders with at work, we learn not only a set of skills but also a perspective on the world.

Most of us eventually become committed to some particular line of work, which often involves trying out various jobs. It also may involve **anticipatory socialization**, learning to play a role before entering it, a sort of mental rehearsal for some future activity. We may read novels about people who work in a career, talk to them, or take a summer internship. This allows us to gradually identify with the role, to become aware of some of its expectations

The workplace—and quite often the fast food industry—is a major socializing agent for teenagers. It also provides an opportunity for young people to interact with older members of the workforce.

and rewards. Sometimes this saves people fruitless years, as with some of the authors' students who tried student teaching, found they couldn't stand it, and moved on to another major more to their liking.

An interesting aspect of work as a socializing agent is that the more you participate in a line of work, the more the work becomes a part of your self-concept. Eventually you come to think of yourself so much in terms of the job that if someone asks you to describe yourself, you are likely to include the job in your self-description, saying "I am a teacher, accountant, nurse" or whatever.

Focus Question
In what ways do we employ anticipatory socialization prior to moving into a particular line of work?

In Sum

Many agents of socialization guide us throughout our lives. From the moment of birth until death, we are encouraged to act, think, and feel in a socially acceptable fashion. The most intimate components of our identity — how we feel love, how we experience grief—are molded by our interactions with family members, with religion, with day care and education, with peers and sports, with the mass media, and with our workplaces. Some agents of socialization are particularly powerful in demanding conformity and punishing deviance. Often our experience with peers forces us to realize the pressure to conform and the perils of being an "outsider." Thus, the socialization process and its agents are powerful determinants of who we are and who we wish to become.

Resocialization

What does a woman who has just become a nun have in common with a man who has just divorced? The answer is that they both are undergoing **resocialization**; that is, they are learning new norms, values, attitudes, and behaviours to match their new situation. In its most common form, resocialization occurs every time we learn something contrary to our previous experiences. A new boss who insists on a different way of doing things is resocializing you. Most resocialization is mild, only a slight modification of things already learned. Resocialization can be intense, however. People who join Alcoholics Anonymous, for example, expose themselves to a barrage of testimony about the destructive effects of excessive drinking. Even more intense is psychotherapy or joining a cult, for these events expose people to ideas that conflict with their previous ways of looking at the world. If these ideas "take," not only does the individual's behaviour change, but he or she also learns a fundamentally different way of looking at life.

The Case of Total Institutions

Relatively few of us experience the powerful agent of socialization Erving Goffman (1961) called the **total institution**. He coined this term to refer to a place in which people are cut off from the rest of society and where they come under almost total control of the officials who run the place. Boot camps, prisons, concentration camps, convents, some religious cults, along with some elite boarding schools, are total institutions.

Resocialization often is a gentle process, as we are gradually exposed to different ways of thinking and doing. Sometimes, however, resocialization can be swift and brutal, as it is for this unwilling inductee to prison boot camp, an alternative to prison for nonviolent offenders.

A person entering a total institution is greeted with a **degradation ceremony** (Garfinkel, 1956), an attempt to remake the self by stripping away the individual's current identity and stamping a new one in its place. This unwelcome greeting may involve fingerprinting, photographing, shaving the head, and banning the person's **personal identity kit** (items such as jewellery, hairstyles, clothing, and other body decorations used to express individuality). Newcomers may be ordered to strip, be examined (often in humiliating, semipublic settings), and then be given a uniform to designate their new status. (For prisoners, the public reading of the verdict and being led away in handcuffs by armed police also form part of the degradation ceremony.)

Total institutions are extremely effective in stripping away people's personal freedom. They are isolated from the public (the walls, bars, or other barriers not only keep the inmates in but also keep outsiders from interfering). They suppress pre-existing statuses (prison inmates, for example, learn that their previous roles such as spouse, parent, worker, or student mean nothing, and that the only thing that counts is their current role). Total institutions suppress the norms of "the outside world," replacing them with their own rules, values, and interpretation of life. They also closely supervise the entire lives of the residents—eating, sleeping, showering, recreation are all standardized. They also control information, which helps the institution shape the individuals' ideas and "picture" of the world. Finally, they control the rewards and punishments. (Under conditions of deprivation, simple rewards for compliance such as sleep, a television program, a letter from home, extra food, or even a cigarette, are powerful incentives in controlling behaviour.) The institution also holds the power to punish rule-breaking—often severely—for example, in prisons by solitary confinement or acceptance of inmate violence and assaults (Kupers, 1999).

The powerful experience leaves an indelible mark on the individual's self that colours the way he or she sees the world. However, the process is not necessarily experienced as oppressive or punishing. As in the case of private boarding schools, participants may come to embrace the total institution as a positive source of self-esteem. Further, total institutions may serve important social functions other than social control of deviants, such as sustaining class solidarity by encouraging friendship and marriage relationships within the particular social class (Maxwell & Maxwell, 1971).

Socialization Through the Life Course

Some compare our lives to an empty canvas on which a series of portraits is painted, others to the seasons of the year. Each analogy depicts an image of personal change as we touch, and are touched by, events in which we are immersed. That series of major events, the stages of our lives from birth to death, is called the **life course** (Heinz & Kruger, 2001).

Analysts have tried to depict the typical stages through which we go, but they have not been able to agree on a standard division of the life course (Levinson, 1978; Schlossberg, 1990; Carr, Ryff, Singer, & Magee, 1995). In the following sketch, a composite of the stages they have proposed, I shall stress the *historical* setting of people's lives in order to emphasize the sociological significance of the life course.

Childhood (From Birth to about Age 12)

It may strike you as strange to say this, but what a child "is" differs from one culture to another. To understand this point, consider how different your childhood would have been if you had grown up during the Middle Ages.

When historian Philippe Ariès (1962) examined European paintings from this period, he noticed that children were always dressed up in adult clothing. If children were not stiffly posed for a family portrait, they were depicted as engaging in adult activities. Ariès concluded that at that time and in that place, childhood was not regarded as a special time of life. Rather, the Europeans considered children miniature adults.

Childhood also used to be harsh. Another historian, Lloyd DeMause (1975), documented the nightmare of childhood in ages past. To beat children used to be the norm. Parents who did not beat their children were considered neglectful of their social duty to keep them off the road to hell. Even teachers were expected to beat their students, and one nineteenth-century German schoolteach-

Sociologists point out that children look up to and emulate role models. However, who is seen as a suitable role model may change dramatically through the course of historical events.

Students often associate the term "socialization" with children and childhood. However, it is important to realize that socialization occurs throughout life and some of the most powerful socialization experiences routinely take place in adulthood. Here are two very different examples of sociological research that explores adult socialization.

Toronto sociologist Bonnie Fox provides a view into the profound transformation men and, especially, women go through when they first become parents. She interviewed 40 heterosexual couples over the course of their first child's birth and babyhood. Not surprisingly, this is a period of momentous personal change, in particular in terms of gender socialization. Fox found that despite the fact these mostly middle-class couples entered into parenthood with a stronger-than-usual commitment to sharing the work and responsibilities of their new child, they soon drifted toward more traditional gender arrangements. In most instances, the women followed societal custom and stayed home, at least initially, with the newborn baby. Much more dependent upon their husbands for financial and emotional support, they became less involved with their personal friends, more involved with catering to their husbands and spent more time creating a "pleasant" home. Given this scenario, it's not surprising to find that the at-home mothers took on the lion's share of housework. In part, this household labour reflected their acceptance of societal standards for the "good mother" and for the protection of the child. Even when their husbands came home, the mothers were more likely to encourage them to "play with the baby" than pitch in with the housework. The end product was often a fairly conventional household where the work and responsibilities of parenting, at least at this point in the life course, fell disproportionately on the women's shoulders (Fox, 2001).

Becoming a parent is only one of many adult socialization experiences that may transform our sense of self and our relationships with others. Sociologists have long been interested in the socialization that occurs through professional education and in employment. Indeed, a number of sociological classics have been devoted to an in-depth examination of the specific process of "becoming a doctor" (Becker, Geer, Strauss, & Hughes, 1961; Haas & Shaffir, 1987). Recent research in Canada suggests that despite a changing student body at medical colleges—more women, older, working-class, gay, lesbian, and visible minorities students—this powerful socialization process remains intact (Beagan, 2001).

As this body of research reveals, medical training is an intense and oner-ous procedure that strives to alter the medical students and their relationship to the social world. Initially, the training inundates the students with an "almost" unmanageable academic program. Faced with constant pressures to perform competently, they slowly acquire techniques to deal with not only a hectic work schedule but also with restrictions on their personal lives and relationships. Importantly, they are also learning that, as a doctor, the expectation is that they appear to know "the answer" even when they don't or they are unsure. As Haas and Shaffir describe it, the students learn to assume the "cloak of competence"— the ability to present themselves to the world as separate and different from their patients in that they are the experts and they are in control. This distinct presentation of self is necessary if they are to be allowed to violate social norms—touching patients' bodies, asking about emotional well-being, and exploring intimate concerns. And, only in the socially constructed "role" of doctor—with its distinctive standards for appearance and communication—can many students themselves accept a self-identity that witnesses death and makes life-and-death decisions. At first, most students struggle with fears of incompetence and a sense of fraudulence, but eventually they learn to incorporate the new subjective reality (Haas & Shaffir, 1987; Beagan, 2001).

er methodically recorded every beating he administered. His record shows 124 000 lashes with a whip, 911 527 hits with a stick, 136 715 slaps with his hand, and 1 115 800 cuffs across the ears.

To keep children in line, parents and teachers also felt it their moral duty to use psychological terror. It was common to terrify children into submission by forcing them to witness gruesome events such as public hangings (DeMause, 1975). A common moral lesson involved taking children to visit the gibbet (an upraised post on which executed bodies were left hanging from chains), where they were forced to inspect rotting corpses hanging there as an example of what happens to bad children when they grow up. Whole classes were taken out of school to witness hangings, and parents would often whip their children after-wards to make them remember what they had seen (DeMause, 1975).

To see children as adults seems strange to us. In some of today's least industrialized nations, however, this reality persists. Visitors to emerging nations are often by struck by the role of children in the economy. It is estimated that globally more than 100 million children under the age of 15 work full-time, often in hazardous and debilitating jobs ("100 million children toil full-time," 1997). Whether engaged in panhandling, mining, or prostitution, their lives are far removed from most Canadians' experience of childhood. For developed regions around the globe, it has been industrialization and the resultant economic surplus that brought fundamental change to the role of children. When children had the leisure to go to school, they came to be

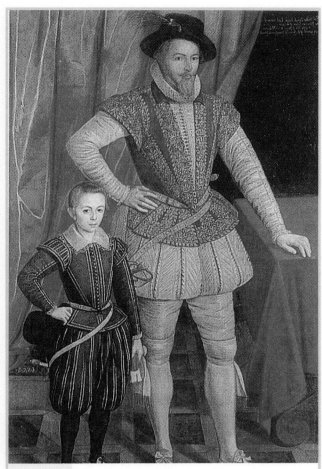

In contemporary Western societies such as Canada, children are viewed as innocent and in need of protection from adult demands such as work and self-support. Historically and cross-culturally, however, ideas of childhood vary. For instance, as illustrated by this painting of Sir Walter Raleigh and son (artist unknown), in fifteenth-century Europe children were viewed as miniature adults who assumed adult roles at the earliest opportunity.

In the United States the use of psychiatric drugs, including Ritalin and anti-depressants, on children aged 2 to 4 years jumped 50 percent between 1991 and 1995 ("Toddlers' use of drugs soars," 2000, p. A1). As a result of these social changes as well as the dramatic changes in the employment patterns of mothers, analysts have voiced concerns that children are being encouraged to grow up too quickly (the 8-year-old Britney Spears wannabes) and that dual career families, television, and educational pressures are robbing boys and girls of the freedom to enjoy being children (McDonnell, 2002). In addition, as more adults opt to be "child-free" there has been a growing popular acceptance of negative attitudes toward children. Joking references to "ankle-biters, crib lizards, and rug rats" appear to reflect an emerging rejection of any romanticized notion of children and childhood (Belkin, 2000).

Childhood, then, is much more than biology (Mandell, 1988). The point in history during which we live, as well as our social location, create a framework that is laid on top of our biological foundation. Although a child's biological characteristics (such as small and dependent) are universal, the child's social experiences (what others expect of the child) are not.

It is also important to keep in mind that there are important variations in childhood experiences. Significant numbers of Canadian children are growing up in poverty, many are in families where both parents are employed, increasing numbers are living in a lone-mother household, and many experience some form of step-parenting or foster parenting (Cheal et al., 1997; Miedema, 1999). In short, the social experience of childhood is a complex and changing reality.

Adolescence (about Ages 13–17)

In earlier centuries, societies did not mark out adolescence as a distinct time of life. People simply moved from childhood into young adulthood, with no stopover in between. The Industrial Revolution brought such an abundance of material surpluses, however, that for the first time millions of teenagers were able to remain outside the labour force. At the same time, the demand for education grew. The convergence of these two forces in industrialized societies created a gap between childhood and adulthood. In the early part of the twentieth century, the term "adolescence" was coined to indicate this new stage in life (G. S. Hall, 1904), one that has become renowned for inner turmoil.

The experience of adolescence has changed dramatically in the past 150 years. This transformation in adolescence is apparent, for example, in terms of sexuality. In the 1890s, the average age of first menstruation for young women was almost 15 years of age. A century later it had decreased to 12.5 years of age. Not only are young people maturing sexually at a younger age, they are becoming sexually active sooner. Over the last half century, the age for initiating vaginal intercourse has been progressively younger with each new birth cohort (Maticka-Tyndale, 2001). While in the

thought of as tender and innocent, as needing more adult care, comfort, and protection. Such attitudes of dependency continued to develop, and today young children are often represented in our culture as needing gentle guidance if they are to develop emotionally, intellectually, morally, socially, even physically. We take our view for granted; after all, it is only "common sense." Yet, as you can see, our view is not "natural," but historically rooted.

Further, as our society changes, so does our conception of childhood. Contemporary social analysts have repeatedly questioned whether modern childhood is being eroded. Certainly, with the advent of television, video games, and the Internet, childhood has been transformed. In the U.S. children are spending on average one-quarter of their free time each week watching TV (Hofferth & Sandberg, 2001, p. 301).

In many societies, manhood is not bestowed upon males simply because they reach a certain age. Manhood, rather, is a standing in the community that must be achieved. Shown here is an initiation ceremony in Indonesia, where boys, to lay claim to the status of manhood, must jump over a barrier.

past late adolescence was a period for exploring sexuality, today younger and younger groups of adolescents are sexually active and dealing with sexual concerns such as birth control and sexually transmitted diseases.

Similarly, there has been a significant shift in adolescent participation in paid employment. Today, more and more adolescents are participating in the paid labour market. Teen years are typically characterized by some participation in part-time work. A recent Ontario survey reported that more than one-third of Grade 10 students and more than half of Grade 11 students hold part-time jobs (Puxley, 2002). Indeed, fast food franchises and retail stores could not survive without the constant supply of teen workers. More work time, higher educational expectations, and more pressure may all translate into a heightened sense of vulnerability.

At the same time, some analysts argue that there is a growing intolerance and mistrust of "teens," as reflected in the introduction of curfews in some areas and restrictions on the presence of teens in malls and stores (Crawford, 2002). As a result, growth toward young adulthood may feel much more uncertain and riskier than in previous generations, and many Canadian adolescents may feel they are set up to fail (Marquardt, 1998).

Young Adulthood (about Ages 18–29)

If society invented adolescence as a special period in life, can it also invent other periods? Historian Kenneth Keniston suggested it could. He noted that industrialized

societies seem to be adding a period of prolonged youth to the life course, in which post-adolescents postpone adult responsibilities and are "neither psychological adolescents nor sociological adults" (Keniston, 1971). From the end of high school through extended education, including vocational schools, university, and even graduate school, many young adults remain free from adult responsibilities, such as a full-time job, marriage, and home ownership.

This shift in patterns of young adulthood is particularly striking in terms of the once-momentous step of "moving out" from the parental home. Now more and more young Canadians are continuing to live with their parents or move out and then back in (the "boomerang kids") as they go through periods of schooling, employment, and family-building. Approximately one in four Canadian young women (age 20 to 34) (up from 16 percent in 1981) and one in three young men (up from 26 percent in 1981) are living with their parents. Clearly, growing educational expectations, along with high rates of youth unemployment and postponement of marriage, have resulted in changes in the life course experiences of Canadian young adults (Boyd & Norris, 1999).

Focus Question
In what ways did industrialization alter the experience of both childhood and adolescence?

The Middle Years (about Ages 30–65)

The Early Middle Years. During the next period, the early middle years (ages 30–49), most people are much surer of themselves and of their goals in life. As with any point in the life course, however, the self can receive severe jolts—in this case from such circumstances as divorce or being fired (Dannefer, 1984). It may take years for the self to stabilize after such ruptures. Because of recent social change, the early middle years pose a special challenge for Canadian women, who increasingly have been given the message, especially by the media, that they can "have it all." They can be superworkers, superwives, and supermoms all at the same time. The reality, however, often consists of too many conflicting pressures, of too little time and too many demands. Something has to give. In short, adjustments continue in this and all phases of life.

The Later Middle Years. During this period (ages 50–65), people attempt to evaluate the past and to come to terms with what lies ahead. They compare what they have accomplished with how far they had hoped to get. Although many do not like the gap they see between where they now are and where they had planned to be, most adjust fairly well (Carr et al., 1995). Looking at the years ahead, most people conclude that they are not likely to get much farther, that their job or career is likely to consist of

This January 1937 photo from Sneedville, Tennessee, shows Eunice Johns, age 9, and her husband, Charlie Johns, age 22. The groom gave his wife a doll as a wedding gift. The new husband and wife planned to build a cabin, and, as Charlie Johns phrased it, "go to housekeeping." This photo illustrates the cultural relativity of life stages, which we sometimes mistake as fixed. It also is interesting from a symbolic interactionist perspective—that of changing definitions—for while our sensibilities are shocked by such marriages, they once were taken for granted (though not common).

"more of the same." During this time of life, many people find themselves caring not only for their own children but also their aging parents. Because of this often crushing set of twin burdens, people in the later middle years are sometimes referred to as the "sandwich generation."

Health and mortality also begin to loom large. People feel physical changes in their bodies, and they may watch their parents become frail and ill, and die. This brings about a fundamental reorientation in thinking—*from time since birth to time left to live* (Neugarten, 1976). This combination of concerns, centring on attainment and mortality, often results in behaviour commonly termed the "mid-life crisis."

In spite of such concerns, many people find the later middle years to be the most comfortable period of their entire lives. They may enjoy job security and a higher standard of living than ever before, a bigger house (perhaps paid for), newer cars, and more exotic vacations. The children are grown, the self is firmly planted, and fewer upheavals are likely to occur.

As they anticipate the next stage of life, however, few people like what they see.

Focus Question
What historical factors have contributed to "boomerang kids," "supermoms," and the "sandwich generation"?

The Older Years (about 66 On)

The Early Older Years. In industrialized societies, the older years begin around the mid-60s. This, too, is recent, for in preindustrial societies, when most people died early, old age was thought to begin around age 40. The improved nutrition, public health, and medical care that industrialization brought, however, delayed the onset of old age. For those in good health, being over 65 is often experienced not as old age, but as an extension of the middle years. People who continue to work or to be active in rewarding social activities are especially unlikely to see themselves as old (Neugarten, 1977). Although frequency of sex declines, most men and women in their 60s and 70s are sexually active (Denney & Quadagno, 1992).

The Later Older Years. As with the preceding periods of life, except the first, there is no precise beginning point to this last stage. For some, the 75th birthday may mark entry into this period of life. For others, that marker may be the 80th or even the 85th birthday. For most, this stage is marked by growing frailty and illness; for all who reach this stage, by death. For some, the physical decline is slow, and a rare few manage to see their 100th birthday mentally alert and in good physical health.

Focus Question
Compare and contrast the experiences of a wealthy and a poor woman moving through early and later old age in contemporary Canada.

In Sum

According to life course analysis, our lives involve a series of stages: childhood, adolescence, young adulthood, the middle years, and the older years. However, how we experience these stages depends on a number of factors, in particular, historical location. Children born during the Middle Ages, for example, were viewed as miniature adults and were often subject to harsh treatment. Needless to say, they did not pass through adolescence. Even a brief difference in historical period may mean the difference between growing up as a child of depression or war rather than a child of affluence and peace. Further, in all the stages of life, social location, such as social class, gender, and race, is also highly significant. Typically, people of the same social class, for example, will have similar experiences. If you are poor, you are likely to age more quickly and be subject to poor health in old age. However, within these complexities, the patterns of human life tend to establish the general boundaries for us at each stage of life. As a result we can

speak of "boomerang kids," "the sandwich generation," "supermoms," or "mid-life crisis" and strike a chord with many Canadians at that particular stage of life. For instance, as we enter the later older years, almost all of us will be coming to terms with common issues such as increasing frailty and the prospect of death.

Summary and Review

GENES OR ENVIRONMENT?

How much of our human characteristics come from "nature" (heredity) and how much from "nurture" (the social environment)?

Observations of isolated and **feral children** help answer this question, as do experiments with monkeys that have been raised in isolation. Language and intimate social interaction, functions of "nurture," appear to be essential to the development of what we consider to be human characteristics. pp. 72–74.

THE SOCIAL DEVELOPMENT OF THE SELF, MIND, AND EMOTIONS

How do we acquire a self?

Humans are born with the capacity to develop a self, but the self must be socially constructed; that is, its contents depend on social interaction. According to Charles Horton Cooley's concept of the **looking-glass self**, our self develops as we internalize others' reactions to us. George Herbert Mead identified the ability to **take the role of the other** as essential to the development of the self. Mead concluded that even the mind is a social product. pp. 74–76.

How do children's thinking processes develop?

Jean Piaget identified four stages children go through as they develop the ability to reason: (1) *sensorimotor*, in which understanding is limited to sensory stimuli such as touching, seeing, and listening; (2) *preoperational*, the ability to use symbols; (3) *concrete operational*, in which reasoning ability is more complex but not yet capable of complex abstractions; and (4) *formal operational*, abstract thinking. Researchers have also found that emotions develop in an orderly sequence. p. 76.

How do sociologists evaluate Freud's psychoanalytic theory of personality development?

Freud viewed personality development as the result of self-centred inborn desires, the **id**, clashing with social constraints. The **ego** develops to balance the id as well as the **superego**, the conscience. In contrast, sociologists do not examine inborn and unconscious motivations, but rather how social factors—social class, gender, religion, education, and so forth—underlie personality development. pp. 76–77.

SOCIALIZATION INTO GENDER

How does gender socialization affect our sense of self?

Gender socialization—sorting males and females into different roles—is a primary means of controlling human behaviour. We

learn **gender roles** beginning in infancy. A society's ideals of sex-linked behaviours are reinforced by its social institutions. pp. 78–82.

AGENTS OF SOCIALIZATION

What are the main agents of socialization?

The main **agents of socialization** are family, religion, day care, school, **peer groups**, the **mass media**, sports, and the workplace. Each has its particular influences in socializing us into becoming full-fledged members of society. pp. 82–86.

RESOCIALIZATION

What is resocialization?

Resocialization is the process of learning new norms, values, attitudes, and behaviours. Intense resocialization occurs in **total institutions**. Most resocialization is voluntary, but some, as with prisoners, is involuntary. pp. 86–87.

SOCIALIZATION THROUGH THE LIFE COURSE

Does socialization end when we enter adulthood?

Socialization occurs throughout the **life course**. In industrialized societies, the life course can be divided into childhood, adolescence, young adulthood, the early middle years, the later middle years, the early older years, and the later older years. Typical patterns include obtaining education, becoming independent from parents, building a career, finding a mate, rearing children, and confronting aging. Life course patterns vary by history and culture, and by social location such as gender, ethnicity, and social class, as well as by individual experiences such as health and age at marriage. pp. 87–92.

Critical Thinking Questions

1. Socialization is intended to turn us into conforming members of society. As a result, we are under considerable pressure to "do the right thing." Explain the actual social forces that push us to act appropriately and then consider how socialization would explain the numerous individuals, from white-collar criminals to wife abusers, who deviate from the social norms.

2. Postmodern feminists are emphasizing that a dualistic (male/female) understanding of gender socialization ignores

the complexities and diversities of gender in our society. Using the gender messages in the mass media, consider the complex and sometimes contradictory ways gender is portrayed.

3. Socialization is presented as such a powerful social process that students sometimes have the impression people are robots whose every action is dictated by social pressures. However, socialization theorists usually accept that each of us is *actively* involved in the social construction of self. Thinking of your own upbringing, consider the ways in which you are not simply a reflection of your family and early childhood experiences.

Key Terms

agents of socialization 82	mass media 79
anticipatory socialization 85	peer groups 85
degradation ceremony 87	personal identity kit 87
ego 77	resocialization 86
feral children 72	self 74
gender roles 78	significant others 75
gender socialization 78	social environment 72
generalized other 75	social inequality 82
id 76	socialization 74
latent functions 84	superego 77
life course 87	taking the role of the
looking-glass self 74	other 74
manifest functions 84	total institution 86

Weblinks

Research on Homeschooling Socialization
learninfreedom.org/socialization.html
A report on a Ph.D. thesis devoted solely to the issue of home-schooling socialization, and on some related research, by Larry Edward Shyers at the University of Florida. The thesis, titled "Comparison of Social Adjustment Between Home and Traditionally Schooled Students," is available from University Microfilms International.

The Looking-Glass Self
wizard.ucr.edu/~bkaplan/soc/lib/coollkgl.html
An excerpt from Charles Horton Cooley, *Human Nature and the Social Order* (New York: Scribner's, 1902), pp. 179–185.

Total and Totalitarian Institutions
faculty.ncwc.edu/toconnor/417/417lec16.htm
This page contains a chart titled "The Difference Between a Total Institution and a Totalitarian Institution." It is part of "Dr. O'Connor's Criminal Justice MegaLinks," one of a group of pages maintained by faculty and staff members, or affiliated organizations, at North Carolina Wesleyan College.

Socialization
www.delmar.edu/socsci/rlong/intro/social.htm
Part of Russell Long's Academic Page on sociology, presented to support various courses and to encourage students to use the Web.

Social Structure and Social Interaction

Chapter 5

Learning Outcomes

After you have studied this chapter, you will be able to

■ distinguish macrosociology from microsociology

■ understand the differences between how functionalists and conflict theorists view social institutions

■ describe the differences between primary and secondary groups

■ discuss how group size affects our attitudes and behaviours

■ discuss the importance of leadership in groups

My curiosity had gotten the better of me. When the sociology convention finished, I climbed aboard the first city bus that came along. I didn't know where the bus was going, and I didn't even know where I was going to spend the night.

Actually, this was my first visit to Washington, D.C. I had no direction, no plans, not even a map. I carried just a driver's licence shoved into my jeans, some pocket change, and a $10 bill tucked into my socks. My goal was simple: If I see something interesting, I'll get off and check it out.

"Nothing but the usual things." I could see myself riding buses the entire night. Then something caught my eye. Nothing spectacular—just groups of people clustered around a large circular area where several streets intersected.

I climbed off the bus and made my way to what turned out to be Dupont Circle. I took a seat on a sidewalk bench and began to observe. I noted several street-corner men drinking and joking with one another. One of the men broke from his companions and sat down next to me. As we talked, I mostly listened.

As night fell, the men said that they wanted to get another bottle of wine. I contributed. They counted their money and asked if I wanted to go with them.

Although I felt a churning inside—emotions combining hesitation and fear—I heard a confident "Sure!" coming out of my mouth. As we left the circle, the three men began to cut through an alley. "Oh, no," I thought. "That's not what I had in mind."

I found myself continuing to walk with the men, but holding back half a step so that none of the three was behind me. As we walked, they passed around the remnants of their bottle. When my turn came, I didn't know what to do. In the semidarkness I faked it, letting only my thumb and forefinger touch my lips and nothing enter my mouth.

When we returned to Dupont Circle, the men finished their new bottle of Thunderbird.

Suddenly one of the men jumped up, smashed the emptied bottle against the sidewalk, and thrust the jagged neck in a menacing gesture. He stared straight ahead at another bench, where he had spotted someone with whom he had some sort of unfinished business. As the other men told him to cool it, I moved slightly to one side of the group—ready to flee, just in case.

Source: The personal experience of J. Henslin.

Levels of Sociological Analysis

Sociologists Elliot Liebow (1997) and Elijah Anderson (1978, 1990, 1997) have written fascinating accounts of men like these. Although street-corner men may appear to be disorganized, simply coming and going as they please and doing whatever feels good at the moment, these sociologists have analyzed how, like us, these men are also influenced by the norms and beliefs of our society. This will become more apparent as we examine the two levels of analysis that sociologists use.

Macrosociology and Microsociology

The first level, **macrosociology**, places the focus on broad features of society. Sociologists who use this approach, especially conflict theorists, functionalists, and many feminist theorists, analyze such things as social class and patriarchy. If macrosociologists were to analyze street-corner men, for example, they would stress that these men are at the bottom of the social class system. Their low status, according to men's feminism, means men will denigrate other men because they possess few skills and little education. As "able-bodied" men, however, they are not eligible for welfare, so they hustle to survive. As a consequence, they spend their lives on the streets. That is, these men are viewed as of little social value and potentially dangerous by other men and women.

Conflict theory, functionalism, and feminism focus on the broader picture and are examples of this macrosociological approach. In these theories, the goal is to examine and interpret the large-scale social forces that influence people.

The second approach sociologists use is **microsociology**. Here the emphasis is placed on **social interaction**, what people do when they come together. Sociologists who use this approach are likely to focus on the men's survival strategies ("hustles"); their rules for dividing up money, wine, or whatever other resources they have; their relationships with girlfriends, family, and friends; where they spend their time and what they do there; their language; their pecking order; and so on. With their focus on face-to-face interaction, symbolic interactionism and feminism that emphasizes the social construction of gender are examples of microsociology.

Postmodernism can be viewed as a recent example of both macrosociology and microsociology. This perspective, developed by Michel Foucault (1972, 1980), J. Lyotard (1984), Roland Barthes (1975), and others, looks at language as the primary social bond in contemporary society. Postmodernists call their emphasis on language *discourse analysis*. Language and culture form the structures within which individuals become social beings. Lyotard (1984) defines the postmodern condition as scepticism toward all universal or absolute truths that have been used to legitimize political and scientific projects such as communism (Marx) or the dominance of the unconscious mind (Freud). Modern technology has brought about this change. Today's world has no need of past or future; it is made up of two "presents"—one that is based in the virtual reality of the new technology and its media partners and the other, "real" present that appears to many as elusive, even borderline. To escape the angst of the "real-world present," for example, a postmodern person could enjoy cybersex with Lulu, the first porn star of Virtual Reality. Or, with the arrival of the "teledildonic" suit made up of a head piece with video and audio inputs connected to a suit that stimulates the erogenous zones, a player can take on any idealized persona and enjoy distant, uncommitted and safe sex (Appignanesi & Garratt, 2000).

With their different emphases, macrosociology and microsociology yield distinctive perspectives, and both are needed to gain a more complete understanding of social life. As we saw in Chapter 1, feminist theories are capable of bringing together both perspectives. We cannot adequately understand street-corner men, for example, without using *macrosociology*. It is essential that we place the men within the broad context of how groups in Canadian society are related to one another—for, as with ourselves, the patriarchal relations and social class of these men helps to shape their attitudes and behaviour. Nor can we adequately understand these men without *microsociology*, for their everyday situations also form a significant part of their lives.

To see how these two approaches help us to understand social life, let's look at each.

The Macrosociological Perspective: Social Structure

Why did the street people in the opening vignette act as they did, staying up all night drinking wine? Why don't *we* act like this? A sociological understanding of social structure helps us answer such questions.

To better understand human behaviour, we need to see how social structure *establishes limits on our behaviour*. **Social structure** is the framework of society that was laid out before you were born; it is the patterns of a society, such as the relationships between men and women or students and teachers that characterize a particular society.

Because the term *social structure* may seem vague, consider first how you personally experience social structure in your own life. As we write this, we do not know whether your background is Caribbean, European, Native Canadian, or East Indian. We do not know your religion. We do not know whether you are young or old, tall or short, male or female. We do not know whether you went to a public high school or an exclusive prep school. But we do know that you are in university. And that alone tells us a great deal about you.

From this one piece of information, we can assume that the social structure of your university is now shaping what you do. For example, let us suppose that today you felt

Sociologists use both macro and micro levels of analysis to study social life. Those who use macrosociology to analyze the homeless—or any human behaviour—focus on broad social forces, such as the economy and social classes. Sociologists who use the microsociological approach analyze how people interact with one another. Note how this scene invites both levels of analysis: Here you have both social interaction and social classes (power and powerlessness).

euphoric over some great news. We can be fairly certain (not absolutely, mind you, but relatively certain) that when you entered the classroom, social structure overrode your mood. That is, instead of shouting at the top of your lungs and joyously throwing this book into the air, you entered the classroom fairly subdued and took your seat.

The same social structure influences your instructor, even if, on the one hand, he or she is facing a divorce or has a child dying of cancer, or, on the other, has just been awarded a promotion or a million-dollar grant. The instructor may feel like either retreating into seclusion or celebrating wildly, but most likely he or she will conduct class. In short, personal feelings and desires tend to be overridden by social structure.

Just as social structure influences you and your instructor, so it also establishes limits for street people. They, too, find themselves in a specific social location in Canadian social structure—although it is quite different from yours or your instructor's. Consequently, they are affected differently —and nothing about their social location leads them to take notes or to lecture. It is just as "natural" in their position in the social structure to drink wine all night as it is for you to stay up studying all night for a crucial examination. It is just as "natural" for you to nod and say, "Excuse me," when you enter a crowded classroom late as it is for them to break off the head of a wine bottle and glare at an enemy.

In short, people learn certain behaviours and attitudes because of their location in the social structure (whether privileged, deprived, or in between), and they act accordingly. This is equally true of street people. *The differences in behaviour and attitudes are not due to biology (race, sex, or any other supposed genetic factors), but to people's location in the social structure.* Switch places with street people and watch your behaviours and attitudes change!

To better understand social structure, read the Down-to-Earth Sociology box on page 103. Because social structure so critically affects who we are and what we are like, let us look in more detail at its major components: culture, social class, social status, roles, groups, and institutions.

Social Institutions

At first glance, the term *social institution* may appear far removed from our personal lives. The term seems so cold and abstract, something remotely "out there." In fact, however, **social institutions**—the organized means that each society develops to meet its basic needs—involve concrete and highly relevant aspects of our lives.

Sociologists have identified nine social institutions: the family, religion, law, politics, economics, education, medicine, science, and military. In industrialized societies, for example, the social institution of education is highly structured, while in preliterate societies education may consist of informally learning expected roles. Figure 5.1 summarizes the basic social institutions. Note that each institution has its own set of roles, values, and norms.

Focus Question
What is a social institution?

The Sociological Significance of Social Institutions

To understand social institutions is to realize how profoundly social structure affects our lives. For example, because of our economic institution, we consider it normal to work a 44-hour week in Canada. There is nothing natural about this pattern, however. Its regularity is only an arbitrary arrangement for dividing work and leisure. Yet this one aspect of a single social institution has far-reaching effects not only on how we structure our time and activities but also on how we deal with family and friends, and how we meet our personal needs and non-work obligations.

Each of the other social institutions also has far-reaching effects on our lives. Social institutions are so significant that if they were different, we would be different people.

Comparing Functionalist, Feminist, and Conflict Perspectives

Let's compare these views.

The Functionalist Perspective. Functionalists stress that every society must meet its basic needs, and they identify five basic needs or **functional requisites** that each society must fulfill if it is to survive (Aberle, Cohen, David, Leng, & Sutton, 1950; Mack & Bradford, 1979).

1. *Replacing members.* Because reproduction is so fundamental to a society's existence and there is such a vital need to protect infants and children, all groups have developed some version of the family. The family also functions to channel people's sex drive, to maintain orderly reproduction, and to give the newcomer to society a sense of belonging by providing a "lineage"—an account of how he or she is related to others.

2. *Socializing new members.* As the primary "bearer of culture," the family is essential to teaching the child what it means to be a full-fledged member of society, but other social institutions, such as religion and education, also contribute to this functional requisite.

3. *Producing and distributing goods and services.* Every society establishes an economic institution, a means of producing basic resources, from food and clothing to shelter and education, along with routine ways to distribute them.

4. *Preserving order.* Societies face two threats of disorder: one internal and the other external. To defend themselves against external conquest, they develop some means of defence, some form of the military. To protect themselves from internal threat, they develop some system of policing themselves, ranging from formal organizations of armed groups to informal systems of gossip.

Figure 5.1 Social Institutions in Industrialized Societies

Social Institution	Basic Needs	Some Groups or Organizations	Some Values	Some Roles	Some Norms
Family	Regulate reproduction, socialize and protect children	Relatives, kinship groups	Sexual fidelity, providing for your family, keeping a clean house, respect for parents	Daughter, son, father, mother, brother, sister, aunt, uncle, grandparent	Have only as many children as you can afford, be faithful to your spouse
Religion	Concerns about life after death, the meaning of suffering and loss; desire to connect with the Creator	Congregation, synagogue, denomination, charitable association	Reading and adhering to holy texts such as the Bible, the Koran, and the Torah; honouring God	Priest, minister, rabbi, worshipper, teacher, disciple, missionary, prophet, convert	Attend worship services, contribute money, follow the teachings
Law	Maintain social order	Provincial police, RCMP, provincial and federal courts, provincial and federal prisions	Trial by one's peers, innocence until proven guilty	Police officer, lawyer, judge defendant, prison guard	Give true testimony, follow the rules of evidence
Politics	Establish a hierarchy of power and authority	Political parties, the Senate, the provinces, Parliament, the monarchy	Majority rule, the right to vote as a sacred trust	Prime minister, provincial premier, MP, MPP, senator	One vote per person, voting as privilege and right
Economics	Produce and distribute goods and services	Credit unions, banks, credit bureaus, credit card companies	Making money, paying bills on time, producing efficiently	Worker, boss, buyer, seller, creditor, debtor, advertiser	Maximize profits, "the customer is always right," work hard
Education	Transmit knowledge and skills across the generations	School, college, university, student senate, sports team, PTA, teachers' union	Academic honesty, good grades, being "cool"	Teacher, student, dean, principal, football player, cheerleader	Do homework, prepare lectures, don't snitch on classmates
Science	Master the environment	Local, provincial, regional, national, and international associations	Unbiased research, open dissemination of research findings	Scientist, researcher, technician, administrator	Follow scientific method, fully disclose research findings
Medicine	Heal the sick and injured, care for the dying	CMA, Health Canada, provincial ministries of health, pharmacies, insurance companies	Hippocratic oath, staying in good health, following doctor's orders	Doctor, nurse, patient, pharmacist, medical insurer	Don't exploit patients, give best medical care available
Military	Protection from enemies, support of national interests	Armed Forces Canada, Royal Military College, military police	To die for one's country is an honour, obedience unto death	Soldier, recruit, enlisted person, officer, prisoner, spy	Be ready to go to war, obey superior officers, don't question orders
Mass Media (an emerging institution)	Disseminate information, mold public opinion, report events	CBC, CTV, Global and other television networks, CRTC, radio stations, publishers	Timeliness, accuracy, large audiences, freedom of the press	Journalist, newscaster, author, editor, publisher	Be accurate, fair, timely, and profitable

5. *Providing a sense of purpose.* For people to cooperate with one another, they need to be convinced that it is worth sacrificing for the common good. All of a society's institutions are actually involved in meeting this functional requisite, for the family provides one part of an interrelated set of answers about the sense of purpose, the school another, and so on.

The Feminist Perspectives. As you read in Chapter 1, there are many variants of feminist theories. Liberal feminists, for example, stress the gendered inequalities between men and women, whether it be in the work force (women get paid much less than men), in the home (the double day of paid work and unpaid housework and child care), or in relationships (date rape, wife abuse, and other forms of violence against women). Marxist and radical feminists emphasize the relationship between patriarchy and social class as the fundamental basis for gender inequality. Multiracial feminists underscore the importance of ethnic and racial characteristics (in addition to social class and patriarchy) in the discrimination and oppression of women and men of colour. The main point recent feminist perspectives have stressed about gender inequality is that gender, too, is an element of social structure, not simply a characteristic of individuals. Gender inequality is built into the organization of work, marriage, politics, religion, the arts, and other cultural institutions such as the mass media. For example, nurses are more likely to be women than men and men who are nurses confront prejudice from those outside the profession. In other words, throughout the world social institutions separate males and females into groups that have unequal access to their society's resources. Solutions to gender inequality, therefore, require social and not individual remedies.

The Conflict Perspective. Conflict theorists stress that a society's institutions are controlled by an elite that manipulates them in order to maintain its own privileged position of wealth and power (Useem, 1984; Domhoff, 1983, 1990, 1997).

As evidence of their position, conflict theorists point out that a fairly small group of people has garnered the lion's share of the nation's wealth. Members of this elite sit on the boards of major corporations and of the country's most prestigious universities. They make strategic campaign contributions to control the nation's politicians, and it is they who influence the major decisions in this society affecting whether to go to war or to refrain from war, to raise or to lower taxes, to raise or to lower interest rates, to pass laws that favour moving capital, technology, and jobs out of the country or not.

The Mass Media in the Information Age

Although not all sociologists agree, the mass media (newspapers, magazines, television, and radio are the principal examples) can be considered a social institution. Far beyond serving simply as sources of information, the media influence our attitudes toward social issues, other people, and even our self-concept. Because the media significantly shape public opinion, all totalitarian governments attempt to maintain tight control over them.

The mass media are a major influence in contemporary life. Until 1436, when Johann Gutenberg invented movable type, printing was a slow process, and printed materials were expensive. Today printed materials are common and often cheap. "Cheap" has a double meaning, with its second meaning illustrated in this photo.

Indeed, one of the most significant questions we can ask about this new social institution is: Who controls it? From a functionalist perspective, we might conclude that the media in a democratic nation represent the varied interests of the many groups that make up that nation. Conflict theorists, however, would see a different scenario: The mass media—at least a country's most influential newspapers and television stations—represent the interests of the political elite, the wealthy and powerful who use the media to mold public opinion.

Since the mass media are so influential, the answer to the question of who controls this vital communications network is of more than passing interest, and further sociological research on it can contribute to our better understanding of contemporary society.

In Sum

Conflict theorists regard our social institutions as having a single primary purpose—to preserve the social order—which they interpret as preserving the wealthy and powerful in their privileged positions. Functionalists, in contrast, view social institutions as working together to meet universal human needs. Feminist perspectives point out the complexities of how our society's social institutions create gender inequality.

Globalization and Changes in Social Structure

This enveloping system that we call social structure, which so powerfully affects our lives, changes as it responds to new technology, to innovative ideas from home and abroad, and to evolving values. In our new era of "globalization," we come into contact with the customs of many other people. This effects profound changes in our basic orientations to life. Nor do social classes remain immune to the winds of global change, for growth and contraction in the economy move people in and out of positions of relative privilege, while shifting relationships between racial, gender, and ethnic groups in the world economy also bring with them changes in relative power and prestige. Similarly, state institutions that did not exist until relatively recently, such as Canada Customs and Revenue Agency (CCRA), formerly Revenue Canada, the body that collects income taxes from Canadian citizens, wield extraordinary power over our lives. It was not always so. In 1917, the federal government passed the *Income War Tax Act* to help raise money to fight World War II. Shortly after, in 1927, the Department of National Revenue was created to administer the collection of income tax in Canada.

What Holds Society Together?

In addition to answering the question "How is society possible with the large numbers of distinct individuals that inhabit its boundaries?" sociologists need to know what keeps a society together. What cements the many different individuals and groups into something larger as they undergo their own dynamics of change? Let us examine two answers to this question.

Mechanical and Organic Solidarity. Sociologist Emile Durkheim (1893/1933) found the key to **social cohesion**—the degree to which members of a society feel united by shared values and other social bonds—in what he called **mechanical solidarity**. By this term Durkheim meant that people who perform similar tasks develop a shared consciousness, a sense of similarity that unites them into a common whole. Members of an agricultural society, for example, are all involved in planting, cultivating, and harvesting. They have so much in common, including the fact that they live close to one another, that it is possible for them to know even the most intimate details about other members of their society.

As societies increase in size, their **division of labour** (how they divide up work) becomes more specialized. Rather than splitting society apart, however, the division of labour makes people depend on one another—for the activities of each contribute to the welfare of the whole. Durkheim called this new form of solidarity based on interdependence **organic solidarity**.

Due to the change from mechanical to organic solidarity, people no longer cooperate with one another because they *feel* alike (mechanical solidarity), but because they *depend* on one another's activities for their own survival (organic solidarity). In the past, societies tolerated little diversity in thinking and attitudes, for their unity depended on similar thinking. With this change to organic solidarity, modern societies can tolerate many differences among people and still manage to work as a whole. Note that both societies are based on social solidarity but that the types of solidarity are remarkably different in each case.

Gemeinschaft **and** *Gesellschaft*. Ferdinand Tönnies (1887/1988) also saw a new type of society emerging. Tönnies used the term *Gemeinschaft* (Guh-MINE-shoft), "intimate community," to describe the traditional type of society in which everyone toes the line because they are acutely sensitive to the opinions of others and know that if they deviate, others will gossip and damage their reputation. Although their lives are sharply controlled by the opinions of others, they draw comfort from being part of an intimate group.

Tönnies saw that industrialization was tearing at this intimate fabric of community life. Instead, short-term relationships, individual accomplishments, and self-interest were being emphasized. Tönnies called this new type of society *Gesellschaft* (Guh-ZELL-shoft), or "impersonal association." In this new world of *Gesellschaft*, however, gossip was ineffective in controlling large numbers of people. To keep people in line, society had to depend on more *formal* agencies, such as the police and courts.

The text contrasts *Gesellschaft* and *Gemeinschaft* societies. The French café represents a *Gemeinschaft* approach to life, where there are warm, ongoing relationships. The cybernet café in Helsinki, Finland, represents the more impersonal *Gesellschaft* orientation. Here people ignore one another in favour of electronic interaction via the Internet. Internet interactions do not easily fit standard sociological models—another instance of cultural lag.

How Relevant Are These Concepts Today? We know that *Gemeinschaft*, *Gesellschaft*, and mechanical and organic solidarity are strange terms and that Durkheim's and Tönnies' observations must seem like a dead issue with no connection to life today. However, in large part, this same concern explains why our world has witnessed the rise of Islamic fundamentalism (Volti, 1995). Islamic leaders fear that their traditional culture will be uprooted by Western values, that cold rationality will replace relationships built on long-term associations between families and clans. Also consider the rise of the Christian Right, particularly in the United States. These religious leaders are fearful of the loss of traditional Christian values in the face of postmodern changes in attitudes and behaviours toward women, gays, and other disenfranchised groups. Although the terms may sound strange, even obscure, the ideas remain a vital part of today's world.

In Sum

The sociological point, again, is that social structure sets the context for what we do, feel, and think. In short, social structure lies at the basis of what kind of people we become.

Focus Question
How is society possible?

Culture

In Chapter 3, we looked in detail at how culture affects us. Sociologists use the term *culture* to refer to a group's language, beliefs, values, behaviours, and even gestures. Culture also includes the material objects used by a group. In short, culture is our social inheritance, what we learn from the people around us. Culture is the broadest framework that determines what kind of people we become. If we are reared in Inuit, Japanese, Russian, or Canadian culture, we will grow up to be like most Inuit, Japanese, Russians, or Canadians. On the outside, we will look and act like them; and on the inside, we will think and feel like them.

Social Class

To understand people, we must examine the particular social locations they hold in life. Especially significant is social class, which is based on income, education, and occupational prestige. Large numbers of people who have similar amounts of income and education and who work at jobs that are roughly comparable in prestige make up a **social class**. We have this in common, then, with the street people described in the opening vignette—both they and we are influenced by our location in the social class structure. Theirs may be a considerably less privileged position, but it has no less influence on their lives. Social class is so significant that we shall spend an entire chapter (Chapter 6) on this topic.

To gain a better idea of what social structure is, think of your high school hockey or soccer team. You know the various positions on a hockey or soccer team. In hockey, there are the following positions: goalie, centre, wingers, and defencemen. In soccer, there are: goalkeeper, strikers, midfielders, and defence. Each is a status; that is, each is a recognized social position. For each of these statuses, there is a role; that is, each of these positions has particular expectations attached to it. In hockey, the centre is expected to win face-offs, the wingers to forecheck, the goalie to stop pucks from going into the net, and so on. Those role expectations guide each player's actions; that is, each player tries to do what his or her particular role requires. Since there are some who can play the role better than others, or who have a particular "style" of play, there is manoeuvrability within each set of expectations about how to perform the role. Individuality emerges from how well or how badly you perform in that social position.

This scenario mirrors social structure. We know that the game does not depend on any particular individual, but rather on the positions the individuals occupy. When someone leaves a position, the game can go on because someone else takes over the position and plays the role.

Social structure is also gendered. In either high school hockey or soccer, there are boys' and girls' teams. What happens when the girls' hockey or soccer team has to be dropped because of municipal or school budget reductions? Can the girls freely compete for a position on the boys' team? Or is it more likely the girls will be faced with opposition to competing for a position on a boys' team? The expectations of sex segregation in sports—girls' and boys' leagues—mirrors the gendered social structure of our society.

In 1988, 15-year-old Justine Blainey broke the ice, so to speak, when she won her case to play goalie in an all-boys hockey league. She was awarded $3000 in damages almost a year after she had been banned from playing in the same league. Most Canadians believed discrimination on the basis of sex in amateur youth sports was to become a thing of the past.

In 1992, the Ontario Soccer Association made history by banning Erin Casselman and Suzanne Ouellet, two teenage girls, from playing in the quarter-finals of the Ontario soccer championships simply because they were girls. So long as there was little chance of the team winning the provincial championships, everything was fine. When it appeared that the team might win, the entire team faced disqualification under the rules sanctioned by the Ontario Soccer Association if the girls continued to play. In November of the following year (1993), an Ontario Human Rights inquiry ordered the Ontario Soccer Association to pay each girl $3500 in damages. What do you think about young girls playing in an all-boys sports team?

Even though you may not play hockey or soccer, you nevertheless live your life within a clearly established gendered social structure. The statuses you occupy and the roles you play were already in place before you were born. However, you need not passively accept your gendered role. Roles and their expectations can and do change. It's all up to you!

Social Status

When you hear the word *status*, you are likely to think of prestige. These two words are welded together in common thinking. Sociologists, however, use **status** in a different way: to refer to the position an individual occupies. That position may have a great deal of prestige, as in the case of a judge or an astronaut, or it may carry very little prestige, as in the case of a gas station attendant or the street people described in the opening vignette. The status may also be looked down on, as in the case of a street person, an ex-convict, or a homeless woman.

We all occupy several positions at the same time. You may be simultaneously a son or daughter, a worker, a date, and a student. Sociologists use the term **status set** to refer to all the statuses or positions you occupy. Obviously your status set changes as your particular statuses change; for example, if you graduate from university and take a full-time job, get married, buy a home, have children, and so on, your status set changes to include the positions of employee, spouse, homeowner, and parent.

The example given earlier of students and teachers doing what others expect of them in spite of their temporary moods is an illustration of how statuses affect our actions—and those of the people around us.

Ascribed Statuses and Achieved Statuses. The first type, **ascribed statuses**, is involuntary. You do not ask for such statuses, nor can you choose them. Some you inherit at birth, such as your race, sex, and the social class of your parents, as well as your statuses as female or male, daughter or son, and granddaughter or grandson. Others, such as teenager and senior citizen, are related to the life course discussed in Chapter 4, and are given to you later in life.

The second type, **achieved statuses**, is voluntary. These statuses you earn or accomplish. As a result of your efforts, you become a business or sociology student, a friend, a spouse, a rabbi, a minister, a priest, or a nun. Or, for lack of effort that others fail to appreciate, you become a school dropout, a former friend, an ex-spouse, or a defrocked priest or nun. In other words, achieved statuses can be either positive or negative; both university president and bank robber represent achieved statuses.

The significance of social statuses for understanding human behaviour is that each status provides guidelines for how people are to act and feel.

Status Symbols. People pleased with their own social status may want others to recognize that they occupy that status. To gain this recognition, they use **status symbols**, signs that identify a status. For example, people wear wedding rings to announce their marital status; or wear uniforms, guns, and badges to proclaim they are police officers and to let you know that their status gives them authority over you; or flaunt their ability to speak both official languages to show they are good citizens.

Some social statuses are negative—and so, therefore, are their status symbols. One example is the conviction held by some English-speaking Canadians living in Quebec that speaking English is a negative status symbol in Quebec while some French-speaking Canadians outside Quebec are just as convinced that speaking French carries a negative status in the rest of the country. Ironically, *bilingualism*, fluency in both English and French, is viewed by most Canadians as a positive achieved status.

We all use status symbols to announce our statuses to others. For example, how does your clothing announce your statuses of sex, age, and university student?

Master Statuses. A **master status** is one that cuts across the other statuses you hold. Some master statuses are ascribed. An example is your sex. Whatever you do, people perceive you as a male or a female. Other master statuses are race and age.

Some master statuses are achieved. If you become very, very wealthy (and it does not matter if your wealth comes from an invention or the lottery—it is still *achieved* as far as sociologists are concerned), your wealth is likely to become a master status.

Similarly, people who become disabled or disfigured can attest to how "disabled" overrides all their other statuses and determines others' perceptions of everything they do.

Although our statuses usually fit together fairly well, sometimes a contradiction or mismatch between statuses occurs; this is known as **status inconsistency (or discrepancy)**. A 14-year-old university student is an example. So is a 40-year-old married woman on a date with a 19-year-old university sophomore.

When statuses mesh well, as they usually do, we know what to expect of people. Status inconsistency, however, upsets our expectations. In the preceding examples, how are you supposed to act? Are you supposed to treat the

Canadian hero Terry Fox is perhaps our best example of someone who had achieved status.

14-year-old as you would a teenager or as you would your university classmate? The married woman as the mother of your friend or as a classmate's date?

Roles

All the world's a stage
And all the men and women merely players.
They have their exits and their entrances;
And one man in his time plays many parts....
—William Shakespeare, *As You Like It*, Act II, Scene 7

Like Shakespeare, sociologists, too, see roles as essential to social life. When you were born, **roles**—the behaviours, obligations, and privileges attached to a status—were already set up for you. Society was waiting to teach you how it expected you to act as a boy or a girl. And whether you were born poor, rich, or somewhere in between, certain behaviours, obligations, and privileges were attached to your statuses.

The difference between role and status is that you occupy a status, but you play a role (Linton, 1936). For example, being a son or daughter is your status, but your expectations of receiving food and shelter from your parents—as well as their expectations that you show respect to them or you are ashamed of them—is your role.

The sociological significance of roles is that they lay out what is expected of people. As Shakespeare put it, people's roles provide "their exits and their entrances" on the stage of life. In short, roles are remarkably effective at keeping people in line—telling them when they should "enter" and when they should "exit," as well as what to do in between.

Social Groups and Societies

Groups are the essence of life in society. Workers in a corporation form a group, as do neighbours on a block. The family is a group, as is the Vancouver Canucks hockey team. The groups to which we belong help to determine our goals and values, how we feel about ourselves, and even how we feel about life itself. Groups can ignite a sense of purpose in life—or extinguish even the spark that makes life seem worthwhile.

Sociologists define a social **group** in many different ways. Albion Small (1905), an early North American sociologist, used this term in a very broad sense to mean people who have some sort of relationship with one another over time. Sociologists Michael Olmsted and Paul Hare (1978) point out that the "essential feature of a group is that its members have something in common and that they believe what they have in common makes a difference." Therefore, a group consists of people who regularly and consciously interact with one another. Just as our actions are influenced by our social class, statuses, and roles, so, too, the groups to which we belong represent powerful forces in our lives. In fact, to belong to a group is to yield to others the right to make certain decisions about our behaviour.

To belong to any group is to relinquish to others at least some control over our lives. Those social groups that provide little option to belong are called *involuntary memberships* (or *involuntary associations*). These include our family and the sexual, ethnic, and racial groups into which we are born. Groups to which we choose to belong are called *voluntary memberships* (or *voluntary associations*). These include the scouts, professional associations such as the Canadian Sociology and Anthropology Association, trade unions such as the Canadian Auto Workers, and recreational clubs such as a local euchre, bowling, or golf league. If we want to remain members in good standing, we must conform to what people in those groups expect of us. The largest and most complex group that sociologists study is **society**, which consists of people who share a culture and a territory. The values, beliefs, and cultural characteristics of a society profoundly affect the smaller groups within it.

For example, Switzerland is probably one of the most successful nations in the world in terms of social cohesion. Why is this so? First and foremost, the Swiss are made up of four different nationalities who have learned to manage their intergroup conflicts or rivalries. Granted, this took a long time to achieve, but for the past 250 years, members of each nationality or canton see themselves as participating in a larger society. Today Switzerland is well known for its stature as a stable multilingual and multicultural society.

> ## Focus Question
> What do you need in order to have a social group?

Groups Within Society

Sociologist Emile Durkheim (1933) viewed small groups as a buffer between the individual and the larger society. He said that by establishing intimate relationships and offering a sense of meaning and purpose to life, small groups serve as a sort of lifeline that helps to prevent *anomie*, a sense of not belonging.

Before we examine groups in more detail, we should distinguish between groups, aggregates, and categories. An **aggregate** consists of individuals who temporarily share the same physical space but who do not see themselves as belonging together, such as people waiting in a checkout line or drivers parked at the same red light. A **category** consists of people who have similar characteristics, such as all university women who wear glasses or all men over six feet tall. Unlike *groups*, the individuals who make up a category neither interact with one another nor take one another into account.

Primary and secondary groups, in-groups and out-groups, reference groups, and social networks are the different types of groups that make up our society. We will also consider a new type of group, the electronic community.

Primary Groups

Charles H. Cooley defines a **primary group** this way: "By primary groups I mean those characterized by intimate face-to-face association and cooperation."

As humans, we have an intense need for face-to-face interaction that provides feelings of self-esteem. By offering a sense of belonging, a feeling of being appreciated, and sometimes even love, primary groups are uniquely equipped to meet this basic need. Primary groups, such as the family, friendship groups, and even gangs, are essential to our emotional well-being. Cooley calls these primary groups the "springs of life."

Another reason primary groups are so significant is even as adults, no matter how far we may have come from our childhood roots, early primary groups remain "inside" us, where they continue to form part of the perspective from which we look out onto the world. Not all primary groups function to positively support the larger society. Three types of dysfunctions can be identified. First, instead of providing emotional support, the members of a primary group may quarrel and humiliate one another. (Note, however, that some members, such as those who dominate a family, may be highly satisfied with such interaction.) Second, a primary group, such as Hells Angels or Rock Machine, may set itself against society. (Note, however, that the group may be dysfunctional for society but highly functional for its members.) The third dysfunction occurs when an essential primary group changes throughout society. An example is the change from primogeniture or the inheritance of the family farm by the first-born male heir, a characteristic of most agricultural societies, to today's conjugal family unit where children establish their "family" in a household separate from either of their parents.

Secondary Groups

Compared with primary groups, **secondary groups** are larger, relatively temporary, more anonymous, formal, and impersonal. Such groups are based on some interest or activity, and their members are likely to interact on the basis of specific roles, such as president, manager, worker, or student. Examples are a university classroom, the Canadian Sociology and Anthropology Association, a factory, or the New Democratic Party.

Although contemporary society could not function without secondary groups, such groups fail to satisfy deep human needs for intimate association. Consequently, *secondary groups tend to break down into primary groups*. For example, at school and work we tend to form friendship cliques, which provide such valued interaction that if it weren't for them we sometimes feel that school or work "would drive us crazy." Just as small groups serve as a buffer between us and the larger society, so the primary groups we form within secondary groups serve as a buffer between us and the demands secondary groups place on us.

In-Groups and Out-Groups

Sometimes group membership is defined as much by what people are *not* as by what they *are*. In other words, the antagonisms some groups feel toward other groups become an integral part of their identity. Groups toward which individuals feel loyalty are called **in-groups**; those toward which they feel antagonisms, **out-groups**.

"I'm surprised, Marty. I thought you were one of us."
Drawing by Ziegler; © 1983 The New Yorker Magazine, Inc.

How our participation in social groups shapes our self-concept is a major focus of symbolic interactionists. In this process, knowing who we are *not* is as significant as knowing who we are.

This fundamental division of the world into in-groups and out-groups has far-reaching consequences for our lives. Because identifying with a group generates a sense of belonging and loyalty, our in-groups exert a high degree of control over us. To maintain status in our in-groups, we may even find ourselves doing things we dislike. How many of us, for example, have put on clothing or worn hairstyles we thought uncomfortable or even a bit strange, but were expected by our in-group?

In-groups also foster ethnocentrism. Measuring ourselves in relationship to out-groups, we are encouraged to judge our own group's accomplishments and characteristics as superior. The result, as sociologist Robert Merton (1968) observed, creates an interesting double standard—the traits of our in-groups come to be viewed as virtues, while those same traits in out-groups are seen as vices. For example, men may perceive an aggressive man as assertive, but an aggressive woman as pushy. A male employee who doesn't speak up may be thought of as "knowing when to keep his mouth shut," but a quiet woman as too timid to make it in the business world.

To divide the world into "we" and "they" sometimes leads to acts directed against out-groups. Such acts may be mild and more esteem-building for the in-group than anything else. For example, in sports rivalries between nearby towns the most extreme act is likely to be travelling to the out-group's territory to steal a mascot, paint a rock, or uproot a goalpost.

Fear and hatred, however, which nourish feelings against out-groups, often give birth to highly destructive acts. During times of economic insecurity, for example, *xenophobia*, or fear of strangers, may grow. The out-group is perceived to have stolen jobs from one's friends and relatives. The result may be *attacks* against immigrants or a national anti-immigration policy.

In short, to divide the world into in-groups and out-groups, a natural part of social life, brings with it both functional and dysfunctional consequences.

Reference Groups

Suppose you have just been offered a good job. It pays double what you hope to make even after you graduate from university. You have just three days to make up your mind. If you accept it, you will have to drop out of university. As you consider the matter, thoughts like this may go through your mind: "My friends will say I'm a fool if I don't take the job … but Dad and Mom will practically go crazy. They've made sacrifices for me, and they'd be crushed if I didn't finish university. They've always said I've got to get my education first, that good jobs will always be there…. But, then, I'd like to see the look on the faces of those neighbours who said I'd never amount to much!"

This is an example of how people use **reference groups**, the groups we use as standards to evaluate ourselves. Reference groups exert tremendous influence over our lives. For example, if you want to become a senior executive of a corporation, you might have your hair cut fairly short, start dressing more formally, try to improve your vocabulary, read the *Financial Post*, take business and law courses at the "right" university, try to obtain a "fast-track" job, and join the local chamber of commerce. In contrast, if you want to become a rock musician, you might wear three earrings in one ear, dress in ways your parents and many of your peers consider outlandish, read *Rolling Stone*, drop out of university, and hang around clubs and rock groups.

From these examples, you can see that the yardsticks provided by reference groups operate as a form of social control. When we see ourselves as measuring up to the yardstick, there is no conflict, but if our behaviour, or even aspirations, do not match the standards held by a reference group, the mismatch can lead to internal turmoil. For example, to want to become a corporate officer would present no inner turmoil for most of us, but it would if you had grown up in an Amish home, for the Amish strongly disapprove of such activities for their children. They ban high school and university education, three-piece suits, the *Financial Post*, and corporate employment. Similarly, if you wanted to become a soldier and had been reared by dedicated pacifists, you likely would experience deep conflict, as such parents, disapproving of violence on principle, hold quite different aspirations for their children.

The "internal recordings" that play contradictory messages from these reference groups, then, are simply one cost of social mobility in a postindustrial society.

Social Networks

If you are a member of a large group, there probably are a few people within that group with whom you regularly associate. In a sociology class one of the authors was teaching, six women chose to work together on a project. They got along well, and began to sit together. Eventually they planned a Christmas party at one of their homes. These clusters, or internal factions, are called **cliques**. The links between people—their cliques, as well as their family, friends, acquaintances, and even "friends of friends"—are called **social networks**. Think of a social network as ties that expand outward from yourself, gradually encompassing more and more people.

Social scientists have wondered just how extensive the connections are between social networks. If you list everyone you know, and each of those individuals lists everyone he or she knows, and you keep doing this, do you think that eventually almost everyone in Canada will be included on those lists?

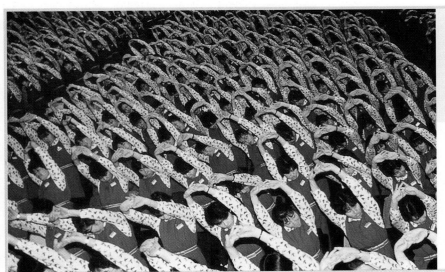

Japanese corporations use many techniques to encourage group identity, such as making group exercise a part of the workday. Sociologically, similarity of appearance and activity helps fuse group identity and company loyalty.

It would be too cumbersome to test this hypothesis by drawing up such lists, but psychologist Stanley Milgram (1967) hit on an ingenious way to find out just how interconnected our social networks are. In what has become a classic experiment, he selected names at random from across the United States. Some he designated as "senders," others as "receivers." Milgram addressed letters to the receivers and asked the senders to mail the letters to someone they knew on a first-name basis whom they thought might know the receiver. This person, in turn, was asked to mail the letter to someone he or she knew who might know the receiver, and so on. The question was: Would the letters ever get to the receivers, and if so, how long would the chain be?

Think of yourself as part of this experiment. What would you do if you are a sender, but the receiver lives in a province in which you know no one? You would send the letter to someone you know who might know someone in that province. And this is just what happened. None of the senders knew the receivers, and in the resulting chains some links broke; that is, after receiving a letter, some people didn't send it on. Surprisingly, however, most letters did reach their intended receivers. Even more surprising, the average chain was made up of only *five* links. This gives us insight into why strangers from different parts of the country sometimes find they have a mutual acquaintance.

Global Considerations. Milgram's experiment shows just how small our world really is. If our social networks are so interrelated that almost everyone in Canada is connected by just five links, how many links connect us to everyone on earth? This experiment has yet to be done.

Networking. The term **networking** refers to using social networks, usually for career advancement. Hoping to establish a circle of acquaintances who will prove valuable to them, people join clubs, churches, synagogues, and political parties. Many networks are hard to break into, such as the "old boy" network, which keeps jobs moving in the direction of male friends and acquaintances.

To break this barrier, many women do *gender networking*, developing networks of working women to help advance their careers. When they reach top positions, some of these women then steer their business to other women. The resulting circle is so tight that the term "new girl" network is being used, especially in certain fields in the social sciences. Like the "old boys" who preceded them, the new insiders also justify their exclusionary practice (Jacobs, 1997).

A New Group: Information Technology and the Emergence of Electronic Communities

In the 1990s, an entirely new type of human group made its appearance. The Internet is a series of millions of computers hooked together worldwide. On the Internet are hundreds of thousands of newsgroups, called usenets, people who communicate on almost any conceivable topic—from donkey racing and bird-watching to sociology and quantum physics. Most newsgroups are only an interesting, new way of communicating, but some meet our definition of *group*: people who interact with one another and think of themselves as belonging together.

Some newsgroups pride themselves on the distinctive nature of their interest and knowledge, factors that give them a common identity, bind them together, and distinguish them from others. Some have even taken on the characteristics we associate with primary groups: People look forward to communicating daily with others in their newsgroup, with whom they share personal, sometimes intimate matters about themselves. This new form of group, the electronic community, is explored in the Sociology and the New Technology box.

Group Dynamics

As you know from your personal experience, the lively interaction *within* groups—who does what with whom—has profound consequences for how you adjust to life. Sociologists use the term **group dynamics** to refer to how groups affect us and how we affect groups. Let's first consider the differences that the size of a group makes, and then examine leadership, conformity, and decision-making.

Before doing this, we should see what sociologists mean by the term **small group**. This is a group small enough for everyone to interact directly with all the other members. Small groups can be either primary or secondary. A wife, husband, and children, as well as workers who take their breaks together, are examples of primary small groups, while bidders at an auction and passengers on a flight from Toronto to Montreal are examples of secondary small groups.

Group Size

Writing at the turn of the twentieth century, sociologist Georg Simmel (1858–1918) noted the significance of group size. He used the term **dyad** for the smallest possible group, which consists of two people. Dyads, he noted, which include partnerships, love affairs, and close friendships, show two distinct qualities. First, they are the most intense or intimate of human groups. Because only two people are involved, the interaction is focused on them. Second, because dyads require the continuing active participation and commitment of both members, they are the most unstable of social groups. If one member loses interest the dyad collapses. In larger groups, in contrast, even if one member withdraws the group can continue, for its existence does not depend on any single member (Simmel, 1950).

A **triad** is a group of three people. As Simmel noted, if you are a member of a triad, you or one of your partners could leave the group but the group will still continue to exist and function as a group. Simmel stated that groups

Sociology and the New Technology

New Forms of Talk: Cybercommunications and the Creation of Electronic Communities

As you have seen from the examples in this chapter, a change in technology alters the way people relate to one another—and, sometimes, even the shape of society itself. *Online communications*—people communicating with one another via computers—is an example of an invention that alters relationships and even the very nature of "talk."

Through most of human history, "talk" meant face-to-face communication. The invention of writing, however, allowed people who were far apart to "talk" to one another—and left a record of what they "said." Another new technology, the printing press, not only multiplied the power of this "long-distance talk," but even changed religion and politics. By putting Bibles in the hands of common people, it weakened the power of the Roman Catholic Church, removing it as the exclusive interpreter of God's Word. As political tracts came off the press, they encouraged independent thinking, which undermined the monarchy and helped bring about constitutional forms of government.

Thus, as sociologist Joshua Meyrowitz (1995) stresses, we should not consider the media as passive channels of information. They are not mere "holders" or "senders" of messages; rather, they shape our lives. Just as when writing and the printing press were new technologies and people saw their relationships change, so our new technologies are bringing forms of "talk" that are also changing our relationships.

A remarkable example is how our new forms of electronic communication, sometimes called the *information superhighway* or *cyberspace*, have made our homes "less-bounded environments." While remaining within the walls of our homes, we now can instantly "travel" electronically to previously remote settings around the world. There, we can share information with people we have never met or seen, and even develop friendships with them. The result is a new type of group known as an **electronic community**. In some cases, the term **electronic primary group** seems more appropriate to refer to this new type of group, for people regularly interact with one another, share personal information, identify with one another, and develop a sense of intimacy—even though they have "met" only electronically.

The implications of cybercommunications for social relationships are still tentative. While our easy access to people in distant localities unites us with them, it also can separate us from people nearby. For example, while some of the authors live in different parts of Canada, we have communicated with one another on numerous occasions via e-mail as quickly as we could contact our next-door neighbours. In fact, our conversations often stray into personal matters—from discussing the attributes of our partners, to vacations, to even writing this book. In contrast, each of us only waves to our next-door neighbour—and only if we happen to be outside at the same time.

It is likely, then, that we are seeing a new form of social intimacy emerging, one in which people have closeness without permanence, depth without commitment, and need never meet one another to identify on a close, personal level (Cerulo, Ruane, & Chayko, 1992). Electronic primary groups, with a changed sense of community, have deep ramifications not only for our social interactions but also for our culture, and even our sense of self.

---

larger than a dyad are inherently stronger because they have the potential to exist for longer periods of time.

Simmel also pointed out that triads, too, are inherently unstable, albeit less so than dyads. Because relationships among a group's members are seldom neatly balanced, they encourage the formation of a **coalition**, in which some group members align themselves against others. In a triad, it is not uncommon for two members to feel stronger bonds with one another, leading them to act as a dyad and leaving the third member feeling hurt and excluded. In addition, triads often produce an arbitrator or mediator, someone who tries to settle disagreements between the other two.

The general principle is that *as a small group grows larger its intensity, or intimacy, decreases and its stability increases.* To see why, look at Figure 5.2. The addition of each person to a group greatly increases the connections among people. In a dyad, there is only 1 relationship; in a triad, 3; in a group of four, 6; in a group of five, 10. If we expand the group to six, we have 15 relationships; while a group of seven yields 21 relationships.

It is not only the number of relationships that makes larger groups more stable. As groups grow, they tend to develop a more formal structure to accomplish their goals. For example, leaders emerge and more specialized roles come into play, ultimately resulting in such formal offices as president, secretary, and treasurer. This structure provides a framework that helps the group survive over time.

Effects on Attitudes and Behaviours.

Imagine you are taking a class with social psychologists John Darley and Bibb Latané (1968) and they have asked you to join a few students to discuss your adjustment to university life. When you arrive, they tell you that to make things anonymous, they would like you to sit unseen in a booth and participate in the discussion over an intercom. You are to speak when your microphone comes on. The professors say they will not listen in, and they leave.

You find the format somewhat strange, to say the least, but you go along with it. You have not seen the other students in their booths, but when they begin to talk about their experiences, you find yourself becoming wrapped up in the problems they

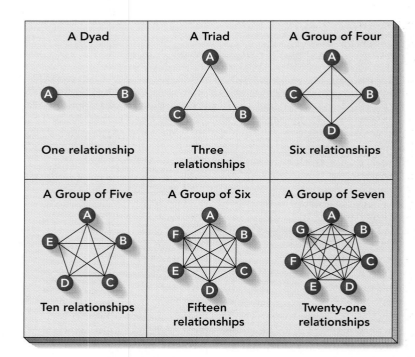

Figure 5.2 The Incremental Effects of Group Size on Relationships

are sharing. One student even mentions how frightening he has found university because of his history of epileptic seizures. Later, this individual begins to breathe heavily into the microphone. Then he stammers and cries for help. A crashing noise follows, and you imagine him lying helpless on the floor. Then there is nothing but an eerie silence. What do you do?

The researchers staged the whole thing, but you don't know that. No one had a seizure. In fact, no students were in the other booths. Everything, except your comments, was on tape.

Some participants were told they would be discussing the topic with just one other student, others with two, others with three, and so on. Darley and Latané found that all students who thought they were part of a dyad rushed out to help. If they thought they were part of a triad, only 80 percent went to help—and they were slower in leaving the booth. In six-person groups, only 60 percent went to see what was wrong—and they were even slower in doing so.

Darley and Latané concluded that students in the dyad clearly knew that it was up to them. In the triad, students felt less personal responsibility, while in the larger group, they felt a *diffusion of responsibility*: It was no more up to them than it was up to anyone else. In general, the smaller the group, the more willing we are to stick our necks out for strangers (Latané & Nida, 1981).

You probably have observed the second consequence of group size first-hand. When a group is small, its members behave informally toward one another. As the group increases in size, however, its members must take a "larger audience" into consideration, and instead of merely "talking," they begin to "address" the group. As their speech becomes more formal, their body language stiffens, too.

The third aspect of group dynamics is also one that you probably have observed many times. In the very early stages of a party, when only a few people are present, almost everyone talks with everyone else. As others arrive, however, the guests soon break into smaller groups despite the host's efforts to get everyone to mix together. The division into small groups is inevitable, because it follows the basic sociological principles we have just reviewed. The addition of each person rapidly increases connections (in this case, "talk lines"). The guests then break into smaller groups where they can see each other and comfortably interact directly with one another.

Leadership

All groups, no matter what their size, have leaders, though they may not hold a formal position in a group. A **leader** is someone who influences the behaviours, opinions, or attitudes of others. Some people are leaders because of their personalities, but leadership involves much more than this, as we shall see.

Types of Leaders. Groups have two types of leaders (Bales, 1950, 1953; Cartwright & Zander, 1968). The first is easy to recognize. This person, called an **instrumental leader** (or task-oriented leader), tries to keep group members from getting sidetracked, reminding them of what they are trying to accomplish. The **expressive leader**, also known as a *socioemotional leader*, in contrast, is likely to crack jokes, to offer sympathy, or to do other things that help lift the group's morale.

Because instrumental leaders are task-oriented, they sometimes create friction as they prod the group to get on with the job. Their actions often cost them popularity. Expressive leaders, in contrast, being peacemakers who stimulate personal bonds and reduce friction, are usually more popular (Olmsted & Hare, 1978). Both types of leadership are essential: the one to keep the group on track, the other to increase harmony and minimize conflicts.

Leadership Styles. Let us suppose the president of your university has asked you to head a task force to determine how the university can reduce discrimination against gays and lesbians on campus. Although this position requires you to be an instrumental leader, you can adopt a number of **leadership styles**, or ways of expressing yourself as a leader. The three basic styles are those of **authoritarian leader**, one who gives orders; **democratic leader**, one who tries to gain a consensus; and **laissez-faire leader**, one who is highly permissive. Which should you choose?

Social psychologists Ronald Lippitt and Ralph White (1958) carried out a classic study of these three leadership styles. Boys, matched for IQ, popularity, physical energy, and leadership, were assigned to "craft clubs" made up of five youngsters each. The experimenters trained adult males in the three leadership styles and rotated them between the clubs.

The authoritarian leaders assigned tasks to the children and set the working conditions. They also praised or condemned their work arbitrarily, giving no explanation for why it was good or bad. The democratic leaders held group discussions and outlined the steps necessary to reach the group's goals. They also suggested alternative approaches to these goals and let the children work at their own pace. When they evaluated the children's projects, they gave "facts" as the bases for their decisions. The laissez-faire leaders were passive, giving the boys almost total freedom to do as they wished. They stood ready to offer help when asked, but made few suggestions. They did not evaluate the children's projects, either positively or negatively.

The results? The boys who had authoritarian leaders grew dependent on the leaders and showed a high degree of solidarity. They also became either aggressive or apathetic, with the aggressive boys growing hostile toward the leader. In contrast, the boys who had democratic leaders were friendlier, more "group-minded," and looked to one another for mutual approval. They did less scapegoating, and when the leader left the room they continued to work at a steadier pace. The boys with laissez-faire leaders asked more questions, but they made fewer decisions. They were notable for their lack of achievement. The researchers concluded that the democratic style of leadership worked best (Olmsted & Hare, 1978).

You may have noted that only males were involved in this experiment. It is interesting to speculate how the results might differ if we repeated the experiment with all-girl groups and with groups of both girls and boys, and used both men and women as leaders. Perhaps you will become the sociologist who performs this research.

Adapting Leadership Styles to Changing Situations. It is important to note that different situations require different styles of leadership. Suppose, for example, that you are leading a dozen backpackers in the Rockies, and it is time to make dinner. A laissez-faire style would be appropriate if everyone had brought their own food—or perhaps a democratic style if the meal were to be communally prepared. Authoritarian leadership——you telling everyone how to prepare their meals—would probably create resentment. This, in turn, would likely interfere with meeting the primary goals of the group, in this case, having a good time while enjoying nature.

Now assume the same group but a different situation: One of your party is lost and a blizzard is on its way. This situation calls for you to take charge and be authoritarian. To simply shrug your shoulders and say, "You figure it out," would invite disaster.

Who Becomes a Leader? Are leaders people born with characteristics that propel them to the forefront of a group? No sociologist would agree with such a premise. In general, people who are seen as strongly representing the group's values or as able to lead a group out of a crisis are likely to become leaders (Trice & Beyer, 1991).

These findings may not be surprising, as such traits appear related to a leadership role. Researchers, however, have also discovered that traits seeming to have no bearing whatsoever on ability to lead are also significant. For example, taller people and those judged better-looking are more likely to become leaders (Stodgill, 1974; Crosbie, 1975). (The taller and more attractive are also likely to earn more, but that is a different issue [Deck, 1968; Feldman, 1972; S. Katz, 1997].)

A simple experiment performed by social psychologists Lloyd Howells and Selwyn Becker (1962) uncovered one of these factors. They formed groups of five people each who did not know one another, seating them at a rectangular table, three on one side and two on the other. After each group had discussed a topic for a set period of time, they chose a leader. The research findings are startling: Although only 40 percent of the people sat on the two-person side, 70 percent of the leaders emerged from that side. The explanation is that we tend to direct more interactions to people facing us than to people to the side of us.

Conformity to Peer Pressure: The Asch Experiment

How influential are groups in people's lives? To answer this, let's look first at *conformity* in the sense of going along with our peers. They have no authority over us, only the influence that we allow.

Imagine you are taking a course with Dr. Solomon Asch (1952) and you have agreed to participate in an experiment. As you enter his laboratory, you see seven chairs, five of them already filled by other students. You are given the sixth. Soon

Figure 5.3 Asch's Cards

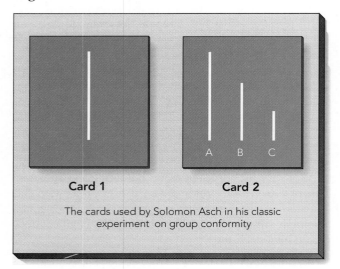

Card 1

Card 2

The cards used by Solomon Asch in his classic experiment on group conformity

the seventh person arrives. Dr. Asch stands at the front of the room and explains that he will first show a large card with a vertical line on it, then another card with three vertical lines. Each of you is to tell him which of the three lines is identical to the line on the first card (see Figure 5.3).

Dr. Asch then uncovers the first card with a single line and the comparison card with the three lines. The correct answer is easy, for two of the lines are obviously wrong, and one exactly right. Each person, in order, states his or her answer aloud. You all answer correctly. The second trial is just as easy. Then on the third trial something unexpected happens. Just as before, it is easy to tell which lines match. The first student, however, gives a wrong answer. The second gives the same incorrect answer. So do the third and the fourth. By now you are wondering what is wrong. How will the person next to you answer? You can hardly believe it when he, too, gives the same wrong answer. Then it is your turn, and you give what you know is the right answer. The seventh person also gives the same wrong answer.

On the next trial, the same thing happens. You know the choice of the other six is wrong. Why aren't they seeing things the same way you are? Something is seriously wrong, and you are no longer sure what to do.

When the eighteenth card is finished, you heave a sigh of relief. The experiment is finally over. Dr. Asch walks over to you, thanks you for participating in the experiment, and then explains that you were the only real subject in the experiment! "I paid them to give those answers," he says. Now you feel real relief. Your eyes weren't playing tricks on you after all.

Now see the account of the Milgram experiments in the Thinking Critically about Social Controversy box that follows.

The results of the Asch (1952) and Milgram experiments leave us with the disturbing question: "How far would *I* go in following authority?" Truly the influence of the group extends beyond what most of us imagine.

Global Consequences of Group Dynamics: Groupthink and Decision-Making

In our era of nuclear weapons, one of the disturbing implications of the Asch and Milgram experiments is **groupthink**. Sociologist Irving Janis (1972) coined this term to refer to the tunnel vision that a group of people sometimes develop—they think alike, and to suggest alternatives is taken as a sign of disloyalty. Groupthink may lead to overconfidence, illusions of invincibility, and blindness to risks (P. Hart, 1991).

The Asch and Milgram experiments let us see how groupthink can develop. Suppose you are a member of the prime minister's inner circle. It is midnight, and the prime minister has just called an emergency meeting to deal with a national crisis. At first, various options are presented. Eventually, these are narrowed to only a few choices, and at some point everyone seems to agree on what now seems "the only possible course of action." At that juncture, expressing doubts will bring you into conflict with *all* the other important people in the room, while actual criticism may mark you as "not a team player." So you keep your mouth shut, with the result that every step commits you—and them—more and more to the "only" course of action.

Preventing Groupthink

Groupthink is a danger that faces any government, for leaders, isolated at the top, can easily become cut off from information that does not support their own opinions. Leaders also foster groupthink by surrounding themselves with an inner circle that closely reflects their own views. Perhaps the key to preventing the mental captivity and paralysis known as groupthink is the widest possible circulation, especially among a nation's top government officials, of research that has been freely conducted by social scientists, and information that has been freely gathered by media reporters.

If this conclusion comes across as an unabashed plug for sociological research and the free exchange of ideas, it is. Giving free rein to diverse opinions can effectively curb groupthink.

The Microsociological Perspective: Social Interaction in Everyday Life

While the macrosociological approach stresses the broad features of society, the microsociological approach has a narrower focus, placing its emphasis on *face-to-face social interaction*, or what people do when they are in each other's presence.

Symbolic Interaction

Symbolic interactionists are especially interested in the symbols people use to define their worlds. They want to know how people look at things and how that, in turn, affects their behaviour.

Imagine that you are taking a course with Dr. Stanley Milgram (1963, 1965), a former student of Dr. Asch's. Assume that you did not take part in Dr. Asch's experiment and have no reason to be wary of these experimenters. You arrive at the laboratory to participate in a study on punishment and learning. You and a second student draw lots for the roles of "teacher" and "learner." You are to be the teacher, he the learner. When you see that the learner's chair has protruding electrodes, you are glad that you are the teacher. Dr. Milgram shows you the machine you will run. You see that one side of the control panel is marked "Mild Shock, 15 Volts," the centre says "Intense Shock, 350 Volts," while the far right side reads, "Danger: Severe Shock."

"As the teacher, you will read aloud a pair of words," explains Dr. Milgram. "Then you will repeat the first word, and the learner will reply with the second word. If the learner can't remember the word, you press this lever on the shock generator. The shock will serve as punishment, and we can then determine if punishment improves memory." You

In the 1960s, U.S. social psychologists ran a series of creative but controversial experiments. Among these were Stanley Milgram's experiments, described in the text. From this photo of the "learner" being prepared for the experiment, you can get an idea of how convincing the situation would be for the "teacher."

nod, now extremely relieved that you haven't been designated a learner.

"Every time the learner makes an error, increase the punishment by 15 volts," Dr. Milgram says. Then, seeing the look on your face, he adds, "The shocks can be extremely painful, but they won't cause any permanent tissue damage." He pauses, and then adds, "I want you to see." You then follow him to the "electric chair," and Dr. Milgram gives you a shock of 45 volts. "There. That wasn't too bad, was it?" "No," you mumble.

The experiment begins. You hope for the learner's sake that she is bright. She gets some answers right, but several are wrong and you have to keep turning up the dial. Each turn of the dial makes you more and more uncomfortable. You find yourself hoping that the learner won't miss another answer. But she does. When she received the first shocks, she let out some moans and groans, but now she is screaming in agony. She even protests that she suffers from a heart condition. How far do you continue turning that dial?

By now, you probably have guessed that there was no electricity attached to the electrodes and that the "learner" was a stooge only pretending to feel pain. The purpose of the experiment, of course, was to find out at what point people refuse to participate. Does anyone actually turn the lever all the way to "Danger: Severe Shock"?

Milgram wanted the answers because of the Nazi slaughter of Jews, gypsies, homosexuals, and others they designated as "inferior." That millions of ordinary people did nothing to stop the deaths seemed bizarre, and Milgram wanted to see how ordinary, intelligent Americans might react in a similar situation.

Milgram was upset by what he found. Many "teachers" broke into a sweat and protested to the experimenter

that this was inhuman and should be stopped. But when the experimenter calmly replied that the experiment must go on, this assurance from the "authority" ("scientist, white coat, university laboratory") was enough for most "teachers" to continue, even though the learner screamed in agony and pleaded to be released. Even "teachers" who were "reduced to twitching, stuttering wrecks" continued to follow orders.

Milgram varied his experiments (D. E. Miller, 1986). He used both males and females and put some "teachers" and "learners" in the same room, where the "teacher" could clearly see the suffering. He had some "learners" pound and kick on the wall during the first shocks and then go silent. The results varied from situation to situation. The highest proportion of "teachers" who pushed the lever all the way to 450 volts—65 percent—occurred when there was no verbal feedback from the "learner." Of those who could see the "learner," 40 percent turned the lever all the way. When Milgram added a second "teacher," a stooge who refused to go along with the experiment, only 5 percent carried out the severe shocking, a result that bears out some of Asch's results.

Milgram's experiments became a stormy basis for rethinking research ethics. Not only were researchers surprised and disturbed at what Milgram found, but they also were alarmed at his methods. Researchers agreed that to reduce subjects to "twitching, stuttering wrecks" was unethical, and almost all deception was banned. Universities began to require that subjects be informed of the nature and purpose of social research.

For Your Consideration

Considering how significant these findings are, do you think the scientific community overreacted to Milgram's experiment? Should we allow such research? Why do you think groups have such a powerful influence over what we do? Can you think of any ways to reduce the power of those in authority to make us do these evil acts?

Stereotypes in Everyday Life. You are familiar with how first impressions set the tone for interaction. When you first meet someone, you cannot help but notice certain highly visible and distinctive features, such as the person's sex, race, age, and physical appearance. Despite the best intentions, your first impressions are shaped by the assumptions you make about such characteristics. You probably also know that these assumptions affect not only your ideas about the person, but also how you act toward that person.

Mark Snyder (1993) wondered if **stereotypes**—the assumptions we make of what people are like—might actually produce behaviours that match the stereotype. He gave university men a Polaroid snapshot of a woman, and told them that they would be introduced to her after they talked with her on the telephone. The photograph, which showed either a physically attractive or an unattractive woman, had been prepared before the experiment began. The one given to the subject had been chosen at random.

As Snyder gave each man the photograph, he asked him what he thought the woman would be like. The men who had been given the photograph of an attractive woman said they expected to meet a poised, humorous, outgoing woman. The men who had been given a photo of an unattractive woman described the person they were going to meet as awkward, serious, and unsociable.

These stereotypes then influenced the men's behaviour. Men who had seen the photograph of an attractive woman were warm, friendly, humorous, and highly animated. Those who had seen the photograph of an unattractive woman were cold, reserved, and humourless.

These differences, in turn, affected the women's behaviour. Although the women did not know about the man's evaluation of their looks, those who were believed to be attractive responded to the men in a warm, friendly, outgoing manner, while those who were perceived as homely became cool, reserved, and humourless. In short, *stereotypes tend to bring out the very kinds of behaviour that fit the stereotype.*

A number of experiments have been conducted to see how stereotypes of gender, race, ability, and intelligence influence people (Snyder, 1993). In one, a welding instructor in a vocational training centre was told that five men in his training program had an unusually high aptitude for welding. Although the five had actually been chosen at random and knew nothing about the experiment, the effects were dramatic. These men were absent less often than other trainees, learned the basics of welding in about half the usual time, and scored 10 points higher than the other men on their final welding test. The difference was noted even by the other trainees, who singled these five out as their preferred co-workers. The men were no different in their initial abilities, but the instructor's stereotype of their abilities changed his behaviour, which brought about a change in the men's performance. This principle is illustrated in Figure 5.4.

Personal Space. Each of us surrounds him- or herself with a "personal bubble" we go to great lengths to protect. We open the bubble to intimates—to close friends, children, parents, and so on—but are careful to keep most people out of this space.

At times we extend our personal space. In the library, for example, you may place your coat on the chair next to you—claiming that space for yourself even though you are not using it. If you want to really extend your space, you

Physical attractiveness underlies much of our social interaction in everyday life. The experiment on stereotypes outlined in the text illustrates how university men modified their interactions on the basis of attractiveness. How do you think women would modify their interactions if they were to meet the two men in these photographs? Would men change their interactions? Would they change them in the same way, or in different ways?

Figure 5.4 *Self-Fulfilling Stereotypes*

| We see features of the person, or hear about the person. | → | We fit what we see or hear into pre-existing stereotypes, and then expect the person to act in certain ways. | → | We act toward the person according to our expectations. | → | From the ways we act, the person gets ideas of how we perceive him or her. | → | The behaviours of the person change to match our expectations, thus confirming the stereotype. |

might even spread books in front of the other chairs, keeping the whole table to yourself by giving the impression that others have just stepped away.

The amount of space people prefer varies from one culture to another.

Anthropologist Edward Hall (1969) observed that North Americans use four different "distance zones."

1. *Intimate distance*. This is the zone that extends to about 45 centimetres from our bodies. We reserve this space for lovemaking, comforting, protecting, wrestling, hugging, and intimate touching.

2. *Personal distance*. This zone extends from 45 centimetres to about 120 centimetres. We reserve it for friends and acquaintances and ordinary conversations.

3. *Social distance*. This zone, extending out from us about 1 to 3.5 metres, marks impersonal or formal relationships. We use this zone for such things as job interviews.

4. *Public distance*. This zone, extending beyond 3.5 metres, marks an even more formal relationship. It is used to separate dignitaries and public speakers from the general public.

Touching. Do you get uncomfortable if a stranger touches you? Many of us do.

Not only does frequency of touching differ across cultures, but so does the meaning of touching within a culture. In general, higher-status individuals do more touching. Thus you are much more likely to see teachers touch students and bosses touch secretaries than the other way around. Apparently, it is considered unseemly for lower-status individuals to put their hands on superiors. An interesting experiment with surgery patients illustrates how touching can have different meanings. When the nurse came in to tell patients about their coming surgery and aftercare, she touched the patients twice, once briefly on the arm when she introduced herself, and then for a full minute on the arm during the instruction period. When she left, she shook the patient's hand.

Men and women reacted very differently. Touching lowered the blood pressure and anxiety of women, both before the surgery and for more than an hour afterward. The touching upset the men, however. Their blood pressure and anxiety rose. Apparently North American men find it harder to acknowledge dependency and fear than women do. For men, then, instead of a comfort, a well-intentioned touch may be a threatening reminder of their vulnerability (Thayer, 1988).

Let us now turn to dramaturgy, a special area of symbolic interactionism.

Social space is one of the many aspects of social life studied by sociologists who have a microsociological focus. What do you see in common in these two photos?

Norms of touching, including kissing, vary widely around the world. Shown here are Palestinian Chairman Yasser Arafat and Monsignor Capucci of the Greek Orthodox Church kissing one another. In North America, in contrast, men shake hands. At most, two male friends, even after a long absence, will hug or clap one another on the back.

Dramaturgy: The Presentation of Self in Everyday Life

Sociologist Erving Goffman (1922–1982) added a new twist to symbolic interactionism when he developed **dramaturgy** (or *dramaturgical analysis*). By this term he meant that social life is like a drama on the stage: Birth ushers us onto the stage of everyday life, and our socialization consists of learning to perform on that stage.

Everyday life, Goffman (1997) said, involves playing our assigned roles. We have **front stages** on which to perform them. Everyday life is filled with them. Where your teacher lectures is a front stage. And if you make an announcement at the dinner table, you are using a front stage. In fact, you spend most of your time on front stages, for a front stage is wherever you deliver your lines. We also have **back stages**, places where we can retreat and let our hair down. When you close the bathroom or bedroom door for privacy, for example, you are entering a back stage.

The same setting can serve as both a back and a front stage. For example, when you get into your car by yourself and look over your hair in the mirror or check your make-up, you are using the car as a back stage. But when you wave at friends or give that familiar gesture to someone who has just cut in front of you in traffic, you are using your car as a front stage.

Roles

Everyday life brings with it many roles. The same person may be a student, a teenager, a shopper, a worker, a date, as well as a daughter or a son. While a role lays down the basic outline for a performance, it also allows a great deal of freedom. The particular emphasis or interpretation that an individual gives a role, the person's "style," is known as **role performance**. Take your role as son or daughter as an example. You may play the role of ideal daughter or son, being very respectful, coming home at the hours your parents set, and so forth. Or that description may not even come close to your particular role performance.

Ordinarily, our roles are sufficiently separated that conflict between them is minimized. Occasionally, however, what is expected of us in one role is incompatible with what is expected of us in another role. This problem, known as **role conflict**, makes us very uncomfortable, as illustrated in Figure 5.5, in which family, friendship, student, and work roles come clashing together. Usually, however, we manage to avoid role conflict by segregating our roles, which in some instances may require an intense juggling act.

Sometimes the *same* role presents inherent conflict, a problem known as **role strain**. Suppose you are exceptionally prepared for a particular class assignment. Although the instructor asks an unusually difficult question, you find yourself knowing the answer when no one else does. If you want to raise your hand, yet don't want to make your fellow students look bad, you will experience role strain. As illustrated in Figure 5.5, the difference between role conflict and role strain is that role conflict is conflict *between* roles, while role strain is conflict *within* a role.

A fascinating characteristic of roles is that *we tend to become the roles we play*. That is, roles become incorporated into the self-concept, especially those for which we prepare long and hard and that become part of our everyday lives. When sociologist Helen Ebaugh (1988) interviewed people who had left marriages, police work, and military, medical, and religious vocations, she found these roles had become so

Shown here are Leonardo Di Caprio and Kate Winslet as passengers on the doomed *Titanic*. In dramaturgy, a specialty within sociology, social life is viewed as similar to theatre. In our everyday lives, we all are actors—we perform roles, use props, and deliver lines to fellow actors.

Figure 5.5 Role Strain and Role Conflict

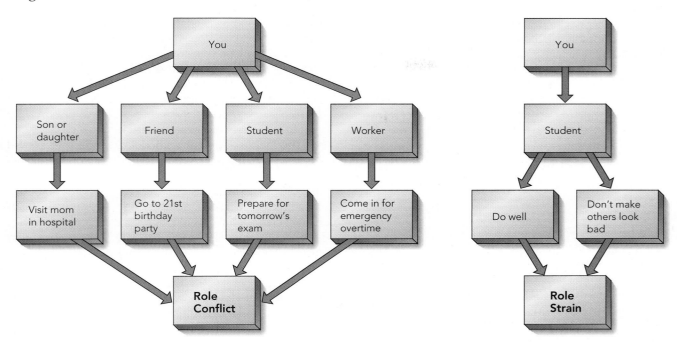

intertwined with the subjects' self-concepts that leaving them threatened their very identity. The question over which they struggled was "Who am I, now that I am not a nun (or physician, wife, colonel, etc.)?" Even years after leaving these roles, in their dreams many continued to perform them.

At the centre of our performances in everyday life is the self and how we want others to think of us. Goffman calls these efforts to manage the impressions others receive of us **impression management**.

To communicate information about the self, we use three types of **sign-vehicles**: the social setting, our appearance, and our manner. The **social setting** is the place where the action unfolds. A social setting might be an office, dorm, living room, church, gym, or bar. It is wherever you interact with others. Your social setting includes *scenery*, the furnishings you use to communicate messages, such as desks, chalkboards, scoreboards, couches, and so on.

The second sign-vehicle is **appearance**, or how we look when we play our roles. Appearance includes *props.* The teacher has books, lecture notes, and chalk, while the football player wears a special costume called a uniform. Although few of us carry around a football, we all use makeup, hairstyles, and clothing to communicate messages about ourselves. Some people use clothing to say that they are university students, others that they are old; some that they are clergy, others that they are prostitutes. Similarly, people use different brands of cigarettes, liquor, and automobiles to convey messages about the self. The Mass Media in Social Life box that follows focuses on a situation in which body size overwhelms other messages about the self.

The third sign-vehicle is **manner**, the attitudes we demonstrate as we play our roles. We use manner to communicate information about our feelings and moods. By communicating anger or indifference, sincerity or good humour, for example, we indicate to others what they can expect of us as we play our roles.

To be a good role player brings positive recognition from others, something that we all want. To accomplish this, said Goffman, we often use **teamwork**, whereby two or more people work together to make certain that a performance goes off as planned. When a performance doesn't come off quite right, however, it may require **face-saving behaviour**. We may, for example, ignore someone's flaws in performance, which Goffman defines as *tact*. Suppose your teacher is about to make an important point. Suppose also that her lecturing has been outstanding and the class is hanging on every word. Just as she pauses for emphasis, her stomach lets out a loud growl. She might then use a face-saving technique by remarking, "I was so busy preparing for class I didn't get breakfast this morning." It is more likely, however, that both class and teacher will simply ignore the sound, both giving the impression that no one heard a thing—a face-saving technique called *studied nonobservance*.

Before closing this section, we should note that impression management is not limited to individuals. Families, corporations, universities, sports teams, in fact probably all groups, try to manage impressions. An interesting example occurred when charges of corruption plagued the International Olympic Committee (IOC) in the first few months of 1999. Many of the 114 delegates of the IOC had been accused of taking bribes—university scholarships, redeeming first-class airline tickets for cash, asking for and getting expensive jewellery—to name but a few "rewards" for their vote. Accusers said this is common practice, part of the organization's culture. We learned about impression management when defenders of the IOC were quick to comment that only a small percentage of IOC members sell their votes, and there are strict policies in place to defend against such behaviour. In addition, this incident provided the public with a brief glimpse into the "backstage" workings of the IOC. We learned, for example, that the octogenarian IOC president, Juan Antonio Samaranch, insisted on being called "your excellency," and we found out something about how the organization may "really work."

Focus Question
What does Erving Goffman mean by "dramaturgy"?

Ethnomethodology: Uncovering Background Assumptions

Ethnomethodologists study how people make sense of life. They try to uncover people's basic assumptions as they interpret their everyday worlds. **Ethnomethodology** means "the study of how people do things." Specifically, ethnomethodologists study how people use common-sense understandings to get through everyday life.

Assumptions about the way life is and the way things ought to work (what ethnomethodologists call **background assumptions**) lie at the root of social life. They are so deeply embedded in our consciousness that we are seldom aware of them, for almost everyone fulfills them unquestioningly.

Let us suppose that you go to a doctor and she says that she doesn't feel like "doing doctoring" today. She then comments on how long your hair is, takes out a pair of scissors, and tries to give you a haircut. This would violate basic assumptions about what doctors are supposed to do. At the very least, we expect our doctor to listen to our medical problems and prescribe medicines. Haircuts, however, are simply not part of our expectations!

The founder of ethnomethodology, sociologist Harold Garfinkel, conducted some interesting exercises to uncover our background assumptions. Garfinkel (1967) asked his students to act as though they did not understand the basic rules of social life. Some tried to bargain with supermarket clerks; others would inch closer to people and stare directly at them. They were met with surprise, bewilderment, even anger. One of the more interesting exercises that Garfinkel's students conducted was to act as though they were boarders in their own homes. When they returned from class they addressed their parents as "Mr." and "Mrs.," asked permission to use the bathroom, sat stiffly, were extremely courteous, and spoke only when spoken to. The other family members were stupefied (Garfinkel, 1967).

Focus Question
What is the difference between ethnomethodology and symbolic interactionism?

Mass Media in Social Life   You Can't Be Thin Enough: Body Images and the Mass Media

When you stand before a mirror, do you like what you see? To make your body more attractive, do you watch your weight? Where do you get your ideas of what you should look like?

Television keeps telling us that something is wrong with our bodies. They aren't good enough, and we've got to improve them. The way to improve them, of course, is to buy the advertised products. Wigs, hair pieces, hair transplants, padded brassieres, diet pills, and exercise equipment. Chuck Norris looks so strong and manly as he touts his full body exerciser, men get the feeling that their body will look like his if they just buy that machine. Female movie stars effortlessly go through tough workouts without even breaking into a sweat. Women get the feeling that men will fight to be near them if they purchase that wonder-working workout machine.

Although we attempt to shrug off these messages, knowing they are designed to sell products, they get our attention. They penetrate our thinking, helping to shape our image of how we "ought" to look. Those models, so attractively clothed and coiffured as they walk down the runway, could they be any thinner? For women, the message is clear: You can't be thin enough. The men's message is clear, too: You can't be strong enough.

Man or woman, your body isn't good enough. It needs to be shaped into something it isn't. It sags where it should be firm. It bulges where it should be smooth. It sticks out where it shouldn't, and it doesn't stick out where it should.

And—no matter what your weight—it's too much. You've got to be thinner.

Exercise takes time, and it's painful getting in shape. Once you do get in shape, it seems to take only a few days for your body to return to its previous slothful, drab appearance if you slack off. You can't let up, you can't exercise enough, and you can't diet enough.

But who can continue at such a pace, striving for what are unrealistic cultural ideas? A few people, of course, but not many. So liposuction is appealing. Just lie there, put up with a little pain, and the doctor will suck the fat right out of you. Surgeons can transform flat breasts into super breasts overnight. They can lower receding hairlines and smooth furrowed brows. They remove lumps with their magical tummy tucks, and take off a decade with their rejuvenating skin peels and face lifts.

With the bosomy girls on *Baywatch* the envy of all, and the impossibly shaped models at *Victoria's Secret* the standard to which they hold themselves, even teens call the plastic surgeon. Parents, anxious lest their child violate peer ideals and trail behind in her race for popularity, foot the bill. In New York City, some parents pay $25 000 to give their daughters a flatter tummy (Gross, 1998).

Although peer pressure to alter the body is high, surgeons keep stoking the fire. A sample ad: "No Ifs, Ands or Butts. You Can Change Your Bottom Line in Hours!"

The thinness craze has moved to the East. Glossy magazines in Japan and China are filled with skinny models and crammed with ads touting diet pills and diet teas. In China, where famine used to abound, a little extra padding was valued as a sign of good health. Today, the obsession is thinness (Rosenthal, 1999). Not-so-subtle ads scream that fat is bad. Some teas come with a package of diet pills. Weight-loss machines, with electrodes attached to acupuncture pressure points, not only reduce fat but also build breasts. Or so the advertisers claim.

Not limited by some of our rules, advertisers in Japan and China push a soap that supposedly "sucks up fat through the skin's pores" (Marshall, 1995). What a dream product! After all, even though those TV models smile as they go through their paces, those exercise machines really do look like a lot of hard work.

In the United States, there is another bottom line. Beauty and attractiveness do pay off. Economists studied physical attractiveness and earnings. The result? "Average-looking" men and women earn more than "plain" people and "good-looking" men and women earn even more. The "ugly" are paid a pittance. "Attractive" women have an added cash advantage—they attract and marry high-er-earning men (Hamermesh & Biddle, 1994).

More popularity *and* more money? Maybe you can't be thin enough. Maybe those exercise machines are a good investment after all. If only we could catch up with the Japanese and develop a soap that would suck the fat right out of our pores. You can practically hear the jingle now.

For Your Consideration

What image do you have of your body? How do cultural expectations of "ideal" bodies underlie your image? Can you recall any advertisement or television program that has affected your body image?

Most advertising and television that focus on weight are directed at women. Women are more concerned than men about weight, more likely to have eating disorders, and more likely to express dissatisfaction with their bodies (Honeycutt, 1995). Do you think the targeting of women in advertising creates these attitudes and behaviours? Or do you think that these attitudes and behaviours would exist even if there were no such ads? Why?

All of us contrast the reality we see when we look in the mirror with our culture's ideal body types. Gwyneth Paltrow represents an ideal body type that has developed in some parts of Western culture. Partly because of such cultural images, large women sometimes find themselves social outcasts. Consequently, as in the photo on the left, some now band together in support groups to help overcome the emotional impact of their unwelcome status.

Postmodernism

Postmodernism assumes that the extensive fragmentation of present-day society causes widespread instability in the meaning of social life. According to postmodernism, language today may be the primary social bond, but, in order to communicate with one another we continually find ourselves playing the almost endless number of "language games" that coincide with the numerous roles we must play in contemporary society. We try to "fake it," or get along with our acquaintances, by communicating the surface reality, the image of ourselves we need to convey at that moment.

Experiencing a postmodern world, according to postmodernists, means that individuals daily confront and communicate only surface realities. There is no need for a past or a future, just the present.

For postmodernists, television and video are the two primary "socializing" agents because we internalize the montage of images they convey about reality (past, present, and possible futures) as the real world. Image and reality become one. Moreover, the television spectacle represented in programs like *Jerry Springer* or *Cops* becomes what is real about the experience of life in a postmodern world. For young people especially, living in a postmodern, urban world means the more sensational the image, or the spectacle, the more intense and fleeting the experience.

In Sum

Symbolic interactionists stress that the events and objects of social life do not come with built-in meanings. Rather, we are constantly interpreting the world around us. Ethnomethodologists explore background assumptions, our taken-for-granted ideas about the world, which underlie our behaviour and are violated only with risk. Postmodernists challenge the manner in which we see and interpret the language and images of contemporary society.

The Social Construction of Reality

Consider the following experience of James Henslin.

On a visit to Morocco, in Northern Africa, I decided to buy a watermelon. When I indicated to the street vendor that the knife he was going to use to cut the watermelon was dirty ("encrusted with filth" would be more apt), he was very obliging. He immediately bent down and began to swish the knife in a puddle on the street. I shuddered as I looked at the passing burros, freely defecating and urinating as they went. Quickly, I indicated by gesture that I preferred my melon uncut after all.

For that vendor, germs did not exist. For Henslin, they did. And each of them acted according to the way they saw matters. Their behaviour did not result from the existence or nonexistence of germs, but rather from their definitions, from their growing up in a group that teaches that germs are real or does not teach this.

Microbes objectively exist, of course, and whether germs are part of our thinking makes no difference in our getting infected by them. Our behaviour, however, depends on the way we define reality—on our **definition of the situation**—not on the objective existence of something.

This is what the **social construction of reality** is. Our society, or the social groups to which we belong, have their particular views of life. From our groups (the social part of this process), we learn specific ways of looking at life—whether that be our view of germs (they exist, they don't exist), or of anything else in life. In short, through our interaction with others, we learn ways of looking at our experiences in life.

Gynecological Examinations. Consider the following example of pelvic examinations that is experienced by women but is difficult for most men to identify with.

A gynecological nurse, Mae Biggs, and James Henslin did research on pelvic examinations. Reviewing about 14 000 cases, they looked at how the medical profession constructs social reality in order to define this examination as nonsexual (Henslin & Biggs, 1997). This desexualization is accomplished by painstakingly controlling the sign-vehicles—the setting, appearance, and manner.

The examination unfolds much like a stage play. We will use "he" to refer to the physician because only male physicians participated in this study. Perhaps the results would be different with female gynecologists.

■ *Scene 1 (the patient as person).* In this scene, the doctor maintains eye contact with his patient, calls her by name, and discusses her problems in a professional manner. He tells a nurse, "Pelvic in room 1." By this statement, he is announcing that a major change will occur in the next scene.

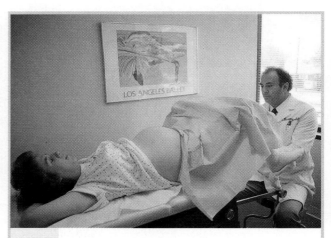

Pelvic examinations provide an excellent illustration of the social construction of reality. As the text explains, this term refers to how people jointly agree that a particular situation has some meaning rather than another.

■ *Scene 2 (from person to pelvic)*. This scene is the depersonalizing stage. In line with the doctor's announcement, the patient begins the transition from a "person" to a "pelvic." The doctor leaves the room, and a female nurse enters to help the patient make the transition. The nurse prepares the "props" for the coming examination and answers any questions the woman might have.

What occurs at this point is essential for the social construction of reality, for *the doctor's absence at this point removes even the suggestion of sexuality.*

The patient also wants to remove any hint of sexuality in the coming interaction, and during this scene she may express concern about what to do with her panties. Most women solve the problem by either slipping their panties under their clothes or placing them in their purse.

■ *Scene 3 (the person as pelvic)*. This scene opens with the doctor entering the room. Before him is a woman lying on a table, her feet in stirrups, her knees tightly together, and her body covered by a drape sheet. The doctor seats himself on a low stool before the woman, tells her, "Let your knees fall apart" (rather than the sexually loaded "Spread your legs"), and begins the examination.

The drape sheet is critical in this process of desexualization, for it *dissociates the pelvic area from the person*: Bending forward and with the drape sheet above his head, the physician can see only the vagina, not the patient's face. Thus dissociated from the individual, the vagina is dramaturgically transformed into an object of analysis. In this critical scene, the patient cooperates in being an object, becoming for all practical purposes a pelvis to be examined. She withdraws eye contact, from the doctor for certain but usually from the nurse as well, is likely to stare at the wall or at the ceiling, and avoids initiating conversation.

■ *Scene 4 (from pelvic to person)*. In this scene, the patient becomes "repersonalized." The doctor has left the examining room; the patient dresses and takes care of any problems with her hair and makeup.

■ *Scene 5 (the patient as person)*. In this scene, the patient is once again treated as a person rather than an object. The doctor makes eye contact with her and addresses her by name. She, too, makes eye contact with the doctor, and the usual middle-class interaction patterns are followed. She has been fully restored.

In Sum

To an outsider to our culture, the custom of women going to a male stranger for a vaginal examination might seem bizarre. But not to us. To sustain this definition as nonsexual requires teamwork—patients, doctors, and nurses working together to jointly produce this definition of reality. Thus, sociologists say that we *socially construct reality.*

Although pelvic examinations are socially constructed as nonsexual, many women still cannot rid themselves of uncomfortable feelings during this procedure, especially if their physician is a man. As the second wave of feminism gathered force in the 1960s and 1970s, women revealed this discomfort to one another. At this time, when less than 10 percent of obstetricians and gynecologists were female, some women decided to "take back control" of their reproductive health. Meeting in "consciousness-raising" groups, they taught themselves how to examine their own bodies.

Since then, the situation has changed somewhat, and today in Canada approximately 40 percent of obstetricians and gynecologists are women. How this changed sex ratio may affect the ways pelvic examinations—and medicine itself—are socially constructed has yet to unfold. Whatever the particulars, the same principles will apply: team players working to maintain agreed-on definitions of the situation.

The social construction of reality is not limited to small segments of social life. Rather, it is an essential part of our everyday lives. Or, as sociologist W. I. Thomas put it, in a classic statement that has become known as the **Thomas theorem**, "If people define situations as real, they are real in their consequences." To understand human behaviour, then, whether that be how people react to pelvic examinations, or to anything else in life, we need to know how people define reality.

The Need for Both Macrosociology and Microsociology

As noted earlier in this chapter, to understand social life adequately, we need both microsociology and macrosociology. Each makes a vital contribution to our understanding of human behaviour.

To illustrate this point, consider the research on two groups of high school boys conducted by sociologist William Chambliss (1973/1997). Both groups attended Hanibal High School. One group was composed of eight promising young students, boys who came from "good" families and were perceived by the community as "going somewhere." Chambliss calls this group the "Saints." The other group consisted of six lower-class boys who were seen as going down a dead-end road. Chambliss calls this group the "Roughnecks."

Both groups were seriously delinquent. Both skipped school, drank a lot, and committed criminal acts, especially fighting and vandalism. The Saints were actually somewhat more delinquent. They were truant more often, and they committed more acts of vandalism. Yet it was the Saints who had the good reputation, while the Roughnecks were seen by teachers, the police, and the general community as no good and heading for trouble.

These reputations followed the boys throughout life. Seven of the eight Saints went on to graduate from university. Three studied for advanced degrees: One finished law school and became active in state politics; one finished medical school and set up a practice near Hanibal; and one went on to earn a Ph.D. The four other university graduates entered managerial or executive training with large firms. After his parents divorced, one Saint failed to graduate from high school on time and had to repeat his senior year. Although this boy tried to go to university by attending night school, he never finished. He was unemployed the last time Chambliss saw him.

In contrast, only four of the Roughnecks even finished high school. Two of these boys did exceptionally well in sports and received athletic scholarships to university. They both graduated from university and became high school coaches. Of the two others who graduated from high school, one became a small-time gambler and the other disappeared "up north" where he was last reported to be driving a truck. Of the two who did not complete high school, each was last heard of serving time in state penitentiaries for separate murders.

To understand what happened to the Saints and the Roughnecks, we need to grasp *both* social structure and social interaction. That is, we need both macrosociology and microsociology. Using *macrosociology*, we can place these boys within the larger framework of a society's social class system. This context reveals how opportunities open or close to people depending on their membership in the middle or lower social class, and how different goals are instilled in youngsters as they grow up in vastly different groups. We can then use *microsociology* to follow their everyday lives. We can see how the Saints used their "good" reputations to skip classes repeatedly and how their access to automobiles allowed them to transfer their troublemaking to different communities and thus prevent damage to their local reputations. In contrast, lacking access to automobiles, the Roughnecks were highly visible. Their lawbreaking activities, limited to a small area, readily came to the attention of the community. Microsociology also reveals how their respective reputations opened doors of opportunity to the first group of boys while closing them to the other.

Thus we need both kinds of sociology, and both will be stressed in the following chapters.

Summary and Review

LEVELS OF SOCIOLOGICAL ANALYSIS

What are the two levels of analysis that sociologists use?

Sociologists use macro- and microsociological levels of analysis. In **macrosociology**, the focus is placed on large-scale features of social life, while in **microsociology**, the focus is on **social interaction**. Functionalists and conflict theorists tend to use a macrosociological approach, while symbolic interactionists are more likely to use a microsociological approach. Feminists and postmodernists are able to bring together both perspectives because feminists concentrate on analyzing gender relations while postmodernists link the culture of society with what makes the individual what he or she is. pp. 96–97.

THE MACROSOCIOLOGICAL PERSPECTIVE: SOCIAL STRUCTURE

How does social structure influence our behaviour?

The term **social structure** refers to a society's framework, which forms an envelope around us and establishes limits on our behaviour. Social structure consists of culture, social class, social statuses, roles, groups, and social institutions; together these serve as foundations for how we view the world. pp. 97–98.

What are social institutions?

Social institutions are the organized and standard means that a society develops to meet its basic needs. Industrialized societies have 10 social institutions—the family, religion, law, politics, eco-

nomics, education, medicine, science, the military, and the mass media. From the functionalist perspective, social institutions meet universal group needs, or **functional requisites**. From the conflict perspective, the elite use social institutions to maintain their privileged position. From the feminist perspective, men dominate the major institutions of society. pp. 98–101.

When societies are transformed by social change, how do they manage to hold together?

In agricultural societies, said Emile Durkheim, people are united by **mechanical solidarity** (similar views and feelings). With industrialization comes **organic solidarity** (people depend on one another to do their jobs). Ferdinand Tönnies pointed out that the informal means of control of *Gemeinschaft* (small, intimate) societies are replaced by formal mechanisms in *Gesellschaft* (larger, more impersonal) societies. pp. 101–102.

What other elements of social structure affect our beliefs and how we behave or misbehave?

Our location in the social structure underlies our perceptions, attitudes, and behaviours. Culture lays the broadcast framework, while **social class** divides people according to income, education, and occupational prestige. Each of us receives **ascribed statuses** at birth; later we add various **achieved statuses**. Our behaviours and orientations are further influenced by **roles** we play, the groups to which we belong, and our experiences with the institutions of our society. These components of society work together to help maintain social order. pp. 102–105.

SOCIAL GROUPS AND SOCIETIES

What is a group?

Sociologists use many definitions of groups, but, in general, *groups* are people who have something in common and who believe that what they have in common is significant. **Societies** are the largest and most complex groups that sociologists study. p. 105.

GROUPS WITHIN SOCIETY

How do sociologists classify groups?

Sociologists divide groups into primary groups, secondary groups, in-groups, out-groups, reference groups, and networks. The cooperative, intimate, long-term, face-to-face relationships provided by **primary groups** are fundamental to our sense of self. **Secondary groups** are larger, relatively temporary, more anonymous, formal, and impersonal than primary groups. **In-groups** provide members with a strong sense of identification and belonging, while **out-groups** help create this identity by showing in-group members what they are *not*. **Reference groups** are groups we use as standards to evaluate ourselves. **Social networks** consist of social ties that link people together. Changed technology has given birth to a new type of group, the **electronic community**. pp. 105–108.

How does a group's size affect its dynamics?

The term **group dynamics** refers to how individuals affect groups and how groups influence individuals. In a **small group**, everyone can interact directly with everyone else. As a group grows larger, its intensity decreases and its stability increases. A **dyad**, consisting of two people, is the most unstable of human groups, but it provides the most intense or intimate relationships. The addition of a third person, forming a **triad**, fundamentally alters relationships. Triads are unstable, as **coalitions** tend to form (the alignment of some members of a group against others). pp. 108–110.

What characterizes a leader?

A leader is someone who influences others. **Instrumental leaders** try to keep a group moving toward its goals, even at the cost of causing friction. **Expressive leaders** focus on creating harmony and raising group morale. Both types are essential to the functioning of groups. pp. 110–111.

What are the three main leadership styles?

Authoritarian leaders give orders, **democratic leaders** try to lead by consensus, and **laissez-faire leaders** are highly permissive. An authoritarian style appears to be more effective in emergency situations, a democratic style works best for most situations, and a laissez-faire style is usually ineffective. p. 111.

How do groups encourage conformity?

The Asch experiment was cited to illustrate the power of peer pressure, the Milgram experiment the influence of authority. Both experiments demonstrate how easily we can succumb to **groupthink**, a kind of collective tunnel vision. Preventing groupthink requires the free circulation of contrasting ideas. pp. 111–112.

THE MICROSOCIOLOGICAL PERSPECTIVE: SOCIAL INTERACTION IN EVERYDAY LIFE

What is the focus of symbolic interactionism?

In contrast to functionalists and conflict theorists, who as macrosociologists focus on "the big picture," symbolic interactionists tend to be microsociologists who focus on face-to-face social interaction. Symbolic interactionists analyze how people define their worlds, and how their definitions, in turn, influence their behaviour. p. 112.

How do stereotypes affect social interaction?

Stereotypes are assumptions of what people are like. When we first meet people, we classify them according to our perceptions of their visible characteristics and our ideas about those characteristics. These assumptions guide our behaviour toward them, which, in turn, influences them to behave in ways that reinforce our stereotypes. p. 114.

Do all human groups share a similar sense of personal space?

In examining how people use physical space, symbolic interactionists stress that each of us is surrounded by a "personal bubble" we carefully protect. People from different cultures have "personal bubbles" of varying sizes, so the answer to the question is no. North Americans typically use four different "distance zones": intimate, personal, social, and public. pp. 114–115.

What is dramaturgy?

Erving Goffman developed **dramaturgy** (or *dramaturgical analysis*), which analyzes everyday life in terms of the stage. At the core of this analysis are the impressions we attempt to make on others. For that, we use the **sign-vehicles** of setting, appearance, and manner. Our performances often call for **teamwork** and **face-saving behaviour**. pp. 116–118.

What is the social construction of reality?

Ethnomethodology is the study of how people make sense of everyday life. Ethnomethodologists try to uncover our **background assumptions**, our basic ideas about the way life is. The phrase **social construction of reality** refers to how we construct our views of the world. p. 118.

POSTMODERNISM

What is postmodernism?

Postmodernism is the study of the contemporary use of language and images in our day-to-day "discourses." Language and culture are macrosociological while images and the individual are microsociological. Mass media and the computer are two primary socializing agents and are the focus of postmodern theoretical and methodological analysis. pp. 120–121.

THE NEED FOR BOTH MACROSOCIOLOGY AND MICROSOCIOLOGY

Why are both levels of analysis important?

Because each focuses on different aspects of the human experience, both microsociology and macrosociology are necessary for us to understand social life.

Sociologists use both macro and micro levels of analysis to study social life. Those who use macrosociology to analyze human behaviour focus on broad social forces, such as the economy and social classes. Sociologists who use the microsociological approach analyze how people interact with one another. pp. 121–122.

Critical Thinking Questions

1. Why do human beings need both verbal and nonverbal means of communication?

2. According to symbolic interactionists, to live together, people must communicate their interpretations of the social situation in which they find themselves at that moment in time. An important part of communication is role-taking, that is, we try to imagine what the other person is experiencing. The next time you are in your sociology class, imagine yourself as the professor looking into the audience of sociology students. How would you emotionally prepare yourself to face this audience?

3. The next time you are in an elevator, instead of standing looking at the floor, try sitting down on the elevator floor. What reactions would you expect to get from those in the elevator? What theory is this a good example of? Can you develop your own assignment for breaking the rules of everyday life?

Key Terms

achieved statuses 103
aggregate 105
appearance 117
ascribed statuses 103
authoritarian leader 111
back stages 116
background assumptions 118
category 105
cliques 107
coalition 109
definition of the situation 120
democratic leader 111
division of labour 101
dramaturgy 116
dyad 108
electronic community 109
electronic primary group 109
ethnomethodology 118
expressive leader 110
face-saving behaviour 117
front stages 116
functional requisites 98
Gemeinschaft 101
Gesellschaft 101
group 105

group dynamics 108
groupthink 112
impression management 117
in-groups 106
instrumental leader 110
laissez-faire leader 111
leader 110
leadership styles 111
macrosociology 96
manner 117
master status 104
mechanical solidarity 101
microsociology 96
networking 108
organic solidarity 101
out-groups 106
postmodernism 97
primary group 105
reference groups 107
role conflict 116
role performance 116
role strain 116
roles 105
secondary groups 106
sign-vehicles 117

small group 108
social class 102
social cohesion 101
social construction of reality 120
social institutions 98
social interaction 96
social networks 107
social setting 117
social structure 97

society 105
status 103
status inconsistency (or discrepancy) 104
status set 103
status symbols 104
stereotypes 114
teamwork 117
Thomas theorem 121
triad 108

Weblinks

Methodological Issues in Conversation Analysis

www.ai.univ-paris8.fr/corpus/papers/tenHave/mica.htm

Conversation analysis, a research tradition that grew out of ethnomethodology, has some unique methodological features. Paul ten Have of the University of Amsterdam describes some of those features in the interest of exploring their grounds.

The Social Construction of Our "Inner" Lives

www.massey.ac.nz/~ALock/virtual/inner.htm

John Shotter of the Department of Communication at the University of New Hampshire explores some aspects of a "rhetorical-responsive" version of social constructionism, and how it might throw some light on the conduct of our "inner" lives.

Microsociology

w1.xrefer.com/entry/344322

This page is part of a site that offers "free access to over 250 000 entries-facts, words, concepts, people, and quotations... Encyclopedias, dictionaries, thesauri, and books of quotations from the world's leading publishers. All cross-referenced, all reliable, all in one place." For example, there is also a page titled "Macrosociology."

Temple of Holy Electronic Media and Unadulterated Slack!

medusa.twinoaks.org/clubs/subgenius/

The Richmond, Virginia, "outpost for organizing world domination by Mutants." The Temple is connected with the satirical Church of the SubGenius. A good example of an electronic community.

part three

Social Inequality

own three radios, two CD players, four telephones (one cellular), two televisions, a camcorder, DVD player, tape recorder, Gameboy, PlayStation, computer, and printer, not to mention two blow dryers, an answering machine, a coffee maker, and an electric toothbrush. This doesn't count the stereo-radio-cassette players in their van and car.

Rick works 40 hours a week as a cable splicer for the telephone company. Patti teaches school part-time. Together they make $60 611, plus benefits. The Kellys can choose from among dozens of super-stocked supermarkets. They spend $5685 for food they eat at home, and another $2895 eating out, a total of about 15 percent of their annual income.

In Canada, the average life expectancy is 78.5 for males, 81.4 for females.

On the Kellys' wish list are two cell phones, a new Jeep, a Pentium III computer, a laser printer, a digital camera, a fax machine, a boat, a camping trailer, and, oh yes, farther down the road, a vacation cabin.

Sources: Menzel (1994); Population Reference Bureau (1995); *Statistical Abstract* (1997), Tables 713, 723; Health Canada (1999).

"Worlds Apart" could be the title for these photos, which illustrate how life chances depend on global stratification. On the left is the Mulleta family of Ethiopia, featured in the opening vignette, standing in front of their home with all their material possessions. On the right is the Skeen family of Texas, surrounded by their possessions.

What Is Social Stratification?

Some of the world's nations are wealthy, others poor, and some in between. This layering of nations, or of groups of people within a nation, is called *social stratification*. Social stratification is one of the most significant topics we shall discuss, for it affects our life chances—from material possessions to the age at which we die.

Social stratification also affects our orientations to life. If you had been born into the Ethiopian family, for example, you would be illiterate and expect your children to be the same. You also would expect hunger to be a part of life and not be too surprised when people die young. To be born into either of the other two families would give you quite different views of the world. Of course, being born a woman (as will be discussed in Chapter 7) would also dramatically affect your life, regardless of which family you were born into.

It is important to emphasize that social stratification does not refer to individuals. It is *a way of ranking large groups of people into a hierarchy that shows their relative privileges.* **Social stratification** is a system in which people are divided into layers according to their relative power, property, and prestige.

Let's examine how the nations of the world became so stratified that, as with these three families, it profoundly affects everyone's chances in life. But first let's review the major systems of social stratification.

Systems of Social Stratification

Every society stratifies its members in some form. Some, such as agricultural societies, draw firm lines that separate group from group, while others, such as hunting and gathering societies, show much greater equality. Regardless of its forms, however, the existence of social stratification is universal. There are four major systems of social stratification: slavery, caste, clan, and class.

Slavery

Let's first look at the broad aspects of slavery—its major causes and conditions—and then at slavery in the New World. As we examine the characteristics of slavery, you will see how remarkably it has varied around the world.

Causes of Slavery. **Slavery**, whose essential characteristic is *ownership of some people by others*, has been common in world history. The Israelites of the Old Testament had slaves, as did the ancient Africans. In classical Greece and Rome, slaves did the work while free citizens engaged in politics and the arts. Slavery was least common among nomads, especially hunters and gatherers, and most common in agricultural societies (Landtman, 1938/1968).

Contrary to popular assumption, slavery was not usually based on racism, but on one of three other factors. The first was debt. In some cultures, an individual who could not pay a debt could be enslaved by the creditor. The second was a violation of the law. Instead of being killed, a murderer or thief might be enslaved by the family of the victim as compensation for their loss. The third was war and conquest. When one group of people conquered another, it was often convenient to enslave at least some of the vanquished (Starna & Watkins, 1991). Historian Gerda Lerner (1986) notes that through this practice the first slaves were women. When premodern men raided a village or camp, they killed the men, raped the women, and then brought the women back as slaves. The women were valued for sexual purposes, for reproduction, and for extra labour. Slavery, then, was a sign of defeat in battle, of crime, or of debt, not the sign of some inherently inferior status.

Slavery in the New World. **Indentured service** represents a fuzzy line between a contract and slavery (Main, 1965; Elkins, 1968). Many people who desired to start a new life in the American colonies were unable to pay their passage. Ship captains would carry them on credit, depending on someone to "buy their paper" when they arrived. This arrangement provided passage for the penniless, payment for the ship's captain, and servants for wealthier colonists for a set number of years. During that specified period, the servants had to serve their master—and could be captured and forcibly returned if they ran away. At the end of the period of indenture, they became full citizens, able to live where they chose and free to sell their labour.

When the colonists found that there were not enough indentured servants to meet their growing need for labour, they tried to enslave Indians. This attempt, however, failed miserably. Among other reasons, when Indians escaped they knew how to survive in the wilderness and were able to make their way back to their tribe. The colonists then turned to Africans, who were being brought to North and South America by the Dutch, English, Portuguese, and Spanish.

Given this background of causes of slavery, some analysts conclude that racism didn't lead to slavery, but, rather, slavery led to racism. Finding it profitable to make people slaves for life, slave owners developed an **ideology**, a system of beliefs that justifies social arrangements. Essential to an ideology that would justify lifelong slavery was the view that the slaves were inferior. Some said that they were locked into a childlike, helpless state, which meant that they needed to be taken care of by superior people—white colonists, of course. Others even concluded that the slaves were not fully human. With these views, the colonists developed elaborate justifications for slavery on the presumed superiority of their own race.

Patterns of legal discrimination did not end after the Civil War. For example, until 1954 the United States operated two separate school systems. Even until the 1950s, to keep the races from "mixing," it was illegal in Mississippi for a white and an African-American to sit together on the same seat of a car! The reason there was no outright ban on both races being in the same car was to allow for African-American chauffeurs.

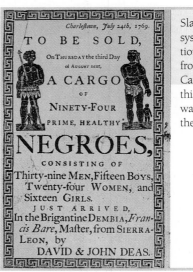

Slavery is an age-old system of social stratification. This 1769 broadside from Charleston, South Carolina, reminds us that this form of stratification was once the custom in the United States.

Caste

The second system of social stratification is caste. In a **caste system**, status is determined by birth and is lifelong. In sociological terms the basis of a caste system is ascribed status (discussed in Chapter 5). Achieved status cannot change an individual's place in this system. Someone born into a low-status group will always have low status, no matter how much that person may accomplish in life.

Societies with this form of stratification try to make certain that the boundaries between castes remain firm. They practise **endogamy**, marriage within their own group, and prohibit intermarriage. To prevent contact between castes, they even develop elaborate rules about *ritual pollution*, teaching that contact with inferior castes contaminates the superior caste.

India. India provides the best example of a caste system. Based not on race but on religion, it has existed for almost 3000 years (Chandra, 1993a, b). India's four main castes, or *varnas*, are depicted in Table 6.1. The four main castes are subdivided into thousands of specialized subcastes, or *jati*, with each *jati* working in a specific occupation. For example, knife-sharpening is done only by members of a certain subcaste.

The lowest group listed on Table 6.1, the Harijan, is actually so low that it is beneath the caste system altogether. The Harijans, along with some of the Shudras, make up India's "untouchables." If someone of a higher caste is touched by one of them, that person becomes unclean. In some cases, even the shadow of an untouchable is contaminating. If anyone becomes contaminated, religion specifies ablution, or washing rituals, to restore purity (Lannoy, 1975).

Although the Indian government declared the caste system abolished in 1949, the force of centuries-old practices cannot be so easily eliminated, and the caste system remains part of everyday life in India (Sharma, 1994). The ceremonies one follows at births, marriages, and deaths, for example, are dictated by caste (Chandra, 1993a). Due to industrialization and urbanization, however, this system is breaking down, for it is difficult to maintain caste divisions in crowded and anonymous cities (I. Robertson, 1976).

Clan

The **clan system** used to be common in agricultural societies. In this system, every individual is linked to a large

Table 6.1 India's Caste System

Caste	Occupation
Brahman	Priests or scholars
Kshatriya	Nobles and warriors
Vaishya	Merchants and skilled artisans
Shudra	Common labourers
Harijan	The outcastes; degrading labour

network of relatives called a **clan**. A clan is like a greatly extended family. Just as in a family, if the clan has a high status, so does the individual. Similarly, the clan's resources—whether few or many—are the individual's. And like a family, allegiance to the clan is a lifelong obligation.

Clans are also like castes in that membership is determined by birth and is lifelong. Unlike castes, however, marriages can cross clan lines. In fact, marriages may be used to forge alliances between clans, for the obligations that a marriage establishes between in-laws can bind clans together (Erturk, 1994).

Just as industrialization and urbanization are eroding the lines that separate the castes of India, so they make clans more fluid, eventually replacing them by social classes.

Class

As we have seen, stratification systems based on slavery, caste, and clan are rigid. The lines marking the divisions between people are so firm that, except for marriage between clans, there is no movement from one group to another. A **class system**, in contrast, is much more open, for it is based primarily on money or material possessions. It, too, begins at birth, when an individual is ascribed the status of his or her parents, but, unlike slavery, caste, and clan, one's social class may change due to what one achieves (or fails to achieve) in life. In addition, there are no laws that specify occupations on the basis of birth or that prohibit marriage between the classes.

A major characteristic of this fourth system, then, is its relatively fluid boundaries. A class system allows for the *possibility* of **social mobility**, that is, movement up or down the class ladder. The potential for improving one's social circumstances, or class, is one of the major forces that drives people to go far in school and to work hard. In the extreme, the family background an individual inherits at birth may bestow such obstacles that the child has little chance of climbing very far—or it may provide such privileges that it is almost impossible to fall very far down the class ladder.

What Determines Social Class?

In the early days of sociology, a disagreement arose about the meaning of social class in industrialized societies. Let's compare how Marx and Weber saw the matter.

Karl Marx: The Means of Production

As discussed in Chapter 1, Karl Marx (1818–1883) personally saw societies in upheaval. When the feudal system broke up, masses of peasants were displaced from their traditional lands and occupations. Fleeing to cities, they competed for the few available jobs. Offered only a pittance for their labour, they dressed in rags, went hungry, and slept under bridges and in shacks. In contrast, the factory owners built mansions, hired servants, and lived in the lap of luxury.

These photos, taken at the end of the nineteenth century, illustrate the different worlds social classes produce within the same society. The boys on the left worked full-time when they could get work. They did not go to school, and they had no home. The children on the right, Cornelius and Gladys Vanderbilt, are shown in front of their parents' estate. They went to school and did not work. You can see how life situations illustrated in these photos would have produced different orientations to life—and, therefore, politics, ideas, and so on—the stuff of which life is made.

Seeing this great disparity between owners and workers, Marx concluded that social class depends on a single factor—the **means of production**—the tools, factories, land, and investment capital used to produce wealth (Marx, 1844/1964; Marx & Engels, 1848/1967).

Marx argued that the distinctions people often make between themselves—such as clothing, speech, education, or relative salary—are superficial matters. They camouflage the only real significant dividing line: People (the **bourgeoisie**) either own the means of production or they (the **proletariat**) work for those who do. This is the only distinction that counts, for these two classes make up modern society. In short, according to Marx, people's relationship to the means of production determines their social class.

Marx did recognize that other groups were part of industrial society: farmers and peasants; a *lumpenproletariat* (marginal people such as migrant workers, beggars, vagrants, and criminals); and a middle class (self-employed professionals). Marx did not consider these groups social classes, however, for they lacked **class consciousness**—common identity based on their position in the means of production. They did not see themselves as exploited workers whose plight could be solved only by collective action. Consequently, Marx thought of these groups as insignificant in the coming workers' revolution that would overthrow capitalism.

Capital will become more concentrated, Marx said, which will make capitalists and workers increasingly hostile. When workers see capitalists as the source of their oppression, they will unite and throw off the chains of their oppressors. In a bloody revolution, they will seize the means of production and usher in a classless society, where no longer will the few grow rich at the expense of the many. What holds back the workers' unity and their revolution is **false consciousness**, workers mistakenly identifying with capitalists. For example, workers with a few dollars in the bank often forget that they are workers and instead see themselves as investors, or as capitalists who are about to launch a successful business.

The only distinction worth mentioning, then, is whether a person is an owner or a worker. This decides everything else, Marx stressed, for property determines people's lifestyles, shapes their ideas, and establishes their relationships with one another.

Max Weber: Property, Prestige, and Power

Max Weber (1864–1920) became an outspoken critic of Marx. He said that property is only part of the picture. Social class, he said, is actually made up of three components—*property*, *prestige*, and *power* (Gerth & Mills, 1958; Weber, 1922/1968). Some call these the three Ps of social class. (Although Weber used the terms "class," "status," and "power," some sociologists find "property," "prestige," and "power" to be clearer terms. To make them even clearer, you may wish to substitute *wealth* for "property.")

Property (or wealth), said Weber, is certainly significant in determining a person's standing in society. On that he agreed with Marx. But, added Weber, ownership is not the only significant aspect of property. For example, some powerful people, such as managers of corporations, *control* the means of production although they do not *own* them. If managers can control property for their own benefit—awarding themselves huge bonuses and magnificent perks—it makes no practical difference that they do not own the property they so generously use for their own benefit.

Prestige, the second element in Weber's analysis, is often derived from property, for people tend to look up to the wealthy. Prestige, however, can also be based on other factors. Olympic gold medallists, for example, may not own property, yet they have very high prestige. Some are even able to exchange their prestige for property—such as being paid a small fortune for saying that they start their day with "the breakfast of champions." In other words, property and prestige are not one-way streets: Although property can bring prestige, prestige can also bring property.

Power, the third element of social class, is the ability to control others, even over their objections. Weber agreed with Marx that property is a major source of power, but he added that it is not the only source. For example, prestige can be turned into power. Perhaps the best example is Ronald Reagan, an actor who became president of the most powerful country in the world. For other interrelationships of property, prestige, and power, see Figure 6.1.

In Sum

For Marx, social class was based solely on a person's position in relationship to the means of production—as a member of either the bourgeoisie or the proletariat—while Weber argued that social class is a combination of property, prestige, and power.

Focus Question

What are some of the differences between Marx's and Weber's approach to social class?

Figure 6.1 Weber's Three Components of Social Class: Interrelationships Between Them

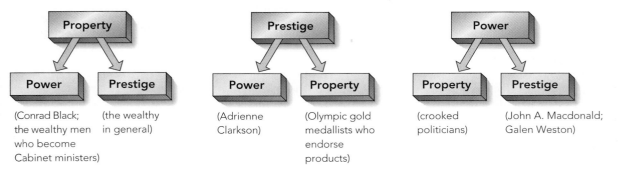

Property → Power (Conrad Black; the wealthy men who become Cabinet ministers)
Property → Prestige (the wealthy in general)

Prestige → Power (Adrienne Clarkson)
Prestige → Property (Olympic gold medallists who endorse products)

Power → Property (crooked politicians)
Power → Prestige (John A. Macdonald; Galen Weston)

The text describes the many relationships among Weber's three components of social class: property, prestige, and power. What mix of the three do you think apply to John A. Macdonald and Adrienne Clarkson?

Defining Social Class

"There are the poor and the rich—and then there are you and I, neither poor nor rich." That is just about as far as most Canadians' consciousness of social class goes. Let's try to flesh this out.

Our task is made somewhat difficult because sociologists have no clear-cut, agreed-on definition of social class. As noted above, most conflict sociologists (of the Marxist orientation) see only two social classes: those who own the means of production and those who do not. The problem with this view, say most sociologists, is that it lumps too many people together. Physicians and corporate executives with incomes of $250 000 a year are lumped together with hamburger flippers working at McDonald's for $10 000 a year.

Most sociologists agree with Weber that there are more components of social class than a person's relationship to the means of production. Consequently, most sociologists use the components Weber identified and define **social class** as a large group of people who rank closely to one another in wealth, power, and prestige. These three elements separate people into different lifestyles, give them different chances in life, and provide them with distinct ways of looking at the self and the world.

Measuring Social Class

We will examine wealth, power, and prestige in the next section, but first let's look at three different ways of measuring social class.

1. *Subjective method.* The **subjective method** is to ask people what their social class is. Although simple and direct, this approach is filled with problems. First, people may deny that they belong to any class, claiming, instead, that everyone is equal. Second, people may classify themselves according to their aspirations—where they would like to be—rather than where they actually are. Third, when asked to what class they belong, most Canadians identify themselves as middle-class, as do most citizens of industrialized nations (Kelley & Evans, 1995; Forcese, 1997). This perception removes the usefulness of the subjective method for most purposes.

2. *Reputational method.* In the **reputational method**, people are asked what class others belong to, on the basis of their reputations. Social anthropologist W. Lloyd Warner (Warner & Hunt, 1941; Warner, Hunt, Meeker, & Eels, 1949) pioneered this method in a study of a community he called "Yankee City." Its use is limited to smaller communities, where people are familiar with one another's reputation.

   Three of Warner's colleagues used this method to study "Old City," a small southern town in the United States (Davis, Gardner, & Gardner, 1941). They found that just as people at each class level see life differently,

Most Canadians identify themselves as middle-class. How would you identify the individuals depicted by artist Duane Hanson in these life-size polyvinyl figures? What status markers do you see?

so they carry around different pictures of society's classes. People see finer divisions at their own class level, but tend to lump people together as a social class recedes from them. Thus people at the top see several groups of people at the top, but tend to lump the bottom into a single unit ("the poor"), while people at the bottom see several distinctions among the poor but tend to see just "the rich" at the top.

3. *Objective method.* In the **objective method**, researchers rank people according to objective criteria such as wealth, power, and prestige. This method has the advantage of letting others know exactly what measurements were made, so that they can test them.

Given the three methods of determining social class, sociologists primarily use the objective method. The studies reported in this chapter are examples of the objective approach.

The Components of Social Class

Let's look at how sociologists measure the three components of social class: wealth, power, and prestige.

Wealth

The primary dimension of social class is **wealth**. Wealth consists of property and income. Property comes in many forms, such as buildings, land, animals, machinery, cars, stocks, bonds, businesses, and bank accounts. Income is money received as wages, rents, interest, royalties, or the proceeds from a business.

Property. Overall, Canadians are worth a hefty sum. The total net wealth of all Canadian households is estimated at about $3 trillion (Yalnizyan, 1998). Most of this wealth is in the form of real estate, corporate stocks, bonds, and business assets. This wealth is highly concentrated. The vast majority, 80 percent, of all corporate stocks and bonds is owned by fewer than 1000 individuals who together make up the inner core of Canada's super-rich. The super-rich constitute less than 2 percent of the Canadian population (Allahar & Coté, 1998).

Clearly, power and wealth are very concentrated within Canadian society. The web of ownership, wealth, power, and property weave a complex network, making it very difficult to indicate precisely the nature of this concentration, although sociologists such as Porter (1965) and Clement (1975), along with journalists Peter Newman (1979) and Diane Francis (1986), have all demonstrated it (Forcese, 1997). Estimates suggest that, for example, one-third of all corporate assets in Canada are controlled by only twelve families and five conglomerates, while about 80 percent of the Toronto Stock Exchange's List of 300 companies are controlled by eight conglomerates (Allahar & Coté, 1998).

Family dynasties hold a prominent place among the wealthy and powerful of Canada. For example, more than 1300 of the largest corporations in Canada in 1983 were owned or controlled by six families (Weston, Black, Desmarais, Irving, Thomson, and Bronfman) (Allahar & Coté, 1998). Most Canadians are unaware of such levels of concentration of wealth and power, but nevertheless are touched by this concentration as they go about their daily routines and activities. As Diane Francis (1986) graphically notes: "everything from your glass of orange juice in the morning, to the clothes you put on, to the office where you work, to the department store and mall where you shop, to that after-work beer and a night at the ball game—are likely to be produced by these families and conglomerates."

Income. How is income distributed in Canada? Very unequally. Income distribution in Canada may be configured into a typical pyramid shape, with a very small percentage of Canadians (1 percent) at the top with very high incomes and the majority residing near the bottom. Economist Paul Samuelson (Samuelson & Nordhaus, 1989, p. 644) put it this way: "If we made an income pyramid out of a child's blocks, with each layer portraying $500 of income, the peak would be far higher than Mount Everest, but most people would be within a few feet of the ground" (see Figure 6.2.).

Figure 6.2 Inequality of Canadian Income

Some Canadians: Higher than Mount Everest

If a 4-centimetre child's block equals $500 of income, the average Canadian is only 2 metres off the ground, and the average family just over 3 metres, while the income of some families propels them past the top of Mount Everest.

2 metres

Average Canadian

Just over 3 metres

Average Canadian Family

Recent evidence suggests there is a growing disparity in incomes, and this mirrors the growing disparity in the distribution of wealth. For example, between 1989 and 1996, the number of millionaires tripled, and it is expected that this number will triple again by 2005 (Yalnizyan, 1998). Individuals without income, in contrast, are experiencing greater difficulty in meeting their basic needs and have been further displaced by the cutbacks in government-sponsored programs and benefits.

The distribution of wealth is more unequal than that of income, and the distribution of inherited wealth is much more unequal than that of wealth in general (Davies, 1999). While income has to be declared for taxation purposes, it is unclear how much wealth there is in Canada. The majority of the population will never inherit significant wealth, and a small minority receives outrageous amounts. This extreme concentration makes inheritance an important determinant of wealth inequality (Davies, 1999).

The typical family on average earned almost $57 000 in 1999. Yet compared with the Mount Everest incomes of a few, these earnings of the typical Canadian family bring it only 3 metres off the ground (Statistics Canada, 1999). The fact that some Canadians enjoy the peaks of Mount Everest while most make it only a few metres up the slope presents a striking image of income inequality in Canada.

Another picture emerges if we consider the percentage of Canadian families distributed within high- and low-income groups. As Table 6.2 shows, 40 percent of families earn less than $40 000 per year and almost 60 percent earn less than the $57 000 Canadian average family income. Families headed by males are better off by far than those headed by females. Among female-headed families in 1996, almost 77 percent earned less than $40 000 and almost 90 percent earned less than the Canadian average of $57 000 (Statistics Canada, 1999). In 1996 the average total income of the poorest 10 percent of Canadian families in which there were children under 18 years of age (including transfers from government income support programs) was $13 522; the average for the richest 10 percent was $138 157 —a ratio of 10:22 (Yalnizyan, 1998).

Table 6.2 Percentage Distribution of Families by Income Group, 1996

	All Families	Male Head	Female Head
Under $20 000	13.0%	8.5%	44.5%
$20 000–$39 999	27.1%	26.4%	32.2%
$40 000–$59 999	23.7%	18.4%	14.7%
$60 000–$79 999	17.2%	18.8%	5.3%
$80 000–$99 999	9.6%	10.8%	1.7%
$100 000 and over	9.4%	10.5%	1.4%

Source: Statistics Canada, *Family Incomes, Census Families*, Catalogue 13-208. Ottawa: Minister of Supply and Services.

Two features of the data available on incomes are outstanding. First, income inequality has remained remarkably consistent through the years. Second, the changes that do occur indicate growing inequality. Since the 1940s, the richest 20 percent of Canadian families have grown richer, while the poorest 20 percent have grown poorer. In spite of numerous social welfare programs, the poorest 20 percent of Canadians receive less of the nation's income today than they did in the 1940s. The richest 20 percent, in contrast, receive more than ever. In 1989, 30 percent of families had an after-tax income of less than $35 000. By 1997, more than 37 percent of families found themselves with this level of income (Yalnizyan, 2000).

A recent (2001) Statistics Canada survey revealed that between 1984 and 1999, the richest 20 percent of family units in Canada increased their wealth by 39 percent (in constant dollars), whereas the bottom 20 percent experienced no increases at all. Demonstrating the tremendous gap between the richest and the poorest families in Canadian society is their total share of wealth: The top 50 percent of family units has 94 percent of wealth, whereas the bottom 50 percent shares the remaining 6 percent (Anderson, 2001). Needless to say, Canadian society is tremendously polarized (Yalnizyan, 2000; Curry-Stevens, 2001).

The most affluent group in Canadian society is the chief executive officers (CEOs) of the nation's largest corporations. Canada's ten top-earning CEOs each took home over $10 million in 1997. The incomes of the six CEOs of the chartered banks totalled $18 million (Yalnizyan, 1998). One of the top-paid CEOs in Canada is Robert Gratton of Power Financial Corporation. His salary in 1997 was $1 758 000. In addition to this hefty sum, he took home a $2 million bonus and over $150 000 in other benefits. But his earnings didn't stop there. He also exercised his stock options, and this added $23.5 million, for a total of $27.4 million in compensation that year. His earnings could have totalled over $78 million had he decided to exercise further options. By contrast, the poorest 10 percent of families with children—almost 390 000 families altogether—took home $71.5 million (Yalnizyan, 1998).

Interestingly, average Canadian CEOs enjoyed double-digit increases in their salaries (15 percent in 1995, 11 percent in 1996, and 13 percent in 1997) in recent years, bringing their average salary (excluding stock options, bonuses, and other forms of compensation) to $862 000. What's interesting is that increases in their incomes do not necessarily match their corporations' overall performance. For example, Galen Weston's 300 percent increase is out of line with the 2 percent growth in George Weston Ltd.'s corporate profit. It is not unusual for CEOs to earn raises even in the face of falling profits or losses (Yalnizyan, 1998).

Across the border in the United States, former Microsoft CEO Bill Gates is wealthier than the bottom 45 percent of American households. In 1997, his wealth surpassed the total GNP of Central America (that's Guatemala, El Salvador, Costa Rica, Panama, Honduras, Nicaragua, and Belize). The following year his wealth had grown to $60 billion, and this was more than the GNPs of Central America, plus Jamaica and Bolivia (Mokhiber & Weissman, 1999).

Imagine how you could live with an income like this. And that is precisely the point. Beyond these cold numbers lies a dynamic reality that profoundly affects people's lives. The difference in wealth between those at the top and the bottom of the Canadian class structure means vastly different lifestyles. For example, a colleague of mine who was teaching at an exclusive eastern university in the United States piqued his students' curiosity when he lectured on poverty in Latin America. That weekend, one of his students borrowed his parents' corporate jet and pilot, and in Monday's class he and his friends reported on their personal observations on the problem. Others, in contrast, must choose whether to spend the little they have at the laundromat or on milk for the baby. In short, divisions of wealth represent not "mere" numbers, but choices that make real differences in people's lives.

Power

Like many people, you may have said to yourself, "Sure, I can vote, but somehow the big decisions are always made in spite of what I might think. Certainly *I* don't make the decision to raise taxes. It isn't *I* who decides to change welfare benefits."

Bill Gates, a co-founder of Microsoft Corporation, is the wealthiest person in the United States. His fortune of US$70 billion continues to increase as his company develops new products. In his Seattle, Washington, home, which cost US$50 million, Gates hung a US$30 million painting in his living room. His fortune is so vast that in 2000, when the Dow Jones Industrial Average dropped, Gates lost US$35 billion.

And then another part of you may say, "But I do it through my representatives in Parliament." True enough—as far as it goes. The trouble is, it just doesn't go far enough. Such views of being a participant in the nation's "big" decisions are a playback of the ideology we learn at an early age—an ideology that Marx said is put forward by the elites to both legitimate and perpetuate their power. Sociologists Daniel Hellinger and Dennis Judd (1991) call this the "democratic façade" that conceals the real source of power in society.

Back in the 1950s, sociologist C. Wright Mills (1956) was criticized for insisting that **power**—the ability to carry out your will in spite of resistance—was concentrated in the hands of the few, for his analysis contradicted an almost sacred ideology of equality. As discussed in Chapter 1, Mills coined the term **power elite** to refer to those who make the big decisions in society.

Mills and others have stressed how wealth and power coalesce in a group of like-minded individuals who share ideologies and values. They belong to the same private clubs, vacation at the same exclusive resorts, and even hire the same bands for their daughters' debutante balls. These shared backgrounds and vested interests all serve to reinforce their view of the world and of their special place in it (Domhoff, 1978, 1997). This elite wields extraordinary power in Canadian society. Although there are exceptions, *most* prime ministers and Cabinet ministers have come from this group—rich white males from families with "old money" (Baltzell & Schneiderman, 1988).

Continuing in the tradition of Mills, sociologist William Domhoff (1990, 1996) argues that this group is so powerful that no major decision of the government is made without its approval. He analyzed how this group works behind the scenes with elected officials to set both the nation's foreign and its domestic policy—from establishing taxes to determining trade tariffs. Although Domhoff's conclusions are controversial—and alarming—they certainly follow logically from the principle that wealth brings power, and extreme wealth brings extreme power.

Prestige

Occupations and Prestige. What would you like to do with the rest of your life? Chances are you don't have the option of lying under palm trees at the beach. Almost all of us have to choose an occupation and go to work.

Why do people give some jobs more **prestige**—respect or regard—than others? Generally, the most prestigious jobs share four elements:

1. They pay more.

2. They require more education.

3. They entail more abstract thought.

4. They offer greater autonomy (freedom or self-direction).

Acceptable display of prestige and high social position varies over time and from one culture to another. Shown here is Elisabeth d'Autriche, queen of France from 1554 to 1592. It certainly would be difficult to outdress her at a party.

Concern with displaying prestige has not let up—for some, it is almost an obsession. Western kings and queens expect curtsies and bows, while their Eastern counterparts expect their subjects to touch their faces to the ground. The prime minister enters a room only after others are present—to show that *he* isn't the one waiting for *them*. Military officers surround themselves with elaborate rules about who must salute whom, while bailiffs, sometimes armed, make certain everyone stands when the judge enters.

The display of prestige permeates society. Addresses in Toronto's Rosedale or Montreal's Westmount are well recognized as among the most prestigious places to live in Canada. Many willingly pay more for clothing that bears a "designer" label. For many, prestige is a primary factor in deciding which university to attend. Everyone knows the prestige of Oxford compares with a degree from Harvard, Princeton, Yale, or Cambridge.

Interestingly, status symbols vary with social class. Clearly, only the wealthy can afford certain items, such as yachts. But beyond affordability lies a class-based preference in status symbols. For example, yuppies ("young upwardly mobile professionals") are quick to flaunt labels and other material symbols to show they have "arrived," while the rich, more secure in their status, often downplay such images. The wealthy see designer labels of the more "common" classes as cheap and showy. They, of course, flaunt their own status symbols, such as the "right" addresses and Rolex watches.

Status Inconsistency

Ordinarily, a person has a similar rank on all three dimensions of social class—wealth, power, and prestige. Such people show **status consistency**. Sometimes the match is not there, however, and someone has a mixture of high and low ranks, a condition called **status inconsistency**. This leads to some interesting situations.

Sociologist Gerhard Lenski (1954, 1966) pointed out that each of us tries to maximize our **status**, or social ranking. Thus individuals who rank high on one dimension of social class but lower on others expect people to judge them on the basis of their highest status. Others, however, trying to maximize their own position, may respond to them according to their lowest status.

A classic study of status inconsistency was done by sociologist Ray Gold (1952). He found that after apartment-house janitors unionized, they made more money than some of the people whose garbage they carried out. Tenants became upset when they saw their janitors driving more expensive cars than they did. Some attempted to "put the janitor in his place" by making "snotty" remarks to him. Instead of addressing him by name, people would say "Janitor." For their part, the janitors took secret pride in knowing "dirty" secrets about the tenants, gleaned from their garbage.

If we turn this around, this means that people give less prestige to jobs that are low-paying, require less preparation or education, involve more physical labour, and are closely supervised. In short, the professions and some white-collar jobs are ranked at the top with regard to prestige, while blue-collar (and pink-collar) jobs are at the bottom.

One of the more interesting aspects of ranking occupations by prestige is how consistent they are across countries and over time. For example, people in every country rank university professors higher than nurses, nurses higher than social workers, and social workers higher than janitors. Similarly, the occupations that were ranked high back in the 1970s are still ranked high today in the new century.

Displaying Prestige. In times past, in some countries only the emperor and his family could wear purple. In France, only the nobility could wear lace. In England, no one could sit while the king was on his throne. Some kings and queens required that subjects walk backward as they left the room—so no one would "turn his (or her) back" on the "royal presence."

Sociologists use income, education, and occupational prestige to measure social class. The term status inconsistency refers to a mismatch of these components. What status inconsistency does Vince Carter, shown here, experience?

Similarly, during the strike of outside workers (including garbage collectors) in July 2002 against the City of Toronto, several media commentaries questioned the rights and motives of these garbage collectors in striking for higher wages and job security. Interestingly, as the stench from the rotting garbage in the summer's heat rose and as the warnings regarding serious health concerns issued by public health officials escalated, few acknowledged the essential contribution these workers make to our communities, our safety, and our well-being.

Individuals with status inconsistency, then, are likely to confront one frustrating situation after another. They claim the higher status, but are handed the lower. The sociological significance of this condition, said Lenski, is that such people tend to be more politically radical. An example is university professors. Their prestige is high, but their incomes are relatively low. Hardly anyone in Canadian society is more educated, and yet university professors don't even come close to the top of the income pyramid. In line with Lenski's prediction, the politics of many professors are left of centre.

Focus Question
What are some of the ways we define or measure social class?

Why Is Social Stratification Universal?

What is it about social life that makes all societies stratified? We shall first consider the explanation proposed by functionalists, which has aroused much controversy in sociology, followed by criticisms of this position. We then explore explanations proposed by conflict theorists.

The Functionalist View of Davis and Moore: Motivating Qualified People

Functionalists take the position that the patterns of behaviour that characterize a society exist because they are functional for that society. They conclude that because social inequality is universal, inequality must help societies survive. Using this principle, sociologists Kingsley Davis and Wilbert Moore (1945, 1953) concluded that stratification is inevitable for the following reasons:

1. Society must make certain that its positions are filled.

2. Some positions are more important than others.

3. The more important positions must be filled by the more qualified people.

4. To motivate the more qualified people to fill these positions, society must offer them greater rewards.

Let's look at some examples to flesh out this functionalist argument. The position of a university president is deemed much more important for society than that of a student, because the president's decisions affect many more people. Any mistakes he or she makes carry implications for a large number of people, including many students. So it is with the general of an army versus privates. The decisions of university presidents and generals affect careers, paycheques, and, in some cases, even life and death.

Positions with greater responsibility also require greater accountability. University presidents and army generals are accountable for how they perform—to boards of trustees and the leader of a country, respectively. How can society motivate highly qualified people to enter such high-pressure positions? What keeps people from avoiding them and seeking only less demanding jobs?

The answer, said Davis and Moore, is that society offers greater rewards for its more responsible, demanding, and accountable positions. If they didn't offer higher salaries, benefits, and greater prestige, why would anyone strive for them? Thus, a salary of $2 million, country club membership, a private jet, and a chauffeured limousine may be necessary to get the most highly qualified people to compete with one another for a certain position, while a $35 000 salary without fringe benefits is enough to get hundreds of people to compete for a less demanding position. Similarly, higher rewards are necessary to recruit people to positions that require rigorous training. Why suffer through taking tests and writing papers in university or graduate school if you can get the same pay and prestige with a high school education?

The functionalist argument is simple and clear. Society works better if its most qualified people hold its most important positions. For example, to get highly talented people to become surgeons—to undergo many years of rigorous training and then cope with life-and-death situations on a daily basis—requires a high payoff.

Tumin: A Critical Response

Note that the Davis-Moore thesis is an attempt to explain why social stratification is universal, not an attempt to *justify* social inequality. Note also that their view nevertheless makes many sociologists uncomfortable, for they see it as coming close to justifying the inequalities of society.

Melvin Tumin (1953) was the first sociologist to point out what he saw as major flaws in the functionalist position. Here are four of his arguments.

First, how do you measure the importance of a position? You can't measure importance by the rewards a position carries, for that argument is circular. You must have an independent measure of importance to test whether the more important positions actually carry higher rewards. For example, is a surgeon really more important to society than a garbage collector, since the garbage collector helps prevent contagious diseases?

Second, if stratification worked as Davis and Moore described it, society would be a **meritocracy**; that is, all positions would be awarded on the basis of merit. Ability, then, should predict who goes to university. Instead, the best predictor of university entrance is family income—the more a family earns, the more likely their children are to go to university. Similarly, while some people do get ahead through ability and hard work, others simply inherit wealth and the opportunities that go with it. Moreover, if a stratification system places most men above most women, it does not live up to the argument that talent and ability are the bases for holding important positions. In short, factors far beyond merit give people their relative positions in society.

Third, Davis and Moore place too much emphasis on money and fringe benefits. These aren't the only reasons people take jobs. An example is university teaching. If money were the main motivator, why would people spend four years in university, then average another six or seven years pursuing a Ph.D.—only to earn slightly more than someone who works in the post office? Obviously, university teaching offers more than monetary rewards: high prestige, autonomy (university professors have considerable discretion about how they do their job), rewarding social interaction (much of the job consists of talking to people), security (when given tenure, professors have a lifetime job), and leisure and the opportunity to travel (many professors work short days, enjoy several weeks of vacation during the school year, and have the entire summer off).

Fourth, if social stratification is so functional, it ought to benefit almost everyone. In actual fact, however, social stratification is *dysfunctional* to many. Think of the people who could have made invaluable contributions to society had they not been born in a slum and had to drop out of school, taking a menial job to help support the family; or the many who, born female, are assigned "women's work," ensuring that they do not maximize their mental abilities (Huber, 1988). In other words, the functionalist perspective of social stratification does not explain why women and members of minority groups are vastly underrepresented amongst those most highly paid in Canada.

The Conflict Perspective and Competition for Scarce Resources

Conflict theorists sharply disagree with the functionalist position. They stress that conflict, not function, is the basis of social stratification. Sociologists such as William Domhoff (1990, 1997), C. Wright Mills (1956), and Irving Louis Horowitz (1966) point out that in every society groups struggle with one another to gain a larger share of their society's limited resources. Whenever some group gains power, it uses that power to extract what it can from the groups beneath it. It also uses the social institutions to keep other groups weak and itself in power. Class conflict, then, is the key to understanding social stratification, for society is far from being a harmonious system that benevolently distributes greater resources to society's supposedly more qualified members.

All ruling groups—from slave masters to modern elites—develop an ideology to justify their position at the top. This ideology often seduces the oppressed into believing that their welfare depends on keeping society stable. Consequently, the oppressed may support laws against their own interests and even sacrifice their children as soldiers in wars designed to enrich the bourgeoisie.

The day will come, Marx said, when class consciousness will overcome ideology. When their eyes are opened, the workers will throw off their oppressors. At first, this struggle for control of the means of production may be covert, showing up as work slowdowns or industrial sabotage, but ultimately it will break out into open resistance. The revolt, though inevitable and bloody, will be difficult, for the bourgeoisie control the police, the military, and even education (where they implant false consciousness in the workers' children).

Some sociologists have refocused conflict theory. C. Wright Mills (1956), Ralf Dahrendorf (1959), and Randall Collins (1974, 1988), for example, stress that groups within the same class also compete for scarce resources—for power, wealth, education, housing, and even prestige—whatever benefits society has to offer. The result is conflict not only between labour unions and corporations, but also between the young and the old, between women and men, and among racial and ethnic groups. Unlike functionalists, then, conflict theorists hold that just beneath the surface of what may appear to be a tranquil society lies overt conflict—only uneasily held in check.

How Do Elites Maintain Social Inequality?

Suppose that you are part of the ruling elite of your society. What can you do to maintain your privileged position? A key lies in controlling ideas and information, in social networks, and in the least effective of all, the use of force.

Ideology Versus Force

Medieval Europe provides a good example of the power of ideology. At that time, land, which was owned by only a small group of people called the "aristocracy," was the primary source of wealth. With the exception of the clergy and some craftsmen, almost everyone was a peasant working for this small group of powerful landowners. The peasants farmed the land, took care of the cattle, and built the roads and bridges. Every year, they had to turn over a designated portion of their crops to their feudal lord. Year after year, for centuries, they did so. Why?

Controlling Ideas. Why didn't the peasants rebel and take over the land themselves? There were many reasons, not the least of which is that the army was controlled by the aristocracy. Coercion, however, only goes so far, for it breeds hostility and nourishes rebellion. How much more effective it is to get the people to *want* to do what the ruling elite desires. This is where *ideology* comes into play, and the aristocracy of that time used it to great effect. They developed an ideology known as the **divine right of kings**—the idea that the king's authority comes directly from God—which can be traced back several thousand years to the Old Testament. The king could delegate authority to nobles, who

as God's representatives also had to be obeyed. To disobey was a sin against God; to rebel meant physical punishment on earth and a sentence to suffer in eternal hell.

The control of ideas, then, can be remarkably more effective than brute force. Although this particular ideology no longer governs people's minds today, the elite in every society develops ideologies to justify its position at the top. For example, around the world schools teach that their country's form of government—*whatever form of government that may be*—is the best. Each nation's schools also stress the virtues of governments past and present, not their vices. Religion also teaches that we owe obedience to authority, that laws are to be obeyed. To the degree that their ideologies are accepted by the masses, political arrangements are stable.

Controlling Information. To maintain their positions of power, elites also try to control information. In dictatorships this is accomplished through the threat of force, for dictators can—and do—imprison editors and reporters for printing critical reports, sometimes even for publishing information unflattering to them (Timerman, 1981). The ruling elites of democracies accomplish the same purpose by manipulating the media through the selective release of information, withholding what they desire "in the interest of national security." But just as coercion has its limits, so does the control of information—especially given its new forms (from satellite communications to fax machines, e-mail, and the Internet) that pay no respect to international borders (Kennedy, 1993).

Social Networks. Also critical in maintaining stratification are *social networks*—the social ties that link people (Higley, Hoffmann-Lange, Kadushin, & Moore, 1991). These networks, expanding outward from the individual to gradually encompass more and more people, supply valuable information and tend to perpetuate social inequality. Sociologists William Domhoff (1983, 1990), John Porter (1965), and Wallace Clement (1975) have documented

The ideology of the *divine right of kings* made the king God's direct representative on earth—so that he could administer justice and punish evildoers. This theological-political concept was supported by the Roman Catholic Church, whose representatives crowned the king. Depicted here is the coronation of Charlemagne by Pope Leo III on Christmas Day A.D. 800, an event that marked the beginning of the period that became known as the Holy Roman Empire.

how members of the elite move in a circle of power that multiplies their opportunities. Contacts with people of similar backgrounds, interests, and goals allow the elite to pass privileges from one generation to the next. In contrast, the social networks of the poor perpetuate poverty and powerlessness.

Technology.   The elite's desire to preserve its position is aided by recent developments in technology, especially monitoring devices. These devices—from "hot telephones" (taps that make your phone a microphone even when off the hook) to machines that can read the entire contents of your computer without leaving a trace—help the elite monitor citizens' activities without their even being aware that they are being shadowed. Dictatorships have few checks on how such technology will be employed, but in democracies checks and balances, such as constitutional rights and the necessity of court orders, at least partially curb their use.

In Sum

Underlying the maintenance of the system of social inequality is control of a society's institutions. In a dictatorship, the elite makes the laws. In a democracy, the elite influences the laws. In both, the legal establishment enforces the laws. The elite also commands the police and military and can give orders to crush a rebellion—or even to run the post office or air traffic control if workers strike. As noted, force has its limits, and a nation's elite generally finds it preferable to maintain its stratification system by peaceful means, especially by influencing the thinking of its people.

Global Stratification: Three Worlds of Development

As noted at the beginning of this chapter, just as the people within a nation are stratified by power, prestige, and property, so are the world's nations. Until recently, a simple model consisting of *First*, *Second*, and *Third Worlds* was used to depict global stratification. "First World" referred to the industrialized capitalist nations, "Second World" to the communist nations, and "Third World" to any nation that did not fit into the first two categories. After the Soviet Union broke up in 1989, these terms became outdated. In addition, although "first," "second," and "third" did not mean "best," "second best," and "worst," they sounded like it. An alternative classification some now use—*developed*, *developing*, and *undeveloped nations*—has the same drawback. By calling ourselves "developed," it sounds as though we are mature, leaving the "undeveloped" nations lacking our desirable trait.

Consequently, we have chosen more neutrally descriptive terms: *most industrialized*, *industrializing*, and *least industrialized nations*. One can measure industrialization with no judgment, even implied, about whether a nation's

industrialization represents "development," ranks them "first," or is even desirable in the first place.

The intention is to depict on a global level social stratification's three primary dimensions: property, power, and prestige. The most industrialized nations have much greater property (wealth), power (they do get their way in international relations), and prestige—rightly or wrongly, they are looked up to as world leaders and as having something worthwhile to contribute to humanity. Internationally, 1.2 billion people live on less than US$1 a day and 2.8 billion on less than US$2. To understand further the tremendous differences between the richest and the poorest people in the world, we consider share of income. The richest 1 percent of people in the world received income equal to 57 percent of the world's poorest people. Further, the income of the world's richest 10 percent of the population was 127.7 times that of the poorest 10 percent of the world's people (Centre for Social Justice, 2001; United Nations, 2001). The three families sketched in the opening vignette provide some insight into the far-reaching effects of global stratification on the citizens of this world, as does the Thinking Critically about Social Controversy box on children as prey.

Over the course of the last two centuries, the gap between the richest and the poorest countries has grown tremendously. In 1820, for example, the richest countries were about 3 times richer than the poorest countries, based on GDP per capita. This ratio rose to 15 by 1950 and to 19 by 1998 (Lee, 2002). As Table 6.3 indicates, the world's richest people's share of total GDP has skyrocketed over the past 40 years. Further, Table 6.4 shows how much the income of the world's poorest people declined between 1988 and 1993 while the income of those at the top rose substantially during the same period.

According to the U.S. Institute for Policy Studies, in 2001 there were 497 billionaires worldwide, with a combined wealth of $1.54 trillion, a figure that exceeds the combined gross national products of all the nations of sub-Saharan Africa or those of the oil-rich regions of the Middle East or North Africa. Moreover, the 497 billionaires' combined wealth is "greater than the combined incomes of the

Table 6.3 Share of Total GDP of World's People: Richest 20 percent Versus Poorest 20 percent

Year	Share of Top 20% Compared to Bottom 20%
1960	30x
1970	32x
1980	45x
1989	59x
1997	74x
In 1997 the top 20 percent received 74 times the income of the bottom 20 percent.	

Source: Based on "The Global Divide: Inequality in the World Economy" by Marc Lee, 2002, *Behind the Numbers: Economic Facts, Figures and Analysis, 4*, No. 2. Ottawa: Canadian Centre for Policy Alternatives. Reproduced from United National Development Program, *Human Development Report 1999.* New York: Oxford University Press, pp. 36–37.

Table 6.4 Global Income Distribution, 1988 and 1993

Percentage of World's Population	Percentage of World Income		Difference (%)
	1988	1993	1988–1993
Top 2%	9.3	9.5	+0.2
Top 5%	31.2	33.7	+2.5
Top 10%	46.9	50.8	+3.9
Bottom 10%	0.9	0.8	-0.1
Bottom 20%	2.3	2.0	-0.3
Bottom 50%	9.6	8.5	-1.1
Bottom 75%	25.9	22.3	-3.6
Bottom 85%	41.0	37.1	-3.9

Source: From "The Global Divide: Inequality in the World Economy" by Marc Lee, 2002, *Behind the Numbers: Economic Facts, Figures and Analysis, 4*, No. 2. Ottawa: Canadian Centre for Policy Alternatives. Reproduced from Branko Milanovic, 1999. "True world income distribution, 1988 and 1993: First calculation based on household surveys alone." *World Bank Research Paper*, Table 18, p. 29.

poorest half of all of humanity" (IPS, quoted in Mokhiber & Weissman, 2002).

Modifying the Model

This classification of nations into most industrialized, industrializing, and least industrialized is helpful in that it pinpoints gross differences among them. But it also presents problems. Just how much industrialization does a nation need in order to be classified as most industrialized or industrializing? Also, several nations have become "postindustrial." Does this new stage require a separate classification? Finally, the oil-rich nations of the Middle East are not industrialized, but by providing the oil and gasoline that fuel the machinery of the most industrialized nations, they have become immensely wealthy. Consequently, to classify them simply as "least industrialized" glosses over significant distinctions, such as their modern hospitals,

---

Thinking Critically about Social Controversy

Open Season: Children as Prey

Sociologist Martha Huggins (1993) reports that in Brazilian slums poverty is so deep that children and adults swarm over garbage dumps to try to find enough decaying food to keep them alive. And you might be surprised to discover that in Brazil the owners of these dumps hire armed guards to keep the poor out—so they can sell the garbage for pig food. And you might be shocked to learn that poor children are systematically killed. Every year, the Brazilian police and death squads murder about 2000 children. Some associations of shop owners even put hit men on retainer and auction victims off to the lowest bidder! The going rate is half a month's salary—figured at the low Brazilian minimum wage.

Life is cheap in the poor nations—but death squads for children? To understand this, we must first note that Brazil has a long history of violence. Brazil has an extremely high rate of poverty, only a tiny middle class, and is controlled by a small group of families who, under a veneer of democracy, make the country's major decisions. Hordes of homeless children, with no schools or jobs, roam the streets. To survive, they wash windshields, shine shoes, beg, and steal. These children, part of the "dangerous classes," as they are known, threaten the status quo.

The "respectable" classes see these children as nothing but trouble. They hurt business, for customers feel uncomfortable or intimidated when they see a group of begging children clustered in front of stores. Some shoplift; others dare to sell items in competition with the stores. With no social institutions to care for these children, one solution is to kill them. As Huggins notes, murder sends a clear message—especially if it is accompanied by ritual torture—pulling out the eyes, ripping open the chest, cutting off the genitals, raping the girls, and burning the victim's body.

Not all life is bad in the poor nations, but this is about as bad as it gets.

The plight of these Brazilian children is replicated around the world. Worldwide, 1.2 billion persons live on a dollar a day or less. Ten of millions of children are on the streets each day, locked out of schools because their parents cannot afford the school fees. And more than a million children die each year from diarrhea because they do not have access to clean drinking water (Mokhiber & Weissman, 2002).

For Your Consideration

Can the most industrialized nations do anything about this situation? Or is it any of their business? Is it, though unfortunate, just an "internal" affair that is up to the Brazilians to handle as they wish?

One of the children killed by death squads operating in Brazil.

Table 6.5 An Alternative Model of Global Stratification

Four Worlds of Development
1. Most industrialized nations
2. Industrializing nations
3. Least industrialized nations
4. Oil-rich, non-industrialized nations

The world's people always have been part of an interconnected system of water and air, and, ultimately, part of a food chain. Now they also are interconnected by a global system of telecommunications. These women in Bangalore, India, are computer programmers.

extensive prenatal care, pure water systems, abundant food and shelter, high literacy, and even computerized banking.

Kuwait, on whose formal behalf the United States and other most industrialized nations fought Iraq in the Gulf War, is an excellent example of the problem. Kuwait is so wealthy that almost none of its citizens is employed. The government simply pays each a generous annual salary just for being citizens. Migrant workers from the poor nations do most of the onerous chores that daily life requires, while highly skilled workers from the most industrialized nations run the specialized systems that keep Kuwait's economy going—and, on occasion, fight its wars, as well. Table 6.5 reflects this significant distinction.

How the World's Nations Became Stratified

How did the globe become stratified into such distinct worlds of development? The obvious answer is that the poorer nations have fewer resources than the richer nations. As with so many other "obvious" answers, however, this one, too, falls short, for many of the industrializing and least industrialized nations are rich in natural resources, while one most industrialized nation, Japan, has few. Four competing theories explain how global stratification came about.

Imperialism and Colonization

The first theory focuses on how the European nations that industrialized earliest got the jump on the rest of the world. Beginning in Great Britain about 1750, industrialization spread throughout Western Europe. This powerful new technology produced great wealth, resulting in surplus capital. According to economist John Hobson (1858–1940), these industrialized nations lacked enough consumers to make it profitable to invest all excess capital there. Consequently, business leaders persuaded their governments to embark on **imperialism**, to take over other countries so they could expand their markets and gain access to cheap raw materials.

Backed by the powerful armaments developed by their new technology, the industrialized nations found others easy prey (Harrison, 1993). The result was **colonization**; that is, these more powerful nations made colonies out of weaker nations. After invading and subduing them, they left a controlling force to exploit their labour and natural

resources. At one point, there was even a free-for-all among these European industrialized nations as they rushed to divide up an entire continent. As Europe sliced Africa into pieces, even tiny Belgium got into the act and acquired the Congo—75 times larger than itself! While the powerful European nations would plant their national flags in a colony and send their representatives to directly run the government, the United States, after it industrialized, usually chose to plant corporate flags in a colony and let these corporations dominate the territory's government. Central and South America are prime examples of U.S. *economic imperialism*. No matter what the form, and whether benevolent or harsh, the purpose was the same—to exploit the nation's people and resources for the benefit of the "mother" country.

Western imperialism and colonization, then, shaped the least industrialized nations (Martin, 1994). In some instances, the most industrialized nations were so powerful that to divide the spoils they drew lines across a map, creating new states without regard for tribal or cultural considerations (Kennedy, 1993). Britain and France did just this in North Africa and parts of the Middle East, which is why the national boundaries of Libya, Saudi Arabia, Kuwait, and other nations are so straight.

World System Theory

Historian Immanuel Wallerstein (1974, 1979, 1984, 1990) proposed a **world system** theory. Since the 1500s, he said, economic and political connections have grown between nations. Today, these connections are so great that they tie most of the world's countries together. Wallerstein identified four groups of interconnected nations. The first group is the *core nations*, those that first embraced capitalism. These nations (Britain, France, Holland, and later Germany) grew rich and powerful. The second group, the nations around the Mediterranean, Wallerstein called the *semiperiphery*. Their economies stagnated because they grew dependent on trade with the core nations. The third group, the *periphery*, or fringe, consists of the eastern European countries. Because they were limited primarily to selling cash crops to the core nations, their economies developed even less. The fourth group, the *external area*, includes most of Africa and Asia. These nations were left out of the development of capitalism and had few economic connections with the core nations.

Capitalism's relentless expansion has given birth to a **capitalist world economy**, which is dominated by the most industrialized nations. This economy is so all-encompassing that today even the nations in the external area are being drawn into its commercial web.

Globalization.   This extensive movement of capital and ideas between the nations of the world ushered in by the expansion of capitalism is called **globalization** (Kanter, 1997b). Although globalization has been under way for several hundred years, today's new forms of communication and transportation have greatly speeded it up. The interconnections have grown so extensive that events in remote parts of the world now affect us all—sometimes immediately, as when a revolution interrupts the flow of raw materials, or, perish the thought, if in Russia's unstable political climate terrorists manage to seize an arsenal of earth-destroying nuclear missiles. At other times, the effects arrive like a slow ripple, as when a government's policies impede its ability to compete in world markets. All of today's societies, then, no matter where they are located, are part of a global social system.

There is substantial evidence that, as capital has moved around the world, poverty has increased and the quality of life of millions has deteriorated. The process of globalization has accelerated the economic competition among countries. To compete with one another in world markets, many nations have responded by lowering wages, eliminating worker support programs and environmental protection, decreasing social spending, and dismantling public health care and other essential services (Brecher & Costello, 1998; McNally, 2002). Sociologists such as James Petras and Henry Veltmeyer (2001) argue that globalization is a modern form of imperialism that advances the interests of the powerful and privileged and neither enhances the quality of life nor extends social justice to the masses.

Dependency Theory

The third theory is sometimes difficult to distinguish from world system theory. **Dependency theory** stresses how the least industrialized nations grew dependent on the most industrialized nations (Cardoso, 1972; Furtado, 1984).

According to this theory, the first nations to industrialize turned other nations into their plantations and mines, harvesting or extracting whatever they needed to meet their growing appetite for raw materials and exotic foods. As a result, many of the least industrialized nations began to specialize in a single cash crop. Brazil became the most industrialized nations' coffee plantation. Nicaragua and other Central American countries specialized in bananas (hence the term "banana republic"). Chile became the primary source of tin, while Zaire (then the Belgian Congo) was transformed into a rubber plantation. And the Mideast nations were turned into gigantic oil wells. A major point of dependency theory is that this domination of the least industrialized nations rendered them unable to develop independent economies.

Culture of Poverty

An entirely different explanation of global stratification was proposed by economist John Kenneth Galbraith (1979), who claimed that it was the least industrialized nations' own cultures that held them back. Building on the ideas of anthropologist Oscar Lewis (1966a, 1966b), Galbraith argued that some nations are crippled by a **culture of poverty**, a way of life that perpetuates poverty from one generation to the next. He explained it in this way: Most of the world's poor live in rural areas, where they barely eke out a living from the land. Their marginal life offers little room for error or risk, so they tend to stick closely to tried-and-true, traditional ways. Experimenting with new farming or manufacturing techniques is threatening, for if these fail, the result could be hunger or death. Their religion also reinforces traditionalism, for it teaches fatalism, the acceptance of their lot in life as God's will.

Evaluating the Theories

Most sociologists find imperialism, world system theory, and dependency theory preferable to an explanation based on a culture of poverty, for this theory places blame on the victim, the poor nations themselves. It points to characteristics of the poor nations, rather than to international arrangements that benefit the most industrialized nations at the expense of the poor nations. But even taken together, these theories yield only part of the picture, as becomes evident from the example of Japan. None of these theories would lead anyone to expect that after World War II, Japan—with a religion that stressed fatalism, with two major cities destroyed by atomic bombs, and stripped of its colonies—would become an economic powerhouse able to turn the Western world on its head.

Each theory, then, yields but a partial explanation, and the grand theorist who will put the many pieces of this puzzle together has yet to appear. However, rather than relying on the possibility of a grand theory to solve the puzzle, looking at detailed socio-historical national studies examining the way in which culture, political structure, and class relations affect global economic positioning may provide us with the clearest understanding of global inequalities.

Focus Question

Which theory do you think most adequately explains global stratification?

Maintaining Global Stratification

Regardless of how the world's nations became stratified, why do the same countries remain rich year after year, while the rest stay poor? Let's look at two explanations of how global stratification is maintained.

Neocolonialism

Sociologist Michael Harrington (1977) argued that colonialism fell out of style and was replaced by **neocolonialism**. When World War II changed public sentiment about sending soldiers and colonists to weaker countries, the most industrialized nations turned to the international markets as a way to control the least industrialized nations. These powerful nations determine how much they will pay for tin from Bolivia, copper from Peru, coffee from Brazil, and so forth. They also move hazardous industries into the least industrialized nations.

As many of us learn, falling behind on a debt often means that we find ourselves dangling at the end of a string pulled by our creditor. So it is with neocolonialism. The *policy* of selling weapons and other manufactured goods to the least industrialized nations on credit turns those countries into eternal debtors. The capital they need to develop their own industries goes instead to the debt, ever bloated with mounting interest. As debtors, these nations are also vulnerable to trading terms dictated by the neocolonialists (Tordoff, 1992; Carrington, 1993).

Thus, although the least industrialized nations have their own governments—whether elected or dictatorships—they remain almost as dependent on the most industrialized nations as they were when those nations occupied them.

Multinational Corporations

Multinational corporations, companies that operate across many national boundaries, also help to maintain the global dominance of the most industrialized nations. In some cases, multinational corporations exploit the least industrialized nations directly. A prime example is the United Fruit Company, which for decades controlled national and local politics in Central America, running these nations as fiefdoms for the company's own profit while the U.S. Marines waited in the wings in case the company's interests needed to be backed up. Most commonly, however, multinational corporations help to maintain international stratification simply by doing business. A single multinational may do mining in several countries, manufacturing in many others, and run transportation and marketing networks around the globe. No matter where the profits are made, or where they are reinvested, the primary beneficiaries are the most industrialized nations, especially the one in which the multinational corporation has its world headquarters. As Michael Harrington (1977) stressed, the real profits are made in processing the products and in controlling their distribution—and these profits are withheld from the least industrialized nations. For more on multinational corporations, see Chapter 11.

Multinational corporations try to work closely with the elite of the least industrialized nations (Lipton, 1979; Waldman, 1995a). This elite, which lives a sophisticated upper-class life in the major cities of its home country, sends its children to Oxford, the Sorbonne, or Harvard to be educated. The multinational corporations funnel investments to this small circle of power, whose members favour projects such as building laboratories and computer centres in the capital city, projects that do not help the vast majority of their people living in poor, remote villages where they eke out a meagre living on small plots of land.

The end result is an informal partnership between multinational corporations and the elite of the least industrialized nations. The elite benefits by receiving subsidies

During a period of exploitation called *colonialism*, European powers acquired as many parts of the globe as they could. Great Britain amassed the most, including Hong Kong, which China ceded in 1842. Shown here is the historic transfer of power that occurred when Hong Kong was returned to Chinese sovereignty on July 1, 1997.

(or payoffs). The corporations gain access to the country's raw materials, labour, and market. Both benefit through political stability, necessary to keep the partnership alive.

This, however, is not the full story. Multinational corporations also play a role in changing international stratification. This is an unintentional by-product of their worldwide search for cheap resources and labour. By moving manufacturing from the most industrialized nations with high labour costs to the least industrialized nations with low labour costs, they not only exploit cheap labour but in some cases also bring prosperity to those nations. Although workers in the least industrialized nations are paid a pittance, it is more than they can earn elsewhere. With new factories come opportunities to develop new skills and a capital base. This does not occur in all nations, but the Pacific Rim nations, nicknamed the "Asian tigers," are remarkable. They have developed such a strong capital base that they have begun to rival the older capitalist nations.

Technology and the Maintenance of Global Domination

The race between the most and least industrialized nations to develop and apply the new information technologies is like a marathon runner competing with a one-legged man. Can the outcome be in doubt? The vast profits piled up by the multinational corporations allow the most industrialized nations to invest huge sums in the latest technology. Gillette, for example, is spending $100 million simply so it can adjust its output "on an hourly basis" (Zachary, 1995). These millions come from just one U.S. company. Many least industrialized nations would love to have $100 million to invest in their entire economy, much less to fine-tune the production of razor blades. In short, in their quest to maintain global domination, the new technologies pile up even more advantages for the most industrialized nations.

Applying Sociological Models of Social Class

The question of how many social classes there are is a matter of debate. Sociologists have proposed various models, but no model has gained universal support. There are two main models: one that builds on Marx, the other on Weber.

Applying Marx

Marx argued that there are just two classes—capitalists and workers—with membership based solely on a person's relationship to the means of production. Sociologists have criticized this view because these categories are too broad. For example, executives, managers, and supervisors are technically workers because they do not own the means of production. But what do they have in common with assembly-line workers? Similarly, the category of "capitalist"

takes in too many types. For example, the decisions of someone who employs a thousand workers directly affect a thousand families. Compare this with a man I know in Calgary, Alberta. Working on cars out of his own backyard, he gained a following, quit his regular job, and in a few years put up a building with five bays and an office. This mechanic is now a capitalist, for he employs five or six other mechanics and owns the tools and building (the "means of production"). But what does he have in common with a factory owner who controls the lives of a thousand workers? Not only is his work different, but so are his lifestyle and the way he looks at the world.

Sociologist Erik Wright (1985) resolved this problem by regarding some people as members of more than one class at the same time. They have what he called **contradictory class locations**. By this Wright means that people's position in the class structure can generate contradictory interests. For example, the automobile-mechanic-turned-business-owner may want his mechanics to have higher wages, since he, too, has experienced their working conditions. At the same time, his current interests—making profits and remaining competitive with other repair shops—lead him to resist pressures to raise wages.

Because of such contradictory class locations, Wright modified Marx's model. As summarized in Table 6.6, Wright identified four classes: (1) *capitalists*, business owners who employ many workers; (2) *petty bourgeoisie*, small business owners; (3) *managers*, who sell their own labour but also exercise authority over other employees; and (4) *workers*, who simply sell their labour to others. As you can see, this model allows finer divisions than the one Marx proposed, yet it maintains the primary distinction between employer and worker.

Applying Weber

Sociologists Dennis Gilbert and Joseph Kahl (1993) developed a six-class model to portray the class structure of the United States and other capitalist countries. Think of their model, illustrated in Figure 6.3, as a ladder. Our discussion will start with the highest rung and move downward. In

Table 6.6 Social Class and the Means of Production

Marx's Class Model (based on the means of production)
1. Capitalists (bourgeoisie)
2. Workers (proletariat)

Wright's Modification of Marx's Class Model (to account for contradictory class locations)
1. Capitalists
2. Petty bourgeoisie
3. Managers
4. Workers

Figure 6.3 The Canadian Social Class Ladder

Source: Based on Gilbert and Kahl (1993); Forcese (1997).

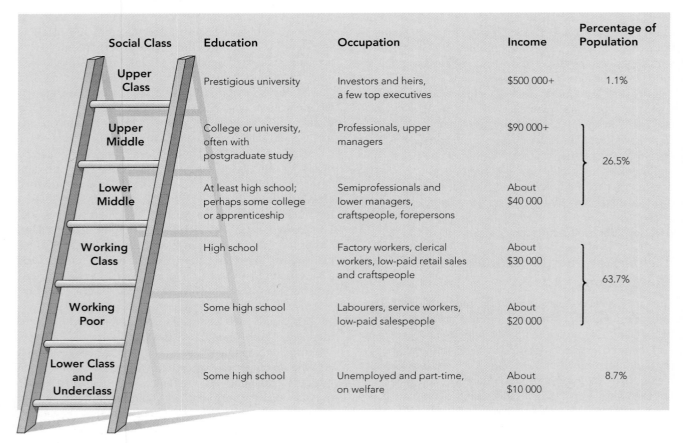

Social Class	Education	Occupation	Income	Percentage of Population
Upper Class	Prestigious university	Investors and heirs, a few top executives	$500 000+	1.1%
Upper Middle	College or university, often with postgraduate study	Professionals, upper managers	$90 000+	26.5%
Lower Middle	At least high school; perhaps some college or apprenticeship	Semiprofessionals and lower managers, craftspeople, forepersons	About $40 000	
Working Class	High school	Factory workers, clerical workers, low-paid retail sales and craftspeople	About $30 000	63.7%
Working Poor	Some high school	Labourers, service workers, low-paid salespeople	About $20 000	
Lower Class and Underclass	Some high school	Unemployed and part-time, on welfare	About $10 000	8.7%

line with Weber, on each lower rung you find less wealth, less power, and less prestige. Note that in this model education is also a primary criterion of class.

The Capitalist Class. The super-rich who occupy the top rung of the class ladder comprise only about 1.1 percent of the population. As mentioned, this 1.1 percent is so wealthy that its members are worth more than the entire bottom 90 percent of the nation. Their power is so great that their decisions open or close jobs for millions of people. Through their ownership of newspapers, magazines, and radio and television stations, and their access to politicians, this elite class even helps to shape the consciousness of the nation. Its members perpetuate themselves by passing on to their children their assets and influential social networks.

Old Money. The capitalist class can be divided into "old" and "new" money (Aldrich, 1989). In general, the longer that wealth has been in a family, the more it adds to the family's prestige. Many people entering the capitalist class have found it necessary to cut moral corners, at least here and there. This "taint" to the money disappears with time, however, and the later generations of Kennedys, Rockefellers, Vanderbilts, Mellons, Du Ponts, Chryslers,

Fords, Eatons, Molsons, Bronfmans, and so on are considered to have "clean" money simply by virtue of the passage of time. Able to be philanthropic as well as rich, they establish foundations and support charitable causes. Subsequent generations attend prestigious prep schools and universities, and male heirs are likely to enter law. These old-money capitalists wield vast power as they use extensive political connections to protect their huge economic empires (Persell, Catsambis, & Cookson, Jr., 1992; Domhoff, 1990, 1997; Clement, 1975; Newman, 1979).

New Money. Those at the lower end of the capitalist class also possess vast sums of money and power, but it is new, and therefore suspect. Although these people may have made fortunes in business, the stock market, inventions, entertainment, or sports, they have not attended the right schools, and they lack the influential social networks that come with old money. The children of the new-monied can ascend into the upper part of the capitalist class if they go to the right schools *and* marry old money.

The Upper Middle Class. Of all the classes, the upper middle is the one most shaped by education. Almost all members of this class have at least a bachelor's degree, and

The Bronfmans are among Canada's oldest wealthy families. Old-money capitalists wield vast power and have numerous political, social, and economic connections that they draw on in order to protect their huge economic empires.

many have postgraduate degrees in business, management, law, or medicine. These people manage the corporations owned by the capitalist class or else operate their own business or profession. As Gilbert and Kahl (1982) say, these positions

> may not grant prestige equivalent to a title of nobility in the Germany of Max Weber, but they certainly represent the sign of having "made it" in contemporary America…Their income is sufficient to purchase houses and cars and travel that become public symbols for all to see and for advertisers to portray with words and pictures that connote success, glamour, and high style.

Consequently, parents and teachers push children to prepare themselves for upper-middle-class jobs.

The Lower Middle Class.

Members of this class follow orders on the job given by those who have upper-middle-class credentials. Their technical and lower-level management positions bring them a good living—albeit one constantly threatened by rising taxes and inflation—and they enjoy a generally comfortable, mainstream lifestyle. They usually feel secure in their positions and anticipate being able to move up the social class ladder.

The distinctions between the lower middle class and the working class on the next lower rung are more blurred than those between other classes. As a result, these two classes run into one another. Members of the lower middle class

work at jobs that have slightly more prestige, however, and their incomes are generally higher.

The Working Class.

This class includes relatively unskilled blue-collar and white-collar workers. Compared with the lower middle class, they have less education and lower incomes. Their jobs are also less secure, more routine, and more closely supervised. One of their greatest fears is being laid off during recessions. With only a high school diploma, the average member of the working class has little hope of climbing up the class ladder. Job changes are usually "more of the same," so most concentrate on getting ahead by achieving seniority on the job rather than by changing their type of work.

The Working Poor.

Members of this class work at unskilled, low-paying, temporary and seasonal jobs, such as migrant farm work, housecleaning, and day labour. Most are high school dropouts. Many are functionally illiterate, finding it difficult to read even the want ads. They are not likely to vote (Gilbert & Kahl, 1993), for they feel that no matter what party is elected to office their situation won't change.

Large numbers among the working poor work full-time (O'Hare, 1996b), but still must depend on help such as food banks to supplement their meagre incomes. It is easy to see how you can work full-time and still be poor. Suppose you are married and have a baby three months old and another three years old. Your spouse stays home to care for them, so earning the income is up to you. But as a high school dropout, all you can get is a minimum wage job. At $6.75 an hour, you earn $270 for 40 hours. In a year, this comes to $14 000—before deductions. Your nagging fear—and daily nightmare—is of ending up "on the streets."

The Underclass.

On the lowest rung, and with next to no chance of climbing anywhere, is the **underclass** (Myrdal, 1962; Kelso, 1995). Concentrated in the inner city, this group has little or no connection with the job market. Those who are employed, and some are, do menial, low-paying, temporary work. Welfare is their main support, and most members of other classes consider these people the ne'er-do-wells of society. Life is the toughest in this class, and it is filled with despair. The children's chances of getting out of poverty are about 50-50 (Gilbert & Kahl, 1982, p. 353).

Below the Ladder: The Homeless

The homeless men described in the opening vignette of Chapter 1, and the women and children like them, are so far down the class structure that their position is even lower than the underclass. Technically, the homeless are members of the underclass, but their poverty is so severe and their condition in life so despairing that we can think of them as occupying an unofficial rung below the underclass.

Most of us feel powerless to help the homeless, especially now as their numbers increase in our major centres.

These are the people whom most Canadians wish would just go away. Their presence on our city streets bothers passersby from the more privileged social classes—which includes just about everyone. "What are those obnoxious, dirty, foul-smelling people doing here, cluttering up my city?" appears to be a common response. Some do respond with sympathy and a desire to do something to help. But what? Almost all of us just shrug our shoulders and look the other way, despairing of a solution and somewhat intimidated by the presence of the homeless.

The homeless are the "fallout" of industrialization, especially our developing postindustrial economy. In another era, they would have had plenty of work. They would have tended horses, worked on farms, dug ditches, shovelled coal, and run the factory looms. Some would have explored and settled the West. Others would have followed the lure of gold to the Yukon, California, Alaska, and Australia. Today, however, with no unsettled frontiers, factory jobs scarce, and even farms becoming technological marvels, we have little need for unskilled labour, and these people are left to wander aimlessly about the city streets.

Consequences of Social Class

Each social class can be thought of as a broad subculture with distinct approaches to life. Of the many ways that social class affects people's lives, we shall briefly review the new technology, physical and mental health, family life, education, religion, politics, and crime.

The New Technology

The higher one goes up the social class ladder, the more technology is a benefit. For the capitalist class, the new technology is a dream come true: global profits through global integration. No longer are national boundaries an obstacle. Rather, a product's components are produced in several countries, assembled in another, and the product marketed throughout the world. The new technology also benefits the upper middle class, for their education prepares them to take a leading role in managing this global system for the capitalist class, or for using the new technology to advance in their chosen professions.

Below these two classes, however, the new technology adds to the uncertainty of life, with the insecurity becoming greater the farther one moves down the ladder. As the new technology transforms the workplace, it eliminates jobs and outdates skills. People in lower management can transfer their skills from one job to another, although in shifting job markets the times between periods of employment can be precarious. Those in crafts are even less secure, for their training is more specific and the changing occupational world can reduce the need for their narrower, more specialized skills.

From this middle point in the ladder down, people are hit the hardest. The working class is ill prepared for the changes ushered in by the new technology, and they are haunted by the spectre of unemployment. The low technical skills of the working poor make them even more vulnerable, for they have even less to offer in the new job market. As unskilled jobs dry up, more and more of the working poor are consigned to the industrial garbage bin. The underclass, of course, with no technical skills, is bypassed entirely.

The playing field is far from level. Some even fear that current trends in exporting Canadian jobs mean that Canadian workers are becoming an expendable luxury, destined to be replaced by low-paid, non-unionized—and more compliant—workers on other continents. In short, the new technology opens and closes opportunities for people largely by virtue of where they are located on the social class ladder.

Physical and Mental Health

Social class even affects our chances of living and dying. The principle is simple: the lower a person's class, the more likely that individual is to die before the expected age. Among the top 25 percent of income earners in Canada, men can expect to live 6.3 years longer and be free of disability for 14.3 years longer while women in this group can expect to live 3 years longer and have about 7.6 more years without disability compared to their lower-income counterparts (Health Canada, 1999). Among status Indians, many of whom have very low incomes, life expectancy was 7 years less than the average for the Canadian population in 1991 (Health Canada, 1999). This principle holds true at all ages. Infants born to the poor are more likely than other infants to die before their first birthday. A recent study found that the rate of infant mortality was twice as high in the poorest neighbourhoods as compared to rates in the richest neighbourhoods within metropolitan areas in urban Canada (Ross, Scott, & Kelly, 1996). In old age—whether 70 or 90—the poor are more likely to die of illness and disease. In Canada the highest life expectancies are found in large metropolitan and urban centres where education levels are high while people in remote northern communities where a large percentage of the population is Aboriginal and where the educational levels are low have the lowest life expectancies (Shields & Tremblay, 2002).

From a comparative global perspective, Canadians enjoy relatively healthy and long lives. A recent report by the World Health Organization placed Canada 12th on a new life expectancy measure. This means that on average Canadians will live about 72 years free of disease or disability while total life expectancy is 78 years. In Japan, the top-ranked country, people might expect to live illness-free 74.5 years while, in contrast, people living in African countries such as Zimbabwe, Botswana, and Sierra Leone can expect less than 35 years of good health. Interestingly, the United States, the most prosperous nation in the world, ranked 23rd on the health-expectancy scale. This relatively poor ranking is explained by the tremendous gap between rich and poor in the United States, where Native Americans, rural blacks, and the inner-city poor enjoy far fewer years free of health problems than others (Philp, 2000).

During both childhood and adulthood, the poor are also more likely to be killed by accidents, fires, and homicide. Underlying these different death rates is unequal access to medical care and nutrition. Despite Canada's government-funded health care system, the higher classes receive better medical treatment. A recent study in Ontario showed that the rate of myocardial infarction (heart attack) was 38 percent higher for those living in the poorest 10 percent of the province's communities, compared with those in the richest 10 percent. Yet those in poorer neighbourhoods were less likely to receive surgery. Relative to the rate of heart disease present, people in wealthy areas received 60 percent more surgery than those living in the poorer areas (Talaga, 1999). Poor people are also less educated concerning nutrition, and their meals tend to be heavy in fats and sugars, neither of which is healthy (Freedman 1990).

Social class also affects mental health. From the 1930s until now, sociologists have found that the mental health of the lower classes is worse than that of the higher classes (Faris & Dunham, 1939; Srole et al., 1978; Brown & Gary, 1988; Lundberg, 1991; Burman, 1996; Capponi, 1997). This difference reflects the greater stresses that those in the lower classes experience, such as unpaid bills, unemployment, dirty and dangerous work, the threat of eviction, unhappy marriages, and broken homes. People higher up the social class ladder also experience stress in daily life, of course, but their stress is generally less and their coping

resources greater. Not only can they afford vacations, psychiatrists, and counsellors, but *their class position gives them greater control over their lives, a key to good mental health.*

The Reach of Social Class

Social class plays a significant role in all aspects of life. The ways in which social class affects various aspects of life, including our personal lives, such as our family life or choice of marital partner, as well as our public lives, such as which school we will attend and for how long, are examined throughout the chapters of this book. Below are some examples of the consequences of social class.

■ *Choice of Husband or Wife.* The capitalist class strongly emphasizes family tradition and continuity. It stresses the family's ancestors, history, and even a sense of purpose or destiny in life (Baltzell, 1979; Aldrich, 1989). Children of this class learn that their choice of husband or wife affects not just themselves but the whole family unit, that their spouse will have an impact on the "family line." Consequently, their field of "eligibles" is much narrower than it is for the children of any other social class. In effect, parents in this class play a greater role in their children's mate selection.

■ *Divorce.* The more difficult life of the lower social classes, especially the many tensions that come from insecure jobs and inadequate incomes, leads to more marital friction and a greater likelihood of both spouse and alcohol abuse. Consequently, the marriages of the poor are more likely to fail and their children to grow up in broken homes.

■ *Child-Rearing.* Sociologist Melvin Kohn (1977) finds significant class differences in child-rearing. Lower-class parents are more concerned that their children conform to conventional norms and obey authority figures. Middle-class parents, in contrast, encourage their children to be more creative and independent, and tolerate a wider range of behaviours (except in speech, where they are less tolerant of bad grammar and curse words).

■ *Education.* As was shown in Figure 6.3, education increases as one goes up the social class ladder. It is not just the amount of education that changes, but also the type of education. Children of the capitalist class bypass public schools entirely in favour of exclusive private schools. Here their children are trained to take a commanding role in society. Prep schools such as Upper Canada College teach upper-class values and prepare their students for prestigious universities (Beeghley, 1996).

■ *Religion.* Classes tend to cluster in different denominations. Anglicans, for example, are much more likely to recruit from the middle and upper classes, Baptists draw heavily from the lower classes, and Methodists are more middle-class. Patterns of worship also follow class lines:

Those that attract the lower classes have more spontaneous worship services and louder music, while the middle and upper classes prefer more "subdued" worship.

■ *Politics.* As has been stressed throughout this text, symbolic interactionists emphasize that people see events from their own corner in life. Political views are no exception to this principle, and the rich and the poor walk different political paths. The working class, which feels much more strongly than the classes above it that government should intervene in the economy to make citizens financially secure, is more likely to vote New Democrat, while those in the higher classes are more likely to vote Progressive Conservative. The Liberal Party is the party of the centre. However, voting patterns and party allegiance are mixed. There is no clear class majority supporting any one party (Forcese, 1997). Although the working class is more liberal on *economic* issues (i.e., they favour government spending), this class is more conservative on *social* issues (such as opposing abortion) (Lipset, 1959; Houtman, 1995). People toward the bottom of the class structure are also less likely to become politically active—to campaign for candidates, or even to vote (Gans, 1991a; Gilbert & Kahl, 1993; Curtis, Grabb, & Guppy, 1999).

■ *Crime and the Criminal Justice System.* If justice is supposed to be blind, it certainly is not when it comes to one's chances of being arrested (Henslin, 1996). In Chapter 16 we will discuss how the upper and lower social classes have different styles of crime. The white-collar crimes of the more privileged classes are more likely to be dealt with outside the criminal justice system, while the street crimes of the lower classes are dealt with by the police. One consequence of this class standard is that poor people, especially poor non-white people, are far more likely to be on probation, on parole, or in jail (National Council of Welfare, 2000; Reiman, 2001). In addition, since people tend to commit crimes in or near their own neighbourhoods, the lower classes are more likely to be robbed, burglarized, or murdered.

Social Mobility

No aspect of life, then—from marriage to politics—goes untouched by social class. Because life is so much more satisfying in the more privileged classes, people strive for upward social mobility. What affects people's chances of climbing the class ladder?

Three Types of Social Mobility

There are three basic types of social mobility: intergenerational, structural, and exchange mobility. **Intergenerational mobility** refers to adult children ending up on a different rung of the social class ladder than their parents—a change that occurs between generations. For example, if the child of someone who sells used cars goes to university and eventually buys a Toyota dealership, that person experiences **upward social mobility**. Conversely, if the child of the dealer's owners parties too much, drops out of university, and ends up selling cars, he or she experiences **downward social mobility**.

We like to think that individual efforts—or faults—are the reason people move up or down the class ladder. In

The term *structural mobility* refers to changes in society that push large numbers of people either up or down the social class ladder. A remarkable example was the Great Depression, during which thousands suddenly lost their jobs and wealth. People who once "had it made" found themselves standing on street corners selling apples or, as depicted here, selling their possessions at fire-sale prices.

Focus Question

In everyday life, what are some of the ways in which social class differences may be observed?

these examples, we can see hard work, sacrifice, and ambition on the one hand, versus indolence and alcohol abuse on the other. Although individual factors do underlie social mobility, sociologists consider **structural mobility** to be the crucial factor. This second basic type of mobility refers to changes in society that cause large numbers of people to move up or down the class ladder.

To better understand structural mobility, think of how opportunities opened when computers were invented. New types of jobs appeared overnight. Huge numbers of people took workshops and crash courses, switching from blue-collar to white-collar work. Although individual effort certainly was involved—for some seized the opportunity while others did not—the underlying cause was a change in the *structure* of work. Or consider the other side, the closing of opportunities in a depression, when millions of people are forced downward on the class ladder. In this instance, too, their changed status is due less to individual behaviour than to *structural* changes in society.

Underlying structural mobility are changes in technology. First there was the change from farming to blue-collar work, and, more recently, the change from blue-collar to white-collar occupations. Huge shifts in the types of work available opened so many doors that it became taken for granted that children could surpass their parents.

The third type, **exchange mobility**, occurs when large numbers of people move up or down the social class ladder, but on balance the proportions of the social classes remain about the same. Suppose a million or so working-class people are trained in computers, and they move up the social class ladder—but a vast surge in imports forces about a million skilled workers into lower-status jobs. Although millions of people change their social class, there is in effect an *exchange* among them. That is, the net result more or less balances out, and the class system remains basically untouched.

Ignoring Women

Sociologists used to focus only on the social mobility of men. For example, major studies of intergenerational mobility concluded that about half of sons moved beyond their fathers, about one-third stayed at the same level, and only about one-sixth fell down the social class ladder (Blau & Duncan, 1967; Featherman & Hauser, 1978; Featherman, 1979).

Fathers and sons? How about the other half of the population? Feminists pointed out this obvious lack (Davis & Robinson, 1988). They also objected that women were assumed to have no class position of their own—they simply were assigned the class of their husbands. The defence was that too few women were in the labour force to make a difference.

With the large numbers of women now working for pay, more recent studies include women (Breen & Whelan, 1995; Beeghley, 1996). Sociologists Elizabeth Higginbotham and Lynn Weber (1992), for example, studied 200 women from working-class backgrounds who became professionals, managers, and administrators in Memphis. They found that almost without exception their parents had encouraged them while they were still little girls to postpone marriage and get an education. This study confirms findings that the family is of utmost importance in the socialization process and that the primary entry to the upper middle class is a university education. At the same time, note that if there had not been a *structural* change in society the millions of new positions that women occupy would not exist.

Gender, Class, and Race

There is a complex interrelationship between gender, race, and class and the ways these relationships are played out within the economy and other social structures such as family, school, media, and politics (McCall, 2001; Brenner, 2000). What is clear from studies of working-class lives is that life's choices are constrained by gender as well as by race and there is a complex relationship between these and social class. Inequalities spring from the complex interaction of social class with race and gender in people's daily lives (Rubin, 1976; Johnson, 2002).

The New Technology and Fears of the Future

The ladder also goes down, of course—precisely what strikes fear in the hearts of many workers. If Canada does not keep pace with global change and remain highly competitive by producing low-cost, quality goods, its economic position will decline. The result will be shrinking opportunities—with Canadian workers facing fewer good jobs and lower incomes. Such a decline would result in children of the next generation having less status than their parents.

Perhaps this decline has already begun. We have lost millions of manufacturing jobs to Mexico, South America, and Asia. These jobs have taken with them the dreams of upward mobility for millions of Canadians. For others, this loss means downward mobility (Dentzler, 1991). Consider Alphonse Brown:

> Twenty-two years ago, his mother, Letitia, the daughter of a migrant worker, easily found work at a parts plant in St. Catharines, Ontario. There she earned good money, built seniority, and enjoyed excellent benefits. Alphonse, in contrast, has given up hope of joining the assembly line. For ten years, he has moved from one low-paying, no-benefits job to another. Letitia says, "There's nobody left with less than 14 years' seniority. We're on our way back to being migrants."

In short, with global competition nipping at the heels of Canadian industry, the richest rewards are reserved for the highly educated or for those who work at jobs sheltered from foreign competition. The result is that millions of workers in the lower half of the Canadian labour force are hitting a brick wall (Swift, 1995).

The foundation of this brick wall is the new technology, especially computers and satellites. When corporations move factories overseas, their top-level managers, through the wonders of satellite-based communications, are able to monitor the production process from the comfort of their U.S. offices. In many instances, this makes North American workers an expendable luxury, replaced by low-paid, non-unionized—and more compliant—workers on other continents.

Of the thousands of examples, consider this:

> Ireland is one of the poorest of European countries. Its workers, though, receive a solid high school education, generally superior to our high schools, and are willing to work for a fraction of what Canadian and American workers make. Consequently, many health insurance claims forms and grocery store redemption coupons are flown overnight to Ireland, where Irish workers efficiently process them, and return them, again overnight, to the United States.

A Matter of Controversy.   Fears of the future are certainly present, but whether social mobility has decreased or not is a matter of heated debate. Although millions of jobs have been exported, millions more have been created. The question to be decided by empirical research is whether the new jobs bring sufficient incomes and status to maintain the social mobility to which Canadians have become accustomed—or do most of them lead to a social-class dead end (Duffy, Glenday, & Pupo, 1997a)? Although this question will not be decided for some time, it is apparent that education remains the key to qualify for the better positions and thus to maintain or improve one's social class.

Poverty

A lot of Canadians find the "limitless possibilities" of the "Canadian Dream" elusive. Between 1993 and 1998, about one in four Canadians experienced low income for at least one year. Almost one in ten (8 percent) of Canadians lived in families who experienced low income for four or more years. Children were, of course, not exempt. More than one-quarter (29 percent) of children under age 6 lived in families that had low incomes for at least one year between 1993 and 1998 (Morissette & Zhang, 2001). The impoverishment of some Canadians is, of course, also evident on our streets in the numbers of homeless and in the proliferation of food banks and food bank users across the nation (Cheadle, 2000). Between 1989 and 2002, the number of Canadians using food banks almost doubled. In March 2002, 718 000 Canadians used a food bank, according to the Canadian Association of Food Banks (Orwen, 2002).

The impoverishment of many Canadians is occurring in the midst of a dramatic growth in the wealth of the richest Canadian families. Between 1984 and 1999, the richest families improved their net worth by 39 percent (or $110 000) while the poorest families lost ground. Indeed, there appears to be a growing chasm between the haves and the have-nots in Canada. The wealthiest 50 percent of the population owned 94 percent of all national wealth, and the poorest 50 percent were left with only 6 percent. The poorest 20 percent of family units has absolutely no net worth and is living month to month, spending all or most of what is earned and having little or nothing to set aside for RRSPs and RESPs (Kerstetter, 2001). Young families with children, single mothers, immigrants, visible minorities, disabled Canadians—all are confronting an increasingly uncertain economic future (Carey, 2001). At the same time, the social welfare net, made up of employment insurance payments, welfare assistance, disability payments, and so on, has grown increasingly bare-boned. Poverty and inequality have taken centre stage in understanding Canadian society.

Drawing the Poverty Line

Most Canadians will be surprised to learn that Canada does not have an "official" poverty line. Indeed, determining who is and is not poor remains a contentious issue (National Council of Welfare, 2001–2002). It is easy to see that homeless, starving children in Guatemala or nineteenth-century Montreal are poor; it is much more difficult to agree upon those present-day Canadians who have so little that they cannot meaningfully participate in Canadian society. According to some analysts, if individuals are not starving, not homeless, and not in immediate physical peril due to their economic plight, they are not *really* poor. For example, in a contentious thesis Christopher Sarlo, under the aegis of the conservative Fraser Institute, argued that if you adopt a "basic needs" approach, "poverty…has been virtually eliminated" in Canada and "is simply not a major problem" (1992, p. 2). This physical survival argument suggests a very narrow understanding of poverty.

Currently, most discussions of poverty in Canada rely on more generous standards of impoverishment. In particular, Statistics Canada's *low-income cut-offs* (LICOs) are frequently employed as informal poverty lines. Adopted in 1973 (and reset in 1992), the LICOs seek to establish a specific income level below which individuals are considered to be living in "straitened circumstances." The assumption underlying the cut-offs is that poor families are those whose income requires them to spend more than 54.7 percent of their gross income on food, clothing, and shelter. Since the average Canadian family spends 34.7 percent of its income on these necessities, it is assumed that an additional 20 percent results in an economic burden (National Council of Welfare, 2001). As a result of these expenditures on absolute necessities, little, if anything, is left over for transportation, health, personal care, education, household operation, recreation, insurance, savings, and so on.

The LICOs are set up so that they vary depending upon the size of the household (how many dependents are supported by the family income) and the size of the town, city, or area (more than 500 000 population, 100 000 to 499 000, and so on) in which the family/individual lives. These calculations result in 35 separate LICOs for all of Canada. For example, a family of three living in Montreal would be poor if the total income for the family was $27 315 or less; the same family living in a rural area would be poor if they received $18 877 or less (National Council of Welfare, 2001, p. 57).

It is important to be aware that there are other "poverty lines" proposed by other organizations. The Canadian Council on Social Development (CCSD), an independent, national, nonprofit organization engaged in social research, policy development, and advocacy, maintains that the LICOs are too restrictive. They argue for a social inclusion approach; that is, a definition which identifies the level at which families and individuals can hope to meaningfully participate in Canadian society. Concretely, they propose that families with three members whose income is half or less of the national average ($57 146 in 1997) should be considered poor. Other analysts have argued for a "market basket measure." This approach, which seeks to create an absolute, long-term measure, develops a basket of necessities for families and then prices the basket in terms of local costs. The net result is a much more restrictive measure of poverty, which, if adopted, would dramatically reduce the number of people who are considered poor in Canada (CCSD, 2000, pp. 14–30).

The definitional struggle is far from resolved. Currently, most of the media reporting on poverty relies on the LICOs; but every now and then, the definitional conflict bursts into the open and there is, as with Sarlo, much discussion of who is "really" poor in Canada.

This is by no means a Canadian problem. Around the world, there are frequent disagreements about who is or is not poor. It is part of the magical sleight-of-hand of modern bureaucracy that a modification in the official measure of poverty instantly adds—or subtracts—millions of people from this category (Sainath, 1996). Governments then use this definition to decide who will receive help and who will not. Using the prevailing definition of poverty in Canada, Statistics Canada's LICOs, let's see who is poor. But before we do this, compare your ideas of the poor with the myths explored in the Down-to-Earth Sociology box here.

Who Are the Poor?

Geography.   Of course, poverty is not evenly distributed across Canada. Reflecting differences in the local economies (and, as a result, opportunities for employment), child poverty rates (the percentage of the population under 18

years of age who fall below the LICOs) in Canada range from a high of 25.3 percent in Newfoundland to a low of 12.5 percent in Prince Edward Island (National Council of Welfare, 2001, p. 9). We know relatively little about the Yukon, Northwest Territories, or Nunavut, since their enumeration in the 1996 census was incomplete. However, the high rates of Aboriginal poverty suggest that impoverishment is a very significant issue in these areas (National Council of Welfare, 2001, pp. 23–26). But the greatest predictor of whether Canadians are poor is not geography, but race/ethnicity, education, and the sex of the person who heads the family. Let's look at these three factors.

Race/Ethnicity.   Despite Canada's official multiculturalism, being a visible minority, immigrant, or Aboriginal Canadian carries with it increased risk of poverty. The national poverty rate among visible minorities is about twice that of other groups, and, in specific provinces such as Newfoundland and Nova Scotia, visible minorities are more likely than other Canadians to be poor. Between 1993 and 1998, at least 21 percent of visible minority Canadians experienced low income for four or more years, compared with only 7 percent of other Canadians (Morissette & Zhang, 2001, p. 26). A recent study of Statistics Canada income data concluded that white Canadians earn about 25 percent more than non-whites (Campbell, 2001).

Predictably, immigrants, especially recent immigrants, are also disadvantaged (Li, 2000). Between 1984 and 1999, when the average Canadian-born family wealth increased by 37 percent, immigrant families who had been in Canada less than 10 years experienced a 16 percent drop in family wealth (Morissette, Zhang, & Drolet, 2002a, p. 18). In part, these difficulties reflect the significantly higher rates of unemployment experienced by recent immigrants to Canada (McDonald & Worswick, 1997).

Not surprisingly, Aboriginal peoples also face increased economic risks. In several provinces in Canada, the poverty rate amongst Aboriginal peoples is more than twice that of non-Aboriginals, and in Saskatchewan and Manitoba more than half of all Aboriginals were living in poverty (CCSD, 2000, pp. 75, 77). The overall Canadian picture is bleak. Almost half (44 percent) of all Canadian Aboriginals and 60 percent of Aboriginal children are reported to be living below the LICOs (Federal, Provincial, and Territorial Advisory Committee, 1999, p. 47).

Education and Poverty.   As you know, education is also a vital factor in poverty. Having a university degree clearly and dramatically reduces your risk of impoverishment. Between 1993 and 1998 only 11 percent of persons with a university degree experienced at least a year of low income. In contrast, 27 percent of those with less than high school experienced a year or more of low income during this period (Morissette & Zhang, 2001). This disparity is also reflected in earnings patterns. When the main wage earner for the family has a high school diploma, the median net

Myth 1: Most poor people are lazy. They are poor because they do not work.

It's important to keep in mind that many of the poor are either too old or too young to work, or disabled and, as a result, limited in their ability to work. In addition, a whole range of societal prejudices, including ageism, racism, and ableism, may stand in the way of finding employment (Jackson, Robinson, Baldwin, & Wiggins, 2000). Even if work is secured, it is no guarantee against poverty. Many poor people are indeed employed but their jobs pay so poorly that their income does not lift them above the low-income cut-offs. In 1997, 56 percent of poor family heads and 55 percent of poor unattached individuals were employed on a full- or part-time basis (National Council of Welfare, 1999a). In 1998, half of poor children were living in families where the major income earner worked part- or full-year and almost one-quarter in families where the major earner worked full-time, full-year (National Council of Welfare, 2001, p. 21). Low-wage and minimum-wage jobs simply do not lift families out of poverty. Finally, poverty rates tend to rise and fall with unemployment rates, which suggests that many poor people grab the chance for paid employment when it is possible.

Myth 2: Most of the poor are single mothers and their children.

Being a single mother with children is a high-risk formula for poverty. In 1998, 53 percent of single-parent mothers were poor. However, mother-headed families make up a minority of poor families. Only 40 percent of poor children are living in mother-headed families. The majority (52 percent) of poor kids are in two-parent families, with a fraction (3 percent) in single-father families (National Council of Welfare, 2001, p. 10).

Myth 3: Poverty is a big-city problem.

Since many Canadians live in large metropolitan areas, it is not surprising to find that many poor individuals also do. In 1997, 71 percent of poor Canadian families and 73 percent of poor unattached individuals lived in cities of 100 000 or more. Only 12 percent of poor families and 7 percent of poor individuals lived in rural areas. However, recent research indicates that "low income intensity" (a measure that combines both poverty and depth of poverty) impacts significantly on both rural and urban areas. Indeed, between 1993 and 1997, rural low-income families experienced a $1800 drop in income while urban families lost only $1000. This drop in income reflects a variety of events, particularly the reduc-

tion in the amount of social assistance provided in a number of provinces and a Canada-wide decline in EI benefits (reflecting greatly restricted access to EI). However, it was particularly in rural and small towns, notably in Atlantic Canada, that the loss of EI impacted on poor families since these areas have been more reliant on government payments and have fewer alternatives in terms of paid employment. In short, poverty is a pressing issue right across Canada, from the countryside and small towns to the largest urban areas (Heisz, 2001).

Myth 4: The poor live on welfare.

In one sense this is true. Living on welfare means living in poverty, since welfare incomes are substantially below the LICOs. However, it is not true that the majority of poor Canadians are living off welfare. In 1998, 43 percent of poor two-parent families with children lived on their earnings from paid employment and 19 percent of poor single mothers lived on their earnings. In addition, 32 percent of poor two-parent families were living on a combination of earnings and welfare or earnings and EI. Similarly, 32 percent of poor single mothers lived on such a combination. Only 38 percent of poor single mothers and a scant 14 percent of poor two-parent families lived on welfare alone (National Council of Welfare, 2001).

---

worth is $62 500; with a bachelor's degree it's $117 500, and with a professional degree (lawyer, dentist) it balloons to $323 000 (Carey, 2001). Ironically, while education may serve as a way out of low income for many, rising tuition costs and mushrooming student-loan debt (which grew by 600 percent between 1984 and 1999) appear to be deterring many students from low-income families from attending postsecondary institutions (Rushowy, 2000).

Education, however, is not a guarantee against bad economic times. Many poor heads of families have education beyond high school and yet still end up in poverty. Between 1993 and 1998, 20 percent of Canadians who had completed some or all of a postsecondary program experienced a year or more of low income (Morissette & Zhang, 2001).

Indeed, in 1998, 46.9 percent of all poor two-parent family major income earners had gone beyond high school (National Council of Welfare, 2001, p. 17). Recent surveys of food bank clients also support the impression that education is not a guarantee against poverty, especially for certain groups of Canadians. According to a 1995 survey by Toronto's Daily Bread Food Bank, only 12 percent of immigrants using food banks had some postsecondary education. In 2002, 59 percent of immigrant users were "highly educated" (Quinn, 2002). This pattern suggests that poverty may be as much a result of too few employment opportunities as too little education.

The data in Table 6.7 also seem to support this view. Although 29.2 percent of poor children are supported by

Table 6.7 The Relationship Between Education and Child Poverty in Canada, 1998

Highest Level of Education Completed by Family Major Income Earner	% of All Poor Children
Less than high school	29.2
High school diploma	14.6
Some postsecondary	16.1
Postsecondary diploma	26.7
University degree	4.0
Unknown	9.4

Source: From National Council of Welfare, *Child Poverty Profile 1998*, 2001 (Summer). Ottawa: Minister of Public Works and Government Services, p. 19.

someone with less than a high school education, 61.4 percent are from families in which the major income earner has a high school diploma or better.

The Feminization of Poverty. The other major predictor of poverty is the sex of the person who heads the family. If we look at the ratio of female to male poverty rates—in other words, the poverty rate of women compared to the poverty rate of men—we consistently find that women are at greater risk of poverty than men. This gender difference has gone up and down over the past two decades, tending to narrow somewhat in tough economic times, but it has consistently favoured men. Between 1993 and 1998, one-quarter of Canadian women experienced a year or more of low income in contrast to one-fifth of men (Morissette & Zhang, 2001, p. 29).

Most of women's greater vulnerability to poverty can be explained by the high poverty rates in three types of families: unattached women under 65, unattached women 65 and older, and single-parent mothers under 65 with children under 18. Women seniors, women on their own, and women who head families are all at greater risk of poverty than their male counterparts.

Single mothers are particularly vulnerable. From 1980 to 1998, between 53 percent and 62 percent of single mothers were living below the poverty line, and they received on average $8950 less than the LICO in 1998 (National Council of Welfare, 2001). The poverty rate for single fathers, a much smaller portion of the population, was about half this rate. Two-parent families living below the poverty line ranged from a low of 9.1 percent to a high of 13.4 percent during the same period.

A variety of social factors contribute to the economic vulnerability of single mothers. Women's work in traditional women's occupations tends to result in less well-paid work with fewer benefits. Women who interrupt their paid work to care for home and family find themselves disadvantaged in the labour market. In the event of divorce, ongoing difficulties receiving child-support payments from non-custodial parents may exacerbate financial problems. Lack of adequate, accessible, and affordable child care may make it difficult for single mothers to improve their financial situation. As one analyst concludes, the simple fact is that single mothers earn less than men, but have the primary responsibility for the custody of the children in the event of marital breakup, and never-married mothers are in an even worse situation (Finnie, 2000, p. 31). Many single mothers turn to social welfare and other government transfer payments in order to maintain their families, and the level of these income transfers guarantees that their families will be living below the low-income cut-offs (CCSD, 2000). In 1998, 38 percent of single mothers were relying solely on welfare payments (as opposed to earnings, EI, or some combination of sources) to support their families (National Council of Welfare, 2001). Not surprisingly, these poor single mothers may find themselves sinking further and further into debt. A recent study reported that, while one in six Canadian families fell behind two months or more on a bill, loan, rent, or mortgage payment, almost one in three single mothers were in the same situation (Pyper, 2002).

Women who are not married and who do not have children at home may also fare poorly. Unattached women under age 65 are more likely than comparable men to be poor. In 1998, the median after-tax income for unattached men was $19 900 and for unattached women, $15 700 (Pyper, 2002). Again, inequalities in the labour market along with work interruptions, divorce, and so on may create these patterns of disparity. Consider, for example, that women 55 to 65 with little experience in the paid labour force and not yet eligible for old age security may find themselves at a significant economic disadvantage.

As women age, the poverty imbalance persists. While, as discussed below, the economic situation for seniors has improved significantly in recent years, it is still the case that women are disproportionately disadvantaged. Between 1993 and 1998, 16 percent of women 65 or older and only 6 percent of comparable men lived at least one year on low income. Since earlier generations of women frequently interrupted their paid labour force participation in order to bear and raise children, they often receive little or no pension income when they retire. Once widowed, divorced, or otherwise single, senior women often find themselves in a financially precarious situation (Morissette & Zhang, 2001).

Disability

Canadians unfortunate enough to be born with or acquire a disability are likely to experience economic difficulties. The 1996 census collected data on the incomes of individuals with disabilities; that is, individuals who have a long-term condition that limits daily activity at home, at work, at school, and in other activities. Currently, there are 4 million Canadians living with a disability (Titchkosky, 2001). Almost 30 percent of disabled men and one-third of disabled women (in contrast to 18 percent of other Canadians) are poor. Discrimination against the disabled in hiring practices, limited accommodations to the disabled in work environments, and inadequate disability benefits all set the stage for this pattern. For example, in Toronto in 2002, the maximum allowance available under the Ontario Disability Support Program for an individual living alone and disabled was $930 a month or $11 160 a year. This sum is a staggering $7211 below the low-income cut-off for a large urban area (CCSD, 2000, p. 76; Morissette & Zhang, 2001, p. 28; Henderson, 2002, pp. L7, 8).

Old Age

The reduction of poverty among seniors is one of the great poverty success stories. Poverty among Canadians 65 and older has dropped significantly throughout the latter years of the twentieth century. In 1997, the poverty rate for seniors hit a record low of 17 percent, down from 33.6 percent in 1980. Between 1993 and 1998 only 6 percent of Canadians 65 and older experienced four or more years of low income. This dramatic improvement is largely the result of changes in government policies. The creation of the Canada Pension Plan and Quebec Pension Plan in 1966, the introduction of the Guaranteed Income Supplement and Old Age Security were all crucial steps. More recent policies have further improved the lives of many seniors (National Council of Welfare, 1999a).

However, seniors are not completely out of the woods. In particular, senior women remain at risk. Women over 65 who are unattached (often widowed) still had a poverty rate of 42 percent in 1997, while unattached male seniors were at 27.2 percent.

Similarly, aged seniors appear to be at a disadvantage. Among older seniors (85+) almost one-third of women and one in seven men are living in poverty regardless of marital status. In short, a substantial number of seniors, especially those not sharing their expenses with a partner, are struggling below the LICOs (National Council of Welfare, 1999a).

Children of Poverty

In 1998, there were 1 353 000 children living below the LICOs in Canada (National Council of Welfare, 2001). That this number of Canadian children are reared in poverty is shocking when one considers the wealth of this country and the supposed concern for the well-being of our children. The tragic aspect of poverty is the topic of the next Thinking Critically about Social Controversy box.

Focus Question
What are some of the popular myths about the poor and why is this misinformation still believed?

Focus Question
Which categories of Canadians are more likely to be poor at some point in their lives?

In Sum

Poverty is a social issue that is not as straightforward as it might first seem. Determining who "qualifies" as poor is a contentious political issue. Understanding the realities of poverty means questioning the popular myths that continue to surround the poor. Finally, it is important to realize that being poor is not simply a result of bad luck. Particular categories of individuals, notably women, seniors, members of racial and ethnic minorities, the disabled, and children whose primary parents are members of these categories are much more likely to be poor. The failure of Canadians and their governments to adequately address poverty over the past three decades does not bode well for the future.

The Dynamics of Poverty

In the 1960s, Michael Harrington (1962) and Oscar Lewis (1966a) suggested that the poor tend to get trapped in a **culture of poverty**. They assumed that the values and behaviours of the poor "make them fundamentally different from other Americans, and that these factors are largely responsible for their continued long-term poverty" (Ruggles, 1989, p. 7). Implied by this approach is the idea that the poor are lazy people who bring poverty on themselves. Is a self-perpetuating culture, transmitted across generations, that locks poor people in poverty the basic reason for poverty? Until recently, we knew little about how long Canadians spend in poverty and how they move in and out of poverty. In the early 1990s Statistics Canada began tracking individuals over six-year stretches to determine how their financial circumstances changed.

As a result, we now have longitudinal information on the financial lives of Canadians, and these data suggest (1) that poverty is much more common amongst Canadians than is often assumed and (2) that long-term poverty impacts disproportionately on certain segments of the poor. We know that although almost one-quarter of Canadians experienced at least one year of low income between 1993 and 1998, it is the clear minority of Canadians who get stuck below the low-income cut-offs. Only 8 percent of Canadians lived in families experiencing low income for four years or more between 1993 and 1998. Predictably, certain segments of the population are particularly vulnerable to long-term impoverishment (see Table 6.8).

In 1989, the House of Commons unanimously resolved to eradicate child poverty in Canada by 2000. In 1991, Canada ratified the United Nations Convention on the Rights of the Child. Successive governments have pledged improvement in the provision of child care. Instead of improvements, the past decade has witnessed a series of disappointing failures. In particular, child poverty rates increased from 14.5 percent in 1989 to 20.8 percent in 1996—the highest rate in 17 years (dropping slightly to 19.2 percent in 1998). In an affluent and progressive country, almost one child in five is living in poverty (National Council of Welfare, 1999a, 1999b, 2001).

This is a particularly sorry record when compared to the efforts of other countries. While the United States, Britain, and Russia have an even more dismal record on child poverty, when we turn our attention to countries such as Sweden, Finland, the Netherlands, and Denmark it is apparent that much more could be accomplished in reducing poverty (Bradshaw, 2002; Federal, Provincial, and Territorial Advisory Committee, 1999). For example, while the poverty rate for lone-parent mothers is 40 percent in Canada and 47 percent

in the United States, in Sweden only 3 percent of lone-parent mothers are impoverished (National Council of Welfare, 2001).

Of course, most children are poor in Canada because they happen to be born into poor families. Their risk of impoverishment simply reflects the patterns of racism, ableism, economic marginalization, and so on, that result in patterns of growing social inequality. For example, child poverty is higher if children's families are headed by young people (under age 25), or have only one parent (especially if this one parent is a mother), or are visible minorities or Aboriginals, or are headed by a disabled adult. Clearly, for more and more poor children, having only one parent to support them is a crucial ingredient in impoverishment. However, keep in mind that many children are the victims of an economy that has generated large numbers of "bad jobs" and high rates of unemployment and a social assistance "net" that is increasingly inadequate.

The statistical profile of child poverty provides a sanitized image. Poverty permeates children's lives. Being born into poverty, for example, means a higher risk of dying at birth and a greater risk of being unhealthy as

you mature. Growing up poor means living in inadequate and unhealthy housing in the midst of unsafe neighbourhoods. Growing up in poverty means less of a chance at a good education, and this in turn reduces the opportunities for satisfying, well-paid employment. Growing up poor may mean being less healthy and having higher rates of hospitalization and heart disease (Raphael, 2001). Growing up poor may mean being seen by social workers, police, and judges alike as less reputable, less trustworthy, and less worthy of lenience (National Council of Welfare, 2000). Not having adequate work leads to insufficient pensions and an old age marked by struggle rather than rest (Federal, Provincial, and Territorial Advisory Committee, 1999).

On a day-to-day basis, being poor may mean not being able to go on the school trip with the other kids, or not having enough to eat, or always feeling on the outside wanting the clothes, vacations, and experiences that others have and the media promote (Hurtig, 1999).

For Your Consideration

Many social analysts—liberals and conservatives alike—are alarmed at this increase in child poverty. They emphasize that it is time to stop blaming the victim; instead we must focus on the structural factors that underlie child poverty. To relieve the problem, they say, we must take immediate steps to establish national programs of child nutrition, child care, health care, and housing. Solutions will require at least these fundamental changes: (1) removing obstacles to employment; (2) improving education; and (3) supporting parents and strengthening the family. To achieve these changes, what specific programs would you recommend?

The number of Canadian children living in poverty is shocking considering the wealth of this country and the concern for the well-being of children and families.

Sources: National Council of Welfare (1999c); Moynihan (1991); C. Murray (1993); Sandefur 1995; *Statistical Abstract* (1997, Tables 22, 736, 739, 1338).

Table 6.8 Percentage of Canadians Vulnerable to Long-Term Low Incomes, 1993–1998

Segment of Population	Percentage with 4 or More Years of Low Income
All Canadians	8%
Lone-parent families	38%
Individuals with a work limitation (disability)	28%
Recent immigrant (after 1986)	28%
Visible minority immigrant	24%
Unattached individuals (divorced, widowed, unmarried)	23%
Individuals with less than high school education	13%
Children under age 6	12%

Source: Statistics Canada, from "Experience low income for several years," by Rene Morissette and Xuelin Zhang, 2001 (Spring), *Perspectives on Labour and Income,* Vol. 2, No. 3, pp. 27, 29, Catalogue no. 75-001-XPE.

Why Are People Poor? Individual Versus Structural Explanations

Two explanations for poverty compete for our attention. The first, which sociologists adopt, focuses on *social structure.* Sociologists stress that *features of society* deny some people access to education or learning job skills. They emphasize racial, ethnic, age, and gender discrimination, as well as changes in the job market—persistent high rates of unemployment, the closing of plants, the drying-up of skilled jobs, and an increase in marginal and part-time jobs that pay poverty wages.

A competing explanation focuses on the *characteristics of individuals* that are assumed to contribute to their poverty. Individualistic explanations that sociologists reject outright as worthless stereotypes are laziness and lack of intelligence, but sociologists acknowledge factors like dropping out of school, bearing children at younger ages, and bearing more children than the other social classes do—though most are reluctant to speak of such factors in this context, for fear of seeming to blame the victim.

The tension between these competing explanations is more than of mere theoretical interest. These explanations affect our perception and have practical consequences, as is illustrated in the Down-to-Earth Sociology and Thinking Critically boxes.

Welfare Reform. After decades of debate, welfare programs across Canada have been reformed. In many provinces welfare incomes, already well below the LICOs, have been further reduced and programs have been introduced so that many of those who receive welfare are required to accept welfare work ("workfare") or participate in training programs in order to qualify for social welfare. At the same time, other government programs that provide assistance to those in economic stress, such as employment insurance, disability payments, and legal aid, have been dramatically cut back in some provinces. Critics call this an attack on the poor, saying that the new rules and restrictions will push many people, notably single mothers, poor kids, and the disabled, deeper into poverty (Bashevkin, 2002). Supporters of welfare reforms claim they rescue people from poverty—transforming them into self-supporting and hard-working citizens—and reduce welfare costs (A. Cohen, 1997). Welfare rolls have dropped but the numbers of homeless in our urban centres have markedly increased. Currently, it is estimated there are more than 1000 homeless people living on the streets of Toronto. It is too soon to know what the long-term results will be.

Down-to-Earth Sociology   Welfare: How to Ravage the Self-Concept

My husband left me shortly after I was diagnosed with multiple sclerosis. At the time, I had five children. My oldest child was 14, and my youngest was 7. My physician, believing I would be seriously disabled, helped get me on Social Security disability. The process took several months, and so it became necessary for me to go on public aid and food stamps.

By the time I needed to depend on my family in the face of a crisis, there weren't any resources left to draw on. My father had passed away and my mother was retired, living on a modest income based on the old age pension and my father's pension. Isn't it funny how there is no social stigma attached to pension benefits for the elderly? People look at this money as an entitlement—"we worked for it." But people who have to depend on public aid for existence are looked at like vermin and accused of being lazy.

I can tell you from my own experience, that a great deal of the lethargy that comes from long periods on welfare is due primarily to the attitudes of the people you have to come into contact with in these programs. I've been through the gamut: from rude, surly caseworkers at public aid, to patronizing nurses at clinics ("You have *how* many children?"), to the accusing tone of the food bank workers when you have to go begging for a handout before the 30-day time span has expired. After a while your dignity is gone, and you start to believe that you really are the disgusting human trash they all make you out to be.

Source: Christine Hoffman, a student in the author's introductory sociology class.

Throughout Canadian history, we have divided the poor into two types: the deserving and the undeserving. The deserving poor are people who, in the public mind, are poor through no fault of their own. Most of the working poor, such as the Lewises, are considered deserving:

> Nancy and Ted Lewis are married, in their late 30s, with two children. Ted works three part-time jobs; Nancy takes care of the children and house. Their total income is $22 000 a year. To make ends meet, the Lewises rely on welfare and food bank support.

The undeserving poor, in contrast, are viewed as having brought on their own poverty. They are freeloaders who waste their lives in sloth, alcohol and drug abuse, and unwed motherhood. They don't deserve help, and, if given anything, will waste it on their dissolute lifestyles. Some people would see Joan as an example:

> Joan's grandmother and her six children were supported by welfare. Joan's parents are alcoholics—and on welfare. Joan started having sex at 13, bore her first child at 15, and, now at 23, with three children, is expecting her fourth. Her first two children have the same father, the third a different father, and Joan isn't sure who fathered her coming child. Joan parties most nights, using both alcohol and whatever drugs are available. Her house is filthy, and social workers have threatened to take away her children.

This division of the poor into deserving and undeserving underlies the heated debate about welfare. "Why should we use *our* hard-earned money to help *them*? They are just going to waste it. Of course, there are those who want to get on their feet, and helping them is okay."

For Your Consideration

Of what use is such a division of the poor into deserving and undeserving? Would we let some people starve because they "brought poverty upon themselves"? Would we let children go hungry because their parents are unmarried, uneducated, and unskilled? Try to go beyond such a simplistic division and use the sociological perspective to explain poverty without blaming the victim. What *social* conditions (conditions of society) create poverty? What *social* conditions produce the lifestyles of which the middle class so vehemently disapproves?

However, reducing the safety net in society while at the same time increasing the gap between rich and poor may have dramatic social consequences.

Deferred Gratification

One consequence of a life of deprivation punctuated by emergencies—*and seeing the future as more of the same*—is a lack of **deferred gratification**, giving up things in the present for the sake of greater gains in the future. It is difficult to practise this middle-class virtue if one does not have a middle-class surplus—or middle-class hope.

Back in 1967, sociologist Elliot Liebow noted this precise problem among African-American street-corner men. Their jobs were low-paying and insecure, their lives pitted with emergencies. With the future looking exactly like the present, and any savings they did manage gobbled up by emergencies—theirs or those of friends and relatives—saving for the future was fruitless. The only thing that made sense from their perspective was to enjoy what they could at the moment. Immediate gratification, then, was not the cause of their poverty, but its consequence. Cause and consequence loop together, however, for their immediate gratification, in turn, helped perpetuate their poverty.

If both causes are at work, why do sociologists emphasize the structural explanation? Reverse the situation for a moment. Suppose that the daily routine of the middle class were an old car that ran only half the time, threats from the utility company to shut off the electricity and heat, and a choice between buying medicine, food, and diapers or paying the rent. How long would they practise deferred gratification? Their orientations to life would likely make a sharp U-turn.

Sociologists, then, look at the behaviours of the poor as more driven by their poverty than as a cause of it. Poor people would love the opportunities that would allow them the chance to practise the middle-class virtue of deferred gratification. They just can't afford it.

"Pull Yourself Up by Your Own Bootstraps": The Social Functions of a Myth

Around the turn of the twentieth century, one of the United States' most talked-about fictional heroes was Horatio Alger, whose rags-to-riches exploits and startling successes in overcoming severe odds motivated thousands of boys of that period. Although he has disappeared from literature, the ideology remains alive and well in the psyche of Canadians. From abundant real-life examples of people from humble origins who climbed far up the social class ladder, Canadians know that anyone can get ahead by really trying. In fact, they believe that most Canadians, including minorities and the working poor, have an average or better-than-average chance of getting ahead—obviously a statistical impossibility (Kluegel & Smith, 1986).

Functionalists would stress that this belief is functional for society. On the one hand, it encourages people to compete for higher positions, or, as the song says, "to reach for the highest star." On the other hand, it places blame for failure squarely on the individual. If you don't make it—in the face of ample opportunities to get ahead—the fault must be your own. The myth helps to stabilize society, then, for since the fault is viewed as the individual's, not society's, current social arrangements are satisfactory. This reduces pressures to change the system.

As Marx and Weber pointed out, social class penetrates our consciousness, shaping our ideas of life and our proper place in society. When the rich look around, they sense superiority and control over destiny. In contrast, the poor see defeat, and a bitter buffeting by unpredictable forces. Both know the dominant ideology, that their particular niche in life is due to their own efforts, that the reasons for success—or failure—lie solely with the self. Like the fish not seeing water, people tend not to see how social class affects their own lives.

A Concluding Note

Let's go back to the three families in the chapter's opening vignette. Remember that these families represent three worlds of development, that is, global stratification. Their life chances—from access to material possessions to the opportunity for education and even the likely age at which their members will die—are profoundly affected by the global stratification reviewed in this chapter. This division of the globe into interconnected units of nations with more or less wealth and more or less power and prestige, then, is much more than a matter of theoretical interest. In fact, it is *your* life we are talking about.

Thinking Critically about Social Controversy

Poverty: A Global Warning

Poverty, of course, has global dimensions. While the industrial countries have long been aware of global inequalities, economic globalization along with the increasing prominence of global organizations such as the World Trade Organization (WTO), the World Bank, and the International Monetary Fund (IMF) have heightened Canadians' awareness of the broader poverty issues. In particular, the events of September 11, 2001, resulted in many analysts pointing to the growing chasm between rich and poor nations as a trigger for international violence and terrorism and a threat to world security.

The issue of global poverty is particularly pressing since the neo-liberal course proposed by the WTO and others has become increasingly suspect. The vision that international investment in the economies of developing countries combined with open markets and more liberalized trade would level the playing field and trickle down to the world's poor has not been fulfilled. Developing countries, in particular in Africa, have made relatively little headway in reducing poverty levels. Indeed, the World Bank suggests that the economic situation for most of Africa is worse today than it was 40 years ago. Although Africa contains about 10 percent of the world population, its gross domestic product (GDP—the value of all goods and services produced annually) is only about 1 percent of the global GDP, and Africa receives less than 1 percent of foreign direct investment. Meanwhile, protectionist policies (tariffs and quotas on foreign imports) in North America and the European Union make it almost impossible for African goods to even enter these markets (Rees, 2002; Khalif, 2002).

The problem is not confined to Africa. Around the globe the rich have become richer and the poor, poorer. In 1970 the richest 10 percent of the world's population earned 19 times the income of the poorest 10 percent. By 1997, the ratio grew to 27:1. By this time the wealthiest 1 percent of the world's population earned as much income as the poorest 57 percent and the 25 million wealthiest Americans (0.4 percent of the global population) received an income larger than that of the poorest 2 billion people on earth (43 percent of the global population) (Rees, 2002). This economic pattern of inequality, of course, translates into a myriad of other inequalities. Currently, 90 percent of the world's medical health research dollars focus on the health problems of 20 percent of the global population. Cancer and heart disease take pre-eminence while the infectious diseases, such as malaria and tuberculosis, which cause half the deaths in developing countries, receive relatively little attention (Calamai, 2002). The AIDS pandemic brings into clear focus the life and death consequences of global inequities. In 2001, 500 000 people in wealthy countries received life-extending drugs and 25 000 died of AIDS. In sub-Saharan Africa, only 30 000 people received antiretroviral medication and 2.2 million died (Donnelly, 2002).

Nor have the rich nations rushed forward to resolve the global inequalities. The IMF is a specialized United Nations agency with 182 member countries, which was created in 1944 to help maintain the world monetary system. The World Bank was set up as a lender of last resort to least industrialized nations. The WTO (which is a successor to other international trade organizations) is intended to bring countries together to improve international trade and, indirectly, to encourage global standards in environmental protections, worker protections, and so on. The history of these various global governing agencies is complex, but suffice it to say that their role remains hotly debated and global inequality is a growing concern.

Even more direct efforts at assisting developing countries through the provision of foreign aid have had limited results and elicited only limited enthusiasm on the part of richer nations. Only Denmark, the Netherlands, Sweden, Norway, and Luxembourg have met the United Nations target of contributing 0.7 percent of their GDP to foreign aid. Canada contributes a scant 0.25 percent, behind much smaller economies such as Portugal and New Zealand. Indeed, Canadian foreign aid contributions are at their lowest level in 30 years. Interestingly, at the bottom of the pack of 22 wealthy nations providing developmental aid to foreign countries is the United States, contributing 0.10 percent of its GDP ("Saturday Special," 2002, p. A25).

Currently, about one in three of the world's 6 billion people live in a state of "extreme poverty" and nearly one in two live on less than US$2 a day. Inhabitants in 21 countries are subsisting on an average income of less than US$1000 a year while at the wealthy end of the scale, citizens of 17 nations average US$20 000 a year. Further, the future for

global poverty appears bleak. The globe is expected to add another 2 billion people over the next 25 years, and 97 percent of these people will living in the poorer countries (Rees, 2002; Crane, 2000).

Critics of the WTO and IMF argue that the wealthy nations are creating and sustaining this pattern of global inequality through their globalization policies because it serves their national interests. In particular, developing countries, deeply in debt to the World Bank, have been forced by the World Bank-IMF to accept structural adjustment programs (SAPs) in order to qualify for loans. For example, Zambia and Tanzania were required to create lean, efficient economies by cutting government payrolls and public subsidies. When the cuts were made, the hoped-for foreign investment did not materialize, and the countries found themselves even deeper in debt, with greater numbers of unemployed and impoverished. Today, analysts are increasingly critical of SAP programs that require impoverished countries to spend much of their national income servicing their debts to

the richer nations, rather than providing improved social services and support for their own citizens. Alternative approaches, including opening the markets in rich countries to products from poorer countries, renegotiating trade pacts, listening to as well as working with local people, and changes in the developed economies' hammerlock on global institutions such as the IMF, are gaining a higher profile (Rees, 2002; Hormeku & Barr, 2002, Langdon, 1999).

Certainly, if the growing strains of global inequalities are not addressed, the negative consequences will likely impact on rich and poor alike. Globalization—with its world trade and world travel in the midst of a world economy—ensures that we all share the outcomes. Ultimately, while the wealthy nations have attempted to create "gated communities," disease and environmental destruction cannot be kept out. If poor countries continue to plunder their natural resources in order to survive and in the process disregard environmental consequences, everyone on the planet will bear the results.

Summary and Review

WHAT IS SOCIAL STRATIFICATION?
The term **social stratification** refers to a hierarchy of relative privilege based on power, property, and prestige. Every society stratifies its members. p. 129.

SYSTEMS OF SOCIAL STRATIFICATION
What are the four major systems of social stratification?
The four major stratification systems are slavery, caste, clan, and class. The essential characteristic of **slavery** is that some people own other people. Initially, slavery was based not on race but on debt, punishment, or defeat in battle. Slavery could be temporary or permanent, and was not necessarily passed on to one's children. In North America, slaves had no legal rights, and the system was gradually buttressed by a racist ideology. In a **caste system**, status is determined by birth and is lifelong. People marry within their own group and develop rules about ritual pollution. In a **clan system**, people's status depends on lineage that links them to an extended network of relatives. A **class system** is much more open than these other systems, for it is based primarily on money or material possessions. Industrialization encourages the formation of class systems. Gender discrimination cuts across all forms of social stratification. pp. 130–131.

What Determines Social Class?
Karl Marx argued that a single factor determines social class: If you own the **means of production**, you belong to the **bourgeoisie**; if you do not, you are one of the **proletariat**. Max Weber argued that three elements determine social class: *property*, *prestige*, and *power*. pp. 131–133.

What is social class, and how do sociologists measure it?
Most sociologists have adopted Weber's definition of **social class** as a large group of people who rank closely to one another in wealth, power, and prestige. There are three ways to measure social class. In the **subjective method**, people assign themselves their own social class. In the **reputational method**, people identify the social class of others on the basis of knowledge of their circumstances. In the **objective method**, researchers assign subjects to a social class on the basis of objective criteria such as wealth, power, and prestige. p. 134.

THE COMPONENTS OF SOCIAL CLASS
What are the three criteria used to measure social class?
Wealth, power, and prestige are most commonly used to measure social class. **Wealth**, consisting of property and income, is con-

centrated in the upper classes. The distribution of wealth in Canada has changed over the past couple of generations: The richest quintile is receiving a larger share of the country's wealth and the poorest quintile a much smaller share, than they did in the 1940s. **Power** is the ability to carry out one's will, even over the resistance of others. C. Wright Mills coined the term **power elite** to refer to the small group that holds the reins of power in business, government, and the military. **Prestige** is often linked to occupational status. People's rankings of occupational prestige have changed little over the decades and are similar from country to country. Globally, occupations that pay more, require more education and abstract thought, and offer greater autonomy are given greater prestige. pp. 134–138.

What is meant by the term *status inconsistency*?

Status is social ranking. Most people are status-consistent; that is, they rank high or low on all three dimensions of social class. People who rank higher on some dimensions than on others are status-inconsistent. The frustrations of status inconsistency tend to produce political radicalism. pp. 138–139.

WHY IS SOCIAL STRATIFICATION UNIVERSAL?

To explain why stratification is universal, functionalists Kingsley Davis and Wilbert Moore argued that to attract the most capable people to fill its important positions, society must offer them higher rewards. Melvin Tumin criticized this view, arguing that if it were correct, society would be a **meritocracy**, with all positions awarded on the basis of merit. Conflict theorists argue that stratification comes about because resources are limited, and groups struggle against one another for them. Gerhard Lenski suggested a synthesis between the functionalist and conflict perspectives. pp. 139–141.

HOW DO ELITES MAINTAIN SOCIAL INEQUALITY?
How do nations maintain social stratification?

To maintain social stratification within a nation, the ruling class uses an ideology that justifies current arrangements. It also controls information, and, when all else fails, depends on brute force. The social networks of the rich and poor also perpetuate social inequality. pp. 141–142.

GLOBAL STRATIFICATION: THREE WORLDS OF DEVELOPMENT
How are the world's nations stratified?

The model presented here divides the world's nations into three groups: most industrialized, industrializing, and least industrialized. This layering represents relative property, power, and prestige. The oil-rich nations are an exception. pp. 142–144.

HOW THE WORLD'S NATIONS BECAME STRATIFIED
Why are some nations rich and others poor?

The main theories that seek to account for global stratification are **imperialism** and **colonization**, **world system** theory, **dependency theory**, and the **culture of poverty**. pp. 144–145.

MAINTAINING GLOBAL STRATIFICATION
How is global stratification maintained?

There are two basic explanations for why nations remain stratified. **Neocolonialism** is the ongoing dominance of the least industrial-ized nations by the most industrialized nations. The second explanation points to the influence of **multinational corporations**, which operate across national boundaries. The new technology gives further advantage to the most industrialized nations. pp. 146–147.

APPLYING SOCIOLOGICAL MODELS OF SOCIAL CLASS
What models are used to portray the social classes?

Two models that portray the social classes were described. Erik Wright developed a four-class model based on Marx: (1) capitalists or owners; (2) petty bourgeoisie or small business owners; (3) managers; and (4) workers. Gilbert and Kahl developed a six-class model based on Weber. At the top is the capitalist or upper class. In descending order are the upper middle class, the lower middle class, the working class, the working poor, and the **underclass**. pp. 147–149.

CONSEQUENCES OF SOCIAL CLASS
How does social class affect people?

Social class leaves no aspect of life untouched. It affects people's chances of benefiting from the new technology, dying early, becoming ill, receiving good health care, and getting divorced. Class membership also affects child-rearing, educational attainment, religious affiliation, political participation, and contact with the criminal justice system. pp. 150–152.

SOCIAL MOBILITY
What are the three types of social mobility?

The term **intergenerational mobility** refers to changes in social class from one generation to the next. **Exchange mobility** is the movement of large numbers of people from one class to another, with the net result that the relative proportions of the population in the classes remain about the same. The term **structural mobility** refers to social changes that affect the social class membership of large numbers of people. pp. 152–154.

POVERTY
Who are the poor?

Poverty is unequally distributed in Canada. Women, seniors, members of racial and ethnic minorities, the disabled, and children whose primary parents are members of these categories are much more likely to be poor. pp. 154–158.

THE DYNAMICS OF POVERTY
What are individual and structural explanations of poverty?

Some social analysts believe that characteristics of individuals, such as a desire for immediate gratification, cause poverty. Sociologists, in contrast, examine structural features of society, such as employment opportunities, to find the causes of poverty. Sociologists generally conclude that life orientations are a consequence, not the cause, of people's position in the social class structure. pp. 158–161.

How is the Horatio Alger myth functional for society?

The Horatio Alger myth-the belief that anyone can get ahead if only he or she tries hard enough-encourages people to strive to get ahead and deflects blame for failure from society to the individual. pp. 161–162.

Critical Thinking Questions

1. What are some of the differences in opportunities and obstacles encountered by the daughter of a fisher living in Newfoundland, the son of a Saskatchewan grain farmer, the daughter of an auto worker in central Canada, and the children of Canada's most prominent families?

2. How is the system of global stratification maintained or reproduced?

3. Despite the existence of a relatively well-developed social welfare system in Canada, why do poverty and social inequality persist?

Key Terms

bourgeoisie 132
capitalist world economy 145
caste system 131
clan 131
clan system 131
class consciousness 132
class system 131
colonization 144
contradictory class locations 147
culture of poverty 145
deferred gratification 161
dependency theory 145
divine right of kings 141
downward social mobility 152
endogamy 131
exchange mobility 153
false consciousness 132
globalization 145
ideology 130
imperialism 144

indentured service 130
intergenerational mobility 152
means of production 132
meritocracy 140
multinational corporations 146
neocolonialism 146
objective method (of measuring social class) 134
power 137
power elite 137
prestige 137
proletariat 132
reputational method (of measuring social class) 134
slavery 130
social class 134
social mobility 131
social stratification 129
status 138
status consistency 138

status inconsistency 138
structural mobility 153
subjective method (of measuring social class) 134

underclass 149
upward social mobility 152
wealth 135
world system 144

Weblinks

Sociology 206E: Social Stratification

www.mcmaster.ca/socscidocs/206_95.htm
A Web course on social stratification that covers the main types of social inequality, such as class, elites, socioeconomic status, education, income, jobs, gender, and race/ethnicity. The dimensions of inequality are illustrated by case studies. Theoretically grounded in the work of classical writers.

National Anti-Poverty Organization

www.napo-onap.ca/
NAPO is a non-profit, non-partisan organization that represents the interests of low-income Canadians. It was founded in 1971 at Canada's first nationwide poor people's conference.

Poverty in Canada

www.fraserinstitute.ca/publications/books/poverty/
Part of the Books Online feature on the Fraser Institute Web site.

National Council of Welfare

http://www.ncwcnbes.net/
The NCCW was established in 1969 as a citizens' advisory body to the federal government on matters of concern to low-income Canadians.

World Bank

www.worldbank.org
Information on emerging economies and development issues.

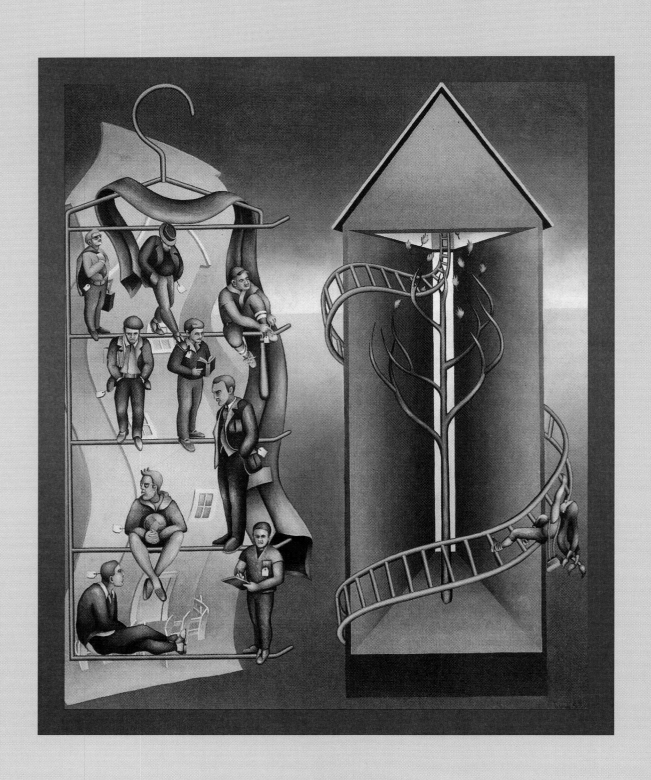

Inequalities of Gender

Learning Outcomes

After you have studied this chapter, you will be able to

■ discuss the overt and hidden ways society is stratified by gender

■ discuss the "nature versus nurture" debate and the ways in which biology and culture may contribute to differences in the behaviours of males and females

■ understand how gender inequality has affected women's chances in education and in the workplace

■ understand how men's dominance and greater access to power is maintained

■ consider the ways in which the worlds of men and women and the experience of gender inequality may be changing

In Tunis, the capital of Tunisia, on Africa's northern coast, I met some postsecondary students, with whom I spent a couple of days. When they said they wanted to see Tunis' red-light district, I wondered if it would be worth the trip. I already had seen other such districts, including the unusual one in Amsterdam where the state licenses the women, requires medical checkups (certificates available for customers to inspect), sets the prices, and pays prostitutes social security at retirement. The women sit behind lighted picture windows while customers, interspersed with tourists and neighbourhood residents, stroll along attractive canalside streets, browsing from the outside.

This time the sight turned my stomach.

We ended up on a narrow street opening onto the Mediterranean. Each side was lined with a row of one-room wooden shacks, the structures touching one another, side wall to side wall. In front of each open door stood a young woman. Peering from outside into the dark interior, I could see a tiny room with a well-worn bed.

The street was crowded with men looking at the women. Many of them wore sailor uniforms from countries that I couldn't identify.

As I looked more closely, I saw runny sores on the legs of some of the women. Incredibly, with such visible evidence of their disease, customers still entered. Evidently the low price (at that time US$2) was too much to resist.

With a sickening feeling to my stomach and the desire to vomit, I kept a good distance between myself and the beckoning women. One tour of the two-block area was more than sufficient.

Out of sight, I knew, was a group of men whose wealth came from these women condemned to a short life punctuated by fear and prolonged by misery.

Issues of Sex and Gender

This chapter examines **gender stratification**—males' and females' unequal access to power, prestige, and property on the basis of sex. Gender stratification is especially significant because it cuts across *all* aspects of social life. No matter what our social class, age, racial or ethnic classification, we are labelled *male* or *female*. The images and expectations attached to these labels guide our behaviour in everyday life. They are especially significant in determining power and privilege. In this chapter's fascinating journey, we shall look at inequality between the sexes in Canada, and to some extent around the world. We shall review such topics as whether it is biology or culture that makes us the way we are, sexual harassment, unequal pay, and violence against women. This excursion will provide a good context for understanding the power differences between men and women that lead to such situations as that just described above. It should also give you insight into your own experiences with gender.

When we consider how females and males differ, the first thing that usually comes to mind is **sex**, the biological characteristics that distinguish males and females. *Primary sex characteristics* consist of a vagina or a penis and other organs related to reproduction; *secondary sex characteristics* are the physical distinctions between males and females that are not directly connected with reproduction. Secondary sex characteristics become clearly evident at puberty when males develop more muscles, a lower voice, and more hair and height while females form more fatty tissue, broader hips, and larger breasts.

Gender, in contrast, is a *social*, not a biological characteristic. Gender varies from one society to another, for it is what a group considers proper for its males and females. Whereas sex refers to male or female, *gender* refers to masculinity or femininity. In short, you inherit your sex, but you learn your gender as you are socialized into behaviours and attitudes thought appropriate for your sex.

The sociological significance of gender is that it is a device by which society controls its members. Gender sorts us, on the basis of sex, into different life experiences. It opens and closes access to power, property, and even prestige. Like social class, gender is a structural feature of society. Cassie Campbell, a member of the Canadian national women's ice hockey team, declares, "I hate the words *feminine* and *masculine,* because who is the person who decides? Who decides who's more feminine than someone and who's more masculine....It's important to be yourself and at the same time know you can go to the gym and sweat. That's okay" (quoted in Doren & Jones, 2000, p. 97).

Before examining inequalities of gender, let's consider why men and women act differently. Are they, perhaps, just born that way?

Biology or Culture? The Continuing Controversy

Why are most males more aggressive than most females? Why do women enter "nurturing" occupations such as nursing in far greater numbers than men? To answer such questions, many people respond with some variation of

Despite the great strides women have made in the work force, there are still many "male" work roles in which society does not easily accept them.

"They're just born that way" or "They have the right characteristics for the job."

Is this the correct answer? Certainly biology is an extremely significant part of our lives. Each of us begins as a fertilized egg. The egg, or ovum, is contributed by our mother, the sperm that fertilizes the egg by our father. At the very moment the egg is fertilized, our sex is determined. Each of us receives 23 pairs of chromosomes from the ovum and 23 from the sperm. The egg has an X chromosome. If the sperm that fertilizes the egg also has an X chromosome, we become female (XX). If the sperm has a Y chromosome, we become male (XY).

That's the biology. Now, the sociological question is: Do these biological differences control our behaviours? Do they, for example, make females more nurturing and males more aggressive and domineering? Almost all sociologists take the side of "nurture" in this "nature versus nurture" controversy, but a few do not, as you can see from the Thinking Critically about Social Controversy sections that follow.

The Dominant Position in Sociology

The dominant sociological position is represented by the symbolic interactionists. They stress that the visible differences of sex do not come with meanings built into them. Rather, each human group determines what these physical differences mean to its members, and on that basis assigns males and females to separate groups. Here, people learn contrasting expectations of life and, on the basis of their sex, are given different access to their society's privileges.

Thinking Critically about Social Controversy

Biology Versus Culture: Culture Is the Answer

For sociologist Cynthia Fuchs Epstein (1986, 1988, 1989), differences between males' and females' behaviour are solely the result of social factors—specifically, socialization and social control. Her argument is as follows:

1. A re-examination of the anthropological record shows greater equality between the sexes in the past than we had thought. In earlier societies, women as well as men hunted small game, made tools for hunting and gathering, and gathered food. Studies of today's hunting and gathering societies show that "both women's and men's roles have been broader and less rigid than those created by stereotypes. For example, the Agta and Mbuti are clearly egalitarian and thus prove that hunting and gathering societies exist in which women are not subordinate to men. Anthropologists who study them claim that there is a separate but equal status of women at this level of development."

2. The types of work that men and women perform in each society are determined not by biology but by social arrangements. Few people, whether male or female, can escape these arrangements and almost everyone works within their allotted narrow range. This gender inequality of work, which serves the interests of men, is enforced by informal customs and formal laws. When these socially constructed barriers are removed, women's work habits are similar to those of men.

3. The human behaviours that biology "causes" are limited to those involving reproduction or differences in body structure. These differences are relevant for only a few activities, such as playing basketball or "crawling through a small space."

4. Female crime rates, which are rising in many parts of the world, indicate that aggression, often considered a biologically dictated male behaviour, is related instead to social rather than biological factors. When social conditions permit, such as when women become lawyers, they also exhibit "adversarial, assertive, and dominant behaviour." Not incidentally, this "dominant behaviour" also appears in scholarly female challenges to the biased views about human nature that have been proposed by male scholars.

In short, rather than "women's incompetence or inability to read a legal brief, perform brain surgery, [or] to predict a bull market," social factors—socialization, gender discrimination, and other forms of social control—are responsible for gender differences in behaviour. Arguments that assign "an evolutionary and genetic basis" to explain differences in sex status are simplistic. They "rest on a dubious structure of inappropriate, highly selective, and poor data, oversimplification in logic and in inappropriate inferences by use of analogy."

Sociologist Steven Goldberg (1974, 1986, 1993) finds it astonishing that anyone should doubt "the presence of core-deep differences in males and females, differences of temperament and emotion we call masculinity and femininity." Goldberg's argument, that it is not environment but inborn differences that "give masculine and feminine direction to the emotions and behaviors of men and women," is as follows:

1. The anthropological record shows that all societies for which evidence exists are (or were) **patriarchies** (societies in which men dominate women). Stories about long-lost **matriarchies** (societies in which women dominate men) are myths.

2. In all societies, past and present, the highest statuses are associated with males. In every society, politics is ruled by "hierarchies overwhelmingly dominated by men."

3. The reason why men dominate societies is that they "have a lower threshold for the elicitation of dominance behavior...a greater tendency to exhibit whatever behavior is necessary in any environment to attain dominance in hierarchies and male-female encounters and relationships." Men are more willing "to sacrifice the rewards of other motivations—the desire for affection, health, family life, safety, relaxation, vacation and the like—in order to attain dominance and status."

4. Just as a six-foot woman does not prove the social basis of height, so exceptional individuals, such as a highly achieving and dominant woman, do not refute "the physiological roots of behavior."

In short, only one interpretation of why every society from that of the Pygmy to that of the Swede associates dominance and attainment with males is valid. Male dominance of society is "an inevitable resolution of the psychophysiological reality." Socialization and social institutions merely *reflect*—and sometimes exaggerate—inborn tendencies. Any interpretation other than inborn differences is "wrongheaded, ignorant, tendentious, internally illogical, discordant with the evidence, and implausible in the extreme." The argument that males are more aggressive because they have been socialized that way is the equivalent of a claim that men can grow moustaches because boys have been socialized that way.

To acknowledge this reality is *not* to defend discrimination against women. Whether one approves of what societies have done with these basic biological differences is not the point. The point is that biology leads males and females to different behaviours and attitudes—regardless of how we feel about this or wish it were different.

Most sociologists find the argument compelling that if biology were the principal factor in human behaviour, around the world we would find women to be one sort of person and men another. In fact, however, ideas of gender—and resulting male-female behaviour—vary greatly from one culture to another. The Tahitians in the South Pacific provide a remarkable contrast to what we expect of gender. They don't give their children names that are identifiable as male or female, and they expect both men and women to be passive, yielding, and to ignore slights. The result of their socialization into gender is reported to be a gentle people where neither men nor women are competitive in trying to attain material possessions (Gilmore, 1990; see Adams, 1997).

Opening the Door to Biology

The matter of "nature versus nurture" is not so easily settled, however, and some sociologists who take the "nurture" side still acknowledge that biological factors may be involved in some human behaviour other than reproduction and child-bearing. Alice Rossi, for example, a feminist sociologist and former president of the American Sociological Association, has suggested that women are better prepared biologically for "mothering" than men. She (1977, 1984) says that women are more sensitive to stimuli such as the infant's soft skin and nonverbal communications. Her basic point is that the issue is not biology or society; it is that nature provides biological predispositions, which are then overlaid with culture (see Renzetti & Curran, 1992).

This argument is supported by the events surrounding a bizarre medical accident.

A Medical Accident. The drama began in 1963, when seven-month-old identical twins were taken to a doctor to be circumcised (Money & Ehrhardt, 1972). The inept physician, who was using electrocautery (a heated needle), turned the electric current too high and accidentally burned off the penis of one of the boys. You can imagine the parents' reaction of disbelief—followed by horror as the truth sank in.

What can be done in a situation like this? The damage was irreversible. The parents were told that the child could never have sexual relations. After months of soul-wrenching agonies and tearful consultations with experts, the parents decided that their son should have a sex change operation. When he was 17 months old, surgeons used the boy's own skin to construct a vagina. The parents then gave the child a girl's name, dressed him in frilly clothing, let his hair grow long, and began to treat him as a girl. Later, physicians gave the child female steroids to promote female pubertal growth.

At first the results were extremely promising. When the twins were 4½ years old, the mother described her daughter as "neat and tidy," "very proud" of her appearance, dainty, and "quite different" from her son (Money & Ehrhardt, 1972).

About a year later, the mother described how their daughter imitated her while their son copied his father:

> I found that my son, he chose very masculine things like a fireman or a policeman.... He wanted to do what daddy does, work where daddy does, and carry a lunch kit. ... And [my daughter] didn't want any of those things. She wants to be a doctor or a teacher.... But none of the things that she ever wanted to be were like a policeman or a fireman, and that sort of thing never appealed to her (Money & Ehrhardt, 1972).

If the matter were this clear-cut, we could use this case to conclude that gender is entirely up to nurture. Seldom are things in life so simple, however, and a twist occurs in this story. In spite of this promising start and her parents' coaching, the twin whose sex had been reassigned did not adapt well to femininity. She rejected dolls and tried to urinate standing up. Classmates called her a "cavewoman" because she walked like a boy (Diamond, 1982). At age 14, in despair over her inner turmoil, she tried to commit suicide. In a tearful confrontation, her father told her about the accident and her sex change. She then chose to stop her hormone therapy, and later had extensive surgery to partially reconstruct a penis. At age 25 he married a woman and adopted her children (Gorman, 1997a; "Sexual Identity Is Inborn Trait," 1997; Wente, 2000).

In another high-profile case, following a successful sex-change operation, Canadian Army Sergeant Sylvia Durand declared, "This is a rebirth. I feel the way I should have felt at my birth. I'm at peace with myself" (quoted in Peritz, 2000).

In Sum

We shall have to await further studies, but what has been published so far is intriguing, indicating that some behaviour we sociologists usually assume to be due entirely to socialization is, in fact, also influenced by biology. The findings are preliminary, but extremely significant. In the years to come, this should prove to be an exciting—and controversial—area of sociological research. One stage will be to document differences that are clearly due to biology. The second stage, of much greater sociological significance, is, in sociologist Janet Chafetz' (1990, p. 30) phrase, to determine "how 'different' becomes translated into 'unequal.'"

Focus Question

What are some of the main arguments in support of the position that differences between males' and females' behaviour are the result of biological factors?

Gender Inequality in Global Perspective

Some analysts speculate that in hunting and gathering societies women and men were social equals (Leacock, 1981; Hendrix, 1994). Apparently, horticultural societies also had much less gender discrimination than our contemporary world does (Collins, Chafetz, Blumberg, Coltrane, & Turner, 1993). In these societies, women may have been equal partners with men. They may even have contributed about 60 percent of the group's total food. Yet, after reviewing the historical record, historian and feminist Gerda Lerner (1986) concluded "there is not a single society known where women-as-a-group have decision-making power over men (as a group)."

Let's have a brief overview of some of this inequality.

Sex Typing of Work

Anthropologist George Murdock (1937), who surveyed 324 premodern societies around the world, found that in all of them activities are **sex-typed**; in other words, every society associates activities with one sex or the other. He also found that activities considered "female" in one society could be considered "male" in another. In some groups, for example, taking care of cattle is women's work, while other groups assign this task to men.

Metalworking was the exception, being men's work in all the societies examined. Three other pursuits—making weapons, pursuing sea mammals, and hunting—were almost universally the domain of men. In a few societies,

Anthropologist George Murdock surveyed 324 traditional societies worldwide. He found that all of them considered some work "men's" and other work "women's." An example of such sex typing of work is shown in this photo of a Quechuan Indian mother and daughter in Cotopaxi Province of Ecuador. The Quechuan Indians consider hoeing "women's work." This photo also illustrates the remarkable power of socialization across generations.

however, women participated in these activities. Although Murdock found no specific work that was universally assigned to women, he did find that making clothing, cooking, carrying water, and grinding grain were almost always female tasks. In a few societies, however, such activities were regarded as men's work.

From Murdock's cross-cultural survey, we can conclude that nothing about biology requires men and women to be assigned different work. Anatomy does not have to equal destiny when it comes to occupations, for as we have seen, pursuits considered feminine in one society may be deemed masculine in another, and vice versa.

Prestige of Work

You might ask whether this division of labour really illustrates social inequality. Does it perhaps simply represent arbitrary forms of dividing up labour, rather than gender discrimination?

That could be the case, except for this finding: *Universally, greater prestige is given to male activities—regardless of what those activities are* (Linton, 1936; Rosaldo, 1974; Ashford, 2001). If taking care of goats is men's work, then the care of goats is considered important and carries high prestige, but if it is women's work, it is considered less important and given less prestige. Or, to take an example closer to home, when delivering babies was "women's work" and done by midwives, it was given low prestige. But when men took over this task, its prestige increased sharply (Ehrenreich & English, 1973). Similarly, when women began to outnumber men as bank tellers and as office workers, wages, along with the prestige accorded these occupations, declined (Lowe, 1987). In short, it is not the work that provides the prestige, but the sex with which the work is associated.

Other Areas of Global Discrimination

Let's briefly consider four additional areas of global gender discrimination. Later, when we focus on Canada, we shall examine these same areas in greater detail.

Education. The following statistics illustrate how extensively females are discriminated against in education: Approximately one billion adults around the world cannot read; two-thirds are women. About 130 million children are not enrolled in grade school; 70 percent are girls (Ashford, 1995). Worldwide, 80 percent of men, compared with 64 percent of women, are literate (Ashford, 2001). While the gender gap in school enrollments closed somewhat during the 1990s, in less developed countries in particular, girls are more likely to quit (or be pressured to quit) school, often for family-related reasons (Ashford, 2001).

Politics. That women lack equal access to national decision-making can be illustrated by this global fact: In no national legislature in the entire world are there as many women as there are men. In 1999 worldwide, women held only 11 percent of seats in parliaments or congresses, and in some countries today, women cannot even vote. In most nations, as in Canada, women hold a minority of national legislative seats (Ashford, 2001).

The Pay Gap. In every nation, women average less pay than men. Despite years of trying to close the gendered pay gap, on average, women in Canada earn less than 73 cents for every dollar earned by Canadian males, while in Bangladesh women make only half of what men earn (Ashford, 2001; Drolet, 2002). Multi-country studies indicate that women usually face the stressful situation of dual responsibilities of work both outside and inside the home. In more developed countries, for example, women spend between 50 and 70 percent as much time as men on paid work, but they spend twice as much time (or more) on unpaid family and household work (Ashford, 2001).

Violence Against Women. A global human rights issue is violence against women (Crossman, 1995). Perhaps the most infamous historical examples are foot binding in China, suttee (burning the living widow with her dead husband's body) in India, and witch burning in

Violence against women has taken many forms throughout history. One of the most ferocious was suttee, in which a living widow was cremated with her dead husband. This painting by Aldo Torchio depicts the riot that ensued at Rajadhar, India, in 1851 when the British police tried to prevent a suttee.

Europe. Rape, wife beating, forced prostitution (as was likely the case in our opening vignette), female infanticide, and female circumcision are prevalent forms of extreme violence against women.

Gender Inequality in Theoretical Perspective

Around the world, gender is *the* primary division between people. Every society sets up barriers to provide unequal access to power, property, and prestige on the basis of sex. Consequently, sociologists classify females as a **minority group**. Because females outnumber males, you may think this strange, but since this term refers to people who are discriminated against on the basis of physical or cultural characteristics, this concept applies to females (Hacker, 1951). For an overview of gender discrimination in a changing society, see the Perspectives box below.

What is the origin of discrimination against women? Let's consider a popular theory. It assumes that patriarchy is universal and, accordingly, to explain its origin it looks to universal conditions—biological factors coupled with social factors.

Childbirth and Social Experiences

This theory points out social consequences of the biology of human reproduction (Lerner, 1986; Friedl, 1990). In early human history, life was short, and to reproduce the human group, many children had to be born. Because only females get pregnant, carry a child nine months, give birth, and nurse, women were limited in activities for a considerable part of their lives. To survive, an infant needed a nursing mother. With a child at her breast or in her uterus, or one carried on her hip or on her back, a woman was physically encumbered. Consequently, around the world women assumed tasks associated with the home and child care, while men took over the hunting of large animals and other tasks that required greater speed and absence from the base camp for longer periods of time (Huber, 1990).

As a consequence, males became dominant. It was the men who left camp to hunt animals, who made contact with other tribes, who traded with these other groups, and who quarreled and waged war with them. It was also men who made and controlled the instruments of death, the weapons used for hunting and warfare. It was they who accumulated possessions in trade and gained prestige by triumphantly returning with prisoners of war or with large animals to feed the tribe. In contrast, little prestige was given to the ordinary, routine, taken-for-granted activities of women—who were not seen as risking their lives for the group. Eventually, men took over society. Their weapons, items of trade, and knowledge gained from contact with other groups became sources of power. Women were transformed into second-class citizens, subject to men's decisions.

Perspectives

Cultural Diversity Around the World: Women in China

Mao, the leader of China's 1949 Communist revolution, is often quoted as saying that women hold up half the sky. By this, he meant that women are as important as men. One of the revolution's goals was to free women from their traditional low status.

Although women never did become the social equals of men, their status under Mao did improve. Today, with China's cautious transition to capitalism, however, the situation of women is deteriorating.

For the first time, factory managers are under pressure to produce a profit. Under the old system, production without profit was the norm: Managers were assigned production goals and given the workers to meet those goals. Now the managers say that with maternity leaves and the requirement that they provide child care centres and rooms for nursing mothers, women workers are more expensive than men. Consequently, women have become the last hired and first fired.

Women are also being encouraged to enter "traditional" women's occupations, which are the least skilled and pay less. Working as nurses, nursery school teachers, grade school teachers, and street sweepers, women are among the least skilled workers and, as such, are poorly paid. Responding to international criticism, China passed a law that guarantees equality for women in employment, education, housing, and property rights. The flaw? There is no mechanism to enforce it. It remains a piece of propaganda.

Westernized ideas have begun to pervade the culture, as is illustrated by an emphasis on appearance rather than on skills. In an adaptation of Western-style advertising, scantily clad women are shown perched on top of sports cars. A new cosmetic surgery industry has sprung up to give Chinese women Western-looking eyes, stencilled eyebrows, and bigger breasts.

While adopting new Westernized ideas of beauty, parts of China maintain a centuries-long tradition of bride-selling. In this blend of old and new worlds, women are commodities for men's consumption. Yet, behind the scenes women have formed study groups. Without slogans or drawing public attention, which could be dangerous, a woman's movement is emerging. As in the West, the political struggle must begin with a changed consciousness of one's status.

Sources: Sun (1993); Chen (1995).

Evaluating the Theory

Does this theory adequately explain women's second-class status? Remember that the answer lies buried in human history, and there is no way of testing it. Male dominance may be due to some entirely different cause.

Another theory, proposed by anthropologist Marvin Harris (1977) argued that universal physical differences between men and women together with universal social conditions account for patriarchy. In other words, because men are more often stronger and larger than women and because hand-to-hand combat was the key to survival for most tribal groups, men were coaxed to become warriors with the promise of rewards for their bravery or with the threat of punishment for their refusal. Ultimately, to entice them to do battle, warriors were rewarded with females for their bravery. For this system to work, it was essential that all women, even those who were as strong as or stronger than some men, be excluded from combat. From birth, men were prepared for their roles in combat while women were socialized into submissiveness.

Frederick Engels' explanation of women's inequality also proposed that social conditions or social structure contributed to women's inequality. He argued that patriarchy (male dominance of a society) developed with the origin of private property (Lerner, 1986). He could not explain why private property should have produced patriarchy, however. Gerda Lerner (1986) suggests that patriarchy may even have had different origins in different places. Whatever its origins, support for patriarchy has been interwoven with culture, custom, ideology, and practice. A closed, circular system of thought evolved. Men developed notions of their own inherent superiority, based on the evidence of their dominant position in society. They then consolidated their power, enshrouded many of their activities with secrecy, and constructed elaborate rules and rituals to avoid "contamination" by the females, whom they openly deemed inferior. Even today, patriarchy is always surrounded with cultural supports to justify male dominance.

As tribal societies developed into larger groups, men, enjoying their power and privileges, maintained their dominance. Long after hunting and hand-to-hand combat ceased to be routine, and even after large numbers of children were no longer needed to reproduce the human group, men held onto their power. Male dominance in contemporary societies, then, is a continuation of a millennia-old pattern whose origin is lost in history.

Focus Question
How do theorists explain women's inequality and male dominance?

Gender Inequality in Canada

Rather than it being some accidental, hit-or-miss affair, the institutions of every society work together to maintain the group's particular forms of inequality. Custom, venerated by history, both justifies and maintains arrangements of gender inequality. Although men have resisted sharing their privileged positions with women, changes are occurring.

Fighting Back: The Rise of Feminism

To see how far we have come, it is useful to see where we used to be. In early Canadian society, the second-class status of women was taken for granted. A husband and wife were legally one person—him (Chafetz & Dworkin, 1986). Women who worked for wages could not even collect their own paycheques—single women were often required to hand them over to their fathers; married women, to their husbands. Women could not serve on juries; nor could they vote, make legal contracts, or hold property in their own name. These conditions were generally seen as part of the *proper* relations of the sexes. How could times have changed so much that such conditions sound like fiction?

A central lesson of conflict theory is that power yields tremendous privilege; that, like a magnet, it draws to the elite the best resources available. Because men held tenaciously onto their privileges and used social institutions to maintain their position, basic rights for women came only through prolonged and bitter struggle (Offen, 1990).

Focus Question
How is patriarchy defined and, according to Engels, how is it supported or maintained?

Feminism, the view that biology is not destiny, and that, therefore, stratification by gender is wrong and should be resisted, met strong opposition—both by men who had privilege to lose and by many women who accepted their status as morally correct. In Great Britain and the United States, for example, women had to directly confront men, who first denied them the right to speak and then ridiculed them when they persisted in speaking in public. Leaders of the feminist movement, then known as *suffragists*, chained themselves to posts and to the iron grillwork of public buildings—and then went on protesting while the police sawed them loose. When imprisoned, they continued to protest by going on hunger strikes. Threatened by such determination and confrontations, men spat on demonstrators for daring to question their place, slapped their faces, tripped them, pelted them with burning cigar stubs, and hurled obscenities at them (J. Cowley, 1969).

Unlike its counterparts in Britain and the United States, where suffragists adopted militant tactics, the "first wave" of the Canadian women's movement was regarded as a war of words. One of the most outspoken suffragists was Nellie McClung, whose passionate statements were strong and compelling.

Although heavily influenced by developments in the United States and Britain, the Canadian women's movement may be characterized as a war of words. The militant tactics of British and American suffragists were not adopted by Canadian feminists, who instead employed a relatively peaceful approach. The Canadian movement upheld Nellie McClung's motto: "Never retract, never explain, never apologize, get the thing done and let them howl" (cited in S. J. Wilson, 1991). These words were strong and compelling, yet moderate. While they may have offended some aspects of the prevailing social etiquette prescribed for women, they were not suggestive of a radical departure from conventional social norms.

This "first wave" of the women's movement had a conservative branch that concentrated on winning the vote for women and a radical branch that wanted to reform all the institutions of society (Chafetz & Dworkin, 1986). Both groups worked toward winning the right to vote, but after the vote was won in 1917 in Canada (and in 1920 in the United States), many declared that the movement had achieved its ultimate purpose, and some argue that this victory left the movement with no unifying goal. However, women continued to struggle for change, by working to establish their voice and presence in trade unions, at the workplace, within the political process, through the courts, and in educational institutions. Every victory was hailed, but feminists realized that barriers to women's social and economic equality, including attitudes and beliefs about women's status and rights, would not be easily changed.

The "second wave" began in the 1960s. Sociologist Janet Chafetz (1990) points out that up to this time most women thought of work as a temporary activity to fill the time between completing school and getting married. When larger numbers of women began to enter the labour force, however, they began to compare their working conditions with those of men. This shift in reference group created a different view of working conditions, launching a "second wave" of protest and struggle against gender inequalities. The goals of this second wave are broad—from changing work roles to changing policies on violence against women.

This second wave is also broken into liberal and conservative factions. Although each holds a different picture of what gender equality should look like, they share several goals, including nondiscrimination in job opportunities and pay. Both liberals and conservatives have a radical wing. The radicals on the liberal side call for hostility toward men, while radicals on the conservative side call for a return to traditional family roles. All factions—whether radical or conservative—claim to represent the "real" needs of today's women. It is from these claims and counterclaims that the women's movement will continue to take shape and affect public policy.

Although women enjoy fundamental rights today, gender inequality continues to play a central role in social life. In some instances, it can even be a life-and-death matter, as with the medical situations discussed in the Down-to-Earth Sociology box that follows.

Let's now look at gender relations in education and everyday life, and then, in greater detail, at discrimination in the world of work.

Gender Inequality in Education

In education, too, a glimpse at the past sheds light on the present. About a century ago, leading educators claimed that women's wombs dominated their minds. This made higher education a burden on women's frail capacities. Dr. Edward Clarke, of Harvard University's medical faculty, expressed the dominant (nineteenth century) sentiment this way:

> A girl upon whom Nature, for a limited period and for a definite purpose, imposes so great a physiological task, will not have as much power left for the tasks of school, as the boy of whom Nature requires less at the corresponding epoch (cited in Andersen, 1988).

Because women were so much weaker, Clarke urged them to study only one-third as much as young men—and not to study at all during menstruation.

Over 200 years ago, in 1792, Mary Wollstonecraft, who is best known among the early feminists, published *A Vindication of the Rights of Woman*, in which she discussed male power as the underlying cause of society's problems (Mackie, 1991, p. 252). She believed that education was the key to liberate both men and women. Although she was heavily criticized as a man-hating crusader, her ideas on the importance of education in contributing to women's equality were not only subsequently echoed by John Stuart Mill and other historical thinkers, but also became part of the foundation of the suffrage movements.

Medical researchers were perplexed. Reports were coming in from all over the country indicating that women, who live longer than men, were twice as likely to die after coronary bypass surgery. Researchers at Cedars-Sinai Medical Center in Los Angeles checked their own hospital's records. They found that of almost 2300 coronary bypass patients, 4.6 percent of the women died as a result of the surgery, compared with only 2.6 percent of the men.

These findings presented a sociological puzzle. To solve it, medical researchers first turned to an answer based on biology. In coronary bypass surgery, a blood vessel is taken from one part of the body and stitched to a coronary artery on the surface of the heart. Perhaps this operation was more difficult to perform on women because of their smaller coronary arteries. To find out,

researchers measured the amount of time surgeons kept patients on the heart-lung machine while they operated. They were surprised to learn that women spent less time on the machine than men, indicating that the operation was not more difficult to perform on women.

As the researchers probed, a surprising answer unfolded—unintended sexual discrimination. Referring physicians had not taken the chest pains of their women patients as seriously as those of their men patients. Physicians, it turned out, were 10 times more likely to give men exercise stress tests and radioactive heart scans. They also sent men to surgery on the basis of abnormal stress tests but waited until women showed clear-cut symptoms of coronary heart disease before sending them to surgery. Being referred for surgery after the disease is further along decreases the chances of survival.

Other researchers wondered if the sex of the physician matters when it comes to ordering Pap smears and mammography. They examined the records of 98 000 patients and found that it does make a difference—women physicians are much more likely to order these screening tests.

For Your Consideration

In short, gender bias is so pervasive that it operates beneath our level of awareness and so severe that it can even be a matter of life or death. It is important to note that the doctors are unaware that they are discriminating. They have no intention of doing so. In what ways does gender bias affect your own perceptions and behaviour?

Sources: Bishop (1990); Lurie, Slater, McGovern, Ekstrum, Quam, & Margolis (1993).

According to Marlene Mackie (1991), the problem of access to higher education was the spark that initiated the Canadian suffrage movement. In the 1860s, schoolteacher Emily Stowe found herself supporting her disabled husband and their three children. Although she managed to save enough money to study medicine, Canadian medical schools denied her admission because of her gender. Eventually she was admitted to an American medical school, and upon her return, she became Canada's first female physician. She continued to struggle with others for the acceptance of women in the professions. As a result, the University of Toronto finally began to admit women in 1886.

Over the years, the situation gradually improved, but discrimination persisted. Through the 1960s, for example, girls were not welcome in shop classes, which were reserved for boys. Instead, they were routed to home economics, considered appropriate for their station in life. (Even today, whenever I attend Toronto Raptors basketball games, I still see an organized group of women, at times scantily clad in short, brightly coloured outfits, wildly cheering from the sidelines. There is no such group of young men leading organized cheers within the WNBA.)

The situation has so changed from what it used to be, however, that some measures of education make it look as though discrimination may be directed against males. For example, more women than men are enrolled in Canadian universities, and women now earn almost 59 percent of all

bachelor's and first professional degrees (Statistics Canada, 2000, Table 37, p. 139).

Probing below the surface, as Table 7.1 reveals, however, degrees follow gender, thus reinforcing male-female distinctions. Extremes at the bachelor's level highlight gender tracking: Men earn 80 percent of bachelor's degrees in engineering and 79 percent in computer science, both considered "masculine" fields, while women are awarded 93 percent of bachelor's degrees in nursing, 85 percent in social work, and 75 percent in languages, traditionally "feminine" fields (Statistics Canada, 2000, Table 37, pp. 136–139). Because gender socialization gives men and women different orientations to life, they enter higher education with gender-linked aspirations. It is this socialization—rather than any presumed innate characteristics—that channels them into different educational paths.

If we follow students into graduate school, with each passing year the proportion of women decreases. Table 7.2 gives us a snapshot of doctoral degrees granted in Canada. Note how accomplishments (doctorates earned) are gender-linked. In all but one of these doctoral programs, men outnumber women, and in *all* of them women are less likely to complete the doctorate. It is significant that the two programs women are least likely to take are considered masculine endeavours, and the one program (education) in which women outnumber men is traditionally regarded as a female-dominated field.

Table 7.1 Bachelor's and First Professional Degrees Granted, by Field of Study and Gender, 1992–1998 (percentage per distribution)

Field of Study	1992 Men	1992 Women	1994 Men	1994 Women	1996 Men	1996 Women	1998 Men	1998 Women
Agricultural and Biological Sciences								
Agriculture	52	48	48	52	43	57	43	57
Biology	45	55	43	57	43	57	40	60
Household science	8	92	7	93	8	92	8	92
Veterinary medicine	37	63	35	65	32	68	31	69
Zoology	43	57	48	52	42	58	32	68
Other	51	49	53	47	51	49	46	54
Total	**41**	**59**	**39**	**61**	**40**	**60**	**37**	**63**
Education								
Education	26	74	26	74	25	75	26	74
Physical education	49	51	48	52	47	53	43	57
Total	**30**	**70**	**30**	**70**	**29**	**71**	**29**	**71**
Engineering and Applied Science								
Architecture	66	34	63	37	65	35	65	35
Landscape architecture	44	56	53	47	48	52	51	49
Engineering	86	14	84	16	81	19	80	20
Forestry	84	16	80	20	76	24	75	25
Total	**84**	**16**	**82**	**18**	**80**	**20**	**79**	**21**
Fine and Applied Arts	**35**	**65**	**34**	**66**	**35**	**65**	**33**	**67**
Health Professions								
Dental studies	62	38	59	41	57	43	56	44
Medical studies	56	44	54	46	49	51	51	49
Nursing	5	95	5	95	6	94	7	93
Pharmacy	36	64	38	62	38	62	35	65
Rehabilitative medicine	15	85	17	83	19	81	22	78
Other	43	57	38	62	38	62	36	64
Total	**29**	**71**	**29**	**71**	**27**	**73**	**28**	**72**
Humanities								
History	53	47	50	50	52	48	51	49
Languages	24	76	25	75	26	74	25	75
Other	44	56	45	55	46	54	44	56
Total	**36**	**64**	**36**	**64**	**37**	**63**	**36**	**64**
Mathematics and Physical Sciences								
Chemistry	64	36	58	42	53	47	56	44
Geology	75	25	68	32	62	38	63	37
Mathematics	58	42	60	40	58	42	56	44
Computer science	78	22	78	22	78	22	79	21
Physics	85	15	81	19	77	23	78	22
Other	64	36	54	46	56	44	67	33
Total	**70**	**30**	**69**	**31**	**68**	**32**	**69**	**31**
Social Sciences								
Business, management, and commerce	53	47	53	47	52	48	51	49
Economics	68	32	65	35	63	37	60	40
Geography	58	42	57	43	58	42	55	45
Law	48	52	48	52	48	52	47	53
Political science	56	44	55	45	53	47	52	48
Psychology	23	77	22	78	23	77	22	78
Social work	16	84	16	84	16	84	15	85
Sociology	26	74	26	74	25	75	24	76
Other	40	60	38	62	37	63	38	62
Total	**45**	**55**	**43**	**57**	**41**	**59**	**40**	**60**
Not reported	**35**	**65**	**33**	**67**	**33**	**67**	**35**	**65**
Grand Total	**43**	**57**	**42**	**58**	**41**	**59**	**41**	**59**

Source: Statistics Canada, *Education in Canada: A Statistical Review*, 2000, Table 41, p. 153, Catalogue No. 81-229.

Table 7.2 Doctorates Earned, by Field of Study and Gender, 1992–1998 (percentage per distribution)

Field of Study	1992		1994		1996		1998	
	Men	Women	Men	Women	Men	Women	Men	Women
Agriculture and biological sciences	72	28	71	29	64	36	64	36
Education	46	54	45	55	40	60	39	61
Engineering and applied sciences	89	11	93	7	89	11	89	11
Fine and applied arts	52	48	60	40	58	42	60	40
Health professions	59	41	60	40	56	44	57	43
Humanities	62	38	59	41	55	45	56	44
Mathematics and physical sciences	83	17	82	18	82	18	78	22
Social sciences	56	44	57	43	57	43	51	49
Not reported	69	31	51	49	61	39	37	63
Total	68	32	69	31	66	34	64	36

Source: Statistics Canada, *Education in Canada*, 2000, Table 41, p. 153, Catalogue No. 81-229.

If we follow those who earn doctoral degrees back into colleges and universities, we find gender stratification in both prestige and income. Throughout Canada, women are less likely to be full professors, the highest, most prestigious rank. It is important also to note that full professors are paid more than the lower ranks (instructor, assistant professor, and associate professor). To see the extent of the stratification, we can note that even when women are full professors, they average less pay than men who are full professors (Canadian Education Statistics Council, 2000).

Some encouraging changes are taking place in higher education. Although we are still a long way from equality, the proportion of professional degrees earned by women has increased sharply. In Canada today, women constitute almost half of all graduates in medical studies and research and are studying dentistry in increasing numbers. In addition, women are now the majority among graduates in two previously male-dominated professional fields, pharmacy and veterinary medicine, outnumbering their male counterparts by almost 2 to 1. (See Table 7.1.)

Gender Inequality in Everyday Life

Of the many aspects of gender discrimination in everyday life that could be examined, we have space to look only at two: the general devaluation of femininity and male dominance of conversation.

General Devaluation of Things Feminine

Leaning against the water cooler, two men—both minor executives—are nursing their cups of coffee, discussing last Sunday's game, postponing for as long as possible the moment when work must finally be faced.

A vice-president walks by and hears them talking about sports. Does he stop and send them back to their desks? Does he frown? Probably not. Being a man, he is far more likely to pause and join in the conversation, anxious to prove that he, too, is "one of the boys," feigning an interest in football that he may very well not share at all. These men—all men in the office—are his troops, his comrades-in-arms.

Now, let's assume that two women are standing by the water cooler discussing whatever you please: women's liberation, clothes, work, any subject—except football, of course. The vice-president walks by, sees them, and moves down the hall in a fury, cursing and wondering whether it is worth the trouble to complain—but to whom?—about all those bitches standing around gabbing when they should be working. "Don't they know," he will ask, in the words of a million men, "that this is an office?" (Korda, 1973, pp. 20–21).

As indicated in this scenario, women's capacities, interests, attitudes, and contributions are not taken as seriously as those of men. Masculinity is valued more highly, for it represents success and strength; while femininity is devalued, for it is perceived as failure and weakness (Schur, 1984).

During World War II, sociologist Samuel Stouffer noted the general devaluation of things feminine. In his classic study of combat soldiers, *The American Soldier*, Stouffer reported that officers used feminine terms as insults to motivate soldiers (Stouffer et al., 1949). To show less-than-expected courage or endurance was to risk the charge of not being a man. An officer might say, "Whatsa matter, Bud—got lace on your drawers?" A generation later, to prepare soldiers to fight in Vietnam, accusations of femininity were still used as motivating insults. Drill sergeants would mock their troops by saying, "Can't hack it, little girls?" (Eisenhart, 1975). In the Marines, the worst insult to male recruits is to compare their performance to a woman's (Gilham, 1989).

The same phenomenon occurs in sports. Sociologist Douglas Foley (1997) notes that football coaches insult boys who don't play well by saying that they are "wearing skirts," and sociologists Jean Stockard and Miriam Johnson (1980), who observed boys playing basketball, heard boys who missed a basket called a "woman." This pattern continues in professional sports, and hockey players who are not rough enough on the ice are called "girls" (Gallmeier, 1988, p. 227). So commonplace is this mocking of boys in feminine terms that it has prompted women athletes to sport T-shirts, popular in women's locker rooms, retorting: "You only wish" (front) … "you played like a girl" (back).

This name-calling is sociologically significant because such insults embody a generalized devaluation of females and there is no comparable phenomenon among women (Stockard & Johnson, 1980, p. 12). Girls' coaches do not ridicule them by calling them "boys." Quite the contrary. In some athletic circles, such as in rowing which demands rigorous strength training, pumping iron and pulling like a man is laudable.

Gender Inequality in Conversation. As you may have noticed in your own life, gender inequality also shows up in everyday talk. Because men are more likely to interrupt a conversation and to control changes in topic, sociologists have noted that talk between a man and a woman is often more like talk between an employer and an employee than between social equals (J. A. Hall, 1984; West & Garcia, 1988; Smith-Lovin & Brody, 1989; Tannen, 1990). Even in college, men interrupt their instructors more often than do women, especially if the instructor is a woman (Brooks, 1982). In short, conversations between men and women mirror their relative positions of power in society.

Derogatory terms and conversation represent only the tip of the iceberg, however, for underlying these aspects of everyday life is a structural inequality based on gender that runs throughout society. Let's examine that structural feature in the workplace.

Gender Relations in the Workplace

To examine the work setting is to make visible basic relations between men and women. Let's consider changes in the labour force, the pay gap, and opportunities for women.

Women's Participation in the Labour Force

While women have always worked, over the past 30 years, there has been a massive movement of women, including those with young children, into the paid labour force. Women's high level of involvement in paid work has prompted sociologists to examine the ways women's employment differs from that of men. This includes comparisons between men's and women's jobs, wages, patterns of employment, and opportunities for promotion, and how their paid work experiences are affected by familial responsibilities and expectations.

Labour force participation rate is the proportion of men and women 16 years and older who are in the labour force, working full- or part-time. A century ago, almost all married women were full-time housewives. While married women were often working in the informal economy (e.g., sewing at home or taking in laundry or boarders), they usually did not participate formally in the labour force. In 1891 two-fifths of employed women were servants or were work-

ing at jobs that mirrored their domestic roles. Eventually the range of occupations open to women widened somewhat and certain jobs became regarded as "women's work." In 1901 about 25 percent of clerical workers were women, but by 1921 more that 40 percent were women (cited in Duffy & Pupo 1992, pp. 15–17). Today, clerical work makes up the largest labour market category for women.

With the demand for workers during and immediately following the world wars, women's labour force participation grew. Women's participation rate increased from 17 percent in 1921 to 20 percent in 1931 and from 24.4 percent in 1939 to 33.5 percent in 1944 (cited in Duffy & Pupo 1992, p. 17). After a decline following World War II, when millions of women left factories and offices to return home as full-time wives and mothers, women's labour force participation steadily climbed from the mid-1950s on. Today almost 60 percent of adult women work for pay (Sunter, 2001).

The Pay Gap

How would you like to earn an extra $800 000 at your job? If this sounds appealing, read on. All you have to do is average an extra $20 000 a year between the ages of 25 and 65.

Is this hard to do? Not if you are a man. Comparing workers who have bachelor's degrees, this is precisely how much more the average man will earn compared to the average woman. Hardly any single factor pinpoints gender discrimination better than this total. This gender gap in earnings shows up at all levels of education. It also exists in all industrialized nations (Blau & Kahn, 1992).

The gender gap in wages is pervasive. On average, women in Canada working full-time, full-year in 1997 were paid 72.5 cents for every dollar their male counterparts earned. Men earned on average $42 600 in 1997 while women earned about $30 900 (Drolet, 2002). While this represents huge gains from the late 1960s, when Canadian women were only earning 58 cents for every dollar earned by males, this gap is persistent, and there is some indication it may be widening among younger workers.

What logic can underlie the gender pay gap? Earlier we saw that university degrees are gender-linked, so perhaps this gap is due to career choices. Maybe women tend to choose lower-paying jobs such as primary school teaching, whereas men are more likely to go into better-paying fields such as business and engineering. Actually, researchers have found that only about *half* the pay gap is due to such factors. The balance, however, is due to gender discrimination (Chaykowski & Powell, 1999; Crompton & Vickers, 2000; Phillips & Phillips, 1993).

Depending on your sex, then, you are likely either to benefit from gender discrimination—or to be its victim. Because the pay gap will be so important in your own work life, let's follow some graduates to see how it takes place. Economists Rex Fuller and Richard Schoenberger (1991) examined the starting salaries of the business majors at the

University of Wisconsin, of whom 47 percent were women. They found that the women averaged 11 percent ($1737) lower pay.

You might be able to think of valid reasons for this initial pay gap. For example, the women might have been less qualified. Perhaps their grades were lower. Or maybe they did fewer internships. If so, they would deserve lower salaries. To find out, Fuller and Schoenberger reviewed the students' college records. To their surprise, it turned out that the women had earned *higher* grades and done *more* internships than the men. In other words, if women were equally qualified, they were offered lower salaries—and if they were more highly qualified, they were offered lower salaries—a classic lose-lose situation.

Struggling for pay equity has paid off for many Canadian women. The settlement of female civil servants in Ontario in 2001 provided each woman about $45 000 in retro pay, and most recently, the settlement with Bell Canada will bring female operators' pay in line with that of their male comparators. These two recent decisions that have been favourable toward mending the gap will continue to pay off for thousands of others waiting to have their cases heard.

What happened after the graduates mentioned above were on the job? Did the starting salaries wash out, so that after a few years the men and women earned about the same? To find out, Fuller and Schoenberger checked their salaries five years later. Instead of narrowing, the pay gap had grown even wider. By this time, the women earned 14 percent ($3615) less than the men.

A Canadian study by Finnie and Wannell (1999) drew similar conclusions. The authors studied university graduates across three cohorts (those who graduated in 1982, 1986, and 1990). They found that the gender pay gap had narrowed overall across the cohorts, due to increases in female graduates' earnings and decreases in male graduates' salaries. However, over time within each cohort, the salary gaps between men and women widened. They concluded that although female graduates in the 1990s may start their careers with salaries similar to those of their male counterparts, they will find their earnings gradually falling behind those of their male classmates. Even when women enter spheres of work traditionally occupied by men, such as engineering, their salaries and chances of advancement lag behind those of their male colleagues (Finnie, Lavoie, & Rivard, 2001).

As a final indication of the extent of the gender pay gap, consider this. Rarely are women appointed chief executive officers. According to a 1993 *Financial Post* survey, less than 2 percent of all CEOs are women. Your best chance to reach the top is to be named—in this order—John, Robert, James, William, or Charles. Edward, Lawrence, and Richard are also advantageous. Amber, Candace, Leticia, and María, however, apparently draw a severe penalty.

Focus Question
What are some of the ways in which women are disadvantaged in the labour force?

These protestors are lobbying for pay equity at Bell Canada. In 1992, the Canadian Human Rights Commission ruled that former female Bell Canada operators had suffered from pay discrimination. The case has been in court ever since, with demands that Bell pay its male and female operators equitably, and that the company pay some 800 former female employees $400 million in pay equity money.

The Glass Ceiling or the Glass Escalator?

The Glass Ceiling. What keeps women from breaking through the "glass ceiling," the mostly invisible barrier that keeps women from reaching the executive suite? Researchers have identified a "pipeline" that leads to the top—marketing, sales, and production—positions that directly add to the corporate bottom line (R. B. Reich, 1995). Stereotyped as better at "support," women often are steered into human resources or public relations. There, successful projects are not appreciated as much as those that bring in corporate profits—and bonuses for their managers.

Another reason the glass ceiling is so powerful is that women lack mentors, successful executives who take an interest in them and show them the ropes. Some men executives fear gossip and sexual harassment charges if they get close to a woman in a subordinate position. Others don't mentor women because of stereotypes of women as less qualified or lacking the necessary commitment to the job. To lack a mentor is no trivial matter, especially since women often experience a "chilly climate" in executive boardrooms or decision-making chambers.

The glass ceiling is cracking, however, and more women are reaching the executive suite (Lublin, 1996). A look at women above the glass ceiling reveals highly motivated women with a fierce competitive spirit who are highly committed to their work and career. Often they play by "men's rules," developing a style that makes men comfortable. In order to play the game successfully, these women establish a support system with their partners or through paid help for household and family work.

The Glass Escalator. Sociologist Christine Williams (1995) interviewed men and women who worked as nurses, elementary school teachers, librarians, and social workers. She found that the men in these traditionally women's occupations, instead of bumping into a glass ceiling, had climbed aboard a *glass escalator*. That is, compared with women the men were accelerated into more desirable work assignments, higher-level positions, and larger salaries. The motor that drives the glass escalator is gender, the stereotype that because someone is male he is more capable.

The "Mommy Track"

Wives are more likely than husbands to be the caretakers of the marriage, to nurture it through the hard times. Most wives also take greater responsibility for taking care of the children and maintaining family ties (such as sending greeting cards), and spend considerably more time doing housework. Consequently, most employed wives face greater role conflict than do their husbands.

The greatest constraint limiting women's labour-force participation or their career advancement is the pressure they face from their family-related roles, expectations, and responsibilities. The burdens of reconciling family and work fall particularly heavily upon the shoulders of mothers with small children whose personal costs (the guilt they feel, not having time for themselves, not living up to the image of the "good mother") for working outside the home are tremendously high. As Tables 7.3 and 7.4 indicate, women are far more engaged than their male partners in housework and child care. Even when both partners work full-time, there is a substantial difference between males and females in the hours they spend on housework and caregiving. A recent case study by Luxton and Corman (2001) of working-class men and women in Hamilton, Ontario, confirms this pattern. Most women in the labour force work a *double day*, that is, a shift of unpaid work at home following or before their shift in their workplace. Not surprisingly, most women at some point face the likelihood of leaving their paid jobs in order to undertake their domestic responsibilities, including caregiving to senior, young, or disabled family members, on a full-time basis.

One of the frustrations felt by many women in the labour force is that no matter what they do, they hit a "glass ceiling." Another is that to succeed they feel forced to abandon characteristics they feel are essential to their self.

After Jill Barad took over the Barbie division of Mattel, Inc., sales soared. In 1997, Barad was elected CEO of Mattel, becoming the first woman to take the reins of a Fortune 500 corporation.

To help resolve this conflict, Felice Schwartz (1989) suggested that corporations offer women a choice of two parallel career paths. The "fast track" consists of the high-powered, demanding positions that may require 60 or 70 hours of work per week—regular responsibilities, emergencies, out-of-town meetings, and a briefcase jammed with work at night and on weekends. Women can opt for this "fast track" if they wish. Or instead they may choose a "mommy track," which would allow for a lower commitment to the firm, freeing time for a higher commitment to family.

What is wrong with this proposal is that a "mommy track" will encourage women to be satisfied with lower aspirations and fewer promotions and confirm men's stereotypes of women executives. Because there is no "daddy track," it also assumes that child-rearing is primarily women's work (Starrels, 1992). To encourage women to slow up in the race to climb the corporate ladder would perpetuate, or even increase, the executive pay gap. The "mommy track," conclude critics, would keep men in executive power and relegate women to an inferior position in corporate life.

Critics suggest that a better way to confront the conflict between work and family is for husbands to take greater responsibility at home and for firms to provide on-site day care, flexible work schedules, and parental leave without loss of benefits (Auerbach, 1990; Galinsky & Stein, 1990; Duffy & Pupo, 1996). Others maintain that the choice between family and career is artificial, that there are ample role models of family-oriented, highly successful women, from Hilary Weston, former Lieutenant-Governor of Ontario, to Judges Rosalie Abella and Louise Arbour, to CEO Christine Magee.

Table 7.3 Male/Female Participation in Housework

	Female (%)	Male (%)
Both spouses employed full-time with children at home		
No hours	1.5	6.6
Less than 5 hours	6.3	24.7
5–14 hours	33.0	42.4
15–29 hours	36.8	19.5
30–59 hours	17.0	5.5
60+ hours	5.5	1.5
	100.0	100.0
	Female (%)	**Male (%)**
Husband employed full-time, wife worked part-time, children at home		
No hours	0.7	7.4
Less than 5 hours	2.6	28.9
5–14 hours	18.1	41.5
15–29 hours	34.1	16.6
30–59 hours	30.5	4.4
60+ hours	14.1	1.2
	100.0	100.0

Source: Statistics Canada, *1996 Census* [CD-ROM], 1997, Ottawa: Minister of Supply and Services.

Parenting and work often bring conflict, some of which we shall examine in Chapter 13. For a controversy surrounding motherhood that has been ushered in by technology, see the next Sociology and the New Technology box.

Table 7.4 Male/Female Participation in Child Care

	Female (%)	Male (%)
Both spouses employed full-time with children at home		
No hours	21.7	27.2
Less than 5 hours	11.2	18.3
5–14 hours	20.4	23.7
15–29 hours	18.0	15.1
30–59 hours	15.6	9.3
60+ hours	13.2	6.5
	100.0	100.0
	Female (%)	**Male (%)**
Husband employed full-time, wife worked part-time, children at home		
No hours	14.6	21.5
Less than 5 hours	8.1	20.2
5–14 hours	15.8	28.0
15–29 hours	15.9	17.5
30–59 hours	18.1	7.9
60+ hours	28.0	4.9
	100.0	100.0

Source: Statistics Canada, *1996 Census* [CD-ROM]. Information contains data selected from Catalogue no. 93F0027XDB96015 in the Nation Series.

Sociology and the New Technology

Rent-a-Uterus: Gender and Reproductive Technology

Breakthroughs in reproductive technology have led to cultural lag. That is, our technology allows forms of reproduction that have outpaced our norms, our standards of right and wrong. Let's look at some real-life examples.

- Consider surrogate motherhood:

  Mary Beth Whitehead of New Jersey signed a contract for which she was paid to be artificially inseminated with the semen of Bill Stern, whose wife was ill. During pregnancy, Whitehead became emotionally attached to her developing child and decided to keep the baby.

  Stern sued Whitehead to enforce the contract. The controversy, known as the "Baby M case," captivated the nation. Should the contract be enforced, or did a "mother's right" supersede the contract? Stern won, not on the basis of the contract, which was ruled illegal, but on the basis of his fathering the baby.

- Consider artificial insemination for the purpose of abortion:

  Rae Leith loved her father, who was suffering the ravages of Alzheimer's disease. She wanted to be inseminated with her father's sperm in order to have an abortion, and then have the brains of the fetus, which would match her father's tissue, transplanted into her father's brain. Her father said no.

- Consider postmortem ventilation (PMV), in which a brain-dead body is kept alive by artificial means:

  Brain-dead pregnant women have been kept in a ventilated state for several months in order to allow their fetuses to have a better chance to survive. In one case, the man who claimed to be the father of the fetus requested PMV, but the husband objected. The court ruled that since the woman was dead, the state had the right to make the decision, which it did, ruling in favour of PMV. Seven weeks later, the baby died after a caesarean delivery.

For Your Consideration

What should the relative roles of men and women be in technological conception? In the first case just described, should contracts for surrogate motherhood be legally enforceable—and be placed higher than a woman's right to motherhood? In the second case, should a woman have an absolute right to do whatever she wishes with her uterus—it making no difference whose sperm is used? In the third case, should the state be able to determine what happens to a woman's womb and fetus if she is brain-dead? Is this the rightful saving of a child's life, or the state's wrongful control over a woman's womb? Finally, on the basis of this last case, since brain-dead women have no legal rights, could they be used as incubators for the embryos of others—which is totally within our technological capacity?

Sources: Overvold (1988); Rothman (1989); J. G. Raymond (1993).

Sexual Harassment

Until the 1970s, women considered it a personal matter when they experienced unwanted sexual comments, touches, looks, or pressure to have sex. The term **sexual harassment**, referring to these activities, especially in occupational or school settings, was unknown. Then in 1979, Catharine MacKinnon, an activist lawyer, published *Sexual Harassment of Working Women: A Case of Sex Discrimination*. MacKinnon stressed that such unwanted sexual advances are a *structural* problem; that is, they are built into the social structure. It is not a case of a man here and a man there doing obnoxious things because they are attracted to a woman; rather, it is a case of men abusing their positions of authority to force unwanted sexual activities on women.

Although the targets of sexual harassment are usually women, the number of male victims has been increasing as women have moved into positions of power. Male victims are less likely than female victims to receive a sympathetic ear, for people tend to find their situations humorous, sort of like a boy's dream come true. Like women victims, however, these men also report that they feel powerless and used. Social norms and symbolic perceptions, we assume, will eventually catch up to this emerging reality of women abusing power and men as victims.

Like other dynamic terms in our language, this one, too, continues to undergo shifts. For example, as the Liberal and Conservative Views on Social Issues box explores, the line between sexual harassment and rape becomes blurred.

Gender and Violence

While most Canadian communities are usually regarded as relatively safe, many are increasingly fearful of robberies, home invasions, assault, kidnappings, and rape. Only a couple of generations ago, Canadians left their homes and cars unlocked. Today, a growing number are having security systems installed in their homes and cars, are escorting their children to and from schools, and are organizing neighbourhood watch networks. Lurking behind these

---

Liberal and Conservative Views on Social Issues
Sexual Harassment and Women in the Military

The news spread like wildfire across the United States. Several male army sergeants at Aberdeen Proving Ground in Maryland were accused of sexually abusing their female trainees (McIntyre, 1997). To become soldiers, female recruits, many in their late teens, had been entrusted to the care of severe, demanding drill sergeants. Nothing new about this, for the Army uses rugged training to socialize its recruits. What was new, however, were widespread accusations of sexual harassment, of using power—including intimidation and threats—to force unwanted sex on unwilling recruits. The accused drill sergeants, who said the sex was consensual, were tried and found guilty of rape. One sergeant, who had pleaded guilty to having consensual sex with 11 trainees (adultery is a crime in the Army), was convicted of raping six trainees a total of 18 times, and sentenced to 25 years in prison.

Conservatives took an "I told you so" attitude. You can't mix the sexes in dormitories unless you're looking for trouble, they said. Those are red-blooded men in the prime of their life, and the recruits are young, desirable, and in

some cases naive. It is absolutely stupid to have them spend the night together under the same roof. If we are going to prepare women for combat, they contended, they need to be trained in separate military camps under the supervision of women. If men are brought in to assist, they must leave at the end of the day or sleep in separate barracks.

Liberals, also shocked by the rapes, took the attitude that the system was fine, but a few sergeants had gone bad. Training men and women together is the only way to assure equality, they insisted. Training must involve all phases of military life. We must impose greater controls on those in charge—expecting a greater sense of responsibility and demanding total accountability. Recruits need to be told to report immediately all violations of touching or even of seductive language.

Then another bombshell hit. After the recruits made their accusations, the Army appointed a blue-ribbon panel to investigate sexual harassment in its ranks. When Sgt. Major Gene McKinney, the highest-ranking of the Army's 410 000 noncommissioned officers, was appoint-

ed to this committee, former subordinates accused him of sexual harassment (Shenon, 1997). McKinney was relieved of his duties and court-martialed.

He was found not guilty, except for one charge of obstruction of justice. His accusers, embittered, claimed that the Army had sacrificed them for McKinney.

Liberals and conservatives reiterated their positions. Liberals insisted women and men continue to be trained together, but that the bad apples should be gotten rid of. Conservatives replied that it isn't bad apples, but human nature; people will abuse power, so stop the nonsense of training women and men together.

Researchers similarly found that violence against women is embedded in the practices and culture of the Canadian military, where wives and workers are subjected to all forms of violence and intimidation. Under the rigid hierarchical power structure in the military and due to the isolation experienced as part of the work and lifestyle, it is very difficult to lay complaints and expose the problem.

Sources: Harrison & Laliberte (1994); Kovitz (2000); O'Hara (1998).

fears is gender inequality of violence—that females are most likely to be victims of males, not the other way around. Let's briefly review this almost one-way street in gender violence.

Violence Against Women

Battering, intimidation, stalking, rape, intimate violence, and physical, emotional, and psychological abuse are among the forms of violence in which the majority of victims are women. Women are more likely than men to experience assault from an intimate male partner, while men are more likely to be assaulted by a stranger (Nelson & Robinson, 1999). There are notable gender differences in rates and patterns of victimization. For example, both in Canada and in the United States, convicted rapists are almost exclusively young men and acts of violence committed by women are likely to occur in their homes, often against their male partners as acts of self-defence or retribution (Nelson & Robinson, 1999; R. Fitzgerald, 1999).

Rape. Prior to changes in the Canadian Criminal Code in 1983, rape was narrowly defined as a sexual act committed by a male upon a female who was not his wife and who did not consent to the act. Under this definition, a man could not be charged with raping or sexually abusing his wife, even if they were separated at the time (Duffy & Momirov, 1997; Nelson & Robinson, 1999). Under the reformed code, rape was renamed "sexual assault" and emphasis is now placed on the violence of the act, including the power and intimidation it entails. Women are no longer exempt as perpetrators under this new definition (Duffy & Momirov, 1997).

Date Rape. What has shocked so many about date rape (also known as *acquaintance rape*) are studies showing that it is not an isolated event here and there. For example, a number of studies concluded that between 50 and 75 percent of college women reported sexual aggression by males while in a dating relationship (Nelson & Robinson, 1999). Date rape most commonly occurs not between relative strangers on first dates, but between couples who have known each other about a year (Muehlenhard & Linton, 1987). Most date rapes go unreported. Those that are reported are difficult to prosecute, for juries tend to believe that if a woman knows the accused she wasn't "really" raped (Bourque, 1989).

Murder. Although men are more than twice as likely as women to become homicide victims (67 percent of homicide victims are male), husbands are about three times more likely to murder their wives than they are to be murdered themselves by their wives. Women are far more likely (by about nine times) to be killed by their husbands than by a stranger (Duffy & Momirov, 1997; Fitzgerald, 1999). Furthermore, the most sensational act of violence in the home, familicide, in which the whole family—women, children, and sometimes other family members—are murdered at the same time, is usually committed by men.

Domestic abuse is one of the most common forms of violence. Until recently, it was treated by the police as a private family matter. Shown here are police pulling a woman from her bathroom window, where she had fled from her armed husband, who was threatening to shoot her.

Violence in the Home. Spouse battering, marital rape, and incest are discussed in Chapter 13.

A Feminist Understanding of Gender Patterns in Violence

Feminist sociologists have been especially effective in bringing violence against women to the public's attention. Some use the perspective of symbolic interactionism, pointing out that to associate strength and virility with violence—as is done in so many areas of Canadian culture—is to produce violence. Others use conflict theory, arguing that as gender relations change, males are losing power, and that some males become violent against females as a way to reassert their power and status.

> ### Focus Question
> According to feminist sociologists, how is violence against women explained?

Solutions

There is no magic solution for this problem, but to be effective any solution must break the connection between violence and masculinity. This would require an educational program that incorporates school, religious institutions,

Spawning a myriad of toys, posters, and other pop culture paraphernalia, *The Simpson's*, one of the longest-running TV shows in North America, is familiar to most Canadian households. Woven through the hundreds of episodes are a number of recurring themes, gently poking at traditional values, structures, and institutions and exposing absurdities in American society. Producer Matt Groening's sarcasm, satire, and wit have extended to schools, policing, local politics, the environment, the church, and the values and practices of capitalism. Through the feisty Lisa, with her intelligence and strong sense of justice, and Marge, housewife and mother, with her quiet commentary, strong moral convictions, fairness, and willingness to engage in local politics, women's place in family and community are exposed and questioned.

In one notable episode, Lisa's concerns over phrases such as "Let's make cookies for the boys," uttered by the popular talking doll, Malibu Stacy (a doll styled with great similarity to Mattel's Barbie), led her to the executive boardroom. There Malibu Stacy's creator, who was recently bought out by a giant competitor, listens to Lisa's concerns over the sexist doll and with Lisa recreates the doll with intelligence. Not surprisingly, the new doll is a bomb.

Along with this candid commentary on gender socialization and sexism in the marketplace, gender tensions are featured throughout the series: When Marge gets a job as a policewoman, she is assigned the toughest tasks to prove that she should be there; when Marge is employed at the nuclear plant, Mr. Burns tries to fire her because she is married; Bart's daring antics are chalked up to the notion that "boys will be boys"; Marge's unpaid household work is unnoticed by Homer and other family members until she is hospitalized with a broken leg. Often the message is that change is difficult and many give up trying. Lisa's enthusiasm for achievement is met with lukewarm welcome, and Marge's ventures into the paid labour force or into local politics are dismal failures.

Underlying many episodes are serious questions about gender relations, opportunities, and roles. Within our society, poking fun at women, trivializing their concerns and contributions to family and society is highly entertaining. While we are also entertained by Homer's stupidity and obsession with food and Bart's boyish pranks, the humour is bounded by different sets of expectations based on gender and position in the family.

How is the issue of gender relations and roles infused in our sense of humour and entertainment within Canadian culture?

homes, the courts, and the media. Many unions offer well-developed anti-violence and sexual harassment awareness programs. Given the breadth of this problem, the tacit acceptance of the many forms of violence, and current messages in the mass media, it is difficult to be optimistic that a change will come soon.

Our next topics, women in politics and women in sports, however, give us much more reason for optimism.

Gender and Change

The Changing Face of Politics

What do these nations have in common?

- Canada
- Argentina, Bolivia, and Nicaragua in Latin America
- Britain, France, Ireland, and Portugal in western Europe
- The Philippines in Asia
- Israel in the Middle East
- Poland in eastern Europe
- India, Pakistan, and Sri Lanka on the subcontinent

The answer is that all have had a woman president or prime minister. To this list we can add even such bastions of male chauvinism as Haiti, Turkey, and Bangladesh (Harwood & Brooks, 1993).

Why don't women, who outnumber men, take political control of the nation? The fact is that, in spite of the political gains women have made in recent elections, they are greatly outnumbered by men in political office.

The reasons for women's underrepresentation? First, they are still underrepresented in law and business, the careers from which most politicians come. Further, many women do not identify themselves as belonging to a class of people who need bloc political action in order to overcome domination. Feminist activists and theorists ask us to look beyond the ways in which women (and other disadvantaged groups) are victimized or further oppressed and examine **agency,** or the ways in which women are responding positively to change their circumstances. When we analyze women's political activities, we see that women are making a difference locally and internationally. Many women are engaged in the politics of their local communities, pressing environmental, educational, health-related, and social justice issues. Postmodern theorists refer to the actions of a number of women, including Judy D'Arcy,

National President of the Canadian Union of Public Employees (CUPE), and Deborah Bourque, National President of the Canadian Union of Postal Workers (CUPW), who have made tremendous gains within their unions, a forum from which they struggle for change, both within their workplace and in the broader society.

The irregular hours needed to run for any type of political office are incompatible with women's role as mothers. Fathers, in contrast, whose ordinary roles are more likely to take them away from home, often do not feel this same conflict. Women are also less likely to have a supportive spouse willing to play an unassuming background role while providing solace, encouragement, child care, and voter appeal. Finally, preferring to hold tightly onto their positions of power, men have been reluctant to incorporate women into centres of decision-making or to present them as viable candidates.

These factors are changing, however, and we can expect more women to seek and gain political office. More are going into law, where they are doing more travelling and making provincial and national contacts. Increasingly, child care is seen as a mutual responsibility of mother and father. And in some areas, party leaders are searching for qualified candidates (read "people with voter appeal and without skeletons in their closets"), regardless of gender. The primary concern in at least some areas today is not gender, but whether a candidate can win. This generation, then, is likely to mark a fundamental change in women's political participation, and it appears only a matter of time until a woman once again occupies 24 Sussex Drive.

Arenas, Gyms, and Courts: Women in Sports

While they were once almost exclusively spectators, cheering for their brothers and boyfriends from the stands, Canadian women are developing a notable presence in communities across the country, in professional, amateur, and school-sponsored sports of all types and at all levels. Hockey, our national sport, is now the domain of both women and men, owing largely to the hard work and success of the Canadian women's ice hockey team, gold medal winners at the 2002 Winter Olympics in Salt Lake City. Many Canadians have followed the triumphs and defeats of athletes such as Silken Laumann, Joanne Malar, Cassie Campbell, and dozens of other women who are role models for novice competitors.

The challenges, however, continue to present themselves. Women's sports are still underfunded and often marginalized compared to men's (Doren & Jones, 2000). Athletes contend with ill-fitting, made-for-males equipment and sometimes raucous and jeering crowds. With the exception of those in some sports, such as figure skating and gymnastics, female athletes are often assumed to be lesbians or tough, out-of-character women, and are treated as such. The image of lean, muscular bodies and a fiercely competitive spirit, for many, does not fit with the likeness of femininity and motherhood.

Such challenges are not keeping young women out of the action. Women's basketball, for example, has been growing by leaps and (re)bounds. According to Janice Deakin, Ontario's chief referee convenor, more girls are starting at a younger age, and the skill level has been increasing remarkably. She has commented that the young women "play like players. They don't play like girls. They know all about good defence and they expect contact" (quoted in T. Fitz-Gerald, 1999). On the horizon for these young women may be a growing number of university scholarships, a place in coaching and mentoring, and recognition earned by exceptional achievement.

Changing Roles of Men

This chapter has provided an introduction to gender dynamics and the social production of gender differences through a feminine lens. From a feminist perspective, sociologists are concerned with finding explanations for gender inequality and with uncovering the ways gender difference and discrimination are embedded in our institutions, laws, customs, behaviours, and practices. We have discussed some of the ways women's social world is changing in response to their historical and ongoing struggles for recognition, rights, access, and equality.

But what has the women's movement meant for men? Has the women's movement raised issues regarding masculinity and the structure of men's gendered lives as well (Connell, 2000)? Is the world of men and boys changing as women's roles shift?

As we see from the next Down-to-Earth Sociology box, young adolescent boys struggle with pushes and pulls of their developing selves. On the one hand, they are pushed to distinguish themselves, although this sometimes means standing out from the rest, often at a price. Men are socialized to avoid emotions (Doyle, 1995). On the other hand, they are pulled to oblivion, to blend with whatever group—skateboarders, jocks, preppies, computer nerds and geeks, druggies—they are most attracted to or that pull them the hardest.

Is the world of boys and men changing? As women have confronted fresh challenges and taken on a wider variety of roles, and as their achievements have become socially recognized, men's world is adapting. On the personal level, over the past few decades there has been a great deal of discussion about development of men's affective side ("Yes, it's okay—real men do cry"). Today, it is becoming more socially acceptable for men to share their intimate feelings and to participate in their children's lives more fully. Images of modern dads gleaned from TV shows like *Full House* incorporate such transformation.

Shaken from what almost became a disastrous end-of-season outing for the season's top 14-year-old Little League pitcher, Chad Esley quietly assessed the emotional roller-coaster he had experienced as he left the baseball diamond on a hot, sticky July evening. Later at home, he related his experience in an e-mail message to all his friends.

Subject: LOVE!LOVE!

It was the top of the 8th and I was going up to the pitcher's mound. I had had a great game so far, with a single, a double, and a few steals, a great play as catcher, and everything! I went up to the mound because it was my turn to pitch.

The first batter was great—I struck him out. Then as the second batter came up, I slightly glanced into the stands only to see a very special person watching me. Talking to myself, telling myself to calm down, I pitched two basketball-looking shots for pitches. I looked over at the person again who this time was looking at me. My coach called me. But I was so damn dazed, he had to call me by two different names four times! And I finally answered. I looked back at the person, and since I had just walked a batter I really wanted to strike this one out. Well, dream on. With the person sitting there watching me, I pitched horribly and the batter hit for a single. I was so mad at myself, I decided not to look at the person until the end of the game. I went on to strike the next two out and we won the game.

As I went to shake hands, I looked again toward the bleachers and there she was, the love of my life, the fire of my eyes. The beat to my heart was sitting there smiling!

How did Chad's friends react? "They laughed and teased me mostly, and of course, deleted it." Even his closest friends were shocked. They did whatever it took to be "cool" with girls, because they feared being rejected, exposing emotions, and especially what others would say. They were astonished by his willingness to open up, to draw attention to himself despite being unsure of the reaction. For most, conformity rules.

Source: Private correspondence, by permission.

On a structural level, more men are finding themselves not working outside the home and having to undertake unpaid domestic work as "househusbands" in ways in which only women had formerly done. Is it by choice or by circumstance? Between 1976 and 1997, researchers estimate that the number of families with a stay-at-home dad increased from 41 000 to 77 000. Among families with a stay-at-home parent, in 1997 fathers "stayed home" in 6 percent of these families, up from 1 percent in 1976. At the same time, stay-at-home fathers are less likely than stay-at-home moms to have very young children at home, perhaps due to gender differences in parental leave policy. Interestingly, stay-at-home fathers spend fewer hours per day in unpaid household work, compared to stay-at-home mothers (K. Marshall, 1998).

"Troubled by an unattainable ideal, boys are learning what girls have long known: it isn't easy living in a *Baywatch* world" (S. S. Hall, 1999). A recent news story on research that concluded that tall men are sexually more active and more attractive to women drew loud complaints from short men who countered with evidence of their own sexual prowess. The two-day media flurry around this story underscored men's deep-seated concern with body image and size. Studies over the past decade indicate that body-image disturbances may be more common in men than was previously believed and that these problems begin during adolescence (Hall, 1999; Connell, 2000).

The boom in the men's cosmetics industry, the promotion and advertising of skin and hair care products and services for men, and the growth in men's clothing lines are signs of change. Previous generations of men, haunted by a fear of being regarded as sensitive—a euphemism for weak or feminine—prided themselves on their apparent lack of interest in their image.

In her book, *Stiffed: The Betrayal of the American Man*, author Susan Faludi (1999) takes a hard look at the male in society, and moves from the conventional explanations of men's behaviour as resulting from a combination of social expectations, biology, reactions to the women's movement, and other structural changes to consider the ways men have been pushed and profoundly betrayed by the very institutions (corporate and political worlds, communities, and families) that promised power, success, recognition, and ultimately fulfillment.

Faludi, along with others, is convinced that men should abandon their "illusions of control" and question the trappings of traditional notions of masculinity. Is there a crisis in masculinity? Do we see emerging a "new man"? While exploring this issue falls outside the purview of this book, many authors discuss changing masculinities as a complex and dynamic process, unfolding as men's experiences and opportunities are challenged and affected by changes in women's lives (Whitehead & Barrett, 2001; Moir & Moir, 1999).

Glimpsing the Future—with Hope

Playing a fuller role in the decision-making processes of our social institutions, women are breaking the stereotypes and role models that lock males into exclusively male activities and push females into roles considered feminine. As structural barriers fall and more activities become degenderized, both males and females will be free to pursue activities more compatible with their abilities and desires as *individuals*.

At present, structural obstacles, accompanied by supporting socialization and stereotypes, cast most males and females into fairly rigid molds along the lines that culture dictates. To overcome these obstacles and abandon traditional stereotypes is to give males and females new perceptions of themselves and one another. Both females and males will then be free to feel and to express needs and emotions that present social arrangements deny them. Females are likely to perceive themselves as having greater access to power and control over their environment. Males are likely to feel and to express more emotional sensitivity—

to be warmer, more affectionate and tender, and to give greater expression to anxieties and stresses that their gender now forces them to suppress. In the future we may discover that such "greater wholeness" of males and females entails many other dimensions of the human personality.

As they develop a new consciousness of themselves and of their own potential, relationships between women and men will change. Certainly, distinctions between the sexes will not disappear. There is no reason, however, for biological differences to be translated into social inequalities. The reasonable goal is appreciation of gender differences coupled with equality of opportunity—which may well lead to a transformed society (Gilman, 1911/1971; Offen, 1990). If so, as sociologist Alison Jaggar (1990) observed, gender equality can become less a goal than a background condition for living in society.

Summary and Review

ISSUES OF SEX AND GENDER
What is gender stratification?

The term **gender stratification** refers to unequal access to power, prestige, and property on the basis of sex. Every society establishes a structure that, on the basis of sex and gender, opens and closes access to the group's privileges. p. 168.

How do sex and gender differ?

Sex refers to biological distinctions between males and females. It consists of both primary and secondary sex characteristics. **Gender**, in contrast, is what a society considers proper behaviours and attitudes for its male and female members. Sex physically distinguishes males from females; gender defines what is "masculine" and "feminine." p. 168.

Why do the behaviours of males and females differ?

In the "nature versus nurture" debate—whether differences between the behaviours of males and females are caused by inherited (biological) or learned (cultural) characteristics—almost all sociologists take the side of nurture. In recent years, however, the door to biology has opened somewhat. pp. 168–171.

GENDER INEQUALITY IN GLOBAL PERSPECTIVE
Is gender stratification universal?

George Murdock surveyed information on premodern societies and found not only that all of them have sex-linked activities, but also that all of them give greater prestige to male activities. **Patriarchy**, or male dominance, does appear to be universal. Besides work, other areas of discrimination include education, politics, and violence. pp. 171–173.

GENDER INEQUALITIES IN THEORETICAL PERSPECTIVE
How did females become a minority group?

The main theory that attempts to explain how females became a **minority group** in their own societies focuses on the physical limitations imposed by childbirth. The origins of this discrimination,

however, are lost in history, and no one knows for sure how this discrimination began. pp. 173–174.

GENDER INEQUALITY IN CANADA
Is the feminist movement new?

In what is called the "first wave," feminists made political demands for change in the early 1900s—and were met with much hostility, and even violence. The "second wave" began in the 1960s and continues today. pp. 174–175.

What forms does gender stratification in education take?

Although more women than men now attend university, each tends to select "feminine" or "masculine" fields. In addition, men outnumber women in most scientific fields. Change is indicated by the growing numbers of women in such fields as law and medicine. pp. 175–178.

Is there gender inequality in everyday life?

Two indications of gender inequality in everyday life are the general devaluation of femininity and the male dominance of conversation. pp. 178–179.

GENDER RELATIONS IN THE WORKPLACE
What gender inequality is there in the workplace?

Over the last century, women have made up an increasing proportion of the work force. Nonetheless, the gender gap in pay characterizes all occupations. For university graduates, the lifetime pay gap runs about $800 000 in favour of men. **Sexual harassment** also continues to be a reality of the workplace. pp. 179–184.

GENDER AND VIOLENCE
What forms does violence against women take?

The victims of battering, rape, incest, and murder overwhelmingly are females. Conflict theorists point out that men use violence to maintain their power. pp. 184–186.

GENDER AND CHANGE

What is the trend in gender inequality in politics?

A strict division of gender roles—women as child care providers and housekeepers, men as workers outside the home—has traditionally kept women out of politics. Although women continue to be underrepresented in Canadian politics, the trend toward greater political equality is firmly in place. pp. 186–188.

GLIMPSING THE FUTURE—WITH HOPE

What progress has been made in reducing gender inequality?

In Canada, women are playing a fuller role in the decision-making processes of our social institutions. Men, too, are re-examining their traditional roles. The ultimate possibility of gender equality is a new conception of the human personality, one that allows both males and females to pursue their individual interests unfettered by gender. pp. 188–189.

Critical Thinking Questions

1. As some forms of work become more and more "faceless" due to advances in technology (Internet businesses, for example), will gender inequalities among workers be minimized?

2. What evidence is there that women's world is beginning to mirror men's world? What factors most significantly contribute to gender inequality?

Key Terms

agency 186	minority group 173
feminism 174	patriarchies 170
gender 168	sex 168
gender stratification 168	sex-typed 171
matriarchies 170	sexual harassment 184

Weblinks

York University Centre for Feminist Research

www.yorku.ca/research/cfr

The Centre for Feminist Research at York University engages in research and education in feminist studies. The Centre links with the Women's Studies programs at York and with women's research networks in Canada and internationally.

Backlash and Battered Husbands

www.vix.com/pub/men/battery/backlash.html

"One way to trivialize and dismiss a point of view is to claim it is part of a backlash. That is the contemptuous and derogatory characterization often applied when the topic of men's issues arises. Domestic violence is a case in point."

Deceptions of a "Gender-Equal Society"

www.vix.com/pub/men/patria/leacock.html

Eleanor Leacock, an anthropologist, published claims of societies that were supposedly egalitarian in regard to both wealth and sex. In her essay "Women In Egalitarian Societies," one of her principal examples was the Montagnais-Naskapi of the Labrador peninsula. The authors argue that it is now clear the gender equality of that society has no basis in fact.

Gender Swapping on the Internet

ftp.media.mit.edu/pub/asb/papers/gender-swapping.ps

The author explains that the Internet, being blind to physical characteristics, has become a way for men and women to make realizations about the stereotypes and treatment of others. However, it hasn't changed the way males and females view each other.

Inequalities of Race and Ethnicity

Learning Outcomes

After you have studied this chapter, you will be able to

■ distinguish between prejudice and discrimination

■ discuss how functionalism, conflict theory, and symbolic interactionism better explain prejudice than any of the psychological theories

■ discuss the six patterns of ethnic stratification—genocide, population transfer, internal colonialism, segregation, assimilation, and multiculturalism

■ discuss the major classifications of ethnicity in Canada—Native peoples, the English and French charter groups, and the other immigrants who entered and settled Canada over the course of the past 100 years or so

Between 800 000 and 1 million Rwandans died in the slaughter. Although the killings were low-tech—most were done with machete—it took just 100 days in the summer of 1994 to complete the state-sanctioned massacres (Gourevitch, 1995).

Rwanda has two major ethnic groups. The Hutus outnumber the Tutsis 6 to 1. Hutus are stocky and round-faced, dark-skinned, flat-nosed, and thick-lipped. The Tutsis are lankier and longer-faced, lighter-skinned, narrow-nosed, and thin-lipped. But the two groups, who speak the same language, have intermarried for so long that they have difficulty telling Hutu from Tutsi. National identity cards, originally issued by the Belgians when Rwanda was its colony, are one sure way of knowing who is who.

During the genocide, a Tutsi card was a passport to death.

The Hutus, who controlled the government, called on all Hutus to kill all Tutsis. It was a national duty, said the Hutu leaders. Obediently, neighbours hacked neighbours to death in their homes. Colleagues hacked colleagues to death at work. Even teachers killed their students.

Nkongoli, a Tutsi who is now the vice-president of the National Assembly, says "One expected to die. Not by machete, one hoped, but with a bullet. If you were willing to pay for it, you could ask for a bullet. Death was more or less normal, a resignation. You lose the will to fight" (Gourevitch, 1995).

At the end of World War II, the world was aghast at the revelations of the Nazi slaughter of Jews, Slavs, gypsies, and homosexuals. Dark images of gas ovens and emaciated bodies stacked like cordwood haunted the world's nations. At Nuremberg, the Allies, flush with victory, put the top Nazis on trial, exposing their heinous deeds to a shocked world. Their public executions, everyone assumed, marked the end of genocide, a shameful aberration of history.

Never again could such a thing happen—that was the general consensus. Yet mass slaughters did occur. By far, the worst was the Khmer Rouge's killing spree in the 1970s, leaving 2 or 3 million Cambodians dead (Markusen, 1995). But this was purely political killing, the ruthless regime and its victims of the same race and ethnicity.

Genocide—the attempt to annihilate a people simply because of their presumed race or ethnicity—continues today, as evidenced from the description above. It grows out of the same impulse of hatred displayed by the Nazis. Although the killings described above lacked swastika and goose-stepping, and machetes replaced poison gas and ovens, the goal was the same.

There were, of course, other reasons for the slaughter. There always are. The Hutus felt threatened by a Tutsi rebel group, and 20 years earlier the Tutsis had killed 100 000 Hutus. What is significant for our purposes is that it happened, even after the world vowed "never again" in 1945.

Laying the Sociological Foundation

Seldom do race and ethnic relations drop to such a brutal low as they did in Nazi Germany and Rwanda, but in our own society, newspaper headlines and television evening news keep race and ethnic relations constantly before us. Sociological findings on this topic, then, can contribute greatly to our better understanding of this aspect of social life. To begin, let us consider to what extent race itself is a myth.

Race: Myth and Reality

With its 6 billion people, the world offers a fascinating variety of human shapes and colours. People see one another as black, white, red, yellow, and brown. Eyes come in various shades of blue, brown, and green. Thick and thin lips. Straight hair, curly hair, kinky hair, black, white, and red hair—and, of course, all hues of brown.

As humans spread throughout the world, their adaptations to diverse climate and other living conditions resulted in this profusion of complexions, colours, and shapes. In this sense the concept of **race**, a group with inherited physical characteristics that distinguish it from another group, is a reality. Humans do, indeed, come in a variety of colours and shapes.

Common Sense Versus Sociology. According to common sense, our racial classifications represent biological differences between people. Sociologists, however, stress that what we call races are *social* classifications, not biological categories.

Sociologists point out that *our "race" depends more on the society in which we live than on our biological characteristics.* The racial categories common in Canada, for example, constitute merely one of numerous ways that people around the world classify physical appearances. Although groups around the world use different categories, each group assumes that its categories are natural, merely a response to visible biology.

But what about the biology? The biological differences are real, regardless of how we categorize them, aren't they? It is true that we humans have numerous physical differences. But if biology is the main element, biologists, of all people, should agree on the numbers and characteristics of human races.

But they do not. Human physical differences are so numerous that biologists cannot even agree on how *many* races there are, much less their characteristics.

In Sum

Race, then, is in the eye of the beholder. Humans show such a mixture of physical characteristics—in skin colour, hair texture, nose shape, head shape, eye colour, and so on—that there is no inevitable, much less universal, way to classify our many biological differences. Because racial classifications are arbitrary, the categories we use change over time. In this sense, then, race is a myth.

Racial Superiority.

The myth of race, however, remains a powerful force in social life. From their basic ethnocentrism, people are inclined to think that their "race" is superior to others. Regardless of the logical arguments just recounted, the idea of racial superiority haunts humanity.

The idea continues its powerful journey even today. As one of the most significant elements of North American culture, it makes an impact on our everyday lives. That race is an arbitrary classification makes little difference to ways of common thinking. "I know what I see, and you can't tell me any different" seems to be the common response. "I know what *they* are like. *They* are (fill in common responses you hear)." For these people, this becomes reality.

As noted in Chapter 5, sociologist W. I. Thomas observed, "If people define situations as real, they are real in their consequences." What makes a difference for social life is what people *believe*, for *people act on beliefs, not facts.* As a result, the ideas of race that are so firmly embedded in our culture—not scientific fact—influence attitudes and behaviour. As you read this chapter, perhaps you will examine some of the racial ideas you learned as you were socialized in your culture.

Ethnic Groups

Whereas people use the term *race* to refer to supposed biological characteristics that distinguish one people from another, **ethnicity** and **ethnic** apply to cultural characteris-

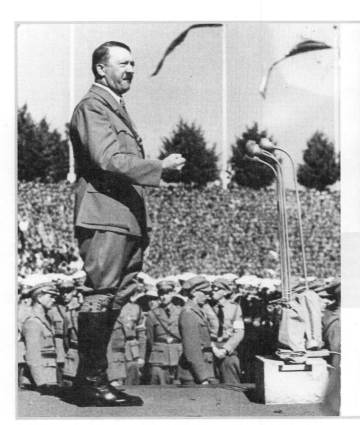

Fanning hatred for Jews—who served as scapegoats for Germany's problems—and preaching the superiority of the supposedly racially pure Aryans, Adolf Hitler put his ideas of race into practice. The result was the Holocaust, the systematic slaughter of Jews and others deemed racially inferior. In the photo on the left, Hitler is addressing a group called Hitler Youth, an organization dedicated to serving Hitler and his ideas. The photo on the right shows the sight that greeted British troops when they entered the concentration camp in Bergen, Germany—60 000 people dying of starvation and diseases amid piles of bodies awaiting burial.

tics. Derived from the Greek *ethnos*, meaning "people" or "nation," these terms refer to people who identify with one another on the basis of common ancestry and cultural heritage. Their sense of belonging may centre on nation of origin, distinctive foods, dress, family names and relationships, language, music, religion, and other customs.

People often confuse the terms *race* and *ethnic group*. For example, many people, including many Jews, consider the Jews a race. Jews, however, are more properly considered an ethnic group, for it is their cultural characteristics, especially religion, that bind them together.

> ## Focus Question
> What is the difference between a race and an ethnic group?

Minority Groups and Dominant Groups

Sociologist Louis Wirth (1945) defined a **minority group** as people who are singled out for unequal treatment *and* who regard themselves as objects of collective discrimination. Either physical (racial) or cultural (ethnic) differences can serve as the basis of the unequal treatment.

Surprisingly, the term *minority group* does not necessarily refer to a *numerical* minority. For example, before India's independence in 1947, a handful of British colonial rulers discriminated against millions of Indians. Similarly, when South Africa practised apartheid, a small group of Dutch discriminated against the black majority. And all over the world, women are a minority group. Accordingly, sociolo-

gists refer to those who do the discriminating not as the *majority*, but, rather, as the **dominant group**, for they have greater power, privileges, and social status.

The dominant group almost always considers its privileged position to be due to its own innate superiority. Possessing political power and unified by shared physical and cultural traits, the dominant group uses its position to discriminate against those with different—and supposedly inferior—traits.

Emergence of Minority Groups. A group becomes a minority in one of two ways. The first is through the expansion of political boundaries. This often occurs as the result of a decisive military victory. When a group expands its political boundaries, however, it produces minority groups if it incorporates people with different customs, languages, values, and physical characteristics into the same political entity. For example, after defeating the French on the Plains of Abraham, the British seized control of New France. Consequently, the French who remained, who had been the dominant group, were transformed into a minority group, a status that has significantly influenced their lives and our own ever since (see the section "The Two Charter Groups" later in this chapter).

The second way a group becomes a minority is by migration. This can be voluntary, as with the millions of people who chose to move to Canada, or involuntary, as with Native Canadians, many of whom were forcibly transported to remote regions of the North (see the Down-to-Earth Sociology box, The Inuit Expulsion, later in this chapter), or the Japanese Canadians who were labelled "Enemy Aliens" during World War II, then stripped of their businesses and livelihoods, forcibly relocated from the West

Because ideas of race and ethnicity are such a significant part of society, all of us are classified according to those ideas. This photo illustrates the difficulty such assumptions posed for Israel. The Ethiopians, shown here as they arrived in Israel, although claiming to be Jews, looked so different from other Jews that it took several years for Israeli authorities to acknowledge this group's "true Jewishness."

Coast, and put in concentration camps throughout Canada. Interestingly, this fate did not befall the many German or Italian Canadians. Instead, cities/towns with identifiable German names were simply renamed.

Shared Characteristics. Anthropologists Charles Wagley and Marvin Harris (1958) identified five characteristics shared by minorities worldwide.

1. Membership in a minority group is an ascribed status; that is, it is not voluntary, but comes through birth.

2. The physical or cultural traits that distinguish minorities are held in low esteem by the dominant group.

3. Minorities are unequally treated by the dominant group.

4. Minorities tend to marry within their own group.

5. Minorities tend to feel strong group solidarity (a sense of "we-ness").

These conditions—especially when combined with collective discrimination—tend to create a shared sense of identity among minorities, and, in many instances, even a sense of common destiny (Chandra, 1993b).

Prejudice and Discrimination

Prejudice and discrimination are common throughout the world. In Mexico, Hispanic Mexicans discriminate against Native-American Mexicans; in Israel, Ashkenazic Jews, primarily of European descent, discriminate against Sephardic Jews from the Muslim world; and in Japan, the Japanese discriminate against just about anyone who is not Japanese, especially immigrant Koreans and the descendants of the Eta caste. A stigma still attaches to the Eta, now renamed the Burakumin, who used to do the society's dirty work—working

Focus Question
What is the difference between prejudice and discrimination?

with dead animals (stripping the hides and tanning the leather) and serving as Japan's executioners and prison guards (Mander, 1992). In some places the elderly discriminate against the young, in others the young against the elderly. And all around the world men discriminate against women.

As you can see from this list, **discrimination** is an *action*—unfair treatment directed against someone. When the basis of discrimination is race, it is known as **racism**, but discrimination can be based on many characteristics other than race—including age, sex, height, weight, income, education, marital status, sexual orientation, disease, disability, religion, and politics. Discrimination is often the result of an *attitude* called **prejudice**—a prejudging of some sort, usually in a negative way. Positive prejudice exaggerates the virtues of a group, such as thinking that some group (usually one's own) is more capable than others. Most prejudice, however, is negative, prejudging a group as inferior.

Individual and Institutional Discrimination

Sociologists stress that we need to move beyond thinking in terms of **individual discrimination**, the negative treatment of one person by another. Although such behaviour certainly creates problems, it is primarily a matter of one individual treating another badly. With their focus on the broader picture, sociologists encourage us to examine **institutional discrimination**; that is, to see how discrimination is woven

In the 1920s, the Ku Klux Klan became a powerful political force in the United States, especially in Indiana, where this photo was taken. Which theories, sociological and psychological, would be most useful to explain this upsurge in racism among ordinary citizens?

into the fabric of society, to such an extent that it becomes routine, sometimes even a matter of social policy. The system once known as apartheid in South Africa, the forced resettlement and expropriation of the property of Japanese Canadians as "Enemy Aliens" during World War II, or the present-day system of reserves for Native Canadians are examples of institutional discrimination.

Theories of Prejudice

Why are people prejudiced? The common-sense explanation is that some member of a group has done something negative to them or to someone they know, and they transfer their feelings to other members of the group. In some cases, this may be true, but as a classic piece of research by psychologist Eugene Hartley (1946) showed, much more is involved. Hartley asked people how they felt about various racial and ethnic groups. Besides blacks, Jews, and so on, his list included the Wallonians, Pireneans, and Danireans—names he had made up. Most people who expressed dislike for Jews and blacks also expressed dislike for these three fictitious groups. The significance of Hartley's study is twofold. First, people who are prejudiced against one racial or ethnic group tend to be prejudiced against other groups. Second, prejudice does not depend on negative experiences with others. People can be, and are, prejudiced against people they have never met—and even against groups that do not exist!

Social scientists have developed several theories to explain prejudice. Let's look first at psychological theories, then at sociological explanations.

Psychological Perspectives

Frustration and Scapegoats. In 1939, psychologist John Dollard suggested that prejudice is the result of frustration. People who are unable to strike out at the real source of their frustration (such as low wages) find someone else to blame. This **scapegoat**, generally a racial, ethnic, or religious minority they unfairly blame for their troubles, becomes a convenient—and safe—target on which to vent their frustrations. Gender and age also provide common bases for scapegoating.

Even mild frustration can increase prejudice. In an ingenious experiment, psychologists Emory Cowen, Judah Landes, and Donald Schaet (1959) measured the prejudice of a sample of students. They then gave the students two puzzles to solve, but made sure they did not have enough time to solve them. After the students had worked furiously on the puzzles, the experimenters shook their heads in disgust and said they could not believe they had not finished. They then retested the students and found higher scores on prejudice. The students had directed their frustrations outward, onto people who had nothing to do with their problem.

The Authoritarian Personality Have you ever wondered if personality is a cause of prejudice—if some people are more inclined to be prejudiced, and others more fair-minded? For psychologist Theodor Adorno, who had escaped from the Nazis, this was no idle speculation. With the horrors he had observed still fresh in his mind, Adorno wondered whether there was a certain type of individual who was more likely to fall for the racist utterances and policies of people like Hitler, Mussolini, and the Ku Klux Klan.

To test this idea, Adorno (1950) developed three scales: a series of statements that measured ethnocentrism, anti-Semitism, and support for strong, authoritarian leaders. Testing about 2000 people, ranging from university professors to prison inmates, Adorno found that people who scored high on one scale also scored high on the other two. For example, people who agreed with anti-Semitic statements also agreed that it was good for a government to be highly authoritarian and that foreign ways of life posed a threat to the "American" way.

Adorno concluded that highly prejudiced people have several things in common. They are insecure, are highly conformist, have deep respect for authority, and are highly submissive to superiors. He termed this the **authoritarian personality**. Individuals who possess an authoritarian personality believe that things are *either* right *or* wrong. When they confront norms and values that differ from their own, especially in matters of religion or sexual orientation, they become anxious. A scapegoat relieves their anxiety, for to define people who are different from themselves as inferior assures them that their own positions are right.

Sociological Perspectives

Sociologists find psychological explanations inadequate. They stress that the key to understanding prejudice is not the *internal* state of individuals, but *factors* outside the individual. Thus, sociological theories focus on how some environments foster prejudice, while others reduce it. Let's compare functionalist, conflict, symbolic interactionist, and feminist perspectives on prejudice.

Functionalism. In a telling scene from a television documentary, journalist Bill Moyers interviewed Fritz Hippler, a Nazi intellectual who at age 29 was put in charge of the entire German film industry. Hippler said that when Hitler came to power the Germans were no more anti-Semitic than the French, probably less so. He was told to create anti-Semitism, which he did by producing movies that contained vivid scenes comparing Jews to rats—their breeding threatening to infest the population.

Why was Hippler told to create hatred? Prejudice and discrimination were functional for the Nazis. The Jews provided a convenient scapegoat, a common enemy around which the Nazis could unite a Germany weakened by defeat in World War I and bled by war reparations and rampant inflation. In addition, the Jews had businesses, bank accounts, and other property to confiscate. They also held key positions (university professors, reporters, judges, and so on), which the Nazis could replace with their own flunkies as they fired Jews. Hatred also showed its dysfunctional side, as the Nazi officials who were sentenced to death at Nuremberg discovered.

Harnessing the state machinery to promote hatred as the Nazis did—the schools, police, courts, mass media, and almost all aspects of the government—makes prejudice practically irresistible.

That prejudice is functional and shaped by the social environment was dramatically demonstrated by Muzafer and Carolyn Sherif (1953) in a simple but ingenious experiment. In a boys' summer camp, they first assigned friends to different cabins and then made the cabin the basic unit of competition. Each cabin competed against the others in sports and for status. In just a few days, strong in-groups had formed, and even former lifelong friends were calling one another "crybaby" and "sissy" and showing intense dislike for one another.

The Sherifs' study illustrates four major points. First, the social environment can be deliberately arranged to generate either positive or negative feelings about people. Second, prejudice can be a product of pitting group against group in an "I win, you lose" situation. Third, prejudice is functional in that it creates in-group solidarity. Fourth, prejudice is dysfunctional in that it destroys community social relationships.

Conflict Theory. Conflict theorists stress that the capitalist class systematically pits group against group. If workers are united, they will demand higher wages and better working conditions. In contrast, groups that fear and distrust one another will work against one another. To reduce workers' solidarity, then, is to weaken their bargaining power, drive down costs, and increase profits. Thus the capitalist class exploits racial and ethnic strife to produce a **dual labour market** (also called a *split labour market*), workers divided along racial, ethnic, and gender lines (Du Bois, 1935/1992; M. Reich, 1972; Lind, 1995). Usually, one ethnic group holds down the good jobs while other identifiable ethnic or racial groups work in low-paying, ordinarily non-unionized jobs.

Unemployment is a useful weapon to help maintain a split labour market. If everyone were employed, the high demand for labour would put workers in a position to demand pay increases and better working conditions. Keeping some people unemployed, however, provides a **reserve labour force** from which owners can draw when they need to expand production. When the economy contracts, these workers are released to rejoin the ranks of the unemployed. Minority workers, including women, are especially useful as members of the reserve army of labour because their presence as potential competitors for "their" jobs poses a threat to the dominant group of workers, usually but never always, white males. (See feminist theories below.)

The consequences are devastating, say conflict theorists. Just like the boys in the Sherif experiments, black Canadians, Native Canadians, Quebecois, anglophones, and so on see themselves as able to make gains only at one another's expense. Thus, their frustration, anger, and hostility are deflected away from the capitalists and directed toward the scapegoats, whom they see as standing in their way. Pitted against one another, racial and ethnic groups learn to fear and distrust one another, instead of recognizing their common class interests and working for their mutual welfare (Blackwelder, 1993).

Symbolic Interactionism. Where conflict theorists focus on the role of the capitalist class in exploiting racial and ethnic inequalities, symbolic interactionists examine how perception and labels produce prejudice.

How Labels Create Prejudice. Words are not simply meaningless labels. Rather, *the labels we learn colour the way we see the world.*

Symbolic interactionists stress that labels are an essential ingredient of prejudice. Labels cause **selective perception**; that is, they lead people to see certain things and blind them to others. Through labels, people look at the members of a group as though they were all alike.

Racial and ethnic labels are especially powerful. They are shorthand for emotionally laden stereotypes. The term *nigger*, for example, is not simply a neutral name. Nor are *honky*, *spic*, *mick*, *kike*, *limey*, *kraut*, *dago*, or any of the other scornful words people use to belittle ethnic groups. Such words overpower us with emotions, blocking out rational thought about the people they refer to (Allport, 1954).

Symbolic interactionists stress that no one is born prejudiced. Instead, we learn our prejudices in interaction with others. At birth each of us becomes a member of some particular family and racial or ethnic group, where we learn our beliefs and values. There, as part of our basic orientations to the world, we learn to like—or dislike—members of other groups and to perceive them positively or negatively. Similarly, if discrimination is the common practice, we learn to practise it routinely. Just as we learn any other attitudes and customs, then, so we learn prejudice and discrimination.

Stereotypes and Discrimination: The Self-Fulfilling Prophecy. The stereotypes we learn not only justify prejudice and discrimination, but they can even produce the behaviour depicted in the stereotype. Let's consider Group X. Negative stereotypes, which characterize Group X as lazy, seem to justify withholding opportunities from this group ("because they are lazy and undependable") and placing its members in inferior positions. The result is a *self-fulfilling prophecy.* Denied jobs that require high dedication and energy, Group X members are confined to "dirty work," for it is seen as more fitting for "that kind" of people. Since much dirty work is irregular, members of Group

X are also liable to be readily visible—standing around street corners. The sight of their idleness then reinforces the original stereotype of laziness, while the discrimination that created the "laziness" in the first place passes unnoticed.

Feminism: Multiracial Feminism and Inequality

Multiracial feminism (otherwise known as multicultural or multiethnic feminism) has emerged from the challenges put forward by women of colour. Simply put, they argue that white men *and women* oppress lower-class women and men of disadvantaged races and ethnicities. However, the inclusion of race and ethnicity with social class inequality complicates the picture. While sex is a dichotomy (generally speaking, you are either a man or a woman), race, ethnicity, and social class are continuums of privileges and disadvantages. Multiracial feminists point out that it is not enough to simply dissect inequality from a woman's point of view. The analysis must include the experiences of women and men of different racial and ethnic groups and their class differences. Therefore, multiracial feminism talks about the outlooks and behaviours of the men and women of different ethnic and racial backgrounds such as black working-class men and women, wealthy white men and women, poor Chinese men and women and so on.

A useful example is eating disorders. Among young, white middle-class women who desire a thin, sexually attractive body, anorexia nervosa and bulima can be the negative consequences of a culture of thinness in Western societies. Much has been written about this social problem and a great deal of television time has been devoted to it. These eating disorders are now defined as a significant social problem. Among many African-American and Hispanic women, binge eating and purges are ways of coping with the traumas of their social lives such as poverty, racism, and sexual abuse. Their eating disorders have not received the same level of attention because of their lower social class position; their lack of access to the levers of power makes their social problems "invisible."

The important point made by multiracial feminism is that a member of a disadvantaged ethnic or racial group (man or woman) is not oppressed because of her/his gender, race, ethnicity, or social class position. They argue that it is a multiple system of domination that requires a multi-faceted strategy to remedy. In contrast to liberal feminists who have focused their energies on the oppression of women ("men versus women") and on raising the status of women through changes in society's laws, and to Marxist and other radical feminists who have argued that women's oppression is linked to working-class political struggles, multiracial feminists point out the complexities of the struggle for equality. It is not "men" who are the enemy, nor simply the "ruling class"; the system of oppression experienced by men and women of colour demonstrates the complexity of these problems of inequality and the difficulty of resolving them (Lorber, 1998, p. 134–47).

> ### Focus Question
> How do sociologists differ from psychologists on the explanations for prejudice?

Global Patterns of Intergroup Relations

In any society that contains minorities, basic patterns develop between the dominant group and the minorities. Let's look at each of the patterns shown in Figure 8.1.

Genocide

The twentieth century's most notorious examples of genocide are Hitler's attempt to destroy all Jews and, as depicted in our opening vignette, the Hutus' attempt to destroy all Tutsis. One of the horrifying aspects of these slaughters is

Figure 8.1 Patterns of Intergroup Relations: A Continuum

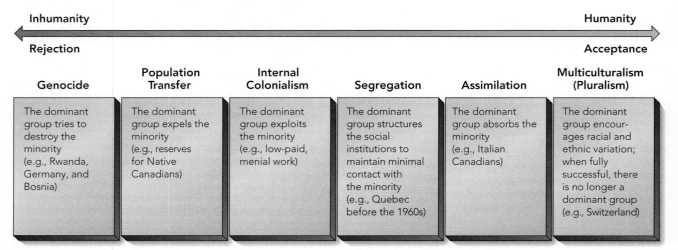

Genocide	Population Transfer	Internal Colonialism	Segregation	Assimilation	Multiculturalism (Pluralism)
The dominant group tries to destroy the minority (e.g., Rwanda, Germany, and Bosnia)	The dominant group expels the minority (e.g., reserves for Native Canadians)	The dominant group exploits the minority (e.g., low-paid, menial work)	The dominant group structures the social institutions to maintain minimal contact with the minority (e.g., Quebec before the 1960s)	The dominant group absorbs the minority (e.g., Italian Canadians)	The dominant group encourages racial and ethnic variation; when fully successful, there is no longer a dominant group (e.g., Switzerland)

that those who participated were ordinary citizens—whose participation was facilitated by labels that singled out the victims as enemies worthy of death.

Labels are powerful forces in human life. Labels that dehumanize others help people to **compartmentalize**—to separate their acts from feelings that would threaten their self-concept and make it difficult for them to participate in killing (Bernard, Ottenberg, & Redl, 1971; Markusen, 1995). Thus, *genocide is facilitated by labelling the targeted group as less than fully human.*

Population Transfer

Population transfer is of two types, indirect and direct. *Indirect* population transfer is achieved by making life so unbearable for members of a minority that they leave "voluntarily." Under the bitter conditions of czarist Russia, for example, millions of Jews made this "choice." *Direct* transfer takes place when a minority is expelled. Examples include the relocation of Native Canadians to reserves and the transfer of Canadians of Japanese descent to relocation camps during World War II.

Internal Colonialism

In Chapter 6, the term *colonialism* was used to refer to how the most industrialized nations exploit the least industrialized nations. Conflict theorists use the term **internal colonialism** to refer to how a dominant group exploits minority groups. The "routine" form is to use the existing social institutions to deny minorities access to the full benefits a society has to offer its citizens. Slavery, reviewed in Chapter 6, is an extreme example of internal colonialism, as was the South African system of *apartheid*. As Simpson

and Yinger (1972) put it, who else would do all the hard work?

Segregation

Segregation—the formal separation of racial or ethnic groups—accompanies internal colonialism. Segregation allows the dominant group to exploit the labour of the minority (butlers, chauffeurs, housekeepers, nannies, street cleaners) while maintaining social distance (P. H. Collins, 1986). In the U.S. South until the 1960s, by law African-Americans and whites had to use separate public facilities such as hotels, schools, swimming pools, bathrooms, and even drinking fountains. In 38 states, laws prohibited interracial marriage. Violators could be punished by one to five years in prison (Mahoney & Kooistra, 1995). The legal structure also upheld residential segregation (Massey & Denton, 1993).

Assimilation

Assimilation is the process by which a minority is absorbed into the mainstream culture. There are two types. In *forced assimilation* the dominant group refuses to allow the minority to practise its religion, speak its language, or follow its customs. Prior to the fall of the Soviet Union, for example, the dominant group, the Russians, required that Armenian schoolchildren be taught in Russian and that Armenians honour Russian, not Armenian, holidays. *Permissible assimilation*, in contrast, permits the minority to adopt the dominant group's patterns in its own way and at its own speed. In Brazil, for example, an ideology favouring the eventual blending of diverse racial types into a "Brazilian stock" encourages its racial and ethnic groups to intermarry.

Segregation is one of the many faces of discrimination. Until the 1940s, major league baseball was reserved for white players. Shown here is Jackie Robinson, who broke the colour barrier in 1947. Voted Rookie of the Year, and then Most Valuable Player two seasons later, Robinson was inducted into the Hall of Fame as soon as he was eligible.

The policy of multiculturalism (or pluralism) permits, or even encourages, racial and ethnic variation—in Canada this allows minority groups to maintain their separate identities but also participate in the country's social institutions.

Multiculturalism (Pluralism)

A policy of **multiculturalism**, also called **pluralism**, permits or even encourages racial and ethnic variation. The minority groups are able to maintain their separate identities, yet participate in the country's social institutions, from education to politics. Switzerland provides an outstanding example of multiculturalism. The Swiss are made up of four separate groups—French, Italian, German, and Romansh—who have kept their own languages, and live peacefully in political and economic unity. Multiculturalism has been so successful that none of these groups can properly be called a minority.

> **Focus Question**
> What is the difference between multiculturalism and assimilation?

The Major Classifications in Canada

Canadians can be classified into three categories: the Native peoples, including status Indians, non-status Indians, Métis, and Inuit; the two "charter groups," the French and English white settlers whose historical relations span over 400 years; and the other immigrants from all over the world who entered and settled in Canada over the course of the past 100 years or so.

Native Peoples

Native peoples comprise a small but extremely disparate constituency. Roughly 3.7 percent of Canada's population, or 1 002 675 people, reported they had Aboriginal ancestry. Native Canadians comprise a rich diversity of customs, languages, and cultural differences that stretch back to pre-European contact (Frideres & Gadacz, 2001). However, not many of them share or have shared in Canada's development. There are wide differences in access to social, health, and education programs, and in levels of development, for Native Canadians both on and off the reserve system.

For this and other reasons, Native Canadians did not consent to the patriation of the Canadian constitution (the *British North America Act*) and even sent a delegation to London, England, to lobby the British parliament not to pass the *Canada Act*.

The federal government has made efforts to gain Native Canadians' support for the Charter of Rights and Freedoms by making provision for their self-government. However, it takes the consent of seven provincial governments to agree to any amendments, and this has yet to be achieved.

Status or registered Indians have the highest profile in Canada. They number 675 499 today, a number expected to rise to approximately three-quarters of a million by 2005. To be considered a member of this category, a person must (1) be admitted to a general registry in Ottawa; (2) be affiliated with one of the 622 bands; (3) be granted the entitlement to reside on band reserve lands; and (4) come under the legal jurisdiction of the *Indian Act* passed in 1876 (see Chapter 3, Table 3.5, p. 61).

The majority of status or registered Indians, 58 percent in 2000, live on reserves created by one of the 61 treaties signed with the British Crown. The federal government allocates approximately $5 billion a year to this group. However, only a very small percentage of this sum, roughly 5 percent, is directed to the economic development of Native reserves. The bulk of the money is monopolized by administrative costs to run the Department of Indian Affairs and Northern Development (or DIAND for short) and social spending.

The interests of status Indians are today represented by 633 chiefs who make up the Assembly of First Nations; however, not all bands belong to it, nor do any Métis.

Part 2 of The Constitution Act of 1982 recognizes Native Indians, Inuit, and Métis. Inuit are Native people whose ancestral home is the Arctic, while Métis are Natives who have married non-Natives. The Charter entrenches "existing aboriginal and treaty rights" (see Ponting, 1986, p. 302). Nevertheless, the use of the term "existing" remains unsatisfactory to many Native groups, because many rights to land that they claim are not recognized by some provincial governments. For example, the government of British Columbia denies that the Native Indians have any historic

Down-to-Earth Sociology — The Inuit Expulsion

The harm that befalls some communities does not necessarily stem from sinister conspiracies. Even the best intentions can lead to suffering and death. The coerced relocation of Native Canadians from one community to another provides an example of how "helping" can dissolve into "hurting." It also alerts us to the possibility of rethinking who is the guilty party in the so-called "Indian" problem.

Native Canadians have been afflicted by about 100 forced removals since Confederation. Take the case of the Inuit. In 1953, southern Canadian bureaucrats dispatched 10 ill-equipped Inuit families, mostly from Quebec, to a life of northern hardship in a bleak and inhospitable environment. The 85 Inuit were identified by dog tags, kept in the cargo hold like livestock throughout the 2000-kilometre trip, separated from their families, abandoned to confront harsh Arctic conditions, left in near-starvation conditions for many years, and discouraged from returning home. The fact that these Inuit had little say in what was happening reflected a callous and arrogant indifference at odds with Canada's increasingly vaunted reputation on the global stage.

The rationale given by the federal government included political expediency, cost-cutting, and human compassion—all justified within the framework of "national interests." Within the federal bureaucracy, the resettlement was viewed as an "experiment" to determine whether the Inuit had gone "soft" or could survive when reunited with a wilderness environment. The government saw Inuit settlements as a bulwark in defence of a de facto sovereignty over the northernmost limits of Canada—a not inconsequential challenge given the U.S. strategic interest in the northern Arctic when there were only 140 permanently settled Canadians to provide evidence of Canada's sovereignty in the far Arctic.

The relocation was also viewed as a way of paring government costs. The solution lay in providing an environment where the Inuit could once again become self-sufficient through resumption of traditional living patterns. However, relief costs were largely underwritten by the Inuit families themselves. Tragically, these Inuit were forced to subsidize their own victimization because they were charged exorbitant prices for necessities but offered reduced payments for the fur pelts they brought to government supply stores. Old colonial practices of exploitation are hard to break!

The injustice in relocation is rarely disputed. The Inuit were little more than pawns in experiments in Canadian society-building. The lack of cultural sensitivity to a people who were deeply attached to their homeland contributed to the sorry outcome. They were powerless to resist and this powerlessness continues to plague many Native communities. Even more unjust is the refusal of the government to provide an apology or a measure of redress commensurate with the gravity of this "white-collar" crime.

Source: Adapted from Fleras & Elliott (1996, pp. 218–219).

---

ownership of land in that province. The Reform Party exploited this sentiment recently in the House of Commons when the federal Liberal government brought in legislation to recognize and award claims to the Nisga'a, who happen to live in British Columbia.

Despite the much-publicized conflicts with Natives such as those related to the James Bay project and the "Oka Crisis" (1990), Quebec in some respects has a better record than the rest of Canada when it comes to its dealings with Native peoples. Evidence can be found in the favourable rate of Native language retention, in the levels of prosperity of Native peoples resident in Quebec compared to other provinces, and in the lower rates of imprisonment as compared to non-Natives.

The Two Charter Groups

In John Porter's *The Vertical Mosaic* (1965) the term *charter groups* was used to characterize the two linguistic and culturally distinct white settler groups, the French and the British. This term gained ready use among academics and policymakers alike. The history of the two charter groups begins with the French colonization of North America in 1534 when Jacques Cartier led the first of three voyages of exploration into the St. Lawrence River region. By the beginning of the eighteenth century, this French colony stretched from Hudson Bay to New Orleans. The British 13 Atlantic colonies, later to become the United States of America, were encircled by the French. However, the nucleus of the French Empire in North America was centred along the St. Lawrence and stretched from Montreal to Quebec City with Louisbourg as the military beachhead on Cape Breton.

The population of "New France," which was the name given this French colony, never exceeded 65 000. The colony depended on the fur trade, a luxury item used in the making of fashion clothing for the aristocracy of Europe. Neither agriculture nor industry of any significant kind was able to develop in New France. Therefore, resources—both material and human—were stretched extremely thin to keep the presence of the French Empire in North America. War with the British Atlantic colonies was inevitable because of the need to expand westward to support a growing and prospering colony. The British succeeded militarily

Down-to-Earth Sociology   The Legacy of Louis Riel

The French Canadians who supported Confederation expected to establish many new communities on the Prairies. This was a realistic vision: The first European explorers on the great plains had been French, and their numbers were increased by the fur trade. The French Canadians and native Cree intermarried, and their offspring were called Métis, who formed a distinctive community with their own language, Michef, a mixture of French and Cree. French-Canadian missionaries converted the region's Native population to Catholicism.

French Canadians and the mixed community, the Métis, were actually the majority of the population when the Prairies entered Confederation through the purchase of the territory from the Hudson's Bay Company.

The first major crisis after Confederation came after the French-Canadian Catholics of the plains protested that they had not been properly consulted regarding the Hudson's Bay Company purchase. This resulted in the "Red River Rebellion," the insistence by

the residents of the area on negotiating their entry into Confederation. They were successful. A new province was created by the *Manitoba Act* (1870), and the French-Canadian majority were guaranteed the right to their own school system.

There was a major difference, however, between the liberal spirit of the *Manitoba Act* and the administration of the new province during its first years. Canadian militia that entered the province terrorized the French-Canadian leaders, prompting many of them to leave before their land claims could be resolved. However, between 1876 and 1881, over 40 000 immigrants, mainly Ontario British, moved into Manitoba, lured by the prospect of profitable wheat farming. Some leaders, notably Louis Riel, moved to the United States. Most Métis went to what is now Saskatchewan. There the "Second Red River Rebellion" or "Riel Rebellion" broke out in 1885 over a concern about the lack of legal protection for French lands and schools. The rebellion was

crushed by 5000 militia. Though Riel was a hero in French Canada, he was vilified in Ontario and executed, despite an appeal for clemency by Queen Victoria. Because the French Canadians were clearly upset about the treatment they were receiving in the West, their migration to the Prairies slowed to a trickle. Instead, they turned north, to "New Quebec," a region inhabited largely by Native peoples.

The story doesn't end there. When Keewatin, a part of the Northwest Territories, was transferred to Manitoba in the latter part of the nineteenth century, no protections were extended for the French Canadians living there. Public opinion in Quebec was outraged by this failure. By way of appeasement, Ungava, a large territory that is now the northern section of the province—later to become the site of the massive James Bay Hydro-Electric Project—was transferred to Quebec.

Source: Adapted from Metta Spencer (1996, p. 379).

---

in expelling the French colonial government from North America in 1763 with the Peace of Paris.

The British alone now controlled North America. The American colonists had been known to grumble for more autonomy from their British overlords before 1763, but they had to worry about the French knocking at their door. Now that the French colonial government was gone, renewed interest in political sovereignty quickly gained momentum. The British government, realizing they could lose it all if they lost a war with their American colonists, passed the Quebec Act of 1774. This act extended extraordinary rights to the newly conquered French Catholic colonists to keep them on side in any conflict with their American counterparts. Among these non-assimilationist rights were the right to keep the French civil law and to practise their Catholic religion. The strategy worked, since the Americans tried but were unsuccessful in gaining support from the French colonists along the St. Lawrence. The Americans did win their war of independence from the British. Unlike the French government, who had lost it all in North America, the British, at least, were successful in keeping the northern tier in their hands.

The nineteenth century was a period of rapid growth in both British immigration into its North American colony and the natural increase of Catholic Quebec. The hundred years leading up to Confederation and beyond witnessed the growth of the two charter groups. Each controlled its own institutional elites—the British controlled commerce and the French Catholics held onto the professions (lawyers, doctors, and the clergy) and farming. This unequal distribution of economic power between the two charter groups was meant to be balanced by political accommodation, especially at the federal level.

As Hubert Guindon (1964, 1968, 1978, 2001) pointed out, this accommodation "worked" as long as there was room for the French Catholics of Quebec to grow. The late nineteenth and the first half of the twentieth century was a time of exploding population in rural Quebec. Quebec had the highest birth rate in the country. When arable land ran out in Quebec by the late nineteenth century, and when the vacant Prairie provinces were closed off to emigration, discontent incubated (see the Down-to-Earth Sociology box on Louis Riel). The solution to the social and political problem of "too many people and not enough arable land" was the industrialization of rural Quebec (see also Hughes, 1943).

Métis leader Louis Riel, who led the "Second Red River Rebellion" in 1885 over a concern about the protection of French lands and schools in the Prairies.

Industrialization was welcomed by the clergy and the people in Quebec. The people had jobs and Quebec's Catholic clergy had parishioners. However, all was not well, especially after World War II. Quebec's government had not kept up with the changing times, and a small group of rogue intellectuals—Pierre Elliott Trudeau, Jean Marchand, and Gerald Pelletier—took on the Quebec government of Maurice Duplessis in a journal called *Cité Libre* ("free city"). Duplessis was accused of corruption and antidemocratic politics. The Catholic Church was also singled out for its support of the Nazis and its authoritarian character. Quebec, so it was argued, had been shackled by the old elites; it was time to modernize her, bring her into the twentieth century as a free, democratic, and secular province.

The death of Maurice Duplessis and his replacement by Paul Sauvé, not Jean Lesage, as Guindon rightly notes, started what has become known as the "Quiet Revolution" in Quebec. It was not and has not been that quiet, nor was it much of a revolution. What it was, was the secularization of Quebec society. Where once the Catholic Church controlled and staffed social welfare, education, and the hospitals, the provincial government took over these responsibilities. The provincial government had access to the resources to effect massive changes in these three areas— health, education, and welfare, and did so by creating jobs in the public sector of the economy. Taking over the hydroelectric power plants in the province by the mid-1960s was tantamount to catching up to Ontario, which had nationalized its hydroelectric power facilities half a century earlier.

At the beginning of the twentieth century, industrialization in rural Quebec had eased the demographic pressure brought on by large family farms by keeping sons and daughters in the province. The post-Duplessis era set the agenda for the secularization of Quebec (the Quiet Revolution) by providing good jobs in the public sector. What about the private sector in Quebec? That preserve was to be left to the largely English-speaking population of the province, who had enjoyed its privileges for over a hundred years. Some Quebecois thought otherwise, and the not-so-quiet politics of language in Quebec has been the result.

The chosen few from the English charter group, according to John Porter (1965), had kept their status as the preeminent economic leaders of the country for several generations. Just as often, though, he found that other members from the English charter group could be found in the country's political elites, the media elites, the upper echelons of the Protestant clergy, and even the trade union elites. Canada was, in Porter's phrase, a "vertical mosaic"— a pyramid in which the apex was composed of one dominant charter group, the English. A select few from the French charter group constituted a subordinate political elite located mostly, but not exclusively, in the province of Quebec. Even as late as the mid-1960s, immigrant minorities had barely touched any significant levers of power or authority in Canada.

However, Porter believed that once Canada expanded and opened its postsecondary educational institutions to all who could qualify, more and more opportunities would be available to a greater number of Canadians. Moreover, he felt that education would help break down the secrecy and exclusivity of Canada's elites and bring about a more democratic society. The economic benefits of modernization and development could be shared among all Canadians: Natives, both charter group members, and the new Canadians coming to this country from all over the world.

Unfortunately, according to Wallace Clement (1975, 1977), a student of Porter who updated his mentor's work, the economic elite has grown more insular and exclusive. While the Canadian economy has expanded since Porter's day, Clement, and now others, see a greater integration of Canada's economic elite with powerful economic interests south of the border. And while many Canadians have benefited from an expanding economy, and many others have access to postsecondary education, not all Canadians share in these benefits (an exception is our publicly funded health care system, in which we all share equally).

Focus Question
Can you describe Canada's two charter groups?

The situation of Canada's ethnic or multicultural minorities is based on their standing as immigrants or descendants of immigrants. Their interests centre more on equality than on political demands.

The Other Ethnic Groups in Canada

Canada's ethnic or multicultural minorities occupy a uniquely different status from either the Native peoples or the twin charter groups. Their situation in Canada is based on their standing as immigrants or descendants of immigrants. Their interests, therefore, centre on equality instead of the more political demands made by the other three groups.

That said, Canada embraces a rich diversity of immigrants and refugees from different parts of the world. At Confederation, barely 8 percent of Canada's population was not British or French. Today, the majority of Canadians have neither British nor French ancestry.

Table 8.1 is based on the 1996 Mini-Census and provides a breakdown of selected characteristics of the nine principal ethnic groups in Canada. All groups, except the Native peoples, reported relatively high levels of educational qualifica-

tions. East and southeast Asians held the highest percentage of university degrees with 22 percent, but Africans were closely behind them with 17 percent. The English and French reported 15 and 13 percent respectively. However, French, English, and western Europeans reported the highest percentage of incomes of $60 000 and over. The discrepancy between income and education could be due to the more recent immigration of those from Africa, the Caribbean, Latin and Central America, and east and southeast Asia to Canada.

According to Metta Spencer (1996), the actual economic experience of moving to and living in Canada has fallen far short of the expectations of many immigrants. The hope of a better life took longer than expected or failed to materialize at all. Faced with unemployment and discrimination, up to 20 percent of some groups, says Spencer, have returned to their native countries. She goes on to say that

Table 8.1 Ethnic Composition of Canada with Selected Ethnic Groups and Characteristics, 1996

Ethnic Category/ Selected Characteristics	British Isles	French	Western European	Southern European	Latin/ Central American	African	Caribbean	East and Southeast Asian	Native/ Aboriginal
Population (000s)	8417	4399	2823	1683	128	150	327	1145	723
Less than Grade 9	6%	13%	8%	21%	10%	6%	8%	13%	15%
University degree	15%	13%	14%	13%	13%	17%	10%	22%	6%
Trades certificate	3.5%	4%	4%	3%	2%	3%	4%	1%	4%
Unemployment rate	8.9%	10.6%	7.4%	9.5%	17.6%	21.1%	16.2%	10.3%	19.9%
$60 000 and over	8%	6%	7%	5%	2%	3%	3%	4%	3%

Source: Statistics Canada, *1996 Census*, 1996 (Catalogue no. 94F0009XDB96192).

Table 8.2 Language and Culture in Canada: Some Important Dates

Federal Initiatives on Language and Culture	Date
Canadian Bill of Rights	1960
Royal Commission on Bilingualism and Biculturalism	1963
Official Languages Act	1969
Promotion of multiculturalism as a national policy (Canada becomes the first country in the world to promote multiculturalism)	1971
Canadian *Human Rights Act*	1977
Canadian Charter of Rights and Freedoms	1982
Multiculturalism Act	1988
Department of Canadian Heritage includes a Secretary of State for Multiculturalism and the Status of Women portfolio	1993
Establishment of the Canadian Race Relations Foundation	1996

while British and American immigrants do well in this country, others are apt to be less successful.

Canada needs immigration in order to continue benefiting from our renewed prosperity. It is no secret that Canada's population is aging and our fertility rate is too low to keep the population at its present level. Any remaining barriers to jobs based on racial or ethnic discrimination must be eradicated. The past is littered with examples of discrimination against immigrants. At first it was probably the Irish or the French who were taking jobs away from "Canadians," then it was the Italians or the Jews, and now it is the Asians or Africans or Caribbeans—all myths with terrible consequences for those who have to bear the brunt of these prejudices. Far from taking employment away from Canadians, immigrants create more jobs than they fill (Dirks, 1995). While it is no easy task, it is time we begin to recognize that in one way or another we are all "immigrants," and the sooner we get over our hang-ups about our fellow human beings, the better our society and ourselves will be for it.

Looking Toward the Future

There will be two major issues facing Canadians as we progress into the twenty-first century. The first is the persistent demand for increased political autonomy, if not outright independence, of Quebec from Canada. Second, we will be faced with new challenges of racial and ethnic diversity due to the immigration of people, including refugees, from the less developed nations of the world. Clearly, there will be increased racial and ethnic diversity and tension, especially in the three major cities Toronto, Montreal, and Vancouver. And for all intents and purposes, it is already here. Neither issue will be simple to resolve.

What we do about each of these two pressing issues depends on our vision of and for Canadian society. If we seek a tolerant, progressive, and pluralistic society, we can achieve one where Native peoples, the two charter groups, and a racially and ethnically diverse population coexist in harmony. We will be the envy of the world and a model for others to follow.

Perspectives   Over Half a Century of Citizenship

Most Canadians do not realize that our citizenship is a relatively new achievement. As late as 1946, Canadians were considered British subjects residing in Canada, not Canadian citizens!

It was not until 1947, with the passage of the first *Citizenship Act*, that the idea of a distinctly Canadian citizenship was introduced. The year 1997 marked the 50th anniversary of Canada taking one more step toward true nationhood.

It was due largely to the efforts of Paul Martin, Sr., father of the present federal Liberal Member of Parliament and prime

ministerial hopeful, that the *Citizenship Act* came into being in the first place. It has been said that, while visiting a military cemetery in France just after World War II, Paul Martin, Sr. was visibly shaken by the rows and rows of wooden crosses that marked the graves of Canadians who had given their lives in the service of their country and for the peace and freedom that everyone now enjoyed.

Mr. Martin was impressed by the various ethnic and religious backgrounds of the names on the graves. Despite their differences, these soldiers had come together in a struggle against

the Nazi dictatorship and fascism and died for what they believed in. When Martin returned to Canada, he set the wheels in motion that led to the establishment of the *Citizenship Act* as a tribute to their memory. On January 1, 1947, Canada took a bold step toward independence when the *Citizenship Act* came into being, and by so doing established a separate Canadian identity, new rights for Canadian women, and our own Canadian passport.

Source: Adapted from Citizenship and Immigration Canada Web site.

Summary and Review

LAYING THE SOCIOLOGICAL FOUNDATION

How is race both a reality and a myth?

In the sense that different groups inherit distinctive physical characteristics, race is a reality. In the sense of one race being superior to another and of there being pure races, however, race is a myth. The *idea* of race is powerful, shaping basic relationships among people. pp. 194–195.

How do race and ethnicity differ?

Race refers to supposed biological characteristics; **ethnicity**, to cultural ones. Ethnic groups identify with one another on the basis of common ancestry and cultural heritage. pp. 195–196.

What are minority and dominant groups?

Minority groups are people singled out for unequal treatment by members of the **dominant group**, the group with more power, privilege, and social status. Minorities originate with the expansion of political boundaries or migration. pp. 196–197.

Why are women a minority?

Women are a minority because they have been singled out for unequal treatment and many regard themselves as objects of collective discrimination. p. 196.

Are prejudice and discrimination the same thing?

Prejudice is an attitude, **discrimination** an act. Some people who are prejudiced do not discriminate, while others who are not prejudiced do. p. 197.

How do individual and institutional discrimination differ?

Individual discrimination is the negative treatment of one person by another, while **institutional discrimination** is discrimination built into a society's social institutions. Institutional discrimination often occurs without the awareness of either the perpetrator or the object of discrimination. pp. 197–198.

THEORIES OF PREJUDICE

How do psychologists explain prejudice?

Psychological theories of prejudice stress frustration displaced toward **scapegoats** and **authoritarian personalities**. p. 198.

How do sociologists explain prejudice?

Sociological theories focus on how different social environments increase or decrease prejudice. Functionalists stress the benefits and costs that come from discrimination. Conflict theorists look at how the groups in power exploit racial and ethnic group divisions in order to hold down wages and otherwise maintain power. Symbolic interactionists stress how labels create **selective perception** and self-fulfilling prophecies. Multiracial feminists argue that white men *and women* oppress lower-class women and men of disadvantaged races and ethnicities. pp. 198–200.

GLOBAL PATTERNS OF INTERGROUP RELATIONS

What are the major patterns of minority and dominant group relations?

Beginning with the least humane, they are **genocide**, **population transfer**, **internal colonialism**, **segregation**, **assimilation**, and **multiculturalism (pluralism)**. pp. 200–202.

THE MAJOR CLASSIFICATIONS IN CANADA

What are the major ethnic groups in Canada?

The major classifications of ethnic groups in Canada are Native Canadians, the two charter groups, and the other ethnic groups in Canada. p. 202.

Why don't all Native peoples in Canada support the Charter of Rights and Freedoms?

The use of the term "existing aboriginal and treaty rights" remains unsatisfactory to many Natives because many land claims are not recognized by some provincial governments. pp. 202–203.

What was the "Quiet Revolution" in Quebec?

Rural industrialization and secularization of religious institutions around health, education, and welfare. pp. 203–205.

Are all immigrants in Canada happy they came to this country?

According to Metta Spencer, the answer is no. She reports that up to 20 percent of some ethnic groups have returned to their native countries. p. 206.

LOOKING TOWARD THE FUTURE

What are the main ethnic issues facing Canada's future?

More political autonomy for Quebec and the challenge of creating a racial and ethnically diverse country. p. 207.

Critical Thinking Questions

1. Is ethnic or cultural assimilation of immigrants to the dominant culture the only workable public policy for a national society such as the United States, France, or Canada?

2. Many sociologists assume a society is held together by the values and beliefs its members hold in common. What beliefs and values today hold Canadian society together?

3. After you have given some thought to what holds Canada together as a society, what are the ethnic or national forces pulling Canada apart? What solutions might you offer to help minimize cultural and national divisions?

4. Does Aboriginal self-government contribute to nation-building in Canada or is it race-based politics that serves to undermine the Canadian state?

Key Terms

assimilation 201
authoritarian personality 198
compartmentalize 201
discrimination 197
dominant group 196
dual labour market 199

ethnic (and ethnicity) 195
genocide 194
individual discrimination 197
institutional discrimination 197
internal colonialism 201

Weblinks

Centre for Ethnic Studies

www.ceetum.umontreal.ca/e/index.html

The University of Montreal's Centre for Ethnic Studies (CEETUM) is a seat of research, training, and the dissemination of knowledge in the area of ethnic studies.

Centre for Refugee Studies

www.yorku.ca/crs/

The Centre for Refugee Studies is engaged in research on refugee issues; it informs public discussion as well as policy development and practice innovation by international, governmental, advocacy, and service organizations; and it supports teaching in refugee and migration studies.

Hate on the Net

www.sociology.org/content/vol003.002/kallen.html

This 1998 paper by Evelyn Kallen of York University shows that messages promoted on the Internet by organized political and religious groups incite hatred and promote harmful action against racial, ethnocultural, religious, and same-sex-oriented minorities. High-tech hate-mongering violates minority members' fundamental right of freedom from group defamation and harassment.

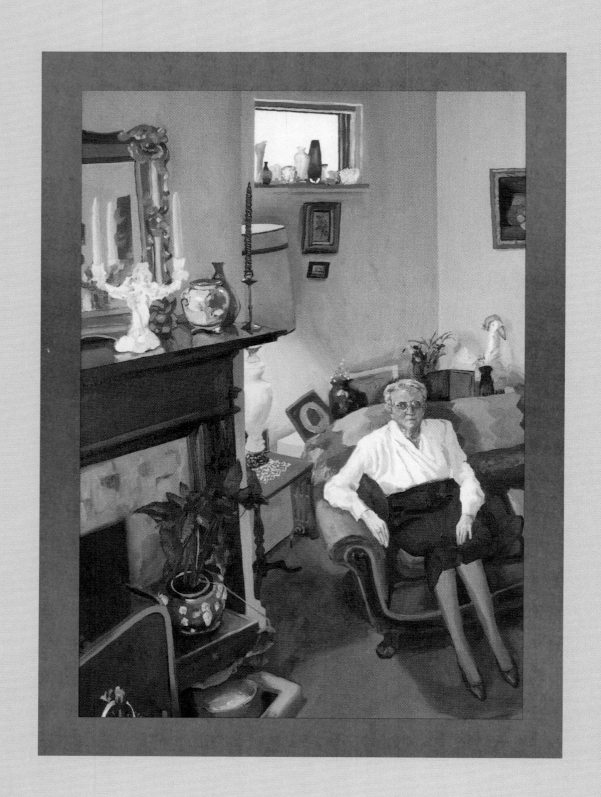

Inequalities of Age

Learning Outcomes

After you have studied this chapter, you will be able to

■ understand the social implications of the dramatic increase in the proportion of seniors in the population in Canada and around the globe

■ look at aging from a variety of useful perspectives: symbolic interactionist, functionalist, feminist, and conflict theory

■ understand the problems that often emerge in finding resources to provide adequate care as seniors become dependent on social and family resources, and how such problems are intensified by poverty and debilitating illnesses

■ see death and dying as social processes that are constructed around social factors

In 1928, Charles Hart, who was working on his Ph.D. in anthropology, did fieldwork with the Tiwi, a preliterate people who live on an island off the northern coast of Australia. Because every Tiwi belongs to a clan, they assigned Hart to the bird (Jabijabui) clan and told him that a particular woman was his mother. Hart describes the woman as "toothless, almost blind, withered," who was "physically quite revolting and mentally rather senile." He then describes this remarkable event:

> [T]oward the end of my time on the islands an incident occurred that surprised me because it suggested that some of them had been taking my presence in the kinship system much more seriously than I had thought. I was approached by a group of about eight or nine senior men, all of whom I knew. They were all senior members of the Jabijabui clan, and they had decided among themselves that the time had come to get rid of the decrepit old woman who had first called me son and whom I now called mother. As I knew, they said it was Tiwi custom, when an old woman became too feeble to look after herself, to "cover her up." This could only be done by her sons and brothers and all of them had to agree beforehand, since once it was done, they did not want any dissension among the brothers or clansmen, as that might lead to a feud. My "mother" was now completely blind, she was constantly falling over logs or into fires, and they, her senior clansmen, were in agreement that she would be better out of the way. Did I agree?
>
> I already knew about "covering up." The Tiwi, like many other hunting and gathering peoples, sometimes got rid of their ancient and decrepit females. The method was to dig a hole in the ground in some lonely place, put the old woman in the hole and fill it in with earth until only her head was showing. Everybody went away for a day or two and then went back to the hole to discover, to their surprise, that the old woman was dead, having been too feeble to raise her arms from the earth. Nobody had "killed" her; her death in Tiwi eyes was a natural one. She had been alive when her relatives last saw her. I had never seen it done, though I knew it was the custom, so I asked my brothers if it was necessary for me to attend the "covering up." They said no and that they would do it, but only after they had my agreement. Of course I agreed, and a week or two later we heard in our camp that my "mother" was dead, and we wailed and put on the trimmings of mourning (C. W. M. Hart, 1970, p. 154).

Aging in Global Perspective

Every society must deal with the problem of people growing old, some of whom grow very frail. Today, many countries around the globe are experiencing a "seniors" boom as life expectancies increase and larger portions of national populations become seniors. Japan, Sweden, the United States, Italy, Germany, and Finland all now have life expectancies beyond age 80 for both men and women. Other emerging nations, notably China with one-quarter of the world's population, are facing a dramatic shift in their age structure owing not only to increases in life expectancy but also to improved control over population growth (such as China's one-child-per-family policy) (Adamchuk, 2001). Although few societies choose to bury seniors alive, all must decide how to allocate limited resources among their citizens. For example, should health care dollars be spent on treating 80-year-old patients or premature babies? With a finite amount of money to be spent, policymakers, and by extension citizens, will be required to decide where to focus their resources.

As publicized during the Second World Assembly on Aging in 2002, evidence from around the globe indicates that at present many seniors are being denied health care, education, and training and often feel excluded from society. As the aging population expands, these problems will intensify rapidly. Analysts predict that by 2050, the proportion of the global population over age 60 will increase by 300 percent to approximately one in five of the earth's inhabitants. As the proportion of the population that is old increases—something that is happening in both industrialized and industrializing nations—decisions about the distribution of societal resources will become more complex and the tensions they create between the generations may deepen ("Forum warned of aging crisis," 2002, p. A14).

The Social Construction of Aging

The example of how the Tiwi treat their frail female elderly reflects one extreme in how societies cope with aging. An extreme in a different direction is illustrated by the Abkhasians, an agricultural people who live in a mountainous region of Georgia, a republic of the former Soviet Union. Rather than "covering up" their elderly, the Abkhasians give them high respect and look to them for guidance. They would no more dispense with one of their elderly in this manner than we would "cover up" a sick child.

The Abkhasian man says he is 115 years old. Reasons for the Abkhasians' apparent longevity are explained in the text. Because birth records in this society do not reach back to the 1800s, however, we cannot be certain of the claims by the Abkhasians.

Central to a group's culture are ways of viewing reality. Living for centuries in isolation on Bathurst and Melville Islands off the northern coast of Australia, the Tiwi, featured in the opening vignette, developed a unique culture. Shown here is Wurarbuti, prior to leading a funeral dance. To be certain that his late uncle's ghost will not recognize him, Wurarbuti is wearing a "shirt" painted with ocher and clay, a topknot of cockatoo feathers, and a beard of goose feathers.

The Abkhasians may be the longest-lived people in the world. Many claim to live past 100—some beyond 120 and even 130 (Benet, 1971). Although it is difficult to document the accuracy of these claims (Haslick, 1974; D. K. Harris, 1990), government records indicate that an extraordinary number of Abkhasians do live to a very old age. Three main factors appear to account for their long lives. The first is their diet, which consists of little meat, much fresh fruit, vegetables, garlic, goat cheese, cornmeal, buttermilk, and wine. The second is their lifelong physical activity. They do slow down after age 80, but even after the age of 100 they still work about four hours a day.

The third factor—a highly developed sense of community—goes to the very heart of the Abkhasian culture. From childhood, every individual is highly integrated into a primary group, and remains so throughout life. There is no such thing as a nursing home, nor do the elderly live alone. Because even into old age they continue to work and contribute to the group's welfare, they aren't a burden to anyone. They don't vegetate, nor do they have the need to "fill time" with bingo and shuffleboard. In short, the elderly feel no sudden rupture between what they "were" and what they "are."

The examples of the Tiwi and the Abkhasians reveal an important sociological principle we shall explore in this chapter—that aging is *socially constructed*. That is, nothing in the nature of aging summons forth any particular set of attitudes. Rather, attitudes toward the aged—and resulting behaviours—are rooted in society, and therefore differ from one social group to another. As we shall also see, even *when* people are considered old depends not on biology, but on culture.

Effects of Industrialization

As noted in previous chapters, industrialization is a worldwide trend. Along with a higher standard of living, with industrialization comes a more plentiful food supply, better public health measures—especially a purer water supply—and a largely successful fight against the diseases that kill people at younger ages. Consequently, when a country industrializes, more of its people reach older ages. In Table 9.1 you can see the dramatic differences in the age distribution in industrial and industrializing countries around the globe. As the industrializing countries catch up, for example, in terms of health care and improved nutrition, the aging of the global population will be intensified.

As the number of a nation's elderly increases, so, too, does the bill its younger citizens pay to provide for their needs. In the most industrialized nations, this bill has become a major social issue. Although Canadians commonly complain that income security taxes are too high, Table 9.2 shows that the Canadian rate is comparatively low. In the least industrialized nations, there are no social security taxes, and families are expected to take care of their own elderly.

Table 9.1 A Comparison of Aging Populations in Selected Industrial and Industrializing Countries Around the Globe

Industrializing Countries	% of Population 65+	Industrial Countries	% of Population 65+
Afghanistan	2.8	Australia	12.5
Brazil	5.5	Canada	12.8
China	7.1	France	16.1
India	4.7	Italy	18.3
Mexico	4.4	Japan	17.5
Pakistan	4.1	Netherlands	13.7
Sudan	2.1	Russia	12.8
Yemen	3.0	United Kingdom	15.7

Source: U.S. Census Bureau, 2001, *Statistical Abstract of the United States* (Washington DC: U.S. Government Printing Office), p. 834.

The Graying of Canada

Table 9.3 shows the notable increase in the number of seniors in the Canadian population. In large measure, this is the result of marked improvements in Canadian **life expectancy**. It is startling to realize that 100 years ago the clear majority of Canadians would not live to see age 65. Indeed, a Canadian woman born in 1901 could expect to live, on average, to age 50 and a man to age 47. Since then, life expectancy has increased so greatly that a Canadian woman born in 1999 can expect to live an average of 81.7 years and a man 76.3 years (Statistics Canada, 2002f). Despite illness, accidents and other factors that may cut life short, the overwhelming majority of Canadians live at least to retirement age. More than 80 percent of men and almost 90 percent of women can expect to live to at least age 65 (Gorrie, 2001; Martel & Belanger, 2000). Further, life expectancy continues to increase, so that every

Table 9.2 Payroll Taxes and the Elderly

Country	Total Population	Percentage over 65	Number over 65	Percentage of Payroll Paid in Taxes to Support the Elderly*
France	59 000 000	16.1	9 500 000	43
Hungary	10 000 000	14.6	1 500 000	40
Holland	16 000 000	13.7	2 200 000	39
Italy	57 000 000	18.2	10 400 000	39
Belgium	10 000 000	17.1	1 700 000	36
Czech Republic	109 000 000	13.8	1 400 000	35
Germany	82 000 000	16.5	13 500 000	34
Greece	11 000 000	17.2	1 900 000	34
Poland	39 000 000	12.2	4 800 000	33
Spain	39 000 000	16.8	6 600 000	29
Mexico	102 000 000	4.3	4 400 000	21
Great Britain	59 000 000	15.7	9 200 000	17
Turkey	67 000 000	6.0	4 000 000	16
Japan	126 000 000	17.0	21 400 000	14
United States	275 000 000	12.6	34 700 000	14
Canada	31 000 000	12.6	3 900 000	11
South Korea	47 000 000	6.9	3 200 000	4
Australia	19 000 000	12.6	2 400 000	2
China	1 256 000 000	7.0	87 900 000	N/A
Indonesia	219 000 000	4.3	9 400 000	N/A
Nigeria	117 000 000	3.0	3 500 000	N/A
Egypt	69 000 000	3.7	2 600 000	N/A
Kenya	29 000 000	2.8	800 000	N/A

*All countries for which the source lists the percentage of labour costs paid in social security taxes, plus five larger countries for comparison.

Source: *Statistical Abstract*, 1999, Tables 1349, 1350, 1384.

Table 9.3 Percentage of Seniors (65+) in the Canadian Population, 1921–2041

Year	Percentage of Canadians 65+
1921	4.8
1931	5.6
1941	6.7
1951	7.8
1961	7.6
1971	8.0
1981	9.6
1991	11.4
1998	12.3
2016*	15.9*
2021*	17.8*
2031*	21.7*
2041*	22.6*

*Projected

Sources: Lindsay, Colin, 1999, *A portrait of seniors in Canada*. 3rd ed. Ottawa: Statistics Canada, Catalogue no. 89-519-XPE; Statistics Canada, 2002, *Population by age groups*. Retrieved February 11, 2002 from **http://www.statcan.ca/english/Pgdb/People/Population/demo31a.htm**; Statistics Canada, 2002, *Population projections for 2001, 2006, 2011, 2016, 2021 and 2026, July 1*. Retrieved February 11, 2002 from **http://www.statcan.ca/english/Pgdb/People/Population/demo23b.htm**.

Table 9.4 Life Expectancy in a Global Context

	Life Expectancy at Birth 1995–2000	
	Women	Men
Southern Africa	56	52
Central America	74	69
Central Asia	71	63
Western Europe	81	75

Source: United Nations, 2000, *The World's Women 2000: Trends and Statistics*. New York: United Nations, p. 54.

five years Canadians can add about another year to their life expectancy.

The term **graying of Canada** has been coined to refer to this increasing proportion of older people in the Canadian population. According to the 2001 census, there are 3.9 million Canadian seniors, or 13 percent of the population. There are also 420 000 Canadians who are 85 and older and 3795 who are 100 and older (Leong, 2002)! Canadian society has become so "gray" that by 2016 there will be more seniors than children aged 14 and younger (Lu, 2001). And the graying is far from complete. Although, as is apparent from Table 9.4, Canada's life expectancy ranks among the highest in the world, other countries, such as Japan and Italy, have surpassed us in terms of the proportion of seniors in the population. As Canada follows suit in the coming years, seniors will take an increasingly prominent place in our population.

Of course, the impact of this aging population has not been felt uniformly across the country. As with so much of Canadian social life, there are important regional differences. There are five regions in particular that have aged considerably: the Okanagan Valley in British Columbia, the Victoria-Vancouver region, a number of townships surrounding Toronto (notably the St. Catharines–Niagara census metropolitan areas), a block of counties in southwest Nova Scotia, and a region that encompasses parts of both Manitoba and Saskatchewan (where more than 17 percent of the popu-

lation are seniors). Clearly, some of this geographic concentration reflects the movement of seniors into areas with attractive climates, affordable housing, services, and proximity to urban areas. In other instances, such as Saskatchewan, there may have been an out-migration of younger people seeking better economic opportunities, leaving behind a concentration of seniors (Statistics Canada, 1999, pp. 73–74).

It is also important to keep in mind that the maximum length of life, the **life span**, has not increased. Experts disagree, however, on what the maximum is and whether it is flexible. We do know that it is possible for a human to live to at least 122, for this was the well-documented age of Jeanne Louis Calment of France at her death in 1997. If the reports on the Abkhasians are correct—which is a matter of controversy—the human life span may exceed even this number by a comfortable margin. Recent genome research with those 100 years of age and older is seeking to unlock some of the genetic components of longevity. With advances in this and other areas of medicine, living to our 100th birthday may become increasingly common.

Aging: Differences by Gender and Ethnicity

Of course, not everyone in society has an equal chance of becoming old. Analysts have long been pointing out that the average Canadian woman can reasonably expect to live longer than the average male. Even though men have been catching up with women in terms of life expectancy since the late 1970s, the latest figures still indicate that there is a gender gap in aging. In 2001, women were likely to live about four years longer than men. Not surprisingly, as a result of this gender pattern, women tend to predominate in the ranks of older Canadians. Currently, women make up 57 percent of Canadians 65 years of age and older and more than 65 percent of those 80 years of age or older (Duchesne, 2002). This greater percentage of women, especially among senior seniors, is one of the reasons aging often draws the attention of feminist researchers. This is discussed in more detail below.

In addition, certain segments of the population have a lower life expectancy. Wherever there are specific populations

Although there was quite an age discrepancy between the late Canadian Prime Minister Pierre Trudeau and his wife Margaret, it was a typical gender age relationship.

subject to higher rates of unemployment, economic marginalization, homelessness, inadequate housing, and so on, these groups are, of course, less likely to enjoy long lives. African-Americans in the United States, for example, have lower life expectancies than other Americans (Henslin, 2001). This same pattern holds true in Canada, where the average Native Canadian is likely to live a shorter life than other Canadians. In 1975, a Canadian male could expect to live to age 70 and a female to 78; in contrast, Native Canadian males could expect to live to 59 years of age and Native Canadian females to age 66. Since then, there have been important improvements in Native life expectancy, largely as a result of lower infant mortality rates among the Native Canadian population. Today, male "registered Indians" can expect to live to 68 and female "registered Indians" can expect to live to 81 (Department of Indian Affairs and Northern Development, 1999, p. 21). Analysts anticipate that further improvements will be made in Native life expectancy in coming years. This improvement, of course, hinges on continuing progress in improving the lives of Canadian Native peoples (Armstrong, 2000).

In Sum

As a result of industrialization and accompanying improvements in sanitation, disease prevention, nutrition, and so on, more and more humans around the globe are living to be old. Not surprisingly, cultures vary in how they treat their elderly and not everyone in a given culture has an equal chance of becoming a senior. In Canada, women are more likely than men to grow old but Aboriginal men and women are at a disadvantage in joining the ranks of the seniors. The impact of being seen to be "old" will vary from culture to culture, ranging from very positive outcomes in some instances to "voluntary" death in other cases.

Focus Question

Why did industrialization have such an impact on the graying of Canada?

The Symbolic Interactionist Perspective

To study how aging is socially constructed, symbolic interactionists examine how the symbols associated with age affect our perceptions. Let's look, then, at how culture underlies our ideas of when a person becomes "old," and then at how negative stereotypes and the mass media affect our perceptions of aging.

Marie-Louise Meilleur of Corbeil, Ontario, was the world's oldest person whose age could be authenticated, until her death on April 16, 1998. Cutting Marie-Louise's 117th birthday cake is former Premier of Ontario Mike Harris.

Labelling and the Onset of Old Age

You probably can remember when you thought a 12-year-old was "old"—and anyone older was beyond reckoning, just "up there" someplace. You were probably 5 or 6 at the time. Similarly, to a 12-year-old, someone of 21 seems "old." At 21, 30 may mark that line, and 40 may seem "very old." And so it keeps on going, with "old" gradually receding from the self. To people who turn 40, 50 seems old; at 50, the late 60s look old (not the early 60s, for at that point in accelerating years they don't seem too far away).

At some point, of course, an individual must apply the label "old" to him- or herself. Often, cultural definitions of age force this label on people sooner than they are ready to accept it. In the typical case, the individual has become used to what he or she sees in the mirror. The changes have taken place very gradually, and each change, if not exactly taken in stride, has been accommodated. (Consequently, it comes as a shock, when meeting a friend one has not seen in years, to see how much that person has changed. At class reunions, no one can believe how much older *the others* appear!)

If there is no single point at which people automatically cross a magical line and become "old," what, then, makes someone "old"? We can point out several factors that spur people to apply that label to themselves.

The first factor is *biology*. One person may experience "signs" of aging much earlier than another: wrinkles, balding, aches, difficulty in doing some things he or she used to take for granted. Consequently, one person will feel "old" at an earlier or later age than others, and only at that time *adopt the role of an "old person"*; that is, begin to act in ways old people in that particular society are thought to act. In short, our experience with and perception of biological changes affects our sense of "self." For example, Laura Hurd Clarke examined the ways in which women's aging bodies—including the deterioration of health and functional abilities—impacted on women's sense of identity. Interestingly, many of her female research participants indicated they came to experience their bodies as both a mask and a prison for their "real" self (2001).

Personal history or biography is a second factor that influences when people consider themselves old. An accident that limits mobility may make one person feel old sooner than others. Or a woman may have given birth at 16 to a daughter, who in turn has a child at 18. When this woman is 34, she is a biological grandmother. It is most unlikely that she will begin to play any stereotypical role—spending the day in a rocking chair, for example—but *knowing* that she is a grandmother has an impact on her self-concept. At a minimum, she must *deny* that she is old.

As discussed in detail below, a third factor determining when people label themselves old is **gender age**. Feminist analysts have pointed out that gender and age intersect with one another and, generally, the negative implications of

Aging depends on much more than biology, and classifying oneself as old depends on many factors, including cultural guidelines and biography. What biographical factors do you think were significant for this woman of the Great Depression?

aging impact more heavily and earlier on women than men. The fourth factor is **timetables**, the signals societies use to inform their members they are old. Since there is no automatic age at which people become "old," these timetables vary around the world and through history (Gilleard, 2002). One group may choose a particular birthday, such as the 60th or 65th, to signal the onset of old age. With increasing longevity in industrialized societies, these social timetables have been amended, and many analysts are now referring to a "third age" (a period of good health, free of many work and family obligations) followed by a "fourth age" (a period when health deteriorates and activity is limited). Further, as discussed below under "Problems of Dependency," it appears that this dependence-free "third age" is expanding as more Canadians adopt a healthy lifestyle (Martel & Belanger, 2000).

The Meaning of Old Age: Cross-Cultural Comparisons

To help pinpoint the extent to which people's experience of old age involves factors beyond biology, let's look at some cross-cultural examples.

Consider first this fictionalized encounter between two Tiwi men:

> Bashti looked in envy at Masta. Masta strutted just a bit as he noticed Bashti glance his way. He knew what Bashti was thinking. Had he not thought the same just 20 years earlier? Then he had no wife; now he had three. Then he had no grand hut. Now he did, plus one for each wife. Then he had no respect, no power, no wealth. Now he was looked up to by everyone. "Ah, the marvels and beauty of gray hair," Masta thought.
>
> Bashti hung his head as he slouched toward the fringe of the group. "But my turn will come. I, too, will grow old," he thought, finding some comfort in the situation.

Why would a Tiwi man look forward to growing old, something that few people in North America do? Traditional Tiwi society was a **gerontocracy**, a society run by the elderly. The old men were firmly entrenched in power and controlled everything. Their power was so inclusive that the old men married *all* the women—both young and old—leaving none for the young men. Only at about the age of 40 was a man able to marry (Hart & Pilling, 1970). (In Tiwi society, females were the pawns, and aging was of no advantage to a woman. Indeed, as we saw in the opening vignette, for a woman aging could be a considerable disadvantage.)

Traditional Inuit society also provides a rich contrast to that of an industrialized society such as Canada.

> Shantu and Wishta fondly kissed their children and grandchildren farewell. Then sadly, but with resignation at the sacrifice they knew they had to make for their family, they slowly climbed onto the ice floe. The goodbyes were painfully made as the large slab of ice inched into the ocean currents. Shantu and Wishta would now starve. But they were old, and their death was necessary, for it reduced the demand on the small group's scarce food supply.
>
> As the younger relatives watched Shantu and Wishta recede into the distance, they knew that their turn to make this sacrifice would come. Each hoped to face it as courageously.

To grow old in traditional Inuit society meant a "voluntary" death. Survival in their harsh environment was so precarious that all, except very young children, had to pull their own weight. The food supply was so limited that nothing was left over to give to anyone who could not participate in the closely integrated tasks required for survival.

Canadian Society: Changing Perceptions

Physician Robert Butler (1975, 1980), when he came to realize how deeply feelings against the elderly can run, coined the term **ageism** to refer to prejudice, discrimination, and hostility directed against people because of their age.

As we have just seen, however, there is nothing inherent in old age to summon forth negative attitudes. Some researchers even suggest that in early Canadian society old age had positive meanings. Due to high death rates, not many people made it to old age. Consequently, growing old was seen as an accomplishment, and the younger generation listened to the elderly's advice about how to live a long life. With no pensions (this was before industrialization), the elderly continued to work. Since their jobs changed little over time, they were a storehouse of knowledge about work skills.

These bases of respect, however, were eroded with the coming of industrialization. Improved sanitation and medical care allowed more people to reach old age, removing the distinction of being elderly. Then, too, the new forms of mass production made young workers as productive as the elderly. Coupled with mass education, this stripped away the mystique that the elderly possessed superior knowledge (Cowgill, 1974; Novak, 1993).

As the social bases that had upheld respect for the elderly crumbled, a new set of images—from those of esteem to those of contempt—emerged. A sign of this shift in meanings is how people lie about their age—they used to claim they were older than they were, but now they say they are younger than they are (Clair, Karp, & Yoels, 1993; Thimm, Rademacher, & Krus, 1998).

It is a basic principle of symbolic interactionism that people perceive both themselves and others according to the symbols of their culture. Thus, as the meaning of old age was transformed—from usefulness to uselessness, from wisdom to foolishness, from an asset to a liability—not only did younger people see the elderly differently, but the elderly, who also internalized the same cultural symbols, came to see themselves in a new light.

The meaning of old age is being transformed once again. The proportion of elderly who are able to take care of themselves financially has grown. They are no longer seen as such a dependent group. In addition, the baby boom generation, the first of whom have now turned 50, has begun to confront the realities of aging. With better health, financial assets, longer lives, and a celebration of a youth culture, this large segment of the population can be counted on to resist being perceived in negative terms. For example, the value of maturity and the possibilities of aging as a process to be appreciated are beginning to be explored. Given their vast numbers and economic clout, they are likely to positively affect our images of the elderly (Friedan, 1993).

However, despite these positive shifts, it is also likely that aging will continue to have a profound meaning for Canadians. It will likely continue to be characterized by dramatic shifts in our sense of self as careers end, as illness and disability become increasing concerns, as important relationships are cut short by death, and as our own death is increasingly confronted. Indeed, in an analogy that is very much in keeping with a symbolic interactionist perspective, Mary Pipher (1999) suggests we need to think of our experience of old age as a trip to a "foreign" country—an unknown landscape in which we will need to learn a new language and a new mode of functioning.

As pointed out by researcher Thomas Walz (2002), the popular media, notably television and movies, have demonstrated an aversion to representing seniors as sexual beings. When they make exceptions to this rule, they frequently present the sexuality of older persons in terms of negative stereotypes. From dirty old men to frigid old women, the message concerning senior sexuality is both contradictory and unflattering. Frequently, seniors are presented as simply sexless—either uninterested in or incapable of sex. In the film *Grumpy Old Men*, for example, the protagonists are portrayed as "talking" about sex while actually spending their time golfing and fishing. When older men or women are presented as sexually driven,

they generally are involved with a younger partner, a pattern in which they run the risk of being presented as sexual predators, as was Humbert in *Lolita* or Mrs. Robinson in the film *The Graduate*. While the popularity of Viagra and the attendant media attention suggest that many older persons are obviously interested in being sexually active, the popularity of Viagra *jokes* in the media speak to the persistent stereotypes. What is missing are images of "truly healthy passionate relationships" between two older persons (Walz, 2002).

This media representation of senior sexuality is particularly interesting since it flies in the face of what we know from sexual research. Over and over,

researchers have documented that the "majority of elderly people remain sexually interested and able and their activity levels would be even greater if losses of partners due to age and infirmity were not so prevalent" (Walz, 2002, p. 109).

It will be fascinating to discover whether the wave of aging baby boomers forces a reconsideration of media stereotypes, a more realistic portrayal of senior sexuality, and a popularization of the sexy senior. A recent edition of the CARP (Canada's Association for the Fifty-Plus) publication *50 Plus* has a cover story entitled "Looking hot after 50" (Righton, 2002). It doesn't appear likely that the boomers are going to accept the traditional stereotypes.

The social position of the elderly differs from one society to another. In Asian cultures, the elderly usually enjoy high respect. Shown here is a Vietnamese-American boy intently learning from his grandfather how to do calligraphy.

The Mass Media: Powerful Sources of Symbols

In Chapter 4, we noted that the mass media help to shape our ideas of gender and relationships between men and women. The media also influence our ideas of the elderly. Like females, the elderly are underrepresented on television, in advertisements, and in most popular magazines. Their

omission implies a lack of social value. The covert message is that the elderly are of little consequence and can be safely ignored. This message is not lost on viewers, who internalize the media's negative symbols and, as they add years, go to great lengths to deny that they are growing old. The mass media then exploit fears of losing youthful vitality to sell hair dyes, skin creams, and innumerable other products that supposedly conceal the appearance of old age (Vernon, Williams, Phillips, & Wilson, 1990; Vasil & Wass, 1993).

It's easy to test the media bias for yourself. Simply pick any popular mass market magazine and look at every identifiable face in an advertisement. Keep track of how many appear to be over 50 or over 60 or over 70. You might simply look for gray in their hair and lines on their face. You will quickly discover that seniors tend to be invisible members of society when viewed through the mass media lens. Consider, for example, recent popular television series— *The West Wing, Friends, Seinfeld, Six Feet Under*—seniors are almost completely invisible. Media images of seniors are, of course, not entirely negative or absent. The popular *Sopranos* television series is an interesting exception to the pattern in that older family members—both male and female—have played a central part in the drama. Further, as the baby boomers grow older, a growing number of specialized magazines and television programming is ensuring that senior interests are represented in the media.

Canadian publications such as *Today's Seniors, The Seniors' Review* and *50 Plus* provide a very positive image of seniors and stress the active, healthy lifestyles enjoyed by many older Canadians. In these media, older individuals

PEANUTS® by Charles M. Schulz

Stereotypes, which play such a profound role in social life, are a basic area of sociological investigation. In contemporary society, the mass media are a major source of stereotypes.

are likely to be portrayed as important and involved members of society who are healthy, capable, and active (Roberts & Zhou, 1997). In addition, these media are often used by organizations such as CARP and the Older Women's Network to lobby for the empowerment of seniors, including more positive media images.

With growing numbers of senior Canadians, it is likely that social pressure will continue to encourage the media to present a more balanced, less stereotyped representation of older men and women (Nelson & Robinson, 2002).

In Sum

Symboic interactionists have drawn our attention to a number of important aspects of aging. First, whether someone is "labelled" old or, indeed, "labels" him- or herself old, depends on a variety of factors, not simply biological age. Physical "signs" of aging such as wrinkles may contribute to the labelling process, but personal history (having grandchildren at a "young" age) and gender (men "mature" while women "age") may also have an impact on how we see ourselves aging. Finally, societies set certain *timetables*, such as retirement at age 65, that tend to be seen as key signals of aging. Given that aging responds to a variety of social factors, it is not surprising that attitudes toward the elderly vary considerably from one society to another; venerated in one society, they may be seen as a troublesome burden in another. Further, these attitudes may shift over time. In early Canadian history, seniors were uncommon, and growing old was seen as an accomplishment. Industrialization served to erode the

notion that seniors were important sources of knowledge and a more negative attitude emerged. In recent times, as the health and wealth of the elderly has improved, a more positive image has again emerged. In this changing image of the elderly, the mass media are playing a key role. On the one hand, seniors have traditionally been ignored, pitied, or trivialized in many media. In recent years, seniors have sought to encourage the media's acceptance of a more positive and inclusive perspective on the elderly.

Focus Question
How do the media influence our attitude toward aging and the elderly, and is that influence likely to change in the near future?

The Feminist Perspective

As women who were active in the modern women's movement moved into their "middle age" in the 1980s and 90s, aging was increasingly included as a feminist issue (Macdonald & Rich, 1991). Many of the most well-known spokeswomen of the movement—Betty Friedan (1993), Germaine Greer (1991), Gloria Steinem (1992)—examined their own personal experiences of growing older and pointed out the inequities faced by older women. In more recent years, as feminists sought to incorporate various patterns of privilege, domination, and oppression (such as sexual orientation, ethnicity, and disability) into the feminist paradigm, aging has emerged as an increasingly important, if contentious, element in feminist analysis (Shaw & Lee, 2001; Reinharz, 1997).

First and foremost, feminist analysts are pointing out that aging exacerbates the problem of power for women (Copper, 2001). As women age they are likely to find themselves increasingly marginalized and dismissed. This is apparent, for example, in patterns of marriage. Around the globe, compared to most women, most men are able to marry much younger spouses. Indeed, the popular media often poke fun at the older man with his much younger "trophy" wife. In part, this pattern of older men with younger wives reflects the belief that men retain their attractiveness and sexuality longer than women. On men, graying hair and even some wrinkles may be seen as signs of "maturing," while on women those same features are likely to be interpreted as signs of being "old." As Canadian sociologists Sharon McIrvin Abu-Laban and Susan McDaniel comment, "Women are said to be older sooner than men. While aging is seen as empowering for many men, it is not seen to be so for women. *His* facial lines are seen as signs of character; her lines are signs of decrepitude and decreasing sexual attractiveness" (1998, p. 79). This difference in the social evaluation of "old women" and "mature men" is also revealed, for example, when older male news anchors are likely to be retained, while female anchors who turn the same age are more likely to be transferred to a less visible position. Similarly, in movies, older men (Sean Connery and Clint Eastwood) are much more likely to play romantic leads—and opposite much younger female rising stars.

Of course, the relative "attractiveness" of women is complexly related to their social and economic positions in society. Many women, who have devoted themselves to home and family and who have interrupted their careers or worked part-time, will not be spending their "mature" years as well-paid corporate chiefs or respected members of the professions. Indeed, many women, particularly if they are divorced or widowed, will find that their economic well-being is problematic. It is likely that these patterns of economic marginalization and insecurity contribute to images of older women as "unattractive."

Needless to say, older women struggling with additional societal prejudices are likely to have even more difficulties. As Abu-Laban and McDaniel comment, "The prospects for women of colour, aboriginal women, women with disabilities, or lesbian women are even worse. Aged women with out-of-date eyewear, bad teeth, unfashionably sized bodies, limited education, and whose only (or main) work experience is raising children on welfare" are even more likely to end up economically and socially peripheralized in old age (1998, p. 87).

There are, of course, exceptions to these general patterns. There are instances in which men marry much older women, and we can point to increasing numbers of female celebrities (Goldie Hawn, Susan Sarandon, Jane Fonda) who are in their 50s and 60s. However, these exceptions,

simply because they are noteworthy, are evidence of the powerful social norms surrounding women and aging. For example, the "mature" women celebrities are outstanding in large measure because of their youthful appearance rather than their age. In an interesting comparison of the media presentations of Jane Fonda (born 1937) and Barbara Bush (born 1925), Myra Dinnerstein and Rose Weitz (2002) point out that Bush with her matronly figure, white hair, and wrinkled face is often presented as a prime candidate for a make-over. Bush herself uses self-deprecating humour to deflect anticipated criticisms of her appearance and often appears defensive when discussing the "naturalness" of her appearance. In contrast, Fonda, who explains her appearance in terms of a commitment to health and fitness along with professional necessity, is presented in magazines as an enviable (if unattainable) role model for aging women. In short, even powerful, respected women find themselves contained by powerful cultural standards of femininity.

The Mass Media: Invisible Women

Much contemporary postmodern feminism has been exploring the ways in which gender and age are reproduced in the discourses embedded in cultural representations such as art, literature, and the mass media. Contemporary efforts to deconstruct these messages reveals how complex and nuanced the meanings attached to gender and age are. However, it is not necessary to deconstruct texts to reveal the messages about gender and aging that are incorporated into contemporary media.

Simply undertaking your own examination of mass media images of older women can be very revealing. This is what U.S. feminist Betty Friedan did when she started research for her book on aging. Not surprisingly, of 290 identifiable faces in *Vogue* she found only one was of a woman who might be over 60. Of 116 identifiable faces in *Vanity Fair* illustrations there were two women over 60—the Queen Mother and Imelda Marcos—and ten older men, all powerful or famous (Friedan, 1993, p. 37). The implicit message is that most seniors, except the rich, famous, and powerful, do not count and that this is especially true of senior women.

Media images of older women are, of course, not entirely negative or absent. Carol Matthews (1996) points out that older women have, on occasion, been portrayed in very positive ways in a variety of Canadian literature. Prominent Canadian authors, including Margaret Laurence, Margaret Atwood, Sylvia Fraser, and Sheila Watson, have represented older women as a powerful presence and significant forces in their novels.

The Functionalist Perspective

Functionalists examine how the parts of society work together. We can consider an **age cohort**—a group of people born at roughly the same time who pass through the life course together—as a component of society. This component affects other parts. For example, if the age cohort nearing retirement is large (a "baby boom" generation), many jobs will open at roughly the same time. If it is small (a "baby bust" generation), fewer jobs will open. A smooth transition at retirement requires a good adjustment among the parts of society.

Disengagement theory and activity theory, which we shall now examine, focus on the adjustments between those who are retiring and society's other components.

Disengagement Theory

Elaine Cumming and William Henry (1961) developed **disengagement theory** to explain how society prevents disruption when the elderly vacate (or disengage from) their positions of responsibility. It would be disruptive if the elderly left their positions only when they died or became incompetent. Consequently, societies use pensions to entice the elderly to voluntarily hand over their positions to younger people. Thus, disengagement is a mutually beneficial agreement between two parts of society, facilitating a smooth transition between the generations.

Cumming (1976) also examined disengagement from the individual's perspective. She pointed out that disengagement begins during middle age, long before retirement, when an individual senses that the end of life is closer than its start. The individual does not immediately disengage, but, realizing that time is limited, begins to assign priority to goals and tasks. Disengagement begins in earnest when children leave home, and continues with retirement and, eventually, widowhood.

Evaluation of the Theory.
Disengagement theory has come under heavy criticism. Anthropologist Dorothy Jerrome (1992) points out that it contains an implicit bias against older people—assumptions that the elderly disengage from productive social roles, and then sort of sink into oblivion. Instead, the elderly in good health spend time in social, recreational, and civic activities. Further, there is increasing evidence that more and more Canadian retirees are remaining active in the labour force. On the one hand, more Canadians are retiring from their jobs earlier. While between 1976 and 1980 the median retirement age was 64.9 years of age, between 1996 and 2000 it dropped to 61.0 years of age. Not surprisingly, many of these younger retirees have the time, energy, and health to continue to hold paid employment. Currently, 60 percent of Canadians aged 65 to 69, and 25 percent of those 70 to 74, are employed (Duchesne, 2002). In short, concerns about the long-term viability of Canadian governmental pension plans along with growing part-time and self-employment opportunities are combining to encourage many senior Canadians to keep "working" (Duffy, Glenday, & Pupo, 1998). In this way, rather than disengaging from society, many seniors are moving on to more flexible, and possibly more challenging, opportunities.

Activity Theory

In contrast, **activity theory** examines whether there is a relationship between social involvement and life satisfaction among retirees. Specifically, it is hypothesized that the more socially active a senior is, the more satisfied the individual will be with life. Although we could consider this theory under other perspectives, because its focus is how disengagement is functional or dysfunctional, it, too, can be considered from a functionalist perspective.

Evaluation of the Theory.
Research suggests that the central hypothesis is frequently supported by real-life experiences. Generally, the more active people are, the more satisfied they also are. Certainly, it is not surprising to find that seniors who enjoy active social ties with family members and friends report a good quality of life (Bess, 1999; Connidis, 1989). However, there are exceptions. For example, a study in France found that some people were happier when they were very active, while others were more content when they were less involved (Keith, 1982). The complexity of this issue is also clearly reflected in individuals' responses to retirement. Although almost half of Canadian retirees (47 percent) believe they got more out of life the year after retirement than the year before (due to the increase in leisure and family time), about one-fifth indicated they enjoyed life less. While some of these individuals were struggling with health issues, others reported that retirement meant less contact with people and, as a result, less overall life enjoyment (Monette, 1996).

To simply count people's activities, then, is far from adequate. We need to examine key variables such as finances, health, and individual orientations. Being active and involved in a fulfilling manner likely hinges on access to adequate financial resources, on healthiness, and on a personal inclination. In order to understand the role of activity in seniors' life satisfaction, the complex interrelationships among these variables must be thoroughly researched.

In Sum

The functionalist perspective draws our attention to the relationship between seniors and the rest of society. Disengagement theory, for example, focuses on the institutionalized patterns that allow seniors to slowly leave their positions of responsibility so the next generation can take over without disruption. However, this theoretical approach tends to ignore the complex contributions and activities of seniors who retire from their main paid employment but remain active in a variety of social contexts. Activity theory points up the potential link between participation in society and personal satisfaction. A variety of evidence does suggest that remaining socially connected—by volunteer activity, part-time employment, friendships, etc.—contributes to the well-being of seniors.

The Conflict Perspective

From the conflict perspective, the guiding principles of social life are competition, disequilibrium, and change. So it is with society's age groups. Whether the young and old recognize it or not, they are part of a basic struggle that threatens to throw society into turmoil. The passage of pension legislation is an example of this struggle.

Pension Legislation

In the 1800s Canada was a largely agricultural and rural nation. Given levels of sanitation, health care, and nutrition, few Canadians lived to old age. The few that did could turn to their large families to provide whatever social and economic support was needed. In the absence of a supportive family, appeals could be made to private charities.

Needless to say, this whole scenario changed with the advent of industrialization and urbanization. Improvements in medicine, sanitation, and nutrition meant more Canadians, particularly women, lived to old age. However, shrinking family size meant that many older Canadians were left impoverished and unsupported. In response, since the 1920s the federal and provincial governments have increasingly introduced policies to provide some measure of economic security for seniors (Oderkirk, 1996).

Currently, Canadian seniors are supported through a three-level retirement income system. At the first level are income security programs funded by the federal, provincial, and territorial governments. The most well known is the Old Age Security pension (OAS), which was first introduced in 1952 and which is paid to most Canadians age 65 or older. This provides Canadian seniors with $442.66 per month (2002). Pensioners receiving OAS, who have little or no other income, are likely to also qualify for the Guaranteed Income Supplement (GIS), which provides up to $526.08 of additional funds. The OAS and GIS are adjusted, depending upon other forms of income, to allow for a maximum yearly income of $12 648. Provincial governments may provide additional small supplements. Finally, the government also provides a Spouse's Allowance (SPA) to low-income spouses of pensioners receiving GIS (Oderkirk, 1996; Crawford, 2002).

At the second level, the Canada and the Quebec Pension Plans (CPP and QPP) were implemented in 1966 to provide pension income (and death and disability benefits) to Canadians employed in the labour force. These plans are financed through contributions from employees and employers. Since not all employers provide an employer-sponsored pension plan, the CPP and the QPP were intended to ensure that everyone who was employed would have some basic income security as seniors (Oderkirk, 1996).

The third level of income support involves private, employer-sponsored pension plans (RPPs) and individual registered retirement savings plans (RRSPs) (introduced in 1957). Currently only 51 percent of Canadian female employees aged 35 to 54 and 67 percent of their male counterparts have some form of pension coverage (Morissette & Drolet, 2001, p. 43). Low-wage workers, many of whom are women, are particularly likely not to be covered by such a plan. For example, only 29 percent of women part-timers (35 to 54 years old) and only 24 percent of women service workers (35 to 54 years old) had some kind of pension coverage (Morissette & Drolet, 2001, p. 43). In short, pension policies do not cover all Canadian workers. However, these policies were not introduced and amended without a struggle. Progressive reformers, poverty activists, and trade unions lobbied long and hard to achieve these guarantees. Indeed, their efforts continue today as reformers call for improvements in existing income security measures and point out that 15.9 percent or more than one in six Canadians 65 or older still live below Statistics Canada's low-income cut-offs (Morissette & Zhang, 2001).

Conflict theorists point out that today's retirement benefits are not the result of generous hearts in Parliament. They are, rather, the result of a struggle between competing interest groups. As conflict theorists stress, equilibrium is only a temporary balancing of social forces, one that is always ready to come apart. Perhaps, then, more direct conflict will emerge in the future.

The Question of Generational Conflict

Many analysts express concern about the future relationships between younger Canadians and the aging "boomers" as they struggle over scarce public resources such as income security, health care, and social services. For example, as a larger and larger proportion of the population is retired, will there be an adequate tax base to continue to support government pension funds (Foot & Stoffman, 1998)? Alarmists predict that younger workers will find themselves contributing to government pension payments to senior Canadians, only to find that when their own retirement comes the pension funds are depleted. From this perspective, some sort of crisis or conflict seems the inevitable result of the aging population (Girard, 2002).

Many point to the dwindling numbers of active workers and the swelling numbers of retirees. The fear is that the number of people who collect government pensions will grow, while the proportion of working people—those who pay for these benefits out of their wages—will shrink. Currently, there are four working taxpayers for every nonworking pensioner. But by 2030 this is expected to drop to a ratio of two to one (Association of Canadian Pension Management [ACPM], 2000). Some see this shift in the **dependency ratio**, the number of workers compared with the number of QPP/CPP recipients, as especially troubling not only in terms of monies available to fund pensions but also in terms of adequate support for the health care system. The Association of Canadian Pension Management comments, for example, "The combined forces of the retirement of the Boomer Generation, rising life expectancies, and falling birth rates will seriously strain, and could possibly rupture our retirement and health care systems in the next 30 years" (ACPM, 2000, p. 2).

In this context it is not surprising that many Canadian sociologists are drawing attention to the tensions between the younger and older generations (Lowe, 2000; Coté & Allahar, 1994; Marquardt, 1998). When many young Canadians face high rates of unemployment and are forced to settle for "McJobs" with low pay and little challenge in the retail or service industries, they feel they are being denied the opportunities enjoyed by their parents and grandparents. For some youth, there is a feeling that the good jobs and the prospects for a prosperous life are being obstructed by a "boomer bottleneck" in which older Canadians continue to hang on to opportunities for privilege and power. The resulting resentment may be compounded by concerns that the younger generation will face the no-win choice of either higher taxes or reduced services in order to provide pensions and health care for the boomer generation.

However, a bitter conflict between old and young is not the only possible future scenario. Analysts argue that as long as there is continued economic growth, the dependency ratio will not pose a problem. Also, there is evidence, as discussed above, that in both Canada and the United States, seniors and "retirees" are continuing to function as productive members of the paid labour force (Bowlby, 2002; Duchesne, 2002). Further, as the population ages there will be cost savings in terms of day care and education, which can then be transferred to other areas of the economy, such as health care (Gorrie, 2002). Finally, research suggests that other social cleavages—gender, race, social class, and political affiliation—are likely to mitigate against any clear-cut divisions by age (Hamil-Luker, 2001).

We have only to look at other industrialized countries, many of which are already experiencing the seniors boom that looms in Canada's future. Italy, Greece, Sweden, Japan, Spain, Belgium, Germany, France, and the United Kingdom already have many more citizens aged 65 and older than Canada. In many of these countries, almost one-fifth of the population is 65 or older, and yet, generational conflict has not become rampant. It appears that by encouraging people to work well past age 65 (by reducing pension benefits, discouraging early retirement, and increasing mandatory retirement ages), providing incentives for direct pension contributions from employees, and facilitating home-based eldercare rather than institutional care, these countries are managing to avoid the pitfalls of bankrupt social security

and health care systems. In the process, these nations appear to have averted future conflict between the interests of young and old (Ross, 2002).

Senior Empowerment

As seniors become an ever more prominent demographic and economic element in society, they have predictably established their own support groups and organizations. Some of these efforts have been intended to provide assistance and support to seniors in terms of specific issues and concerns, while others are intended more generally to provide a sense of community and solidarity. The first significant step in this direction was taken in the 1960s when Margaret Kuhn helped establish the Gray Panthers in the United States. This organization played a foundational role in both advocating on seniors' issues and providing a locus for seniors mobilizing around a variety of social issues. Since that time, a growing number of organizations have flourished in both Canada and the United States. For example, in 1973 the Fédération de l'Âge d'Or du Québec was created. The Fédération lobbies the government on seniors' issues, publishes a newspaper, and writes briefs to the government on senior concerns. Similarly, Albertans established the Alberta Council of Aging in the 1970s to identify seniors' needs and mobilize senior leaders to act (Novak, 1993).

In the following years, a wide variety of groups have emerged. For example, there is an organization, Grandparents Raising Grandchildren, that provides support and advocacy for grandparents who become primary caregivers for their grandchildren. Across the country, there are organizations that target elder abuse—for example, the Ontario Network for the Prevention of Elder Abuse—and seek to both educate the public and provide support for victims (Community Information Centre of Metropolitan Toronto, 1997).

A telling example of the ability of Canadian seniors to mobilize effectively and quickly around a social issue was the seniors' response to the 1985 government efforts to de-index government pensions. Under pressure from the business community to cut government spending and reduce the national debt, Finance Minister Michael Wilson proposed that the Old Age Security (OAS) and Guaranteed Income Supplement (GIS) pensions no longer be automatically increased in response to increases in the cost of living (the Consumer Price Index). Rather, he suggested that pension payments would only be increased once the cost of living rose by more than 3 percent. For example, if the cost of living increased by 5 percent, then pensions would be increased by 2 percent. If it rose by 3 percent, there would be no increases in pensions. The government predicted that this policy—scheduled to be implemented on January 1, 1986—would save the government $1.6 billion in 1990–91. However, the policy would effectively reduce the income of all seniors—rich and poor—since they would have to make up any 3 percent increases in living costs.

The response from seniors across the country was immediate and overwhelming. Drawing on all the traditional methods of protest, seniors and their supporters made pension de-indexation a front-page issue. Petitions were circulated, news conferences held, politicians confronted. The nationwide efforts were capped in the summer of 1985 with a massive protest on Parliament Hill. A wide variety of other social advocacy groups also marshalled their support and urged the government not to fight the deficit on the backs of seniors, especially poor seniors. Anti-poverty advocates pointed out that the proposed changes would consign hundreds of thousands of low-income seniors to poverty. In the face of five weeks of these protests, the federal government backed down and abandoned the legislation (Novak, 1993).

This episode speaks eloquently to the ability of seniors to mobilize effectively and rapidly across the country in response to particularly important issues. In the following years, seniors have become not only more numerous but better organized. The Canadian Association of Retired Persons (CARP, now known as Canada's Association for the Fifty-Plus) has launched a vigorous Canada-wide campaign against age discrimination. In Ontario, working with the Ontario Human Rights Commission, the group has helped to create a province-wide campaign to increase public awareness of ageism and its impact. Its resulting publications point out, for example, that discrimination against older workers is counterproductive since older workers are highly productive, have on-the-job experience, and have lower absenteeism and turnover rates than younger workers (Pasternak, 2002). Other initiatives, such as demanding improvements in the health care system and challenging efforts to increase long-term institutional care costs, reflect the dynamism of this and other senior organizations. In short, it is clear that Canadian seniors have in place a number of organizations through which they can ensure that their voices are heard and their interests protected.

In Sum

Conflict theorists point out that we all do not share common interests, and the interests of the young may be in direct opposition to those of seniors. For example, as a society we must decide on the allocation of resources. Seniors might prioritize health care issues such as Alzheimer's disease and other dementia research; younger generations might want to focus resources on fertility and childhood illnesses. With finite resources, difficult decisions must be made. One source of potential conflict is the provision of social support (pensions) for seniors. With growing concern about the cost of providing pension income for senior baby boomers, the conflict of interest may become more apparent in the near future. Generational conflict may emerge as an important sociological issue in the next several decades. However, the experiences in

CARP (Canada's Association for the Fifty-Plus), in collaboration with the Ontario Human Rights Commission, has developed a campaign to combat age discrimination.

other, "grayer" nations suggest it is possible to employ social policies to avert such clashes. Future conflict between young and old may hinge on the introduction of innovative social policies.

Focus Question

Why might the interests of young Canadians (25 to 35) be at odds with the interests of senior Canadians (65+)?

Problems of Dependency

"Will I be able to take care of myself? Will I become frail and not be able to get around? Will I end up poor and in some nursing home somewhere, in the hands of strangers who don't care about me?" These are some concerns of people as they grow older. Let's examine the dependency of the elderly: isolation, disability, nursing homes, abuse, and poverty.

Isolation and Gender

Most Canadian elderly are not isolated. The majority are living with their immediate family (spouse) and a few with their extended family. Further, the majority of seniors who have had children are in weekly contact with their adult children (Townsend-Batten, 2002). However, a significant minority (17 percent of senior men and 38 percent of senior women) do live on their own. Further, their numbers are expanding rapidly with a 200 percent increase between 1971 and 2001 in the number of widowed seniors living alone. Not surprisingly, by 2001, the more than one million widowed seniors comprised the largest group of Canadians living alone (Clark, 2002; Carey, 2002c). Predictably, given women's longevity and patterns of age at marriage, women are much more likely to end up on their own. If they have married, they are likely to outlive their spouse and to spend some portion of their senior years as a widow living on their own (see Figure 9.1). As women age, this pattern intensifies. More than half (58 percent) of women 85 and older live by themselves (Lindsay, 1999). Of course, this pattern has long been reflected in the stereotype of the senior widow as, at best, sad and lonely, or, worse, the witch or "old hag."

However, despite these stereotypes, living alone does not necessarily mean living in lonely isolation. An increasing variety of research indicates that many seniors, even older seniors, live energetic, active lives. According to the 2001 census, 10 percent of seniors 75 to 79 are employed as are 5 percent of those 80 and above (Carey, 2002d). In addition, they volunteer, they have hobbies, and they are learning new things (Morris, 2001). The mass media are filled with stories about industrious and vigorous 90-year-olds who shovel snow and chop wood. It is often the onset of serious illness or disability that leads to a sense of isolation and loneliness.

Disability, Dementia, and Seniors

Health increasingly becomes a concern as we age. The clear majority of Canadian seniors living at home report relatively good health and research indicates that there have been significant improvements in seniors' (68 to 85) health over the past 20 years (Crompton, 2000). However, a large num-

ber of seniors (81 percent) also indicate they have at least one chronic health problem—heart disease, diabetes, rheumatism, or arthritis—as diagnosed by a health professional and 25 percent indicate that they are living with chronic pain (Lindsay, 1999; Crompton, 2000).

In addition, one-third of Canadian seniors living at home report cognitive difficulties; that is, forgetfulness or difficulty thinking (Lindsay, 1999). For some, these concerns will evolve into a serious disability. As there are more seniors and, especially, more senior seniors in the Canadian population, the number of elderly Canadians with some form of dementia (Alzheimer's disease and vascular dementia) will rapidly increase. Currently, 300 000 Canadians suffer from degenerative, incurable Alzheimer's disease (Hurst, 2000). With the aging of the Canadian population the numbers will mushroom. By 2031, it is estimated that the number of Canadian seniors with dementia—many of them women—will increase by 300 percent to almost one million Canadians (Burke, Lindsay, McDowell, & Hill, 1997).

Caring for Disabled Seniors

As anyone familiar with disease and disability will agree, caring for an individual suffering from an incapacitating aliment such as Alzheimer's disease or chronic arthritis is a stressful and intense responsibility. Currently, care for ill or disabled seniors is provided by an uneven mix of home care, hospital care, and institutional care. However, it is not clear that these arrangements will be manageable as the baby boomers age.

Analysts anticipate that seniors will place increasingly onerous demands on the health care system. Currently about 5 percent of seniors (65 or older) and 18 percent of those 80 or older were being cared for in an institution (Crompton, 2000). At the lowest level of need, institutional care costs $12 504 a year and at the highest level (including 24-hour nursing) it averages $41 023 (Hurst, 2000). Predictably, there are concerns that these and other health-care costs will become unsupportable as the size of the

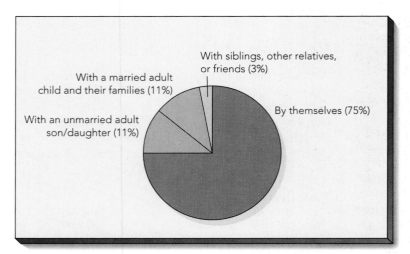

Figure 9.1 Canadian Widows 65+ Living Alone
N = 661 000

Source: Statistics Canada, from Irwin Bess, "Widows Living Alone," *Canadian Social Trends* 53 (Summer 1999), pp. 2–6, Catalogue no. 11-008.

"I'm ready," shouted Clay from the bedroom.

"That was fast," thought Virginia, his wife of 48 years. "He never gets ready for church that fast."

Virginia walked into the bedroom, and there, smiling and ready to leave for church, stood Clay—absolutely naked except for three watches strapped to his left wrist. Virginia told me this story later that morning when I asked her how things were going.

As people age, among their fears is that of "losing their mind." By this they mean senility, or, more technically, Alzheimer's disease.

How do we care for people when they get like Clay?

Clay, of course, is just fine. His wife is still healthy, and she lovingly makes certain that he eats nourishing meals, is included in social events—and wears clothes when he goes out.

But what about the many who don't have close, caring relatives? For them, senility means institutionalization—which, even if it does not mirror the horror stories we all have heard, is certainly a far cry from the tender love and con-

Former U.S. president Ronald Reagan suffers from Alzheimer's disease. This disease devastates the thinking process, making its victims unable to carry out the ordinary routines on which everyday life depends. As the percentage of the aged in our society increases, so will the number of people who suffer from this disease—and the caregiving that will become necessary.

sideration that someone like Virginia gives.

Institutionalization, however, can be positive. For an example we can turn to Sweden, which since the 1980s has been pioneering group homes for victims of Alzheimer's disease (Malmberg & Sundström, 1996). The group homes consist of six to eight small apartments fanning outward from a shared kitchen and living room. Residents have their own accommodations, but a care staff is available around the clock. The goal is to provide a supportive home environment in which residents participate in everyday activities. In addition to receiving humane care, residents find that secondary problems associated with Alzheimer's—depression, restlessness, and anxiety—are apparently lessened.

For Your Consideration

The group home model pioneered by Sweden is exemplary, but expensive. In Canada, what chance do you think we have of providing similar group homes for victims of Alzheimer's disease? Since we could hardly afford such homes for all victims, how should they be rationed?

senior population grows. From their perspective many seniors would, of course, prefer to avoid institutional care. They fear the loss of independence and autonomy and prefer caregiving provided by friends and family (Crompton, 2000). However, personal caregiving, while less financially costly, has its own pitfalls. First, although many daughters, and to a lesser degree sons, are providing care for their aging parents, it often falls to the elderly wife to care for her husband. Ironically, the elderly wife is likely to outlive her husband and end up being cared for herself in an institution (Burke et al., 1997).

Second, family members may also find it difficult to manage eldercare. By the late twentieth century, 2.1 million Canadians were providing care to senior family members or friends with long-term health problems. Since two-thirds (61 percent) of these caregivers were women, concerns have been raised about the gender inequity in shouldering responsibility for senior care. Not only are women (typically aged 30 to 59) more likely than men to be providing eldercare, they spend much more time than men (five hours per week) on that care (Townsend-Batten, 2002; Frederick & Fast, 1999).

There are several other serious drawbacks to these informal arrangements. Few adult women and men, most of whom have their own family and paid work responsibilities, can afford the time and energy necessary to provide informal care to a seriously disabled senior family member. As research constantly reveals, most employed mothers are already "time crunched." Further, the caregiving work itself may be physically and emotionally exhausting. Research with caregivers reveals "Difficulty balancing work and family, lack of free time, wishing that someone else would take over, and anger with the person they were looking after ..." (Frederick & Fast, 1999; Keating, Fast, Frederick, Cranswick, & Perrier, 1999). Many find that their own physical and emotional health deteriorates—reflected in sleeplessness, crying episodes, and fatigue. The demands may also jeopardize personal relationships with friends and other family members, leaving the caregiver isolated. Even when community service providers are called upon to assist caregivers, problems often emerge in terms of frequent changes of staff, inadequately trained staff, and inconsistent performance of tasks (Hawranik & Strain, 2002). Clearly current informal caregiving arrangements may not benefit either the seniors or their caregivers.

Elder Abuse and Neglect: The Silent Crime

By the 1980s, activists working on family violence issues—child abuse, wife abuse, and so on—increasingly recognized that seniors were also subject to violence, both within the family and outside it. The first national survey of elder abuse in 1992 estimated that between 4 and 10 percent of elderly Canadians experienced some form of abuse, but more recent analyses suggest that the higher estimate (10 percent subject to physical, psychological, and/or financial abuse) may be more accurate (Brennan, 2002). Currently, we must rely on research based upon self-reported accounts of violence and police statistics to gauge the extent of senior abuse. Of course, both of these methods may underrepresent the dimensions of the problem.

According to the 1999 General Social Survey on Victimization, 7 percent of seniors stated that they had experienced some form of financial or emotional abuse as well as physical and sexual violence by children, caregivers, and spouses in the preceding five years. Not surprisingly, police statistics reveal that few instances of abuse are reported. In 2000, there were 1006 reports of seniors being victimized by a family member. According to these data, women are the most likely victims of abuse, accounting for 65 percent of older victims of family violence. The perpetrators of this violence against senior women are commonly spouses or adult children. Not surprisingly, many refer to abuse of older women as wife abuse grown old. In contrast, senior men are more likely to be abused by their adult children. (Statistics Canada, 2002e; Vann, 2002).

Why do children, spouses, and other relatives abuse their own elderly? Apparently, one precipitating cause of this form of violence may be situational: stress from caring for a person who is highly dependent, demanding, and in some cases violent (Pillemer & Suitor, 1992). Others suggest that a history of family violence may lay the foundation for violence against seniors. Recently, analysts have been pointing out the relevance of feminist analysis to elder abuse. Canadian researchers, for example, suggest that a feminist perspective (focusing on gender inequalities and the subordination of women) along with a situational model are most helpful in understanding which elderly individuals are more likely to be victims of physical abuse (Pittaway, Westhues, & Peressini, 1995; Whittaker, 1995). Being a woman is an important ingredient in patterning the victimization of seniors.

Of course violence against seniors may occur outside the parameters of the family. Indeed, many seniors have been found to be abused by professional caregivers, who were overmedicating them, keeping them under restraint, or using physical violence to control and intimidate them. As increasing numbers of seniors come to rely on both our families and our institutions, there will be growing concern about the adequacy of our protections for some of the most vulnerable and dependent members of our society.

The Elderly Poor

When we look at the income security plans provided to Canadian seniors it is easy to understand why many elderly live in nagging fear of poverty. Since they do not know how long they will live, nor what the rate of inflation will be, they are uncertain whether their money will last as long as they will. Government sources—GIS, OAS—will not necessarily lift them out of poverty, especially if they live alone in one of Canada's large urban centres.

Despite these concerns, in some respects poverty trends among Canadian seniors are a success story (Morissette,

In old age, as in other stages in the life course, having enough money for one's needs and desires makes life more pleasant and satisfying. This homeless woman is not likely to find her old age satisfying. Income, however, is hardly the sole determinant of satisfaction during this time of life. As indicated in the text, integration in a community in which one is respected is a crucial factor. Thus, these elderly men, although poor, are likely to find their old age much more satisfying than the isolated homeless woman.

2002; Myles, 2000). In 1989 more than one-quarter (27.9 percent) of seniors were living below the Statistics Canada low-income cut-offs. By the end of the twentieth century (thanks in large measure to improved government income support for seniors), those figures have been dramatically reduced. Today, only one in five (20.8 percent) of seniors are living in poverty (Statistics Canada, 2001, p. 214). The societal benefits of lifting seniors out of poverty are numerous and include not only a better quality of life for seniors but also improved health, since seniors in the upper-middle and upper income brackets are more likely to enjoy good health (Crompton, 2000).

However, this progress clearly does not imply complete eradication of poverty. Many seniors still live in poverty and near the poverty line, and the economic well-being of certain groups of seniors is particularly precarious. There are, for example, disturbing reports of increased homelessness and food bank use among seniors living in the Greater Toronto Area (Henderson, 2000). Other research indicates that senior women living alone continue to be particularly vulnerable to poverty. About one in five of all seniors who are living on their own live on low income. Almost half (49 percent) of single, widowed, and divorced women 65 or over and 60 percent of those 75 and older are poor (Morissette, 2002; Black, 2000; Gorrie, 2001). Further, senior women appear much more vulnerable not only to poverty but to long-term poverty (four or more years) than their male counterparts (Morissette & Zhang, 2001). In short, being old, being a woman, and being on one's own are still key risk factors for impoverishment. Not surprisingly, additional factors such as advanced age, visible minority status, and recent immigration simply intensify the likelihood that older women will be poor (Brotman, 1998).

In Sum

Inevitably, seniors must tackle concerns about becoming frail and dependent. Although men and women confront this issue, it is particularly women who are likely to end up on their own and potentially isolated from the larger society. Isolation may become a serious issue when coupled with disability, particularly dementia. Chronic illness requires intense support from families and/or from health care institutions. With growing numbers of seniors, senior disability is likely to become an increasingly important social issue. Certainly, the health care system is already experiencing severe pressures, and the burden of family support is often found to fall disproportionately on adult women. In this context, it is troubling to note that elder abuse and neglect may be important issues. Isolated seniors and disabled seniors may be particularly vulnerable to abuse from both professional and family caregivers. These concerns may be compounded by the economic vulnerability of seniors. Although government policies have improved the financial situation of many Canadian seniors, many still live in or near poverty.

Focus Question

Why do disability and dementia among seniors threaten to be a problem for both the individual family and the health care system?

The Sociology of Death and Dying

In a fascinating sub-field of sociology, death and dying, sociologists stress how death, like old age, is much more than a biological event. They examine how culture shapes the ways people experience death. Let us look at some of their findings.

Effects of Industrialization and the New Technology

In preindustrial societies, the sick were taken care of at home, and they died at home. Because life was short, during childhood most people saw a sibling or parent die (Blauner, 1966). Corpses were even prepared for burial at home.

Industrialization radically altered the circumstances of dying. With modern medicine, dying was transformed into an event to be managed by professionals in hospitals. Consequently, most Canadians have never seen anyone die. Fictional deaths on television are the closest most come to witnessing death. In effect, dying has become an event that takes place behind closed doors—isolated, disconnected, remote.

In consequence, the process of dying has become strange to us. To help put on a mask of immortality, we hide from the fact of death. We have even developed elaborate ways to refer to death without using the word itself, which uncomfortably reminds us of our human destiny. We carefully construct a language of avoidance, using terms such as "gone," "passed on," "no longer with us," "gone beyond," "passed through the pearly gates," and "at peace now."

New technologies not only have removed the dying from our presence, but they also are bringing a new experience of death. They have produced what sociologists Karen Cerulo and Janet Ruane (1996) call *technological lifespace*— a form of existence that is neither life nor death as we usually define them. The self of a brain-dead person, for example, is gone—dead—yet due to technology the body lives on. The boundaries between life and death are now becoming murky, for technological lifespace is a kind of bridge between life and death.

As people grow older, death becomes a less distant event. The elderly see many friends and relatives die, and much of their talk centres on those persons. Often fears about dying focus more on the "how" of death than on death itself. The elderly are especially fearful of dying alone or in pain. One of their biggest fears is cancer, which seems to strike out of the blue.

Death as a Process

Through her interviews with people who had been informed that they had an incurable disease, psychologist Elisabeth Kübler-Ross (1969, 1981) found that coming face to face with one's own death sets in motion a five-stage process:

1. *Denial.* In this first stage, people cannot believe that they are really going to die. ("The doctor must have made a mistake. Those test results can't be right.") They avoid the topic of death and any situation that might remind them of it.

2. *Anger.* In this second stage, they acknowledge their coming death but see it as unjust. ("I didn't do anything to deserve this. So-and-so is much worse than I am, and he's in good health. It isn't right that I should die.")

3. *Negotiation.* Next, the individual tries to get around death by making a bargain with God, with fate, or even with the disease itself. ("I need one more Christmas with my family. I never appreciated them as much as I should have. Don't take me until after Christmas, and then I'll go willingly.")

4. *Depression.* In this stage, people are resigned to the fact that death is inevitable, but they are extremely unhappy about it. They grieve because their life is about to end, and they have no power to change the course of events.

5. *Acceptance.* In this final stage, people come to terms with the certainty of impending death. They are likely to get their affairs in order—to make wills, pay bills, give instructions to children on what kind of adults they should become and of how they should take care of the surviving parent, and express regret at not having done certain things when they had the chance. Devout Christians are likely to talk about the hope of salvation and their desire to be in heaven with Jesus.

Kübler-Ross noted that not everyone experiences all these stages, and that not everyone goes through them in this precise order. Some people never come to terms with their death and remain in the first or second stage throughout the process of dying. Others may move back and forth, vacillating, for example, between acceptance, depression, and negotiation.

Hospices

In earlier generations, when not many people made it to age 65 or beyond, death at an early age was taken for granted—much as people take it for granted today that most people *will* see 65. In fact, due to advances in medical technology and improved health practices by many Canadians, *most* deaths in Canada do occur after age 65. With technology reducing the swift deaths that come from infectious diseases and giving us earlier detection of fatal illnesses even before the symptoms are felt, the time of "dying" has also been lengthened (J. A. Levy, 1994).

The effects of technology on disease and dying have led to a greater concern about the *how* of dying. Few elderly people want to burden their children with their own death. They also want to die with dignity and with the comforting presence of friends and relatives. Hospitals, to put the matter bluntly, are awkward places in which to die. There, experiencing what sociologists call *institutional death,* patients are surrounded by strangers in formal garb, in an organization that puts its routines ahead of their needs.

Hospices emerged as a solution to these problems. These institutions, which originated in Great Britain, attempt to reduce the emotional and physical burden on children and other relatives and to lower costs. Above all, hospices are intended to provide dignity in death and to make people comfortable in what Kübler-Ross (1989) called *the living-dying interval,* that period between discovering death is imminent and death itself. The term **hospice** originally referred to a place, but it also refers to services that are brought into a dying person's home—from intricate counselling to such down-to-earth help as providing babysitters or driving the person to a lawyer (Levy, 1994). In the United States, the number of hospices has grown from one in 1974 to 1800 today (Busby, 1993).

Whereas hospitals are dedicated to prolonging life, hospices are dedicated to bringing comfort and dignity to a dying person's last days or months. In the hospital the patient is the unit, but in the hospice the unit becomes the dying person and his or her friends and family. In the hospital, the goal is to make the patient well; in the hospice, it is to relieve pain and suffering. In the hospital, the primary concern is the individual's physical welfare; in the hospice, although medical needs are met, the primary concern is the individual's social—and in some instances, spiritual—well-being.

While these explanations of hospice care emphasize the positive, it is also important to examine the ways hospices protect friends and families from "dirty dying." Recent research with hospice patients in England finds that patients are most likely to be sent to hospices when the physical boundaries established by Western society—the retention and control over bodily fluids and so on—break down. Since in the West, bodily fluids are typically viewed as "filth," family caregivers find it particularly difficult to deal with death and dying involving a disruption of bodily boundaries. In this sense, hospice care can be seen as a particular extension of our societal desire to hide the death process. In this instance, we are hiding the particularly troublesome experience of "dirty dying" (Lawton, 1998).

Suicide and the Elderly

In the light of many of the issues discussed above, it may be surprising to learn that senior Canadians report themselves happy. Despite more health problems, reduced incomes, and higher rates of widowhood, nearly 60 percent of a sample of Canadians 75 and over reported a positive sense of well-being. This is only slightly less than the 67 percent of Canadians aged 15 to 74 who described themselves as happy (Prasil, 1993). However, for a small minority of seniors, life is apparently a troublesome burden and they opt for suicide to escape.

In Chapter 1, we noted that Durkheim analyzed suicide as much more than an individual act. He stressed that every country has its own suicide rate and that these rates remain quite stable year after year. This same stability can be seen in the age, sex, and race of people who kill themselves.

There was a general trend toward an increasing suicide rate from the 1920s to the 1980s, and the elderly were part of it. More recently—1979 to 1998—the total number of suicide deaths has remained fairly stable (Langlois & Morrison, 2002). Within this general pattern, women's rates have typically been much lower than men's, regardless of age. The suicide rate for Canadian women 60 to 74 is 5.0 suicides per 100 000 population. For men of the same age, the rate is approximately *four times higher* (21.1 suicides per 100 000 population). For those 75 and older, the gender difference is even more pronounced with 24.5 male suicides to 5 female suicides per 100 000 population (Langlois & Morrison, 2002). Indeed, in nearly all the industrialized countries the highest rates of suicide are reported for males aged 75 and older (Pearson, Conwell, Lindesay, Takahasi, & Caine, 1997). Figure 9.2 reveals the distinct gender differences in Canadian suicide rates.

Sociologists have attempted to explain why the elderly would commit suicide and why women, regardless of age, are less likely to commit suicide. Research, for example, has suggested that some seniors may have stronger feelings of lack of meaning in life. Typically, as we age we lose social roles and social relationships. Friends and family members die, children grow up and may move away, marriages end,

retirement puts an end to employment, and friends and family move. The net result may be a feeling of isolation and even loneliness. In conjunction with other factors, notably ill health, these factors may contribute to an increased risk of suicide (Novak, 1993).

As far as elderly women are concerned, it seems that despite the fact that women are more likely than men to end up on their own, they enjoy some protection from suicide. Concrete evidence suggests that gender socialization that has encouraged women to emphasize social relationships and social skills benefits women when they find themselves alone. Recent surveys of senior widows in Canada found that they have typically developed a strong support network—"many of them have lived in the same home for a long time and have close relationships with friends and their adult children" (Bess, 1999). Despite other problems, such as economic vulnerability and reduced physical capability, many women draw crucial sustenance from this social network.

However, for both men and women there may come a time, perhaps as a result of illness or loss, when life does not feel worth living. Not surprisingly, as more and more Canadians age, there is growing discussion of whether or not those who desire to end their suffering should be assisted. The issues surrounding the "right to die," including voluntary **euthanasia**, or mercy killing, and assisted suicide, are contentious and unclear. Currently, right-to-die advocates are urging that we must create social policies that recognize that the terminally ill and those who suffer from debilitating, irreversible, and slow-moving diseases have the right to a "timely death." At present, only the Netherlands and the state of Oregon in the U.S. (1997) allow assisted suicides. Given the mushrooming number of elderly, the dramatic increases in health care costs, and

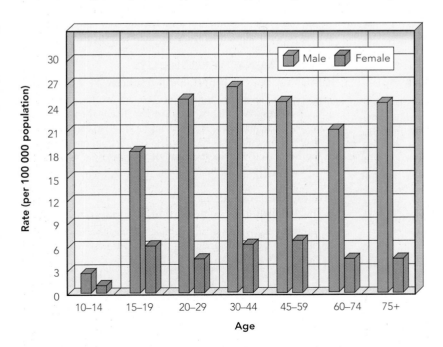

Figure 9.2 Suicide Rates by Age and Gender 1998, Canada (per 100 000 population)

Source: Statistics Canada, from Stephanie Langlois & Peter Morrison, "Suicide deaths and attempts," *Canadian Social Trends*, 2002, (Autumn), p. 21, Catalogue no. 11-402.

improvements in medicine's ability to prolong biological life, along with polls indicating that three-quarters of Canadians support doctor-assisted suicide for the terminally ill, control over one's own death will likely become a focus for public debate (Pollard, 2001). Of course, the very existence of this debate in Canadian society speaks strongly to the fact that death and dying are socially constructed events.

In Sum

Sociologists approach death, too, as a socially constructed reality. The ways you die and the meaning you attach to death will vary with the culture you are born into and the historical moment of your death. We live in a society where technology has produced an increasingly complex understanding of the line between alive and dead. For individuals knowing they are going to die, coming to terms with death is also a socially constructed process. In Canada, this process of dying has been altered by the introduction of hospices, which allow individuals to die outside the hospital setting while also protecting the family from the worse aspects of "dirty dying."

For some seniors, dying becomes a more purposive act—they take their own lives. Although most seniors report a positive sense of well-being, a constant minority, particularly of men, opt for suicide. Given the gender and age pattern, it is clear that even in this instance dying is socially constructed. If current efforts to legalize euthanasia succeed, then the social construction of death in Canada will be importantly altered.

> ### Focus Question
> What evidence supports sociologists' argument that death and dying are socially constructed processes?

Summary and Review

AGING IN GLOBAL PERSPECTIVE

How are the aged treated around the world?

No single set of attitudes, beliefs, or policies regarding the elderly characterizes the world's nations. Rather, they vary, from exclusion and killing to integration and honour. Globally, and especially in industrialized nations, the trend is for more people to live longer. pp. 212–213.

What does the term "graying of Canada" mean?

The phrase **graying of Canada** refers to the growing proportion of Canadians who reach old age. The cost of health care for the elderly has become a social issue, and sentiment about the elderly may be shifting. pp. 213–216.

THE SYMBOLIC INTERACTIONIST PERSPECTIVE

What factors influence perceptions of aging?

Symbolic interactionists stress that, by itself, reaching any particular age has no meaning. They identify four factors that influence when people label themselves as "old": biological changes, biographical events, gender age, and cultural timetables. Cross-cultural comparisons—for example, the traditional Tiwi and the Inuit—demonstrate the role of culture in determining how individuals experience aging. **Ageism**, negative reaction to the elderly, is based on stereotypes, which, in turn, are influenced by the mass media. pp. 216–220.

THE FEMINIST PERSPECTIVE

How does aging affect men and women differently?

Feminist analysts have extensively documented the fact that the aging process impacts on men and women differently. Aging women are more likely to be socially marginalized and dismissed as evidenced by the popular beliefs that men are more attractive and sexual at an older age than women. Women are also likely to find themselves economically disadvantaged, particularly if they have taken 'time out' to devote themselves to their home and family. Finally, older women who are also members of minority groups—aboriginal women, lesbians, disabled women—are likely to experience additional societal prejudices. pp. 220–221.

THE FUNCTIONALIST PERSPECTIVE

How is retirement functional for society?

Functionalists focus on how the withdrawal of the elderly from positions of responsibility benefits society. **Disengagement theory** examines retirement as a device for ensuring that a society's positions of responsibility will be passed smoothly from one generation to the next. **Activity theory** examines how people adjust when they disengage from productive roles. pp. 221–222.

THE CONFLICT PERSPECTIVE

Is there conflict among different age groups?

Government legislation is an example of one generation making demands on another generation for limited resources. As the

dependency ratio, the number of workers who support one retired person, decreases, workers may become resentful. pp. 223–225.

PROBLEMS OF DEPENDENCY

What are some of the problems that today's elderly face?

Due to differences in mortality and work histories, women are more likely to live alone and to be poor. pp. 225–229.

THE SOCIOLOGY OF DEATH AND DYING

How does culture affect the meaning—and experience—of death and dying?

Like old age, death is much more than a biological event. Industrialization, for example, brought modern medicine, and with it hospitals and the custom of dying in a formal setting surrounded by strangers. Kübler-Ross identified five stages in the dying process, which, though insightful, do not characterize all people. **Hospices** are a cultural device of recent origin, designed to overcome the negative aspects of dying in hospitals. Suicide shows distinct patterns by age, sex, and race. pp. 229–232.

Critical Thinking Questions

1. How has the process of becoming old and dying changed in Canada over the past 100 years?

2. What are the important gender differences in aging and dying?

3. How would symbolic interactionists, functionalists, feminists, and conflict theorists explain the differences between men's and women's experiences of aging?

4. Are media images of older men and women changing for the better?

5. Is conflict between seniors and younger members of society likely to intensify in coming years?

Key Terms

activity theory 222
age cohort 221
ageism 218
dependency ratio 224
disengagement theory 222
euthanasia 231
gender age 217

gerontocracy 218
graying of Canada 215
hospice 230
life expectancy 214
life span 215
timetable 217

Weblinks

All URLs listed are current as of the printing of this book. URLs are often changed. Please check our Web site **www.abacon.com/ henslin** for updates.

Canada's Association for the Fifty-Plus (CARP)

www.fifty-plus.net
Contains information and links of interest to Canadians 50 and over.

Elderweb

www.elderweb.org
An online community of older adult computer users.

Division of Aging and Seniors

www.hc-sc.gc.ca/seniors-aines/
The Division of Aging and Seniors of Health Canada provides federal leadership in areas pertaining to aging and seniors, and serves as a focal point for information and as a centre of expertise.

Canadian Association on Gerontology

www.cagacg.ca/
The Canadian Association on Gerontology (CAG-ACG) is a national, multidisciplinary association established to provide leadership in matters relating to the aging population in Canada. CAG fosters research, education, and policy aimed at improving the quality of life of the elderly in Canada.

Alzheimers.com

www.alzheimers.com/
Alzheimers.com is dedicated to preventing and treating the cognitive decline of Alzheimer's disease, and to providing practical, up-to-the-minute information that empowers caregivers to manage the disease more confidently, effectively, and economically.

Aging in a Social Context

userpages.umbc.edu/~vdotte1/index.html
This page is meant to help sociology students and others interested in aging to find information about aging, gerontology, and the political, social, and economic aspects of aging.

Statistics Canada

www.hc-sc.gc.ca/seniors-aines/pubs/factoids/en/no1.htm
Statistical snapshots of Canada's seniors.

part four

Social Institutions

Chapter 10

Bureaucracy and Formal Organizations

Learning Outcomes

After you have studied this chapter, you will be able to

- understand transformations in people's thinking and practices that brought about the rationalization of society

- describe the characteristics of a bureaucracy and how different organizations, such as a profit-making corporation and a publicly funded high school, share similar practices and organizational designs

- discuss who has power within a formal organization

- understand how hidden values and expectations in the workplace affect people's chances of success and their levels of satisfaction with their work

- describe some of the ways in which efficiency-driven bureaucracies may be humanized

This was the most exciting day Jennifer could remember. Her first day at university. So much had happened so quickly. Her senior year had ended with such pleasant memories: the prom, graduation—how proud she had felt at that moment. But best of all had been her final term's marks. Everyone, especially Jennifer, had been surprised at the results—she had outscored everyone in her class.

"Yes, they're valid," her advisor had assured her. "You can be anything you want to be."

Those words still echoed in Jennifer's mind. "Anything I want to be," she thought.

Then came the scholarship! Full tuition for four years. It went beyond anything Jennifer had ever dreamed possible. She could hardly believe it, but it was really hers.

"Your social insurance number, please!"

These abrupt words snapped Jennifer out of her reverie. After an hour, she had reached the head of the line. Jennifer quickly mumbled the nine digits destined to stay with her to the grave.

"What?" asked the clerk. Jennifer repeated the numbers more clearly.

"I can't give you a class card. You haven't paid your fees."

"What do you mean? I'm on scholarship."

"Evidently not, or else you'd be in the computer," replied the clerk, rolling her eyes.

"But I am."

"If you were, it would say so here."

"But I really am. Look," Jennifer said as she took the prized letter out of her purse.

"I can't help what it says there," replied the clerk, "The only thing that counts is what it says here," she said, gesturing toward the computer. "You'll have to go to Administration Hall to clear it up." Then looking past Jennifer, the clerk said, "Next."

Jennifer felt thoroughly confused. Dejected, she crossed the quadrangle to Administration Hall and joined a double line of students that stretched from the building to the courtyard.

No one told Jennifer that this was the line for deferring tuition. The "problem" line was in the basement.

The Rationalization of Society

You can understand Jennifer's dismay. Things could have been clearer—a lot clearer. The problem is that many universities must register thousands of students, most of whom are going to start classes on the same day. To do so, they have broken the registration process into tiny bits, with each piece making a small contribution to getting the job done. Of course, as Jennifer found out, things don't always go as planned.

This chapter looks at how society is organized to "get its job done." As you read it, you may be able to trace the source of some of your frustrations to this social organization, as well as see how your welfare depends on it.

Over the course of history, societies have undergone transformations so extensive that whole new types of societies emerged. In addition to these transformations, a major development has been **rationality**—the acceptance of rules, efficiency, and practical results as the right way to approach human affairs. Let's examine how this approach to life—which we today take for granted—came about.

The Contribution of Max Weber

Max Weber (1864–1920), a sociologist whose studies incorporated an amazingly broad sweep of world history, concluded that until recently the world's groups and nations had been immersed in a **traditional orientation** to life—the idea that the past is the best guide for the present. In this view, what exists is good because it has passed the test of time. Customs—and relationships based on them—have served people well and should not be lightly abandoned. A central orientation of a traditional society is to protect the status quo. Change is viewed with suspicion, and comes but slowly, if at all.

Such a traditional orientation stands in the way of industrialization, which requires the willingness—even eagerness—to change. If a society is to industrialize, a deep-seated shift must occur in people's thinking—from wanting to hold onto things as they are to seeking the most efficient way to accomplish matters. With the "bottom line" (results) replacing the status quo, rule-of-thumb methods give way to explicit rules and procedures for measuring results. This change requires an entirely different way of

Until the 1500s, the world's societies had a traditional orientation to life. The way things had "always" been was the guide to decision-making. Change, which came very slowly, was viewed with suspicion, and one generation was very similar to the next. In this painting from 1416 by Französische Buchmalerei, *Les Très Riches Heures du Duc de Berry*, you can see the slow pace of life. The rise of capitalism, however, changed this orientation, and for much of the West, rationality became the new guide to decision-making.

looking at life. It flies in the face of human history, for it is opposed to the basic orientation of all human societies until the time of industrialization. How, then, did what Weber called the **rationalization of society**—a widespread acceptance of rationality and a social organization largely built around this idea—come about? How did people break through their profound resistance to change?

To Weber, this problem was like an unsolved murder is to a detective. Weber's primary clue was that capitalism thrived only in certain parts of Europe. If he could determine why this was so, he was convinced that he could discover the root of this fundamental change in human society.

As Weber pursued the matter, he concluded that religion held the key, for it was in Protestant countries that capitalism flourished, while Roman Catholic countries held onto tradition and were relatively untouched by capitalism.

But why should Roman Catholics have continued to hold onto the past, while Protestants embraced change, welcoming the new emphasis on practical results? Weber's answer to this puzzle has been the source of controversy ever since he first proposed it in his highly influential book, *The Protestant Ethic and the Spirit of Capitalism* (1904–1905/1958). He concluded that essential differences between the two religions held the answer. Roman Catholic doctrine emphasized the acceptance of present arrangements, not change: "God wants you where you are. You owe primary allegiance to the Church, to your family, to your community and country. Accept your lot in life and remain rooted." But Protestant theology was quite different, Weber argued, especially Calvinism, a religion he was intimately familiar with from his mother. Calvinists (followers of the teachings of John Calvin, 1509–1564) believed that before birth people are destined to go either to heaven or to hell—and they would not know their destiny until after they died. Weber believed that this teaching filled Calvinists with an anxiety that pervaded their entire lives. Salvation became their chief concern in life—they wanted to know now where they were going after death.

To resolve their spiritual dilemma, Calvinists came up with an ingenious solution: God did not want those chosen for heaven to be ignorant of their destiny. Consequently, he would bestow signs of approval on them. But what signs? The answer, they claimed, was found not in mystical, spiritual experiences, but in tangible achievements that people could see and measure. The sign of God's approval became success: Those whom God had predestined for heaven would be blessed with visible success in this life.

This idea transformed Calvinists' lives, serving as an extraordinary motivation to work hard. Because Calvinists also believed that thrift is a virtue, their dedication to work led to an accumulation of money. Calvinists could not spend the excess on themselves, however, for to purchase items beyond the basic necessities was considered sinful. **Capitalism**, the investment of capital in the hope of producing profits, became an outlet for their excess money, while the success of those investments became a further sign of God's approval. Worldly success, then, became transformed into a spiritual virtue, and other branches of Protestantism, although less extreme, adopted the creed of thrift and hard work. Consequently, said Weber, Protestant countries embraced capitalism.

Now, what has this to do with rationalization? Simply put, capitalism demands *rationalization*, the careful calculation of practical results. If profits are your goal, you must compute income and expenses. You must calculate inventories and wages, the cost of producing goods, and how much

A central characteristic of formal organizations is the division of labour. Bureaucracies, for example, divide tasks into very small segments. Prior to capitalism and industrialization, however, there was little division of labour, and few formal organizations existed. In this woodcut of money coiners in Germany during the Middle Ages, you can see an early division of labour and perhaps the emergence of a formal organization.

they bring in. You must find ways to lower your costs, and often this means finding ways to decrease labour costs. For example, you might require that workers produce more units per hour or that work be intensified in such a way that fewer workers are needed to do the job. You must determine "the bottom line." In such an arrangement of human affairs, efficiency, not tradition, becomes the drum to which you march. Traditional ways of doing things, if inefficient, must be replaced, for what counts are the results.

Focus Question

How did Marx and Weber differ in their views on rationality and how it came to permeate society?

Marx on Rationalization

Another sociologist, Karl Marx, also noted that tradition had given way to rationality. When he analyzed the problem, however, Marx came up with an entirely different explanation. He didn't think religion had anything to do with breaking the bondage of tradition. Rather, Marx concluded that the switch to rationality was due to capitalism itself. When people saw that capitalism was more efficient, that it produced things they wanted in much greater abundance, they embraced rationality, giving up their traditional thinking. Thus Marx reversed the equation: The change to capitalism, he said, changed the way people thought about life, not the other way around.

The power of the traditional way of life prior to the arrival of capitalism is still evident from the dominating position of Hradcany Cathedral in Prague. Max Weber wrote that the rise of capitalism and the type of society it produced—one based on rationality versus tradition—emerged in response to the Protestant ethic, especially the Calvinist doctrine of predestination. Karl Marx saw things differently. He believed that capitalism itself was responsible for the breakdown of traditional society and the rise of rationality.

Marx criticized capitalism's rationality and emphasis on efficiency. He argued that the values and practices of capitalism contributed to feelings of alienation. The needs of workers became secondary to the interests of capital and the capitalists' persistent pursuit of profit—often profit at any cost.

Who is correct? Weber, who concluded that Protestantism produced rationality, which then paved the way for capitalism? Or Marx, who concluded that capitalism produced rationality? No analyst has yet reconciled these two opposing answers to the satisfaction of sociologists. The two views still remain side by side.

Formal Organizations and Bureaucracy

Regardless of whether Marx or Weber was right about its cause, rationality was a totally different way of thinking that came to permeate society. This new orientation transformed the way in which society is organized. As a result, **formal organizations**, secondary groups designed to achieve explicit objectives, have become a central feature of contemporary society. Most of us are born within them, we are educated in them, we spend our working lives in them, and we are buried by them (Volti, 1995).

Formal Organizations

Prior to industrialization, only a few formal organizations existed. The guilds of western Europe during the twelfth century are an example. People who performed the same type of work organized to control their craft in a local area. They set prices and standards of workmanship (Bridgwater, 1953; Volti, 1995). Much like modern unions, guilds also prevented outsiders (those who were not members of the guild) from working at the particular craft. Another example of an early formal organization is the army, with its structure of senior officers, junior officers, and ranks. Formal armies, of course, go back to early history.

With industrialization, secondary groups became common. Today we take their existence for granted, and, beginning with grade school, all of us spend a good deal of time in them. Formal organizations tend to develop into bureaucracies, and in general, the larger the formal organization, the more likely it is to be bureaucratic.

The Essential Characteristics of Bureaucracies

 Although a police department, the post office, a university, and General Motors may not seem to have much in common, they are all bureaucracies. As Weber (1913/1947) analyzed them, these are the essential characteristics of a **bureaucracy**:

1. *A hierarchy with assignments flowing downward and accountability flowing upward.* The organization is divided into clear-cut levels. Each level assigns responsibilities to the level beneath it, while each lower level is accountable to the level above for fulfilling those assignments. The bureaucratic structure of a typical university is shown in Figure 10.1.

2. *A division of labour.* Every member of a bureaucracy has a specific task to fulfill, and all the tasks are then coordinated to accomplish the purpose of the organization. In a university, for example, a professor does not run the heating system, the president does not teach, and a secretary does not evaluate textbooks. These tasks are distributed among people who have been trained to do them.

3. *Written rules.* In their attempt to become efficient, bureaucracies stress written procedures. In general, the longer a bureaucracy exists and the larger it grows, the more written rules it has. The rules of some bureaucracies cover just about every imaginable situation. In the university, for example, often the rules are bound in handbooks: separate ones for faculty, students, administrators, service workers, etc. The guiding principle generally becomes: "If there isn't a written rule covering it, it is allowed."

4. *Written communications and records.* Records are kept of much of what occurs in a bureaucracy. ("Fill that out in triplicate.") Consequently, workers in bureaucracies spend a fair amount of time sending memos and e-mail messages back and forth, the proverbial paper trail. They also produce written reports detailing their activities. Universities, for example, require that each faculty member keep his or her curriculum vitae up to date and that departments write an annual report listing what was accomplished in teaching, research, and service. These materials go to committees whose task it is to evaluate the relative performance of the departments and the courses offered.

5. *Impersonality.* It is the office that is important, not the individual who holds the office. You work for the organization, not the replaceable person who heads some post in the organization. Consequently, members of a bureaucracy owe allegiance to the office, not to particular people. If you work in a bureaucracy, you become a small cog in a large machine. Each worker is a replaceable unit, for many others are available to fulfill each particular function. For example, when a professor retires or dies, someone else is appointed to take his or her place.

These five characteristics not only help bureaucracies reach their goals but also allow them to grow and endure.

If the head of a bureaucracy dies, retires, or resigns, the organization continues, ordinarily hardly skipping a beat, for, unlike a "mom and pop" operation, the functioning of

Figure 10.1 Typical Bureaucratic Structure of a Medium-Sized University

This is a scaled-down version of a university's bureaucratic structure. The actual lines of authority of a university are likely to be much more complicated than those depicted here. A university may have a chancellor and several vice-presidents under the chancellor, each responsible for a certain campus. Although extensions of authority are given in this figure only for the Vice-president for academic affairs and the Faculty of social sciences, each of the other vice-presidents and faculties has similar positions. If the figure were to be extended, departmental secretaries would be shown, and eventually, somewhere, even students.

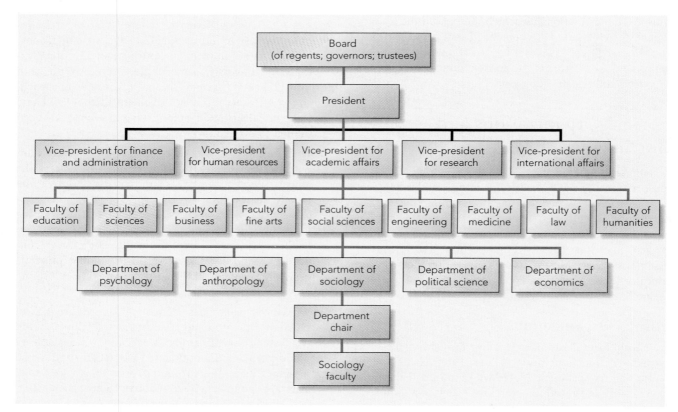

This 1907 photo indicates one way technology has changed our lives. The little drawers the women are searching contain customer records of the Metropolitan Life Insurance Company. Today, this entire bank of records could be stored on a personal computer. We could also use the computer to search or modify the records, which is infinitely faster—and certainly much easier on the legs—than standing on a ladder.

The McDonaldization of Society

Sociologist George Ritzer (1993) sees the thousands of McDonald's restaurants that dot the North American landscape—and increasingly, the world—as having much greater significance than the convenience of fast hamburgers and milkshakes. He coined the term "the McDonaldization of society" to refer to the increasing rationalization of the routine tasks of everyday life. In coining this term, Ritzer argues that the modern fast food restaurant presents us with a better paradigm for rationalization than Weber's conceptualization of bureaucracy (Ritzer, 1998).

He points out that Ray Kroc, the founder of McDonald's, applied the principles developed by Henry Ford to the preparation and serving of food. A 1958 operations manual spelled out the exact procedure:

> It told operators exactly how to draw milk shakes, grill hamburgers, and fry potatoes. It specified precise cooking times for all products and temperature settings for all equipment. It fixed standard portions on every food item, down to the quarter ounce of onions placed on each hamburger patty and the thirty-two slices per pound of cheese. It specified that french fries be cut at nine thirty-seconds of an inch thick....Grill men... were instructed to put hamburgers down on the grill moving from left to right, creating six rows of six patties each. And

McDonald's in Tokyo, Japan

because the first two rows were farthest from the heating element, they were instructed (and still are) to flip the third row first, then the fourth, fifth, and sixth before flipping the first two.

Ritzer stresses that "McDonaldization" does not refer just to the robotlike assembly of food. Rather, this process, occurring throughout society, is transforming our lives. Shopping malls are controlled environments of approved design, logo, colours, and opening and closing hours. Travel agencies transport middle-class tourists to 10 European capitals in 14 days, each visitor experiencing exactly the same hotels, restaurants, and other predictable settings. No one need fear meeting a "real" native. Television produces the same bland, instant news—in short, unanalytic

pieces that can be taken in between gulps of the McShake or the McBurger.

Is all this bad? Not necessarily. Efficiency does bring reduced prices. But at a cost, a loss of something difficult to define, a quality of life washed away by rationalization. If you travel, for example, and take packaged tours, you may never have the enjoyable, eye-opening experiences that add to your appreciation of human diversity.

In any event, the future has arrived. The trend is strongly toward the McDonaldization of human experience. For good or bad, our social destiny is to live in such prepackaged settings. When education becomes rationalized—which is now in process—our children will no longer have to put up with the idiosyncrasies of real professors, those people who think that ideas must be discussed endlessly and who never come to decisive answers anyway. What we want are instant, preformed solutions to social issues, like those we find in mathematics and engineering. Fortunately, our children will be able to be instructed in computerized courses, in which everyone learns the same answers, the approved, "politically correct," precise, and proper ways to think about social issues. This certainly will be efficient—as well as proof that the "iron cage" of bureaucracy that Weber said would entrap us, has.

a unit does not depend on the individual who heads it. The expansion (some would say domination) of bureaucracies in contemporary society is illustrated by the Down-to-Earth Sociology box above.

Another company that has attracted interest across the globe is Nike. The infamous Nike swoosh has, in many ways, symbolized global economic power, linking production facilities in Indonesia, China, and Vietnam where workers are paid subsistence wages, to mass-consumption markets in Canada, the United States, western Europe, and Japan. By 1996 Nike had captured 36 percent of the world market for sports equipment. It took over Canstar Sports, a famous Canadian company that sold hockey equipment worldwide. CEO Phil Knight's fourth-quarter dividend earnings in 1997 totalled US$80 million while Nike's revenue that year totalled US$9.19 billion. In contrast, a Nike

contract worker in Indonesia made about US$2.60 per day, and working 10 hours a day, six days a week earned about US$811 that year (LaFeber, 1999).

"Ideal" Versus "Real" Bureaucracy

Just as people often act quite differently from the way the norms say they should, so it is with bureaucracies. The characteristics of bureaucracies identified by Weber are ideal types; that is, they are a composite of characteristics based on many specific examples. Think of a judge at a dog show. He or she has a mental image of what a certain breed of dog should look like, and judges each dog according to that mental image. No one dog will have all the characteristics, but all dogs of that breed put together have them. Thus, a particular organization may be ranked high or low on some characteristic and still qualify as a bureaucracy.

One bureaucracy's rules may clash with another's, creating situations in which it is impossible for people to have their needs met fairly. Bureaucratic dysfunctioning may inadvertently place people who question or challenge rules, policies, or procedures at tremendous disadvantage, even jeopardize their opportunities or threaten their well-being.

Consider the case of high school student and athlete, Jackie B. After graduating with honours from the local public middle school, Jackie left behind her friends to attend the separate secondary school in her area. Her reason was simple, she thought. She was a highly competitive soccer player and she wanted to take up the sport of rowing. The separate school supported not only a rowing team, but also the most highly successful and well regarded girls' soccer program in the province.

Jackie's Grade 9 school year started with all the usual awkwardness experienced by most freshmen. But soon after the school year began, Jackie found herself a victim of bullying and harassment. At first she ignored it and fully expected that it would end as she continued to prove herself on the field and as an outstanding newcomer to the rowing crew. As the year went on, she became increasingly despondent. She found herself alone and depressed and her marks began to drop. She feared reporting the bullies. The situation was brought to the attention of the school's senior administration, and when pressed, Jackie

divulged the name of one of the leading bullies. However, the situation was poorly handled, and Jackie's sense of security both within the school and in public places, such as the movie theatres, was threatened. For many, the solution would be simple: Transfer to the public high school. For an athlete, however, this simple solution is very costly.

To prevent coaches from "shopping" for star athletes and luring students from one school to another, either inside or outside home boundaries, the provincial athletic association has a rule on transfers. If a student transfers schools, she or he will not be allowed to participate in any sport (falling under the association's umbrella) in which she or he was involved in during the previous school year. Jackie was devastated by the situation in which she found herself. Transferring schools would possibly mean sitting out of her sports for a year, while staying put would be increasingly difficult to deal with. However, there were exceptions to this rule, and there would be opportunity for her to appeal her case. Her chances of winning were slim but would improve considerably if she were able to obtain a statement by an official from the separate school that she was a victim of bullying and harassment and transferred because of it.

Jackie's coaches and teachers at her new school were highly accommodating and helped her and her parents with the appeal. Nevertheless, they ran into a major roadblock. No one from Jackie's previous school would help her out. Her

parents' phone calls were not returned and the situation was swept under the carpet. Even several teachers who were very well aware of the problems Jackie had experienced refused to help her. It seems that they were under strict orders from the principal not to involve themselves. Worried that perhaps their careers might suffer, they turned a blind eye to Jackie's plight, despite their knowledge of the situation and their willingness to agree that bullying and harassment are serious problems in schools and that steps should be taken to eliminate the problem.

Without the supporting documents from the separate school, Jackie lost her appeal. She paid the price for being on the receiving end of bullies' actions. And it would cost her, whether or not she chose to transfer. If she remained at the separate school, she would continue to be victimized at the expense of her well-being and her marks. Her decision to transfer to the public high school was supported by her family and friends as her only reasonable choice, but the price she paid for this decision was clearly outrageous.

For Your Consideration

How was Jackie limited by bureaucratic decision-making? What does Jackie's situation tell us about bureaucratic alienation, careerism, communication within or between bureaucracies, and lines of authority? What message does this incident give to the bullies?

Instead of labelling a particular organization as a "bureaucracy" or "not a bureaucracy," it probably makes more sense to think in terms of the *extent* to which an organization is bureaucratized (Udy, 1959; R. H. Hall, 1963).

As with culture, then, a bureaucracy often differs from its ideal image. The actual lines of authority ("going through channels"), for example, may be quite different from those portrayed on organizational charts, such as that shown in Figure 10.1. For example, suppose that before being promoted, the university president taught in the history department. As a result, friends from that department may have direct access to him or her. In giving their "input" (ranging

from opinions about how to solve problems to personal grievances or even gossip), these individuals may skip their chairperson or even the dean of their faculty altogether.

Dysfunctions of Bureaucracies

Although no other form of social organization has been found to be more efficient in the long run, as Weber recognized, his model accounts for only some of the characteristics of bureaucracies. They also have a dark side and do not always operate smoothly. The Thinking Critically about Social Controversy box above presents a teenager's dilemma as she is caught between bureaucracies and their policies. Let's look at some of bureaucracy's dysfunctions—red tape, lack of communication, alienation, goal displacement, and incompetence.

Red Tape: A Rule Is a Rule.
As Jennifer in the opening vignette discovered, bureaucracies can be filled with so much red tape that they impede the purpose of the organization. In New York, Mother Teresa spotted a structurally sound abandoned building in the Bronx, and wanted to turn it into a homeless shelter. But she ran head-on into a rule: The building must have an elevator for the handicapped homeless. Not having the funds for the elevator, Mother Teresa struggled to get permission to bypass this rule. Two frustrating years later, she gave up. The abandoned building is still an abandoned building (Tobias, 1995).

Obviously, this well-intentioned rule about elevators was not meant to stop Mother Teresa from ministering to the down and out. But, hey, rules are rules!

Lack of Communication Between Units.
Each unit within a bureaucracy performs specialized tasks, which are designed to contribute to the organization's overall goals. At times, these units fail to communicate with one another and end up working at cross-purposes. In Granada, Spain, for example, the local government was concerned about the rundown appearance of buildings along one of its main roads. Consequently, one unit of the government fixed the fronts of these buildings, painting and repairing concrete, iron, and stonework. The results were impressive, and the unit was proud of what it had accomplished. The only problem was that another unit of the government had slated these same buildings for demolition (Arías, 1993). With neither unit of this bureaucracy knowing what the other was doing, a huge expense and effort ended in a heap of rubble.

Bureaucratic Alienation.
Many workers find it disturbing to deal with others in terms of roles, rules, and functions rather than as individuals. Similarly, they may dislike writing memos instead of talking to people face to face. It is not surprising, then, that workers in large organizations sometimes feel more like objects than people, or, as Weber (1922/1978) put it, "only a small cog in a ceaselessly moving mechanism which prescribes to [them] an endlessly fixed routine…." Because workers must deal with one another in such formal ways, and because they constantly perform routine tasks, some come to feel that no one cares about them and that they are misfits in their surroundings.

Marx termed these reactions **alienation** and attributed them to the fact that workers are cut off from the finished product of their labour. Although assigning workers to repetitive tasks makes for efficient production, Marx argued that it also reduces their satisfaction by limiting their creativity and sense of contribution to the finished product. Underlying alienation is the workers' loss of control over their work because they no longer own their own tools. Before industrialization, individual workers used their own tools to produce an entire product, such as a chair or table. Now the capitalists own the machinery and tools and assign each worker only a single step or two in the entire production process. Relegated to repetitive tasks that seem remote from the final product, workers lose a sense of identity with what they produce. Ultimately, they come to feel estranged not only from their products but from their whole work environment.

Today's armies, no matter from what country, are bureaucracies. They have a strict hierarchy of rank, division of labour, and impersonality (an emphasis on the office, not the person holding it), and they stress written records, rules, and communications—essential characteristics identified by Max Weber. This army in India, though its outward appearance may differ from Western standards, is no exception to this principle.

Resisting Alienation. Alienation, of course, is not a pleasant experience. Because workers want to feel valued and want to have a sense of control over their work, they resist alienation. Forming primary groups at work is a major form of that resistance. They band together in informal settings—at lunch, around desks, for a drink after work. There they give one another approval for jobs well done and express sympathy for the shared need to put up with cantankerous bosses, meaningless routines, and endless rules. Here they relate to one another not just as workers, but as people who value one another. They laugh and tell jokes, talk about their families, their problems, their goals, and, often, their love life. Adding this multidimensionality to their work relationships restores their sense of being persons rather than mere cogs in an endlessly moving machine. When workers decide to take collective action about their workplace struggles, they form a union.

Consider a common sight. You are visiting an office, and you see work areas decorated with family and vacation photos. The sociological implication is that of workers striving to overcome alienation. By staking a claim to individuality, the workers are rejecting an identity as mere machines performing functions.

The Alienated Bureaucrat. Not all workers succeed in resisting alienation, however, and some become extremely alienated. They remain in the organization because they see no viable alternative or because they have "only so many years until retirement." They hate every minute of it, however, and it shows—in their attitudes toward clients, toward fellow workers, and especially toward authority in the organization. The alienated bureaucrat does not take initiative, will not do anything for the organization beyond what he or she is absolutely required to do, and uses rules to justify doing as little as possible. If Jennifer in this chapter's opening vignette had come across an alienated bureaucrat behind the registration window, she might have been told: "What's the matter with you—can't you read? Everyone else manages to pay their fees on time, why can't you? I don't know what kind of students they are sending us nowadays." If the worker had been alienated even more, he or she might even have denied knowledge of where to get the problem taken care of.

In spite of poor attitude and performance, alienated workers often retain their jobs, because they have seniority, or know the written rules backward and forward, or threaten expensive, time-consuming, and embarrassing legal action if anyone tries to fire them. Some alienated workers are shunted off into small bureaucratic corners, where they do trivial tasks and have little chance of coming in contact with the public. This treatment, of course, only alienates them further.

Managers might find ways to challenge workers who have lost interest in their jobs. They could provide these workers with an opportunity to have input into decisions in order to rekindle their commitment and to develop more congenial work relations.

Goal Displacement. Bureaucracies sometimes take on a life of their own, adopting new goals in place of old ones. In this process, called **goal displacement**, even when the goal of the organization has been achieved and there no longer is any reason for it to continue, continue it does. A good example is the national foundation for the March of Dimes, organized in the 1930s to fight polio, a crippling disease that strikes without warning (Sills, 1957). The origin of polio was a mystery to the medical profession, and the public was alarmed and fearful. All sorts of rumours ran rampant about its cause. Overnight, a healthy child would

The March of Dimes was founded by U.S. President Franklin Roosevelt in the 1930s to fight polio. The Ontario March of Dimes was established in 1951. When a vaccine for polio was discovered in 1955, the organization did not declare victory and disband. Instead, it kept the organization intact by adopting a new goal—fighting birth defects. Sociologists use the term *goal displacement* to refer to this process of adopting new goals. "Fighting birth defects" is now being replaced by something even vaguer, "Breakthroughs for Babies." This new goal displacement may guarantee the organization's existence forever, for it is a goal so elusive it can never be reached. (Can we ever run out of the need for "breakthroughs"?)

be stricken. Parents were fearful, because no one knew whose child would be next. The March of Dimes began to publicize individual cases. An especially effective strategy was placing posters of a child on crutches near cash registers in almost every store. The public took the goals of the organization to heart and contributed heavily.

The organization raised money beyond its wildest dreams. Then during the 1950s, when Dr. Jonas Salk developed a vaccine for polio, this threat was wiped out almost overnight. The public breathed a collective sigh of relief. What then? Did the organization fold? After all, its purpose had been fulfilled. But, as you know, the March of Dimes is still around. Faced with the loss of their jobs, the professional staff that ran the organization quickly found a way to keep the bureaucracy intact by pursuing a new enemy—birth defects. Their choice of enemy is particularly striking, for it is doubtful that we will ever run out of birth defects—and thus unlikely that these people will ever run out of jobs.

Bureaucratic Incompetence.   In a tongue-in-cheek analysis of bureaucracies, Laurence Peter proposed what has become known as the **Peter principle**: Each employee of a bureaucracy is promoted to his or her *level of incompetence* (Peter & Hull, 1969). People who perform well in a bureaucracy come to the attention of those higher up the chain of command and are promoted. If they again perform well, they are again promoted. This process continues until finally they are promoted to a level at which they can no longer handle the responsibilities well; this is their level of incompetence. There they hide behind the work of others, taking credit for what those under their direction accomplish. Although the Peter principle contains a grain of truth, if it were generally true bureaucracies would be staffed entirely by incompetents, and none of these organizations could succeed. In reality, bureaucracies are remarkably successful.

> **Focus Question**
> What are some of the ways bureaucracies become inefficient and dysfunctional?

The Sociological Significance of Bureaucracies

Perhaps the main sociological significance of bureaucracies is that they represent a fundamental change in how people relate to one another. When work is rooted in social relationships, much more is at stake than efficiency in performing tasks and keeping an eye on the bottom line. Seeing that all family members are employed, or that everyone in the community has a chance to make a living, for example, may be the determining factors in making decisions. Bureaucracies, or the rationalization of society, changed all this (Volti, 1995).

Voluntary Associations

Although bureaucracies have become the dominant form of organization for large, task-oriented groups, even more common are **voluntary associations**, groups made up of volunteers who organize on the basis of some mutual interest. Let us examine their essential characteristics.

Back in the 1830s, a Frenchman travelled across the United States, observing the customs of this new nation. Alexis de Tocqueville wrote a widely read book about his observations, *Democracy in America* (1835/1966), which is still quoted for its insights into character. As an outsider, de Tocqueville was able to see patterns that people immersed in them could not. One of de Tocqueville's observations was that Americans joined a lot of voluntary associations.

Like their American neighbours, Canadians are very proud of their commitment to voluntary associations. Visitors entering small towns across the country are often greeted with a sign proclaiming which volunteer associations that particular town has: Girl Scouts, Boy Scouts, Kiwanis, Lions, Knights of Columbus, Chamber of Commerce, Canadian Legion, Little League, and perhaps a host of others. One form of voluntary association is so prevalent that a separate sign usually indicates which varieties are present in the town: Roman Catholic, Jewish, Muslim, Buddhist, Lutheran, Anglican, and so on. Not listed on these signs are many other voluntary associations, such as political parties, unions, health clubs, social planning councils, minor hockey associations, the National Action Committee on the Status of Women, the National Anti-Poverty Organization, Alcoholics Anonymous, the Canadian Cancer Society, and Citizens United For or Against This and That.

One of the groups in Canada most heavily involved in volunteering is the growing population of seniors (age 55+). According to the National Survey of Volunteer Activity, Canadians aged 35 to 44 have the highest rate of volunteerism, but seniors who volunteer their time spend more hours per week than others. In 1997, on average almost 30 percent of 55-to-64-year-olds and almost 26 percent of those aged 65 to 74 participated formally through a group or organization in volunteer work. Seniors donate about 15 hours of their time per month, in contrast to all other groups who volunteer for approximately 12 hours a month (Jones, 1997). They work in a variety of settings: They organize community events, fundraise, campaign, canvass, and sit on boards. With cutbacks in funding to hospitals and social service agencies, volunteer work has become essential in meeting many public organizations' service goals. Major organizations, such as hospitals, sometimes hire full-time volunteer coordinators who provide training and support to this army of unpaid workers. Although most volunteers describe their work as personally rewarding, from a critical perspective it is sometimes argued that these workers are not valued highly enough for their contributions and are exploited by administrators and governments whose primary concern is cost-saving.

Canadians love voluntary associations, using them to express a wide variety of interests, goals, opinions, and even dissatisfactions. Some groups are local, consisting of only a few volunteers; others are national, with a paid professional staff. Some are temporary, organized to accomplish a specific task such as arranging a town's next Labour Day parade; others, such as the Scouts and political parties, are permanent, large, secondary organizations with clear lines of command—and they are also bureaucracies.

Shared Interests

Voluntary associations, then, represent no single interest or purpose. They can be reactionary, dragged screaming into the present as their nails claw the walls of the past, or they can lead the vanguard for social change, announcing their vision of a better world. The anti-globalization movement, for example, extends across the globe, bringing together scientists and activists who question policies such as NAFTA and raise awareness of human rights, labour, and environmental issues while examining the decisions of organizations such as the World Bank and International Monetary Fund.

In spite of their amazing diversity, however, a thread does run through all voluntary associations. That thread is mutual interest. Although the particular interest varies from group to group, shared interest in some view or activity is the tie that binds each group's members together.

Although members are united by shared interests, their motivations for joining the group differ widely. Some join because they have strong convictions concerning the stated purpose of the organization, others simply because

membership gives them a chance to make contacts that will help them politically or professionally. Some even join for social reasons. Others, like seniors, derive satisfaction and a sense of pride by using their skills and experience in a meaningful way.

With motivations for joining voluntary associations and commitment to their goals so varied, these organizations often have a high turnover. Some people move in and out of groups almost as fast as they change clothes. Within every organization, however, is an inner core of individuals who stand firmly behind the group's goals, or at least are firmly committed to maintaining the organization itself. If this inner core loses commitment, the group is likely to fold.

The Problem of Oligarchy

Most organizations are run by only a few of their members (Cnaan, 1991). Building on the term *oligarchy*, a system in which many are ruled by a few, sociologist Robert Michels (1876–1936) coined the term the **iron law of oligarchy** to refer to how formal organizations come to be dominated by a small, self-perpetuating elite. The majority of the members become passive, and an elite inner group keeps itself in power by passing the leading positions from one clique member to another.

What many find depressing about the iron law of oligarchy is that it applies even to organizations strongly committed to democratic principles. Even Canadian political parties, for example, supposedly the backbone of the nation's representative government, have fallen prey to it. Run by an inner group that may or may not represent the community, they pass their leadership positions from one elite member to another.

Voluntary organizations are extremely popular. Across Canada, clubs such as Kiwanis, Canadian Legion, Lions, Little League, and Rotary are widely recognized. Local branches are linked to headquarters where the organization's overall goals and objectives are set. In addition to such national bodies, numerous smaller local organizations, whose volunteers help run food banks, shelters for battered women, and programs for homeless people, for example, contribute to the spirit and well-being of communities.

The iron law of oligarchy is not without its limitations, of course. Members of the inner group must remain attuned to the opinions of the other members, regardless of their personal feelings. If the oligarchy gets too far out of line, it runs the risk of a grassroots rebellion that would throw this elite group out of office. It is this threat that often softens the iron law of oligarchy by making the leadership responsive to the membership. In addition, because not all organizations become captive to an elite, this is a tendency, not an inevitability (J. Fisher, 1994).

Focus Question
How is the power structure within most formal organizations described?

Careers in Bureaucracies

Since you are likely to end up working in a bureaucracy, let's look at how its characteristics may affect your career.

The Corporate Culture: Consequences of Hidden Values

Who gets ahead in a large corporation? Although we might like to think that success is the consequence of intelligence and hard work, many factors other than merit underlie salary increases and promotions. Historically, in Canada family ties have secured many individuals to the power structure, or what author Peter C. Newman refers to as the "Canadian Establishment." Although a number of these historically dominant family dynasties, such as the Eatons, have recently tumbled, others, such as the Irvings, Sobeys, Ganongs, Molsons, and McCains, maintain control over their corporate empires (Newman, 1999). A few among the group of Canada's most wealthy and powerful may trace their roots back to more humble origins. Paul Desmarais, CEO of Power Corporation, started his career by revitalizing a small one-route bus line in Sudbury, Ontario; Jean Coutu and Murray Koffler, retail pharmacy magnates, each started with one corner drugstore; and diving for salvage was the first job of Newfoundland's premier businessman, Craig Dobbin, a lumberjack's son (Newman, 1999).

While hard work and a cunning business sense certainly helped a number of Canada's most prominent corporate executives, the largest group has succeeded through familial and social interrelations. Some have even enjoyed continued prosperity despite incompetence. Senior executives with companies such as Bell Canada, Dofasco Inc., Montreal Trust, Confederation Life, and others, have, at one time or another, misjudged business prospects, and for their poor decision-making were actually promoted and given raises with bonuses (Newman, 1999). As sociologist Rosabeth Moss Kanter (1977, 1983) stresses, the **corporate culture**, the orientation that characterizes a corporate work setting, is crucial in determining people's corporate fate. She explains how a corporation's "hidden values"—those not officially part of the organization, but which nevertheless powerfully influence its members—operate as self-fulfilling stereotypes. The elite holds ideas about who are the best workers and colleagues, and those who fit this mold get better access to information and networking, and are put in "fast-track" positions. Not surprisingly, these people perform better and become more committed to the organization, thus confirming the initial expectation. In contrast, those judged to be outsiders find opportunities closing up. They tend to work at a level beneath their capacity, come to think poorly of themselves, and become less committed to the organization.

The hidden values that created this self-fulfilling prophecy remain invisible to most. What are visible are the promotions of people with superior performances and greater commitment to the company, not the self-fulfilling prophecy that produced these attitudes and work performances.

The Down-to-Earth Sociology box on page 248 explores how ideas often are judged in corporations not by their merit, but according to *who* expresses them. You can see how such hidden values contribute to the iron law of oligarchy, for the corporate elite, the tight inner group that heads a corporation, sets in motion a self-fulfilling prophecy that tends to reproduce itself with people who "look" like its members, generally white and male. Although women and minorities, who don't match the stereotype, are often "showcased"—placed in highly visible positions with little power in order to demonstrate to the public and affirmative action officials how progressive the company is (Benokraitis & Feagin, 1991)—they often occupy "slow-track" positions, where accomplishments seldom come to the attention of top management.

While a number of sociologists have discussed the ways in which women are overlooked in their pursuit of upward social mobility and how organizations may become more open to promoting women, Kathy Ferguson, in her 1984 book *The Feminist Case Against Bureaucracy*, identifies the power structures within bureaucratic capitalist society as a

Sociologist Rosabeth Moss Kanter has written extensively about corporations, including such titles as *Men and Women of the Corporation, Innovation: Breakthrough Thinking*, and *World Class: Thriving Locally in the Global Economy*.

I work for a large insurance company. Of its 2500 employees, about 75 percent are women. Only 5 percent of the upper management positions, however, are held by women.

I am one of the more fortunate women, for I hold a position in middle management. I am also a member of the twelve-member junior board of directors, of whom nine are men and three are women.

Recently, one of the female members of the board suggested that the company become involved in Horizons for Tomorrow, a program designed to provide internships for disadvantaged youth. Two other women and I spent many days developing a proposal for the company's participation.

The problem was how to sell the proposal to the company president. From past experiences, we knew that if he saw it as a "woman's project" it would be shelved into the second tier of "maybes." He hates what he calls

"aggressive bitches."

We three decided, reluctantly, that the proposal had a chance only if it were presented by a man. We decided that Bill was the logical choice. We also knew that we had to "stroke" Bill if we were going to get his cooperation.

We first asked Bill if he would "show us how to present our proposal." (It is ridiculous to have to play the role of the "less capable female" today, but, unfortunately the corporate culture sometimes dictates this strategy.) To clinch matters, we puffed up Bill even more by saying, "You're the logical choice as the next chair of the board."

Bill, of course, came to our next planning session, where *we* "prepped" *him* on what to say.

At our meeting with the president, we had Bill give the basic presentation. We then backed *him* up, providing the background and rationale for why the president should endorse the project. As

we answered the president's questions, we carefully deferred to Bill.

The president's response? "An excellent proposal," he concluded, "an appropriate project for our company."

To be successful, we had to manoeuvre through the treacherous waters of the "hidden culture" (actually not so "hidden" to women who have been in the company for a while). The proposal was not sufficient on its merits, for the "who" behind a proposal is at least as significant as the proposal itself.

"We shouldn't have to play these games," Laura said, summarizing our feelings.

But we all know that we have no choice. To become labelled "pushy" is to commit "corporate suicide"—and we're no fools.

Source: Written by an insurance executive in Henslin's introductory sociology class who, out of fear of retaliation at work, chooses to remain anonymous.

---

primary source of oppression for both women and men. She advocates elimination, rather than amelioration, of these structures (Ferguson, 1984). Moreover, it is important to develop a critical approach to organizations that focuses on inequalities of power and opportunity within hierarchical structures and to examine how women, minorities, Aboriginal people, and the working class are disadvantaged within organizations (Mills & Simmons, 1999).

Kanter found that the level people reach in the organization also shapes their behaviour, and even their attitudes toward themselves and others. In general, the higher people go, the higher their morale. "This is a good company," they say to themselves. "They recognize my abilities." With their greater satisfaction, people in higher office also tend to be more helpful to subordinates and flexible in their style of leadership. In contrast, people who don't get very far in the organization are frustrated and tend to have lower morale. A less apparent result of their blocked opportunity, however, is that they are likely to be rigid supervisors and strong defenders of whatever privileges they have. Because the workers in a corporation tend to see only the level that is readily visible, they usually ascribe differences in behaviours and attitudes to people's personalities. Sociologists probe beneath this level, however, to examine

how corporate culture shapes people's attitudes, and, by extension, the quality of their work.

One of the major issues in bureaucracies is how to adapt to a changing work force. A controversial solution that some corporations have chosen is discussed in the Liberal and Conservative Views on Social Issues box.

Management Strategies and the Corporate Culture

Bureaucracies have transformed society by harnessing people's energies to specific goals and monitoring progress to those goals. Weber (1946a) predicted that because bureaucracies were so efficient and had the capacity to replace themselves indefinitely, they would come to dominate social life. More than any prediction in sociology, this one has withstood the test of time (Rothschild & Whitt, 1986; Perrow, 1991).

Scientific Management

During the late 1880s, Frederick Winslow Taylor, an American industrial engineer, developed the **principles of scientific management**, which sought to reduce waste and inefficiency in production. Using these principles,

Some of the signs: Almost 80 percent of Canadian workers are minorities, immigrants, and women (cited in Henslin & Nelson, 1996). Diversity includes ethnicity, gender, age, religion, social class, and sexual orientation.

The huge successes of the women's movement and of civil rights activism have encouraged pride in one's heritage and made many Canadians comfortable with being different from the dominant group. Consequently, people are now less amenable to **assimilation**, the process by which minorities are absorbed into the dominant culture. Assimilation involves relinquishing distinctive cultural patterns of behaviour in favour of those of the dominant culture. Realizing that assimilation is probably not the wave of the future, most major companies, unions,

and public service commissions sponsor "diversity training," sending workers to lectures and workshops to learn to work with colleagues of diverse cultures and racial/ethnic backgrounds.

In general, liberals welcome diversity training. They see it as an effective means of coming to grips with the new reality of the workplace. Consequently, say liberals, diversity training is needed so we can develop an appreciative understanding of our differences and work together to meet common goals.

Critical approaches to the study of organizations suggest that diversity training programs alone will not eliminate the problems confronting racial and ethnic minorities within organizations today. In fact, critics argue that diversity training and multiculturalism may gloss over

underlying sentiments of racism. It is not enough to respect or to know about various cultures; it is necessary to ensure that each has equal access to positions, rewards, and statuses within an organization (Mills & Simmons, 1999).

Conservatives, in general, see a negative side to diversity training. They believe it stimulates the stereotypes and divisiveness it is meant to alleviate. Consequently, say conservatives, we must de-emphasize group differences and instead stress the behavioural qualities that lead to success—especially responsibility and pride in one's work. Then we can work together as a team to meet common goals.

Sources: R. R. Thomas (1990); Piturro (1991); Sowell (1993a); Reibstein (1996).

Some members of the "Canadian Establishment," such as Paul Desmarais, CEO of Power Corporation, trace their roots to humble origins and owe their powerful positions to their own entrepreneurial efforts. Others have secured their positions within the Canadian power structure through family ties.

management was able to regulate work precisely by controlling the pace of work, the level of production, and all decisions pertaining to the labour process. In order for management to maintain or re-establish control over work, Taylor recommended dividing complex tasks into a number of sub-tasks and separating knowledge or conceptual work from the execution of the tasks. He used a series of time and motion studies to detail the exact movements required by workers to carry out the task and the length of time needed to complete each task. The data were then used by management to specify exactly how the work was to be done, and it was the worker's responsibility to carry out his or her assigned task to management's precise specifications. By adopting the principles of scientific management, employers were able to hire less skilled, lower-paid workers (Braverman, 1974). While Taylor's principles were originally applied in factories, eventually these rules were utilized in offices, call centres, fast food restaurants, and reservation services, and in Canada Post and Air Canada (Ritzer, 1998; Schlosser, 2002; Shalla, 1997).

Humanizing Work

Bureaucracies appear likely to remain our dominant form of social organization, and most of us, like it or not, are destined to spend our working lives in bureaucracies. Many people have become concerned about the negative side of bureaucracies, however, and would like to make them more humane. **Humanizing a work setting** means organizing work in such a way that it develops rather than impedes human potential. Such work settings offer access to opportunities on the basis of ability and contributions rather than personal characteristics, distribute power more equally, and have less rigid rules and more open decision-making. In short, more people are involved in making decisions, their contributions are more readily recognized, and individuals feel freer to participate.

Can bureaucracies adapt to such a model? Contrary to some popular images, not all bureaucracies are unyielding, unwieldy monoliths. There is nothing in the nature of bureaucracies that makes them *inherently* insensitive to people's needs or that prevents them from humanizing corporate culture.

Moreover, to humanize corporate culture does not require huge expense. Kanter (1983) compared 47 companies that were rigidly bureaucratic with competitors of the same size that were more flexible. It turned out that the more flexible companies were also more profitable—probably because their greater flexibility encouraged greater company loyalty, creativity, and productivity.

Quality Circles

In the light of such findings, many corporations have taken steps to humanize their work settings, motivated not by any altruistic urge to make life better for their workers but by self-interest, the desire to make their organization more competitive. Companies—from the smallest to the largest—have begun to reform their work organizations. Some have developed **quality circles**, which consist of perhaps a dozen workers and a manager or two who meet regularly to try to improve the quality of both the work setting and the company's products.

However, many companies report that quality circles have yielded few benefits. Disappointed with the results, companies such as Whirlpool and GE have abandoned the idea. (Part of the reason may be that they set up quality circles for reasons of publicity, not intending to take employee suggestions seriously.) Both companies continue to solicit ideas from their employees, however. GE now uses town-hall-type meetings and rewards workers with cash and stock options (Naj, 1993).

Employee Stock Ownership

Many companies offer an opportunity for their employees to purchase the firm's stock at a discount or as part of their salary, and numerous Canadian companies, including Canadian Tire Corporation, are now partially owned by their employees. Because each employee typically owns only a tiny amount of stock in the company, such "ownership" is practically meaningless. In a small percentage of these companies, however, the employees own the majority of the stock. On average, companies with at least 10 percent of stock owned by employees are more profitable than other firms, probably because the workers are more committed and managers take a longer-term view (White, 1991).

One might think that employee ownership of a company's stock would eliminate problems between workers and management. Profitability, however, not ownership, appears to be the key to reducing these problems. Unprofitable firms put more pressure on their employee-owners, creating tension between workers and managers, while profitable companies resolve problems more quickly.

Small Work Groups

Pioneered in the computer industry to increase productivity and cut down on absenteeism, small work groups, or self-managed teams, are now becoming increasingly common. Small work groups stimulate creative ideas and imaginative solutions to problems, and employees who work in them feel a greater sense of loyalty to the company, work harder, and reduce their absenteeism. Workers in these groups also react more quickly to threats posed by technological change and competitors' advances. No less a behemoth than IBM has found that people work more effectively in a small group than in a distant, centralized command structure (Drucker, 1992).

The small work group establishes primary relationships among its members, and workers' identities become

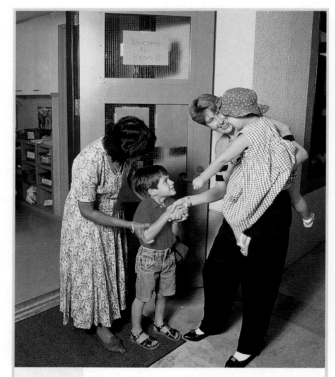

"Humanizing" the work setting—the attempt to make working conditions match human needs—has taken many forms. One (used by only a minority of corporations) is to offer on-site day care. Shown here is a working mother dropping her little girl off at the company-run day care centre. Such services cost companies less than they appear to, for they reduce worker turnover.

tied up with their group. This reduces alienation, for rather than being lost in a bureaucratic maze, here their individuality is appreciated, their contributions more readily recognized. The group's successes become the individual's successes—as do its failures—reflecting positively or negatively on the individual. As a consequence of their expanded personal ties, workers make more of an effort. The results have been so good that, in what is known as "worker empowerment," some self-managed teams even replace bosses in controlling everything from schedules to hiring and firing (Lublin, 1991).

Workplace Day Care

Another way to humanize the work setting is to set up day care facilities at work. This eases the strain on parents, especially on new mothers, who are then able to go to work and still keep an eye on a baby or young child. Parents are also able to spend time with their children during breaks and lunch hours. Mothers can even nurse a child at these times.

Granted global competition, can firms afford child care? Accountable to its stockholders, the Union Bank of Monterey, California, decided to measure the net cost of its day care. They found that the turnover of employees who used the centre was only 2.2 percent, in contrast to 9.5 percent of those who did not use it. Users of the centre were also absent from work almost two days a year less than the non-users, and their maternity leaves were shorter. The net cost? After subtracting what it cost to open the centre and to run it, the bank saved over $200 000 (Solomon, 1988).

A measure in between the company providing such services and offering no child care is to provide quality emergency backup child care. Parents use their own babysitter, but when the sitter can't make it the centre's services allow the parent to get to work—and to work without worry (Nayaran, 1994). Today, with fewer families with a stay-at-home parent, there may be more and more pressure on firms to offer child care services as part of a benefits package to attract and hold capable workers.

Developing an Alternative: The Cooperative

While measures such as those described above generally make the workplace more hospitable to workers, these management strategies are ultimately aimed at increasing profit and productivity. In the 1970s, many workers across North America, especially those opposed to capitalism and what they considered to be the deadening effects of bureaucracy, began to seek an alternative organizational form. They began to establish cooperatives—organizations owned by members who collectively make decisions, determine goals, evaluate resources, set salaries, and assign work tasks. The tasks are all carried out without a hierarchy of authority, for all members can participate in the decisions of the organization. In Canada there are approximately 300 worker-managed companies, with about 6000 members altogether (Rinehart, 1996).

As sociologists Joyce Rothschild and Allen Whitt (1986) pointed out, cooperatives are not new. Farmers' cooperatives, once popular in western Canada, have a long and rich history. Cooperatives attempt to achieve some specific social good (such as lowering food prices and improving food quality) and to provide a high level of personal satisfaction for their members as they work toward that goal. Most self-managed enterprises are small companies in which workers are ultimately concerned with controlling their own labour. Some companies were bought out by the workers in order to save their jobs. One such company is Northern Breweries in Sault Ste. Marie, Ontario (Rinehart, 1996). Because all members can participate in decision-making, cooperatives spend huge amounts of time deciding even routine matters.

The economic results of cooperatives are mixed. Many are less profitable than private organizations, others more so. A few have been so successful that they have been bought out by major corporations.

Say Hello to the New Taste in Town

There is a rich vein of gold in Northern Ontario. That liquid gold is St. Joseph Island maple syrup and it is as much a part of life today as it was when it was first tapped generations ago. The sterling reputation of St. Joe Island as a source of world-class maple syrup is well deserved. The region boasts plentiful sugar maples, rooted in limestone-rich soil, growing in just the right climate.

Red Maple Premium Lager is made using amber maple syrup from St. Joe Island producers. Its characteristic maple flavour gently balances the natural bitterness created by the blend of imported hops. When combined with premium black roasted barley malt, and pure Pre-Cambrian Shield waters of Lake Superior, the result is an uncommonly smooth beer with a uniquely Northern character. In essence, Red Maple Premium Lager is a gift of nature, from the North.

 NORTHERN BREWERIES SINCE 1876

503 Bay Street, Sault Ste. Marie

OPEN Mon.-Sat. 9 a.m. to 11 p.m.
Sunday 11 a.m. to 6 p.m.

Debit card, Visa, MasterCard, American Express accepted.

Cooperatives provide workers with an alternative work arrangement. As owners, organization members collectively make decisions, determine goals and policies, and set salaries and work tasks. Decision-making, even on routine matters, is often very time-consuming, since all members participate. Cooperatives strive to provide members with a high level of satisfaction for work performed.

The Conflict Perspective

Conflict theorists point out that the basic relationship between workers and owners is confrontational regardless of how the work organization is structured (R. Edwards, 1979; Derber & Schwartz, 1988; Rinehart, 1996). Each walks a different path in life, the one exploiting workers to extract a greater profit, the other trying to resist that exploitation. Since their basic interests are fundamentally opposed, these critics argue, employers' attempts to humanize the work setting (or to manage diversity) are mere window dressing, efforts to conceal their fundamental goal to exploit workers. If these efforts are not camouflage, then they are worse—attempts to manipulate workers into active cooperation in their own exploitation. This analysis does not apply to cooperatives because they are owned by the workers.

Technology and the Control of Workers

The microchip is rapidly changing our lives. Many people rejoice over the computer's capacity to improve their quality of life. They are pleased with the quality control of manufactured goods and the reduction of drudgery. Records are much easier to keep, and we can type just one letter and let the computer print and address it to 10 people—or 10 000.

Computers also hold the potential for severe abuse. They may allow governments to operate a police state, monitoring our every move. The Big Brother in Orwell's classic novel, *1984*, may turn out to be a computer. Technology has, in many ways, transformed work into a "Brave New World," according to writer and activist Heather Menzies. In the new workplace, individuals play a secondary role to advanced technologies that not only are capable of levels of production and efficiency beyond human capability, but also simultaneously connect to and manage facilities and labour forces across the globe (Menzies, 1996). The technologically advanced workplace has the capacity to eliminate and de-skill workers, resulting in high levels of unemployment and a deep sense of insecurity experienced by workers in various settings (Noble, 1995).

Whether this happens or not, the computer certainly does allow managers to achieve much greater control over workers. Social psychologist Shoshana Zuboff (1991) reports how computers allow managers to increase surveillance without face-to-face supervision. They let managers know the number of strokes a word processor makes every minute or hour, or inform supervisors how long each telephone operator takes per call. Operators who are "underperforming" are singled out for discipline. It does not matter that the slower operators may be more polite or more helpful, only that the computer reports slower performance.

As sociologist Gary Marx (1985, 1986, 1995) says, with computers able to measure motion, air currents, vibrations, odours, pressure changes, and voice stress, accompanied by video cameras that need only a pinhole for their spying eye, we may be moving to a "maximum-security" workplace. When workers at a leading hotel punch in, a device scans their eyes, comparing their retina with computerized data on file. This prevents employees from punching in one another's time cards. A truck driver at Safeway used to enjoy his job. He says, "No one was looking over your shoulder, and you felt like a human being." But now he says he feels "pushed around." A small computer in the dashboard of his truck (called, appropriately, a Tripmaster) keeps track of his speed, shifting, excessive idling, and even reports when and how long he stops for lunch or a coffee break. The driver says he will retire early.

"Maximum-security workplace" seems an apt term for what is coming. And, as many fear, with the computer's awesome capacities, this kind of workplace may be just one part of a "maximum-security society" (Marx, 1995).

> **Focus Question** From the worker's perspective, what are some of the advantages and disadvantages of the various techniques or strategies employed by managements to "humanize" the corporate culture?

The Japanese Corporate Model

How were the Japanese able to arise from the defeat of World War II, including the nuclear destruction of two of their main cities, to become such a giant in today's global economy? Some analysts trace part of the answer to the way their major corporations are organized. Let's look at the conclusions of William Ouchi (1981), who pinpointed five major ways Japanese corporations differ from those in the North America.

Hiring and Promotion

In *Japan*, postsecondary graduates hired by a corporation are thought of as a team working toward the same goal, namely the success of the organization. They are all paid about the same starting salary and are rotated in the organization to learn its various levels. Not only do they work together as a team, but also they are promoted as a team. Team members cooperate with one another, for the welfare of one represents the welfare of all. They also develop intense loyalty to one another and to their company. Only in later years are individuals singled out for recognition. When there is an opening in the firm, outsiders are not even considered.

In *Canada*, an employee is hired on the basis of what the firm thinks that individual can contribute. Employees try to outperform others, regarding salary and position as a sign of success. The individual's loyalty is to himself or herself, not to the company. When there is an opening in the firm, outsiders are considered.

Lean Production

The Japanese production technique is often referred to as *lean production*. Unlike Fordist production, which relies on enormous inventories of parts and massive warehouse space, and requires large workspaces to house parts and repair areas to deal with problems in assembly, lean production employs a **just-in-time (JIT) strategy**. Under this system, parts inventories are reduced to the amount needed at the time, reducing the demand for huge parts warehouses and large work stations. Work is flexible. Workers easily rotate through the various jobs and share job classifications. Overall there are fewer problems with faulty assemblies and poor-quality production (Rinehart, 1996).

Central to the process of lean production is work standardization. The Japanese model incorporates the practice of **kaizen**, which means continuous improvement. Under kaizen, production techniques are constantly evaluated in search of more efficient and improved methods. While workers are involved in discussions around these improvements, ultimately the goal of kaizen and lean production is to reduce the labour force, minimizing inefficiency. Lean production is particularly pertinent in the auto industry, and the success of Toyota has attracted the attention of the North American auto industry. In Canada, the CAMI plant in Ingersoll, Ontario, a joint venture of General Motors and Suzuki, is organized according to lean production techniques. Despite the reputation of lean production strategies for minimizing labour disputes, in 1992 workers at the CAMI plant went on strike after realizing that work rotation and continuous improvement in practice eliminated jobs and intensified their work (Rinehart, 1996).

Lifetime Security

In *Japan*, lifetime security is taken for granted. Once hired, employees can expect to work for the same firm for the rest of their lives. Similarly, the firm expects them to be loyal to the company, to stick with it through good times and bad. On the one hand, employees will not be laid off or fired; on the other hand, they do not go job shopping, for their careers—and many aspects of their lives—are wrapped up in this one firm.

In *North America*, lifetime security is unusual, being limited primarily to some university professors (who receive what is called *tenure*). A company is expected to lay off workers in slow times, and if it reorganizes it is not unusual for whole divisions to be fired. Given this context, workers "look out for number one," and that includes job shopping and job hopping, constantly seeking better pay and opportunities elsewhere.

Patterns of shorter job tenure and the phenomenon of moving from job to job among Canadians are relatively

For a time, North Americans were in awe of the Japanese corporate model. Research (as well as the passage of time that revealed problems with competitiveness), however, has uncovered several serious flaws. Lifetime job security, for example, is a myth. These homeless men are living in the Shinjuko train station in Tokyo. Note how they have followed the Japanese custom of placing their shoes outside before entering their "home."

recent. Past generations of workers (typically males) prided themselves on their long-term employment with the same company and were commonly rewarded with a gold watch for 25 years or more of service. Retirees became members of their workplaces' "Quarter Century Club," an honour bestowed for their loyalty. Today's seniors—among them dads who spent 35 years at General Motors, in the steel plant, or in the local fire department—worry that their sons and grandsons are disloyal as they continually seek out newer and better places of employment.

Almost Total Involvement

In *Japan*, work is like a marriage. The employee and the company are committed to each other. The employee supports the company with loyalty and long hours of dedicated work, while the company, in turn, supports the worker with lifetime security, health services, recreation, sports and social events, even a home mortgage. Involvement with the company does not stop when workers leave the building. They are likely to spend evenings with co-workers in places of entertainment, and perhaps to be part of a company study or exercise group.

In *North America*, the work relationship is assumed to be highly specific. An employee is hired to do a specific job, and employees who have done their jobs have thereby fulfilled their obligation to the company. The rest of their hours are their own. They go home to their private lives, which are highly separated from the firm.

Broad Training

In *Japan*, employees move from one job to another within the corporation. Not only are they not stuck doing the same thing over and over for years on end, but they gain a broader picture of the corporation and how the specific jobs they are assigned fit into the bigger picture.

In *North America*, employees are expected to perform one job, to do it well, and then to be promoted upward to a job with more responsibility. Their understanding of the company is largely tied to the particular corner they occupy, and it may be difficult for them to see how their job fits into the overall picture.

Decision-Making by Consensus

In *Japan*, decision-making is a lengthy process involving every person to be affected by a decision. The Japanese believe that after lengthy deliberations, everyone will agree on which suggestion is superior. This process broadens decision-making, allowing workers to feel that they are an essential part of the organization, not simply cogs in a giant wheel.

In *North America*, whoever has responsibility for the unit in question does as much consulting with others as he or she thinks necessary and then makes the decision.

Limitations of the Model

This model of corporate life in Japan has always struck some sociologists as too idealized to accurately reflect reality. And, indeed, to peer beneath the surface gives a different view of this ideal image, as is illustrated in the Perspectives box here, with which we shall close this chapter.

> ### Focus Question
> What are some of the features of the Japanese corporate model?

Perspectives

Cultural Diversity Around the World: Cracks in the Corporate Facade

- The Japanese are more productive than Canadians.
- The living standard of North Americans has fallen behind that of the Japanese.
- All Japanese workers enjoy lifetime job security.
- The Japanese work for cheaper wages than Canadians.

What is wrong with these statements? Nothing, except that they are untrue.

In recent years, the Japanese economic behemoth seemed unstoppable. Many nations felt threatened by it, and there was even talk that though Japan had lost World War II it was winning a new, undeclared economic war. Impressed with the success of the Japanese, many nations copied parts of their economic model. A closer look, however, reveals that not everything about the Japanese corporate system is as it seems.

One element that would be difficult for Canadians to accept is that at age 60, workers are dismissed. Although early retirement may sound attractive, the problem is that retirement income does not begin until workers reach 65. Facing five years without income, these workers must depend on savings, part-time low-paying jobs, and family and friends to get by until their retirement pay kicks in.

Other cracks in the seamless surface have also become visible. It turns out that only employees of major corporations have lifetime job security, perhaps a third of Japanese workers. And Japan has found that paying the same wages to almost everyone in the same age group is costly and inefficient. Diligent but uninspired executives are compensated more by seniority than by output. Bottom-up decision-making is also too slow to adjust to rapidly changing worldwide markets. Although still small by Western standards, unemployment has grown, while industrial output has fallen. Japanese labour costs have soared, while their much-vaunted productivity actually lags behind that of U.S. industry.

In a surprise move, Japan turned to U.S. corporations to see why they are more efficient. Flying in the face of their traditions, Japanese corporations now lay off workers and use merit pay. Toyota and Honda, for example, give bonuses to managers who meet their goals (a standard policy in the United States and Canada, to be sure, but strange and innovative in Japan). And to meet the challenges of international markets, instead of waiting for "bottom-up" results, some managers now initiate decisions.

Perhaps the biggest surprise was Ford's takeover of Mazda. After huge losses, Mazda creditors decided that Ford knew more about building and marketing cars than Mazda and invited Ford to manage the company. Just a few years earlier, the Japanese auto industry had seemed invincible.

We will have to await the results, but we know that the Japanese were remarkably successful in their initial adapting of the West's manufacturing techniques to their culture. If they make the adjustment of this second phase as successfully, we can predict that a much leaner, meaner Japanese production machine will emerge.

The real bottom line is that we live in a global marketplace—of ideas as well as products. The likely result of global competition will be that the West and Japan will feed off each other—the one learning greater cooperation in the production process, the other greater internal competition.

Sources: Besser (1992); Naj (1993); Schlesinger & Sapsford (1993); Schlesinger, Williams, & Forman (1993); Shill (1993); Reitman & Suris (1994); Shirouzu & Williams (1995); Kanabayashi (1996).

Summary and Review

THE RATIONALIZATION OF SOCIETY

How did the rationalization of society come about?

Weber used the phrase **rationalization of society** to refer to transformation in people's thinking and behaviours—the change from protecting time-honoured ways to a concern with efficiency and practical results. Weber traced the rationalization of society to Protestant theology, which he said brought about capitalism, while Marx attributed the rationalization to capitalism itself. pp. 236–239.

FORMAL ORGANIZATIONS AND BUREAUCRACY

What are formal organizations?

Formal organizations are secondary groups designed to achieve specific objectives. Their dominant form is the **bureaucracy**, which Weber characterized as consisting of a hierarchy, a division of labour, written rules, written communications, and impersonality of positions—characteristics that allow bureaucracies to be efficient and enduring. pp. 239–242.

What dysfunctions are often associated with bureaucracies?

The dysfunctions of bureaucracies include alienation, red tape, lack of communication between units, **goal displacement**, and incompetence (as seen in the **Peter principle**). In Weber's view, the impersonality of bureaucracies tends to produce **alienation** among workers—the feeling that no one cares about them and that they do not really fit in. Marx's view of alienation is somewhat different—workers are separated from the product of their labour because they participate in only a small part of the production process. pp. 242–245.

VOLUNTARY ASSOCIATIONS

What are the functions of voluntary associations?

Voluntary associations are groups made up of volunteers who organize on the basis of common interests. These associations further mutual interests, provide a sense of identity and purpose, help to govern and maintain order, mediate between the government and the individual, give training in organizational skills, help provide access to political power, and pave the way for social change. pp. 245–246.

What is the "iron law of oligarchy"?

Sociologist Robert Michels noted that formal organizations have a tendency to become controlled by a small group that limits leadership to its own inner circle. The dominance of a formal organization by an elite inner circle that keeps itself in power is called the **iron law of oligarchy**. pp. 246–247.

CAREERS IN BUREAUCRACIES

How does the corporate culture affect workers?

The term **corporate culture** refers to an organization's traditions, values, and unwritten norms. Much of corporate culture, such as its hidden values, is not readily visible. Often, a self-fulfilling prophecy is at work: People who match a corporation's hidden values are put on tracks that enhance their chance of success, while those who do not match these values are set on a course that minimizes their performance. pp. 247–248.

MANAGEMENT STRATEGIES AND THE CORPORATE CULTURE

What does humanizing a work setting mean?

Humanizing a work setting means organizing it in a way that develops rather than impedes human potential. Among the characteristics of more humane bureaucracies are expanded opportunities on the basis of ability and contributions rather than personal characteristics, a more even distribution of power, less rigid rules, and more open decision-making. Attempts to modify bureaucracies include quality circles, small work groups, and self-management teams. Employee ownership plans give workers a greater stake in the outcomes of their work organizations. These humanizing techniques are management strategies designed to increase productivity and profit and are not real alternatives. Cooperatives are an alternative to bureaucracies. Conflict theorists see attempts to humanize work as a way of manipulating workers. pp. 248–252.

THE JAPANESE CORPORATE MODEL

How do Japanese and North American corporations differ?

The Japanese corporate model contrasts sharply with the North American model in its hiring and promotion practices, lifetime security, worker involvement outside the work setting, broad training of workers, and collective decision-making. This model, however, has been idealized and does not adequately reflect the reality of Japanese corporate life today. pp. 252–254.

Critical Thinking Questions

1. To what extent has Canadian society become over-rationalized?

2. What are some of the difficulties cooperative organizations might encounter in their interactions with hierarchically structured organizations?

3. Why is it difficult for many Canadians to adjust to the expectations and culture of cooperative or alternative organizational structures?

Key Terms

alienation 243
assimilation 249
bureaucracy 239
capitalism 237
corporate culture 247
formal organizations 239
goal displacement 244
humanizing a work setting 249
iron law of oligarchy 246

just-in-time (JIT) strategy 253
kaizen 253
Peter principle 245
principles of scientific management 248
quality circles 250
rationality 236
rationalization of society 237
traditional orientation 236
voluntary associations 245

Weblinks

All URLs listed are current as of the printing of this book. URLs are often changed. Please check our Web site **www.abacon.com/henslin** for updates.

Formal Organization

www.spc.uchicago.edu/ssr1/PRELIMS/orgs.html
Summaries of classic studies in formal organization from the University of Chicago.

Organizational Learning Resources

choo.fis.utoronto.ca/fis/OrgCog/
A selection of Web-based resources on organizational learning, organizational cognition, information management, knowledge management, environment scanning, and scenario planning.

The Many Virtues of the Virtual Office

www.reengineering.com/articles/apr96/VIRTOFC.htm
An article by Stephen Bouvet on how phone, fax, and e-mail create new workplace alternatives. Includes useful tips for employers and employees considering virtual offices outside the formal office.

Center for the Study of Work Teams

www.workteams.unt.edu/
The Center, based at the University of North Texas, stimulates education and research in all areas of collaborative work systems.

Chapter 11
The Economy: Money and Work

Learning Outcomes

After you have studied this chapter, you will be able to

■ discuss the differences between preindustrial, industrial, and postindustrial societies

■ understand the differences between laissez-faire and welfare capitalism

■ describe the main features of the Canadian economy

■ understand the differences between the symbolic interactionist, feminist, functionalist, and conflict perspectives on work

The alarm pounded in Kim's ears. "Not Monday already," she groaned. "There must be a better way of starting the week." She pressed the snooze button on the clock (from Germany) to sneak another 10 minutes' sleep. In what seemed just 30 seconds, the alarm shrilly insisted she get up and face the week.

Still bleary-eyed after her shower, Kim peered into her closet and picked out a silk blouse (from China), a plaid wool skirt (from Scotland), and leather shoes (from India). She nodded, satisfied, as she added a pair of simulated pearls (from Taiwan). Running late, she hurriedly ran a brush (from Mexico) through her hair. As Kim wolfed down a bowl of cereal (from Canada), topped with milk (from Canada), bananas (from Costa Rica), and sugar (from the Dominican Republic), she turned on her kitchen television (from Korea) to listen to the weather forecast.

Gulping the last of her coffee (from Brazil), Kim grabbed her briefcase (from Wales), purse (from Spain), and jacket (from Malaysia), and quickly climbed into her car (from Japan). As she glanced at her watch (from Switzerland), she hoped the traffic would be in her favour. She muttered to herself as she glimpsed the gas gauge at a street light (from Great Britain). She muttered again when she paid for the gas (from Saudi Arabia), for the price had risen once more. "My cheque never keeps up with prices," she moaned to herself as she finished the drive to work.

The office was abuzz. Six months ago, Vancouver headquarters had put the company up for sale, but there had been no takers. The big news this Monday was that both a Japanese and an American corporation had put in bids over the weekend. No one got much work done that day, as the whole office speculated about how things might change.

The Transformation of Economic Systems

Today, the term *market* means much more than the personal touch you get when local farmers sell you fruits, vegetables, and meats, or when you are shopping at a flea market or buying something at a yard or garage sale. It has kept its original meaning of buying and selling, but it now refers to things much more impersonal. The **market**, the mechanism by which we establish values in order to exchange goods and services, today means the Toronto, Montreal, or Vancouver Stock Exchange, the Dow Jones Industrial Average in New York City, and the Nikkei Index in Tokyo. "Market" also means the movement of vast amounts of goods across international borders, even across oceans and continents. Market means brokers taking orders for IBM, speculators trading international currencies, and futures traders making huge bets on whether oil, wheat, and pork bellies will go up or down.

People's lives have always been affected by the dynamics of the market, or as sociologists prefer to call it, the **economy**. Today, the economy, which many sociologists believe is the most important of our social institutions, differs radically from all but our most recent past. Economic systems have become impersonal and global. The products we buy such as Swatches, Nikes, or Tommy Hilfiger clothes make it apparent that today's economy knows no national boundaries. The economy is essential to our welfare, for it means inflation or deflation, high or low interest rates, high or low unemployment, economic recession or economic boom. The economy affects our chances of buying a new home, of having to work at a dead-end job, or of being on a fast track in an up-and-coming company.

To better understand the Canadian economy and its relative standing in history, let's begin with a review of sweeping historical changes.

Preindustrial Societies: From Equality to Inequality

The earliest human groups, hunting and gathering societies, had a simple **subsistence economy**. Groups of perhaps 25 to 40 people lived off the land, gathering what they could find and moving from place to place as their food supply ran low. With no excess to accumulate, everybody possessed about the same as everyone else.

People discovered how to breed animals and cultivate plants, which then produced a surplus and ushered in social inequality because some people were able to keep more of the surplus for themselves. Due to the more dependable food supply, humans settled down in a single place. Human groups grew larger, and for the first time some people became leather workers, others weapon makers, and so on. This new division of labour produced a variety of items that were available for trade. The primary

Although the term *market* now refers to the mechanisms by which people establish value so they can exchange goods and services, its original meaning referred to a direct exchange of goods, as shown in this photo of a market in Chiapas, Mexico. In peasant societies, where such markets are still a regular part of everyday life, people find the social interaction every bit as rewarding as the goods and money that they exchange.

sociological significance of surplus and trade was that they fostered *social inequality*, for some people now accumulated more possessions than others and passed them on to their children. The effects of that change remain with us today.

The next major change was due to the invention of the plow, which made land much more productive. As *agricultural societies* developed trade expanded, and trading centres came into being. As trading centres turned into cities, power passed from the heads of families and clans to a ruling elite. The result was even greater social, political, and economic inequality.

Industrial Societies: The Birth of the Machine

Industrial societies, which are based on machines powered by fuels, created a surplus unlike anything the world had seen. The early part of the Industrial Revolution magnified social inequalities, as some individuals found themselves able to exploit the labour of many others and to manipulate the political machinery for their own purposes. Later on, bloody battles occurred as workers unionized to improve their working conditions.

As the surplus increased, the emphasis changed from the production of goods to their consumption. Sociologist Thorstein Veblen (1912) used the term **conspicuous consumption** to describe this fundamental change in people's orientations. By this term, Veblen meant that the Protestant ethic identified by Weber—an emphasis on hard work, savings, and a concern for salvation (discussed in Chapter 10)—had been replaced by an eagerness to show off wealth by the "elaborate consumption of goods." The most recent product or device became a significant "marker" for a person's or a family's social status.

Postindustrial Societies: The Birth of the Information Age

In 1973, sociologist Daniel Bell noted that an entirely new type of society was emerging. To refer to it, he coined the term *postindustrial society*. He identified six characteristics of such a society: (1) a service sector so large that it employs the majority of workers; (2) a huge surplus of goods; (3) even more extensive trade among nations; (4) a wider variety and quantity of goods available to the average person; (5) an "information explosion"; and (6) a "global village"—that is, the globe becomes linked by instantaneous communications, transportation, and trade.

Perhaps the "information explosion" and the global village are the key elements of the postindustrial society. Although few people are needed to produce food or basic materials and few people to process them, the information explosion demands that large numbers of people do "knowledge work"—managing information and designing and servicing products. Almost all of us who graduate from university will be doing some form of "knowledge work."

The consequences of this information explosion that is transforming the world are unevenly distributed. Most of us who graduate from university will become as comfortable with the new society as our predecessors became with theirs. But not everyone will find a comfortable niche in this new global village.

You can think of the global village as divided into three large neighbourhoods—the three worlds of development, which we reviewed in Chapter 6. Due to political and economic arrangements, some nations are socially destined to live in the poor part of the village, where citizens barely eke out a living from menial work. Some will even starve to

One of the negative consequences of early industrialization in the West was the use of child labour. In the photo on the left, of the U.S. textile industry in the 1800s, you can see spindle boys at work in a Georgia cotton mill. Today's least industrialized nations are experiencing the same negative consequences as they industrialize. The photo on the right shows boys at work in a contemporary textile factory in Varanas, India. About the only improvement is that the child workers in India are able to sit down as they exhaust their childhood.

death while fellow villagers in another neighbourhood feast on the best that the globe has to offer.

Within each neighbourhood in the village, gross inequalities also show up, for both the wealthy and the poor neighbourhoods have citizens who are well off and those who are poor. In preceding chapters, we examined inequalities—from global stratification to inequalities of social class, gender, race, and age in Canada. There is little to add to that extensive presentation, but an overall snapshot of how the income of Canada is distributed may be useful.

See the inverted pyramid shown in Figure 11.1. The proportion of the nation's income going to the wealthiest fifth of the Canadian population is at the top, the proportion going to the poorest fifth at the bottom. Note that *47 percent* of the whole country's income goes to just one-fifth of Canadians,

while only *3 percent* goes to the poorest fifth. Rather than bringing equality, then, the postindustrial society has perpetuated the income inequalities of the industrial society.

While the percentage of income going to each fifth of the population resembles the skewed distribution in the United States, the inequalities between the richest and poorest Canadians are still less than they are in the United States, largely due to the federal government's transfers to individuals.

Focus Question
What are the differences between preindustrial, industrial, and postindustrial societies?

Figure 11.1 The Inverted Income Pyramid: The Proportion of Income Received by Each Fifth of the Canadian Population

Source: Based on Statistics Canada, 1997: *Income Distributions by Size in Canada*, Catalogue no. 13-207, Table 60.

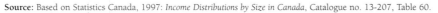
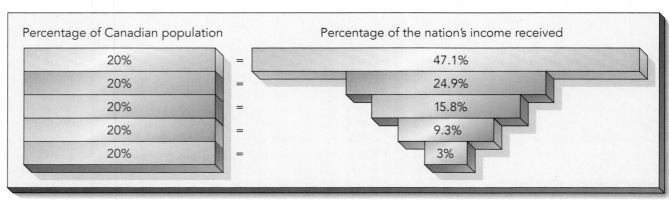

Percentage of Canadian population		Percentage of the nation's income received
20%	=	47.1%
20%	=	24.9%
20%	=	15.8%
20%	=	9.3%
20%	=	3%

The Transformation of the Medium of Exchange

As each type of economy evolved, so too did the **medium of exchange**, the means by which people value and exchange goods and services.

Earliest Mediums of Exchange

As noted, the lack of surplus in hunting and gathering societies meant that there was little to trade. Whatever trading did occur was by **barter**, the direct exchange of one item for another.

Medium of Exchange in Agricultural Societies

Although bartering continued in agricultural societies, people increasingly came to use **money**, a medium of exchange by which items are valued. In most places, money consisted of gold and silver coins, their weight and purity determining the amount of goods or services that could be purchased. In some places people made purchases with **deposit receipts**, receipts that transferred ownership of a specified number of ounces of gold, bushels of wheat, or amount of other goods that were on deposit in a warehouse or bank. Toward the end of the agricultural period, deposit receipts became formalized into **currency** (paper money), each piece of paper representing a specific amount of gold or silver on deposit in a central warehouse. Thus currency (and deposit receipts) represented **stored value**, and no more currency could be issued than the amount of gold or silver that the currency represented. Gold and silver coins continued to circulate alongside the deposit receipts and currency.

Medium of Exchange in Industrial Societies

With but few exceptions, bartering became a thing of the past in industrial societies. Gold was replaced by paper currencies, which, in the United States, could be exchanged for a set amount of gold stored at Fort Knox. This policy was called the **gold standard**, and as long as each dollar represented a specified amount of gold the number of dollars that could be issued was limited. By the late 1960s, U.S. paper money could no longer be exchanged for gold or silver, resulting in **fiat money**, currency issued by a government that is not backed by stored value.

One consequence of the move away from stored value was that coins made of precious metals disappeared from circulation. In comparison with fiat money, these coins were more valuable, and people became unwilling to part with them. Gold coins disappeared first, followed by the largest silver coin, the dollar. Then, as inferior metals (copper, zinc, and nickel) replaced the smaller silver coins, people began to hoard them, too, and silver coins also disappeared from circulation.

Even without a gold standard that restrains the issuing of currency to stored value, governments have a practical limit on the amount of paper money they can issue. In general, prices increase if a government issues currency at a rate higher than the growth of its **gross national product (GNP)**, the total goods and services a nation produces. This condition, **inflation**, means that each unit of currency will purchase fewer goods and services. Governments try to control inflation, for it is a destabilizing influence.

In industrial societies, chequing accounts held in banks became common. A cheque is actually a type of deposit receipt, for it is a promise that the writer of the cheque has enough currency on deposit to cover the cheque. Then came the **credit card**, a device that allows its owner, who has been approved for a set amount of credit, to purchase goods without an immediate exchange of money—either metal or currency. The credit card owner is later billed for the purchases and is charged interest.

Medium of Exchange in Postindustrial Societies

During the first part of the postindustrial society, paper money becomes less common as it is gradually replaced by credit cards and the **debit card**, a device by which a purchase is charged against the purchaser's bank account. The debit card, too, is a type of deposit receipt, for it is a guarantee that its user has enough currency on deposit to cover the purchase.

Increasingly, spending in the postindustrial society means not an exchange of physical money—whether paper or coins—but rather the electronic transfer of numbers residing in computer memory banks. In effect, the new medium of exchange is itself a part of the information explosion.

World Economic Systems

Now that we have outlined the main economic changes in history, let's compare capitalism and socialism.

Capitalism

If we distill the businesses of Canada to their basic components, we see that **capitalism** has three essential features: (1) **private ownership of the means of production** (individuals own the land, machines, and factories, and decide what shall be produced); (2) the pursuit of profit (selling something for more than it costs); and (3) **market competition** (an exchange of items between willing buyers and sellers).

Welfare (or State) Capitalism Versus Laissez-Faire Capitalism. Pure capitalism, known as **laissez-faire capitalism** (loosely, "leave alone"), means that **market forces** operate without interference from the government. Such is not the case in Canada or the United States, where many restraints to the laissez-faire model are in force. The current

Figure 11.2 The Five Largest Federal and Provincial Crown Corporations, 2002

Source: The Globe and Mail, July 2002, *Report on Business Magazine.*

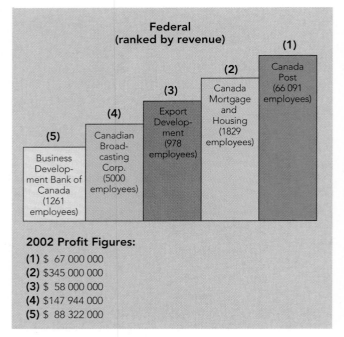

Federal
(ranked by revenue)

(5) Business Development Bank of Canada (1261 employees)

(4) Canadian Broadcasting Corp. (5000 employees)

(3) Export Development (978 employees)

(2) Canada Mortgage and Housing (1829 employees)

(1) Canada Post (66 091 employees)

2002 Profit Figures:
(1) $ 67 000 000
(2) $345 000 000
(3) $ 58 000 000
(4) $147 944 000
(5) $ 88 322 000

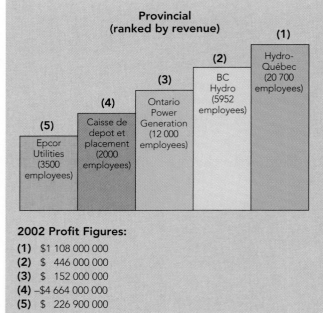

Provincial
(ranked by revenue)

(5) Epcor Utilities (3500 employees)

(4) Caisse de depot et placement (2000 employees)

(3) Ontario Power Generation (12 000 employees)

(2) BC Hydro (5952 employees)

(1) Hydro-Québec (20 700 employees)

2002 Profit Figures:
(1) $1 108 000 000
(2) $ 446 000 000
(3) $ 152 000 000
(4) –$4 664 000 000
(5) $ 226 900 000

form of Canadian capitalism is **welfare or state capitalism**, in which private citizens acting as individuals or in groups such as credit unions, cooperatives, or the *caisses populaires* ("people's banks") in Quebec and Ontario, together with the provincial and federal governments, own the means of production and pursue profits in a system of laws designed to protect the welfare of the population.

For example, there are a number of Crown corporations—companies owned by the provincial or federal government but managed at "arm's length" from the government (see Figure 11.2). The largest federal Crown corporation is Canada Post, which reported a profit of $67 million in 2002 and employed over 66 000 employees.

Before the provincial government passed legislation that broke it up into separate entities, the largest provincial Crown corporation was Ontario Hydro, with 1998 profits of almost $2 billion and 26 000 persons on the payroll. The largest is now Hydro-Québec, with a 2002 profit of more than $1.1 billion and a work force numbering 20 000.

Suppose that you have discovered what you think is a miracle tonic: It will grow hair, erase wrinkles, and dissolve excess fat. If your product works, you will become an overnight sensation—not only a millionaire, but also the toast of television talk shows.

Before you count your money—and your fame—you must reckon with **market restraints**, the laws and regulations of welfare capitalism that limit your capacity to sell

what you produce. First, you must comply with municipal, provincial, and federal rules. You must register your company's name with the provincial registry—or, better yet, obtain a charter of incorporation from the province, a business licence from the municipality if you are operating a store in the town or city where you live, and a GST number from the federal government that allows you to buy untaxed purchases.

Second, you cannot simply take your item to local stores and ask them to sell it; you must first seek approval from federal agencies that monitor compliance with the *Food and Drug Act* (FDA). In addition, the *Hazardous Products Act* forbids the advertising, sale, or import of unsafe products that went into either your "miracle" cure or the product itself. This means you must prove that your product will not cause harm to the public. Moreover, you must be able to substantiate your claims—or face being shut down by provincial and federal agencies that monitor the market for fraud.

Suppose you succeed in overcoming these obstacles, your business starts to prosper, and you begin hiring. Other provincial and federal agencies will monitor your compliance with regulations concerning employment. For example, if your employees are not unionized you must comply with the provincial *Employment Standards Act*. On the other hand, if they become unionized, relations with your employees falls under the *Labour Relations Act* of your

Canada's state capitalism at work: Pictured here is one of the newer "convenience store" postal outlets of Canada Post. Canada Post is the largest Canadian federal Crown corporation; in 2002 it reported a profit of $67 million and had a staff of 66 091 employees.

province. The provincial and federal human rights statutes cover discrimination in the workplace on the basis of sex, race, or ethnicity and, at the federal level and in almost every province, sexual orientation. Income tax, employment insurance, and CPP contributions are handled by the federal government, and on occasion the Supreme Court of Canada has adjudicated issues dealing with unionized workplaces (see Glenday, 1997).

In Sum

As currently practised, capitalism is far from the classical laissez-faire model. Canada's economic system encourages the first two components of capitalism, the private ownership of the means of production and the pursuit of profit. But a vast system of government regulations both protects and restricts the third component, market competition.

As illustrated by this scene in Havana, Cuba, poverty is not limited to any particular economic system. The cause of the poverty shown here, however, is as complex as the relationship between economic systems, for economic sanctions by the United States directed against Fidel Castro certainly have not helped Cubans thrive.

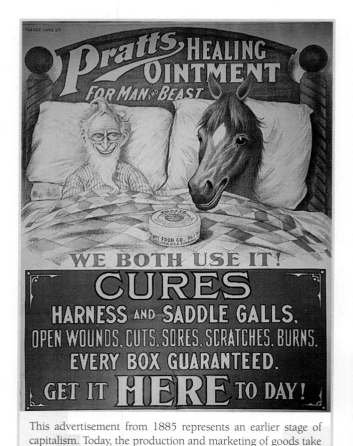

This advertisement from 1885 represents an earlier stage of capitalism. Today, the production and marketing of goods take place under detailed, complicated government regulations.

Socialism

Socialism also has three essential components: (1) the public ownership of the means of production; (2) central planning; and (3) distribution of goods without a profit motive.

In socialist economies, the government owns the means of production—not only the factories, but also the land, railroads, oil wells, and gold mines. In a socialist economy, *everyone* in the economic chain works for the government. By narrowing the huge pay gaps that characterize capitalist nations, however, socialist nations were able to establish considerably greater equality of income.

Democratic Socialism. Dissatisfied with the greed and exploitation of capitalism and the lack of freedom and individuality of socialism, some Western nations (most notably Sweden and Denmark) developed **democratic socialism**, or welfare socialism. In this form of socialism, both the state and individuals engage in production and distribution.

Criticisms of Capitalism and Socialism

The primary criticism levelled against capitalism is that it leads to social inequality. Capitalism, say its critics, pro-

duces a tiny top layer consisting of wealthy, powerful people, who exploit a vast bottom layer of poorly paid workers, many of whom are unemployed and underemployed (**underemployment** is having to work at a job beneath one's training and abilities or being able to find only part-time work). Another major criticism is that the tiny top layer wields vast political power. To further their own wealth, the few who own the means of production and reap huge profits are able to get legislation passed that goes against the public good.

The primary criticism levelled against socialism is that it does not respect individual rights (Berger, 1991). In the case of China, the government even controls how many children families may have (Mosher, 1983). Critics also argue that central planning is grossly inefficient (Kennedy, 1993) and that socialism is not capable of producing much wealth.

Changes in Capitalism and Socialism

Changes in Capitalism. Over the years, Canada adopted several public policy practices such as universal

Throughout most of the twentieth century, capitalism and communism were pitted against one another in a deadly struggle. Each thought of itself as the correct economic form, and the other as an evil obstacle to be eradicated. In support of this view of essential goodness and evil, proponents of each system launched global propaganda campaigns. Shown here is a painting of Vladimir Lenin, leader of the worldwide workers' revolution. This 1930 painting by Alexander Gerassimow (1881–1963) hangs in the Tretyakov Gallery in Moscow.

Advertising is such an integral part of contemporary life that it almost appears to be our natural state to be deluged with ads. We open a newspaper or magazine and expect to find that a good portion of its pages proclaim the virtues of products and firms. We turn on the television and on most stations are assailed with commercials for about 10 minutes of every half-hour. Some social analysts even claim that the purpose of television is to round up an audience to watch the commercials—making the programs a mere diversion from the medium's real objective of selling products!

A fascinating potential of advertising is its ability to increase our desire to consume products for which we previously felt no need whatsoever. Our kitchens, filled with gadgets that slice and dice and machines that turn anything into a sandwich, attest to this power.

But advertising's power to make people gluttons for consumption goes beyond kitchen gadgets soon consigned to back drawers and later to garage sales. Many North Americans today would not think of going out in public without first shampooing, rinsing, conditioning, and blow-drying their hair. Many also feel the need to apply an underarm deodorant so powerful that it overcomes the body's natural need to sweat. For many women, public appearance also demands the application of foundation, lipstick, eye shadow, mascara, rouge, powder, and perfume. For many men, aftershave lotion is essential. And only after covering the body with clothing bearing suitable designer labels do North Americans feel that they are presentable to the public.

Advertising also penetrates our consciousness to such an extent that it determines not only what we put on our bodies, what we eat, and what we do for recreation, but to a large degree also how we feel about ourselves. Our ideas of whether we are too fat, too skinny, too hippy, too buxom, whether our hair is too oily or too dry, our body too hairy, or our skin too rough are largely a consequence of advertising. As we weigh our self-image against the idealized pictures that constantly bombard us in our daily fare of commercials, we conclude that we are lacking something. Advertising, of course, assures us that there is salvation—some new product that promises to deliver exactly what we lack.

The creation of constant discontent —dissatisfaction with ourselves compared to ideal images that are impossible to match in real life—is, of course, intentional. As designed, it leaves most of us vulnerable to consuming more of the never-ending variety of products that the corporations have for sale—and decided that we need.

health care and accessible and free public education in which the federal and provincial governments redistribute tax dollars to pay for benefits given to all Canadians, no matter where they may live in the country. Besides health care and education, there is Employment Insurance (formerly Unemployment Insurance, established in 1940), welfare, the Canada Pension Plan (1966), and Old Age Security (1952).

Changes in Socialism. For its part, in 1989 the Soviet Union, which headed an eastern European bloc of nations (East Germany, Czechoslovakia, and Hungary, among others), concluded that its system of central planning had failed. Suffering from shoddy goods and plagued by shortages, the former Soviet Union began to reinstate market forces.

Although most people under communist rule lived in poverty, they were assured jobs that provided very basic food and shelter. Today, with the transition to capitalism, citizens of the former Soviet Union no longer have that assurance. Shown here is a scene in Sverdlosk, Russia, where people are learning capitalism, that is, to buy and sell for profit.

The second major socialist power, China, watched in dismay as its one-time mentor abandoned the basic principles of socialism (Szelenyi, 1987). In 1989, at the cost of many lives and despite world opposition, Chinese authorities, in what is called the Tiananmen Square massacre, stood firm, putting down a hunger strike by students and workers who were demanding greater freedom and economic reforms. Despite this repressive measure, however, China, too, began to endorse capitalism. Its leaders also solicited Western investments and encouraged farmers to cultivate their own plots on the communal farms. They allowed the use of credit cards, approved a stock market, and even permitted bits of that symbol of China itself, the Great Wall, to be sold as souvenirs—for profit (McGregor, 1992). While still officially proclaiming Marxist-Leninist-Maoist principles, the Communist party, under the slogan "One China, two systems," is trying to make Shanghai the financial centre of East Asia (McGregor, 1993; Schlesinger, 1994). One consequence—besides the new and brash advertisements for Avon and Head and Shoulders—is a rapidly rising standard of living.

Convergence Theory. The socialist nations, then, have embraced profit while the capitalist nations have adopted socialistic programs designed to redistribute wealth. Will the two systems continue to adopt features of the other until they converge, creating a sort of hybrid economic system? This, at least, is the bare-bones outline of the prediction made by **convergence theory** (Form, 1979; Kerr, 1960, 1983).

The evidence for this theory seems impressive. Since the pursuit of profits will produce greater wealth and an inevitably higher standard of living, it will be almost impossible for socialist leaders to erase profits from their economic system. Similarly, the citizens of capitalist nations have become so used to socialistic features built into their system that they cannot imagine a government that does not protect the unemployed, guarantee a minimum wage, and so on. Leaders and citizens of both systems may quarrel about the details, but they have embraced the opposing principles.

The matter, however, is not this simple. The systems remain far from "converged," and the struggle between them continues. Russian and Polish citizens, for example, longing for greater stability, have voted communists back into top government positions. At the same time, the federal Alliance Party and to a greater or lesser extent the federal and provincial Progressive Conservatives, Liberals, and even NDP (witness Bob Rae's Ontario NDP) have all tried to roll back public policies introduced as part of welfare capitalism in Canada.

Focus Question
What makes Canada a welfare capitalist society?

In Sum

At this historical point, we must note that there is no pure capitalism (and likely never was). Today, then, capitalism speaks in a variety of accents, some softer than others, with the versions in China, the former Soviet Union, Great Britain, Japan, Germany, Sweden, Canada, and the United States each differing from the others.

Capitalism in a Global Economy

Today, large multinational corporations dominate the national and international economic systems. Because of increasing exposure to the globalization of capitalism, the Canadian economy and economies around the world are being profoundly reorganized.

Corporate Capitalism

A **corporation** is a business that is treated in law as a person. Its liabilities and obligations are separate from those of its owners. For example, each shareholder of Bell Canada—whether the owner of 1 or 100 000 shares—owns a portion of the company. Bell Canada is a legal entity, and can buy and sell, sue and be sued, make contracts, and incur debts. It is the corporation, however—not its individual owners—that is responsible for the firm's liabilities, such as paying debts and fulfilling contracts.

One of the most significant aspects of corporations is the *separation of ownership and management*. Unlike most businesses, it is not the owners, those who own the company's stock, who run the day-to-day affairs of the company (A. Walters, 1995). Rather, a corporation is run by managers who are able to treat it *as though it were their own* (Cohen, 1990). The result is the "ownership of wealth without appreciable control, and control of wealth without appreciable ownership" (Berle & Means, 1932).

At the annual stockholders' meeting, the owners consider broad company matters including the selection of a board of directors and a firm to audit the company's books. As long as management reports a handsome profit, the stockholders rubber-stamp its recommendations.

The world's largest corporations wield immense power. Forming **oligopolies**—several large companies that dominate a single industry, such as gasoline, breakfast cereal, or light bulbs—they dictate pricing, set the quality of their products, and protect their markets. Oligopolies also use their political connections to support legislation that gives them special tax breaks or protects their industry from imports. Corporations have so changed capitalism that the term **corporate capitalism** is used to indicate that giant corporations dominate the economic system. Of the hundreds of thousands of businesses and tens of thousands of corporations in the United States, a mere 500 dominate the economy. These firms, called the Fortune 500 (after *Fortune* magazine's annual profile of the 500 largest companies), make annual profits that represent 10 percent of that country's entire gross national product (*Statistical Abstract,* 1997, Tables 698, 874).

Interlocking Directorates

One way the wealthy use corporations to wield power is by means of **interlocking directorates** (Mizruchi & Koenig, 1991). The elite serve as directors of several companies. Their fellow members on those boards also sit on the boards of other companies, and so on. Like a spider's web that starts at the centre and then fans out in all directions, eventually the top companies in the country are interlocked into a network (Mintz & Schwartz, 1985). The chief executive officer of a firm in Great Britain, who also sits on the board of directors of half-a-dozen other companies, noted:

> If you serve on, say, six outside boards, each of which has, say, ten directors ...who you meet automatically each month, you're joining a club, a very good club (Useem, 1984).

As we saw in Chapter 8, John Porter in *The Vertical Mosaic* (1965) was the first Canadian sociologist to identify the highly concentrated nature of Canada's corporate elite. Just 10 years later, and following in his mentor's footsteps, Wallace Clement in *The Canadian Corporate Elite* (1975) and *Continental Corporate Power: Economic Elite Linkages Between Canada and the United States* (1977) showed that corporate power in Canada had concentrated even further. Jorge Niosi in his *Canadian Capitalism: A Study of Power in the Canadian Business Establishment* (1981) went so far as to conclude that Canada's economy was dominated by just 13 families!

More recently, R. Jack Richardson (1993) compared corporate concentration in several developed economies and concluded that the level of corporate concentration in Canada was over twice that found in Germany, Japan, and the United States. Since Porter's and Clement's studies, the concentration has proceeded unabated. While the 17 largest companies in 1978 controlled 64 percent of the assets of corporate Canada, this figure had climbed to 75 percent just nine years later in 1987. Richardson notes that 10 of the 30 largest corporations in 1978 had been taken over by just four corporate giants, the largest of which, EdperBrascan, then controlled no fewer than 421 companies. Table 11.1 offers a glimpse into the corporate connections of the 10 most powerful capitalists (all men) in Canada.

The resulting concentration of power minimizes competition, for a director is not going to approve a plan that will be harmful to another company in which he or she (mostly he) has a stake. The top executives of the largest Canadian enterprises (Porter, 1965; Clement, 1975, Niosi, 1981) also meet in recreational settings, where they renew their sense of solidarity, purpose, and destiny.

Table 11.2 shows the 10 highest annual compensation packages for the top-paid men in corporate Canada. While profits were down, the compensation paid to the top 10 executives was also down, believe it or not! These exorbitant amounts are seen as justified in a capitalist economy. However, they say more about the ostentatious appetites of Canada's ruling oligarchy.

Multinational Corporations

Outgrowing national boundaries, the larger corporations have become more and more detached from the interests and values of their country or origin. They move investments and production from one part of the globe to another—with no concern for consequences other than profits. As the Cold War trading barriers broke down and the global economy became more integrated, these corporations took on an increasingly significant role in global life (Kennedy, 1993).

The domination of world trade shows an interesting pattern. After World War II, with Germany destroyed and France in shambles, the United States eclipsed Great Britain and became the major player in international business. Figure 11.3 shows the extent of the global reach of U.S.

Table 11.1 Corporate Power in Canada: The Top 10

Rank	Name	Corporate Directorships and Advisory Boards
1	Paul Desmarais, Jr.	Too many, including financial, resource, and media companies in Canada, the United States, France, etc.
2	Guy Saint-Pierre	Royal Bank, Bell Canada, BCE Inc., Alcan Aluminum, General Motors of Canada
3	Paul Tellier	Alcan Aluminum, Bell Canada, Bombardier, McCain Foods
4	Conrad Black	CIBC, EdperBrascan Corp., Sotheby Holdings Inc., *Advisory:* Council on Foreign Relations
5	John A. Tory	Hudson's Bay, Rogers Communications, Royal Bank, Thomson Corp., Abitibi Consolidated
6	Jean Monty	Bombardier, CGI Group Inc., Nortel Networks, Teleglobe Inc.
7	J. Edward Newall	Royal Bank, BCE Inc., Alcan Aluminum, Canadian Pacific Ltd.
8	William G. Davis	CIBC, Algoma Steel, Dylex Ltd., Magna International, Power Corp. of Canada, Seagrams
9	J. Trevor Eyton	Barrick Gold Corp., Imax Corp., MediSolution, Noranda Inc., Trilon Financial
10	André Desmarais	Canadian Pacific, Seagrams, Bombardier, *Advisory:* China Business Council, Business Council of National Issues

Source: *The Globe and Mail,* July 1999, *Report on Business Magazine,* p. 120.

Table 11.2 Top 10 Paid Executives in Canada

Rank	Executive and Company	Base Salary	Annual Bonus	Long-Term Incentive	TOTAL
1	Frank Stronach, Chairman, Magna	$310 000	$2 323 000	$55 546 000	$58 178 000
2	Travis Engen, President & CEO Alcan	$1 858 000	$1 858 000	$14 778 000	$18 494 000
3	Jean Monty, Chairman & CEO, BCE	$1 300 000	$1 500 000	$15 589 000	$18 389 000
4	Frank Dunn, President, CEO, Nortel	$1 277 000	$0	$16 889 000	$18 166 000
5	Donald Walker, President & CEO, Magna	$408 000	$7 228 000	$10 383 000	$18 020 000
6	Gerald Schwartz, Chairman & CEO, Onex	$975 000	$16 271 000	$0	$17 245 000
7	William Fatt, Director & CEO, Fairmont Hotels & Resorts	$557 000	$775 000	$14 971 000	$16 304 000
8	Christopher Mackenzie, President & CEO, TrizecHahn Corp.	$3 019 000	$2 594 000	$10 301 000	$15 974 000
9	Irving Weiser, Chair & CEO, RBCdain Rauscher, Royal Bank	$374 000	$4 645 000	$10 236 000	$15 255 000
10	Don Wright, Vice-Chairman, TD Bank Financial Group	$413 000	$8 600 000	$5 702 000	$14 716 000

Source: *The Globe and Mail*, July 2002, *Report on Business Magazine*.

Figure 11.3 The Globalization of Capitalism: U.S. Ownership in Other Countries

Source: *Statistical Abstract*, 1999, Table 1317.

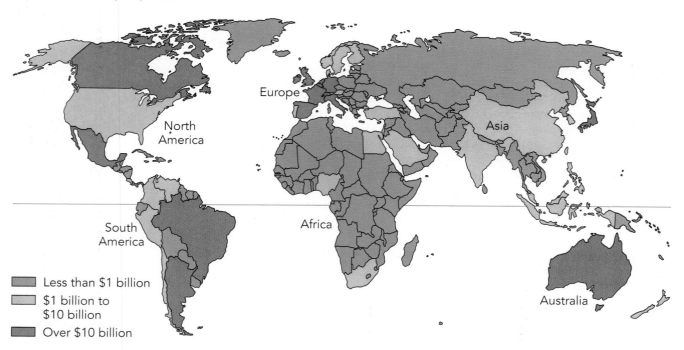

Less than $1 billion

$1 billion to $10 billion

Over $10 billion

capitalism today. Canada, Mexico, Australia, Great Britain, western Europe, and most of South America are where U.S. corporations are concentrated. Recently, the Japanese, also using the multinational corporate model, gained huge markets across the globe.

By comparison, Table 11.3 depicts the top 20 corporations in Canada. The top three positions are taken by Canada's banks. With the exception of Bell Canada, the top six positions are banks. Natural resources—but in particular petroleum—corporations, insurance and financial service corporations also dominate the corporate landscape.

Unlike the U.S. economy, the major players in Canada are largely restricted to the primary and tertiary sectors of the economy. Canada's economy and the Canadian owned and controlled corporate structure are unique to Western economies.

Focus Question

In 2001, how many of Canada's banks were in the top 10 corporations (by profits) in Canada?

Table 11.3 The Top 20 Corporations in Canada, 2001

Profits Rank 2001	Company	Group Affiliation
1	Royal Bank of Canada	Financial Services
2	Bank of Nova Scotia	Financial Services
3	Canadian Imperial Bank of Commerce	Financial Services
4	Bell Canada	Telecommunications
5	Bank of Montreal	Financial Services
6	Toronto Dominion Bank	Financial Services
7	EnCana Corp.	Diversified
8	Imperial Oil	Petroleum
9	Thomson Corp.	Media
10	Manulife Financial	Financial Services
11	Shell Canada	Petroleum
12	PetroCanada	Petroleum
13	Magna International	Auto
14	Sun Life Financial	Financial Services
15	Power Financial	Financial Services
16	Onex Corp.	Diversified
17	Talisman Energy	Natural Resources
18	Canadian National Railway	Transportation
19	Canadian Natural Resources	Natural Resources
20	Husky Energy	Petroleum

Source: *The Globe and Mail*, July 2002, *Report on Business Magazine.*

The sociological significance of global capitalism is that the multinational corporations owe allegiance only to profits and market share, not to any nation, nor even to any particular culture. As a U.S. executive said, "The United States does not have an automatic call on our resources. There is no mindset that puts the country first" (Kennedy, 1993). This fundamental shift in orientation is so new that its implications are unknown at present. Certainly the millions of workers whose jobs have been pulled out from under them know the negative consequences. On the positive side, these corporations' global interconnections may be a force for peace, for they are removed from tribal loyalties and national boundaries. The downside, however, may be a "new world order" dominated by a handful of corporate leaders reminiscent of George Orwell's *1984* or the dark and intriguing film *Bladerunner.*

Applying Sociological Theories

We shall now apply the theoretical perspectives of sociology to our economic life.

The Symbolic Interactionist Perspective

As we apply the symbolic interactionist perspective, let's consider what distinguishes a job from a profession.

Profession or Job? Work as a Status Symbol. We know that selling hamburgers from a drive-in window is not a profession, but why isn't selling shoes? Sociologists who adopt a symbolic interactionist perspective on work identify five characteristics of **professions** (Parsons, 1954; W. J. Goode, 1960; Greenwood, 1962; Etzioni, 1969).

1. *Rigorous education.* Today the professions require not only a university degree but also completion of graduate school. Ordinarily, those years are followed by an examination that determines whether you will be allowed into the profession.

2. *Theory.* The education is theoretical, not just "hands-on." In other words, concepts or objects that cannot be seen are used to explain what can be seen. For example, in medicine, microbes, viruses, and genetics are used to explain disease, while in sociology, social structure and social interaction are used to explain human behaviour.

3. *Self-regulation.* Members of the profession claim that only they possess sufficient knowledge to determine the profession's standards and to certify those qualified to be admitted. As sociologist Ernest Greenwood (1962) put it, "a person who assumes the title of physician or attorney without having earned it conventionally becomes an imposter." The group's members also determine who shall be decertified because of incompetence or moral problems.

4. *Authority over clients.* Members of a profession claim authority over clients on the basis of their specialized

In its march toward globalization, capitalism is undergoing major changes. Such fundamental change is exemplified by companies that locate their corporate headquarters in one country, manufacture basic components in a different country, assemble them in still another, and sell them throughout the world. In this photo, Nike soccer balls are being assembled in Pakistan—illustrating an old standby of economic systems—the use of child labour.

education and theoretical understanding. Unlike carpentry, in which any of us can see that the nail is bent, members of the profession claim that the matter is complex and therefore entreat the client to follow the professional's instructions.

5. *Professional culture.* The public good, or service to society, not self-interest, lies at the heart of a professional culture. Although some car salespeople may make preposterous claims about serving the public good, we all know that they sell cars to make money. In contrast, the professions claim that they exist "to provide service to whomever requests it, irrespective of the requesting client's age, income, kinship, politics, race, religion, sex, [sexual orientation,] and social status" (Greenwood, 1962; Hall, 1994).

Today, we expect the basic motivation of a physician to be not unlike an automobile mechanic—that is, to make money. However, the educational credentials, membership in professional associations, and the professional culture of a physician distinguish her or his work from that of an automobile mechanic.

As we see from Table 11.4, there has been a significant gain in employment among the better educated, and a net loss of jobs among the less educated, in Canada in the past decade. This trend is indicative of the increase in status of many new jobs created as the result of the information explosion, something we have discussed already and which will continue to be a point of interest later in this chapter and in subsequent chapters.

The Functionalist Perspective

Work is functional for society. It is only because people work that we have electricity, hospitals, schools, automobiles, and homes. Beyond this obvious point, however, lies a basic sociological principle: *Work binds us together.* Let us review Durkheim's principles of mechanical and organic solidarity introduced in Chapter 5.

Table 11.4 The Education—Job Market Connection

Level of Education	Change in Number of People Employed, 1990–2001 (25–65 years old)
Grade 8 or less	−285 000
Some high school	−560 000
High school graduate	−198 000
Some postsecondary	−32 800
Postsecondary certificate	+834 000
University degree (bachelor's)	+1 110 300
Above bachelor's degree	+172 600
Total	**+1 040 200 jobs**

Source: Statistics Canada, March 2002, *Labour Force Historical Review 2001* (revised edition). Catalogue no. 71F0004XCB.

Mechanical Solidarity. In preindustrial societies, people do similar work and directly share most aspects of life. Because of this, they look at the world in similar ways. Durkheim used the term **mechanical solidarity** to refer to this sense of unity that comes from doing similar activities.

Organic Solidarity. As societies industrialize, however, a division of labour develops, and people work at different occupations. Consequently, they feel less solidarity with one another. Wheat farmers in Saskatchewan, for example, may feel little in common with manufacturers of aircraft in Ontario. Yet, like an organism, each is part of the same economic system, and the welfare of each depends on the others. Durkheim called this economic interdependence **organic solidarity**.

The Global Division of Work. Organic solidarity has expanded far beyond anything Durkheim envisioned. Today it engulfs the world, and as for Kim in our opening vignette, our daily life now depends on workers around the globe. People who live in Vancouver or Calgary—or even St. John's, Newfoundland—depend on workers in Tokyo to produce cars. Tokyo workers, in turn, depend on Saudi Arabian workers for oil, South American workers to operate ships, and South African workers for palladium for their catalytic converters. Although we do not feel unity with one another—in fact, we sometimes feel threatened and hostile—interdependence links us all in the same economic web.

Driving this global interdependence is the dominance of capitalism. As capitalism globalizes, the world's nations are being divided into three primary trading blocs: North and South America dominated by the United States, Europe dominated by Germany, and Asia dominated by Japan. The multinational corporate giants, benefiting from this new world structure, are promoting free trade. If free trade is put into practice worldwide, its functions will include greater competition over scarce resources on a global scale. Another dysfunctional consequence—already felt by millions of U.S., U.K., French, and German workers—is the vast loss of production jobs in the most industrialized nations. Another consequence may be a decrease in nationalistic ties as identity expands from the nation to a global region. This change—considered by some a function, by others a dysfunction—may be part of the New World Order discussed in Chapter 12.

The Conflict Perspective

Central to conflict theory is an emphasis on how the wealthy benefit at the expense of workers. Conflict theorists' analysis includes the impact of technology and the economic and political power of capitalism's inner circle.

Technology: Who Benefits? Conflict theorists point out that the jobs the new technologies destroy are not located at the top levels of the multinationals, nor are they held by the wealthy individuals who own large blocs of stock. For the most part, these people are immune from such disruptions. For them, by lowering production costs, the new technology increases profits and fattens their dividend cheques. The people who bear the brunt of the change are low-level workers who live from paycheque to paycheque. It is they who suffer the ravages of uncertainty, the devastation of job loss, and, often, the wrenching adjustments that come with being forced into jobs that pay lower wages.

The Inner Circle of Power. The multinational corporations are headed by a group that Michael Useem (1984) calls the *inner circle*. Members of this inner circle, though in competition with one another, are united by an interest in preserving capitalism (Mizruchi & Koenig, 1991). Within their own country, they consult with high-level politicians, promote legislation favourable to big business, and serve as trustees for foundations and universities. They also promote political candidates who stand firmly for the private ownership of property. On a global level, they fiercely promote the ideology of capitalism and move capital from one nation—or region—to another in their relentless search for greater and more immediate profits.

As stressed in previous chapters, conflict theorists focus on power. Although multinational corporations enshroud much of their activities in secrecy, on occasion their subterranean abuse of power comes to light. As Lord Acton said, "Power tends to corrupt, and absolute power corrupts absolutely." The more power a corporation has, then, the greater the temptation to misuse that power. One of the most notable examples occurred in 1973 when a U.S. multinational, the International Telephone & Telegraph Company (ITT), joined the CIA in a plot to unseat Chile's elected government. They first attempted to bring about the economic collapse of Chile. When this failed, they plotted a coup d'état, which resulted in the assassination of the Chilean president, Salvador Allende (Coleman, 1995).

The Feminist Perspectives

As we saw in Chapter 1, there are different feminist theories that tackle the various issues facing women in the world today. In some respects, these differences correspond to the distinctive stages or "waves" of feminism. The "first-wave" feminists were primarily concerned with the political right of voting and were known as "suffragists." In Canada and the United States, women were granted the right to vote after World War I. In France, it wasn't until after World War II that Charles de Gaulle enfranchised women for their courage and determination in the underground fight against the Nazis and the collaborationist Vichy government. In some Muslim countries today, women still cannot vote, leave the house without their husband's permission, drive cars, or appear in public unveiled.

Rights concerned with property ownership, earning a living, and achieving higher education, many of which were granted at the end of the nineteenth century, contributed to increasing women's economic independence in twentieth-century Canada and the United States.

Second-wave feminism is believed to have begun with the publication in France in 1949 of Simone de Beauvoir's *The Second Sex*. She argued that men were the first sex because they dominated the economic realm and set the standards and values women were to follow. Men led and women followed. De Beauvoir insisted that this inequality was not due to biological differences but was a *social creation*. It wasn't until the 1960s, however, that second-wave feminism took hold and the struggle for equality in the workplace gained momentum. Equal pay for equal work and employment equity (in Canada) or Affirmative Action (in the United States), became the rallying cry of women for several decades. While many women have made advances in the world of work and entrepreneurship, job (pink) ghettoes and glass ceilings remain in force. **Job ghettoes** (also called **pink ghettoes**) are those employment areas where women dominate such as nursing, elementary school teachers, child care workers, and so on. **Glass ceiling** refers to the barriers to social advancement that many women face in some organizations.

Third-wave feminism concentrates on sex, sexuality, and gender and offers very little to our understanding of inequality in the workplace. Today, the feminist view of what makes women and men unequal is less unified than it was with first-wave feminism, in large part because of a new focus on the complexity of gender inequality.

> **Focus Question**
> What are the differences between the functionalist, feminist, and conflict perspectives on work?

Work in Canadian Society

Let's now turn our focus onto work in Canadian society. To understand the present situation, we must first review the large-scale changes in what are called *economic sectors*.

Three Economic Sectors

Sociologists divide economic life into three sectors: primary, secondary, and tertiary. In the **primary sector**, workers extract natural resources from the environment. Canadians who fish for a living or mine copper in northern Ontario and Quebec work in the primary sector. So do hunters, cattle raisers, farmers, and lumberjacks. In the **secondary sector**, workers turn raw materials into manufactured goods. They package fish, process copper into electrical wire, and turn trees into lumber and paper. The secondary sector dominates industrial economies.

The main focus of the **tertiary sector** is providing services. Some workers, such as computer technicians and automobile mechanics, install or service products. Others, such as private detectives and cab drivers, provide personal services. Although most of the labour force in postindustrial societies works in the tertiary sector, all three sectors exist side by side. Take the common lead pencil as an example. People who extract lead and cut timber work in the primary sector, those who turn the wood and lead into pencils are in the secondary sector, and those who advertise and sell the pencils work in the tertiary sector.

Farming provides a remarkable example of the change in sector employment in Canada (Drucker, 1987, 1994). Table 11.5 shows the dramatic decline in employment in farming (the primary sector) since World War II in Canada from a high of almost 20 percent in 1951 to its present low of 2 percent! There has been a similar trend in the other primary sector (logging, mining, oil, and natural gas) of the Canadian economy. Manufacturing (the secondary sector) also shows a decline in employment from two in seven workers in 1951 to only one in seven today. In both cases, the declines in

employment have come about because technological changes in the way food is grown and goods produced dramatically increased crop yields and manufacturing output. For example, while the production of steel in Canada has increased threefold to almost 14.5 million tonnes a year since 1960, the number of people employed has fallen from 36 500 to 27 200 in 2002 (*Maclean's*, January 23, 1995, p. 32).

Although a postindustrial society requires fewer people to produce food or basic materials and fewer people to process them, the information explosion demands that large numbers of people work in the tertiary sector. Consequently, we have experienced a surge in "knowledge and information work"—managing information and designing, servicing, and marketing products—that require higher levels of education, as shown in Table 11.4 on page 272.

Table 11.5 shows that between 1961 and 1971 a major transition occurred in Canada. Employment in community, business, and personal services grew rapidly and continues to be the major engine of job growth in the Canadian economy.

On the other hand, the reported average weekly earnings of people employed in the mining and petroleum businesses

Table 11.5 Employment by Industry, 1951–2001 (percentage of total employed), and Average Weekly Earnings, April 2002

Industry	1951	1961	1971	1981	1991	1997	2001	Average Weekly Earnings, April 2002
Agriculture	18.4%	11.2%	6.3%	4.3%	3.4%	1.9%	2.1%	N/A
Other primary (logging and forestry)	4.4%	3.0%	2.8%	3.0%	2.4%	1.8%	1.9%	$870.36
Mining								$1084.90
Crude petroleum and natural gas								$1403.94
Manufacturing	26.5%	24.0%	22.2%	19.5%	15.4%	15.0%	15.1%	$886.35
Autos								$1236.42
Pulp and paper								$1043.38
Construction	6.8%	6.2%	6.1%	6.3%	6.5%	5.6%	5.5%	$799.58
Transportation, communication, and utilities	8.8%	9.3%	8.7%	8.2%	7.4%	7.1%	N/A	—
Transportation								$761.05
Utilities								$1019.78
Trade	14.1%	16.9%	16.5%	17%	17.5%	16.5%	15.8%	$539.98
Finance, insurance, and real estate	3.0%	3.9%	4.8%	5.3%	5.9%	5.3%	N/A	—
Finance and insurance								$842.97
Real estate								$613.94
Community, business, and personal service	18%	19.5%	26.2%	29.6%	35.0%	36.6%	N/A	N/A
Amusement, gambling, and recreational services								$476.78
Personal services (excluding private household)								$423.36
Accommodation, food/beverages services								$298.35
Information and Cultural Industries								$821.47
Public administration	—	5.9%	6.4%	6.8%	6.5%	5.4%	5.1%	$768.05
Federal administration								$841.12
Provincial administration								$788.39
Local administration								$709.16
Total	100%*	100%*	100%*	100%*	100%*	100%*	—	
Total Number Employed in Canada (000)	5097	6055	8078	12 131	14 083	15 354	—	$598.26

*When totals do not add up to 100%, unclassified workers make up the remainder.
Source: Labour Division, Statistics Canada, *Labour Force Annual Averages*, Catalogues 71-529, 71-201; *Employment Earnings and Hours*, Catalogue 72-002.

and such manufacturing sectors as the auto and pulp and paper industries are considerably higher than the average weekly earnings of those in the booming tourist and food services enterprises. This difference is due in large part to two major factors: the increased productivity of technological changes and the highly unionized nature of the work force.

Focus Question
What are the three highest-paying jobs in Canada (by average weekly earnings)?

Women and Work

One of the chief characteristics of the Canadian work force has been the steady increase in the number of women in paid employment outside the home. In the early 1900s, only one in six women were in the paid labour force, while today the proportion is one in two! As Figure 11.4 shows, this ratio is one of the highest in the industrialized world.

How likely a woman is to be in the labour force depends on several factors. One factor is the influence of marital status. In a recent study by Statistics Canada, families in which the wife reported employment income had higher incomes than other types of family structure. In 1995, less than 5 percent of these had a total income of less than $20 000 while 14 percent had an income of over $100 000. These findings stand in contrast to families in which the wife did not receive income, where 21 percent had incomes of less than $20 000 and less than 5 percent reported incomes of at least $100 000 (Statistics Canada, 1998a, pp. 12–17).

Researchers have found some major distinctions between women and men in the world of work. For one, women tend to be more concerned than men with maintaining a balance between their work and family lives (Statham, Miller, & Mauksch, 1988). For another, men and women tend to follow different models for success: Men tend to emphasize individualism, power, and competition, while women are much more likely to stress collaboration, persuasion, and helping (Miller-Loessi, 1992). A primary concern of many women is the extent to which they must adopt the male model of leadership in order to be successful in their careers. Note that these findings represent tendencies only and many people diverge from them.

"The Quiet Revolution." Because the changes it has caused have been both gradual and profound, sociologists in the United States use the term **quiet revolution** to refer to the higher and higher proportion of women in the labour force. This trend has transformed consumer patterns, relations at work, self-concepts for both men and women, and relationships with husbands and children. One of the most significant aspects of the quiet revolution is the increased proportion of women with preschool children who work for wages. In 1981, 47 percent of married women in Canada were employed; by 1997 that proportion had increased to 57 percent. As we saw above, dual-income families tend to be better off than single-income families, and they are becoming an increasing characteristic of the Canadian labour force. The implications of these and other related changes to Canada's families are discussed in Chapter 13.

The Underground Economy

The underground economy. It has a sinister ring—suggestive of dope deals struck in alleys and wads of dollar bills hastily exchanged. The underground economy is this, but it is a lot more—and usually a lot more innocent. If you pay the plumber with a check made out to "cash," if you purchase a pair of sunglasses from a street vendor or a kitchen gadget at a yard sale, if you so much as hand a neighbor's kid a $20 bill (or if you accept it) to mow the lawn or to baby sit, you are participating in the underground economy. (Pennar & Farrell, 1993)

Figure 11.4 Percentage of Labour Force Made Up by Women in Most Industrialized Countries

Source: *Statistical Abstracts*, 1997, Tables 624, 1362.

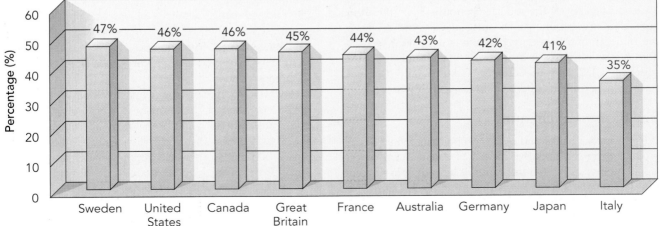

The term underground economy has a sinister ring to it. Part of the underground economy does consist of drug deals furtively transacted in back alleys, but the term refers to any unreported, untaxed commercial transaction. Most are as innocuous, and common, as that depicted in this photo.

The **underground economy**, also known as the *informal economy* and the *off-the-books economy*, consists of economic activities—legal or illegal—that people don't report to the government. What interests most of us is not unreported babysitting money, but the illegal activities that people cannot report even if they want to. As a 20-year-old child care worker who also works as a prostitute two or three nights a week said, "Why do I do this? For the money! Where else can I make this kind of money in a few hours? And it's all tax-free" (Jim Henslin's files). Drug dealing is perhaps the largest single source of illegal income, for billions of dollars flow from users to sellers and their networks of growers, importers, processors, transporters, dealers, and enforcers. These particular networks are so huge that every year more than a million Americans are arrested for illegal drug activities (*Statistical Abstract,* 1997, Table 328).

Because of its subaltern nature, no one knows the exact size of Canada's underground economy, but it is probably 15 to 20 percent of the regular economy. Since the 2002 gross domestic product (GDP) of Canada is $940 billion, the underground economy probably runs over $140 billion! It is so huge that it distorts the official statistics of the country's GDP, and the Canada Customs and Revenue Agency loses millions of dollars in taxes each year.

Shrinking Paycheques

While Canada's banks and other corporations report record profits, one might think that the pay of Canadian employees would be increasing. On the contrary, according to a recent study, household income growth has declined dramatically in the past 20 years (*Financial Post,* November 13, 1998, p. C7). As we saw from Table 11.5, the average weekly earnings of workers in 2002 appeared high in some sectors of the Canadian economy such as mining, autos, crude petroleum, and natural gas. However, even with the sharp rise in the number of working mothers, the study concludes that the standard of living of average Canadians is falling relative to much of the rest of the industrial world. GDP per capita fell below the OECD average in 1993, and the decline continues. Canadian consumers have responded by going increasingly into debt. This is not a recipe for a financially secure future.

Some workers, however, aren't able to bring home even these shrinking paycheques. Could you imagine making payments on rent, car, food, and, if you had anything left over, entertainment, on the approximately $300 a week provided to employees in the accommodation and food/beverages services industries (see Table 11.5)? That's why many young people have two or more jobs and "bunk up" with others their age, or they return home to their parents to live. The Perspectives box looks at some of the problems Canadians are having in today's job market.

Patterns of Work and Leisure

Trends in Leisure. **Leisure** is time not taken up by work or required activities such as eating and sleeping. It is not the activity itself that makes something leisure, but the purpose for which it is done. Consider driving a car. If you do it for pleasure, it is leisure, but if you are an on-duty police officer or commuting to the office, it is work. If done for enjoyment, horseback riding and reading a book are leisure—but these activities are work for jockeys and students.

Patterns of leisure change with the life course, following the U-curve shown in Figure 11.5. Young children enjoy the most leisure, but teenagers still have considerably more leisure than their parents. Parents with small children have the least leisure, but after the children leave home, leisure picks up again. After the age of 60 or so, the amount of leisure for adults peaks.

Work in the Postindustrial Society. While some workers today enjoy far more leisure time, more and more Canadian workers are feeling the stress of working more but enjoying life less. Over the past several decades, unionization helped many Canadians increase the amount of time spent in leisure activities. Today, the assault on trade unions by business and government alike makes increasing vacation time for their members a luxury when faced with more pressing issues such as job security.

However, shortening the work week is one way to increase employment. In Germany, for example, the work week is presently 35 hours, with Friday afternoons usually off. Volkswagen was the world's first global corporation to adopt a 30-hour work week (Rifkin, 1995). In addition, German workers are guaranteed six weeks of paid vacation each year. Unlike western Europe, however, the trend in Canada and the United States is opposite: Canadian workers now average 2036 hours of work a year, with U.S.

What is it like for some people in Canada to find work? Below are two typical stories that shed light on the personal problems faced by more and more Canadians, young and old alike.

On March 2, 1990, Garrie Manser punched out at the north-end picture-frame plant for the last time. K-D Manufacturing had closed and moved across the river to Watertown, New York. Manser, with 21 years as a painter at K-D, remembers the exact date three years later. He can also remember his first day at K-D, November 13, 1968. He was 22 at the time.

After K-D shut down, Manser managed to find work with Dustbusters (a contract cleaning outfit) and the Ministry of Transport. He liked the government job; it involved painting highway guardrails, and he could use his experience. But both jobs ended soon after they started. He also got in six weeks at a door and window maker, but left because chemicals in the wood preservative gave him an unbearable rash.

"There's so darn many people out of work, they don't know who to pick," Garrie Manser says. His 21 years working in one place doesn't seem to carry any weight. "They want a Grade 12 edu-

cation. The jobs you see in the paper are for bartenders, cooks, and like that. They want experience."

Russ Jackson is typical of his generation. His father commuted every day to work in Ford's Windsor foundry. Born in nearby Chatham in 1959, Russ married Brenda Ritchie, the girl next door, after teaching her how to drive the family car. At age 18 he followed his father and started work at the Ford foundry, then watched as his parents and their friends retired and began spending half the year in winter homes purchased in Florida. Before he was to be laid off in 1979, he took a job at a newly opened foundry, Brant Casting, that supplied forged engine parts to the Big Three. Ten years after he signed on at Brant Casting, Jackson and his mates punched out for the last time when the plant closed permanently, one of the first of many factories to feel the first bite of the recession that began in 1990. For 10 years Jackson had been living from cheque to cheque, saving little. By this time, Brenda was working as a molder in a plastic factory run by the Complax company. She had started back to work when she felt her youngest daughter was ready to be left with a caregiver. Less than a half a year later the Complax plant, though new,

also closed down. "There is no other plant in Canada or in the U.S. with the high technology we have," company president Ralph Zarboni had bragged when the plant first opened in the 1980s. "It's state of the art," Brenda Jackson says. She is still proud of her former workplace.

"The days of getting hired somewhere and spending 30 years there are done," Russ Jackson says. "Now you'll be jumping from job to job. You can feel it in the town, the insecure feeling that most people have. It's affected our kids." He tells how his daughter wanted to go ice skating but couldn't because her skates didn't fit. "She didn't want to ask for the ten bucks for another pair." In 10 years at Brant Castings Russ Jackson managed to put $600 into an RRSP, and now he can't rely on getting a pension. "People who jump from job to job don't have that. That's the scary part. We're all going to get older. How will we live then?" The very notion of retirement—to say nothing of the "early" retirement now aimed at saving the jobs of young employees—was only being invented when Russ Jackson's dad started work.

Source: Glenday, Duffy, & Pupo (1997).

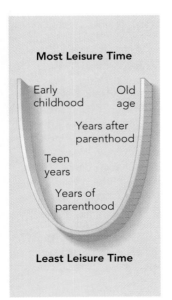

Figure 11.5 Leisure and the Life Course: The "U" Curve of Leisure

Most Leisure Time

Early childhood

Old age

Years after parenthood

Teen years

Years of parenthood

Least Leisure Time

workers averaging 1948 hours. For Japanese workers, the total is 2120 hours.

The Future: Facing the Consequences of Global Capitalism

A little over a decade and a half ago, a small number of sociologists in Great Britain and France were celebrating the coming "Leisure Revolution" (Sherman, 1985; Jenkins & Sherman, 1981; Gorz, 1982, 1985). We were told then that, within our lifetime, the application of the new microelectronics-based technology by business and governments would steer us all into a future where the nature of work and the work ethic would be defined by what we did in our leisure time, be it simple relaxation or starting our own business. True, we would still have to work at something that was not of our own choosing. However, there would be limitations on the length of time we would be exposed to this kind of work.

As one of the "Paths to [this] Paradise," André Gorz (1985) spoke of a lifetime work schedule of 20 000 hours. Can you believe working for only 20 years and only for 6 hours a day, 4 days a week, and 42 weeks a year? Imagine starting employment after university with a four-day work week, two-and-a-half months' paid vacation, and retiring before your 45th birthday!

Clearly, however, this is not our present-day reality, nor is it likely to become reality in the immediate future. What happened to the transformation of work? Is the idea of a shortened work week and meaningful jobs an impossible utopia?

It is true that jobs are being transformed and new jobs created everywhere, but the new realities of work deal with the nature of jobs and skills-based change. The transformation of work has witnessed the rise of a knowledge/information/service economy based on the universal application of microelectronics technology that creates new occupational categories—a rush of change that has left in its wake thousands of lost jobs, while most of the remaining positions have become "retooled."

What does this mean for the future of occupational choice for young Canadians? When governments are divesting themselves of their people and their assets and large companies are shedding their "excess" human resources, what are the prospects for the future? Will there be enough good service jobs created by the private sector in this country? What would it take to rescue the dream of the "Leisure Revolution"?

If politics make strange bedfellows, so do economics. The animosity felt by U.S. politicians toward Vietnam's economic system was once so fierce that they sacrificed hundreds of thousands of lives and billions of dollars in a wasted effort to extinguish "the enemy." This photo from Ho Chi Minh City, the capital of Vietnam, illustrates how this former "enemy of death" is now in the process of becoming an economic partner of the United States.

The Thinking Critically about Social Controversy box that follows focuses on the far-reaching implications of this global transformation of our economy.

Thinking Critically about Social Controversy

New Technology and the Restructuring of Work: What Type of New Society?

What are we to base prospective discussions on, when debating the new realities of work? Economic nationalism is no longer on the political agenda in Canada. As a modest beginning, let us explore two possible scenarios.

The first scenario reflects the changes taking place in Canadian society today with large, lean, or agile corporations such as General Motors or Northern Telecom continuing their strategy of cost-cutting, otherwise known as "downsizing" or "reengineering," with layoffs, redundancies, and early retirement of their unionized or non-unionized employees and large segments of lower and middle management. Included in this "economic necessity" are governments, at all levels, "fighting inflation" and "tackling the debt" by slashing jobs and eliminating, privatiz-

ing, or contracting out public services.

Nowadays, it is not uncommon for us to see television personalities, business consultants, government bureaucrats, and many others point out that today's redundant blue- and white-collar employees will need time to adjust to the new realities of work in an information age. Often this means acquiring new skills through retraining programs, or upgrading existing skills, or even getting a basic education. Just as often, new entrants into the labour market are told that to be competitive, computer skills, the ability to work in teams, and networking are prerequisites for that increasingly elusive good job. While many of these skills are necessary for getting a job, the competition is such that landing a job remains a gamble for many. The insecurity about the future

breeds suspicion, anxiety, and frustration for ever-larger numbers of young Canadians. The sign of these times is the flatter, leaner, and meaner corporation and government, where all levels of the work force are multiskilled and where government employees and corporate citizens alike are "working more for less."

The ruling orthodoxy maintains the promise of new and better jobs for the casualties of corporate restructuring and government reengineering. We are told it is information technology that has eliminated all those good jobs in traditional industries, especially manufacturing, but that new jobs in the service sector are being created rapidly, and that the private sector, if unfettered by government regulations, will create more and better jobs than those lost in manufacturing and the public sector. University graduates are told that they will be sought after by those companies Edward Luttwak calls "the New Titans" of the information age—Microsoft and Intel. Yet, as Luttwak (1996) rightly points out, Microsoft and Intel, whose value on Wall Street is much greater than that of General Motors, had a combined total of only 48 100 employees worldwide, while Ford alone payrolled 325 000 employees! Clearly, the good jobs from the "New Titans" are just not there.

What's more, the answer today to the question of what comes after school/university is not the one promising good jobs and plenty of leisure time for most Canadians. There is little prospect of a secure future with better-compensated leisure time. On the contrary, everyone is being told we can't afford our lifestyle, that governments have to cut and corporations must become global and more competitive. While our retail stores carry a wider variety of products available for consumption than at any previous time in recorded history—from Benetton clothes to Ikea furniture, Macintosh computers, and Toyota Camrys—these products are being made in various parts of the globe but with a shrinking proportion of well-paid factory and office workers.

If this scenario holds, Canada's occupational structure could take on the appearance of a bottom-heavy hourglass, replacing the traditional pyramid—otherwise known as the "shrinking middle." This New Society would restrict access to the limited numbers of good jobs or careers defined by a high degree of employment security, high pay, and relatively decent working conditions, while promoting a burgeoning secondary sector comprising openly competitive, insecure, and nonstandard "work arrangements." It will consist of entrenched bipolar occupational estates that offer less and less opportunity for advancement into the good jobs and could give rise to a new set of dangerous populist politics.

The second scenario involves the promise of a better, prosperous life that is also the result of the revolution in new information technologies—a promise kept alive by characters like *The Jetsons* or the vision of Gene Roddenberry's *Star Trek* where poverty has been eliminated and ethnic violence is a forgotten memory.

The basis for this second and more optimistic scenario, too, is the dramatic increase in the productive capacity of the world economy generated by microelectronics-based information technology. The capability to produce so much more so cheaply could mean more people would be freed from wage slavery. The drudgery, danger, and pain associated with factory, longshore, mining, and forestry jobs would be dramatically reduced. Instead of men, women, and children destroying themselves while at work, the microelectronics-based information revolution could bring almost everyone a chance for self-fulfillment and meaning.

This dream of a liberated future has been superseded by an uncertain present. For most Canadians, holding a steady, full-time job is probably more important now than it was 30 years ago. Nevertheless, some analysts have argued that the disruptions brought about by the sustained advance to an information-based, service economy are much like the dramatic changes in the world's economic livelihood brought about by the Industrial Revolution. Time was needed for those displaced from their agricultural way of life to adapt to the discipline of the factory regime. Our society is in a period of transition, they contend. Eventually all the good jobs will appear!

However, can the more positive scenario be realized by simply waiting and leaving well enough alone? Or will it require Canadians, Americans, the British, the French, and citizens in other developed and less developed countries to pressure their governments to step in and challenge the path chosen by those who wield economic and political power?

For Your Consideration

Given the discussion in this chapter about (1) the effects of the new technologies on work and (2) the direction of capitalism, especially the globalization of trade and the growing power of multinationals, which of these futures appears more likely?

As conflict theorists stress, in order to keep labour costs low and profits high, capitalist economies need a *reserve labour force* that pits one worker against another. This poorly paid gold miner in South Africa, working under debilitating conditions, is an expendable part of the profit system that drives the economic machinery called capitalism. If this worker protests his working conditions, he will be fired immediately, for waiting in the wings are thousands of unemployed workers eager to take his place.

Summary and Review

THE TRANSFORMATION OF ECONOMIC SYSTEMS

How are economic systems linked to types of societies?

The earliest societies, hunting and gathering societies, were **subsistence economies**: Small groups lived off the land and produced little or no surplus. Economic systems grew more complex as people discovered how to domesticate and cultivate, farm (agricultural societies), and manufacture (industrial societies). Each of these methods allowed people to produce a *surplus*, which fostered trade. Trade, in turn, brought social inequality as some people began to accumulate more than others. pp. 260–262.

THE TRANSFORMATION OF THE MEDIUM OF EXCHANGE

How has the medium of exchange evolved?

A **medium of exchange** is any means by which people exchange goods and services. In hunting and gathering societies, people **bartered** goods and services. In agricultural societies, **money** came into use, which evolved into **currency**, or paper representing a specific amount of gold or silver. Postindustrial societies rely increasingly on electronic transfer of funds in the form of **credit cards** and **debit cards**. p. 263.

WORLD ECONOMIC SYSTEMS

How do the major economic systems differ?

The world's two major economic systems are capitalism and socialism. In **capitalism**, private citizens own the means of production and pursue profits. In **socialism**, the state owns the means of production and determines production with no goal of profit. Adherents of each have developed ideologies that defend their own systems and paint the other as harmful. Following **convergence theory**, in recent years each system has adopted features of the other. pp. 263–268.

CAPITALISM IN A GLOBAL ECONOMY

What is the role of the corporation in capitalism?

The term **corporate capitalism** indicates that giant corporations dominate capitalism today. At the top of the major corporations is an inner circle, whose mutual interests make certain corporate capitalism is protected. The primary sociological significance of global capitalism is that the interests of the inner circle lie beyond national boundaries. pp. 268–271.

APPLYING SOCIOLOGICAL THEORIES

How do four of the major sociological perspectives apply to work?

Symbolic interactionists analyze meanings and self-perceptions, asking why work is a job or a profession, what gives work status, and what makes work satisfying. From the *functionalist perspective*, work is a basis of social solidarity. Preindustrial societies foster **mechanical solidarity**, identifying with others who perform similar tasks. With industrialization comes **organic solidarity**, economic interdependence brought about by the division of labour. *Conflict theorists*, who focus on worker exploitation and alienation, note how the new technology and global capitalism affect workers and owners. Workers lose jobs to automation, while the inner circle maintains its political power and profits from these changes. *Feminist theories* concentrate on gender inequality and how men dominate the more important good jobs while women can be found in **pink ghettoes**. Those that do enter the mostly male occupations tend to experience **glass ceilings**. pp. 271–273.

WORK IN CANADIAN SOCIETY

What are the three economic sectors of the labour force?

In the **primary sector** workers extract raw materials from the environment. In the **secondary sector** workers turn raw products into manufactured goods. In the **tertiary sector** workers produce services. Most Canadians now work in the tertiary, or service, sector. pp. 273–275.

How has the ratio of women in the work force changed?

In 1921, one in five Canadian women were in paid employment. Today, this figure is almost one in two, one of the highest ratios in the industrialized world. p. 275.

What is the underground economy?

The **underground economy** consists of any economic activity not reported to the government, from babysitting to prostitution. The size of the underground economy is perhaps 10 to 15 percent of the regular economy. pp. 275–276.

How have patterns of work and leisure changed?

Industrialization initially brought a dramatic decrease in **leisure**, but workers have gained some back. Among the industrialized nations, currently only the Japanese work more hours per year than Canadian workers. p. 276.

THE FUTURE: FACING THE CONSEQUENCES OF GLOBAL CAPITALISM

Expanding global trade, new technologies, and downsizing will continue to force a restructuring of work. Choices made now can lead to either a better society or a fortress mentality. pp. 277–279.

Critical Thinking Questions

1. For some sociologists and most public officials, microelectronics-based, computer technologies hold the promise of a better future for most Canadians. Do you believe this is an accurate assessment?

2. Most students today work while going to university. Describe the ways you would make your workplace a better place to work. Why can't you implement your ideas? Do you think having a trade union in your workplace would matter?

3. Some sociologists believe work is important because it provides all of us with status and meaning. It is not uncommon to hear someone say "I am a sociologist" or "I am a university student" or "I am a teacher." If work is so important for our well-being, why is it that so many people hate their jobs and can't wait to retire?

Key Terms

barter 263
capitalism 263
conspicuous consumption 261
convergence theory 268
corporate capitalism 268
corporation 268
credit card 263
currency 263
debit card 263
democratic socialism 266
deposit receipts 263
economy 260
fiat money 263
glass ceiling 273
gold standard 263
gross national product (GNP) 263
inflation 263
interlocking directorates 269
job ghettoes 273
laissez-faire capitalism 263
leisure 276

market 260
market competition 263
market forces 263
market restraints 264
mechanical solidarity 272
medium of exchange 263
money 263
oligopolies 268
organic solidarity 272
pink ghettoes 273
primary sector 273
private ownership of the means of production 263
professions 271
quiet revolution 275
secondary sector 273
socialism 266
stored value 263
subsistence economy 260
tertiary sector 274
underemployment 266
underground economy 276
welfare (state) capitalism 264

Weblinks

All URLs listed are current as of the printing of this book. URLs are often changed. Please check our Web site **www.abacon.com/henslin** for updates.

Centre for Research on Work and Society (CRWS)

www.yorku.ca/crws
The Centre for Research on Work and Society at York University brings together academic researchers with labour movement partners to engage in research and education on work and labour matters. One of the Centre's most recent projects is an electronic journal, entitled *Just Labour*. You can reach the Just Labour Web site through the CRWS home page.

Canadian Business: Performance 2000

www.canadianbusiness.com/CB500/p500.htm
An annual corporate ranking—the most complete and authoritative list of Canada's most successful companies.

Socialism.org: The Socialism Organization

www.socialism.org/
A nonprofit research project site whose main aim is to form an online rendezvous for those who share the vision of building a peaceful and ordered socialist society.

Capitalism.org

www.capitalism.org/
"Capitalism is a social system based on the principle of individual rights. The term 'capitalism' is used here in the broader philosophical political sense, and not in the narrower economic sense, i.e., a free-market."

Ed Brown's Political Economy Archive

www.stile.lut.ac.uk/~gyedb/STILE/index.html
The bibliography section of this site consists of over 500 entries organized under a series of topic headings. Most entries provide a description of the article or book referenced and some also contain comments. The e-mail archive consists of an extensive collection of documents collected from the Internet.

Institute for International Economics Homepage

www.iie.com/
The Institute for International Economics is a private, nonprofit, nonpartisan research institution devoted to the study of international economic policy. Since 1981 the Institute has provided timely, objective analysis and concrete solutions to key international economic problems.

Chapter 12

Politics: Power and Authority

Learning Outcomes

After you have studied this chapter, you will be able to

■ describe Max Weber's three bases for authority—traditional, rational-legal, and charismatic

■ understand the differences between democracy, monarchy, and oligopoly

■ describe the parliamentary system of government in Canada

■ understand the social basis for the rise of the sovereignty movement in Quebec

■ discuss the reasons for war as a means to achieve political objectives

In the 1930s, George Orwell wrote *1984*, a novel about a future in which the government, known as "Big Brother," dominates society, dictating almost every aspect of everyone's life. To love someone is considered a sinister activity, a betrayal of the unquestioning allegiance all citizens owe Big Brother.

Two characters, Winston and Julia, fall in love. Because of Big Brother, they meet furtively, always with the threat of discovery and punishment hanging over their heads. When informers turn them in, expert interrogators separate Julia and Winston. They swiftly proceed to break their affection—to restore their loyalty to Big Brother.

Then follows a remarkable account of Winston and his tormentor, O'Brien. Winston is strapped so tightly into a chair that he can't even move his head. O'Brien explains that inflicting pain is not always enough, but that everyone has a breaking point, some worst thing that will push them over the edge.

O'Brien tells Winston that he has discovered his, Winston's, worst fear. He sets on the table next to Winston a cage with two giant, starving sewer rats, then picks up a mask connected to the door of the cage and places it over Winston's head. In a quiet voice, O'Brien explains that when he presses the lever, the door of the cage will slide up, and the rats will shoot out like bullets and bore straight into Winston's face. Winston's eyes, the only part of his body that he can move, dart back and forth, revealing his terror. Still speaking so quietly that Winston has to strain to hear him, O'Brien adds that the rats sometimes attack the eyes first, but sometimes they burrow through the cheeks and devour the tongue. When O'Brien places his hand on the lever, Winston realizes that the only way out is for someone to take his place. But who? Then he hears his own voice screaming, "Do it to Julia! ...Tear her face off, strip her to the bones. Not me! Julia! Not me!"

Orwell does not describe Julia's interrogation, but when Julia and Winston see each other later they realize that each has betrayed the other. Their love is gone. Big Brother has won. Although Orwell pictures an extreme form of totalitarianism, politics is always about power and authority, the focus of this chapter.

Micropolitics and Macropolitics

Although the images that come to mind when we think of politics are those of government—kings, queens, coups, dictatorships, running for office, voting—politics, in the sense of power relations, is also an inevitable part of everyday life (M. Schwartz, 1990). As Weber (1922/1968) said, **power** is the ability to carry out your will in spite of resistance, and in every group, large or small, some individuals have power over others. Symbolic interactionists and feminists use the term **micropolitics** to refer to the exercise of power in everyday life. Routine situations in which people jockey for power include several employees' trying to impress the new boss—who is going to decide which one of them will be promoted to manager—and efforts by parents to enforce their curfew on a reluctant daughter or son, and the struggle over the remote control to the television. *Every group, then, is political, for in every group there is a power struggle of some sort.*

In contrast, **macropolitics**—the focus of this chapter-refers to the exercise of large-scale power over a large group. Governments, whether the dictatorship faced by Winston in the opening vignette, or the elected forms in the United States and Canada, are examples of macropolitics.

Power, Authority, and Violence

For a society to exist, it must have a system of leadership. As Max Weber (1913/1947) pointed out, however, we perceive power as either legitimate or illegitimate. Weber used the term **authority** to refer to legitimate power—that is, power that we accept as right. In contrast, illegitimate power—**coercion**—is power that we do not accept as just.

> ### Focus Question
> What is the difference between power and authority?

Imagine you are driving to university to take a sociology exam, and on the way you stop to buy a CD player on sale for $250. As you approach the store, a man jumps out of the alley and shoves a gun in your face. He demands your money. Frightened for your life, you hand it over. After filing a police report, you are running late. Afraid you might miss the test, you step on the gas. As the needle hits 130, you see flashing blue and red lights in your rearview mirror. Your explanation about the robbery doesn't faze the officer—or the judge who hears your case a few weeks later. She first lectures you on safety and then orders you to pay $50 court costs plus $200 for travelling 30 kilometres per hour over the speed limit. You pay the $250.

What's the difference? The mugger, the police officer, and the judge—each has power, and in each case you part with $250. The difference is that the mugger has no authority. His power is illegitimate—he has no *right* to do what he did. In contrast, you acknowledge that the officer has the right to stop you and that the judge has the right to fine you. Theirs is authority, or legitimate power.

Authority and Legitimate Violence

As sociologist Peter Berger observed, it makes little difference whether you willingly pay the fine the judge levies or refuse to pay. The court will get its money one way or another.

> If all the warnings are disregarded, the last thing that will happen is that a couple of cops show up at the door with handcuffs. Even the cop who hands out the initial traffic ticket is likely to wear a gun—just in case. (Berger, 1963).

The **state**, then—a term synonymous with government—claims a monopoly on legitimate force or violence within some designated territory. This point, made by Max Weber (1946a, 1922/1968)—that the state claims the exclusive right to use violence and the right to punish everyone else who does—is critical to our understanding of macropolitics. If someone owes you a debt, you cannot imprison that person or even forcibly take the money. The state can. As Berger (1963) summarized this matter, *"Violence is the ultimate foundation of any political order."*

Before we explore the origins of the modern state, let us first look at a situation in which the state loses legitimacy.

The Collapse of Authority. Sometimes the state oppresses its people, and they resist their government just as they do a mugger. **Revolution**, armed resistance with the intention to overthrow a government, is not only a people's rejection of a government's claim to rule over them but also a rejection of its monopoly on violence. The American Revolution of 1776, the Russian Revolution of 1917, which resulted in the establishment of the Soviet Communist regime and lasted until 1989, or the Chinese Communist Revolution are examples of the use of violence to achieve a fundamental change in government.

What some see as coercion, however, others see as authority. Consequently, some people remain loyal to a government, willingly defend it, perhaps even die for it, although others are ready to take up arms against it. *The more its power is seen as legitimate, then, the more stable a government is.* The Canadian system of democracy is seen by most Canadians as legitimate, and therefore the people do not seek a radical transformation in how our government runs.

But just why do people accept power as legitimate? Max Weber (1922/1968) identified three sources of authority: traditional, rational-legal, and charismatic.

Focus Question
What are Max Weber's three bases for authority?

Traditional Authority

Throughout history, the most common form of authority has been tradition. **Traditional authority** is based on custom. For example, because of birth a particular individual becomes the chief, king, or queen. As far as members of that society are concerned, this is the right way to determine who shall rule because "It's always been done this way."

Gender relations in most human groups are a good example of traditional authority, for they are based on custom. For example, in the villages of Spain and Portugal widows are expected to wear only black until they remarry—which generally means they wear black for the rest of their lives. Tradition, decreeing black, is so strong that if a widow were to violate the dress code, she would be seen as having profaned the memory of her deceased husband and would be ostracized by the community.

When a traditional society changes, it undermines traditional authority. For example, as a society industrializes, people have new experiences. This opens up new perspectives on life, and no longer does traditional authority go unchallenged. Thus, in Spain and Portugal you can still see old women dressed in black from head to toe—and you immediately

For centuries, widows in the Mediterranean area were expected to dress in black. Their long dresses were matched by black stockings, black shoes, and black head coverings. Widows conformed to this socially defined expression of ongoing sorrow for the deceased husband not because of law, but because of custom. Today, however, as industrialization erodes traditional authority, few widows follow this practice.

know their marital status. Younger widows, however, are likely to be indistinguishable from other women.

Even in postindustrial societies, parental authority provides an excellent example of traditional authority (M. Schwartz, 1990). From generations past, we inherit the idea that not only are parents responsible for providing their children with food and shelter, but also they have the right to discipline them, choose their doctors and schools, and teach them religion and morality.

Rational-Legal Authority

The second type of authority identified by Weber, **rational-legal authority**, is not based on custom but on written rules. "Rational" means reasonable, and "legal" means part of law. The matters agreed to may be as broad as a constitution that specifies the rights of all members of a society or as narrow as a contract between two individuals. Because bureaucracies are based on written rules, rational-legal authority is also called *bureaucratic authority*.

Rational-legal authority comes from the position an individual holds, not from the person who holds the position. In a democracy, for example, the prime minister's authority comes from the office, as specified in a written constitution, not from custom or the individual's personal characteristics.

One of the best examples of charismatic authority is Joan of Arc, shown here at the coronation of Charles VII, whom she was instrumental in making king. Uncomfortable at portraying Joan of Arc wearing only a man's coat of armour, the artist has made certain she is wearing plenty of makeup, and also has added a ludicrous skirt.

Charismatic authorities can be of any morality, from the saintly to the most bitterly evil. Like Joan of Arc, Adolf Hitler attracted throngs of people. This poster from the 1930s, entitled *Es Lebe Deutschland* ("Long Live Germany") illustrates the qualities of leadership that Germans of the period saw in Hitler.

Charismatic Authority

A charismatic individual is someone to whom people are drawn because they believe that person has been touched by God or has been endowed by nature with exceptional qualities (Lipset, 1993). Joan of Arc is an example of such **charismatic authority**, the third type of authority Weber identified. (*Charisma* is a Greek word that means a gift freely and graciously given [Arndt & Gingrich, 1957].) People followed her because they were drawn to her outstanding traits. They saw her as a messenger of God, fighting on the side of justice, and accepted her leadership because of these appealing qualities.

The Threat Posed by Charismatic Leaders. To what do charismatic leaders owe allegiance? Because their authority is based only on their personal ability to attract followers, charismatic leaders pose a threat to the established political system. Accordingly, they can inspire followers to disregard—or even overthrow—traditional and rational-legal authorities.

Authority as Ideal Type

Weber's classifications—traditional, rational-legal, and charismatic—represent ideal types of authority. Any given leader, then, may show a combination of characteristics.

Pierre Elliott Trudeau at the 1968 Liberal leadership convention. He is a good example of someone who combined rational-legal and charismatic authority.

Charismatic and traditional authority can also overlap. The Ayatollah Khomeini of Iran, for example, was a religious leader, holding the traditional position of ayatollah. His embodiment of the Iranian people's dreams, however, as well as his austere life and devotion to principles of the Koran, gave him such mass appeal that he was also a charismatic leader. Khomeini's followers were convinced he had been chosen by God, and his speeches could arouse tens of thousands of followers to action.

The Transfer of Authority

The orderly transfer of authority from one leader to another is critical for social stability. Under traditional authority, people generally know who is next in line. Under rational-legal authority, people may not know who the next leader will be, but they do know how that person will be selected. South Africa provides a remarkable example of the orderly transfer of authority under a rational-legal organization. In spite of this country being ripped apart by decades of racial strife, accompanied by not only deep suspicions and hatreds but also many murders committed on each side, through maintaining its rational-legal authority the country was able to peacefully transfer power from the white minority group led by President de Klerk to the black majority group led by Nelson Mandela.

Charismatic authority, however, has no such rules of succession, which makes it inherently less stable than either traditional or rational-legal authority. Because charismatic authority is built around an individual, the death or incapacitation of a such a leader can mean a bitter struggle for succession. Consequently, some charismatic leaders make arrangements for an orderly transition of power by appointing a successor. This does not guarantee orderly succession, of course, for the followers may not perceive the designated heir in the same way as they did the earlier leader. A second strategy is for the charismatic leader to build an

An example is Pierre Elliott Trudeau, who combined rational-legal and charismatic authority. As the elected head of the Canadian government, Trudeau represented rational-legal authority. Yet his mass appeal, especially in English-speaking Canada, was so great that his public speeches could arouse feelings of patriotism and national identity.

Crucial for society is the orderly transfer of power. One of the most remarkable transfers occurred in South Africa. Under this country's constitutional system, power was transferred from the white dominated government headed by Fredrik Willem de Klerk (on the right) to Nelson Mandela (on the left).

organization, which then develops a system of rules or regulations, thus transforming itself into a rational-legal leadership. Weber used the term **routinization of charisma** to refer to this transition of authority from a charismatic leader to rational-legal authority.

Types of Government

How do the various types of government—monarchies, democracies, dictatorships, and oligarchies—differ?

Monarchies: The Rise of the State

City-states were the first type of government. Each had its own **monarchy**, a king or queen whose right to rule was considered hereditary. If you drive through Spain, France, or Germany, you can still see evidence of former city-states. In the countryside you will see only scattered villages. Farther on, your eye will be drawn to the outline of a castle on a faraway hill. As you get closer, you will see that the castle is surrounded by a city. Several miles further, you will see another city, also dominated by a castle. Each city, with its castle, was once a centre of power.

Although the city controlled the immediate area around it, the areas between cities remained in dispute. City-states often quarrelled, and wars were common. The victorious ones extended their rule, and eventually a single city-state was able to wield power over an entire region. As the size of these regions grew, the people slowly developed an identity with the larger region. That is, they began to see distinct inhabitants as a "we" instead of a "they." What we call the state—the political entity that claims a monopoly on the use of violence within a territory—came into being.

Democracies: Citizenship as a Revolutionary Idea

Both Canada and the United States have governments that are called **democracies**. (The word *democracy* is derived from two Greek words—*kratos* [power] and *demos* [common people]—thus it literally means "power to the people.")

The democracies of the two countries differ in that the government of the United States grew out of a revolutionary past with Great Britain, while Canada's grew out of accepting our colonial heritage with Great Britain and pre-Revolutionary France.

Because of their small size, tribes and cities were able to practise **direct democracy**. That is, they were small enough for the eligible voters to meet together, express their opinions, and then vote publicly—much like a town hall meeting today. Direct democracy is not possible with the large populations of Canada and the United States. Therefore, **representative democracy** was invented.

Today we take the idea of citizenship for granted. However, there is nothing natural about citizenship—it is simply one way in which people choose to define themselves. Throughout most of human history, people were thought to *belong* to a clan, to a tribe, or even to a ruler. The idea of **citizenship**—that by virtue of birth and residence people have basic rights—is quite new to the human scene (B. Turner, 1990).

The concept of representative democracy based on citizenship was revolutionary. Its implementation meant *the reversal of traditional ideas, for the government was to be responsive to the people's wishes, not the people to the wishes of the government.*

The idea of **universal citizenship**—of everyone having the same basic rights by virtue of being born in a country (or by immigrating and becoming a naturalized citizen)—flowered very slowly, and came into practice only through fierce struggle. At first only certain citizens (male land owners) in Canada voted for men to represent them, at first in Montreal, which was the first city of representative government in British North America, and only later in Ottawa.

Today it seems inconceivable to us that anyone on the basis of gender or race/ethnicity should not have the right to vote, hold office, make a contract, testify in court, or own property. For earlier generations of Canadians, however, it seemed just as inconceivable that the poor, women, Native Canadians, or Asian Canadians should have such rights. See Table 12.1 for the evolution of the right to vote in Canada.

Over the years, then, rights have been extended, and in Canada citizenship and its privileges now apply to all. No longer does property, sex, or ethnicity determine the rights just mentioned.

> ### Focus Question
> Why is the parliamentary system in Canada a form of democracy?

Dictatorships and Oligarchies: The Seizure of Power

A government run by a single person who has seized power is known as a **dictatorship**. If a small group seizes power, the government is called an **oligarchy**. Although one individual may be named president, it is often a group of high-ranking military officers, working behind the scenes, that makes the decisions. If their designated president becomes uncooperative, they remove him from office and designate another.

Monarchies, dictatorships, and oligarchies vary in the amount of control they exert over their people. **Totalitarianism** is almost *total* control of a people by the government. As our opening vignette demonstrated, totalitarian regimes tolerate no opposing opinion. In Nazi Germany, for example, Hitler kept the populace in tight control through the Gestapo, a ruthless secret police force that looked for any sign of dissent. Control was so thorough that spies even watched moviegoers' reactions to newsreels,

Table 12.1 Women, Equity, and the Right to Vote

Year	Event
1867	British North America Act excludes women's right to vote.
1873	Women property owners in British Columbia become the first women to gain the right to vote in a municipal election.
1885	Sir John A. Macdonald introduces, then withdraws, an elections act amendment giving women the vote.
1894	House of Commons votes down the Women's Christian Temperance Union petition for women's suffrage.
1914	Flora Denison publishes the first suffrage journal, entitled *War and Women*.
1916	Women in Manitoba become the first in Canada to win the vote in provincial elections. In March and April, Saskatchewan and Alberta follow Manitoba's lead.
1918	On May 24, women vote in federal elections but must be 21 years or older, not be alien-born, and meet the property requirements in the province where they reside.
1919	Electoral law amended so that women can stand for federal office.
1920	Federal law amended to include universal female and male suffrage regardless of provincial law.
1921	The first federal election in which women vote under universal franchise.
1940	Women gain the provincial franchise in Quebec.
1948	Disqualifications based on race eliminated from federal election law.
1955	Final restrictions based on religion removed from federal elections act.
1960	Diefenbaker's government extends the franchise to "Registered Indians."
1970	Voting age lowered to 18. Eighteen-year-olds vote for the first time in the 1972 federal election.
1982	Charter of Rights and Freedoms entrenches the right to vote.
1992	People with disabilities are ensured access to the vote.
1993	Special ballot for Canadians living or travelling abroad who can't vote on election day.
1996	National Register of Electors eliminates door-to-door enumeration.

Source: Elections Canada, 2000, Catalogue no. CA1 TB #52, ISSN 12022454. Adapted with the permission of the Minister of Public Works and Government Services Canada.

reporting those who did not respond "appropriately" (Hippler, 1987). A more recent example is the armed squads in Taliban-ruled Afghanistan who patrolled the streets looking for any who transgressed the religious rules of the regime.

People around the world find the ideas of citizenship and of representative democracy appealing. Those who have no say in their government's decisions, or who face prison for expressing dissent, find in these ideas the hope for a brighter future. With today's electronic communications, people no longer remain ignorant of whether they are more or less privileged politically than others. This knowledge produces pressure for greater citizen participation in government. With continued development in communications, the future will continue to step up this pressure.

The Canadian Political System

The Canadian system of government can be described as a parliamentary democracy. Parliament is constitutionally the supreme national lawmaking authority for all matters that fall within its jurisdiction. Examples of Parliament's powers include interprovincial and international trade, communications, banking and finance, and some criminal matters. However, in Canada, the provinces have evolved a number

of separate and significant powers of their own. Examples include control over natural resources, most labour legislation (approximately 90 percent of trade unions' members come under provincial jurisdiction), and some criminal matters.

Canada is a democracy, since the people elect their politicians through periodic elections. Since World War II, between 70 and 80 percent of Canadians have participated in the electoral process (see Table 12.2). This contrasts with only 50 to 55 percent of Americans voting for their president and less than a majority of eligible voters casting ballots for their representatives to Congress. Since the 1990s, however, a downward trend may be evidence of a growing cynicism toward our political system among the electorate in Canada. Canada has a federal system of government. This means that some areas of legal jurisdiction or real powers of enforcement are reserved for the federal parliament and other, residual powers are distributed among the provincial and municipal governments.

Canada's federal form of government is unlike a **unitary state** in which all power resides with the central government. Neither does Canada's parliamentary democracy resemble a **confederal union** in which the provinces have most of the powers and the central government has little authority to enforce national decisions on the "sovereign" provinces.

Canada has evolved a system of government that is somewhere in between these two extremes. Nevertheless, to most Canadians the year 1867 is commonly known as that of "Confederation." As Garth Stevenson notes, the use of that term to denote our system of government is inaccurate. At the time of "Confederation," Quebec, New Brunswick, Nova Scotia, and Prince Edward Island were all interested in preserving their distinctive cultural and social qualities and meeting the particular economic needs of their province. This could only be accomplished if they could retain control over matters that would allow them to preserve their local character and institutions. Therefore, a unitary national state of any kind was out of the question, while a confederal union was appealing to Quebec and the Maritime provinces. He goes so far as to say that the use of the word "Confederation" to denote our federal system of government was purposely encouraged to "confuse those [such as the people of the Maritimes and Quebec] who might find such a project [a unitary state] alarming" (1987, p. 9).

What Is the Parliamentary System in Canada?

Constitutionally, there are three major levels of national government in Canada: the Queen, the Senate, and Parliament. However, the Queen has no powers to make laws in Canada, and the Senate, an appointed body, is a minor player in the lawmaking process. Therefore, only Parliament has the ultimate power to make law in Canada.

While Parliament makes the laws, there are limits to what Parliament can do. Parliament cannot make laws in areas reserved exclusively to the provinces. And, since 1982, Parliament's formal powers have been limited by the Charter of Rights and Freedoms.

Most Canadians, however, realize that the lion's share of the federal government's policymaking authority comes from the prime minister's office and the Cabinet. The power to spend money and to introduce tax legislation is limited to the Cabinet, while the prime minister has the exclusive power to open, postpone, and dissolve Parliament. Ultimately, it is the prime minister who wields the real power in Canada's federal government. He or she appoints the Cabinet, whose members become the heads of the various federal government departments such as Finance, Human Resources, Transportation, and so on.

The role of the opposition parties is basically adversarial. That is, during Question Period, they debate the government's policies and other, related matters. However, there are rules to follow, and all Members of Parliament must conduct themselves in an appropriate manner. The Speaker of the House presides over but is not permitted to participate in the debates in the House of Commons. In the 2002 House of Commons, the governing party was the Liberal Party and the opposition parties were: the Reform/Alliance Party as the Official Opposition, the Bloc Québécois, the New Democratic Party, and the Progressive Conservative Party.

Table 12.3 provides a chronology of all the prime ministers in Canada since Confederation; their political party affiliations, the dates they held office, and the lengths of their tenure as prime minister are also displayed. (The only woman prime minister in Canada's history has been Kim Campbell, whose short-lived status as the head of government in Canada came after Brian Mulroney left the post late in his second term of office as prime minister.)

Table 12.2 Voter Turnout at Federal Elections

Date of Election	Population	Number of Electors	Total Ballots Cast	Voter Turnout (%)
March 31, 1958	16 073 970	9 131 200	7 357 139	79.4
June 18, 1962	18 238 247	9 700 325	7 772 656	79.0
April 8, 1963	18 238 247	9 910 757	7 958 636	79.2
November 8, 1965	18 238 247	10 274 904	7 796 728	74.8
June 25, 1968	20 014 880	10 860 888	8 217 916	75.7
October 30, 1972	21 568 311	13 000 778	9 974 661	76.7
July 8, 1974	21 568 311	13 620 353	9 671 002	71.0
May 22, 1979	22 992 604	15 233 653	11 541 000	75.7
February 18, 1980	22 992 604	15 890 416	11 015 514	69.3
September 4, 1984	24 343 181	16 774 941	12 638 424	75.3
November 21, 1988	25 309 331	17 639 001	13 281 191	75.3
October 25, 1993	27 296 859	19 906 796	13 863 135	70.9
June 2, 1997	28 846 761	19 662 522	13 171 628	67.0
November 27, 2000	30 769 669	21 243 473	12 997 185	61.2

Source: Adapted from *A History of the Vote in Canada*, Elections Canada, 1997. Reproduced with the permission of the Minister of Public Works and Government Services, 2002, and courtesy of Elections Canada.

Table 12.3 Prime Ministers of Canada from Confederation to the Present

Prime Minister	Political Party	Dates in Office	Tenure
John A. Macdonald	Liberal-Conservative	1867–1873	
John A. Macdonald	Conservative	1878–1891	19 years
Alexander Mackenzie	Liberal	1873–1878	5 years
John Abbott	Conservative	1891–1892	1 year
John Thompson	Conservative	1892–1894	2 years
Mackenzie Bowell	Conservative	1894–1896	1 year
Charles Tupper	Conservative	1896	2 months
Wilfrid Laurier	Liberal	1896–1911	15 years
Robert Borden	Conservative	1911–1920	9 years
Arthur Meighen	Conservative	1920–1921	2 years
William Lyon Mackenzie King	Liberal	1921–1930	
William Lyon Mackenzie King	Liberal	1935–1948	22 years
R. B. Bennett	Conservative	1930–1935	5 years
Louis St. Laurent	Liberal	1948–1957	9 years
John Diefenbaker	P.C.	1957–1963	6 years
Lester Pearson	Liberal	1963–1968	5 years
Pierre Elliott Trudeau	Liberal	1968–1979	
Pierre Elliott Trudeau	Liberal	1980–1984	15 years
Joe Clark	P.C.	1979–1980	9 months
John Turner	Liberal	1984	2 months
Brian Mulroney	P.C.	1984–1993	9 years
Kim Campbell*	P.C.	1993	2 months
Jean Chrétien	Liberal	1993–present	—

*Canada's first woman prime minister.

The Evolution of the Political Party System in Canada: From the Two-Party to the Multiple-Party System

John A. Macdonald was Canada's first prime minister (1867–1873). He headed a coalition Conservative government made up of Ontario Tories and Quebec Liberals or *Bleus*, as they were called. His first term in office as head of this Liberal-Conservative coalition ended in scandal (the "Pacific Scandal"), when it was revealed he and a number of his colleagues had accepted large sums of money as kickbacks from the promoters of the Canadian Pacific Railway. By 1878, there were two political parties in Canada—the Conservatives and the Liberals.

Canada, in 1867, comprised only five provinces. In 1870 Manitoba was added, and in 1871 British Columbia. Alberta and Saskatchewan did not enter Confederation until 1905. As Canada was still in the process of nation-state building, the two-party system of the Liberals and the Conservatives dominated Canadian politics until well into the twentieth century.

The end of World War I (1914–1918) saw the emergence of a coalition of farmers' organizations based in Alberta but extending to Ontario that became known as the Progressive Movement. It was populist in ideology (i.e., grassroots democracy with regional agricultural-based policies) and had a short life nationally. However, the party continued to dominate western provincial governments until World War II. The end of the Progressive era in Canadian politics came when the Manitoba premier, John Bracken, moved to the federal Conservative party in 1942 on the condition that it change its name to the Progressive Conservative Party!

The demise of the Progressive movement in the West led to the dramatic election in the 1935 Alberta legislature of another grassroots, populist protest party known as Social Credit. Unlike the Progressive Movement, the Social Credit Party was able to achieve a beachhead in Quebec with its sister party known as the Ralliement des Créditistes under the leadership of Réal Caouette, a Rouyn-Noranda, Quebec, radio commentator. Except for a one-time electoral success of the Ralliement des Créditistes in the 1962 federal election (26 seats from rural Quebec), Social Credit remained a provincial party contender in Manitoba, Alberta, and British Columbia until the early 1970s when it disappeared for good from Canada's political landscape.

The CCF (Cooperative Commonwealth Federation), later the NDP (New Democratic Party), was founded by representatives from the cooperative movement, labour leaders, and academics in Regina, Saskatchewan, in 1933. The founding principles of the party are contained in the Regina Manifesto. The party remains Canada's national social democratic party. Its provincial strongholds are Saskatchewan, Manitoba, and British Columbia. While never achieving a majority in the House of Commons, the NDP did form a coalition government with the Liberals for two years from 1972–1974.

The Reform/Alliance Party is a recent addition to the House of Commons. Like the Progressive Movement and the Social Credit Party, the Reform/Alliance Party is a right-wing protest party that has its roots in Alberta. Preston Manning, the son of E. C. Manning, who had been the Social Credit Premier of Alberta for many years, used his political roots to help him on the road to founding the Reform/Alliance Party in 1987. Deborah Grey was the first elected Reform MP in March 1989. Today, the Canadian Alliance is the Official Opposition, and in January 2000 Preston Manning led the charge to establish a new coalition of right-wing supporters first under the leadership of Stockwell Day and now led by Stephen Harper.

Finally, first elected in 1990, the Bloc Québécois is the newest political party on the national scene in Canada. Its roots are exclusively in the province of Quebec. Unlike the Reform Party, the Bloc Québécois was formed from a coalition of dissident Quebec MPs who left the Liberal and Progressive Conservative parties. It upholds a social democratic platform of policies and is committed to increased sovereignty for Quebec. The party was initially led by Lucien Bouchard, the one-time Minister of the Environment in Brian Mulroney's Cabinet. Lucien Bouchard left the Bloc (now led by Gilles Duceppe) to become the leader of the Parti Québécois and the premier of Quebec.

The Structure of the Canadian Bureaucracy

Today, employees of the federal government who work for one of the ministries are called *public servants*. Under the 1967 *Public Service Employment Act*, public servants were allowed the right to bargain collectively with their employer. However, *public sector employees* in Canada are a much larger group, which includes both federal and provincial public servants and employees of Crown corporations, the military, and other nondepartmental agencies of the government. Taken together, all categories of public sector employees at all levels of government make up over 40 percent of the total labour force.

The *federal bureaucracy* comprises employees in the armed forces, the RCMP, the various government agencies, and the public service. At the federal level, the main categories of the bureaucracy are government departments, departmental corporations, Crown corporations, the Canadian Armed Forces (115 000 employees), and the RCMP (with 20 000 employees).

Quebec: The Social Basis for the Quiet Revolution and the Rise of the Sovereignty Movement

Politically, the Quiet Revolution in Quebec began with the death of Maurice Duplessis and his replacement by Paul Sauvé, his right-hand man in the Union Nationale Party. Premier Sauvé died after only a hundred days in office but began the process of modernization in the province. The election of the provincial Liberal Party under the leadership of Jean Lesage in 1960 carried forward the initiatives begun by Sauvé: the creation of professionally qualified jobs in the modernizing sectors of the health, education, and welfare bureaucracies of the provincial government and the eventual nationalization of the hydroelectric power companies under Hydro-Québec.

The social basis for the rapid expansion of the public sector in Quebec during the 1960s began with the industrialization of rural Quebec in the first half of the twentieth century. During this time, rural Quebec came under the pressure of a "demographic contradiction"; that is, there were too many people and not enough arable land to settle. Where was the surplus population to go? Some went to northern Quebec and northern Ontario to work in the mines; others went in search of work in Montreal and towns such as Drummondville that were springing up in the Eastern Townships; still others went to the New England states of Vermont, New York, and New Hampshire. And the only employment open to the children of rural farmers was labouring jobs in the factories owned by foreign or English Canadian capital.

Everett Hughes, in his classic study of the industrialization of rural Quebec entitled *French Canada in Transition* (1943), paints a graphic picture of what he calls an "ethnic division of labour" in which the bosses in the factories were all English-speaking and Protestant while the workers were all French-speaking and Catholic. Contrary to what one might expect, Hughes argued that it was not the rural Quebecois working class who had difficulty adapting to their new situation; it was, for example, the traditional Quebec middle class of lawyers and doctors who had the most difficulty. According to Hughes, so long as Quebec remained rural and agricultural, members of the small middle class could survive by passing on to their sons (and some daughters) the education and class privileges they themselves held. Industrialization changed all this because the workers' sons and daughters would soon require better education and would be able to compete for the small number of middle-class jobs once held by their class "betters." The only remedy for the situation was expanding the number of middle-class jobs available to the growing number of educated children of Quebec's working and middle classes. Modernizing and professionalizing the Quebec government bureaucracy was the only viable solution. Moreover, and equally important, these jobs in the public sector would ensure the continuation of the French language and culture (but not religion) in the decades subsequent to the Quiet Revolution. However, this was not an easy task, and it had to wait until Maurice Duplessis' death and the election of Jean Lesage and the provincial Liberal Party.

The Quiet Revolution gave hope to many Quebecois seeking to modernize their province through the expansion of health, education, and welfare bureaucracies while taking on other, more daring projects such as nationalizing the province's hydroelectric power companies. It unleashed a tidal wave of energy in the province that included the rise of the terrorist group known as the FLQ (Front de Libération du Québec) and the creation of the Parti Québécois.

By 1970, the bubble had burst with the FLQ kidnappings of James Cross, the British attaché in Montreal, and Pierre Laporte, the Minister of Labour in the ruling provincial Liberal Party. Prime Minister Trudeau invoked the *War Measures Act* in October 1970, the first time these extraordinary powers were used in peacetime.

This was an unsettling period for many Canadians both inside and outside Quebec. The fact that the kidnappers were found by means of conventional police methods strongly indicated to many that the invocation of the *War Measures Act* was at best an overreaction on the part of Pierre Trudeau and the federal Liberals, and at worst a disguised attempt to undermine the credibility of the Parti Québécois and the sovereignty movement in the province. In any event, the tide shifted back toward the sovereignty movement when, in 1976, the Parti Québécois was elected for the first time. One of the first pieces of legislation passed by the newly formed PQ government was Bill 101—"the language law."

Language at work had become a major political issue in Quebec before 1976. Starting with the Report of the Royal Commission on Bilingualism and Biculturalism in 1968, the stage was set for a lingering feud over language in Quebec that continues into the present. The passage of Bill 22 by the Liberal Party of Quebec in 1972 and Bill 101 by the Parti Québécois should have been a wake-up call to the rest of Canada, a reminder that language and culture are significant social issues that go beyond petty party politics.

What is the social basis for the politics of language in Quebec? For those of us in the rest of Canada to begin to understand, we need to set aside the complex political wrangling over the repatriation of the Constitution in 1982 and the "failures" of the Meech Lake Accord (1987) and the Charlottetown Accord (1992). Instead, we need to see the preservation of language and culture in Quebec as tied to "jobs." Speaking at work, not speaking at school, is the primary vehicle for sustaining a language and culture. It is at work that you constantly exercise your language, and it is at work that language and cultural experiences are shared and grow. Therefore, making French the language of work for everyone in Quebec makes sense to the majority who are French-speaking. On the other hand, the English-speaking minority recognizes the significance of work for language preservation and struggles against the majority's language bills.

Focus Question

Why are language and culture so important for many Quebecois?

This is the essence of the political strife in Quebec. The struggles over language in Quebec are just as much struggles over who get which jobs. In other words, the social basis of language and culture is a necessary starting point for all of us if we hope to achieve an understanding of the growing complexity of the politics of Quebec, either in or out of Canada. To bury our heads in the sand or to fall back on old and tired clichés will not resolve our difficulties as a maturing nation. We, as Canadians, need to begin an intelligent and reasonable discussion of the issues if we are to participate in their resolution.

A French-only sign in Quebec. The language debate has been escalating in that province since the Report of the Royal Commission on Bilingualism and Biculturalism in 1968.

Democratic Systems in Europe

We tend to take our political system for granted and assume that any other democracy looks like ours. Such is not the case. To achieve a comparative understanding, let us look at the European system.

Most European countries base their elections on a system of **proportional representation**; that is, the seats in the national legislature are divided according to the proportion of votes received by each political party. If one party wins 51 percent of the vote, for example, that party is awarded 51 percent of the seats; a party with 49 percent of the votes receives 49 percent of the seats.

Second, proportional representation encourages minority parties. The proportional representation followed in most European countries means that if a party gets 10 percent of the voters to support its candidate, it will get 10 percent of the seats. This system encourages the formation of **noncentrist parties**, those that propose less popular ideas.

Three main results follow from being able to win even just a few seats in the national legislature. First, if a minority party has officeholders, it gains access to the media throughout the year, receiving publicity that helps keep its issues alive. Second, because many parties compete in the elections, no single party is likely to gain a majority of the seats in the national legislature. To muster the required votes to make national decisions, the party with the most seats must align itself with one or more of the smaller parties and form a **coalition government**. A party with only 10 or 15 percent of the seats, then, may be able to trade its vote on some issues for the larger party's support on others. Third, because coalitions break down, the governments tend to be less stable. Italy, for example, has had 51 different governments since World War II, in contrast to the 10 prime ministers of Canada (see Table 12.3).

Who Rules Canada?

The Functionalist Perspective: Pluralism

Functionalists view the state as having arisen out of the basic needs of the social group. People must perform a balancing act between having no government—which would lead to what functionalists view as **anarchy**, a state in which disorder and violence reign—and having a government to protect them from violence, but that may itself turn against them. When functioning well, then, the state is a balanced system that protects its citizens—from one another *and* from government.

Functionalists say that **pluralism**, a diffusion of power among many interest groups, prevents any one group from gaining control of the government and using it to oppress the people (Polsby, 1959; Huber & Form, 1973; Dahl, 1961, 1982).

From the functionalist perspective, ethnic groups, women, men, farmers, the unemployed, and the retired are all parts of our pluralist society. As special-interest groups

such as women or the disabled negotiate with one another and reach compromises, conflict is minimized, and the resulting policies gain wide support. In other words, the Canadian government functions like a healthy human body.

The Conflict Perspective: Power Elite/Ruling Class

Conflict theorists come up with a different answer. The important question is who holds the power that determines the overarching policies for Canada. For example, who determines how many Canadians will be out of work by raising or lowering interest rates? Who sets policies that transfer jobs from Canada to the United States or countries with low-cost labour? And the ultimate question of power: Who is behind decisions to go to war?

C. Wright Mills (1956) took the position that the decisions that have the greatest impact on the lives not only of Americans—but of Canadians and people across the face of the globe—are made by a coalition of individuals whose interests coincide and who have access to the centre of political power in the United States. Mills called them the **power elite**. As depicted in Figure 12.1, the power elite consists of the top leaders of the largest corporations, the most powerful generals and admirals of the armed forces, and certain elite politicians. It is they who wield power, who make the decisions that direct the country—and shake the world (Hellinger & Judd, 1991; Ferguson, 1995).

Conflict theorists point out that we should not think of the ruling class as a group that meets together and agrees on specific matters. Their behaviour stems not from some grand conspiracy to control the country, but rather from mutual interests in solving problems that face large businesses (Useem, 1984). It consists of people whose backgrounds and orientations to life are so similar—they attend prestigious private schools, belong to exclusive private clubs, and are millionaires many times over—that they automatically share the same values and goals.

As has been mentioned in other chapters, in *The Vertical Mosaic* (1965) John Porter identified several elites in Canadian society, not just the industrial-military complex identified by C. Wright Mills for the United States. In addition to the economic elite, he identified elites in the media, religion, organized labour, and the political sector of Canadian society.

The common characteristics discovered by Porter were similar to those found by C. Wright Mills. The Canadian economic elite, for example, attended similar if not the same private schools and completed their education at the "right" universities. British Protestants (primarily Anglican) still dominate, with very few French-Canadians, Jews, or Catholics. The members of the economic elite attend the same social (private) clubs and recruit one another to serve on various boards of directors.

Wallace Clement's (1975, 1977, 1983) studies classified three components of Canada's corporate elite: a Canadian

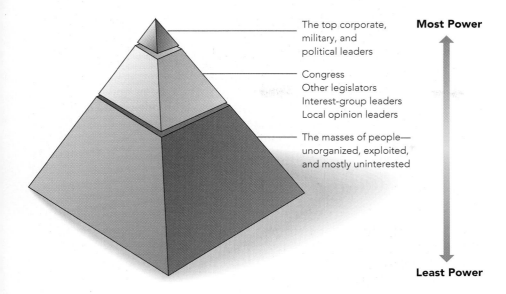

The top corporate, military, and political leaders

Congress
Other legislators
Interest-group leaders
Local opinion leaders

The masses of people—unorganized, exploited, and mostly uninterested

Most Power

Least Power

Figure 12.1 Power in the United States: The Model Proposed by C. Wright Mills

Source: Based on Mills (1956).

component based mainly in banking, insurance, and other related financial institutions; a foreign (mainly U.S.) component that predominates in the manufacturing and natural resource sectors of the economy; and a component Clement calls a *comprador* elite: native-born directors and senior managers of foreign-controlled corporations operating in Canada.

Dennis Olsen (1980), another graduate student of John Porter's, studied the Canadian state elite. While Olsen discovered that members of the federal bureaucratic elite (judges, politicians, and senior federal and provincial bureaucrats such as deputy ministers) were more open to recruitment and were a much larger group than the economic elite, most came from middle-class backgrounds and were channelled to executive positions through "acceptable" bureaucratic means; they were able to stay in regular contact through what Olsen calls "executive federalism."

Unfortunately, very little recent research has been carried out to investigate the changing social characteristics of Canada's political elites.

The Feminist Perspectives: Gender Reform, Resistance, and Rebellion

Current feminist theorizing about the nature of gender inequality is linked to whether the theorists would seek reform from the present system, or struggle to achieve some fundamental change. That is, the main reasons given for women having a lesser social status and fewer advantages than men of similar education, class background, race/ethnicity, and religion lead to proposed solutions or remedies, including political ones. Proponents of liberal feminism, for example, hold the current system of democratic government as legitimate. They have been instrumental in making visible the pervasiveness of overt discrimination. The solutions they have proposed such as pay and employment equity in

Canada and Affirmative Action in the United States have sparked debate and discussion.

Employment Equity. Since the 1970s, the Canadian government has attempted to change the manner by which employees are recruited into the federal bureaucracy. The major policy initiative has been employment equity, or recruitment targeting the designated groups of women, Aboriginal people, visible minorities, and the physically disabled. Table 12.4 provides a portrait of the "success" of this policy at the "executive category" level.

Clearly, women have made important strides over the short period from the early 1990s to the present, though women remain underrepresented at the "executive level." Aboriginal numbers remain small, at only 2 percent, and visible minorities have made only small advances, holding just 3.4 percent of executive-level positions in 2001.

In addition, the number of jobs at this level is decreasing, from a high of 4155 in 1993 to a low of 3421 in 1999,

Table 12.4 Employment Equity at the "Executive Category" Level in the Federal Civil Service

Executive Employment Category	1993		1999		2001	
	Number	%	Number	%	Number	%
Women	731	17.6	919	26.9	1057	30
Aboriginal people	44	1.1	64	1.9	70	2
People with disabilities	81	1.9	101	3.0	125	3.5
Visible minority	N/A	—	103	3.0	118	3.4
Total executive category	**4155**		**3421**		**3522**	

Source: Adapted from Treasury Board of Canada, Employment Equity in the Federal Public Service—Annual Report, Ottawa, Communications and Coordination Directorate, 1994–present.

a drop of nearly 20 percent in six years. The number rose somewhat between 1999 and 2001, although it is still 15 percent lower than in 1993. The difficulties this decrease in employment poses to those who seek greater equality in the federal public service have yet to be determined.

Gender resistance feminisms such as radical and lesbian feminisms claim that the gender order cannot be made gender-neutral by seeking legislative changes. Instead, these feminists propose a woman-centred society and seek to create a women-oriented culture, ethics, and even religion. Finally, gender rebellion feminisms such as multiracial and postmodern and queer theory attack the gender order directly by undermining the boundaries that separate men from women, male from female, and homosexual from heterosexual. Using the language of postmodernism, these feminists deconstruct the categories of sex, sexuality, and gender and thereby undermine the legitimacy of favouring one group over another.

War and Terrorism: A Means to Implement Political Objectives

As we have noted, an essential characteristic of the state is that it claims a monopoly on violence. **War**, armed conflict between nations or politically distinct groups, is often part of national policy.

Is War Universal?

War is simply one option that groups may choose for dealing with disagreements; but not all societies choose this option. The Mission Indians of North America, the Arunta of Australia, the Andaman Islanders of the South Pacific, and the Inuit of the Arctic, for example, had procedures to handle aggression and quarrels, but they did not have organized battles that pitted one tribe or group against another. These groups do not even have a word for war (Lesser, 1968).

During war, countries harness their most advanced technology in the attempt to destroy their enemies. Shown here in a classic photo from World War II is a B-26 Marauder dropping 26 bombs on Nazi installations in France.

Why Nations Go to War

Sociologist Nicholas Timasheff (1965) identified three essential conditions of war. The first is a cultural tradition of war. Because their nation has fought wars in the past, the leaders of a group see war as an option for dealing with serious disagreements with other nations. The second is an antagonistic situation in which two or more states confront incompatible objectives. For example, each may want the same land or resources. The third is a "fuel" that heats the antagonistic situation to a boiling point, so that people cross the line from thinking about war to actually engaging in it.

Timasheff found that war is likely if a country's leaders see the antagonistic situation as an opportunity to achieve one of the following objectives:

1. To exact revenge or settle "old scores" from previous conflicts.

2. To dictate their will to a weaker nation.

3. To enhance the nation's prestige or save the nation's "honour."

4. To unite rival groups within their country.

5. To protect or exalt their own position.

6. To satisfy the national aspirations of ethnic groups, bringing under their rule "our people" who are living in another country.

7. To forcibly convert others to religious and ideological beliefs.

> ### Focus Question
> Which countries are the "chief merchants of death"?

Sowing the Seeds of Future Wars

With incredible hypocrisy, the most industrialized nations lament the regional conflicts that can escalate into larger wars while zealously pursuing profits by selling advanced war technology to the least industrialized nations. When one least industrialized nation buys high-tech weapons, its neighbours get nervous, sparking an arms race among them (Cole & Lubman, 1994; Ricks, 1994).

Table 12.5 shows that the United States is the chief merchant of death even though the Cold War is over and it can no longer claim the "communist threat" as a reason for arming the free world. The seeds of future wars are also sown by nuclear proliferation, and several least industrialized nations such as India, Pakistan, and China now have nuclear weapons. Always a threat to the world's safety, these weapons in the hands of a dictator can mean blackmail or attack to settle personal or nationalistic grudges.

Table 12.5 The Business of Death

The Five Largest Arms Dealers, 1999*	
United States	$23.5 billion
Great Britain	$6.1 billion
France	$3.2 billion
Germany	$0.8 billion
China	$0.6 billion
The 10 Largest Arms Consumers	
Saudi Arabia	$9.8 billion
Japan	$2.4 billion
Egypt	$1.8 billion
Kuwait	$1.7 billion
Great Britain	$1.5 billion
Turkey	$1.4 billion
Australia	$1.3 billion
United States	$1.1 billion
South Korea	$1.1 billion
Israel	$0.9 billion

*Russia used to be listed in the source as a top exporter of arms, but it no longer appears on this list. Either Russia no longer exports many arms, or it is excluded for some other reason.

Source: *Statistical Abstract*, 1999, Table 582.

Terrorism

With hatreds fanned through the generations, a continuing danger is terrorism directed against a civilian population.

One of the few options open to a weaker group looking to retaliate against a powerful country for its suppression is "suicide terrorism"—which usually involves bombs capable of blowing up only a few people at a time. However, as we witnessed on September 11, 2001, suicide terrorism can also strike on a grander scale, killing thousands.

War and Dehumanization

Proud of his techniques, the U.S. trainer was demonstrating to the South American soldiers how to torture a prisoner. As the victim screamed in anguish, the trainer was interrupted by a phone call from his wife. His students could hear him say, "A dinner and a movie sound nice. I'll see you right after work." Hanging up the phone, he then continued the lesson. (Stockwell, 1989)

War exacts many costs in addition to killing people and destroying property. One is its effect on morality. Exposure to brutality and killing often causes **dehumanization**, the process of reducing people to objects that do not deserve to be treated as humans.

As we review findings on dehumanization and see how it breeds callousness and cruelty, perhaps we can better understand how O'Brien in the opening vignette could have unleashed rats into someone's face. Consider the four characterizations of dehumanization (Bernard, Ottenberg, & Redl, 1971):

1. *Increased emotional distance from others.* Instead of people, they are seen as subhuman, "the enemy," or objects of some sort.

War takes many forms, only one of which is armed conflict officially declared between countries. More common is terrorism. This particular example is from Algiers, the capital of Algeria, but it might as well be from Ireland, Angola, Sri Lanka, India, Pakistan, Israel, Paris, Madrid, and so on.

Cultural Diversity Around the World: The Rise of
Nationalism Versus the Globalization of Capitalism—
Implications for a New World Order

The world has about 5000 nations. What makes each a *nation* is that its people share a language, culture, territory, and political organization. A *state*, in contrast, claims a monopoly on violence over a territory. A state may contain many nations. The Kayapo Indians are but one nation within the state called Brazil. The Chippewa and Sioux are two nations within the state called the United States and, to some, Quebec is a nation within Canada. To nation peoples, group identity transcends political affiliation. The world's nations have existed for hundreds, some even for thousands, of years. In contrast, most of the world's 194 states have been around only since World War II.

Most modern states are empires, and they are increasingly seen as such by the nations that have been incorporated into them—usually by conquest. Some states have far better records than others, but overall, no ideology, left or right, religious or sectarian, has protected nations or promoted pluralism much better or worse than any other. In fact, the twentieth century has probably seen more genocides and ethnocides (the destruction of an ethnic group) than any other.

Clearly, the Palestinians who live within Israel's borders will not soon identify themselves as Israelis. The 22 million Kurds don't consider themselves first and foremost Turks, Iranians, Iraqis, or Syrians. There are about 130 nations in the former USSR, 180 in Brazil, 90 in Ethiopia, 450 in Nigeria, 350 in India. That so many nations are squeezed into

Nourished by family, centuries-old hatreds are passed from one generation to the next. To avenge wrongs and kill "the enemy" becomes a duty, a righteous calling, inherited with one's language, the air one breathes, the dreams of one's people.

so few states is, in fact, the nub of the problem.

In most states, power is in the hands of a few elites, who operate by a simple credo: winner take all. They control foreign investment and aid, and use both to reinforce their power. They set local commodity prices, control exports, levy taxes—and buy the weapons. They confiscate the resources of the nations, whether it be Indian land in North and South America or oil from the Kurds in Iraq. When nations resist, the result is open conflict.

About half of the debt of the least industrialized states and nearly all debt in Africa comes from the purchase of weapons for states to fight their own citizens. Most of the world's 12 million refugees are the offspring of such conflicts, as are most of the 100 million internally displaced people who have

been uprooted from their homelands.

A vicious cycle forms. The appropriation of a nation's resources leads to conflict, conflict leads to weapons purchases, weapons purchases lead to debt, and debt leads to the appropriation of more resources. This self-feeding cycle helps ensure the cooperation of the elites of the least industrialized states as the most industrialized states divide the globe's resources among themselves.

The fly in the ointment in the march to the "new world order" is the appearance of fierce **nationalism**—identity with and loyalty to a nation. Nationalism, with its loyalty to small groups, threatens to undermine the developing new order. Based on nationalism, the shooting wars increase—fought over issues, grudges, and animosities rooted in long history, only faintly understood by those who are not a party to the events but vividly alive in the folklore and collective memory of these nations. These wars threaten the yet fragile coalitions of the powerful states that are dividing up the world's resources.

Currently, then, we witness an oppositional struggle: nationalism versus the formation of global coalitions. We are likely to see many more seemingly contradictory fruits of these two forces: the globe divided into huge regional trading blocs controlled by the most industrialized states, matched by the simultaneous outbreak of small-scale shooting wars as nations struggle for independence.

Sources: Clay (1990); Kanter (1995); Ohmae (1995); Jáuregui (1996); Marcus (1996).

2. *An emphasis on following procedures.* People are likely to say, "I don't like doing this, but it is necessary to follow procedures," or "We all have to die some day. What difference does it make if these people die now?"

3. *Inability to resist pressures.* Fears of losing one's job, losing the respect of one's peers, or having one's integrity and loyalty questioned take precedence over individual moral decisions.

4. *A diminished sense of personal responsibility.* People see themselves as not responsible for what they do, because they are simply following orders.

A Vietnam vet who read this section remarked, "You missed the major one we used. We killed kids. Our dehumanizing technique was a saying: 'The little ones are the soldiers of tomorrow.'"

As sociologist Tamotsu Shibutani (1970) stressed, dehumanization is helped along by the tendency for prolonged conflicts to be transformed into a struggle between good and evil. The enemy, of course, represents evil in the equation. Dehumanization does not always insulate the self from guilt, however, and its failure to do so can bring severe personal consequences. During the war, while soldiers are surrounded by army buddies who agree that the enemy is less than human and deserves inhuman treatment, such definitions ordinarily remain intact. After returning home, however, the dehumanizing definitions more easily break down. Many soldiers then find themselves seriously disturbed by what they did during the war. Although most eventually adjust, some cannot.

A New World Order?

The globalization of capitalism, accompanied by the worldwide flow of information, capital, and goods discussed in the previous chapter, is little affected by national boundaries. The United States, Canada, and Mexico have formed a North American Free Trade Association, to which all of South America will eventually belong. Most European countries have formed an economic and political unit (the European Union) that supersedes their national boundaries. Similarly, the United Nations, transcending national borders and moderating disputes between countries, can authorize the use of international force against individual nations—as it has done against North Korea in 1950, Iraq in 1990, and on a smaller scale Somalia in 1993 and Bosnia in 1994 and 1997.

Will this process continue until there is but one state or empire that envelops the earth itself? This is a possibility. Set against it is the demand for self-determination and self-government from nations within the bosom of states in the developed part of the world. Examples include Scottish and Quebec independence, the Palestinians, Aboriginals, and so on. And as borders shift, as occurred with the breakup of the Soviet Union, previously unincorporated nations such as Lithuania and Azerbaijan demand their independence and the right to full statehood. The Perspectives box here explores this rising tension between nations and states.

If global political and economic unity does come about, it is fascinating to speculate on what type of government will result. If Hitler had had his way, his conquests would have resulted in world domination—by a world dictator and a world totalitarian regime based on racial identification. If a world order does emerge from current trends—that's a big "if"—the potential for human welfare is tremendous.

Summary and Review

MICROPOLITICS AND MACROPOLITICS

What is the difference between micropolitics and macropolitics?

The essential nature of politics is **power**, and every group is political. The term **micropolitics** refers to the exercise of power in everyday life, **macropolitics** to large-scale power, such as governing a nation. p. 284.

POWER, AUTHORITY, AND VIOLENCE

How are authority and coercion related to power?

Authority is power that people view as legitimately exercised over them, while **coercion** is power they consider unjust. The **state** is a political entity that claims a monopoly on violence over a particular territory. If enough people consider a state's power illegitimate, **revolution** is possible. pp. 284–285.

What kinds of authority are there?

Max Weber identified three types of authority. Power in **traditional authority** derives from custom—patterns set down in the past serve as rules for the present. Power in **rational-legal authority** (also called *bureaucratic authority*) is based on law and written procedures. In **charismatic authority**, power is based on loyalty to an individual to whom people are attracted. Charismatic authority, which undermines traditional and rational-legal authority, has built-in problems in transferring authority to a new leader. pp. 285–288.

TYPES OF GOVERNMENT

How are the types of government related to power?

In a **monarchy**, power is based on hereditary rule; in a **democracy**, power is given to the ruler by citizens; and in a **dictatorship**, power is seized by an individual or small group. pp. 288–289.

THE CANADIAN POLITICAL SYSTEM

What are the main characteristics of the Canadian political system?

Canada is a federal state with a parliamentary democracy. Sometimes, though rarely, Canada's parliamentary system can have a **coalition government** that is unlike the "winner take all" system of the United States. Most European democracies have **proportional representation** with legislative seats divided among political parties according to the percentage of votes each receives. If no single party wins a majority of votes, proportional representation creates the need for a coalition government. pp. 289–290.

What political parties are there at present in the House of Commons?

The Liberal Party, the Reform/Alliance Party, the Bloc Québécois, the New Democratic Party, and the Progressive Conservative Party. pp. 291–292.

What is at the root of the political strife in Quebec politics?

We need to see the preservation of language and culture in Quebec as tied to "jobs." Speaking at work is the primary vehicle for sustaining a language and culture. It is at work that you constantly exercise your language, and it is at work that language and cultural experiences are shared and grow. This is the essence of the political strife in Quebec. pp. 292–294.

WHO RULES CANADA?

Is Canada controlled by a ruling class?

In a view known as **pluralism**, functionalists say that no one group holds power, that the country's many competing interest groups balance one another. Conflict theorists, who focus on the top level of power, say that Canada is governed by a **power elite**, a ruling class made up of the top corporate, military, and political leaders. In Canada, John Porter, Wallace Clement, and Dennis Olsen describe Canada's power elites. Feminst perspectives include liberal feminism, which seeks to fight overt discrimination from within the system by winning such legislative advances as employment equity, and radical forms of feminism that believe change must be much more fundamental. pp. 294–295.

How successful has employment equity been as a federal public policy?

Clearly, women have made important strides over the short period from the early 1990s to the present, though women remain underrepresented at the "executive level." Visible minorities, on the other hand, have made the smallest advance. pp. 295–296.

WAR AND TERRORISM: A MEANS TO IMPLEMENT POLITICAL OBJECTIVES

How is war related to politics, and what are its costs?

War, common in human history, is a means of attempting to reach political objectives. The least industrialized nations, which can least afford it, spend huge amounts on technologically advanced weapons. Another cost is **dehumanization**, whereby people no longer see others as worthy of human treatment. pp. 296–299.

A NEW WORLD ORDER?

Is humanity headed toward a one-world political order?

The global expansion of communications, transportation, and trade; the widespread adoption of capitalism and the retreat of socialism; and the trend toward larger political unions may indicate that a world political system is developing. The oppositional trend is a fierce **nationalism**. If a new world order develops, the possible consequences for human welfare range from excellent to calamitous. p. 299.

Critical Thinking Questions

1. According to Max Weber, the state is an organization with a monopoly on the legitimate use of violence. In a democracy, what other forms of power are there for citizens to express their point of view?

2. Some sociologists point out that democracy as a form of government and capitalism as an economic system are two sides of the same coin. Is it true that democracy and capitalism are directly related?

3. The democratic institutions we have inherited in Canada are apparently unable to resolve some of the political demands being made by Quebec nationalists. Is Quebec sovereignty inevitable? Can you think of any public policy alternatives to the present dilemma, or do we need to completely change the way we practise politics in Canada?

Key Terms

anarchy 294
authority 284
charismatic authority 286
citizenship 288
city-states 288
coalition government 294
coercion 284
confederal union 289
dehumanization 297
democracy 288
dictatorship 288
direct democracy 288
macropolitics 284
micropolitics 284
monarchy 288
nationalism 298
noncentrist party 294

oligarchy 288
pluralism 294
power 284
power elite 294
proportional representation 294
rational-legal authority 286
representative democracy 288
revolution 284
routinization of charisma 288
state 285
totalitarianism 288
traditional authority 285
unitary state 289
universal citizenship 288
war 296

Weblinks

All URLs listed are current as of the printing of this book. URLs are often changed. Please check our Web site **www.abacon.com/henslin** for updates.

Anarchy Archives

dwardmac.pitzer.edu/Anarchist_Archives/
The goals of this archive are to provide at one site the collected works of the major anarchists and an online history of anarchists and anarchist movements worldwide.

The MoJo Wire: Daily News and Resources for the Skeptical Citizen

www.mojones.com/
Mother Jones is a magazine of investigation and ideas for independent thinkers. Provocative and unexpected articles inform readers and inspire action toward positive social change.

Canadian Political Parties

home.ican.net/~alexng/can.html

A comprehensive array of links to parties and to other indexes. Highly recommended.

Political Science: A Net Station

www.library.ubc.ca/poli/cpweb.html

A starting point for researchers working their way through cyberspace, enabling them to quickly locate interesting sites of information on Canadian politics, government, public policy, foreign relations, etc.

The Family: Initiation into Society

Learning Outcomes

After you have studied this chapter, you will be able to

■ explain why the question of "what is a family" is much more complex than we might think

■ understand the important features of family life from the very different and sometimes opposing theoretical orientations of the functionalist, conflict (in particular feminist), and symbolic interactionist approaches to sociology

■ explain patterns within the diversity of family life experiences—for example, how social class generally affects them

■ appreciate the variety of family forms in Canada, and important changes that are taking place

■ understand the problems of abuse, battering, rape, and incest faced by children and women

■ be aware of the ingredients for a good marriage

"Hold still. We're going to be late," said Samira as she tried to put shoes on two-year-old Kabir, who kept squirming away.

Finally succeeding with the shoes, Samira turned to four-year-old Sasha, who was trying to pull a brush through her hair. "It's stuck, Mom," Sasha said.

"Well, no wonder. Just how did you get gum in your hair? I don't have time for this, Sasha. We've got to leave."

Getting to the van 15 minutes behind schedule, Samira strapped the kids in, and then herself. Just as she was about to pull away, she remembered that she had not checked the fridge for messages.

"Just a minute, kids. I'll be right back."

Running into the house, she frantically searched for a message from Mohammed. She vaguely remembered him mumbling something about being held over at work. She grabbed the Post-It and ran back to the van.

"He's picking on me," complained Sasha when her mother climbed back in.

"Oh, shut up, Sasha," Samira said. "He's only two. He can't pick on you."

"Yes, he did," Sasha said, crossing her arms defiantly, as she stretched out her foot to kick her brother's seat.

"Oh, no! How did Kabir get that smudge on his face? Did you do that, Sasha?"

Sasha crossed her arms again, pushing out her lips in her classic pouting pose.

As Samira drove to the day-care centre, she tried to calm herself. "Only two more days of work this week, and then the weekend. Then I can catch up on housework and have a little relaxed time with the kids. And Mohammed can finally cut the lawn and buy the groceries," she thought. "And maybe we'll even have time to make love. Boy, that's been a long time."

At a traffic light, Samira found time to read Mohammed's note. "Oh, no. That's what he meant. He has to work Saturday. Well, there go those plans."

What Samira didn't know was that her mother-in-law also had made plans for Samira's Saturday. And that the van would break down on the way home from work. And that Kabir was coming down with chicken pox. And that Sasha would follow next. And that …

That there isn't enough time to get everything done is a common complaint of most of us. But it is especially true for working parents of young children who find themselves without the support services taken for granted just a generation ago: stay-at-home moms who were the centre of the neighbourhood, a husband whose sole income was enough to support a wife and several children, a safe neighbourhood where even small children could play outside, even a grandma who could pitch in during emergencies.

Those days are gone forever. Today, more and more families are like Samira and Mohammed's. They are harried, pressured, working more and seemingly making less, and, certainly, having less time for one another—and for their children. In this chapter, we shall try to understand what is happening to the Canadian family and families worldwide.

Marriage and Family in Global Perspective

To better understand Canadian patterns of marriage and family, let's first sketch a cross-cultural portrait. The perspective it yields will give us a context for interpreting our own experience in this vital social institution.

Defining Family

"What is a family, anyway?" asked William Sayres (1992) at the beginning of an article on this topic. By this question, he meant that although the family is so significant to humanity that it is universal—every human group in the world organizes its members in families—the world's cultures display so much variety that the term *family* is difficult to define. For example, although the Western world long assumed a family consisted of a husband, wife, and children, other groups have family forms in which men have more than one wife (**polygyny**) or women more than one husband (**polyandry**).

To try to define the family as the approved group into which children are born overlooks the Banaro of New Guinea. Among this group a young woman must give birth before she can marry, and she cannot marry the father of her child (Murdock, 1949).

And so it goes. For just about every element you might consider essential to marriage or family, some group has a different custom. Even the sex of the bride and groom may not be what you expect. Although in almost every instance the bride and groom are female and male, there are exceptions, rare though they may be. In some Native American tribes, for example, a man or woman who wanted to be a member of

Often one of the strongest family bonds is that of mother-daughter. The young artist, an eleventh-grader, wrote, "This painting expresses the way I feel about my future with my child. I want my child to be happy and I want her to love me the same way I love her. In that way we will have a good relationship so that nobody will be able to take us apart. I wanted this picture to be alive; that is why I used a lot of bright colours."

the opposite sex went through a ceremony (*berdache*) and was *declared* to be of that sex. From then on, the "new" man or woman not only did the tasks associated with that sex, but also was allowed to marry—in which case the husband and wife were of the same biological sex. In the contemporary Western world, Denmark, Holland, Norway, and Sweden have legalized same-sex marriages, and in Canada there are vigorous campaigns to follow suit (Thompson, 2002).

Even to say that the family is the unit in which children are disciplined and their parents are responsible for their material needs is not universally true. Among the Trobriand Islanders, the wife's eldest brother is responsible for making certain that his sister's children are fed and are properly disciplined when they get out of line (Malinowski, 1927). Finally, even sexual relationships don't universally characterize a husband and wife. The Nayar of Malabar never allow a bride and groom to have sex. After a three-day celebration of the marriage, they send the groom packing—and never *allow* him to see his bride again (La Barre, 1954). (In case you are wondering, the groom comes from another tribe, and Nayar women are allowed to have sex, but only with approved lovers—who can never be the husband. This system keeps family property intact—along matrilineal lines.)

Focus Question

What might the following families have in common: a refugee family, recently arrived from Pakistan, living in downtown Toronto; a single-parent Native family living in Northern Alberta; and a childless gay couple living in a Victoria retirement community?

Common Cultural Themes

In spite of this diversity, several common themes do run through marriage and family. Table 13.1 illustrates the ways in which traditional and industrial/postindustrial societies typically pattern mate selection, descent, inheritance, and family authority.

These patterns, however, are situated in history, which means they are also changing. Modern Egypt, by most standards a traditional country, recently revolutionized its divorce laws by allowing women to seek a unilateral, no-questions-asked divorce (United Nations Population Fund, 2000, p. 55).

Norms of Mate Selection. Every human group establishes formal or informal norms to govern who marries whom. Norms of **endogamy** specify that people should marry within their own group. Groups may prohibit interracial marriages, for example. In contrast, norms of **exogamy** specify that people must marry outside their group. The best example is the *incest taboo*, which prohibits sex and marriage between designated relatives. Even when informal, these norms are powerful. For example, in North America most people marry within their own "racial" and social class groups.

Reckoning Patterns of Descent. How are you related to your father's father or your mother's mother? The explanation is found in your society's **system of descent**, the way people trace kinship over generations. To us, a **bilateral** system seems logical—and natural—for we think of ourselves as related to both our mother's and our father's side of the family. "Doesn't everyone?" you might ask. Interestingly, this is only one logical way to reckon descent. In a **patrilineal** system, descent is traced only on the father's side, and children are not considered related to their mother's relatives. In a **matrilineal** system, descent is figured only on the mother's side, and children are not considered related to their father's relatives.

Rights of Inheritance. Marriage and family—in whatever form is customary in a society—are also used to compute rights of inheritance. In the bilateral system, property is passed to both males and females, in the patrilineal system only to males, and in the matrilineal system (the rarest form) only to females. Each system matches a people's ideas of justice and logic.

Patterns of Authority. Historically, some form of **patriarchy**, a social system in which men dominate women, has formed a thread running through all societies. As noted in Chapter 7, there are no historical records of a true **matriarchy**, a social system in which women as a group dominate men as a group. Our marriage and family customs, then, developed within a framework of patriarchy. Although Canadian family patterns are becoming more **egalitarian**, or equal, many customs practised today point up their patriarchal origin. Naming patterns, for example, reflect patriarchy.

Table 13.1 Common Cultural Themes: Marriage in Traditional and Industrial Societies

Characteristic	Traditional Societies	Industrial (and Postindustrial) Societies
What is the structure of marriage?	*Extended* (marriage embeds spouses in a large kinship network of explicit obligations)	*Nuclear* (marriage brings fewer obligations toward the spouse's kin)
What are the functions of marriage?	Economic production, socialization, care of the sick and aged, recreation, sexual control, and reproduction	More limited (many traditional social functions are fulfilled by other institutions)
Who holds authority?	Highly *patriarchal* (authority is held by males)	Although some patriarchal features remain, authority is more evenly divided
How many spouses at one time?	Most have one spouse (*monogamy*), while some have several (*polygamy*)	One spouse
Who selects the spouse?	The parents, usually the father	Individuals choose their own spouse
Where does the couple live?	Most commonly with the groom's family (*patrilocal residence*), less commonly with the bride's family (*matrilocal residence*)	In a new home (*neolocal residence*)
How is descent figured?	Most commonly from male ancestors (*patrilineal kinship*); less commonly from female ancestors (*matrilineal kinship*)	From male and female ancestors equally (*bilateral kinship*)
How is inheritance figured?	Rigid system of rules; usually patrilineal, but may be matrilineal	Highly individualistic; usually bilateral

In spite of recent trends, the typical bride (outside the province of Quebec) still takes the groom's last name; children, too, are usually given the father's last name (Arichi, 1999). For information on a society that systematically promotes equality in marriage, see the Perspectives box here.

Focus Question

What are some of the fundamental differences in family life as it is lived around the globe?

Perspectives

Cultural Diversity Around the World: Family Life in Sweden

Swedish lawmakers hold a strong image of what good family life is. That image is of total equality in marriage and the welfare of children. They bolster this image with laws designed to put women and men on equal footing in marriage, to have mothers and fathers share responsibility for the home and children, and to protect the financially weaker party in the event of divorce.

At the centre of family laws is the welfare of children. Health care for mothers and children, for example, is free. This includes all obstetric care and all health care during pregnancy. Maternity centres offer free health checks and courses in preparation for childbirth. Fathers are encouraged to attend the childbirth classes.

When a child is born, the parents are eligible for 15 months' leave of absence with pay. The leave and compensation are available for either or both parents. Both cannot receive compensation at the same time, and the parents decide how they will split the leave between them. For the first 12 months the state pays 90 percent of gross income, and then a generous fixed rate for the remaining three months. The paid leave does not have to be taken all at once, but can be spread over eight years. The parents can stay at home full-time, or they can work part-time for a longer period. Because most mothers take all the leave, the law now includes a "father's month," one month that cannot be transferred to the mother.

Local governments are required to provide free counselling to any parent who requests it. If both parties agree and if they have no children under the age of 16, a couple is automatically entitled to a divorce. Otherwise the law requires a six-month cooling-off period, so the couple can more calmly consider what is best for their children. Joint custody of children is automatic, unless one of the parents opposes it. The children may live only with one of the parents. The parent who does not live with the children is required to pay child support in proportion to his or her finances. If the parent fails to do so, the social security system makes the payments.

For Your Consideration

How does the Swedish system compare with that of Canada? What "system" for watching out for the welfare of children does Canada have, anyway?

Source: Based on The Swedish Institute (1992); Froman (1994).

Definitions of the Family: The Problem of the Monolithic Bias

Social researchers have tended to downplay the amazing diversity in family life and to focus on common cultural themes. As a result, they are able to arrive at a very broad definition of the **family** as two or more people who consider themselves related by blood, marriage, or adoption. A **household**, in contrast, consists of all people who occupy the same housing unit—a house, apartment, or other living quarters. Within these broad categories, some sociologists then classify families as **nuclear** (husband, wife, and children) and **extended** (including people such as grandparents, aunts, uncles, and cousins in addition to the nuclear unit). Sociologists also refer to the **family of orientation** (the family in which an individual grows up) and the **family of procreation** (the family formed when a couple have their first child). Finally, regardless of its form, **marriage** can be viewed as a group's approved mating arrangements—usually marked out by a ritual of some sort (the wedding) to indicate the couple's new public status.

While it is important to be aware of this terminology in the sociology of the family literature, it is also crucial to realize that many Canadian sociologists have explicitly rejected this approach to the family as a **monolithic structure**. In particular, noted Canadian sociologist Margrit Eichler has developed an extensive critique of this approach to family studies (1988a, 1997). As she suggests, the popular definition of the nuclear family appears to support a very limited view of family life. If we assume that all or most families include a mother and a father who are married to one another, who live together, and who have biological children who reside with them, we are of course ignoring the hundreds of thousands of Canadians who live in single-parent families, or who do not have children, or do not have children living at home, or have stepchildren, or have adopted children, or are working so that their children can join them as immigrants to Canada (Thomas, 2001). We would also tend to overlook in our research gay and lesbian families, families in which the couple are joined by common-law marriage, families in which the partners live apart for significant periods of time (immigrating families, commuting couples, truck drivers, military personnel), and adults and children who are residing not with family but in institutional settings (prisons, group homes, hospitals, and so on). Indeed, the list of exceptions seems to become longer and longer as we examine the complex realities of family life.

This **monolithic bias** not only lends itself to a very incomplete approach, but also tends to support a **conservative bias**. The monolithic approach implies that the "normal" and "natural" family is the one composed of two heterosexual adults who reside with and raise their biological (or adopted) children. On the one hand, this perspective tends to ignore the numerous difficulties and shortcomings attached to many "normal" nuclear families —for example, child abuse, woman abuse, incest, and so on—and on the other, it tends to devalue or dismiss families that exist outside these boundaries—gay and lesbian families, families of culturally or ethnically nondominant groups in Canada, and so on. This conservative bias is particularly evident in the structural-functionalist theoretical perspective on the family.

> ### Focus Question
> Why does Canadian sociologist Margrit Eichler reject the monolithic approach to the family?

In Sum

Clearly, the question of "what is a family" is much more complex than we might think. Not only is there tremendous variation in family life around the globe, there are important diversities within the North American family. Further, certain definitions of the family may carry an unspoken agenda. If the "real" family is restricted to heterosexual couples with male breadwinners, female housewives, children living at home, and so on, then the majority of Canadians are, according to this narrow definition, not living in a family.

Marriage and Family in Theoretical Perspective

The Functionalist Perspective: Functions and Dysfunctions

As noted in Chapter 1, functionalists stress that to survive, a society must meet certain basic needs, or functions. When functionalists look at family, they examine how it is related to other parts of society, especially how it contributes to the well-being of society.

Why the Family Is Universal. Functionalists argue that, although the form of the family may vary from one human group to another, the family is universal because it fulfills six needs basic to every society's well-being. As described in Table 13.1, these needs, or functions, are economic production, socialization of children, care of the sick and aged, recreation, sexual control, and reproduction.

As Eichler would be quick to point out, many groups that consider themselves "families" do not in fact fulfill all or even most of these "basic needs" (1997). Childless couples and couples whose children are grown up do not actively socialize children, yet will likely consider themselves members of a family. In some families, the socialization of children is entirely the responsibility of others; for example, children placed in homes for young offenders or sent to boot camps, and those who attend private residential schools or

Mass Media in Social Life

The Role of the Media in Promoting Family Roles and Family Forms

Not surprisingly, the media are an important source of our images of family life.

Researcher Gayle Kaufman, for example, examined the portrayal of fathers and husbands in television commercials. Not surprisingly, she found that, following a very traditional gender division, advertisements were more likely to portray women at home and men away from home. In terms of activities, advertisements contained more images of women engaged in cooking, cleaning, washing dishes, and shopping than of men doing these activities.

She also found few representations of men taking care of a child and, in those instances that did exist, the child was a boy. When men are shown interacting with children they are typically shown teaching, reading, talking, eating, and playing with children rather than taking care of children. The portrayal of a man cooking for his children is an absolute rarity, although men are often shown playing sports or sharing technical knowledge with children.

In a computer advertisement, for example, the man is apparently teaching his son to use the computer but becomes completely engrossed with the screen while his son jumps up and down for attention. This is an interesting combination of two important themes—men as both teacher and playmate.

Kaufman concluded that contemporary television commercials reinforce traditional notions by portraying the "dirty work" of home and children as primarily women's responsibility, while men's role is to be a "good provider" to his family, with some added contributions as a "playmate" to his children.

Source: Kaufman (1999).

---

who are raised by nannies. Similarly, families do not necessarily provide a medium for legitimate sexual activity. Some families, as discussed below, engage in illegal and/or socially stigmatized sexual behaviour such as marital rape, child sexual abuse, or "swinging." In some families, the "couple" have no sexual relations or only have sexual relations with partners outside the family relationship. The examples are endless.

Clearly, the notion that families are structures which necessarily perform certain functions in society is not borne out in everyday experience. Conversely, the notion that groups that do not perform these functions are not "normal" families runs contrary to our common-sense understanding of family life. It is useful to keep this criticism in mind when considering the remaining elements in the structural functional perspective on the family.

Functions of the Incest Taboo. Functionalists argue that by specifying which people are too closely related to have sex or to marry, the incest taboo helps families avoid role confusion. This, in turn, facilitates the socialization of children. For example, if father-daughter incest were allowed, how should a wife treat her daughter—as a daughter, as a subservient second wife, or even as a rival? Should the daughter act toward her mother as a mother or as a rival? Would her father be a father or a lover? And would the wife be the husband's main wife, a secondary wife—or even "the mother of the other wife" (whatever role that might be)? Maternal incest would also lead to complications every bit as confusing as these.

Another function of the incest taboo according to functionalists is to force people to look outside the family for marriage partners. Anthropologists theorize that exogamy was especially functional in tribal societies, for it forged alliances between tribes that otherwise might have killed each other off. Today, exogamy extends a bride's and groom's social networks beyond the nuclear family, building relationships with their spouse's family.

Connection to Other Parts of Society. Functionalists stress that the family is not an isolated unit, but vitally connected to other parts of society. They note, for example, that industrialization made the family more fragile. It ushered in formal organizations, some of which began to replace the family's traditional functions. Medical treatment began to be provided by hospitals, recreation by businesses, and sex education by schools. To weaken family functions is to weaken the "ties that bind," to reduce the motivation to struggle together against hardships. One consequence is more divorce. From the functionalist perspective, then, increased divorce does not represent "incompatible personalities." Rather, changes in other parts of society affect intimate relationships.

Isolation and Emotional Overload. Functionalists also analyze the dysfunctions that arise from the relative isolation of today's nuclear family (another consequence of industrialization). Unlike extended families in traditional societies, which are enmeshed in kinship networks, members of nuclear families can count on fewer people for material and emotional support. This makes nuclear families vulnerable to "emotional overload." That is, the stress that comes with crises such as the loss of a job—or even the routine stress of a harried life, as described in our opening vignette—is spread around among fewer people. This puts a greater strain on each family member. In addition, the relative isolation of the nuclear family makes it vulnerable to a "dark side"—incest and various other forms of abuse—which we examine later in this chapter.

The Conflict Perspective: Gender, Conflict, and Power

As you recall, central to conflict theory is the struggle over scarce resources. The recurring struggle over who does housework is actually a struggle over scarce resources—time, energy, and the leisure to pursue interesting activities. In particular, feminist sociologists have drawn attention to the social issues surrounding housework.

The Power Struggle over Housework. When the second wave of feminism swept over North America and western Europe in the 1960s, social researchers began to realize that who washed the dishes and who diapered the baby were significant social issues. In particular, American feminist Betty Friedan developed a stinging indictment of a society that produced extremely well-educated women and then sequestered them as unpaid housewives for the majority of their adult lives (Friedan, 1963). Canadian sociologists working from a conflict perspective quickly picked up on this issue, and developed a wealth of material on the experience of Canadian women. Among the most notable work was that of Meg Luxton, an anthropologist who lived for several years in Flin Flon, Manitoba, and chronicled the day-to-day lives of women in the community (1980). From this and other research, it became clear that in Canada, as elsewhere, women were doing the lion's share of housework and child care. The implicit agreement in many Canadian families, especially in the 1950s and 1960s, was that the husband would "bring home the bacon" and the wife would take care of home and children.

Unfortunately, as the research record increasingly documented, this unspoken arrangement contained significant drawbacks for women. Like many forms of low-paid, semiskilled work, housework was often tedious, time-consuming, repetitive, and boring. Women with young children reported shouldering onerous amounts of work while receiving little support within their family or community (Duffy, Mandell, & Pupo, 1989). Indeed, for many women

housework and child care was an isolating experience in which some felt completely cut off from adult stimulation. These problems were, of course, intensified for women who were poor or recent immigrants or disabled. Most importantly, unlike other work, housework and child care was unpaid, and, in a variety of ways, this reality could have devastating implications in women's lives. Women whose marriages failed or who became widows (as most eventually would) often found that years of cooking, cleaning, and care translated into impoverishment when they were on their own (see Chapter 9).

Of course, the 1950s, when many families could afford to have a full-time homemaker working at home, were short-lived. Growing financial pressure on family resources has meant few families can any longer afford a full-time parent in the home; indeed the total workday (paid and unpaid work) of parents has increased by almost one hour over the past decade as parents cut back on personal care and leisure activities (Fast, Frederick, Zukewich, & Franke, 2001, p. 21). As part of this general shift toward more work time, wives and mothers have moved increasingly into the paid labour force (see Figure 13.1).

Interestingly, the movement of women into paid work has not resolved the struggle over who does the housework. The research record continues to document that women are undertaking the lion's share of unpaid domestic work (Leonard, 2001). On average, Canadian women spend almost twice as much time per week (15.2 hours) as men on housework and more than twice as many hours (18.9 compared to men's 8.3 per week) on child care. Not surprisingly, becoming parents intensifies the gendered division of labour even in the dual-earner family. Employed mothers spend about 3 hours more than employed fathers on unpaid work and 3 hours less on paid work. A similar pattern has been documented with regard to elder care. When the families undertake the unpaid care of aging relatives, the majority of the care and time is provided by women (Milan, 2000, p. 9). For women the problem is

ARLO & JANIS ® by Jimmy Johnson

The cartoonist has beautifully captured the reduction-of-needs strategy discussed by Hochschild.

what American sociologist Arlie Hochschild terms the "the second shift" (1989). Many women are returning from a day of paid employment to find that groceries still have to be bought, meals prepared, children looked after, dishes washed, laundry done, and so on and so on.

Hochschild's research suggests that at least part of the problem is continued male resistance to household equality. For example, according to her series of in-depth interviews with about 50 American families, many men never volunteer to do chores around the house or they passively resist the work by responding glumly or with irritation when asked to "help out." A number of men "play dumb"; that is, they burn the dinner or lose the grocery list or forget to stop off at the dry cleaners. Some men use a "needs reduction" strategy in which they tell their wives not to bother to iron their clothes because they don't mind walking around in a wrinkled shirt; or that they don't need to tidy up because they don't mind the mess; or, when on their own, that they have a bowl of cereal for supper because that's all they want. When this strategy works, women feel guilty and self-conscious—they want their husband and their home to appear neat and tidy. They then provide the tidying, the ironed shirts, or the cooked dinner. Finally, in some cases, men offer appreciation and rewards—expressing admiration for their wife's ability to manage the double day and providing her with a dishwasher to help out with the dishes—rather than actually increasing their own labour contribution to the home.

Of course, the problem does not rest solely with resistant husbands. Many 60-hour-week professional careers—held by men and women—allow little time to attend to family responsibilities. Further, the research does suggest that over the last several years, Canadian fathers have been reorienting some of their paid "work" time to child care, household maintenance, and meal preparation (and mothers are directing more time to paid work). However, we remain far from equity in the typical Canadian family. Men now average 3.5 hours of unpaid work (domestic chores, child care) a day and women 6.1 (Fast et al., 2001). In a dual-earner family with young children, the mother spends an average of 147 minutes a day caring for the children, while the father averages only 85 minutes (Clark, 2001, p. 6). As a result, the unequal division of this unpaid work remains a potential source of conflict and stress in many Canadian homes.

Focus Question
Compare the ways in which functionalists and feminist conflict theorists would approach women's participation in paid employment.

Not surprisingly, the burden of the second shift creates deep discontent among wives. These problems, as well as how wives and husbands cope with them, are discussed in the next Thinking Critically about Social Controversy box.

Focus Question
Why is it that employed mothers still assume most of the responsibility for household work?

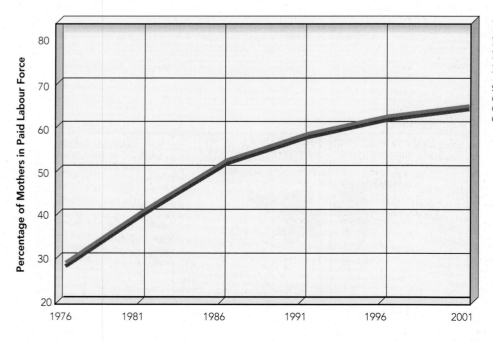

Figure 13.1 Employment Rate of Canadian Women with Partners and Children under Age 3, 1976–2001

Source: Statistics Canada, 2002, *Women in Canada: A Gender-Based Statistical Report.* Ottawa: Minister of Industry, p. 119, Catalogue no. 89-503-XPE.

The Symbolic Interactionist Perspective: Gender and the Meanings of Marriage

As noted in Chapter 1, symbolic interactionists focus on the meanings that people give to their lives. Let's apply this perspective to some surprising findings about marriage.

Housework, Paycheques, and Masculinity. The first finding is probably what you'd expect—the closer a husband's

---

From the 1970s to the end of the 1990s, the Canadian family mobilized more and more income earners. Not only wives and mothers but also teenage family members moved into the paid labour force. Also, employed mothers are returning quickly to their paid work after childbirth. Almost 90 percent of women who gave birth in 1993 and 1994 were back at work within a year and one in five were back by the end of the first month ("Most women return to work," 2000, p. 26). Much has been made of the reasons why family members, particularly mothers, have become so deeply involved with paid work, particularly when it often results in considerable time stress for mothers of young children (Frederick, 1993). While financial considerations are only one element in the mix, it is important to recognize that the Canadian family has been under considerable economic pressure.

Family incomes have grown only minimally for almost two decades. Average after-tax income for Canadian households rose from $41 000 in 1982 to $42 500 in 1999, an increase of only 4 percent. Meanwhile, spending increased by 10 percent and, not surprisingly, by 1999 family debt was hitting record highs while savings were at record lows (Kremarik, 2002). It seems that the dearth of secure, well-paying, full-time jobs continues to take a toll on the average Canadian family (Carey, 2000, p. D26). At the same time as income has stagnated, costs incurred by families, such as for housing and postsecondary education, have increased substantially, and government transfer payments, such as employment insurance and social welfare support, have dropped markedly. Even financially well-to-do families have been facing a 40 percent increase in spending on recreation (Kremarik, 2002). In this econom-

ic context, it is not surprising to see many families, rich and poor, mobilizing every available wage-earner.

Currently, employed wives are contributing on average about 30 percent of family income. Consider what it would mean to your family to lose almost one-third of its income. For many Canadian families, the result would be impoverishment. Analysts calculate that the poverty rate would double to 21.4 percent of Canadian families if employed wives returned to full-time homemaking (National Council of Welfare, 1998, pp. 87–88). While many Canadian families could "survive" without women's income and many women work for reasons other than economic survival, it is important to realize the role played by economic pressures.

It is precisely this issue that is addressed in Meg Luxton and June Corman's award-winning book, *Getting By in Hard Times* (2001). Based on a case study conducted from 1980 to 1996 among families where at least one person was employed at Stelco's steel manufacturing plant in Hamilton, Ontario, their work reveals a great deal about the impact of international economic shifts—such as economic restructuring—on the day-to-day realities of family life. Economic restructuring, including the movement of many industrial jobs to other countries with lower labour costs, the loss of industrial jobs to technological innovation, and the growth of poorly paid service jobs, shook the traditional family to its core. Where once a job at the steel plant had promised lifelong economic security, now families were faced with layoffs and insecurity.

Not surprisingly, Luxton and Corman found that many of their working-class families moved away from a pattern in which women were full-time housewives and men were income earn-

ers to one where women were also income earners. For many, standards of living needed to be lowered, and family members, especially mothers, needed to intensify their unpaid work at home to help make ends meet.

The resultant upheaval reverberated through family and personal life. Tensions over the division of household work and child care intensified. These pressures on individual families and their members, in turn, affected the larger community. There was little in the way of time or energy to direct toward strong friendship networks and community organizations or to organize protest movements. The day-to-day demands of the family took precedence, and opportunities for collective actions—from the union movement to local community initiatives—were undermined.

Further, frustration with increasing economic insecurity led to increased racial, ethnic, and gender conflict. Immigrants in general, along with specific ethnic groups and women's organizations, were blamed for putting obstacles in the employment paths of white, able-bodied men. Affirmative action policies were seen as evidence of increasing patterns of unfairness in which "others" were always the first to get the jobs.

By locating family life in the midst of these crucial larger social issues, Luxton and Corman dramatically expose the complex ways in which economic pressures, exacerbated by cutbacks in government services, can force the family to turn inward, away from possibilities of progressive social change.

For Your Consideration

Identify the sources of economic pressures in the contemporary Canadian family. Consider strategies that family members might employ to lessen these pressures.

Researchers June Corman and Meg Luxton, pictured here, have chronicled the impact of large social trends, such as economic restructuring, on ordinary Canadian families.

and wife's earnings, the more likely they are to share housework. (Although husbands in such marriages don't share housework equally, they do more than other husbands.) This next finding, however, may be surprising: *Husbands who earn less than their wives* (and about 20 percent of husbands in dual-earner families do earn less than their wives) *do the least housework* (Statistics Canada, 2000). And this one: Most husbands who get laid off *reduce* their housework.

How can we explain this? You would think husbands who earn less than their wives would want to balance things out—do more around the house, not less. Researchers suggest that the key is gender role. If a wife earns more than her husband, this threatens his masculinity—he takes it as a sign that he has failed in his traditional manly role of provider. To do housework—"women's work" in his eyes—threatens it even further. By avoiding housework, he "reclaims" his masculinity (Hochschild, 1989; Brines, 1994).

Two Marriages in One. Another interesting finding of symbolic interactionists is how husbands and wives perceive their marriage. When asked how much housework each does, they give different answers. They even disagree about whether they fight over doing housework (Sanchez, 1994). Groundbreaking sociologist Jessie Bernard, who studied this marital gulf, noted in a classic work (1972) that when researchers

> ask husbands and wives identical questions about the union they often get quite different replies. There is usually agreement on the number of children they have and a few other such verifiable items, although not, for example, on length of premarital acquaintance and of engagement, on age at marriage and interval between marriage and birth of first child.

Why don't husbands and wives agree on such a basic matter as how frequently they have sex? The answer lies in differing *perceptions* of lovemaking. It appears that in the typical marriage the wife desires greater emotional involvement from her husband, while the husband's desire is for more sex (Komter, 1989; Barbeau, 1992). When questioned about sex, then, the husband, feeling deprived, tends to underestimate it, while the wife, more reluctant to participate in sex because of unsatisfied intimacy needs, overestimates it (Bernard, 1972).

Symbolic interactionists conclude that because husbands and wives hold down such different corners in marriage they perceive marriage differently. Their experiences contrast so sharply that *every marriage contains two separate marriages—his and hers.*

In Sum

Working from very different and sometimes opposing theoretical orientations, sociologists of the family have focused on a number of important features of family life. Functionalists tend to emphasize the interconnections between the family and other social institutions and the ways the family functions to serve other areas of society such as the education system and the economy. The conflict perspective, and feminist sociologists in particular, have emphasized the conflicts of interests that often emerge in family life. Nowhere is this strain more apparent than in the struggle over who should be responsible for housework, particularly in the dual-earner family. Finally, symbolic interactionists explore the meaning family members attach to family life. Not surprisingly, given differences in gender socialization, men and women approach the meaning of family activities in very different ways. This is so much the case that it is reasonable to refer to "his" marriage and "her" marriage.

Focus Question In what way do male and female perceptions of lovemaking and housework reveal the differences between "his" and "her" marriage? What are the implications?

The Family Life Cycle

Thus far we have seen that the forms of marriage and family vary widely, and we have examined marriage and family from different sociological perspectives. Now let's discuss love, courtship, and the family life cycle.

Love and Courtship in Global Perspective

Until recently, social scientists thought romantic love originated in western Europe during the medieval period (Mount, 1992). When anthropologists William Jankowiak and Edward Fischer (1992) surveyed the data available on 166 societies around the world, they found that this was not so. **Romantic love**—people being sexually attracted to and idealizing one another—showed up in 88 percent (147) of these groups. The role of love, however, differs sharply from one society to another. For example, in India people don't expect love to occur until *after* marriage—if then.

Romantic love usually begins with sexual attraction. We find ourselves sexually attracted to someone and spend time with that person. If we discover mutual interests, we may eventually label our feelings "love." Apparently, then, romantic love has two components. The first is emotional, a feeling of sexual attraction. The second is cognitive, a label we attach to our feelings. If we do attach this label, we describe ourselves as being "in love."

Focus Question
Using a functional perspective, explain why notions of romantic love vary from one culture to another.

Marriage

In the typical case, marriage in Canada is preceded by "love," but contrary to folklore, whatever love is, it certainly is not blind. That is, love does not hit anyone willy-nilly.

The Social Channels of Love and Marriage. When we marry, we generally think we have freely chosen our spouse. With few exceptions, however, our choices follow highly predictable social channels, especially age, education, social class, race, and religion (Tucker & Mitchell-Kerman, 1990; Kalmijn, 1991). A young woman with a university degree whose parents are both physicians is likely to fall in love with and marry a young man slightly older than herself who has graduated from university. Similarly, a female high school dropout whose parents are on welfare is likely to fall in love with and marry a male who comes from a background similar to hers.

Sociologists use the term **homogamy** to refer to the tendency of people with similar characteristics to marry one another. Homogamy occurs largely as a result of *propinquity*, or spatial nearness. That is, we tend to fall in love with and marry people who live near us or whom we meet at school, church, or work. The people with whom we associate are far from a random sample of the population, for social filters produce neighbourhoods, schools, and churches that follow racial-ethnic and social class lines.

Of course, it is not simply the case that people tend to marry others who are like them. There are also gender considerations. Traditionally, women have tended to marry men with strong economic prospects, while women's marriageability was seen to be determined by other factors, notably her physical attractiveness and her potential as a wife and mother. These old patterns hinged on an image of marriage in which a woman was looking for a partner who would support his family at a desirable standard while she maintained the home "front." With women's increasing economic contributions to the marriage along with increased rates of marriage breakdown, it is likely that old considerations in mate selection are breaking down and other factors, such as a prospective wife's economic and career prospects, may figure more prominently in modern love and marriage (Sweeney, 2002).

Childbirth

The popular image is that the arrival of a baby makes a couple deliriously happy. The facts are somewhat different.

Marital Satisfaction. A sociological finding that surprises many is that marital satisfaction usually *decreases* with the birth of a child (Whyte, 1992; Bird, 1997). To understand why, recall from Chapter 5 that a dyad (just two persons) provides greater intimacy than a triad (after adding a third person, interaction must be shared). To move from the theoretical to the practical, think about the implications of coping with a newborn—less free time (feeding, soothing, and diapering), less sleep, and heavier expenses.

Focus Question
Why would marital satisfaction decline with the birth of a child, and why might social class affect this decline?

Child-Rearing

Who's minding the kids while the parents are at work? A while back such a question would have seemed ridiculous, for the mother was at home taking care of the children. That assumption, however, no longer holds. In Canada, two-thirds of Canadian wives with young children (under age six) are working for pay and almost 90 percent of employed women are back at the job within a year of giving birth (Statistics Canada, 2002; Marshall, 1999). Clearly, many children are spending some portion of their lives being cared for by someone other than their mother or father. Not surprisingly, research suggests that when both parents work, children grow up spending more time out of the home, and have less free play time at home (Hofferth & Sandberg, 2001). However, research also suggests that the children of employed parents do feel loved and valued, provided they know they are their parents' priority (Galinsky, 1999). Further, recent research indicates that employed mothers are spending as many hours a week with their children as stay-at-home moms did in 1981, and fathers are spending more time with their children, up from 19 hours a week in 1981 to 24 in 1997 ("Kids Spending More Time with Parents," 2001, p. M10). So, while non-familial child care is important, child-rearing still remains an important aspect of family life.

Table 13.2 illustrates the dramatic increase in the number of licensed day-care spaces in Canada from 1971 to 1996.

Day Care. Research suggests that more than half of infants and nearly two-thirds of toddlers spend at least part of the week in non-parental care (Che-Alford, Allan, & Butlin, 1994, p. 37). However, many of these children are being cared for in unlicensed situations. In 1996, for example, while there were 300 000 day-care spaces available for preschool-age children, there were 900 000 families where there was at least one preschool child and where both parents or the lone parent was employed (Statistics Canada, 2000, p. 101). These figures suggest several social phenomena. First, for many young Canadians the process of growing up is changing. For the majority, some portion of childhood is spent in child care or at the babysitter's. As discussed in Chapter 4, the impact of this experience will vary with the quality of the care provided. High-quality, stimulating, and supportive child care benefits children. However, it is often difficult for parents to gauge the quality

of the care provided, particularly if the provider is unlicensed. Given the abysmally low salaries of child care workers and babysitters, there is little economic motivation to improve the current uneven quality of care.

Nannies. Of course, more well-to-do parents can afford the personal care provided by a nanny. In large metropolitan areas such as Toronto, nannies have become increasingly common among upper-middle-class parents, since they provide the round-the-clock at-home care that is most beneficial to professional men and women. Indeed, around the globe, immigrant and minority women are increasingly called upon to provide much of the housecleaning and nanny work needed by affluent families (Hondagneu-Sotelo, 2001). However, this arrangement has numerous drawbacks. The burden that falls to the nannies may be overwhelming and oppressive. Often leaving their own family and children in their country of origin, nannies may find in Canada a heavy routine of domestic work and child care isolated from any support network. While they may share their cultural background with the children they care for, their position in the household may also communicate some very problematic lessons to children regarding race and social inequality. The working conditions for Canadian nannies have been so unfavourable that the government stepped in to upgrade their wages and employment conditions (Silvera, 1989). Not surprisingly, the parents who employ nannies are often not completely satisfied, sometimes becoming jealous at the bond between their children and their caregiver or, conversely, being concerned about the patterns of discipline and punishment that occur when the parents are absent (Ansberry, 1993).

Social Class. Childhood experiences are also affected by social class. Sociologists have long pointed out that parents tend to socialize their children according to the norms of their work worlds (M. L. Kohn, 1959). Because members of the working class are more closely supervised and are expected to follow explicit rules laid down for them by others, their concern is less with their children's motivation and more with outward conformity. They are more apt to use physical punishment. In contrast, middle-class parents, who are expected to take more initiative on the job, are more concerned that their children develop curiosity, self-expression, and self-control. They also are more likely to withdraw privileges or affection than to use physical punishment.

Birth Order. Birth order may also be significant. Parents tend to discipline their firstborns more than their later children and to give them more attention. When the second child arrives, the firstborn competes for attention. Researchers suggest that this instills in firstborns a greater drive for success, which is why they may be more likely than their siblings to earn higher grades in school, to go on to postsecondary education, and to go further there. Although subsequent children may not go as far, most are inclined to be less anxious about being successful and more

Table 13.2 Number of Licensed Day-Care Spaces in Canada, 1971–1996

Year	Number of Licensed Day-Care Spaces
1971	17 391
1975	69 952
1980	109 141
1985	192 374
1990	298 083
1995	394 788
1996	435 478

Source: Statistics Canada, 2000, *Women in Canada: A Gender-Based Statistical Report.* Ottawa: Minister of Industry, p. 120, Catalogue no. 89-503-XPE.

relaxed in their relationships (Snow, Jacklin, & Maccoby, 1981; Goleman, 1985). Firstborns are also somewhat more likely to defend the status quo and to support conservative causes, while later-borns may be more predisposed to upset the apple cart and support liberal causes (Sulloway, 1997).

The Family in Later Life

The later stages of family life bring their own pleasures to be savoured and problems to be solved. Let's look at the empty nest, "boomerang kids," and widowhood.

The Empty Nest. Families that once had children and now are empty-nesters are the largest and fastest-growing type of family without children in Canada. According to the 1996 census, 37 percent of all Canadian families were empty-nesters, and as the population ages this trend is likely to grow (Statistics Canada, 1998, p. 184).

When the last child leaves home, the husband and wife are left, as at the beginning of the marriage, alone together. They can expect to live as much as 20 or 30 years together as empty-nesters. This situation was once thought to signal a difficult time of adjustment for women—especially those who have not worked outside the home—because they have devoted so much energy to a child-rearing role that is now gone. Sociologist Lillian Rubin (1992a), who interviewed both career women and homemakers, found that this picture is largely a myth. Contrary to the stereotype, she found that women's satisfaction generally *increases* when the last child leaves home. A typical statement was made by a 45-year-old woman, who leaned forward in her chair as though to tell Rubin a secret:

> To tell you the truth, most of the time it's a big relief to be free of them, finally. I suppose that's awful to say. But you know what, most of the women I know feel the same way.

Similar findings have come from other researchers, who report that most mothers feel relieved at finally being able to spend more time on themselves (Whyte, 1992). Many couples also report a renewed sense of intimacy at this time (Mackey & O'Brien, 1995). This closeness appears to stem from four causes: The couple is free of the many responsibilities of child-rearing; they have more leisure; their income is at its highest; and they have fewer financial obligations.

While the positive possibilities of the empty nest are important to recognize, some experts claim that the long periods of time "alone together" may also contribute to the divorce rate. People are not willing to "wait it out" in an unhappy marriage (Statistics Canada, 1998, p. 184).

Boomerang Kids. Of course, the empty nest may not be that empty. Sociologists are pointing to a very important shift in life cycle patterns. Between 1971 and 1981, young adults tended to increasingly move out on their own. From 1981 to 2001, there was a dramatic 27 percent increase in the numbers of adult children who were living

at home. In 2001, 64 percent of men aged 20 to 24 and 52 percent of same-age women lived with their parents. Even among those 25 to 29, 29 percent of men and 19 percent of women were living at home (Tustin and Walton, 2002, p. A6).

Once, adult children went off to form their own lives by taking a job and getting married. Given high rates of youth unemployment, drops in the income rates for youth, and periods of economic recession in the 1980s and 1990s, it is not surprising to find that many young adults opt to remain in their family home, even when they are married. Economic pressures, as well as growing patterns of postponed child-bearing and prolonged education, all contribute to the "boomerang kids" phenomenon (Boyd & Norris, 1999).

This trend clearly signals an important shift in family life experiences. At this point we are only starting to evaluate its implications. Recent research suggests that the clear majority of parents have very positive responses to their adult children living at home. They enjoy the companionship and the help. However, there is also evidence of an uneasy undercurrent. Two-thirds of the parents in this "positive" study indicated that they sometimes felt "taken advantage of" by their returned children. Additional research is needed to fully understand the impact on the family and its members (Mitchell, 1998).

Widowhood. Women are more likely than men to face widowhood and its wrenching problems. Not only does the average wife live longer than her husband, but also she has married a man older than herself. The death of a spouse tears at the self, clawing at identities that had merged through the years (DiGiulio, 1992). Now that the one who had become an essential part of the self is gone, the survivor, as in adolescence, is forced once again to wrestle with the perplexing question "Who am I?"

However, despite the fact that most Canadian women can expect to end up on their own and that many will be struggling with economic vulnerability (see Chapter 9), widows do more than simply endure. A recent survey of the 887 000 widows in Canada aged 65 and older found that three-quarters are living on their own. Typically, they have created a strong social network and have frequent social contact, often with a group of other women their own age. About half of the women in this survey had four or more friends they felt strongly attached to. Many, having lived in the same home for a long time, enjoyed long-standing friendships with neighbours. Adult children and other family members also helped provide social support. The notion of a lonely, isolated widowhood does not appear to be the norm for Canadian women (Bess, 1999).

In Sum

Following the family through the life course—from romance and courtship to widowhood and death—provides us with an appreciation for the complexities of family life. Certainly, not every family follows the same path, and indeed an examination of other cultures and other historical periods reveals profoundly different experiences of love, childbirth, and child-rearing. However, within this diversity there are interesting patterns. For example, social class generally affects our family life experiences. Young men and women typically fall in love with members of the same class. Similarly, social class affects child-rearing options: Well-to-do children may be cared for by a nanny while working-class children are under the supervision of their grandmother. Regardless of class, most couples find that childbirth and child-rearing are difficult stages in their marriage. Similarly, as we saw in Chapter 4, many Canadian families are finding their child-rearing stage extended, as adult children return "home" to search for employment or accumulate economic resources.

> **Focus Question** Considering recent changes in Canadian family life, speculate on what life might be like for a husband and wife from age 50 to their death.

Diversity in Canadian Families

It is important to realize that there is no such thing as *the* Canadian family. Rather, family life varies widely throughout Canada.

Racial and Ethnic Diversities

For generations, Canada has been based in immigration. This is becoming increasingly the case as the birth rate decreases. For a number of years Canadian fertility has been below the "replacement level"; that is, the numbers of children born to Canadians are not sufficient to maintain the population size. Coupled with the "aging" of the Canadian population and the increased number of retirees, the continuing need for immigrant labour is clear. Between 1945 and 1966, 125 000 immigrants arrived yearly in the country. Throughout the 1970s and 1980s, the pattern remained much the same. In the 1990s, immigration soared to more than 200 000 annually, and in 1993 more than a quarter of a million immigrants arrived. Although immigration has levelled off since then, it is not surprising to learn that there are members of more than 100 different ethnic groups in Canada and that immigrants make up 17.4 percent of our population and 19 percent of wage-earners (Statistics Canada, 2001).

Given the increasing diversity of immigrants, it is also not surprising to find that more than one in 10 Canadians are visible minorities (usually Chinese, South Asian, or black) and it is projected that by 2016 almost one-fifth (19 percent) of the Canadian population will be members of

A First Nations wedding reception. In 1996, 800 000 people on the census reported that they were North American Indian, Métis, or Inuit.

visible minorities. Meanwhile, the proportions of the Canadian population identifying with the traditional British-only and French-only have shrunk to 17 percent and 9 percent, respectively (Statistics Canada, 1998).

All of these statistics underscore the continuing importance of recognizing the diversity of cultures that influence Canadian families. Some differences, as in national costume or dates of religious events, may seem trivial, but many, such as differences in mother tongue or cultural beliefs and values, may have a profound impact on almost every aspect of family life. Depending on their cultural background, families embrace varying views on the rights and responsibilities of family members. Issues as crucial and diverse as whether marriages should be arranged or whether wives should have paid employment will be approached differently depending upon ethnic origins. Similarly, the lives of Canadian families will be variously influenced by patterns of discrimination and economic inequality (Driedger & Halli, 2000).

Consider, for example, the family lives of Canada's First Nations. On the 1996 census, 800 000 people reported that they were North American Indian, Métis, or Inuit (totalling 3 percent of the Canadian population). There is of course considerable diversity within this population, since these individuals are divided among 48 First Nations, ranging from the 120 000-member Cree to the 85-member Potawatomi, and some are living in large metropolitan areas while others are on remote reserves. However, family life for members of the First Nations is still conditioned by long-standing patterns that have tended to marginalize Native Canadians economically and socially (Ponting, 1998). While individual lives vary, simply by reason of being a Native Canadian you are more likely to be in a low-income category, more likely to commit suicide, more likely to have a variety of serious illnesses, and less likely to have high levels of formal education. For example, at least 44 percent of the Aboriginal population in Canada and 60 percent of Aboriginal children under age six live below the poverty line (Federal, Provincial, and Territorial Advisory Committee, 1999, p. 47). Clearly, these patterns are in turn likely to affect the day-to-day realities of family life.

Another example of the impact of ethnicity on family life is in terms of three-generation households and numbers of children. Needless to say, there are relatively few Canadian families in which grandparents, children, and grandchildren all live in the same home. However, between 1986 and 1996 the number of three-generation families in Canada increased by 39 percent to 208 000. It appears that this trend is a reflection of increased numbers of Asian immigrants to Canada. By the 1996 census, almost half of three-generation families were headed by immigrants, and between 1986 and 1996, Asians made up three-quarters of three-generation household heads (Che-Alford & Hamm, 1999). There is also evidence that recent immigrants, many of whom were born outside Europe and the United States, are more likely to have three or more children. Compared to Canadian-born women, fertility rates of immigrant women born outside Europe and the United States are 50 percent higher (Belanger, 1999). In short, evidence suggests that recent immigrants, notably Asian immigrants, have brought with them a cultural tradition of living in a large, extended family system, and have transplanted that family configuration into the Canadian context. Here, once again, ethnic origin can be seen to directly affect the most basic realities of family life.

Finally, the family lives of members of various racial and ethnic groups are also affected by the explicit responses of the dominant culture. Members of visible minorities, including both immigrants and Native peoples, have often been subjected to direct and indirect manifestations of discrimination and cultural domination that have impacted the quality and even the possibility of family life among minority communities. Historically, immigration policies have intentionally blocked family formation among working-class Chinese, South Asian, and Japanese men and women, and more recently black Caribbean women. Policies sought to ensure that these visible immigrants remained "single," provided temporary labour, and then returned to their country of origin. Missionary-led residential schools and, later, non-Native child-welfare agencies similarly undermined family life among Canadian Native peoples by removing children from their Native communities, by undermining familial relationships, especially between child and parent, and by terminating Native cultures, languages, religions, education, and economies (Das Gupta, 2000). As Canada becomes ever more multicultural, it is increasingly important to pay attention to differences in both the history and the current day-to-day realities of Canada's ethnically and racially diverse families.

One-Parent Families

From TV talk shows to government officials, one-parent families have become a matter of general concern. The increase is no myth, although it is often over-stated since in the early 1930s more than one family in 10 was a single-parent family. However, the overwhelming majority of those families were created by the death of a parent. As the adult death rate lessened so did the proportion of single-parent families. By 1961, there were only 347 400 single-parent families in Canada. Then came the enormous increase. As of the 1996 census, there were 1.1 million such families in Canada! A clear majority (83 percent) of these single-parent families are headed by women (Vanier Institute, 2000). Needless to say, these figures have a momentous import for child-rearing.

Not only have the absolute numbers of single parents increased, the social causes of one-parent families have changed. Where once, most lone parents were widows or widowers, today the overwhelming majority of one-parent families are the result of divorce. In addition, a small but increasing number of lone parents (22 percent in 1996) are never-married singles who have opted for parenting without a partner.

Not surprisingly, this shift in family configuration has triggered a heated debate on the implications of divorce and single-parent families for children (see below).

To understand many one-parent families, we need to view them through the lens of poverty, for that is often the primary source of strain. The results are serious, not just for these parents and their children but for society as a whole. Children from poor families are penalized in terms of physical, mental, and social health. Level of income is clearly related to a sense of identity and purpose, social contacts, and opportunities for personal growth. For example, children from low-income families are likely to achieve lower levels of education and this, in turn, is likely to translate into higher levels of unemployment (Federal, Provincial, and Territorial Advisory Committee, 1999). Although poverty does not inevitably repeat itself generation after generation, children of poor families are certainly not set up to succeed.

Families Without Children

Why do some couples not have children? Sociologist Kathleen Gerson (1985) found that some women see their marriage as too fragile to withstand the strains a child would bring. Other women believe they would be stuck at home—bored and lonely and with diminishing career opportunities. Many couples see a child as too expensive or feel that having a child would limit their options in life. With trends firmly in place—more education and careers for women; technological advances in contraception, abortion, sterilization; the high cost of rearing children—the proportion of women who never bear children is likely to increase.

Currently, 41 percent of Canadian families have no children under age 25 in the home (Statistics Canada, 2002b). However, many of these families would be empty-nesters whose children have gone off to establish families of their own (Berry et al., 1999, p. 72). Research suggests that about 10 percent of Canadian women never give birth (Nelson & Robinson, 2002). In part, this reflects the intentions of some men and women not to have children. According to recent research, 4 percent of women and 6 percent of men aged 20 to 29 intend to remain childless. By age 30 to 39, 8 percent of both women and men are committed to a child-free family (Dupuis, 1998).

It appears that there has been a shift toward greater social acceptability of both fewer numbers of children in the family and families/women who choose to remain child-free. Certainly, researchers are drawing more attention to voluntary childlessness as a life option and challenging the pronatalist views that all women want to become mothers (Gillespie, 2000). Indeed, several social groups have emerged that are devoted to extolling the virtues of adults-only communities, vacation spots, and so forth. For example, the nonprofit social club "No Kidding" provides support for couples who don't have or ever want children. Created in 1984, the organization now has 70 chapters throughout North America with 7000 members and a very active Web site (McNeely, 2002).

Many couples, however, are not childless by choice. Some adopt. For example, in 1998, 2223 children were adopted from countries outside Canada (Belanger, 1999). Other families turn to the solutions featured in the Sociology and the New Technology box here.

Focus Question

In what ways are the social responses experienced by one-parent families and families without children both similar and different?

Blended Families

An increasingly significant type of family formation found in Canada is the **blended family**, one whose members were once part of other families. Two divorced people who marry and bring their children into a new family unit become a blended family. With divorce common, many children spend some of their childhood in blended families; that is, living in families with step-parents, step-siblings and, often, half-siblings. In addition, they may have biological parents living elsewhere with new partners and new half-siblings. Research suggests that only half of children born today will live in a household with their original parents; indeed, one in five Canadian children are not born into the "traditional" family of mother, father, and joint children (Carey, 2001b, p. D3; Mclanahan, 2002). Evidence of the pervasiveness and complexity of this experience is provided by the 1995 General Social Survey, which indicated there are approximately 430 000 stepfamilies in Canada. Slightly more than half are made up of a mother, her children, and a stepfather. About 10 percent are made up of a father, his children, and a stepmother, and about a third are made up of the father and his children, the mother and her children, and/or the children of the new couple (cited in Nelson & Robinson, 1999, p. 421).

No, this is not a preschool, though it may look like one. These six children, all born within a few minutes of one another, have the same parents. One consequence of fertility drugs is multiple births. Shown here are the Dilley sextuplets of Indianapolis, Indiana: Ian, Adrian, Claire, Brenna, Quinn, and Julian.

Imagine a child being able to claim five people as parents. First, there's the woman who provided the egg. Second, there's the man who donated the sperm. Third, there's the woman who carried the child, "in utero," and gave birth. Fourth and fifth are the man and woman who took the child home from the hospital to rear her or him (Eichler, 1997).

Welcome to the brave—and very real—new world of high-tech reproduction. Although to date most children conceived with the aid of high-tech procedures claim only two parents, and a minority claim three, reproductive technologies—especially procedures such as *in vitro fertilization (IVF)*—make this scenario possible. IVF is a technique in which a woman's eggs are surgically removed from an ovary and placed in a laboratory dish along with a man's sperm. A fertilized egg is then inserted into the woman's uterus. The sperm can be anyone's—the husband's or a donor's—which complicates parentage.

The first successful IVF took place in 1978, when a woman in England gave birth to Louise, the world's first "test-tube baby." Well over 250 000 children worldwide have been born as a result of this procedure since then (T. Harper, 2000, pp. L1, L3). The vast majority of these children are the biological offspring of the same parents who rear

them. In some instances, however, single women, lesbian and heterosexual, have purchased sperm from sperm banks; the resulting child does not know the identity of the biological father.

If a woman cannot produce viable eggs, *donor* eggs can be used; that is, her husband's sperm are mixed with eggs removed from a fertile woman—the donor (Harper, 2000, pp. L1, L3). The resulting embryo is implanted in the infertile woman's uterus. In this instance, the child is related biologically to the father who rears her or him, but not to the mother who does so.

In some instances of donor IVF a woman can produce viable eggs, but suffers from miscarriage and cannot carry a child to term. Her eggs are mixed with her husband's sperm, and the embryo is implanted in a surrogate, who agrees to carry it to term and then relinquish the baby. In this instance, the child is related biologically to the two parents who rear him or her, but not to the woman who gave birth to her or him.

Needless to say, these technological advances have generated heated public debate over the ethical implications. Should 65-year-old women be allowed to use this technology to become mothers? Who should "own" the frozen embryos of deceased couples? Should donors and surrogates be allowed to "sell" their services?

Which fertility services—IVF costs about $7000 (including required medication)—should be covered by the government-funded health insurance program? Since the treatment is often unsuccessful, how many attempts should be allowed? And so on. Since each year an estimated 330 000 Canadian couples seek fertility assistance, this is an important social issue.

For Your Consideration

- Is it ethical for physicians, clinics, donors, and surrogates to make a profit by providing fertility services?
- Is fertility a basic health right that should be funded by government health care funds?
- Should children who are the result of donor eggs or donor sperm be allowed to contact their "biological" parents?
- Should society bear the brunt of multiple births and increased numbers of birth defects that are the consequences of some fertility procedures?
- Why do prospective parents bear the risks, expenses, and low success rates of fertility treatments when enormous numbers of children are available for international adoption?
- Should there be limits on parents' ability to "choose" their children's genetic profile—in terms of sex, intelligence, appearance, and so on?

Not surprisingly, the result of this pattern may be more complicated family relationships (Eichler, 1997, p. 67). Unfortunately, the complexity of family relations may not be the only problem. Blended families appear to be at greater risk of family breakup. Perhaps because one of the adult members has already made the decision to end a marriage, the decision to separate or divorce may seem easier. Certainly, the lack of social support for blended families and the stress resulting from the lack of established guidelines for family relations may increase the overall instability (Carey, 2001, p. D3).

Focus Question
What kinds of issues might emerge when a blended family celebrates a family member's birthday?

Gay Families

In 1989, Denmark was the first country to legalize marriage between people of the same sex. Since then, the Netherlands, Norway, and Sweden have made same-sex marriages legal. In 2001, the Netherlands provided same-sex couples with the right to marriage, adoption, and divorce, placing them at the vanguard of gay rights internationally (Deutsch, 2000). In this same year in the Netherlands, six men and two women became the first same-sex couples to be legally married anywhere in the world. In recent years the Canadian federal and provincial governments have moved increasingly toward legally recognizing gay families. In 1996, the government amended the Canadian Human Rights Code, adding sexual orientation as a prohibited ground of discrimination. Health care benefits have been extended to same-sex partners and the term "common-law spouse" in collective agreements has been interpreted to include same-sex couples. In 1998, British Columbia became the first jurisdiction in North America to give same-sex couples the same privileges and obligations as opposite-sex couples (including custody, access, and child support) (O'Brien & Goldberg, 2000). On July 12, 2002, the Ontario Superior Court ruled that the current legal definition of marriage is discriminatory and ordered it changed to include recognition of same-sex marriages. Currently, the Canadian federal government is appealing this ruling (Thompson, 2002, p. A2).

These changes, of course, reflect great social acceptance of 34 200 same sex couples enumerated in the 2001 census (Richer, 2002, p. A7). For example, in 1999 more than one-third of Canadians (36 percent) indicated they accepted the idea of same-sex marriages (up from 24 percent in 1992). A similar proportion of Canadians believe that gays and lesbians should be allowed to adopt children (up from 25 percent in 1988) (Edwards & Mazzuca, 1999a).

What are gay and lesbian relationships like? Same-sex couples cannot be painted with a single brushstroke. As with opposite-sex couples, social class is highly significant, and orientations to life differ according to education, occupation, and income. Some sociologists have pointed out that gay and lesbian relationships are more egalitarian than heterosexual relationships. For example, decision-making and financial arrangements are based on a greater measure of sharing than in same-sex couples (O'Brien & Goldberg, 2000).

However, gay and lesbian relationships are also directly affected by the often hostile social context in which they are lived out. There has, of course, been a long tradition of legal discrimination against gays and lesbians in Canada. Growing up gay continues to be a difficult and stressful process, since negative social stereotypes of gays and lesbians continue to abound. Not surprisingly, gays and lesbians must often rely on their communities to provide support to survive as relationships and as families in this negative social climate.

Intentional Families

The segmented relationships of contemporary society make many of us feel emotionally aloof, disconnected from others. Many would like to find a solution to this problem—to enjoy long-term relationships and to feel closer to others. To overcome such problems of loneliness, some have started **intentional families**. The members, though not related by blood or marriage, declare themselves a family. They live separately, but near one another. They meet regularly and share experiences, which adds satisfaction to their lives. The first intentional family, formed in Providence, Rhode Island, has been together for 25 years (Graham, 1996). While some might say that they are not a "real" family, they consider themselves a family. A sign of their family-like intimacy is evident when the 18 members get together for their Sunday suppers—they walk into the house without knocking.

> ### Focus Question
> What sort of family diversities should the typical Canadian grade-school teacher expect in the classroom?

In Sum

It is very important to keep in mind not only the patterning of family life, but also the diversity of experiences within this pattern. Here we have considered racial and ethnic diversities, one-parent families, families without children, families formed through reproductive technology, blended families, gay families, and intentional families. Of course, many families combine these diversities. Consider, for example, the one-parent family headed by a gay parent or the blended family in which one or several members are racial or ethnic minorities. In addition, there are diversities that are not included here but that we should be aware of, such as adoptive families, families with foster children, and families in which one or several family members are disabled. Families in each of these categories may share certain experiences. For example, one-parent families frequently confront an education and employment system that simply assumes there are two parents in the home. Sociologists are quick to point out that "the family" does not exist and that we must remain aware of the variety of family forms.

Trends in Canadian Families

Marriage and family life patterns in Canada are in the midst of fundamental shifts. The traditional North American household composed of a married couple with children is increasingly scarce. By 1998, it made up only 26 percent of North American households, down from 45 percent in 1972. Meanwhile, the most common living arrangement (33 percent of all households up from 16 percent in 1972) consisted of unmarried people and no children. Indicators of these changes include the postponement of marriage, increases in common-law marriage, single motherhood, divorce, and remarriage.

Postponing Marriage and Parenting

After declining since the 1920s, the average age of first-time brides and grooms turned upward in the 1980s. In 1925, the average bride was 25 and her groom was almost 30. By 1975, the brides averaged 22 years of age and grooms only 24. Today, the average bride is older than at any time in the twentieth century and the average groom is back to where he was in 1925 (see Table 13.3). Further, men and women are now closer in age at the time of their first marriage, suggesting a move to greater equality (Milan, 2000).

Table 13.3 Changes in the Average Age of Marriage, Canada, 1925–1998

	Average Age of Marriage	
	Brides	**Grooms**
1925	25.3	29.8
1930	25.0	29.2
1935	25.0	29.0
1940	24.4	27.7
1945	25.5	29.0
1950	25.3	28.5
1955	25.1	28.0
1960	24.7	27.7
1965	24.5	27.2
1970	24.9	27.3
1975	22.0	24.4
1980	22.8	25.0
1985	24.1	26.2
1990	25.5	27.4
1995	27.1	29.0
1998	27.6	29.7

Source: Statistics Canada.

At the same time, since the mid-1970s, there has been a steady decrease in the nuptiality rate in Canada—that is, the number of marriages per 1000 Canadians. Despite increases in the number of Canadians, the number of marriages has declined so dramatically that, in 1998, the marriage rate was at an all-time low (Milan, 2000). The trend was particularly marked in Quebec, where the marriage rate per 1000 population dropped from 640 in 1976 to 345 in 1997. It is intriguing to note that the decline has not been so precipitous in the United States, where the marriage rate is 1.5 times that of Canada (Statistics Canada, 2001, p. 189).

Not only marriage but also child-rearing is being postponed. Table 13.4 reveals the clear shifts in child-bearing patterns. Younger women, particularly those under 30 years of age, are having fewer babies, while women over age 30 have increased their fertility rate. In the mid-1980s, only 14 percent of first-time mothers were over age 30; today, almost one-third of first births are to women aged 30 or more. Overall, of course, there has been a dramatic decrease in the number of births in each age group. Today, it is estimated the average woman will have 1.49 children

in her lifetime; this marks the lowest fertility rate in Canadian history (Statistics Canada, 2002d). Interestingly, this is in sharp contrast to the United States fertility rate, which is 2.2. Although young women in both Canada and the United States indicate that they would like to have, on average, 2.2 children, Canadian women are having fewer children.

Analysts argue that there is a strong economic motivation behind these trends. Research indicates that Canadian women who had children earlier than the average of 27.1 years of age earned at least 6 percent less a year than those that waited until later in life. Even postponing child-rearing one year beyond the average resulted in significant improvements in income. It appears that promotions, wage increases, and training all come early in a career. Clearly, a woman without children is better able to take advantage of these opportunities and also more willing to relocate and travel, all of which may lead to career progression. If these are sacrificed in the interests of child-rearing, the woman's career may never recover (Carey, 2002a, p. A2).

The motivation to postpone child-bearing may also be related to patterns of youth unemployment. Analysts argue that the high rate of youth unemployment in Canada (higher by half than in the United States) has meant declining income for young men through the past two decades. If young people find it difficult to integrate into the labour market, it is argued, then young women will postpone marriage and delay children. By delaying having children, they dramatically increase the likelihood they will have fewer children (Carey, 2002b, p. A8).

However, as discussed below, the postponement of marriage and parenthood does not mean Canadians are avoiding relationships. Instead of marriage, more and more Canadians are opting for common-law relationships.

Common-Law Marriage

At one time, Canadians would have rejected the notion of two people living together without a formal married union. Today, 14 percent of all couples are common-law, and, if trends continue, by 2022 the number of common-law couples will be equal to the number of married couples. In Quebec, where common-law relationships are most popular, 30 percent of all couples are common-law unions (Anderssen, 2002).

Table 13.4 Changes in Fertility Rates* Among Canadians, 1961–1999

	15–19 Years	20–24 Years	25–29 Years	30–34 Years	35–39 Years	40–44 Years
1961	58.2	233.6	219.2	144.9	81.1	28.5
1981	31.8	100.2	125.3	68.1	19.8	3.3
1991	28.6	78.1	118.6	85.8	30.1	4.2
1999	14.6	64.6	98.4	88.5	35.6	6.0

*Fertility rate is calculated by dividing the number of live births in each age group by the total female population (in thousands) in each age group.

Source: Statistics Canada, from Alain Belanger, *Report on the Demographic Situation in Canada 1998–1999: Current Demographic Analysis.* Ottawa: Ministry of Industry, Catalogue no. 91-209-XPE, Statistics Canada 1998.

Table 13.5 Percentage of All Canadians in Various Living Arrangements, by Sex, 2001

	Men	Women
Single	46.6	39.5
Married*	47.4	46.9
Widowed	1.8	8.0
Divorced	4.2	5.5

*Includes persons legally married, legally married and separated, persons living common-law.

Source: Derived from Statistics Canada, 2002, *CANSIM II*, Table 051-0010.

Reflecting a shift in social values, increasing numbers of common-law unions include children. In 2001, almost half of common-law families involved children, and more than one in 10 (13 percent) children across Canada were living in a common-law family (Anderssen, 2002).

For some common-law couples, their relationship is a trial run. They live together as long as the relationship works, and if it sours, they can move out. In line with this pattern, first common-law relationships are twice as likely as first marriages to end in separation. Not surprisingly, children of separated parents are more likely to opt for this kind of trial run, and, also not surprisingly, almost half of common-law relationships end within five years. Further, those common-law couples who do marry are more likely to divorce than those who did not cohabit first (Statistics Canada, 2002c).

> **Focus Question**
> Does the postponement of marriage and child-rearing, along with increases in divorce, signal a disillusionment with family life?

The Sandwich Generation and Eldercare

The term "sandwich generation" refers to people who find themselves sandwiched between two generations, responsible for the care of their children as well as their own aging parents. Typically, they are between the ages of 40 and 55, and frequently they are women. A recent survey of eldercare in Canada found that women made up the majority (61 percent) of eldercare-givers and provided much more time than men on care-related activities. Indeed, many women were caring for more than two seniors, and women were more likely than men to be the primary caregiver (Frederick & Fast, 1999, p. 27).

Not surprisingly, feeling responsible both for children and for aging and/or ill parents can result in guilt and anger because people can be in only one place at a time (Shellenbarger, 1994a). Indeed, research in Canada suggests that although eldercare is seen as an act of love, the more time that must be devoted to care of the elderly, the more stress the caregivers experience (Frederick & Fast, 1999).

Concerns about the sandwich generation and eldercare have gained the attention of the corporate world, and about 25 percent of large companies offer some kind of eldercare assistance to their employees (Hewitt Associates, 1995), and increasing numbers of collective agreements are including "eternity care" (care for terminally ill elderly) in their discussions. Assistance for the caregiver may include seminars, referral services, and flexible work schedules in order to help employees meet their responsibilities without missing so much work (Shellenbarger, 1994b).

Some experts believe that companies may respond more positively to the issue of eldercare than to child day care. Why? Most CEOs are older men whose wives stayed home to take care of their children, so they lack an understanding of the stresses of balancing work and child care. Nearly all have aging parents, however, and many have faced the turmoil of trying to cope with work, children, and aging parents.

> **Focus Question**
> Explain the "sandwich generation" and discuss its particular relevance for women.

Divorce and Remarriage

Discussion of the family would not be complete without considering marriage breakup. Many analysts have pointed to increases in divorce as evidence not only that the family is in decline but that our society and its basic social values are in jeopardy. Certainly, divorce may be a catastrophic event in the family, with long-term negative consequences for all family members. For example, recent research suggests that divorced men are almost twice as likely as other men to commit suicide. However, it is also important to place increases in divorce rates in the larger context of continued societal commitment to both marriage and child-rearing. A clear majority (over 75 percent) of Canadian young people plan to marry and an overwhelming majority (about 95 percent) intend to have children (Dupuis, 1998). Indeed, an overwhelming majority of Canadians (80 percent) are currently involved in family life in some way-as husbands, wives, common-law partners, lone parents, or children (Statistics Canada, 1998, p. 181). Finally, it is important to be aware of the fact that although many marriages end in divorce, most divorces (except in Quebec) end in remarriages (Nelson & Robinson, 2002, p. 347). When marriages fail, Canadian men and women frequently try again.

In the past, divorce was a distinctly uncommon phenomenon. From the time of Confederation until 1968, adultery was the only grounds for divorce in most of Canada. Not surprisingly, few couples petitioned on these scandalous grounds. However, this did not mean that marriages did not break down. Formal divorces were uncommon, but informal separations and family desertions provided a way out for many unhappy husbands and wives.

Finally, in 1968, under growing social pressure, the *Divorce Act* was changed, the grounds for divorce were expanded, and a number of "no-fault, no-blame grounds" were added. In particular, if the couple could demonstrate that they had lived separately for three or more years, they could petition for divorce.

Predictably, this change in the law opened the floodgates to a backlog of divorce actions. Couples who had been informally divorced made their status official and legitimate. In 1985 the *Divorce Act* was amended again: A couple living separately for a period of not less than one year, as well as adultery or mental or physical cruelty were viewed as indicative of marriage breakdown and legitimate grounds for divorce (Nelson & Robinson, 2002, pp. 343–344).

These changes in the law were reflected in dramatic increases in the number of Canadians obtaining divorces. Table 13.6 reveals the increases from 1925 to the mid-1980s and the more recent levelling-off. From 1990 to 1995, the number of divorces plateaued and then dropped in 1996 and 1997. In 1998, the divorce rate increased again. Today over one-third (36 percent) of marriages are expected to end in divorce within 30 years of marriage. The average length of marriage ending in divorce increased to 14 years and the average age at divorce rose to 42 for men and 29 for women. Only 31 percent of divorces involve custody orders, with 60 percent of primary custody being awarded to mothers, 10 percent to fathers, and 30 percent joint custody ("Happily ever after?" 2001, p. 22).

Divorce is, of course, not a distinctly Canadian phenomenon. Indeed, our neighbour to the south has the highest divorce rate in the industrialized world with 20 out of every 1000 adult women indicating they have been divorced and one million children a year learning that their parents are divorcing (Henslin, 2001, p. 466). In contrast, Canada reports 11 per 1000 women and Italy a mere 2. Further, there are likely to be continued changes in the global patterns of divorce. Despite the prevailing impression that Muslim countries are conservative and oppose women's rights within marriage, significant shifts are occurring in the Muslim world. Tunisia and, more recently Egypt (March 2000), enacted laws that would allow women to seek a unilateral, no-questions-asked divorce; in short, women have gained divorce rights similar to those of men (United Nations Population Fund, 2000, p. 55). As we saw in Canada, changes in divorce law often precede dramatic changes in the rates of divorce.

In the meantime, the rate of remarriage in Canada is levelling off. From the 1970s to the 1990s, as numbers of divorced men and women increased, the number of remarriages grew. By the mid 1990s, one third of marriages involved a previously married groom and/or bride (Vanier Institute, 2000; Nelson & Robinson, 2002, p. 391). In recent years, this pattern has reversed, and by 1995 one marriage in four involved at least one partner who was married previously (Statistics Canada, 1998, pp. 187–188).

For a variety of reasons—including the tendency of men to marry younger women and the greater longevity of women—men are more likely to remarry and remarry more quickly than women. This may reflect not only the smaller pool of potential partners for women, but also men's greater motivation to remarry. Research has consistently indicated that men derive greater benefit from marriage—for example, in terms of increased life expectancy—than women. Presumably, men derive considerable benefit from the familial gender roles in which women are expected to bring to the marriage companionship skills as well as housekeeping abilities. In line with this, women who possess very high levels of education and income are less likely to remarry than their less-educated, less well-to-do counterparts (Nelson & Robinson, 2002, pp. 347–348). Apparently, women who are more educated and more independent (no children) can afford to be more selective.

Children of Divorce

From the 1970s to the end of the 1990s, the number of young Canadian children witnessing divorce increased by 300 percent (Gorlick, 2000, p. 265). Most divorcing parents become so wrapped up in their own problems that they are unable to prepare their children for the divorce—even if they knew how to do so in the first place. When the break comes, children often become confused and insecure. For security, many cling to the unrealistic idea that their parents will be reunited (Wallerstein & Kelly, 1992). To help resolve the conflict, they may side with one parent and reject the other. Needless to say, social researchers are concerned that children will suffer long-term negative effects from divorce.

A Statistics Canada survey of 23 000 children, which generated considerable media attention, claimed that "living with a single parent has a devastating effect on children physically, mentally and emotionally" (Carey, 1998, p. A2).

Table 13.6 Rates of Divorce* in Canada, 1925–2000

1925	0.06
1930	0.09
1975	2.22
1980	2.59
1985	2.44
1990	2.80
1995	2.60
2000	2.30

*Rate of divorce indicates the number of divorces per 1000 population.

Source: Statistics Canada.

 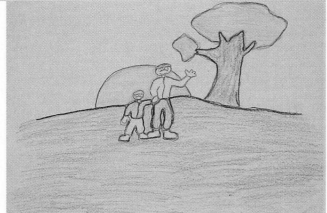

It is difficult to capture the anguish of children of divorce, but these lines by the fourth-grader who drew these two pictures are eloquent:

Me alone in the park …
All alone in the park.
My Dad and Mom are divorced
That's why I'm all alone.

This is me in the picture with
my son. We are taking a walk in the park.
I will never be like my father.
I will never divorce my wife and kid.

According to initial findings from this 18-year study, children from lone-parent families have poorer scores in terms of academic achievement, health, behaviour, and relationships. Similarly, American research suggests that girls raised away from a biological parent are more likely to become sexually active at a younger age and to have a child outside marriage while their male counterparts are more likely to have trouble getting employment. Both boys and girls are more likely to drop out of high school, more likely to leave home earlier, more likely to rely on Income Assistance as adults, and also more likely to work at low-paying jobs. Furthermore, adult children of divorce are more likely to put off marriage and have a higher chance of marital instability (Mclanahan, 2002).

Not surprisingly, the more frequently children experienced disruptions (divorce, death) in the parental structure of the family (800 000 adult Canadians have experienced two or more such disruptions), the less likely they are as adults to report they had a very happy childhood (Williams, 2001). There is likely a complex interplay of emotional and economic issues here, since children of divorce who end up supported by single mothers are likely to experience severe economic pressures.

Certainly the research does not present an unqualifiedly negative impression of the impact of divorce on children. A recent study that compared the lives of 518 divorced or separated mothers to 502 married mothers and many of their children concluded that single mothers are functioning very well as parents and are able to protect their children against many of the stresses of divorce. The researcher suggests that with the dramatic increases in numbers of single parents, some of the stigma attached to being a divorced single parent has gone, and institutions in society, notably schools, have become more sensitive to the diversity of family forms (Habib, 2000). Other researchers report, from interviews with children of divorce, that although parental divorce is experienced as a crisis in children's lives, many are able to become active, competent participants in the changing family and regain a new sense of balance (Butler, Scanlan, Robinson, Douglas, & Murch, 2002). Clearly, the impact of divorce on children is a complex and dynamic process.

Economics is an important piece of this complexity. The negative impacts of divorce on children likely have much to do with the fact that so many single-parent families are poor. Since the overwhelming majority of single parents are women, they are handicapped by the tendency of women to be segregated into low-wage "women's jobs." Most divorced women earn less than their former husbands, and their financial problems may be compounded by difficulties in securing child-support payments. In this context, it is not surprising to learn that almost half of mother-headed one-parent families and one-quarter of father-headed one-parent families live in poverty (Vanier Institute, 2000, p. 114). It is likely that this economic deprivation then intensifies other problems that emerge as a result of the disruption of household routines and increased pressures on the mother-child relationship (Mclanahan, 2002).

It is interesting to note that although Canadians express concerns about the impact of divorce on children, the prevailing values support ending an unhappy marriage. Whatever our concerns about the well-being of children, most of us are not willing to stay in an unhappy relationship simply for the sake of the children. Six out of 10 Canadians indicated in a recent survey that they would not stay married for the kids' sake. Women, who are often the front-line parent in families, were less inclined than men to stay married in order to protect the children's happiness. Only one woman in three indicated she would stay in a bad marriage for her children (Frederick & Hamel, 1998, p. 10).

> ## Focus Question
> Divorce has a very different impact on men, on women, and on children. Explain some of these differences.

In Sum

Not only is it vital to appreciate the variety of family forms in Canada, we must recognize that families are in the midst of important changes. More and more Canadians are postponing marriage and parenting. They are also much more likely to enter into common-law relationships. As more and more Canadians become seniors, middle-aged Canadians are finding that family responsibilities involve providing care for aging parents. Finally, although divorce statistics appear to have hit a plateau, Canadians are finding that divorce is an increasingly common ingredient of family life.

Two Sides of Family Life

Let's first look at situations in which marriage and family have gone seriously wrong and then try to answer the question of what makes marriage work.

The Dark Side of Family Life: Child Abuse, Battering, and Incest

The dark side of family life involves events that people would rather keep in the dark. In Canada and around the globe, family life is often marred by violence and abuse. We shall look at child abuse, battering, and incest.

Child Abuse. Most of us are bothered by child abuse—helpless children being victimized by their own parents, the adults who are supposed to love, protect, and nurture them. The most gruesome of these cases make the evening news—for example, the four-year-old girl beaten and raped by her mother's boyfriend, who passed away after three days in a coma, or the six-to-ten-year-old children video-

taped in sex acts by their stepfather. But few of the less-sensational child abuse cases come to our attention: the children who live in filth, those who are neglected, those who are left alone for hours or days at a time, those who are beaten with extension cords, and those who are kept in a plywood box perforated with holes.

At present, we do not have statistics that capture the full extent of child abuse across Canada or around the globe (Duffy & Momirov, 1997, p. 61). Police statistics provide a glimpse, but only recently have more accurate reporting by police along with legislated requirements for mandatory coroner inquests improved our knowledge base. Crime figures provide us with part of the picture. In 1996, when children under 18 made up 24 percent of the Canadian population, they were the victims in 23 percent of violent crime reported to police. Sixty-one percent of the sexual assaults reported to police were against children and 30 percent were perpetrated by a family member (Statistics Canada, 2002e).

In Ontario, recent research suggests evidence of a dramatic surge in the number of confirmed cases of child abuse reported by children's aid societies. In 1998, 24 000 children were identified as abused compared with half this number five years earlier. Further, the proportion of these cases that resulted in criminal charges almost doubled in that same time frame (2100 in 1993 and 4000 in 1998) (Orwen, 2002). It is interesting to note that the majority of cases investigated by agencies involve neglect and emotional maltreatment, with exposure to family violence the most common form of suspected emotional abuse. Severe physical abuse, which requires medical treatment, is relatively rare (Infantry, 2001, p. A3). Even opinion polls provide important information here. A recent poll of Canadians found that 17 percent of respondents had personal knowledge of child abuse (physical abuse of children by their parents). Alarmingly, the largest segment of respondents did nothing in response to these incidents (Edwards & Mazzuca, 1999).

While physical abuse and murder capture the headlines, it's important to realize that numerous Canadian children are abused by being neglected or exposed to growing up in a violent home. Recent research suggests that when children simply witness physical fights between adults or teenagers in their home, they become more likely to be physically aggressive, to commit property offences, and to display emotional disorders ("The harm that family violence does to children," 2001, p. 19). At the other end of the spectrum, some children suffer the ultimate abuse and are murdered by family members. In 2000, 55 children (under age 18) were killed in Canada, with parents being charged in 31 of these deaths (Statistics Canada, 2002e, p. 36).

Globally, we know that in some countries accepted social practices result in the routine abuse of children, especially female children. Infanticide and neglect (along with

Ironically, social research into the patterns of family violence has led to disputes about who is the "real" victim. Despite media coverage indicating that both men and women engage in violence in intimate relationships, it is important to keep in mind that it is typically women who are the victims of severe violence, and even of murder, in violent heterosexual relationships.

sex-selective abortion) are reported to have resulted in the elimination of 60 million girls from Asian populations. Honour killings (or rapes) of young girls who are suspected of dishonouring their families by losing their virginity or acting in an "unchaste" manner are a socially sanctioned form of child murder. Female genital mutilation, which has been performed on at least 130 million girls and often results in persistent gynecological problems, may be viewed as a socially accepted expression of child sexual abuse. Child labour, particularly in the form of child prostitution, is a culturally embedded practice that destroys childhoods around the world. It is estimated that 2 million girls between the ages of 5 and 15 are introduced, often by family members, to the commercial sex market each year, some ending up on the streets of Toronto and Vancouver (United Nations Population Fund, 2000). Child abuse, when viewed from this perspective, is a complex, growing, and global reality.

Battering. Thanks in large measure to Statistics Canada's landmark 1993 *Canadian Violence Against Women Survey* and the now yearly family violence statistical profiles, we have excellent national statistics concerning wife battering. In the1993 survey, almost one woman in three (29 percent) who had ever married or lived in a common-law relationship revealed at least one episode of violence by a husband or live-in partner (H. Johnson, 1996). According to the 1999 General Social Survey on Victimization, 1.2 million women and men have experienced "spousal violence during the past five years." Not surprisingly, it is women who experience more frequent and severe violence, seek medical attention, and fear for their lives because of this violence. When domestic violence turns to murder, women are three times more likely than men to be the victim ("Family violence," 2000, p. 28).

The global picture is alarmingly similar. A quick review of the information at hand indicates that violence against women in intimate relationships remains commonplace. In South Africa 20 percent, in Ethiopia 45 percent, and in Switzerland 21 percent of adult women reported physical assault by a male partner. In some countries, the violence is amplified by a cultural tolerance for violence against women—a view shared by men and women alike. In rural Egypt, for example, 80 percent of women surveyed said that beatings were common and justified, especially if the woman refused her partner sex. In some countries (such as the case of dowry murder in India), prevailing laws and practices mean that the male attackers will seldom be punished and women have little access to alternative shelter (United Nations Population Fund, 2000; Rudd, 2001).

Violence against women is clearly related to the sexist structure of society, which we reviewed in Chapter 7, and to the socialization we reviewed in Chapter 4. Growing up with norms that encourage aggression and the use of violence, many men feel it is their right to control women. When frustrated in a relationship—or even by causes outside it—many men turn violently on their wives and lovers. The basic sociological question is how to socialize males to handle frustration and disagreements without resorting to violence (Rieker et al., 1997). We do not yet have this answer.

Having discussed woman abuse among heterosexual couples, it's important to point out that gays and lesbians are not immune from partner abuse. Canadian researcher Janice Ristock (2002) reports that lesbians, like straight women, may be subjected to severe physical, verbal, and sexual abuse. Unlike heterosexual women, they may be afraid to use shelters, crisis counselling, or support groups and may live in fear of being "outed" by their abuser.

According to Ristock's interviews, when lesbians did turn to police their complaints were often minimized or laughed off. In short, while violence is often gendered among heterosexual couples, it is not simply a heterosexual phenomenon.

Incest. Sexual relations between relatives, such as brothers and sisters or parents and children, called **incest**, are most likely to occur in families that are socially isolated (B. A. Smith, 1992). As with marital rape, sociological research has destroyed assumptions that incest is not common. Sociologist Diana Russell (n.d.) found that incest victims who experience the most difficulty are those who have been victimized the most often, over longer periods of time, and whose incest was "more intrusive," for example, sexual intercourse as opposed to sexual touching.

Who are the offenders? Russell found that uncles are the most common offenders, followed by first cousins, then fathers (stepfathers especially), brothers, and, finally, relatives ranging from brothers-in-law to stepgrandfathers. Other researchers report that brother-sister incest is several times more common than father-child incest (Canavan, Meyer, & Higgs, 1992). Incest between mothers and sons is rare.

As with other forms of child abuse, sexual abuse appears to be on the rise. It is likely this increase reflects improved reporting as well as increased research in the field. In 1998, there were approximately 3800 confirmed cases of sexual abuse in Ontario, up from slightly less than 2000 in 1993 (Orwin, 2002).

> **Focus Question**
> How is violence in the family connected to the sexist structure of society?

The Bright Side of Family Life: Successful Marriages

After examining divorce and family abuse, one could easily conclude that marriages seldom work out. That would be far from the truth. To find out what makes marriage successful, sociologists Jeanette and Robert Lauer (1992) interviewed 351 couples who had been married 15 years or longer. Fifty-one of these marriages were unhappy but the couple stayed together for religious reasons, family tradition, or "the sake of the children." Of the others, the 300 happy couples, all:

1. think of their spouse as their best friend;
2. like their spouse as a person;
3. think of marriage as a long-term commitment;
4. believe that marriage is sacred;
5. agree with their spouse on aims and goals;
6. believe that their spouse has grown more interesting over the years;
7. strongly want the relationship to succeed;
8. laugh together.

Not surprisingly there are some general social factors that also help predict "lasting" marriages. Being wealthy, religious, college-educated, not living common-law before marriage, and postponing marriage to at least age 20 are all factors associated with low rates of divorce ("U.S. study tries to unravel mysteries of lasting marriages," 2002, p. A12).

The Future of Marriage and Family

What can we expect of marriage and family in the future?

Certain trends are firmly in place. Cohabitation, mother-headed families, and age at first marriage will increase. More married women will join the work force, and they will continue to gain marital power. Equality in marriage, however, is not even on the horizon. The number of elderly will continue to increase, and more couples will find themselves sandwiched between caring for their parents and their own children. The reduction in our divorce rate is another matter entirely. At this point we don't know whether it is just a breather from which an even higher rate will be launched, the prelude to a long-term decline, or even an indication that we have reached the saturation point and divorce will remain flat.

Finally, our culture will continue to be haunted by distorted images of marriage and family: the bleak ones portrayed in the mass media and the rosy ones painted by cultural myths. Sociological research can help correct these distortions and allow us to see how our own family experiences fit into the patterns of our culture. Sociological research also can help to answer the big question of how to formulate social policy that will support and enhance family life.

> **Focus Question**
> What will the Canadian family look like in 20 years?

In Sum

Social researchers are increasingly aware that numerous families are often troubled and even violent. The abuse is particularly troublesome when the victims are children, since they are often trapped by the power of their parental "caregivers." Women are also common victims of family violence and these assaults may put the victims at significant risk. Given that family life may go tragically wrong, it is important to be aware of the ingredients for a good marriage. Although as a society, we are increasingly aware of family dynamics, in the immediate future many families are likely to continue to struggle with issues of inequality and conflict.

Summary and Review

MARRIAGE AND FAMILY IN GLOBAL PERSPECTIVE

What is a family—and what themes are universal?

Family is difficult to define. For just about every element one might consider essential, there are exceptions. Consequently, **family** is defined broadly—as two or more people who consider themselves related by blood, marriage, or adoption. Sociologists and anthropologists have documented extensive variation in family customs—from cultures in which babies are married to those in which husbands and wives refrain from sexual relations for years at a time. Universally, **marriage** and family are mechanisms for governing mate selection, reckoning descent, and establishing inheritance and authority. pp. 304–307.

MARRIAGE AND FAMILY IN THEORETICAL PERSPECTIVE

What is the functionalist perspective on marriage and family?

Functionalists examine the functions of families, analyzing such matters as the incest taboo. They also examine consequences of weakening family functions, and the dysfunctions of the family. pp. 307–308.

What is the conflict perspective on marriage and family?

Conflict theorists examine how marriage and family help perpetuate inequalities, especially the subservience of women. Power struggles in marriage, such as those over housework, are an example. pp. 309–310.

What is a symbolic interactionist perspective on marriage and family?

Symbolic interactionists examine how the contrasting experiences and perspectives of men and women are played out in marriage. They stress that only by grasping the vastly different perspectives of wives and husbands can we understand their behaviour. pp. 311–312.

THE FAMILY LIFE CYCLE

What are the major elements of the family life cycle?

The major elements are love and courtship, marriage, childbirth, child-rearing, and the family in later life. Most marriages follow predictable patterns of age, social class, race, and religion. Childbirth and child-rearing patterns also vary by social class. pp. 313–316.

DIVERSITY IN CANADIAN FAMILIES

How significant are race and ethnicity in family life?

The primary distinction is social class, not race or ethnicity. Families of the same social class are likely to be similar, regardless of their racial or ethnic makeup. pp. 316–317.

What other diversity in Canadian families is there?

Also discussed were one-parent, childless, **blended**, and gay families. Although each has its own unique features, social class is also significant in determining each one's primary characteristics. Poverty is especially significant for one-parent families, most of which are headed by women. pp. 317–320.

TRENDS IN CANADIAN FAMILIES

What major changes characterize Canadian families?

Two changes are postponement of first marriage and an increase in common-law marriages. With more people living longer, many middle-aged couples find themselves sandwiched between caring for their own children and caring for their own parents. pp. 320–322.

How do children and their parents adjust to divorce?

Divorce is especially difficult for children, whose adjustment problems often continue into adulthood. Financial problems are usually greater for the former wives. Although most divorced people remarry, their rate of remarriage has slowed considerably. pp. 322–325.

TWO SIDES OF FAMILY LIFE

What are the two sides of family life?

The dark side is family abuse—child abuse, spouse battering, and incest, activities that revolve around the misuse of family power. The bright side is families that provide intense satisfaction for spouses and their children. pp. 325–327.

What is the likely future of marriage and family?

We can expect cohabitation, births to unmarried mothers, and age at marriage to increase. The growing numbers of women in the work force will likely continue to shift the marital balance of power. p. 327.

Critical Thinking Questions

1. How would the participants in "successful" marriages address the issue of the division of household work?

2. How are the interconnections between the family and other societal institutions—the economic system, the education system—likely to change in the near future?

3. Given that the Canadian family is going through a number of important changes, what particular family issues confront children and adolescents today?

Key Terms

bilateral (system of descent) 305	family of procreation 307
blended family 318	homogamy 313
conservative bias 307	household 307
egalitarian 305	incest 327
endogamy 305	intentional families 320
exogamy 305	marriage 307
extended family 307	matriarchy 305
family 307	matrilineal (system of descent) 305
family of orientation 307	monolithic bias 307

Weblinks

All URLs listed are current as of the printing of this book. URLs are often changed. Please check our Web site **www.abacon.com/ henslin** for updates.

National Clearinghouse on Family Violence

www.hc-sc.gc.ca/hppb/familyviolence/
The National Clearinghouse on Family Violence is a national resource centre for all Canadians seeking information about violence inside the family and looking for new resources being used to address it. The Clearinghouse seeks to help Canadian communities work toward the eventual elimination of all forms of family violence.

Family Relations

www.personal.psu.edu/faculty/n/x/nxd10/family3.htm
Information about families put together by Pennsylvania State University students in the course "Human Development & Family Studies 418."

Family Sociology Resources

osiris.colorado.edu/SOC/RES/family.html
Part of the WWW Resources for Sociologists site of the Department of Sociology, University of Colorado at Boulder.

Vanier Institute of the Family

www.vifamily.ca
The Vanier Institute of the Family was established in 1965 under the patronage of their Excellencies Governor General Georges P. Vanier and Madame Pauline Vanier. It is a national voluntary organization dedicated to promoting the well-being of Canada's families through research, publications, public education, and advocacy. The Web site is a very useful resource for publications examining trends in Canadian families.

Children's Defense Fund

www.childrensdefense.org/
The mission of the Fund is to "ensure every child a Healthy Start, a Head Start, a Fair Start, a Safe Start, and a Moral Start in life and successful passage to adulthood with the help of caring families and communities."

Abstracts on Work and Family Interactions

www.cyfc.umn.edu/Work/abstracts.html
A series of abstracts of current literature on work and family interactions created as a project of a University of Minnesota course called Work Family Relationships. Part of Work-Family-Life Interactions is a collection of information, research, and opinion on work and family issues that aims to provide ongoing electronic access to information resources that assist in balancing and integrating our work and personal lives.

Chapter 14

Education and Religion

◼ 331

Learning Outcomes

After you have studied this chapter, you will be able to

- ■ discuss why there is an emphasis on credentialism within contemporary Canadian society
- ■ analyze the functions of education and the meaning of the "hidden curriculum"
- ■ discuss the relationship between access to education and social inequality
- ■ understand how functionalist, symbolic interactionist, conflict, and feminist theories explain religion
- ■ describe the religious differences between Canada and the United States
- ■ explain the process by which a cult is transformed into an organized religion

Neha still feels resentment when she recalls the memo that greeted her that Monday morning:

> With growing concern about international competition for our products, the management is upgrading several positions. The attached listing of jobs states the new qualifications that must be met.

Neha quickly scanned the list. The rumours had been right, after all. The new position the company was opening up—the job she had been slated to get—was listed.

After regaining her composure somewhat, but still angry, Neha marched to her supervisor's office. "I've been doing my job for three years," she said. "You always gave me good evaluations, and you said I'd get that new position."

"I know, Neha. You'd be good at it. Believe me, I gave you a high recommendation. But what can

I do? You know what the higher-ups are like. If they decide they want someone with a university degree, that's just what they'll get."

"But I can't go back to university now, not with all my responsibilities. It's been five years since I was in university, and I still have a year to go."

The supervisor was sympathetic, but she insisted that her hands were tied. Neha would have to continue working at the lower job classification—and stay at the lower pay.

It was Neha's responsibility to break in Melissa, the newcomer with the freshly minted university degree. Those were the toughest two weeks Neha ever spent at work—especially since she knew that Melissa was already being paid more than she was.

Education: Transferring Knowledge and Skills

Today's Credential Society

Sociologist Randall Collins (1979) observed that industrialized nations have become **credential societies**, that employers use diplomas and degrees to determine who is eligible for a job. In many cases, the diploma or degree is irrelevant for the work that must be performed. The new job that Neha wanted, for example, did not suddenly change into a task requiring a university degree. Her immediate supervisor knew Neha's abilities well and was

sure she could handle the responsibility just fine—but the new company policy required a credential that Neha didn't have. Similarly, is a high school diploma necessary to pump gas or to sell shoes? Yet employers routinely require such credentials.

In fact, it is often on the job, not at school, that employees learn the specific knowledge or skills a job requires. A high school diploma teaches no one how to sell tacos or to be polite to customers. Neha had to teach Melissa the ropes. Why, then, do employers insist on diplomas and degrees? Why don't they simply use on-the-job training?

A major reason credentials are required is the larger size, urbanization, and consequent anonymity of industrial societies. Diplomas and degrees serve as automatic sorting devices. Because employers don't know potential workers personally or even by reputation, they depend on schools to weed out the capable from the incapable. By hiring graduates, the employer assumes that the individuals are responsible people; for evidently they have shown up on time for numerous classes, have turned in scores of assignments, and have demonstrated basic writing and thinking skills. The specific job skills that a position requires can then be grafted onto this base certified by the academic institution.

In other cases, specific job skills must be mastered before an individual is allowed to do certain work. As a result of change in technology and in knowledge, simple on-the-job training will not do for physicians, engineers, and airline pilots. That is precisely why doctors so prominently display their credentials. Their framed degrees declare that they have been certified by an institution of higher learning, that they are qualified to work on our bodies.

In general, unemployment rates are lower among the more highly educated. In Canada in 1999 the unemployment rate among university graduates was 4.3 percent. In contrast, 7.5 percent of high school graduates were unemployed, while 13.5 percent of those who did not finish high school and 12.8 percent of Canadians over age 15 who had eight or fewer years of schooling were unemployed (Statistics Canada, 2001, Table 71, p. 200).

Without the right credentials, you won't get hired. It does not matter that you can do the job better than someone else. You will never have the opportunity to prove what you can do, for, like Neha, you lack the credentials even to be considered for the job.

The Development of Modern Education

Credentialing is only one indicator of how central the educational institution is in our lives. Before exploring the role of education in contemporary society, let us first look at education in earlier societies, and then trace the development of universal education.

Education in Earlier Societies

In earlier societies there was no separate social institution called education. There were no special buildings called schools, and no people who earned their living as teachers. Rather, as an integral part of growing up children learned what was necessary to get along in life. If hunting or cooking were the essential skills, then people who already possessed those skills taught them. *Education was synonymous with* **acculturation**, the transmission of culture from one generation to the next—as it still is in today's preliterate groups.

In some societies, when a sufficient surplus developed—as in Arabia, China, North Africa, and classical Greece—a separate institution developed. Some people then devoted

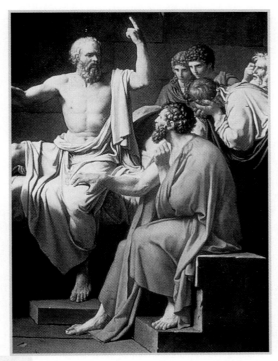

One of the first great educators was Socrates, depicted here in a 1787 painting by Jacques Louis David. Education can be a dangerous thing, for it often challenges conventional beliefs. Socrates, who taught in Greece 400 years before the birth of Christ, was forced to take poison because his views challenged those of the establishment.

themselves to teaching, while those who had the leisure—the children of the wealthy—became their students. In ancient China, for example, Confucius taught a few select pupils, while in Greece, Aristotle, Plato, and Socrates taught science and philosophy to upper-class boys. **Education**, then, came to be something quite distinct from informal acculturation; education is a group's *formal* system of teaching knowledge, values, and skills. Such instruction stood in marked contrast to the learning of traditional skills such as farming or hunting, for it was clearly intended to develop the mind.

The flourishing of education during the period roughly marked by the birth of Christ, however, slowly died out. During the Dark Ages of Europe, the candle of enlightenment was kept burning by monks, who, except for a handful of the wealthy and nobility, were the only ones who could read and write. Although they delved into philosophy, the intellectual activities of the monks centred on learning Greek, Latin, and Hebrew so that they could read early texts of the Bible and writings of the church fathers. Similarly, Jews kept formal learning alive as they studied the Torah.

Formal education, however, remained limited to those who had the leisure to pursue it. (In fact, school comes from a Greek word meaning "leisure.") Industrialization transformed this approach to learning, for the new machinery and new types of jobs brought a general need to be able to read, to write, and to work accurately with figures—the classic "three R's" of the nineteenth century ("Reading, 'Riting, and 'Rithmetic").

Democracy, Industrialization, and Universal Education

The development of universal education is linked to industrialization. Let's see how free, universal education was developed in Canada.

Prior to Confederation, it was mainly religious groups who were most involved in education. Their primary goal was to "civilize" Native Canadians along with other children by teaching them a curriculum based on the "three R's." The church's influence on education, however, was significant and lessons usually included guidance in morality and obedience. Both Catholic and Protestant (or public) school systems had been created even before Confederation. The *School Act* of 1851 provided Roman Catholics with public funds for their schools, a topic of ongoing controversy even today. The development of higher education was also linked to religious bodies. North America's oldest institution of higher learning, Laval University in Quebec City, was founded by Jesuit priests in 1636. The founders of both University of Toronto and McGill University were linked to the Church of England.

By the time of Confederation, the makings of a free and universal education system had been firmly entrenched. A number of school acts were passed throughout Upper and Lower Canada, for example, providing for schools within bounded areas, and school attendance gradually began to increase as the value of education was recognized across communities. Commitment to education was regarded not only as a personal benefit, but also as a civic responsibility, since schooling the masses was considered the means to social improvement. Education was a matter of **political socialization**, the way young people would be inculcated with beliefs, ideas, and values and would embrace the civil order, all of which was necessary for the developing capitalist and industrial order. A universal system of schooling based on standardized texts would instill patriotism and teach the principles of democratic government.

In Ontario, Reverend Egerton Ryerson, who was the province's superintendent of schools from 1844 to 1876, was instrumental in establishing the system of free, publicly supported schools. His work in Ontario was eventually followed by that of educational activists throughout Canada. Prior to Ryerson's work, formal education was optional for working-class children. Most children learned from their parents in and around the home or in the small workshops that dotted the Canadian landscape. Upper-class children attended costly private schools or were taught in their home by tutors. In 1871, schooling was made compulsory and the relationship between the school and the state tightened. The common school became "a public institution in the modern sense of the term, an institution not only paid for out of public funds, but with publicly defined goals" (Prentice, 1977, p. 17). It is no coincidence that universal education and industrialization occurred simultaneously. Seeing that the economy was undergoing fundamental change, political and civic leaders recognized the need for an educated work force. They also feared the influx of foreign values and looked on public education as a way to socialize immigrants to the Canadian way of life.

Over time, the amount of education considered necessary continued to expand. By 1920, most provinces had

Figure 14.1 Educational Attainment Among Canadians Aged 15+, 1999

Source: Statistics Canada, 2001, *Education in Canada 2000*. Ottawa: Minister of Industry, Catalogue no. 81.22-XPB.

Note: Population (est.): 11 768 000 men; 12 201 000 women.

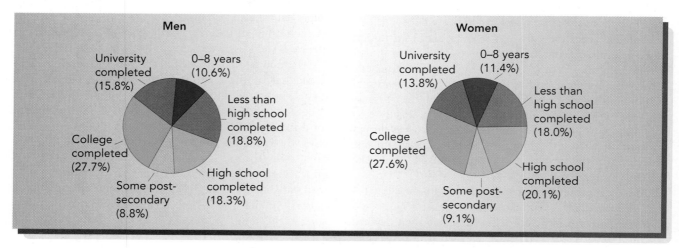

compulsory education laws requiring children to attend school, usually until they had completed the eighth grade or turned 16, whichever came first. In the early 1900s, graduation from the eighth grade was considered to be a full education for most people. "Dropouts" at that time were students who did not complete grade school. High school, as its name implies, was viewed as a form of "higher" education.

As industrialization progressed and as fewer people made their living from agriculture, formal education came to be thought of as essential to the well-being of society. Industrialized nations then developed some form of the credential society described earlier. Graduation with a postsecondary certificate or university degree is more and more common in Canada. As you can see from Figure 14.1, 42.5 percent of the Canadians aged 15 and over completed college or university. It is not surprising that those who have not completed high school are between the ages of 15 and 19 or are over the age of 55. Today, men are only slightly more likely than women to hold degrees or diplomas.

Canadians who don't make it through high school, however, are condemned to a difficult economic life. On average, the unemployment rate among high school leavers is higher, their wages are lower, and they are less likely to work full-time, full-year compared to high school graduates (Clark, 1997). For example, in families in which the major income earner did not graduate from high school, the family's median net worth was $62 000, but this rate soared to $117 500 when the major income earner had a Bachelor's degree. When the major income earner in a family had a professional degree in law, medicine, veterinary medicine, or optometry, then the family's median net worth jumped to $323 000 (Anderson, 2001). The rates of high school graduation are not evenly distributed across the provinces. Relatively higher numbers in Newfoundland, the Northwest Territories, Prince Edward Island, and Saskatchewan leave school before completing high school. To some degree the rates of school leaving correlate with the distribution of poverty within the provinces, with the relatively poorer provinces having a higher number of school leavers and the relatively well-off having greater numbers of university graduates.

Canada ranks fourth among developed countries for the percentage of its labour force holding a university degree (20 percent). Canada is behind the United States (28 percent), the Netherlands (27 percent), and Korea (21 percent), and ahead of Australia (17 percent), the United Kingdom (15 percent), and Sweden (13 percent), among others (Centre for Educational Research and Innovation, 1998).

> **Focus Question**
> How are education and industrialization linked?

The Functionalist Perspective: Providing Social Benefits

As stressed in previous chapters, a central position of functionalism is that when the parts of society are working properly, each contributes to the well-being or stability of that society. The intended consequences of people's actions are known as **manifest functions**, while those that are not intended are called **latent functions**. As we examine the functions of education, both its manifest and its latent functions will become evident.

Teaching Knowledge and Skills

Education's most obvious manifest function is to teach knowledge and skills, whether those be the traditional three R's or their more contemporary versions such as computer literacy. Every society must train the next generation to fulfill its significant positions. From a functionalist perspective, this is the reason schools are founded, parents support them, and taxes are raised to finance them.

Cultural Transmission of Values

At least as significant as teaching knowledge and skills is a function of education called **cultural transmission**, a process by which schools pass on a society's core values from one generation to the next. In addition to responding to the demands of the economy, the need to produce an informed electorate, and the desire to "Canadianize" immigrants, how else does the educational system reflect—and transmit—cultural values?

Schools are such an essential part of Canadian culture that it is difficult even to know where to begin. For example, outside Quebec, instruction takes place primarily in English, reflecting the dominant British influence on Canadian institutions and culture. In 1998–1999, only 151 800 students outside Quebec were enrolled in minority official (French) instruction. While this number had decreased by 6000 since 1994–1995, during the same period enrollment in English schools in Quebec had increased (Statistics Canada, 2001). Similarly, the architecture of school buildings themselves reflects Western culture, their often distinctive appearance identifying them as schools on sight, unlike, for example, the thatched-roof schools of some tropical societies.

With almost 5.4 million students attending elementary and high schools, and almost 1 million enrolled in community colleges and universities (Statistics Canada, 2001), Canadian education is big business. Education at all levels has become a major employer, providing relatively well-paid work for thousands of professionals. In addition to the classroom teachers and university professors, thousands more work in classroom support as aides, administrators, bus drivers, janitors, and secretaries. Others earn their living in industries that service schools—from building schools to manufacturing pencils, paper, computers, and desks, to providing insurance, cleaning supplies, and food. Overall, Canada spent about $60.5 billion in 1998–1999 on education. This figure represents just under $2000 per capita (Canadian Education Statistics Council, 2000, p. 54). In 1995–1996 Canada spent 7 percent of gross domestic product (GDP) on education and this was the highest expenditure on education among the G-7 countries (Canadian Education Statistics Council, 2000, p. 59).

To better understand the connection between education and values, let's look at how the educational system transmits individualism, competition, and patriotism.

Individualism. Individualism forms a thread integrally woven into the Canadian educational system. Unlike their Japanese counterparts, Canadian teachers and students seldom focus on teamwork. Where Japanese schools stress that the individual is only one part of a larger, integrated whole, Canadian students learn that the individual is on his or her own. Pervasive but often subtle, such instruction begins in the early grades when teachers point out the success of a particular student. They might say, for example, "Everyone should be like Joey," or "Why can't you be like María, who got all the answers right?" In such seemingly innocuous statements, the teacher thrusts one child ahead of the rest, holding the individual up for praise. Schools continue to select class valedictorians, reward high achievers, sponsor athlete-of-the-year banquets, and participate in science fairs, math competitions, and spelling bees. From each of these events, in the end, usually only one student takes home the coveted prize.

Competition. Competitive games in the classroom and the schoolyard provide an apt illustration of how schools transmit this core value. In the classroom, a teacher may divide the class into competitive groups for a spelling bee, while on the playground children are encouraged to play hard-driving competitive games and sports. The school's formal sports program—baseball, football, basketball, soccer, hockey, volleyball, and so on—pits team against team in head-to-head confrontations, driving home the lesson that the competitive spirit is highly valued. Although organized sports stress teamwork, the individual is held up for praise. The custom of nominating an "outstanding player" (emphasizing which of these persons is the best) reinforces the related lesson of individualism.

Patriotism. Finally, as in schools around the world, schools in North America teach patriotism. Canadian students are taught that Canada is the best country in the world; Russians learn that no country is better than Russia; and French, German, British, Spanish, Japanese, Chinese, Afghani, and Egyptian students all learn the same about their respective countries. To instill patriotism, elementary school teachers in every country extol the virtues of the society's founders, their struggle for freedom from oppression, and the goodness of the country's basic social institutions.

Sociologist Randle Nelsen (2002) argues that, in today's schools, education has become infused with popular culture in such a way that education has become "edu-tainment" and that the corporate presence at schools and on college and university campuses represents the encroachment of the corporate agenda into the curriculum and therefore into the heart of education. It's not only that schools, and particularly university and college campuses, have taken on a "shopping mall" appearance, but also that the transformation in the appearance of the "ivy walls" represents long-term contracts and agreements the institutions have struck with big business—and it is these relationships that have affected dominant values, ideas, and experiences within schools.

Corporations can sometimes play a significant role in the education system. Over the years, some schools have negotiated agreements with specific corporations in return for funding, however, while students may benefit from the extra money their school has managed to acquire in this way, the students' ideas, values, and overall school experiences are often influenced by that company's corporate agenda, as well.

Social Integration

Schools also perform the function of social integration, helping to mold students into a more or less cohesive unit. Indeed, as we just saw, forging a national identity by integrating immigrants into a common cultural heritage was one of the manifest functions of establishing a publicly funded system of education in Canada. When children enter school, they come from many different backgrounds. Their particular family and social class may have taught them speech patterns, dress, and other behaviours or attitudes that differ from those generally recognized as desirable or acceptable. In the classroom and on the playground, those backgrounds take new shape. The end result is that schools help socialize students into the mainstream culture.

Peer culture is especially significant, for most students are eager to fit in. From their peers, they learn ideas and norms that go beyond their family and little corner of the world. Guided by today's powerful mass media, students in all parts of the country choose to look alike by wearing, for example, the same brands and styles of jeans, shirts, skirts, shoes, and jackets. Peer culture molds not only the youths' appearance but even their ideas, speech patterns, and interaction with the opposite sex (Thorne & Luria, 1993). Peer culture may also turn awry, with those not seen as fitting in becoming targets for insults, pranks, or more serious and violent words and actions, as we see with the increased incidence of bullying in Canadian schools (see the Thinking Critically about Social Controversy box in Chapter 10, p. 242). As well-publicized cases in British Columbia and at Columbine High School in the United States indicate, bullying in its extreme form has pushed many to suicide and others to violent actions, including murder.

The classroom itself helps to produce social integration. As students learn about Confederation and the Canadian Charter of Rights and Freedoms, and as they sing "O Canada," for example, they become aware of the "greater government," and their sense of national identity grows. One indicator of how education promotes political integration is the millions of immigrants who have attended Canadian schools, learned mainstream ideas, and given up their earlier national and cultural identities as they became Canadians. They have done so despite the emphasis in Canada on multiculturalism. Schools also socialize students politically by the ways they incorporate and emphasize, however subtly, dominant values, ideas, and experiences. Teaching is primarily from a white, middle-class, male, non-Native perspective. Many critics have exposed the ways structural barriers, such as racism, classism, and sexism, operate within the Canadian school system to limit the level of participation and success of minority students (C. James, 1999).

How significant is this integrative function of education? It goes far beyond similarities of appearance or speech. To forge a national identity is to stabilize the polit-

Schools socialize students politically by incorporating, however subtly, dominant values, ideas, and experiences. Most school lessons are taught primarily from a white, middle-class, male, non-Native perspective.

ical system. If people identify with a society's social institutions and perceive them as the basis of their welfare, they have no reason to question or rebel. This function is especially significant when it comes to the working classes, in which the greatest desire for and the strongest pursuit of social and political change ordinarily develops. The wealthy already have a vested interest in maintaining the status quo, but to get the working classes to identify with the Canadian social system as it is goes a long way to preserving the system as it is.

Gatekeeping

Gatekeeping, or determining which people will enter what occupations, is another major function of education. Credentialing, the subject of the opening vignette, is an example of gatekeeping. Because Neha did not have the credentials, but Melissa did, education closed the door to the one and opened it to the other. Yet, as sociologist David Livingstone (1999) argues, many workers are vastly underemployed, and this may be so because we usually focus on the question of how schools should prepare students for work, rather than how work might make use of people's education, continuing learning capacities, and knowledge.

Essential to the gatekeeping function is **tracking**, sorting students into different educational programs on the basis of real or perceived abilities. Tests are used to determine which students should be directed into "university-bound" programs, while others are put onto a vocational track. The impact is lifelong, for as we saw with Neha and Melissa, throughout adulthood opportunities for jobs, raises, and promotions open or close on the basis of education.

Tracking begins in grade school, where on the basis of test results most students take regular courses, but some are placed in advanced sections of English and mathematics. In high school, tracking becomes more elaborate. In many schools, students are funnelled into university-bound, non-university-bound, or vocational programs. All students who complete their sequence of courses receive a high school diploma, but not all graduates are eligible to go on to higher education. Those in vocational or non-academic streams are most likely to go to work after high school or perhaps will take a vocational or trade course; those in the academic streams enter university; and those in between may attend a community college to obtain a diploma or certificate in one of a number of semiprofessional, technological, or vocational fields.

In a study of Ontario schools, the authors conclude that children whose parents are in unskilled jobs are 10 times more likely than children whose parents are professionals to be directed toward non-college-or-university-bound high school programs. Also, working class children are far less likely than others from higher social class backgrounds to go to university, and this is the result of the ways in which the school system sorts students. Not only is this a shameful waste of human potential, but it discriminates against working class and poor children (Curtis, Livingstone, & Smaller, 1992).

Besides academic achievement, which many suggest is related to social class, students are provided with opportunities on the basis of other characteristics, such as gender. Today, educational attainment of females in Canada is roughly equivalent to that of males. For example, in 1996, 37.9 percent of males and 36.2 percent of females in the labour force had a high school education. Among those with university degrees, women outnumbered men: 10.3 percent of women compared to 9 percent of men in the labour force had graduated from university (Krahn & Lowe 1998). Overall, women earned almost 59 percent of all bachelor's and first professional degrees granted in Canada in 1998 (Statistics Canada, 2001).

However, some fields, such as engineering, are clearly male-dominated. Males earn over 79 percent of engineering degrees and, in addition, at the undergraduate level, women are underrepresented in mathematics and the physical sciences. At the same time, men are underrepresented in nursing, rehabilitation medicine, social work, languages, education, and a number of the social sciences, including psychology and sociology (Statistics Canada, 2001). Considering these patterns, we might conclude that males and females are sent down separate gender-specific career pathways and that these pathways are to some degree mapped out by their school-related experiences, including advice from guidance counsellors, encouragement from teachers, and reception from other students.

Gatekeeping sorts people on the basis of merit, say functionalists. Sociologists Talcott Parsons (1940), Kingsley Davis,

and Wilbert Moore (1945), who pioneered this view, also known as **social placement**, argue that a major task of society is to fill its positions with capable people. Some positions, such as that of physician, require a high intellect and many years of arduous education. Consequently, to motivate capable people to postpone immediate gratification and to submit to many years of rigorous education, high income and prestige are held out as rewards. Other jobs require far fewer skills and can be performed by people of lesser intelligence. Thus, functionalists look on education as a system that, to the benefit of society, sorts people according to their abilities.

Promoting Personal Change

Learning critical thinking skills helps to promote personal change. Schools teach students to "think for themselves"— to critically evaluate ideas and social life. One consequence is that the further people go in school, the more open they tend to be to new ways of thinking and doing things. People with more education tend to hold more liberal ideas, while those with less education tend to be more conservative.

Promoting Social Change

The educational institution also contributes to social change by sponsoring research. Most university professors, for example, are given time off from teaching so that they can do research. Their findings become part of a body of accumulated knowledge that stimulates social change. Sociologists, for example, presented conclusions from sociological research before the Supreme Court that helped bring about pay equity decisions. Some academic research has had an explosive impact on society—literally, in the case of the atomic and hydrogen weapons that were developed in part from university research. Nobody remains untouched by this function of education. For example, medical research conducted in universities across the world is partially responsible for the likelihood that you will reach old age.

Mainstreaming

A new function of education is **mainstreaming**, incorporating people with disabilities into regular social activities. As a matter of routine policy, students with disabilities used to be placed in special schools. Educators concluded that in these settings disabled students learned to adjust only to a world of the disabled, leaving them ill-prepared to cope with the dominant world. The educational philosophy then changed to having disabled students attend regular schools.

Mainstreaming is easiest for students whose disabilities are minor, of course, for they fit more easily into regular schools. For people who cannot walk, schools (and other public facilities) have been required to build wheelchair ramps; for those who cannot hear, "signers" (interpreters who use their hands) may attend classes with them. Most blind students still attend special schools, as do people with severe learning disabilities.

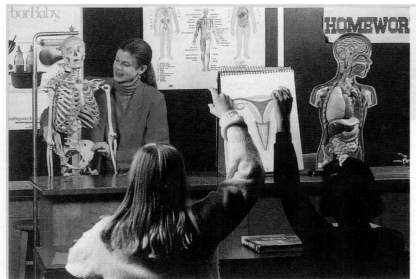

Education has replaced several functions of the family. In most areas, parents have quietly acquiesced. Sex education, however, has remained a source of continuing controversy. Many parents object to the schools' usurping their role, as well as to their children being taught values that violate their own. Many would condemn a graphic presentation of how to put on a condom.

Replacing Family Functions

Canadian schools have become a rival for some family functions. Child care is an example. Grade schools do double duty as babysitters for parents who both work, or for single mothers in the work force. Child care always has been a *latent* function of formal education, for it was an unintended consequence of schooling. Now, however, since most families have two wage earners, child care has become a manifest function. Some schools even offer child care both before and after formal classes. Another example is providing sex education and birth control advice, which has stirred controversy, for some families resent this function being taken from them.

Other Functions

Education also fulfills many other functions. For example, because most students are unmarried, high schools and universities effectively serve as *matchmaking* institutions. It is here that many young people find their future spouses. The sociological significance of this function of schools is that they funnel people into marriages with mates of similar background, interests, and education. Schools also establish *social networks*. Some older adults maintain friendship networks from high school and university, while others become part of business or professional networks that prove highly beneficial to their careers. Finally, schools also help to *stabilize employment*. In the most industrialized nations, keeping millions of young people out of the labour market keeps positions open for older workers.

Focus Question

What is political socialization and how does it take place through education?

Focus Question

How does the educational system transmit values of individualism and competition?

The Conflict Perspective: Reproducing the Social Class Structure

Unlike functionalists, who see education as a social institution that performs functions for the benefit of society, conflict theorists see the educational system as a tool used by those in the controlling sector of society to maintain their dominance.

The Hidden Curriculum

The term **hidden curriculum** refers to the unwritten rules of behaviour and attitudes, such as obedience to authority and conformity to cultural norms, that are taught in the schools in addition to the formal curriculum (Gillborn, 1992). Conflict theorists note how this hidden curriculum perpetuates social inequalities.

To better understand this central point, consider the values and work habits that students are taught in school: obedience to the teacher, punctuality, and turning in neat work on time. These traits are highly desired by employers, who want dependable, docile, subordinate workers. Or consider just the emphasis on "proper" English. Members of the elite need people to run their business empires, and they are more comfortable if their managers possess the "refined" language and manners that they themselves are used to. Consequently, middle-class schools, whose teachers know where their pupils are headed, stress "proper" English and "good" manners. In contrast, because few

Sociologist Harry Gracey (1997), who did participant observation in a kindergarten, concluded that kindergarten is a sort of boot camp for the entire educational system. Here, tender students are drilled in the behaviours and attitudes deemed appropriate for the "student role," which, he argued, is to follow classroom routines. The goal of kindergarten is to mold many individuals from diverse backgrounds into a compliant group that will, on command, unthinkingly follow classroom routines.

Kindergarten's famous "show and tell," for example, does not merely allow children to be expressive. It also teaches them to talk only when they are asked to speak. ("It's 'your turn,' Jarmay.") The format also teaches children to request permission to talk ("Who knows what Letitia has?") by raising a hand and being acknowledged. Finally, the whole ritual teaches children to acknowledge the teacher's ideas as superior. (She is the one who has the capacity to evaluate students' activities and ideas.)

Gracey found a similar hidden curriculum in the other activities he observed. Whether it was drawing pictures, listening to records, snack time, or rest time, the teachers would quiet talkative students, even scolding them at times, while giving approval for conforming behaviours. In short, the message is that the teacher—and, by inference, the entire school system—is the authority.

The purpose of kindergarten, Gracey concluded, is to teach children to "follow orders with unquestioning obedience." To accomplish this, kindergarten teachers "create and enforce a rigid social structure in the classroom through which they effectively control the behaviour of most of the children for most of the school day." This produces three kinds of students: (1) "good" students, those who submit to school-imposed discipline and come to identify with it; (2) "adequate" students, those who submit to the school's discipline but do not identify with it; and (3) "bad" students, those who refuse to submit to school routines. This third type is also known as "problem children." To bring them into line, a tougher drill sergeant, the school psychologist, is called in.

Learning the student role prepares children for grade school, where they "will be asked to submit to systems and routines imposed by the teachers and the curriculum. The days will be much like those of kindergarten, except that academic subjects will be substituted."

Gracey adds that these lessons extend well beyond the classroom, that they prepare students for the routines of the work world, whether those be of the assembly line or the office. Mastering the student role prepares them to follow unquestioningly the routines imposed by "the company."

children from working class or minority backgrounds will occupy managerial positions, their teachers allow street language in the classroom, and are less concerned with students' grammatical skill.

To reproduce the social class structure, then, means to prepare students to work in positions similar to those of their parents. Some children, socially destined for higher positions, need to learn "refined" speech and manners. Others simply need to be taught to obey rules so they can take their place in the closely supervised, low-status positions for which they are socially destined (Bowles & Gintis, 1976; Olneck & Bills, 1980). From this conflict perspective, even kindergarten has a hidden curriculum, as the Down-to-Earth Sociology box illustrates.

Tilting the Tests: Discrimination by IQ

Even intelligence tests play their part in keeping the social class system intact. For example, how would you answer the following question?

A symphony is to a composer as a book is to a(n)

paper _____
sculptor _____
musician _____
author _____
man _____

You probably had no difficulty coming up with "author" as your choice. Wouldn't any intelligent person have done so?

In point of fact, this question raises a central issue in intelligence testing. Not all intelligent people would know the answer, because this question contains cultural biases. In other words, children from some backgrounds are more familiar with the concepts of symphonies, composers, sculptors, and musicians than other children. Consequently, the test is tilted in their favour (Turner, 1972; Ashe, 1992).

Perhaps asking a different question will make the bias clearer. How would you answer this question?

If you throw dice and "7" is showing on top, what is facing down?

seven _____
snake eyes _____
box cars _____
little Joes _____
eleven _____

This question, suggested by Adrian Dove (n.d.), a social worker in Watts, is slanted toward a working-class experience. It surely is obvious that this *particular* cultural bias tilts the test so that children from some social backgrounds will perform better than others.

It is no different with IQ (intelligence quotient) tests that use such words as *composer* and *symphony*. A working-class child may have heard about rap, rock, hip hop, or jazz but not about symphonies. In other words, IQ tests measure not only intelligence but also culturally acquired knowledge. Whatever else we can say, the cultural bias built into the IQ tests used in schools is clearly *not* tilted in favour of the working classes.

A second inadequacy of IQ tests is that they focus on mathematical, spatial, symbolic, and linguistic abilities. Intelligence, however, consists of more than these components. The ability to compose music, to be empathetic to the feelings of others, or to be humorous or persuasive are also components of intelligence.

The significance of these factors, say conflict theorists, is that culturally biased IQ tests favour the middle classes and discriminate against students from lower-class backgrounds. These tests, used to track students, assign disproportionate numbers of minorities and the poor to non-university-bound tracks (Kershaw, 1992). This outcome, as we have seen, destines them for lower-paying jobs in adult life. Thus, conflict theorists view IQ tests as another weapon in the arsenal designed to maintain the social class structure over the generations (Postman, 1992).

Stacking the Deck: Unequal Funding

Conflict theorists stress the central role that funding for education plays in perpetuating social inequalities. Funding is a scarce resource unequally distributed among rich and poor students. The vast regional inequality in Canada affects education. Analyzing 1991 census data, sociologists Scott Davies and Neil Guppy concluded that a greater percentage of the population over age 25 in the relatively richer provinces have university degrees, while at the other end, the relatively poorer provinces have the highest proportion of adults with less than a Grade 9 education. For example, Yukon Territory had the highest percentage of residents (14.8 percent) with a university degree, followed by Ontario (14.6 percent) and Alberta (13.7 percent). More than 31 percent of 15- to 24-year-olds living in the Northwest Territories, compared to only 2 percent in Ontario, had completed less than Grade 9 (A. Humphreys, 1998). Moreover, a greater percentage of Aboriginal students compared to non-Aboriginal students drop out of school although there are fewer dropping out today as compared to the numbers who dropped out in earlier decades (Canadian Education Statistics Council, 2000).

The low rate of school completion in the Northwest Territories in part reflects the abysmal way schooling has been provided for Aboriginal Canadians. Under the residential school system, formally operated by the Canadian government through the *Indian Act* of 1876 from 1892 to 1969, Native children were separated from their families, often by force, and taken to boarding schools where they were stripped of their Indianness. They were not allowed to speak in their Native languages, nor were they provided with opportunities to learn from within and about their

own culture. Many students suffered sexual, physical, and emotional abuse in these schools, which were eventually abolished (MacKinnon, 1999). Overall, about 130 000 Native children were taken into the country's 130 residential schools. After 1969 some of the schools remained in operation, but were run by churches and then eventually by band councils. Akaitcho Hall in Yellowknife, the last residential school to remain open, was finally closed in 1994 (Mironowicz, 2002).

Since then, overall education levels on reserves have increased, but there are still wide gaps between levels of school completion for Native populations and those for Canada as a whole. For example, in 1991, 5 percent of the reserve population compared to 0.8 percent of all Canadians 15 years of age or older had no schooling or kindergarten only (DIAND, 1997).

Among Canadians aged 24 in 1995, 15 percent were school leavers. In general, school leavers face a number of labour market challenges. Not only are they less likely to find work, but the jobs they do find typically have lower wages, higher rates of unemployment, and less security than those of high school or postsecondary graduates (Clark, 1997). Across Canada, the rate of dropping out varies, with "have-not" provinces (Newfoundland, Prince Edward Island, Quebec) having a higher rate compared with "have" provinces (Alberta, British Columbia, Ontario) (Taylor, 1998; Canadian Education Statistics Council, 2000). According to analysts, school leavers tend to be from lower socioeconomic backgrounds, often from single- and no-parent families, and usually experience pressures to enter the labour market. They are also more likely to be married and have dependent children (Clark, 1997; Taylor, 1997).

The disparities across Canada in educational attainment may be explained by a variety of additional factors. Education is a provincial matter and there are vast economic differences between provinces in the tax bases from which funding is drawn. Decisions made by local school boards may also account for variations between and within provinces. Some provinces have larger urban areas, and generally rural areas are relatively poorer. In urban areas, the demand for higher educational credentials is higher and relates to the types of industries and work available. Provinces such as Ontario, for example, house high-profile law and medical schools that attract students from across Canada. The existence of a degree-granting institution within a community is a drawing card for a highly educated work force. The Northwest Territories does not have a university. Many young residents who leave never return, eventually settling in the community where they graduated (A. Humphreys, 1998).

Conflict theorists go beyond these observations, however. They stress that in each province and community the deck is stacked against the poor. Because public schools are largely supported by local property taxes, the richer communities (where property values are higher) have more to spend on their children, while the poorer communities end up with much less. Consequently, the richer communities are able to offer higher salaries (and take their pick of the most highly qualified and motivated teachers), afford the latest textbooks and computers, teach additional courses in languages, music, and arts, and provide better opportunities for young athletes interested in sports programs. Because schools so closely reflect the Canadian social class system, then, the children of the privileged emerge from elementary and middle schools best equipped for success in high school. In turn, they come out of high school best equipped for success in university. Their greater likelihood of success in university, and in high-status professional programs such as medicine and law, in turn, serves to maintain their dominance.

The Correspondence Principle

Conflict sociologists Samuel Bowles and Herbert Gintis (1976) used the term **correspondence principle** to refer to the ways schools reflect the social structure of society. This term means that what is taught in a nation's schools corresponds to the characteristics of that society. Thus education helps to perpetuate a society's social inequalities. The following list provides some examples.

Characteristics of Society	Characteristics of Schools
1. Capitalism	1. Promote competition
2. Social inequality	2. Unequal funding of schools, track the poor to job training
3. Racial-ethnic prejudice	3. Make minorities feel inferior, track minorities to job training
4. Bureaucratic structure of the corporation	4. Provide a model of authority in the classroom
5. Need for submissive workers	5. Make students submissive
6. Need for dependable workers	6. Promote punctuality
7. Need to maintain armed forces and agents of control	7. Promote nationalism (to fight for capitalism)

Thus, conclude conflict theorists, the Canadian educational system is designed to produce dependable workers who will not question their bosses, and produce some individuals who will go on to be innovators in thought and action but can still be counted on to be loyal to the social system as it exists (Olneck & Bills, 1980).

The Bottom Line: Family Background and the Educational System

The end result of unequal funding, IQ tests, and so on is that family background proves more important than test scores in predicting who attends university. Back in 1977, sociologist Samuel Bowles compared the college attendance of the brightest 25 percent of high school students in the United States with the intellectually weakest 25 percent. Of the brightest 25 percent of high school students, 90 percent of those from affluent homes went to college, while only half of those from low-income homes did so. Of the weakest students, 26 percent from affluent homes went to college, while only 6 percent from poorer homes did so.

Canadian sociologists also found that in Canada students from a higher class background were far more likely to go to university than poorer students within the same cohort (Porter, Porter, & Blishen, 1979). And today? This same general relationship still holds. If you rank families from the poorest to the richest, as the income increases the likelihood that the children will attend institutions of higher learning also increases (Manski, 1992–1993; Curtis, Livingstone & Smaller, 1992).

Conflict theorists point out that the educational system reproduces the wealth-poverty divide within the Canadian social class structure. Like Neha in the opening vignette, those without degrees have less access to jobs with better pay and potential for advancement. Then, too, there is program and the type of institution attended. Wealthy Canadians are more likely than others to attend private schools and prestigious and internationally renowned universities.

The purpose of the educational system, stress conflict theorists, is to reproduce inequality, to help keep the social class structure intact from one generation to the next. Consequently, most children of the less privileged are funnelled into job training programs, while children of the middle classes attend universities and community colleges. The offspring of the elite, in contrast, attend exclusive private schools, such as Upper Canada College, where their learning environment includes small classes and well-paid teachers (Persell et al., 1992). Here they inherit a cozy social network between the school's advisors and the admissions officers of the nation's and the world's most elite institutions. Some of these networks are so efficient that a majority of these private schools' graduating classes are admitted to McGill, University of Toronto Law School, and University of Western Ontario's Business School, or to Harvard, Yale, and Princeton.

Focus Question

What are some of the ways the education system reproduces inequality?

The Symbolic Interactionist Perspective: Teacher Expectations and the Self-Fulfilling Prophecy

Whereas functionalists look at how education functions to benefit society and conflict theorists examine how education perpetuates social inequality, symbolic interactionists study face-to-face interactions inside the classroom. They have found that the expectations of teachers have profound consequences for their students.

The Rist Research

Symbolic interactionists have uncovered some of the dynamics of educational tracking. In what has become a classic study, sociologist Ray Rist did participant observation in an African-American grade school with an African-American faculty. Rist (1970) found that after only eight days in the classroom, the kindergarten teacher felt that she knew the children's abilities well enough to assign them to three separate worktables. To Table 1, Mrs. Caplow assigned those she considered to be "fast learners." They sat at the front of the room, closest to her. Those whom she saw as "slow learners," she assigned to Table 3, located at the back of the classroom. She placed "average" students at Table 2, in between the other tables.

This pattern seemed strange to Rist. He knew that the children had not been tested for ability, yet the teacher was certain that she could differentiate between bright and slow children. Investigating further, Rist found that social class was the underlying basis for assigning the children to the different tables. Middle-class students were separated out for Table 1, children from poorer homes to Tables 2 and 3. The teacher paid the most attention to the children at Table 1, who were closest to her, less to Table 2, and the least to Table 3. As the year went on, children from Table 1 perceived that they were treated better and came to see themselves as smarter. They became the leaders in class activities and even ridiculed children at the other worktables, calling them "dumb." Eventually, the children at Table 3 disengaged themselves from many classroom activities. Not surprisingly, at the end of the year only the children at Table 1 had completed the lessons that prepared them for reading.

This early tracking stuck. When these students entered the first grade, their new teacher looked at the work they had accomplished and placed students from Table 1 at her Table 1. She treated her tables much as the kindergarten teacher had, and the children at Table 1 again led the class.

The children's reputations continued to follow them. The second-grade teacher reviewed their scores and also divided her class into three groups. The first she named the "Tigers," and, befitting their name, gave them challenging readers. Not surprisingly, the Tigers came from the original Table 1 in kindergarten. The second group she called the "Cardinals." They came from the original Tables 2 and 3. Her third group consisted of children she had failed the previous year, whom she called the "Clowns." The Cardinals and Clowns were given less advanced readers.

Rist concluded that *the child's journey through school was determined at the eighth day of kindergarten!* What had occurred was a **self-fulfilling prophecy**, a term coined by sociologist Robert Merton (1949/1968) to refer to an originally false assumption of what is going to happen that comes true simply because it was predicted. For example, if people believe an unfounded rumour that a bank is in trouble and assume that they won't be able to get their money out, they all rush to the bank to demand their money. The prediction—*although originally false*—is now likely to be true.

In this case, of course, we are dealing with something more important than money, the welfare of little children. Labels are powerful. They can set people on courses of action that affect the rest of their lives. That, of course, is the significance of Rist's observations of these grade school children.

How Do Teacher Expectations Work?

How do teacher expectations work? Observations of classroom interaction give us some idea (Leacock, 1969; Rist, 1970; Buckley, 1991; Farkas, 1996; Farkas, Sheehan, & Grobe, 1990b; Farkas, Grobe, Sheehan, & Shuan, 1990a). The teacher's own middle-class background comes into play, for teachers are pleased when middle-class students ask probing questions. They take these as a sign of intelligence. When working-class students ask similar questions, however, teachers are more likely to interpret their questions as "smart aleck." In addition, working-class children are more likely to reflect a subculture that "puts down" intellectual achievements, an attitude that causes teachers to react negatively.

We do not yet have enough information on how teachers form their expectations, how they communicate them to students, or exactly how these expectations influence teacher-student interaction. Nor do we know very much about how students "signal" messages to teachers. (As discussed in the Sociology and the New Technology box here, technology is producing new forms of student-teacher interaction and "signalling.") Perhaps you will become the educational sociologist who will shed more light on these everyday but significant aspects of human behaviour.

Rethinking Schools: Problems and Solutions

To conclude this section on education, let's list some of the major problems facing Canadian education today—and consider potential solutions.

Distance learning, courses taught to students who are not physically present with their instructor, is not new. For decades, we have had correspondence courses.

Today, however, distance learning refers to something much more than this. Joe Martin, a 41-year-old executive, is enrolled in a university MBA program. On his lunch hour or at night in his bedroom, Martin logs onto the Internet and does homework assigned by a professor whom he has never met. He also listens to lectures on the Internet and chats with classmates in China and Brazil and from across Canada and the United States (Hamilton & Miller, 1997).

Telecommunications—satellites, computers, television, and CD-ROMs—are changing the face of education. With computer linkups, students in remote parts of the North earn BAs from universities in the South. What is now a flow will become a torrent, and cybercolleges soon may be part of mainstream education.

In the past, distance learning often meant a TV screen that replaced a live teacher in a classroom. Consequently, some critics say that the only real change has been an increased capacity to bore: Instead of a live teacher boring a few students in a single classroom, that person's image bores thousands simultaneously (Thornburg, 1994). Certainly, until now, most distance learning has been either slow (a correspondence course) or one-way (students passively receiving instruction, usually providing feedback only through tests). The new technology, such as teleconferencing, however, permits students and teachers to see one another, to talk with one another, and to share documents worldwide.

The potential is staggering. Why, indeed, should our learning be limited to walled classrooms? When studying human culture, for example, wouldn't it be intriguing to be able to compare notes on eating, dating, or burial customs with fellow students in Thailand, Iceland, South Africa, Germany, Egypt, China, and Australia? Or even to write a joint paper comparing your cross-cultural experiences with those described in the text, and then submitting that paper to your mutual instructor?

Will we eventually go from kindergarten to grad school, proceeding at our own pace, with classmates from around the world? While this may sound intriguing, no walls also means no flirting after class, no joking in the hallway or dorm, and no keg parties.

The Rising Tide of Mediocrity

While more and more Canadians are staying in school longer, a significant number of Canadians experience illiteracy. At the same time, dropout rates have declined significantly across Canada. Teachers' groups may claim that teachers are doing a better job! Teachers are getting more students to stay in high school and to go on to university. Is it possible that higher retention rates today mean that fewer students are failing due to poorer standards and a deflation in expectations?

In the United States, researchers have suggested that Scholastic Aptitude Test (SAT) scores have declined because children find television and video games more appealing than reading (Rigdon & Swasy, 1990). Students who read little acquire a smaller vocabulary and less rigour in thought and verbal expression. Sociologists Donald Hayes and Loreen Wolfer (1993a, b) are convinced that the culprit is the "dumbed down" textbooks that pervade schools. Some point their fingers at other low standards: "frill" courses, less homework, fewer term papers, grade inflation, and burned-out teachers who often find themselves working under dismal classroom conditions due to recent cutbacks and restructuring in many areas of the school system. Professors in Canadian universities often find students in their classes who experience great difficulties in summarizing researchers' findings in social science courses, who read too slowly or without adequate comprehensive skills to keep up with weekly reading assignments, or who are unable to write well.

Cheating and Essay-Writing Mills

Almost every year, stories of essay-writing services are uncovered in major centres. These services offer recycled or hastily prepared essays for sale. With enough cash, students may purchase a made-to-order term paper that conforms more closely to the particular requirements of the course. These illegal operations boom at peak periods during the academic year, and the arrogance of their proprietors is demonstrated by their bold advertisements littering Canadian campuses.

In addition to buying these services, some students engage in other forms of academic dishonesty, including plagiarism, cheating, and misrepresentation at examinations. The extent of such problems is unknown, possibly due to difficulties in detection.

Grade Inflation, Social Promotion, and Functional Illiteracy

At the same time that learning may be declining, grades are going up. In the 1960s, high school teachers gave out about twice as many C's as A's, but now the A's exceed the C's. Grade inflation in the face of declining standards has been accompanied by social promotion, the practice of passing students from one grade to the next even though they have not mastered basic materials. One unfortunate result is functional illiteracy, difficulty with reading and writing even though one has graduated from high school. Some high school graduates cannot fill out job applications; others can't figure out if they are given the right change at the grocery store.

Peer Groups

A team of two psychologists and a sociologist studied 20 000 high school students in California and Wisconsin (Steinberg, Dornbusch, & Brown, 1996). They found that of all the influences affecting these teenagers, peer group is the most important. Simply put, those who hang out with good students tend to do well; those who hang out with poor students tend to do poorly. The subcultures students develop include informal norms about educational achievement; some groups set up norms of classroom excellence, others sneer at getting good grades. What's cool or not so cool according to the group is the guiding code of conduct. The question that arises from this research, of course, is how to build educational achievement into student culture.

Violence in Schools

> James Murphy was teaching his government class at Dartmouth High, in a town 80 kilometres south of Boston, when two Dartmouth students and a third teenager suddenly burst through the door. One brandished a bat, another a billy club, and the third a hunting knife. When they asked for Shawn Pina, Jason Robinson made the fatal mistake of asking why they wanted him. When Murphy saw one go after Robinson with the bat, he wrestled the assailant to the floor. Another plunged his knife into Robinson's stomach, killing him (Toch, 1993).

The above incident, and the shooting spree at Columbine High School in the spring of 1999, in many ways represent the intensity of the violence many young people live with on a daily basis. Many U.S. schools have deteriorated to the point where basic safety is an issue, putting students' lives at risk, a condition that only a few years back would have been unimaginable. In some schools, uniformed guards have become a fixture, while in others students can gain entrance only after passing through metal detectors. Some even supplement the traditional fire drills with "drive-by shooting drills" (Toch, 1993; Grossman, 1995).

While Canadian schools are much safer, the growing number of incidents of violence, including the possession and use of weapons, beatings, drug trafficking, and other serious offences, have prompted school boards to adopt "zero tolerance" policies, which expel or suspend students at their first offence for even minor infractions. Without programs in place to prevent students from committing the "offensive" behaviour in the first place, critics say that such policies are too punitive and may backfire, turning students away from school altogether (Canadian Press, 2002, p. A3).

A secure learning environment is basic to a good education. The growing number of violent incidents in Canadian schools has prompted school boards to confront the problem with strict, no-nonsense policies, such as "zero tolerance."

Teenage Pregnancy

Students who lack a high school diploma face a severe handicap in life. As already noted above, they are more likely to experience unemployment and poor job prospects. Females who left school had the highest unemployment rates (30 percent), and their family responsibilities affected their job searches and their availability for work (Clark, 1997). Consequently, single mothers, especially teenage mothers, often experience the cycle of poverty. Not only do these young women, some still girls, have the expense and responsibility of caring for a child, but they also are unlikely to complete high school, thus perpetuating a cycle of poverty and interrupted education.

Solutions: Retention, Safety, Standards, and Other Reforms

It is one thing to identify problems, quite another to find solutions for them.

A Secure Learning Environment. The first criterion for a good education is security, to guarantee students' physical safety and freedom from fear (Shanker, 1995). Fortunately, most Canadian schools are relatively trouble-free, and those that are not can be changed. School administrators and teachers can reclaim the schools by expelling all students who threaten the welfare of others and by refusing to tolerate threats, violence, drugs, and weapons (Toby, 1992). However, what is surfacing today is the extent of problems such as bullying and harassment. These are difficult issues to address and, unfortunately, many school administrators seem to "bury their heads in the sand" when it comes to confronting these problems head on.

Higher Standards. Within a secure learning environment, then, steps can be taken to improve the quality of education.

Students perform better when they are expected to do well. To this, you might want to reply "Of course. I knew that. Who wouldn't?" Somehow, however, such a basic principle seems to be lost on many teachers, who end up teaching at a low level—and on most school administrators, who accept low student performance. The reason, actually, is probably not their lack of awareness of such basics, but rather the constraints in which they find themselves organizationally, the bureaucracies in which ritual often replaces performance. To understand this point better, you may wish to review Chapter 10.

Ultimately, then, it is not only of students that we must expect more, but also of teachers and administrators.

Reform in anything needs a guiding principle. We suggest that this serve as the guiding principle in reforming education: The problem is not the ability of the students, but rather the educational system itself. That this is true becomes apparent when we consider the results reported in the Thinking Critically about Social Controversy box with which we close this section.

Thinking Critically about Social Controversy

Breaking Through the Barriers: The Jaime Escalante Approach to Restructuring the Classroom

Called "the best teacher in America," Jaime Escalante taught in an East Los Angeles inner-city school plagued with poverty, crime, drugs, gangs, and the usual miserably low student scores. In this self-defeating environment, he taught calculus. His students scored so highly on national tests that test officials, suspecting cheating, asked his students to retake the test. They did. Again they passed—this time with even higher scores.

How did Escalante overcome such odds? His success is *not* due to a recruitment of the brightest students. Students' poor academic performance does not stand in the way of being admitted to the math program. The *only* requirement is an interest in math. What did Escalante do right, and what can we learn from his approach?

"Success starts with attitude" could be Escalante's motto. Few Latino students were taking math. Most were tracked into craft classes and made jewellery and birdhouses. "Our kids are just as talented as anyone else. They just need the opportunity to show it. And for that, they must be motivated," he said. "They just don't think about becoming scientists or engineers."

To say that today's schoolchildren can't learn as well as previous schoolchildren is a case of blaming the victim. Jaime Escalante, shown here, demonstrated that teachers can motivate even highly deprived students to study hard and to excel in learning. His experience challenges us to rethink our approach to education.

Here are the keys to what Escalante accomplished. First, teaching and learning can't take place unless there is discipline. For that the teachers, not gangs, must control the classroom. Second, the students must believe in themselves. The teacher must inspire students with the idea that they *can* learn (remember teacher expectations). Third, the students must be motivated to perform, in this case to see learning as a way out of the barrio, the path to good jobs.

Escalante uses a team approach. He has his students think of themselves as a team, of him as the coach, and the national exams as a sort of Olympics for which they are preparing. To stimulate team identity, the students wear team jackets, caps, and T-shirts with logos that identify them as part of the team. Before class, his students do "warmups" (hand-clapping and foot-stomping to a rock song).

His team has practice schedules as rigorous as a championship football team. Students must sign a contract that binds them to participate in the summer program he has developed, to complete the daily homework, and to attend Saturday morning and after-school study sessions. To get into his class, even the students' parents have to sign the contract. To keep before his students the principle that self-discipline pays off, Escalante covers his room with posters of sports figures in action—Michael Jordan, Jerry West, Babe Ruth, and Tiger Woods.

The sociological point is that the problem was not the ability of the students. Their failure to do well in school was not due to something within them. The problem was the system, the way classroom instruction is arranged. When Escalante changed the system of instruction, both attitudes and performance changed. Escalante makes this very point—that student performance does not depend on the charismatic personality of a single person, but on how we structure the learning setting.

For Your Consideration

What principles discussed in this or earlier chapters did Escalante apply? What changes do you think we can make in education to bring about similar results all over the country?

Sources: Barry (1989); Meek (1989); Escalante & Dirmann (1990); Hilliard (1991).

Religion: Establishing Meaning

With his mother's call, Tom's world had begun to crumble. Amid sobs, she had told him that she had left his father. After 22 years, their marriage was over! Why? It just didn't make sense. Tom knew that his mother and father had problems, that they argued quite a bit. But they always had. And didn't every married couple? Where was he going to go for the summer? His parents had put the house up for sale, and each had moved to a small apartment. There was no home anymore.

Life seemed a little brighter when Tom met Amy in English class. She was the only one he could talk to about his feelings—Amy's parents had divorced three years before, and she understood. When Amy was invited to a meeting of the Unification Church, Tom agreed to go with her.

The meeting was a surprise. Everyone was friendly, and everything was low-key. And everyone seemed so sure. They all believed that Judgment Day was just around the corner.

Amy and Tom found the teachings rather strange, but, since the people had been so friendly, they came back. After Tom and Amy attended meetings for about a month, they became good friends with Marcia and Ryan. Later they moved into an apartment house where Marcia, Ryan, and other Moonies lived. After a while, they dropped out of university and immersed themselves in a new life as Moonies.

What Is Religion?

Sociologists who do research on religion analyze the relationship between society and religion and study the role religion plays in people's lives. They do not seek to make value judgments about religious beliefs. Nor is their goal to verify or to disprove anyone's faith. Religion is a matter of faith; sociologists deal with empirical matters, things they can observe or measure. Thus sociologists can measure the extent to which people are religious, and they can study the effects of religious beliefs and practices on people's lives. They can analyze how religion is organized and how systems of belief are related to culture, stratification systems, and other social institutions.

In 1912 Emile Durkheim published an influential book, *The Elementary Forms of the Religious Life*, in which he tried to identify the elements common to all religions. He found that all religions, regardless of their name or teaching, separate the sacred from the profane. By **sacred**,

From his review of world religions, Durkheim concluded that all religions have beliefs, practices, and a moral community. Part of Hindu belief is that the Ganges is a holy river and bathing in it imparts spiritual benefits. Every year, millions of Hindus participate in this rite of ablution (purification).

Durkheim referred to aspects of life having to do with the supernatural that inspire awe, reverence, deep respect, even fear. By **profane**, he meant aspects of life that are not concerned with religion or religious purposes but, instead, are part of the ordinary aspects of everyday life. Durkheim also found that all religions develop a community around their practices and beliefs. He summarized his findings as follows:

> A religion is a unified system of beliefs and practices relative to sacred things, that is to say, things set apart and forbidden-beliefs and practices which unite into one single moral community called a Church ....

Thus, he argued, a **religion** is defined by three elements:

1. *beliefs* that some things are sacred (forbidden, set off from the profane);

2. *practices* (rituals) centring around the things considered sacred;

3. *a moral community* (a church) resulting from a group's beliefs and practices. (1912/1965)

Durkheim used the word **church** in an unusual sense, to refer to any "moral community" centred on beliefs and practices regarding the sacred. In Durkheim's sense, church refers to Buddhists bowing before a shrine, Hindus dipping in the Ganges River, and Confucianists offering food to their ancestors. Similarly, the term *moral community* does not imply morality in the sense familiar to most of us. A **moral community** is simply people united by their religious practices—and that would include Aztec priests or Jehovah's Witnesses.

To better understand the sociological approach to religion, let's see what pictures emerge when we apply the major theoretical perspectives.

The Functionalist Perspective

Functionalists examine the functions and dysfunctions of religion. Let us look at some of their conclusions.

Functions of Religion

Around the world, religions provide answers to perplexing questions about ultimate meaning—such as the purpose of life, why people suffer, and the existence of an afterlife.

Similarly, religious rituals that enshroud critical events such as illness and death provide emotional comfort at times of crisis. The individual knows others care and can find consolation in following familiar rituals.

Religious teachings and practices unite believers into a community that shares values and perspectives ("we Jews," "we Christians," "we Muslims"). The religious rituals that surround marriage, for example, link the bride and groom with a broader community that wishes them well. So do other religious rituals, such as those that celebrate birth and mourn death. The Ten Commandments, for example, provide instructions on how to live everyday life, from how to get along with parents, employers, and neighbours to warnings about lying, stealing, and adultery.

Religion not only provides guidelines for everyday life, but also controls people's behaviours. An example is religious teachings that are incorporated into criminal law. In Ontario, for example, laws once prohibited the sale of alcohol before noon on Sunday.

Religion can help people adapt to new environments. By keeping their native language alive and preserving familiar rituals and teachings, religion provides continuity with immigrants' cultural past.

Most religions provide support for the government. An obvious example is the Canadian flag prominently displayed in many Anglican and other churches. Another example is the Queen (or King) of England's coronation as head of state (for Great Britain and Canada) which means she (or he) is also the head of the Church of England.

Although religion is often so bound up with the prevailing order that it resists social change, occasionally religion spearheads change. In Canada, a notable example is J. S. Woodsworth's religious movement that began in Saskatchewan and eventually led to the founding of the Cooperative Commonwealth Federation (the CCF), now known as the New Democratic Party (NDP).

Dysfunctions of Religion

Functionalists also examine ways in which religion can be dysfunctional; that is, how it can bring about harmful results. Two main dysfunctions are war and religious persecution.

War. History is filled with wars based on religion. Between the eleventh and fourteenth centuries, for example, Christian monarchs conducted nine bloody Crusades in an attempt to wrest control of the Holy Land from the Muslims. Unfortunately, such wars are not just a relic of the past. Even in recent years, we have seen Protestants and Catholics kill one another in Northern Ireland, while Jews and Muslims in Israel and Christians and Muslims in Bosnia have done the same thing.

Persecution. Beginning in the 1200s and continuing into the 1800s, in what has become known as the Inquisition, special commissions of the Roman Catholic church tortured women to elicit confessions that they were witches, and burned them at the stake. In 1692, Protestant leaders in Salem, Massachusetts, drowned women who were accused of being witches. (The last execution for witchcraft was in Scotland in 1722 [Bridgwater, 1953]). In short, religion has been used to justify oppression and any number of brutal acts.

The Symbolic Interactionist Perspective

Symbolic interactionists focus on the meanings people give their experiences, especially how they use symbols. Let's apply this perspective to religious symbols, rituals, and beliefs to see how they help to forge a community of like-minded people.

Religious Symbols

All religions use symbols to provide identity and social solidarity for their members. A symbol is a condensed way of communicating. In other words, for Muslims, the primary symbol is the crescent moon and star, for Jews the Star of David, for Christians the cross. For members, these are not ordinary symbols, but sacred symbols that evoke feelings of awe and reverence.

Rituals

Rituals, that is, ceremonies or repetitive practices, are also symbols that help unite people into a moral community. Some rituals, such as the bar mitzvah of Jewish boys and

Many think Pope John Paul II's visit to communist Cuba in 1998 stimulated social change in that island nation. Shown here is the Pope meeting with Fidel Castro.

Holy Communion of Christians, are designed to create in the devout a feeling of closeness with God and unity with one another. Rituals include kneeling and praying at set times, bowing, crossing oneself, singing, lighting candles and incense, a liturgy, scripture readings, processions, baptisms, weddings, funerals, and so on.

Beliefs

Symbols, including rituals, develop from beliefs. The belief may be vague ("God is") or highly specific ("God wants us to prostrate ourselves and face Mecca five times each day"). Religious beliefs include not only **values** (what is considered good and desirable in life—how we ought to live) but also a **cosmology**, a unified picture of the world. For example, the Jewish, Christian, and Muslim belief that there is only one God, the Creator of the universe, who is concerned about the actions of humans and who will hold us accountable for what we do, is a cosmology. It presents a unifying picture of the universe.

Community

Finally, the shared meanings that come through symbols, rituals, and beliefs (and for some, a religious experience) unite people into a moral community. People in a moral community feel a bond with one another, for their beliefs and rituals bind them together while at the same time separating them from those who do not share their unique symbolic world. Mormons, for example, feel a "kindred spirit" (as it is often known) with other Mormons. So do Baptists, Jews, Jehovah's Witnesses, and Muslims with members of their respective faiths.

This woodcut commemorates a dysfunction of religion, the burning of witches at the stake. This particular burning occurred at Derneburg, Germany, in 1555. (Woodcuts were used to illustrate books shortly after the printing press was invented.)

The removal of community is a serious matter for people whose identity is bound up in the community. Sociologists John Hostetler (1980), William Kephart, and William Zellner (1994) describe the Amish practice of *shunning*—ignoring an offender in all situations. Persons who are shunned are treated as though they do not exist. The shunning is so thorough that even family members, who themselves remain in good standing in the congregation, are not allowed to talk to the person being shunned.

The Conflict Perspective

The conflict perspective has an entirely different focus. Conflict theorists examine how religion supports the status quo, and helps to maintain social inequalities.

Opium of the People

In general, conflict theorists are highly critical of religion. Karl Marx, an avowed atheist, set the tone for conflict theorists with his most famous statement on this subject: "Religion is the sigh of the oppressed creature, the sentiment of a heartless world. ... It is the opium of the people" (Marx, 1844/1964). By this statement, Marx meant that oppressed workers, sighing for release from their suffering, escape into religion. For them, religion is like a drug that helps them forget their misery. By diverting their eyes to future happiness in a coming world, religion takes their eyes off their suffering in this one, thereby greatly reducing the possibility that they will rebel against their oppressors.

Symbolic interactionists stress that a basic characteristic of humans is that they attach meaning to objects and events and then use representations of those objects or events to communicate with one another. Some religious symbols are used to communicate feelings of awe and reverence. Michelangelo's *Pietà*, depicting Mary tenderly holding her son, Jesus, after his crucifixion, is one of the most acclaimed symbols in the Western world, admired for its beauty by believers and nonbelievers alike.

A Reflection of Social Inequalities

Conflict theorists stress that religious teachings and practices are a mirror of a society's inequalities. Gender inequality illustrates this point. In the mid-nineteenth century when Canada was evolving into a nation, the church, like Parliament and other institutions of society that were dominated by men, ordained only men, limiting women to such activities as teaching children Sunday school or preparing meals for congregational get-togethers, which were considered appropriate "feminine" activities. As women's roles in the broader society changed, however, religion reflected those changes. First, many religious groups allowed women to vote. Then, as women attained prominent positions in the business world and professions, some Protestant and Jewish groups allowed women to be ordained. Similarly, just as women still face barriers in secular society, so some congregations still refuse to ordain women. In some congregations the barriers remain so high that women are still not allowed to vote.

A Legitimation of Social Inequalities

Not only does religion mirror the social inequalities of the larger society, conflict theorists say, but also it legitimates them. By this, they mean that religion, reflecting the interests of those in power, teaches that the existing social arrangements of a society represent what God desires.

In what is perhaps the supreme technique of legitimating the social order, the religion of ancient Egypt held that the Pharaoh was a god. The Emperor of Japan was similarly declared divine. If this were so, who could even question his decisions?

Conflict theorists point out many other examples of how religion legitimates the social order. One of the more remarkable took place in the decades before the U.S. Civil War. Southern ministers used scripture to defend slavery, saying it was God's will—while northern ministers legitimated *their* region's social structure and used scripture to denounce slavery as evil (Ernst, 1988; Nauta, 1993; White, 1995). In India, Hinduism supports the caste system by teaching that an individual who tries to change caste will come back in the next life as a member of a lower caste—or even as an animal.

The Feminist Perspective

Female Spirituality

According to Johanna Stuckey (1998), there are a number of reasons to study female spirituality from a feminist perspective. First, the feminist commitment to diversity leads to an acceptance of exploring the positive spiritual experience of women. Second, feminist endorsement of the personal should recognize that the spiritual is deeply personal. Third, spirituality and its manifestations in religion help to reveal how this male-dominated system controls both women and men. Fourth, the separation of mind and body or rationality and spirituality is a fabrication of Western male epistemologies (i.e., theories of knowledge), which feminists must avoid. And fifth, half the human population, that is, women, have been neglected in religious studies. It is time to include women's religious roles, women's understanding of spirituality, and women-centred religious symbols.

Stuckey (1998) outlines four main categories of the feminist study of spirituality. **Revisionists** are those who believe that the basic message of the major religions is liberating. The major changes to the teachings revisionists would defend include replacing sexist prose with sex-neutral language. **Reformists** advocate revealing the "liberating core" of religious teachings with female imagery and exposing and refusing to accept rituals that are clearly sexist. **Revolutionaries** seek to change the established orthodoxy by importing language, images, and rituals from other traditions. Finally, **rejectionists** are feminists who judge the traditional teachings to be hopelessly sexist and have abandoned them in order to establish a new spiritual tradition. Most practise "Feminist Goddess Worship," which is understood to be completely different from any other religious expressions of spirituality.

Themes in Christian Feminism

Several themes have been expressed by feminists interested in female spirituality within the Christian tradition. First is overcoming sexism by taking account of women's experiences in the church. Second, and a very productive area of Christian feminism, is the recovery of Christian women's histories. Rescued names and lives of women of the past include the twelfth-century prophet Hildegard of Bingen, Shaker Ann Lee, and Roman Catholic social activist Dorothy Day. Third is exploring the meaning of Jesus, a debate that has produced heated encounters. One telling example is the statue "Crucified Woman" that stands outside Emmanuel College at the University of Toronto (Dyke, 1991). Fourth, the issue of Christian feminist ethics has produced a burgeoning literature by tackling issues such as abortion, homophobia, power and sexuality, and suffering and evil.

Themes in Judaism and Feminism

Jewish feminists, like their counterparts within Christianity, have been questioning the male dominance of their religion and the masculinity of God. For the most part, Jewish feminists are revisionists in that they believe in the core meanings of Judaism and seek to change Judaism from the inside by challenging blatantly sexist rituals and teachings. They have fought to take part in public rituals and to fill leadership roles. Within non-Orthodox Judaism, for example, there are a number of female rabbis. In Conservative, Reform, and Reconstructionist Judaism, women read the Torah in public and can take part in the *minyan*, the formerly "10 males" prayer ceremony (Elwell, 1996).

Feminist spirituality is a recent development within second-wave feminism. However, the thrust of feminist spirituality resides in the Christian and Jewish traditions and is only now beginning to have an impact on Islam and other world religions. For the most part, feminists interested in spirituality have not given up on their religious upbringing. Very few profess rejectionist sentiments. Most are working for change from within an established religious tradition.

> ## Focus Question
> What explanations are provided by the functionalist, symbolic interactionist, conflict, and feminist perspectives for the existence of religion in society?

Religion and the Spirit of Capitalism

Weber was intrigued with the question of why some societies embraced capitalism while others clung to their traditional ways. Tradition is strong and holds people in check, yet some societies had been transformed by capitalism, while others remained untouched. As he explored this problem, Weber concluded that religion held the key to **modernization**—the transformation of traditional societies to industrial societies.

To explain his conclusions, Weber wrote *The Protestant Ethic and the Spirit of Capitalism* (1904-1905/1958). His explanation is briefly summarized here.

1. Capitalism represents a fundamentally different way of thinking about work and money. To accumulate money (capital) as an end in itself and to consider it a duty to invest money in order to make profits, Weber called the **spirit of capitalism**.

2. Why did the spirit of capitalism develop in Europe, and not, for example, in China or India, where the people had similar intelligence, material resources, education, and so on? According to Weber, *religion was the key*.

3. What was different about Protestantism, especially Calvinism? Calvinists concluded that church members had a duty to prove that they are one of God's elect, and to live as though they are predestined to heaven. This conclusion motivated Calvinists to lead highly moral lives *and* to work hard, to not waste time, and to be frugal—for idleness and needless spending were signs of worldliness. Weber called this hard-working, self-denying approach to life the **Protestant ethic**.

4. As people worked hard and spent money only on necessities, they accumulated money. This capital, in turn, since it couldn't be spent, was invested—which led to a surge in production.

5. Thus, a change in religion to Protestantism, especially Calvinism, led to a fundamental change in thought and behaviour (the *Protestant ethic*). The result was the *spirit of capitalism*. Hence capitalism originated in Europe, and not in places where religion did not encourage capitalism's essential elements: the accumulation of capital through frugality and hard work, and its investment and reinvestment.

At this point in history, the Protestant ethic and the spirit of capitalism are not confined to any specific religion or even part of the world. Rather, they have become cultural traits that have spread to societies around the world (Greeley, 1964; Yinger, 1970). Canadian Catholics have about the same approach to life as Canadian Protestants. In addition, Hong Kong, Japan, Malaysia, Singapore, South Korea, and Taiwan—not exactly Protestant countries—have embraced capitalism (M. J. Levy, 1992).

The World's Major Religions

Of the thousands of religions in the world, most people practise either Judaism, Christianity, Islam, Hinduism, Buddhism, or Confucianism. Let us briefly review each.

Judaism

The founding of Judaism marked a fundamental change in religion, for it was the first religion based on **monotheism**, the belief that there is only one God. Prior to Judaism, religions were based on **polytheism**, the belief that there are many gods. In Greek religion, for example, Zeus was the god of heaven and earth, Poseidon the god of the sea, and Athena the goddess of wisdom. Other groups followed **animism**, believing that all objects in the world have spirits, some of which are dangerous and must be outwitted.

Contemporary Judaism comprises three main branches: Orthodox, Reform, and Conservative. Orthodox Jews adhere to the laws espoused by Moses. They eat only foods prepared in a designated manner (kosher), observe the Sabbath in a traditional way, and segregate males and females in their religious services. During the 1800s, a group that wanted to make its practices more compatible with the secular (nonreligious) culture broke from this tradition. This liberal group, known as Reform Judaism, mostly uses the vernacular (a country's language) in its religious ceremonies and has reduced much of the ritual. The third branch, Conservative Judaism, falls somewhere between the other two.

The history of Judaism is marked by conflict and persecution. The Israelites were conquered by Babylon and made slaves. After returning to Israel and rebuilding the temple, they were later conquered by Rome, and after their rebellion at Masada in A.D. 70 failed, they were dispersed for almost 2000 years into other nations. During those centuries, they faced prejudice, discrimination, and persecution (called **anti-Semitism**) by many peoples and rulers. The most horrendous example is Hitler's attempt to eliminate the Jews as a people in the Nazi Holocaust of World War II. Under the Nazi occupation of Europe and North Africa, about 6 million Jews were slaughtered, perhaps half dying in gas ovens constructed specifically for this purpose.

Christianity

Christianity, which developed out of Judaism, is also monotheistic. Christians believe that Jesus Christ is the Messiah. Jesus was born in poverty, and—traditional Christians believe—to a virgin. At about the age of 30, he began a preaching and healing ministry.

His increasingly popular teachings threatened members of the religious establishment, some of whom convinced the Romans that he endangered the civil order, a crime punishable by death. The 12 main followers of Jesus, called *the apostles*, believed that Jesus afterward rose from the dead. The new religion spread rapidly, and after initial hostility from imperial Rome—persecution included feeding Christian believers to lions in the Coliseum—in A.D. 317 Christianity became the empire's official religion.

During the first 1000 years of Christianity, there was only one church organization, directed from Rome. During the eleventh century, after disagreement over doctrine and politics, Greek Orthodoxy was established. It was headquartered in Constantinople (now Istanbul, Turkey). During the Middle Ages, the Roman Catholic Church aligned with the political establishment.

Although Martin Luther's original goal was to reform the Church, not divide it, the Reformation began a splintering of Christianity. The schism coincided with the breakup of feudalism and the beginning of capitalism. More and more, people clamoured for independence not only in political but also religious thought.

Today, Christians are divided into hundreds of groups, some with doctrinal differences so slight that only members of the group can appreciate the extremely fine distinctions that, they feel, significantly separate them from others.

Islam

Islam, whose followers are known as Muslims, began in the same part of the world as Judaism and Christianity. Islam is the world's third monotheistic religion. It was founded by Muhammad, who was born in Mecca (now in Saudi Arabia) about A.D. 570. His teachings were written down in a book called the Koran. When he found out that there was a plot to murder him, Muhammad fled to Medina, where he found a more receptive audience. There he established a *theocracy* (a government based on the principle that God is the ruler, his laws the statutes of the land, and priests his earthly administrators), and founded the Muslim empire. In A.D. 630 he returned to Mecca, this time as a conqueror (Bridgwater, 1953).

After Muhammad's death, a struggle for control over the empire he had founded split Islam into two branches that remain today, the Sunni and the Shi'ite. The Shi'ites, who believe that the *imam* (the religious leader) is inspired as he interprets the Koran, are generally more conservative and inclined to **fundamentalism**, the belief that modernism threatens religion and that the faith as it was originally practised should be restored. The Sunni, who do not share this belief, are generally more liberal.

Like the Jews, Muslims trace their ancestry to Abraham. For Muslims, also, Jerusalem is a holy city. The Muslims consider the Bibles of the Jews and the Christians to be sacred but take the Koran as the final word. They believe that the followers of Abraham and Moses (Jews) and Jesus (Christians) changed the original teachings and that Muhammad restored their purity. It is the duty of each Muslim to make a pilgrimage to Mecca during his or her lifetime.

Hinduism

Unlike the other religions described, Hinduism has no specific founder. Going back about 4000 years, Hinduism is the chief religion of India. The term *Hinduism*, however, is Western, and in India the closest term is *dharma* (law). Unlike Judaism, Christianity, and Islam, Hinduism has no texts thought to be inspired by God. Instead, several books, including the *Brahmanas*, *Bhagavad-Gita*, and *Upanishads*, expound on moral qualities that people should strive after.

Hindus are *polytheists*; that is, they believe there are many gods. They believe one of these gods, Brahma, created the universe. Brahma, along with Shiva (the Destroyer) and Vishnu (the Preserver), form a triad at the centre of modern Hinduism. A central belief is *karma*, spiritual progress. There is no final judgment but, instead, **reincarnation**, a cycle of life, death, and rebirth. Death involves only the body, and every person's soul comes back in a form that matches the individual's moral progress in the previous life (which centres on proper conduct in following the rules of one's caste). If an individual reaches spiritual perfection, he or she has attained *nirvana*. This marks the end of the cycle of death and rebirth, when the soul is reunited with the universal soul. When this occurs, *maya*, the illusion of time and space, has been conquered.

Buddhism

About 600 B.C., Siddhartha Gautama founded Buddhism. (*Buddha* means "enlightened one," a term Gautama was given by his disciples.) Gautama was the son of an upper-caste Hindu ruler in an area north of Benares, India. At the age of 29, he renounced his life of luxury and became an ascetic. Through meditation, he discovered the following

The most famous Buddhist symbol is the Buddha, which is depicted in many forms, including female. Shown here is a Buddhist monk in Sri Lanka praying before the world-famous Buddha at Anuradhapura.

century A.D., Buddhism reached the height of its popularity in India, after which it died out. Buddhism, however, had been adopted in Sri Lanka, Myanmar, Tibet, Laos, Cambodia, Thailand, China, Korea, and Japan, where it flourishes today.

Confucianism

About the time that Gautama lived, K'ung Fu-tsu (551–479 B.C.) was born in China. Confucius (his name strung together in English), a public official, was distressed by the corruption that he saw in government. Unlike Gautama, who urged withdrawal from social activities, Confucius urged social reform and developed a system of morality based on peace, justice, and universal order. His teachings were incorporated into writings called the *Analects*.

The basic moral principle of Confucianism is to maintain *jen*, sympathy or concern for other humans. The key to jen is to maintain right relationships—being loyal and placing morality above self-interest. In what is called the "Confucian Golden Rule," Confucius stated a basic principle for jen: to treat those who are subordinate to you as you would like to be treated by people superior to yourself. Confucius taught that right relationships within the family (loyalty, respect) should be the model for society. He also taught the "middle way," an avoidance of extremes.

Confucianism was originally atheistic, simply a set of moral teachings without reference to the supernatural. As the centuries passed, however, local gods were added to the teachings, and Confucius himself was declared a god. Confucius' teachings became the basis for the government of China (Bridgwater, 1953). Following the Communist revolution of 1949, political leaders attempted to weaken the people's ties with Confucianism.

Types of Religious Groups

Sociologists have identified four types of religious groups. The summary presented here is a modification of analyses by sociologists Ernst Troeltsch (1931), Liston Pope (1942), and Benton Johnson (1963). (Figure 14.2 illustrates the relationship between each of these four types of religious groups.)

Cult

Cults sometimes make instant headlines around the world, as did the ones described in the Down-to-Earth Sociology box on page 356. Cults, however, are not necessarily weird, and few practise "brainwashing" or bizarre rituals. In fact, *all religions began as cults* (R. Stark, 1989).

Cults often begin with the appearance of a **charismatic leader**, an individual who inspires people because he or she seems to have extraordinary qualities. Finding something highly appealing about the individual, people feel drawn to both the person and the message.

"four noble truths," all of which emphasize self-denial and compassion:

1. Existence is suffering.
2. The origin of suffering is desire.
3. Suffering ceases when desire ceases.
4. The way to end desire is to follow the "noble eightfold path."

The noble eightfold path consists of

1. right belief
2. right resolve (to renounce carnal pleasure and to harm no living creature)
3. right speech
4. right conduct
5. right occupation or living
6. right effort
7. right-mindedness (or contemplation)
8. right ecstasy

Buddhism spread rapidly. In the third century B.C., the ruler of India adopted Buddhism and sent missionaries throughout Asia to spread the new teaching. By the fifth

Figure 14.2 A Cult-Sect-Church-Ecclesia Continuum

Source: Troeltsch (1931); Pope (1942); Johnson (1963).

Note: Any religious organization can be placed somewhere on this continuum, on the basis of its having "more" or "less" of these characteristics.

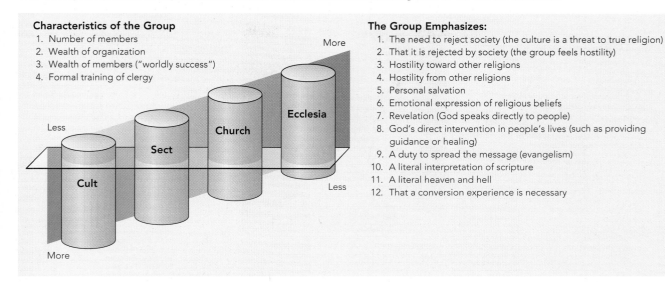

Characteristics of the Group
1. Number of members
2. Wealth of organization
3. Wealth of members ("worldly success")
4. Formal training of clergy

Less

More

Ecclesia

Church

Sect

Cult

More

Less

The Group Emphasizes:
1. The need to reject society (the culture is a threat to true religion)
2. That it is rejected by society (the group feels hostility)
3. Hostility toward other religions
4. Hostility from other religions
5. Personal salvation
6. Emotional expression of religious beliefs
7. Revelation (God speaks directly to people)
8. God's direct intervention in people's lives (such as providing guidance or healing)
9. A duty to spread the message (evangelism)
10. A literal interpretation of scripture
11. A literal heaven and hell
12. That a conversion experience is necessary

A **cult**, then, is simply a new or different religion, with few followers, whose teaching and practices put it at odds with the dominant culture and religion. Because the term "cult" has such negative meanings in the public mind, however, some scholars prefer to use *new religion* instead.

Every cult meets with rejection from society. Its message is considered bizarre, its approach to life, strange. Its members antagonize the majority, who are convinced that they have a monopoly on the truth. The new message may claim revelation, visions, visits from God and angels, some form

of enlightenment, or seeing the true way to God. The cult demands intense commitment, and its followers, confronting a hostile world, pull into a tight circle, separating themselves from nonbelievers.

Most cults fail. Not many people believe the new message, and the cult fades into obscurity. Some, however, succeed and make history. Over time, large numbers of people may come to accept the message, and become followers of the religion. If this happens, the new religion changes from a cult to a *sect*.

The sociological and common-sense meanings of the term *cult* differ radically. Shoko Asahara of Japan, left, matches the public's image of a crazed cult leader. Asahara headed a cult that, on March 20, 1995, released a nerve gas, sarin, in the Tokyo subway during rush hour (right). The attack left 10 people dead and 4700 injured. As the text explains, the sociological meaning of *cult*, in contrast, is neutral.

The news made instant headlines around the world. Thirty-nine bodies in an exclusive San Diego neighbourhood draped in purple, diamond-shaped shrouds. Some of the men had been castrated. No sign of a struggle.

Reports followed on the beliefs of those who died. A spaceship was hiding behind the Hale-Bopp comet ready to transport them to a new life. To be beamed aboard, they had to leave their "containers" behind. That meant suicide. For their space travels, each cult member put on new Nike sneakers. Each also packed a bag with clothing, $5 bills, and quarters—and a passport.

Then there is the garbage-eating Brotherhood led by an ex-Marine who claims he is Jesus. His long-haired followers rummage through dumpsters, carefully removing any mould before dining on rotting scraps of the material world they so disdain. They blame their stomachaches on Satan (O'Neill, 1997).

Other Messiahs have been just as influential. Back in the 1970s, hundreds followed Jim Jones to Guyana. More than 900 committed suicide—or were murdered. In the 1990s, 74 members of

Marshal Applewhite, pictured here, was able to persuade 38 men to commit suicide with him in order to be beamed aboard a spaceship. The text explains how such bizarre events can occur.

the Solar Temple in Switzerland, France, and Canada arranged themselves in the shape of a cross and set themselves afire. They believed they would be transported to the star Sirius (Lacayo, 1997).

Why would anyone fall for such "obvious" deception? Finding *meaning* in life lies at the centre of religion.

Always, people seek to satisfy their spiritual longings. And with today's rapid social change, our traditional meanings are constantly challenged and sometimes uprooted. Most significantly, cult teachings are learned among a group of people who satisfy deep needs of belonging, who provide a life-enhancing sense of community. Newcomers are isolated, cut off from family and friends who would provide a balancing perspective on reality. As the group's views are regularly confirmed by people one has come to like and respect, the bizarreness of these beliefs gradually wears off. Instead, cult members come to be viewed as "insiders" privy to secret messages beyond the grasp of ordinary people.

Heaven's Gate, and its many counterparts throughout the world, matches the public's image of cults—bizarre people with strange teachings whose followers act in repugnant ways. As has been stressed, however, the *sociological* meaning of "cult" is different. All new religions begin as cults. Some grow and become sects. Others even develop into churches and ecclesias.

Sect

A **sect** is a group larger than a cult. Its members still feel a fair amount of tension with the prevailing beliefs and values of the broader society. The sect may even be hostile to the society in which it lives. At the very least, its members remain uncomfortable with many of the emphases of the dominant culture, while nonmembers, in turn, tend to be uncomfortable with members of the sect.

Ordinarily, sects are loosely organized and fairly small. They emphasize personal salvation, and clapping, shouting, dancing, and extemporaneous prayers are hallmarks of sects. Like cults, sects also stress **evangelism**, the active recruitment of new members.

If a sect grows, its members gradually tend to make peace with the rest of society. They become more respectable in the eyes of the majority and feel much less hostility and little, if any, isolation. To appeal to the new, broader base, the sect shifts some of its doctrines, redefining matters to remove some of the rough edges that created tension between it and the rest of society. If a sect follows

this course and becomes larger and more integrated into society, it changes into a *church*.

Church

At this point, the religious group is highly bureaucratized—probably with national and international headquarters that give directions to the local congregations, enforce rules about who can be ordained, and control finances. Written prayers, for example, are now likely to be read before the congregation, and sermons to be much more formal. Rather than being recruited from the outside by fervent, personal evangelism, most new members now come from within, from children born to existing members. At some designated age, children may be asked to affirm the group's beliefs in a confirmation or bar mitzvah ceremony.

Ecclesia

Finally, some groups become so well integrated into a culture, and so strongly allied with their government, that it is difficult to tell where one leaves off and the other takes over. In these state religions, also called **ecclesias**, the government and religion work together to try to shape society. The majority of the society, however, may belong to the religion in name only. How extensively religion and government intertwine in an ecclesia is illustrated by Sweden, where in the 1800s all citizens had to memorize Luther's *Small Catechism* and be tested on it yearly (P. Anderson, 1995). Today, Lutheranism is still the state religion, but most Swedes come to church only for baptisms, marriages, and funerals.

Examples of ecclesias include the Church of England (whose very name expresses alignment between church and state), the Lutheran church in Sweden and Denmark, Islam in Iran and Iraq, and, during the time of the Holy Roman Empire, the Roman Catholic Church, which was the official religion for what is today Europe.

Variations in Patterns

Obviously, not all religious groups go through all these stages—from cult to sect to church to ecclesia. Some die out because they fail to attract enough members. Others, such as the Amish, remain sects. And, as is evident from the short list of countries that have state religions, very few religions ever become ecclesias.

In addition, these classifications are not perfectly matched in the real world. For example, although the Amish are a sect, they place little or no emphasis on recruiting others. The early Quakers, another sect, shied away from emotional expressions of their beliefs. Finally, some groups that become churches may retain a few characteristics of sects, such as an emphasis on evangelism.

Although all religions began as cults, not all varieties of a given religion may have done so. For example, some **denominations**—"brand names" within a major religion, such as Methodism or Reform Judaism—may begin as splinter groups. A large group within a church may disagree with *some aspects* of the church's teachings (not its major message) and break away to form its own organization.

When Religion and Culture Conflict

As we have seen, cults and sects represent a break with the past. Consequently, they challenge the social order. Three major patterns of adaptation occur when religion and the culture in which it is embedded find themselves in conflict.

First, the members of a religion may reject the dominant culture and have as little as possible to do with nonmembers of their religion. Like the Amish, they may withdraw into closed communities.

In the second pattern, a cult or sect rejects only specific elements of the prevailing culture. Most elements of the main culture, however, are accepted. Although specific activities are forbidden, members of the religion are able to participate in most aspects of the broader society. They resolve this mild tension either by adhering to the religion or by "sneaking," doing the forbidden acts on the sly.

In the third pattern, the society rejects the religious group and may even try to destroy it. The early Christians are an example. The Roman emperor declared them enemies of Rome and ordered all Christians hunted down and destroyed.

Characteristics of Religion in Canada

How can we generalize about religion in Canada, with its hundreds of denominations and sects? What do these many religious groups have in common? It certainly isn't doctrine, but doctrine is not the focus of sociology. Sociologists, rather, are interested in the relationship between society and religion, and the role religion plays in people's lives. To better understand religion in Canadian society, then, we shall focus first on characteristics of members of religious groups, then on the groups themselves.

The picture for religion in Canada is a changing one—but one that recognizes diversity and a degree of continuity with the past.

Historically, Canada has been predominantly Christian. Most of the population has been divided between Protestants, living mostly outside the province of Quebec, and Roman Catholics, of whom the majority continue to live in the province of Quebec. Between 1986 and 1996, Roman Catholics remained at approximately 46 percent of the adult population in Canada while established Protestants such as Anglican, United, and so on dropped

While attendance at religious services in Canada has declined over the past five decades, the vast majority of Canadians still retain a belief in God.

Table 14.1 Religion in Canada, 1986–1996
(in millions)

Religion	1986	1991	1996
Roman Catholic	9.0	9.3	10.4
Eastern Orthodox	0.3	0.2	0.2
Established Protestants	5.6	5.0	4.8
Right-wing Protestants	1.2	1.1	1.4
Other Protestants	0.7	0.7	1.2
Jewish	0.2	0.2	0.2
Eastern non-Christian	0.3	0.5	0.7
No religion	2.0	3.5	3.4
Not stated	0.4	0.5	1.2

Source: Statistics Canada, *General Social Survey*, 1996.

from 28 percent to 20 percent of the adult population in the country. However, the more right-wing, conservative Protestants continue to draw approximately 6 percent of the population.

The only religious group that has grown to any significant degree over this time period is the Eastern, non-Christian religions of Islam, Hinduism, and Buddhism. While the proportion is small—3 percent of the adult Canadian population—the numbers have increased from approximately 300 000 in 1986 to over 700 000 in 1996 or a percentage increase of over 130 percent in 10 years! (See Table 14.1.)

Next, what is changing in Canada in terms of religion and religious identity? Since the 1961 census, the incidence of those reporting "No religion" has increased dramatically from a low of less than 1 percent in 1961 to over 18 percent at the beginning of this millennium. It would appear that this group of Canadians continues to grow. Compared to the United States, proportionally more Canadians profess not to be part of any religious tradition, and this trend appears to be growing.

Another significant change has been the proportion of Canadians who have been attending religious services. Since the post–World War period, Canadians have been attending religious services on a less frequent basis. For example, over two-thirds of Canadians in 1951 stated they attended religious services during the previous week. The General Social Survey in 1996 reported that fewer than 20 percent of adult Canadians attend religious services every week.

While this is true for all age groups in Canada, over a third of seniors aged 65 and over attended religious services weekly in 1996. This percentage is twice that reported for 15- to 24-year-olds.

While attendance at religious services may be down and there is a growing trend toward Canadians expressing no religious affiliation, Reginald Bibby, in his 1995 Project Canada survey, found that the vast majority of Canadians— 81 percent—still believe in God. Thus, while attendance at

religious services is dramatically down, and Canadians appear less religious, apparently the vast majority of Canadians have retained their belief in God.

When compared to Americans, Canadians show a dramatic difference when it comes to the non-religious category. In 1996, Queen's University conducted a North American survey entitled "God and Society in North America." In that survey, those expressing no religious affiliation are broken down into the following categories: "Agnostic," "Atheist," "Nothing," and "Don't know." In each category, Canadians scored higher (in percentage terms) than Americans. In total, almost a quarter (23.4 percent) of Canadians fell into these categories, while only one in seven (14 percent) of Americans expressed these sentiments. (See Table 14.2.)

> **Focus Question** What are the religious differences between Canada and the United States?

While established and non-established Christian religions continue to dominate the Canadian religious landscape, questions about spirituality or the human spirit are increasing.

The Future of Religion

Marx was convinced religion would crumble when the workers threw off their chains of oppression. When the workers usher in a new society based on justice, he argued, there will no longer be a need for religion, for religion is the refuge of the miserable, and people will no longer be miserable. Religion will wither away, for people will see that thoughts about an afterlife are misdirected. In its place, they will put their energies into developing a workers' paradise here on earth (De George, 1968).

Table 14.2 Expressions of Religious Tradition for Canada and the United States, 1996

Religious Tradition	Canada	United States
Christian	69.0% (2070)	76.5% (2313)
Jewish	1.0% (29)	2.1% (63)
Muslim	0.4% (13)	0.3% (9)
Other non-Christian	0.8% (23)	1.2% (36)
Agnostic	3.1% (92)	2.1% (64)
Atheist	3.2% (97)	0.9% (26)
Nothing	16.0% (481)	10.1% (304)
Something	5.4% (162)	6.0% (180)
Don't know	1.1% (33)	0.9% (28)

Source: Adapted from *God and Society in North America Survey*, Queen's University, 1996, with the permission of the American Religious Data Archive.

PEANUTS® by Charles M. Schulz

In its common usage, to "evangelize" means to make converts. As *Peanuts* so humorously picks up, evangelization is sometimes accomplished through means other than pronouncements.

After communist countries were established, however, people continued to be religious. At first, the leaders thought this was simply a remnant of the past that would eventually dwindle to nothing. Old people might cling to the past, but the young would give it up, and with the coming generation religion would cease to exist.

The new Marxist states, avowing atheism, were not content to let this withering occur on its own, and they tried to eradicate religion from their midst. (Keep in mind that Marx said that he was not a Marxist. He did not advocate the persecution of religion, for he felt that religion would crumble on its own.) The Communist government in the Soviet Union confiscated church buildings and turned them into museums or government offices. The school curriculum was designed to ridicule religion, and a civil marriage ceremony was substituted for the religious ceremony (complete with an altar and a bust of Lenin), while a ceremony dedicating newborns to the state was substituted for baptism. Ministers and priests were jailed as enemies of the state, and parents who dared to teach religion to their children were imprisoned or fired from their jobs, their children taken from them to be reared by the state where they would learn the "truth."

In spite of severe, extended persecution, religion remained strong, even among many of the youth. Table 14.3 shows results of the first scientific sampling of the Russian population since the collapse of the Soviet Union. Three out of four Russians believe there is a God, and one out of three believes there is a heaven.

Science simply never can replace religion. Nor can political systems, as demonstrated by the experience of socialist and communist countries. Science can describe death and compute consequences, but it cannot dictate the moral superiority of any action.

There is no doubt that religion will last as long as humanity lasts—or until humans develop adequate functional alternatives. And even though such alternatives do come, would they not be religion under a different name?

Table 14.3 Religious Beliefs in Russia

Percentage of Russians Who Believe in the Following:	
God	74%
Life after death	40%
Miracles	33%
Heaven	33%
Hell	30%

Source: Greeley (1994).

Summary and Review

EDUCATION: TRANSFERRING KNOWLEDGE AND SKILLS

TODAY'S CREDENTIAL SOCIETY

What is a credential society, and how did it develop?

A **credential society** is one in which employers use diplomas and degrees to determine who is eligible for a job. One reason that credentialism developed is that large, anonymous societies lack the personal knowledge common to smaller groups; educational certification provides evidence of a person's ability. pp. 332–333.

THE DEVELOPMENT OF MODERN EDUCATION

How did modern education develop?

In most of human history, education consisted of informal learning, equivalent to **acculturation**. In some earlier societies, centres of formal education did develop, such as among the Arabians, Chinese, Greeks, and Egyptians. Because modern education came about in response to industrialization, formal education is much less common in the least industrialized nations. pp. 333–335.

THE FUNCTIONALIST PERSPECTIVE: PROVIDING SOCIAL BENEFITS

What is the functionalist perspective on education?

Among the functions of education are the teaching of knowledge and skills, **cultural transmission** of values, social integration, **gatekeeping**, promoting personal and social change, and **mainstreaming**. Functionalists also note that education has replaced some traditional family functions. pp. 335–339.

THE CONFLICT PERSPECTIVE: REPRODUCING THE SOCIAL CLASS STRUCTURE

What is the conflict perspective on education?

The basic view of conflict theorists is that education reproduces the social class structure; that is, through such mechanisms as unequal funding and operating different schools for the elite and for the masses, education reinforces a society's basic social inequalities. pp. 339–342.

THE SYMBOLIC INTERACTIONIST PERSPECTIVE: TEACHER EXPECTATIONS AND THE SELF-FULFILLING PROPHECY

What is the symbolic interactionist perspective on education?

Symbolic interactionists focus on face-to-face interaction. In examining what occurs in the classroom, they have found a **self-fulfilling prophecy**: that student performance tends to conform to teacher expectations, whether they are high or low. p. 343.

RETHINKING SCHOOLS: PROBLEMS AND SOLUTIONS

What are the chief problems that face Canadian education?

The major problems are low achievement, grade inflation, social promotion, functional illiteracy, violence, and teen pregnancy. pp. 343–345.

What are the primary solutions to these problems?

The primary solution is to restore high educational standards, which can be done only after providing basic security for students. Any solution for improving quality must be based on raising standards and expecting more of students and teachers alike. pp. 345–347.

RELIGION: ESTABLISHING MEANING

WHAT IS RELIGION?

Durkheim identified three essential characteristics of **religion**: beliefs that set the **sacred** apart from the **profane**, **rituals**, and a **moral community** (a church). pp. 347–348.

THE FUNCTIONALIST PERSPECTIVE

What are the functions and dysfunctions of religion?

Among the functions of religion are answering questions about ultimate meaning, providing emotional comfort, social solidarity, guidelines for everyday life, social control, adaptation, support for the government, and fostering social change. Groups or activities that provide these same functions are called functional equivalents of religion. Among the dysfunctions of religion are war and religious persecution. pp. 348–349.

THE SYMBOLIC INTERACTIONIST PERSPECTIVE

What aspects of religion do symbolic interactionists study?

Symbolic interactionists focus on the meanings of religion for its followers. They examine religious symbols, rituals, beliefs, experiences, and the sense of community provided by religion. pp. 349–350.

THE CONFLICT PERSPECTIVE

What aspects of religion do conflict theorists study?

Conflict theorists examine the relationship of religion to social inequalities, especially how religion is a conservative force that reinforces a society's social stratification. pp. 350–351.

THE FEMINIST PERSPECTIVE

What aspects of religion do feminists study?

Feminists focus on female spirituality. There are four main categories of the feminist study of spirituality: **revisionists**, **reformists**, **revolutionaries**, and **rejectionists**. All attempt to eliminate sexist ritual and teachings. pp. 351–352.

RELIGION AND THE SPIRIT OF CAPITALISM

What does the spirit of capitalism have to do with religion?

Max Weber disagreed with Marx's conclusion that religion impedes social change. In contrast, Weber saw religion as a primary source of social change. He analyzed how Protestantism gave rise to the **Protestant ethic**, which stimulated what he called the **spirit of capitalism**. The result was capitalism, which transformed society. p. 352.

THE WORLD'S MAJOR RELIGIONS

What are the world's major religions?

Judaism, Christianity, and Islam, all **monotheistic** religions, can be traced to the same Old Testament roots. Hinduism, the chief religion of India, has no specific founder, as do Judaism (Abraham), Christianity (Jesus), Islam (Muhammad), Buddhism (Gautama), and Confucianism (K'ung Fu-tsu). Specific teachings and history of these six religions are given in the text. pp. 352–354.

TYPES OF RELIGIOUS GROUPS

What types of religious groups are there?

Sociologists divide religious groups into cults, sects, churches, and ecclesias. All religions began as **cults**. Those that survive tend to develop into **sects** and eventually into **churches**. Sects, often led by **charismatic leaders**, are unstable. Some are perceived as a threat and persecuted by the state. **Ecclesias**, or state religions, are rare. pp. 354–357.

CHARACTERISTICS OF RELIGION IN CANADA

What are the main trends in religion in Canada?

Most Canadians are either Protestants or Roman Catholics. The only religious group that has grown to any significant degree in the past decade and a half is the Eastern non-Christian religions of Islam, Hinduism, and Buddhism. Second, since 1961, the incidence of those reporting "No religion" has increased dramatically from a low of less than 1 percent to an approximate high today of over 18 percent. pp. 357–358.

What is one of the principal differences between Canada and the United States with regard to religion?

When compared to Americans, Canadians show a dramatic difference when it comes to the non-religious affiliation category. Almost a quarter (23.4 percent) of Canadians reported no religious affiliation, while only one in seven (14 percent) of Americans expressed these sentiments. p. 358.

THE FUTURE OF RELIGION

Because science and political systems cannot answer questions about ultimate meaning, the need for religion will remain. In any foreseeable future, religion—or its functional equivalents—will prosper. pp. 358–359.

Critical Thinking Questions

1. With technology providing greater out-of-classroom educational opportunities (courses through the Internet, for example), will education's role in reproducing inequality be diminished?

2. How might education become a liberator for the poor and other minority groups?

3. What are some of the pressures high school students experience in today's economy and how might these pressures contribute to growing violence within the schools?

4. Compared to Americans, a much larger percentage of Canadians report that they have no religious affiliation. What do you think accounts for this difference? Do Weber's ideas of secularization have any merit?

5. Generally speaking, why do you think people from different classes in Canada also differ in their religious preferences? Compare the religious affiliation of small businessmen with the rich and the more underprivileged members of Canadian society.

Key Terms

acculturation 333
animism 352
anti-Semitism 353
charismatic leader 354
church 348
correspondence principle 342
cosmology 349
credential societies 332

cult 355
cultural transmission 335
denominations 357
ecclesias 357
education 333
evangelism 356
fundamentalism 353
gatekeeping 337

hidden curriculum 339
latent functions 335
mainstreaming 338
manifest functions 335
modernization 352
monotheism 352
moral community 348
political socialization 334
polytheism 352
profane 348
Protestant ethic 352
reformists 351
reincarnation 353

rejectionists 351
religion 348
revisionists 351
revolutionaries 351
rituals 349
sacred 348
sect 356
self-fulfilling prophecy 343
social placement 338
spirit of capitalism 352
tracking 337
values 349

Weblinks

All URLs listed are current as of the printing of this book. URLs are often changed. Please check our Web site **www.abacon.com/ henslin** for updates.

Canadian Montessori Academy

www.montessori-academy.com/about_montessori.htm
This page explains the philosophy of the Montessori Method of early education, in which the teacher creates a prepared environment supported by specialized materials that help children teach themselves.

AskERIC

ericir.syr.edu/
The Educational Resources Information Center (ERIC) is a national information system that provides (through its 16 subject-specific clearinghouses, associated adjunct clearinghouses, and support components) a variety of services and products on a broad range of education-related issues.

CampusNewsOnCults.com

www.campusnewsoncults.com/
Disseminates information about high-pressure, manipulative cults on university campuses in an effort to counteract their influence.

WebCircle

www.brewich.com/webcircle/
"WebCircle is a ring of Pagan sites around the web.... [These sites] hope to help others find their way to the Old Gods. The pages in the circle are carefully chosen. Not all who apply are accepted."

Chapter 15

Medicine: Health and Illness in Canada

Learning Outcomes

After you have studied this chapter, you will be able to

■ understand the social production of illness

■ describe the publicly funded health care system in Canada

■ provide some explanation for the gendered experience of health and illness

■ show why extra-billing of patients for medical services is not a good idea

■ discuss the latest developments in AIDS research

Rudy Johnson had a problem—how to transport a long extension ladder on a short pickup truck. Against her better judgment, his wife, Norma, consented to sit on the ladder while Rudy moved it. That worked out just fine—until Rudy took a curve too fast and she and the ladder spilled out.

This was not Norma's lucky day. She landed on her head.

An emergency medical team answered the 911 call. Determining that the unconscious woman was near death, the team ordered a helicopter to fly Norma to a trauma centre, where emergency specialists sprang into action. The trauma surgeon ordered X-rays, which revealed a haziness in her lungs, probably from aspirated vomit. A CAT scan revealed a brain hemorrhage and a skull fracture. When a blood test showed that the oxygen level in her blood had fallen to a dangerously low level, an anesthesiologist inserted a breathing tube into Norma's trachea and administered 100 percent oxygen.

Norma's condition worsened. The trauma surgeon inserted a tube into her chest to expand a collapsed lung. The cardiologist pushed an ultrasound probe down her throat to take pictures of her beating heart and to evaluate its pumping efficiency. The neurosurgeon drilled a hole in Norma's skull and inserted a pressure gauge to monitor her swollen brain.

To improve the blood flow to her lungs, that night a special bed rocked Norma from side to side. Her condition stabilized, and she lived. Norma vowed never again to ride in the back of a pickup—at least not on top of an extension ladder.

Source: Based on J. J. Miller (1995).

Sociology and the Study of Medicine

The technology that saved Norma Johnson's life, available in only a few places on earth, opens up fascinating possibilities in health care. It also contributes to skyrocketing medical costs and creates such dilemmas as whether or not such expensive technology should be rationed, topics we shall explore in this chapter.

As we look at such issues, the role of sociology in studying **medicine**—a society's standard ways of dealing with illness and injury—will become apparent. For example, medicine is a profession, a bureaucracy, and a publicly funded institution in Canada. Indeed, in the midst of our publicly funded, universally accessible medicare system in Canada stands what we could call the Health-Industrial Complex. The Health-Industrial Complex comprises the pharmaceutical industries, the private health insurance companies such as Blue Cross and Green Shield that provide extra medical coverage for Canadians, the privately operated home care industries, and the many other for-profit industries that extend over the health and medicine sector of our economy.

Sociologists study how this important and extensive sector of our economy and society is influenced by ideas of self-regulation, the bureaucratic structure, and public policy in Canada. Sociologists also study how illness and health are much more than biological matters—how, for example, they are intimately related to cultural beliefs, lifestyle, and social class. Because of such emphases, the sociology of medicine is one of the applied fields of sociology.

> **Focus Question**
> Why do sociologists study health and illness?

The Symbolic Interactionist Perspective

The Role of Culture in Defining Health and Illness

Clearly, there are biological components of health—a nutritious diet, exercise, the use of antibiotics, and so on. However, there is an important cultural dimension to physical well-being that is the focus of the sociology of health and medical sociology.

Consider mental "illness" and mental "health." If a Canadian talks aloud to spirits that no one else can see, and takes direction from them, he or she is likely to be defined as being mentally ill. In some tribal societies, someone who talks to invisible spirits might be honoured for being in close contact with the spiritual world—and, for everyone's good, be declared a **shaman** (or witch doctor) who will diagnose and treat medical problems.

Around the world, every culture provides guidelines its people use to determine whether they are "healthy" or "sick." This is another example of the vital role the social construction of reality plays in our lives.

What Is Health?

In 1941, international health experts identified three components of **health**: physical, mental, and social (World Health Organization, 1946). (See Figure 15.1. In consideration of recent feminist interest in the "spiritual" side of well-being and our previous discussion on religion, we have added a spiritual component to the diagram.)

As symbolic interactionists stress, an important concern of sociologists is not to define what "true" health or "true" illness is. Instead, it is to analyze the effects people's ideas of health and illness have on their lives.

The Functionalist Perspective

If society is to function well, its people need to be healthy enough to perform their normal roles. This means societies must establish ways to control sickness. One level is the system of medical care societies develop. But there is also another level—making rules to keep too many people from "being sick."

The Sick Role

Do you remember when your throat began to hurt and when your mom or dad took your temperature the thermometer registered 102°F? Your parents took you to the doctor, and despite your protests that tomorrow was (your birthday or the first day of vacation), you had to spend the next three days in bed taking medicines. You were forced to play what sociologists call the **sick role**. What do they mean by this term?

Health practices vary widely around the world. Many cultures have *shamans*, who treat both mental and physical illnesses. Shown here are shamans in Nepal, performing a ceremony as part of their patients' treatment.

Elements of the Sick Role. Talcott Parsons (1953), the functionalist who first analyzed the sick role, pointed out that it has four elements—that you are not held responsible for being sick, that you are exempt from normal responsibilities, that you don't like the role, and that you will get competent help so you can return to your routines. People who don't seek competent help are denied the right to claim sympathy from others and to be excused from their normal routines. The one is given sympathy and encouragement, the other a cold shoulder for wrongfully claiming the sick role.

Ambiguity in the Sick Role. Instead of a fever of 102°F, suppose the thermometer registers 99.3°F. Do you then "become" sick or not? That is, do you decide to claim the sick role? Because clear-cut events such as heart attacks and limb fractures are rare, decisions to claim the sick role often are based more on social considerations than physical conditions. Let's also suppose that you are facing a midterm for which you are drastically underprepared, and you are allowed to make it up. The more you think about the test, the worse you are likely to feel—legitimating to yourself the need to claim the sick role. Now assume that you have no test, but your friends are coming over to take you out to celebrate your 21st birthday. You are much less likely to play the sick role. Note that in the two cases your physical condition is the same.

Gatekeepers to the Sick Role. Parents and physicians are the primary gatekeepers to the sick role. That is, they mediate between our feelings of illness and our claim to

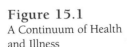

Figure 15.1
A Continuum of Health and Illness

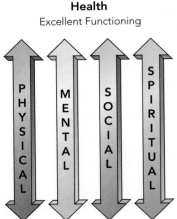

Health
Excellent Functioning

PHYSICAL MENTAL SOCIAL SPIRITUAL

Poor Functioning
Illness

being sick. Before parents call the school to excuse a child's absence, they decide whether the child is faking or has genuine symptoms serious enough to allow him or her to remain home from school. For adults, physicians are the main gatekeepers of the sick role. A "doctor's excuse"—actually official permission to play the sick role—removes the need for employers and teachers to pass judgment on the individual's claim.

The Conflict Perspective

As stressed in earlier chapters, the primary focus of conflict theorists is how people struggle over scarce resources. Since medical treatment is one of those resources, let's examine this competition in global perspective.

Effects of Global Stratification on Health Care

Our review in Chapter 6 of how the globe became stratified stressed how the nations that industrialized obtained the economic and military power that allowed them to become rich and dominate the globe. One consequence is the global stratification of medical care.

Our opening vignette is an example. The least industrialized nations cannot even begin to afford the technology that saved Norma Johnson's life. Life expectancy also illustrates global stratification. Whereas most people in the industrialized world can expect to live to about 75, *most* people in Afghanistan, Angola, Cambodia, Haiti, and Rwanda die before they reach 50. The infant mortality rates shown in Figure 15.2 also tell the story. This figure lists the world's countries where fewer than 7 out of every 1000 babies die before they are a year old. *All* of them are industrialized nations. The contrast is stark—close to 150 of every 1000 babies born in Afghanistan and Angola never reach their first birthday (*Statistical Abstract*, 1997, Table 1336).

Global stratification, then, is a matter of life and death. Suppose you were born in a least industrialized nation located in the tropics. During your much shorter life, you would face illness and death from four major sources: malaria (from mosquitoes), internal parasites (from contaminated water), diarrhea (from food and soil contaminated with human feces), and malnutrition. That is, a longer life expectancy in the developed industrial nations depends on the diseases you are not likely to contract that could kill you early in life. Or, if you do come down with malaria or diarrhea, for example, there are "cures" available to you.

> **Focus Question**
> What are the differences between the functionalist and the conflict perspectives on health?

The Feminist Perspective

As stressed in earlier chapters, the primary focus of feminist theorists is how sexism pervades our social institutions and social life. Since medical treatment is one important institution in our society, let's examine how sexism works in medicine and health.

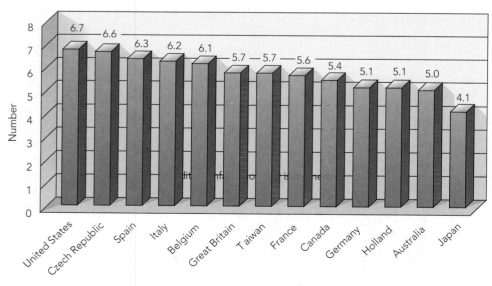

Figure 15.2 How Many Babies Die Before Their First Birthday?

Note: The figure shows all countries listed in the source that had an infant mortality rate below that of the United States (6.7). Infant mortality is defined as the number of babies who die before their first birthday, per 1000 live births.

Source: *Statistical Abstract*, 1999, Table 1352.

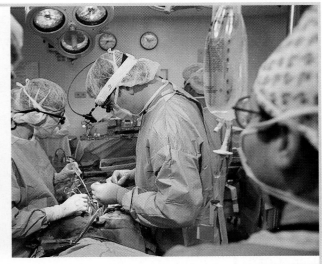

Global stratification in health care is starkly contrasted in these two photographs. It is difficult to believe, but the photo on the left is a hospital scene. It was taken in Ruhengeri Hospital in Rwanda, one of the poorest countries in the world. The photo on the right, of a heart transplant operation, illustrates the kind of medical treatment available in the most industrialized nations. Not all of their citizens, however, have equal access to such technology.

Sexism in Medicine

Although usually quite subtle, often even below people's awareness, sexism in medicine can carry serious consequences. As we saw in the Down-to-Earth Sociology box in Chapter 7, physicians don't take women's health complaints as seriously as men's. As a result, women are operated on at a later stage in heart disease, making it more likely they will die from their surgery.

Bias *against* women's reproductive organs has also been reported. Sue Fisher (1986) did participant observation in a hospital. When she heard doctors recommend total hysterectomy (removal of both the uterus and the ovaries) although no cancer was present, she asked why. The doctors explained that the uterus and ovaries are "potentially disease-producing" organs. Also, they said, they are unnecessary after the child-bearing years, so why not remove them?

To "convince" a woman to have this surgery, the doctor tells her that, unfortunately, the examination has turned up fibroids in her uterus—and they *might* turn into cancer. This statement is often sufficient, for it frightens women, who can picture themselves ready to be buried. What the surgeon does *not* say is that the fibroids probably will not turn into cancer and that many nonsurgical alternatives are available.

Underlying this sexism is male dominance of medicine in Canada. This is not a worldwide phenomenon. For example, in the former Soviet Union three out of four physicians were women (Knaus, 1981). Following changes in gender relations, the percentage of Canadian medical degrees earned by women has risen from only 24.3 percent in 1975 to 40.5 percent today (Altman, 1993). This changing sex ratio should help to reduce sexism in medical practice.

Although usually quite subtle, sexism does exist in Canadian medicine. Male dominance of the profession here does not translate to the rest of the world: For example, while less than 30 percent of Canadian physicians are women, in the former Soviet Union three out of four physicians were women.

The Gendered Experience of Health and Illness: Some Explanations

There are gender differences in causes of death (discussed in the next section) and, while the gap is narrowing, in life expectancy (see Chapter 9). Moreover, we know that men and women experience health and illness differently. For example, having social support is a more important predictor of good health for women than for men.

Leonard Stein (1988), a physician who observed nurses and doctors for many years, analyzed their interactions in terms of a game. Because physicians have higher status, nurses must try to give the impression that the doctor is always "in control." Although nurses spend more time with patients and, therefore, are often more familiar with their needs, nurses can never be perceived as giving recommendations to a doctor. Consequently, nurses disguise their recommendations. Consider the following dialogue between a nurse and a resident physician whom the nurse has called at 1 a.m. The rotating resident does not know the patient.

"This is Dr. Jones." (*An open and direct communication.*)

"Dr. Jones, this is Nurse Smith on 2W. Mrs. Brown learned today that her father died, and she is unable to fall asleep." (*This apparently direct, open com-munication of factual information—that the patient is unable to sleep and has learned of a death in the family—contains a hidden recommendation. The nurse has diagnosed the cause of the sleeplessness and is suggest-ing that a sedative be prescribed.*)

The conversation continues: "What sleeping medication has been helpful to Mrs. Brown in the past?" (*This communi-cation, supposedly a mere request for facts, is actually a request for a recommendation of what to prescribe.*)

"Pentobarbital, 100 milligrams, was quite effective the night before last." (*This is actually a specific recommendation from the nurse to the physician, but it comes disguised in the form of factual informa-tion.*)

"Pentobarbital, 100 milligrams before bedtime, as needed for sleep. Got it?" (*This communication is spoken with audible authority—a little louder, a little firmer.*)

"Yes, I have, and thank you very much, doctor."

The two have successfully played the doctor-nurse game. The lower-status person has made a recommendation to the higher-status person in a covert man-ner that requires neither of them to acknowledge what really occurred and does not threaten their relative statuses.

According to Stein, the doctor-nurse game is breaking down because of the larger number of men in nursing, the feminist movement challenging male authority, and the larger number of women physicians. As a consequence, nurses are less subservient, and physi-cians are less able to exert unquestioned authority.

Some version of the game will con-tinue to be played, however, as long as status differences remain. The rules will simply be modified to meet changing circumstances.

What could account for these and other gendered dif-ferences? Leaving aside any biological answers, there are five sociological explanations for gender differences in the experience of health and illness.

1. First, there is *role accumulation*. This theory suggests that the more roles, the better the person's health. However, this simple explanation fails to take into account the kinds of roles a woman performs. For example, the benefits of being married and having a job such as increased income and social support may be off-set by the added burdens of the parental role. Therefore, modifications to this explanation have centred on the kinds of roles women and men perform.

2. A second explanation put forward for the gendered dif-ferences in health and illness concentrates on the negative effects of women's roles on their health and well-being. The demands of the *double day* (i.e., family and employ-ment responsibilities) leads to increased stress and exces-sive demands on women's time and energy.

3. *Social acceptability*, or explanation three, suggests that due to the socialization of women into traditional roles, women are more willing than men to admit to being sick and accept help in dealing with their health prob-lems. On the other hand, men are socialized to control their experiences of pain or illness and so are reluctant to adopt the sick role, and as a result, talk about their health. Therefore, women are more likely to share infor-mation about the types of symptoms they are experi-encing. Finally, while men rely on their spouses for social support, women tend to turn to their friends and their children for help.

4. The fact that women experience more illness than men is explained by the *nurturing* tendencies of women. In their role as primary caregiver for their spouses, chil-dren, and aging parents, women experience consider-able stress with little, if any, time left for themselves. As a result, they may neglect their own health.

5. Finally, there is the suggestion that men are socialized to take more risks than women while women are social-ized to be cautious. This *competitive* view of gender role differences sees men engaging in more risky behaviours such as smoking, alcohol, and accidents while women take on more preventive and protective behaviours such as seeking help early.

All these theories have been advanced in order to make sense of the complex differences between the social charac-teristics of men and women and their impact on gendered experience of health and illness.

Focus Question
Is there a gendered experience of health and illness?

Historical Patterns of Health

How have patterns of health and illness in Canada changed? The answer to this question takes us into the field of **epidemiology**, the study of how medical disorders are distributed throughout a population.

Physical Health

Table 15.1 provides recent data for the leading causes of death among Canadians. Clearly, the top three causes of death—cancer, heart disease, and cerebrovascular diseases such as stroke—were similar for both males and females. Gender differences are most pronounced when it comes to suicide, which ranked 9th among males but only 13th among females, with four times as many males as females committing suicide. Unintentional deaths such as motor vehicles accidents ranked 4th for males and 5th for females. While males accounted for the majority of fatal accidents for 1997 (69 percent), the rate of death has been dropping steadily since the late 1970s. Finally, a substantial drop in the number of Canadians dying from AIDS was reported, with 81 dying in 1997 compared to 1482 in 1995, or a decline of over 1800 percent! However, the number of reported positive HIV cases continues to remain high. In recent years, over 2000 cases a year have been reported. While the incidence of positive HIV cases has steadily declined among gay males over the past few years, young women between the ages of 15 and 29, blacks, and Aboriginals have witnessed a sharp increase. Clearly, the danger of AIDS remains an important social and medical issue in Canada.

Interprovincially, Quebec reported the highest mortality rates for lung and colon cancer, while Alberta reported the lowest lung and British Columbia the lowest colon cancers. While deaths due to suicide have declined in all provinces except Saskatchewan, Alberta, and Quebec, Quebec's rate not only remained the highest but exceeded the margin set the year before for all the provinces and territories in Canada.

The reason or reasons for this cause of death is a matter of serious research and public policy remedies in Quebec. Having said this, the highest rates of suicide in Canada remain those of our Aboriginal populations, especially those located in the Yukon and the Northwest Territories. This must become the highest priority for the federal Department of Indian Affairs and Northern Development (DIAND).

Were Canadians Healthier in the Past? Mortality rates help us to answer this question. Because most people today live longer than their ancestors, we can conclude that contemporary Canadians are healthier.

Mental Health

When it comes to mental health, we have no rational basis at all for making comparisons. All groups have had their share of mental problems—and common-sense beliefs that mental illness is worse today represent perceptions, not measured reality. Since we don't even know how extensive mental illness is today (M. W. Miller, 1993), we certainly can't judge how much there was in the past.

Issues in Health Care

Health Care in Canada

While the provision of health care in Canada is a provincial responsibility, the federal government has played a major role in financing the health care services available to all Canadians.

The primary purpose of national health insurance in Canada is the elimination of financial barriers to health care. Universal, government-funded medical, hospital, and other related health insurance has been available only since 1971 even though there was a federal hospital insurance program in the 1950s and a federal medical insurance program covering physicians and related services in the mid-1960s.

Table 15.1 Leading Causes of Death in Canada and Age-Standardized Mortality Rates for Males and Females, 1997

Causes by Rank	Number Males	Number Females	Mortality Rate*	
			Males	Females
1. Cancer	31 555	27 148	1. 229.7	1. 148.5
2. Heart disease	23 824	19 702	2. 180.8	2. 94.0
3. Cerebrovascular diseases	6675	9376	3. 52.8	3. 43.9
4. Unintentional injuries	5810	3558	4. 41.2	5. 19.5
5. Other chronic airways obstructions	4517	3028	5. 36.0	10. 15.1
6. Pneumonia/influenza	3749	4283	6. 31.5	6. 19.2
7. Heart failure	3572	4610	7. 29.3	4. 20.9
8. Suicide	2914	767	10. 19.5	13. 4.9
9. Hereditary and degenerative diseases of the central nervous system	2843	3714	8. 21.9	7. 18.2
10. Diabetes	2767	2932	9. 20.6	8. 14.8
11. Diseases of the arteries	2505	2262	10. 19.5	9. 10.6

*Age-standardized rank order for males and females.

Source: Adapted from Statistics Canada, *Mortality—Summary List of Causes*, 1997, July 1999. Catalogue no. 82-221-XCB.

Under Canada's medicare system, hospitals are financed on the basis of annually negotiated planned-for budgets. Physicians are reimbursed on a fee-for-service basis (as is the case in the United States). However, these fees are determined by provincewide, negotiated, uniform fee schedules. Private insurance companies offer coverage only for various forms of additional services such as private-room accommodation in hospitals, eyeglasses (up to a certain dollar limit, since the eye examination is covered by medicare), and pharmaceutical drugs.

By 1977, the rapidly escalating costs for medicare led the federal government to establish upper limits on the percentage increases to hospital and medical insurance costs that it would share with the provinces. Under the new program, Established Programs Financing (EPF), the federal government provided equal per capita entitlements to all provinces for the three established programs—health insurance, extended health care, and postsecondary education. Quebec received a tax transfer as part of its contracting-out of the hospital insurance program.

In 1984, the *Canada Health Act* came into force to ensure that necessary health services would be available to all Canadians regardless of their financial circumstances. The Act sets out a national standard for the provision of Canada's health care with which the provinces are obligated to comply under penalty of withholding transfer payments.

Table 15.2 outlines the five basic criteria: comprehensive scope, universal coverage, public administration, portability, and accessibility.

Beginning in 1996–1997, as part of the federal government's strategy of deficit reduction, the EPF was replaced by the Canada Health and Social Transfer program (CHST). Unlike the EPF, which was divided into separate categories, the CHST is a block transfer payment to the provinces. This makes determining the federal share of health costs extremely difficult. However, we do know that the federal government's share of health care funding has been dramatically cut and only now, when there is a budget surplus, is the federal government open to increasing its share of health care funding.

Table 15.3 reports federal government expenditures on health care. Hospital care, medical care, and preventive care are the three main categories of health services in Canada. It is clear from the data presented here that the federal government transfers to the provinces under EPF disappear for the years 1997–1999. Unfortunately, it is unknown how much of the federal subsidy (via CHST) goes to provincial health care systems. The 1999 amount of $1607 million, for example, is made up almost entirely of federal expenditures on Aboriginal health on reserves that include (1) preventive medicine, counselling, and education and (2) medical and dental treatment via nursing stations, visiting physicians, and patient evacuations.

Data for the 2000–2001 fiscal year reveal a total transfer to the provinces and territories under CHST of almost $33 billion! What amounts go directly to medical health care and what goes to social spending is determined mainly by the individual provinces and territories.

One issue that occasionally surfaces is the use of *extra billing* or charging patients "a little extra" as a means of cutting down on "unnecessary" visits by patients to general practitioners. As early as 1968–1972, Saskatchewan instituted a regime of modest extra billing. This measure was devastating to the poor and the elderly, but little evidence could be found to support the contention that extra billing cut down on unnecessary visits to doctors. On the contrary, R. G. Evans, a health care economist, concluded from his study of the province's "experiment" in extra billing that it involved "perverse wealth transfers from the ill to the healthy and from low-to-high income classes" (Barer, Evans, & Stoddart, 1979, p. 111).

More recently, British Columbia, Alberta, Newfoundland, Manitoba, and Nova Scotia experimented with extra billing. However, under the *Canada Health Act*, the federal government penalized each province. Alberta, for example, lost almost $4 million while Newfoundland was penalized $270 000, Nova Scotia $157 000, and Manitoba $1.3 million before banning user fees.

Focus Question

Describe the publicly funded health care system of Canada.

Table 15.2 *Canada Health Act*, 1984

Criterion	Description
Comprehensive	A province must cover all services provided by physicians (general practitioners and specialists)
Universal	A province must provide insured services to all insured residents and must not impose a residential or waiting period longer than three months
Public administration	A provincial plan must be administered and operated on a nonprofit basis by a public authority
Portability	The benefits must be available to insured persons temporarily absent from the province (e.g., on vacation) and to those who move to another province until such time as they qualify for medicare benefits in that province
Accessibility	A province's health care services must be reasonably accessible to all insured persons

Table 15.3 Federal Expenditures on Health, 1989–1999

Year	Total Millions of $	Hospital Care	Medical Care	Preventive Care	Other
1989	$7723	$5435	$1342	$235	$711
1990	7818	5344	1435	293	745
1991	7397	4739	1435	338	885
1992	8081	5314	1523	327	919
1993	9803	6832	1677	323	971
1994	8913	5801	1783	315	1014
1995	9392	6122	1829	368	1072
1996	9024	5770	1812	316	1126
1997	1177	−44	316	247	658
1998	1328	26	347	247	708
1999	1607	17	343	316	931

Source: Adapted from Statistics Canada, CANSIM Database, Table 385-0002.

The Development of the Sociology of Health in Canada

The sociology of health in Canada has passed through at least two major stages. During the 1970s, or stage one, the sociology of health in Canada focused on matters related to the complexity of the health care system, such as the changing relationships between health care professionals, the challenges posed by nurses and chiropractors to the dominance of the traditional model of medicine, and the dynamics of the sick role and patient illness behaviour. During the 1980s, the second stage brought the inclusion of other themes, such as the impact of population aging on health and health care delivery.

In 1993, the sociology of health in Canada boasted its first journal, *Health and Canadian Society*. The principal focus of the research in the field of health care has been the use of large surveys to gauge the health status of Canadians. The most recent is the ongoing longitudinal *National Population Health Survey*, conducted by both Health Canada and Statistics Canada. This large survey, begun in 1994 and continuing every second year thereafter, is an important source of information about the health and health behaviours of Canadians. In the studies that have been conducted to date, the most significant finding centres on the *causal* links between social status and health status. That is, social factors such as socioeconomic status (e.g., income and education) and gender, age, and ethnicity play a vital part in determining how healthy Canadians are. In addition to these, studies have confirmed that the organization of work and family life are important predictors of the health status of Canadians.

> ### Focus Question
> What is the sociology of health in Canada?

Depersonalization

One of the main criticisms levelled against the medical profession is **depersonalization**, the practice of dealing with people as though they were cases and diseases, not individuals. Many patients get the impression they are being treated by a physician who, while talking to them, is impatiently counting minutes and tabulating dollars so that he or she can move on to the next customer and more dollars. After all, extra time spent with a patient is money down the drain.

Participant observation of medical students at McMaster University by sociologists Jack Haas and William Shaffir (1978/1993) provides insight into how physicians learn to depersonalize patients. Haas and Shaffir found that students begin medical school wanting to "treat the whole person." As vast amounts of material are thrown at them, their feelings for patients are overpowered by the need to be efficient. These students' statements pick up on the change:

> Somebody will say, "Listen to Mrs. Jones' heart." It's just a little thing flubbing on the table. And *you forget about the rest of her* … The advantage is that *you can go in a short time and see a patient, get the important things out of the patient, and leave* [italics added].
>
> … Someone comes in who has croaked (died) [and you say], "Well, come on. Here is a chance to practise your intubation" [inserting a tube in the throat].

Medicalization of Society

As we have seen, women's reproductive organs have become defined as medical matters. Sociologists use the term **medicalization** to refer to the process of turning something that was not previously considered medical into a medical matter. Examples include balding, weight, wrinkles, acne, anxiety, depression, a sagging chin or buttocks, small breasts, and even the inability to achieve orgasm. There is nothing inherently medical in such human condi-

Proponents of euthanasia base their claim on "people's right to die." "If someone wants to be disconnected from feeding tubes," they say, "he or she should be able to die in peace. And if someone wants to commit suicide, that person should have the right to do so. What right does the rest of society have to interfere?"

If the issue is framed this way, many Canadians would agree that euthanasia should be permitted. "The problem," say its opponents, "is that most euthanasia involves other types of dying."

The best example, critics point out, is the Netherlands, which has allowed euthanasia for over 20 years. According to Dutch law, a physician can assist a patient in dying if the patient makes "a free, informed, and persistent request."

Euthanasia must be a "last resort," and physicians are accountable to the courts for following the letter of the law.

A Dutch government committee, however, has found that the practice is very different from what the law specifies. Although only about 150 cases of euthanasia are reported annually to government officials, this doesn't come even close to the actual number. The committee found 2300 cases of "voluntary" euthanasia and 400 assisted suicides. They also found 8750 deaths due to the physicians withholding or withdrawing treatment—*in not one of these cases did the patients consent to their deaths.* Doctors killed another 8100 people by giving them pain-killing drugs—and more than half of these patients had *not* consented to their deaths.

Leading Dutch physicians who practise euthanasia oppose its legalization in the United States, which has a private, for-profit health care system (unlike Canada and the Netherlands, where health care is publicly funded). Said one, "If euthanasia were allowed in the United States, I would not want to be a patient there. In view of the financial costs that the care of patients can impose on relatives and society under the United States health care system, the legalization of euthanasia in America would be an open door to get rid of patients."

For Your Consideration

What do you think?

Sources: Gomez (1991); Markson (1992); Angell (1996).

tions, yet we have become so used to medicalization that we tend to consider them somehow naturally medical concerns. As Susan Sontag (1994) says, even many criminal behaviours have become matters to be medically understood and treated.

Medically Assisted Suicide

I started the intravenous dripper, which released a salt solution through a needle into her vein, and I kept her arm tied down so she wouldn't jerk it. This was difficult as her veins were fragile. And then once she decided she was ready to go, she just hit the switch and the device cut off the saline drip and through the needle released a solution of thiopental that put her to sleep in ten to fifteen seconds. A minute later, through the needle flowed a lethal solution of potassium chloride.

This is how Jack Kevorkian described his "death machine" (Denzin, 1992). Kevorkian, a retired pathologist who introduced his machine on a TV talk show, is known by some as "Dr. Death." He has helped over 100 people commit suicide. One side defends Kevorkian as a courageous trailblazer, while another side decries his acts as perverted. Some even call him "Jeffrey Dahmer in a lab coat" (Morganthau, 1993). A how-to book on suicide, *Final Exit*, sold over a half million copies. The Hemlock Society, a group advocating voluntary **euthanasia**—mercy killing—for terminally ill people, has grown to 80 chapters. The case of "Nancy B" became the first celebrated one of euthanasia in Canada.

With new technology that can keep the body alive even after the heart, lungs, and other vital organs no longer function on their own, a burning question, yet undecided, is "Who has the right to pull the plug?" Should someone's body be kept alive for years although the person's mind can no longer work? To resolve this issue, some people sign a **living will**—a declaration they make while in good health of what they want medical personnel to do in case they become dependent on artificial life support systems.

Our technology and the acts of Kevorkian have brought us face to face with matters of death that are both disturbing and unresolved. Should "medically assisted suicide" be legal? Few find this medical-ethical issue easy to resolve. The Thinking Critically about Social Controversy box above explores these issues.

Threats to Health

Let's look at these threats to health: AIDS, the globalization of disease, drugs, and disabling environments.

AIDS

Perhaps one of the most pressing health issues today in Canada—and globally—is AIDS (acquired immune deficiency syndrome). Let's look at some of its major characteristics.

Origin. The origin of AIDS is unknown. The most prevalent theory is that the virus was first present in monkeys in

Africa and then transmitted to humans. If so, just how the transmission to humans took place remains a matter of conjecture. It may have occurred during the 1920s and 1950s when, in a peculiar experiment for malaria, people were inoculated with blood from monkeys and chimpanzees. The blood may have been infected with viral ancestors of HIV (Rathus & Nevid, 1993). Since monkeys are considered food in several parts of Africa, another possibility is that the virus was transmitted through inadequately cooked meat. Some suggest the opposite route, that the disease originated in Europe or the United States and was somehow transmitted to Africa (Rushing, 1995).

The Transmission of AIDS. AIDS is known to be transmitted by the exchange of blood and semen, and, in rare cases, by mother's milk to newborns. Since the virus can be present in all bodily fluids, including sweat, tears, spittle, and urine, some people think AIDS can also be transmitted in these forms. The U.S. Centers for Disease Control, however, says that AIDS cannot be transmitted by casual contact in which traces of these fluids would be exchanged (Edgar, 1994). One study has indicated that oral sex is risky when engaged in frequently. (See Figure 15.3.)

The Stigma of AIDS. One of the most significant sociological aspects of AIDS is its stigma, another example of how social factors are essential to health and illness. From the outset, the notion of "AIDS as a gay disease" was spread rapidly by television evangelists and other Christian conservatives in Canada and the United States. Even today, in many parts of the world including our own, some remain convinced that AIDS is a "divine" message from God. Some people even refuse to be tested because they fear the stigma they would have to bear if they tested positive. One unfortunate consequence is the further spread of AIDS by people who "don't want to know." The stigma is so great in some Asian countries that government officials refuse to acknowledge how widespread AIDS is. Burying their heads in the sand, however, makes them unable to sponsor preventive measures, and so the epidemic grows (Shenon, 1995). If this disease is to be brought under control, its stigma must be overcome: AIDS must be thought of as being, like other lethal diseases, simply the work of a destructive biological organism.

The Globalization of AIDS. Today's global travel has brought the globalization of this disease. Africa has been hit the hardest, and we can expect 20 million deaths there (Haub, 1997). In some countries ravaged by AIDS, life expectancy may be cut in half (Olshansky, Carnes, Rogers, & Smith, 1997). Botswana, Uganda, and Zimbabwe are likely to lose a quarter of their populations (Stout, 1992).

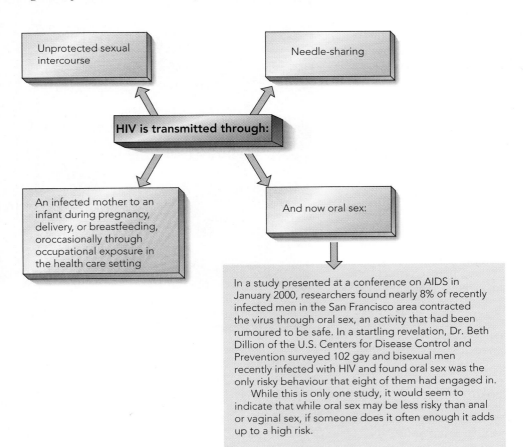

Figure 15.3 How Do I Get HIV/AIDS?

Source: Information on oral sex adapted from Reuters.

Unprotected sexual intercourse

Needle-sharing

HIV is transmitted through:

An infected mother to an infant during pregnancy, delivery, or breastfeeding, oroccasionally through occupational exposure in the health care setting

And now oral sex:

In a study presented at a conference on AIDS in January 2000, researchers found nearly 8% of recently infected men in the San Francisco area contracted the virus through oral sex, an activity that had been rumoured to be safe. In a startling revelation, Dr. Beth Dillion of the U.S. Centers for Disease Control and Prevention surveyed 102 gay and bisexual men recently infected with HIV and found oral sex was the only risky behaviour that eight of them had engaged in.

While this is only one study, it would seem to indicate that while oral sex may be less risky than anal or vaginal sex, if someone does it often enough it adds up to a high risk.

In Kampala and Kigali, a third of all pregnant women have AIDS (Scommegna, 1996). In the former Soviet Union AIDS is multiplying, primarily due to the rise in prostitution and drug use since the fall of communism (Kaminski & Palchikoff, 1997). AIDS is also flourishing in Asia, partly because of its huge sex industry.

Is There a Cure For AIDS? As has been mentioned, the number of deaths due to AIDS in Canada began to decline in 1996. Does this mean we have found a cure for AIDS? With thousands of scientists searching for a cure, the media have heralded every new breakthrough in research as a possible cure, but this has yet to appear.

The most promising treatment to date, the one that lies behind the reduction in deaths, was spearheaded by David Ho, a virologist (virus researcher). If patients in the very early stages of the disease take a "cocktail" of drugs (a combination of protease inhibitors, AZT, and 3TC), the "visible" signs of the virus can be erased from their bodies. Their immune systems then rebound (C. Gorman, 1997b). No one is yet calling this a cure, however. What is not known is whether the virus could be hiding undetected in some part of the body, and if it, too, will rebound unexpectedly.

While most praise this new treatment, some researchers have issued a dire warning (Rotello, 1996). They suggest that the cocktail may become this decade's penicillin. When penicillin was introduced, everyone was ecstatic with its results. But over the years the microbes it targets mutated, producing "super bugs" against which we have no protection. If this is the case with AIDS, then a new, "super AIDS" virus may hit the world with more fury than the first devastating wave.

The Globalization of Disease

In the movie *Outbreak*, when a new disease threatened the world, government epidemiologists were transformed into Indiana Jones heroes in order to save it. But aside from its overdramatization, the movie's depiction of the rapid spread of disease is not too far from reality. Modern travel has wiped out the frontiers that used to contain diseases.

As mentioned earlier, older diseases have mutated and produced "super bugs" immune to antibiotics. Antibiotics are also ineffective against many of the 28 new diseases that have recently appeared on the world scene. Because some of these new diseases are lethal, we may have to resort to an old remedy—sending people to asylums. The only way ebola, with its particularly hideous death, could be contained was to isolate an entire region in Zaire. Apparently some U.S. patients with new strains of deadly tuberculosis have already been quietly removed from the population (Olshansky et al., 1997).

Drugs: Alcohol and Nicotine

Let's examine some of the health consequences of alcohol and nicotine, the most frequently used drugs in Canada.

Alcohol. Alcohol is the standard recreational drug of Canadians. Is it bad for the health? This beverage cuts both ways. About two drinks a day for men and one drink for women reduce the risk of heart attacks and blood vessel diseases. (Women weigh less on average and produce fewer enzymes that metabolize alcohol.) Beyond these amounts, however, alcohol increases the risk of a variety of diseases, from cancer to stroke. It also increases the likelihood of birth defects.

Nicotine. Of all drugs, nicotine is the most harmful to health. Sociologist Erich Goode (1989) points out smokers are three times as likely as nonsmokers to die before reaching the age of 65. Smokers in their 30s are six times as likely to have heart attacks as nonsmokers of the same age (Winslow, 1995). Smoking doubles the risk of blindness in old age (Lagnado, 1996). It also causes progressive emphysema and several types of cancer that kill an increasing number of Canadians every year. Between 1991 and 2001, deaths due to smoking increased from over 41 000 to almost 47 000, or over 20 percent of *all* deaths in Canada.

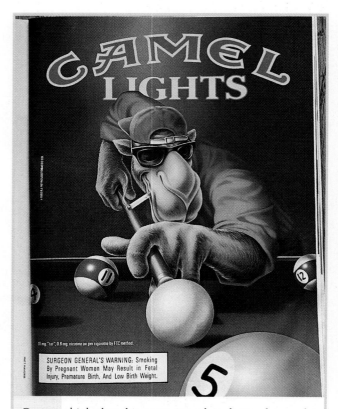

Do you think that this magazine ad is designed to make cigarettes appealing to male youths? Although tobacco industry officials denied they were trying to entice youth to smoke, evidence such as this ad is overwhelmingly against them. After pressure from the U.S. Congress, in 1997 Camel agreed to terminate its Joe Camel ads.

It has been estimated that smoking kills *three times* more Canadians prematurely than car accidents, suicides, drug abuse, murder, and AIDS combined! By far, nicotine is the most lethal of all recreational drugs.

Stressing the health hazards of smoking and of second-hand smoke, an anti-tobacco campaign is being waged successfully in Europe and North America. It has ended smoking on Canadian airlines and brought about smoking and nonsmoking areas in restaurants and offices. It is even illegal to light up in a bar in British Columbia.

Yet many people persist. Why, when it is so destructive to their health? There are two major reasons: addiction and advertising. Nicotine may be as addictive as heroin (Tolchin, 1988). And even though cigarette ads were banned from television in the 1980s, cigarettes continue to be heavily advertised on billboards and in print; the industry targets youth, often by associating cigarette smoking with success, high fashion, and independence.

Disabling Environments

A **disabling environment** is one harmful to health. The health risk of some occupations is evident: lumberjacking, mining, and the construction industry are obvious examples. In many occupations, however, people become aware of the risk only years after they worked at jobs they thought were safe. For example, several million people worked with asbestos during and after World War II. Now the government estimates that one-quarter of them will die of cancer from having breathed asbestos dust. It is likely that many other substances we have not yet identified also cause slowly developing cancers—including, ironically, some asbestos substitutes (Meier, 1987).

Although industrialization has increased the world's standard of living, it also threatens to disable the basic environment of the human race, posing what may be the greatest health hazard of all time. The burning of vast amounts of carbon fuels is leading to the *greenhouse effect*, a warming of the earth that may change the globe's climate, melt its polar icecaps, and flood the earth's coastal shores. Use of fluorocarbon gases in such items as aerosol cans, refrigerators, and air conditioners is threatening the *ozone shield*, the protective layer of the earth's upper stratosphere that screens out a high proportion of the sun's ultraviolet rays. High-intensity ultraviolet radiation is harmful to most forms of life. In humans, it causes skin cancer. The pollution of land, air, and water, especially through nuclear waste, pesticides, herbicides, and other chemicals, poses additional risks to life on our planet.

To identify environmental threats to world health is only the first step. The second is to introduce short- and long-term policies to reduce such problems. The sociology of the environment is discussed in Chapter 17.

The Search for Alternatives

What alternatives are there to the way medicine is usually practised? The suggestion we shall explore here is that we shift the emphasis away from the treatment of disease to prevention.

Treatment or Prevention?

Effects of Values and Lifestyles.   Prevention implies both an individual and a group responsibility. On the individual level, doing exercises regularly, eating nutritious food, having protected sex, and avoiding smoking and alcohol abuse go a long way to preventing disease. Following these guidelines can add years to our lives.

Awareness of disabling environments has grown—from air pollution to asbestos and harmful food additives. Coping mechanisms are also taking many forms, from reducing auto emissions and eating organically grown foods to what is depicted here—Tokyo shoppers "stopping off for a quick one," in this case a hit of pure oxygen.

Visiting a doctor or a hospital today is not without risk, but the risk is small compared with the times when physicians bled and purged their patients. Today's physicians are well trained, and medical care is supported by scientific studies. Our new technology even allows us to cure medical conditions that just a short time ago doomed people to premature deaths. In other instances, the medical condition remains, but the patient is able to live a long life.

And there's the rub. Some technology is limited, and there isn't enough to go around to everyone who needs it.

Other technology is so costly that it would bankrupt society if it were made available to everyone who has a particular condition. Who, then, should receive the benefits of our new medical technology?

At the heart of this issue of how to spend limited resources lie questions not only of costs, but also of fairness, of how to distribute equitably the benefits of advanced medical technology.

For Your Consideration

The dilemma is harsh: If we choose medical rationing, many sick people

will be allowed to die. If we don't, we may go bankrupt. In more specific terms: Should a federal Cabinet minister who is an alcoholic be given a liver transplant when he is already dying of cancer? Use ideas, concepts, and principles presented in this and other chapters to develop a reasonable answer to this pressing issue. Also note how this dilemma changes shape if you view it from the contrasting perspectives of conflict, functionalism, and symbolic interactionism.

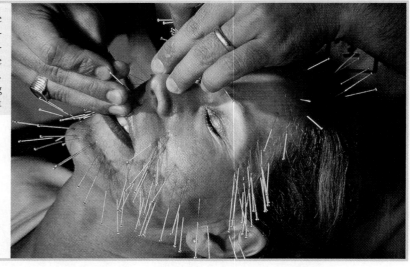

Every culture makes basic assumptions about the causes and cures of medical problems. The traditional assumptions of Eastern medical practitioners, usually ridiculed by Western physicians, are now being examined seriously by some. Acupuncture, for example, is gradually gaining acceptance in the West, although it does not fit Western assumptions of cause and cure.

On the group level, one alternative is preventive medicine. Instead of the treatment of disease, medicine could have "wellness" as its goal. What would it require to implement a national policy of "prevention, not intervention?" This would require a program of education in the schools and the media showing how some practices of nutrition, exercise, sex, and drug use pay off with healthier lives. For example, diet is a significant factor in many types of cancer, and an educational program to replace fatty, low-fibre foods with a diet rich in fruits, vegetables, and green tea would go a long way in saving lives. Unfortunately, rather than making such basic changes

most Canadians still seem to prefer that their doctors prescribe drugs.

On yet a broader scale is comprehensive prevention—eliminating disabling environments and the use of harmful drugs. Some businesses continue to spew industrial wastes into the air and to use rivers and oceans as industrial sewers, while others use advertising to seduce youths to use harmful drugs. These acts are unconscionable. Finally, since we now live in a global village, the creation and maintenance of a health-producing environment require international controls and cooperation.

Summary and Review

SOCIOLOGY AND THE STUDY OF MEDICINE
What is the role of sociology in the study of medicine?
Sociologists study medicine as a social institution. As practised in Canada, three of its primary characteristics are professionalization, bureaucracy, and public policy. p. 364.

THE SYMBOLIC INTERACTIONIST PERSPECTIVE
What is the symbolic interactionist perspective on health and illness?
Health is not only a biological matter, but also intimately related to society. Illness is not only an objective matter; it can be viewed from the framework of culture, and such definitions vary from one group to another. pp. 364–365.

THE FUNCTIONALIST PERSPECTIVE
What is the functionalist perspective on health and illness?
The **sick role** is society's permission to not perform one's usual activities. In return for this permission, the individual assumes responsibility to seek competent help and to cooperate in getting well so he or she can quickly resume normal activities. pp. 365–366.

THE CONFLICT PERSPECTIVE
What is the conflict perspective on health and illness?
Health care is one of the scarce resources over which groups compete. On a global level, health care follows the international stratification we studied in Chapter 6, with the best health care available in the industrialized nations and the worst in the least industrialized nations. p. 366.

THE FEMINIST PERSPECTIVE
What is the feminist perspective on health and illness?
Sexism is one source of gender inequality in medicine. More recently, five explanations have been advanced to account for the gendered experience of health and illness: role accumulation, double day, social acceptability, nurturing tendencies of women, and competition. pp. 366–368.

HISTORICAL PATTERNS OF HEALTH
What are the gender differences in the causes of death?
The three leading causes of death—cancer, heart disease, and cerebrovascular diseases such as stroke—are the same for both men and women in Canada. Men, however, are more apt to die from suicides than women. The number of Canadians dying from AIDS has dropped significantly in recent years. p. 369.

ISSUES IN HEALTH CARE
Which level of government in Canada is responsible for health care?
While the provision of health care in Canada is a provincial responsibility, the federal government has played a major role in financing the health care services available to all Canadians. pp. 369–370.

Is extra billing a good idea for cutting costs to the health care system in Canada?
Research showed that, although extra billing meant the poor and the elderly were dissuaded from going to their general practitioner, there was no support for the contention that extra billing cut down on unnecessary visits to doctors. p. 370.

What are the five provisions of the *Canada Health Act* (1984)?
The five provisions of the *Canada Health Act* (1984) are comprehensive scope, universal coverage, public administration, portability, and accessibility. p. 371.

What is one of the major findings of the sociology of health research in Canada?
The most significant finding centres on the *causal* links between social status and health status of Canadians. p. 371.

Why is medically assisted suicide an issue now?
Due to advanced technology, people can be kept technically alive even when they have no brain waves. Physicians who openly assist in suicides have come under severe criticism. Research findings on **euthanasia** in the Netherlands have fuelled this controversy. p. 372.

THREATS TO HEALTH
What are some threats to the health of Canadians?
Discussed here are AIDS; alcohol and nicotine, the most lethal drugs used by Canadians; and **disabling environments**, environments harmful to health such as work-related diseases or pollution of air and water. pp. 372–375.

THE SEARCH FOR ALTERNATIVES
Are there alternatives to our current health care system?
The primary alternative discussed here is a change from treatment to the prevention of disease. pp. 375–376.

Critical Thinking Questions

1. Canadians are not all equally likely to become sick or suffer an injury. Some are more likely to develop particular diseases or disabilities. Why do you think there are differences in the health and illness of Canadians based on sex and class?

2. Virtually everyone recognizes the life-saving value of medicine and the advances being made in medical research on such diseases as cancer and AIDS. However, are there any social factors that negatively contribute to our physical, mental, and spiritual well-being?

3. Is the medicalization of society a good thing? Apply the functionalist and conflict perspectives to help answer this question.

Key Terms

depersonalization 371
disabling environment 375
epidemiology 369
euthanasia 342
health 365

living will 342
medicalization 371
medicine 364
shaman 364
sick role 365

Weblinks

All URLs listed are current as of the printing of this book. URLs are often changed. Please check our Web site **www.abacon.com/ henslin** for updates.

World Health Organization (WHO)

www.who.int/
WHO's objective is the attainment by all peoples of the highest possible level of health—defined in the WHO constitution as a state of complete physical, mental, and social well-being and not merely the absence of disease or infirmity.

Centers for Disease Control and Prevention

www.cdc.gov/
An agency of the U.S. Department of Health and Human Services, located in Atlanta, Georgia. Its mission is to "promote health and quality of life by preventing and controlling disease, injury, and disability."

AIDS Treatment News Archive Online

www.immunet.org/immunet/atn.nsf/homepage
Complete archive, including the current issue, of *AIDS Treatment News,* an internationally recognized newsletter for persons living with HIV/AIDS and looking for information on new therapies. *AIDS Treatment News* has been published twice a month since 1986.

JHPPL Home Page

www.jhppl.org/
The *Journal of Health Politics, Policy and Law* is a multidisciplinary publication published bimonthly by Duke University Press. Its articles contain original scholarship in a variety of issues related to health.

part five

Social Change

Chapter 16

Social Deviance and Social Control

Learning Outcomes

After you have studied this chapter, you will be able to

■ understand that it is more important to know who is defining social deviance than to rely on "common sense"

■ understand that socialization, whether in the family or in a peer group, is a fundamental part of social control, which includes keeping members of our society's subculture "in line"

■ understand that men use violence against their female partners primarily to maintain control over them

■ discuss the four major theories of social deviance

In just a few moments I was to meet my first Yanomamo. What would it be like? I looked up (from my canoe) and gasped when I saw a dozen burly, naked, hideous men staring at us down the shafts of their drawn arrows. Immense wads of green tobacco were stuck between their lower teeth and lips, making them look even more hideous, and strands of dark-green slime dripped or hung from their noses. We arrived at the village while the men were blowing a hallucinogenic drug up their noses.

The whole situation was depressing, and I wondered why I ever decided to switch from civil engineering to anthropology in the first place. … [Soon] I was covered with red pigment, the result of a dozen or so complete examinations. … These examinations capped an otherwise grim day. The Indians would blow their noses into their hands, flick as much of the mucus off that would separate in a snap of the wrist, wipe the residue into their hair, and then carefully examine my face, arms, legs, hair, and the contents of my pockets. I said (in their language), "Your hands are dirty"; my comments were met in the following way: they would "clean" their hands by spitting a quantity of slimy tobacco juice into them, rub them together, and then proceed with the examination.

Source: Chagnon (1977).

Gaining a Sociological Perspective on Social Deviance

So went Napoleon Chagnon's eye-opening introduction to the Yanomamo tribe of the rain forests of Brazil. His ensuing months of fieldwork continued to bring surprise after surprise, and often Chagnon (1977) could hardly believe his eyes—or his nose.

How Norms Make Social Life Possible

Norms make social life possible by making behaviour predictable. Only because we can count on most people most of the time to meet the expectations of others can social life as we know it exist.

You can depend on grocery clerks to sell you milk. You also can depend on paying the same price as everyone else and not being forced to attend a party in the store. Why can you depend on this? Because we are socialized to follow norms, to play the basic roles society assigns to us.

Norms lay out the basic guidelines for how we play our roles and how we interact with others. In short, norms allow **social order**, a group's usual and customary social arrangements. Our lives are based on these arrangements, which is why social deviance is often seen as so threatening, for it undermines predictability, the foundation of social life. Consequently, human groups develop a system of **social control**, formal and informal means of enforcing norms.

Comparing Biological, Psychological, and Sociological Explanations

Since norms are essential for society, why do people violate them? To better understand the reasons, it is useful to know first how sociological explanations differ from biological and psychological ones, and then to examine how the four sociological perspectives explain social deviance.

Psychologists and *sociobiologists* explain social deviance by looking for answers *within* individuals. They assume that something in the makeup of people leads them to become socially deviant. By contrast, sociologists look for answers in factors *outside* the individual. They assume that something in the environment influences people to become socially deviant.

Biological explanations focus on **genetic predispositions** to such social deviance as juvenile delinquency and crime (Lombroso, 1911; Sheldon, 1949; Glueck & Glueck, 1956; Wilson & Hernstein, 1985; Kamin, 1975, 1986; S. Rose, 1986). Biological explanations include (but are not restricted to) the following three theories: (1) intelligence—low intelligence leads to crime; (2) the "XYY" theory—an extra Y chromosome in males leads to crime; and (3) body type—people with "squarish, muscular" bodies are more likely to commit **street crime**, acts such as mugging, rape, and burglary.

How have these theories held up? Some criminals are very intelligent, and most people of low intelligence do not commit crimes. Most criminals have the normal "XY" chromosome combination, and most men with the "XYY" combination do not become criminals; in addition, no women have this combination of genes, so it wouldn't even deal with female criminals. Criminals also run the range of the body types exhibited by humanity, and most people with "squarish, muscular" bodies do not become street criminals. In short, these supposed "causes" of social deviance are even more common among the general population of people who do not commit crimes. Therefore, the causes of social deviance cannot be answered by biology alone. For example, some of the expectations of the masculine role in

Canadian society—to be braver, tougher, more independent, and less tolerant of insult—increase the likelihood that males will become involved in violence.

Psychologists focus on abnormalities *within* the individual, on what are called **personality disorders**. Their supposition is that deviating individuals have deviating personalities (Kalichman, 1988; M. H. Stone, 1989; Heilbrun, 1990). That is, various unconscious urges drive people to social deviance. No specific negative childhood experience, however, is invariably linked with social deviance. For example, children who had "bad toilet training," "suffocating mothers," or "dysfunctional families" may become embezzling bookkeepers—or good accountants. Just as students, teachers, and police officers represent a variety of bad—and good—childhood experiences, so do social deviants. In short, there is no inevitable outcome of particular childhood experiences, and social deviance is not associated with any particular personality or unconscious "urges."

Sociologists, in contrast, search for factors *outside* the individual. Since social deviance is relative, they ask, why should we expect to find anything constant within people to account for a behaviour that is conforming in one society and socially deviant in another? Sociologists also look for social influences that "recruit" some people rather than others to break norms. To account for why people commit crimes, for example, sociologists examine such external influences as socialization, subcultural membership, and social class. *Social class*, a concept discussed in depth in Chapter 6 and the next two chapters, refers to people's relative standing in terms of education, occupation, and especially income and wealth.

The Relativity of Social Deviance

Sociologists use the term **social deviance** to refer to any violation of norms—whether the infraction is as minor as jaywalking, as serious as murder, or as humorous as Chagnon's encounter with the Yanomamo. This deceptively simple definition takes us to the heart of the sociological perspective of social deviance, which sociologist Howard S. Becker (1966) identified this way: *It is not the act itself, but the reactions to the act, that make something deviant.* In other words, people's behaviours must be viewed from the framework of the culture in which they take place. What was deviant to Chagnon was *conforming* to the Yanomamo. From their viewpoint, you *should* check out strangers as they did—and nakedness is good, as are hallucinogenic drugs.

Chagnon's abrupt introduction to the Yanomamo allows us to see the *relativity of social deviance*. Thus, acts perfectly acceptable in one culture—or in one group within a society—may be considered socially deviant in another culture, or in another group within the same society. This idea is explored in the Perspectives box on the following page.

Unlike the general public, sociologists use the term *deviance* nonjudgmentally, to refer to any act to which people respond negatively. To sociologists, then, all of us are social deviants of one sort or another, for we all violate norms from time to time.

To be considered socially deviant, a person may not even have to *do* anything. Sociologist Erving Goffman (1963) used the term **stigma** to refer to attributes that discredit people. These attributes include violations of norms of ability (blindness, deafness, mental handicaps) and norms of appearance (a facial birthmark, obesity). They also include involuntary membership in groups, such as being the victim of AIDS or the brother of a rapist. The stigma becomes a person's *master status*, defining him or her as socially deviant. Recall from Chapter 5 that a master status cuts across all other statuses that a person occupies.

Knowing how relative social deviance is, sociologists wonder why anyone would expect to find factors within people to explain social deviance. For example, because **crime** is the violation of norms that have been written into law, what a crime is varies from one human group to another. Why, then, should we expect to find anything constant within people to account for crime—or any other behaviour that is conforming in one group but socially deviant in another?

Who Defines Social Deviance?

If social deviance does not lie in the act, but in definitions of the act, where do those definitions come from? To see how sociologists explain social deviance, especially criminal behaviour, let's contrast the four sociological perspectives—symbolic interactionism, functionalism, feminism, and conflict theory.

> **Focus Question**
> What is social deviance?

In Sum

In sociology, the term *social deviance* refers to all violations of social rules, regardless of their seriousness. The term is not a judgment about the behaviour. Social deviance is relative, for what is socially deviant in one group may be conformance in another. Consequently, we must consider social deviance from within a group's own framework, for it is *their* meanings that underlie their behaviour.

The Symbolic Interactionist Perspective

As we examine symbolic interactionism, it will become more evident why sociologists are not satisfied with explanations rooted in biology or personality. A basic principle of symbolic interactionism is that each of us interprets life through the symbols that we learn.

Anthropologist Robert Edgerton (1976) reports how differently human groups react to similar behaviours. Of the many examples he cites, let's look at suicide and sexuality to illustrate how a group's *definitions* of a behaviour, not the behaviour itself, determine whether it will be considered deviant.

Suicide

In some societies, suicide is seen not as social deviance but as a positive act, at least under specified conditions. In traditional Japanese society, hara-kiri, a ritual disembowelment, was considered the proper course for disgraced noblemen or defeated military leaders. Similarly, kamikaze pilots in World War II who crashed their explosives-laden planes into U.S. warships were admired for their bravery and sacrifice. Traditional Inuit approved the suicide of individuals no longer able to contribute their share to the group. Sometimes an aged father would hand his hunting knife to his son, asking him to drive it through his heart. For a son to refuse this request would be considered deviant.

Sexuality

Norms of sexual behaviour vary so widely around the world that what is considered normal in one society may

Suicide is not inherently deviant; it is deviant only when that meaning is assigned to it. During World War II, some Japanese pilots were trained for kamikaze, or suicide, missions. Their planes were loaded with bombs, and their mission was to ram U.S. ships, killing themselves in the process. Shown here are six kamikaze pilots after their training.

be considered deviant in another. The Pokot people of northwestern Kenya, for example, place high emphasis on sexual pleasure and fully expect that both a husband and his wife will reach orgasm. If a husband does not satisfy his wife, he is in serious trouble. Pokot men often engage in adulterous affairs, and should a husband's failure to satisfy his wife be attributed to his adultery, when her husband is asleep his wife will bring in female friends and tie him up. The women will then shout obscenities at him, beat him, and, as a final gesture of

their utter contempt, slaughter and eat his favourite ox before releasing him. His hours of painful humiliation are assumed to make him henceforth more dutiful concerning his wife's conjugal rights.

Ideal Versus Covert Norms

People can also become deviants for failing to understand that the group's ideal norms may not be its real norms. As with many groups, the Zapotec Indians of Mexico expect sexual activity to take place exclusively between husband and wife. Yet the only person in one Zapotec community who had had no extramarital affairs was considered deviant. Evidently these people have a covert, commonly understood norm that married couples will engage in discreet extramarital affairs, for when a wife learns that her husband is having an affair she does the same thing. One Zapotec wife, however, did not follow this informal pattern. Instead, she continually threw her virtue into her husband's face—and claimed headaches. Worse, she also informed the other husbands and wives in the village who their spouses were sleeping with. As a result, this virtuous woman was condemned by everyone in the village. In other words, the official norms do not always represent the real norms—another illustration of the gap between ideal and real culture.

Differential Association Theory

The Theory. Contrary to theories of biology and personality, sociologist Edwin Sutherland stressed that people *learn* social deviance. He coined the term **differential association** to indicate that learning to deviate or to conform to society's norms is influenced most by the people with whom we associate (Sutherland, 1924, 1947; Sutherland & Cressey, 1974; Sutherland, Cressey, & Luckenbill, 1992). On the most obvious level, boys and girls who join street gangs learn a way of looking at the world that is more likely to get them in trouble with the law than boys and girls who join the scouts.

Sutherland's theory is actually more complicated than this, but he stressed that learning social deviance is like learning anything else—which goes directly against the thinking that social deviance is biological or due to deep personality needs.

Families. If we learn attitudes from others, then one's family should make a big difference. To see if delinquents are more likely to come from families who themselves get in trouble with the law, researchers examined the family history of 25 000 delinquents locked up in high-security state institutions (Beck, Kline, & Greenfield, 1988). They

Unlike biology and psychology, which look *within* individuals for explanations of human behaviour, sociological explanations focus on *external* experiences, such as people's associations or group memberships. Sociological explanations of human behaviour have become widely accepted and now permeate society, as illustrated by this teenager.

found that 25 percent have a father who has been in prison, 25 percent a brother or sister, 9 percent a mother, and 13 percent some other relative. This study suggests that families involved in crime tend to provide an environment conducive to criminal behaviour.

Friends and Neighbourhoods.   The longer someone has delinquent friends the more likely he or she is to be delinquent (Warr, 1993). Since delinquency is clustered in certain neighbourhoods, children from those neighbourhoods are likely to become delinquent (Miller, 1958; Wolfgang & Ferracuti, 1967). This, of course, comes as no surprise to parents, who generally are eager to get their kids out of "bad" neighbourhoods and away from "bad" friends, for, although they may not know the term "differential association," they know how it works.

Subcultures.   All subcultures contain particular attitudes about social deviance and conformity, and their members learn those attitudes. Sociologist Ruth Horowitz (1983, 1987), who did participant observation in a Chicago Chicano neighbourhood, reports that the formula was simple: A man must have honour. An insult is a threat to one's

honour. Therefore, not to stand up to someone is to be less than a real man. Now suppose you were a young man growing up in this neighbourhood. You would likely do a fair amount of fighting, for you would see many statements and acts as infringing on your honour. You might make certain that you carried a knife or had access to a gun, for words and fists won't always do. Along with members of your group, you would define fighting, knifing, and shooting quite differently from the way most people do.

For members of the Mafia, ideas of manliness are also intertwined with social deviance. For them, *killing is a primary measure of their manhood*. Not all killings are accorded the same respect, however, for "the more awesome and potent the victim, the more worthy and meritorious the killer" (Arlacchi, 1980). Some killings are very practical matters. A member of the Mafia who gives information to the police, for example, has violated the Mafia's *omerta* (the vow of secrecy its members take). Such an offence can never be tolerated, for it threatens the very existence of the group. This example further illustrates just how relative social deviance is. Although the act of killing is socially deviant to mainstream society, for them, *not* killing after certain rules are broken, such as "squealing" to the cops, is the socially deviant act.

Prison or Freedom?   Symbolic interactionists stress that we are not mere pawns in the hands of others. We are not destined by our group membership to think and behave as our groups dictate. Rather, *we help produce our own orientations to life*. Our choice of membership (differential association), for example, helps to shape the self. One university student may join a feminist group that is trying to change the treatment of women in university; another may associate with a group of women who smokes cigarettes. Their choice of groups points them in two different directions. The one who associates with cigarette smokers may or may not find herself becoming a smoker, while the one who joins the feminist group may develop an even greater interest in producing social change.

> **Focus Question**
> According to symbolic interactionists, are we mere pawns in the hands of others when we socialize with "bad people?"

Labelling Theory

Labelling theory focuses on the significance of the labels (names, reputations) given to people. Labels tend to become a part of the self-concept. Depending on the kind of pressure coming from others, these labels help set people on paths that propel them into or divert them from social deviance.

Rejecting Labels: How People Neutralize Social Deviance.   Most people resist the negative labels others try to pin on them. Some are so successful that even though

Mainstreaming of social deviance occurs when people or activities that generally are disapproved of move into the mainstream, or become more socially acceptable. An example is the Beastie Boys, whose music and message have brought them fame and wealth. In years past, this group's audience would have been limited to a small following.

they persist in social deviance, they still consider themselves conformists. For example, even though they beat up people and vandalize property, some delinquents consider themselves conforming members of society. How do they do it?

Sociologists Gresham Sykes and David Matza (1988), studied boys in this exact situation. They found that they used these five **techniques of neutralization** to help them deflect society's norms:

1. *Denial of responsibility*. The youths frequently said, "I'm not responsible for what happened because ..." and then were quite creative about the "becauses." The act may have been an "accident," or they may see themselves as "victims" of society, with no control over what happened—like billiard balls shot around the pool table of life.

2. *Denial of injury*. Another favourite explanation of the boys was "What I did wasn't wrong because no one got hurt." They would define vandalism as "mischief," gang fighting as a "private quarrel," and stealing cars as "borrowing." They might acknowledge that what they did was illegal, but claim that it was "just having a little fun."

3. *Denial of a victim*. Sometimes the boys thought of themselves as avengers. To vandalize a teacher's car is only to get revenge for an unfair grade, while to shoplift is to even the score with "crooked" store owners. In short, they protect their self-concept by claiming that the people "deserved what they got."

4. *Condemnation of the condemners*. Another technique the boys used was to deny that others had the right to judge them. They might accuse people who pointed their fingers at them of being "a bunch of hypocrites": The police

are "on the take," teachers have "pets," and parents cheat on their taxes. In short, they say, "Who are *they* to accuse *me* of something?"

5. *Appeal to higher loyalties*. A final technique the boys used to justify antisocial activities was to consider loyalty to the gang more important than following the norms of society. They might say, "I had to help my friends. That's why I got in the fight."

In Sum

These five techniques of neutralization have implications far beyond these boys, for it is not only delinquents who try to neutralize the norms of mainstream society. Look again at these five techniques: (1) "I couldn't help myself." (2) "Who really got hurt?" (3) "Don't you think she deserved that, after what *she* did?" (4) "Who are *you* to talk?" and (5) "I had to help my friends—wouldn't you have done the same thing?" Don't such statements have a familiar ring? All of us attempt to neutralize some of the labels we are taught to carry with us.

Rejecting Labels: Becoming a Prostitute. Sociologist Nanette Davis (1978), who interviewed young women to find out how they had become prostitutes, noted that they had experienced a gradual slide from sexual promiscuity to prostitution. Their first acts of selling sex were casual. At this point, the girls were in a stage of social deviance that sociologist Edwin Lemert (1972) calls **primary social deviance**—fleeting acts that do not become part of the self-concept. The young women did not think of themselves as prostitutes. As one girl said, "I never thought about it one way or another."

Why are these women selling their bodies on the streets of Toronto instead of working at "respectable" jobs or studying sociology and other academic subjects in university?

Girls who are engaged in the "business" for a longer time, however, come to think of themselves as prostitutes. When this occurs, they have entered **secondary social deviance**.

The movement from primary to secondary social deviance may be gradual. Through *self-labelling*, bit by bit the social deviance becomes part of the self-concept. Often the reactions of others facilitate this transition. Self-jarring labels such as "pervert" and "whore" tend to lock people out of conforming groups and push them into contact with others like themselves.

In **tertiary social deviance**, socially deviant behaviour is normalized by *relabelling* it nondeviant (Kitsuse, 1980; de Young, 1989). Most people in this stage simply reject the judgment that the behaviour is wrong. For example, prostitutes in the United States have formed an organization called Coyote (Call Off Your Old Tired Ethics) (Hughes, 1995). This group takes the position that prostitutes perform a service to society. Therefore it is a reasonable occupational choice and legislation should allow prostitutes to operate without interference from the government.

Inviting Labels: The Embrace of Social Deviance. Although most of us resist attempts to label us as socially deviant, there are those who revel in a socially deviant identity. Some teenagers, for example, make certain by their choice of clothing, music, and hairstyles that no one misses their intentional rejection of adult norms. Their status among fellow members of a subculture, within which they are almost obsessive conformists, is vastly more important than any status outside it.

One of the best examples of a group that embraces social deviance is motorcycle gangs. Sociologist Mark Watson (1988) did participant observation with outlaw bikers. He rebuilt Harleys with them, hung around their bars and homes, and went on "runs" (trips) with them. He concluded that outlaw bikers see the world as "hostile, weak, and effeminate," while they pride themselves on looking "dirty, mean, and generally undesirable"—and take great pleasure in provoking shocked reactions to their appearance. Holding the conventional world in contempt, they also pride themselves on getting into trouble, laughing at death, and treating women as lesser beings whose primary value is to provide them with services—especially sex.

Outlaw bikers are of sociological interest because they reject the labels society holds out as desirable and in an "in-your-face" approach replace them with their own labels of approval. What outward signs of this phenomenon are visible in this photo?

The Power of Labels: The Saints and the Roughnecks. We can see how powerful labelling is by referring back to the study of the "Saints" and the "Roughnecks" cited in Chapter 5. As you recall, both groups of high school boys were "constantly occupied with truancy, drinking, wild parties, petty theft, and vandalism." Yet their teachers looked on the Saints as "headed for success" and the Roughnecks as "headed for trouble." By the time they finished high school, not one Saint had been arrested, while the Roughnecks had been in constant trouble with the police.

Why did the community see these boys so differently? Chambliss (1973/1997) concluded that this double vision was due to their family background, especially *social class*. The Saints came from respectable, middle-class families, while the Roughnecks came from less respectable, working-class families. Because of their respective backgrounds, teachers and other authorities expected good, law-abiding behaviour from the Saints and trouble from the Roughnecks. And like the rest of us, both teachers and police see what they expect to see.

Social class had allowed the Saints' lawbreaking to be *less visible*. The Saints had automobiles, and they made their drinking and vandalism inconspicuous by spreading it around neighbouring towns. Without cars, the Roughnecks could not even make it to the edge of town. Day after day, they hung around the same street corners, where their boisterous behaviour made them conspicuous, confirming the negative ideas that the community held about them.

Another significant factor was also at work. The boys' different social backgrounds had equipped them with distinct *styles of interaction*. When questioned by police or teachers, the Saints put on apologetic and penitent faces. Their deferential behaviour elicited such positive reactions that they escaped serious legal problems. In contrast, the Roughnecks' attitude was "almost the polar opposite." They expressed open hostility to the authorities, and even when they pretended to show respect, the veneer was so thin that it fooled no one. Consequently, while the police let the Saints off with warnings, they came down hard on the Roughnecks, interrogating and arresting them when they had the chance.

While a lifetime career often is not determined by a label alone, the Saints and Roughnecks did live up to the labels that the community gave them. As you recall, all but one of the Saints went on to university, after which one earned a doctorate and one became a lawyer, one a doctor, and the others business managers. In contrast, only two of the Roughnecks went to university, both on athletic scholarships, after which they became coaches. The other Roughnecks did not fare so well. Two of them dropped out of high school, later became involved in separate killings, and received long prison sentences. One became a local bookie, and no one knows the whereabouts of the other.

How do labels work? While the matter is extremely complex since it involves the self-concept and individual reactions, we can note that labels open and close the doors of opportunity.

Focus Question

How does labelling help us understand the persistence of social deviance?

In Sum

Symbolic interactionists examine how people's definitions of the situation underlie their rejection of or conformity to social norms. They focus on group membership (differential association) and the significance of the labels placed on people (labelling theory).

The Functionalist Perspective

When we think of social deviance, its dysfunctions are likely to come to mind. Functionalists, in contrast, are as likely to stress the functions of social deviance as its dysfunctions.

How Social Deviance Is Functional for Society

According to Emile Durkheim (1893/1933, 1895/1964), social deviance, including crime, is functional for society. Its three main functions are as follows:

1. *Deviance clarifies moral boundaries and affirms norms.* A group's ideas about how people should act and think mark its *moral boundaries*. Social deviance challenges those boundaries. To call a socially deviant member to account, saying in effect, "You broke an important rule, and we cannot tolerate that," affirms the group's norms and clarifies the distinction between conforming and deviating behaviour.

2. *Deviance promotes social unity.* To affirm the group's moral boundaries fosters a "we" feeling among the group's members. In saying, "You can't get away with that," the group collectively affirms the rightness of its own ways.

3. *Deviance promotes social change.* Groups do not always agree on what to do with people who push beyond their acceptable ways of doing things. Boundary violations that gain enough support become new, acceptable behaviours. Thus, social deviance may force a group to rethink and redefine its moral boundaries, helping groups, and whole societies, to change their customary ways.

Focus Question

Is social deviance always bad for society?

Functionalism and Social Control. Functionalists stress how the many groups in a pluralistic society coexist. Although tensions between them may appear from time to time, the balancing of these tensions produces the whole that we call society. If some group threatens to upset the equilibrium, efforts are made to restore balance. For example, in a pluralistic society the central government often plays a mediating role between groups. In Canada, the federal and provincial governments and the Supreme Court of Canada mediate the demands of the various groups that make up society, preventing groups whose basic ideas deviate from those held by most members of society from taking political control (Porter, 1965). This view of mediation and balance among competing groups is broadly representative of what may be called the **pluralistic theory of social control**.

Strain Theory: How Social Values Produce Crime

Functionalists argue that crime is a *natural* part of society, not an aberration or some alien element in our midst. Indeed, they say, some crime represents values that lie at the very core of society. This concept sounds strange at first. To understand how the acceptance of mainstream values can generate crime, consider what sociologists Richard

Social control refers to messages that persuade—such as the above—or to law enforcement and military intervention.

Cloward and Lloyd Ohlin (1960) identified as the crucial problem of the industrialized world: the need to locate and train the most talented people of every generation— whether born in wealth or in poverty—so they can take over the key technical jobs of modern society. When children are born, no one knows which ones will have the abilities to become dentists, nuclear physicists, or engineers. To get the most talented people to compete with one another, society tries to motivate everyone to strive for success. It does this by arousing discontent—making people feel dissatisfied with what they have so that they will try to "better" themselves.

Most people, then, end up with strong desires to achieve **cultural goals** such as wealth or high status. Not everyone, however, has equal access to society's **institutionalized means**, the legitimate ways of achieving that success. Some people, for example, find their path to education and good jobs blocked. These people experience *strain* or frustrations, which may motivate them to take a socially deviant path.

This perspective, known as **strain theory**, was developed by sociologist Robert Merton (1956, 1968). Because the dominant norms (work, education) don't seem to be getting them anywhere, they have a difficult time identifying with them. They may even feel wronged by the system, and its rules may seem illegitimate (E. Anderson, 1978).

Merton's classic outline of how people react to cultural goals and institutionalized means is depicted in Table 16.1 below. The first reaction, which Merton said is the most common, is *conformity*, using socially acceptable means to strive to reach cultural goals. In industrialized societies most people try to get good jobs, a good education, and so on. If well-paid jobs are unavailable, they take less desirable jobs. Others take night classes and attend vocational schools. In short, most people take the socially acceptable road.

Four Socially Deviant Paths. The remaining four responses represent reactions to strain. Let's look at each. *Innovators* are people who accept the goals of society but use illegitimate means to try to reach them. Drug dealers, for instance, accept the goal of achieving wealth but reject the legitimate avenues for doing so. Other examples are embezzlers, robbers, and con artists.

Table 16.1 How People Match Their Goals to Their Means

Feel Strain That Leads to Anomie?	Mode of Adaptation	Cultural Goals	Institutionalized Means
No	Conformists	Accept	Accept
Yes	Innovators	Accept	Reject
	Ritualists	Reject	Accept
	Retreatists	Reject	Reject
	Rebels	Reject/accept	Reject/accept

Down-to-Earth Sociology

Mean Streets and Hard Time: Youth Unemployment and Crime in Canada

Newspaper headlines from western Canada have told us that "Tough Times Drive Kids out of Class, into Crime" (*Winnipeg Free Press*, September 5, 1993). A few months earlier, the same newspaper reported that "Young Canadians have the highest unemployment rate, account for a large share of criminal activity and are especially vulnerable to economic downturns" (March 16, 1993, p. A3). Also according to the same article, students who work more than 15 hours a week are more likely to drop out of school. Even those who stay in school see grim prospects for good jobs. Corey, a 15-year-old, said "there are more offers from gangs than offers of jobs."

Among Canadian criminologists, the link between unemployment and property crimes has been ignored in favour of more "sophisticated" theories. "Dysfunctional" family background is often used by more conservative theorists who point out single-parent households or a parent's alcoholism as negatively affecting the children's actions. Others are more prone to differential association theory—that is, a person's prior exposure to socially deviant beliefs—and/or labelling theory—that is, a person's passage through successive stages of negative stigmatization.

Clearly, youth unemployment affects different young people differently. In Great Britain, the increase in suicide rates among young people has been linked with prolonged periods of unemployment (*Calgary Herald*, April 2, 1993). That said, the relationship between youth unemployment and crime is also real. But what types of crime are associated with prolonged periods of unemployment?

It is crimes against property that are most commonly related to unemployment. Prostitution is another course of action, especially for teenage girls and boys who have nothing to eat and nowhere to go. However, for many young adults, poorly paid part-time work and/or seasonal work, a growing sector of the economy and population, can lead many young adults to commit property crimes such as robbery, larceny, auto theft, and burglary. Or, to paraphrase from Gary O'Bireck's (1993) ethnographic study of Toronto youth, "Why work at McDonalds when you can sell drugs or steal stereos?"

What's the answer to prolonged periods of youth and young adult unemployment and property crimes? Better and more secure jobs for young adults, not prison time.

For Your Consideration

What do you think? Which theory or theories do you feel helps explain property crimes among Canada's young people?

Source: From *Not a Kid Anymore, Canadian Youth, Crime, and Subcultures* by O'Bireck, PHD. © 1996. Reprinted with the permission of Nelson, a division of Thomson Learning: www.thomsonlearning.com.

The second socially deviant path is taken by people who become discouraged and give up on achieving cultural goals, but who still cling to conventional rules of conduct. Merton called this response *ritualism*. Although ritualists have given up on excelling and advancing in position, they survive by following the rules. Teachers who suffer from "burnout" but continue to go through the motions of classroom performance after their idealism is shattered are examples of ritualists.

People who choose the third socially deviant path, *retreatism*, reject both cultural goals and the institutionalized means of achieving them. Those who drop out of the pursuit of success by way of membership in mystical religious sects are retreatists. Such people do not even try to appear as though they share the goals of their society.

The final type of socially deviant response is *rebellion*. Convinced that the society in which they live is corrupt, rebels, like retreatists, reject both society's goals and its institutionalized means. Unlike retreatists, however, they seek to replace existing goals with new ones. Revolutionaries are the most committed type of rebels.

Strain theory underscores the main sociological point about social deviance, namely, that social deviants are not pathogenic individuals, but the product of society. Due to their social location, some people experience greater pressures to deviate from society's norms. Simply put, if a society emphasizes the goal of material success, groups deprived of access to this goal will be more involved in property crime. During periods of economic recession, we can expect to find an increase in property crimes simply because there aren't enough good jobs to go around to all who want or need them, especially hard-hit young males. See the Down-to-Earth Sociology box above.

Illegitimate Opportunity Theory: Explaining Social Class and Crime

Social class position is an important predictor of economic success in our society. And just as different classes carry different cultures of dress, speech, and mannerisms, so too do social classes have distinct styles of crime.

The Poor and Crime. Functionalists point out that industrialized societies have no trouble socializing the poor into wanting to possess things. Like others, they, too, are bombarded with messages urging them to buy everything from designer jeans to new cars. The vivid images in movies and on television of the middle class enjoying luxurious lives reinforce the myth that all Canadians can afford society's many goods and services. This bombardment of messages also unintentionally produces the idea that they have a *right* to these items.

This 1871 wood engraving depicts children as they are being paid for their day's work in a London brickyard. In early capitalism, most street criminals came from the marginal working class, as did these children. It is the same today.

The school system, however, which constitutes the most common route to success, fails the poor. It is run by the middle class, and when the children of the poor enter it, already at an educational disadvantage, they confront a bewildering world for which their background ill prepares them. Their grammar and nonstandard language—liberally punctuated by what the middle class considers obscene and foul words and phrases—their ideas of punctuality and neatness, and their lack of preparation in paper-and-pencil skills are a mismatch with their new environment. Facing these barriers, the poor drop out of school in larger numbers than their more privileged counterparts. Educational failure, in turn, closes the door on many legitimate avenues to financial success.

Not infrequently, however, a different door opens to them, one that sociologists Richard Cloward and Lloyd Ohlin (1960) called **illegitimate opportunity structures**. Woven into the texture of life in poor urban neighbourhoods are gambling and other remunerative crimes, commonly called "hustles" (Liebow, 1967; E. Anderson, 1978, 1990; Bourgois, 1994). For many of the poor, the "hustler" is a role model—glamorous, in control, the image of "easy money," and one of the few people in the area who comes close to the cultural goal of success. For some, then, such illegal income-producing activities are functional—they provide income—and they attract disproportionate numbers of the poor.

White-Collar and Street Crime. The more privileged social classes are not crime-free, of course, but they find a different illegitimate opportunity structure beckoning. The more privileged encounter "opportunities" for income tax evasion, bribery of public officials, stock manipulation, embezzlement, false advertising, and so on. Sociologist Edwin Sutherland (1949) used the term **white-collar crime** to refer to crimes that people of respectable and high social status commit in the course of their occupations.

Although the general public seems to think that the lower classes are more crime-prone, numerous studies show that white-collar workers also commit many crimes (Weisburd, Wheeler, & Waring, 1991; Zey, 1993). This difference in perception is largely based on visibility. While crimes committed by the poor are given much publicity, the crimes of the more privileged classes seldom make the evening news and go largely unnoticed. Yet the dollar cost of "crime in the suites" is considerably higher than "crime in the streets." It actually totals in the billions of dollars a year. These totals refer only to dollar costs. No one has yet figured out a way to compare, for example, the suffering of a rape victim with the pain experienced by an elderly couple who lose their life savings to white-collar fraud.

Although white-collar crime is not as dramatic as a street killing or an abduction and rape—and therefore usually considered less newsworthy—it, too, can involve physical harm, and sometimes death. Unsafe working conditions, for example, many the result of executive decisions to put profits ahead of workers' safety, kill about 1000 Canadians each year. Of five countries surveyed for the International Labour Organization (ILO), Canada's record for occupational injuries at work was the worst in all three economic sectors surveyed—manufacturing, mining, and construction (Glenday, 1996). Nevertheless, Canadians are becoming more and more worried about street crime, since the media is diligent about reporting any and almost all encounters with violence on the street.

In Sum

Functionalists conclude that much street crime is the consequence of socializing the lower social classes into equating success with material possessions, while denying them the means to attain that success. People from higher social classes encounter different opportunity structures to commit crimes.

The Conflict Perspective

Class, Crime, and the Criminal Justice System

Conflict theorists stress that the state's machinery of social control, which includes the **criminal justice system**—the police, courts, and prisons that deal with people who are accused of having committed crimes—represents the interests of the wealthy and powerful. This group determines the basic laws whose enforcement is essential to preserving its own power.

The Law as an Instrument of Oppression

According to conflict theorists, the idea that the law is a social institution that operates impartially and administers a code shared by all is a cultural myth promoted by the capitalist class. In contrast, they see the law as an instrument of oppression, a tool designed to maintain the powerful in their privileged position (Spitzer, 1975; Ritzer, 1992; MacDonald, 1995). Because the working class holds the potential of rebelling and overthrowing the current social order, when its members get out of line they are arrested, tried, and imprisoned.

Conflict Theory and Social Control. Conflict theorists stress that every society is dominated by a group of elite, powerful people, and that the basic purpose of social control is to maintain the current power arrangements. The group that holds power must always fend off groups that desire to replace it and take over the society themselves. If another group does gain power, it, too, immediately tries to neutralize competing groups. Some groups are much more ruthless than others; for example, before and during World War II the Nazis in Germany and the communists in the Soviet Union systematically eliminated individuals and groups they deemed a threat to their vision of the ideal society. In more recent years, the Khmer Rouge did the same in Cambodia. Other dominant groups may be less ruthless, but they, too, are committed to maintaining power.

Although political power is not as naked in Canada as it is in dictatorships, conflict theorists note that an elite group of wealthy, largely white males maintains power, working behind the scenes to control the federal government by making certain the group's interests are represented in Cabinet (Porter, 1965; Clement & Myles, 1994; Olsen, 1980; McQuaig, 1995). Thus, it is this group's views of capital and property, the basis of its power, that are represented in the laws of society. This means that **official social deviance**—the statistics on victims, lawbreakers, and the outcomes of criminal investigations and sentencing—centres on maintaining their interests. Other norms, such as those that govern informal behaviour (chewing with a closed mouth, appearing in public with combed hair, and so on), may come from other sources, but they simply do not count for much. Although they influence everyday behaviour, they do not determine prison sentences.

The Trouble with Official Statistics

Both the findings of symbolic interactionists concerning the authorities' reactions to such groups as the Saints and the Roughnecks and the conclusions of conflict theorists that the criminal justice system exists to serve the ruling elite demonstrate the need for caution in interpreting official

As conflict theorists stress, the enforcement of norms is always about power: About 2000 years ago, the norms of the Romans and Christians clashed, with the Romans using violence to enforce its norms. Interestingly, the "powerless" group won the struggle. Shown here is a Hollywood version of Christians facing lions and gladiators in Rome's Coliseum. The clip is from *Quo Vadis?*, a 1951 movie, with Peter Ustinov playing Emperor Nero.

You probably have no difficulty telling which of these photos shows upper-middle-class youths and which portrays working-class youths. In spite of similarities of social identifiers by which both groups of students proclaim that they are teenagers, they also use status markers to signal their social class background. As the text explains, this information is of crucial importance, for it affects perception, social interaction, and ultimately life chances.

crime statistics. Statistics are not objective, tangible objects, like apples in a supermarket, waiting to be picked up. They are a human creation, produced within a specific social and political context for some particular purpose.

According to official statistics, working-class boys clearly emerge as much more delinquent than middle-class boys. Yet, as we have seen, who actually gets arrested for what is directly affected by social class, a point that has far-reaching implications. As symbolic interactionists point out, the police use a symbolic system as they enforce the law. Their ideas of "typical criminals" and "typical good citizens," for example, permeate their work. The more a suspect matches their ideas of the "criminal profile," the more likely that person is to be arrested. Police discretion, the decision whether or not to arrest someone or even to ignore a matter, is a routine part of police work. Consequently, official crime statistics always reflect these and many other biases.

For this reason, the criminal justice system does not focus on the owners of corporations and the harm they do to the masses with unsafe products, wanton pollution, and price manipulations but, instead, directs its energies against violations by the working class (Gordon, 1971; Platt, 1978; Coleman, 1989). The violations of the capitalist class cannot be totally ignored, however, for if they became too outrageous or oppressive, the appearance of fairness is revealed to be a sham. To prevent this, a flagrant violation by a member of the capitalist class is occasionally prosecuted. The publicity given to the case helps to stabilize the social system by providing visible evidence of the "fairness" of the criminal justice system.

Usually, however, the powerful bypass the courts altogether, appearing instead before some agency with no power to imprison. Most cases of illegal sales of stocks and bonds, price-fixing, restraint of trade, collusion, and so on are handled by "gentlemen overseeing gentlemen," for such agencies are directed by people from wealthy backgrounds who sympathize with the intricacies of the corporate world. It is not surprising, then, that the typical sanction is a token fine. In contrast, the property crimes of the masses are handled by courts that do have the power to imprison. The burglary, armed robbery, and theft by the poor not only threaten the sanctity of private property but, ultimately, the positions of the powerful.

In Sum

From the perspective of conflict theory, the small penalties imposed for crimes committed by the powerful are typical of a legal system designed to mask injustice, to control workers, and, ultimately, to stabilize the social order. From this perspective, law enforcement is a cultural device through which the capitalist class carries out self-protective and oppressive policies (Silver, 1977).

The Feminist Perspective

Feminist theories stress the importance of gender inequality in society. Patriarchy implies male power over women and social deviance from a feminist perspective evokes male violence against women. Let's examine this aspect of social deviance.

Feminist Theories and Male Violence Against Women

As has been mentioned in previous chapters, there are several feminist theories—Marxist feminist theories, liberal feminist theories, non-Marxist radical feminist theories, and postmodern feminist theories. However, when it comes to feminist theories of social deviance, more specifically, male violence against women, a number of common principles are shared by all feminist theories, of which the most important is patriarchy.

First and foremost, **patriarchy** is characterized as a "sexual system of power in which the male possesses superior power and economic privilege" (Eisenstein, 1980, p. 16). Michael Smith (1990) has identified two related forms of patriarchy, the "social" and the "familial." The first refers to male domination at the societal level, whereas the latter pertains to male control in domestic arrangements including dating and nonmarriage or common-law relationships.

When it comes to male violence against women, virtually all feminist theorists agree that men assault their female partners to maintain control over them and, if they happen to live in a relationship, their "domestic" situation. Control over women has been measured as (1) sexual fidelity, (2) obedience, (3) respect, (4) loyalty, (5) dependency, and (6) sexual access.

Several studies have been conducted that confirm the relationship of a patriarchal ideology of control and male violence against women (D. E. Smith, 1987, 1990). Feminist contributions to our understanding of male violence against women are pioneering. However, this approach is not without its detractors and progressive critics. Conservative critics, for example, are quick to regard theories of patriarchy as political philosophies rather than social scientific theories (Gelles & Cornell, 1985; Levinson, 1989). The empirical work of Smith and others challenges this notion.

More serious criticisms come from those who point out that feminist theories ignore the effects of class and ethnicity/race on violence against women. It is too simple to point to some empirical studies that have shown violence against women is more prevalent among lower-class males. And, as we have seen in this chapter, official statistics tend to hide as much as they may reveal about criminal activity. These critics entreat feminists to explain how certain class-based cultural characteristics interact with gender relations and how these circumstances put some women more at risk than others.

Ethnicity/race is another significant factor in assessing male violence against women. For example, Aboriginal women are especially prone to violence against their male partners. Also, the experiences of black women in Canada are seldom analyzed. Finally, feminist theories and researchers are only now becoming sensitive to the issue of violence in same-sex relationships, whether gay or lesbian. The fact that there is little research on violence in these relationships does not signify its absence. Same-sex relationships may be an accepted social fact among many urban-based gays and lesbians in Canada, but violence in such relationships is probably still in the closet.

Feminist Theories and Issues of Public Policy in Canada

Four strategies for coping with male violence against women are discussed below—policing, job creation, social services, and antisexist male collectives. The first involves raising the sensitivity of police to the reality of male violence against women. Where once police officers, most of whom are males, would not want to arrest or lay charges against a man, today there has been a change in attitude and training across Canada. This change has been largely due to feminist research findings and effective lobbying. This is not to say all is well. Far from it. For example, while arrests are up for violence against women, some feminists charge that simply enforcing arrest policies can make a bad situation even worse. They point out that many women do not want to report their husbands, companions, or boyfriends simply because the women believe their partner's arrest will destroy the relationship. They suggest that following only aggressive charging policies fails to address the wider issues of patriarchy, including many women's economic dependence on men.

The second strategy includes all levels of government participating in good job creation programs. DeKeseredy and Hinch (1991), for example, argue that economic policy reforms such as paid work leaves, flexible hours (flextime), pay equity, and improving the quality of work available to disadvantaged people, to name just a few, can lower the rate of male violence against women.

The need for expanded social services such as short-term emergency shelters and housing assistance is the third strategy for coping with male violence against women. Since 1979, the number of Canadian women's shelters has tripled. Nevertheless, most emergency shelters in this country are usually overcrowded and understaffed. All levels of government, in their cost-cutting frenzy, were quick to knife these essential social services. Instead of returning to their violent partners, women who find themselves with little money and are unable to buy a house or rent an apartment should be assured of some measure of safety and autonomy by living in state-subsidized housing or co-ops.

Antisexist self-help groups for violent men are beneficial so long as the men are attending for the right reasons.

If the men are attending because they were told to change before returning home, or were caught by the police and ordered to take counselling by a judge, the success of these programs may be jeopardized. Only if there is a genuine willingness to change can the issues have any hope of being resolved. Examples of antisexist male self-help groups include AMEND, EMERGE, New Directions, and Vivre sans Violence.

The costs for these initiatives should not come from the limited amount of money available for the victims of violence. Shelters for women and other social services are also beneficial and necessary to cope with male violence against women. Instead, governments must adequately fund both initiatives.

The Need for Multiple Theories

All these theories have merit. Feminist theories, differential association, labelling, blocked opportunities, illegitimate opportunities, and the privileged position of the elite—all help explain social deviance, including crime.

Reactions to Social Deviance

Whether it be cheating on a sociology quiz or drinking under the legal age, any violation of norms invites reaction. Let's look first at reactions by others, and then at how people react to their own social deviance.

Sanctions

Responding to social deviance is vital to the welfare of groups, for groups must maintain their boundaries if they are to continue to claim a unique identity. Disapproval of social deviance, called **negative sanctions**, ranges from frowns and gossip for breaking folkways to imprisonment and capital punishment for breaking mores. **Positive sanctions**, in contrast—from smiles to formal awards—are used to reward people for conforming to norms. Getting a raise is a positive sanction, being fired a negative sanction. Getting an A in basic sociology is a positive sanction, getting an F a negative one.

Degradation Ceremonies

Sociologist Harold Garfinkel (1956) called formal attempts to mark an individual with the status of an outsider **degradation ceremonies**. The individual is called to account before the group, witnesses denounce him or her, the offender is pronounced guilty, and, most importantly in sociological terms, steps are taken to *strip the individual of his or her identity as a group member*. Following a court martial, for example, officers found guilty stand at attention before their peers while the insignia of rank are ripped from their uniforms. A priest may be defrocked before a congregation, a citizen forced to wear a prison uniform. These procedures indicate that the individual is no longer a member of the group—no longer able to command soldiers, to preach or offer sacraments, or to move about freely.

Imprisonment

Today, the prison experience follows a degradation ceremony involving a public trial and the public pronouncement that the person is "unfit to live among decent, law-abiding people" for some specified period of time.

> **Focus Question**
> What is the more important strategy for reducing crime—punishment or rehabilitation?

Alabama has brought back chain gangs. These men, chained together, do hard physical labour. Some chain gangs merely break rocks with sledge-hammers all day long. Do you think the purpose is retribution, deterrence, rehabilitation, or incapacitation?

There are substantial differences between the United States and Canada in terms of rates of violent crime and other forms of social deviance. According to James Henslin, between 1970 and 1995, the population of the United States grew by 28 percent, while the prison population grew 20 times as fast, increasing by 560 percent! If the number of prisoners had increased at the same rate as the general population, there would be about 250 000 people in prison, about one-fifth of the actual number. By contrast, the increase in the prison population in Canada between 1980 and 1990 was 12 percent or 81.1 to 92.1 per 100 000.

These differences in incarceration or imprisonment have been explained in a number of ways. A widely recognized explanation was offered by Seymour Martin Lipset (1990) who pointed to our counterrevolutionary history and its traditions of respect for institutional authority. The revolutionary history of the United States, by contrast, boasts of traditions respecting "rugged individualism" and irreverence for authority. What is more, the U.S. constitution guarantees every individual the right to life, to liberty, to the pursuit of happiness, and to bear arms. This makes for a lethal cultural cocktail. On the other hand, in Canada, the British North America Act promises peace, order, and good government while the Charter of Rights and Freedoms contains provisions for both individual and collective rights.

Canadian economic history has also been used to explain the cultural differences between the two countries. Canada has relied much more on large commercial enterprises such as the Canadian Pacific Railroad for nation-building, while major U.S. industries were frequently begun by individuals, often "robber barons" known to bend the rules on their way to fame and fortune. Because of the size of Canadian enterprises, our economic development relied more heavily on government subsidies than that of our U.S. capitalist counterparts. Therefore, the government and the police were active in the settlement of western Canada, in contrast to the "frontier spirit" of conquest over nature and people that symbolized U.S. westward expansion.

In Sum

Reactions to social deviants vary from such mild sanctions as frowns and stares to such severe responses as imprisonment and death. Some sanctions are formal— court hearings, for example—although most are informal, as when friends refuse to talk to each other. One sanction is to label someone a social deviant, which can have powerful consequences for the person's life, especially if the label closes off conforming activities and opens up socially deviant ones. The degradation ceremony, in which someone is publicly labelled "not one of us," is a powerful sanction. So is imprisonment. Official statistics must be viewed with caution, for they reflect a strong social class bias.

The Medicalization of Social Deviance: Mental Illness

Another way society deals with social deviance is to *medicalize* it. To medicalize something is to make it a medical matter, to classify it as a form of illness that properly belongs in the care of physicians.

Neither Mental nor Illness? For the past 100 years or so, especially since the time of Sigmund Freud (1856–1939), the Viennese physician who founded psychoanalysis, there has been a growing tendency toward the **medicalization of social deviance**. In this view, social deviance, including crime, is a sign of mental sickness. Rape, murder, stealing, cheating, and so on are external symptoms of internal disorders, consequences of a confused or tortured mind.

Thomas Szasz (1986, 1996), a renegade in his profession of psychiatry, argues that *mental illnesses are neither mental nor illnesses. They are simply problem behaviours.* Some forms of so-called mental illnesses have organic causes; that is, they are physical illnesses that result in unusual perceptions and behaviour. Some depression, for example, is caused by a chemical imbalance in the brain, which can be treated by drugs. The depression, however, may show itself as crying, long-term sadness, and the inability to become interested in anything. When a person becomes socially deviant in ways that disturb others, and these others cannot find a satisfying explanation for why the person is "like that," they conclude that a "sickness in the head" causes the inappropriate, unacceptable behaviour.

All of us have troubles. Some of us face a constant barrage of problems as we go through life. Most of us continue the struggle, encouraged by relatives and friends, motivated by job, family responsibilities, and life goals. Even when the odds seem hopeless, we carry on, not perfectly, but as best we can.

Some people, however, fail to cope well with the challenges of daily life. Overwhelmed, they become depressed, uncooperative, or hostile. Some strike out at others, while some, in Merton's terms, become retreatists and withdraw into their apartments or homes and won't come out. These are *behaviours, not mental illnesses*, stresses Szasz. They may be inappropriate coping devices, but they are coping devices, nevertheless, not mental illnesses. Thus, Szasz concludes that "mental illness" is a myth foisted on a naive public by a medical profession that uses pseudoscientific jargon to expand its area of control and force nonconforming people to accept society's definitions of "normal."

Szasz's extreme claim forces us to look anew at the forms of social deviance called mental illness. To explain behaviour that people find bizarre, he directs our attention not to "things hidden deep within the subconscious," but, instead, to how people learn such behaviours. To ask "What is the origin of inappropriate or bizarre behaviour?" then becomes similar to asking "Why do some women steal?" "Why do some men rape?" "Why do some teenagers cuss their parents and stalk out of the room slamming doors?" *The answers depend on people's particular experiences in life, not some illness in their mind.* In short, some sociologists find Szasz's renegade analysis refreshing because it indicates that *social experiences,* not some illness of the mind, underlie bizarre behaviours—as well as social deviance in general.

The Homeless Mentally Ill

Jamie was sitting on the low wall surrounding the landscaped, open-air eating area of an exclusive restaurant. She appeared unaware of the stares elicited by her many layers of mismatched clothing, her dirty face, and the ever-present shopping cart overflowing with her meagre possessions.

Every once in a while Jamie would pause, concentrate, and point to the street, slowly moving her finger horizontally. I asked her what she was doing.

"I'm directing traffic," she replied. "I control where the cars go. Look, that one turned right there," she said, now withdrawing her finger.

"Really?" I said.

After a while she confided that her cart talked to her.

"Really?" I said again.

"Yes," she replied. "You can hear it, too." At that, she pushed the shopping cart a bit.

"Did you hear that?" she asked.

When I shook my head, she demonstrated again. Then it hit me. She was referring to the squeaking wheels!

I nodded.

When I left Jamie, she was looking toward the sky, her finger upraised, for, as she told me, she also controlled the flight of airplanes.

To most of us, Jamie's behaviour and thinking are bizarre. They simply do not match any reality we know. Jamie might be mentally ill. Some organic problem, such as a chemical imbalance in her brain, might underlie her behaviour. But perhaps not. Could you or I become Jamie?

Suppose for a bitter moment that you are homeless and have to live on the streets. You have no money, no place to

The homeless are located at the bottom of the Canadian social class ladder. Why do you think a society as wealthy as Canada has homeless people?

sleep, no bathroom, do not know *if* you are going to eat, much less where, have no friends or anyone you can trust, and live with the constant threat of rape and violence. Do you think this might be enough to drive you "over the edge"?

Consider just the problems involved in not having a place to bathe. (Shelters are often so dangerous that the homeless prefer to take their chances sleeping in public settings.) At first, you will try to wash in the toilets of gas stations, bars, the bus station, or a shopping centre. But you are dirty, and people stare when you enter, and they call the management when they see you wash your feet in the sink. You are thrown out, and told in no uncertain terms to never come back. So you get dirtier and dirtier. Eventually you come to think of being dirty as a fact of life. Soon, maybe, you don't even care. No longer do the stares bother you— at least not as much.

No one will talk to you, and you withdraw more and more into yourself. You begin to build a fantasy life. You talk openly to yourself. People stare, but so what? They stare anyway. Besides, they are no longer important to you.

How long would it take us to engage in bizarre behaviours if we were homeless? What if we were homeless and hopeless for years? The point is that *just being on the streets can cause mental illness*—or whatever we want to label socially inappropriate behaviours that we find difficult to classify (McCarthy, 1983; Belcher, 1988; R. K. Nelson, 1989). *Homelessness and mental illness are reciprocal:* Just as "mental illness" can cause homelessness, so the trials of being homeless, of living on cold, hostile streets, can lead to unusual and unacceptable thinking and behaviours.

The Need for a More Humane Approach

As Durkheim (1895/1938, pp. 68–69) pointed out, social deviance is inevitable—even in a group of saints.

> Imagine a society of saints…. Crimes, properly so called, will there be unknown; but faults which appear [invisible] to the layman will create there the same scandal that the ordinary offense does in ordinary [society].

With social deviants inevitable, one measure of a society is how it treats them. Social class position remains an important predictor for how we treat our socially deviant citizens. White-collar criminals continue to get by with a slap on the wrist while street criminals are severely punished. Taking refuge in shelters and cardboard boxes in city streets is not a humane answer to homelessness. Neither is enforcing arrest policies the answer for violence against women. Although no one has *the* answer, it does not take much reflection to see that there are more humane approaches than these.

With social deviance inevitable, the larger issues are how to protect people from socially deviant behaviours that are harmful to themselves or others, to tolerate those that are not, and to develop systems of fairer treatment for social deviants. In the absence of the fundamental changes that would bring about a truly equitable social system, most efforts are, unfortunately, Band-Aid work. What is needed is a more humane social system, one that would prevent the social inequalities that were the focus of Chapters 6 to 9.

Summary and Review

GAINING A SOCIOLOGICAL PERSPECTIVE ON SOCIAL DEVIANCE

How do sociologists view social deviance?

From a sociological perspective, **social deviance**—defined as the violation of norms—is relative. What people consider socially deviant varies from one culture to another and from group to group within the same society. Consequently, as symbolic interactionists stress, it is not the act itself, but the reactions to the act, that make something socially deviant. All groups develop systems of **social control** to punish social deviants, those who violate its norms. pp. 382–383.

How do biological, psychological, and sociological explanations of social deviance differ?

To explain why people deviate, biologists and psychologists look for reasons *within* the individual, such as **genetic predispositions** or **personality disorders**. Sociologists, in contrast, look for explanations *outside* the individual, in social relations. pp. 382–383.

THE SYMBOLIC INTERACTIONIST PERSPECTIVE

How do symbolic interactionists explain social deviance?

Symbolic interactionists have developed several theories to explain social deviance such as **crime** (the violation of norms written into law). According to **differential association** theory, people learn to deviate from associating with others. **Labelling theory** focuses on how labels (names, reputations) help to propel people into or divert people from social deviance. Many people commit socially deviant acts and still think of themselves as conformists. They apparently use five **techniques of neutralization**. Studies of prostitutes show three ways in which the self-concept is involved in socially deviant acts. In **primary social deviance**, the acts are fleeting and have little effect on the self-concept. In **secondary social deviance**, people incorporate their socially deviant acts into their self-concept. In **tertiary social deviance**, acts commonly considered socially deviant are relabelled as normal. Although most people resist being labelled socially deviant, some embrace social deviance. pp. 383–388.

THE FUNCTIONALIST PERSPECTIVE

How do functionalists explain social deviance?

Functionalists point out that social deviance, including criminal acts, is functional for society. Functions include affirming norms and promoting social unity and social change. According to **strain theory**, societies socialize their members into desiring **cultural goals**, but many people are unable to achieve these goals in socially acceptable ways—by **institutionalized means**. Social deviants, then, are people who either give up on the goals or use socially deviant means to attain them. Merton identified five types of responses to cultural goals and institutionalized means: conformity, innovation, ritualism, retreatism, and rebellion. Illegitimate opportunity theory stresses that some people have easier access to illegal means of achieving goals. pp. 388–391.

THE CONFLICT PERSPECTIVE

How do conflict theorists explain social deviance?

Conflict theorists see power and social inequality as the primary characteristics of society. They stress that the state's machinery of social control, which includes the **criminal justice system**—the police, courts, and prisons that deal with the accused—represents the interests of the wealthy and powerful, a group that determines the basic laws essential to preserving its own power. p. 392.

Are official statistics on crime reliable?

The conclusions of both symbolic interactionists (that the police operate with a large measure of discretion) and conflict theorists (that the legal system is controlled by the capitalist class) cast doubt on the accuracy of official crime statistics. pp. 392–393.

FEMINIST THEORIES AND MALE VIOLENCE AGAINST WOMEN

Why do men commit acts of violence against women?

When it comes to male violence against women, virtually all feminist theorists agree that men assault their female partners to maintain control over them and, if they happen to live in a relationship, their "domestic" situation. Control over women has been measured as (1) sexual fidelity, (2) obedience, (3) respect, (4) loyalty, (5) dependency, and (6) sexual access. p. 394.

What can be done about male violence against women?

Four strategies for coping with male violence against women are: (1) training the police to identify and charge offenders; (2) good job creation strategies; (3) social services such as shelters and co-op housing; and (4) antisexist male collectives. DeKeseredy and Hinch, for example, argue that economic policy reforms such as paid work leaves, flexible hours (flextime), pay equity, and improving the quality of work available to disadvantaged people, to name just a few, can lower the rate of male violence against women. pp. 394–395.

REACTIONS TO SOCIAL DEVIANCE

How do societies react to social deviance?

Deviance results in **negative sanctions**, acts of disapproval ranging from frowns to capital punishment. Some groups use **degradation ceremonies** to impress on their members that certain violations will not be tolerated. pp. 395–396.

What is the *medicalization of social deviance*?

The medical profession has attempted to **medicalize** many forms of social deviance, claiming that they represent mental illnesses. Thomas Szasz disagrees, claiming that they are just problem behaviours, not mental illnesses. Research on homeless people illustrates how problems in living can lead to bizarre behaviour and thinking. pp. 396–398.

THE NEED FOR A MORE HUMANE APPROACH

Deviance is inevitable, so the larger issues are how to protect people from social deviance that harms themselves and others, to tolerate social deviance that is not harmful, and to develop systems of fairer treatment for social deviants. p. 398.

Critical Thinking Questions

1. According to Robert K. Merton, when people lack the opportunities to legitimately pursue culturally approved goals, they may turn to crime. Two ways of circumventing this are to (1) teach people to be satisfied with less and (2) provide more legitimate opportunities. If you alone had the means to decrease crime in Canadian society, which strategy would you pursue and why?

2. According to one of the authors of this book (Glenday), Canadian criminologists have largely ignored the link between unemployment and property crimes in Canada. Instead, they have focused on more "sophisticated" theories that suggest "dysfunctional family backgrounds" as the cause for property crimes or differential association and labelling theories. Why do you think Canadian criminologists have ignored the link between unemployment and property crimes?

3. Probation officers and social workers usually want to identify "young offenders" as early as possible so that they may be "treated" before their "socially deviant" character is firmly established. Is this the right or wrong approach to take for young offenders?

Key Terms

crime 383
criminal justice system 392
cultural goals 389
degradation ceremonies 395
differential association 384
genetic predispositions 382
illegitimate opportunity structures 391
institutionalized means 389
labelling theory 385
medicalization of social deviance 396
negative sanctions 395
official social deviance 392
patriarchy 394
personality disorders 383

pluralistic theory of social control 389
positive sanctions 395
primary social deviance 386
secondary social deviance 387
social control 382
social deviance 383
social order 382
stigma 383
strain theory 389
street crime 382
techniques of neutralization 386
tertiary social deviance 387
white-collar crime 391

Weblinks

All URLs listed are current as of the printing of this book. URLs are often changed. Please check our Web site **www.abacon.com/ henslin** for updates.

Journal of Prisoners on Prisons: Front Page

www.jpp.org/
A prisoner-written, academically oriented journal, whose purpose is "to bring the knowledge and experience of the incarcerated to bear upon more academic arguments and concerns and to inform public discourse about the current state of our carceral institutions."

Shadows

sacrilege.com/~shadows/
Focuses on social deviance in a manner different from that of the average academic site. "This page exists to promote a more sophisticated understanding of society as a vast array of systems of shared meanings, each with its own internal logic; an understanding of society that is not threatened by deviant belief systems or social norms, but which seeks to understand them. ..."

Internet Crime Archives

www.mayhem.net/Crime/archives.html

Information on all manner of illegal deviant behaviour.

American Society of Criminology

www.asc41.com/

This is an international organization concerned with criminology, embracing scholarly, scientific, and professional knowledge concerning the etiology, prevention, control, and treatment of crime and delinquency.

Art Crimes: The Writing on the Wall

www.graffiti.org/

A gallery of graffiti art from cities around the world, providing cultural information and resources and aiming to preserve and document the constantly disappearing paintings. "We do not advocate breaking the law, but we think art belongs in public spaces and that more legal walls should be made available for this fascinating art form."

Population, Urbanization, and the Environment

Chapter 17

Learning Outcomes

After you have studied this chapter, you will be able to

■ describe the feminist viewpoint on the population debate

■ explain why the least industrialized nations have so many children

■ understand the different models of urban growth

■ describe the main categories of Canada's immigration policy

■ contrast the environmental with the traditional sociological view of society

The image still haunts me. There stood Celia, age 30, her distended stomach obvious proof that her 13th child was on its way. Her oldest was only 14 years old! A mere boy by our standards, he had already gone as far in school as he ever would. Every morning, he joined the men to work in the fields. Every evening around twilight, we saw him return home, exhausted from hard labour in the sun.

My wife and I, who were living in Colima, Mexico, had eaten dinner in Celia and Angel's home, which clearly proclaimed the family's poverty. A thatched hut consisting of only a single room served as home for all 14 members of the family. At night, the parents and younger children crowded into a double bed, while the eldest boy slept in a hammock. As in many other homes in the village, the others slept on mats spread on the dirt floor.

The home was meagrely furnished. It had only a gas stove, a cabinet where Celia stored her cooking utensils and dishes, and a table. There being no closets, clothes were hung on pegs in the walls. There were no chairs, not even one. This really startled us. The family was so poor that they could not afford even a single chair.

Celia beamed as she told us how much she looked forward to the birth of her next child. Could she really mean it? It was hard to imagine that any woman would want to be in her situation.

Yet Celia meant every word. She was as full of delightful anticipation as she had been with her first child—and with all the others in between.

Source: Based on the personal experience of James Henslin.

Population in Global Perspective

How could Celia have wanted so many children—especially when she lived in such poverty? Celia's story takes us into the heart of **demography**, the study of the size, composition, growth, and distribution of human populations. It brings us face to face with the question: Will our planet be able to support its growing population? Or is chronic famine and mass starvation the sorry fate that awaits most of us in this millennium? Let's look at how this concern began, and then at what today's demographers say about it.

A Planet with No Space to Enjoy Life?

Sometimes the cultural diffusion of a simple item can have far-reaching consequences on nations. An example is the potato, which the Spanish Conquistadors found among the natives of the Andes. When the Spanish brought this food back to Europe, the people there came to gradually accept it. Eventually, the potato became the principal food of the lower classes. With more abundant food, fertility increased, and the death rate dropped. As a result, Europe's population soared, almost doubling during the 1700s (McKeown, 1977).

This rapid growth alarmed Thomas Malthus (1766–1834), an English Protestant theologian. He saw it as a sign of coming doom. In 1798, he wrote a book that became world-famous, *An Essay on the Principle of Population*. In it, Malthus proposed what became known as the **Malthus theorem**. He argued that while population grows geometrically (from 2 to 4 to 8 to 16 and so forth), the food supply increases only arithmetically (from 1 to 2 to 3 to 4 and so on). This meant, he claimed, that if births go unchecked, the population of a country, or even of the world, will outstrip its food supply. War and famine would be the inevitable result.

The New Malthusians

Was Malthus right? One group, which can be called the "New Malthusians," is convinced that today's situation is at least as grim as, if not grimmer than, Malthus ever imagined. Figure 17.1 shows how fast the world's population is growing. *In just the time it takes you to read this chapter, another 15 000 to 20 000 babies will be born!*

The New Malthusians point out that the world's population is following an **exponential growth curve**. To illustrate, sociologist William Faunce (1981) told a parable about a man who saved a rich man's life. The rich man was grateful and said that he wanted to reward the man for his heroic deed.

The man replied he would like his reward to be spread out over a four-week period, with each day's amount being twice what he received on the preceding day. He also said he would be happy to receive only one penny on the first day. The rich man immediately handed over the penny and congratulated himself on how cheaply he had gotten by. At the end of the first week, the rich man owed only $1.27….On the twenty-first day, however, the rich man was surprised to find that the total had grown to $20 971.51. When the twenty-eighth day arrived the rich man was shocked to discover that he owed $1 342 177.28 for that day alone and that the total reward had jumped to $2 684 354.56!

In earlier generations, large farm families were common. Having many children was functional—there were many hands to help with crops, food production, and food preparation. As the country industrialized and urbanized, this changed—children became expensive and nonproducing. Consequently, the size of families shrank as we entered Stage 3 of the *demographic transition* (see p. 406), and today Canadian families with 10 children are practically non-existent.

Figure 17.1 How Fast Is the World's Population Growing?

Source: "Population Update," January 2000, *Population Today, 28,* 1.

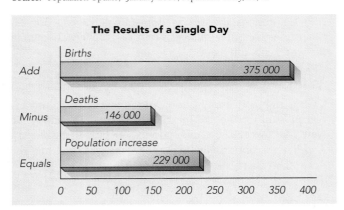

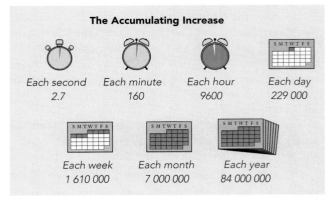

This is precisely what alarms the New Malthusians. Figure 17.2 shows why they think the day of reckoning is just around the corner. They point out that it took all of human history for the world's population to reach its first billion around 1800. It then took about 130 years (1930) to add the second billion. Just 30 years later (1960), the world population hit three billion. The time needed to reach the fourth billion was cut in half, to only 15 years (1975). Right now, the world population has reached six billion (Haub & Yinger, 1994; Cohen, 1996).

The Anti-Malthusians

It does seem obvious, and no one wants to live in a shoulder-to-shoulder world and fight for scraps. How, then, can anyone argue with the New Malthusians?

A much more optimistic group of demographers, whom we can call the "Anti-Malthusians," claim that such an image of the future is ridiculous. Anti-Malthusians, such as economist Julian Simon (1992, 1996) and anthropologist Steven Mosher (1994, 1997), argue people simply do not blindly reproduce until there is no room left.

The Anti-Malthusians believe that Europe's **demographic transition** provides a more accurate picture of the future. This transition is diagrammed in Figure 17.3. During most of its history, Europe was in Stage 1. High birth rates offset by high death rates led to a fairly stable population. Then came Stage 2, the "population explosion" that so upset Malthus. Europe's population surged because birth rates remained high, while death rates went down. Finally, Europe made the transition to Stage 3—the

Figure 17.2 World Population Growth over 2000 Years

Source: Adapted from Piotrow (1973, p. 4).

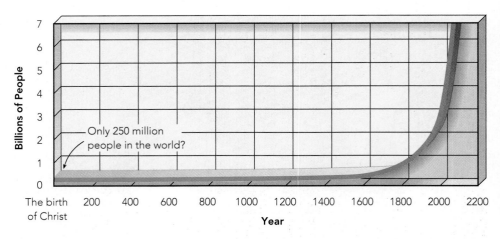

population stabilized as people brought their birth rates into line with their lower death rates.

This, continue the Anti-Malthusians, is precisely what will happen in the least industrialized nations. Their current surge in growth simply indicates that they have reached the second stage of the demographic transition. Hybrid seed and modern medicine imported from the most industrialized nations have cut their death rates, but their birth rates remain high. When they move into the third stage, we will wonder what all the fuss was about.

Some Anti-Malthusians go even further (Mosher, 1997). As shown by the far right part of Figure 17.3, they foresee a "demographic free fall." They predict that the world's population will peak at about seven billion around the year 2030, then begin a long descent. As countries industrialize women become more educated, postpone marriage, and reduce the number of children they bear. The result will be **population shrinkage**.

The shrinking population of Europe—Germany and Italy already fill more coffins than cradles—has begun to alarm policymakers. Closer to home, the demographic picture of

Quebec society over the past 50 years illustrates this Anti-Malthusian claim. Quebec went from having the highest birth rate in the country to the lowest in just two generations. The two main concerns for Anti-Malthusians are not enough young workers to support a rapidly growing elderly population, and race-ethnic problems that develop as workers from other parts of the world migrate to depopulating countries. Coming as a surprise to almost everyone, this fourth stage of the demographic transition has also begun to hit Asia: Japan and South Korea do not produce enough children to maintain their populations (Chesnais, 1997). In short, stress the Anti-Malthusians, the world's problem will not be a population explosion, but *population shrinkage*—too few children in the world, not too many.

Who Is Correct?

Who is right? It simply is too early to tell. Like the proverbial pessimists who see the glass of water half empty, the New Malthusians interpret population growth negatively. And like the optimists who see the same glass half full, the Anti-Malthusians view the figures positively.

Figure 17.3
The Demographic Transition

Note: The standard demographic transition is depicted by Stages 1–3. Stage 4 has recently been suggested by some Anti-Malthusians.

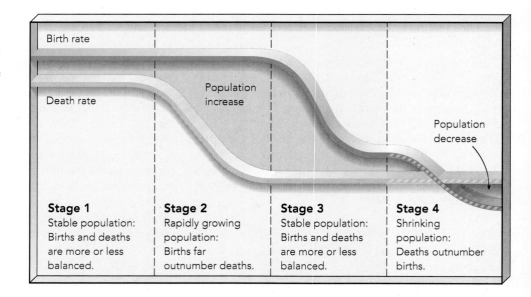

However, in addition to the Mathusian debate, we should consider another perspective, namely feminism and population control.

Feminism and the Population Debate

Feminists rejected the "solutions" favoured by the New Malthusians to limit population growth in the industrializing and least industrialized countries. The New Malthusians proposed, for example, forced sterilization of women in the industrializing and least industrialized countries. This idea and others like it were rightly analyzed as patriarchal policies. That is, these heavy-handed decisions, thought up by governments, are mainly rules created by older men to be imposed on younger men, women, and children. Feminists objected to these policies because they deprive women of the freedom to make decisions for themselves—decisions about their own bodies.

The feminist perspective on the topic of population control begins with the emancipation of women from patriarchal decision-making. They argue that women's rights, especially the right to decide about one's reproductive future, must be recognized as basic human rights. Unlike their Victorian predecessors who rejected contraception, the contemporary feminist perspective recognizes the importance of birth control.

How to achieve population control? Provide women with economic opportunities, education about birth control, and rights. Women who work, especially in cities, generally want to limit the number of children they will bear. This is a "policy" that does not have to be imposed; it simply involves making available opportunities for employment. There is strong evidence to support the argument that educating women is another important step. Women who can read are better able to care for their children, leading to lowered infant mortality rates and lower fertility rates.

For most feminists, the course of action is clear. Empower women by giving them opportunities to find and get meaningful employment, provide free public education, and enshrine women's rights in national and international legislation, and they will voluntarily lower their fertility.

> **Focus Question**
> What is the feminist viewpoint on the population debate?

Why Are People Starving?

Pictures of starving children haunt us. We live in such abundance, while these children and their parents starve before our very eyes. Why don't these children have enough food?

The basic question is this: Does the world produce enough food to feed everyone? Here, the Anti-Malthusians make a point that seems irrefutable. As Figure 17.4 shows, *the amount of food produced for each person in the world is now much more than it was in 1950*. Although the

Photos of starving people, such as this mother and child, haunt Canadians and other citizens of the most industrialized nations. Many of us wonder why, when some are starving, we should live in the midst of such abundance, often overeating and even casually scrapping excess food. The text discusses reasons for such unconscionable disparities.

Figure 17.4 How Much Food Does the World Produce per Person?

Note: 1979–1981=100. Years 1975–1991 are UN figures; years prior to 1975 have been recomputed from Simon to 1979–1981 base; years beyond 1993 are the authors' projections.

Sources: Simon (1981, p. 58); *United Nations Statistical Yearbook,* 1985–1986, Table 7, and 1990–1991, Table 4; *Statistical Abstract,* 1999, Table 1394 and earlier years.

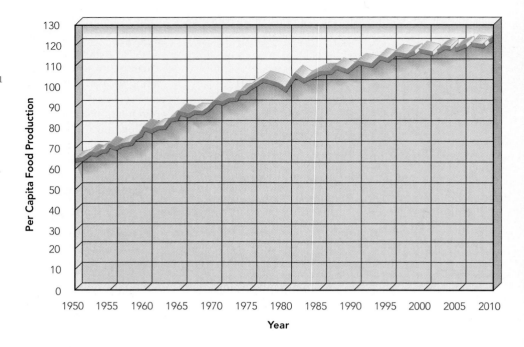

world's population has more than doubled during this time, improved seeds and fertilization have made more food available for every person on earth.

Then why do people die of hunger? From Figure 17.4, we can conclude that some countries produce more food than their people can consume, others less than they need for survival. In short, the cause of starvation is an imbalance between supply and demand. It is important to understand the underlying cause of such human misery, some of which could certainly be alleviated by transferring food from nations that have a surplus.

One of the most notable examples is that at the same time as widespread famine is ravishing West Africa, Canadian farmers are having trouble selling their grain on the global market. The result: The lack of adequate incomes from these cash crops has forced many Western Canadian family farmers to give up and leave for the city.

Africa has been the site of recent pockets of starvation. The images presented to us in the media leave the impression that Africa is overpopulated. Why else would all those people be starving? The truth, however, is far different. Africa has 22 percent of the earth's land surface, but only 10.5 percent of the earth's population (Nsamenang, 1992). In fact, Africa contains some of the world's largest untapped land suitable for agriculture. The reason for famines in Africa, then, certainly is not too many people living on too little land (Bender & Smith, 1997). Rather, these famines are due to two primary causes: outmoded farming techniques and political instability—revolutions and other warfare—that disrupt harvests and food distribution.

Population Growth

Even if famines are due to a maldistribution of food rather than world overpopulation, the fact remains that the least industrialized nations are growing *15 times faster* than the most industrialized nations. At these rates, it will take 564 years for the average most industrialized nation to double its population, but just 38 years for the average least industrialized nation to do so (Haub & Cornelius, 1997). Why do those who can least afford it have so many children?

Why the Least Industrialized Nations Have So Many Children

To understand why the population is increasing so much more rapidly in the least industrialized nations, let's figure out why Celia is so happy about having her 13th child. Let us consider three reasons that bearing many children plays a central role in the lives of millions of poor people around the world.

First of all, in the least industrialized nations, the more children a woman bears, the more she is thought to have achieved the purpose for which she was born—motherhood. Similarly, a man proves his manhood by fathering children. The more children he fathers, especially sons, the better—for through them his name lives on.

Second, the community views children as a sign of God's blessing and encourages a couple to have many children. The barren woman, not the woman with a dozen children, is to be pitied.

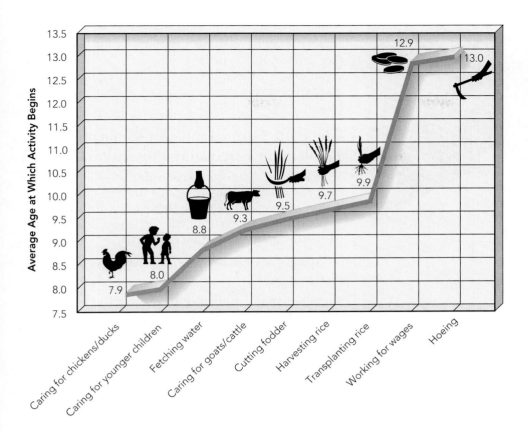

Figure 17.5 Why the Poor Need Children

Surviving children are an economic asset in the least industrialized nations. This figure, based on a survey in Indonesia, shows that boys and girls can be net income earners for their families by the age of nine or ten.

Source: U.N. Fund for Population Activities.

Third, poor people in the least industrialized nations consider children economic assets. They have no social insurance or medical and employment insurance. As a result, when parents become sick or too old to work—or when no work is to be found—the more children they have, the broader their base of support. Moreover, like the eldest son of Celia and Angel, children begin contributing to the family income at a young age. Figure 17.5 illustrates how children can be net income earners for a least industrialized nations family. For example, consider the following incident, reported by a government worker in India:

> Thaman Singh [a very poor man, a water carrier] … welcomed me inside his home, gave me a cup of tea, and said: "You were trying to convince me in 1960 that I shouldn't have any more sons. Now, you see, I have six sons and two daughters and I sit at home in leisure. They are grown up and they bring me money. *You told me I was a poor man and couldn't support a large family. Now, you see, because of my large family I am a rich man*" (Mamdani, 1973, italics added).

Feminists offer a different view of why women in the poor nations bear so many children. They stress that in these cultures men dominate women in all spheres of life, including that of reproduction. Feminists argue that Celia has internalized values that support male dominance. For example, in Latin America *machismo* is common. This emphasis on male virility and dominance includes fathering many children as a means of achieving status in the community. From a feminist perspective, then, the reason poor people have so many children is that men control women's reproductive choices.

Estimating Population Growth: The Three Demographic Variables

It is important to accurately project the future of human populations. Educators want to know how many schools to build. Manufacturers want to anticipate changes in demand for their products. The government needs to know how many doctors, engineers, and executives to train, as well as how many people will be paying taxes and how many young people will be available to fight a war.

To project population trends, demographers use three **demographic variables**: fertility, mortality, and net migration.

Fertility. The **fertility rate** is the number of children the average woman bears. A term sometimes confused with fertility is **fecundity**, the number of children that women are *capable* of bearing. The fecundity of women around the world is around 20 children each. Their fertility rate, however (the actual number of children they bear), is much

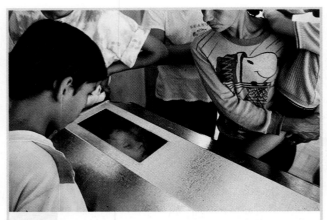

Although all humans face mortality (the second demographic variable), the conditions of death vary from one culture to another. In the most industrialized nations, the death of a child is rare, whereas in the least industrialized nations it is common. Shown here are mourners at the funeral of a child in South America.

lower. The world's overall fertility rate is 3.0, which means that the average woman in the world bears 3 children during her lifetime. At 1.8, the fertility rate of Canadian women is considerably less.

To compute the fertility rate of a country, demographers figure the country's **crude birth rate**, the annual number of live births per 1000 population.

Mortality.   The second demographic variable, **crude death rate**, is the number of deaths per 1000 population.

Migration.   The third major demographic variable is the **net migration rate**, the difference between the number of *immigrants* (people moving in) and *emigrants* (people moving out) per 1000 population. To understand migration, we need to look at both *push* and *pull* factors. The push factors are the things people want to escape—poverty, the lack of religious and political freedoms, even political persecution. The pull factors are the magnets that draw people to a new land, such as a chance for higher wages and better jobs.

Around the world, the flow of migration is from the least industrialized nations to the more industrialized countries (Kalish, 1994). After "migrant paths" are established, immigration often accelerates as networks of kin and friends become further magnets that attract more people from the same nation—and even from the same villages.

Table 17.1 shows the demographic profile of Canada from the first census taken in 1851 to the present. Look at the rapid increase in births just after World War II, signalling the beginning of the "baby boom" generation. Also take note of the final three periods on the table (1986–1991, 1991–1996, and 1996–2001). The number of

deaths increased due to an aging population, while the number of births remained stagnant over the 1986–1996 time period but *declined significantly* over the last five years (1996–2001). Immigration to Canada is the key to supporting population growth and with it sustaining our standard of living.

The Basic Demographic Equation and Problems in Forecasting Population Growth

The total of the three demographic variables—fertility, mortality, and net migration—gives us a country's **growth rate**, the net change after people have been added to and subtracted from a population. What demographers call the **basic demographic equation** is quite simple:

Growth rate = Births − Deaths + Net migration

With such a simple equation, it might seem that it also would be a simple matter to project a country's future population. But social factors—economic booms and busts, wars, plagues, and famines—push rates up or down.

The primary factor that influences a country's growth rate is its rate of industrialization. *In every country that industrializes the growth rate declines.* Not only does industrialization open up economic opportunities, but it also makes children more expensive. Significantly, the basis for conferring status also changes—from having children to attaining education and displaying material wealth. People like Celia and Angel then begin to see life differently, and their motivation to have many children drops sharply. Not knowing how rapidly industrialization will progress or how quickly changes in values and reproductive behaviour will follow adds to the difficulty of making accurate projections.

Because of such complications, demographers play it safe by making several projections of population growth (Haub, 1997). For example, what will the population of Canada be in the year 2010? Perhaps we will be at **zero population growth**, with every 1000 women giving birth to 2100 children. (The extra 100 children make up for those who do not survive.) Will a larger proportion of women go to university? (The more education women have, the fewer children they bear.) How will immigration change during the coming years? Will AIDS be brought under control? Will some other horrible disease appear? What will happen to the global economy?

The Challenge of the Twenty-First Century

Let's look at a different aspect of population, where people live. Since the world is rapidly becoming urban, we shall concentrate on urban trends and urban life.

Table 17.1 Demographic Profile of Canada from the First Census in 1851–2001 (thousands)[1]

Period	Total Population Growth[2]	Births	Deaths	Immigration	Emigration	Population of Canada at the End of the Period
1851–1861	793	1 281	670	352	170	3230
1861–1871	460	1370	760	260	410	3689
1871–1881	636	1480	790	350	404	4325
1881–1891	508	1524	870	680	826	4833
1891–1901	538	1548	880	250	380	5371
1901–1911	1835	1925	900	1550	740	7207
1911–1921	1581	2340	1070	1400	1089	8788
1921–1931	1589	2420	1060	1200	970	10 377
1931–1941	1130	2294	1072	149	241	11 507
1941–1951	2141	3186	1214	548	379	13 648
1951–1956	2071	2106	633	783	185	16 081
1956–1961	2157	2362	687	760	278	18 238
1961–1966	1777	2249	731	539	280	20 015
1966–1971	1553	1856	766	890	427	21 568
1971–1976	1488	1755	824	1053	496	23 550
1976–1981	1371	1820	843	771	377	24 820
1981–1986	1280	1872	885	677	384	26 101
1986–1991	1930	1933	946	1189	256	28 031
1991–1996	1641	1936	1027	1170	480	29 672
1996–2001	1409	1660	1114	1137	321	31 081

1. Includes Newfoundland since 1951.
2. Figures are approximate.

Source: Statistics Canada, *Annual Demographic Statistics*, 2001 (corrected), catalogue no. 91-213-XPB.

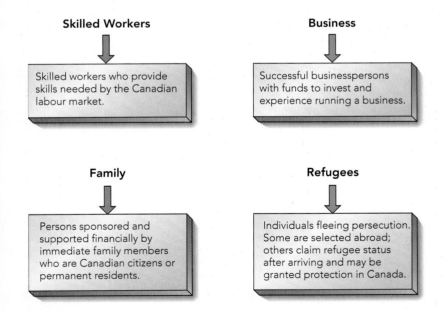

Skilled Workers

Skilled workers who provide skills needed by the Canadian labour market.

Business

Successful businesspersons with funds to invest and experience running a business.

Family

Persons sponsored and supported financially by immediate family members who are Canadian citizens or permanent residents.

Refugees

Individuals fleeing persecution. Some are selected abroad; others claim refugee status after arriving and may be granted protection in Canada.

Figure 17.6 How Are Immigrants Chosen?

Source: Based on data taken from the Heritage Canada Web site (**www.cic.gc.ca/english/immigr/ihav-e.html**).

"The Mysterious Case of the Missing Girls" could have been the title of this box. Around the globe, for every 100 girls about 105 boys are born. In China, however, for every 100 girl babies, there are 111 boy babies. With China's huge population, this imbalance indicates that about 400 000 baby girls are missing each year. What is happening to them?

The answer is rooted in deep sexism—the preference for boy babies. To ensure the birth of boys, for millennia people have experimented with a variety of folk techniques, none of which has worked. Only in recent years, with the development of technology that separates semen, has a technique become available, which is 80 percent effective. China, however, is not technologically advanced. Have the Chinese, then, stumbled on some effective folk technique?

The answer points in a different direction—to the ancient practice of *female infanticide*, the killing of girl babies. When a Chinese woman goes into labour, village midwives sometimes grab a bucket of water. If the newborn is a girl, she is plunged into the water before she can draw her first breath.

At the root of China's infanticide is economics. The people are extremely poor, and they have no pensions. When parents can no longer work, sons support them. In contrast, a daughter must be married off, at great expense, and at that point her obligations transfer to her husband and his family.

In the past few years, the percentage of boy babies has grown. The reason, again, is economics, but this time with a new twist. As China opened the door to capitalism, travel and trade opened up—but primarily to men, for it is not thought appropriate for women to travel alone. Thus men find themselves in a better position to bring profits home to the family—one more push toward preferring male children.

By no means is female infanticide limited to China. Although the British banned this practice in India in 1870, it continues. Western technology has even been put to work. Many Indian women use amniocentesis to learn the sex of their child, and then decide whether to abort. In 99.9 percent of these abortions, the fetus is female.

This use of amniocentesis for sex selection led to a public outcry in India. The indignation was not due to outrage about female infanticide, however; nor was it due to some anti-abortion movement. Rather, the public became indignant when a physician mistakenly gave the parents wrong information and aborted a *male* baby!

It is likely that the preference for boys, and the consequent female infanticide, will not disappear until the social structures that perpetuate sexism are dismantled. This will not take place until women hold as much power as men, a time that—if it ever occurs—apparently lies far in the future.

Sources: Lagaipa (1990); McGowan (1991); Polumbaum (1992); Renteln (1992); Greenhalgh & Li (1995).

Thinking Critically about Social Controversy

What Are the Prospects for Population Growth in Twenty-First Century?

There is no doubt that Malthus' pessimistic predictions were wrong—for his time, that is. Malthus could not foresee the new technology of the Industrial Revolution, which created new wealth and caused national products to skyrocket.

But what about today, as we enter the twenty-first century? Economist Paul Kennedy (1993) says that our greatest challenge is how to use modern technology to free the least industrialized nations from "the growing Malthusian trap of malnutrition, starvation, resource depletion, unrest, enforced migration, and armed conflict—developments that will also endanger the richer nations, if less directly."

The past, unfortunately, may not provide guidelines for the future. During the last century, both the population and technology exploded in the same place, the British Isles. Today, however, technology is exploding in one part of the world, population in another. In the most industrialized nations, which have the technology explosion, population is slow-growing and in some places even declining. The areas with the population explosion, however, find themselves with "limited technological resources, very few scientists and skilled workers, inadequate investment in research and development ... and cultural and ideological prejudices are much more tilted against change than they were in the England of the Industrial Revolution" (Kennedy, 1993). To complicate matters even more, adds Kennedy, overgrazing and erosion are also concentrated in these countries, reducing their agricultural resources just as their populations are mushrooming.

For Your Consideration

As we move into the twenty-first century, then, we face a severe challenge—with the fate of millions, if not billions, of people hanging in the balance. Considering the materials so far in this chapter, do you think we should open our borders to anyone and everyone who wants to immigrate? Or would closing them entirely and concentrating on taking care of our own problems be a better approach? Do you think the population problem is so severe that the most industrialized nations should subsidize world condom distribution? Or pay people to be sterilized? What solutions do feminists offer? Finally, how do you think the most industrialized nations can harness their vast technologies to benefit today's global community?

Urbanization

The Development of Cities

Perhaps as early as 7000 to 10 000 years ago people built small cities with massive defensive walls, such as the biblically famous Jericho (Homblin, 1973).

The key to the origin of cities is the development of more efficient agriculture (Lenski & Lenski, 1987). Only when farming produces a surplus can some people stop being food producers and gather in cities to spend time in other pursuits. The invention of the plow between 5000 and 6000 years ago created widespread agricultural surpluses, stimulating the development of towns and cities (Curwin & Hart, 1961). A **city**, in fact, can be defined as a place in which a large number of people are permanently based and do not produce their own food.

Most early cities were tiny by comparison with those of today, merely a collection of a few thousand people in agricultural centres or on major trade routes. The most notable exceptions are two cities that reached one million for a brief period of time before they declined—Changan in China about A.D. 800 and Baghdad in Persia about A.D. 900 (Chandler & Fox, 1974). Even Athens at the peak of its power in the fifth century B.C. had fewer than 200 000 inhabitants. Rome, at its peak, may have had a million or more (Flanagan, 1990).

Urbanization, Metropolises, and Megalopolises

Although cities are not new to the world scene, urbanization is. **Urbanization** refers to masses of people moving to cities, giving cities a growing influence on society. Urbanization is worldwide. Just 200 years ago, in 1800, only 3 percent of the world's population lived in cities (Hauser & Schnore, 1965). Today about 45 percent do: about 75 percent of people in the industrialized world and 37 percent of those who live in the least industrialized nations (Haub & Cornelius, 1999).

To understand the city's attraction, we need to consider the "pull" of urban life. Due to its exquisite division of labour, the city offers incredible variety—music ranging from rock and rap to country and classic, diets for vegetarians and diabetics as well as imported delicacies from around the world. Cities also offer anonymity, which so many find highly refreshing in the light of the much tighter controls of village and small-town life. And, of course, the city offers work.

The term **metropolis** refers to a central city surrounded by smaller cities and their suburbs. They are connected economically, sometimes politically through county boards and regional governing bodies, and physically by ties of transportation and communication.

Some metropolises have grown so large and influential that the term **megalopolis** is used to describe them. This term refers to an overlapping area consisting of at least two metropolises and their many suburbs.

Urban Patterns in Canada

In 1871 only 18 percent of the Canadian population lived in what could be called small cities. Industrialization had not taken off in Canada, so these early cities were geographically small with limited transportation routes connecting the various districts. By 1921, however, in a period of rapid industrialization and the influx of thousands of European

Early cities were small economic centres surrounded by walls to keep out enemies. Pictured here is Carcasonne, a restored medieval city in southern France.

immigrants, the percentage of Canadians living in cities had jumped to almost half the population. Today, over four-fifths of Canadians live in cities.

However, not all cities are the same size, nor do they grow at the same rate or carry the same commercial or financial weight. There is a hierarchy of urban centres in Canada.

One measure of the importance of cities in Canada is based on the population size and its rate of growth over a period of time. In some instances, several towns expand until they run together and form a continuous urban area even though their municipal governments are still separate. Federal statisticians classify a continuous, built-up region of this kind with a population of 100 000 or more as a census metropolitan area (CMA).

Between 1996 and 2001, six of the 10 fastest-growing census metropolitan areas were located in Ontario: Oshawa, Toronto, Kitchener, Windsor, Ottawa-Hull, and Hamilton in that order. The remaining CMAs were Edmonton (third place), Vancouver (fourth place), Abbotsford (Quebec), and Ottawa-Hull (Quebec part). For 2001, the CMAs with the largest populations were Toronto (4 682 897), Montreal (3 426 350), Vancouver (1 986 965), Ottawa-Hull (1 063 664), and Calgary (951 395). The combined population of these five urban agglomerations accounted for nearly 40 percent of Canada's total population!

Models of Urban Growth

In the early 1920s a University of Chicago sociologist, Robert Park, coined the term **human ecology** to describe how people adapt to their environment (Park & Burgess, 1921a; Park,

1936). (This concept is also known as *urban ecology*.) Let us look at the three main models of urban growth.

The Concentric Zone Model

To explain how cities expand, sociologist Ernest Burgess (1925) proposed a *concentric-zone model*. As shown in segment A of Figure 17.7, Burgess noted that a city expands outward from its centre.

Burgess noted, however, that no "city fits perfectly this ideal scheme." Some cities have physical obstacles, such as a lake, river, or railroad, which cause their expansion to depart from the model (Palen, 1987; Milbank, 1995a).

The Sector Model

Sociologist Homer Hoyt (1939, 1971) noted that a city's concentric zones do not form a complete circle, and he modified Burgess' model of urban growth. As shown in segment B of Figure 17.7, a concentric zone might contain several sectors—one of working-class housing, another of expensive homes, a third of businesses, and so on, all competing for the same land.

What sociologists call an **invasion-succession cycle** is an example of this dynamic competition of urban life. When poor immigrants or migrants enter a city, they settle in the lowest-rent area they can. As their numbers swell, they spill over into adjacent areas. Upset at their presence, the middle class moves out, thus expanding the sector of low-cost housing. The invasion-succession cycle is never complete, for later another group will replace this earlier one, or it may be gentrified by other migrants. **Gentrification** is the movement of middle-class people into rundown areas of a city. They are attracted by the low prices for quality housing that can be restored. Montreal's famous St. Urban/St. Lawrence Boulevard corridor

Figure 17.7 Models of Urban Growth

Source: Cousins & Nagpaul (1970).

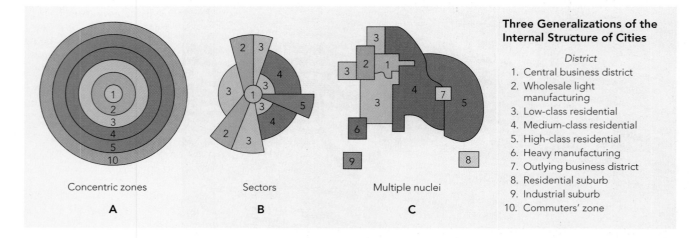

Concentric zones
A

Sectors
B

Multiple nuclei
C

Three Generalizations of the Internal Structure of Cities

District

1. Central business district
2. Wholesale light manufacturing
3. Low-class residential
4. Medium-class residential
5. High-class residential
6. Heavy manufacturing
7. Outlying business district
8. Residential suburb
9. Industrial suburb
10. Commuters' zone

has been the home of Jewish, Italian, Portuguese, Spanish, and other ethnic groups over the course of the past 100 years. Toronto's Cabbagetown and Spadina Avenue corridor are other examples.

The Multiple-Nuclei Model

Geographers Chauncey Harris and Edward Ullman noted that some cities have several centres or nuclei (Harris & Ullman, 1945; Ullman & Harris, 1970). As shown in segment C of Figure 17.7, each nucleus is the focus of some specialized activity. A familiar example is the clustering of fast food restaurants in one area and automobile dealerships in another. Other clustering occurs because some activities, such as factories and expensive homes, are incompatible with one another. Thus, push-pull factors separate areas by activities, and services are not evenly spread throughout an urban area.

Critique of the Models

These models tell only part of the story of how cities develop. They are time-bound, for medieval cities didn't follow these patterns (see the photo earlier in this chapter). They also are geography-bound. England, for example, has planning laws that preserve green belts (trees, farmlands) around the city. This prevents urban sprawl: Wal-Mart cannot buy land outside the city and put up a store, but instead must locate in the downtown area with the other stores. Norwich, England, for example, has 250 000 people; yet the city suddenly ends, and in its green belt pheasants skitter across plowed fields while sheep graze in verdant meadows (Milbank, 1995b). The models, then, do not account for urban planning policies.

The models also fall short when it comes to the cities of the least industrialized nations. Here the wealthy often claim the inner city, where fine restaurants and other services are readily accessible. Tucked behind tall walls and protected from public scrutiny, they enjoy luxurious homes and gardens. In contrast, the poor, especially rural migrants, settle unclaimed fringe areas outside the city (see the Perspectives box on page 416).

> ### Focus Question
> What are the three models of urban growth?
> What are their limitations?

City Life

Cities are intended to be solutions to problems. They are human endeavours to improve life collectively, to develop a way of life that transcends the limitations of farm and village. Cities hold out the hope of gaining employment, education, and other advantages. The perception of such opportunities underlies mass migration to cities throughout the world.

Just as cities provide opportunities, however, they also create problems. Humans not only have physical needs—food, shelter, and safety—but also a need for **community**, a feeling of belonging—the sense that others care what happens to you, and that you can depend on the people around you. Some people find this sense of community in the city; others find only its opposite, *alienation*, a sense of not belonging, and a feeling that no one cares what happens to you. Let's look at these two aspects of city life.

Alienation

Why should the city be alienating? In a classic essay, "Urbanism as a Way of Life," sociologist Louis Wirth (1938) argued that the city undermines kinship and neighbourhood, which are the traditional sources of social control and social solidarity.

Wirth built on the ideas of *Gemeinschaft* and *Gesellschaft* discussed in Chapter 5. *Gemeinschaft*, the sense of community that comes from everyone knowing everyone else, is ripped apart as a country industrializes. What emerges is a new society based on *Gesellschaft*, secondary, impersonal relationships. The end result can be alienation so deep that people can sit by while someone else is being murdered. Lacking identification with one another, people develop an attitude of "It's simply none of *my* business." In short, the very sense of personal freedom that the city provides comes at the cost of alienation.

Community

Such attitudes, however, do not do justice to the city. The city is more than a mosaic of strangers who feel disconnected and distrustful of one another. It is also made up of a series of smaller worlds, within which people find *community*, a sense of belonging. Here they live, work, shop, and play. Even slums, which to outsiders seem so threatening, can provide a sense of belonging. In a classic study, sociologist Herbert Gans noted:

> After a few weeks of living in the West End [of Boston], my observations—and my perceptions of the area—changed drastically. The search for an apartment quickly indicated that the individual units were usually in much better condition than the outside or the hallways of the buildings. Subsequently, in wandering through the West End, and in using it as a resident, I developed a kind of selective perception, in which my eye focused only on those parts of the area that were actually being used by people.
>
> Since much of the area's life took place on the street, faces became familiar very quickly. I met my neighbours on the stairs and in front of my building. And, once a shopping pattern developed, I saw the same storekeepers frequently, as well as the area's "characters" who wandered through the streets every day on a fairly regular route and schedule. In short, the exotic quality of the stores and the residents also wore off as I became used to seeing them.

Images of the least industrialized nations that portray serene pastoral scenes distort today's reality. In these nations, poor rural people have flocked to the cities in such numbers that the nations now contain most of the world's largest cities. In general, the world's industrialization preceded urbanization, but here urbanization is preceding industrialization. Their limited technology makes it difficult to support the mushrooming urban populations.

When rural migrants and immigrants move to U.S. cities, they usually settle in the low-rent districts, mostly deteriorating housing located near the city's centre. The wealthy reside in exclusive suburbs and luxurious city enclaves. In contrast, migrants in the least industrialized nations settle in squatter settlements outside the city. There they build shacks from scrap boards, cardboard, and bits of corrugated metal. Even flattened tin cans are considered valuable building material. The squatters enjoy no city facilities—roads, transportation lines, water, sewers, or garbage pickup.

After thousands of squatters have settled in an area, the city runs bus lines to it, acknowledging their de facto right to live there. Eventually the city runs a water line to the area and several hundred people use a single spigot. About four million of Mexico City's inhabitants live in such conditions.

Reflecting on conditions in its cities, India's leading news magazine published the following report.

[The city is] heading for a total breakdown. The endless stream of migrants pour in, turning metropolises into giant slums. A third of the urban population lives in ramshackle huts with gunny sacks as doors and pavements for toilets. Another half of the populace is squeezed into one-room tenements or lives in monotonous rows of multi-storeyed flats (Singh, 1988).

Why are people rushing to these cities? Basically, the rural way of life is breaking down. As the second leg of the demographic transition—low death rates and high birth rates—kicks in, rural populations are multiplying, and no longer is there enough land to divide up among descendants. There are also the pull factors discussed in this chapter—from jobs, education, and better housing to a more stimulating life.

Will cities of the least industrialized nations satisfy the people's longing for a better life? As miserable as life for the poor is in these cities, for many it is an improvement over what they left behind. If not, they would flee the city to return to pastoral pleasures. If the Anti-Malthusians are right, this second stage of the demographic transition will come to an end, and the population of the least industrialized nations will stabilize. In the meantime, however, the least industrialized nations cannot catch up with their population explosion—or their urban growth.

Sources: Palen (1987); Singh (1988); Huth (1990); Kasarda & Crenshaw (1991); Chen (1996).

The least industrialized nations are facing massive upheaval as they rapidly urbanize, resulting in disparities such as those depicted here. Lacking the infrastructure to support their many newcomers, cities in the least industrialized nations, already steeped in poverty, face the daunting task of developing jobs, housing, sewage and electrical systems, roads, schools, and so on.

Living in the West End, Gans gained an insider's perspective. Gans had located a community in the West End, discovering that its residents visited back and forth with relatives and were involved in extensive networks of friendships and acquaintances. Gans therefore titled his book *The Urban Villagers* (1962).

The city dwellers whom Gans identified as *ethnic villagers* find community in the city. Living in tightly knit neighbourhoods, they know many other residents. Some first-generation immigrants have even come from the same village in the "old country."

Types of Urban Dwellers

Whether you find alienation or community in the city largely depends on who you are, for the city offers both. People from different backgrounds experience the city differently. Gans (1962, 1968, 1991a) identified the types of people who live in the city. The first three types live in the city by choice, where they find a sense of community.

The Cosmopolitans.   The cosmopolitans are the city's students, intellectuals, professionals, musicians, artists, and entertainers. They have been drawn to the city because of its conveniences and cultural benefits.

The Singles.   Young, unmarried people, who may team up to rent an apartment, come to the city seeking jobs and entertainment. Businesses and services such as singles bars, singles apartment complexes, and computer dating cater to their needs. Their stay in the city often reflects a temporary stage in their life course, for most move to the suburbs after they marry and have children.

The Ethnic Villagers.   These people live in tightly knit neighbourhoods that resemble villages and small towns. United by race/ethnicity and social class, their neighbourhoods are far from depersonalized or disorganized. Placing an emphasis on family and friendship, the ethnic villagers try to isolate themselves from what they view as the harmful effects of city life.

The Trapped.   This group of people have little choice about where they live. Outcasts of industrial society, they are alienated and always skirting the edge of disaster. They consist of four subtypes: those who could not afford to move when their neighbourhood was "invaded" by another ethnic group; elderly people who are not wanted elsewhere; alcoholics and other drug addicts; and the "downwardly mobile," people who have fallen from a higher social class. The trapped suffer high rates of assault, mugging, robbery, and rape. The homeless are made up of all four types of urban dwellers.

Gans' typology provides insight into the great variety of ways urban dwellers experience the city. Some find the streets a stimulating source of cultural contrasts. For others, however, the same events pose a constant threat as they try to survive in what for them amounts to an urban jungle.

Urban Sentiment: Finding a Familiar World

Sociologists note that *the city is divided into little worlds* that people come to know down to their smallest details. Gregory Stone (1954) and Herbert Gans (1970) observed how city people create a sense of intimacy for themselves by *personalizing* their shopping. By frequenting the same stores, they become recognized as "regulars," and after a period of time customers and clerks greet each other by name. Particular taverns, restaurants, laundromats, and shops are more than just buildings in which to purchase items and services. They become meeting places where neighbourhood residents build social relationships with one another and share informal news about the community.

Spectator sports also help urban dwellers find a familiar world (Hudson, 1991). When the Hamilton Tiger Cats won the Grey Cup in 1999, the city of Hamilton celebrated the victory of "their" team with a downtown parade and week-long festivities. Sociologists David Karp and William Yoels (1990) note that such identification is so intense that long after moving to other parts of the country many people maintain an emotional allegiance to the sports teams of the city in which they grew up.

As sociologists Richard Wohl and Anselm Strauss (1958) pointed out, city dwellers even develop strong feelings for particular objects and locations in the city, such as buildings, rivers, lakes, parks, and even trees and street corners. In some cases, objects become a type of logo that represents the city—for example, Kensington Market in Toronto, the Latin Quarter in Montreal, or Granville Island in Vancouver.

> For those who live in these respective cities, such objects and places do not merely identify the city; they are also sources for personal identification with the city (Karp, Stone, & Yoels, 1991).

Urban dwellers find their community, then, not in buildings and space, but in their social relationships. Regardless of where they live in the city, people who are not integrated into social networks find alienation, while those who are integrated find community.

Suburbanization

Suburbanization, which refers to people moving from cities to **suburbs**, the communities located just outside a city, is not new. The dream of a place of one's own with green grass, a few trees, and kids playing in the yard was not discovered by this generation (Riesman, 1970). For the past 100 years or so, as transportation became more efficient, especially with the development of automobiles, people have moved to towns next to the cities in which they work.

Focus Question
Why has the world's population tended to move into urban settlements?

Deindustrialization and Globalization

The development of a global market has left a heavy imprint on Canadian cities. As sociologist Victor Rodríguez (1994) points out, to compete in the global market many industries have abandoned local communities and moved their factories to places where labour costs are lower. This process has eliminated millions of manufacturing jobs, locking many poor people out of the postindustrial economy engulfing some cities in Canada. Left behind in the inner cities, many live in despair as a distant economy charges into the uncharted waters of a brave new world without them (see Perspectives: Finding Work, in Chapter 11, page 277).

The Environment

The Natural Environment

Environmental Problems of Past Civilizations

Contrary to common assumptions, environmental problems are not new on the human scene. Several civilizations destroyed themselves by destroying the environment on which their very existence depended.

The most famous is the fall of Mesopotamia, a civilization located in the lush river basin of the Tigris and Euphrates in what is now Iraq. About 3000 years before Christ, this civilization flourished because the people had developed an extensive irrigation system that provided abundant food. This irrigation system, however, had no drainage. The water constantly evaporated, gradually growing saltier. Over the

Figure 17.8 Urban Growth and Urban Flight

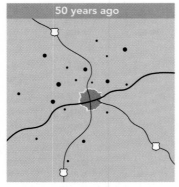

At first, the city and surrounding villages grew independently.

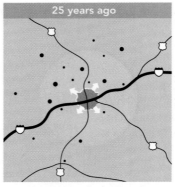

As city dwellers fled urban decay, they created a ring of suburbs.

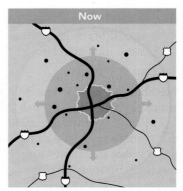

As middle-class flight continues outward, urban problems are arriving in the outer rings.

centuries, the underground water table rose, and the land became too salty to grow crops. The Mesopotamians had unwittingly destroyed the agricultural base on which their civilization depended (Jacobsen & Adams, 1958). What once was a beautiful, lush, green land producing fruits, vegetables, and grains in abundance is now desert.

Environmental Problems in the Most Industrialized Nations

Although environmental degradation is not new, the frontal assault on the natural environment did not begin in earnest until nations industrialized. The more extensive the industrialization, the better it was considered for a nation's welfare, and the slogan for the most industrialized nations has been "Growth at any cost."

Industrial growth did come, but at a high cost to the natural environment. Today many formerly pristine streams are polluted sewers, and the water supply of many cities is unfit to drink. Most major Canadian cities have information on their daily air pollution index. Montreal's McGill subway station, for example, posts the changing daily pollution count on an overhead electronic bulletin board for commuters to easily see. During the summer months, nearly all Canadian radio and television news programs report on the sun's ultraviolet radiation by telling listeners/viewers how long it is safe for us to stay outside without sunscreen protection.

Of all the consequences of pollution we could discuss, we shall consider—due to space limitations—just the implications of fossil fuels.

Fossil Fuels and Environmental Degradation. The burning of fossil fuels for factories, motorized vehicles, and power plants has been especially harmful. Fish can no longer survive in some lakes in Canada and the northeastern United States because of **acid rain**—the burning fossil fuels release sulfur dioxide and nitrogen oxide, which react with moisture in the air to become sulfuric and nitric acids (Luoma, 1989).

An invisible but more serious consequence is the **greenhouse effect**. Like the glass of a greenhouse, the gases emitted from burning fossil fuels allow sunlight to enter the earth's atmosphere freely, but inhibit the release of heat. It is as though the gases have closed the atmospheric window through which our planet breathes. Not all scientists agree that a greenhouse effect exists or that we face an imminent danger globally (Robinson & Robinson, 1997). Most scientists say, however, that the resulting **global warming** may melt the polar icecaps and inundate the world's shorelines, cause the climate boundaries to move about 644 kilometres north, and make many animal and plant species extinct (Smith & Tirpak, 1988; P. Thomas, 1988; Weisskopf, 1992). Alarmed, in 1997, 160 nations approved an environmental treaty that requires a reduction of "greenhouse gases."

The Energy Shortage, Internal Combustion Engines, and Multinational Corporations. If you ever read about an energy shortage, you can be sure it is false. There is no energy shortage, nor can there ever be. The earth holds the potential of producing unlimited low-cost power, which can help raise the living standards of humans across the globe. The sun, for example, produces more energy than humanity could ever use. Boundless energy is also available from the tides and the winds. In some cases, we need better technology to harness these sources of energy; in others, we need only apply technology we already have.

Since burning fossil fuels in internal combustion engines is the main source of pollution in the most industrialized nations, and vast sources of alternative energy are available, why don't we develop the technology to use these alternative sources of energy? From a conflict perspective, these abundant sources of energy threaten the multinationals' oil monopoly. To maintain their profits, these corporations make certain that internal combustion engines remain dominant. The practical development and widespread use of alternative sources of power will wait until the multinationals have cornered the market on the technology that will harness them—so they can continue reaping huge profits.

Environmental Problems in the Industrializing Nations

Negative environmental consequences of industrialization, such as ozone depletion, the greenhouse effect, and global warming, cannot be laid solely at the feet of the most industrialized nations. With their rush to be contenders in global competition, the lack of funds to purchase pollution controls, and few antipollution laws, the industrializing nations make their own enormous contributions to this problem. Breathing the polluted air of Mexico City, for example, is the equivalent of smoking two packs of cigarettes a day (Durbin, 1995).

The former Soviet Union is a special case. Until this empire broke up, pollution had been treated as a state secret. Scientists and journalists were forbidden to mention pollution in public. Even peaceful demonstrations to call attention to pollution could net participants two years in prison (Feshbach, 1992). With protest stifled and no environmental protection laws, environmental pollution could be found everywhere: Almost half of Russia's arable land has been made unsuitable for farming, about a third of Russians live in cities where air pollution is over 10 times greater than levels permitted in Canada, and half of Russia's tap water is unfit to drink. Pollution is so severe that the life expectancy of Russians has dropped, a lesson that should not be lost on the rest of us as we make decisions on how to treat our environment.

Environmental Problems in the Least Industrialized Nations

Their greater poverty and swelling populations, combined with almost non-existent environmental regulations destine the least industrialized nations to become major sources of pollution.

Their lack of environmental protection laws has not gone unnoticed by opportunists in the most industrialized nations, who have seized the opportunity to use these countries as garbage dumps for hazardous wastes and for producing chemicals that their own nations will no longer tolerate (LaDou, 1991; C. S. Smith, 1995). Alarmed at the growing environmental destruction, the World Bank, a monetary arm of the most industrialized nations, has put pressure on the least industrialized nations to reduce pollution and soil erosion (Lachica, 1992). Understandably, the basic concern of these nations is to produce food and housing first, and to worry about the environment later.

Rain Forests and Extinction. Holding unknown consequences for the future of humanity is the extinction of numerous plant and animal species as tropical rain forests are relentlessly cleared for lumber, farms, and pastures. Although the rain forests cover just 7 percent of the earth's land area, they are home to half of its plant species. With the rain forests disappearing at a rate of nearly *2500 acres (1012 hectares) every hour* (McCuen, 1993), it is estimated that 10 000 species become extinct every year—about one per hour (Durning, 1990). As the rain forests are destroyed, so are the native communities that live in them.

The Bottom Line: The Growth Machine Versus the Earth

Underlying today's environmental decay is the globalization of capitalism. To maintain their dominance and increase their wealth, the most industrialized nations, spurred by multinational corporations, continue to push for economic growth.

The industrializing nations don't like second place, and, playing catch-up, are striving to develop their economies. Meanwhile, the least industrialized nations, eyeing the wealth of the others, are anxious to enter the race. Starting from far behind, however, they have to push for even faster growth if they have any hope of catching up.

Some scientists are convinced that the earth cannot withstand such onslaught (Krupp, 1995). Our global economic production creates extensive pollution, and faster-paced production means faster-paced destruction of our environment. If the goal is a **sustainable environment**, a world system in which we use our physical environment to meet our needs without destroying humanity's future, we cannot continue to trash the earth's natural resources.

The Environmental Movement

Concern about environmental problems has produced a worldwide social movement. In some countries, political parties built around environmental concerns, called *green parties*, campaign in local and national elections. In Europe,

especially Germany, green parties have become a political force and have won seats in the national legislatures.

Activists in the environmental movement generally seek solutions in politics, legislation, and education. Seeing that pollution continues, the rain forests are still being cleared, and that species are becoming extinct, some activists are convinced that the planet is doomed unless immediate steps are taken. Choosing a more radical course, they use extreme tactics to try to arouse indignation among the public and thus force the government to act. Convinced that they stand for morality, many are willing to break the law and go to jail for their actions. Such activists are featured on the following page, in the Thinking Critically about Social Controversy box.

Environmental Sociology

Environmental sociology, which examines the relationship between human societies and the environment, emerged as a subdiscipline of sociology about 1970 (Dunlap & Catton 1979, 1983; Buttel, 1987; Freudenburg & Gramling, 1989; Laska, 1993). Its main assumptions are:

1. The physical environment is a significant variable in sociological investigation.

2. Human beings are but one species among many that are dependent on the natural environment.

3. Because of intricate feedbacks to nature, human actions have many unintended consequences.

4. The world is finite, so there are potential physical limits to economic growth.

5. Economic expansion requires increased extraction of resources from the environment.

6. Increased extraction of resources leads to ecological problems.

7. These ecological problems place restrictions on economic expansion.

8. Governments create environmental problems by trying to create conditions for the accumulation of capital.

As you can see, the goal of environmental sociology is not to stop pollution or nuclear power, but, rather, to study how humans (their cultures, values, and behaviours) affect the physical environment and how the physical environment affects human activities. Environmental sociologists, however, generally are also environmental activists.

> **Focus Question**
> What is the relationship between our physical environment and sociological theory?

Chaining oneself to a giant Douglas fir slated for cutting; pouring sand down the gas tank of a bulldozer; tearing down power lines and ripping up survey stakes; driving spikes into redwood trees; and sinking whaling vessels—are these the acts of dangerous punks, intent on vandalism and with little understanding of the needs of modern society? Or are they the acts of brave men and women willing to put their freedom, and even their lives, on the line on behalf of the earth itself?

How many 3000-year-old trees remain on this planet? Do fences and picnic tables for backyard barbecues justify cutting them down? It is questions like these, as well as the slaughter of seals, the destruction of the rain forests, and the drowning of dolphins in mile-long drift nets that spawned Earth First! and other organizations devoted to preserving the environment, such as Greenpeace, Sea Shepherds, and the Ruckus Society.

"We feel like there are insane people who are consciously destroying our environment, and we are compelled to fight back," explains a member of one of the militant groups. "No compromise in defense of Mother Earth!" says another. "With famine and death approaching, we're in the early stages of World War III," adds another.

The dedication of some of these activists has brought them close to martyrdom. When Paul Watson, founder of the Sea Shepherds, sprayed seals with green dye, which destroys the value of their pelts but doesn't hurt the animals, hunters hog-tied him, dragged him

As concern about the environment has grown, a social movement to try to change the course of events has developed. Protest groups have rallied around numerous issues, including the seal hunt, whaling, and the destruction of old growth forests on Canada's west coast.

across the ice, and threatened to toss him into the sea. "It's no big deal," says Watson, "when you consider that 100 million people in this century have died in wars over real estate."

Radical environmentalists represent a broad range of activities and purposes. They are united on neither tactics nor goals. Some want to stop a specific action, such as the killing of whales, or to destroy all nuclear weapons and disman-

tle nuclear power plants. Others want everyone to become vegetarians. Still others want the earth's population to be reduced to one billion, roughly what it was in 1800. Some even want humans to return to hunting and gathering bands. Most espouse a simpler lifestyle that will consume less energy and put less pressure on the earth's resources. These groups are so splintered that the founder of Earth First!, Dave Foreman, quit his own organization when it became too confrontational for his tastes.

Among their successes, the radical groups count a halt to the killing of dolphins off Japan's Iki Island, a ban on whaling, trash recycling in many communities, and hundreds of thousands of acres of uncut trees.

For Your Consideration

Who, then, are these people? Should we applaud ecosaboteurs or jail them? As symbolic interactionists stress, it all depends on your definition. And as conflict theorists emphasize, your definition likely depends on your location in the economic structure. That is, if you are the owner of a lumber company you will see ecosaboteurs differently from the way many Native Canadians view the destruction of Mother Earth. How does your own view of ecosaboteurs depend on your life situation? What effective alternatives to ecosabotage are there for people convinced we are destroying the life support system of our planet?

Sources: Russell (1987); Borrelli (1988); Guha (1989); Carpenter (1990); Eder (1990); Foote (1990); Martin (1990); Parfit (1990); Reed & Benet (1990); Courtney (1995).

Kathleen Riel is an environmental sociologist in Canada and has written extensively on matters affecting our environment. In Table 17.2, she provides us with contrasting views of society as seen from environmental and traditional sociological perspectives.

Ecofeminism and the Environment

Ecofeminists believe human beings are connected to one another and to the nonhuman world whether it is animal, vegetable, or mineral. They point out that we do violence to

Table 17.2 Comparison of Competing Paradigms, Selected Items

New Environmental Paradigm	Dominant Sociology Paradigm
I. *High valuation of nature*	I. *Lower valuation of nature*
▪ Environmental protection over economic growth	▪ Human domination over nature
II. *Generalized compassion*	II. *Compassion only for those near and dear*
▪ Concern for other species, peoples, and generations	▪ Concern for present generation only
III. *Careful planning and acting to avoid risk*	III. *Acceptance of risk to maximize wealth*
▪ Regulation to protect nature and humans—government's responsibility	▪ Deregulation by governments—individual responsibility
IV. *Limits to growth*	IV. *No limits to growth*
▪ Conservation	▪ Production and consumption
V. *Completely new society*	V. *Present society fine (maintain the status quo)*
▪ Openness and participation	▪ Competition and emphasis on the market
VI. *New Politics*	VI. *Old Politics*
▪ Emphasis on foresight and planning	▪ Emphasis on market control

Source: *Canadian Society: Meeting the Challenges of the Twenty-First Century,* 2001, Dan Glenday and Ann Duffy, eds. Toronto: Oxford University Press, copyright © 2001.

each other and to nature while congratulating ourselves on providing material abundance for some while militarily protecting our self-interests in the exploitation of the earth's natural resources such as fossil fuels and other valuable minerals and ores.

They explain the harm done to humanity and the environment by pointing to patriarchy's hierarchical, dualistic, and oppressive ways of thinking. For example, women are "naturalized" when they are described in animal terms such as "foxes, cows, chicks, bird-brains" and so on while nature is "feminized" when "she" is "raped, conquered, mastered, penetrated, subdued" or "worshipped" as the grandest "mother" of them all. In biblical terms, man is lord over nature and over nature's analogue, woman. These dualistic, hierarchical, and oppressive ways of thinking have brought humanity to the brink of disaster by disrespecting nature and women.

Ecofeminists disagree on the proper "solutions" to this social problem, but most agree that a fundamental and radical change in our thinking must be a necessary start. We can begin individually by respecting ourselves and nature and conserving resources through, for example, recycling and refusing to eat animals that have been grown under cruel conditions, and collectively by supporting environmental causes.

At this point in global capitalism, the goal of achieving a harmonious relationship with our environment is not even on the horizon. In 1997, pollution in Malaysia was so bad that for many months people wore masks as they went about their everyday lives. Shown here are surgical masks for sale from a roadside vendor.

Technology and the Environment: The Goal of Harmony

It is inevitable that humans will continue to develop new technologies. But the abuse of our environment by those technologies is not inevitable.

If we are to have a world that is worth passing on to coming generations, we must seek harmony between technology and the natural environment. This will not be easy. At one extreme are people who claim that to protect the environment we must eliminate industrialization and go back to some sort of preindustrial way of life. At the other extreme are people unable to see the harm being done to the natural environment, who want the entire world to con-tinue industrializing at full speed. Somewhere, there must be a middle ground, one that recognizes that industrialization is here to stay but that we can control it, for it is our creation. Industrialization, controlled, can enhance our quality of life. As a parallel to the development of tech-nologies, then, we must develop systems to reduce or elim-inate their harm to the environment. This includes mechanisms to globally monitor the production, use, and disposal of technology. The question, of course, is whether we have the resolve to take the steps that will preserve the environment for future generations. The stakes—no less than the welfare of the entire planet—are surely high enough to motivate us to make the correct choices.

Summary and Review

POPULATION IN GLOBAL PERSPECTIVE

A PLANET WITH NO SPACE TO ENJOY LIFE?

What debate did Thomas Malthus initiate?

In 1798, Thomas Malthus analyzed the surge in Europe's popula-tion. His conclusion, called the **Malthus theorem**, was that because the population grows geometrically but food only arith-metically, the world population will outstrip its food supply. The debate between today's New Malthusians and those who disagree, the Anti-Malthusians, continues, while feminists offer their own analysis and solutions. pp. 404–407.

Why are people starving?

Starvation is not due to a lack of food in the world, for there now is more food for each person in the entire world than there was 50 years ago. Starvation is due, rather, to a maldistribution of food. pp. 407–408.

POPULATION GROWTH

Why do the poor nations have so many children?

In the least industrialized nations, children are generally viewed as gifts from God, cost little to rear, and represent the parents' social security. Consequently, people are motivated to have large fami-lies. pp. 408–409.

What are the three demographic variables?

To compute population growth, demographers use *fertility*, *mor-tality*, and *migration*. The **basic demographic equation** is Births – Deaths + Net migration = Growth rate. pp. 409–410.

Why is forecasting population difficult?

A nation's growth rate is affected by unanticipated variables—from economic conditions, wars, plagues, and famines to government policies and industrialization. p. 410.

What population challenges do we face today?

The population explosion is occurring in those nations that have the least wealth and technology. The challenge is how to use tech-nology to help the least industrialized nations avoid starvation and resource depletion. p. 411.

URBANIZATION

What is the relationship of cities to farming?

Cities can develop only if there is a large agricultural surplus, which frees people from food production. The primary impetus to the development of cities was the invention of the plow about 5000 or 6000 years ago. p. 413.

What are metropolises and megalopolises?

Urbanization is so extensive that some cities have become **metropolises**, dominating the area adjacent to them. The areas of influence of some metropolises have merged, forming a **megal-opolis**. p. 413.

MODELS OF URBAN GROWTH

What models of urban growth have been proposed?

The primary models are a concentric zone model, a sector model, and a multiple-nuclei model. These models fail to account for medieval cities, as well as many European cities and those in the least industrialized nations. pp. 414–415.

CITY LIFE

Is the city inherently alienating?

Some people experience alienation in the city; others find **commun-ity** in it. What people find depends largely on their background and urban networks. The types of people who live in cities are cos-mopolitans, singles, ethnic villagers, and the trapped. pp. 416–418.

THE ENVIRONMENT

THE NATURAL ENVIRONMENT

What are the environmental problems of the most industrialized nations?

The environmental problems of the most industrialized nations are severe, ranging from city smog and **acid rain** to the greenhouse effect. Scientists debate whether the greenhouse effect is real; if it is, it may cause **global warming** that will fundamentally affect social life. The burning of fossil fuels in internal combustion engines lies at the root of many environmental problems, but alternative sources of energy are unlikely to be developed until the multinational corporations can turn them to a profit. pp. 418–419.

What are the environmental problems of the industrializing and least industrialized nations?

Some of the worst environmental problems are found in the former Soviet Union, a legacy of the unrestrained exploitation of resources by the Communist Party. The rush of the least industrialized nations to industrialize is adding to our environmental decay. The world is facing a basic conflict between the lust for profits through the exploitation of the earth's resources and the need to produce a **sustainable environment**. pp. 419–420.

What is the environmental movement?

The environmental movement is an attempt to restore a healthy environment for the world's people. This global movement takes many forms, from peacefully influencing the political process to *ecosabotage*, sabotaging the efforts of people thought to be harming the environment. p. 420.

What is environmental sociology?

Environmental sociology is not an attempt to change the environment, but a study of the relationship between humans and the environment. Environmental sociologists are generally also environmental activists. pp. 420–421.

ECOFEMINISM AND THE ENVIRONMENT
What is ecofeminism?

While there are several variants of *ecofeminism*, they all agree the human and nonhuman worlds are interconnected. Patriarchy's hierarchical, dualistic, and oppressive ways of thinking explain the environmental predicament facing our planet today. pp. 421–422.

Critical Thinking Questions

1. Should governments try to limit population growth by using such traditional techniques as family planning?

2. Is it true, as some believe, that famine, overpopulation, and disease are rapidly destroying the social fabric of our planet?

3. All major municipalities in Canada have urban planners. However, their advice for more urban green space, for example, is often ignored because it conflicts witho powerful economic interests who benefit from the increases in the price of land that result from building huge skyscrapers, stadiums, or other concrete structures in our cities. How would you try to resolve these conflicts of interest if you were an urban planner promoting the public use of a segment of waterfront or riverfront property in your city?

4. Why is there such a shortage of affordable housing in booming cities like Vancouver, Calgary, and Toronto?

Key Terms

acid rain 419
basic demographic equation 410
city 413
community 416
crude birth rate 410
crude death rate 410
demographic transition 405
demographic variables 409
demography 404
environmental sociology 420
exponential growth curve 404
fecundity 409
fertility rate 409
gentrification 414

global warming 419
greenhouse effect 419
growth rate 410
human ecology 414
invasion-succession cycle 414
Malthus theorem 404
megalopolis 413
metropolis 413
net migration rate 410
population shrinkage 406
suburbanization 418
suburbs 418
sustainable environment 420
urbanization 413
zero population growth 410

Weblinks

All URLs listed are current as of the printing of this book. URLs are often changed. Please check our Web site **www.abacon.com/ henslin** for updates.

WWICS Comparative Urban Studies Project

wwics.si.edu/THEMES/URBAN/CUSPWEB1.HTM
This project of the Woodrow Wilson International Center for Scholars brings together scholars and policymakers to discuss problems of urban management from a multidisciplinary, multiregional perspective. Participants organize international conferences and disseminate findings through policy briefs, occasional papers, books, and other publications.

Office of Population Research, Princeton University

opr.princeton.edu/
The oldest population research centre in the United States. Many of its graduates occupy important professional positions in developing countries; others are on university faculties worldwide.

Network for Change

envirolink.netforchange.com/
Network for Change is part of EnviroLink Network: The Online Environmental Community. When completed, it will be a comprehensive resource for individuals, organizations, and businesses working for social and environmental change.

Deep Ecology

www.envirolink.org/enviroethics/deepindex.html
An article about the most radical wing of the environmental movement. Presented by EnviroLink Network: The Online Environmental Community.

Chapter 18

Social Movements and Social Change

Learning Outcomes

After you have studied this chapter, you will be able to

■ understand why sociologists describe social movements as a form of rational behaviour

■ distinguish between social movements and other forms of collective behaviour such as rumours, urban legends, fads, and fashions

■ discuss the many reasons for joining a social movement

■ explain how new technologies, defined as both the tools and the skills to make and use these tools, influence the changes in our society

The news spread like wildfire. A police officer had been killed. In just 20 minutes, the white population was armed and heading for the cabin. Men and mere boys, some not more than 12 years old, carried rifles, shotguns, and pistols.

The mob, now about 400, surrounded the log cabin of a local black man. Tying a rope around the man's neck, they dragged him to the centre of town. While the men argued about the best way to kill him, the women and children shouted their advice—some to hang him, others to burn him alive.

Someone pulled a large wooden box out of a store and placed it in the centre of the street. Others filled it with straw. Then they lifted the man, the rope still around his neck, and shoved him head first into the box. One of the men poured oil over him. Another lit a match.

As the flames shot upward, the man managed to lift himself out of the box, his body a mass of flames. Trying to shield his face and eyes from the fire, he ran the length of the rope, about 20 feet, when someone yelled, "Shoot!" In an instant, dozens of shots rang out. Men and boys walked to the lifeless body and emptied their guns into it.

They dragged the man's body back to the burning box, then piled on more boxes from the stores, and poured oil over them. Each time someone threw more oil onto the flames, the crowd roared shouts of approval.

Standing about 75 feet away, I could smell the poor man's burning flesh. No one tried to hide their identity. I could clearly see town officials help in the burning. The inquest, dutifully held by the coroner, concluded that the man met death "at the hands of an enraged mob unknown to the jury." What else could he conclude? Any jury from this town would include men who had participated in the man's death.

They dug a little hole at the edge of the street, and dumped in it the man's ashes and what was left of his body.

The man's name was Sam Pettie, known by everybody to be quiet and unoffensive. I can't mention my name. If I did, I would be committing suicide.

Source: A May 1914 letter to *The Crisis*.

Collective Behaviour

Why did the people in this little town "go mad"? These men—and the women who watched in agreement—were ordinary, law-abiding citizens. Even some of the "pillars of the community" joined in the vicious killing of Sam Pettie, who may have been innocent.

Lynching is a form of **collective behaviour**, a group of people bypassing the usual norms that guide their behaviour and doing something unusual (Turner & Killian, 1987; Lofland, 1993). Collective behaviour is a very broad term, for it includes not only such violent acts as lynchings and riots, but also panics, rumours, fads, and fashions. Before examining its specific forms, let us look at theories that seek to explain collective behaviour.

Early Explanations: The Transformation of the Individual

When people can't figure something out, they are apt to say, "She went 'off her rocker'; that's why she drove her car off the bridge." "He must have 'gone nuts,' or he wouldn't have shot into the crowd." Early explanations of collective behaviour were not far from such assumptions. Let's look at how these ideas developed.

Charles Mackay and Gustave LeBon: How the Crowd Transforms the Individual

The field of collective behaviour began when Charles Mackay (1814–1889), a British journalist, noticed that "country folks," who ordinarily are reasonable sorts of people, sometimes "went mad" and did "disgraceful and violent things" when they got in a crowd. The best explanation Mackay (1852) could come up with was that people had a "herd mentality"—they were like a herd of cows that suddenly stampede.

About 50 years later, Gustave LeBon (1841–1931), a French psychologist, built on this initial idea. In an 1895 book, LeBon stressed how crowds make people feel anonymous, as though they are not accountable for what they do. In a crowd, people even develop feelings of invincibility, and come to think that they can do almost anything. A **collective mind** develops, he said. Then contagion, something like mass hypnosis, takes over, releasing the destructive instincts that society has so carefully repressed.

see from Figure 18.1, Blumer (1939) identified five stages that precede what he called an **acting crowd**, an excited group that moves toward a goal. This model still dominates today's police manuals on crowd behaviour (McPhail, 1989).

1. *Tension or unrest.* At the root of collective behaviour is a background condition of tension or unrest. An example of a background condition of tension occurred when the PC government of Mike Harris decided in 1997 to place control of Ontario's $14 billion public education system firmly in the hands of the provincial government, and by so doing, eliminate between 7500 and 10 000 jobs and cut billions of dollars from the education budget. As a result, the five unions representing 126 000 teachers pulled their members out of the classroom and onto the streets of Ontario's cities and towns. This was the first Ontario-wide teachers' strike in more than two decades (Jenish, 1997, p. 18).

2. *Exciting event.* An exciting event occurs, one so startling that people become preoccupied with it. An example would be the cutting of billions of dollars from public education by Premier Harris and his Ontario Cabinet in 1997.

3. *Milling.* Next comes **milling**, people standing or walking around, talking about the exciting event. A circular reaction then sets in. That is, as people pick up cues to the "right" way of thinking and feeling, they reinforce them in one another.

4. *A common object of attention.* In this stage, people's attention becomes riveted on some aspect of the event. They get caught up in the collective excitement.

U.S. race relations have gone through many stages, some of them very tense. They sometimes have exploded into violence, as with the lynchings in the 1920s and 1930s. This gruesome photo was taken on August 7, 1930, in Marion, Indiana. The victims, Thomas Shipp and Abram Smith, were accused of rape.

Herbert Blumer: The Acting Crowd

Herbert Blumer (1900–1987) synthesized LeBon's ideas with those of another sociologist, Robert Park. As you can

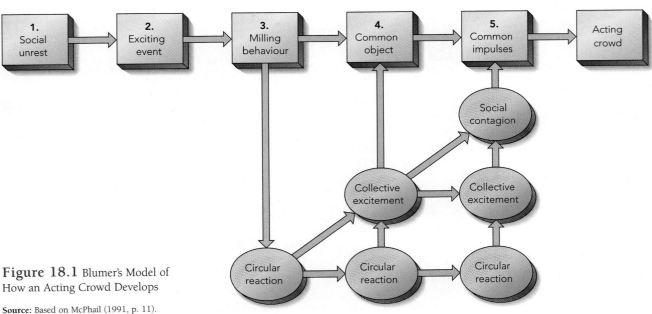

Figure 18.1 Blumer's Model of How an Acting Crowd Develops

Source: Based on McPhail (1991, p. 11).

5. *Common impulses*. A sense of collective agreement about what should be done emerges. What stimulates these common impulses is social contagion, a sense of excitement that is passed from one person to another. In the vignette at the beginning of the chapter, people concluded that the killer had to be punished, and that only an immediate, public death would be adequate vengeance—as well as a powerful warning for other African-Americans who might even think about getting "out of line."

Acting crowds aren't always negative or destructive, as this one was, for they also include spontaneous demonstrations or sit-ins directed against oppression, such as Amnesty International's efforts to free political prisoners in many parts of the globe. Nor are they all serious—even "food fights" are acting crowds!

The Contemporary View: The Rationality of the Crowd

If we were to witness a lynching—or a screaming mob or prison riot—most of us probably would agree with LeBon that some sort of "madness" had swept over the crowd. Sociologists today, however, point out that crowds are actually quite rational. By this, they mean that crowds take deliberate steps to reach some desired goal.

Richard Berk: The Minimax Strategy

A general principle of human behaviour is that we try to minimize our costs and maximize our rewards. Sociologist Richard Berk (1974) calls this a **minimax strategy**. The fewer costs and the more rewards we anticipate from some-

thing, the more likely we are to do it. For example, if we believe that others will approve an act, the likelihood that we will do it increases. Whether in yelling for the referee's blood at a bad call in football, or shouting for the release of a political prisoner, this principle applies

Ralph Turner and Lewis Killian: Emergent Norms

Sociologists Ralph Turner and Lewis Killian (1987) point out that life usually goes much as we expect, and our usual norms are adequate. When an unusual event disrupts our usual ways of doing things, however, our ordinary norms may not cover the new situation. People then may develop *new* norms to deal with the new situation. Sometimes they even produce new definitions of right and wrong that *under the new circumstances* justify actions that they would otherwise consider wrong. Turner and Killian use the term **emergent norms** to describe this change.

To understand how new norms emerge, we need to keep in mind that not everyone in a crowd has the same point of view (Snow, Zurcher, & Peters, 1993; Rodríguez, 1994). As Turner and Killian (1987) point out, there are five kinds of crowd participants:

1. The *ego-involved* feel a personal stake in the extraordinary event.

2. The *concerned* have a personal interest in the event, but less so than the ego-involved.

3. The *insecure* care little about the particular issue, but they join the crowd because it gives them a sense of power and security.

4. The *curious spectators* also care little about the issue, but they are inquisitive about what is going on.

This protest against imports by farmers in Marseilles, France, illustrates several sociological principles. Among them are emergent norms (behaviour otherwise disapproved becomes acceptable) and different types of crowd participants (the curious spectators are especially evident; the photographer could be an exploiter).

5. The *exploiters* do not care about the event, but are entrepreneurial and use it for their own purposes, such as hawking food or T-shirts.

The various attitudes, motives, and emotions of these different types of participants significantly influence the emergence of new norms. The most important role goes to the "ego-involved": some make suggestions about what should be done, while others take action. As the "concerned" join in, they, too, help to set the crowd on a particular course of action. The "insecure" and the "curious spectators" may then join in. Although the "exploiters" are unlikely to participate, they do lend the crowd passive support. Once a common mood develops, emergent norms are likely to replace the usual norms of accepted behaviour. Activities "not OK" in everyday life may now seem "OK"—whether throwing bottles at the cops or protesting the provincial government's cuts to public education or health care.

Focus Question

Why don't all sociologists describe collective behaviour in terms of emotions?

Forms of Collective Behaviour

Sociologists, then, treat collective behaviour the same as other forms of behaviour (Turner & Killian, 1987; Lofland, 1993; Turner, 1993). They view it as ordinary people responding to extraordinary situations (Rodríguez, 1994). They ask their usual questions about interaction, such as: How do people influence one another? What is the significance of the members' age, gender, and social class? What role do pre-existing attitudes play? Just how do people's perceptions get translated into action?

Collective behaviour takes many forms, including riots, panics, moral panics, rumours, fads, fashions, and urban legends. Let's look at each.

Riots or Demonstrations

White Los Angeles police officers had been caught on videotape beating an African-American traffic violator with their nightsticks. Television stations around the United States—and the world—broadcast the pictures to stunned audiences.

When the officers went on trial 14 months later for beating the man identified as Rodney King, how could the verdict be anything but guilty? Yet a jury consisting of eleven whites and one Asian-American found the officers innocent of using excessive force. The result was a **riot**—violent crowd behaviour aimed against people and property. Within minutes of the verdict, angry crowds began to gather in Los Angeles. That night, mobs set fire to businesses in south-central Los Angeles, and looting and arson

Most of the demonstrators at the APEC Conference in Vancouver came from middle-class backgrounds. One of their goals was to increase public awareness of the corporate agenda of this transnational organization.

began in earnest. The rioting spread to other cities, including Atlanta, Georgia; Tampa, Florida; and even Madison, Wisconsin and Las Vegas, Nevada. Whites and Koreans were favourite targets of violence.

On the third night, after 4000 fires had been set and more than 30 people killed, President George Bush announced on national television that the U.S. Justice Department had appointed prosecutors to investigate possible federal charges against the police officers for violating the civil rights of Rodney King. He then stated that he had ordered the Seventh Infantry, SWAT teams, and the FBI into Los Angeles. He also placed the California National Guard under the command of Gen. Colin Powell, the African-American chairman of the Joint Chiefs of Staff. Even Rodney King went on television and tearfully pleaded for peace.

The Los Angeles riot was the bloodiest in recent U.S. history. Before it was over, 54 people lost their lives, 2328 people were treated in hospital emergency rooms, thousands of small businesses were burned, and about $1 billion of property was destroyed. Two of the police officers were later sentenced to 2½ years in prison on federal charges, and King was awarded several million dollars in damages (Rose, 1992; Stevens & Lubman, 1992; Holden & Rose, 1993; Cannon, 1998).

Urban riots usually are caused by frustration and anger at deprivation. Frustrated at being kept out of mainstream society—limited to a meagre education, denied jobs and justice, and kept out of good neighbourhoods—frustration builds to such a boiling point that it takes only a precipitating event to erupt in collective violence. In the Los Angeles riot all these conditions existed, with the jury's verdict the precipitating event.

Sociologists have found that it is not only the deprived, however, who participate in riots or **demonstrations**. During the November 1997 demonstration against the APEC (Asia Pacific Economic Cooperation) summit in Vancouver, over four dozen people were arrested while many others were hosed with pepper spray by the RCMP. APEC is a group of 18 member nations that comprise half the world's economic strength and whose aims include "free trade" among member states by the year 2020. The APEC demonstrators were part of the 700 delegates from around the world attending the People's Summit on APEC. Most of the demonstrators were university students, environmentalists, trade unionists, educators, and others who came from stable middle-class backgrounds. Why would middle-class people participate in demonstrations? The answer, says sociologist Victor Rodríguez (1994), is a sense of frustration that many feel with being treated as second-class citizens even when they are gainfully employed and living stable lives.

Panics

In 1938, on the night before Halloween, a radio program of dance music was interrupted with a report that explosions had been observed on the surface of Mars. The announcer breathlessly added that a cylinder of unknown origin had been discovered embedded in the ground on a farm in New Jersey. The radio station then switched to the farm, where an alarmed reporter gave details of horrible-looking Martians coming out of the cylinder. Their death-ray weapons had destructive powers unknown to humans. An interview with an astronomer confirmed that Martians had invaded the Earth.

Perhaps six million North Americans heard this broadcast. About one million were frightened, and thousands panicked. Unknown numbers burst into tears, while thousands more grabbed weapons and hid in their basements or ran into the streets.

Of course, there was no invasion. This was simply a dramatization of H. G. Wells' *War of the Worlds*, starring Orson Welles. There had been an announcement at the beginning of the program and somewhere in the middle that the account was fictional, but apparently many people missed it. Although the panic reactions to this radio program may appear humorous to us today, to anyone who is in a panic the situation is anything but. **Panic** occurs when people become so fearful that they cannot function normally, and may even flee.

Why did people panic? Psychologist Hadley Cantril (1941) attributed the result to widespread anxiety about world conditions. The Nazis were marching in Europe. War jitters, he said, created fertile ground for the broadcast to touch off a panic.

Contemporary analysts, however, question whether there even was a panic. Sociologist William Bainbridge (1989) acknowledges that some people did become frightened. But he says that most of this famous panic was an invention of the news media. Reporters found a good story and milked it, exaggerating as they went along.

Natural disasters often provide examples of collective behaviour. A primary finding of disaster research is that people act rationally. Typically, they first check on the safety of their loved ones, then organize to overcome the effects of the disaster. Although this man appears dazed after a tornado destroyed his home, predictably, he soon will participate in organized efforts to recover from the disaster.

Bainbridge points to a 1973 event in Sweden. To dramatize the dangers of atomic power, Swedish Radio broadcast a play about an accident at a nuclear power plant. Knowing about the 1938 broadcast in the United States, Swedish sociologists were waiting to see what would happen. Might some people fail to realize that it was a dramatization and panic at the threat of ruptured reactors spewing out radioactivity? The sociologists found no panic. A few people did become frightened. Some telephoned family members and the police—reasonable responses, considering what they thought had occurred.

The Swedish media, however, reported a panic! Apparently, a reporter had telephoned two police departments and learned that each had received calls from concerned citizens. With a deadline hanging over his head, the reporter decided to gamble. He reported that police and fire stations were jammed with citizens, that people were flocking to the shelters, and that others were fleeing south (Bainbridge, 1989).

Panics do occur, of course—which is why nobody has the right to shout "Fire!" in a public building when no such danger exists—for if people fear immediate death, they will lunge toward the nearest exit in a frantic effort to escape. Such a panic occurred on January 7, 1995, at a 30-storey apartment building in suburban North York, Ontario. In the early morning hours, around 5 a.m., residents were awoken by a fire alarm. Most on the lower floors were able to race out of the building while others screamed from balconies as the acrid smoke from the fire that had started on the 5th floor slowly gripped the whole building. In the end, six bodies—two men and four women, one of whom had been six months pregnant, were found dead in the smoke-filled stairwell. One eyewitness, who lived on the 18th floor, decided to leave her apartment and descend the stairwell to the ground floor. By the time she reached the 11th floor, she says,

The stairwell was full of panicking, half-asleep people carrying their pets, and then the smoke became so thick we couldn't go any further—everybody was choking—I knew we had to turn back, but we had to get everybody turned around because the stairwells were lined. It became even harder to breathe because you're puffing from climbing the stairs (Canadian Press Newswire, January 5, 1995).

Sociologists have found what other researchers have discovered in analyzing other disasters. *Not everybody panics.* In disturbances many people continue to act responsibly. Sociologists us the term **role extension** to describe these actions. Especially important are primary group bonds. Parents help their children, for example (Morrow, 1995). Gender roles also persist, and more men help women than women help men (N. R. Johnson, 1993). Even work roles continue to guide some behaviour.

Moral Panics

Moral panics occur when large numbers of people become intensely concerned, even fearful, about some behaviour thought to threaten morality, and the fear is out of proportion to any supposed danger (Cauthen & Jasper, 1994; Goode & Ben-Yehuda, 1994). The threat is seen as enormous, and hostility builds toward those thought responsible. The most infamous of moral panics is the fear of witches in Europe between 1400 and 1650, resulting in the Inquisition—investigations, torture, and burning at the stake of people accused of witchcraft.

Another example is Joan of Arc—Luc Besson's recent film *The Messenger* captured the moral panic she caused among France's religious and political leaders after her successful military campaigns against the English.

Focus Question
Why aren't all crowds destructive mobs?

Today, moral panics are fuelled by the media. Like other panics, moral panics centre around a sense of danger. Moral panics are further fuelled by **rumour**, information for which there is no discernible source and which is usually unfounded. For example, a rumour, still continuing, is that missing children are sold to Satanists who abuse them sexually and then ritually murder them. This rumour is intensely believed by some, and has been supported by testimony from people who claim to have been involved in such sacrifices. Investigations by the police, however, have uncovered no evidence to substantiate it.

Moral panics thrive on uncertainty and anxiety. Today's changing family serves up a rich plateful of anxiety. Concerns that children are receiving inadequate care because so many mothers left home to join the work force become linked with thoughts of dangers to children from sinister sources lurking almost everywhere.

Rumours

In *Aladdin*, the handsome young title character murmurs, "All good children, take off your clothes." In *The Lion King*, Simba, the cuddly lion star, stirs up a cloud of dust that, floating off the screen, spells S-E-X. Then there is the bishop in *The Little Mermaid*, who, presiding over a wedding, becomes noticeably aroused.

Thriving in conditions of ambiguity, rumours function to fill in missing information (Turner, 1964; Shibutani, 1966). In response to the rumour, Disney reports that Aladdin really says "Scat, good tiger, take off and go." The line is hard to hear clearly, however, leaving enough ambiguity for others to continue to hear what they want, even to insist that it is an invitation to a teenage orgy. Similar ambiguity remains with Simba's dust and the aroused bishop.

Most rumours are short-lived. They arise in a situation of ambiguity, only to dissipate when they are replaced by factual information—or by another rumour. For example, despite a publication ban about the brutal killing of Leslie Mahaffy and Kristin French during the 1993 trial of Karla Homolka and Paul Bernardo, rumours about the details of the crimes were said to be available on the Internet for those curious enough to find them.

Why do people believe rumours? Three main factors have been identified. First, rumours deal with a subject that is important to an individual. Second, they replace ambiguity with some form of certainty. Third, they are attributed to a creditable source. An office rumour may be preceded by "Jane has it on good authority that …," or "Bill overheard the boss say that. …" Ambiguity or uncertainty is especially important in giving life to rumours.

Fads and Fashions

A **fad** is a novel form of behaviour that briefly catches people's attention. The new behaviour appears suddenly and spreads by suggestion, imitation, and identification with people already involved in the fad. Publicity by the mass media also helps to spread the fad (Aguirre, Quarantelli, & Mendoza, 1993).

Fads are one of the fascinating aspects of life that sociologists study. Body piercing, whose origins reach back into antiquity, has become popular in the Western world. It is unlikely, however, that body piercing will enter the mainstream culture. Certainly its extremes won't.

Sociologist John Lofland (1985) identified four types of fads. First are object fads, such as the Hula Hoop of the 1950s, the pet rocks of the 1970s, the Rubik's Cube and Cabbage Patch Dolls of the 1980s, and the pogs, beanie babies, and Pokémon of the 1990s. Second are activity fads, such as eating goldfish in the 1920s and bungee jumping and body piercing in the 1990s. Third are idea fads, such as astrology. Fourth are personality fads, such as Elvis Presley, Princess Diana, and Wayne Gretzky. Some fads are extremely short-lived, such as "streaking" (running naked in a public place). When a fad lasts, it is called a **fashion**. Some fashions, as with clothing, are the result of a coordinated international marketing system that includes designers, manufacturers, advertisers, and retailers. Billions of dollars worth of clothing are sold by manipulating the tastes of the public. Fashion, however, also refers to hairstyles, home decorating, even the design and colours of buildings. Sociologist John Lofland (1985) pointed out that fashion even applies to language, as demonstrated by these roughly comparable terms: "Neat!" in the 1950s, "Right on!" in the 1960s, "Really!" in the 1970s, "Awesome!" in the 1980s, and "Bad!" and the resurrection of "Cool" and "buddy" in the 1990/2000s.

Urban Legends

Jerry [or whoever] went to a nightclub last weekend. He met a good-looking woman, and they hit it off. They spent the night in a motel, and when he awoke the next morning, the woman was gone. When he went into the bathroom, he saw a message scrawled on the mirror in lipstick: "Welcome to the wonderful world of AIDS."

Urban legends are stories with an ironic twist that sound realistic but are false. Although untrue, they usually are told by people who believe that they happened.

Another urban legend that has made the rounds is "Kentucky Fried Rat."

One night, a woman didn't have anything ready for supper, so she and her husband went to the drive-through at Kentucky Fried Chicken. While they were eating in their car, the wife said, "My chicken tastes funny."

Her husband said, "You're always complaining about something." When she insisted that the chicken didn't taste right, he put on the light. She was holding fried rat—crispy style. The woman went into shock and was rushed to the hospital.

A lawyer from the company offered them $100 000 if they would sign a release and not tell anyone. This is the second case they have had.

Folklorist Jan Brunvand (1981, 1984, 1986) reported that urban legends are passed on by people who think that the event happened just one or two people down the line of transmission, often to a "friend of a friend." Brunvand views urban legends as "modern morality stories," with each teaching a moral lesson about life.

If we apply Brunvand's analysis to these two urban legends, three major points emerge. First, their moral serves as a warning. "The Wonderful World of AIDS" warns young people that they should be careful about where they go, with whom they go, and what they do. The world is an unsafe place, and "messing around" is risky. "Kentucky Fried Rat" contains a different moral: Do you *really* know what you are eating when you buy food from a fast food outlet?

Second, each story is related to social change: "The Wonderful World of AIDS" to changing sexual morality; "Kentucky Fried Rat" to changing male-female relationships, especially changing sex roles at home. Third, each is calculated to instill guilt and fear: guilt—the wife failed in her traditional role of cooking supper, and she gets punished—and fear, the dangerous unknown, whether unprotected sex or fast food. The ultimate moral of these stories is that we should not abandon traditional roles or the safety of the home.

Social Movements

Social movements consist of large numbers of people who organize to promote or resist social change. They have strong ideas about what is wrong with the world—or some part of it—and how to make things right. Examples include the temperance movement, the women's movement, the animal rights crusade, the Quebec sovereignty movement, and the environmental movement.

At the heart of social movements lie grievances and dissatisfactions. For some people, a current condition of society is intolerable, and their goal is to *promote* social change. Theirs is called a **proactive social movement**. In contrast, others feel threatened because some condition of society is changing, and they organize to *resist* that change. Theirs is a **reactive social movement**.

To further their goals, people develop **social movement organizations**. Those whose goal is to promote social change develop such organizations as the over 700-member National Action Committee on the Status of Women, the Council of Canadians, and the National Indian Brotherhood. In contrast, for those who are trying to resist these changes, the National Citizens Coalition, the Western Guard, and REAL Women of Canada serve this purpose. To recruit followers and sympathizers, leaders of social movements use various attention-getting devices, from marches and protest rallies to sit-ins and boycotts. To publicize their grievances, they also may try to stage "media events" (see the following Perspectives box).

The Quiet Revolution in Quebec, which began in the early 1960s, was a response to the two-decades-long failure of Maurice Duplessis' Union Nationale government to modernize the state institutions of health, education, and welfare in that province. But the Quiet Revolution also unleashed many other social movements, including the *indépendence* movement and the FLQ or Front de Libération du Québec.

Perspectives

Which Side of the Barricades? The Pros and Cons of Trade Unions in Canada

Trade unions in Canada are important social movements with a clearly defined organization and goals. However, the role trade unions should play in Canadian society has never been clear. Often, trade unions are portrayed in the media as adversarial organizations hell-bent on pitting management against employees and sometimes worker against worker. Advocates, on the other hand, argue that unions provide employees with an effective voice to express their views and achieve positive resolutions to their grievances against the many arbitrary decisions made by management.

The views of the two sides could not be more incompatible. Those who favour trade unions' contribution to Canadian society look at the over three million trade union members as examples of men and women exercising their basic human right of organizing for a better life and national community.

Those who gather round the anti-union banner see unions as harmful to society because union leaders fight for their own members' interest at the expense of everyone else.

For those on either side of the barricade, there is little likelihood of reconciling such contrary attitudes. Each sees the other as unreasonable and extremist. And each uses propaganda by focusing on either worst- or best-case scenarios; anti-unionists point out the examples of corruption and undemocratic factions within specific unions; pro-unionists point out that trade unions have been in the forefront of the struggle for maintaining, even strengthening, universal social programs such as health care and government pensions.

As each side fights in the political arena for what it considers basic rights, each encounter reinvigorates the other camp. When in 1982, the Charter of

Rights and Freedoms came into effect, trade unions across Canada were to face formidable challenges from their adversaries. The Canadian Labour Congress (CLC) did not participate in the original discussions, due largely to the determination of senior Quebec Federation of Labour officials. As a result, the "rights" of trade unionists were never seriously discussed for possible inclusion in the Charter. Several Supreme Court of Canada cases later, each side has won and lost some battles. So the contest continues.

Because the two sides see reality in very different ways, the advocates and the detractors of the trade union movement in Canada are not likely to give up their struggle in the foreseeable future. Nothing, then, to such committed activists is ever complete. Rather, each action is only a way station in a prolonged struggle.

Types and Tactics of Social Movements

Let's see what types of social movements there are and then examine their tactics.

Types of Social Movements

Since social change is always their goal, we can classify social movements according to their *target* and the *amount of change* they seek. Figure 18.2 summarizes the classification developed by sociologist David Aberle (1966). If you read across, you will see that the target of the first two types of social movements is *individuals*. **Alterative social movements** seek only to alter some particular behaviour of people. An example of a powerful social movement today is Mothers Against Drunk Driving (MADD), whose goal is to get people to stop driving if they have drunk any alcohol. Its members are convinced that if they could stop drunk drivers there would be many fewer deaths on our highways. **Redemptive social movements** also target individuals, but here the aim is for *total* change. An example is a religious social movement that stresses conversion. In fundamentalist Christianity, for example, when someone converts to a particular view of Jesus Christ, the entire person is supposed to

Figure 18.2 Types of Social Movements

Source: Aberle (1966).

Amount of Change

	Partial	Total
Individual	Alterative 1	Redemptive 2
Society	Reformative 3	Transformative 4

Target of Change

change, not just some specific behaviour. The individual becomes a "true believer" of that religious sect or cult.

The target of the next two types of social movements is *society*. **Reformative social movements** seek to *reform* some specific aspect of society. The environmental movement, for example, seeks to reform the ways society treats the environment, from its disposal of garbage and nuclear wastes to its use of forests and water. **Transformative social movements**, in contrast, seek to *transform* the social order itself and to replace it with a new version of the good society. Revolutions such as those in the American colonies, France, Russia, and Cuba are examples.

A new twist in social movements is the global orientation of some. Rather than focusing on changing a condition within a specific country, the goal is to change this condition throughout the world. The women's, environmental, and animal rights movements are examples. Because of this new focus, some sociologists refer to them as **new social movements** (McAdam, McCarthy, & Zald, 1988).

Tactics of Social Movements

The leaders of a social movement can choose from a variety of tactics. Should they peacefully boycott, march, or hold an all-night candlelight vigil? Or should they bomb a building, blow up an airplane, or assassinate a key figure? To understand why the leaders of social movements choose their tactics, we need to examine a group's membership, the publics it addresses (or audience), and its relationship to authorities.

Membership. Figure 18.3 shows the composition of social movements. At the centre is the inner core, those people most committed to the movement. This inner core sets the group's goals, timetables, and strategies, and inspires the other members. Those at the second level are also committed to the movement. People at this level, however, can be counted on to show up for demonstrations and to do the grunt work—to do mailings, pass out petitions and leaflets, make telephone calls. At the third level is a

Nellie McClung and Emmeline Pankhurst in 1916. What kind of tactics did the sufragettes use in their social movement?

Figure 18.3 The Membership and Publics of Social Movements

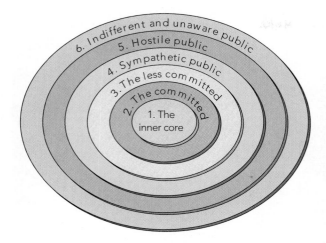

6. Indifferent and unaware public
5. Hostile public
4. Sympathetic public
3. The less committed
2. The committed
1. The inner core

Women participating in a Take Back the Night march, which takes place annually in communities across Canada and throughout the world.

wider circle of people who are less committed and less dependable. Their participation is primarily a matter of convenience. If an activity does not interfere with something else they want to do, they participate.

The predispositions and backgrounds of the inner core are essential in the choice of tactics. Because of their background, the inner core of some groups is predisposed to use peaceful means, others prefer confrontational means, while still others prefer violence. Tactics also depend on the number of committed members. Different tactics are called for if the inner core can count on 700 committed members to show up—as opposed to, say, seven.

The Publics. Lying outside the membership is the **public**, a dispersed group of people who usually have an interest in the issue. Just outside the third circle of members, and blending into it, is the sympathetic public. Sympathy with the movement's goals makes this public fertile ground for recruiting new members. The second public is hostile; it is keenly aware of the group's goals and dislikes them. This public wants to stop the social movement, for the movement's values go against its own. The third public consists of disinterested people. They are either unaware of the social movement, or if aware, indifferent to it.

Relationship to Authorities. The movement's relationship to authorities is also significant in determining tactics—especially in choosing peaceful or violent tactics. If a social movement is *institutionalized*—accepted by authorities—violence will not be directed against the authorities, for they are on the same side. This, however, does not rule out violence directed against the opposition. If authorities are hostile to a social movement, aggressive or even violent tactics are more likely.

Other Factors. Sociologist Ellen Scott (1993), who studied the movement to stop rape, discovered that close friendships, race, and even size of town are important in determining tactics.

Social Movements and the Media

In selecting tactics, the leaders of social movements are keenly aware of their effects on the mass media (Zald, 1992). Their goal is to influence **public opinion**, how people think about some issue. Pictures of bloodied, dead baby seals, for example, go a long way toward getting one group's message across.

A key to understanding social movements, then, is **propaganda**. Although this word often evokes negative images, it actually is neutral. Propaganda is simply the presentation of information in the attempt to influence people. Its original meaning was positive, for *propaganda* referred to a committee of cardinals of the Roman Catholic Church whose assignment was the care of foreign missions. (They were to *propagate* the faith.)

Propaganda, then, in the sense of organized attempts to manipulate public opinion, is a regular part of modern life. Advertisements, for example, are a form of propaganda, for they present a one-sided version of reality. Underlying effective propaganda are seven basic techniques, discussed in the Down-to-Earth Sociology box on page 439. Perhaps by understanding these techniques, you will be able to resist

The use of propaganda is popular among those committed to the goals of a social movement. They can see only one side to the social issue they are so upset about. Do you think there is another side to this social issue?

one-sided appeals—whether they come from social movements or from hawkers of some new product.

The mass media play a crucial role in social movements. They have become, in effect, the gatekeepers to social movements. If those who control and work in the mass media—from owners to reporters—are sympathetic to some particular "cause," you can be sure that it receives sympathetic treatment. If the social movement goes against their biases, it will either be ignored or receive unfavourable treatment. If you ever get the impression that the media are trying to manipulate your opinions and attitudes on some particular social movement—or some social issue—you are probably right. Far from doing unbiased reporting, the media are under the control and influence of people who have an agenda to get across. To the materials in the Down-to-Earth Sociology box on propaganda, then, we need to add the biases of the media establishment. TV, radio, newspapers, magazines, and so on select the issues to which they choose to give publicity, those they ignore, and whether they will present favourable or unfavourable treatment of issues and movements.

Sociology can be a liberating discipline (Berger, 1963). It sensitizes us to the existence of *multiple realities*; that is, for any single point of view on some topic, there likely are competing points of view, which some find equally as compelling. Consequently, although the committed members of a social movement are sincere, and perhaps even sacrificing for "the cause," theirs is but one view of the way the world is. If other sides were presented, the issue would look quite different.

Why People Join Social Movements

As we have seen, social movements arise from the conviction that some condition of society is no longer tolerable. Not everyone, however, who feels strongly dissatisfied about an issue joins a social movement. Let's look at three explanations for why some people join social movements.

> **Focus Question**
> Who joins social movements and why?

Mass Society Theory

To explain why people are attracted to social movements, sociologist William Kornhauser (1959) proposed **mass society theory**. Kornhauser argued that **mass society**—an impersonal, industrialized, highly bureaucratized society—makes many people feel isolated. Social movements fill a void by offering people a sense of belonging. In geographical areas where social ties are supposedly weaker, such as western Canada, one would then expect to find more social movements than in areas where traditional ties are supposedly stronger, such as in Atlantic Canada.

This theory seems to match common-sense observations. Certainly, social movements seem to proliferate on the Prairies and the West Coast. But sociologist Doug McAdam (McAdam et al., 1988), who interviewed people who had

Sociologists Alfred and Elizabeth Lee (1939) found that propaganda relies on seven basic techniques, which they termed "tricks of the trade." To be effective, the techniques should be subtle, with the audience remaining unaware of just which part of their mind or emotions is being manipulated. If propaganda is effective, people will not know *why* they support something, only that they do.

1. *Name calling*. This technique aims to arouse opposition to the competing product, candidate, or policy by associating it with a negative image. By comparison, one's own product, candidate, or policy appears attractive. Political candidates who call an opponent "soft on crime" are using this technique.

2. *Glittering generality*. Essentially the opposite of the first, this technique surrounds the product, candidate, or policy with "virtue words," phrases that arouse positive feelings. "She's a *real* New Democrat" has little meaning, but it makes the audience feel that something has been said. "He stands for individualism" is so general that it is meaningless, yet the audience thinks that it has heard a specific message about the candidate.

3. *Transfer*. In its positive form, this technique associates the product, candidate, or policy with something the public respects or approves; in its negative form, with something of which it disapproves. Let's look at the positive form: You might not be able to get by with saying "Labatt's is cool," but surround a beer with happy, outgoing young people, and beer drinkers will get the idea that they too can be cool, young, and carefree if they drink this brand of beer rather than its rival.

4. *Testimonials*. Famous and admired individuals are used to endorse a product, candidate, or policy. Wayne Gretzky lends his name to Tylenol, Esso, and CIBC, while Candice Bergen does the same for Sprint. In the negative form of this technique, a despised person is associated with the competing product. If propagandists could get away with it, they would show Saddam Hussein drinking a competing beer or announcing support for an opposing candidate.

5. *Plain folks*. Sometimes it pays to associate the product, candidate, or policy with "just plain folks." "If Mary or John Q. Public like it, you will, too." A political candidate who kisses babies, dons a hard hat, and has lunch at McDonald's while photographers "catch him or her in the act"—is using the "plain folks" strategy. "I'm just a regular person" is the message of the political candidate posing for photographers in jeans and work shirt—while making certain that the Mercedes and chauffeur are not visible in the background.

6. *Card stacking*. The aim of this technique is to present only positive information about what you support, only negative information about what you oppose. Make it sound as though there is only one conclusion a rational person can draw. Use falsehoods, distortions, and illogical statements if you must.

7. *Bandwagon*. "Everyone is doing it" is the idea behind this technique. After all, "20 million Frenchmen can't be wrong," can they? Emphasizing how many others buy the product or support the candidate or policy conveys the message that anyone who doesn't join in is on the wrong track.

The Lees (1939) added, "Once we know that a speaker or writer is using one of these propaganda devices in an attempt to convince us of an idea, we can separate the device from the idea and see what the idea amounts to on its own merits."

---

risked their lives in the civil rights movement, found that these people were firmly rooted in families and communities. It was their strong desire to right wrongs and overcome injustices, not their isolation, which motivated their participation. Ironically, the homeless, among the most isolated, generally do not join anything—except food lines.

Deprivation Theory

A second explanation to account for why people join social movements is *deprivation theory*. According to this theory, people who are deprived of things deemed valuable in society—whether money, justice, status, or privilege—join social movements in the hope of redressing their grievances. This theory may seem so obvious as to need no evidence. Aren't the Mohawk warriors who occupied their land for 78 days in what became known across Canada as "The Oka Crisis" ample evidence that the theory is true?

Deprivation theory does provide a starting point. But there is more to the matter than this. We must also pay attention to what Alexis de Tocqueville (1856/1955) noted almost 150 years ago. The peasants of Germany were worse off than the peasants of France, and from deprivation theory we

The "Oka Crisis," during which Mohawk warriors occupied their land for 78 days in Quebec, is perhaps an example of deprivation theory.

would expect the Germans to have rebelled and overthrown their king. Revolution, however, occurred in France, not Germany. The reason, said de Tocqueville, is *relative* deprivation. French peasants had experienced improving living conditions and could imagine even better conditions, while German peasants, having never experienced anything but depressed conditions, had no comparative basis for feeling deprived.

According to **relative deprivation theory**, then, it is not people's actual negative conditions (their *absolute* deprivation) that matters. Rather, the key to participation is *relative* deprivation—that is, what people *think* they should have relative to what they once had, hope to have, or what others have. This theory, which has provided excellent insight into revolutions, also holds a surprise. Because improving conditions fuel human desires for even better conditions, in some instances *improving* conditions can spark revolutions.

Moral Issues and Ideological Commitment

Some people join because of *moral shock*—a sense of outrage at finding out what is "really" going on (Jasper & Poulsen, 1995). They feel they must choose sides and do what they can to make a difference. As sociologists put it, they join because of *ideological commitment* to the movement.

Many members on both sides of the Quebec sovereignty issue see their involvement in such terms. Similarly, most activists in the animal rights movement are convinced that

there can be no justification for animals to suffer in order to make safer products for humans. For others, matters of the environment are moral issues, and not to act would be an inexcusable betrayal of future generations. The *moral* component of a social movement, then, is a primary reason for some people's involvement.

A Special Case: The Agent Provocateur

A unique type of social movement participant is the **agent provocateur**, an agent of the government or even of a rival social movement, whose job is to spy on the leadership and perhaps sabotage the group's activities. Some are recruited from the membership itself and betray their movement's goals for money, while others are members of the police or a rival group who go underground and join the movement.

Since the social change that some social movements represent is radical, threatening the power elite, the use of agent provocateurs is not surprising. What may be surprising, however, is that some agents get converted to the social movement on which they are spying. Sociologist Gary Marx (1993) explains that, to be credible, agents must share at least some of the class, age, gender, ethnic, racial, or religious characteristics of the group. This, however, makes the agents more likely to sympathize with the movement's goals and become disenchanted with trying to harm the group. What also may be surprising is how far some agents go. During the 1960s, when a wave of militant social movements rolled across Quebec, the RCMP and other police were busy recruiting agent provocateurs. To sabotage groups, these agents provoked illegal activities that otherwise would not have occurred, setting the leadership up for arrest (Sawatsky, 1980).

In Sum

Perhaps most commonly, people join a social movement because they have friends and acquaintances already in the movement (McCarthy & Wolfson, 1992; Snow, Zurcher, & Ekland-Olson, 1993). Some join because of moral convictions, others to further their own careers, because it is fun, or because they achieve recognition or find a valued identity. As we just saw, police officials may join social movements in order to spy on them and sabotage their activities. In no social movement, then, is there a single cause for people joining.

On the Success and Failure of Social Movements

Large industrial societies produce the fertile ground of discontent that spawns social movements, but most social movements are not successful. Let's look at the reasons for their success or failure.

The Life Course of Social Movements

Social movements have a life course; that is, they go through different stages as they grow and mature. Sociologists have identified five stages of social movements (Lang & Lang, 1961; Mauss, 1975; Spector & Kitsuse, 1977; Tilly, 1978; Jasper, 1991).

1. *Initial unrest and agitation.* During this first stage, people are upset about some condition in society and want to change it. Leaders emerge who verbalize people's feelings and crystallize issues. Most social movements fail at this stage. Unable to gain enough support, after a brief flurry of activity they quietly die.

2. *Resource mobilization.* The crucial factor that enables social movements to make it past the first stage is **resource mobilization**. By this term, sociologists mean the mobilization of resources such as time, money, people's skills, technologies such as direct mailing and fax machines, attention by the mass media, and even legitimacy among the public and authorities (Oliver & Marwell, 1992; Buechler, 1993).

3. *Organization.* A division of labour is set up. The leadership makes policy decisions, and the rank and file carry out the daily tasks necessary to keep the movement going.

4. *Institutionalization.* At this stage, a movement has developed a *bureaucracy*, the type of formal hierarchy described in Chapter 10. The collective excitement is gone, and control lies in the hands of career officers, who may care more about their own position in the organization than the movement for which the organization's initial leaders made sacrifices. They may move the group's headquarters to a "good" location, for example, furnish it with expensive furniture and art work, and take pains to be seen with the "right" people in the "right" places.

5. *Organizational decline and possible resurgence.* At this point, instead of working on the issues, the leadership may waste its energies on managing the day-to-day affairs of the organization. With no strong, committed group united by a common cause, the movement may wither away and finally disappear. Its diehards always linger, grasping at any straw in hopes there will be a resurgence.

And appearances can be deceiving. Even if most participants desert and those most committed flounder with little support, this does not necessarily mean the end of a movement. After suffragists won the right to vote in Canada in 1919, their movement declined until nothing but a shell remained. During a period researchers call *abeyance*, only a handful of committed organizers were left, and the best they could do was to desperately keep the flame burning.

Yet the women's movement was re-energized, and again thrust into national prominence (Taylor, 1997).

The Thinking Critically about Social Controversy box on page 442 provides an example of the building of a social movement.

> ### Focus Question
> Do all social movements have a sociological life (i.e., birth, maturation, and eventual death)?

An Overview of Social Change

Social change is brought about by people organized into social movements. Before we can interpret these changes, whether they are progressive, or even whether there is such a thing as progress, it is necessary to make a few introductory comments about the importance of technology in any theory of social change.

How Technology Changes Society

As you may recall from Chapter 3, **technology** carries a double meaning. It refers to both *tools*, items used to accomplish tasks, and the *skills or procedures* to make and use those tools. This broad concept includes in its first meaning tools as simple as a comb and as complicated as computers. Its second meaning refers in this case not only to the skills or procedures used to manufacture combs and computers but also to those required to "produce" an acceptable hairdo or to gain access to the Internet. Apart from its particulars, technology always refers to *artificial means of extending human abilities.*

All human groups make and use technology, but the chief characteristic of postindustrial societies (also called **postmodern societies**) is technology that greatly extends our ability to analyze information, communicate, and travel. These *new technologies*, as they are called, allow us to do what had never been done in history: probe space and other planets, communicate almost instantaneously anywhere on the globe, travel greater distances faster, and store, retrieve, and analyze vast amounts of information.

This level of accomplishment, though impressive, is really very superficial. As we look at how technology spreads, we shall stress this sociological aspect of technology—how it affects people's lives.

Modernization

The term given to the sweeping changes ushered in by the Industrial Revolution is **modernization**. Table 18.1 reviews these changes. This table is an *ideal type* in Weber's sense of

On September 25, 1997, Saskatoon, Saskatchewan's Broadway Theatre was the site of the first large-scale rally in Canada against the Multilateral Agreement on Investment (MAI). So how is it possible for an apparently invisible issue to become so visible?

This can be attributed to the organizing that had gone on previously in the community. Two months earlier, a small group got together to talk about the way the MAI was being secretly negotiated, how to break the code of secrecy and build resistance to it. Organizers decided to concentrate on the negative impacts of the MAI, such as potential job losses, increased regional disparities, and the loss of national sovereignty.

The second stage of the organizing grew out of an agreement to work toward a major public event in September. Another organizing meeting was held in August. People from different social justice, antinuclear, development, church, labour, farm, health, and other organizations in Saskatoon attend-ed. Various people and organizations took on tasks such as distributing posters, developing leaflets, issuing press releases, and getting more groups to support the coming rally. As well, two Saskatoon organizers wrote articles on the MAI for the local *Saskatoon Star Phoenix*.

Another event helped to spur things forward. A conference of the Asia Pacific Economic Cooperation Forum (APEC) was held in Saskatoon in early September 1997. Because of the short notice, only about 30 protestors gathered at the hotel where the conference was being held. As small as it was, the demonstration did receive positive press coverage; however, as a result of this experience, organizers decided that it was very important to have an active phoning tree.

To keep the momentum growing, the organizing group agreed to meet on a weekly basis leading up to the Broadway Theatre event. Finally, an afternoon workshop on dismantling the corporate agenda was held just prior to the event at the Broadway.

After the rally, participants met at the Broadway Theatre where they endorsed a People's Charter in opposition to the MAI. Two hundred people signed letters calling for a full and open public debate in the House of Commons and the provincial legislatures; the letters were sent to Prime Minister Jean Chrétien and Premier Roy Romanow.

Certainly, the key organizing question is how to keep this social movement alive. Participants at the September rally were invited to attend an organizing meeting to be held the next month.

For Your Consideration

Typically, the last stage of a social movement is decline. Does the last stage apply to this social movement? Under what conditions will this social movement decline?

Source: Cram & Kossick (1997).

the term, for no society exemplifies to the maximum degree all the traits listed here. For example, although most Canadians now work in the service sector of the economy, over two million still work in the natural resource and manufacturing sectors. Thus all characteristics shown in Table 18.1 should be interpreted as "more" or "less" rather than "either-or."

As technology from the industrialized world is introduced into traditional societies, we are able to witness how far-reaching the changes are. Take just modern medicine as an example. Its introduction into the least industrialized nations helped reduce death rates while birth rates remained high. As a result, the population exploded, bringing hunger and starvation, mass migration to cities, and mass migration to the industrialized nations.

Ogburn's Theory of Social Change

Technology, sociologist William Ogburn (1922, 1961, 1964) said, can lead to social change through invention, discovery, and diffusion.

Invention. Ogburn defined **invention** as a combining of existing elements and materials to form new ones. Although we think of inventions as being only material, such as computers, there also are *social* inventions, such as capitalism and the corporation.

Discovery. Ogburn's second process of change is **discovery**, a new way of seeing reality. However, a discovery brings extensive change only when it comes at the right time.

Diffusion. The spread of an invention or discovery from one area to another, called **diffusion**, can have far-reaching effects on human relationships. For example, when missionaries introduced steel axes to the aborigines of Australia, it upset their whole society. Before this, the men controlled the making of axes, using a special stone available only in a remote region and passing axe-making skills from one man to another. Women had to request permission to use the stone axe. When steel axes became common, women also possessed them, and the men lost both status and power (L. Sharp, 1995).

Diffusion also includes the spread of ideas. The idea of citizenship, for example, changed the political structure, for no longer was the monarch an unquestioned source of authority. Today, the concept of gender equality is circling the globe, with the basic idea that it is wrong to withhold rights on the basis of someone's sex. This idea, though now

Table 18.1 Comparing Traditional and Modern Societies

Characteristics	Traditional Societies	Modern Societies
General Characteristics		
Social change	Slow	Rapid
Size of group	Small	Large
Religious orientation	More	Less
Formal education	No	Yes
Place of residence	Rural	Urban
Demographic transition	First stage	Third stage
Family size	Larger	Smaller
Infant mortality	High	Low
Life expectancy	Short	Long
Health care	Home	Hospital
Temporal orientation	Past	Future
Material Relations		
Industrialized	No	Yes
Technology	Simple	Complex
Division of labour	Simple	Complex
Economic sector	Primary	Tertiary
Income	Low	High
Material possessions	Few	Many
Social Relationships		
Basic organization	*Gemeinschaft*	*Gesellschaft*
Families	Extended	Nuclear
Respect for elders	More	Less
Social stratification	Rigid	More open
Statuses	More ascribed	More achieved
Gender equality	Less	More
Norms		
View of reality, life, and morals	Absolute	Relativistic
Social control	Informal	Formal
Tolerance of differences	Less	More

taken for granted in a few parts of the world, is revolutionary. Like citizenship, it is destined to transform basic human relationships and entire societies.

Cultural Lag. As noted in Chapter 3, Ogburn coined the term **cultural lag** to describe the situation in which some elements of a culture adapt to an invention or discovery more rapidly than others.

Evaluation of Ogburn's Theory

Some find Ogburn's analysis too one-directional, saying it makes technology the cause of almost all social change. They point out that adapting to changing technology is only one part of the story. The other part consists of people taking control over technology—developing the technology they need.

Technology and social change, then, actually form a two-way street: Just as technology leads to social change, so social change leads to new technology. For example, as the numbers of elderly in our society have grown, their needs have stimulated the development of medical technologies to treat Alzheimer's disease. Changing ideas about the disabled have stimulated the development of new types of wheelchairs that allow people who cannot move their legs to play basketball, participate in the Special Olympics, and enter races.

Transforming Society

As discussed in the Sociology and the New Technology box on the following page, it is easy to misguess the consequences of a new technology. Let's look at five ways technology can change society.

Transformation of Existing Technologies. The first impact is felt by the technology that is being displaced. For example, IBM electric typewriters, "state of the art" equipment just a decade ago, have been rendered practically useless by the desktop computer.

Changes in Social Organization. Technology also changes social organization. For example, machine technology gave birth to the factory. Then it was discovered that workers could produce more items if each did a specialized task. Henry Ford then built on this innovation by developing the assembly line: Instead of workers moving to the parts, a machine moved the parts to the workers. In addition, the parts were made interchangeable and easy to attach (Womack, Jones, & Roos, 1991).

Changes in Ideology. Technology also spurs new ideologies. For example, Karl Marx saw the change to the factory system as a source of **alienation**. He noted that workers who did repetitive tasks on just a small part of a product no longer felt connected to the finished product. They became alienated from the product of their labour, which bred dissatisfaction and unrest.

Transformation of Values. Today, for example, Canadians and Americans brag about cars, hot tubs, and jacuzzis—and make certain their jeans have the right labels prominently displayed. In short, the particular emphasis on the social value of materialism often depends on the state of technology.

Transformation of Social Relationships. Technology can also change social relationships. New technological changes flourish in our largest cities. And these cities are growing ever larger. Thriving, vibrant cities provide sufficient social space for individuals living in diverse communities to flourish. Ironically, the bigger the city, the "freer" the individual is to be him- or herself and to pursue his or her interests, often with minimal social pressure. In the age of globalization,

Almost everybody wants to know the future—from the work we'll be doing five years from now to how much money we'll have in 10 years.

So it is with technology. Futurists guesstimate the social ramifications of new technologies, predicting far-reaching—and sometimes dire—consequences. Consider the following *totally wrong* predictions:

A new century is at hand. Our new technology will practically annihilate time and space. It will let people live and work wherever they please, creating dynamic new communities linked by electronics. Because of this new technology, many people will move out of cities, doing their work from their homes.

Some social class barriers will crumble, for people will have the power to summon almost anyone. It may even save the family farm by linking farmers with others.

In this amazing future, people will be able to dial up symphonies, presidential speeches, and even three-dimensional Shakespeare plays.

The new technology is not without risk, however. Novels and movie theatres may vanish, people may lose their privacy, and its illicit use can spark a crackdown by the government.

How can I say with such certainty that these predictions are *totally wrong*? After all, we are only in the initial stages of the communications revolution, and they all may prove true. Perhaps. But the problem is that these predictions were made 100 years ago—and not about the computer, but about the telephone!

To all the guesstimates of futurists, a reasonable response seems to be, "Let's wait and see." Plenty of predictions in the past didn't see the light of day. We do know that our way of life depends on technology and that new technology can transform society. Changes there will be—that we can count on; what we don't know are the exact directions and implications of those changes. For that, we must let the future itself unfold—taking us with it—sometimes willingly, sometimes reluctantly.

Sources: Marvin (1988); Fischer (1995); Pearl (1995a).

---

new social relationships sparked by living in big cities with people from all walks of life and from all parts of the globe lead to the explosion of new ideas and new inventions.

The Automobile

If we try to pick a single item that has had the greatest impact on social life this past century, among the many candidates the automobile stands out. Let us look at some major effects of this innovation.

Displacement of Existing Technology. In the beginning, people considered the automobile to be cleaner, safer, more reliable, and more economical than horses. Cars also offered the appealing prospect of lower taxes, for no longer would the public have to pay to clean up the tonnes of horse manure that accumulated on the city streets each day.

The automobile also replaced a second technology. Canada had developed a vast system of urban transit, with electric streetcar lines radiating outward from the centre of our cities. As the automobile became affordable and more dependable, Canadians demonstrated a clear preference for the greater convenience of private transportation. Instead of walking to a streetcar and then having to wait for one to arrive, people were able to travel directly from home on their own schedule.

Effects on Cities. The decline in the use of streetcars actually changed the shape of most North American cities, as it stimulated mass suburbanization.

Changes in Architecture. The automobile's effects on commercial architecture are clear—from the huge parking lots that decorate malls to the drive-up windows of banks and restaurants. But the automobile also fundamentally altered the architecture of North American homes (Flink, 1990). First, new homes were built with a detached garage, located, like the stable, at the back of the home. Second, as the automobile became a more essential part of the North American family, the garage was incorporated into the home by moving it from the backyard to the side of the house, and connecting it by a breezeway. In the final step, the breezeway was removed and the garage integrated into the home so that people could enter their automobiles without even going outside.

Changed Courtship Customs and Sexual Norms. By the 1920s, the automobile was used extensively in dating. In 1925, Jewett introduced cars with a foldout bed, as did Nash in 1937. The Nash version became known as "the young man's model" (Flink, 1990). Since the 1970s, mobile lovemaking has declined, partly because urban sprawl (itself due to the automobile) left fewer safe trysting spots, and partly because changed sexual norms made beds more accessible (see Chapter 3).

Effects on Women's Roles. The automobile may also lie at the heart of the changed role of women in Canadian society. Because automobiles required skill rather than strength, women were able to drive as well as men. This new mobility freed women physically from the narrow confines of the home. As Flink (1990) observed, the automobile changed women "from producers of food and clothing into consumers of national-brand canned goods, prepared foods, and ready-made clothes. The automobile permitted shopping at self-serve supermarkets outside the neighborhood and in combination with the electric refrigerator made buying food a weekly rather than a daily activity." When women began to do the shopping, they gained greater control over the family budget, and as their horizons extended beyond the confines of the home, they also gained different views of life.

In short, the automobile helped change women's roles at home, including their relationship with their husband, and facilitated their participation in areas of social life not connected with the home.

In Sum

With changes this extensive, it would not be inaccurate to say the automobile also shifted basic values and changed the way we look at life. No longer isolated, women and teenagers began to see the world differently. So did husbands and wives, whose marital relationship had also been altered. The automobile even transformed views of courtship, sexuality, and gender relations. No one attributes such fundamental changes solely to the automobile, of course, for many historical events, as well as other technological changes, occurred during this same period, each making its own contribution to social change.

The Computer

The second candidate for bringing the greatest social change is the computer. Let's consider its effects.

None of us is untouched by the computer. Although the computer has intruded into our daily lives, most of us never think about it. Our grades are computerized, and probably our paycheques as well. When we buy groceries, a computer scans our purchases and presents a printout of the name, price, and quantity of each item. Essentially the computer's novelty has given way to everyday routine; it is simply another tool.

At this point, let's consider how the computer is changing medicine, education, and the workplace, then its likely effects on social inequality.

Medicine. The patient's symptoms were mystifying. After exercise, one side of his face and part of his body turned deep red, the other chalky white. He looked as though someone had taken a ruler and drawn a line down the middle of his body.

Stumped, the patient's physician consulted a medical librarian who punched a few words into a personal computer to search for clues in the world's medical literature. Soon, the likely answer flashed on the screen: Harlequin's disease (Winslow, 1994).

The computer was right, and a neurosurgeon was able to correct the patient's nervous system. With computers, physicians can peer within the body's hidden recesses to determine how its parts are functioning or to see if surgery is necessary. Today, one million tiny fragments of genetic DNA can be crammed onto a disposable microchip. Read by a laser scanner, in just a few minutes the chip reveals such things as whether a patient carries the cystic fibrosis gene or has grown resistant to AIDS drugs (King, 1994).

As the future rushes in, the microchip is bringing even more technological wonders. In what is called *telemedicine*, patients have their hearts and lungs checked with a stethoscope—by doctors in another province or country. The data are transmitted by fibre-optic cable (Richards, 1996). Soon a surgeon in Halifax or Vancouver, using a remote-controlled

Most of us take computers for granted, but they are new on the world scene—as are their effects on our lives. This photo captures a significant change in the evolution of computers. The laptop held by the superimposed model has more power than the room-sized ENIAC of 1946.

robot and images relayed via satellite to computers, will be able to operate from almost any place or circumstance in the world.

Education. Almost every grade school in Canada introduces its students to the computer. Successful educational programs use a game-like, challenging format that makes students forget they are "studying." Most classrooms are wired to the Internet ("Cyberschool Makes Its Debut," 1996).

The question of social inequality becomes significant in this context. Those schools most able to afford the latest in computer technology are able to better prepare their students for the future, thus helping to perpetuate social inequalities that arise from the chance of birth.

The computer has already transformed the university. Students at Mount Allison University in Sackville, New Brunswick, are provided a laptop computer free of charge (if it should be required for their studies) upon their acceptance at the university. And in every university in Canada, students have direct access to the Internet and are provided with free e-mail accounts. Overall, "surfing the Net" for research and fun is a mainstay of student life at Canadian universities. If you wish, you can use the CD included with this text to give yourself a test—at your chosen level of difficulty—so you can immediately check your mastery of the material.

The Workplace. The computer has also transformed the workplace. In some cases it has returned the work location to the home—an arrangement called *telework*. Already millions of people perform their jobs at home. As discussed earlier, industrialization caused work to shift from home to factory and office; since workers can now be "networked" (linked by computers), for many public and private sector workers this historic change is being reversed.

On the negative side are increased surveillance of workers and depersonalization. As a telephone information operator said:

> The computer knows everything. It records the minute I punch in, it knows how long I take for each call … I am supposed to average under eighteen seconds per call…. Everything I do is reported to my supervisor on his computer, and if I've missed my numbers I get a written warning. I rarely see the guy. … It's intense. It's me and the computer all day. I'm telling you, at the end of the day I'm wiped out. Working with computers is the coal mining of the nineties (Mander, 1992, p. 57).

Cyberspace and Social Inequalities in the Twenty-First Century

The term *information superhighway*, which evokes the idea of information travelling at high speed between homes and businesses, is most apt for what is occurring at present around the world. Just as a highway allows physical travel from one place to another, so homes and businesses are being connected by the rapid flow of information. Already about 300 million people around the world are able to communicate by Internet, which allows electronic access to libraries of information. Some programs sift, sort, and transmit scanned images, sound, even video. E-mail allows people to fire off messages without regard to national boundaries. This is the shape of the future: a world linked by almost instantaneous communication, with information readily accessible around the globe, and with few places being considered remote.

But the implications of the information superhighway for national and global stratification are severe. On the national level, we may end up with "information have-nots," thereby perpetuating present inequalities. On the global level, the question is: Who will control the information superhighway? The answer, of course, is obvious, for it is the most industrialized nations that are developing the system. This leads to one of the more profound issues of the twenty-first century—will such control destine the least industrialized nations to endless pauper status?

If the answer is yes, how can we reduce the social inequalities this revolution will create on a global scale? There are no easy answers.

Contemporary Theories of Social Change

Table 18.2 categorizes the principal contemporary theories about the causes of social change.

1. *Evolutionary theories* presuppose that societies are moving from the same starting to some similar ending point. Unilinear theories, which assume the same path for every society, have been replaced with multilinear theories, which assume that different paths can lead to the same stage of development.

2. *Marxist conflict theories* are similar to evolutionary theories of progress except that the final stage, communism—otherwise known as "the end of history"—is the ultimate stage of development.

3. *Cyclical theories*, in contrast, view civilizations as going through a process of birth, youth, maturity, decline, and death.

4. *Feminist theories* assume that all societies, except possibly for the earliest hunting-and-gathering tribes, are dominated by patriarchy; and only by women achieving equality of condition and taking action on global human rights can the privileges and liabilities of patriarchy be overcome.

Table 18.2 Contemporary Theories of Social Change

Theories of Social Change	Assumptions	Path(s) of Social Change
Evolutionary Theories of Social Change	All societies progress from simple to more complicated forms of material organization.	From elementary beginnings to more complex stages of development.
1. Unilinear evolution	All societies follow the same path of development.	One road out of a small village that leads to a town, then a city and beyond.
2. Multilinear evolution	Different routes can lead to a similar stage of development.	Multiple roads out of a small village that lead to a town, then a city and beyond.
Marxist Conflict Theories of Social Change	Similar to evolutionary theories of progress, except communism is the last stage of development, otherwise known as "the end of history."	Multiple roads out of a small village that lead to a town, next a city, and ending in Paradise.
Cyclical Theories of Change	Civilizations such as the Greek, Egyptian, or Western, not one particular society, are like organisms; they are born, experience an exuberant youth, mature, and finally decline and die.	Airborne fireworks display that begins with the trail upward, then a sudden burst, followed by beautiful colours, and ending with the long trail downward to the earth.
Feminist Theories of Social Change	Except for possibly the earliest hunting-and-gathering communities, all societies have been dominated by patriarchy.	A "tug of war" in which more and more women are added to one side of the rope until there is an eventual stalemate.
Postmodern Theories of Social Change	There is no progress or purpose or continuity of values, beliefs, and disbeliefs, since the confidence in the association between science and morality has been broken.	A rushing river with multiple currents and fast-moving water, light sparkling off the top of the water and the surface glimmer being all one sees or wants to see.

5. *Postmodern theories* assume the present, so that there is no progress or continuity in values, beliefs, and disbeliefs; belief in scientific progress has been replaced with a belief in appearance or form. To postmodernists, all change is ephemeral.

The Difficult Road to Success

In spite of their significance in contemporary society, social movements as agents of social change seldom solve all of society's social problems. Resource mobilization helps to explain why. To mobilize resources, a movement must appeal to a broad constituency. For example, the fact that workers at one particular plant are upset about their low wages is not adequate to recruit the broad support necessary for a social movement. At best, it will result in local agitation. The low wages and unsafe working conditions of millions of Canadian workers, however, have a chance of becoming the focal point of a social movement.

Many social movements, however, do vitally affect society. The Quebec sovereignty movement comes quickly to mind. Some, such as trade unions in Canada, become powerful forces for social change. They highlight problems and turn the society onto a path that solves the problem. Others become powerful forces in resisting the social change that its members—and the public it is able to mobilize—consider undesirable.

By their very nature, broad social problems are entrenched in society and not easy to solve. They require more than merely tinkering with some small part. Just as the problem touches many interrelated components of society, so the solutions require changes in those many parts. Social movements and new technology are among the forces that change society.

> **Focus Question**
> Do all sociologists hold the view that humankind is making progress and will keep getting better?

Summary and Review

COLLECTIVE BEHAVIOUR

EARLY EXPLANATIONS: THE TRANSFORMATION OF THE INDIVIDUAL

How did early theorists explain the effects of crowds on individuals?

Early theorists argued that individuals are transformed by crowds. Charles Mackay used the term *herd mentality* to explain why people did wild things when they were in crowds. Gustave LeBon said that a **collective mind** develops, and people are swept away by suggestions. p. 428.

What stages of crowd behaviour are there?

Herbert Blumer identified five stages that crowds go through before they become an **acting crowd**: social unrest, an exciting event, **milling**, a common object of attention, and common impulses. pp. 429–430.

THE CONTEMPORARY VIEW: THE RATIONALITY OF THE CROWD

What is the current view of crowd behaviour?

Current theorists view crowds as rational. Richard Berk stresses a **minimax strategy**; that is, people try to minimize their costs and maximize their rewards, whether or not they are in crowds. Ralph Turner and Lewis Killian analyze how new norms emerge that allow people to do things in crowds that they otherwise would not do. pp. 430–431.

FORMS OF COLLECTIVE BEHAVIOUR

What forms of collective behaviour are there?

Some of the major forms of collective behaviour are **demonstrations**, **riots**, **panics**, **moral panics**, **rumours**, **fads**, **fashions**, and **urban legends**. Conditions of discontent or uncertainty provide fertile ground for collective behaviour, and each form provides a way of dealing with these conditions. pp. 431–435.

SOCIAL MOVEMENTS

TYPES AND TACTICS OF SOCIAL MOVEMENTS

What types of social movements are there?

Social movements consist of large numbers of people who organize to promote or resist social change. Depending on their target (individuals or society) and the amount of social change desired (partial or complete), social movements can be classified as **alterative**, **redemptive**, **reformative**, and **transformative**. p. 436.

How do social movements select their tactics?

Tactics are chosen on the basis of a group's membership, its publics (audience), and its relationship to authorities. The three levels of membership are *the inner core*, *the committed*, and *the less committed*. The predispositions of the inner core are crucial in choosing tactics, but so is the public they wish to address. If relationships with authorities are bad, the chances of aggressive or violent tactics increase. Friendship, size of city, and race of movement participants and their targets may also be significant. pp. 436–437.

How are the mass media related to social movements?

Because the mass media are gatekeepers for social movements, their favourable or unfavourable coverage greatly affecting a social movement, tactics are chosen with the media in mind. Social movements also make use of **propaganda** to further their cause. pp. 437–438.

WHY PEOPLE JOIN SOCIAL MOVEMENTS

Why do people join social movements?

There is no single, overriding reason why people join social movements. According to **mass society theory**, social movements relieve feelings of isolation created by an impersonal, bureaucratized society. According to **relative deprivation theory**, people join movements in order to address their grievances. Morality, values, and ideological commitment also motivate people to join social movements. The **agent provocateur** illustrates that even people who hate a cause can end up participating in it. pp. 438–440.

ON THE SUCCESS AND FAILURE OF SOCIAL MOVEMENTS

Why do social movements succeed or fail?

Social movements go through several stages—initial unrest and agitation, mobilization, organization, institutionalization, and finally organizational decline with possible resurgence. Groups that appeal to few people cannot succeed. But to appeal broadly in order to accomplish **resource mobilization**, the movement must focus on very broad concerns, problems deeply embedded in society, which also makes success extremely difficult. pp. 440–441.

HOW TECHNOLOGY CHANGES SOCIETY

What is Ogburn's theory of social change?

Ogburn identified technology as the basic cause of social change, which comes through three processes: invention, discovery, and diffusion. The term **cultural lag** refers to symbolic culture lagging behind changes in technology. pp. 442–443.

What types of technology are there, and what effects can a changed technology have on society?

Because technology is an organizing force in social life, when technology changes its effects can be profound. The automobile and the computer were used as extended examples. The automobile changed the development of cities, buying patterns, architecture, and even courtship and women's roles. We looked at how the computer is changing the way we practise medicine, learn, and work. The information superhighway is likely to perpetuate social inequalities on both a national and a global level. pp. 444–446.

CONTEMPORARY THEORIES OF SOCIAL CHANGE

What are the contemporary theories of social change?

Evolutionary theories presuppose that societies are moving from the same starting to some similar ending point. *Marxist conflict theories* are similar except that communism is the ultimate stage of development. *Cyclical theories* view civilizations as going through a process of birth, youth, maturity, decline, and death. *Feminist theories* assume that societies are mostly dominated by patriarchy, to be overcome by achieving equality of opportunity for women and securing global human rights. In *postmodern theories*, belief in scientific progress has been replaced with a belief in appearance or form; all change is ephemeral. pp. 446–447.

Critical Thinking Questions

1. To understand the social pressures of a social group or social movement, imagine yourself at a hockey game. When the Canadian national anthem is sung, instead of standing up with all the other members of the audience, you stay seated. How do you feel when you don't join in with all the other members of the audience? Who is behaving rationally in this situation? You or everyone else?

2. How do the media influence the creation or the development of social movements?

3. All too often, sociologists describe social movements as examples of social problems and not as solutions to social problems. Do social movements such as trade unions serve any useful functions in Canadian society?

4. While it is true that technology influences the broad nature of social change, human beings also contribute to the direction of a society's transformation. After having read this book, you should know what sociology is and whether it has anything further to offer you. Do you think sociologists should use their skills and knowledge to directly influence Canadian public policy?

Key Terms

acting crowd 429
agent provocateur 440
alienation 443
alterative social movements 436
collective behaviour 428
collective mind 428
cultural lag 443
demonstrations 432
diffusion 442
discovery 442
emergent norms 430
fad 434

fashion 434
invention 442
mass society 438
mass society theory 438
milling 429
minimax strategy 430
modernization 441
moral panic 433
new social movements 436
panic 432
postmodern societies 441
proactive social movement 435

propaganda 437
public 437
public opinion 437
reactive social movement 435
redemptive social movements 436
reformative social movements 436
relative deprivation theory 440
resource mobilization 441

riot 431
role extension 433
rumour 433
social change 441
social movement 435
social movement organizations 435
technology 441
transformative social movements 436
urban legends 434

Weblinks

All URLs listed are current as of the printing of this book. URLs are often changed. Please check our Web site **www.abacon.com/henslin** for updates.

Collective Behaviour and Social Movements

www.abacon.com/sociology/soclinks/collect.html
A list of useful links on this topic; part of the Allyn and Bacon Sociology Links site.

American Sociological Association's Section on Collective Behavior and Social Movements

www.u.arizona.edu/~jearl/cbsm.html
Crowds, social movements, disasters, riots, fads, strikes, and revolutionary movements are a few of the areas explored in this site.

Social Movements

www.unm.edu/~lorstone/mov.html
This site is an ongoing project. The section on research has information on methods and a list of electronic journals and newsletters; the section on theory presents various theoretical perspectives; the archives section has topical and thematic links; the engines section includes searchable sites from around the world; the material manifestations section has online galleries and museums and links related to the topic.

Social Change

www.abacon.com/sociology/soclinks/schange.html
A list of useful links on this topic; part of the Allyn and Bacon Sociology Links site.

Glossary

acculturation: the transmission of culture from one generation to the next

achieved statuses: positions that are earned, accomplished, or that involved at least some effort or activity on the individual's part

acid rain: rain containing sulfuric and nitric acids

acting crowd: Herbert Blumer's term for an excited group that collectively moves toward a goal

activity theory: the view that satisfaction during old age is related to a person's level and quality of activity

age cohort: a group of people born at roughly the same time who pass through the life course together

ageism: prejudice, discrimination, and hostility directed against people because of their age; can be directed against any age group, including youth

agency: individual or collective actions upon social structures and circumstances

agent provocateur: someone who joins a group in order to spy on it and to sabotage it by provoking its members to commit illegal acts

agents of socialization: people or groups that affect our self-concept, attitudes, or other orientations toward life

aggregate: individuals who temporarily share the same physical space but do not see themselves as belonging together

alienation: Marx's term for workers' lack of connection to the product of their labour; caused by their being assigned repetitive tasks on a small part of a product

alterative social movement: a social movement that seeks to alter only particular aspects of people

anarchy: a condition of lawlessness or political disorder caused by the absence or collapse of governmental authority

animal culture: learned, shared behaviour among animals

animism: the belief that all objects in the world have spirits, some of which are dangerous and must be outwitted

anomie: Durkheim's term for a condition of society in which people become detached, cut loose from the norms that usually guide their behaviour

anticipatory socialization: learning part of a future role because one anticipates it

anti-Semitism: prejudice, discrimination, and persecution directed against Jews

appearance: how an individual looks when playing a role

applied sociology: the use of sociology to solve problems—from the micro level of family relationships to the macro level of crime and pollution

ascribed statuses: positions an individual either inherits at birth or receives involuntarily later in life

assimilation: the process whereby a minority group is absorbed into the mainstream culture

authoritarian leader: a leader who leads by giving orders

authoritarian personality: Theodor Adorno's term for people who are prejudiced and rank high on scales of conformity, intolerance, insecurity, respect for authority, and submissiveness to superiors

authority: power that people accept as rightly exercised over them; also called legitimate power

back stage: where people rest from their performances, discuss their presentations, and plan future performances

background assumptions: deeply embedded common understandings, or basic roles, concerning our view of the world and of how people ought to act

barter: the direct exchange of one item for another

basic demographic equation: growth rate = births − deaths + net migration

basic sociology: see *pure or basic sociology*

bilateral (system of descent): a system of reckoning descent that counts both the mother's and the father's side

blended family: a family whose members were once part of other families

bourgeoisie: Karl Marx's term for capitalists, those who own the means to produce wealth

bureaucracy: a formal organization with a hierarchy of authority; a clear division of labour; emphasis on written rules, communications, and records; and impersonality of positions

capitalism: an economic system characterized by the private ownership of the means of production, the pursuit of profit, and market competition; the investment of capital with the goal of producing profits

capitalist class: the wealthy who own the means of production and buy the labour of the working class

capitalist world economy: the dominance of capitalism in the world along with the international interdependence that capitalism has created

caste system: a form of social stratification in which one's status is determined by birth and is lifelong

category: people who have similar characteristics

causation: if a change in one variable leads to a change in another variable, causation is said to exist

charismatic authority: authority based on an individual's outstanding traits, which attract followers

charismatic leader: an individual who inspires people because he or she seems to have extraordinary qualities

church: according to Durkheim, one of the three essential elements of religion—a moral community of believers or a large, highly organized group with formal, sedate worship services and little emphasis on personal conversion

citizenship: the concept that birth (and residence) in a country impart basic rights

city: a place in which a large number of people are permanently based and do not produce their own food

city-state: an independent city whose power radiates outward, bringing the adjacent area under its rule

clan: an extended network of relatives

clan system: a form of social stratification in which individuals receive their social standing through belonging to an extended network of relatives

class conflict: Marx's term for the struggle between the proletariat and the bourgeoisie

class consciousness: Karl Marx's term for awareness of a common identity based on one's position in the means of production

class system: a form of social stratification based primarily on the possession of money or material possessions

clique: a cluster of people within a larger group who choose to interact with one another; an internal faction

closed-ended questions: questions followed by a list of possible answers to be selected by the respondent

coalition: the alignment of some members of a group against others

coalition government: a government in which a country's largest party aligns itself with one or more smaller parties

coercion: power that people do not accept as rightly exercised over them; also called illegitimate power

collective behaviour: extraordinary activities carried out by groups of people; includes lynchings, rumours, panics, urban legends, and fads and fashions

collective mind: Gustave LeBon's term for the tendency of people in a crowd to feel, think, and act in extraordinary ways

colonization: the process by which one nation takes over another nation, usually for the purpose of exploiting its labour and natural resources

common sense: those things that "everyone knows" are true

community: a place people identify with, where they sense that they belong and that others care what happens to them

compartmentalize: to separate acts from feelings or attitudes

confederal union: system of government in which the provinces have most of the powers and the central government has little authority

conflict theory: a theoretical framework in which society is viewed as composed of groups competing for scarce resources

conservative bias: the tendency of analysts to downplay evidence of historical change and to reject evidence of challenges to traditional social patterns

conspicuous consumption: Thorstein Veblen's term for a change from the Protestant ethic to an eagerness to show off wealth by the elaborate consumption of goods

contradictory class location: Erik Wright's term for a position in the class structure that generates contradictory interests

control group: the group of subjects not exposed to the independent variable

convergence theory: the view that as capitalist and socialist economic systems each adopt features of the other, a hybrid (or mixed) economic system will emerge

corporate capitalism: the domination of the economic system by giant corporations

corporate culture: the orientation that characterizes a corporate work setting

corporation: the joint ownership of a business enterprise, whose liabilities and obligations are separate from those of its owners

correlation: the simultaneous occurrence of two or more variables

correspondence principle: the sociological principle that schools correspond to (or reflect) the social structure of society

cosmology: teachings or ideas that provide a unified picture of the world

counterculture: a group whose values, beliefs, and related behaviours place its members in opposition to the broader culture

credential society: the use of diplomas and degrees to determine who is eligible for jobs, even though the diploma or degree may be irrelevant to the actual work

credit card: a device that allows its owner to purchase goods but to be billed later

crime: the violation of norms that are written into law

criminal justice system: the system of police, courts, and prisons set up to deal with people accused of having committed a crime

crude birth rate: the annual number of births per 1000 population

crude death rate: the annual number of deaths per 1000 population

cult: a new or different religion, with few followers, whose teachings and practices put it at odds with the dominant culture and religion

cultural diffusion: the spread of cultural characteristics from one group to another

cultural goals: the legitimate objectives held out to the members of a society

cultural lag: William Ogburn's term for human behaviour lagging behind technological innovations

cultural levelling: the process by which cultures become similar to one another, and especially by which Western industrial culture is imported and diffused into developing nations

cultural relativism: understanding a people from the framework of its own culture

cultural transmission: in reference to education, the ways schools transmit a society's culture, especially its core values

cultural universal: a value, norm, or other cultural trait that is found in every group

culture: the language, beliefs, values, norms, behaviours, and even material objects passed from one generation to the next

culture of poverty: the assumption that the values and behaviours of the poor make them fundamentally different from other people, that these factors are largely responsible for their poverty, and that parents perpetuate poverty across generations by passing these characteristics on to their children

currency: paper money

debit card: a device that allows its owner to charge purchases against his or her bank account

deferred gratification: forgoing something in the present in the hope of achieving greater gains in the future

definition of the situation: the way we look at matters in life; the way we define reality or some particular situation

degradation ceremony: a term coined by Harold Garfinkel to describe an attempt to remake the self by stripping away an individual's self-identity and stamping a new one in its place; a ritual designed to strip an individual of his or her identity as a group member—for example, a court martial or the defrocking of a priest

dehumanization: the act or process of reducing people to objects that do not deserve the treatment accorded humans

democracy: a system of government in which authority derives from the people; derived from two Greek words that translate literally as "power to the people"

democratic leader: a leader who leads by trying to reach a consensus

democratic socialism: a hybrid economic system in which capitalism is mixed with state ownership

demographic transition: a three-stage historical process of population growth: first, high birth rates and high death rates; second, high birth rates and low death rates; and third, low birth rates and low death rates

demographic variables: the three factors that influence population growth: fertility, mortality, and net migration

demography: the study of the size, composition, growth, and distribution of human populations

demonstration: a public meeting, march, etc. for a political or moral purpose

denomination: a "brand name" within a major religion, for example, Methodist or Baptist

dependency ratio: the number of paid workers required so that dependent individuals, usually seniors and children, can be adequately supported

dependency theory: the view that the Least Industrialized Nations have been unable to develop their economies because they have grown dependent on the Most Industrialized Nations

dependent variable: a factor that is changed by an independent variable

depersonalization: dealing with people as though they were objects—in the case of medical care, as though patients were merely cases and diseases, not persons

deposit receipts: a receipt stating that a certain amount of goods is on deposit in a warehouse or bank; the receipt is used as a form of money

dictatorship: a form of government in which power is seized by an individual

differential association: Edwin Sutherland's term to indicate that associating with some groups results in learning an "excess of definitions" of social deviance, and, by extension, in a greater likelihood that one will become socially deviant

diffusion: the spread of invention or discovery from one area to another; identified by William Ogburn as the final of three processes of social change

direct democracy: a form of democracy in which the eligible voters meet together to discuss issues and make their decisions

disabling environment: an environment harmful to health

discovery: a new way of seeing reality; identified by William Ogburn as the second of three processes of social change

discrimination: an act of unfair treatment directed against an individual or a group

disengagement theory: the view that society prevents disruption by having the elderly vacate (or disengage from) their positions of responsibility so the younger generation can step into their shoes

divine right of kings: the idea that the king's authority comes directly from God

division of labour: the splitting of a group's or a society's tasks into specialties

documents: in its narrow sense, written sources that provide data; in its extended sense, archival material of any sort, including photographs, movies, and so on

dominant group: the group with the most power, greatest privileges, and highest social status

downward social mobility: movement down the social-class ladder

dramaturgy: an approach, pioneered by Erving Goffman, analyzing social life in terms of drama or the stage; also called dramaturgical analysis

dual labour market: workers split along racial, ethnic, gender, age, or any other lines; this split is exploited by owners to weaken the bargaining power of workers

dyad: the smallest possible group, consisting of two people

ecclesia (plural ecclesias): a religious group so integrated into the dominant culture that it is difficult to tell where the one begins and the other leaves off; also referred to as *state religion*

economy: a system of distribution of goods and services

education: a formal system of teaching knowledge, values, and skills

egalitarian: authority more or less equally divided between people or groups, for example, between husband and wife in a family

ego: Freud's term for a balancing force between the id and the demands of society

electronic community: individuals who more or less regularly interact with one another on the Internet

electronic primary group: individuals who regularly interact with one another on the Internet, who see themselves as a group, and who develop close ties with one another

emergent norms: Ralph Turner's and Lewis Killian's term for the development of new norms to cope with a new situation, especially among crowds

endogamy: the practice of marrying within one's own group

environmental sociology: a subdiscipline of sociology that examines how human activities affect the physical environment and how the physical environment affects human activities

epidemiology: the study of disease and disability patterns in a population

ethnic (and ethnicity): having distinctive cultural characteristics

ethnocentrism: the use of one's own culture as a yardstick for judging the ways of other individuals or societies, generally leading to a negative evaluation of their values, norms, and behaviours

ethnomethodology: the study of how people use background assumptions to make sense out of life

euthanasia: mercy killing

evangelism: an attempt to win converts

exchange mobility: about the same numbers of people moving up and down the social class ladder, such that, on balance, the social class system shows little change

exogamy: the practice of marrying outside one's group

experiment: the use of control groups and experimental groups and dependent and independent variables to test causation

experimental group: the group of subjects exposed to the independent variable

exponential growth curve: a pattern of growth in which numbers double during approximately equal intervals, thus accelerating in the latter stages

expressive leader: an individual who increases harmony and minimizes conflict in a group; also known as a socioemotional leader

extended family: a nuclear family plus other relatives, such as grandparents, uncles, and aunts, who live together

face-saving behaviour: techniques used to salvage a performance that is going sour

fad: a temporary pattern of behaviour that catches people's attention

false consciousness: Karl Marx's term to refer to workers identifying with the interests of capitalists

family: two or more people who consider themselves related by blood, marriage, or adoption

family of orientation: the family in which a person grows up

family of procreation: the family formed when a couple's first child is born

fashion: a pattern of behaviour that catches people's attention and lasts longer than a fad

fecundity: the number of children women are theoretically *capable* of bearing

feminist theories: all three types of feminist theories—Marxist, liberal, and radical—hold that women are oppressed by gender roles that are products of social, historical, and cultural factors

feral children: children assumed to have been raised by animals, in the wilderness isolated from other humans

fertility rate: the number of children the average woman bears

fiat money: currency issued by a government that is not backed by stored value

folkways: norms that are not strictly enforced

formal organization: a secondary group designed to achieve explicit objectives

front stage: where performances are given

functional analysis: a theoretical framework in which society is viewed as composed of various parts, each with a function that, when fulfilled, contributes to society's equilibrium; also known as functionalism and structural functionalism

functional requisites: the major tasks a society must fulfill if it is to survive

fundamentalism: the belief that true religion is threatened by modernism and that the faith as it was originally practised should be restored

gatekeeping: the process by which education opens and closes doors of opportunity; another term for the *social placement* function of education

Gemeinschaft: a type of society dominated by intimate relationships; a community in which everyone knows everyone else and people share a sense of togetherness

gender: the social characteristics that a society considers proper for its males and females; masculinity or femininity

gender age: the relative vales of men's and women's ages in a particular culture

gender role: the behaviours and attitudes considered appropriate because one is a female or a male

gender socialization: the ways society sets children on different courses in life because they are male or female

gender stratification: males' and females' unequal access to power, prestige, and property on the basis of their sex

generalizability: the extent to which the findings from one group (or sample) can be generalized or applied to other groups (or populations)

generalized other: the norms, values, attitudes, and expectations of "people in general"; the child's ability to take the role of the generalized other is a significant step in the development of a self

genetic predispositions: inborn tendencies, in this context, to commit socially deviant acts

genocide: the systematic annihilation or attempted annihilation of a people based on their presumed race or ethnicity

gentrification: the displacement of the poor by the relatively affluent, who renovate the former's homes

gerontocracy: a society (or some other group) run by the elderly

Gesellschaft: a type of society dominated by impersonal relationships, individual accomplishments, and self-interest

gestures: the ways in which people use their bodies to communicate with one another

glass ceiling: barriers to social advancement that many women face in some organizations

global warming: an increase in the earth's temperature due to the *greenhouse effect*

globalization: the extensive movement of capital and ideas between nations due to the expansion of capitalism

goal displacement: replacement of one goal by another; in this context, the adoption of new goals by an organization; also known as *goal replacement*

gold standard: paper money backed by gold

graying of Canada: a term that refers to the rising proportion of older people as a percentage of the Canadian population

greenhouse effect: the buildup of carbon dioxide in the earth's atmosphere that allows light to enter but inhibits the release of heat; believed to cause *global warming*

gross national product (GNP): the amount of goods and services produced by a nation

group: defined differently by various sociologists, but in a general sense, people who have something in common and who believe that what they have in common is significant; also called a *social group*

group dynamics: the ways individuals affect groups and the ways groups influence individuals

groupthink: Irving Janis' term for a narrowing of thought by a group of people, leading to the perception that there is only one correct answer, and a situation in which to even suggest alternatives becomes a sign of disloyalty

growth rate: the net change in a population after adding births, subtracting deaths, and either adding or subtracting net migration

health: a human condition measured by four components: physical, mental, social, and spiritual

hidden curriculum: the unwritten goals of schools, such as obedience to authority and conformity to cultural norms

homogamy: the tendency of people with similar characteristics to marry one another

hospice: a place, or services brought into someone's home, for the purpose of bringing comfort and dignity to a dying person

household: all people who occupy the same housing unit

human ecology: Robert Park's term for the relationship between people and their environment (natural resources such as land)

humanizing a work setting: organizing a workplace in such a way that it develops rather than impedes human potential

hypothesis: a statement of the expected relationship between variables according to predictions from a theory

id: Freud's term for our inborn basic drives

ideal culture: the ideal values and norms of a people, and the goals held out for them

ideal type: a composite of characteristics based on many specific examples ("ideal" in this case means a description of the abstracted characteristics, not what one desires to exist)

ideology: beliefs about the way things ought to be that justify social arrangements

illegitimate opportunity structures: opportunities for crime that are woven into the texture of life

imperialism: a nation's attempt to create an empire; its pursuit of unlimited geographical expansion

impression management: the term used by Erving Goffman to describe people's efforts to control the impressions others receive of them

incest: sexual relations between specified relatives, such as brothers and sisters or parents and children

indentured service: a contractual system in which someone sells his or her body (services) for a specified period of time in an arrangement very close to slavery, except that it is voluntarily entered into

independent variable: a factor that causes a change in another variable, called the dependent variable

individual discrimination: the negative treatment of one person by another on the basis of that person's perceived characteristics

inflation: an increase in prices

in-groups: groups toward which one feels loyalty

institutional discrimination: negative treatment of a minority group that is built into a society's institutions; also called systemic discrimination

institutionalized means: approved ways of reaching cultural goals

instrumental leader: an individual who tries to keep the group moving toward its goals; also known as a task-oriented leader

intentional family: people who declare themselves a family and treat one another as members of the same family; originated in the late twentieth century in response to the need for intimacy not met due to distance, divorce, and death

intergenerational mobility: the change that family members make in social class from one generation to the next

interlocking directorates: the same people serving on the board of directors of several companies

internal colonialism: the policy of economically exploiting minority groups

interview: direct questioning of respondents

invasion-succession cycle: the process of one group of people displacing a group whose racial-ethnic or social class characteristics differ from their own

invention: the combination of existing elements and materials to form new ones; identified by William Ogburn as the first of three processes of social change

iron law of oligarchy: Robert Michels' phrase for the tendency of formal organizations to be dominated by a small, self-perpetuating elite

job ghettoes: also known as *pink ghettoes*, employment areas dominated by women (and usually lower paid than areas dominated by men)

just-in-time (JIT) strategy: a Japanese way of organizing production that minimizes inventory and storage at the production site—components are produced and moved between plants on a just-in-time basis

kaizen: continuous improvement—production techniques are continuously evaluated in search of more efficient and improved methods

labelling theory: the view, developed by symbolic interactionists, that the labels people are given affect their own and others' perceptions of them, thus channelling their behaviour into either social deviance or conformity

laissez-faire capitalism: unrestrained manufacture and trade (loosely, "leave alone" capitalism)

laissez-faire leader: an individual who leads by being highly permissive

language: a system of symbols that can be combined in an infinite number of ways and can represent not only objects but also abstract thought

latent functions: the unintended consequences of people's actions that help keep a social system in equilibrium

leader: someone who influences other people

leadership styles: ways people express their leadership

leisure: time not taken up by work or required activities such as eating, sleeping, commuting, child care, and housework

life course: the sequence of events that we experience as we journey from birth to death

life expectancy: the number of years an average newborn can expect to live

life span: the maximum length of life of a species

living will: a statement people in good health sign that clearly expresses their feelings about being kept alive on artificial life support systems

looking-glass self: a term coined by Charles Horton Cooley to refer to the process by which our self develops through internalizing others' reactions to us

macro-level analysis: an examination of large-scale patterns of society

macropolitics: the exercise of large-scale power, the government being the most common example

macrosociology: analysis of social life focusing on broad features of social structure, such as social class and the relationships of groups to one another; an approach usually used by functionalist and conflict theorists

mainstreaming: helping people become part of the mainstream of society

Malthus theorem: an observation by Thomas Malthus that although the food supply increases only arithmetically (from 1 to 2 to 3 to 4 and so on), population grows geometrically (from 2 to 4 to 8 to 16 and so forth)

manifest function: the intended consequences of people's actions designed to help some part of a social system

manner: the attitudes people show as they play their roles

market: any process of buying and selling; on a more formal level, the mechanism that establishes values for the exchange of goods and services

market competition: the exchange of items between willing buyers and sellers

market force: the law of supply and demand

market restraints: laws and regulations that limit the capacity to manufacture and sell products

marriage: a group's approved mating arrangements, usually marked by a ritual of some sort

mass media: forms of communication, such as radio, newspapers, and television, directed to mass audiences

mass society: industrialized, highly bureaucratized, impersonal society

mass society theory: an explanation for participation in social movements based on the assumption that such movements offer a sense of belonging to people who have weak social ties

master status: a status that cuts across the other statuses an individual occupies

material culture: the material objects that distinguish a group of people, such as their art, buildings, weapons, utensils, machines, hairstyles, clothing, and jewellery

matriarchy: authority vested in females; female control of a society or group; a society in which women dominate men

matrilineal (system of descent): a system of reckoning descent that counts only the mother's side

means of production: the tools, factories, land, and investment capital used to produce wealth

mechanical solidarity: Durkheim's term for the unity that comes from being involved in similar occupations or activities

medicalization: the transformation of something into a matter to be treated by physicians

medicalization of social deviance: to make social deviance a medical matter, a symptom of some underlying illness that needs to be treated by physicians

medicine: one of the major social institutions that sociologists study; a society's organized ways of dealing with sickness and injury

medium of exchange: the means by which people value goods and services in order to make an exchange, for example, currency, gold, and silver

megalopolis: an urban area consisting of at least two metropolises and their many suburbs

meritocracy: a form of social stratification in which all positions are awarded on the basis of merit

metropolis: a central city surrounded by smaller cities and their suburbs

micro-level analysis: an examination of small-scale patterns of society

microsociology: analysis of social life focusing on social interaction; an approach usually used by symbolic interactionists

middle-range theories: explanations of human behaviour that go beyond a particular observation or research but avoid sweeping generalizations that attempt to account for everything

milling: a crowd standing or walking around as they talk excitedly about some event

minimax strategy: Richard Berk's term for the effort people make to minimize their costs and maximize their rewards

minority group: a group discriminated against on the basis of its members' physical or cultural characteristics

modernization: the process by which a *Gemeinschaft* society is transformed into a *Gesellschaft* society; the transformation of traditional societies into industrial societies

monarchy: a form of government headed by a king or queen

money: any item (from seashells to gold) that serves as a medium of exchange; today, currency is the most common form

monolithic bias: the tendency to ignore the diversity contained within a phenomenon and to focus, instead, on the most general exterior features. When applied to the family, the bias results in a failure to recognize that traditional notions of the family—male breadwinner, housewife, and biological children—have been supplanted by an amazing diversity of family forms and experiences

monolithic structure: the representation of structure as homogeneous and undiversified. For example, if the family is represented as a monolithic structure, the representation ignores the complex diversity of types and forms incorporated into contemporary experiences of the family

monotheism: the belief that there is only one God

moral community: people united by their religious practices

moral panic: a fear that grips large numbers of people that some evil group or behaviour threatens the well-being of society, followed by intense hostility, sometimes violence, toward those thought responsible

mores: norms that are strictly enforced because they are thought essential to core values

multiculturalism (also called pluralism): a philosophy or political policy that permits or encourages ethnic variation

multinational corporations: companies that operate across many national boundaries; also called *transnational corporations*

nationalism: a strong identity with a nation, accompanied by the desire for that nation to be dominant

natural sciences: the intellectual and academic disciplines designed to comprehend, explain, and predict events in our natural environment

negative sanction: an expression of disapproval for breaking a norm, ranging from a mild, informal reaction such as a frown to a formal prison sentence or an execution

neocolonialism: the economic and political dominance of the Least Industrialized Nations by the Most Industrialized Nations

net migration rate: the difference between the number of immigrants and emigrants per 1000 population

networking: the process of consciously using or cultivating networks for some gain

new social movements: social movements with a new emphasis on the world, instead of on a condition in a specific country

new technology: the emerging technologies of an era that have a significant impact on social life

noncentrist party: a political party that represents less popular ideas

nonmaterial culture: a group's ways of thinking (including its beliefs, values, and other assumptions about the world) and doing (its common patterns of behaviour, including language and other forms of interaction)

nonverbal interaction: communication without words through gestures, space, silence, and so on

norms: the expectations or rules of behaviour that develop out of values

nuclear family: a family consisting of a husband, wife, and child(ren)

objective method (of measuring social class): a system in which people are ranked according to objective criteria such as their wealth, power, and prestige

objectivity: total neutrality

official social deviance: a society's statistics on lawbreaking; its measures of crimes, victims, lawbreakers, and the outcomes of criminal investigations and sentencing

oligarchy: a form of government in which power is held by a small group of individuals; the rule of the many by the few

oligopoly: the control of an entire industry by several large companies

open-ended questions: questions that respondents are able to answer in their own words

operational definitions: the way in which a variable in a hypothesis is measured

organic solidarity: Durkheim's term for the interdependence that results from people needing others to fulfill their jobs; solidarity based on the interdependence brought about by the division of labour

out-groups: groups toward which one feels antagonism

panic: the condition of being so fearful that one cannot function normally, and may even flee

participant observation (or fieldwork): research in which the researcher participates in a research setting while observing what is happening in that setting

patriarchy: authority vested in males; male control of a society or group; a society in which men dominate women

patrilineal (system of descent): a system of reckoning descent that counts only the father's side

patterns: recurring characteristics or events

peer group: a group of individuals roughly the same age linked by common interests

personal identity kit: items people use to decorate their bodies

personality disorders: the view that a personality disturbance of some sort causes an individual to violate social norms

Peter principle: a bureaucratic "law" according to which the members of an organization are promoted for good work until they reach their level of incompetence, the level at which they can no longer do good work

pink ghettoes: also knows as *job ghettoes*, employment areas dominated by women (and usually lower paid than areas dominated by men)

pluralism: the diffusion of power among many interest groups, preventing any single group from gaining control of the government

pluralistic society: a society made up of many different groups

pluralistic theory of social control: the view that society is made up of many competing groups, whose interests manage to become balanced

political socialization: the way in which young people are inculcated with beliefs, ideas, and values that embrace the civil order through the education system

polyandry: a marriage in which a woman has more than one husband

polygyny: a marriage in which a man has more than one wife

polytheism: the belief that there are many gods

population: a target group to be studied

population shrinkage: the process by which a country's population becomes smaller because its birth rate and immigration are too low to replace those who die and emigrate

population transfer: involuntary movement of a minority group

positive sanction: a reward or positive reaction for approved behaviour, for conformity

positivism: the application of the scientific approach to the social world

postmodern society: another term for postindustrial society; its chief characteristic is the use of tools that extend the human abilities to gather and analyze information, communicate, and travel

postmodernism: analysis of contemporary social life where the use of images to convey meaning replaces social reality.

power: the ability to carry out one's will, even over the resistance of others

power elite: C. Wright Mills' term for those who rule the country: the top people in the leading corporations, the most powerful generals and admirals of the armed forces, and certain elite politicians, who make the nation's major decisions

prejudice: an *attitude* of prejudging, usually in a negative way

prestige: respect or regard

primary group: a group characterized by intimate, long-term, face-to-face association and cooperation

primary sector: that part of the economy which extracts raw materials from the environment

primary social deviance: Edwin Lemert's term for acts of social deviance that have little effect on the self-concept

principles of scientific management: also referred to as Taylorism, scientific management sought to reduce waste and inefficiency in production by measuring every movement and regulating every step of the work process

private ownership of the means of production: the ownership of machines and factories by individuals who decide what shall be produced

proactive social movement: a social movement that promotes some social change

profane: Durkheim's term for common elements of everyday life

profession: (as opposed to a job) an occupation characterized by rigorous education, a theoretical perspective, self-regulation, authority over clients, and a professional culture that stresses service to society

proletariat: Karl Marx's term for the exploited class, the mass of workers who do not own the means of production

propaganda: in its broad sense, the presentation of information in the attempt to influence people; in its narrow sense, one-sided information used to try to influence people

proportional representation: an electoral system in which seats in a legislature are divided according to the proportion of votes each political party receives

Protestant ethic: Weber's term to describe the ideal of a self-denying, highly moral life, accompanied by hard work and frugality

public: a dispersed group of people who usually have an interest in the issue on which a social movement focuses; the sympathetic and hostile publics have such an interest, but a third public is either unaware of the issue or indifferent to it

public opinion: how people think about some issue

pure or basic sociology: sociological research whose only purpose is to make discoveries about life in human groups, not to make changes in those groups

qualitative or field interview: an interview in which the researcher is a participant in a conversation with the subject being interviewed

qualitative research methods: research in which emphasis is placed on observing, describing, and interpreting people's behaviour

quality circles: refer to the involvement of rank-and-file workers in detecting and correcting defects and inefficiencies in products and services

quantitative research methods: research in which emphasis is placed on precise measurement, numbers, and statistics

questionnaire: a list of questions to be asked

quiet revolution: the fundamental changes in society that occur as a result of vast numbers of women entering the work force

race: inherited physical characteristics that distinguish one group from another

racism: prejudice and discrimination on the basis of race

random sample: a sample in which everyone in the target population has the same chance of being included in the study

rapport: a feeling of trust between researchers and subjects

rationality: the acceptance of rules, efficiency, and practical results as the right way to approach human affairs

rationalization of society: a widespread acceptance of rationality and a social organization largely built around this idea

rational-legal authority: authority based on law or written rules and regulations; also called *bureaucratic authority*

reactive social movement: a social movement that resists some social change

real culture: the norms and values that people actually follow

redemptive social movement: a social movement that seeks to change people totally

reference groups: the groups we use as standards to evaluate ourselves

reformative social movement: a social movement that seeks to change only particular aspects of society

reformists: a category of study of feminist spirituality represented by those who advocate revealing the "liberating core" of religious teachings with female imagery and exposing and refusing to accept rituals that are clearly sexist

reincarnation: in Hinduism and Buddhism, the return of the soul after death in a different form

rejectionists: a category of study of feminist spirituality represented by those who judge the traditional teachings to be hopelessly sexist and have left it to establish a new spiritual tradition

relative deprivation theory: in this context, the belief that people join social movements on the basis of their evaluations of what they think they should have compared with what others have

reliability: the extent to which data produce consistent results

religion: according to Durkheim, beliefs and practices that separate the profane from the sacred and unite its adherents into a moral community

replication: repeating a study in order to test its findings

representative democracy: a form of democracy in which voters elect representatives to govern and make decisions on their behalf

reputational method (of measuring social class): a system in which people who are familiar with the reputations of others are asked to identify their social class

research method (or research design): one of seven procedures sociologists use to collect data: surveys, participant observation, qualitative interviews, secondary analysis, documents, unobtrusive measures, and experiments

reserve labour force: the unemployed; unemployed workers are thought of as being "in reserve"—capitalists take them "out of reserve" (put them back to work) during times of high production and then lay them off (put them back in reserve) when they are no longer needed

resocialization: the process of learning new norms, values, attitudes, and behaviours

resource mobilization: a theory that social movements succeed or fail on the basis of their ability to mobilize resources such as time, money, and people's skills

respondents: people who respond to a survey, either in interviews or by self-administered questionnaires

revisionists: a category of study of feminist spirituality represented by those who believe that the basic message of the major religions is liberating

revolution: armed resistance designed to overthrow a government

revolutionaries: a category of study of feminist spirituality represented by those who seek to change the established orthodoxy by importing language, images, and rituals from other traditions

riot: violent crowd behaviour aimed against people and property

rituals: ceremonies or repetitive practices; in this context, religious observances or rites, often intended to evoke awe for the sacred

role: the behaviours, obligations, and privileges attached to a status

role conflict: conflicts that someone feels *between* roles because the expectations attached to one role are incompatible with the expectations of another role

role extension: the incorporation of additional activities into a role

role performance: the ways in which someone performs a role within the limits that the role provides; showing a particular "style" or "personality"

role strain: conflicts that someone feels *within* a role

romantic love: feelings of erotic attraction accompanied by an idealization of the other

routinization of charisma: the transfer of authority from a charismatic figure to either a traditional or a rational-legal form of authority

ruling class: another term for the power elite

rumour: unfounded information spread among people

sacred: Durkheim's term for things set apart or forbidden that inspire fear, awe, reverence, or deep respect

sample: the individuals intended to represent the population to be studied

sanctions: expressions of approval or disapproval given to people for upholding or violating norms

Sapir-Whorf hypothesis: Edward Sapir and Benjamin Whorf's hypothesis that language creates ways of thinking and perceiving

scapegoat: an individual or group unfairly blamed for someone else's troubles

science: the application of systematic methods to obtain knowledge and the knowledge obtained by those methods

scientific method: the use of objective, systematic observations to test theories

secondary analysis: the analysis of data already collected by other researchers

secondary group: compared with a primary group, a larger, relatively temporary, more anonymous, formal, and impersonal group based on some interest or activity, whose members are likely to interact on the basis of specific roles

secondary sector: that part of the economy which turns raw materials into manufactured goods

secondary social deviance: Edwin Lemert's term for acts of social deviance incorporated into the self-concept, around which an individual orients his or her behaviour

sect: a group larger than a cult that still feels substantial hostility from and toward society

segregation: the policy of keeping racial or ethnic groups apart

selective perception: seeing certain features of an object or situation, but remaining blind to others

self: the unique human capacity of being able to see ourselves "from the outside"; the picture we gain of how others see us

self-administered questionnaires: questionnaires filled out by respondents

self-fulfilling prophecy: Robert Merton's term for an originally false assertion that becomes true simply because it was predicted

sex typing: the association of behaviours with one sex or the other

sexual harassment: the abuse of one's position of authority to force unwanted sexual demands on someone

shaman: the healing specialist of a preliterate tribe who attempts to control the spirits thought to cause a disease or injury; commonly called a *witch doctor*

sick role: a social role that excuses people from normal obligations because they are sick or injured, while at the same time expecting them to seek competent help and cooperate in getting well

significant other: an individual who significantly influences someone else's life

sign-vehicles: the term used by Erving Goffman to refer to how people use social setting, appearance, and manner to communicate information about the self

slavery: a form of social stratification in which some people own other people

small group: a group small enough for everyone to interact directly with all the other members

social change: the alteration of culture and societies over time

social class: a large number of people with similar amounts of income and education who work at jobs roughly comparable in prestige; according to Weber, a large group of people who rank closely to one another in wealth, power, and prestige; according to Marx, one of two groups: capitalists who own the means of production or workers who sell their labour

social cohesion: the degree to which members of a group or a society feel united by shared values and other social bonds

social construction of reality: the process by which people use their background assumptions and life experiences to define what is real for them

social construction of technology: the view (opposed to technological determinism) that culture (people's values and special interests) shapes the use and development of technology

social control: a group's formal and informal means of enforcing its norms

social deviance: the violation of rules or norms

social environment: the entire human environment, including direct contact with others

social facts: Durkheim's term for the patterns of behaviour that characterize a social group

social inequality: a social condition in which privileges and obligations are given to some but denied to others

social institutions: the organized, usual, or standard ways by which society meets its basic needs

social integration: the degree to which people feel a part of social groups

social interaction: what people do when they are in one another's presence

social location: the group memberships that people have because of their location in history and society

social mobility: movement up or down the social-class ladder

social movement: a large group of people who are organized to promote or resist social change

social movement organization: an organization developed to further the goals of a social movement

social network: the social ties radiating outward from the self that link people together

social order: a group's usual and customary social arrangements, on which its members depend and on which they base their lives

social placement: a function of education that funnels people into a society's various positions

social sciences: the intellectual and academic disciplines designed to understand the social world objectively by means of controlled and repeated observations

social setting: the place where the action of everyday life unfolds

social stratification: the division of large numbers of people into layers according to their relative power, property, and prestige; applies both to nations and to people within a nation, society, or other group

social structure: the framework that surrounds us, consisting of the relationship of people and groups to one another, which gives direction to and sets limits on behaviour

socialism: an economic system characterized by the public ownership of the means of production, central planning, and the distribution of goods without a profit motive

socialization: the process by which people learn the characteristics of their group: the attitudes, values, and actions thought appropriate for them

society: a term used by sociologists to refer to a group of people who share a culture and a territory

sociological perspective: an approach to understanding human behaviour that entails placing it within its broader social context

sociology: the scientific study of society and human behaviour

spirit of capitalism: Weber's term for the desire to accumulate capital as a duty—not to spend it, but as an end in itself—and to constantly reinvest it

state: a political entity that claims monopoly on the use of violence in some particular territory; commonly known as a *country*

status: social ranking; the position someone occupies in society or a social group

status consistency: ranking high or low on all three dimensions of social class

status inconsistency (or discrepancy): ranking high on some dimensions of social class and low on others; a contradiction or mismatch between statuses

status set: all the statuses or positions an individual occupies

status symbols: items used to identify a status

stereotype: assumptions of what people are like, based on previous associations with them or with people who have similar characteristics, or based on information, whether true or false

stigma: "blemishes" that discredit a person's claim to a "normal" identity

stockholders' revolt: the refusal of a corporation's stockholders to rubber-stamp decisions made by its managers

stored value: the backing of a currency by goods that are stored and held in reserve

strain theory: Robert Merton's term for the strain engendered when a society socializes large numbers of people to desire a cultural goal (such as success) but withholds from many the approved means to reach that goal; one adaptation to the strain is crime, the choice of an innovative means (one outside the approved system) to attain the cultural goal

stratified random sample: a sample of specific subgroups of the target population in which everyone in the subgroups has an equal chance of being included in the study

street crime: crimes such as mugging, rape, and burglary

structural mobility: movement up or down the social-class ladder that is attributable to changes in the structure of society, not to individual efforts

structured conversation: see qualitative or field interview

structured interviews: interviews that use closed-ended questions

subculture: the values and related behaviours of a group that distinguish its members from the larger culture; a world within a world

subjective meanings: the meanings that people give their own behaviour

subjective method (of measuring social class): a system in which people are asked to state the social class to which they belong

subsistence economy: a type of economy in which human groups live off the land with little or no surplus

suburbanization: the movement from the city to the suburbs

suburbs: the communities adjacent to the political boundaries of a city

superego: Freud's term for the conscience, the internalized norms and values of our social groups

survey: the collection of data by having people answer a series of questions

sustainable environment: a world system that takes into account the limits of the environment, produces enough material goods for everyone's needs, and leaves a heritage of a sound environment for the next generation

symbol: something to which people attach meanings and then use to communicate with others

symbolic culture: another term for nonmaterial culture

symbolic interactionism: a theoretical perspective in which society is viewed as composed of symbols that people use to establish meaning, develop their views of the world, and communicate with one another

system of descent: how kinship is traced over the generations

taboo: a norm so strong that it brings revulsion if violated

taking the role of the other: putting oneself in someone else's shoes; understanding how someone else feels and thinks and thus anticipating how that person will act

teamwork: the collaboration of two or more persons interested in the success of a performance to manage impressions jointly

techniques of neutralization: ways of thinking or rationalizing that help people deflect society's norms

technological determinism: the view that technology determines culture, that technology takes on a life of its own and forces human behaviour to follow

technology: often defined as the applications of science, but can be conceptualized as tools (items used to accomplish tasks) and the skills or procedures necessary to make and use those tools

tertiary sector: that part of the economy which consists of service-oriented occupations

tertiary social deviance: the normalizing of behaviour considered socially deviant by mainstream society; relabelling the behaviour as non-deviant

theory: a general statement about how some parts of the world fit together and how they work; an explanation of how two or more facts are related to one another

Thomas theorem: William I. Thomas's classic formulation of the definition of the situation: "If people define situations as real, they are real in their consequences."

timetables: the signals societies use to inform their members that they are old; these timetables vary around the world

tool: an object created or modified for a specific purpose

total institution: a place in which people are cut off from the rest of society and are almost totally controlled by the officials who run the place

totalitarianism: a form of government that exerts almost total control over the people

tracking: the sorting of students into different educational programs on the basis of real or perceived abilities

traditional authority: authority based on custom

traditional orientation: the idea—characteristic of tribal, peasant, and feudal societies—that the past is the best guide for the present

transformative social movement: a social movement that seeks to change society totally

triad: a group of three people

underclass: a small group of people for whom poverty persists year after year and across generations

underemployment: the condition of having to work at a job beneath one's level of training and abilities, or of being able to find only part-time work

underground economy: exchanges of goods and services that are not reported to the government and thereby escape taxation

unitary state: form of government in which all power resides with the central government

universal citizenship: the idea that everyone has the same basic rights by virtue of being born in a country (or by immigrating and becoming a naturalized citizen)

unobtrusive measures: various ways of observing people who do not know they are being studied

unstructured interviews: interviews that use open-ended questions

upward social mobility: movement up the social-class ladder

urban legend: a story with an ironic twist that sounds realistic but is false

urbanization: the process by which an increasing proportion of a population lives in cities

validity: the extent to which an operational definition measures what was intended

value cluster: a series of interrelated values that together form a larger whole

value contradictions: values that contradict one another; to follow the one means to come into conflict with the other

value-free: an ideal condition in which a sociologist's personal values or biases do not influence social research

values: the standards by which people define what is desirable or undesirable, good or bad, beautiful or ugly; attitudes about the way the world ought to be

variable: a factor or concept thought to be significant for human behaviour, which varies from one case to another

Verstehen: a German word used by Weber that is perhaps best understood as "to have insight into someone's situation"

voluntary association: a group made up of volunteers who have organized on the basis of some mutual interest

war: armed conflict between nations or politically distinct groups

wealth: property and income

welfare (state) capitalism: an economic system in which individuals own the means of production, but the state regulates many economic activities for the welfare of the population

white-collar crime: Edwin Sutherland's term for crimes committed by people of respectable and high social status in the course of their occupations; for example, bribery of public officials, securities violations, embezzlement, false advertising, and price-fixing

working class: those who sell their labour to the capitalist class

world system: economic and political connections that tie the world's countries together

zero population growth: a demographic condition in which women bear only enough children to reproduce the population

100 million children toil full time, forum told. (1997, October 28). *Toronto Star*, p. A5.

Aberle, D. F., Cohen, A. K., David, A. K., Leng, M. J. Jr., & Sutton, F. N. (1950, January). The functional prerequisites of a society. *Ethics, 60,* 100–111.

Aberle, D. (1960). *The Peyote religion among the Navaho.* Chicago: Aldine.

Abramson, J., & Rogers, D. (1991, January 10). The Keating 535. *Wall Street Journal,* pp. A1, A8.

Abu-Laban, S. M., & McDaniel, S. A. (1998). Beauty, status, and aging. In N. Mandell, (Ed.), *Feminist issues: Race, class and sexuality* (2nd ed., pp. 78–102). Scarborough, ON: Prentice Hall Allyn and Bacon Canada.

Adamchuk, D. J. (2001). The effects of age structure on the labor force and retirement in China. *The Social Science Journal, 38,* pp. 1–11.

Adams, M. L. (1997). *The Trouble With Normal: Post-War Youth and the Making of Heterosexuality.* Toronto: University of Toronto Press.

Addams, J. (1981). *Twenty years at Hull-House.* (First published 1910). New York: Signet.

Adler, P. A., Kless, S. J., & Adler, P. (1992, July). Socialization to gender roles: Popularity among elementary school boys and girls. *Sociology of Education, 65,* 169–187.

Adorno, T. W., Frenkel-Brunswick, E., Levinson, D. J., & Sanford, R. N. (1950). *The authoritarian personality.* New York: Harper & Row.

Aguirre, B. E., Quarantelli, E. L., & Mendoza, J. L. (1993). The collective behavior of fads: The characteristics, effects, and career of streaking. In R. L. Curtis, Jr., & B. E. Aguirre (Eds.), *Collective behavior and social movements* (pp. 168–182). Boston: Allyn and Bacon.

Ahlburg, D. A., & De Vita, C. J. (1992, August). New realities of the American family. *Population Bulletin, 47*(2), 1–44.

Albert, E. M. (1963). Women of Burundi: A study of social values. In D. Paulme (Ed.), *Women of tropical Africa* (pp. 179–215). Berkeley: University of California Press.

Aldrich, N. W., Jr. (1989). *Old money: The mythology of America's upper class.* New York: Vintage Books.

Allahar, A. L., & Coté, J. E. (1998). *Richer and poorer: The structure of inequality in Canada.* Toronto: James Lorimer & Co.

Allen, K. R., & Demo, D. H. (1995, February). The families of lesbians and gay men: A new frontier in family research. *Journal of Marriage and the Family, 57,* 111–127.

Allport, F. (1954). *Social Psychology.* Boston: Houghton Mifflin.

Alpert, H. (1939). *Emile Durkheim and his sociology.* New York: Columbia University Press.

American Sociological Association. (1989, August 14; 1997, Spring). *Code of ethics.* Washington, D.C.: American Sociological Association.

Andersen, M. L. (1988). *Thinking about women: Sociological perspectives on sex and gender.* New York: Macmillan.

Anderson, E. (1997). Streetwise. In J. M. Henslin (Ed.), *Down to earth sociology: Introductory readings* (9th ed., pp. 170–179). New York: Free Press.

Anderson, E. (1978). *A place on the corner.* Chicago: University of Chicago Press.

Anderson, E. (1990). *Streetwise.* Chicago: University of Chicago Press.

Anderson, J. (2001, March). *Wealth divide grows in rich country.* Toronto: Centre for Social Justice. Accessed at: http://www.socialjustice.org/media/releases/wealthgap.html.

Anderson, N. (1966). *Desert saints: The Mormon frontier in Utah.* Chicago: University of Chicago Press. (First published 1942).

Anderson, P. (1995, Autumn). God and the Swedish immigrants. *Sweden and America,* 17–20.

Anderssen, E. (2002, October 23). Junior's at home and grandma's alone. *The Globe and Mail,* p. A1.

Angell, M. (1996, November 28). Euthanasia in the Netherlands—Good news or bad? *New England Journal of Medicine, 335,* 22.

Angell, R. C. (1965). The sociology of human conflict. In E. B. McNeil (Ed.), *The Nature of Human Conflict.* Englewood Cliffs, NJ: Prentice Hall.

Ansberry, C. (1988, November 29). Despite federal law, hospitals still reject sick who can't pay. *Wall Street Journal,* pp. A1, A4.

Ansberry, C. (1993, May 21). Nannies and mothers struggle over roles in raising children. *Wall Street Journal,* pp. A1, A6.

Anybody's son will do. (1983). National Film Board of Canada, KCTS, and Films, Inc.

Aptheker, H. (1990). W.E.B. Du Bois: Struggle not despair. *Clinical Sociology Review, 8,* 58–68.

Arías, J. (1993, January 2). La Junta rehabilita en Grenada casas que deberá tirar por ruina. *El Pais,* p.1.

Arichi, M. (1999). Is it radical? Women's right to keep their own surnames after marriage. *Women's Studies International Forum, 22*(4), 411–415.

Ariès, P. (1962). *Centuries of childhood: A social history of family life* (R. Baldick, Trans.). New York: Vintage.

Arlacchi, P. (1980). *Peasants and great estates: Society in traditional Calabria.* Cambridge, England: Cambridge University Press.

Armitage, R. L. (1989, February 7). Red army retreat doesn't signal end of U.S. obligation. *Wall Street Journal,* p. A20.

Armstrong, R. (2000). Mapping the conditions of First Nations communities. *Canadian Social Trends* (Vol. 3, pp. 28–32). Toronto: Thompson Educational Press.

Arndt, W. F., & Gingrich, F. W. (1957). *A Greek-English lexicon of the New Testament and other early Christian literature.* Chicago: University of Chicago Press.

Arnold, T. (2002, October 23). Two-parent households are waning. *The National Post,* p. A1.

Asch, S. (1952). Effects of group pressure upon the modification and distortion of judgments. In G. Swanson, T. M. Newcomb, & E. L. Hartley (Eds.), *Readings in social psychology.* New York: Holt, Rinehart and Winston.

Ashe, A. (1992, February 27). A zero-sum game that hurts Blacks. *Wall Street Journal,* p. A10.

Ashford, L. S. (1995, March). New perspectives on population: Lessons from Cairo. *Population Bulletin, 50*(1), 1–44.

Ashford, L. S. (2001, March). New population policies: Advancing women's health and rights. *Population Bulletin, 56*(1).

Association of Canadian Pension Management (ACPM). (2000, January). *Dependence or self-reliance: Which way for Canada's retirement income system?* Retrieved October 12, 2000 from, www.acpm.com/ACPMenglish/documents/dep_selfreliance.htm

Aubin, B. (2001–2002, December 31–January 7). Where the solitudes meet. *Maclean's* (Toronto Edition), *114*(53), p. 32.

Auerbach, J. D. (1990, December). Employer-supported child care as a women-responsive policy. *Journal of Family Issues, 11*(4), 384–400.

Bainbridge, W. S. (1989). Collective behavior and social movements. In R. Stark, *Sociology* (pp. 608–640). Belmont, CA: Wadsworth.

Bales, R. F. (1950). *Interaction Process Analysis*. Reading, MA: Addison-Wesley. Bales, R. F. (1953). The equilibrium problem in small groups. In T. Parsons et al. (Eds.), *Working papers in the theory of action* (pp. 111–115). New York: Free Press.

Baltzell, E. D., & Schneiderman, H. G. (1988, September/October). Social class in the Oval Office. *Society, 25,* 42–49.

Baltzell, E. D. (1964). *The Protestant establishment: Aristocracy and caste in America.* New York: Vintage.

Baltzell, E. D. (1979). *Puritan Boston and Quaker Philadelphia.* New York: Free Press.

Bannon, L. (1995, October 24). How a rumor spread about subliminal sex in Disney's "Aladdin." *Wall Street Journal,* pp. A1, A6.

Barbeau, C. (1992) The man–woman crisis. In J. M. Henslin (Ed.), *Marriage and Family in a Changing Society* (4th ed.). New York: Free Press, pp. 193–199.

Barnes, F. (1995, June 14). How to rig a poll. *Wall Street Journal,* p. A14.

Barnes, H. E. (1935). *The history of Western civilization* (Vol. 1). New York: Harcourt, Brace.

Barnes, J. A. (1990, December 12). Canadians cross border to save their lives. *Wall Street Journal,* p. A14.

Baron, R., & Greenberg, G. (1990). *Behavior in organizations.* Boston: Allyn and Bacon.

Barry, P. (1989, Fall). Strong medicine: A talk with former principal Henry Gradillas. *College Board Review,* 2–13.

Barthes, R. (1975). *The pleasure of the text* (R. Miller, Trans., with a note on the text by R. Howard). New York: Hill and Wang.

Bashevkin, S. (2002, May 27). Warning: Duty state under construction. *Toronto Star,* p. A21.

Baudrillard, J. (1983). *Simulations* (P. Foss, P. Patton, & P. Beitchman, Trans.). New York: Semiotext.

Baudrillard, J. (1993). *The transparency of evil: Essays on extreme phenomena* (J. Benedict, Trans.). London; New York: Verso.

Baudrillard, J. (1995). *The Gulf War did not take place* (P. Patton, Trans. and intro.). Bloomington: Indiana University Press.

Beagan, B. L. (2001). Even if I don't know what I'm doing I can make it look like I know what I'm doing: Becoming a doctor in the 1990s. *The Canadian Review of Sociology and Anthropology, 38,* pp. 275–292.

Beals, R. L., & Hoijer, H. (1965). *An introduction to anthropology* (3rd ed.). New York: Macmillan.

Beck, A. J., Kline, S. A., & Greenfeld, L. A. (1988, September). Survey of youth in custody, 1987. Washington, DC: U.S. Department of Justice.

Beck, S. H., & Page, J. W. (1988). Involvement in activities and the psychological well-being of retired men. *Activities, Adaptation, & Aging, 11*(1), 31–47.

Becker, H. S. (1966). *Outsiders: Studies in the sociology of deviance.* New York: Free Press.

Becker, H. S., Geer, B., Strauss, A. L., and Hughes, E. C. (1961). *Boys in white: Student culture in medical school.* Chicago: University of Chicago Press.

Beckett, P. (1996, September 11). Even piñatas sold in Mexico seem to originate in Hollywood now. *Wall Street Journal,* p. B1.

Beeghley, L. (1996). *The structure of social stratification in the United States* (2nd ed.). Boston: Allyn and Bacon.

Belanger, A. (1999). *Report on the demographic situation in Canada 1998–1999: Current demographic analysis.* Ottawa: Minister of Industry.

Belcher, J. R. (1988, Fall). Are jails replacing the mental health system for the homeless mentally ill? *Community Mental Health Journal, 24*(3), 185–195.

Belkin, L. (2000, June 23). Your kids are their problem. *The New York Times Magazine,* 30ff.

Bell, D. (1973). *The coming of post-industrial society: A venture in social forecasting.* New York: Basic Books.

Benales, C. (1973, January 1). 70 days battling starvation and freezing in the Andes: A chronicle of man's unwillingness to die. *New York Times,* p. 3.

Bender, W., & Smith, M. (1997, February). Population, food, and nutrition. *Population Bulletin, 51*(4), 1–47.

Benet, S. (1971, December). Why they live to be 100, or even older, in Abkhasia. *New York Times Magazine,* 26.

Bennett, N. G., Blanc, A. K., & Bloo, D. E. (1988). Commitment and the modern union: Assessing the link between premarital cohabitation and subsequent marital stability. *American Sociological Review, 53,* 127–138.

Benokraitis, N. V., & Feagin, J. R. (1991). Sex discrimination—Subtle and covert. In J. M. Henslin (Ed.). *Down to Earth Sociology: Introductory Readings* (6th ed., pp. 334–343). New York: Free Press.

Berger, P. L. (1963). *Invitation to sociology: A humanistic perspective.* New York: Doubleday.

Berger, P. L. (1967). *The sacred canopy: Elements of a sociological theory of religion.* Garden City, NY: Doubleday.

Berger, P. L. (1991). *The capitalist revolution: Fifty propositions about prosperity, equality, and liberty.* New York: Basic Books.

Berger, P. L. (1992). *A far glory: The quest for faith in an age of credulity.* New York: Free Press.

Berger, P. L. (1997). Invitation to sociology. In J. M. Henslin (Ed.). *Down to Earth Sociology: Introductory Readings* (9th ed., pp. 3–7). New York: Free Press.

Berk, R. A. (1974). *Collective behavior.* Dubuque, Iowa: Brown.

Berle, A. Jr., & Means, G. C. (1980). *The modern corporation and private property* (Original work published 1932, New York: Harcourt, Brace and World). As cited in Useem, 44.

Bernard, J. (1972). *The Future of Marriage.* New York: Bantam.

Bernard, J. (1992). The good-provider role. In J. M. Henslin, (Ed.). *Marriage and family in a changing society* (4th ed., pp. 275–285). New York: Free Press.

Bernard, V. W., Ottenberg, P., & Redl, F. (1971). Dehumanization: A composite psychological defense in relation to modern war. In R. Perucci & M. Pilisuk (Eds.). *The triple revolution emerging: Social problems in depth* (pp. 17–34). Boston: Little, Brown.

Berry, L. et al. (1999). *Canadian global almanac 2000.* Toronto: Macmillan Canada.

Bess, I. (1999, Summer). Widows living alone. *Canadian Social Trends, 53*(20), 2–6.

Besser, T. L. (1992, May). A critical approach to the study of Japanese management. *Humanity and Society, 16*(2), 176–195.

Bibby, R. W. (1995). *The Bibby report: Social trends Canadian style.* Toronto: Stoddart.

Bijker, W. E., Hughes, T., & Pinch, T. (1987). *The social construction of technological systems.* Cambridge, MA: MIT Press.

Bird, C. E. (1997, August). Gender differences in the social and economic burdens of parenting and psychological distress. *Journal of Marriage and the Family, 59,* 1–16.

Bishop, J. E. (1990, April 16). Study finds doctors tend to postpone heart surgery for women, raising risk. *Wall Street Journal,* p. B4.

Black, D. (2000, October 13). Older women prepare to battle government. *Toronto Star,* p. E4.

Blackwelder, S. P. (1993). Duality of structure in the reproduction of race, class, and gender inequality [Paper presented at the 1993 meetings of the American Sociological Association].

Blau, F. D., & Lawrence M. K. (1992, December). The gender earnings gap: Some international evidence [Working Paper No. 4224, National Bureau of Economic Research].

Blau, P. M. (1994). Social structure and life chances. *Current Perspectives in Social Theory, 5*(Supplement 1), 177–190.

Blau, P. M. & Duncan, O. D. (1967). *The American Occupational Structure.* New York: John Wiley.

Blauner, R. (1966). Death and social structure. *Psychiatry, 29,* 378–394.

Blumer, H. G. (1939). Collective behavior. In R. E. Park (Ed.). *Principles of Sociology,* (pp. 219–288). New York: Barnes and Noble.

Blumer, H. (1966). Sociological implications of the thought of George Herbert Mead. *American Journal of Sociology, 71,* 535–544.

Blumer, H. (1990). *Industrialization as an agent of social change: A critical analysis;* D. R. Maines & T. J. Morrione, (Eds.). Hawthorne, NY: Aldine de Gruyter.

Bogardus, E. S. (1929). *A history of social thought* (2nd ed.). Los Angeles: Jesse Ray Miller.

Borrelli, P. (1988, Spring). The ecophilosophers. *Amicus Journal,* 30–39.

Bourgois, P. (1994). Crack in Spanish Harlem. In J. Curtis & L. Tepperman (Eds.), *Haves and have-nots: An international reader on social inequality* (pp. 131–136). Englewood Cliffs, NJ: Prentice Hall.

Bourque, L. B. (1989). *Defining rape.* Durham, NC: Duke University Press.

Bowlby, G. (2002, Spring). The labour-market: Year-end review 2001. *Perspectives on Labour and Income, 14,* pp. 7–14.

Bowles, S., & Gintis, H. (1976). *Schooling in capitalist America.* New York: Basic Books.

Boyd, M. (1989). Immigration and income security policies in Canada: Implications for elderly immigrant women. *Population Research and Policy Review, 8,* 5–24.

Boyd, M., & Norris, D. (1999, Spring). The crowded nest: Young adults at home. *Canadian Social Trends, 52,* 2–5.

Bradley, M. B., Green, N. M. Jr., Jones, D. E., Lynn, M., & McNiel, L. (1992). *Churches and church membership in the United States 1990.* Atlanta: Glenmary Research Center.

Bradshaw, J. (2002). Child poverty and child outcomes. *Children and Society, 16,* pp. 131–140.

Brajuha, M., & Hallowell, L. (1986, January). Legal intrusion and the politics of fieldwork: The impact of the Brajuha case. *Urban Life, 14*(4), 454–478.

Brauchli, M. W. (1993a, May 10). A satellite TV system is quickly moving Asia into the global village. *Wall Street Journal,* pp. A1, A8.

Braverman, H. (1974). *Labor and monopoly capital: The degradation of work in the twentieth century.* New York: Monthly Review Press.

Bray, R. L. (1995, November–December). Rosa Parks: A legendary moment, a lifetime of activism. *Ms., 6*(3), 45–47.

Brecher, J., & Costello, T. (1998). *Global Village or Global Pillage: Economic Reconstruction From the Bottom Up.* Cambridge, Mass: South End Press.

Breen, R., & Whelan, C. T. (1995, February). Gender and class mobility: Evidence from the Republic of Ireland. *Sociology, 29*(1), 1–22.

Brennan, R. (2002, March 29). $4.3 million campaign targets elder abuse. *Toronto Star,* p. A3.

Brenner, J. (2000). *Women and the Politics of Class.* New York: Monthly Review Press.

Bretos, M. A. (1994, May 22). Hispanics face institutional exclusion. *Miami Herald.*

Bridgman, A. (1994, April 6). Report from the Russian front. *Education Week,* pp. 22–29.

Bridgwater, W. (Ed.). (1953). *The Columbia Viking desk encyclopedia.* New York: Viking Press.

Brilliant, A. E. (1964). *Social effects of the automobile in Southern California during the 1920s* [Unpublished doctoral dissertation]. University of California at Berkeley.

Brines, J. (1994, November). Economic dependency, gender, and the division of labor at home. *American Journal of Sociology, 100*(3), 652–688.

Bromley, D. G. (1991, May–June). The Satanic cult scare. *Culture and Society,* 55–56.

Bronfenbrenner, U. (1992). Principles for the healthy growth and development of children. In J. M. Henslin (Ed.), *Marriage and family in a changing society* (4th ed., pp. 243–249). New York: Free Press.

Brooks, V. R. (1982). Sex differences in student dominance behavior in female and male professors' classrooms. *Sex Roles, 8*(7), 683–690.

Brotman, S. (1998, Summer). The incidence of poverty among seniors in Canada: Exploring the impact of gender, ethnicity and race. *Canadian Journal of Aging, 17*(2), 166–185.

Brown, D. R., & Gary, L. E. (1988). Unemployment and psychological distress among Black American women. *Sociological Focus, 21,* 209–221.

Brunvand, J. H. (1981). *The vanishing hitchhiker: American urban legends and their meanings.* New York: Norton.

Brunvand, J. H. (1984). *The choking Doberman and other "new" urban legends.* New York: Norton.

Brunvand, J. H. (1986). *The study of American folklore.* New York: Norton.

Bryant, C. D. (1993). Cockfighting: America's invisible sport. In J. M. Henslin (Ed.), *Down to earth sociology: Introductory readings* (7th ed.). New York: Free Press.

Buckley, S. (1991, June 17). Shrugging off the burden of a brainy image. *Washington Post,* p. D1.

Budiansky, S. (1987, February 9). The trees fell—and so did the people. *U.S. News and World Report,* p. 75.

Buechler, S. M. (1993). Beyond resource mobilization: Emerging trends in social movement theory. *Sociological Quarterly, 34*(2), 217–235.

Burgess, E. W. (1925). The growth of the city: An introduction to a research project. In R. E. Park, E. W. Burgess, & R. D. McKenzie (Eds.), *The city* (pp. 47–62). Chicago: University of Chicago Press.

Burgess, E. W., & Locke, H. J. (1945). *The family: From institution to companionship.* New York: American Book.

Burke, M. A., Lindsay, J., McDowell, I., & Hill, G. (1997, Summer). Dementia among seniors. *Canadian Social Trends, 45,* 24–27.

Burke, M. A., Crompton, S., Jones, A., & Nessner, K. (1994). Caring for children. In *Canadian Social Trends: A Canadian Studies Reader* (Vol. 2, pp. 209–212). Toronto: Thompson Education Press.

Burman, P. (1996). *Poverty's bonds: Power and agency in the social relations of welfare.* Toronto: Thompson Educational Publishing.

Busby, J. (1993, January). Hospices: Help for the dying. *Current Health,* 30–31.

Bush, D. M., & Simmons, R. G. (1990). Socialization processes over the life course. In M. Rosenberger & R. H. Turner (Eds.), *Social psychology: Sociological perspectives* (pp. 133–164). New Brunswick, NJ: Transaction.

Butler, I., Scanlan, L., Robinson, M., Douglas, G., & Murch, M. (2002). Children's involvement in their parent's divorce: implications for practice. *Children and Society, 26,* pp. 89–102.

Butler, R. N. (1980, Winter). Ageism: Another form of bigotry. *Gerontologist, 9,* 243–246.

Butler, Robert N. *Why Survive? Being Old in America.* New York: Harper & Row, 1975.

Buttel, F. H. (1987). New directions in environmental sociology. In W. R. Scott & J. F. Short, Jr., (Eds.), *Annual Review of Sociology, 13,* 465–488. Palo Alto, CA: Annual Reviews.

Calamai, P. (2002, September 28). 10 biotech breakthroughs lifesavers for poor. *Toronto Star,* p. A19.

Calvert, S. L., Kondla, T. A., Ertel, K. A., & Meisel, D. S. (2001). Young Adults' Perceptions and Memories of a Televised Woman Hero. *Sex Roles, 45,* pp. 31–52.

Campbell, M. (2001, May 4). Study links racism, wage gap. *Toronto Star,* p. A19.

Canadian Council on Social Development (CCSD). (2000). *The Canadian Fact Book on Poverty.* Ottawa: CCSD.

Canadian Education Statistics Council. (2000, February). *Education Indicators in Canada: Report of the Pan-Canadian Education Indicators Program 1999*. Ottawa: Canadian Education Statistics Council.

Canadian Press. (2002, July 22). Suspensions soar in schools: Critics are alarmed at trend of punishing young for minor offences. *The Toronto Star*, p. A3.

Canadian Sociology and Anthropology Association. (1995). *Code of ethics*. Montreal.

Canavan, M. M., Meyer, W. J. III, & Higgs, D. C. (1992). The female experience of sibling incest. *Journal of Marital and Family Therapy, 18*(2), 129–142.

Cannon, L. (1998). *Official negligence: How Rodney King and the riots changed Los Angeles and the LAPD*. New York: Times Books.

Cantril, H. (1941). *The psychology of social movements*. New York: Wiley.

Caplow, T. (1991). The American way of celebrating Christmas. In J. M. Henslin (Ed.), *Down to earth sociology: Introductory readings* (6th ed., pp. 88–97). New York: Free Press.

Capponi, P. (1997). *Dispatches from the poverty line*. Toronto: Penguin Books.

Cardoso, F. H. (1972, July–August). Dependent capitalist development in Latin America. *New Left Review, 74*, 83–95.

Carey, E. (1998, October 28). One-parent families under fire. *The Toronto Star*, p. A2.

Carey, E. (1999a, October 6). "Cookie-sharing" children credited with crime drop. *The Toronto Star*, p. A5.

Carey, E. (1999b, July 27). Despite upturn, families are no better off. *The Toronto Star*, pp. D1, D26.

Carey, E. (2000, January 13). Family incomes on national downward slide. *The Toronto Star*, p. A7.

Carey, E. (2000, January 21). Smoking by teens on increase. *Toronto Star*, p. A20.

Carey, E. (2001, March 16). Rich, poor are even wider apart. *Toronto Star*, pp. A1, A10.

Carey, E. (2001a, December 11). Baby can wait, couples find. *Toronto Star*, p. A20.

Carey, E. (2001b, April 3). Stress, instability mark of 'blended' families. *Toronto Star*, p. D3.

Carey, E. (2002a, May 2). Delaying childbirth boosts earning power. *Toronto Star*, p. A2.

Carey, E. (2002b, July 4). Drop in Canada's birth rate attributed to 20-somethings. *Toronto Star*, p. A8.

Carey, E. (2002c, September 18). Home alone: A growing reality for Canadians. *Toronto Star*, p. A7.

Carey, E. (2002d, May 18). Many seniors stay on job, study says. *Toronto Star*, p. A12.

Carpenter, B. (1990, September 17). Redwood radicals. *U.S. News & World Report, 109*(11), 50–51.

Carr, D., Ryff, C. D., Singer, B., & Magee, W. J. (1995). Bringing the "life" back into life course research: A "person-centered" approach to studying the life course. Paper presented at the 1995 meetings of the American Sociological Association.

Carrington, T. (1993, September 20). Developed nations want poor countries to succeed on trade, but not too much. *Wall Street Journal*, p. A10.

Carroll, P. N., & Noble, D. W. (1977). *The free and the unfree: A new history of the United States*. New York: Penguin.

Cartwright, D., & Zander, A. (Eds.), (1968). *Group dynamics* (3rd ed.). Evanston, IL: Peterson.

Cauthen, N. K., & Jasper, J. M. (1994, September). Culture, politics, and moral panics. *Sociological Forum, 9*(3), 495–503.

Centre for Educational Research and Innovation. (1998). *Education at a glance: OECD indicators 1998*. Paris: OECD.

Centre for Social Justice. (2001). *New UN report shows Canada low-down in poverty ranking*. Toronto: Centre for Social Justice.

Cerulo, K. A., & Ruane, J. M. (1996). Death comes alive: Technology and the re-conception of death. In *Science as Culture*.

Cerulo, K. A., Ruane, J. M., & Chayko, M. (1992, February). Technological ties that bind: Media-generated primary groups. *Communication Research, 19*(1), 109–129.

Chafetz, J. S., & Dworkin, A. G. (1986). *Female revolt: Women's movements in world and historical perspective*. Totowa, NJ: Rowman & Allanheld.

Chafetz, J. S. (1974). *Masculine/feminine or human? An overview of the sociology of sex roles*. Itasca, IL: Peacock.

Chafetz, J. S. (1990). *Gender equity: An integrated theory of stability and change*. Newbury Park, CA: Sage.

Chagnon, N. A. (1977). *Yanomamo: The fierce people* (2nd ed.). New York: Holt, Rinehart and Winston.

Chambliss, W. J. (1997). The saints and the roughnecks. In J. M. Henslin (Ed.), *Down to earth sociology: Introductory readings* (9th ed., pp. 246–260). New York: Free Press. [First published in *Society, 11*, 1973].

Chandler, D. (1995). Technological or media determinism. Internet, Media and Communication Studies Page, from dgc(a)aberystwyth.ac

Chandler, T., & Fox, G. (1974). *3000 years of urban growth*. New York: Academic Press.

Chandra, V. P. (1993a). Fragmented identities: The social construction of ethnicity, 1885–1947 [Unpublished paper].

Chandra, V. P. (1993b). The present moment of the past: The metamorphosis [Unpublished paper].

Chavez, L. (1990, November 19). Rainbow Collision. *New Republic* pp. 14–16.

Chaykowski, R. P., & Powell, L. M. (Eds.). (1999). *Women and Work*. Kingston: McGill-Queen's University Press.

Cheadle, B. (2000, October 17). Food bank users double in 10 years. *Toronto Star*, p. A1.

Cheal, D., et al. (1997, Spring). Canadian children in the 1990s: Selected findings of the national longitudinal survey of children and youth. *Canadian Social Trends, 44*, 2–9.

Che-Alford, J., & Hamm, B. (1999, Summer). Under one roof: Three generations living together. *Canadian Social Trends, 53*, 6–9.

Che-Alford, J., Allan, C., & Butlin, G. (1994). *Families in Canada*. Scarborough, ON: Prentice-Hall and Statistics Canada.

Chen, E. (1979, December 9). Twins reared apart: A living lab. *New York Times Magazine*, 112.

Chen, K. (1995, August 28). China's women face obstacles in workplace. *Wall Street Journal*, pp. B1, B5.

Chen, K. (1996, January 4). Chinese are going to town as growth of cities takes off. *Wall Street Journal*, pp. A1, A12.

Cheng, T. O. (1999). Teenage smoking in China. *Journal of Adolescence, 22*, 607–620.

Chesnais, J.-C. (1997, January). The demographic sunset of the west? *Population Today, 25*(1), 4–5.

Chodorow, N. J. (1990). What is the relation between psychoanalytic feminism and the psychoanalytic psychology of women? In D. L. Rhode (Ed.), *Theoretical perspectives on sexual difference* (pp. 114–130). New Haven, CT: Yale University Press.

Chui, T. (1996, Autumn). Canada's population: Charting into the 21st century. *Canadian Social Trends, 42*, 3–7.

Clair, J. M., Karp, D. A., & Yoels, W. C. (1993). *Experiencing the life cycle: A social psychology of aging* (2nd ed.). Springfield, IL: Thomas.

Clark, S. D. (1942). *The social development of Canada: An introductory study with select documents*. Toronto: University of Toronto Press.

Clark, W. (1997, Spring). School leavers revisited. *Canadian Social Trends*. (Statistics Canada, Catalogue 11-008-XPE, Number 44, 10–12).

Clark, W. (2000). Patterns of religious observance. *Canadian Social Trends 59*, pp. 23–27.

Clark, W. (2001). Economic gender equality indicators 2000. *Canadian Social Trends, 60*, pp. 1–8.

Clark, W. (2002, Autumn). Time alone. *Canadian Social Trends*, pp. 2–6.

Clarke, L. H. (2001). Older women's bodies and the self: The construction of identity in later life. *Canadian Review of Sociology and Anthropology, 38*, pp. 441–464.

Clay, J. W. (1990, November–December). What's a nation? *Mother Jones, 28*, 30.

Clement, W. (1975). *The Canadian corporate elite: An analysis of economic power.* Toronto: McClelland and Stewart.

Clement, W. (1977). *Continental corporate power: Economic elite linkages between Canada and the United States.* Toronto: McClelland and Stewart.

Clement, W. (1983). *Class, power and property: Essays on Canadian society.* Toronto: McClelland and Stewart.

Clement, W., & Myles, J. (1994). *Relations of ruling: Class and gender in postindustrial societies.* Montreal: McGill-Queen's University Press.

Cloward, R. A., & Ohlin, L. E. (1960). *Delinquency and opportunity: A theory of delinquent gangs.* New York: Free Press.

Cnaan, R. A. (1991, December). Neighborhood-representing organizations: How democratic are they? *Social Science Review,* 614–634.

Cohen, A. (1997, April 21). The great American welfare lab. *Time,* 74–76, 78.

Cohen, J. E. (1996, January). How many people can the earth support? *Population Today,* 4–5.

Cohen, S. M. (1990, December). Hey NCR—we're the shareholders, you work for us. *Wall Street Journal,* p. A16.

Cole, J., & Lubman, S. (1994, January 28). Weapons merchants are going great guns in post-Cold War era. *Wall Street Journal,* pp. A1, A4.

Coleman, J. W. (1989). *The criminal elite: The sociology of white collar crime.* New York: St. Martin's Press.

Coleman, J. W. (1995). Politics and the abuse of power. In J. M. Henslin (Ed.), *Down to earth sociology: Introductory readings* (8th ed., pp. 442–450). New York: Free Press.

Collins, P. H. (1986, December). Learning from the outsider within: The sociological significance of Black feminist thought. *Social Problems, 33*(6), 514–532.

Collins, R. (1974). *Conflict sociology: Toward an explanatory science.* New York: Academic Press.

Collins, R. (1979). *The credential society: An historical sociology of education.* New York: Academic Press.

Collins, R. (1988). *Theoretical sociology.* San Diego: Harcourt, Brace Jovanovich.

Collins, R., Chafetz, J. S., Blumberg, R. L., Coltrane, S., & Turner, J. H. (1993). Toward an integrated theory of gender stratification. *Sociological Perspectives, 36*(3), 185–216.

Community Information Centre of Metropolitan Toronto. (1997). *55 plus Ontario: A handbook on services for older adults.* Toronto: The Community Information Centre.

Conahan, F. C. (1994, September 28). Human experimentation: An overview on Cold War era programs (1–11). Washington, DC: U.S. General Accounting Office.

Connell, R. W. (2000). Masculinities and globalization. In M. Zinn, P. Hondagneu-Sotelo, & M. Messner (Eds.), *Gender through the prism of difference* (2nd ed., pp. 49–62). Boston: Allyn and Bacon.

Connell, R. W. (2000). *The men and the boys.* Berkeley: University of California Press.

Connell, R. W. (2002). *Gender.* Malden, Mass.: Polity.

Connidis, I. A. (1989). *Family ties and aging.* Toronto: Butterworths.

Cooley, C. H. (1902). *Human nature and the social order.* New York: Scribner's.

Cooley, C. H. (1962). *Social organization.* New York: Schocken. [First published by Scribner's, 1909].

Copper, B. (2001). Voices: On becoming old women. In S. Shaw and J. Lee (Eds.), *Women's Voices, Feminist Visions: Classic and Contemporary Readings* (pp. 94–97). Mountain View, California: Mayfield Publishing Company.

Coser, L. A. (1977). *Masters of sociological thought: Ideas in historical and social context* (2nd ed.). New York: Harcourt Brace Jovanovich.

Coté, J. E., & Allahar, A. (1994). *Generation on hold: Coming of age in the late twentieth century.* Toronto: Stoddart.

Courtney, K. (1995). Two sides of the environmental movement: Radical Earth First! and the Sierra Club. [Paper presented at the 1995 meetings of the American Sociological Association].

Cousins, A., & nagpaul, H. (1970). *Urban man and society.* New York: McGraw-Hill.

Covell, K., & Howe, R. B. (2001). *The Challenge of Children's Rights for Canada.* Waterloo: Wilfrid Laurier University Press.

Cowen, E. L., Landes, J., & Schaet, D. E. (1959, January). The effects of mild frustration on the expression of prejudiced attitudes. *Journal of Abnormal and Social Psychology,* 33–38.

Cowgill, D. (1974). The aging of populations and societies. *Annals of the American Academy of Political and Social Science, 415,* 1–18.

Cowley, G. (1996, November 16). Attention: Aging men. *Newsweek, 66*–75.

Cowley, J. (1969). *Pioneers of Women's Liberation.* New York: Merit.

Cox, P. (1997, November 17). Cyberdegrees. *Wall Street Journal,* p. R26.

Cram, K. & Kossick, D. (1997, November). *Briarpatch 26* (9), pp. 13–14.

Crane, D. (2000, September 17). Poverty guarantees a nastier world. *Toronto Star,* p. B6.

Crawford, T. (2002, April 13). Moving down in the world. *Toronto Star,* pp. L1, L2, L3.

Crawford, T. (2002, February 16). Under Suspicion: Society is laying down the lay and hobbling teenagers with intolerance and mistrust. *Toronto Star,* pp. M1, 2, 4.

Croal, N., & Hughes, J. (1997, November 10). Lara Croft, the bit girl. *Newsweek,* 82, 86.

Crompton, S. (2000, Winter). 100 years of...health. *Canadian Social Trends,* pp. 12–17.

Crompton, S., & Vickers, M. (2000, Summer). One hundred years of labour force. *Canadian Social Trends,* pp. 2–13.

Crosbie, P. V., (Ed.). (1975). *Interaction in small groups.* New York: Macmillan.

Crossen, C. (1991, November 14) *Wall Street Journal,* pp. A1, A7.

Crossman, D. K. (1995). Global structural violence against women. [Paper presented at the 1995 meetings of the American Sociological Association].

Cumming, E. (1976). Further thoughts on the theory of disengagement. In C. S. Kart & B. B. Manard (Eds.), *Aging in America: Readings in social gerontology* (pp. 19–41). Sherman Oaks, CA: Alfred Publishing.

Cumming, E., & Henry, W. E. (1961). *Growing old: The process of disengagement.* New York: Basic Books.

Curry-Stevens, A. (2001). *When Markets Fail People: Exploring the Widening Gap Between Rich and Poor in Canada.* Toronto: Centre for Social Justice.

Curtis, B., Livingstone, D. W., & Smaller, H. (1992). *Stacking the Deck: The Streaming of Working-Class Kids in Ontario Schools.* Montreal: Our Schools/Our Selves Education Foundation.

Curtis, J., Grabb, E., & Guppy, N. (Eds.). (1999). *Social Inequality in Canada: Patterns, Problems, and Policies,* 3rd Ed. Toronto: Prentice-Hall.

Curwin, E. C., & Hart, G. (1961). *Plough and pasture.* New York: Collier Books.

Cyberschool makes its debut. (1996, January). *The American Schoolboard, 183,* 1, A11.

Dahl, R. A. (1961). *Who governs?* New Haven, CT: Yale University Press.

Dahl, R. A. (1982). *Dilemmas of pluralist democracy: Autonomy vs. control.* New Haven, CT: Yale University Press.

Dahrendorf, R. (1959). *Class and class conflict in industrial society.* Palo Alto, CA: Stanford University Press.

Dannefer, D. (1984, February). Adult development and social theory: A reappraisal. *American Sociological Review, 49*(1),100–116.

Darley, J. M., & Latané, B. (1968). Bystander intervention in emergencies: Diffusion of responsibility. *Journal of Personality and Social Psychology, 8*(4), 377–383.

Darnell, V. (1971, May). Qualitative-quantitative content analysis of graffiti in the public restrooms of St. Louis, Missouri, and Edwardsville, Illinois [Master's thesis]. Edwardsville, IL: Southern Illinois University.

Darwin, C. (1859). *The origin of species.* Chicago: Conley.

Das Gupta, T. (2000). Families of Native people, immigrants and people of colour. In N. Mandell & A. Duffy, *Canadian families: Diversity, conflict and change* (pp. 146–187). Toronto: Harcourt Brace & Company, Canada.

Davies, Scott. (1999). Stubborn disparities: Explaining class inequalities in schooling. In J. Curtis, E. Grubb, and N. Guppy, (Eds.), *Social Inequality in Canada: Patterns, Problems, Policies.* Toronto: Prentice-Hall.

Davis, A., Gardner, B. B., & Gardner, M. R. (1941). *Deep south: A social-anthropological study of caste and class.* Chicago: University of Chicago Press.

Davis, F. (1959, September). The cabdriver and his fare: Facets of a fleeting relationship. *American Journal of Sociology, 65,* 158–165.

Davis, K. (1940, January). Extreme social isolation of a child. *American Journal of Sociology, 45*(4), 554–565.

Davis, K. (1997). Extreme isolation. In J. M. Henslin (Ed.), *Down to earth sociology: Introductory readings* (9th ed., pp. 121–129). New York: Free Press.

Davis, K., & Moore, W. E. (1945). Some principles of stratification. *American Sociological Review, 10,* 242–249.

Davis, K., & Moore, W. E. (1953). Reply to Tumin. *American Sociological Review, 18,* 394–396.

Davis, L. J. (1996). Medscam. In L. M. Salinger (Ed.), *Deviant Behavior 96/97* (pp. 93–97). Guilford, CT: Dushkin.

Davis, N. J., & Robinson, R. V. (1988, February). Class identification of men and women in the 1970s and 1980s. *American Sociological Review, 53,* 103–112.

Davis, N. J. (1978). Prostitution: Identity, career, and legal-economic enterprise. In J. M. Henslin & E. Sagarin (Eds.), *The sociology of sex: An introductory reader* (rev. ed., pp. 195–222). New York: Schocken Books.

De George, R. T. (1968). *The new Marxism: Society and East European Marxism since 1956.* New York: Pegasus.

Deck, L. P. (1968). Buying brains by the inch. *Journal of the College and University Personnel Association, 19,* 33–37.

Deegan, M. J. (1988, Winter). W. E. B. Du Bois and the women of Hull-House, 1895–1899. *American Sociologist,* 301–311.

DeKeseredy, W., & Hinch, R. (1991). *Woman Abuse: Sociological Perspectives.* Toronto: Thompson Educational Publishers.

DeMartini, J. R. (1982). Basic and applied sociological work: Divergence, convergence, or peaceful co-existence? *The Journal of Applied Behavioral Science, 18*(2), 203–215.

DeMause, L. (1975, April). Our forebears made childhood a nightmare. *Psychology Today 8*(11), 85–88.

Denney, N. W., & Quadagno, D. (1992). *Human sexuality* (2nd ed.). St. Louis: Mosby.

Dentzler, S. (1991, April 22). The vanishing dream. *U.S. News and World Report,* 39–43.

Denzin, N. K. (1992, July–August). The suicide machine. *Society,* 7–10.

Department of Indian Affairs and Northern Development (DIAND). (1997). *Socioeconomic indicators in Indian reserves and comparable communities.* Ottawa: DIAND.

Department of Indian Affairs and Northern Development (DIAND). (1999). *Basic departmental data.* Ottawa: First Nations and Northern Statistics Section, Corporate Information Management Directorate, Information Management Branch.

Department of Indian Affairs and Northern Development (DIAND). (2001). Basic departmental data. Accessed March 2002 at http://www.ainc-inac.gc.ca/pr/sts/bdd01/bdd01_e.pdf.

Derber, C., & Schwartz, W. (1988). Toward a theory of worker participation. In F. Hearn (Ed.), *The transformation of industrial organization: Management, labor, and society in the United States* (pp. 217–229). Belmont, CA: Wadsworth.

Deutsch, A. (2000, September 13). Dutch bill gives gays right to marry. *Toronto Star,* p. A13.

deYoung, M. (1989, March). The world according to NAMBLA: Accounting for deviance. *Journal of Sociology and Social Welfare, 16*(1), 111–126.

Diamond, M. (1982). Sexual identity: Monozygotic twins reared in discordant sex roles and a BBC follow-up. *Archives of Sexual Behavior, 11*(2), 181–186.

Dickson, T., & McLachlan, H. V. (1989). In search of "the spirit of capitalism": Weber's misinterpretation of Franklin. *Sociology, 23*(1), 81–89.

Dietz, T. L. (1998, March). An examination of violence and gender role portrayals in video games: Implications for gender socialization and aggressive behaviour. *Sex Roles, 38,* 425–442.

DiGiulio, R. C. (1992). Beyond widowhood. In J. M. Henslin (Ed.), *Marriage and family in a changing society* (4th ed., pp. 457–469). New York: Free Press.

Dinnerstein, M., & Weitz, R. (2002). Jane Fonda, Barbara Bush and other aging bodies: Femininity and the limits of resistance. In K. S. Ratcliff (Ed.), *Women and Health: Power, Technology, Inequality, and Conflict in a Gendered World,* (pp. 180–190). Boston: Allyn and Bacon.

Dirks, G. E. (1995). *Controversy and Complexity: Canadian Immigration Policy During the 1980s.* Montreal: McGill-Queen's University Press.

Dobriner, W. M. (1969a). The football team as social structure and social system. In *Social Structures and Systems: A Sociological Overview* (pp. 116–120). Pacific Palisades, CA: Goodyear.

Dobriner, W. M. (1969b). *Social Structures and Systems.* Pacific Palisades, CA: Goodyear.

Dollard, J., et al. (1939). *Frustration and aggression.* New Haven, CT: Yale University Press.

Domhoff, G. W. (1967). *Who rules America?* Englewood Cliffs, NJ: Prentice Hall.

Domhoff, G. W. (1978). *Who really rules? New Haven and community power reexamined.* New Brunswick, NJ: Transaction.

Domhoff, G. W. (1979). *The powers that be.* New York: Random House.

Domhoff, G. W. (1983). *Who rules America now? A view of the '80s.* Englewood Cliffs, NJ: Prentice Hall.

Domhoff, G. W. (1990). *The power elite and the state: How policy is made in America.* Hawthorne, NY: Aldine de Gruyter.

Domhoff, G. W. (1997). The Bohemian grove and other retreats. In J. M. Henslin (Ed.), *Down to earth sociology: Introductory readings* (9th ed., pp. 340–352). New York: Free Press.

Domhoff, G. William. 1996 *State Autonomy or Class Dominance? Case Studies on Policy Making in America.* Hawthorne, N.Y.: Aldine de Gruyter.

Donnelly, J. (2002, July 4). Global AIDS pandemic worse than thought, UN study says. *Toronto Star,* p. A3.

Doren, K., & Jones, C. (2000). *You Go Girl! Winning the Woman's Way.* Kansas City: Andrews McMeel Publishing.

Dove, A. (n.d.). Soul folk "chitling" test or the Dove counterbalance intelligence test. (Mimeo)

Doyle, J. A. (1995). *The male experience* (3rd ed.). Madison, WI: WCB Brown & Benchmark Publishers.

Driedger, L., & Halli, S. S. (Eds.). (2000). *Race and Racism: Canada's Challenge.* Montreal: McGill/Queen's University Press.

Drolet, M. (2002, Spring). The male-female wage gap. *Perspectives on Labour and Income,* Statistics Canada, Catalogue 75-001-XPE.

Drucker, P. F. (1987, April 22). The rise and fall of the blue-collar worker. *Wall Street Journal,* p. 36.

Drucker, P. F. (1992, February 11). There's more than one kind of team. *Wall Street Journal,* p. A16.

Drucker, P. F. (1994, November). The age of social transformation. *Atlantic Monthly, 274*(5), 53+.

Du Bois, W. E. B. (1966). *Black reconstruction in America: An essay toward a history of the part which Black folk played in the attempt to reconstruct democracy in America, 1860–1880.* New York: Frank Cass. (First published 1935).

Du Bois, W. E. B. (1992). *Black reconstruction in America, 1860–1889.* New York: Atheneum. (First published 1935).

Duchesne, D. (2002, Summer). Seniors at work. *Perspectives on Labour and Income, 14,* pp. 33–44.

Duffy, A. (1996). Bad girls in hard times: Canadian female juvenile offenders. In G. M. O'Bireck (Ed.), *Not A Kid Anymore: Canadian Youth, Crime and Subcultures* (pp. 203-220). Toronto: Nelson Canada.

Duffy, A. (1997). The part-time solution: Toward entrapment or empowerment. In A. Duffy, D. Glenday, N. Pupo, (Eds.), *Good jobs, bad jobs, no jobs: The transformation of work in the 21st Century.* Toronto: Harcourt Brace Canada, 166–188.

Duffy, A., & Mandell, N. (forthcoming). Poverty in Canada today. In D. Glenday & A. Duffy (Eds.), *Canadian Society.* Toronto: Oxford University Press.

Duffy, A., & Momirov, J. (1997). *Family violence: A Canadian introduction.* Toronto: Lorimer.

Duffy, A. & Pupo, N. (1992). *The part-time paradox: Connecting gender, work and family.* Toronto: McClelland and Stewart.

Duffy, A. & Pupo, N. (1996). Family-friendly organizations and beyond: proposals for policy directions with women in mind. National Forum on Family Security. Ottawa: Canada Council on Social Development.

Duffy, A., Glenday, D., & Pupo, N. (Eds.). (1997a). *Good Jobs, Bad Jobs, No Jobs: The Transformation of Work in the 21st Century.* Toronto: Harcourt Brace.

Duffy, A., Glenday, D. G., & Pupo, N. (1998, Fall). Seniors in the part-time labour force: Issues of choice and power. *International Journal of Canadian Studies, 18,* 133–152.

Duffy, A., Mandell, N. & Pupo, N. (1989). *Few choices: Women, work and family.* Toronto: Garamond Press.

Dundes, L. (2001). Disney's modern heroine Pocahontas: Revealing age-old gender stereotypes and role discontinuity under a façade of liberation. *The Social Science Journal, 38,* pp. 353–365.

Dunlap, R. E., & Catton, W. R., Jr. (1979). Environmental sociology. *Annual Review of Sociology, 5,* 243–273.

Dunlap, R. E., & Catton, W. R., Jr. (1983). What environmental sociologists have in common whether concerned with "built" or "natural" environments. *Sociological Inquiry, 53*(2/3), 113–135.

Dupuis, D. (1998, Spring). What influences people's plans to have children? *Canadian Social Trends, 48,* 2–5.

Durbin, S. (1995, July–August). Mexico. *Population Today,* 7.

Durkheim, E. (1933). *The division of labor in society* (G. Simpson, Trans.). New York: Free Press. (First published 1893).

Durkheim, E. (1938, 1958, 1964). *The Rules of sociological method* (S. A. Solovay & J. H. Mueller, Trans.). New York: Free Press. (First published 1895).

Durkheim, E. (1965). *The elementary forms of the religious life.* New York: Free Press. (First published 1912).

Durkheim, E. (1966). *Suicide: A study in sociology* (J. A. Spaulding & G. Simpson, Trans.). New York: Free Press. (First published 1897).

Durning, A. (1990). Cradles of life. In L. W. Barnes (Ed.), *Social Problems 90/91* (pp. 231–241). Guilford, CT: Dushkin.

Dyke, D. J. (1991). *Crucified women.* Toronto: United Church.

Easterbrook, G. (1987 January 26). The revolution in modern medicine. *Newsweek, 109,* 40–74.

Ebaugh, H. R. F. (1988). *Becoming an ex: The process of role exit.* Chicago: The University of Chicago Press.

Eder, K. (1990). The rise of counter-culture movements against modernity: Nature as a new field of class struggle. *Theory, Culture & Society, 7,* 21–47.

Edgar, G. (1994, March 28). Author's interview with Gary Edgar of the Surveillance Branch of the CDC.

Edgerton, R. B. (1976). *Deviance: A cross-cultural perspective.* Menlo Park, CA: Benjamin/Cummings.

Edgerton, R. B. (1992). *Sick societies: Challenging the myth of primitive harmony.* New York: Free Press.

Edwards, G., & Mazzuca, J. (1999, August 12). Canadians' awareness and perception of child abuse. *The Gallup Poll, 59*(50), 1–3.

Edwards, G., & Mazzuca, J. (1999a, May 21). A third of Canadians accepting of same sex marriages, adoption. *The Gallup Poll, 59*(32), 1–4.

Edwards, R. (1979). *Contested terrain: The transformation of the workplace in the twentieth century.* New York: Basic Books.

Ehlers, T. (2000). Debunking Marianismo: Economic vulnerability and survival strategies among Guatemalan wives. In M. Zinn, P. Hondagneu-Sotelo, & M. Messner (Eds.), *Gender Through the Prism of Difference,* 2nd Edition (pp. 478–489). Boston: Allyn and Bacon.

Ehrenreich, B., & English, D. (1973). *Witches, midwives, and nurses: A history of women healers.* Old Westbury, NY: Feminist Press.

Ehrlich, P. R., & Ehrlich A. H. (1997). *Betrayal of science and reason: How anti-environmental rhetoric threatens our future.* Washington, DC: Island Press.

Eibl-Eibesfeldt, I. (1970). *Ethology: The biology of behavior.* New York: Holt, Rinehart, and Winston.

Eichler, M. (1988a). *Families in Canada today: Recent changes and their policy consequences* (2nd ed.). Toronto: Gage Educational Publishing.

Eichler, M. (1988b). *Nonsexist research methods: A practical guide.* New York: Routledge.

Eichler, M. (1997). *Family shifts: Families, policies and gender equality.* Toronto: Oxford University Press.

Eisenhart, R. W. (1975, Fall). You can't hack it, little girl: A discussion of the covert psychological agenda of modern combat training. *Journal of Social Issues, 31,* 13–23.

Ekman, P., Friesen, W. V., & Bear, J. (1984, May). The international language of gestures. *Psychology Today,* 64.

Elkins, S. M. (1968). *Slavery: A problem in American institutional and intellectual life* (2nd ed.). Chicago: University of Chicago Press.

Elwell, S. (1996). Women's voices: The challenges of feminism to Judaism. In C. Wessenger (Ed.), *Religious institutions and women's leadership: New roles inside the mainstream* (pp. 331–43). Columbia, SC: University of South Carolina.

Emerson, B. (2001, July 14). Boys judged by their walk: Study. *Toronto Star,* p. M4.

Engels, F. (1942). *The origin of the family, private property, and the state.* New York: International Publishing. (First published in 1884).

Epstein, C. F. (1986, September–October). Inevitabilities of prejudice. *Society,* 7–15.

Epstein, C. F. (1988). *Deceptive distinctions: Sex, gender, and the social order.* New Haven, CT: Yale University Press.

Epstein, C. F. (1989, January 26). Letter to the author.

Erik, J. (1982, January 3). China's policy on births. *New York Times,* pp. IV, 19.

Ernst, E. G. (1988). The Baptists. In C. H. Lippy & P. W. Williams (Eds.), *Encyclopedia of the American religious experience: Studies of traditions and movements* (Vol. 1, pp. 555–577). New York: Scribners.

Erturk, Y. (1994). The status of Moslem women in Turkey and Saudi Arabia. In J. Curtis & L. Tepperman (Eds.), *Haves and have-nots: An* international reader on social inequality (pp. 288–293). Englewood Cliffs, NJ: Prentice Hall.

Escalante, J., & J. Dirmann. (1990, Summer). The Jaime Escalante math program. Journal of Negro Education, 59(3), 407–423.

Etzioni, A. (Ed.). (1969). The semi-professions and their organization. New York: Free Press.

Faludi, S. (1999). Stiffed: The betrayal of the American man. New York: William Morrow & Company.

Family violence. (2000, Winter). Canadian Social Trends, 59, p. 28.

Faris, R.E. L., & Dunham, W. (1939). Mental disorders in urban areas. Chicago: University of Chicago Press.

Farkas, G. (1996). Human capital or cultural capital?: Ethnicity and poverty groups in an urban school district. New York: Walter DeGruyter.

Farkas, G., Sheehan, D., & Grobe, R. P. (1990, Winter). Coursework mastery and school success: Gender, ethnicity, and poverty groups within an urban school district. American Educational Research Journal, 27(4), 807–827.

Farkas, G., Grobe, R. P., Sheehan, D., & Shuan, Y. (1990, February). Cultural resources and school success: Gender, ethnicity, and poverty groups within an urban school district. American Sociological Review, 55, 127–142.

Fast, J., Frederick, J., Zukewich, N., & Franke, S. (2001, Winter). The time of our lives… Canadian Social Trends, 63, pp. 20–23.

Faunce, W. A. (1981). Problems of an industrial society, (2nd ed.). New York: McGraw-Hill.

Featherman, D.L. (1979). Opportunities are expanding. Society, 13, 4–11.

Featherman, D. L., & Hauser, R. M. (1978). Opportunity and change. New York: Academic Press.

Federal, Provincial, and Territorial Advisory Committee on Population Health. (1999). Statistical report on the health of Canadians. Ottawa: Health Canada.

Federal, Provincial, and Territorial Advisory Committee on Population Health for the Meeting of Ministers of Health. (1999). Toward a healthy future: Second report on the health of Canadians. Ottawa: Minister of Public Works.

Feldman, S. D. (1972). The presentation of shortness in everyday life— Height and heightism in American society: Toward a sociology of stature. [Paper presented at the 1972 meetings of the American Sociological Association].

Ferguson, K. E. (1984). The Feminist Case Against Bureaucracy. Philadelphia: Temple University Press.

Ferguson, T. (1995). Golden Rule. Chicago: University of Chicago.

Ferguson, T., & Dunphy, J. S. (1991). Answers to the mommy track: How wives and mothers in business reach the top and balance their lives. New York: New Horizon Press.

Ferri, B. A., & Gregg, N. (1998). Women with disabilities: Missing voices. Women's Studies International Forum, 21 (4), pp. 429–439.

Feshbach, M., & Friendly, A., Jr. (1992). Ecocide in the USSR: Health and nature under siege. New York: Basic Books.

Finnie, R. (2000, September). The dynamics of poverty in Canada. C.D. Howe Institute Commentary, 145.

Finnie, R. & Wannell, T. (1999). The gender earnings gap amongst Canadian Bachelor's level university graduates: A cross-cohort, longitudinal analysis. In R. Chaykowski & L. Powell (Eds.), Women and work. Kingston, ON: John Deutsch Institute for the Study of Economic Policy.

Finnie, R., Lavoie, M., & Rivard, M.-C. (2001). Women in engineering: The missing link in the Canadian knowledge economy. Education Quarterly Review, 7(3), Statistics Canada, Catalogue 81-003.

Fischer, C. S. (1995). Technology and community: Historical complexities. [Paper presented at the 1995 meetings of the American Sociological Association.]

Fisher, J. (1994, February). Is the iron law of oligarchy rusting away in the third world? World Development, 22(2), 129–143.

Fisher, S. (1986). In the patient's best interest: Women and the politics of medical decisions. New Brunswick, NJ: Rutgers University Press.

Fitz-Gerald, T. (1999, December 11). Girls' club hoops hitting new heights. The Hamilton Spectator.

Fitzgerald, R. (1999). Family Violence in Canada: A Statistical Profile. Ottawa: Statistics Canada, Catalogue No. 85-224-XPE.

Flanagan, W. G. (1990). Urban sociology: Images and structure. Boston: Allyn and Bacon.

Flavel, J. H., et al. (1968). The development of role-taking and communication skills in children. New York: Wiley.

Fleming, J. D. (1974). The state of the apes. Psychology Today, 7, 31–38.

Fleras, A., & Elliott, J. L. (1996). Unequal Relations: An Introduction to Race, Ethnic, and Aboriginal Dynamics in Canada. 2nd ed. Scarborough, Ontario: Prentice Hall.

Flexner, A. (1910). Medical education in the United States and Canada: A report to the Carnegie Foundation for the Advancement of Teaching. Bulletin No. 4. Boston: Merrymount Press.

Flink, J. J. (1990). The automobile age. Cambridge, MA: MIT Press.

Foley, D. E. (1997). The great American football ritual. In J. M. Henslin (Ed.), Down to earth sociology: Introductory readings (9th ed., pp. 412–475). New York: Free Press.

Foley, L. A., Evancic, C., Karnik, K., King, J., & Parks, A. (1995, February). Date rape: Effects of race of assailant and victim and gender of subjects on perceptions. Journal of Black Psychology, 21(1), 6–18.

Foot, D. K., & Stoffman, D. (1998). Boom, bust and echo 2000. Toronto: Macfarlane, Walter and Ross.

Foote, J. (1990, February 5). Trying to take back the planet. Newsweek, 115(6), 24–25.

Forcese, D. (1997). The Canadian class structure (4th ed.). Toronto: McGraw-Hill Ryerson.

Form, W. (1979). Comparative industrial sociology and the convergence hypothesis. In A. Inkeles, J. Coleman, & R. H. Turner (Eds.). Annual Review of Sociology, 5, 1.

Forum warned of aging crisis. (2002, April 8). Toronto Star, p. A14.

Foucault, M. (1972). The archaeology of knowledge (A. M. S. Smith, Trans.). New York: Pantheon Books.

Foucault, M. (1980). The History of Sexuality (3 Vols, R. Hurley, Trans.). New York: Vintage Books.

Fox, B. (2001, November). The formative years: How parenthood creates gender. The Canadian Review of Sociology and Anthropology, 38, pp. 373–390.

Fox, E., & Arquitt, G. E. (1985). The VFW and the "iron law of oligarchy." In J. M. Henslin (Ed.), Down to earth sociology (4th ed., pp. 147–155). New York: Free Press.

Francis, D. (1986). Controlling interest: Who owns Canada? Toronto: Macmillan.

Frederick, J. (1993, Winter). Tempus Fugit…Are you time crunched? Canadian Social Trends 31, pp. 6–10.

Frederick, J. A. (1995). As time goes by: Time use of Canadians. General Social Survey (Catalogue 89-544E). Ottawa: Minister of Industry.

Frederick, J. A., & Fast, J. E. (1999, Autumn). Eldercare in Canada: Who does how much? Canadian Social Trends, 54, 26–30.

Frederick, J. A., & Hamel, J. (1998, Spring). Canadian attitudes to divorce. Canadian Social Trends, 48, 6–11.

Freedman, A. M. (1990, December 18). Amid ghetto hunger, many more suffer eating wrong foods. Wall Street Journal, pp. A1, A8.

Freudenburg, W.R., & Gramling, R. (1989, November). The emergence of environmental sociology: Contributions of Riley E. Dunlap and William R. Catton, Jr. Sociological Inquiry, 59(4), 439–452.

Frideres, J., & Gadacz, R. (2001). Aboriginal Peoples in Canada: Contemporary Conflicts, 6th ed. Toronto: Prentice Hall.

Friedan, B. (1963). The feminine mystique. New York: Dell Publishing Co., Inc.

Friedan, B. (1993). *The Fountain of Age*. New York: Simon and Shuster.

Friedl, E. (1990). Society and sex roles. In J. P. Spradley & McCurdy, D. W. (Eds.), *Conformity and conflict: Readings in cultural anthropology* (pp. 229–238). Glenview, IL: Scott, Foresman.

Froman, I. (1994, November). Sweden for women. *Current Sweden, 407,* 1–4.

Fuller, R., & Schoenberger, R. (1991, December). The gender salary gap: Do academic achievement, internship experience, and college major make a difference? *Social Science Quarterly, 72*(4), 715–726.

Furnham, A., & Mak, T. (1999). Sex-role stereotyping in television commercials: A review and comparison of fourteen studies done on five continents over 25 years. *Sex Roles, 41*(5/6), 413–437.

Furtado, C. (1984). *The economic growth of Brazil: A survey of colonial to modern times.* Westport, CT: Greenwood Press.

Galanter, M. (1989). *Cults: Faith, healing, and coercion.* New York: Oxford University Press.

Galbraith, J. K. (1979). *The nature of mass poverty.* Cambridge MA: Harvard University Press.

Galinsky, E. (1999). *Ask the children: What America's children really think about working parents.* New York: William Morrow and Company.

Galinsky, E., & Stein, P. J. (1990, December). The impact of human resource policies on employees: Balancing work/family life. *Journal of Family Issues, 11*(4), 368–383.

Galliher, J. F. (1991). *Deviant behavior and human rights.* Englewood Cliffs, NJ: Prentice Hall.

Gallmeier, C.P. (1988). Methodological issues in qualitative sport research: Participant observation among hockey players. *Sociological Spectrum, 8,* 213–235.

Gans, H. J. (1962). *The urban villagers.* New York: Free Press.

Gans, H. J. (1968). *People and plans: Essays on urban problems and solutions.* New York: Basic Books.

Gans, H. J. (1970). Urbanism and suburbanism. In A. N. Cousins & H. Nagpaul (Eds.), *Urban man and society: A reader in urban ecology* (pp. 157–164). New York: Knopf.

Gans, H. J. (1991a). *People, plans, and policies: Essays on poverty, racism, and other national urban problems.* New York: Columbia University Press.

Gardner, R. A., & Gardner, B. T. (1969). Teaching sign language to a chimpanzee. *Science, 165,* 664–672.

Garfinkel, H. (1956, March). Conditions of successful degradation ceremonies. *American Journal of Sociology, 61*(2), 420–424.

Garfinkel, H. (1967). *Studies in ethnomethodology.* Englewood Cliffs, NJ: Prentice Hall.

Gecas, V. (1990). Context of soicalization. In M. Rosenberg & Turner, R. H. (Eds.), *Social psychology: Sociological perspectives* (pp. 165–199). New Brunswick, NJ: Transaction.

Gee, E. M., & Kimball, M. M. (1987). *Women and aging.* Toronto: Butterworths.

Geis, G., Meier, R. F., & Salinger, L. M. (1995). *White-collar crime: Classic and contemporary views* (3rd ed.). New York: Free Press.

Gelles, R. J. (1980). The myth of battered husbands and new facts about family violence. In R. L. David (Ed.), *Social problems 80–81,* Guilford, CT: Dushkin.

Gelles, R. J., & Cornell, C. P. (1985). *Intimate violence in families.* Beverly Hills, California: Sage Publications.

Gerson, K. (1985). *Hard choices: How women decide about work, career, and motherhood.* Berkeley: University of California Press.

Gerth, H. H., & Mills, C. W. (1958). *From Max Weber: Essays in sociology.* New York: Galaxy.

Giddens, A. (1978). *Emile Durkheim.* New York: Penguin Books.

Gilbert, D., & Kahl, J. A. (1982). *The American class structure: A new synthesis.* Homewood, IL: Dorsey Press.

Gilbert, D., & Kahl, J. A. (1993). *The American class structure: A new synthesis* (4th ed.). Homewood, IL: Dorsey Press.

Gilham, S. A. (1989). The marines build men: Resocialization in recruit training. In R. Luhman (Ed.), *The sociological outlook: A text with readings* (2nd ed., pp. 232–244). San Diego, CA: Collegiate Press.

Gillborn, D. (1992). Citizenship, "race" and the hidden curriculum. *International Studies in the Sociology of Education, 2*(1), 57–73.

Gilleard, C. (2002, March). Aging and old age in Medieval society and the transition of modernity. *Journal of Aging and Identity, 7,* pp. 25–41.

Gillespie, R. (2000). When no means no: disbelief, disregard and deviance as discourses of voluntary childlessness. *Women's Studies International Forum, 23,* pp. 223–234.

Gilligan, C. (1982). *In a different voice.* Cambridge, MA: Harvard University Press.

Gilman, C. P. (1971). *The man-made world or, our androcentric culture.* New York. (First published 1911).

Gilmore, D. D. (1990). *Manhood in the making: Cultural concepts of masculinity.* New Haven, CT: Yale University Press.

Girard, D. (2002, July 20). The picture if we don't do anything is quite depressing. *Toronto Star,* pp. E1, E3.

Gitlin, T. (1997). *The twilight of common dreams: Why America is wracked by culture wars.* New York: Metropolitan Books.

Glenday, D. (1996). Mean streets and hard time: Youth unemployment and crime in Canada. In G. O'Bireck (Ed.), *Not a kid anymore: Canadian youth, crime and subcultures* (pp. 147–174). Toronto: Nelson.

Glenday, D. (1997). Lost horizons, leisure shock: Good jobs, bad jobs, uncertain future. In D. Glenday, *Good jobs, bad jobs, no jobs: The transformation of work in the 21st century* (pp. 8–34). Toronto: Harcourt Brace.

Glenday, D., & Duffy, A. (Eds.). (2001). *Canadian society: Meeting the challenges of the twenty-first century.* Toronto: Oxford University Press.

Glenday, D., Duffy, A., & Pupo, N. (Eds.). (1997). *Good jobs, bad jobs, no jobs: The transformation of work in the 21st century.* Toronto: Harcourt Brace.

Glenday, D., & McMullan, J. (1970). *An historical examination into the history of the sociology of Québec.* Paper presented to the Canadian Sociology and Anthropology Association meetings. Newfoundland.

Glueck, S., & Glueck, E. (1956). *Physique and delinquency.* New York: Harper & Row.

Goffman, E. (1959). *The presentation of self in everyday life.* New York: Doubleday.

Goffman, E. (1961). *Asylums: Essays on the social situation of mental patients and other inmates.* Chicago: Aldine.

Goffman, E. (1963). *Stigma: Notes on the management of spoiled identity.* Englewood Cliffs, NJ: Prentice Hall.

Goffman, E. (1977). The arrangement between the sexes. *Theory and Society, 4,* 301–331.

Goffman, E. (1997). The presentation of self in everyday life. In J. M. Henslin (Ed.), *Down to earth sociology: Introductory readings* (9th ed., pp. 106–116). New York: Free Press.

Gold, R. (1952). Janitors versus tenants: A status–income dilemma. *American Journal of Sociology, 58,* 486–493.

Goldberg, S. (1986, September–October). Reaffirming the obvious. *Society,* 4–7.

Goldberg, S. (1974). *The inevitability of patriarchy* (Rev. ed.). New York: Morrow.

Goldberg, S. (1993). *Why men rule: A theory of male dominance.* Chicago: Open Court.

Goldberg, S., & Lewis, M. (1969, March). Play behavior in the year-old infant: Early sex differences. *Child Development, 40,* 21–31.

Goleman, D. (1993, September 7). Pollsters enlist psychologists in quest for unbiased results. *New York Times,* pp. C1, C11.

Goleman, D. (1985, May 28). Spacing of siblings strongly linked to success in life. *New York Times,* pp. C1, C4.

Gomez, C. F. (1991). *Regulating death: Euthanasia and the case of the Netherlands.* New York: Free Press.

Goode, E. (1989). *Drugs in American society* (3rd ed.). New York: Knopf.

Goode, E. (1996). The ethics of deception in social research: A case study. *Qualitative Sociology, 19*(1), 11–33.

Goode, E., & Ben-Yehuda, N. (1994). Moral panics: Culture, politics, and social construction. *Annual Review of Sociology, 20,* 149–171.

Goode, W. J. (1960, December). Encroachment, charlatanism, and the emerging profession: Psychology, sociology, and medicine. *American Sociological Review, 25*(6), 902–914.

Gooden, A. M., & Gooden, M. A. (2001, July). Gender Representation in Notable Children's Picture Books: 1995–1999. *Sex Roles,* pp. 89–99.

Goodwin, C. (2000, January 30). Misogyny is alive and well. *Toronto Star,* p. D4.

Goodwin, G. A., Horowitz, I. L. & Nardi, P. M. (1991, May). Laud Humphreys: A pioneer in the practice of social science. *Sociological Inquiry, 61,* 2, 139–147.

Gordon, D. M. (1971, Summer). Class and the economics of crime. *The Review of Radical Political Economics, 3,* 51–57.

Gorlick, C. A. (2000). Divorce: Options available, constraints forced, pathways taken. In N. Mandell & A. Duffy (Eds.), *Canadian families: Diversity, conflict and change* (pp. 260–289). Toronto: Harcourt Brace Canada.

Gorman, C. (1997, January 6). The disease detective. *Time,* 56–65.

Gorman, C. (1997, March 24). A boy without a penis. *Time,* 83.

Gorrie, P. (2001, June 16). Is Harris right about seniors? *Toronto Star,* p. A17.

Gorrie, P. (2002, July 20). Ultimately an aging society is a victory. *Toronto Star,* pp. E1, E3.

Gorz, A. (1982). *Farewell to the working class. An essay in post-industrial socialism.* London: Pluto Press.

Gorz, A. (1985). *Paths to paradise: On the liberation from work.* London: Pluto Press.

Gotlieb, R. (2000, October 28). Many retirees are stepping back into rat race. *Toronto Star,* p. P7.

Gourevitch, P. (1995, December 18). After the genocide. *New Yorker,* 78–94.

Gracey, H. L. (1997). Learning the student role: Kindergarten as academic boot camp. *Down to earth sociology: Introductory readings* (9th ed., pp. 376–388). New York: Free Press.

Graham, E. (1996, March 4). Craving closer ties, strangers come together as family. *Wall Street Journal,* pp. B1, B6.

Grant, K. R. (1984, April). The inverse care law in the context of universal free health insurance in Canada: Toward meeting health needs through social policy. *Sociological Focus, 17*(2), 137–155.

Graves, F. L., Dugas, T., & Beauchamp, P. (In press). Identity and National Attachments in Contemporary Canada. In H. Lazar & T. McIntosh (Eds.), *Canada: The State of the Federation 1998–99: Vol. 13. How Canadians Connect.* IIGR.

Greeley, A. M. (1964, Spring). The Protestant ethic: Time for a moratorium. *Sociological Analysis, 25,* 20–33.

Greeley, A. (1994, September). A religious revival in Russia. *Journal for the Scientific Study of Religion, 33*(3), 253–272.

Green, S. J. (1999, July 10). Rituals of renewal. *Toronto Star,* p. J2.

Greenhalgh, S., & Li, J. (1995, Spring). Engendering reproductive policy and practice in peasant China: For a feminist demography of reproduction. *Signs, 20*(3), 601–640.

Greenwood, E. (1962). Attributes of a profession. In S. Nosow & W. H. Form (Eds.), *Man, work, and society: A reader in the sociology of occupations* (pp. 206–218). New York: Basic Books.

Greer, G. (1991). *The Change: Women Aging and the Menopause.* New York: Fawcet Columbine.

Gross, J. (1998, November 29). In the quest for the perfect look, more girls choose the scalpel. *New York Times.*

Grossman, L. K. (1995). *The electronic republic: Reshaping democracy in the information age.* New York: Viking.

Guha, R. (1989, Spring). Radical American environmentalism and wilderness preservation: A third world critique. *Environmental Ethics, 11*(1), 71–83.

Guindon, H. (1964, Summer). Social unrest, social class, and Québec's bureaucratic revolution. *Queen's Quarterly,* pp. 12–32.

Guindon, H. (1967). Two Cultures: An essay on nationalism, class, and ethnic tension. In R. H. Leach (Ed.), *Contemporary Canada.* Duke, N.C.: Duke University Press.

Guindon, H. (1978). The modernization of Québec and the legitimacy of the Canadian state. In D. Glenday, H. Guindon, and A. Turowetz (Eds.), *Modernization and the Canadian State* (pp. 212–246). Toronto: Macmillan.

Guindon, H. (2001). Québec's social and political evolution since 1945: A view from within. In D. Glenday and A. Duffy, (Eds.), *Canadian Society: Meeting the Challenges of the Twenty-First Century* (pp. 281–320). Toronto: Oxford University Press.

Haas, J. (1972). Binging: Educational control among high-steel iron workers. *American Behavioral Scientist, 16,* 27–34.

Haas, J., & Shaffir, W. (1987). *Becoming Doctors: The Adoption of a Cloak of Competence.* Greenwich, Conn.: JAI Press.

Haas, J., & Shaffir, W. (1993). The cloak of competence. In J. M. Henslin (Ed.), *Down to earth sociology: Introductory readings* (7th ed., pp. 432–441). New York: Free Press. (First published 1978).

Habib, Marlene. (2000, February 12). Single mothers deal well with stress, study finds. *The Toronto Star,* p. P8.

Hacker, H. M. (1951, October). Women as a minority group. *Social Forces, 30,* 60–69.

Hakansson, S. (1994, January). New ways of financing and organizing health care in Sweden. *International Journal of Health Planning and Management, 9*(1), 103–124.

Hall, E.T. (1969). *The hidden dimension.* Garden City, NY: Anchor Books.

Hall, G. S. (1904). *Adolescence: Its psychology and its relations to physiology, anthropology, sociology, sex, crime, religion, and education.* New York: Appleton.

Hall, J. A. (1984). *Nonverbal sex differences: Communication accuracy and expressive style.* Baltimore: Johns Hopkins University Press.

Hall, O. (1994). Work: The sociology of work in Canada. In A. Wipper (Ed.), *Papers in Honour of Oswald Hall.* Ottawa: Carleton University Press.

Hall, R. H. (1963, July). The concept of bureaucracy: An empirical assessment. *American Journal of Sociology, 69,* 32–40.

Hall, S. S. (1999, August 22). The bully in the mirror. *The New York Times Magazine,* 30–35, 58, 62, 64–65.

Halle, D. (1984). *America's working man: Work, home, and politics among blue-collar property owners.* Chicago: University of Chicago Press.

Hamermesh, D. S., & Biddle, J. E. (1994, December). Beauty and the Labor Market. *American Economic Review, 84* (5), pp. 1174–1195.

Hamil-Luker, J. (2001). The prospects of age war: Inequality between (and within) age groups. *Social Science Research, 30,* pp. 386–400.

Hamilton, K., & Miller, S. (1997, March 10). Internet U—No ivy, no walls, no keg parties. *Newsweek,* 12.

Hamilton, R. (2000). An examination of the Marxist and feminist theories. In B. A. Crow & L. Gotell (Eds.), *Open Boundaries: A Canadian Women's Studies Reader* (pp. 6–16). Toronto: Prentice Hall Allyn and Bacon Canada.

Hanson, D. J. (1973, April–July). A note on sociology and infrahuman culture. *International Journal of Contemporary Sociology, 10*(2 & 3), 121–124.

Happily ever after? (2001, Spring). *Canadian Social Trends, 60,* p. 22.

Harlow, H. F., & Harlow, M. K. (1962). Social deprivation in monkeys. *Scientific American, 207,* 137–147.

Harlow, H. F., & Harlow, M. K. (1965). The affectional systems. In A. M. Schrier, H. F. Harlow, & F. Stollnitz (Eds.), *Behavior of nonhuman primates: Modern research trends* (Vol. 2, pp. 287–334). New York: Academic Press.

The harm that family violence does to children. (2001, Winter). *Canadian Social Trends, 63,* p. 19.

Harper, T. (1999, November 5). One in five seniors now living in poverty. *The Toronto Star,* p. A6.

Harper, T. (2000, January 15). Law of the seed. *The Toronto Star,* pp. L1, L3.

Harrington, M. (1962). *The other America: Poverty in the United States.* New York: Macmillan.

Harrington, M. (1977). *The vast majority: A journey to the world's poor.* New York: Simon & Schuster.

Harris, C., & Ullman, E. (1945). The nature of cities. *Annals of the American Academy of Political and Social Science, 242,* 7–17.

Harris, D. K. (1990). *The sociology of aging.* New York: Harper.

Harris, M. (1977, November 13). Why men dominate women. *New York Times Magazine, 46,* 115, 117–123.

Harrison, D. & Laliberte, L. (1994). *No life like it: Military wives in Canada.* Toronto: James Lorimer and Company.

Harrison, P. (1993). *Inside the third world: The anatomy of poverty* (3rd ed.). London: Penguin Books.

Hart, C.W. M., & Pilling, A. R. (1970). *The Tiwi of North Australia.* New York: Holt, Rinehart, and Winston.

Hart, P. (1991). Groupthink, risk-taking and recklessness: Quality of process and outcome in policy decision making. *Politics and the Individual, 1(1),* 67–90.

Hartley, E. (1946). *Problems in prejudice.* New York: King's Crown Press.

Harvey, D. (1989). *The condition of postmodernity.* Oxford; New York: Blackwell.

Harwood, J., & Brooks, G. (1993, December 14). Other nations elect women to lead them, so why doesn't U.S.? *Wall Street Journal,* pp. A1, A9.

Haslick, L. (1974). *Gerontologist, 14,* 37–45.

Haub, C. (1997, April). New UN projections depict a variety of demographic futures. *Population Today, 25(4),* 1–3.

Haub, C., & Cornelius, D. (1997). World population data sheet. Washington, DC: Population Reference Bureau.

Haub, C., & Cornelius, D. (1999). *World Population Data Sheet.* Washington D.C.: Population Reference Bureau.

Haub, C., & Yinger, N. (1994). The UN long-range population projections: What they tell us. Washington, DC: Population Reference Bureau.

Hauser, P., & Schnore, L. (Eds.). (1965). *The study of urbanization.* New York: Wiley.

Hawranik, P., & Strain, L. (2002, Spring). Always on-call: The health of informal caregivers for seniors. *Centres of Excellence for Women's Health Research Bulletin, 3,* pp. 8–13.

Hayes, D. P., & Wolfer, L. T. (1993a). Have curriculum changes caused SAT scores to decline? Paper presented at the annual meetings of the American Sociological Association.

Hayes, D. P., & Wolfer, L. T. (1993b). Was the decline in SAT-verbal scores caused by simplified schoolbooks? (Technical Report Series 93-8). Ithaca, NY: Cornell University Press.

Haynes, R. M., & Chalker, D. M. (1997, May). World class schools. *American School Board Journal, 20,* 22–25.

Haynie, D. (2001). *American Journal of Sociology.*

Health Canada. (1999). *Statistical Report on the Health of Canadians.* Ottawa: Minister of Public Works and Government Services.

Heilbrun, A. B. (1990). Differentiation of death-row murderers and life-sentence murderers by antisociality and intelligence measures. *Journal of Personality Assessment, 64,* 617–627.

Heinz, W. R., & Kruger, H. (2001). Life course: Innovations and challenges for social research. *Current Sociology, 49* (2), pp. 29–45.

Heisz, A. (2001, Autumn). Low income intensity: Urban and rural families. *Perspectives on Labour and Income, 13,* pp. 14–16.

Hellinger, D., & Judd, D. R. (1991). *The Democratic Facade.* Pacific Grove, CA: Brooks/Cole.

Henderson, H. (2000, April 29). Rent hikes are pushing pensioners to the limit. *Toronto Star,* p. J4.

Henderson, H. (2002, June 22). Disabled are living below poverty line. *Toronto Star,* pp. L7–L8.

Hendrix, L. (1994, August). What is sexual inequality? On the definition and range of variation. *Gender and Society, 28(3),* 287–307.

Henley, N., Hamilton, M., & Thorne, B. (1985). Womanspeak and manspeak. In A. G. Sargent (Ed.), *Beyond sex roles.* St. Paul, MN: West.

Henry, T. (1995, January 17). Day care on the upswing globally. *USA Today,* p. 6D.

Henslin, J. M. (1967, September). *The cab driver: An interactional analysis of an occupational culture.* Washington University Ph.D. dissertation.

Henslin, J. M. (1990a). It's not a lovely place to visit, and I wouldn't want to live there. In R. G. Burgess (Ed.), *Studies in qualitative methodology, a research annual: Reflections on field experiences* (pp. 51–76). Greenwich, CT: JAI Press.

Henslin, J. M. (1992). Centuries of childhood. In J. M. Henslin (Ed), *Marriage and family in a changing society* (4th ed., pp. 214–225). New York: Free Press.

Henslin, J. M. (1993). Trust and cabbies. In J. M. Henslin (Ed), *Down to earth sociology: Introductory readings* (7th ed., pp. 183–196). New York: Free Press.

Henslin, J. M. (1996). *Social Problems* (4th ed.). Englewood Cliffs, NJ: Prentice Hall.

Henslin, J. M. (1997a). On becoming male: Reflections of a sociologist on childhood and early socialization. In J. M. Henslin (Ed), *Down to earth sociology: Introductory readings* (9th ed., pp. 130–140). New York: Free Press.

Henslin, J. M. (1997b). Sociology and the social sciences. In J. M. Henslin (Ed), *Down to earth sociology: Introductory readings* (9th ed., pp. 8–18). New York: Free Press.

Henslin, J. M. (1997c). The survivors of the F-227. In J. M. Henslin (Ed), *Down to earth sociology: Introductory readings* (9th ed., pp. 237–245). New York: Free Press.

Henslin, J. M. (2001). *Sociology: A Down-To-Earth Approach,* 5th edition. Boston: Allyn and Bacon.

Henslin, J. M., & Biggs, M. A. (1997). Behavior in pubic places: The sociology of the vaginal examination. In J. M. Henslin (Ed), *Down to earth sociology: Introductory readings* (9th ed., pp. 203–214). New York: Free Press. (Original version published 1971 as Dramaturgical desexualization: The sociology of the vaginal examination in J. M. Henslin (Ed.), *Studies in the sociology of sex,* (pp. 243–272). New York: Appleton-Century-Crofts.)

Henslin, J. M., & Nelson, A. (1996). *Sociology: A down-to-earth approach* (3rd ed.). Scarborough, ON: Allyn & Bacon Canada.

Hertzler, J. O. (1965). *A sociology of language.* New York: Random House.

Hewa, S. (1993). Sociology and public policy: The debate on value-free social science. *International Journal of Sociology and Social Policy, 13(1–2),* 64–82.

Hewitt Associates. (1995). *Summary of work and family benefits report.* Lincolnshire, IL: Hewitt Associates.

Higginbotham, E., & Weber, L. (1992, September). Moving with kin and community: Upward social mobility for Black and White women. *Gender and Society, 6(3),* 416–440.

Higley, J., Hoffmann-Lange, U., Kadushin, C., & Moore, G. (1991, May). Elite integration in stable democracies: A reconsideration. *European Sociological Review, 7(1),* 35–53.

Hilliard, A., III. (1991, September). Do we have the *will* to educate all children? *Educational Leadership, 49,* 31–36.

Hillyer, B. (1997). *Feminism and Disability*. Norman, Oklahoma: University of Oklahoma Press.

Hippler, F. (1987). Interview in a television documentary with Bill Moyers in *Propaganda,* in the series "Walk Through the 20th Century."

Hochschild, A. (1989). *The second shift: Working parents and the revolution at home.* New York: Viking.

Hofferth, S., & Sandberg, J. E. (2001, May). How American children spend their time. *Journal of Marriage and the Family, 63,* pp. 295–308.

Hofstede, G. H. (1980). *Culture's consequences: International differences in work-related values.* Beverly Hills, CA: Sage Publications.

Holden, B. A., & Rose, F. (1993, August 5). Two policemen get 2½ year jail terms on U.S. charges in Rodney King case. *Wall Street Journal,* p. B2.

Homblin, D. J. (1973). *The first cities.* Boston: Little, Brown, Time-Life Books.

Hondagneu-Sotelo, P. (2001). *Domestica: Immigrant Workers Cleaning and Caring in the Shadows of Affluence.* Berkeley: University of California Press.

Honeycutt, K. (1995). Disgusting, pathetic, bizarrely beautiful: Representations of weight in popular culture. [Paper presented at the 1995 meetings of the American Sociological Association].

Hormeku, T., & Barr, G. (2002, May 3). Africans left out of plan for future. *Toronto Star,* p. A21.

Horowitz, I. L. (1966). *Three worlds of development: The theory and practice of international stratification.* New York: Oxford University Press.

Horowitz, R. (1983). *Honor and the American dream: Culture and identity in a Chicano community.* New Brunswick, NJ: Rutgers University Press.

Horowitz, R. (1987, December). Community tolerance of gang violence. *Social Problems, 34*(5), 437–450.

Hostetler, J. A. (1980). *Amish society* (3rd ed.). Baltimore: Johns Hopkins University Press.

Houtman, D. (1995). What exactly is a "social class"?: On the economic liberalism and cultural conservatism of the "working class." [Paper presented at the 1995 meetings of the American Sociological Association].

Howe, H., Lyne, J, Gross, A. VanLente, H., Rip, A., Lewontin, R., et al. (1992, April–June). Gene talk in sociobiology. *Social Epistemology, 6*(2), 109–163.

Howell, P. (2000, March 18). Act like a man. *Toronto Star,* pp. M1, M9.

Howells, L. T., & Becker, S. W. (1962, February). Seating arrangement and leadership emergence. *Journal of Abnormal and Social Psychology, 64,* 148–150.

Hoyt, H. (1939). *The structure and growth of residential neighborhoods in American cities.* Washington, DC: Federal Housing Administration.

Hoyt, H. (1971). Recent distortions of the classical models of urban structure. In L. S. Bourne (Ed.), *Internal structure of the city: Readings on space and environment* (pp. 84–96). New York: Oxford University Press.

Huber, J. (1988). From sugar and spice to professor. In J. M. Henslin (Ed.), *Down to earth sociology: Introductory readings* (5th ed., pp. 92–101). New York: Free Press.

Huber, J. (1990, February). Micro-macro links in gender stratification. *American Sociological Review, 55,* 1–10.

Huber, J., & Form, W. H. (1973). *Income and Ideology.* New York: Free Press.

Hudson, J. R. (1991). Professional sports franchise locations and city, metropolitan and regional identities. [Paper presented at the annual meetings of the American Sociological Association].

Huggins, M. K. (1993). Lost childhoods: Assassinations of youth in democratizing Brazil. [Paper presented at the annual meetings of the American Sociological Association].

Hughes, E. C. (1943). *French Canada in transition.* Chicago: University of Chicago Press.

Hughes, H. S. (1962). *Oswald Spengler: A critical estimate* (Rev. ed.). New York: Scribner's.

Hughes, J. (1995, November 7). A legend returns. *SF Bay Guardian.*

Humphreys, A. (1998, February 10). The inequality of educating Canada. *The Hamilton Spectator.*

Humphreys, L. (1971). Impersonal sex and perceived satisfaction. In J. M. Henslin (Ed.), *Studies in the Sociology of Sex* (pp. 351–374). New York: Appleton-Century-Crofts.

Humphreys, L. (1975). *Tearoom trade: Impersonal sex in public places* (Enlarged ed.). Chicago: Aldine.

Hurst, L. (2000, September 23). How the boomers will go bust. *Toronto Star,* p. A29.

Hurtig, M. (1999). *Pay the rent or feed the kids: The tragedy and disgrace of poverty in Canada.* Toronto: McClelland and Stewart.

Huth, M. J. (1990). China's urbanization under communist rule, 1949–1982. *International Journal of Sociology and Social Policy, 10*(7), 17–57.

Infantry, A. (2001, March 14). Children feel sting of emotional abuse: study. *Toronto Star,* p. A3.

Infants at greatest murder risk, most killed by parents. (2000, Spring). *Canadian Social Trends, 56,* p. 26.

Itard, J. M. G. (1962). *The wild boy of Aveyron* (G., & M. Humphrey Trans.). New York: Appleton-Century-Crofts.

Jackson, A., Robinson, D., Baldwin, B., & Wiggins, C. (2000). *Falling Behind: The State of Working Canada 2000.* Ottawa: Canadian Centre for Policy Alternatives.

Jackson, J. D. (1975). *Community & conflict: A study of French-English relations in Ontario.* Toronto: Holt, Rinehart & Winston of Canada.

Jacobs, M. A. (1997, March 4). "New girl" network is boon for women lawyers. *Wall Street Journal,* pp. B1, B7.

Jacobsen, T., & Adams, R. M. (1958, November 21). Salt and silt in ancient Mesopotamian agriculture. *Science,* 1251–1258.

Jaggar, A. M. (1990). Sexual difference and sexual equality. In D. L. Rhode (Ed.), *Theoretical perspectives on sexual difference* (pp. 239–254). New Haven, CT: Yale University Press.

James, C. (1999). *Seeing ourselves: Exploring race, ethnicity, and culture* (2nd ed.). Toronto: Thompson Educational Publishing.

Janis, I. (1972). *Victims of groupthink.* Boston, MA: Houghton Mifflin.

Jankowiak, W. R., & Fischer, E. F. (1992, April). A cross-cultural perspective on romantic love. *Journal of Ethnology, 31*(2), 149–155.

Jasper, J. M. (1991). Moral dimensions of social movements. [Paper presented at the annual meetings of the American Sociological Association].

Jasper, J. M., & Poulsen, J. D. (1995, November). Recruiting strangers and friends: Moral shocks and social networks in animal rights and anti-nuclear protests. *Social Problems, 42*(4), 493–512.

Jáuregui, G. (1996, July 19). El poder y la soberana en la aldea global. *El Pais.* 11.

Jenish, D'Arcy. (1997, November 10). *Maclean's, 110* (45), p. 18.

Jenkins, C., & Sherman, B. (1981). *The Leisure Shock.* London: Eyre Methuen.

Jerrome, D. (1992). *Good company: An anthropological study of old people in groups.* Edinburgh, UK: Edinburgh University Press.

Johnson, B. (1963). On church and sect. *American Sociological Review, 28,* 539–549.

Johnson, H. (1996). *Dangerous domains: Violence against women in Canada.* Toronto: Nelson Canada.

Johnson, J. (2002). *Getting By on the Minimum: The Lives of Working-Class Women.* New York: Routledge.

Johnson, N. R. (1993). Panic at "The Who concert stampede": An empirical assessment. In R. L. Curtis, Jr., & B. E. Aguirre (Eds.), *Collective behavior and social movements* (pp. 113–122). Boston: Allyn and Bacon.

Jones, F. (1999, Autumn). Are children going to religious services? *Canadian Social Trends, 54,* 13–16.

Jones, F. (1997, Autumn). Seniors who volunteer. *Perspectives on Labour and Income, 11*(3), 9–17.

Kagan, J. (1984). The idea of emotions in human development. In C. E. Izard, J. Kagan, & R. B. Zajonc (Eds.), *Emotions, cognition, and behavior* (pp. 38–72). New York: Cambridge University Press.

Kalichman, S. C. (1988, November). MMPI profiles of women and men convicted of domestic homicide. *Journal of Clinical Psychology, 44*(6), 847–853.

Kalish, S. (1994, March). International migration: New findings on magnitude, importance. *Population Today, 22*(3), 1–2.

Kalmijn, M. (1991, December). Shifting boundaries: Trends in religious and educational homogamy. *American Sociological Review, 56,* 786–800.

Kamin, L. J. (1975). *The science and politics of IQ.* Hillsdale, NJ: Erlbaum.

Kamin, L. J. (1986, February). Is crime in the genes? The answer may depend on who chooses what evidence. *Scientific American,* 22–27.

Kaminski, M., & Palchikoff, K. (1997, April 14). The crisis to come. *Newsweek,* 44–46.

Kanabayashi, M. (1996, August 20). Work week. *Wall Street Journal,* p. A1.

Kanter, R. M. (1977). *Men and women of the corporation.* New York: Basic Books.

Kanter, R. M. (1983). *The change masters: Innovation and entrepreneurship in the American corporation.* New York: Simon & Schuster.

Kanter, R. M. (1997). *World class: Thriving locally in the global economy.* New York: Touchstone Books.

Kanter, R. M., Wiersema, F., & Kao, J. J. (Eds.). (1997). *Innovation: Breakthrough thinking at 3M, DuPont, GE, Pfizer, and Rubbermaid.* New York: HarperBusiness.

Karnow, S., & Yoshihara, N. (1992). *Asian Americans in transition.* New York: Asia Society.

Karp, D. A., Stone, G. P., & Yoels, W. C. (1991). *Being urban: A sociology of city life* (2nd ed.). New York: Praeger.

Karp, D. A., & Yoels, W. C. (1990). Sport and urban life. *Journal of Sport and Social Issues, 14*(2), 77–102.

Kart, C. S. (1990). *The realities of aging: An introduction to gerontology* (3rd ed.). Boston: Allyn and Bacon.

Kasarda, J. D., & Crenshaw, E. M. (1991). Third world urbanization: Dimensions, theories, and determinants. *Annual Review of Sociology, 17,* 467–501.

Katz, S. (1997). The importance of being beautiful. In J. M. Henslin (Ed.), *Down to earth sociology: Introductory readings* (9th ed., pp. 307–313). New York: Free Press.

Kaufman, G. (1999). The portrayal of men's family roles in television commercials. *Sex Roles, 41*(5/6), 439–458.

Kaufmann, C. (1994). Rights and the provision of health care: A comparison of Canada, Great Britain, and the United States. In H. D. Schwartz (Ed.), *Dominant issues in medical sociology* (3rd ed., pp. 376–396). New York: McGraw-Hill.

Keating, N., Fast, J., Frederick, J., Cranswick, K. & Perrier, C. (1999). *Eldercare in Canada: Context, content and consequences.* Ottawa: Minister of Industry.

Keith, J. (1982). *Old people, new lives: Community creation in a retirement residence* (2nd ed.). Chicago: University of Chicago Press.

Kelley, J., & Evans, M. D. R. (1995, April). Class and class conflict in six Western nations. *American Sociological Review, 60,* 157–178.

Kelso, W. A. (1995). *Poverty and the underclass: Changing perceptions of the poor in America.* New York: New York University Press.

Keniston, K. (1971). *Youth and dissent: The rise of a new opposition.* New York: Harcourt, Brace, Jovanovich.

Kennedy, P. (1993). *Preparing for the twenty-first century.* New York: Random House.

Kephart, W. M., & Zellner, W. W. (1994). *Extraordinary groups: An examination of unconventional life-styles* (5th ed.). New York: St. Martin's Press.

Kerr, C. (1983). *The future of industrialized societies.* Cambridge, MA: Harvard University Press.

Kerr, C., et al. (1960). *Industrialism and industrial man: The problems of labor and management in economic growth.* Cambridge, MA: Harvard University Press.

Kershaw, T. (1992, September). The effects of educational tracking on the social mobility of African Americans. *Journal of Black Studies, 23*(1), 152–169.

Kerstetter, S. (2001, March 25). Radical change necessary to aid poor. *Toronto Star,* p. A 13.

Khalif, M. H. (2002, April 30). Bridging the prosperity gap. *Toronto Star,* p. A24.

Kids spending more time with parents. (2001, May 19). *Toronto Star,* p. M10.

King, M. L., Jr. (1958). *Stride toward freedom: The Montgomery story.* New York: Harper & Brothers.

King, R. T., Jr. (1994, October 25). Soon a chip will test blood for diseases. *Wall Street Journal,* pp. B1, B11.

Kitsuse, J. I. (1980, October). Coming out all over: Deviants and the politics of social problems. *Social Problems, 28*(1), 1–13.

Kluegel, J. R., & Smith, E. R. (1986). *Beliefs about inequality: America's views of what is and what ought to be.* Hawthorne, NY: Aldine de Gruyter.

Knaus, W. A. (1981). *Inside Russian medicine: An American doctor's first-hand report.* New York: Everest House.

Kohfeld, C. W., & Leip, L. A. (1991, April). Bans on concurrent sale of beer and gas: A California case study. *Sociological Practice Review, 2*(2), 104–115.

Kohn, M. L. (1959). Social class and parental values. *American Journal of Sociology, 64,* 337–351.

Kohn, M. L. (1963). Social class and parent–child relationships: An interpretation. *American Journal of Sociology, 68,* 471–480.

Kohn, M. L. (1976). Occupational structure and alienation. *American Journal of Sociology, 82,* 111–130.

Kohn, M. L. (1977). *Class and conformity: A study in values* (2nd ed.). Homewood, IL: Dorsey Press.

Kohn, M.L., & Schooler, C. (1969). Class, occupation, and orientation. *American Sociological Review, 34,* 659–678.

Kohn, M.L., & Schooler, C. (1983). *Work and personality: An inquiry into the impact of social stratification.* New York: Ablex Press.

Kohn, M. L., Slomczynski, K. M., & Schoenbach, C. (1986). Social stratification and the transmission of values in the family: A cross-national assessment. *Sociological Forum, 1*(1), 73–102.

Komter, A. (1989, June). Hidden power in marriage. *Gender and Society, 3*(2), 187–216.

Korda, M. (1973). *Male chauvinism: How it works.* New York: Random House.

Kornhauser, W. (1959). *The politics of mass society.* New York: Free Press.

Kotlowitz, A. (1992, February 25). A businessman turns his skills to aiding inner-city schools. *Wall Street Journal,* pp. A1, A6.

Kovitz, M. (2000, Winter). The enemy within: Female soldiers in the Canadian armed forces. *Canadian Woman Studies, 19*(4), 36–41.

Krahn, H., & Lowe, G. (1998). *Work, industry, and Canadian society.* Scarborough: Nelson Canada.

Kraybill, D.B. (1989). *The riddle of Amish culture.* Baltimore: Johns Hopkins University Press.

Kremarik, F. (2002, Spring). The changing recreational spending patterns of Canadian families. *Canadian Social Trends, 64,* pp. 13–18.

Krupp, H. (1995). European technology policy and global Schumpeter dynamics: A social science perspective. *Technological Forecasting and Social Change, 48,* 7–26.

Kübler-Ross, E. (1969). *On death and dying*. New York: Macmillan.

Kübler-Ross, E. (1981). *Living with death and dying*. New York: Macmillan.

Kübler-Ross, E. (1989). *Death: The final stage of growth*. Englewood Cliffs, NJ: Prentice Hall.

Kupers, T. A. (1999). *Prison madness: The mental health crisis behind bars and what we must do*. San Francisco: Josey-Bass.

La Barre, W. (1954). *The human animal*. Chicago: University of Chicago Press.

Lacayo, R. (1997, April 7). The lure of the cult. *Time, 45–46*.

Lachica, E. (1992, May 18). Third world told to spend more on environment. *Wall Street Journal*, p. A2.

LaDou, J. (1991, July). Deadly migration: Hazardous industries' flight to the third world. *Technology Review, 94*(5), 46–53.

LaFeber, W. (1999). *Michael Jordan and the new global capitalism*. New York: W. W. Norton & Company.

Lagaipa, S. J., (1990). Suffer the little children: The ancient practice of infanticide as a modern moral dilemma. *Issues in Comprehensive Pediatric Nursing, 13*, 241–251.

Lagnado, L. (1996, October 9). Another peril: Smoking doubles risk of old-age blindness, two studies say. *Wall Street Journal*, p. B8.

Landtman, G. (1968). *The origin of the inequality of the social classes*. New York: Greenwood Press. (First published 1938.)

Lang, K., & Lang, G. E. (1961). *Collective Dynamics*. New York: Crowell.

Langdon, S. (1999). *Global poverty, democracy and North-South change*. Toronto: Garamond Press.

Langlois, S., & Morrison, P. (2002, Autumn). Suicide deaths and attempts. *Canadian Social Trends*, pp. 20–25.

Lannoy, R. (1975). *The speaking tree: A study of Indian culture and society*. New York: Oxford University Press.

LaPiere, R. T. (1934, December). Attitudes versus action. *Social Forces, 13*, 230–237.

Larson, J. H. (1988, January). The marriage quiz: College students' beliefs in selected myths about marriage. *Family Relations*, 3–11.

Laska, S. B. (1993, September). Environmental sociology and the state of the discipline. *Social Forces, 72*(1), 1–17.

Latané, B., & Darley, J. M. (1970). *The unresponsive bystander: Why doesn't he help?* New York: Appleton-Century-Crofts.

Latané, B., & Nida, S. (1981). Ten years of research on group size and helping. *Psychological Bulletin, 89*(2), 308–324.

Lauer, J., & Lauer, R. (1992). Marriages made to last. In J. M. Henslin (Ed.), *Marriage and family in a changing society* (4th ed., pp. 481–486). New York: Free Press.

Lawton, J. (1998, March). Contemporary hospice care: The sequestration of the unbounded body and "dirty dying." *Sociology of Health and Illness, 20*(2), 121–143.

Lazarsfeld, P. F., & Reitz, J. G. (1989). History of applied sociology. *Sociological Practice, 7*, 43–52.

Leacock, E. (1969). *Teaching and learning in city schools*. New York: Basic Books.

Leacock, E. (1981). *Myths of male dominance*. New York: Monthly Review Press.

LeBon, G. (1895). *Psychologie des foules (The psychology of the crowd)*. Paris: Alcan. (Various editions in English.)

Lee, A. M., & Lee, E. B. (1939). *The fine art of propaganda: A study of Father Coughlin's speeches*. New York: Harcourt Brace.

Lee, F. R. (1996, January 9). Infertile couples forge ties within society of their own. *New York Times*, p. A1.

Lee, M. (2002, April 18). The Global Divide: Inequality in the World Economy. In Canadian Centre for Policy Alternatives, *Behind the Numbers: Economic Facts, Figures and Analysis, 4* (2).

Lemert, C. (1994). A classic from the other side of the veil: Du Bois's *Souls of Black folk*. *Sociological Quarterly, 35*(3), 383–396.

Lemert, E. M. (1972). *Human deviance, social problems, and social control* (2nd ed.). Englewood Cliffs, NJ: Prentice Hall.

Lenski, G. (1954). Status crystallization: A nonvertical dimension of social status. *American Sociological Review, 19,* 405–413.

Lenski, G. (1966). *Power and privilege: A theory of social stratification*. New York: McGraw-Hill.

Lenski, G., & Lenski, J. (1987). *Human societies: An introduction to macrosociology* (5th ed.). New York: McGraw-Hill.

Leonard, M. (2001). Old wine in new bottles? Women working inside and outside the household. *Women's Studies International Forum, 24*, pp. 67–78.

Leong, M. (2002, July 17). 'Outliving your money' a new concern for seniors. *Toronto Star*, p. A6.

Lerner, G. (1972). *Black women in white America: A documentary history*. New York: Pantheon Books.

Lerner, G. (1986). *The creation of patriarchy*. New York: Oxford.

Lesser, A. (1968). War and the state. In M. Fried, M. Harris, & R. Murphy (Eds.), *War: The anthropology of armed conflict and aggression* (pp. 92–96). Garden City, NY: Natural History.

Levinson, D. J. (1978). *The seasons of a man's life*. New York: Knopf.

Levy, J. A. (1994). The hospice in the context of an aging society. In R. B. Enright, Jr., (Ed.), *Perspectives in social gerontology* (pp. 274–286). Boston: Allyn and Bacon.

Levy, M. J., Jr. (1992, May–June). Confucianism and modernization. *Society, 24*, (4), 15–18.

Lewis, O. (1966a, October). The culture of poverty. *Scientific American, 115*, 19–25.

Lewis, O. *La Vida*. (1966b). New York: Random House.

Li, P. S. (2000, August). Earning disparities between immigrants and native-born Canadian. *Canadian Review of Sociology and Anthropology, 37*, pp. 289–311.

Liebow, E. (1967). *Tally's corner: A study of Negro streetcorner men*. Boston: Little, Brown.

Liebow, E. (1997). Tally's corner. In J. M. Henslin (Ed.), *Down to earth sociology: Introductory readings* (9th ed., pp. 330–339). New York: Free Press.

Lind, M. (1995). *The next American nation: The new nationalism and the fourth American Revolution*. New York: Free Press.

Lindsay, C. (1999, Spring). Seniors: A diverse group aging well. *Canadian Social Trends, 52,* 24–26.

Lindsay, C. (1999). *A portrait of seniors in Canada*, 3rd ed. Ottawa: Statistics Canada, Catalogue 89-519-XPE.

Linton, R. (1936). *The Study of Man*. New York: Appleton-Century-Crofts.

Lippitt, R., & White, R. K. (1958). An experimental study of leadership and group life. In E. E. Maccoby, T. M. Newcomb, & E. L Hartley (Eds.), *Readings in social psychology* (3rd ed., pp. 340–365). New York: Holt, Rinehart and Winston. (As summarized in Olmsted and Hare (1978), pp. 28–31.)

Lipset, S. M. (1959). Democracy and working-class authoritarianism. *American Sociological Review, 24,* 482–502.

Lipset, S. M. (1990). *Continental divide: The values and institutions of the United States and Canada*. Washington, DC: Canadian-American Committee.

Lipset, S. M. (1993). The social requisites of democracy revisited. Presidential address to the American Sociological Association, Boston, MA.

Lipton, M. (1979). *Why poor people stay poor: Urban bias in world development*. Cambridge, MA: Harvard University Press.

Livingstone, D. W. (1999). *The education-jobs gap: Underemployment or economic democracy*. Toronto: Garamond Press.

Lofland, J. F. (1985). *Protest: Studies of collective behavior and social movements*. New Brunswick, NJ: Transaction Books.

Lofland, J. F. (1993). Collective behavior: The elementary forms. In R. L. Curtis, Jr., & B. E. Aguirre (Eds.), *Collective behavior and social movements* (pp. 70–75). Boston: Allyn and Bacon.

Lombroso, C. (1911). *Crime: Its causes and remedies* (H. P. Horton, Trans.). Boston: Little, Brown.

Lopez, J. A. (1992, March 3). Study says women face glass walls as well as ceilings. *Wall Street Journal*, pp. B1, B8.

Lorber, J. (1994). *Paradoxes of gender.* New Haven, CT: Yale University Press.

Lorber, J. (1998). *Gender inequality: Feminist theories and politics.* Los Angeles: Roxbury.

Lowe, G. S. (1987). *Women in the administrative revolution.* Toronto: University of Toronto Press.

Lowe, G. S. (2000). *The quality of work: A people-centred agenda.* Toronto: Oxford University Press.

Lu, V. (2001, March 14). More seniors than children by 2016. *Toronto Star*, p. A8.

Lu, V. (2002, June 20). Tobacco use will kill 1 billion, group warns. *Toronto Star*, p. A18.

Lublin, J. S. (1991, February 13). Trying to increase worker productivity, more employers alter management style. *Wall Street Journal*, pp. B1, B7.

Lublin, J. S. (1996, February 28). Women at top still are distant from CEO jobs. *Wall Street Journal*, p. B1.

Lucas, K., & Lloyd, B. (1999). Starting smoking: Girls' explorations of the influence of peers. *Journal of Adolescence, 22,* 647–655.

Lundberg, O. (1991). Causal explanations for class inequality in health—An empirical analysis. *Social Science and Medicine, 32*(4), 385–393.

Luoma, J. R. (1989). Acid murder no longer a mystery. In T. D. Goldfarb (Ed.), *Taking sides: Clashing views on controversial environmental issues* (3rd ed., pp. 186–192). Guilford, CT: Dushkin.

Lurie, N., Slater, J., McGovern, P., Ekstrum, J., Quam, L., & Margolis, K. (1993, August 12). Preventive care for women: Does the sex of the physician matter? *New England Journal of Medicine, 329,* 478–482.

Luttwak, E. (1996). Buchanan has it right. *London Review of Books, 18*(9), 6–8.

Luxton, M. (1980). *More than a labour of love.* Toronto: Women's Press.

Luxton, M. (1995). Two hands for the clock: Changing patterns in the gendered division of labour in the home. In E. Nelson & B. Robinson (Eds.), *Gender in the 1990s: Images, realities and issues* (pp. 288–301). Toronto: Nelson Canada.

Luxton, M., & Corman, J. (2001). *Getting By in Hard Times: Gendered Labour at Home and on the Job.* Toronto: University of Toronto Press.

Lyotard, J. F. (1984). *The postmodern condition: A report on knowledge* (G. Bennington & B. Massumi, Trans.; F. Jameson, Foreword). Minneapolis: University of Minnesota Press.

Macdonald, B., with Rich, C. (1991). *Look me in the eye: Old women aging and ageism.* Minneapolis: Spinsters Ink.

MacDonald, H. (1995, November 8). Law school humbug. *Wall Street Journal*, p. A23.

MacDonald, J. (2002, March 2). Doctor of love. *Saturday Post*, pp. SP1, 6, 7.

Mack, R. W., & Bradford, C. P. (1979). *Transforming America: Patterns of social change* (2nd ed.). New York: Random House.

Mackay, C. (1852). *Memories of extraordinary popular delusions and the madness of crowds.* London: Office of the National Illustrated Library.

Mackey, R. A., & O'Brien, B. A. (1995). *Lasting marriages: Men and women growing together.* Westport, CT.

Mackie, M. (1987). *Constructing women and men: Gender socialization.* Toronto: Holt, Rinehart and Winston of Canada Limited.

Mackie, M. (1991). *Gender relations in Canada: Further explorations.* Toronto: Butterworths.

MacKinnon, C. A. (1979). *Sexual harassment of working women: A case of sex discrimination.* New Haven, CT: Yale University Press.

MacKinnon, M. (1999, March 1). The lowest incomes in Canada are found on Native reserves. *The Globe and Mail.*

MacLennan, H. (1946). *Two solitudes.* London: Cresset Press.

Mahoney, J. S., Jr., & Kooistra, P. G. (1995). Policing the races: Structural factors enforcing racial purity in Virginia (1630–1930). (Paper presented at the 1995 meetings of the American Sociological Association.)

Mahran, M. (1978). *Proceedings of the third international congress of medical sexology.* Littleton, MA: PSG Publishing.

Maher, F. A., & Tetreault, M. K. T. (2001). *The feminist classroom: Dynamics of gender, race and privilege.* Expanded Edition. London: Rowman & Littlefield Publishers, Ltd.

Main, J. T. (1965). *The social structure of revolutionary America.* Princeton, NJ: Princeton University Press.

Malinowski, B. (1927). *Sex and repression in savage society.* Cleveland, OH: World.

Malinowski, B. (1945). *The dynamics of culture change.* New Haven, CT: Yale University Press.

Malmberg, B., & Sundström, G. (1996, January). Age care crisis in Sweden? *Current Sweden, 412,* 1–6.

Malson, L. (1972). *Wolf children and the problem of human nature.* New York: Monthly Review Press.

Malthus, T. R. (1926). *First essay on population 1798.* London: Macmillan. (Originally published 1798.)

Mamdani, M. (1973). The myth of population control: Family, caste, and class in an urban village. New York: Monthly Review Press.

Mandell, N. (1988). The child question: Links between women and children in the family. In N. Mandell & A. Duffy (Eds.), *Reconstructing the Canadian family: Feminist perspectives* (pp. 49–81). Toronto: Butterworths.

Mander, J. (1992). *In the absence of the sacred: The failure of technology and the survival of the Indian nations.* San Francisco, CA: Sierra Club Books.

Manno, B. V. (1995, September 13). The real score on the SATs. *Wall Street Journal*, p. A14.

Manski, C. F. (1992–1993, Winter). Income and higher education. *Focus, 14*(3), 14–19.

Marcus, A. D. (1996, September 5). Mideast minorities: Kurds aren't alone. *Wall Street Journal*, p. A12.

Markson, E. W. (1992, July–August). Moral dilemmas. *Society,* 4–6.

Markusen, E. (1995). Genocide in Cambodia. In J. M. Henslin (Ed.), *Down to earth sociology* (8th ed., pp. 355–364). New York: Free Press.

Marolla, J., & Scully, D. (1986). Attitudes toward women, violence, and rape: A comparison of convicted rapists and other felons. *Deviant Behavior, 7*(4), 337–355.

Marquardt, R. (1998). *Enter at your own risk: Canadian youth and the labour market.* Toronto: Between the Lines.

Marshall, G. (1982). *In search of the spirit of capitalism: An essay on Max Weber's Protestant ethic thesis.* New York: Columbia University Press.

Marshall, K. (1998, Spring). Stay-at-home Dads, *Perspectives on Labour and Income, 10*(1), 9–15.

Marshall, K. (1999, Autumn). Employment after childbirth, 1993/94. *Perspectives on Labour and Income, 8,* 3.

Marshall, S. (1995, November 2). It's so simple: Just lather up, watch the fat go down the drain. *Wall Street Journal*, p. B1.

Martel, L., & Belanger, A. (2000, Autumn). Dependence-free life expectancy in Canada. *Canadian Social Trends*, pp. 26–29.

Martin, M. (1990, Winter). Ecosabotage and civil disobedience. *Environmental Ethics, 12*(4), 291–310.

Martin, W. G. (1994, Spring). The world-systems perspective in perspective: Assessing the attempt to move beyond nineteenth-century Eurocentric conceptions. *Review, 17*(2), 145–185.

Martineau, H. (1962). *Society in America.* Garden City, NY: Doubleday. (First published 1837.)

Marvin, C. (1988). *When old technologies were new: Thinking about electronic communication in the late nineteenth century.* New York: Oxford University Press.

Marx, G. T. (1985, May–June). The new surveillance. *Technology Review,* 43–48.

Marx, G. T. (1986, November–December). Monitoring on the job: How to protect privacy as well as property. *Technology Review,* 63–72.

Marx, G. T. (1993). Thoughts on a neglected category of social movement participant: The agent provocateur and the informant. In R. L. Curtis, Jr., & B. E. Aguirre (Eds.), *Collective Behavior and Social Movements* (pp. 242–258). Boston: Allyn and Bacon.

Marx, G. T. (1995). The road to the future. In *Triumph of discovery: A chronicle of great adventures in science* (pp. 63–65). New York: Holt.

Marx, K. (1964). Contribution to the critique of Hegel's philosophy of right. In T. B. Bottomore (Ed.), *Karl Marx: Early writings,* (p. 45). New York: McGraw-Hill. (First published 1844.)

Marx, K., & Engels, F. (1967). *Communist manifesto.* New York: Pantheon. (First published 1848.)

Massey, D. S. (2002, February). A brief history of human society: The origin and role of emotion in social life. *American Sociological Review, 67,* pp. 1–29.

Massey, D. S., & Denton, N. A. (1993). *American apartheid: Segregation and the making of the underclass.* Cambridge, MA: Harvard University Press.

Maticka-Tyndale, E. (2001, Spring). Sexual health and Canadian youth: How do we measure up? *The Canadian Journal of Human Sexuality, 10* (1–2), pp. 1–17.

Matthews, C. (1996, Summer). A powerful presence: Images of the grandmother in Canadian literature. *Canadian Journal of Aging, 15*(2), 264–273.

Mauss, A. (1975). *Social problems as social movements.* Philadelphia: Lippincott.

Maxwell, K. A. (2002). Friends: The role of peer influence across adolescent risk behaviours. *Journal of Youth and Adolescence, 32* (4), pp. 267–278.

Maxwell, M. P., & Maxwell, J. D. (1971). Boarding school: Social control, space and identity. In D. I. Davies & K. Herman (Eds.), *Social space: Canadian perspectives.* Toronto: New Press.

Mayo, E. (1966). *Human problems of an industrial civilization.* New York: Viking.

McAdam, D., McCarthy, J. D., & Zald, M. N. (1988). Social movements. In N. J. Smelser (Ed.), *Handbook of sociology* (pp. 695–737). Newbury Park, CA: Sage.

McCabe, J. T., & Ellis, J. E. (1990). Pastoralism: Beating the odds in arid Africa. In J. P. Spradley & D. W. McCurdy (Eds.), *Conformity and conflict: Readings in cultural anthropology* (pp. 150–156). Glenview, IL: Scott, Foresman.

McCall, L. (2001). *Complex Inequality: Gender, Class and Race in the New Economy.* New York: Routledge.

McCall, M. (1980). Who and where are the artists? In W. B. Shaffir, R. A. Stebbins, & A. Turowetz (Eds.), *Fieldwork experience: Qualitative approaches to social research* (pp. 145–158). New York: St. Martin's.

McCarthy, C. (1983, March 5). America's homeless: Three days down and out in Chicago. *Nation, 236*(9), 1, 271.

McCarthy, J. D., & Wolfson, M. (1992). Consensus movements, conflict movements, and the cooperation of civic and state infrastructures. In A. D. Morris & C. M. Mueller (Eds.), *Frontiers in social movement theory* (pp. 273–297). New Haven, CT: Yale University Press.

McCarthy, J. D., & Zald, M. N. (1977). Resource mobilization and social movements: A partial theory. *American Journal of Sociology, 82*(6), 1212–1241.

McCarthy, M. J. (1993, August 25). James Bond hits the supermarket: Stores snoop on shoppers' habits to boost sales. *Wall Street Journal,* pp. B1, B8.

McCoy, E. (1985). Childhood through the ages. In J. M. Henslin (Ed.), *Marriage and family in a changing society* (2nd ed., pp. 386–394). New York: Free Press.

McCuen, G.E. (Ed.). (1993). *Ecocide and genocide in the vanishing forest: The rainforests and native people.* Hudson, WI: GEM Publications.

McDonald, J. T., & Worswick, C. (1997). Unemployment incidence of immigrant men in Canada. *Canadian Public Policy, 23* (4), pp. 367–371.

McDonald, L., Hornick, J. P., Robertson, G. B., & Wallace, J. E. (1991). *Elder abuse and neglect in Canada.* Toronto: Butterworths.

McDonnell, K. (2002, March). The hurried child. *The New Internationalist, 343,* pp. 22–23.

McGowan, J. (1991, August 9). Little girls dying: An ancient & thriving practice. *Commonweal,* 481–482.

McGregor, J. (1992, March 20). China's aging leader seems set to carve reformist idea in stone. *Wall Street Journal,* p. A9.

McGregor, J. (1993, September 24). Running bulls. *Wall Street Journal,* p. R16.

McIntyre, J. (1997, April 30). Army rape case renews debate on coed training. CNN Internet article.

McKeown, T. (1977). *The modern rise of population.* New York: Academic Press.

McLanahan, S. (2002, Spring). Life without father: What happens to the children? *Contexts, 1* (1), pp. 35–44.

McLanahan, S., & Sandefur, G. (1994). *Growing up with a single parent: What hurts, what helps.* Cambridge, MA: Harvard University Press.

McLuhan, M. (1964). *Understanding media: The extensions of man.* New York: Mentor.

McMahon, A. (1998). Blokus domesticus: The sensitive new age guy in Australia. *Journal of Australian Studies, 56,* 147–157.

McNally, D. (2002). *Another world is possible: Globalization and anti-capitalism.* Winnipeg: Arbeiter Ring Publishers.

McNeely, S. (2002, May 21). Childless—and loving it. *Toronto Star,* pp. C1, C3.

McPhail, C. (1989). Blumer's theory of collective behavior: The development of a non-symbolic interaction explanation. *Sociological Quarterly, 30*(3), 401–423.

McPhail, C. (1991). *The myth of the madding crowd.* Hawthorne, NY: Aldine de Gruyter.

McQuaig, L. (1995). *Shooting the hippo: Death by deficit and other Canadian myths.* Toronto: Viking.

Mead, G. H. (1934). *Mind, self and society.* Chicago: University of Chicago Press.

Mead, M. (1950). *Sex and temperament in three primitive societies.* New York: New American Library. (First published in 1935.)

Meek, A. (1989, February). On creating "ganas": A conversation with Jaime Escalante. *Educational Leadership, 46*(5), 46–47.

Meier, B. (1987, May 12). Health studies suggest asbestos substitutes also pose cancer risk. *Wall Street Journal,* pp. 1, 21.

Meltzer, B. N., Petras, J. W. & Reynolds, L. T. (1975). *Symbolic interactionism: Genesis, varieties, and criticism.* London: Routledge & Kegan Paul.

Menaghan, E. G., Kowaleski-Jones, L, & Mott, F. L. (1997, March). The intergenerational costs of parental social stressors: Academic and social difficulties in early adolescence for children of young mothers. *Journal of Health and Social Behavior, 38,* 72–86.

Menzel, P. (1994). *Material world: A global family portrait.* San Francisco: Sierra Club.

Menzies, H. (1996). *Whose brave new world? The information highway and the new economy.* Toronto: Between the Lines.

Merton, R. K. (1949). *Social theory and social structure.* Glencoe, IL: Free Press. (Enlarged ed., 1968.).

Merton, R. K. (1956). The social-cultural environment and *anomie.* In H. L. Witmer & R. Kotinsky (Eds.), *New perspectives for research on* juvenile delinquency (pp. 24–50). Washington, DC: U.S. Department of Health, Education, and Welfare.

Messner, M. (1990, January). Boyhood, organized sports, and the construction of masculinities. *Journal of Contemporary Ethnography, 18*(4), 416–444.

Meyrowitz, J. (1995). Shifting worlds of strangers: Medium theory and changes in "them" vs "us." (Paper presented at the 1995 meetings of the American Sociological Association.)

Miedema, B. (1999). *Mothering and the state: The paradox of fostering.* Halifax: Fernwood Publishing.

Milan, A. (2000, Spring). One hundred years of families. *Canadian Social Trends, 56,* pp. 2–12.

Milbank, D. (1995a, May 3). Guarded by greenbelts, Europe's town centers thrive. *Wall Street Journal,* pp. B1, B4.

Milbank, D. (1995b, August 9). Working poor fear welfare cutbacks aimed at the idle will inevitably strike them, too. *Wall Street Journal,* p. A10.

Milburn, S. S., Carney, D. R,. & Ramirez, A. M. (2001). Even in modern media, the picture is still the same: A content analysis of clipart images. *Sex Roles, 44* (5/6), pp. 277–294.

Milgram, S. (1963). Behavioral study of obedience. *Journal of Abnormal and Social Psychology, 67*(4), 371–378.

Milgram, S. (1965, February). Some conditions of obedience and disobedience to authority. *Human Relations, 18,* 57–76.

Milgram, S. (1967). The small world problem. *Psychology Today, 1,* 61–67.

Milkie, M. A. (1994, October). Social world approach to cultural studies. *Journal of Contemporary Ethnography, 23*(3), 354–380.

Miller, D. E. (1986). Milgram redux: Obedience and disobedience in authority relations. In N. K. Denzin (Ed.), *Studies in Symbolic Interaction* (pp. 77–106). Greenwich, CT: JAI Press.

Miller, J. J. (1995, May 25). Don't close our "golden door." *Wall Street Journal,* p. A14.

Miller, M. W. (1993, December 2). Dark days: The staggering cost of depression. *Wall Street Journal,* pp. B1, B6.

Miller, W.B. (1958). Lower class culture as a generating milieu of gang delinquency. *Journal of Social Issues, 14*(3), 5–19.

Miller-Loessi, K. (1992). Toward gender integration in the workplace: Issues at multiple levels. *Sociological Perspectives, 35*(1), 1–15.

Mills, A. J., & Simmons, T. (1999). *Reading organization theory: A critical approach to the study of organizational behaviour and structure.* Toronto: Garamond Press.

Mills, C. W. (1956). *The power elite.* New York: Oxford University Press.

Mills, C. W. (1959). *The sociological imagination.* New York: Oxford University Press.

Minister of Public Works and Government Services Canada. (1997). *A history of the vote in Canada.* Ottawa.

Minkler, M., & Robertson, A. (1991, March). The ideology of "age/race wars": Deconstructing a social problem. *Ageing and Society, 11*(1), 1–22.

Mintz, B. A., & Schwartz, M. (1985). *The power structure of American business.* Chicago: University of Chicago Press.

Mironowicz, M. (2002, July 19). Native forum probes legacy of residential schools. *The Hamilton Spectator.*

Mitchell, B. (1998, Winter). Too close for comfort? Parental assessments of "boomerang kids" living arrangements. *Canadian Journal of Sociology, 23*(1), 21–46.

Mizruchi, M. S., & Koenig, T. (1991, June). Size, concentration, and corporate networks: Determinants of business collective action. *Social Science Quarterly, 72*(2), 299–313.

Moir, A., & Moir, B. (1999). *Why Men Don't Iron: The New Reality of Gender Differences.* New York: Harper Collins.

Mojab, S. (2000, Winter). Vengeance and violence: Kurdish women recount the war. *Canadian Woman Studies, 19*(4), 89–94.

Mokhiber, R., & Weissman, R. (1999, May 4). A moment of silence. *Multinational Monitor—A Web-Based Newsletter.*

Mokhiber, R., & Weissman, R. (2002, May 28). The age of inequality. *Focus on the Corporation.* Accessed October 11, 2002 at http://www. corporatepredators.org.

Monette, M. (1996). *Canada's changing retirement patterns: Findings from the general social survey.* Ottawa: Minister of Industry.

Money, J., & Ehrhardt, A. A. (1972). *Man and woman, boy and girl.* Baltimore: Johns Hopkins University Press.

Monsebraaten, L. (1998, November 18). Politicians fail on child care, group told. *The Toronto Star,* p. B7.

Montagu, M. F. A. (1964). *The Concept of Race.* New York: Free Press.

Montgomery, S. (2000, January 14). Quebec's 'universal' day care lottery for the lucky. *Toronto Star,* p. A17.

More Inuit children smoke. (2002, January 31). *Toronto Star,* p. A6.

Morganthau, T. (1993, March 8). Dr. Kevorkian's death wish. *Newsweek,* 46–48.

Morissette, R. (2002, Summer). Families on the financial edge. *Perspectives on Labour and Income, 14,* pp. 9–20.

Morissette, R., & Drolet, M. (2001, Summer). Pension coverage and retirement savings. *Perspectives on Labour and Income, 13,* pp. 39–46.

Morissette, R., & Zhang, X. (2001, Summer). Experience low income for several years. *Perspectives on Labour and Income, 13,* pp. 25–36.

Morissette, R., Zhang, X., & Drolet, M. (2002a, Autumn). Are families getting richer? *Canadian Social Trends, 14,* pp. 15–19.

Morissette, R., Zhang, X., & Drolet, M. (2002b, Spring). Wealth inequality. *Perspectives on Labour and Income, 14,* pp. 15–22.

Morris, C. (2001, June 21). Study shatters myths about over-80s. *Toronto Star,* p. A3.

Morris, J. R. (1991, March). Racial attitudes of undergraduates in Greek housing. *College Student Journal, 25*(1), 501–505.

Morrow, B. H. (1995). Urban families as support after disaster: The case of Hurricane Andrew. (Paper presented at the 1995 meetings of the American Sociological Association.)

Mosca, G. (1939). *The ruling class.* New York: McGraw-Hill. (First published 1896).

Moscos, C. C., & Butler, S. (1997). *All that we can be: Black leadership and racial integration the army way.* New York: Basic Books.

Mosher, S. W. (1983, July 25). Why are baby girls being killed in China? *Wall Street Journal,* p. 9.

Mosher, S. W. (1994). *A mother's ordeal: One woman's fight against one-child China.* New York: HarperCollins.

Mosher, S. W. (1997, February 10). Too many people? Not by a long shot. *Wall Street Journal,* p. A18.

Most women return to work after childbirth. (2000, Spring). *Canadian Social Trends, 56,* p. 26.

Mount, F. (1992). *The subversive family: An alternative history of love and marriage.* New York: Free Press.

Moyers, B. (1989). Propaganda. In the series A walk through the 20th century. (video)

Moynihan, D. P. (1991, September 14). Social justice in the *next* century. *America,* 132–137.

Mudry, A. (1996). *World enough and time: Conversations with Canadian women at midlife.* Toronto: Dundurn Press.

Muehlenhard, C. L., & Linton, M. A. (1987). Date rape and sexual aggression in dating situations: Incidence and risk factors. *Journal of Counseling Psychology, 34*(2), 186–196.

Murdock, G. P. (1937, May). Comparative data on the division of labor by sex. *Social Forces, 15*(4), 551–553.

Murdock, G. P. (1945). The common denominator of cultures. In R. Linton (Ed.), *The science of man and the world crisis.* New York: Columbia University Press.

Murdock, G. P. (1949). *Social structure.* New York: Macmillan.

Murray, C. (1993, October 29). The coming White underclass. *Wall Street Journal,* p. A16.

Murray, G. W. (1935). *Sons of Ishmael.* London: Routledge.

Myles, J. (2000, Winter). Incomes of seniors. *Perspectives on Labour and Income, 12,* pp. 23–32.

Myrdal, G. (1962). *Challenge to Affluence.* New York: Pantheon Books.

Nachman, S. (1991). Elder abuse and neglect substantiations: What they tell us about the problem. *Journal of Elder Abuse and Neglect, 3*(3), 19–43.

Naj, A. K. (1993, May 7). Some manufacturers drop efforts to adopt Japanese techniques. *Wall Street Journal,* pp. A1, A12.

Narayan, S. (1994, December 5). A first in child care. *Boston Globe,* pp. 19–20.

National Council of Welfare. (1998–99). *A new poverty line: Yes, no or maybe?* Ottawa: Minister of Public Works and Government Services.

National Council of Welfare. (1999). *A pension primer.* Ottawa: Minister of Public Works and Government Services.

National Council of Welfare. (1999a). *Poverty profile 1997.* Ottawa: Minister of Public Works and Government Services.

National Council of Welfare. (1999b). *Preschool children: Promises to keep.* Ottawa: Minister of Public Works and Government Services.

National Council of Welfare. (1999c). *Children first.* Ottawa: Minister of Public Works and Government Services.

National Council of Welfare. (2000, Spring) *Justice and the poor.* Ottawa: Minister of Public Works and Government Services.

National Council of Welfare. (2001, Summer). *Child poverty profile 1998.* Ottawa: Minister of Public Works and Government Services.

National Council of Welfare. (2001–02, Winter). *The cost of poverty.* Ottawa: Minister of Public Works and Government Services.

Nauta, A. (1993). That they all may be one: Can denominationalism die? Paper presented at the annual meetings of the American Sociological Association.

Nelsen, R. W. (2002). *Schooling as entertainment: Corporate education meets popular culture.* Kingston: Cedarcreek Publications.

Nelson, A., & Robinson, B. W. (2002). *Gender in Canada,* 2nd Edition. Toronto: Prentice Hall.

Nelson, E. D., & Robinson, B. W. (1999). *Gender in Canada.* Scarborough: Prentice Hall Allyn and Bacon Canada.

Nelson, R. K. (1989, November 2). Letter to the editor. *Wall Street Journal,* p. A23.

Neugarten, B. L. (1976). Middle age and aging. In B. B. Hess (Ed.), *Growing old in America* (pp. 180–197). New Brunswick, NJ: Transaction.

Neugarten, B. L. (1977). Personality and aging. In J. E. Birren & K. W. Schaie (Eds.), *Handbook of the psychology of aging* (pp. 626–649). New York: Van Nostrand Reinhold.

Newman, P. C. (1979). *The Canadian establishment* (Vol. 1). Toronto: McClelland and Stewart.

Newman, P.C. (1999). *Titans: How the new Canadian establishment seized power.* Toronto: Penguin Books Canada Ltd.

Niebuhr, H. R. (1929). *The social sources of denominationalism.* New York: Holt.

Niosi, J. (1981). *Canadian capitalism: A study of power in the Canadian business establishment* (R. Chodos, Trans.). Toronto: Lorimer.

Noah, T. (1994, January 4). White House forms panel to investigate Cold War radiation tests on humans. *Wall Street Journal,* p. A12.

Noble, D. F. (1995). *Progress without people: New technology, unemployment, and the message of resistance.* Toronto: Between the Lines.

Norland, J. A. (1994). *Focus on Canada: Profile of Canada's seniors.* Ottawa: Statistics Canada and Prentice Hall Canada, Inc.

Novak, M. (1993). *Aging and society: A Canadian perspective* (2nd ed.). Toronto: Nelson Canada.

Nsamenang, A. B. (1992). *Human development in cultural context: A third world perspective.* Newbury Park, CA: Sage.

Oberschall, A. (1973). *Social conflict and social movements.* Englewood Cliffs, NJ: Prentice Hall.

O'Bireck, G. M. (1993). *Gettin' tall: Cocaine use within a subculture of Canadian professional musicians: An ethnographic inquiry.* Toronto: Canadian Scholars' Press.

O'Brien, C.-A., & Goldberg, A. (2000). Lesbians and gay men inside and outside families. In N. Mandell & A. Duffy (Eds.), *Canadian families: Diversity, conflict and change* (pp. 115–145). Toronto: Harcourt Brace Canada.

O'Brien, J. E. (1975). Violence in divorce-prone families. In S. K. Steinmetz & M. A. Straus (Eds.). *Violence in the family* (65–75). New York: Dodd, Mead.

Oderkirk, J. (1996, Spring). Government sponsored income security programs for seniors: An overview. *Canadian Social Trends, 40,* 2–15.

Offen, K. (1990). Feminism and sexual difference in historical perspective. In D. L. Rhode (Ed.), *Theoretical perspectives on sexual difference* (pp. 13–20). New Haven, CT: Yale University Press.

Ogburn, W. F. (1922). *Social change with respect to culture and human nature.* New York: W. B. Huebsch. (Other editions by Viking 1927, 1938, and 1950).

Ogburn, W. F. (1961). The hypothesis of cultural lag. In T.Parsons, E. Shils, K. D. Naegele, & J. R. Pitts (Eds.), *Theories of society: Foundations of modern sociological theory* (Vol. 2, pp. 1270–1273). New York: Free Press.

Ogburn, W. F. (1964). *On culture and social change: Selected papers,* O. D. Duncan (Ed.) Chicago: University of Chicago Press.

O'Hara, J. (1998, May 25). Rape in the military. *Maclean's, 3*(21), 14–21.

O'Hare, W. P. (1996b, October). U.S. poverty myths explored: Many poor work year-round, few still poor after five years. *Population Today: News, Numbers, and Analysis, 24*(10), 1–2.

Ohmae, K. (1995). *The end of the nation state: The rise of regional economies.* New York: Free Press.

Oliver, P. E., & Marwell, G. (1992). Mobilizing technologies for collective action. In A. D. Morris & C. C. Mueller (Eds.), *Frontiers in social movement theory* (pp. 251–272). New Haven, CT: Yale University Press.

Olmsted, M.S., & Hare, A. P. (1978). *The small group* (2nd ed.). New York: Random House.

Olneck, M. R., & Bills, D. B. (1980). What makes Sammy run? An empirical assessment of the Bowles-Gintis correspondence theory. *American Journal of Education, 89,* 27–61.

Olsen, D. (1980). *The state elite.* Toronto: McClelland and Stewart.

Olshansky, S. J., Carnes, B., Rogers, R. G., & Smith, L. (1997, July). Infectious diseases—New and ancient threats to world health. *Population Bulletin, 52*(2), 1–51.

O'Neill, H. (1997, April 6). Strange, strange worlds. *Alton Telegraph,* A10.

Oosthoek, S. (1999, September 13). Is greed fuelling the need for two-income families? *The Toronto Star,* p. E6.

Ortega, S. T., & Corzine, J. (1990). Socioeconomic status and mental disorders. *Research in Community and Mental Health, 6,* 149–182.

Orwell, G. (1949). *1984.* New York: Harcourt Brace.

Orwen, P. (1999, September 11). How day care crisis traps Moms. *Toronto Star,* pp. A1, A30.

Orwen, P. (2002, May 8). Child abuse caseload 24 000 and growing. *Toronto Star,* p. A2.

Orwen, P. (2002, June 10). Canada not keeping pledge to halve hunger. *Toronto Star,* p. A17.

Ouchi, W. (1981). *Theory Z: How American business can meet the Japanese challenge.* Reading, MA: Addison-Wesley.

Ouchi, W. (1993). Decision-making in Japanese organizations. In J. M. Henslin (Ed.), *Down to earth sociology: Introductory readings* (7th ed., pp. 503–507). New York: Free Press.

Overvold, A. Z. (1988). *Surrogate parenting*. New York: Pharos.

Pagelow, M. D. (1992, March). Adult victims of domestic violence: Battered women. *Journal of Interpersonal Violence, 7*(1), 87–120.

Palen, J. J. (1987). *The Urban World* (3rd ed.). New York: McGraw-Hill.

Parfit, M. (1990, April). Earth First!ers wield a mean monkey wrench. *Smithsonian, 21*(1), 184–204.

Park, R. E., & Burgess, E. W. (1921a). *Human ecology*. Chicago: University of Chicago Press.

Park, R. E., & Burgess, E. W. (1921b). *Introduction to the science of sociology*. Chicago: University of Chicago Press. (As quoted in McPhail 1991: 6).

Park, R. E. (1936, July). Human ecology. *American Journal of Sociology, 42*(1), 1–15.

Parsons, T. (1940). An analytic approach to the theory of social stratification. *American Journal of Sociology, 45,* 841–862.

Parsons, T. (1953). Illness and the role of the physician: A sociological perspective. In C. Kluckhohn & H. A. Murray (Eds.). *Personality in nature, society, and culture* (2nd ed., pp. 609–617). New York: Knopf.

Parsons, T. (1954). The professions and social structure. In T. Parsons (Ed.), *Essays in Sociological Theory* (Rev. ed., pp. 34–49). New York: Free Press.

Parsons, T. (1975, Summer). The sick role and the role of the physician reconsidered. *Milbank Memorial Fund Quarterly/Health and Society, 53*(3), 257–278.

Pasternak, J. (2002, October). Definition of ageism. *50 Plus*, pp. 99–100.

Pearl, D. (1995a, September 7). Futurist Schlock: Today's cyberhype has a familiar ring. *Wall Street Journal,* :A1, A6.

Pearson, J. L., Conwell, Y., Lindesay, J., Takahasi, Y., & Caine, E. D. (1997, May). Elderly suicide: A multi-national view. *Aging and Mental Health, 1*(2), 107–111.

Peart, K. N. (1993, October 22). Converts to the faith. *Scholastic Update, 126*(4), 16–18.

Pennar, K., & Farrell, C. (1993, February 15). Notes from the underground economy. *Business Week*, 98–101.

Peritz, I. (2000, February 22). Sex-change Soldier Hails Canada's Liberal Attitudes. *The Globe and Mail*, pp. A1, A17.

Perrin, K. (1994). Rationing health care: Should it be done? In R. B. Enright, Jr. (Ed.), *Perspectives in social gerontology* (pp. 309–314). Boston: Allyn and Bacon.

Perrow, C. (1991, December). A society of organizations. *Theory and Society, 20*(6), 725–762.

Persell, C. H, Catsambis, S. & Cookson, P. W., Jr. (1992). Family background, school type, and college attendance: A conjoint system of cultural capital transmission. *Journal of Research on Adolescence, 2*(1), 1–23.

Peter, L. J., Hull, R. (1969). *The Peter Principle: Why things always go wrong*. New York: Morrow.

Petras, J., & Veltmeyer, H. (2001). *Globalization unmasked: Imperialism in the 21st century*. Halifax: Fernwood Books.

Phillips, J. L., Jr. (1969). *The origins of intellect: Piaget's theory*. San Francisco: Freeman.

Phillips, P., & Phillips, E. (1993). *Women and work: Inequality in the Canadian Labour Market*. 2nd Edition. Toronto: James Lorimer.

Philp, M. (2000, June 5). Canadians enjoy long and healthy lives: But 12th-place ranking lags behind nations with more aggressive programs. *The Globe and Mail*.

Piaget, Jean. (1950). *The psychology of intelligence*. London: Routledge & Kegan Paul.

Piaget, J. (1954). *The construction of reality in the child*. New York: Basic Books.

Pillemer, K., & Suitor, J. J. (1992). Violence and violent feelings: What causes them among family caregivers? *Journal of Gerontology, 47*(4), 165–172.

Pillemer, K., & Wolf, R. S. (1987). *Elder abuse: Conflict in the family*. Dover, Mass.: Auburn House.

Pilling, D., & Pringle, M. K. (1978). *Controversial issues in child development*. London: Paul Elek.

Pines, M. (1981, September). The civilizing of Genie. *Psychology Today, 15,* 28–34.

Piotrow, P. T. (1973). *World population crisis: The United States' response*. New York: Praeger.

Pipher, M. (1999). *Another Country: Navigating the Emotional Terrain of Our Elders*. New York: Riverhead Books.

Pittaway, E.D., Westhues, A., & Peressini, T. (1995, Summer). Risk factors for abuse and neglect among older adults. *Canadian Journal of Aging, 14*(Supplement 2), 20–44.

Piturro, M. (1991, May–June). Managing diversity. *Executive Female,* 45–46, 48.

Piven, F. F, & Cloward, R. A. (1988). *Why Americans don't vote*. New York: Pantheon Books.

Platt, T. (1978). "Street" crime—A view from the left. *Crime and Social Justice: Issues in Criminology,* 9, 26–34.

Pollard, J. (2001, Fall). The Impact of Religious Affiliation and Religious Practices on Attitudes toward Euthanasia. *York University Institute for Social Research Newsletter,* 16, pp. 1–4.

Polsby, N. W. (1959, December). Three problems in the analysis of community power. *American Sociological Review, 24*(6), 796–803.

Polumbaum, J. (1992, September–October). China: Confucian tradition meets the market economy. *Ms.*, 12–13.

Ponting, J. R. (Ed.). (1986). *Arduous Journey: Canadian Indians and Decolonization*. Toronto: McClelland and Stewart.

Ponting, J. R. (1994). Turning up the heat. In D. Glenday & A. Duffy (Eds.), *Canadian society: Understanding and surviving the 1990s* (pp. 86–116). Toronto: McClelland and Stewart.

Ponting, J. R. (1998). Racism and Stereotyping of First Nations. In V. Satzewich (Ed.), *Racism and Social Inequality in Canada: Concepts, Controversies and Strategies of Resistance* (pp. 269-298). Toronto: Thompson Educational Publishing, Inc.

Pope, L. (1942). *Millhands and preachers: A study of Gastonia*. New Haven, CT: Yale University Press.

Population, consumption, and the earth's future. (1996, April). *Population Today,* 4.

Population Reference Bureau. (1995, May). World information data sheet. Washington, DC.

Population update. (1997, April). *Population Today, 25*(4), 6.

Porter, J. (1965). *The vertical mosaic: An analysis of social class and power in Canada*. Toronto: University of Toronto Press.

Porter, J., Porter, M., & Blishen, B. (1979). *Does money matter?* (Rev. ed.). Toronto: Macmillan.

Portés, A., & Rumbaut, R. G. (1990). *Immigrant America*. Berkeley: University of California Press.

Postman, N. (1992). *Technopoly: The surrender of culture to technology*. New York: Knopf.

Prasil, S. (1993, Autumn). Seniors 75+ lifestyles. *Canadian Social Trends,* 26–29.

Prentice, A. (1977). *The school promoters: Education and social class in mid-nineteenth century Upper Canada*. Toronto: McClelland and Stewart.

Pupo, N. (1997). Always working, never done: The expansion of the double day. In A. Duffy, D. Glenday, & N. Pupo (Eds.), *Good jobs, bad jobs, no jobs: The transformation of work in the 21st century* (pp. 144–165). Toronto: Harcourt Brace & Company Canada.

Puxley, C. (2002, January 25). Students hard at work outside of class, study finds. *Toronto Star*, p. A4.

Pyper, W. (2002, Autumn). Falling behind. *Perspectives on Labour and Income,* 14, pp. 21–27.

Quinn, J. (2002, March 31). Food bank clients often well-educated immigrants. *Toronto Star*, p. A12.

Raphael, D. (2001, August 20). Poverty is at root of heart disease. *Toronto Star*, p. A17.

Rathus, S., & Nevid, J. (1993). *Human Sexuality in a World of Diversity*. Boston: Allyn and Bacon.

Raymond, C. (1990, December 19). New studies by anthropologists indicate Amish communities are much more dynamic and diverse than many believed. *Chronicle of Higher Education*, pp. A1, A9.

Raymond, J. G. (1993). *Women as wombs: Reproductive technologies and the battle over women's freedom*. New York: HarperCollins.

Read, P. P. (1974). *Alive. The story of the Andes survivors*. Philadelphia: Lippincott.

Reed, S., & Benet, L. (1990, April 16). Ecowarrior Dave Foreman will do whatever it takes in his fight to save Mother Earth. *People Weekly, 33*(15), 113–116.

Rees, W. E. (2002, April 22). Squeezing the poor. *Toronto Star*, p. A17.

Reibstein, L. (1996, November 25). Managing diversity. *Newsweek*, 50.

Reich, M. (1972). The economics of racism. In R. C. Edwards, M. Reich, & T. E. Weiskopf (Eds.), *The capitalist system* (pp. 313–321). Englewood Cliffs, NJ: Prentice Hall.

Reich, R. B. (1995, March). *Good for business: Making full use of the nation's human capital, the environmental scan*. Washington, DC: U.S. Department of Labor.

Reiman, J. (2001). *The Rich Get Richer and the Poor Get Prison: Ideology, Class and Criminal Justice*. Boston: Allyn and Bacon.

Reinharz, S. (1997). Friends or foes: Gerontological and feminist theory. In M. Pearsall (Ed.), *The Other within Us: Feminist Explorations of Women and Aging* (pp. 73–94). Boulder, Colo.: Westview.

Reitman, V., Suris, O. (1994, November 21). In a cultural u-turn, Mazda's creditors put Ford behind the wheel. *Wall Street Journal*, pp. A1, A4.

Renteln, A. D. (1992). Sex selection and reproductive freedom. *Women's Studies International Forum, 15*(3), 405–426.

Renzetti, C. M., & Curran, D. J. (1992). *Women, men, and society* (2nd ed.). Boston: Allyn and Bacon.

Requena, F. (2001). Family, socialization and development in Spain: A cross-national comparison with the United States. *International Journal of Comparative Studies, XLII* (4), pp. 369–387.

Reynolds, C. (1998). The educational system. In N. Mandell (Ed.), *Feminist issues: Race, class and sexuality* (pp. 233–248). Scarborough: Prentice Hall Allyn and Bacon Canada.

Richards, B. (1996, January 17). Doctors can diagnose illnesses long distance, to the dismay of some. *Wall Street Journal*, pp. A1, A8.

Richer, S. (2002, October 23). Gay couple welcomes recognition in census. *The Globe and Mail*, p. A7.

Ricks, T. E. (1994, February 14). Pentagon considers selling overseas a large part of high-tech weaponry. *Wall Street Journal*, p. A16.

Rieker, P. P., Bird, C. E., Bell, S., Ruducha, J., Rudd, R. E., & Miller, S. M. (1997). Violence and women's health: Toward a society and health perspective. Unpublished paper.

Riesman, D. (1970). The suburban dislocation. In A. N. Cousins & H. Nagpaul (Eds.), *Urban man and society: A reader in urban ecology* (pp. 172–184). New York: Knopf.

Riessman, C. K. (1994). Women and medicalization: A new perspective. In H. D. Schwartz (Ed.), *Dominant issues in medical sociology* (3rd ed., pp. 190–211). New York: McGraw-Hill.

Rifkin, J. (1995). *The end of work: The decline of the global labor force and the dawn of the post-market era*. New York: Putnam.

Rigdon, J. E., & Swasy, A. (1990, October 1). Distractions of modern life at key ages are cited for drop in student literacy. *Wall Street Journal*, pp. B1, B3.

Righton, B. (2002, October). Well Done. *50 Plus*, pp. 42–46.

Riley, N. E. (1997, May). Gender, power, and population change. *Population Bulletin, 52*(1), 1–47.

Rinehart, J. (1996). *The tyranny of work: Alienation and the labour process* (3rd ed.). Toronto: Harcourt Brace.

Rist, R. C. (1970, August). Student social class and teacher expectations: The self-fulfilling prophecy in ghetto education. *Harvard Educational Review, 40*(3), 411–451.

Ristock, J. (2002). *No More Secrets: Violence in Lesbian Relationships*.

Ritzer, G. (1992). *Sociological theory*, (3rd ed.). New York: McGraw-Hill.

Ritzer, G. (1993). *The McDonaldization of society: An investigation into the changing character of contemporary life*. Thousand Oaks, CA: Pine Forge Press.

Ritzer, G. (1997). The McDonaldization of society. In J. M. Henslin (Ed.), *Down to earth sociology: Introductory readings* (9th ed., pp. 492–504). New York: Free Press.

Ritzer, G. (1998). *The McDonaldization Thesis: Explorations and Extensions*. London: Sage Publications.

Roberts, S. D. & Zhou, N. (1997, June). The 50 and older characters in advertisements of modern maturity: Growing older, getting better. *Journal of Applied Gerontology, 16*(2), 208–220.

Robertson, I. (1976). Social stratification. In D. E. Hunter & P. Whitten (Eds.), *The study of anthropology*, New York: Harper & Row.

Robertson, I. (1987). *Sociology* (3rd ed.). New York: Worth.

Robertson, R. (1992). *Globalization: Social theory and global culture*. London: Sage.

Robinson, A.B., & Robinson, Z. W. (1997, December 4). Science has spoken: Global warming is a myth. *Wall Street Journal*, p. A22.

Rodríguez, V. M. (1994, Spring). Los Angeles, USA 1992: A house divided against itself.... *SSSP Newsletter*, 5–12.

Roethlisberger, F. J., & Dickson, W. J. (1939). *Management and the worker*. Cambridge, MA: Harvard University Press.

Rosaldo, M. Z. (1974). Women, culture and society: A theoretical overview. In M. Z. Rosaldo & L. Lamphere (Eds.). *Women, culture, and society*, Stanford: Stanford University Press.

Rose, F. (1992, May 5). Los Angeles tallies losses; curfew is lifted. *Wall Street Journal*, pp. A3, A18.

Rose, S. (1986). Stalking the criminal chromosome. *Nation, 242*(20), 732–736.

Rosenberg, C. E. (1987). *The care of strangers: The rise of America's hospital system*. New York: Basic Books.

Rosenthal, E. (1996, January 1). From lives begun in lab, brave new joy. *New York Times*, p. A1.

Rosenthal, E. (1999, December 9). China's chic waistline: Convex to concave. *New York Times*.

Rosenthal, R., & Jacobson, L. (1968). *Pygmalion in the classroom: Teacher expectation and pupils' intellectual development*. New York: Holt, Rinehart, and Winston.

Ross, David P., Scott, K, & Kelly, M. (1996). *Child poverty: What are the consequences?* Ottawa: Canadian Council on Social Development.

Ross, D. P., Scott, K. J., & Smith, P. J. (2000). *The Canadian fact book on poverty*. Ottawa: Canadian Council on Social Development.

Ross, O. (2002, July 20). World shows Canada how to cope with elderly. *Toronto Star*, p. E8.

Rossi, A. S. (1977). A biosocial perspective on parenting. *Daedalus, 106*, 1–31.

Rossi, A. S. (1984). Gender and parenthood. *American Sociological Review, 49*, 1–18.

Rossi, P. H. (1989). *Down and out in America: The origins of homelessness*. Chicago: University of Chicago Press.

Rossi, P. H. (1991). Going along or getting it right? *Journal of Applied Sociology, 8*, 77–81.

Rossi, P. H., Fisher, G. A., & Willis, G. (1986, September). *The condition of the homeless of Chicago*. Amherst: University of Massachusetts.

Rossi, P.H., Wright, J. D., Fisher, G. A. & Willis, G. (1987, March 13). The urban homeless: Estimating composition and size. *Science, 235,* 1136–1140.

Rotello, G. (1996, July 14). The risk in a "cure" for AIDS. *New York Times.*

Rothman, B. K. (1989). *Recreating motherhood: Ideology and technology in a patriarchal society.* New York: Norton.

Rothschild, J., & Whitt, J. A. (1986). *The cooperative workplace: Potentials and dilemmas of organizational democracy and participation.* Cambridge, England: Cambridge University Press.

Rubenstein, C. (1992). Is there sex after baby? In J. M. Henslin (Ed.), *Marriage and family in a changing society* (4th ed., pp. 235–242). New York: Free Press.

Rubin, L. B. (1976). *Worlds of pain: Life in the working-class family.* New York: Basic Books.

Rubin, L. B. (1992a). The empty nest. In J. M. Henslin (Ed.), *Marriage and family in a changing society* (4th ed., pp. 261–270). New York: Free Press.

Rubin, L. B. (1992b). Worlds of pain. In J. M. Henslin (Ed.), *Marriage and family in a changing society* (4th ed., pp. 44–50). New York: Free Press.

Rudd, J. (2001). Dowry-Murder: An example of violence against women. *Women's Studies International Forum, 24,* pp. 513–522.

Ruggles, P. (1989, June). Short and long term poverty in the United States: Measuring the American "underclass." Washington, DC: Urban Institute.

Rushing, W. A. (1995). *The AIDS epidemic: Social dimensions of an infectious disease.* Boulder, CO: Westview Press.

Rushowy, K. (2000, March 23). Tuition deters poor, study finds. *Toronto Star,* p. A8.

Russell, D. E. H. Preliminary report on some findings relating to the trauma and long-term effects of intrafamily childhood sexual abuse. Unpublished paper.

Russell, D. E. H. (1990). *Rape in marriage.* Bloomington: Indiana University Press.

Russell, D. (1987, Fall). The monkeywrenchers. *Amicus Journal,* 28–42.

Sainath, P. (1996). *Everybody loves a good drought.* London: Review.

Salazar, L. P., Schludermann, S. M., Schuldermann, E. H., & Huynh, C.-L. (2001). Canadian Filipino adolescents report on parental socialization for school involvement. *Canadian Ethnic Studies, XXXIII* (2), pp. 52–77.

Samuelson, P. A., & Nordhaus, W. D. (1989). *Economics* (13th ed.). New York: McGraw-Hill.

Sanchez, L. (1994, December). Gender, labor allocations, and the psychology of entitlement within the home. *Social Forces, 13*(2), 533–553.

Sandefur, G. D. (1995, Summer). Children in single-parent families: The roles of time and money. *Focus, 17*(1), 44–45.

Sapir, E. (1949a). The status of linguistics as science. In D. G. Mandelbaum (Ed.), *Culture, language, and personality.* Berkeley, CA: University of California Press.

Sapir, E. (1949b). Selected writings of Edward Sapir. In D. G. Mandelbaum (Ed.), *Culture, language, and personality.* Berkeley, CA: University of California Press.

Sarlo, C. (1992). *Poverty in Canada.* Vancouver: The Fraser Institute.

Saturday Special. (2002, March 23). *Toronto Star,* pp. A24, 25.

Sawatsky, J. (1980). *Men in the Shadows: The RCMP Security Service.* Toronto: Doubleday Canada.

Sayres, W. (1992). What is a family anyway? In J. M. Henslin (Ed.), *Marriage and family in a changing society* (4th ed., pp. 23–30). New York: Free Press.

Scarce, R. (1993a, June 12–13). Rik Scarce responds: A clear-cut case of academic freedom at risk. *Daily News* (Moscow-Pullman), p. 1B.

Scarce, R. (1993b, June 15). Turnabout: Jailed for no crime at all. *Morning Tribune* (Lewiston).

Scarce, R. (1994, July). (No) trial (but) tribulations. *Journal of Contemporary Ethnography, 23*(2), 123–149.

Scarr, S., & Eisenberg, M. (1993). Child care research: Issues, perspectives, and results. *Annual Review of Psychology, 44,* 613–644.

Schaefer, R. T. (1979). *Racial and ethnic groups.* Boston: Little Brown.

Schaefer, R. T. (1989). *Sociology* (3rd ed.) New York: McGraw-Hill.

Schlesinger, J. M. (1994, January 31). For what ails Japan, some think the cure is a good hot slogan. *Wall Street Journal,* pp. A1, A7.

Schlesinger, J. M., & Sapsford, J. (1993, December 1). Japan, shaken by plunging stocks, mulls further economic measures. *Wall Street Journal,* p. A14.

Schlesinger, J. M., Williams, M. & Forman, C. (1993, September 29). Japan inc., wracked by recession, takes stock of its methods. *Wall Street Journal,* pp. A1, A4.

Schlossberg, N. (1990). *Overwhelmed: Coping with life's ups and downs.* Boston: Lexington Books.

Schlosser, E. (2002). *Fast food nation: The dark side of the all-American meal.* New York: Perennial Books.

Schrieke, B. J. (1936). *Alien Americans.* New York: Viking.

Schur, E. M. (1984). *Labeling women deviant: Gender, stigma, and social control.* New York: Random House.

Schwartz, F. N. (1989, January–February). Management women and the new facts of life. *Harvard Business Review, 89*(1), 65–76.

Schwartz, M. A. (1990). *A sociological perspective on politics.* Englewood Cliffs, NJ: Prentice Hall.

Scommegna, P. (1996, August). Teens' risk of AIDS, unintended pregnancies examined. *Population Today, 24*(8), 1–2.

Scott, E. K. (1993, August). How to stop the rapists: A question of strategy in two rape crisis centers. *Social Problems, 40*(3), 343–361.

Scully, D. (1990). *Understanding sexual violence: A study of convicted rapists.* Boston: Unwin Hyman.

Scully, D. (1994). Negotiating to do surgery. In H. D. Schwartz (Ed.), *Dominant issues in medical sociology* (3rd ed., pp. 146–152). New York: McGraw-Hill.

Scully, D., & Marolla, J. (1984, June). Convicted rapists' vocabulary of motive: excuses and justifications. *Social Problems, 31*(5), 530–544.

Scully, D., & Marolla, J. (1985, February). Riding the bull at Gilley's: Convicted rapists describe the rewards of rape. *Social Problems, 32*(3), 251–263.

Searle, J. R. (1995). *The construction of social reality.* New York: Free Press.

Seaver, W. J. (1973). Effects of naturally induced teacher expectancies. *Journal of Personality and Social Psychology, 28,* 333–342.

Selvan, M. S., Ross, M. W., Kapadia, A.S., Mathai, R., & Hira, S. (2001). Study of perceived norms, beliefs and intended sexual behaviour among higher secondary school students in India. *AIDS CARE,* 13 (6), pp. 779–788.

Sennett, R., & Cobb, J. (1972). *The hidden injuries of class.* New York: Knopf.

Sennett, R., & Cobb, J. (1988), Some hidden injuries of class. In J. M. Henslin (Ed.), *Down to earth sociology: Introductory readings* (5th ed., pp. 278–288). New York: Free Press.

Seubert, V. R. (1991, Fall–Winter).Sociology and value neutrality: Limiting sociology to the empirical level. *American Sociologist,* 210–220.

Sexual identity is inborn trait, according to study. (1997, March 16). *Alton Telegraph,* p. A6.

Shalla, V. (1997). Technology and the deskilling of work: The case of passenger agents at Air Canada. In A. Duffy, D. Glenday, & N. Pupo (Eds.), *Good jobs, bad jobs, no jobs: The transformation of work in the 21st century.* Toronto: Harcourt Brace.

Shanker, A. (1995, September 15). Education contract with America. *Wall Street Journal,* p. A10.

Sharma, S. S. (1994). Untouchables and Brahmins in an Indian village. In J. Curtis & L. Tepperman (Eds.), *Haves and have-nots: An international reader on social inequality* (pp. 299–303). Englewood Cliffs, NJ: Prentice Hall.

Sharp, L. (1995). Steel axes for stone-age Australians. In J. M. Henslin (Ed.), *Down to earth sociology: Introductory readings* (8th ed., pp. 453–462). New York: Free Press.

Shaw, S. M., & Lee, J. (2001). *Women's voices, feminist visions: Classic and contemporary readings*. Mountain View, California: Mayfield Publishing Company.

Sheldon, W. (1949). *Varieties of delinquent youth: An introduction to constitutional psychiatry*. New York: Harper.

Shellenbarger, S. (1994a, February 16). The aging of America is making "elder care" a big workplace issue. *Wall Street Journal*, pp. A1, A8.

Shellenbarger, S. (1994b, February 16). How some companies help with elder care. *Wall Street Journal*, p. A8.

Shellenbarger, S. (1995a, February 6). Child care is worse than believed, with safety jeopardized, study suggests. *Wall Street Journal*, p. A7.

Shenon, P. (1995, January 2). AIDS epidemic, late to arrive, now explodes in populous Asia. *New York Times*, pp. A1, A12.

Shenon, P. (1997, August 26). Arguments conclude in army sex hearing. [Electronic version]. *New York Times*

Sherif, M., & Sherif, C. (1953). *Groups in harmony and tension*. New York: Harper & Row.

Sherman, B. (1985). *Working at Leisure*. London: Methuen.

Shibutani, T. (1966). *Improvised news: A sociological study of rumor*. Indianapolis, IN: Bobbs-Merrill.

Shibutani, T. (1970). On the personification of adversaries. In T. Shibutani (Ed.), *Human nature and collective behavior*. Englewood Cliffs, NJ: Prentice Hall.

Shields, M., & Tremblay, S. (2002). *The Health of Canada's Communities*. Statistics Canada: Supplement to Health Reports, 13, Catalogue 82-003.

Shill, W. (1993, November 1). Lessons of the Japanese mavericks. *Wall Street Journal*, p. A18.

Shirouzu, N., & Williams. M. (1995, July 25). Pummeled by giants, Japan's small firms struggle with change. *Wall Street Journal*, pp. A1, A5.

Signorielli, N. (1989). Television and conceptions about sex roles: Maintaining conventionality and the status quo. *Sex Roles, 21*(5/6), 341–360.

Signorielli, N. (1990). Children, television, and gender roles: Messages and impact. *Journal of Adolescent Heath Care, 11*, 50–58.

Sills, D. L. (1957). *The Volunteers*. Glencoe, IL: Free Press.

Sills, D. L. (1968). Voluntary associations: Sociological aspects. In D. L. Sills (Ed.), *International Encyclopedia of the Social Sciences, 16* (pp. 362–379). New York: Macmillan.

Silver, I. (1977, March–April). Crime and conventional wisdom. *Society, 14*(9), 15–19.

Silvera, M. (1989). *Silenced*. Toronto: Sister Vision.

Simmel, G. (1950). *The sociology of Georg Simmel* (K.H. Wolff, Ed. and Trans.). Glencoe, Ill.: Free Press. (First published between 1902 and 1917)

Simon, D. R., & Eitzen, D. S. (1993). *Elite deviance* (4th ed.). Boston: Allyn and Bacon.

Simon, J. L. (1981). *The ultimate resource*. Princeton, NJ: Princeton University Press.

Simon, J. L. (1986). *Theory of population and economic growth*. New York: Blackwell.

Simon, J. L. (1992). Population growth is not bad for humanity. In K. Finsterbusch & G. McKenna (Eds.), *Taking sides: Clashing views on controversial social issues* (p. 347–352). Guilford, CT: Dushkin.

Simon, J. L. (1996). *The ultimate resource 2*. Princeton, NJ: Princeton University Press.

Simpson, G. E., & Yinger, J. M. (1972). *Racial and cultural minorities: An analysis of prejudice and discrimination* (4th ed.). New York: Harper & Row.

Singh, A. (1988). Urbanism, poverty, and employment: The large metropolis in the third world. Unpublished monograph, Cambridge University. As quoted in Giddens, A. (1991).*Introduction to Sociology* (p. 690). New York: W. W. Norton.

Sloat, L. (1998). Incubus: Male songwriters' portrayal of women's sexuality in pop metal music. In J. S. Epstein (Ed.), *Youth culture: Identity in a postmodern world* (pp. 286–301). Malden, MA: Blackwell.

Small, A. W. (1905). *General sociology*. Chicago: University of Chicago Press. As cited in Olmsted and Hare (1978) p. 10.

Smart, B. (1990, August). On the disorder of things: Sociology, postmodernity and the "end of the social." *Sociology, 24*(3), 397–416.

Smith, B. A. (1992). An incest case in an early 20th-century rural community. *Deviant Behavior, 13*, 127–153.

Smith, C. S. (1995, October 9). China becomes industrial nations' most favored dump. *Wall Street Journal*, p. B1.

Smith, D. E. (1987). *The everyday world as problematic: A feminist sociology*. Boston: Northeastern University Press.

Smith, D. E. (1990). *Texts, facts and femininity: Exploring the relations of ruling*. London: Routledge.

Smith, D. E. (1999). *Writing the social: Critique, theory, and investigations*. Toronto: University of Toronto Press.

Smith, D. A., & Brame, R. (1994). On the initiation and continuation of delinquency. *Criminology, 32*(4), 607–629.

Smith, J. B., & Tirpak, D. A. (1988, October). *The potential effects of global climate change in the United States*. Washington, DC: U.S. Environmental Protection Agency.

Smith, L. (1987, July 20). The war between the generations. *Fortune*, 78–82.

Smith, M., (Ed.). (1990). *Breaking chains: Social movements and collective action*. New Brunswick, NJ: Transaction Publishers.

Smith, T. M. (1996). *The condition of education 1996*. Washington, DC: U.S. Government Printing Office.

Smith-Lovin, L. & Brody, C. (1989). Interruptions in group discussions: The effects of gender and group composition. *American Sociological Review, 54*, 424–435.

Snow, D. A., Zurcher, L. A., & Peters, R. (1993). Victory celebrations as theater: A dramaturgical approach to crowd behavior. In R. L. Curtis, Jr., & B. E. Aguirre (Eds.), *Collective behavior and social movements* (pp. 194–208). Boston: Allyn and Bacon.

Snow, D. A., Zurcher, L. A., & Ekland-Olson, S. (1993). Social networks and social movements: A microstructural approach to differential recruitment. In R. L. Curtis, Jr., & B. E. Aguirre (Eds.), *Collective behavior and social movements* (pp. 323–334). Boston: Allyn and Bacon.

Snow, M. E., Jacklin, C. N. & Maccoby, E. E. (1981). Birth-order differences in peer sociability at thirty-three months. *Child Development, 52*, 589–595.

Snyder, M. (1993). Self-fulfilling stereotypes. In J. M. Henslin (Ed.), *Down to earth sociology: Introductory readings* (7th ed., pp. 153–160). New York: Free Press.

Solomon, J. (1988, December 29). Companies try measuring cost savings from new types of corporate benefits. *Wall Street Journal*, p. B1.

Sontag, S. (1994). As quoted in C. K. Riessman, Women and medicalization: A new perspective. In H. D. Schwartz (Ed.), *Dominant issues in medical sociology* (3rd ed., pp. 190–211). New York: McGraw-Hill.

Sowell, T. (1993a, September 27). Effrontery and Gall, Inc. *Forbes, 52*.

Specter, M. (1995, August 1). Plunging life expectancy puzzles Russians. *New York Times*, pp. A1, A6.

Spector, M., & Kitsuse, J. (1977). *Constructing social problems*. Menlo Park, CA: Cummings.

Spencer, H. (1884). *Principles of sociology* (3 vols.). New York: Appleton.

Spencer, M. (1996). *Foundations of modern sociology*, 7th Edition. Toronto: Prentice Hall.

Spitzer, S. (1975, June). Toward a Marxian theory of deviance. *Social Problems, 22*, 608–619.

Srole, L., et al. (1978). *Mental health in the metropolis: The midtown Manhattan study.* New York: New York University Press.

Stark, E. (1989). Friends through it all. In J. M. Henslin (Ed.). *Marriage and family in a changing society* (3rd ed., pp. 441–449). New York: Free Press.

Stark, R. (1989). *Sociology* (3rd ed.). Belmont, CA: Wadsworth.

Starna, W. A., & Watkins, R. (1991, Winter). Northern Iroquoian slavery. *Ethnohistory, 38*(1), 34–57.

Starrels, M. (1992, September). The evolution of workplace family policy research. *Journal of Family Issues, 13*(3), 259–278.

Statham, A., Miller, E. M., & Mauksch, H. O. (1988). The integration of work: Second-order analysis of qualitative research. In A. Statham, E. M. Miller, & H. O. Mauksch (Eds.), *The worth of women's work: A qualitative synthesis* (pp. 11–35). Albany, NY: State University of New York Press.

Statistical Abstract of the United States. (Published annually). Washington DC: Bureau of the Census.

Statistics Canada. (Selected years). *General Social Survey.*

Statistics Canada (1995). *Women in Canada: A statistical report* (3rd ed.). Ottawa: Minister of Industry.

Statistics Canada. (1997). *Income Distributions by Size in Canada*, Catalogue no. 13-207.

Statistics Canada (1997). 1996 census (CD-ROM). Ottawa: Minister of Supply and Services.

Statistics Canada (1998). *Education in Canada* (Catalogue 81-229). Ottawa: Minister of Supply and Services.

Statistics Canada (1998a). *Family incomes* (Catalogue 13-208). Ottawa: Minister of Supply and Services.

Statistics Canada (1998). *Labour force annual averages* (Catalogue 71-220). Ottawa: Minister of Supply and Services.

Statistics Canada (1999). *Historical labour force statistics 1998* (CD-ROM, 71 FOOO 4XCB). Ottawa: Minister of Supply and Services.

Statistics Canada. (1999). *Income in Canada.* Ottawa: Statistics Canada, Catalogue No. 75-202.

Statistics Canada (1999). *The 1999 Canada year book.* Ottawa: Minister of Industry.

Statistics Canada (2000). *Women in Canada 2000: A gender-based statistical report.* Ottawa: Minister of Industry.

Statistics Canada. (2000, May). *Education in Canada, 2000.* Ottawa: Minister of Supply and Services, Catalogue 81-229-XPB.

Statistics Canada. (2001). *Canada Year Book 2001.* Ottawa: Minister of Industry.

Statistics Canada. (2002). *CANSIM II*, Table 051-0010.

Statistics Canada. (2002). *Population by age groups.* Retrieved February 11, 2002 from http://www.statcan.ca/english/Pgdb/People/Population/demo31a.htm.

Statistics Canada. (2002). *Population projections for 2001, 2006, 2011, 2016, 2021 and 2026, July 1.* Retrieved February 11, 2002 from http://www.statcan.ca/english/Pgdb/People/Population/demo23b.htm.

Statistics Canada. (2002, March). *Labour force historical review 2001.* Catalogue no. 71F0004XCB.

Statistics Canada. (2002, April 26). Childcare services industry. *The Daily*, p. 1.

Statistics Canada. (2002f, May 7). *The Daily.* Ottawa: Minister of Industry.

Statistics Canada. (2002a). *Women in Canada: Work chapter updates.* Ottawa: Minister of Industry, Catalogue 89F0133XIE.

Statistics Canada. (2002b, October 22). *The Daily.* Ottawa: Minister of Industry.

Statistics Canada. (2002c, July). *General social survey—Changing conjugal life in Canada.* Ottawa: Minister of Industry, Catalogue 89-576-XIE.

Statistics Canada. (2002d, September 26). *The Daily.* Ottawa: Minister of Industry.

Statistics Canada. (2002e). *Family violence: A statistical profile.* Ottawa: Minister of Industry, Catalogue 85-224-XIE.

Stein, L. I. (1988). The doctor–nurse game. In J. M. Henslin (Ed.), *Down to earth sociology: Introductory readings* (5th ed., pp. 102–109). New York: Free Press.

Steinberg, L., Dornbusch, S., & Brown, B. (1996). *Beyond the classroom.* New York: Simon & Shuster.

Steinem, G. (1992). *Revolution from within.* Boston: Little, Brown and Company.

Stevens, A., & Lubman, S. (1992, May 1). Deciding moment of the trial may have been five months ago. *Wall Street Journal*, p. A6.

Stevenson, G. (1987). *The politics of Canada's airlines from Diefenbaker to Mulroney.* Toronto: University of Toronto Press.

Stinnett, N. (1992). Strong families. In J. M. Henslin (Ed.), *Marriage and family in a changing society* (4th ed., pp. 496–507). New York: Free Press.

Stockard, J., & Johnson, M. M. (1980). *Sex roles: Sex inequality and sex role development.* Englewood Cliffs, NJ: Prentice Hall.

Stockwell, J. (1989, February). The dark side of U.S. foreign policy. *Zeta Magazine*, 36–48.

Stodgill, R. M. (1974). *Handbook of leadership: A survey of theory and research.* New York: Free Press.

Stone, G. P. (1954, November). City shoppers and urban identification: Observations on the social psychology of city life. *American Journal of Sociology, 60*, 276–284.

Stone, M. H. (1989, September). Murder. *Psychiatric Clinics of North America, 12*(3), 643–651.

Stouffer, S.A., Lumsdaine, A. A., Lumsdaine, M. H., Williams, R. M. Jr., Smith, M. B., Janis, I. L., et al. (1949). *The American soldier: Combat and its aftermath* (Vol. 2). New York: Wiley.

Stout, H. (1992, June 4). Harvard team says that AIDS is accelerating. *Wall Street Journal*, p. B10.

Straus, R. A. (1991). The sociologist as a marketing research consultant. *Journal of Applied Sociology, 8*, 65–75.

Stryker, S. (1990). Symbolic interactionism: Themes and variations. In M. Rosenberg & R. H. Turner (Eds.), *Social psychology: Sociological perspectives* New Brunswick, NJ: Transaction.

Sulloway, F. J. (1997). *Born to rebel: Birth order, family dynamics, and creative lives.* New York: Vintage Books.

Sumner, W. G. (1906). *Folkways: A study in the sociological importance of usages, manners, customs, mores, and morals.* New York: Ginn.

Sun, L. H. (1993, February 16). A great leap back: Chinese women losing jobs, status as ancient ways subvert socialist ideal. *Washington Post*, p. A1.

Sunter, D. (2001, Spring). Demography and the Labour Market. *Perspectives on Labour and Income*, Catalogue 75-001-XPE.

Suslova, M. I. (2001, October). On the Socialization of young handicapped people. *Education and Society*, 43, pp. 64–69.

Sutherland, E. H. (1924). *Criminology.* Philadelphia: Lippincott.

Sutherland, E. H. (1947). *Principles of criminology* (4th ed.). Philadelphia: Lippincott.

Sutherland, E. H. (1949). *White collar crime.* New York: Dryden Press.

Sutherland, E. H., & Cressey, D. (1974). *Criminology* (9th ed.). Philadelphia: Lippincott.

Sutherland, E.H., Cressey, D. R., & Luckenbill, D. F. (1992). *Principles of criminology* (11th ed.). Dix Hills, NY: General Hall.

Swedish Institute, The. (1992, February). Fact sheets on Sweden.

Swedish Institute, The. (1990, July). Health and medical care in Sweden (pp. 1–4).

Sweeney, M. M. (2002, February). Two decades of family change: The shifting economic foundations of marriage. *American Sociological Review, 67*, pp. 132–147.

Sweezy, P. M., & Magdoff, H. (1992, March). Globalization—to what end? Part II. *Monthly Review, 43*(10), 1–19.

Swift, J. (1995). *Wheel of fortune: Work and life in the age of falling expectations*. Toronto: Between the Lines.

Sykes, G. M., & Matza, D. (1988). Techniques of neutralization. In J. M. Henslin (Ed.). *Down to earth sociology: Introductory readings* (5th ed., pp. 225–231). New York: Free Press. (First published 1957)

Szasz, T. S. (1986). *The myth of mental illness* (Rev. ed.). New York: Harper & Row.

Szasz, T. S. (1996). Mental illness is still a myth. In L. M. Salinger (Ed.), *Deviant behavior 96/97* (pp. 200–205). Guilford, CT: Dushkin.

Szelenyi, S. (1987). Social inequality and party membership: Patterns of recruitment in the Hungarian Socialist Workers' Party. *American Sociological Review, 52*, 559–573.

Talaga, T. (1999, September 26). How poor are caught in heart-attack trap. *The Toronto Star*, pp. A1, A8.

Tannen, D. (1990). *You just don't understand: Women and men in conversation*. New York: Morrow.

Taylor, R. J. (1998). *Education databank*. Waterloo: R. L. Taylor Publishing.

Taylor, V. (1997). Social movement continuity: The women's movement in abeyance. In D. McAdam & D. A. Snow (Eds.), *Social movements: Readings on their emergence, mobilization, and dynamics* (pp. 409–420). Los Angeles: Roxbury Publishing.

Thayer, S. (1988, March). Encounters. *Psychology Today*, 31–36.

Thimm, C, Rademacher, U., & Krus, L. (1998, February). Age stereotypes and patronizing messages: Features of age-adapted speech in technical instructions to the elderly. *Journal of Applied Communication Research, 26*(1), 66–82.

Thomas, D. (2001, Summer). Evolving family living arrangements of Canada's immigrants. *Canadian Social Trends, 61*, pp. 16–22.

Thomas, P. (1988, October 21). EPA predicts global impact from warming. *Wall Street Journal*, p. B5.

Thomas, P. (1991, October 22). U.S. examiners will scrutinize banks with poor minority-lending histories. *Wall Street Journal*, p. A2.

Thomas, R. R., Jr. (1990, March–April). From affirmative action to affirming diversity. *Harvard Business Review, 90*(2), 107–117.

Thompson, A. (2002, July 30). Ottawa will fight ruling on same-sex marriages. *Toronto Star*, p. A2.

Thompson, W. E. (1995). Hanging tongues: A sociological encounter with the assembly line. In J. M. Henslin (Ed.), *Down to earth sociology: Introductory readings* (9th ed., pp. 193–202). New York: Free Press.

Thornburg, D. (1994, November–December). Why wait for bandwidth? Schools can teleconference even with ordinary phone lines. *Electronic Learning, 14*(3), 20.

Thorne, B. (1990). Children and gender: Constructions of difference. In D. L. Rhode (Ed.), *Theoretical perspectives on sexual difference* (pp. 100–113). New Haven, CT: Yale University Press.

Thorne, B. (2000). Children and gender: Constructions of difference. In M. Zinn, P. Hondagneu-Sotelo, & M. Messner (Eds.), *Sex and gender through the prism of difference* (2nd ed., pp. 30–41). Boston: Allyn and Bacon.

Thorne, B., & Luria, Z. (1993). Sexuality and gender in children's daily worlds. In J. M. Henslin (Ed.), *Down to earth sociology: Introductory readings* (7th ed., pp. 133–144). New York: Free Press.

Tilly, C. (1978). *From mobilization to revolution*. Reading, MA: Addison-Wesley.

Timasheff, N. S. (1965). *War and revolution* (J.F. Scheuer, Ed.). New York: Sheed & Ward.

Timerman, J. (1981). *Prisoner without a name, cell without a number*. New York: Knopf.

Timmermans, S. (1998, March). Resuscitation technology in the emergency department: Towards a dignified death. *Sociology of Health and Illness, 20*(2), 144–167.

Tinkler, P. (2001). Rebellion, modernity and romance: Smoking as a gendered practice in popular young women's magazines, Britain 1918–1939. *Women's Studies International Forum, 24* (1), pp. 111–122.

Titchkosky, T. (2001, May). Disability: A rose by any other name? 'People-first' language in Canadian society. *Canadian Review of Sociology and Anthropology, 38*, pp. 125–140.

Tobias, A. (1995, May 31). The "don't be ridiculous" law. *Wall Street Journal*, p. A14.

Toby, J. (1992, March 23). To get rid of guns in schools, get rid of some students. *Wall Street Journal*, p. A12.

Toch, T. (1993, November 8). Violence in schools. *U.S. News & World Report, 115*(18), 31–36.

Tocqueville, A. de. (1966). *Democracy in America* (J. P. Mayer & M. Lerner, Eds.). New York: Harper & Row. (First published 1835)

Tocqueville, A. de. (1955). *The old regime and the French Revolution* (S. Gilbert,Trans.). Garden City, NY: Doubleday Anchor. (First published 1856).

Toddlers' use of drugs soars. (2000, February 23). *Toronto Star*, p. A1.

Tolchin, M. (1988, May 17). Surgeon general asserts smoking is an addiction. *New York Times*, pp. A1, C4.

Tönnies, F. (1988). *Community and society (Gemeinschaft und Gesellschaft)*, with a new introduction by J. Samples. New Brunswick, NJ: Transaction (First published 1887).

Tordoff, W. (1992). The impact of ideology on development in the third world. *Journal of International Development, 4*(1), 41–53.

Totten, M. D. (2000). *Guys, gangs and girlfriend abuse*. Peterborough, Ontario: Broadview Press.

Townsend-Batten, B. (2002, Spring). Staying in touch: Contact between adults and their parents. *Canadian Social Trends*, pp. 9–12.

Treiman, D. J. (1977). *Occupational prestige in comparative perspective*. New York: Academic Press.

Trice, H. M., & Beyer, J. M. (1991, May). Cultural leadership in organization. *Organization Science, 2*(2), 149–169.

Troeltsch, E. (1931). *The social teachings of the Christian churches*. New York: Macmillan.

Tucker, B. M., & Mitchell-Kernan, C. (1990). New trends in Black American interracial Marriage: The social structural context. *Journal of Marriage and the Family, 52*, 209–218.

Tumin, M. M. (1953, August). Some principles of social stratification: A critical analysis. *American Sociological Review 18*, 394.

Turnbull, C. M. (1995). The mountain people. In K. Finsterbusch (Ed.), *Sociology 95/96* (pp. 6–15). Sluice Dock, CT: Dushkin. (First published 1972)

Turner, B. S. (1990, May). Outline of a theory of citizenship. *Sociology, 24*(2), 189–217.

Turner, J. H. (1978). *The structure of sociological theory*. Homewood, IL: Dorsey.

Turner, R. H. (1964). Collective behavior. In R. E. L. Faris (Ed.), *Handbook of modern sociology* (pp. 382–425). Chicago: Rand McNally.

Turner, R. H. (1993). Race riots past and present: A cultural-collective behavior approach. Paper presented at the annual meetings of the American Sociological Association.

Turner, R. H., & Killian, L. M. (1987). *Collective behavior* (2nd ed.). Englewood Cliffs, NJ: Prentice Hall.

Tustin, E., & Walton, D. (2002, October 23). Twentysomethings cling to nest. *The Globe and Mail*, p. A6.

Two-parent families growing scarcer, study finds. (1999, December 18). *The Toronto Star*, p. N8.

U.S. Census Bureau. (2001). *Statistical Abstract of the United States*. Washington, D.C.: U.S. Government Printing Office.

U.S. study tries to unravel mysteries of lasting marriages. (2002, July 25). *Toronto Star*, p. A12.

Udy, S. H., Jr. (1959, December). Bureaucracy and rationality in Weber's organizational theory: An empirical study. *American Sociological Review, 24,* 791–795.

Ullman, E., & Harris, C. (1970). The nature of cities. In A. N. Cousins & H. Nagpaul (Eds.), *Urban man and society: A reader in urban ecology* (pp. 91–100). New York: Knopf.

United Nations. (2000). *The world's women 2000: Trends and statistics.* New York: United Nations.

United Nations. (2001). *Human development report 2001.* New York: United Nations.

United Nations Population Fund. (2000). *Lives together, worlds apart: Men and women in a time of change.* New York: United Nations.

Useem, M. (1984). *The inner circle: Large corporations and the rise of business political activity in the U.S. and U.K.* New York: Oxford University Press.

Van Lawick-Goodall, J. (1971). *In the shadow of man.* Boston: Houghton Mifflin.

Vande Berg, L. R., & Streckfuss, D. (1992, Spring). Prime-time television's portrayal of women and the world of work: A demographic profile. *Journal of Broadcasting and Electronic Media,* 195–208.

Vann, K. (2002, March 2). Elderly murder-suicides on rise. *Toronto Star*, p. C9.

Vasil, L., & Wass, H. (1993, January–February). Portrayal of the elderly in the media: A literature review and implications for educational gerontologists. *Educational Gerontology, 19*(1), 71–85.

Veblen, T. (1912). *The Theory of the Leisure Class.* New York: Macmillan.

Vernon, J. A., Williams, J. A. Jr., Phillips, T., & Wilson, J. (1990). Media stereotyping: A comparison of the way elderly women and men are portrayed on prime-time television. *Journal of Women and Aging, 2*(4), 55–58.

Volti, R. (1995). *Society and technological change* (3rd ed.). New York: St. Martin's Press.

Von Hoffman, N. (1970, May). Sociological snoopers. *Transaction 7*(4), 6.

Wagley, C., & Harris, M. (1958). *Minorities in the new world.* New York: Columbia University Press.

Waldholz, M. (1991, December 2). Computer "brain" outperforms doctors in diagnosing heart attack patients. *Wall Street Journal,* p. 7B.

Waldholz, M. (1996, January 30). Three-drug therapy may suppress HIV. *Wall Street Journal,* pp. B1, B6.

Waldman, P. (1995a, June 12). Riots in Bahrain arouse ire of feared monarchy as the U.S. stands by. *Wall Street Journal,* pp. A1, A8.

Wallerstein, I. (1974). *The modern world system: Capitalist agriculture and the origins of the European world-economy in the sixteenth century.* New York: Academic Press.

Wallerstein, I. (1979). *The capitalist world-economy.* New York: Cambridge University Press.

Wallerstein, I. (1984). *The politics of the world-economy: The states, the movements, and the civilizations.* Cambridge, UK: Cambridge University Press.

Wallerstein, I. (1990). Culture as the ideological battleground of the modern world-system. In M. Featherstone (Ed.), *Global culture: Nationalism, globalization, and modernity* (pp. 31–55). London: Sage.

Wallerstein, J. S., & Kelly, J. B. (1992). How children react to parental divorce. In J. M. Henslin (Ed.), *Marriage and family in a changing society* (4th ed., pp. 397–409). New York: Free Press.

Walters, A. (1995, October 31). Let more earnings go to shareholders. *Wall Street Journal,* p. A23.

Walters, J. (1990, May 18–20). Chimps in the mist. *USA Weekend,* p. 24.

Walz, T. (2002, June). Crones, dirty old men, sexy seniors: Representations of the sexuality of older persons. *Journal of Aging and Identity,* 4, p. 112.

Ward, L. (2002, June 14). *The First Nations Governance Act.* CBC News Online. Accessed at http://cbc.ca/news/features/indian_act.html.

Warner, W. L., & Hunt, P. S. (1941). *The social life of a modern community.* New Haven, CT: Yale University Press.

Warner, W. L, Hunt, P. S., Meeker, M., & Eels, K. (1949). *Social class in America.* New York: Harper.

Warr, M. (1993). Age, peers, and delinquency. *Criminology, 31*(1), 17–40.

Watson, J. M. (1988). Outlaw motorcyclists. In J. M. Henslin (Ed.), *Down to earth sociology: Introductory readings* (5th ed., pp. 203–213). New York: Free Press.

Webb, E. J., Campbell, D.T., Schwartz, R. D., & Sechrest, L. (1966). *Unobtrusive measures: Nonreactive research in the social sciences.* Chicago: Rand McNally.

Weber, M. (1946). *From Max Weber: Essays in sociology* (H. Gerth & C. Wright Mills, Trans. and Ed.). New York: Oxford University Press.

Weber, M. (1947). *The theory of social and economic organization* (A. M. Henderson & T. Parsons, Trans., T. Parsons, Ed.). Glencoe, IL: Free Press. (First published 1913)

Weber, M. (1958). *The Protestant ethic and the spirit of capitalism.* New York: Scribner's. (First published 1904–1905)

Weber, M. (1968). *Economy and society* (E. Fischoff, Trans.). New York: Bedminster Press. (First published 1922)

Weber, M. (1978). *Economy and society* (G. Roth & C. Wittich, Eds.). Berkeley: University of California Press. (First published 1922)

Weeks, J. R. (1994). *Population: An introduction to concepts and issues* (5th ed.). Belmont, CA: Wadsworth.

Weisburd, D., Wheeler, S., & Waring, E. (1991). *Crimes of the middle classes: White-collar offenders in the federal courts.* New Haven, CT: Yale University Press.

Weisskopf, M. (1992). Scientist says greenhouse effect is setting in. In Washington Post Writers Group (Eds.), *Ourselves and others: The Washington Post sociology companion* (pp. 297–298). Boston: Allyn and Bacon.

Wente, M. (2000, January 29). How David found his manhood. *The Globe and Mail.*

West, C., & Garcia, A. (1988). Conversational shift work: A study of topical transitions between women and men. *Social Problems, 35,* 551–575.

White, J. E. (1995, July 3). Forgive us our sins. *Time,* 29.

White, J. A. (1991, February 13). When employees own big stake, it's a buy signal for investors. *Wall Street Journal,* pp. C1, C19.

Whitehead, S. M., & Barrett, F. J. (Eds). (2001). *The Masculinities Reader.* Cambridge: Polity Press.

Whittaker, T. (1995, March). Violence, gender and elder abuse: Towards a feminist analysis and practice. *Journal of Gender Studies, 4*(1), 35–45.

Whorf, B. (1956). *Language, thought, and reality* (J. B. Carroll, Ed.). Cambridge, MA: MIT Press.

Whyte, M. K. (1992, March–April). Choosing mates—The American way. *Society,* 71–77.

Whyte, W. H. (1989). *The city: Rediscovering the center.* New York: Doubleday.

Whyte, W. H. (1997). Street corner society. In J. M. Henslin (Ed.), *Down to earth sociology: Introductory readings* (9th ed., pp. 59–67). New York: Free Press.

Williams, C. L. (1995). *Still a man's world: Men who do women's work.* Berkeley: University of California Press.

Williams, C. (2001, Autumn). Family disruptions and childhood happiness. *Canadian Social Trends,* 62, pp. 2–4.

Williams, R. M., Jr. (1965). *American society: A sociological interpretation* (2nd ed.). New York: Knopf.

Willie, C. V. (1991). Caste, class, and family life experiences. *Research in Race and Ethnic Relations, 6,* 65–84.

Wilson, E. O. (1975). *Sociobiology: The new synthesis.* Cambridge, MA: Harvard University Press.

Wilson, J. Q., & Hernstein, R. J. (1985). *Crime and human nature.* New York: Simon & Schuster.

Wilson, S.J. (1991). *Women, families, and work.* Toronto: McGraw-Hill Ryerson.

Wilson, W. J. (1996). *When work disappears: The world of the new urban poor.* Chicago: University of Chicago Press.

Winslow, R. (1994, October 7). More doctors are adding online tools to their kits. *Wall Street Journal,* pp. B1, B4.

Winslow, R. (1995, August 18). Smoking increases heart-attack risk five-fold for people in their 30s and 40s. *Wall Street Journal,* p. B5.

Wirth, L. (1938, July). Urbanism as a way of life. *American Journal of Sociology, 44,* 1–24.

Wirth, L. (1945). The problem of minority groups. In R. Linton (Ed.), *The science of man in the world crisis.* New York: Columbia University Press.

Wohl, R. R., & Strauss, A. (1958, March). Symbolic representation and the urban milieu. *American Journal of Sociology, 63,* 523–532.

Wolfgang, M. E., & Ferracuti, F. (1967). *The subculture of violence: Toward an integrated theory in criminology.* London: Tavistock.

Womack, J. P., Jones, D. T. & Roos, D. (1991). *The machine that changed the world: The story of lean production.* New York: Harper Perrenial.

World Health Organization. (1946). *Constitution of the World Health Organization.* New York: World Health Organization Interim Commission.

Wotherspoon, T. (2000). Transforming Canada's education system: The impact on educational inequalities, opportunities, and benefits. In B. S. Bolaria (Ed.), *Social issues and contradictions in Canadian society* (3rd ed.). Toronto: Harcourt, Brace.

Wright, E. O. (1985). *Class.* London: Verso.

Yalnizyan, A. (1998). *The growing gap: A report on growing inequality between the rich and poor in Canada.* Toronto: Centre for Social Justice.

Yalnizyan, A. (2000). *Canada's great divide: The politics of the growing gap between rich and poor in the 1990s.* Toronto: Centre for Social Justice.

Yearbook of American and Canadian Churches (Various editions.) Nashville, TN: Abingdon.

Yinger, J. M. (1965). *Toward a field theory of behavior: Personality and social structure.* New York: McGraw-Hill.

Yinger, J. M. (1970). *The scientific study of religion.* New York: Macmillan.

Young, L. E. (1995). The overlooked contributions of women to the development of American sociology: An examination of AJS articles from 1895–1926. Paper presented at the 1995 meetings of the American Sociological Association.

Zachary, G. P. (1995, November 22). Behind stocks' surge is an economy in which big U.S. firms thrive. *Wall Street Journal,* pp. A1, A5.

Zakuta, L. (1989). Equality in North American marriages. In J. M. Henslin (Ed.), *Marriage and family in a changing society* (3rd ed., pp. 105–114). New York: Free Press.

Zald, M. N. (1992). Looking backward to look forward: Reflections on the past and the future of the resource mobilization research program. In A. D. Morris & C. M. Mueller (Eds.), *Frontiers in social movement theory* (pp. 326–348). New Haven, CT: Yale University Press.

Zellner, W. W. (1995). *Countercultures: A sociological analysis.* New York: St. Martin's.

Zerubavel, E.. (1991). *The fine line: Making distinctions in everyday life.* New York: Free Press.

Zey, M. (1993). *Banking on fraud: Drexel, junk bonds, and buyouts.* Hawthorne, NY: Aldine de Gruyter.

Zou, H. F. (1994, July). "The spirit of capitalism" and long-run growth. *European Journal of Political Economy, 10*(2), 279–293.

Zuboff, S. (1991). New worlds of computer-mediated work. In J. M. Henslin (Ed.), *Down to earth sociology: Introductory readings* (6th ed., pp. 476–485). New York: Free Press.

Flink, J.J., 444
Foley, D., 179
Foley, L.A., 42
Foot, D.K., 223
Foote, J., 421
Forcese, D., 134, 135, 148, 152
Form, W., 268
Form, W.H., 294
Forman, C., 254
Foucault, M., 97
Fox, Bonnie, 88
Fox, G., 413
Francis, D., 135
Franke, 309, 310
Frederick, 309, 310
Frederick, J., 227
Frederick, J.A., 227, 311, 322, 325
Freedman, A.M., 151
Freud, S., 76–77, 97, 396
Freudenburg, W.R., 420
Frideres, J., 202
Friedan, B., 218, 221, 309
Friedl, E., 173
Friesen, W.V., 51
Froman, I., 306
Fuller, R., 180
Furnham, A., 79
Furtado, C., 145

G
Gadacz, R., 202
Galbraith, J.K., 145
Galinsky, E., 182, 314
Galliher, J., 12
Gallmeier, C.P., 179
Gans, H.J., 152, 415–416, 417
Garcia, A., 179
Gardner, A., 64
Gardner, B., 64
Gardner, B.B., 134
Gardner, M.R., 134
Garfinkel, H., 87, 118, 395
Garratt, 97
Gary, L.E., 151
Gecas, V., 82
Geer, B., 88
Gelles, 394
Gerin, 54
Gérin, L., 14
Germain, S., 15
Gerson, K., 317
Gerth, H., 132
Giddens, A., 10
Gilbert, D., 148, 149, 152
Gilham, S.A., 178
Gillborn, D., 339
Gilleard, 217
Gillespie, 318
Gilligan, C., 77
Gilman, C.P., 13, 15, 79, 189
Gilmore, D.D., 170
Gingrich, F.W., 286
Gintis, H., 340, 342
Girard, 223
Gitlin, T., 9
Glenday, D., 14, 37, 154, 222, 265, 277, 390, 391, 422
Glueck, E., 382

Glueck, S., 382
Goffman, E., 83, 86, 116, 117, 118, 383
Gold, R., 138
Goldberg, A., 320
Goldberg, S., 79, 170
Goleman, D., 31, 315
Gomez, C.F., 372
Goodall, J., 64
Goode, E., 375, 433
Goode, W.J., 271
Gooden, A.M., 80
Gooden, M.A., 80
Goodwin, C., 82
Goodwin, G.A., 41
Gordon, D.M., 393
Gorlick, C.A., 323
Gorman, C., 171, 374
Gorrie, 215, 224, 229
Gorz, A., 277, 278
Gourevitch, P., 194
Grabb, 152
Gracey, H., 340
Graham, E., 320
Gramling, R., 420
Graves, F.L., 59
Greeley, A.M., 352, 359
Green, S.J., 84
Greenberg, G., 34
Greenfield, L.A., 385
Greenhalgh, S., 412
Greenwood, E., 271, 272
Gregg, A., 56, 59
Gregg, N., 82
Grobe, R.P., 343
Grossman, L.K., 345
Guha, R., 421
Guindon, H., 205, 221
Guppy, 152
Guppy, N., 341

H
Haas, J., 88, 371
Habib, M., 324
Hacker, H.M., 173
Hall, 272
Hall, E., 115
Hall, G.S., 90
Hall, J.A., 179
Hall, S.S., 188
Halle, D., 56
Halli, 317
Hallowell, L., 40
Hamel, J., 325
Hamermesh, 119
Hamil-Luker, 224
Hamilton, 77
Hamilton, A., 15
Hamilton, K., 344
Hamilton, M., 9
Hamm, B., 317
Hanson, D.J., 64
Hare, A.P., 105, 111
Harlow, H., 73, 74
Harlow, M., 73, 74
Harper, T., 319
Harrington, M., 146, 158
Harris, C., 415
Harris, D.K., 213

Harris, M., 174, 197
Harrison, D., 184
Harrison, P., 144
Hart, C., 212
Hart, C.W.M., 218
Hart, G., 413
Hart, P., 112
Hartley, E., 198
Harvey, D., 17, 20
Harwood, J., 186
Haslick, L., 213
Haub, C., 374, 405, 408, 410, 413
Hauser, P., 413
Hauser, R.M., 153
Hawranik, 227
Hayes, D., 344
Haynes, R.M., 9
Haynie, D., 85
Heilbrun, A.B., 383
Heinz, W.R., 87
Hellinger, D., 137, 294
Hendrix, L., 171
Henley, N., 9
Henry, T., 83
Henry, W., 222
Henslin, J.M., 4, 5, 13, 28, 32, 38, 40, 48, 49, 55, 56, 79, 120, 152, 216, 248, 249, 276, 323, 396, 404, 428
Hernstein, R.J., 382
Hertzler, J.O., 55
Hewa, S., 12
Higginbotham, E., 153
Higgs, D.C., 327
Higley, J., 142
Hill, G., 226
Hilliard, A. III., 347
Hillyer, B., 82
Hinch, 394
Hippler, F., 289
Hira, S., 85
Ho, D., 374
Hobson, J., 144
Hochschild, A.R., 310, 312
Hofferth, S., 89, 314
Hoffman, C., 160
Hoffmann-Lange, U., 142
Hofstede, G.H., 56
Hoijer, H., 63
Holden, B.A., 432
Homblin, D.J., 413
Hondagneu-Sotelo, P., 314
Honeycutt, K., 119
Hormeku, 163
Horowitz, I.L., 41, 140
Horowitz, R., 385
Hostetler, J., 350
Houtman, D., 152
Howe, R.B., 76
Howells, L., 111
Hoyt, H., 414
Huber, J., 173, 294
Hudson, J.R., 418
Huggins, M., 143
Hughes, E.C., 14, 31, 88, 204, 293
Hughes, J., 387
Hughes, T., 66
Hull, R., 245
Humphreys, A., 341

patterns of, after U.S. Civil War, 130
prevalence of, 197
stereotypes and, 199–200
disengagement theory, 222
distance zones, 115
diversity training, 249
divine right of kings, 141
division of labour, 101, 239
divorce, 151, 322–323, 325
doctors, 88
documents, 33
dominant groups, 196
double day, 368
down-to-earth sociology
adult socialization, 88
boys, and the struggle for expression and
self, 188
cults, 356
doctor-nurse game, 368
gendered social structure, 103
Hawthorne experiments, 34
high school hockey and soccer, 103
how not to do research, 31
Inuit expulsion, 203
kindergarten as boot camp, 340
legacy of Louis Riel, 204
marketing research, 35
Mcdonaldization of society, 241
old elephant story, updated, 7
online shorthand, 53
propaganda, 439
sociological findings *vs.* common sense
(quiz), 8, 9
teenagers and sex at home, 54
welfare, and self-concept, 160
women in male-dominated business
world, 248
youth unemployment and crime in
Canada, 390
downward social mobility, 152
dramaturgy, 116
Du Bois, W.E.B., 15
dual labour market, 199
Durkheim, Emile, 10–11, 13, 18
dyad, 108

E
early middle years, 90
early older years, 91
eating disorders, 200
ecclesia, 357
ecofeminism, 421–422
economic imperialism, 144
economic life
conflict perspective, 272–273
education-job market connection, 272
feminist perspectives, 273
functionalist perspective, 272
global division of work, 272
inner circle of power, 273
mechanical solidarity, 272
organic solidarity, 272
symbolic interactionist perspective,
271–272
technology, who benefits from, 272–273
work, as status symbols, 271–272
work in Canadian society, 273–277
economic systems
capitalism. *See* capitalism
economy, 260
industrial societies, 261

market, 260
postindustrial societies, 261–262
socialism. *See* socialism
subsistence economy, 260–261
transformation of, 260–262
world economic systems, 263–268
economics, 6
economy, 260
ecosabotage, 421
education
see also school
the computer, 446
conflict perspective, 339–342
correspondence principle, 342
cultural transmission of values, 335–336
in earlier societies, 333–334
educational tracking, 343
and family background, 342
functionalist perspective, 335–339
gatekeeping, 337–338
and gender inequality, 172, 175–178
hidden curriculum, 84, 339–340
high school leavers, 335
industrialization and, 334–335
Internet university, 344
job market connection, 272
latent functions, 84
mainstreaming, 338
manifest functions, 84
modern, development of, 333–335
other functions of, 339
personal change, 338
and population growth, 410
and poverty, 155–157
professional wrestling, study of, 60
replacement of family functions, 339
Rist research, 343
social benefits of, 335–339
social change, 338
and social class, 151
social class and, 343
social integration, 337
and social mobility, 154
symbolic interactionist perspective, 343
teacher expectations, 343
teaching knowledge and skills, 335
today's credential society, 332–333
unequal funding, 341–342
universal schooling in 19th century, 65
egalitarian family patterns, 306
ego, 77
Egypt, divorce in, 305
elder abuse and neglect, 228
eldercare, 322
the elderly
payroll taxes and, 214
electronic communities, 108, 109
electronic primary group, 109
The Elementary Forms of the Religious Life
(Durkheim), 348
elites
controlling ideas, 141
controlling information, 141
divine right of kings, 141
ideology *vs.* force, 141
and maintenance of social inequality,
141–142
social networks, 141–142
technology, use of, 142
emergent norms, 430–431

emotions, social development of, 74–78
employee stock ownership, 250
employment equity, 295–296
empty nest, 315
endogamy, 131, 305
the environment
acid rain, 419
concern for, as value, 62
ecofeminism, 421–422
ecosabotage, 421
energy shortage, 419
fossil fuels and environmental
degradation, 419
global warming, 419
greenhouse effect, 419
industrializing nations, 419
least industrialized nations, 419–420
most industrialized nations, 419
multinational corporations, 419
past civilizations, 418–419
rain forests and extinction, 420
sustainable environment, 420
technology and, 423
environmental influences. *See* social
environment
environmental movement, 420
environmental sociology, 420
epidemiology, 369
An Essay on the Principle of Population (Malthus),
404
ethics
Brajuha research, 40
deception in research, 113
Humphreys research, 40–41
Milgram experiment, 113
in research, 38–41
Scarce research, 40
Ethiopia, 128
ethnic, 196
ethnicity
and aging, 215–216
defined, 196
diversity in Canadian families, 316–317
and poverty, 155
ethnocentrism, 49
ethnomethodology, 118
European democratic systems, 294
euthanasia, 232, 372
exchange mobility, 153
exogamy, 305
experimental group, 33
experiments
and cause and effect, 33
control group, 33
dependent variable, 33
experimental group, 33
independent variable, 33
exponential growth curve, 404
expressive leaders, 110–111

F
face-saving behaviour, 117
fads, 434
false consciousness, 132
family
see also marriage
as agent of socialization, 82–83
authority patterns, 305–306
battering, 326–327
child abuse, 325–326
common cultural themes, 305–306

and popular music, 81
and television, 80
and video and computer games, 80
gender stratification, 168
see also gender inequality
gendered social structure, 103
generalizability, 32
generalized other, 75
generational conflict, 223–224
genetic predispositions, 382
genetics, *vs.* social environment, 72–74
Genie, 73
genocide, 194, 201
gentrification, 415
gerontocracy, 218
Gesellschaft, 101–102, 415
gestures, 51–52
Getting By in Hard Times (Luxton and Corman), 311
glass ceiling, 181, 273
glass escalator, 181
glittering generality, 439
global capitalism, 270–271, 298, 299
global division of work, 272
global stratification
children as prey, 143
colonization, 144
culture of poverty, 145
dependency theory, 145
development of, 144–145
dimensions of, 142
global income distribution, 143
and globalization, 145
health care and, 366
imperialism, 144
maintenance of, 146–147
modifying the model, 143–144
and multinational corporations, 146–147
neocolonialism, 146
technology, and global domination, 147
theory evaluation, 145
world system theory, 144–145
global village, 66, 261–262
global warming, 419
globalization
of AIDS, 373–374
defined, 145
of disease, 374
and global stratification, 145
and social structure, 101
urbanization, effect on, 418
goal displacement, 244–245
gold standard, 263
government
city-states, 288
coalition government, 294
confederal union, 290
democracies, 288
dictatorships, 288–289
monarchies, 288
oligarchy, 288–289
totalitarianism, 289
unitary state, 290
graying of Canada, 214–215
green parties, 420
greenhouse effect, 419
gross national product (GNP), 263
group dynamics, 108–110, 112
groups, 105
vs. aggregate, 105

attitudes, effects on, 109–110
behaviours, effect on, 109–110
vs. category, 105
cliques, 107
coalition formation, 109
dominant, 196
dyad, 108
electronic communities, 108, 109
electronic primary group, 109
groupthink, 112
in-groups, 106–107
intergroup relations. *See* intergroup relations
leadership, 110–111
minority, 196–197
out-groups, 106–107
peer pressure, conformity to, 111–113
primary, 105–106
reference, 107
secondary, 106
size, 108–110
small group, 108
social networks, 107–108
within society, 105–108
triad, 109
groupthink, 112
growth rate, 410
gynecological examinations, 120–121

H
Hawthorne experiments, 34
health and illness
conflict perspective, 366
culture and, 364–365
feminist perspective, 366–368
functionalist perspective, 365–366
gendered experience of, 367–368
health, components of, 365
historical patterns of health, 369
mental health patterns, 369
mental illness. *See* mental illness
physical health patterns, 369
sick role, 365–366
symbolic interactionist perspective, 364–365
health care
in Canada, 369–370
depersonalization, 371
and global stratification, 366
living will, 372
medicalization of society, 371–372
medically assisted suicide, 372
sociology of health in Canada, 371
treatment *vs.* prevention, 375–376
health threats
AIDS, 372–374
alcohol, 374
disabling environments, 375
drugs, 374–375
globalization of disease, 374
nicotine, 375
hidden curriculum, 84, 339–340
Hinduism, 353
the homeless, 4, 36, 149–150, 397–398
hospices, 230
household, 307
housework
husbands, and paycheque size, 312
power struggle over, 309–310
hypothesis, 38

I
"I," 76
ideal culture, 63, 77
ideological commitment, 440
ideology
changes in, 443
defined, 130
vs. force, 141
illegitimate opportunity structures, 391
illegitimate opportunity theory, 390–391
imitation/preparatory stage, 75
immigrants in Canada, 206–207
imperialism, 8, 144
impression management, 117, 118
imprisonment
Canadian *vs.* American, 396
vs. freedom, 385
as reaction to social deviance, 395
in-groups, 106–107
incest, 327
incest taboo, 63, 305, 308
income
distribution in Canada, 135–136
global income distribution, 143
and wealth, 135–137
indentured service, 130
independent variable, 33
India
caste system in, 131
female infanticide, 412
Indian Act (1876), 59–61
indirect population transfer, 201
individual discrimination, 198
individualism, 336
Industrial Revolution, 7, 261, 442
industrial societies, 261, 263
industrialization
and aging, 213
death and dying, 229
deindustrialization, effect of, 418
and education, 334–335
and growth rate, 410
negative environmental consequences, 419
traditional orientation and, 237
industrializing nations
environmental problems, 419
as term, 142
inflation, 263
informal economy, 276
information explosion, 261
information highway, 446
information technology, 108
inheritance rights, 305
inner circle of power, 273
institutional death, 230
institutional discrimination, 198
institutionalized means, 389
instrumental leaders, 110–111
intelligence tests, 340–341
intentional families, 320
intergenerational mobility, 152
intergroup relations
assimilation, 201
genocide, 201
global patterns of, 200–201
internal colonialism, 201
multiculturalism, 202
patterns of, 200–202
pluralism, 202

Photo Credits

Chapter Opener Art Credits

Chapter 1: *Unity Rally III, Montreal,* by Evangeline Murray. Photo Courtesy of Donald Murray.

Chapter 2: *Untitled* by Diana Ong, 1995. Diana Ong/SuperStock.

Chapter 3: *Bus Stop in Beijing* by Phoebe Beasley, 1983.

Chapter 4: *Le Bingo Paroissial* by Helen Beck.

Chapter 5: *Patria B* by Alejandra Xul Solar, 1925. Christie's Images/SuperStock.

Chapter 6: *Globes Interconnected* by Pete Whyte, 1996. Pete Whyte/SIS.

Chapter 7: *Dissension* by Wendy Seller, 1993. 1993 Wendy Seller. In the collection of Robert and Elayne Simardi.

Chapter 8: *Un Certain Soir de Mai* by Therese Joyce-Gagnon. Photo by Daniel Roussel.

Chapter 9: *Lady in Her Living Room* by Joanna Strong.

Chapter 10: *Conference in Color* by Diana Ong, 1997. Diana Ong/SuperStock.

Chapter 11: *Workers Walking in a City Landscape* by Harvey Chan, 1996. Harvey Chan SIS.

Chapter 12: *Judgement After the War* by Tsing-Fang Chen, 1977. Lucia Gallery, New York City/TF Chen, 1977.

Chapter 13: *Looking in Simpson's Window* by Marlene Siomra.

Chapter 14: *School Bus, Conception Bay* by Reginald Shepard.

Chapter 15: *Doctor and Patient* by Connie Hayes, 1996. Connie Hayes/SIS.

Chapter 16: *Generation X, Sequence I* by Therese Joyce Gagnon, 1994.

Chapter 17: *New York, Going to Work* by Ralph Fasanella, 1980. Courtesy ACA Galleries, New York.

Chapter 18: *Petroushka* by Paraskeva Clark.

Photo Credits

Chapter 1

p. 5 Victor Last/Geographical Visual Aids; p. 8 Mary Evans Picture Library; p. 9 North Wind Picture Archive; p. 10 (left) Corbis/Bettmanm; (right) Reuter's/San Diego Sheriff's Dept./Archive Photos; p. 11 (top left) Zigy Kaluzny/Tony Stone Images; (bottom left) Mike Yamashita/Woodfin Camp & Associates; (right) The Granger Collection; p. 13 The Granger Collection; p. 14 Courtesy of Wallace Clement; p. 15 (left) Liza McCoy, Photographer; (right) North Wind Picture Archive; p. 16 University of Chicago Library.

Chapter 2

p. 29 (left) Andrew Lichtenstein/Impact Visuals; (right) Canapress/Mary Butkus; p. 30 Reproduced by permission of Johnny Hart and Creators Syndicate Inc.; p. 32 Micheal Newman/Photo Edit; p. 33 Rhonda Sidney/The Image Works; p. 36 Benali/Gamma-Liaison; p. 40 Cameron Davidson/Comstock.

Chapter 3

p. 49 (top left) Alison Wright/The Image Works; (top right) Fourmy/REA; p. 50 Canapress/Ryan Remiorz; p. 51 (top left) Benali/Gamma-Liaison; (top right) Bob Daemmrich/Tony Stone Images; p. 56 Mirror Syndication International; p. 57 (top) Canapress/AP/Elaine Thompson; (bottom) Canapress/Jonathan Hayward; p. 64 Micheal Nichols/Magnum; p. 65 *The Wall Street Journal,* permission Cartoon Features Syndicate; p. 66 Canapress Photos; p. 67 Scott Houston/ Corbis Sygma.

Chapter 4

p. 73 Harlow Primates Laboratory/University of Wisconsin; p. 75 Charles Thatcher/Tony Stone Images; p. 77 Jack Smith/AP/Wide World Photos; p. 78 Malcolm Mayes/Artizans.com; p. 79 (left) FPG/Jacques Copeau; (right) W.P. Wittman Limited; p. 81 (left) Eidos Interactive Limited; (right) G.Short/HO/AP/Wide World Photos; p. 84 George Mars Cassidy/The Picture Cube; p. 85 Anne Dowie; p. 86 (left) Al Harvey/The Slide Farm; (right) Bill Cooke/Saba; p. 87 Steve Neace/*The Toronto Star*; p. 89 The Granger Collection; p. 90 Micheal MacIntyre/The Hutchinson Library; p. 91 AP/Wide World Photos.

Chapter 5

p. 97 Canapress/Tom Hanson; p. 102 (left) Charles Gupton/The Stock Market; (right) I.Uimonen/Corbis Sygma; p. 104 Canapress/Jann Van Home; p. 106 Drawing by Ziegler 1983, *The New Yorker* Magazine, Inc.; p. 107 Fujifotos/The Image Works; p. 113 1965 by Stanley Milgram. From the film *Obedience,* distributed by Pennsylvania State University, Audio Visual Services; p. 114 (left) 2000 James Darell/Stone; (right) Mark C. Burnett/Stock, Boston/Picture Quest; p. 115 (left) Alain Evrard/Photo Researchers Inc.; (right) Franz Lanting/Minden Pictures; p. 116 (left) J.C. Francolon/Gamma Liason; (right) AP/Wide World Photos; p. 119 (left) Andrew Ramey/Woodfin Camp & Associates; (right) Photo Richard Corkery/*NY Daily News*; p. 120 Mark Walker/ The Picture Cube.

Chapter 6

p. 129 (left) Shawn G. Henry/Material World; (right) Peter Ginter/Material World; p. 130 The Granger Collection; p. 132 (top left) Jacob Riis, *Two Ragamuffins,* "Didn't Live Nowhere,".ca. 1898. The Jacob A. Riis Collection, #DE. The Museum of the City of New York; (top right) Corbis-Bettman; p. 133 (bottom left) PHC Archives NAC Image; (bottom right) Canapress/Tom Hanson; p. 134 Courtesy of the Helander Gallery; p. 137 AP/Wide World Photos; p. 138 Jean Clouet, *Elizabeth of Austria, Queen of France.* Musee du Loubre, Paris. Photo: Erich Lessing/Art Rosource; p. 139 Frank Gunn/Canadian Press; p. 141 *The*

Crowning of Charlemagne, medieval manuscript. Bibliotheque de l'Arsenal, Paris. Photo: Scala/Art Resource; p. 143 J.L. Bulcao/Gamma-Liason; p. 146 Peter Turnley/Black Star; p. 149 Ryan Remiorz/Canadian Press; p. 150 Canapress/Frank Gunn; p. 152 UPI/Corbis-Bettman; p. 159 Canapress/Gary Hebbard.

Chapter 7

p. 169 SuperStock/Kai Chiang; p. 171 Jeremy Horner/Panos Pictures; p. 172 Mary Evans Picture Library; p. 175 National Archives of Canada; p. 180 CEP; p. 181 Reprinted by permission of United Features Syndicate, Inc.; p. 182 Daniel Simon/Gamma-Liason; p. 185 Lannis Waters/*The Palm Beach Post.*

Chapter 8

p. 195 (bottom left) AP/Wide World Photos; (bottom right) Archive Photos; p. 196 Jim Hollander/Reuters/Archive Photos; p. 197 Corbis-Bettmann; p. 210 UPI/Corbis-Bettmann; p. 202 *The Toronto Star*; p. 205 PHC Archives/NAC; p. 206 PHC Archives/*Halifax Chronicle Herald.*

Chapter 9

p. 213 (left) Sovfoto/Novosti; (right) Charles P. Mountford/National Geographic Society; p. 216 (left) Canapress/Peter Bregg; (right) *The Nugget*, Denis Dubois/AP/Wide World Photos; p. 217 Dorothea Lange, *Migrant Mother,* Nipomo California (1936); p. 219 Lawrence Migdale/Tony Stone Images; p. 220 PEANUTS reprinted by permission of United Features Syndicate, Inc.; p. 225 Human Rights Commission; p. 227 AP/Wide World Photos; p. 228 (left) Canapress/Ward Perrin; (right) Stephanie Maze/Woodfin Camp & Associates.

Chapter 10

p. 237 The Limbourg Brothers, "March," from *Les tres riches heurse du Duc de Berry.* Photo AKG London; p. 238 (top) North Wind Picture Archive; (bottom) Rafael Macia/Photo Reseachers; p. 240 Courtesy MetLife Archives; p. 241 AP Wide World Archives; p. 243 Charlyn Zlotnick/Woodfin Camp & Associates; p. 244 Courtesy of the March of Dimes Birth Defects Foundation; p. 246 Dick Hemmingway; p. 247 Photo: Peter Simon/Courtesy of Rosabeth Moss Kanter; p. 249 Phil Norton/Montreal Gazette; p. 250 Billy Hustace/Tony Stone Images; p. 251 *Courtesy of Northern Breweries Ltd.*; p. 253 Micheal Wolf/Visum/SABA.

Chapter 11

p. 261 Doranne Jacobson; p. 262 (left) Lewis Hine/Corbis Bettmann; (right) Lindsey Hebbard/Woodfin Camp & Associates; p. 265 (top) Dick Hemmingway; (bottom) Micheal J. O'Brien/Panos Pictures; p. 266 (left) The Granger Collection; (right) Photo AKG London; p. 267 Shepard Sherbell/Saba; p. 271 Marie Dorigny/R.E.A./Saba; p. 276 Grosset Simon/ Spooner/ Liason Agency; p. 278 Louis De Matteis; p. 279 A.Aarhus/Sipa Press.

Chapter 12

p. 285 Woodfin Camp & Associates; p. 286 (left) Jean-Auguste-Dominique Ingres, *Jeanne D'Arc,*1854. Musee du Louvre, Paris. Photo AKG London; (right) Photo AKG London; p. 287 (top)

PHC Archives; (bottom) AP/Wide World Photos; p. 293 Victor Last/Geographical Visual Aids; p. 296 UPI/Corbis-Bettmann; p. 297 Sygma; p. 298 Noel Quidu/Gamma-Liason.

Chapter 13

p. 305 Courtesy of the National Parenting Association (NPA), NY 1994 by the NPA; p. 309 ARLO AND JANIS reprinted by permission of Newspaper Enterprise Association Inc.; p. 316 Greg Locke/Stray Light; p. 318 Dean Musser Jr./*Fort Wayne Journal Gazette*/Sygma; p. 324 Courtesy of the National Parenting Association (NPA), NY 1994 by the NPA; p. 326 Dusen Petricic/*The Toronto Star.*

Chapter 14

p. 333 Corbis-Bettman; p. 336 Tricia Yourkevich; p. 337 Canapress/Winnipeg Free Press/Mark Gallant; p. 339 Will and Deni McIntyre/Tony Stone Images; p. 345 Canapress/Mike Ridewood; p. 346 Andy Freeberg; p. 348 Jehangir Gazdar/Woodfin Camp & Associates; p. 349 Sygma; p. 350 (top) The Granger Collection; (bottom) Scala/Art Resource; p. 354 Hugh Sitton/Tony Stone Images; p. 355 (left) Epix/Sygma; (right) Asahi Shimbun/Sipa Press; p. 356 Sygma; p. 357 SuperStock/Liz Strenk; p. 359 PEANUTS reprinted by permission of United Features Syndicate, Inc.

Chapter 15

p. 365 Nazima Kowall/Corbis; p. 367 (top left) Noel Guidu/Liaison Agency; (top right) Mark Peterson/SABA; (bottom) Gary Buss 1997; p. 374 David Younge-Wolff/Photo Edit; p. 375 Paul Chesley/Tony Stone Images; p. 376 J.P. Laffont/Sygma.

Chapter 16

p. 384 Hulton-Deutsch Collection/Corbis; p. 385 James Henslin; p. 386 Lynn Goldsmith/Corbis; p. 387 (top) McKenna/Toronto Sun Syndicate; (bottom) George Shelley/Black Star; p. 389 Courtesy of MADD; p. 391 The Granger Collection/New York; p. 392 Photofest; p. 393 (left) Barbara Filet/Tony Stone Image; (right) Micheal Newmann/PhotoEdit; p. 395 John Levy/Gamma-Liason; p. 397 Robert Harbison.

Chapter 17

p. 405 Archive Photos; p. 407 (left) Reuters/Archive Photos; (right) 2000 Anthony Blake/Stone; p. 410 Ben Gibson/Woodfin Camp & Associates; p. 413 Jonathan Blair/Woodfin Camp & Associates; p. 416 Ron Giling/Panos Pictures; p. 417 Rudi Von Briel/Photo Edit; p. 421 Cunningham/Greenpeace; p. 422 S. Thinakran/AP/Wide World Photos.

Chapter 18

p. 429 AP/Wide World Photos; p. 430 Paris/R.E.A./Saba; p. 431 Canapress/Chuck Stoody; p. 432 Kerr/Toronto Sun Syndicate; p. 434 Sean Sprague/Stock, Boston; p. 436 Provincial Archives, Victoria, BC; p. 437 Canapress/Tony Caldwell; p. 438, Filipacchi/Gamma-Liaison ; p. 440 Canapress/Shaney Komulainen CP; p. 445 Courtest the Computer Museum History Centre/Model photo Dennis Bourke.